Europe

R. Chapple/PIX

P. Czeslaw /PIX

On the western tip of Asia, the smallest of all the continents is a world apart. Its sky is a huge battlefield where, year after year, the Azores anticyclone triumphs over the cold air from the north and east. The shores and hinterland of the Mediterranean are still bathed in the same incomparable light as in ancient times, when it was the centre of the world. Further inland, heavy clouds from the Atlantic bring refreshing rain. The North Sea warmed by the Gulf Stream washes the Scandinavian coast and opens into the Baltic by a series of little straits.
In the east, the Black Sea laps the shores of Ukraine, Romania, Bulgaria and Turkey, and is connected to the Sea of Marmara by the Bosphorus. Its sandy eastern coastline is dotted with resorts renowned in this part of Europe for their sun and sea.
This rich range of climates and contrasting topography, a bottomless melting pot of peoples, have produced a multitude of civilisations, both brilliant and refined.
Europe was named after Europa, daughter of Agenor, King of Phoenicia. One day, while she was tending her father's flock near Tyre, a splendid, milk-white bull appeared before her. The beautiful Europa decked its horns with flowers and, as she stroked it, mounted its broad back. The bull stood up and plunged with her into the sea, then swam to the Island of Crete. The bull, who was no other than Zeus, vanished and re-appeared to Europa in his godlike form. From their union was born Minos, the civilising king of Crete and, later judge of Hades.
It was in memory of this princess who had involuntarily come to their continent that the Ancients named this part of the world Europe.

M. Guillot /MICHELIN

Contents

Key

★★★ **Worth a journey**

★★ **Worth a detour**

★ **Interesting**

Tourism

- Admission Times and Charges listed at the end of the guide
- Sightseeing route with departure point indicated
- Ecclesiastical building
- Synagogue – Mosque
- Building (with main entrance)
- Statue, small building
- Wayside cross
- Fountain
- Fortified walls – Tower – Gate
- Visit if time permits
- AZ B — Map co-ordinates locating sights
- Tourist information
- Historic house, castle – Ruins
- Dam – Factory or power station
- Fort – Cave
- Prehistoric site
- Viewing table – View
- Miscellaneous sight

Recreation

- Racecourse
- Skating rink
- Outdoor, indoor swimming pool
- Marina, moorings
- Mountain refuge hut
- Overhead cable-car
- Tourist or steam railway
- Waymarked footpath
- Outdoor leisure park/centre
- Theme/Amusement park
- Wildlife/Safari park, zoo
- Gardens, park, arboretum
- Aviary, bird sanctuary

Additional symbols

- Motorway (unclassified)
- Junction: complete, limited
- Pedestrian street
- Unsuitable for traffic, street subject to restrictions
- Steps – Footpath
- Railway – Coach station
- Funicular – Rack-railway
- Tram – Metro, Underground
- Bert (R.)... — Main shopping street
- Post office – Telephone centre
- Covered market
- Barracks
- Swing bridge
- Quarry – Mine
- B F — Ferry (river and lake crossings)
- Ferry services: Passengers and cars
- Foot passengers only
- ③ — Access route number common to MICHELIN maps and town plans

Abbreviations and special symbols

D, G, L, P	Local authority offices
H, R	Town hall
J	Law courts
M	Museum
POL.	Police station
T	Theatre
U	University
	Police station (Gendarmerie)
	Hotel

Book well in advance as vacant hotel rooms are often scarce in high season.

Using this Guide

Your Green Guide is a mine of information containing:

- **Theme maps** – Principal sights, Major European destinations and transport. In addition to this, the map on the back cover of the guide gives the numbers of complementary Michelin guides.

- **Introducing Europe** – Find out more about the continent's landscape, history and art before you leave or once you are on your way.

- **Which destination?** – A presentation of the countries in alphabetical order, together with major towns and cities and the most important tourist sites. Place names are given in the language of the country in question to make it easier for you to find your way about.

- **Practical information** – Useful addresses, moving about, theme tours, accommodation, restaurants, major events etc.

- An **Index** at the back of the guide – the quick way to find a description of a town or site or information about a prominent figure or important historical event.

We are interested in what you think. If you have any ideas or criticisms, write and tell us about them when you get back. Let us know, too, about any good places you have discovered. Bibendum is waiting to hear from you at *Michelin Tyre PLC, Tourism Department, 38 Clarendon Road - Watford Herts WD 1 1SX, United Kingdom*, or on the Internet at www.michelin-travel.com, and wishes you

Bon voyage!

J.-C. Saturnin/Michelin

Principal sights

ROMA ***ALPES***		Outstanding site
AVIGNON ***VESUVIO***	★★★	Worth a journey
Lund ***Mývatn***	★★	Worth a detour
Malmö *Shetland I.*	★	Interesting

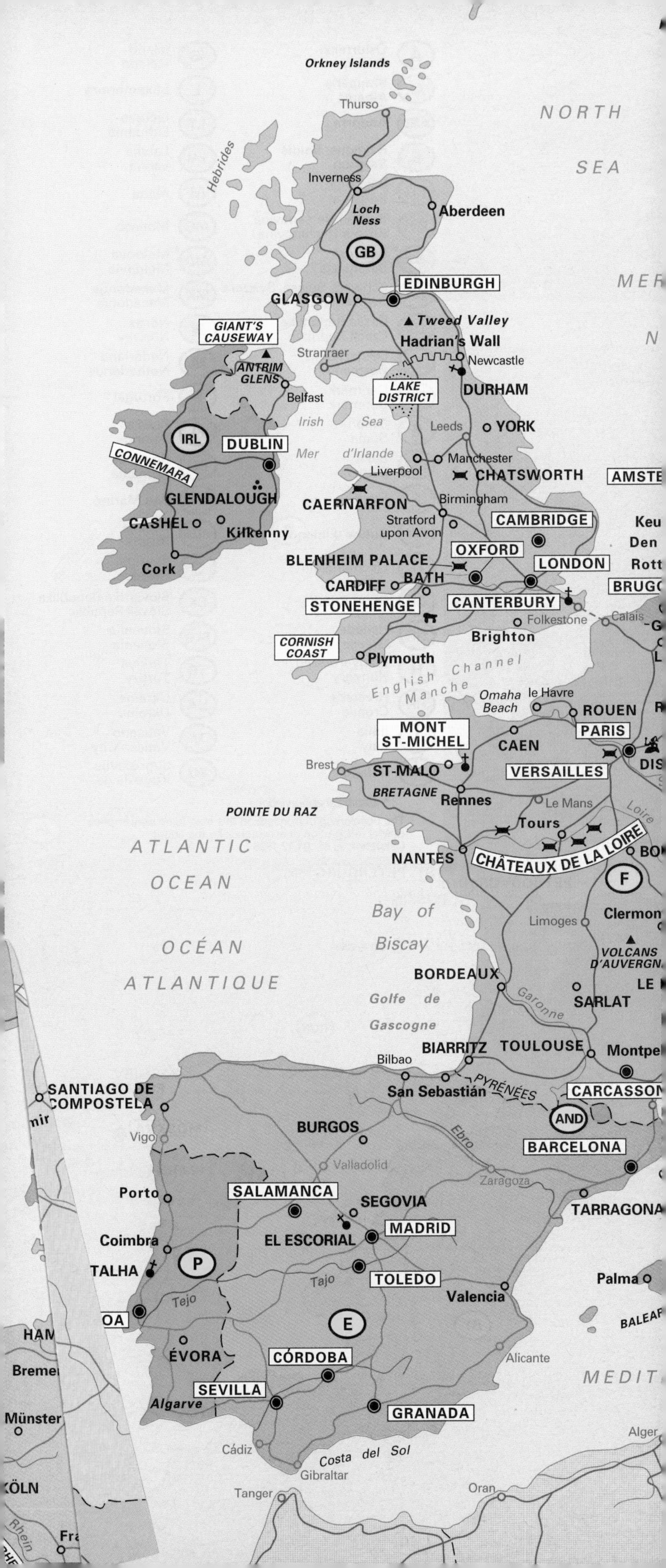
Orkney Islands
Thurso
NORTH
SEA
Hebrides
Inverness
Loch Ness
Aberdeen
GB
EDINBURGH
GLASGOW
Tweed Valley
GIANT'S CAUSEWAY
Hadrian's Wall
Stranraer
Newcastle
ANTRIM GLENS
LAKE DISTRICT
DURHAM
Belfast
Irish Sea
YORK
Leeds
IRL
DUBLIN
Mer d'Irlande
Manchester
CONNEMARA
Liverpool
CHATSWORTH
GLENDALOUGH
CAERNARFON
Birmingham
CASHEL
Kilkenny
Stratford upon Avon
CAMBRIDGE
Cork
BLENHEIM PALACE
OXFORD
LONDON
CARDIFF
BATH
STONEHENGE
CANTERBURY
Folkestone
Calais
CORNISH COAST
Brighton
Plymouth
English Channel
Manche
Omaha Beach
le Havre
ROUEN
MONT ST-MICHEL
PARIS
CAEN
Brest
ST-MALO
VERSAILLES
BRETAGNE
Rennes
Le Mans
POINTE DU RAZ
Loire
Tours
ATLANTIC OCEAN
NANTES
CHÂTEAUX DE LA LOIRE
F
Bay of Biscay
Limoges
OCÉAN ATLANTIQUE
VOLCANS D'AUVERGNE
BORDEAUX
Golfe de Gascogne
Garonne
SARLAT
BIARRITZ
TOULOUSE
Bilbao
San Sebastián
PYRÉNÉES
SANTIAGO DE COMPOSTELA
AND
BURGOS
Ebro
Vigo
BARCELONA
Valladolid
Zaragoza
Porto
SALAMANCA
SEGOVIA
TARRAGONA
Coimbra
EL ESCORIAL
MADRID
P
Tajo
TOLEDO
Palma
Tejo
Valencia
E
ÉVORA
CÓRDOBA
Alicante
SEVILLA
Algarve
GRANADA
Cádiz
Costa del Sol
Gibraltar
Alger
Tanger
Oran
Bremen
Münster
KÖLN
Rhein

Hardangerfjord
Västerås
STOCKHOLM
Skien
Örebro
Stavanger
Vänern
Norrköping
Vättern
Kristiansand
Göteborg
Gotland
Jönköping
BALTIC
Frederikshavn
Ålborg
MER BALTIQUE
Öland
Karlskrona
DU
Århus
DK
KØBENHAVN
Lund
Roskilde
Malmö
Ystad
ORD
Odense
Bornholm
Kiel
Gdańsk
LÜBECK
Rostock
Szczecin
HAMBURG
Groningen
RDAM
NL
Elbe
Bremen
Poznan
Hannover
BERLIN
HET LOO
PL
POTSDAM
Münster
Oder
Kinderdijk
D
Łódź
Eindhoven
Weser
Leipzig
CZĘSTOCHOWA
Weimar
DRESDEN
Wroclaw
ANTWERPEN
KÖLN
KARLOVY VARY
BRUXELLES
PRAHA
Katow
Rhein
Frankfurt
B
Bamberg
Plzeň
CZ
Ostrava
RHEINTAL
Luxembourg
ROTHENBURG
Olomouc
L
Nürnberg
Brno
Heidelberg
Regensburg
NANCY
Stuttgart
Donau
SK
STRASBOURG
Ulm
MÜNCHEN
MELK
WIEN
Bratislava
SCHWARZWALD
BOURGOGNE
DEUTSCHE ALPENSTRAẞE
SALZBURG
Sopron
BASEL
ZÜRICH
SALZKAMMERGUT
BUDAPEST
DIJON
Bodensee
Innsbruck
A
Arlberg
LUZERN
Graz
Balaton
BERN
FL
DAVOS
GENÈVE
CH
INTERLAKEN
DOLOMITI
SLO
Pécs
Ljubljana
LYON
REGIONE DEI LAGHI
Zagreb
VERONA
POSTOJNA
Mt Blanc
Trieste
ALPES
MILANO
VENEZIA
HR
Grenoble
Torino
Po
BIH
Genova
Bologna
RAVENNA
Rhône
AVIGNON
FIRENZE
S. Marino
NICE
PORTOFINO
CANNES
RSM
SPLIT
Trogir
MONACO
PISA
Adriatic
MC
SIENA
Mer
ASSISI
MARSEILLE
Pescara
DUBROVNIK
Adriatique
CORSE
ROMA
Sea
Ajaccio
VATICANO
I
V
BONIFACIO
Bari
NAPOLI
Olbia
NETTUNO
VESUVIO
POMPEÏ
Taranto
SARDEGNA
Mer Tyrrhénienne
Tyrrhenian Sea
Cagliari
Messina
Reggio di Calabria
PALERMO
ETNA
TAORMINA
RRANEAN SEA
AGRIGENTO
SIRACUSA
SICILIA
Constantine
Tunis
VALLETTA
M
Sfax
MER

PETRODVOREC
PUŠKIN
Tallinn
EST
Čudskoje Ozero
Novgorod
Rybinskoje Vodochranilišče
Rybin
Pärnu
Ozero Il'men
Jarosla
Saaremaa
Pskov
RUS
Volga
Tver'
SERGIEV POSAD
LV
Riga
Daugava
Velikijé Luki
MOSKVA
Daugavpils
Klaipéda
LT
Dnepr
Nemunas
Kaunas
Vicebsk
Smolensk
RUS
Vilnius
Kaliningrad
Oka
Minsk
Mahilëŭ
Br'ansk
Hrodna
Or'ol
Białystok
BY
Dnjapro
Homel'
WARSZAWA
Brest
Pinsk
Kursk
Černihiv
Wisła
Lublin
Kyïvs'ke Vodoschovyšče
Sumy
Rivne
Kyïv
KRAKÓW
Žytomyr
Charkiv
UA
L'viv
Vinnycja
Kremenčuc'ke Vodoschovyšče
Poltava
Čerkasy
Dnister
Tatry
Pivdennyj Buh
Dnipropetrovs'k
Košice
Černivci
Kryvyj Rih
Zaporižža
Miskolc
BUCOVINA
MD
CARPATTI
Cluj-Napoca
Iași
Chișinău
Cherson
Odesa
Dnipro
Melitopol'
H
RO
Timișoara
BRAȘOV
SINAIA
Galați
DELTA DUNARII
Sevastopol'
Beograd
Srbija
București
Constanța
Craiova
Dunav
Ruse
BLACK SEA
MER NOIRE
YU
VELIKO TĂRNOVO
Varna
SOFIA
BG
PLOVDIV
Burgas
Podgorica
RILA
Skopje
TR
Tiranë
MK
ISTANBUL
OHRID
AL
Thessaloníki
Bursa
Ankara
METÉORA
Lárissa
Mer Égée
Aegean Sea
KÉRKIRA
GR
DELFÍ
ATHÍNA
Izmir
Kórinthos
AKRÍ SOÚNIO
OLIMBIÁ
EPÍDAVROS
Antalya
KIKLÁDES
RÓDOS
Nicosia
Iráklio
KRÍTI
MÉDITERRANÉE

Major European destinations

For further information see the Practical Information chapter at the end of the guide
Oulu
Gulf of Bothnia
Golfe de Botnie
Tahko
Koli
Åre
FIN
S
Savonlinna
Idre
Lappeenranta
Lillehammer
Mora
Naantali
HELSINKI
G. of Finland
G. de Finlande
Oslo
Hanko
ST. PETERBURG
STOCKHOLM
Tallinn
Vänern
EST
Strömstad
Vättern
SEA
RUS
BALTIQUE
Göteborg
LV
Varberg
Riga
Ronneby
BALTIC
KØBENHAVN
Malmö
LT
MER
Vilnius
MOSKVA
Sopot
RUS
Rügen
Gdańsk
Usedom
Travemünde
Minsk
BY
Poznań
WARSZAWA
BERLIN
PL
Harz
Dresden
Częstochowa
Kyïv
Karlovy Vary
PRAHA
Kraków
Bayreuth
CZ
Zakopane
UA
Mariánské Lázně
Tatry
SK
MÜNCHEN
WIEN
Bratislava
MD
Garmisch-Part.
Salzburg
BUDAPEST
A
Kitzbühel
Odesa
Innsbruck
Badgastein
Balatonfüred
RO
Hévíz
Cortina d'Ampezzo
Velden
H
MER NOIRE
Poiana Braşov
Carpatii
SLO
Verona
VENEZIA
Zagreb
HR
Sinaia
Abano-T.
Beograd
Mamaia
Bucureşti
BIH
Salsomaggiore-T.
Opatija
Olimp-Neptun
Montecatini-T.
Sarajevo
Rimini
YU
Zlatni Pjasăci
FIRENZE
BLACK SEA
Mer Adriatique
Adriatic Sea
Viareggio
BG
Sofia
Slăncěv Brjag
I
Assisi
Peschici
Skopje
ROMA
ISTANBUL
Fiuggi
Mattinata
MK
Tiranë
NAPOLI
Tyrrhenian Sea
AL
Positano
Ischia
Thessaloníki
Mer Tyrrhénienne
Capri
GR
TR
Kérkira
Aegean Sea
Mer Egée
Mer Ionienne
Ionian Sea
Izmir
Palermo
ATHÍNA
Pátra
Sicilia
Taormina
Náfplio
Míkonos
Porto Empedocle
Santoríni
MER MÉDITERRANÉE
Malta
Ródos
Kriti
MEDITERRANEAN SEA

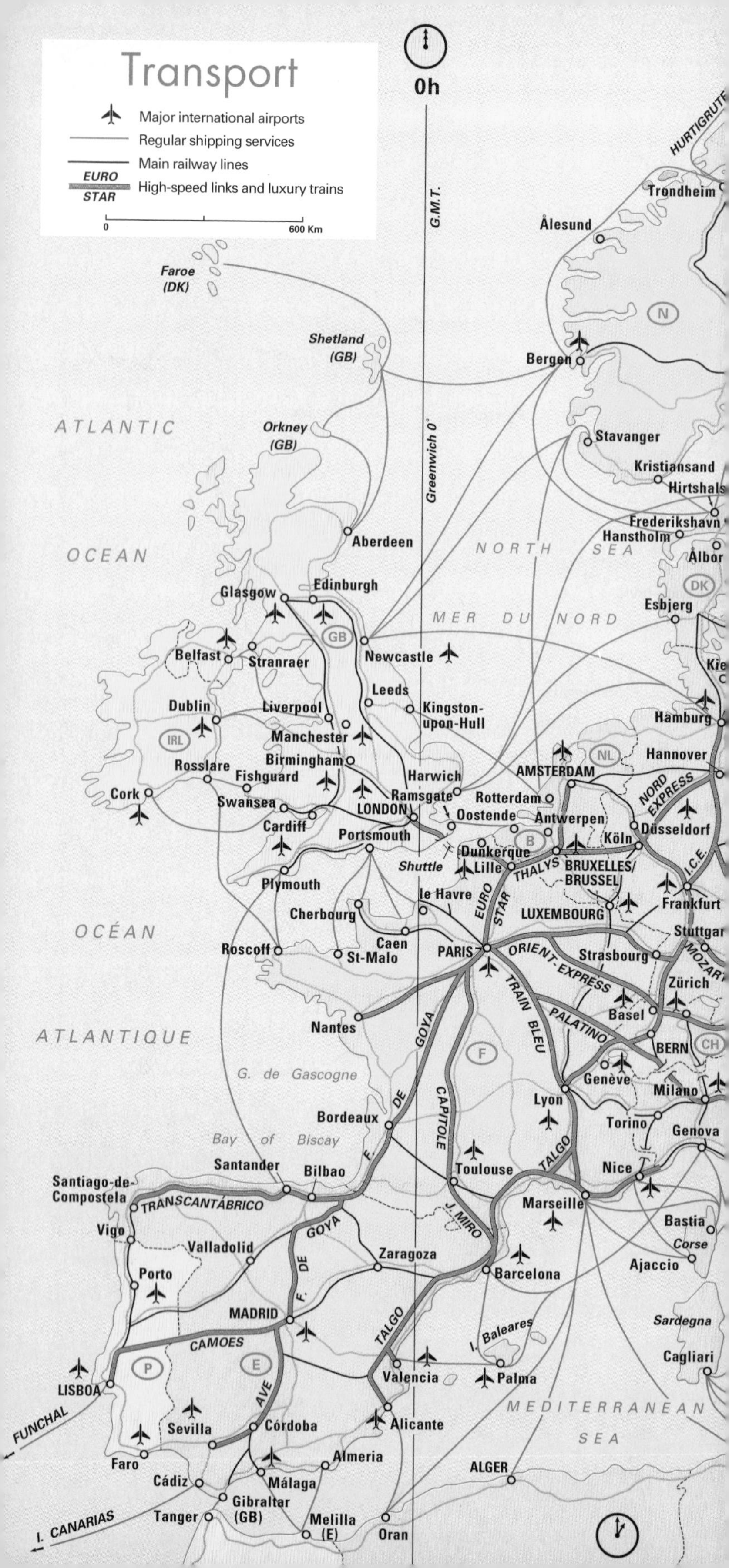
Transport
Major international airports
Regular shipping services
Main railway lines
EURO STAR
High-speed links and luxury trains
0
600 Km
0h
G.M.T.
Greenwich 0°
HURTIGRUTE
Trondheim
Ålesund
Faroe (DK)
N
Shetland (GB)
Bergen
ATLANTIC
Orkney (GB)
Stavanger
Kristiansand
Hirtshals
Frederikshavn
Hanstholm
Aberdeen
NORTH SEA
OCEAN
Ålborg
DK
Edinburgh
Glasgow
Esbjerg
MER DU NORD
GB
Belfast
Stranraer
Newcastle
Kiel
Leeds
Dublin
Liverpool
Kingston-upon-Hull
Hamburg
IRL
Manchester
NL
Hannover
Birmingham
AMSTERDAM
Rosslare
Fishguard
Harwich
NORD EXPRESS
Cork
Swansea
Ramsgate
Rotterdam
Cardiff
LONDON
Ostende
Antwerpen
Düsseldorf
Portsmouth
Dunkerque
B
Köln
Shuttle
Lille
THALYS
BRUXELLES/BRUSSEL
I.C.E.
Plymouth
le Havre
EURO STAR
Frankfurt
Cherbourg
LUXEMBOURG
Stuttgart
OCÉAN
Caen
PARIS
ORIENT-EXPRESS
Roscoff
St-Malo
Strasbourg
MOZART
TRAIN BLEU
Zürich
Basel
Nantes
PALATINO
ATLANTIQUE
GOYA
F
BERN
CH
G. de Gascogne
Genève
Milano
Lyon
CAPITOLE
Torino
DE
Bordeaux
Genova
Bay of Biscay
TALGO
F.
Nice
Santander
Toulouse
Bilbao
Santiago-de-Compostela
TRANSCANTÁBRICO
Marseille
J. MIRO
Bastia
Vigo
Corse
GOYA
Valladolid
Zaragoza
Ajaccio
DE
Porto
Barcelona
F.
MADRID
Sardegna
TALGO
I. Baleares
CAMOES
Cagliari
E
P
Valencia
Palma
LISBOA
AVE
MEDITERRANEAN
FUNCHAL
Sevilla
Córdoba
Alicante
SEA
Almeria
Faro
Málaga
ALGER
Cádiz
Gibraltar (GB)
I. CANARIAS
Tanger
Melilla (E)
Oran

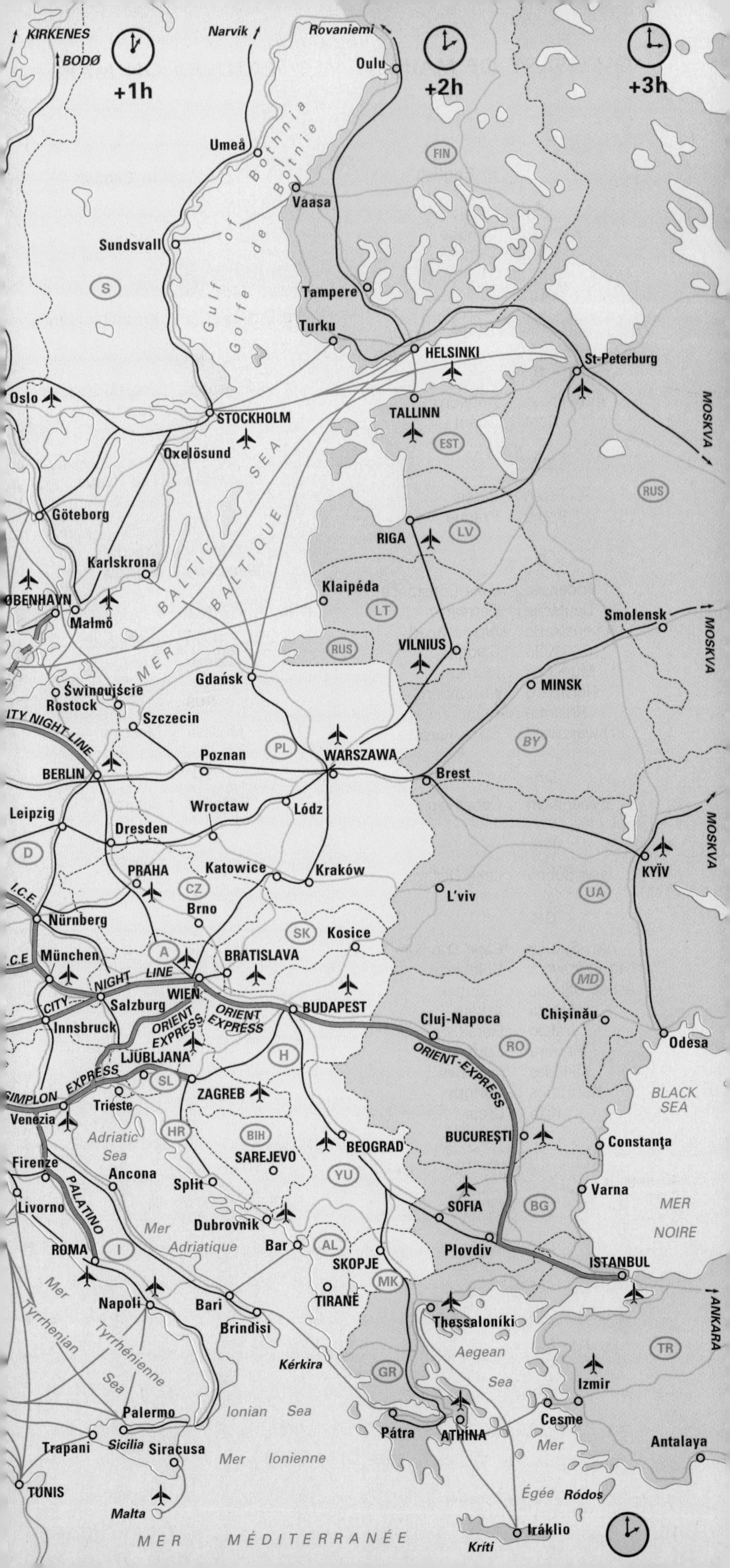
KIRKENES
BODØ
Narvik
Rovaniemi
Oulu
+1h
+2h
+3h
Umeå
Gulf of Bothnia
Golfe de Botnie
Vaasa
FIN
Sundsvall
S
Tampere
Turku
HELSINKI
St-Peterburg
Oslo
STOCKHOLM
TALLINN
EST
MOSKVA
Oxelösund
BALTIC SEA
MER BALTIQUE
RUS
Göteborg
RIGA
LV
Karlskrona
Klaipéda
LT
KØBENHAVN
Malmö
Smolensk
MOSKVA
RUS
VILNIUS
Gdańsk
MINSK
Świnoujście
Rostock
Szczecin
CITY NIGHT LINE
PL
BY
Poznan
WARSZAWA
BERLIN
Brest
Leipzig
Wroctaw
Lódz
MOSKVA
Dresden
D
KYÏV
PRAHA
Katowice
Kraków
CZ
UA
L'viv
I.C.E.
Nürnberg
Brno
SK
Kosice
I.C.E
München
A
BRATISLAVA
NIGHT
LINE
MD
CITY
Salzburg
WIEN
BUDAPEST
Cluj-Napoca
Chişinău
Innsbruck
ORIENT EXPRESS
ORIENT EXPRESS
Odesa
LJUBLJANA
H
RO
ORIENT-EXPRESS
SIMPLON EXPRESS
SL
ZAGREB
BLACK SEA
Trieste
Venezia
HR
BIH
BUCUREŞTI
Constanţa
Adriatic Sea
BEOGRAD
SAREJEVO
Firenze
YU
Ancona
Split
Varna
Livorno
SOFIA
PALATINO
MER NOIRE
Mer Adriatique
Dubrovnik
BG
ROMA
I
Bar
AL
Plovdiv
SKOPJE
ISTANBUL
MK
TIRANË
ANKARA
Napoli
Bari
Thessaloníki
Brindisi
Tyrrhenian Sea
Mer Tyrrhénienne
Aegean Sea
TR
Kérkira
GR
Izmir
Palermo
Ionian Sea
Cesme
Pátra
ATHÍNA
Trapani
Sicilia
Siracusa
Mer Ionienne
Mer Égée
Antalaya
TUNIS
Ródos
Malta
MER MÉDITERRANÉE
Iráklio
Kríti

GLOSSARY OF MAIN NAMES FEATURED ON MAPS

	In English
A	
Donau	Danube
Wien	Vienna
AL	
Tiranë	Tirana
B	
Antwerpen	Antwerp
Gent	Ghent
CZ	
Plzeň	Pilsen
Praha	Prague
D	
Bodensee	Lake Constance
Deutsche	German
Alpenstraße	Alpine Road
Köln	Cologne
München	Munich
Nürnberg	Nuremberg
Rheintal	Rhine Valley
Schwarzwald	Black Forest
DK	
København	Copenhagen
FIN	
Järvi Suomi	Lake District
GR	
Akrí Soúnio	Cape Sounion
Arhéa Epídavros	Epidauros
Arhéa Olimbía	Olympia
Athína	Athens
Iráklio	Heraklion
Kérkira	Corfu
Kiklådes	Cyclades
Kórinthos	Corinth
Kríti	Crete

	In English
H	
Duna	Danube
IS	
Vestmannaeyjar	Westman Islands
N	
Hurtigruten	Coastal steamer
Nordkapp	North Cape
NL	
Den Haag	The Hague
PL	
Kraków	Cracow
Warszawa	Warsaw
RO	
Bucuresti	Bucharest
Dunav	Danube
RUS	
Moskva	Moscow
YU	
Beograd	Belgrade

THE EURO

On 1 January 1999, eleven European Union countries (Austria, Belgium, Finland, France, Germany, Ireland, Italy, the Grand Duchy of Luxembourg, the Netherlands, Portugal and Spain) adopted the Euro as their single currency and prices are now shown in the national currencies and in Euros in these countries.

1 Euro	Austria	13,7603	ATS
1 Euro	Belgium	40,3399	BEF
1 Euro	France	6,55957	FRF
1 Euro	Germany	1,95583	DEM
1 Euro	Ireland	0,787564	IEP
1 Euro	Italy	1936,27	ITL
1 Euro	Luxembourg	40,3399	BEF
1 Euro	Finland	5,94573	FIM
1 Euro	The Nederlands	2,20371	ATS
1 Euro	Portugal	200,482	PTE
1 Euro	Spain	166,386	PTE

On 1 January 2002, coins and notes in Euros will be introduced. These will replace the national currencies in the short term and the latter will gradually be withdrawn from circulation. Each coin and note will have one side identifying its country of origin, while the other will be common to the European Union. The Euro will be divided into 100 cents.

Coins: 1, 2, 5, 10, 20 and 50 cents; 1 and 2 Euros.

Notes: 5, 10, 20, 50, 100, 200 and 500 Euros.

Messerschmidt/VLOO

Introducing Europe

Facts about Europe

NATURAL BOUNDARIES

In geographic terms, Europe appears as a peninsula of the Asian continent. It is situated in the Northern Hemisphere between latitudes 35° and 71° N, covering a surface area of 10 million km²/3.86 million sq mi. It stretches 4000km/2480mi from north to south and 5500km/3410mi from east to west. All in all, Europe accounts for only 8% of the Earth's land.
The boundary between Asia and Europe traditionally runs along the Ural Mountains. But that frontier is arbitrary and inaccurate. In the north, Europe extends to the junction between the Arctic and North Atlantic Oceans including the Azores and Iceland. Europe's southern edge is easier to define even though the continental land mass is broken up into islands and archipelagos across the Mediterranean Sea.
Although Europe is the globe's smallest continent, its physical geography is the most varied. Diverse natural environments create Europe's political and territorial complexity. More than 40 countries compose the continent. Continuous tensions arise from the instability of international frontiers and the demands of minority groups. But **balkanisation** is counterbalanced by a process of economic unification within the **European Union**. The recent collapse of the Eastern Bloc's communist system and the disappearance of the Iron Curtain give a new impetus to integration, reinvigorating the long sought-after concept of an economically and politically unified Europe extending from the Atlantic to the Urals.
Europe's land area is largely habitable. It contains abundant natural resources and numerous concentrations of wealth production. Densely populated and developed, the European continent has exerted a crucial influence on global history. Patterns of political, economic, social and legislative organisation first established within Europe are now adopted throughout the world. In addition, a number of widely spoken languages have their origins in Europe, providing an indispensable basis for world wide communication.

Gontscharoff

Irancy and its vineyards, France

A MOSAIC OF VARIED TOPOGRAPHY

Europe's moderate average altitude, 340m/1115ft, offers little hint of the varied and contrasted nature of its land, the result of a long and complex geological history.

Northwest Europe's Caledonian belt – Rocks more than 1 billion years old formed a **shield** on Europe's northwestern fringe from Ireland to Lapland. About 400 million years ago, the Caledonian massifs were uplifted during the major folding of mid-Paleozoic times. Worn down by repeated erosion, these massifs are now relatively gentle. In certain areas such as the Scottish Highlands and the Scandinavia mountains, the Caledonian belt was rejuvenated at the end of the Tertiary Era, producing some steeper inclines.

Morteratsch Glacier, Switzerland

Glaciers cut wide and deep U-shaped valleys before being flooded by the sea to form majestic **fjords**. **Moraines** were deposited around the edges of the vast inland ice cap. **Inlandsis** occupied the Scandinavian Peninsula, resulting in astounding landscapes where water and land intermingle.

In the centre, Hercynian Europe – Ancient mountains mark Western and Central Europe from Wales to Russia. The Hercynian folding took place from about 320 million years ago at the end of the Paleozoic Era. These mountains formed areas of jagged relief. **Peneplanation** then smoothed out the land surface. The Hercynian massifs trace Europe's backbone. Their broad rounded summits of medium altitude rarely exceed 1 500m/4 920ft, forming a vast W-shaped belt that starts in the British Isles and continues through France's Massif Central and Spain's Castilian Meseta. They also produced Germany's Rhenish Massif and the Czech Republic's Bohemian hills. Eventually, these Hercynian massifs join the Urals in Russia.
During the Tertiary Era, repercussions from Alpine folding produced fractures or **rift valleys**. The Rhine Graben between the Vosges and the Black Forest resulted. These upheavals led to abundant volcanic activity, as recorded in the now-extinct volcanoes of the French Massif Central.
At the same time, **sedimentary basins** were created in the London and Paris basins. This terrain displays a succession of plains, hills and low plateaux.

Towards the east, a continent of vast plains – Vast plains characterise the European landscape. This North European Plain extends from Flanders to the Urals and covers more than half of the continent. It attains its maximum width in Russia and Ukraine where it stretches 1 500km/930mi from north to south. The plain rarely rises more than 200m/656ft above sea level; ice sheet covered large areas about 18 000 years ago leaving behind this flat topography scattered with moraine hills and strings of lakes. To the north, marshland, coastal lagoons and **beach ridges** border the Baltic and North Seas. The rivers Rhine, Elbe, Oder and Vistula end here. Through the construction of **polders**, lowland inhabitants have struggled against the instability of their coastline and regained some territory from the sea.
Farther south, violent Ice Age winds led to the accumulation of fine-grained sand called **loess**. This ensures high fertility in certain regions such as the Borde Plain near Hanover in Germany and the Ukrainian Plain.

In the south, a continent of high mountain ranges – Young fold mountains run from the Iberian Peninsula to Georgia. The intensity of the relief is due to a major upheaval of the Earth's crust during the Tertiary Era beginning about 65 million years ago when the Eurasian and African **tectonic plates** collided. The Sierra Nevada, Pyrenees, Alps, Apeninnes, Carpathians, as well as the Balkan and Caucasus mountains all resulted from this paroxysm; their summits often rise more than 3 000m/9 848ft, forming sharp peaks covered in permanent snow and residual **glaciers**. Mont Blanc in the Western Alps is Europe's highest mountain at 4 807m/15 767ft. Mount Elbruz, 5 633m/18 476ft, is the highest peak of the Caucasus, lying at the limits of Eastern Europe.

EUROPEAN LANDSCAPES

North Cape
Varanger Fjord
Barents Sea
Finnmark
Mourmansk
Narvik
L. Inari
Kola
Peninsula
2411
LAPLAND
White Sea
Oulu
Archangelsk
Norrland
Gulf of Bothnia
KARELIA
Dvina
Finnish
Lakeland
L. Onega
Lake
Ladoga
Svealand
Åland
Helsinki
Gulf of Finland
St Petersburg
Mälaren
Stockholm
Tallinn
Rybinsk Reservoir
L. Peipous
Gotland
BALTIC
L. Ilmen
Gorky Reservoir
Volga
CENTRAL RUSSIAN PLAIN
Riga
Öland
Moscow
BALTIC SEA
REPUBLICS
Bornholm
Vilnius
Niemen
Minsk
Masuria
Pomerania
EUROPEAN PLAIN
Dniepr
Warsaw
Vistula
Don
Oder
Kiev
Sudeten
Silesia
UKRAINE
Prague
Bohemia
Tatras 2655
Dniestr
Vienna
CARPATHIANS
Bukovina
Rostov
Budapest
L. Balaton
Moldavia
Odessa
Drava
Plain
Hungarian
Sea of Azov
Transylvania
Crimean
Peninsula
Zagreb
Vojvodine
Iron
Gate
Bucharest
Sava
Belgrade
Walachia
Sarajevo
Dalmatia
Danube
BLACK SEA
Adriatic Sea
BALKANS
Sofia
2914
Abruzzi
Montenegro
Rhodope
Istanbul
Bosphorus
Albania
Pontic Mountains
Macedonia
Apulia
Ankara
Vesuvius
2917
Olympus
Aegean Sea
ANATOLIAN PLATEAU
Stromboli
Corfu
Thessalonia
3916
Calabria
Ionian
Sea
Izmir
Taurus
Athens
Dodecanese
Etna
3340
Straits of Messina
Peloponnese
Cyclades
Sicily
Malta
Rhodes
Crete
Cyprus
NEAN SEA

The Alpine chain enjoys majestic features including pyramidal peaks, such as the Matterhorn, **cirques**, high-altitude lakes and deep eroded **U-shaped valleys**. Communications are facilitated by numerous passes providing links between the glacial valleys.
Narrow coastal plains are often found at the foot of mountain ranges. However, some basins such as the Po Basin and Hungarian Plain are wide, and corridors surround rivers such as the Rhône and Danube.

Volcanic zones – These zones exhibit **volcanic activity**. Smouldering deposits of ash are found along the Mid-Atlantic ridge in the Azores, and Iceland, as well as in the extreme south, in Southern Italy and Greece. Catastrophic **earthquakes** periodically strike these southern countries where the Earth's crust remains unstable. Africa is advancing beneath the European land plate at a rate of 0.7cm/.27 in per year, a high speed compared with normal geological processes.

A TEMPERATE CLIMATE

Most of Europe enjoys a temperate climate. However, the extreme north of Scandinavia and Russia reside in a **sub-polar** region deprived of a true summer season, except for the **midnight sun** during the solstice period. Europe's overall advantageous position in latitude allows it to avoid extremes in weather.
Cold polar **air masses** from the north come up against warm tropical air masses from the south. These air masses meet along the **polar front**, giving rise to **depressions** responsible for weather instabilities across Western Europe. Europe's east-west mountainous relief favours the passage of westerly winds and enables these depressions to penetrate into the continental interior. The **North Atlantic Drift**, a northerly extension of the Gulf Stream, carries tropical waters, protecting Europe from extreme North American or Asian cold or hot weather.
Meteorological influences and geographical setting distinguish four main Europe climates.

West Maritime – Europe's Atlantic is subject to **western ocean airs**. Frequent **light rain** or showers throughout the year characterise its cool and humid **maritime climate**. The winters are not severe, and the summers relatively cool. **Mist** and **fog** are common. Winds intensify **storms** in winter. Frost and snow are rare except farther north in Scandinavia.

Transitional or Semi-Continental – Towards the interior, annual temperatures increase and precipitation decreases. This **transition** between maritime and continental climates occurs between the Paris Basin and the River Oder.

F. Jourdan/EXPLORER

Kolovesi National Park, Finland

C. Vaisse/HOA QUI

West coast of Majorca, Spain

Continental climates in the east – These climates predominate in areas to the east of the River Oder. Harsh weather takes strong seasonal contrasts. The **Siberian anti-cyclone** causes a long winter. During this stable period of **cold dry** weather, **snow** covers the ground, **frost** occurs everywhere and **ice jams** block rivers and streams. In spring, the **ice breaks up** and causes sudden flooding hindering transport. A brief hot summer is broken by thunder showers.

In the south, Mediterranean climates – It concerns the Mediterranean and the Black Sea coasts. These regions are sheltered from southward flowing air by the surrounding mountains. Tropical air and warm seas add to the temperate influences. Consequently, mild winters and **hot, very dry** summers predominate. Large amounts of **sunshine** and a remarkable **clarity of the light** exist, particularly when strong winds blow from inland. Precipitation is concentrated in spring and autumn. **Heavy showers** often transform rivers and streams into **destructive torrents**.

A DIVERSITY OF NATURAL ENVIRONMENTS

From the icy wastes of the far north to the arid hills of Spain, Europe displays a varied palette of natural environments. More than in any other part of the world, human habitation has modified original landscapes. During the past few decades, ecological problems have increased. Environmental catastrophes such as the 1986 Chernobyl disaster in Ukraine do not represent a direct threat to continental ecosystems. However, environmental deterioration has caused the majority of European countries to establish **natural reserves** for protecting flora and fauna. Examples include Gran Paradiso in Italy, Coto Doñana in Spain, Puszcza Biazowieska in Poland and the Danube delta in Romania.

In the west – Near the Atlantic seaboard in the west, moist and mild climatic conditions favour vegetation growth throughout the year. **Deciduous forests** composed of oak and beech have managed to escape massive land clearance. **Moorland** has developed where excess humidity or wind strength prevents the growth of trees. **Peat bogs** thrive in moist ground.

In the east – Away from maritime influence in the east, the vegetation is divided into clear **zones**. A narrow belt of Arctic **tundra** lies within the sub-polar far north. It consists of short-cropped moss and lichen grazed by reindeer. The ground is frozen permanently to a maximum depth of 400m/1 312ft.
Further south, the **taiga** contains a vast forest of conifers and birch established on acid **podzol** soil. The land is unsuitable for agriculture. Deer run wild. However, the number of large animals that traditionally inhabit these forests is dwindling.
A **deciduous forest** belt extends over most of the North European Plain. It is made up of sessile or oak, hornbeam, and is more or less mixed with conifers. Being mostly cleared, this forest has given way to cultivated land.
Accumulations of loess cover a zone on the southern borders of the North European Plain. The excellent soil is called **chernozem**. These soils produce **grassland** composed of graminaceous and low bulb plants. Again, the original vegetation has been almost completely replaced by cultivated land or pasture.

In the south – Erosion has weakened the soil on slopes around the Mediterranean. The **terra rossa** is a type of red clay soil.
Mediterranean-type vegetation, with its leaves and elongated roots, releases a scented odour and exhibits a wealth of imaginative adaptations to the summer drought. These flora include the evergreen forest, mainly composed of pines, holm-oak, cork-oak and olive trees. Repeated land clearance, overgrazing and forest fires, have caused devastation. Much of the evergreen forest has given way to sparse scrub on limy soils (**garrigue**) or dense bushy vegetation on acid soils (**maquis**). Snakes, lizards and tortoises like this type of environment, whereas the deltas and lagoons of coastal areas attract vast numbers of migrating birds.

At high altitude – Mountain vegetation resists the cold and the snow. Up to about 2500m/8200ft, a **succession** of beech, firs, spruce, larch and silver pine finally give way to grass. Higher still, broken rocks and persistent snow dominate the landscape. The upper limit of vegetation is higher on the sunny southern slopes than on the northern shaded slopes.

AN ASSORTMENT OF DIFFERENT POPULATIONS

High population concentration – In the final decade of the century, Europe is home to 700 million inhabitants. The average population density is 67 per km^2/176 per sq mi, but it is spread unevenly. The highest densities, with more than 200 per km^2/526 per sq mi, run in a diagonal belt from England to the Po Valley in Italy. This arc has the Rhine Valley as its backbone and coincides with a series of rich agricultural plains and a cluster of major urban and industrial regions. The embryonic **megalopolis** links London, Rotterdam, Brussels, Paris, Frankfurt, Munich, and Milan. Other concentrations of population occur along the coast and around some isolated urban centres such as Barcelona, Athens, Rome, Berlin, Vienna, Moscow, and St-Petersburg.
In contrast, some mountainous regions have a severe climate, whereas certain rural areas are poorly provided with modern means of communication. Such sparsely populated areas are found in the interior of the Iberian Peninsula, the Scottish Highlands and in Northern Scandinavia.

The most urbanised continent – Three out of four Europeans live in cities. More than 30 urban agglomerations have a population exceeding one million. **Urbanisation** reaches a record 97% intensity in Belgium. The **rural-urban migration** continues to depopulate the countryside. Rural communities remain more populous than city dwellers in only a few cases such as Albania and ex-Yugoslavia.
City centres are being restored and embellished. Their architectural heritage represents an inestimable value. **Suburbs** continue to expand at the expense of cultivated land. Unchecked development often raises serious questions about living conditions. A desire to escape from urban congestion has fuelled the phenomenon of **re-urbanisation** in countryside near major cities.

A senior citizen boom – This phenomenon is occurring as Europe's population **growth** slows. Population growth has even become negative in Germany, Italy and the Netherlands. The **birth rate** has dropped sharply following the rise in the cost of living, increased urbanisation, and the spread of contraception. At present, fewer than two children are born per woman. Under these conditions, the proportion of Europeans in the world population – one in eight in 1900 – has undergone a spectacular decline. It will only be one in 125 by the year 2000!
At the same time, improved standards of living and progress in medicine have extended life expectancy beyond 70 years.
The marked aging of the European population will produce consequences beyond the need to care for increasing numbers of retirees.

A service boom and unemployment scourge – Europe's economic growth depends more and more on services rather than agriculture and manufacturing. A post-industrial society is emerging. Apart from some local exceptions, the **service sector** employs more than half of the working population. It represents the only economic activity capable of sustaining a **positive balance of employment**.
Since the beginning of the 1970s, a series of recessions and economic changes has caused a rise in unemployment. On average, 10% of Europeans are without work. In Eastern Europe, unemployment made its official appearance along with the market economy. It now is just as virulent as in the rest of Europe. Even in countries enjoying good economic growth, companies searching for profits are undergoing massive lay-offs.

A multilingual and multidenominational continent – Successive invasions and migrations have provided Europe with remarkable ethnic and linguistic diversity. The **Indo-European** peoples established the common roots of most European languages, subdivided into several branches: Celtic, Germanic (English, German, and Dutch.), Latin or Romance (Italian, French, and Spanish), Slavonic, Baltic, Greek and Albanian. Some languages, including Finnish, Hungarian and Estonian, belong to the **Finno-Ugric** subfamily. Still others, such as Basque, resist all classification.
In certain countries such as Switzerland, Belgium and Finland, several languages coexist officially, whereas in many other countries various non-official languages or dialects are common.

PER CAPITA INCOME IN SOME COUNTRIES IN 1995

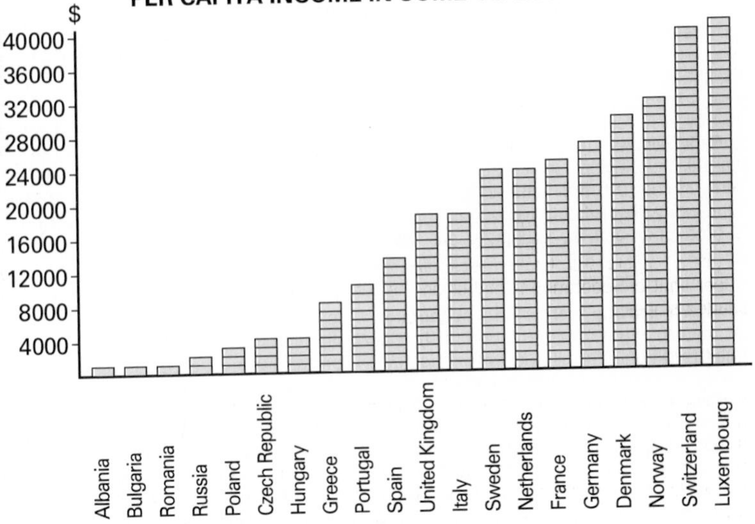

Each culture is characterised by its religious choice. The vast majority of Europeans are Christians, with the Protestant Church predominant in the Germanic North, the Roman Catholic Church in the Latin South and the Orthodox Church in the Slavic East. Several groups fall outside this general pattern: Poles are Catholic Slavs, whereas the Latin Romanians belong to the Orthodox Church. Judaism is widely diffused throughout Europe. Islam is practised notably in Bosnia, Albania and Turkey.

States, nationalities and minorities – National boundaries within Europe do not always coincide with the frontiers between states. **Minorities** remain distinguished from the rest of the population by their language, history or traditional customs. Liberated minorities in post-communist Eastern Europe are now demanding some level of autonomy or independence. The Slovak nationalist movement recently obtained a velvet divorce separating them from the Czech Republic. For similar reasons, deep unrest shakes the ex-member states of the Soviet Union, while civil war engulfs the former Yugoslavia. Such tensions threaten the entire continent's stability.
Affluent Western European countries have attracted a wave of **immigrants**, creating new minorities and social tensions. Despite the presence of numerous official border controls, the movement of migrant workers has proved difficult to stem. The collapse of communism provides new impetus to this immigration.

ECONOMIC CHANGES

Although on the whole prosperous, Europe nevertheless exhibits strong disparities in living standards. Switzerland and Albania represent the two extremes in wealth; the difference in average income per inhabitant ranges from one to 30. The rich countries are mostly located in the northwest, whereas the less well off are found notably in the south and southeast.

Agriculture is carried out over most of the continent. Since the end of the Second World War, agriculture has undergone profound modernisation, creating the tractor revolution. Western Europe, apart from a few oil-rich states bordering the North Sea, is dependent on energy imports, primarily **hydrocarbon fuels**. This handicap weighs on national economies. **Coal** deposits which previously ensured the economic wealth of Germany and the United Kingdom are now exhausted and play only a minor role. On the contrary, Eastern Europe possesses immense resources, albeit poorly developed. Electricity generated from **nuclear power** can only partially fill Europe's energy shortage. The powerful European **industrial base** produces a wide range of specialised products and services: chemicals, automotive engineering, railway equipment, machine tools, electronic equipment, aerospace industries, telecommunications, and biotechnology. More and more industrial plants are being located close to ports so they can import raw materials and semi-manufactured goods and then export their finished articles. As in the US and the Far East, research and development occupies an increasingly important place. Europe plays a leading role in **international commerce**. It is served by the world's most comprehensive **transport and communications network**. Every day, large swarms of businessmen pass through the airports of London, Paris and Frankfurt. Competition and the trend towards larger and larger ships fuel growing activity at the ports of London, Hamburg, Antwerp and, above all, Rotterdam, the busiest port in the world. Communication networks are becoming international. Witness the Channel Tunnel and the initial steps along the information highway. **Trans-border economic zones** are being established such as the Regio Basilensis around Basel in Switzerland.

Finally, Europe is the world's most important **tourist** destination, thanks to the richness of its artistic, historical and natural heritage.

Europe's developed northwest – Here large modern farms dominate agriculture. They achieve high yields through intensive animal grazing and farming of cereals, sugar beet, oil-bearing and vegetables grown under glass. These farmers are so successful that they constantly produce surpluses.
Northwest Europe's industrial fabric is complex and varied. In a number of regions known as **Black Countries**, the crisis in heavy industry and textiles comes on top of problems in coal mining. Regions such as Cumbria and Lancashire in England have become wastelands. In contrast, restructuring has been successfully carried out in regions such as the Ruhr Valley. **New industrial regions** have grown up around the North Sea, linked to offshore oil production and the Groningen gas field in the Netherlands. The **Rhine Valley** connects the heart of Europe with the rest of the world. A new link with the River Danube reinforces the Rhine's status as the most economically valuable river on the face of the Earth.

Southern Europe's emerging economies – Countries bordering the Mediterranean are undergoing a transformation of their agriculture along with an industrial take-off. Small traditional farms and **latifundia** stand in contrast with modern estates. Irrigated **huertas** grow high-yielding **specialised crops** such as fruit, vegetables and rice. Vineyards produce both mass market and high-quality wines.
Industry in Southern Europe is handicapped by the paucity of mineral resources, the weakness of technical innovation, and the over-dependence on foreign capital. Still, after a long delay and persistent inertia in Portugal and Greece, development is getting under way. Italy and Spain are catching up with their northern neighbours. Major companies in high-wage economy countries have **moved production** towards countries with weaker currencies and low labour costs.
The Mediterranean coast profits as Europe's region of sun and sea. It has become one of the world's leading **tourist destinations**. Spain and Italy welcome the highest numbers of tourists. Millions of visitors are attracted to the **seaside**.

Eastern Europe's uncertain future – After decades of Soviet domination and **socialist central planning**, the countries of Eastern Europe are reforming their political institutions and disorganised economies. The transformation to a **market economy**

requires an immense financial outlay, as well as a change from quantity to quality in production. Both shock therapy in the ex-German Democratic Republic and Poland and the more gradual approach such as in the Czech Republic and Hungary have caused a drop in industrial production and the rise of unemployment and inflation. Living standards have plunged and social inequality widened.
Enormous farms derived from collectivisation are being divided up. Rural areas are impoverished. The shortage of modern infrastructure makes for mediocre crop yields. Russian oil, gas and iron ore, together with coal from Poland, represent a colossal wealth of energy and minerals. However, these resources have been devastated by heavy industry hungry for **raw materials**. Western firms are helping build a new industrial fabric.

THE EUROPEAN UNION – THE WAY FORWARD?

The European Community was founded in 1957 as a **common market**. The original goal was economic, but the long term aim was political union. This community is now known as the **European Union**. It comprises most of Western Europe *(see economic map)*. The community has grown in successive stages. Its economy is currently the **world's second largest**. A high priority has been placed on integrating nuclear energy (Euratom), fisheries and especially agriculture. Industry does not yet come under a common policy, but individual agreements envisage cooperation between European companies.
The European Union is above all the world's **most important trading power**. It accounts for more than half the volume of international commerce. The abolition of internal frontiers in 1993 and the creation of a large **single market** stimulated trade. A **common currency**, the Euro, will come into existence in 2002 in 11 European Union countries (Germany, Austria, Belgium, Spain, Finland, France, Ireland, Italy, Luxembourg, the Netherlands and Portugal) replacing the national currencies. This new common currency should boost trade. The creation of a **European economic area**, bringing together the European Union countries and the dwindling number of members of the European Free Trade Association, will finally mark a new stage in Europe's organisation.
The European Union remains fragile. Nonetheless, it expresses hope for the future of the Old World divided by disparities in development and national rivalries. For this reason, most European countries are striving to become part of the Union.

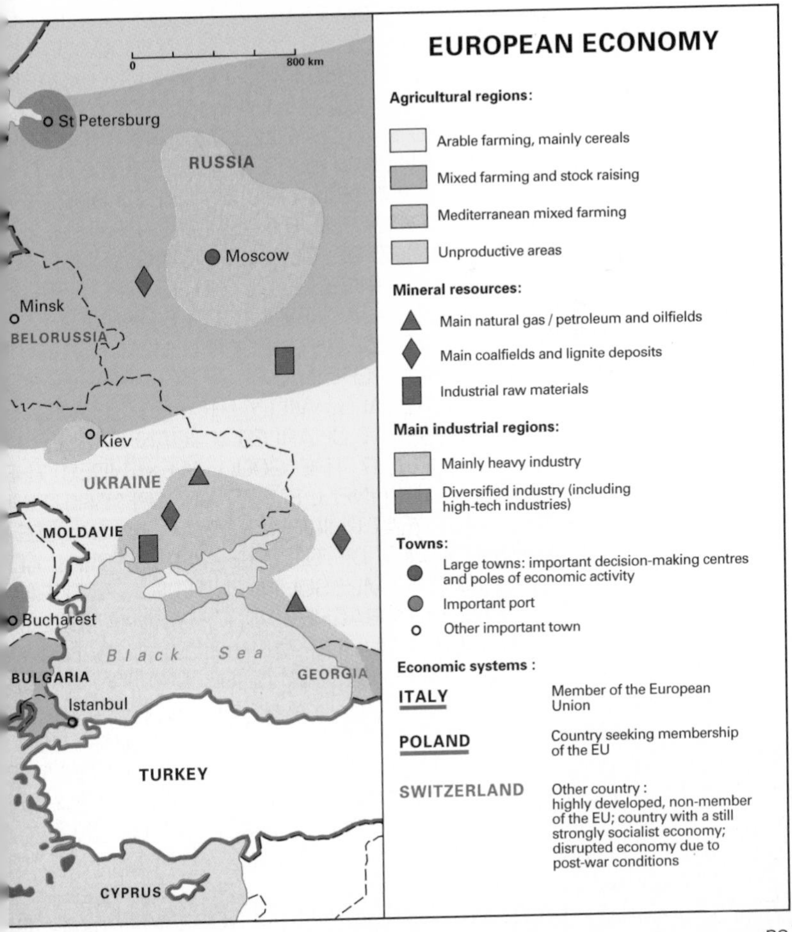

LIC LEOPOLD I QUEEN VICTORIA GARIBALDI WILLY BRANDT CLOVIS J
BETH I CHARLEMAGNE PETER THE GREAT CHARLES V JUAN CARLOS
BISMARCK HENRI VIII HADRIAN PHILIP THE GOOD ALEXANDER TH
THERESA OF HABSBURG DANIEL O'CONNELL FRANZ JOSEPH BREZHN
CROMWELL TITO CATHERINE THE GREAT PHILIP II GENERAL DE GAULLE
RICK BARBAROSSA LENIN WILLIAM II OF ORANGE NAPOLEON I A
LEON III KHRUSHCHEV WILLIAM I MUSSOLINI HITLER FREDERIC
NZOLLERN MARGARET THATCHER GORBACHEV VICTOR EMMANUEL I
PERICLES WILLIAM THE CONQUEROR JULIUS CAESAR LOUIS XIV LECH
CIS I OTTO I METTERNICH CHURCHILL FERDINAND OF ARAGON ISABE
LIC LEOPOLD I QUEEN VICTORIA GARIBALDI WILLY BRANDT CLOVIS J
ETH I CHARLEMAGNE PETER THE GREAT CHARLES V JUAN CARLOS
BISMARCK HENRI VIII HADRIAN PHILIP THE GOOD ALEXANDER TH
THERESA OF HABSBURG DANIEL O'CONNELL FRANZ JOSEPH BREZHN
CROMWELL TITO CATHERINE THE GREAT PHILIP II GENERAL DE GAULLE
RICK BARBAROSSA LENIN WILLIAM II OF ORANGE NAPOLEON I AD
EON III KHRUSHCHEV WILLIAM I MUSSOLINI HITLER FREDERIC
NZOLLERN MARGARET THATCHER GORBACHEV VICTOR EMMANUEL II
PERICLES WILLIAM THE CONQUEROR JULIUS CAESAR LOUIS XIV LECH
IS I OTTO I METTERNICH CHURCHILL FERDINAND OF ARAGON ISABE
LIC LEOPOLD I QUEEN VICTORIA GARIBALDI WILLY BRANDT CLOVIS JU
ETH I CHARLEMAGNE PETER THE GREAT CHARLES V JUAN CARLOS I
BISMARCK HENRI VIII HADRIAN PHILIP THE GOOD ALEXANDER TH
THERESA OF HABSBURG DANIEL O'CONNELL FRANZ JOSEPH BREZHN
CROMWELL TITO CATHERINE THE GREAT PHILIP II GENERAL DE GAULLE
RICK BARBAROSSA LENIN WILLIAM II OF ORANGE NAPOLEON I AD
EON III KHRUSHCHEV WILLIAM I MUSSOLINI HITLER FREDERIC
NZOLLERN MARGARET THATCHER GORBACHEV VICTOR EMMANUEL II
PERICLES WILLIAM THE CONQUEROR JULIUS CAESAR LOUIS XIV LECH
S I OTTO I METTERNICH CHURCHILL FERDINAND OF ARAGON ISABE
LIC LEOPOLD I QUEEN VICTORIA GARIBALDI WILLY BRANDT CLOVIS JU
ETH I CHARLEMAGNE PETER THE GREAT CHARLES V JUAN CARLOS I
BISMARCK HENRI VIII HADRIAN PHILIP THE GOOD ALEXANDER THE
THERESA OF HABSBURG DANIEL O'CONNELL FRANZ JOSEPH BREZHN
CROMWELL TITO CATHERINE THE GREAT PHILIP II GENERAL DE GAULLE
RICK BARBAROSSA LENIN WILLIAM II OF ORANGE NAPOLEON I AD
EON III KHRUSHCHEV WILLIAM I MUSSOLINI HITLER FREDERICK
NZOLLERN MARGARET THATCHER GORBACHEV VICTOR EMMANUEL II
PERICLES WILLIAM THE CONQUEROR JULIUS CAESAR LOUIS XIV LECH
S I OTTO I METTERNICH CHURCHILL FERDINAND OF ARAGON ISABE
LIC LEOPOLD I QUEEN VICTORIA GARIBALDI WILLY BRANDT CLOVIS JU
ETH I CHARLEMAGNE PETER THE GREAT CHARLES V JUAN CARLOS I
BISMARCK HENRI VIII HADRIAN PHILIP THE GOOD ALEXANDER THE
THERESA OF HABSBURG DANIEL O'CONNELL FRANZ JOSEPH BREZHNE
CROMWELL TITO CATHERINE THE GREAT PHILIP II GENERAL DE GAULLE
ICK BARBAROSSA LENIN WILLIAM II OF ORANGE NAPOLEON I AD
ON III KHRUSHCHEV WILLIAM I MUSSOLINI HITLER FREDERICK
ZOLLERN MARGARET THATCHER GORBACHEV VICTOR EMMANUEL II
PERICLES WILLIAM THE CONQUEROR JULIUS CAESAR LOUIS XIV LECH
S I OTTO I METTERNICH CHURCHILL FERDINAND OF ARAGON ISABEL
IC LEOPOLD I QUEEN VICTORIA GARIBALDI WILLY BRANDT CLOVIS JU
TH I CHARLEMAGNE PETER THE GREAT CHARLES V JUAN CARLOS I
BISMARCK HENRI VIII HADRIAN PHILIP THE GOOD ALEXANDER THE
THERESA OF HABSBURG DANIEL O'CONNELL FRANZ JOSEPH BREZHNE
ROMWELL TITO CATHERINE THE GREAT PHILIP II GENERAL DE GAULLE
CK BARBAROSSA LENIN WILLIAM II OF ORANGE NAPOLEON I AD
ON III KHRUSHCHEV WILLIAM I MUSSOLINI HITLER FREDERICK
ZOLLERN MARGARET THATCHER GORBACHEV VICTOR EMMANUEL II
PERICLES WILLIAM THE CONQUEROR JULIUS CAESAR LOUIS XIV LECH

THE EUROPEAN UNION

The Treaty of Maastricht, which was signed on 7 February 1992 and took effect on 1 November 1993, set up the European Union. Since 1 January 1995, the EU has been composed of 15 Member States: Austria, Belgium, Denmark, Finland, France, Germany, Great Britain, Greece, Republic of Ireland, Italy, Grand Duchy of Luxembourg, the Netherlands, Portugal, Spain and Sweden. The EU is required to seek political cooperation on a European scale and cooperation in the fields of justice and the internal affairs of individual States.

The flag is azure blue with 12 gold stars (the number is invariable and symbolises perfection and plenitude) set in a circle. It was selected in 1955.

The European anthem is the prelude to the Ode to Joy in Beethoven's 9th Symphony. The version used is an arrangement by Herbert von Karajan adopted in 1972.

Wysocki/EXPLORER

Europe throughout the centuries

ORIGINS: FROM PREHISTORIC MAN TO ANCIENT CIVILISATION

About one and a half million years ago, the first humans **(Homo Erectus)** apparently came from Africa and settled in the southern regions of Europe. The presence of **Neanderthal man**, named after the excavations in the Neander valley in Germany, dates from about 150 000 years ago. Numerous archeological artefacts provide us with information: Neanderthal man was short in stature, with an elongated cranium and an upright stance. He made flint tools, hunted, lived in small tribes and used fire. He buried the dead, but did not create any works of art. About 35 000 years ago, the **Cro-Magnon** (site of the excavations in France) **species** to which we belong, began to spread over the entire continent. A large skull and articulate speech distinguished this intelligent branch of Homo Sapiens. Cro Magnon man lived in organised communities, became skilled in tool-making and hunting, and learned to paint caves.

The Stone Age

4000 - 2000 BC	From the Paleolithic to the Neolithic Age. The first megaliths and stone tombs (menhirs, dolmens, tumuli and cromlechs) are erected in Western Europe. The most important of these are Stonehenge in England, Newgrange in Ireland, Carnac in France, the Hunebedden in Holland, and Knebel and Kivick in Scandinavia. These monumental tombs have enabled ethnographers to study the religious customs of an agrarian and sedentary society.
c. 2500 2400 2300 BC	Era of the pyramids of Egypt.

The Bronze Age

During this period, a civilisation spanning more than 20 centuries leaves a strong mark on European history.

The second millennium witnesses the use of bronze (a copper and tin alloy), which originated in the East and spread along with trade throughout the Mediterranean in Europe. **Crete**, through the mighty organisation of its palace Knossos, becomes the first state founded in Europe. The island's intense economic and cultural activity results in the **Minoan civilisation**, called after King Minos, whose name occurs in numerous legends. Influenced by Egypt, the Cretans adopt hieroglyphic script, make vases, statues and jewels, develop advanced architecture and practise the cult of the mother goddess.

1900 - 1400 BC	The Minoan civilisation reaches its zenith. The first wave of Indo-Europeans (Achaeans, Aeolians and Ionians) settle in Greece. Contact between Indo-Europeans and Mediterranean populations gives birth to the Mycenean civilisation.
1250 BC	The prosperous and powerful cities of Mycenae, Pylos and Tiryns reach their zenith. The kings of Homer's *Iliad* rule these islands, constructed from huge blocks of stone known as **Cyclopean**.
1193 – 1150 BC	The Trojan War erupts. The mythical poet Homer describes these events in the *Iliad* and the *Odyssey*. The Greeks destroy Troy in order to gain access to the Black Sea.
1150 BC	The second Indo-European migration begins with the arrival of the Dorians.
1100 BC	The Aeolians, Ionians, and then the Dorians, colonise Asia Minor.
1100 – 750 BC	The destruction of the Mycenaean cities results in economic and political decline known as the Greek Dark Age. During this austere period, the use of iron spreads throughout Europe and replaces the golden period of the Bronze Age civilisation.
776 BC	The first official celebration of the Olympic Games takes place at Olympia.

The Iron Age

8C BC	Greece assumes a key role in the history of Europe.
725 –480 BC	First Iron Age: the **Hallstatt civilisation** (named after the village in the Tyrol where over 20 000 objects were found scattered throughout numerous burial sites) and Celtic civilisation dominate Central Europe. During this period, Gaul develops trade between the Celts and the Mediterranean populations. Greek and Etruscan influences predominate in the arts.

6C BC | The **Etruscans** flourish: this seafaring people, attracted to Tuscany by its iron deposits, rule Latium from as early as the 7C and found Rome. Etruscan kings govern the city from 616 to 509 BC.

753 BC | Legendary date of Rome's founding.

5C - 2C BC | Second Iron Age: the **civilisation of La Tène** (a Swiss archeological site) marks the summit of Celtic culture which spreads throughout the Balkans, Greece (capture of Delphi in 270 BC), Asia Minor and the whole of Gaul.
Celtic tribes governed by prosperous warrior chiefs dominate Europe from the River Danube to the Atlantic Ocean.
The Celts do not build an empire, but rapidly assimilate with the existing population, giving rise to the Celtiberians in Spain and the Gallo-Greeks in Asia. Their society, divided into three classes (the warrior aristocracy, the common people and the Druids), is united by language and religion. From the 2C, Rome reduces Celtic culture to small enclaves in Brittany, Cornwall, Wales, northwest Scotland and Ireland.

750 - 600 BC | The second Greek colonisation of the Mediterranean takes place. Towards the end of the Dark Ages, Greece once again becomes a cultural power and the focus of economic activity for four centuries. It experiences a population explosion which prompts it to establish colonies on the Mediterranean and Black Sea coasts, particularly in southern Italy and Sicily. This expansion sparks rivalry with Carthage.

GREEKS AND PHOENICIANS

- Phoenician colonies (9-6C BC)
- Greek colonies (8-6C BC)
- The Celtic World (and its main sites)

ANCIENT NAMES → PRESENT NAMES

Byzantium (Constantinople): Istanbul
Carthago Nova: Cartagena
Gades: Cadix
Hipo Regius: Annaba
Massalia: Marseille
Neapolis: Naples
Nicaea: Nice
Panormos: Palermo
Tingis: Tangier

The splendour of Athens

600 BC | A class struggle erupts between the powerful aristocracy, a new merchant middle class, the peasants and the immigrant slaves. In certain cities, legislation is reformed to eliminate the worst injustices.
In Athens, Solon (594 BC), Peisistratus (560 and 527 BC) and Cleisthenes (507 BC) enact reforms.

5C BC | Tensions mount between the vast Persian Empire under Xerxes and the Greeks led by Themistocles, culminating in the **Persian Wars** (500 to 480 BC).

490 BC | The Greeks defeat the Persians for the first time at **Marathon**.

480 BC | The King of Sparta Leonidas dies at **Thermopylae**.
The Greeks defeat the Persians for the second time at **Salamis**.

495 – 429 BC | Under **Pericles**, Athens expands into a resplendent metropolis of civilisation and Classical art. Aided by the architect Phidias, Pericles transforms the Acropolis and develops the port of Piraeus.

To counter Persian attacks, numerous Greek cities unite in the **league of Delos** led by Athens. A man who prized equality, yet who possessed near absolute power, Pericles initiates direct democracy in Athens. However, a large segment of the Athenian people do not enjoy access to citizenship. The stateless include slaves, women and foreigners. Democratic institutions are divided into the people's assembly *(ekklesia)*, open to any male citizen from the age of 18, The Council *(boulé)* comprising 500 men selected by lot, 50 of whom are councillors *(prutaneis)* exercising executive power, and lastly the tribunal of jurors elected by the people *(heliaea)* holding judiciary power.
The law becomes the highest authority and citizens are bound by the collective will of the city *(polis)*. Following Athens' example, other cities adopt democratic principles. There exists, however, oligarchic opponents of democracy who look to conservative **Sparta**.
These oligarchic cities unite and form the Peloponnesian League.

431 – 404 BC The **Peloponnesian War** breaks out between two former allies: Athens and Sparta. The Peloponnesian League and Sparta's severe military discipline prove superior in withstanding the ordeals of war.
In 404 BC, Athens capitulates, surrenders its navy, dissolves the League of Delos and demolishes the walls protecting the city.

End of 5C BC-beginning of 4C BC After the Peloponnesian War, Greece enters a period of decadence. In the east, an all-powerful sovereign rules the Persian Empire. In the west, Rome begins its expansion, and in the north the Celts extend their influence. The Greek cities finally lose their autonomy when Philip of Macedonia conquers southern Greece.

438 BC Philip II of Macedonia becomes master of Greece.

356 – 323 BC His son **Alexander the Great** (pupil of Aristotle) conquers the entire Persian Empire all the way to the Indian frontier. In this empire, a common culture, **Hellenism**, combines Persian and Greek elements. However, Hellas soon loses its economic power to Rome, a new state which conquers Greece in 146 BC.

Under the banner of Rome

from 146 BC Greece becomes a Roman province. The first great universal European empire emerges: the western Roman Empire. Over 1 000 years elapse between the legendary date of the founding of Rome (753 BC) and the empire's collapse (476 AD); in the course of this long period, Roman civilisation unites Europe and leaves an indelible mark upon certain regions.

509 BC The Tarquin royal dynasty falls. The **Republic** is established and the power of the king transferred to two consuls elected annually.

4 and 3C BC Start of the Roman Conquest: Rome engages a war against its neighbours and gradually conquers all of Italy as far as the River Arno and River Rubicon.

241 BC The first **Punic War** ends: Carthage, the oldest Phoenician colony, surrenders Sicily to the Romans.

218 – 201 BC The second Punic War takes place. The two greatest generals of all time, Hannibal and Scipio dominate the fighting. Hannibal crosses the Alps and defeats the Romans at Lake Trasimene, crushing them at Cannae in Apulia. But he fails to march against Rome and settles in Capua.
In 210 BC, Scipio extends the war to Spain and Africa. Hannibal is recalled to Carthage and defeated by Scipio at Zama in 202 BC.

149 – 146 BC Carthage is destroyed, Greece becomes a Roman province, and Spain is occupied in the Third Punic War. Rome, towards the end of the 2C BC, reigns as mistress of most of the Mediterranean world with the creation of new provinces in southern Gaul, in Asia and Africa. The Mediterranean becomes Mare Nostrum.

2C - 1C BC The exceptional valour of the Roman legions and their generals lead to victory after victory. However, rapid growth creates problems: republican institutions are no longer adapted to this colonisation. New Agrarian laws fail. A change in thinking takes place; imaginative Greek mythology infects the austere Roman religion. Out of this century of crisis and civil wars comes the imperial regime.

81-79 BC Sulla seizes power by military means and imposes a dictatorship. His conquest follows the successive failure of reforms advocated by Tiberius and Gaius Gracchus, and Marius. Marius defeats Jugurtha, King of Numidia and repels the Cimbrian and Teutonic invasions.

Exceptional men: the Caesars

70 BC The elected consuls, Pompey and Crassus, become masters of Rome.

60 BC First triumvirate: Pompey, Crassus, Caesar.
Julius Caesar, soldier and statesman, orator and writer, and a remarkable example of an autocratic personality, lays the foundations of the Roman Empire.

59 – 45 BC During his consulship, Caesar embarks on his campaigns in Gaul (surrender of Vercingétorix at Alésia in 52 BC), crosses the Rubicon and drives Pompey out of Rome. He then triumphs over his rivals and his supporters in Spain, Greece and Egypt.

55 BC Roman invasion of Britain but the Romans never invaded Ireland.

44 BC After being appointed dictator for life, Caesar is assassinated by republican devotees, one of whom, Brutus, is his adopted son.

43 BC Second triumvirate: Octavius (Caesar's nephew and heir), Mark Anthony and Lepidus. With his delicate constitution, Octavius, at the age of 19, is not a renowned soldier; he soon proves himself a master of peerless self-control, tenacity and political genius.

31 BC An open conflict pits Octavius against Mark Anthony who had drifted into the arms of Cleopatra and the languorous East. Finally Mark Anthony is beaten at Actium.

The century of Augustus

27 BC The Senate awards Octavius, sole master of the Empire, the title of Augustus, exalting him to the position of a god. Augustus guarantees the frontiers and organises the administration of the provinces by creating a road network and an imperial postal service. The length of his reign enables him to establish a new Greco-Roman civilisation combining piety, a sense of civic duty and respect for the community.
After the Pax Romana, the Empire wages almost no more civil or foreign wars. However, this attempt at legal and moral uniformity soon clashes with the individual character of each culture. Peasants are virtually kept in a state of serfdom and the prosperity of the towns contributes little to the welfare of the countryside.
Architecture becomes monumental; so do the religious and economic demands of Augustus. Cities sprawl. The new urban population requires the construction of colossal structures, aqueducts, public baths and amphitheatres.

14 Augustus dies.

14-37 Reign of Tiberius. Roman army at war in Germany under the generalship of Germanicus.

54-68 Nero reigns. He puts to death Britannicus, his mother Agrippina, his wives Octavia and Poppea. He also sets fire to Rome and persecutes the Christians.

68 The Julio-Claudian dynasty of Tiberius, Caligula, Claudius, and Nero, ends. Despite their savagery and cruelty, their rule generated overall prosperity.

69-96 The Flavian dynasty of Vespasian, Titus and Domitian takes over and the emperor amasses excessive power.

96-192 Nerva, Trajan, Antonius, Marcus Aurelius and Commodus compose the Antonine dynasty.
The Golden Age of the Antonines marks the Empire's zenith. Under the happy rule of **Trajan** and **Hadrian**, the Roman world experiences its greatest expansion with the conquest of Dacia, annexation of Mesopotamia, Armenia and Arabia Petraea. It extends over nearly three and a half million km^2 (over 2 million sq mi), with an estimated population of 70 million inhabitants.
The Empire's centre of gravity remains in the Mediterranean. But frontier fortifications such as Hadrian's Wall, the Antoninus Pius Wall and the Rhine boundary, do not prevent the Barbarians from endangering the Empire. Although the Roman legions stop at the Rhine and the Danube they still maintain a major influence over the primary part of the Germanic, Scandinavian, Slav and Irish populations.

166 In 170, Germanic tribes cross the Danube to reach the port of Aquileia on the Adriatic, beginning a series of regular migrations that would continue over three centuries.

193-284 During the Severus dynasty, a troubled military period occurs, typifying the crisis of the 3C and heralding the Roman Empire's decline. A new Europe is forged in the wake of extensive invasions and the spread of Christianity.

Christian Rome, decline of the Empire, invasions and transformations

284-305 **Diocletian** institutes a tetrarchy, entrusting government to a college of four. He also persecutes the Christians (303).

306-337 **Constantine** makes Christianity the official state religion – a decisive turning point in the history of Christian Europe. The decree embodied in the edict of Milan (313) proclaims freedom of worship, and convenes the Council of Nicaea (325). By naming Constantinople (the New Rome) as the Empire's capital, Constantine hopes to thwart any risk of attack by the Barbarians and Sassanids. The decision lays the foundations for the future Byzantine Empire.

354-430 St Augustine proclaims the doctrine of a universal Church and advocates monastic rule, inspiring the creation of great religious orders.

375 The **Huns** invade Europe, driving the Germanic peoples into the Empire.

379-395 **Theodosius**, the last emperor to reign over the Roman empire after its conversion to Christianity, forbids heathen practices, destroys temples or transforms them into churches, and suppresses the Olympic Games. At his death, the Empire is divided into two (East and West). Roman unity no longer exists.

397 Saint Martin, who converted Gaul to Christianity, dies.

5C This is a time of **invasions** and **transformations**.
The Germanic kings had long served an empire and never ceased to admire it. But they now destroy Rome and change the face of Europe. A gradual interaction between the Roman and the Germanic worlds develops.
In 406, the Vandals, Sueves and Alans invade Gaul. Alaric, King of the Visigoths seizes Rome (410) which is soon sacked again in 455 by the Vandals under Genseric. In 476, **Odoacer**, ruler of the Heruli, deposes the last western emperor who is still a child, and sends the imperial insignia back to Constantinople. The Western Roman Empire is dead.
However, the Germanic rulers still wish to perpetuate Roman civilisation. In 450, Romans and Goths band together against **Attila**'s Huns, expelling them from Gaul. Having settled in Aquitaine, then in Spain, the Visigoths found the Kingdom of Toledo which is recognised by the Latin populations. In 481, **Clovis** makes Paris the capital of the Frankish Kingdom and succeeds in amalgamating Frankish and Roman traditions. **Theodoric the Great**, King of the Ostrogoths, wins the agreement of the Eastern Emperor and drives Odoacer from Italy. He installs his capital at Ravenna, in 493. Rome's influence, including its language, persists in these western regions, but is obliterated from Brittany and England. Germanic tribes invade northern England via the North Sea; Gaels from Ireland found the Scottish Kingdom of Scotland, and from the 5C to the 9C, the Anglo-Saxon nations come into being. Wales, Cornwall and Brittany (formerly Armorica) avoid Germanisation and become havens of Celticism.

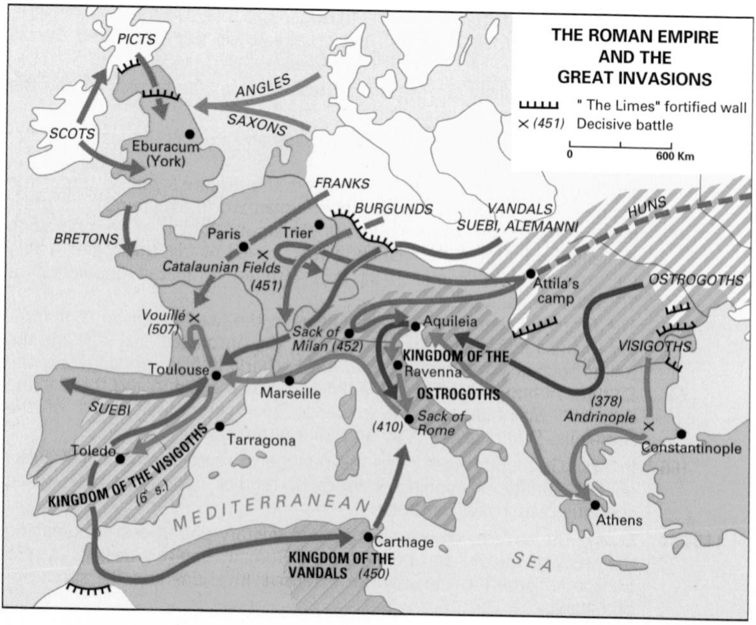

449-452 **Attila and the Huns threaten the West.** The Huns, a Mongolian people, crossed the Volga as early as 370, provoking a series of great invasions. Having conquered all the territories in their path, they settle in present-day Hungary and embark upon the great invasion of Gaul in 406, destroying the Burgundian Kingdom and laying waste to the Eastern Empire. United by Attila into a vast empire extending from the Danube to the Dniepr, the Huns invade the Balkans and pose a threat to Constantinople (448). After being defeated in Gaul (451), they plunder northern Italy before retreating east. Attila's sudden death (453) precipitates the dissolution of their empire.

5C The first monasteries appear. In 461, St Patrick converts Ireland which in the 6C would become a fervent centre of religious and intellectual activity, producing such brilliant minds as Colombanus, Fiachra and Colomba. During the same period, the Benedictine rule founded by St Benedict of Nursia in Italy spreads throughout Western Europe.

THE WEST AND BYZANTIUM (6 TO 10C)

481-511 Clovis reigns in Gaul establishing the Merovingian dynasty. Under his rule and that of his sons, the Frankish Catholic Kingdom extends to the Garonne, comprising Burgundy, Provence, Thuringia and Bavaria.

527-565 **Emperor Justinian** reigns. Aided by his wife Theodora and his generals Narses and Belisarius, he attempts to rebuild the Roman Empire with all its territories and with its uniformity of religion and institutions. But his attempt to impose Christian orthodoxy precipitates a revival of paganism and heresy. He recaptures most of North Africa from the Vandals (533), Italy from the Ostrogoths (535, 552), and Andalusia from the Visigoths (550-554). The Mediterranean once more becomes a Roman lake. But the Empire is frail, under constant threat following the resumption of the Persian War in 540 and Hun and Slav invasions in the Balkans. To resist the Barbarians, Justinian is forced to increase fortifications at strategic points on the frontiers and to pay heavy tributes. This severe fiscal strain undermines administrative reforms and shifts policy in favour of the major landowners; the impoverished masses rebel in 532 against such despotic power. Nevertheless, the 6C is known as Justinian's century. The first great monuments of Byzantine civilisation are built; they include St-Sophia in Constantinople, San Vitale in Ravenna. The Justinian Code, a sophisticated legal system influenced by Roman law, is also formulated.

568 The Lombards, a Germanic people, settle in northern Italy.

590-604 **Pope Gregory the Great** strengthens the power of the Papacy, organises the defence against the Lombards and sends the monk Augustine (later to become Archbishop of Canterbury) to convert the Saxons in Great Britain.

7C Under Byzantine administrative dependency, the Bulgars settle in lower Mesia, the Serbs in provinces near the Danube, the Croats in Dalmatia, and the Avars in the Balkans.

8C and 9C Religious unity, political stability and the predominance of Hellenic elements mark these centuries in the Byzantine empire. However, Byzantium still faces its old problems - and new adversaries.

8C In 717 and 718, the **Arabs** besiege Constantinople without success. But in 929 they succeed in founding an independent emirate in Cordoba in Spain.

In the Mediterranean, towards the end of the 9C, the Saracens conquer Crete and launch piratical raids against Byzantium and the West. Meanwhile, the Bulgars embark upon violent conflicts with Byzantium (762, 792, 811) before signing a peace treaty in 813.

Finally, during the 8C and 9C, new States emerge in Europe: the Papal States which contribute to the loss of Byzantium's Italian possessions and reinforce the power of the Roman Church as well as that of the Carolingian State, the Scandinavian countries and Great Britain.

732 Charles Martel repels the Arabs at Poitiers. His Frankish kingdom, which since the 6C had made its mark on a large section of Western and Central Europe, soon reaches the summit of its influence. Under the leadership of Charlemagne, it is transformed into the great **Carolingian Empire**, a serious threat to Byzantium's interests.

751 The Papal States are created.

768-814 **Charlemagne** is crowned Emperor of the West in Rome on December 25 in the year 800. Charlemagne's Empire no longer centres on the Mediterranean, but extends over a new geopolitical zone from the North Sea to central Italy, from the Pyrenees to the Elbe.

843 In the partition of Verdun, the Carolingian Empire is divided between the three sons of Louis the Pious, Charlemagne's successor. West Francia goes to Charles the Bald, East Francia to Louis the German and the central area from the North Sea to Italy to Lothair.

End of 9C - beginning of 10C The last Carolingians prove powerless against invasions and their authority weakens. Even the Papacy feels threatened by Saracen invasions. A strong candidate to take over the empire is missing. Confronted with this power vacuum, local families, Capetians in Francia, Saxons and Ottonians in Germania consolidate their control.

9C **The Scandinavians invade:** the Swedes settle in the east, first along the Baltic Sea, then in Russia where, together with the Varangians, they found principalities such as Kiev and Novgorod and trade with Constantinople. The Norwegians and Danes known as **Normans** head west and south, ravaging everything in their path, terrorising the population. They reach Iceland, Ireland, Great Britain, Germania, Holland, France and even the Mediterranean Hellenic territories. Their commercial acumen brings prosperity to Northern Europe. Their chiefs, the **Vikings**, are formidable sailors and warriors. They lay waste to England later reconquered in 855 by Alfred the Great, founder of the first real Kingdom of England. They also settled in France, where in 911, the Danish chief, Rollo, was recognised as Duke of Normandy.

9C and 10C **Saracen and Hungarian invasions:** Southern Europe is subjected to Arab Saracen raids. They invade Corsica, Sicily, southern Italy, Rome in 846 and in 900 settled in Provence. Arab influence extends over the western Mediterranean. In the east, the Hungarians, from Asia, launch expeditions westwards.

910 The Abbey of Cluny in Burgundy is founded. In an unstable, disorientated and unscrupulous political and social world, Cluny provides great assistance to the Papacy, helping it to fulfil its aim of reforming the Church.

10C and 11C The zenith of Byzantium coincides with a cultural and economic Renaissance that sees the Empire recovering some of the grandeur of the Justinian period, and succeeding in administering its frontiers efficiently. Prestigious emperors such as Basil II recapture Crete (961), Bulgaria (1018) and reassert the Byzantine presence on the Black and Aegean Seas. The situation remains less favourable in the Mediterranean, an area coveted successively by the Arabs, Otto I's Holy German Empire and the Normans. From 1025 to 1055, the first signs of the Byzantine Empire's decline appear. Endangered by the settling of Seljuk Turks in Asia Minor and Normans at Bari, by a lax administration and a weak army, the Empire verges on collapse.

The 9C, 10C and 11C are imbued with a policy of Christianisation carried out by Byzantine or Germanic emperors. This policy has a considerable influence on the history of the European States. Great monasteries are founded, playing a crucial role in economic, cultural and political life. At the same time, a gap widens between the empires of Rome and Constantinople, with their different religious denominations.

972 The Orthodox monastery of Grand Lavra is founded on Mount Athos in Greece; its far-reaching influence extends well beyond the Empire.

936-973 Otto I, Emperor of the Holy Germanic Empire, defender of the Church, reigns.

Numerous reforms and an impressive renewal of intellectual life occur the Ottonian Renaissance.

955 Otto checks the expansion of the Hungarians at Lechfeld and compels them to settle in present-day Hungary.

987 Hugh Capet is elected King of the Franks. The Capetian dynasty lasts for more than eight centuries.

1014-1035 Canute seizes the throne of England, uniting Norway, Denmark and England. His successors elect an Anglo-Saxon king, Edward the Confessor (1042-1066) who reintroduces the Saxon dynasty, divides the kingdom into counties and establishes relations with Normandy.

THE CHRISTIAN MIDDLE AGES (11C TO 13C)

The new medieval European civilisation signals a break with the Ancient World's Mediterranean civilisation. Several trends explain this shift: the arrival of the Arabs and the 8C expansion of Islam end Mediterranean unity, the western Church becomes autonomous and provokes a decisive rupture with the eastern Church, the Carolingian Empire is created and finally the Norman, Saracen and Hungarian invasions of the 9C and 10C divide Europe. Towards the year 1000, the concept of Christianity becomes more precise, bringing western Christians in conflict not only with heathens but also with eastern Christians. During the Carolingian period, the Emperor appoints bishops

and is crowned by the Pope. However, after 1030, a reform movement led by the monks of Cluny gains strength; it calls in question imperial authority and brings about radical changes to the relationship between the Papacy and the empire.
Feudalism makes its first appearance during the 8C. This new political system based on the existence of fiefs and seigneuries becomes widespread in the 11C, with knights embarking on crusades to impose respect for the peace of God.
The Middle Ages experiences a spectacular increase in population, an agricultural revolution (fields replace forests), and a new town lay-out based on commercial principles. At the same time, new roads are built, used by merchants and pilgrims to travel to centres such as Rome, and Santiago de Compostela.

10C and beginning of 11C	Throughout the European territory, trade develops, led by the Venetians and the Amalfians. The Flemish towns of Ghent and Bruges become renowned as centres of woollen cloth production.
1054	A final rupture occurs between the churches of Rome and Constantinople, creating a schism between the Orthodox and Catholic religions.
1059	Pope Nicholas II entrusts the election of the Pope to the cardinals instead of the Emperor.
1075	Pope Gregory VII institutes with Emperor Henry IV the election of the bishops to the chapter of canons. This causes the quarrel, known as the war of the Investitures.
1066	At Hastings, William, Duke of Normandy, defeats Harold, Edward the Confessor's successor. **William the Conqueror** becomes King of England (1066-1087). Under the Normans (1066-1154) England becomes one of the most prosperous countries in Western Europe. Administration is feudal and centralised. Fiefs (expropriated from the Saxons) are granted to barons. Civil law is unified (Common Law) and a survey carried out (Doomsday Book); culture and language are Gallicised.
11C	**Reconquista:** Christians recapture Toledo from the Muslims (1085). After being ruled by the Arabs and the Byzantines, Sicily and southern Italy are invaded by the Normans in 1090.
1095-1099	Urban II launches the first crusade. Thirty thousand crusaders seize Jerusalem and establish a feudal kingdom defended by soldier-monks, the Templars and Knights Hospitallers.
12C	Increasing trade encourages the building of new roads: the road to Rome benefits Lucca, Asti and Sienna. Merchants also use the roads of Mont-Cenis, Grand-Saint-Bernard and the Simplon and Tarvis passes. At the famous fairs of Champagne, Mediterranean and Nordic merchants meet to sell spices, metal, silk and wool cloth. Two centuries later, Flanders loses its monopoly on the production of wool cloth, and the fairs move south to Geneva and Lyon. During the 12C, universities make their first appearance in the cities of Salerno, Bologna, Paris, Oxford, Cambridge, Palencia, Salamanca, and Padua.
1098	Robert de Molems founds a great abbey at Côteaux.
1147-1149	At Vézelay, St Bernard, one of the spiritual leaders of the Middle Ages, preaches in favour of the second crusade, but after the siege of Damascus, it fails.
1152-1190	Frederick Barbarossa is crowned Emperor. He attempts to destroy the economic activity of the Communes flourishing in Italy. The struggle between the Empire (Ghibellines) and the Papacy (Guelphs) is renewed. In 1167, the Lombard League is created to fight the Emperor.
1152	Louis VII, King of France, repudiates Eleanor of Aquitaine who in the same year marries Henry Plantagenet, Duke of Normandy, Count of Anjou and suzerain Lord of Touraine and Maine. When the Plantagenet King inherits the English Crown as Henry II, a struggle between the French and the English results. It will last three centuries.
1170	In his attempt to control the English Church, Henry II orders the assassination of Thomas Becket, Archbishop of Canterbury.
1180-1223	Philippe II (Augustus) is King of France.
1189-1199	Richard I the Lionheart is King of England.
1189-1191	The third crusade led by Frederick I fails after the emperor's death.
1198-1216	During the papacy of Innocent III, papal power reaches its zenith.
1204	The Venetians spearhead the fourth crusade, seizing Constantinople and provisionally ending the Byzantine Empire.

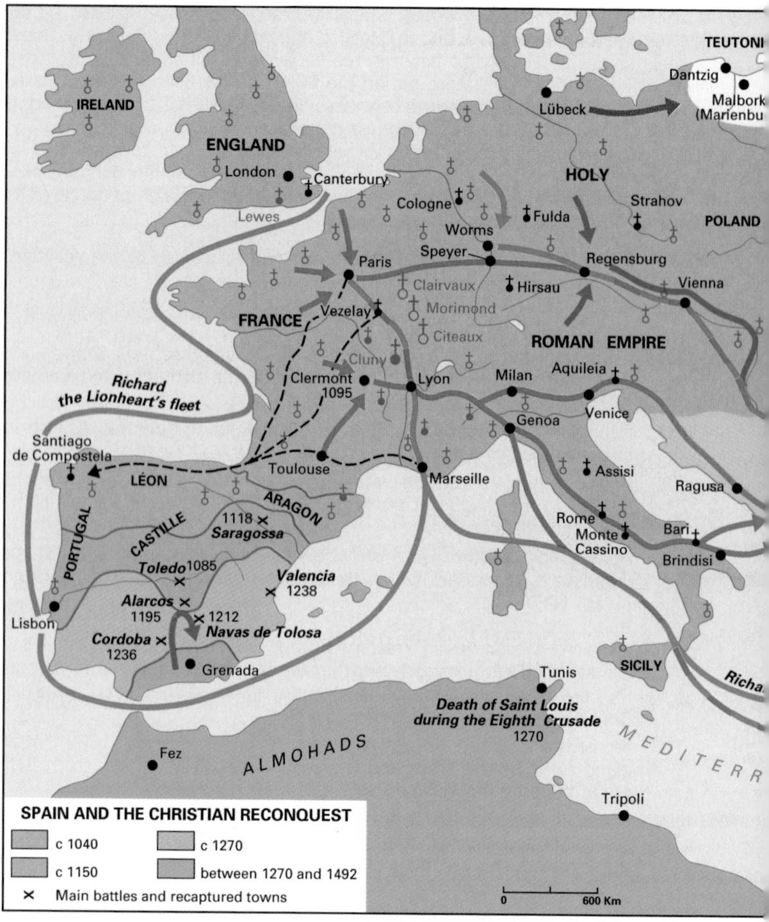

1214 After the Battle of Bouvines, the French monarchy succeeds in reducing the English fiefdoms in France to the Bordeaux region.

1215 England's King John moves to quell rebellious lords by granting them the Magna Carta, upon which the British Parliament's supremacy is based.

1212-1250 The Emperor Frederick II of Hohenstaufen renews the struggle between the empire and the Papacy. The Papacy once again triumphs.
In 1230, Teutonic knights conquer Prussia.

1249 King Louis IX (St Louis) of France is imprisoned in Egypt while leading the seventh crusade.

Middle of the 13C New merchant cities are built around the Baltic. Lübeck, Hamburg, Danzig and Riga form a commercial association known as the **Hanseatic League**. In 1252, the Florentine florin becomes a gold coin in current use on international exchanges.

1270 During the eighth crusade, France's King Louis IX dies close to Tunis.

1273-1291 Rudolf I, founder of the Habsburg dynasty, reigns.

1291 The Swiss federation is born after a permanent alliance is forged between the three cantons of Uri, Schwyz and Unterwalden.

CALAMITIES AND TRANSFORMATIONS (14C AND 15C)

A series of calamities – famine, epidemics of plague, wars, religious strife, social turmoil – replace the splendid unity prevailing in 13C Europe. This country knows a prompt economic decline, a decrease in population, the weakening of imperial power. However, by the end of the 14C, sovereign states had succeeded the feudal parcelling out of land. Efficient administration, trade and industry acquire a new impetus. Religious unity is also re-established. Conditions are ripe for a new cultural flowering, as illustrated by the Flemish Primitives and the Italian Renaissance.

1309-1378 The great Schism occurs, splitting the Church for four years, and the popes settle in Avignon (from Clement V to Gregory XI, who returned to Rome at the request of St Catherine of Sienna).

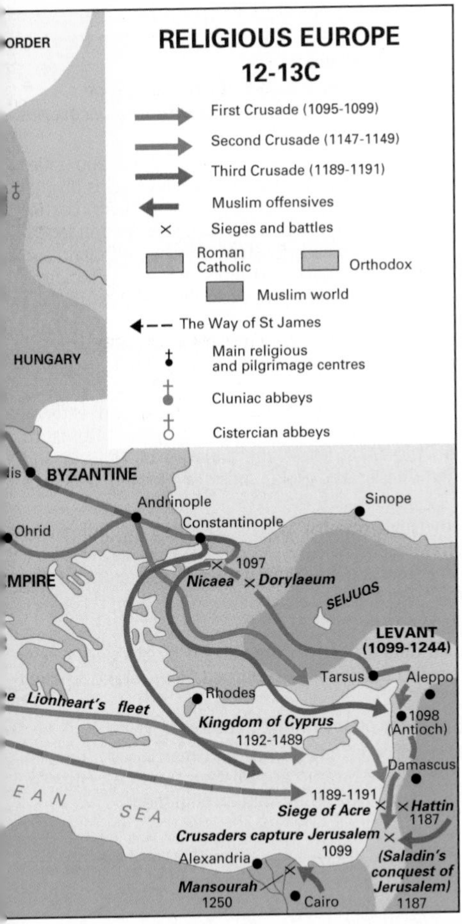

St Bernard

It was precisely to fight against the luxury and the slack discipline among the monks of Cluny that St Bernard spoke out. This young nobleman born at the château of Fontaine near Dijon, followed an unexpected destiny when at the age of twenty-one he renounced all riches and honours and went with thirty-two companions to the monastery of Cîteaux in search of God's mercy.

1316 Europe experiences a great famine. The agrarian crisis forces villages to be abandoned and land left fallow, particularly in England where it was used as pasture for sheep.

1328 Emperor Louis II of Bavaria's intervention in Italy fails, and the Germanic Holy Roman Empire loses its supremacy to the great western Christian kingdoms of France and England.

1337-1453 The **Hundred Years War** erupts, both a political confrontation between the Plantagenets and the Capetians and a struggle about feudal rights. From the outset the French suffered crushing defeats in Flanders (1340), at Crécy (1346), Calais (1347) and Poitiers (1356) before resigning themselves to a treaty in 1360 (Peace of Brétigny) that puts the whole of southwest France as well as Calais under English dominance. Under Charles V, Du Guesclin's campaigns restore order. In France as in England, internal difficulties abound. In 1395, hostilities are resumed with the civil war between the Armagnacs and the Burgundians. After the disaster of Agincourt (1415), John the Fearless, Duke of Burgundy, switches to the English side.
With the Treaty of Troyes in 1420, the French surrender their country to the English.
The epic tale of Joan of Arc (1429-1431) the liberator of Orléans, restores the Dauphin's confidence; he is crowned at Reims. After the civil war, Charles VII assembles an army and drives the English out of France in 1453.

1347-1374 The Great Plague causes a decline in the population from 73 million men in 1300 to 45 million in 1400. From 1347 to 1351, the Black Death kills a third of all Europeans. In England, life expectancy falls from 25 years in 1348 to 17 years in 1376. In a state of panic, people turn Jews into scapegoats and persecute them. A wave of mysticism sweeps over Europe.

1359-c 1450 In 1359, the Hanseatic League reaches its peak. It comprises about 70 towns which, under the aegis of Lübeck, supervise trade on the Baltic and in northern Europe. During this period, the lucrative trade in bills of exchange develops. Rich banking families possess considerable power (the Medici and the Strozzi in Italy, the Fuggers and Welsers in the Holy Empire and Jacques Coeur in France).

1378-1382 Due to the rural crisis, insurrections explode throughout Europe. Peasants are reduced to begging or organise themselves into *Jacqueries* to protest against taxes.

14C - beginning of 15C European territories evolve. Italy consists of small states and cities governed by great families, often at war. The Iberian Peninsula is divided into three kingdoms: Aragon (already a great maritime power), Castille (with which it shares a common cause against the Moors) and independent Portugal. Principalities are formed in Eastern Europe: in Poland and Lithuania, which soon unite, in Hungary and Moscow, and in Moldavia and Wallachia. With his religious reforms, Jean Hus fights for the freedom of Bohemia, a precursor of the future Czech State.
In 1380, Russia regains its independence by driving out the Mongols.
In Scandinavia, Norway, Denmark and Sweden are brought together at the Union of Kalmar in 1397.
The Duchy of Burgundy becomes a new political entity and extends towards the north: Philip the Bold acquires Limburg and rights to Brabant. In 1428, Philip the Good seizes the counties of Holland and Zealand. In 1473, under Charles the Bold, most of Holland falls into Burgundian hands.

1400 The Italian Renaissance (Quattrocento) begins, sparked by humanists such as Dante, Petrarch, and Boccacio.
In the Low Countries, Philip the Bold's sumptuous court encourages the blossoming of the Flemish Primitives.

1410 Poland defeats the Teutonic Order.

1414- 1418 The Council of Constance puts an end to the Schism by electing a new Pope acceptable to all. In 1415, John Hus is burned at the stake, ending the Hussite revolt.

1434 Gutenberg invents the printing press, printing the Bible in 1455.

1440-1493 Frederick III establishes a policy of inheritance and marriages by which the Habsburgs gain the highest rank in Western Europe. His son Maximilian becomes the first to benefit by this arrangement.

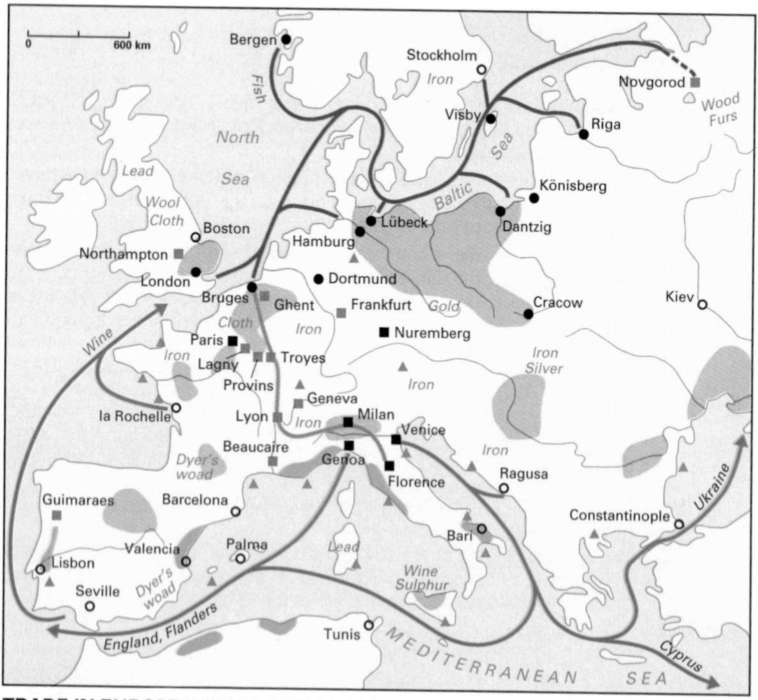

TRADE IN EUROPE DURING THE 12-13C

■ Trading centre
■ Fairs
● Hanseatic town
Mont Cenis route
Genoese and Venetian maritimes routes
Hanseatic maritime routes
Cereals
Olive oil
Salt ▲

1442 Alfonso V, King of Aragon, is crowned King of the two Sicilies.

1453 Constantinople, capital of eastern Christianity, falls into the hands of the Turks led by Mohammed II.

1455-1483 The War of the Roses pits York against Lancaster in England.

1461-1483 Louis XI founds the modern French state.

1469 The marriage of Ferdinand of Aragon and Isabella of Castille unifies Spain.

1485-1509 The Tudor dynasty begins in England. Henry VII rebuilds the country's economy and strengthens the power of the monarchy, weakened by the War of the Roses.

EUROPEAN EXPANSION

Starting in the 15C, the frontiers of the known world are pushed back. Curiosity for new territory increases in Spain, Italy and above all in Portugal. Courageous adventurers embark upon the conquest of the African Continent and the Atlantic Ocean. Lisbon and Seville, which are at the head of two enormous colonial empires, gradually see a decrease in power, whereas Antwerp followed by Amsterdam become Europe's greatest financial centres in the 17C. England, France and Holland, countries with great maritime traditions, want to break the Iberian monopoly and organise large expeditions to found their own colonial empires.
They engage in the triangular trade (European products-slaves-colonial produce) bringing great wealth to the northern European ports. The discoveries lead to a European expansion which revolutionised world history; the arena of trade passes from the cities of the Mediterranean to the Atlantic. Southern Europe is eclipsed by Northern Europe.

1415 The Portuguese capture Ceuta, giving them control of the Straits of Gibraltar and enhancing their prestige with the Spaniards who had already taken possession of the Canary Islands.
At Sagres, the Infante of Portugal, Henry the Navigator founds a school for navigators, aiming to find a southern route between the Indies and Europe. With the help of improved astrolabes and quadrants, he ushers in the era of celestial navigation.
The Portuguese, ahead of their time in cartography, succeed in building a radical new ship, the caravel. A sternpost rudder gives it increased manoeuvrability.

1445 Dinis Dias arrives at Cape Verde and Senegal.

1460-1474 The Portuguese reach Gambia, Guinea and Sierra Leone. From these wealthy regions in Africa, they establish commercial links and begin trafficking in slaves, gold or ivory which they exchange for European products.

1488 Bartholomeu Dias sails past the Cape of Tempests, renamed Cape of Good Hope by King John II.

1492 Christopher Columbus discovers America. Some years before, this Genoese navigator, married to a Portuguese, had the idea of reaching the Indies by sailing west. After his proposal was rejected in Lisbon, he discovers the New World under the sponsorship of the Castillian Catholic kings.

1497 John Cabot, an Italian navigator, in the service of England, lands on the North American coast.

1498 The Portuguese admiral Vasco da Gama sails from Lisbon in May 1497 to discover the famous sea route to India. He arrives in Callicut, after reaching Mozambique and crossing the Indian Ocean.

1499 The Spaniard Amerigo Vespucci arrives at the Gulf of Maracaibo.

1500 Pedro Alvarez Cabral discovers Brazil. He establishes Portuguese "captaincies", coveted by the French and Dutch. Brazil becomes the world's greatest producer of sugar cane, requiring numerous slaves imported from Africa.

1501 Gaspard Corte Real arrives in Newfoundland. But King Manuel is more interested in Asia. In a few years, the Portuguese explore the Asian coast. By 1515 they control the Indian Ocean, with strongholds such as Goa, seized by Alfonso de Albuquerque in 1510. In 1540 they forge business links with China, then Siam, Indonesia and the Philippines.

1519 The Spanish conquistadors embark upon the conquest of America. In Mexico, Hernan Cortez vanquishes the powerful Aztecs. In 1531, Francisco Pizzaro lands in Peru and, after seizing the empire of the Incas, founds Lima as the new Peruvian capital. The navigator Pedro de Mendoza establishes Buenos Aires in 1535. In 1541, Pedro Valdivia takes possession of Chile. The Spanish Crown, through the agency of the Consejo de la Indias and the Casa de Contratation, exploits these colonies for their gold, silver and precious stones. The Spanish introduce the cultivation of European plants and attract settlers by granting them land worked by Indians (Encomiendas System).

1519-1521 Fernando de Magellan, a Portuguese navigator in the service of Spain, embarks upon the first circumnavigation of the globe.
From the second half of the 16C, northern European navigators take advantage of Iberia's loss of economic power and its political vulnerability. England, France and Holland construct colonial empires on mercantilist principles; large companies control all overseas trade. 17C Anglo-Dutch rivalry is replaced during the 18C by an Anglo-French struggle for naval supremacy.

1534-1541 A Frenchman, Jacques Cartier, reaches the Gulf of St-Lawrence and discovers Canada.

1579 The Union of Utrecht is framed binding together the northern part of the Netherlands into the United Provinces. Due to their prestigious cartography, the sophistication of their weapons and their excellent navy, the Dutch soon gain naval supremacy.

1580 Philip II of Spain annexes Portugal and its overseas territories.

1586-1590 Cavendish, in the service of England, carries out a third voyage round the globe.

1587 The Englishman Sir Walter Raleigh founds a colony in America which he names Virginia.

1595 The Dutchman Houtmann arrives in Indonesia.

1602-1621 The United Provinces create the East India and West India Companies which conduct a flourishing trade in spices and other commodities in areas previously occupied by the Spaniards and Portuguese.

1608-1615 The French explorer Champlain makes several expeditions to North America and founds Quebec.

1610 The Englishman Hudson sails along the American Coast and discovers the Bay now bearing his name.

1620 English immigrants from the Mayflower establish a colony in Massachusetts. As the number of English settlers increases, they require slaves to work the plantations. The British found syndicates in Madras in the Indian Ocean.

1621 The Dutch establish Batavia on the island of Java, soon to become the centre of trade in the East. They also establish numerous syndicates in America: West Indies, Guyana, Venezuela (Curaçao) and create New-Amsterdam (the future New York).

1638 French colonisation spreads to Morocco and Black Africa, with the founding of Saint-Louis in Senegal and Fort-Dauphin in Madagascar (1641).

1642-1644 The Dutchman Tasman arrives in New Zealand. He also discovers the Tonga, Fiji and Solomon Archipelagos.

1682 Louisiana, one of the first French colonies, is founded, followed by Guadeloupe, Martinique and Haiti.
During the 18C, voyages become scientific and interest focuses on the Pacific Ocean. New observation instruments appear such as the octant, azimuth needle and chronometer. These facilitate progress in geography.

1725-1741 Bering explores the northern coasts of Asia and America, reaching the Strait now bearing his name.

1763 With the Treaty of Paris, France surrenders most of its overseas territories, including Senegal, Quebec, the West Indies, and India to Britain which becomes the world's most powerful colonial and maritime state.

1766-1779 Bougainville makes the first French voyage of circumnavigation.

RENAISSANCE, WARS OF RELIGION AND ABSOLUTISM (16C AND 17C)

During the 16C, the Renaissance attains its zenith. It spreads throughout Europe, a continent in the midst of economic expansion, growing rich with gold and silver from the Americas. A first type of commercial capitalism is born. The development of the banking system furthers the growth of modern states. Monarchs receiving credit from bankers, interfere increasingly in the management of the national economy. However, momentous discoveries and the disclosure of new peoples give rise to religious questions; were the inhabitants of the New World tainted like ourselves by original sin? The Reformation, for which the humanists claim responsibility, results from troubled consciences and the emergence of a spirit of criticism, as well as from the unbridled luxury of the Papal court. It brings to an end the unity of western Christianity, and initiates a long period of religious wars dividing Europe. Religious, social and political turmoil encourage the rise of absolute monarchy in the second half of the 17C, most notably in Louis XIV's France. Only in England and the Netherlands do the liberal ideas of great political thinkers make their mark. The Declaration of Rights is proclaimed in England in 1689.

1478-1479 A special papal bull leads to the founding in Spain of the tribunal of the Inquisition; Torquemada later becomes its Inquisitor-General. This religious and political institution created to suppress heresy lasts until the 19C. In 1479, the first step towards Spanish unity is taken when Ferdinand becomes King of Aragon.

1512 Navarre is conquered by the Duke of Alva, achieving Spanish unity.

1494-1512 Three generations of French kings, Charles VIII, Louis XII and Francis I resolve to recapture the Kingdom of Naples, inherited from the House of Anjou by Louis XI. Attracted by Italy, they become the main initiators of the French Renaissance.

1515 Francis I comes to the throne. He signs a permanent peace with Switzerland. Rivalry erupts between Francis I and the future Charles V. At the Battle of Marignano, Milanese Lombardy is restored to France and Naples to Spain.

1517 Martin Luther, a German monk troubled by problems of salvation and faith, nails to the doors of the church in Wittenberg 95 theses against the sale of Indulgences. In 1521, he burns the papal bull threatening him with excommunication. When he refuses to recant at the Diet of Worms convened by the young Charles V, the Empire outlaws him and orders his works burnt.

1519 After the death of Maximilian of Austria, Charles I of Spain is elected Emperor of the Holy Roman Empire under the name of Charles V. He rules over Spain, Naples, Sicily, Sardinia, the American territories, in addition to Germany, Austria, Franche-Comté and the Netherlands.

1521-1556 The emperor encounters constant opposition from France, irredentism from the German princes and a threat from Turkey.
Charles V wages five wars against France for European hegemony. In the first four, he defeats Francis I, taking him prisoner at Pavia in 1525. During the fifth one, he routs the new French King, Henry II, and takes possession of Milanese Lombardy.

1523 The communal congress adopts the religious doctrines of Zwingli, resembling those of Luther.

1524 War of the peasants erupts in Germany.

1527 The imperial armies sack Rome.

1529 Charles V beats back the Turkish advance outside Vienna. Under the leadership of Suleiman the Magnificent, the Turks had seized Belgrade (1521), vanquished the Hungarians (1526) and threatened the Spaniards in the Mediterranean.

1530 On behalf of the Lutherans Melanchthon draws up the Augsburg Confession, the first systematic presentation of Protestant theology.

1531 German Protestant princes, supporters of the Lutheran movement, unite against the emperor in the Smalkaldic League.

1534 The Anglicans break away. King Henry VIII becomes head of the Church of England, proclaims his own divorce, dissolves the monasteries, redistributes the land and severely represses the opposition.
In Europe, new religious orders emerge to counter Protestantism. In Spain, a wave of mysticism (St John of the Cross, St Teresa of Avila) leads to the founding by the Spaniard Ignatius Loyola of the **Society of Jesus**. Jesuits are active on behalf of the Catholic Counter-Reformation and establish missions throughout the world for example St Francis Xavier in India and in Japan.

1536 Frenchman John Calvin publishes, in Latin, *The Institutes of the Christian Religion*. He wishes to break with the delights of the Renaissance and to prevent the Reformation from fragmenting into numerous sects – 24 years after Martin Luther's 95 theses – by asserting its universal character. Calvinism spreads rapidly through Switzerland, England (under Edward VI), Scotland, Italy, Spain, France and the Netherlands, then to Hungary, Bohemia and Poland in the 17C.

1545-1563 The **Council of Trent** initiates a renewal of Catholicism and reaffirms papal authority.

1547 In Russia, Ivan IV the Terrible assumes the title of Csar and engages in a violent struggle against the boyars; the practice of serfdom helps him assert his power.

1555 After a fruitless struggle against the German Reformation, Charles V signs a compromise with the Protestants, the **Peace of Augsburg**, and abdicates in 1556 in favour of his son **Philip II**. The Empire is divided: Philip II receives Spain, Portugal, Northern Italy, Naples and Sicily, the Netherlands and Burgundy; Charles V's brother, **Ferdinand I of Habsburg**, founds the Austrian monarchy and also rules Bohemia and Hungary.

EUROPE DURING THE 17C

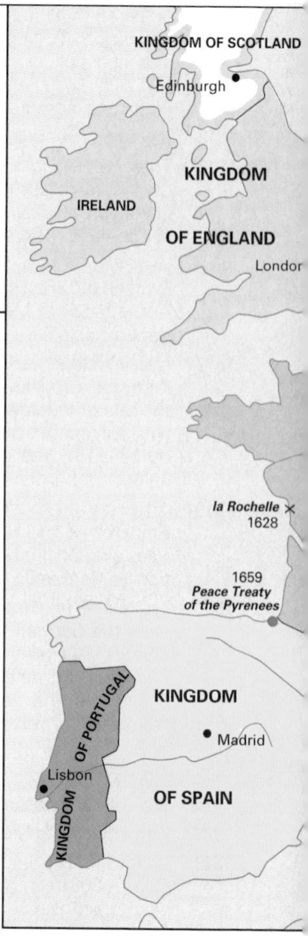

1559 The Treaty of Cateau-Cambrésis brings an end to the long standing Franco-Spanish dispute.

1562 Religious wars erupt, swamping France in blood for 36 years. Spain supports the Catholic Holy League, formed by the Guises and the Montmorencys. England backs the Huguenot Bourbons, Condés and Colignys.

1563 After Mary Tudor's savage reimposition of Catholicism, Elizabeth I reinstates the Anglican Church's prerogatives. The reformed English church meets with hostility from some Catholics, Puritans and Presbyterians (Church founded in Scotland in 1561 by John Knox) because of its allegiance to royal authority.

1571 The Holy League of Spain, Venice and Rome defeats the Turks at **Lepanto**.

1572 Three thousand Huguenots are assassinated in Paris in what becomes known as St Bartholomew's Massacre.

1576 After Spanish troops sack Antwerp, the 17 Catholic and Protestant Dutch provinces resume their struggle for freedom.

1579 The Netherlands is divided in half: the Union of Arras grants freedom to the 10 southern Catholic provinces, and the Union of Utrecht freedom to the seven northern Protestant provinces. In 1581, these northern provinces become the independent Republic of the United Provinces.

1588 Philip II sends his **Invincible Armada** against Protestant England, which is supporting the Netherlands. Its destruction finishes Spain as a maritime power.

1593 The French King, Henry IV, renounces Protestantism.

1598 Henry IV issues the Edict of Nantes, proclaiming liberty of conscience and bringing peace to the French kingdom.

1613 Michael Romanov ascends to the throne in Russia after driving the Poles from Moscow.

1618 The **Thirty Years War** begins. Antagonism between Protestants and Catholics and European fears of the House of Hapsburg's political ambitions provoke the bloodbath. Bohemia rises against its emperor, only to lose its freedom for over two centuries. German Protestants, threatened by the Catholics, appeal to the Danish King. But the Danes abdicate and sign the Peace of Lübeck in 1629. Between 1630 and 1635, the Swedes intervene under Gustavus Adolphus's leadership. He is victorious at Leipzig and Lâtzen, but the Swedes and the Protestant princes are defeated at Nordlingen in 1635. French intervention and the Battle of Rocroi in 1643 signal the *coup de grâce* to Spanish power in Europe.

1638 Galileo, an Italian, asserts that motion obeys mathematical laws.

1648 The **Treaties of Westphalia** bring the Thirty Years War to an end. They mark the failure of the Habsburgs attempt to take over Germany, confirm Holland's independence, recognise France's claims to Alsace (excepting Strasbourg and Mulhouse), and establish French as the language of diplomacy.

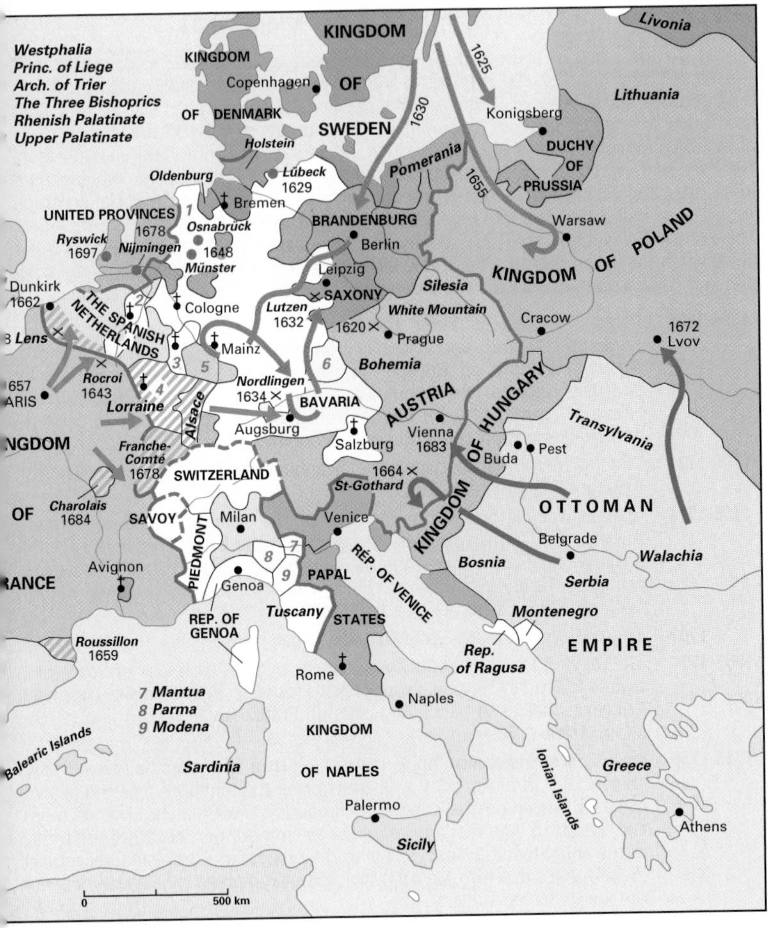

1642-1649 Civil war breaks out in England. **Cromwell** unites the Puritan Parliamentary armies against the tyrannical policies of King Charles I. Twice he defeats the royalist armies, before condemning to death and beheading the monarch in 1649. Parliament then proclaims a Republican state, the Commonwealth, led for 11 years by the Lord Protector Cromwell.
At Cromwell's death in 1660, the English restore the monarchy. Charles II Stuart ensures individual freedom for everyone by approving the law of **Habeas Corpus** in 1679.

1643-1715 **Louis XIV** rules for 72 years as the Sun King, leaving a strong mark on France and Europe.

1659 The **Peace of the Pyrenees** ends war between France and Spain. Philip IV gives his daughter Maria Theresa in marriage to King Louis XIV.

1665 **Louis XIV** launches his expansionist plans, which bring French power to its zenith in 1680. This absolute monarch affirms divine right and, aided by his minister Colbert, also pursues a vigorous domestic policy.

1667-1668 During the War of Devolution, Spain loses some Flemish territories to France.

1672-1678 In the Dutch War, Louis XIV's generals, Turenne and Vauban, defeat Spain. Peace is signed in 1678 with the Treaty of Nijmegen.

1685 The revocation of the Edict of Nantes precipitates the War of the League of Augsburg by pitting France against Austria, Spain, Sweden and various German princes. It ends with French victories and the Treaty of Ryswick in 1697. The revocation of the Edict of Nantes also leads to the emigration of Huguenots to Switzerland, Brandenburg, the United Provinces and Ireland. Similarly, some Irish Catholics attempt to avoid oppression from the British Crown by going into exile in Catholic countries during the 17C and 18C.

1687 The Englishman Newton discovers the law of universal gravity.

1689 In England, the Glorious Revolution ends with William III of Orange and his wife Mary, upholders of the Protestant religion, crowned as sovereigns. They approve the Declaration of Rights.

THE AGE OF ENLIGHTENMENT (1700-1815)

During the 18C, rich or aristocratic young men make a Grand Tour to complete their education. They discover the marvels of Versailles, Amsterdam, Italy, and sometimes Northern or Central Europe. Rulers and the nobility share a common culture, but fight each other in wars of succession. During the second half of the 18C, the philosophers of the Enlightenment call society into question, prizing above all else Nature and Reason. Thinkers such as Voltaire rebel against the *Ancien régime's* absolutism. Jean-Jacques Rousseau passionately advocates the freedom of the individual and the social contract. John Locke and other British writers detail the right of nations to self-determination. The French Revolution, itself inspired by the American Revolution, provokes a great upheaval in European society. These new ideas were echoed by nationalists in the colonies and several Spanish colonies win independence in 1816 followed by Brazil in 1822.

1694-1725	Peter I, known as Peter the Great, reigns in Russia. After visiting England, Holland and Vienna incognito, he founds St Petersburg, Russia's window on Europe. In his wish to Europeanise Russia, he launches reforms with tyrannical authority to modernise the country. However, continual wars for control of the Baltic, increase in serfdom and heavy taxation check Russia's economic expansion in the early 18C.
1700-1721	The Northern War between the Scandinavian countries ends Swedish hegemony in Northern Europe.
1702-1714	Charles II leads Spain into the war of the Spanish Succession, where Austria, the German princes, England and the United Provinces form a coalition against France. Austria, supported by the United Provinces, occupies present-day Belgium. Philip V of Bourbon is proclaimed King of Spain and rules from 1714 to 1745.
1707	England and Scotland unite to form Great Britain.
1733-1774	The reign of France's Louis XV is marked by the Polish War of Succession from 1733 to 1738. Louis supports his father-in-law, Stanislas Leczinski; Emperor Charles VI backs Augustus III. France acquires Lorraine (1766) and Corsica (1769).
1740-1786	**Frederick II of Hohenzollern** takes power. In just a few years he gives Prussia an efficient administration and transforms the kingdom into the second greatest power on the continent. Frederick the Great, a lover of music and literature who made primary school compulsory, becomes the model of the enlightened despot, enjoying the respect of European intellectuals. Prussia owes much to his rule, which is also marked by alliance between the king and the nobility.
1740-1748	During the War of Austrian Succession, France and Austria dispute Maria **Theresa of Habsburg**'s title to the imperial Crown. Louis XV invades the United Provinces which by the Treaty of Aix-la-Chapelle are restored to Maria Theresa, now sovereign. Frederick II annexes Silesia.
1756-1763	A reversal of European alliances results in the Seven Years War: Austria becomes allied with lifelong enemy France, and Russia, Saxony and Sweden against Britain and Prussia. In the end, Prussia succeeds in retaining Silesia.
1762-1796	Catherine II of Russia, patron of the arts and literature, a friend of Voltaire and Diderot, reigns in Russia. Under her rule, Russia's economic, industrial and cultural influence increases.
1772	Diderot publishes his Encyclopaedia. An abortive rising of the Polish Patriots against Russian intervention is followed by the first partition of Poland between Russia, Prussia and Austria.
1783	The United States of America wins independence at the Peace of Versailles.
1789-1799	The French Revolution signals a decade long crisis, ending the Ancien Régime and exposing Europe to democracy. Philosophers' protest against the absolute power of the Crown, and the institutions and privileges left over from feudalism ferment the Revolution, which is accelerated by a disastrous financial crisis.
May 5, 1789	The Estates General meet and declare themselves the National Assembly responsible for giving France a constitution.
July 4, 1789	The Bastille falls.
August 4, 1789	French feudalism and all aristocratic privileges are abolished.
August 23, 1789	The Declaration of the Rights of Man and the Citizen is proclaimed.
June, 1791	King Louis XVI flees. He is identified at Varenne, brought back to Paris and suspended on September 30.
August 1791	Leopold II and Frederick William II of Prussia issue the Declaration of Pilnitz calling on European rulers to support the French monarchy.

April 20, 1792 — The Revolutionary wars start. At Valmy, the courage of the French sans-culottes stop the Prussians from invading France.

September 21, 1792 — After the deposition of Louis XVI, suspected of allying himself with Prussia and Austria to return to power, a national convention proclaims the French Republic.

January 21, 1793 — Louis XVI is executed. The Chouans, inhabitants of Vendée rebel under the leadership of the Catholic royalist army against the revolutionary government. The ensuing civil war is brutally crushed in winter 1794.
Following the death of Louis XVI, the majority of the European states form the First Coalition and declare war on revolutionary France.

1795 — After the victories of Jemmapes (1792) and Fleurus (1794), France annexes the Austrian Netherlands. For the third time, Poland is partitioned between Prussia, Austria and Russia. The Polish State disappears from the map, and numerous patriotic nationals disperse throughout Europe.

1797 — France and Austria sign the Treaty of Campo-Formio. Austrian Netherlands, present-day Belgium, goes to France, the Venetian Republic to Austria.

November 9, 1799 — The Coup d'Etat of 18 Brumaire ends the French Directoire and ushers in the Consulate.

December 2, 1804 — **Napoleon I** is crowned Emperor of the French by Pope Pius VII. Napoleon must now fight to retain the conquests of the Revolution.

1805 — Napoleon abandons his camp at Boulogne where the invasion of Britain was planned. After the French defeat at Trafalgar, Britain re-establishes its naval supremacy. But Napoleon is victorious at Ulm and Austerlitz. When Charles V of Spain abdicates, Napoleon proclaims his brother Joseph as King of Spain. He also transforms the Italian Republic into a kingdom, assuming the Iron Crown of the Lombard kings.

1806 — Napoleon imposes a blockade against England to ruin the country and sends his army to Portugal; it becomes a British dependency (1807-1821).
Napoleon enters Berlin. Emperor Francis I of Austria abdicates the Crown of the Germanic Holy Roman Empire, and the **Rhenish Confederation** is created under a French presidency.

1808 — The people of Madrid rise up against the French troops. The ensuing war of Spanish Independence lasts until 1814. In that year, Wellington defeats Napoleon, and returns Ferdinand VII to the throne. In 1812, the Spanish Patriots draft the Constitution of Cadiz, a liberal document.

1809 The Papal States unite with France.

1812 Napoleon's downfall accelerates: after his disastrous campaign in Russia and the defeat of Leipzig in 1813, all of Europe unites against the French Emperor. Paris falls on 20 April, 1814 and Napoleon abdicates in favour of King Louis XVIII.

1814 After Napoleon's downfall, Belgium and Holland form the Kingdom of the Netherlands governed by William I of Orange who also becomes Grand Duke of Luxembourg.

1814-1815 The victorious Allies refashion Europe at the **Congress of Vienna**.

1815 The **German Confederation** is founded between 35 autonomous German states represented by a Diet of 11 members designated by the governments. Metternich, the Austrian Chancellor, acts as arbiter, turning it into a federation whose antiquated formula disappoints the German liberals who dream of a greater national presence.

THE INDUSTRIALISATION OF EUROPE (19C)

As Malthus forecasted, 19C Europe experiences a population explosion. In 1800, the continent numbers about 190 million inhabitants. By 1900, the population has reached about 420 million.

Although agriculture remains static, the urban population booms. In Britain, the most urbanised and soon the richest country in the world, nine out of ten inhabitants live in towns. New methods of transport, canals, railways, toll-free roads, and steamships, come of age, particularly in the British Midlands, giving birth to the Industrial Revolution. Britain soon exports its technical knowledge to other European countries. Industrialisation initiates mathematics, physics, chemistry, and technical progress. Old inventions make way for mechanisation, utilising hydroelectric power and steam. Coal basins and steel mines develop in Belgium, then France (Le Creusot with the brothers Schneider), and in Germany (the Ruhr with the Krupp family) and Silesia.

This modernisation exacerbates social problems, poverty, epidemics, lack of hygiene. In the long term, though, it encourages improvements in living conditions, education, and the position of women.

Nationalist and liberal movements, seeking to promote the ideals of the French Revolution, are repressed. Nevertheless, towards the end of the 19C, new nation-States, political parties and social reforms arise in Europe.

1819 In Britain, after a cavalry charge breaks up a meeting of Manchester workers in the so-called Peterloo Massacre, strict laws are promulgated restricting political demonstrations.

In Germany, the Carlsbad decrees forbid meetings and introduce press censorship.

1820 After Riego's liberal insurrection in Cadiz, Spain's 1812 constitution is re-established. However, in 1823, Ferdinand VII of Spain requests aid. The Hundred Sons of St Louis Army intervenes on the King's side to restore absolutism (up to 1833).

1821 Greek Orthodoxians, led by the secret society Philike Hetairia and supported by Russia, rebel against the Turkish authorities. In 1827, France and Great Britain intervene, destroying the Turkish fleet at Navarino. After the War of Greek Independence, also known as the National Revolution, Greece becomes independent in 1830. In 1843, the Greeks revolt against the absolute power of their king and obtain parliamentary rule.

1823 The Irish agitate for the repeal of the Act of Union (1800) under the leadership of Daniel O'Connell, known as the Liberator.

1829 The Roman Catholic Emancipation Act allows the election of Irish Catholics to Parliament.

1830 A first wave of revolution sweeps France.

In England, peasants revolt against large landowners.

In France, the Bourbons are driven out in the July Revolution, inspiring other European liberals.

Brussels' revolt against its Dutch monarch leads, to Belgian independence. Under Leopold I (1831-1865), Belgium fights another war against Holland in 1839.

In Portugal, a civil war (1828-1834) breaks out between liberals and absolutists, supported sometimes by France, sometimes by Britain.

In Italy, the *carbonari* patriots rise against the Austrian occupants and Mazzini establishes the Young Italy association. This popular movement soon inspires sister movements such as Young Germany, Young Poland, and Young Ireland. Mazzini himself hopes to forge a Young Europe movement.

The Polish insurrection against czarist oppression is violently quelled. Numerous Poles emigrate to France.

1832 Great Britain's Reform Act leads to the establishment of a modern parliamentary system.

1833- 1839 The liberals win the First Carlist war against the traditionalists in Spain.

1834-1837 Insurrections erupt in Genoa in the kingdom of the Two Sicilies.

1837-1901 **Queen Victoria**'s long reign, austere and puritanical, marks the apogee of Great Britain as a world power. In 1838, the Chartists agitate for an increase in the representative power of the House of Commons and universal suffrage. Friedrich Engels publishes in 1844 *The Condition of the Working Classes in England.*

1845-1849 After the great famine which caused 800 000 deaths, some one million Irishmen emigrate to England, Canada, and the United States.

1848 A second wave of revolutions sweep Europe, most of which are violently repressed.
After the French king, Louis Philippe's forced abdication, Louis Napoleon is elected by universal suffrage President of the French Republic.
In the wake of riots, a short-lived (1848-1849) German national Parliament meets in Frankfurt.
In Vienna, the Hungarian rising led by the nationalist Kossuth is repressed with the assistance of Russia but the Austrian conservative chancellor Metternich is forced to flee.
Franz-Joseph I ascends the throne. During his long reign (1848-1916), he restored the influence of the Habsburg dynasty and laid the foundations of a powerful and centralised State. However, he was rapidly confronted with the minority problem that led to the decline of the Austro-Hungarian Empire.
In Italy, the first war of Italian independence against Austria takes place. The liberal King Victor Emmanuel II, assisted by his minister Cavour, use Piedmont as their base.
After the troubles in Switzerland, a new constitution (revised in 1874), still in force today, is established, defining the country's federal political system.
The second Carlist war in Spain (1847-1849) ends with Isabella II's victory. A succession of uprisings by progressives and moderates disrupts her reign.
In England, Chartism comes to an end. Meanwhile, in Ireland a peasants revolt fails.
In Poland, insurrections in Cracow (1846) and Poznan (1848) are violently repressed.
Karl Marx, assisted by Friedrich Engels, writes the *Communist Party Manifesto.*

1851 The First Great Universal Exhibition is held in London.

1852 Napoleon III intervenes on the side of Piedmont against Austria. Austria loses Lombardy, after its defeats at Magenta and Solferino.

1854-1856 In the Crimean War, the Turks, aided by the French, British and Piedmontese, emerge victorious over the Russians. However, the Russian threat continues to menace Eastern Europe and the Balkans.

1858 The Irish Republican Brotherhood is founded.

1859 France supports the second war of Italian Independence. In 1860, supported by Cavour's complicity and the thousand Redshirts, Garibaldi frees Sicily and southern Italy from Bourbon rule. The Kingdom of Italy is proclaimed in 1861. Savoy and the county of Nice are given to France.

1861 Russia abolishes serfdom. Land is placed under collective ownership of the village, or in Russian, the *mir.*

1862 The Kingdom of Romania is created.

1862-1870 In eight years, **Bismarck** imposes by fire and by sword a centralised Germany governed by Prussia. He frustrates Austrian attempts to form a federation of the various States into a Great Germany extending from the North Sea to the Adriatic. Austria then directs its energies to the Balkans.

1863 Henri Dunant founds the international Red Cross in Switzerland. An Englishman, Thomas Cook, organises his first conducted tour in Switzerland.

1864 The First International meets in London.

1867 Driven out of Germany, the Habsburgs create the Dual Austro-Hungarian monarchy. The army, foreign policy, and finance remain under the rule of Vienna. Karl Marx publishes the first volume of his *Das Kapital.*

1868 France establishes freedom of the press.
The Spanish Revolution led by Prim brings Isabella's reign to an end.
The German Workers' Party is founded. In 1875, it becomes the Social Democratic Party.

1870 France declares war on Prussia. The fall of Sedan on 1 September marks the end of France's Second Empire, the birth of the Third Republic and the last phase of Italian and German unification. After a plebiscite, Rome is declared capital of a united Italy. On 18 January 1871, William I proclaims the **German Empire** at Versailles. Germany acquires Alsace and Lorraine and remains a federal state. However, Prussia holds almost total power.

1870-1900 Unions are organised to represent workers in European political life.

1873 Spain's Third Carlist War (1872-1876) leads to the king's abdication and the proclamation of a republic by the National Assembly.

From 1880 Following the German model, Social Democratic Parties emerge in Belgium, Holland, Austria, Poland, Hungary and Russia. Europeans begin to adopt social laws including pensions and public health insurance.

1882 Italy, Germany and Austria-Hungary sign the **Triple Alliance**.

1886 On 1 May, the American government reduces the working day to eight hours.

1889 In Paris, the Eiffel Tower is constructed for the Universal Exhibition. The Second International Congress is held.

1890 Emperor William II engineers Bismarck's resignation, just when Germany has experienced an industrial and demographic boom. Members of the Pan-German League push for expansion. William II's reckless foreign policy earns him the hostility of Britain, Russia and France.
Luxembourg proclaims its independence and is ruled by the Grand Duke Adolph of Nassau.
The Belle Époque begins in France and lasts throughout Europe until 1914.

1896 Frenchman Pierre de Coubertin organises the first modern Olympic games in Athens.

1899 Twenty-six states discuss disarmament at the First Peace Conference in The Hague.

CONFLICTS AND A UNITED EUROPE (20C)

1900 to 1945: Self-destruction

At the start of the century, the United States is already challenging Europe's technological and scientific supremacy. Then in less than half a century, the Old Continent is battered by two global wars, the massive economic crisis of 1929, and the turmoil of the 1917 revolution which transforms the Czarist Empire into the USSR. As a result, Europe ceases to dominate the world.
Social divisions divide the continent. The working class, while increasing in political power, remains impoverished. Only one sentiment succeeds in erasing social divisions: nationalism. Unfortunately, nationalism often produces dangerous dictatorships. An arms race ignites. Although some supporters of a united Europe attempt to ensure peace, they do not succeed

Social tensions, international crises:

1900 In Italy an anarchist assassinates King Humbert I. Victor Emmanuel III ascends to the throne in Italy.
The working classes remain very poor but gain political strength on a European scale. The Workers' International holds regular congresses (1900, 1904, 1907, 1910, and 1912).

1901 Alfred Nobel, the inventor of dynamite, establishes the Nobel Peace Prize. The inaugural award goes to Henri Dunant, founder of the Red Cross.

1904 France and Britain form the **Entente Cordiale**, and Italy moves close to them.

1905 Norway separates from Sweden.

1907 France, Britain, and Russia form the **Triple Entente**.

1910 Two years after the assassination in Lisbon of King Charles I, Portugal becomes a Republic.

1912-1913 War explodes in the Balkans. Under the leadership of Venizelos, the Greek Army liberates Macedonia and Turkish Epirus. Crete also comes under Greek control.

1914-1918 The **First World War** pits Germany, Austria, Turkey and Bulgaria against Serbia, Russia, Romania, France, Britain, Italy and the United States.

1914 The assassination in Sarajevo on June 28 of the Austrian Archduke Franz Ferdinand by a Serb nationalist precipitates the cataclysm. Austria's entry into war against Serbia leads to the general mobilisation of Europe's armies. On 1 August, Germany declares war on Russia then on 3 August against France. Germany's invasion of neutral Belgium prompts Britain's entry into the war on 4 August. The German offensive on the Western Front is halted at the Marne when Paris taxis assure the resupply of the French army. However, more than 700 000 German and French perish. A murderous land war now begins in the trenches, marked by deadly new weapons, gas, machine guns, aeroplanes, and submarines.

1915 Italy enters into the war on the side of the Allies.

February 1916 At the heroic battle of Verdun, French generals Pétain and Nivelle repel the German offensive.

1916 Bulgaria enters into the war on the side of Germany.

1917 After the Czar's abdication, Russia plunges into the throes of the **Bolshevik October Revolution**. **Lenin** asks for an armistice. The United States, whose merchant navy was attacked by German submarines, enter the war. Spain, which remained neutral during the conflict, experiences a general strike, harshly repressed.

1918 Wilson, President of the United States, proposes 14 points as a basis for peace in Europe, including disarmament and the founding of a **League of Nations**.
In October, an Allied counterattack finally subdues the Germans. Behind the line, revolution explodes in the Reich. On 11 November, the new German government represented by the People's Council, signs the **Armistice in Rethondes.**

1919 A series of Peace Conferences are held:
The Treaty of Versailles with Germany calls for occupation of the River Rhine's left bank for 15 years. Germany also relinquishes its colonies and a seventh of its territory and must pay heavy reparations.
The Treaty of St-Germain with Austria separates Austria from Hungary, awards Istria and Trentino to Italy, and recognises the independence of Czechoslovakia, Poland, Hungary and Yugoslavia.
The Treaty of Neuilly with Bulgaria gives Thrace and Smyrna to Greece.

1920 **The Treaty of Trianon** forces Hungary to relinquish Slovakia to Czechoslovakia, Transylvania to Romania, and the Banat to Yugoslavia.
The Treaty of Sèvres with Turkey assures international control of the Straits.
The Treaty of Turku with Russia guarantees the independence of Finland and the Baltic states.
The **League of Nations** is launched, comprising France, Great Britain, Italy and Japan as permanent members.

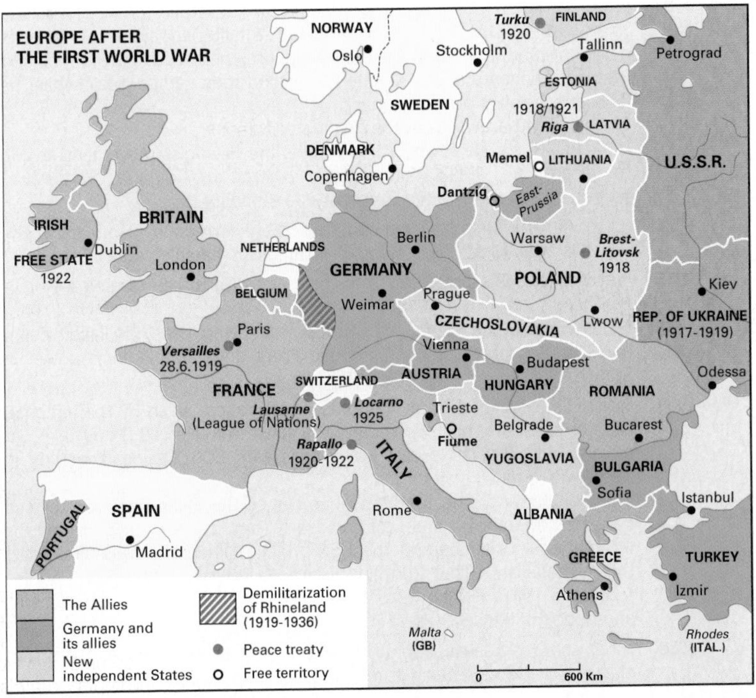

1919-1922 Conflict between Turkey and Greece leads to the emigration of 1.5 million Greeks from Asia Minor to Europe.

1922 The **Free State of Ireland** is founded. Independence follows the Easter Rising of 1916 in Dublin, the reorganisation of Sinn Fein in 1917, the declaration of independence in 1919, the anti-British campaign led by the IRA between 1919 and 1921, and civil war between the Free State Army and the Republicans.
In Italy, the fascist party marches upon Rome. **Mussolini** becomes head of the government, then Duce.
A brutal civil war ends in the creation of the Union of Soviet Socialist Republics (USSR). The Comintern (Communist International), based in Moscow, attempts to instigate a world revolution.
Belgium and Luxembourg form an economic union.

1923 France and Belgium occupy the Ruhr to force the Germans to pay reparations. Hitler, leader of the National Socialist German Workers' Party, attempts a putsch at Munich on 8-9 November. It fails. In Spain, with the king's support, General Primo de Rivera proclaims a dictatorship. However, opposition mounts.

1924 Stalin takes over after Lenin and launches a period of rapid industrialization of the USSR. Hitler publishes *Mein Kampf* in a climate of general indifference.

1925 to 1928: International détente

1925 After the evacuation of the Ruhr, the Pact of Locarno peacefully settles European disagreements.

1926 The Weimar German Republic joins the League of Nations.

1928 Fifty-four countries sign the Briand-Kellog Pact outlawing war.

1929 to 1939: Rise of the dictatorships

1929 The October Wall Street crash precipitates a massive world wide economic crisis.
Rome and the Papacy sign the Lateran Agreements.

1930 In Spain, General Berenguer replaces Primo de Ribera's dictatorship.

1931 In the Spanish general elections of April, the Republicans triumph in Catalonia and in the Basque country. The Second Republic is proclaimed after the king's departure. The right strongly opposes agrarian reforms, including the expropriation of large estates.

1933 **Hitler**, the last hope of six million unemployed, becomes chancellor of the Third Reich. The Führer constructs a totalitarian state. He arrests 4000 communists after the Reichstag fire, persecutes the Jews, and interns opponents of the regime in concentration camps. Meanwhile, he launches a policy of rearmament.
Germany withdraws from the League of Nations.
In Spain, Primo de Rivera's son founds the Falangist movement hostile to separatism. Totalitarian regimes emerge in Bulgaria, Yugoslavia, Austria, Poland, Portugal, Romania and Hungary.

1934 Catalonia proclaims its independence. The insurrection of miners in the Asturias against the right-wing government is harshly repressed.

1936 Italy occupies Ethiopia. Italy draws closer to Germany, forging a Rome-Berlin Axis.
Hitler violates the treaty of Locarno, occupying the Rhineland. Berlin hosts the Olympic Games. A Popular Front government takes power in France.

1936-1939 **Spanish Civil War:** on 18 July 1936, General Franco, aided by the nationalists, organises a military rebellion against the elected Popular Front government. A terrible civil war begins with 500000 dead, ending in 1939 with Franco's victory.
The Republicans, one tenth the number of the Falangists, are divided between anarchists and communists. They receive help from the International Brigades and the USSR, while Hitler and Mussolini assist the Nationalists. The Germans bomb Guernica. Appointed Caudillo (guide) in 1938, Franco restores the monarchy in Spain with an iron will, and appoints himself regent for life.

1938 Hitler annexes Austria, and at the Munich Conference, obtains the return of the Czech Sudetenland from the British and French.

1939 War becomes inevitable: after the dismantling of Czechoslovakia in March, Germany attacks Poland on 1 September, forcing the Allies to honour their guarantees.

1940-1945 The **Second World War** pits Hitler's Germany, Mussolini's Italy and Japan against France, Great Britain, the United States and the USSR.

June 1940 A formidable offensive *(Blitzkrieg)* enables the Germans to conquer most of Western Europe. The British alone, secure on their island, resist thanks to the heroic defence of their air force. Despite the armistice signed on 17 June, the Free French, comprising troops from Norway and volunteers from the French colonial empire, rally to General de Gaulle's call from London on 18 June, and continue the war on the side of the Allies.

1941 While Rommel pursues his offensive in Africa and the Balkans are conquered, Hitler invades Russia without warning. After Japan's attack on the American bases in **Pearl Harbour** in December, the Americans enter the conflict. The war has become a world war.

1942 The Third Reich reaches the summit of its power. Heroic resistance movements take shape in the occupied countries. But many choose to collaborate such as Pétain in France.

1943 A Soviet counter-offensive results in the victory of Stalingrad. Americans and British planes bomb German cities. The Allied armies land in Sicily. Mussolini is dismissed and arrested and Italy enters the war against Germany.

1944 The Allies land in Normandy in June and liberate Paris. The Red Army continues its difficult advance in the east towards Berlin.

1945 After the Führer's suicide on 30 April, Germany, now a vast expanse of ruins, capitulates at Reims on 8 May. The liberation of the death camps reveals to a horrified world the reality of the Nazi extermination policy. Six million Jews are dead.
Mussolini is executed. The United States drop the first atomic bombs in August on Hiroshima and Nagasaki.
At the **Yalta conference** in February between **Roosevelt**, **Stalin** and **Churchill**, Germany is divided into four occupied zones, Poland partitioned once more and Soviet nationals repatriated back to the USSR.
After 1945, millions of Europeans flee from communist regimes.

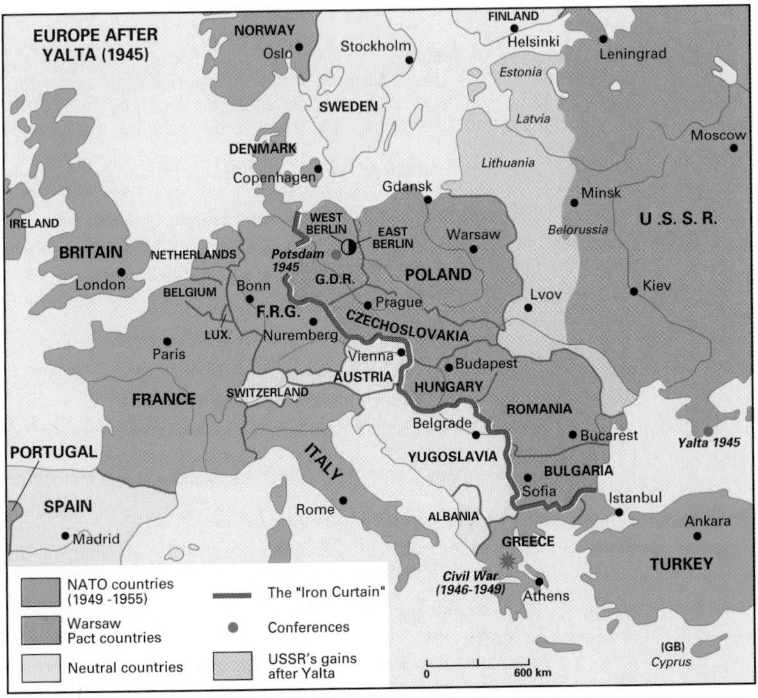

1945 TO 1992: TOWARDS RECONSTRUCTION

No other war created so many victims. Between 50 to 60 million perished of whom a large proportion were civilians. These horrific crimes against humanity underline the barbarity existing in a Europe once considered civilised.
In 1945, the old continent is drained and exhausted, while the United States and the USSR compete for world hegemony. In 1947, a final break occurs between Eastern Europe under Soviet control and Western Europe under the American influence.
After the loss of its colonial empires, Western Europe aspires to unification and succeeds in rebuilding a flourishing capitalist economy. The 1973 oil crisis exposes the weaknesses of the consumer society, while the socialist systems of Eastern Europe move towards self-destruction.
In recent years, the European Union has played an increasingly active role, while the communist Eastern Bloc has disintegrated. The dream of a united Europe, Gorbachev's homeland from the Urals to the Atlantic, has become a real possibility. Will the idea ever be realised?

1945 to 1960: Attempts to rebuild a vanquished and divided Europe

1947 Lord Mountbatten negotiates the independence of India. Pakistan is founded.
The USSR and its satellites refuse the Marshall Aid offered by America to all European countries that have suffered in the Second World War. As predicted by Churchill, the **Iron Curtains** splits Europe in two and the Cold War begins. The Cominform strengthens Soviet political and military pressure on Eastern Bloc countries but Soviet hegemony meets with resistance in Greece, Czechoslovakia and Yugoslavia.

1946-1949 After repelling the 1940 Italian invasion in Epirus, and resisting the German occupation, Greece is torn by civil war between pro-Americans and Communists.

1948 The Communists take power in Czechoslovakia in the Prague Coup of 25 February.
In Yugoslavia, independent **Marshall Tito** is accused of revisionism and breaks with Stalin.
In Germany, the United States, France and Great Britain unify their three zones of occupation and create a common monetary unit: the Deutschemark. In reprisal, the Soviets blockade the western sectors of Berlin.
The European Organisation for Economic Cooperation (OEEC which in 1961 is superseded by the OECD) is created to allocate American aid among the 16 countries benefiting from the Marshall Plan.
Belgium, the Netherlands and Luxembourg form the Benelux Customs union.

1949 Two Germanies are founded. The German Federal Republic comprises the three western zones. Under **Adenauer**, who remains Chancellor until 1963, West Germany experiences a spectacular economic recovery and normalizes its international relations. The Soviet zone becomes the German Democratic Republic.
NATO and the **Council of Europe**, which in 1950 promoted a European Convention for human rights, are founded.
Somalia, Libya, the Irish Republic and Indonesia gain independence.

1951 The **Treaty of Paris** establishes a coal and steel union and an independent high level European Authority representing governments.

1952 Elizabeth II's reign begins in Great Britain.

1953 Stalin dies on 5 March.

1954 Italy and Germany join the Union of Western Europe.
The French defeat at Dien Bien Phu marks the end of the eight-year-long war in Indochina and of French influence in Southeast Asia.

1955 Spain ends its diplomatic isolation under Franco and joins the UN at the same time as Ireland.
In response to Germany's entry into NATO, the **Warsaw Pact** is formed on 14 May.

1956 **Khrushchev** presides over the 20th Congress of the Soviet Communist Party in February. It launches de-Stalinisation and the abolition of the Cominform, but the USSR harshly represses nationalist insurrections in Warsaw and Budapest in October and November.
Nasser nationalises the Suez Canal, ending French and British influence in the Middle East.
After a referendum, the Sarre decides to become part of the German Federal Republic.

1957 The **Treaty of Rome** creates the **European Economic Community**. The founding Europe of Six consists of Luxembourg, Italy, France, Germany, the Netherlands, and Belgium.
In 1959, Britain, which had been excluded, creates EFTA, the European Free Trade Association.

1960 to 1974: Stagnation in the East, Prosperity in the West

1960 Marshall Tito is reconciled with the USSR.
The Belgian Congo gains independence.

1961 The Berlin Wall is erected on 13 August to stop the flow of refugees to the West.
The Belgrade Conference proclaims the policy of non-alignment promoted by Nehru, Nasser and Tito.

1962 In response to the decline in Christianity, the Pope launches the Second Vatican Council.
In France, a referendum establishes the election of the President of the Republic by universal suffrage.
The Evian Agreements end a ten-year-long war and recognise the Algerian Republic. French control of North Africa is finished. More than 800 000 Europeans are repatriated.

23 January 1964 Conrad Adenauer and Charles de Gaulle sign the Élysée Treaty solemnising Franco-German partnership.

1964 After attempts by Khrushchev at liberalisation, **Brezhnev** comes to power and tightens Soviet rule on its satellites.

1967-1974 A military dictatorship rules Greece.

May 1968 In France, students demonstrate with the support of workers on strike. This crisis reflects the anti-establishment youth movement against society.

August 1968 The Prague Spring is repressed by the tanks of the Warsaw Pact countries with the exception of Romania, which refused to send troops.

1969 The Irish Troubles erupt. British troops are dispatched to Northern Ireland to protect the Roman Catholic minority against the Unionist extremists. In 1971, the IRA sets off bombs to force the British out of Northern Ireland.

1970 Polish police repress riots in Gdansk.

1972 East and West Germany sign a treaty. Chancellor Brandt pursues an open door policy towards the East: Ostpolitik.

1973 Great Britain (after being opposed by Général de Gaulle in 1963 and 1967), Ireland, Northern Ireland and Denmark become members of the European Community.

1974 to 1985: The crisis years

1974 In Portugal's Revolution of the Carnations, the Army seizes power.
Greece disposes its military dictatorship and becomes a Republic.
The devaluation of the dollar and the increase in oil prices precipitate a European economic crisis, with unemployment, xenophobic movements and terrorist activity.

1974-1975 Portugal's African territories, Angola and Mozambique, win independence.

1975 Following Franco's death, Juan Carlos becomes King of Spain.

1976 The European Council decides to elect a European Parliament by universal suffrage.

1977 Adolfo Suarez is reelected president of the government in the Spanish general elections. In 1978, a new constitution is approved by referendum. Catalonia, the Basque Country and Galicia are awarded autonomy.
Ecologist movements gain strength, particularly the Greens in the German Federal Republic.

1978 The Red Brigades assassinate Italy's Christian Democrat president, Aldo Moro.
The Archbishop of Krakow, Karol Wojtyla, is elected Pope and takes the name of John Paul II.
The first Ariane rocket blasts off.

1980 In Gdansk, Lech Walesa, founder of the free union Solidarity, urges the workers to rebel against social and religious oppression.

1981 Greece joins the European Community.
A military coup fails in Spain on 23 February. In the 1982 general elections, Felipe Gonzalez is elected president of the Socialist government.
In France, Socialist François Mitterrand is elected President of the Republic.

1982 Christian Democrat Helmut Kohl becomes Chancellor of the German Federal Republic.

1983 Twelve million are unemployed in the EEC.

1985 to 1992: The end of Yalta's frontiers - the new Europe

1985	After a government crisis, Mikhail Gorbachev is elected General Secretary of the Soviet Communist Party. He launches *perestroika* (reform) and *glasnost* (openness).
1986	Portugal and Spain enter the EEC.
1987	The ERASMUS programme is launched in an attempt to initiate a European culture.
1989	The Eastern Bloc disintegrates: Poland, Hungary, then the GDR, Czechoslovakia, Bulgaria, Romania (execution of the dictator Ceaucescu and his wife) free themselves from the communist yoke.
10 November 1990	Berlin's **wall of shame** falls.
1990	The GDR holds free elections in May and its Parliament ratifies the treaty of reunification.
Spring 1991	The Federal Socialist Republic of Yugoslavia collapses. Slovenia and Croatia declare independence. Serbia and Montenegro constitute the new Yugoslavia or Federal Yugoslav Republic. A terrible civil war explodes.
7 February 1992	Europe's leaders sign the Treaty of Maastricht.
11 November 1992	The synod of the Anglican Church decides to accept the ordination of women. An increasing number of countries (Austria, Norway, Switzerland, Turkey, Sweden, Malta) request admission to the European Community which, despite disagreements between member States, has become an acknowledged political and economic power.
1 January 1995	Austria, Finland and Sweden become members of the European Union which now counts 15 member States.
December 1995	The Dayton Peace Treaty is signed in Paris ending the war between Croatia, Serbia and Bosnia.
September 1997	Municipal elections take place in Bosnia-Herzegovina.
8-9 July 1997	NATO conference in Madrid accepting in principle membership of Poland, Hungary and the Czech Republic.
10 April 1998	Signature of the Belfast Peace Accord aimed at ending hostilities between Protestants and Catholics in Northern Ireland. Hungarians vote to join NATO.
1 January 1999	In 11 European Union countries (Austria, Belgium, Finland, France, Germany, Ireland, Italy, the Grand Duchy of Luxembourg, the Netherlands, Portugal and Spain), prices are shown in the national currency and in Euros.
13 March 1999	Hungary, Poland and the Czech Republic join NATO.
2002	In 11 European Union countries, the Euro will be the only currency. Coins and notes in Euros will shortly replace the national currencies.

*The **Michelin Maps** scale 1:200,000 for this region are shown in the diagram below the table of contents*

The text refers to the maps which, owing to their scale or coverage, are the clearest and most appropriate in each case

Do you know where to find these masterpieces?

1 Guernica by Pablo Picasso
2 Mona Lisa by Leonardo da Vinci
3 Death and Fire by Paul Klee
4 The Night Watch by Rembrandt
5 Music and Dance by Matisse
6 The Birth of Venus by Botticelli
7 Church at Auvers by Van Gogh
8 The Four Apostles by Albrecht Dûrer
9 The Burning of the Houses of Parliament by Turner
10 The Scream by Edvard Munch
11 The Ambassadors by Holbein the Young
12 Descent from the Cross by Rubens
13 The Clothed Maja and Naked Maja by Goya
14 Artemision Poseidon (bronze statue)
15 The Kiss by Gustav Klimt
16 The Maids of Honour (Las Meninas) by Velazquez
17 The Old Testament Trinity by Andrei Rublev
18 Polyptych of the Adoration of St Vincent by Nuno Gonçalves
19 Icon of the Black Madonna
20 Descent from the Cross by Caravaggio

Answers on p 83

The Fine Arts in Europe

PREHISTORY

Prehistoric art in Europe did not appear until the **Upper Paleolithic** period. Specialists separate personal art such as carved bone and wood, anthropomorphic statuettes, and decorated everyday objects from wall art, mainly identified in the Spanish Levant and in the south of France. Encampments dating from the Paleolithic Period have been discovered in Mezerich (Russia) and Pavlov (Moravia) as well as a few rare European sites.
During the **Neolithic period** (c 6500 BC), permanent settlements, livestock raising and ceramics became widespread throughout Europe. While the Danubian civilisation spread to the Atlantic seaboard, the Mediterranean world was a different, more advanced Neolithic culture, particularly with regard to urbanisation. Megalith sculpture, carved or rough-hewn menhirs and dolmens, took root in Western Europe.
From 3000 BC, metallurgy developed in Western Europe, causing a rapid expansion of techniques and handicrafts. Initially, metallurgy was most intensive in southern Spain (Río Tinto) and Ireland (Mount Gabriel). Jewellery and weapon making predominated.

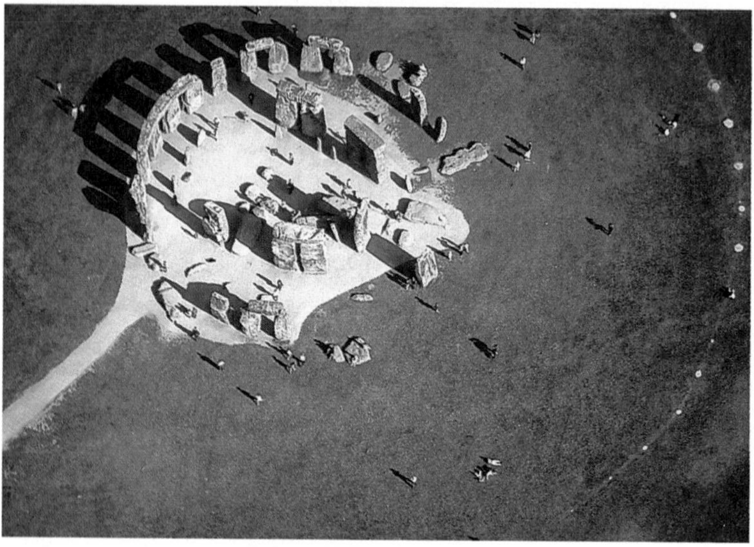

A Howarth/EXPLORER

Aerial view of Stonehenge, Great Britain

The art of metal-making progressed and reached its peak with the Celtic culture. Originally from the steppes, the Celts settled throughout Europe at the end of the bronze age and the iron age. This warlike people buried their dead in chariot tombs. The Roman conquest put an end to this civilisation, while integrating certain Celtic traits.

GRECO-ROMAN ART, THE BASIS OF WESTERN ART

Greek art

Development of Greek art – Cretan and Mycenaen influences played an important role. But Greek Art did not come into its own until the 9C BC. **Ceramics** with geometrical motifs were produced for everyday use and funerals. The Greeks exported their art throughout the Mediterranean and Greek traders played a principal role in hellenising western art.

Sculpture developed in the Archaic Era from 700 to 480 BC. *Kouros* (young nude man) and *Koré* (young woman) provided the main subjects for primitive sculptures based on pharaonic funerary statues.
In the 8C BC, two orders of **architecture** appeared, Doric and Ionic. The Corinthian and Composite orders did not appear until later.
In the 5C, Athens asserted its political and cultural hegemony, launching ambitious architectural and urban projects, particularly the development of the Acropolis. The sculptor **Pheidias** and great politician Pericles dominated the century. The harmony of proportions in this golden era of art provided a constant model for future western art.

Greek and Roman Art

Ministry of Culture, Athens.

The Theatre, Epidauros (Greece)

P. Roy / EXPLORER.

The Laocoon (Vatican Museums)

Römermuseum, Augst

Romain mosaic in Augst (Switzerland)

A. Abbe / VLOO.

Roman theatre in Merida (Spain)

Between the death of Alexander in 323 BC and the Roman conquest in the 1C BC, artistic creation moved towards the eastern provinces of the Greek Empire. This period's "**Hellenistic**" art represents a sculptural milestone. The Romans executed countless copies, creating future sources of European academic sculpture. Knowledge of Greek models has been kept alive in Europe through writings such as Pausanias' guide book, architectural plans and engravings.

Architecture, sculpture, bas-reliefs – The **Greek temple** is not a place of worship. It contains the statue of a god, but sacrifices take place outside. Initially built of perishable materials, temples were constructed of stone from the 7C BC. Although temple plans vary, they usually consists of a *cella* (containing the cult image), a *pronaos* (a sort of antechamber to the cella) and an *opisthodomos* (behind the *cella*).
The Greek temple's façade presents a row of columns, topped with a triangular pediment. The temple is surrounded by one peripteral temple or two rows of dipteral columns. Temples built on a circular plan are called tholos – for example, the tholos of Delphi. This type of circular building was popular during the Renaissance.
The **theatre** consisted of a circle of tiered seating *(cavea)*. Below, a circular area *(orchestra)* was separated by a low wooden barrier forming the stage. The theatres of Epidaurus in Greece and Pergamos in Eastern Turkey are the best preserved.

Bas-reliefs and **sculpture** represent the main ornaments of Greek buildings. Ionic temples are decorated with a frieze around the outside wall of the *cella*. The Great Panathenia Procession frieze on the Parthenon, executed by Pheidias' studio – today kept in the Louvre in Paris and the British Museum in London – and the Pergamon altar decoration – in the Staatliche Museum in Berlin – are the most famous pieces of monumental Greek decoration.
Greek statuary is mainly known through Roman replicas. During Classical times, in 5C BC, **Polyclitus** defined his Canon. It said the height of the body is equal to seven times that of the head. During the Hellenistic Era, **Lysippus** modified the canon to eight times the height of the head. The male body is depicted nude, with a slight sway of the hips, or dressed as a philosopher from Classical Antiquity with the end of his cloak held over his arm. Women are dressed in a tunic and cloak; the female nude only became widespread in Greek art during the Hellenistic Era. During this period, sculpture became expressionistic and oriental. It showed in exaggerated realism not only pain, but also movement. The *Laocoon* in the Vatican Museum and the *Winged Victory of Samothrace* in the Louvre represent good examples of this style.

Roman art

When the Romans began their conquests on the Italian peninsular and later around the Mediterranean Basin, they were enemies of luxury and showed little interest in the arts. Contact with the Greek civilisation changed Roman values. Although dependent on Greek models, Roman art distinguishes itself by the use of brick for utilitarian architecture and the importance of public art.

Public architecture: religious and civil – The Roman **temple**, in its plan and elevation, is derived from the Greek model. However, a few changes are visible: the pediment is rarely sculpted and the columns along the outside wall of the cella can be set against the wall.
In Rome, as in most of the towns in the Empire, monumental decoration consisted of a series of temples, baths, a theatre, and a circus.
The **baths** played an important role in Roman social lives. They included the cold rooms *(frigidarium)*, warm rooms *(tepidarium)* and hot rooms *(caldarium)*. The baths generally included a built-in gymnasium called *palaestra*, and sometimes a library such as at Caracalla's and Diocletian baths in Rome.
The Roman **theatre** differed from that of the Greek theatre. The cavea was part of the stage wall; the orchestra was not circular, but semicircular. The stage wall, a palace façade of colonnades and statuary, served as a backdrop for performances. The Merida theatre in Spain and the Orange theatre in France are well preserved.

Private architecture: Roman villas and palaces – Roman **villas** varied in style but followed certain rules. A rich villa, such as that of the Fauna in Pompeii, always had a peristyle, an open courtyard surrounded by a portico, and an atrium around which the bedrooms and *tablinium* (private apartment) were organised. Large country villas were composed of a *pars urbana* (apartments) and a *pars rustica* (functional buildings such as barns).
Palace architecture ranged from Nero's gold house in Rome and Hadrian's Villa in Tivoli. But the ceremonial rooms and garden landscaping were always of great importance. The houses and palaces were richly decorated with frescoes often utilising *trompe l'œil*. **Mosaics**, for which the techniques varied from one workshop to the other, covered the floors and sometimes the walls.

Public art – Official events, often military, were celebrated in triumphal arches, equestrian and pedestrian statues, monumental trophies and columns.

Sculpture and portraits – Roman portraits followed the conventions of Greek portraiture but could be distinguished by a concern with naturalism, sometimes even caricature. In sculpture, the Romans copied or carried out pastiches of Hellenistic originals.

BYZANTINE ART

In the 4C, the Roman emperor, Constantine reunited the Western and Eastern Empires and transferred his capital to Byzantium, renamed Constantinople, in 330. Christianity, which had become the State religion, demonstrated its fervour in its art. The Paleo-Christian monuments adopted the well-known forms of Roman architecture (a basilica with apsidal chapels or centrally-planned mausoleum) and later the richly ornamental features mastered by the Byzantine civilisation (Rome and Ravenna, 5C and 6C). Byzantine art continued this merger of Early Christian art and Greco-Oriental art. It is characterised by a highly-developed sense of the sacred expressed in the magnificent mosaics and frescoes which decorate the domes, walls and columns of the religious buildings, and icons, or painted objects of veneration. Hieratic and mystical, this sumptuous art spread from south eastern Europe to Italy (from Venice to Sicily), as well as Central Europe and Russia. This was subsequently the area in which the Orthodox faith was adopted after its separation from Rome in the 11C.

THE MIDDLE AGES

The barbarian invasions resulted in a decisive rupture with Roman tradition. The invention of printing, the discovery of America and the fall of Grenada all influenced art of the Middle Ages.

Art at the time of the Barbarian kingdoms

After the barbarians sacked Rome in 410, they brought new elements to western art, particularly in colours and gold and silver ware. They invented the cloisonné enamel technique. In Italy, the Lombard civilisation produced the altar of the Duke of Ratchis in Cividale Cathedral and the gold and silver ware in the Monza Cathedral Treasury. The Visigoth capitals of the Church of San Pedro de la Nave in Spain represent a good example of the barbarian style of representing anatomy. The Quarrazar treasure in the Madrid Archeological Museum shows the perfection of Visigoth gold and silver ware. In France, the hypogeum of the Dunes in Poitiers is a funerary chamber of Gallo-Roman tradition. Serpents carved on the steps indicate German inspiration.
Ireland, a refuge for the Latin tradition during the Barbarian invasions in continental Europe, developed its monastic art during the 6C and 7C. It incorporated decorative elements crucial to the formal, iconographic Roman heritage.

The Carolingian Renaissance and the end of Barbarian art – Charlemagne's rise to power and his desire to unify Europe brought a deliberate return to ancient art forms: centrally planned buildings such as in Aachen and gatehouses modelled on imperial arches such as at Lorsch Abbey. The Carolinian religious buildings have a double chancel and a double transept to the east and west. They are based on the abbey church of St-Riquier in France. This facilitated the cult of relics.

Development of Romanesque art

Around the year 1000, European art split into two distinct trends. The Germanic area remained faithful to Carolinian traditions of Ottonian art, while Southern Europe developed Romanesque art.

Ottonian art – The Carolinian buildings served as a model for major Ottonian works of art such as St Michael's in Hildesheim (now restored to its original state) and the abbey of Hersfeld. The decoration closely resembles Carolinian frescoes such as the painted cycle of St George of Oberzell on Reichenau Island in Lake Constance.
Ottonian art was rich in religious gold and silver ware; the cross of Abbess Mathilda in Essen Cathedral consists of embossed gold sheet, enamel and filigree work.

Romanesque art – In the rest of Europe, particularly in Italy, Northern Spain and the Southwest France, new architectural experiments took place in the organisation of volumes and the execution of external decorative features. At the San Paragorio in Noli, Italy, the chevet is enclosed by two small apses, and walls decorated with pilaster-strips and festoons. At St Cecilia of Montserrat (Spain), an attempt at stone vaulting was extended to the whole of the building. In France, monumental sculpture appeared on the lintel of Saint-Genis-les-Fontaines (Roussillon).

Characteristics of Romanesque building – The most common basilica plan consisted of a nave completed by a chancel, with or without a transept. The chancel of Romanesque churches varied. Sometimes it was straight with staggered apses, and sometimes festooned with radiating chapels. Although timber vaulting is still found on occasions such as in Peterborough, England, stone vaulting, either barrel or dome, characterised most Romanesque building.
External buttressing reinforced the walls. Sculpture was located outside on the tympanum, arches and compound piers, and inside on the capitals. The subjects were generally taken from the Bible.
The frame law required that the depicted form follow the contours of its frame. It is the main aesthetic principle of Romanesque art.

GOTHIC ART

Genesis of Gothic art in Europe – As the Romanesque style peaked in the early 12C, Gothic art began to appear in France and England. In Durham, rib vaulting was used to cover the nave. In St Denis, outside Paris, rib vaulting in the narthex was combined with important innovations on the façade: statue-columns and sculptures appeared in covings. These innovations soon spread throughout Europe. Ribs appeared at Limburg-on-the-Lahn in Germany, Pórtico de la Gloria in Santiago de Compostela in Spain, and Rochester and Chichester in England. Shortly before 1200, two major innovations signalled the coming of Classical Gothic: the use of flying buttresses on Notre-Dame in Paris and inscription of the theme of the Virgin Mary on the portal of Notre-Dame-de-Senlis in France.

Classical Gothic peaked in Europe between about 1180 and 1270 with the reconstruction of the Cathedral of Chartres in France. The unequal-sided quadrilateral plan was used for the rib vaulting, three storeys articulated the interior elevation. In the Sainte Chapelle in Paris, a rose window created an illusion of light, brightening up the inside of the building.

From the 13C, the Gothic style prevailed throughout Europe, with each nation developing its own particular tone. In Spain, despite the adoption of French models, windows were sometimes converted into oculi as in Barcelona Cathedral.

In England, the decomposition of the vault gave rise to the decorative style in the chancel of Exeter Cathedral and the fan vaults in the Gloucester cloisters. The screen façades in Wells Cathedral differ from those of the Chartres tradition.

In Northern and Eastern Germany, the execution in brick of the Backsteingothik in Lübeck, and the unusual plan of hall churches lent originality to the Gothic style.

In Italy, the Gothic style developed with some difficulty. The taste for polychrome and mosaics, the alternate use of coloured marbles or **pietra serena** and white stone in the façade of Orvieto Cathedral, and the custom of separating the campanile and baptistery are specifically Italian traits.

During the 14C, Gothic architecture did not develop any further in its principles, but the ornamental vocabulary resulted in a plethora of stone lace details – pinnacles, gables, outer fillets, and flames. This Flamboyant Gothic produced St-Maclou in Rouen, Henri VII Chapel in Westminster, and the Burgos Cathedral in Spain. It was referred to as *gótico florido* and in Germany as *Spätgotik*. The carved wood altarpieces, painted and gold-leafed, are grandiose and exuberant, particularly in Flanders and Spain.

Gothic sculpture and painting – As the statue-columns on the cathedral portals were freed from their architectural context, they gained in movement and expressiveness. The representations of the *Church* and the *Synagogue* on the portal of Bamberg Cathedral in Germany are good examples.

Peter Parler (Prague Cathedral) and **Claus Sluter** *(Le Puits de Moïse* in the Champmol Charter house in Dijon, France) represent the main 14C sculptors. A painful, macabre realism also characterises some of the works of the time such as the *Pietà Roettgen* in the Rhenish Museum of Bonn, Germany.

In the 14C, easel painting began. A good example is the portrait of Jean le Bon in the Louvre Museum. But in Italy, **Giotto** developed the science of perspective and representation.

At the turning point between the Gothic and the Renaissance styles, the 15C art of the Flemish Primitives was enamoured of colour and descriptive realism. The Flemish excelled in miniature. The greatest painter was **Jan van Eyck** (after 1441). He invented oil painting. After him came the Bruges School, including **Petrus Christus, Memling** and **Gerard David**. In Tournai, France, **Robert Campin**, sometimes called the Master of Flémalle, trained **Rogier van der Weyden**. Mysticism infuses Van der Weyden's heart-rending compositions whereas his sharp, precise drawings resulted in remarkable portraits. His pupil, **Thierry Bouts**, produced impassive expressions tempered by rich colours and crowded backdrops.

Hieronymus Bosch (1450-1516), although in contact with Flemish masters such as Bouts, remained an isolated personality. He demonstrated great fineness and precision of touch and, in particular, an inexhaustible surrealistic imagination.

THE RENAISSANCE

The Italian Renaissance, model for Europe's Renaissance

While Gothic art dominated the rest of Europe, the Renaissance swept Italy.

New Style art in Florence in the 15C – Innovative artists emerged in Florence in the early 15C benefiting from the important patronage of the Medici family. A return was made to the sobriety of ancient art.

Brunelleschi introduced the use of mathematical perspective into architecture. In particular, he designed the portico of the Foundlings' Hospital with semicircular arcades and regular bays. He also created the square module at San Lorenzo. The other major architect of the period was Michelozzo. He built the Palazzo Medici, a model for Renaissance palaces of the Tuscan type.

Romanesque and Gothic art

Gauthier / PIX.

Statues on the doorway of St-Trophime, Arles (France)

S. Chirol.

Amiens Cathedral, quadripartite vaulting around the transept crossing (France)

LAUROS / GIRAUDON.

Doorway of Glory, Santiago de Compostela (Spain)

HUBER / Garmisch-Partenkirchen

Cross of Lothair (990), Ottonian Art, Aachen (Germany)

GIRAUDON

Chartres Cathedral, The Three Kings (detail) 12C (France)

Finally, the treatises of architect **Alberti** enjoyed considerable influence on 16C Europe. His Palazzo Rucellai superposed Greek and Roman orders to decorate the façade. Palatial architecture underwent a decisive evolution with construction of the suburban villa of Poggio a Caiano by **Guiliano da Sangallo**. The gardens, the square plan, found again at Chambord in France, for example, the symmetrical layout of the rooms and the portico terrace demonstrate total independence of medieval traditions.

In sculpture, **Donatello** abandoned Gothic conventions in his bronze *David*. The figure, with slightly turned hips, was the first ancient-style nude of the Renaissance. Originally placed in the courtyard of the Palazzo Medicio, it now stands in the Bargello in Florence.

In painting, **Masaccio** made the major innovations. He avoided gilt backgrounds, substituting realism, a more systematic use of perspective, and a humanist vision of sacred history. In his wake, the 15C Florentine School divided into two main branches. The first was powerful, sculptural and sometimes austere, always preoccupied in particular with volume and represented by painters such as **Paolo Uccello, Andrea del Castagno, Piero della Francesca** and ultimately **Michelangelo**. The second was more flowery, anecdotal and gentle, concerned with beauty of lines, **Fra Angelico, Ghirlandaio**, a painter of upper middle class society, the **Lippi** family and, above all, **Botticelli,** who was attached to the Medici Court.

In this creative melting pot, the surprising, polymorphous personality of **Leonardo da Vinci** made its mark. His work was aimed at expressing perfect, timeless beauty in which the contours and backgrounds are suffused with blurred outlines and bluish mists.

SCALA

Donatello: *David*, Bargello Museum, Florence (Italy)

SCALA

Michelangelo: *the tomb of Lorenzo de Medici*, New Sacristy of San Lorenzo, Florence (Italy)

Rome in the first decades of the 16C – From 1500, Florence's power and artistic influence gave way to Rome. Pope Julius II commissioned the major artists of the time – **Bramante, Michelangelo** and **Raphael** – to work on the Sistine Chapel, the Vatican and St Peter's. This period marks the peak of humanism, characterised by references to Greco-Roman art, the search for anatomical truth and the expansion of secular culture. Outside Rome, numerous cities came into their own, particularly Venice, the creative home of great painters such as **Titian, Tintoretto** and **Veronese**.

The Italian style spreads throughout Europe

From the middle of the century, other Europeans imitated the Italian example. Each nation, however, maintained and developed its own originality.

The French Renaissance – Francis I introduced the Italian style into the French court, although Louis XII had already brought several Lombard artists back to France. Initially, the Italian manner only affected the architectural decoration with its plethora of shells, foliage, and little angels called *putti*. Princely residences discarded the

SCALA

Veronese:The Meal in the House of Levi, Academy of Fine Arts, Venice (Italy)

defensive function of the castle and gave full rein to pomp and splendour at Chenonceau and Azay-le-Rideau. The vast royal projects of Blois Château continued this trend, basing the loggias on the façade with examples from the Vatican.
Italians **Primaticcio, Rosso** and **Nicoló dell'Abate** established the Fontainebleau School, and finished perhaps the most striking Italian decoration in France in Fontainebleau Palace. During the second part of the century, French art moved away from Italian models. **Pierre Lescot** (Hôtel Carnavalet in Paris), **Philibert Delorme** (Anet Château) and the sculptors **Jean Goujon** and **Germain Pilon**, developed a new style.

The German Renaissance – In Germany, the Italian influence was highly accentuated. The Palatine electors of Heidelberg rebuilt the castle and turned it into a pleasure palace. The Othon-Henry Wing boasts a rich decor of pilasters, and foliated scrolls. In Munich, Albert V hired an Italian architect to built the first extension to the castle outside the medieval walls, the Antiquarium. Finally the Landshut Residence resembled the Palazzo del Té in Mantua.
In painting, **Albrecht Dürer** was the greatest artist of the period and known as the prince of German artists. **Matthias Grünewald** and **Lucas Cranach** remained, in some ways, close to Gothic conventions.

Spain and Portugal – In the Moorish Calahorra Castle, an Italian-style interior court was built by artists from Genoa and Lombardy. **Machuca**, an artist trained in Raphael's studio, designed Charles V's palace in the Alhambra in Grenada. He used the vocabulary of the Renaissance, a plan on a square module, interior colonnade, and superposition of orders.
However, Spanish art developed a unique **Plateresque** style, blending the ornamental vocabulary of Flamboyant Gothic and traditions of Islamic origin. Good examples include the Alcazar in Toledo, the Salamanca University façade and the Grego de Valladolid College.
In painting, **El Greco** (1541-1614), trained in Italy and scorned by the Spanish court, developed a powerful personal art in Toledo. Elongated figures, and cold, contrasting colours characterise his work.
In Portugal, **Manueline** art flowered during the reign of Manual I (1495-1521). This art marked the transition from the local Gothic style (which was infused with Islamic elements) to the Renaissance style. In the Batalha Monastery and that of Jerónimos in Lisbon, the decor consisting of plants, repeated geometrical and calligraphic themes remain far more important than the volume.

England and the Netherlands – England remained outside the innovative European movement. Wollatton Hall, near Nottingham in England, is the most important example of the era. The German painter, **Holbein the Younger**, finished his career in London in the service of Henry VIII.
In the Netherlands, civil architecture blossomed. The Antwerp Town Hall by **Cornelius Floris** has arcades on the ground floor and upper floors decorated with pilasters; the central body evokes a traditional bell-tower.
Brussels was the production centre of tapestries for all of Europe. Pope Leo X ordered a series based on cartoons by Raphael and later, Henry IV set up a workshop of Flemish weavers in Paris.
In the 16C, **Quentin Massys** (1466-1530) became the first Flemish painter to draw inspiration from the Renaissance, developing an art of delicacy and refinement. He was noted for religious subjects and portraits.

Pieter Bruegel the Elder (c 1525-1569), an emulator of Hieronymus Bosch, produced cheerful paintings full of picturesque observation. His son, Pieter, known as **Hell Brueghel**, imitated him with talent.

The Renaissance

Château d'Azay-le-Rideau

3bis / MICHELIN.

Brussels (Belgium): Tapestry of the *Legend of Notre-Dame-du-Sablon*

Musées Royaux d'Art et d'Histoire.

Plateresque decoration Colegio de San Gregorio, Valladolid, Spain

Ch. Sappa / CEDRI.

Matthias Grünewald: *Isenheim Altarpiece*, Colmar, France

GIRAUDON.

THE SEVENTEENTH CENTURY

The Birth of Classicism and Baroque

Roman artistic circles fostered the two main artistic movements of the 17C – Classicism and Baroque.

Roman Classicism – During the last few years of the 16C and up until the end of the first quarter of the 17C, Roman art reacted against Mannerism. The Council of Trent, completed in 1563, called for messages to be comprehensible. Along with the search for archeological verity, major repercussions were felt on religious art.

St-Paul's Cathedral, London, Great Britain

PICTOR

In painting, different genres practised landscapes, still lives, and historical paintings. **Annibale Carracci** pioneered new Classicism; on the ceiling of Palazzo Farnese in Rome, he painted love fables from Ovid as a manifesto of a new art. The decorative system of the vaulted ceiling juxtaposed illusionist architecture, *quadri riportati* and stucco: it foreshadowed Italian ceiling decoration in 17C Europe. Carracci's draughtsmanship shows the attentive study of ancient sarcophagi: his frieze composition, with little depth, focuses on order, clarity and legibility.

In architecture, a similar trend is visible in religious buildings such as **Carlo Moderno**'s St-Suzanna Church. The simple structure of the façade contrasts with the complexity of the Mannerist buildings. In Milan, Saint Charles Borromeo spread the classicist style and **Fabbio Mangone**, in accordance with his austere spirituality, erected the Helvetic College. Ionic colonnades line the courtyard of this monument.

Classicism's impact varied throughout Europe. The Farnese Palace's decorative vaulted roof was imitated in private French mansions such as the gallery of the Hôtel de la Vrillière or Tuileries Palace in Paris. Unfortunately, both have been destroyed. Painters **Guido Reni** and **Domenichino** worked for European courts propagating Classical ideas.

In architecture, **Palladio** followed in the footsteps of Bramante in Venezia and exalted the elegance of Roman and Greek styles, building churches, palaces and luxurious villas.

Inigo Jones, a great admirer of Palladio, introduced the Renaissance vocabulary into England. His Queen's Pavilion in Greenwich represented Britain's first Palladian villa. Its façade was studded with orders and inside a split-level drawing room and loggia gave out onto the garden. After the Civil War, **Sir Christopher Wren** extended the classicist style in his plans for St Paul's Cathedral.

Realism – During the first decade of the 17C, realism developed in Rome. **Caravaggio** initiated this stylistic reform which refused idealization and practised chiaroscuro. Caravagesque lighting defines a dramatic, intense space. Caravaggio also reformed religious iconography, drawing inspiration from everyday lives.

Caravaggio: *The Fortune-Teller*, The Louvre, France

RMN

After the artist's death, Caravagism underwent rapid expansion in Europe, particularly in Utrecht with **Honthorst** and **Ter Brugghen**, in France with **Claude Vignon**, in Lorraine with **Georges de la Tour**, and in Spain with the early works by **Velasquez**.

Roman Baroque – Towards the middle of the century, a new group of artists moved away from Classicism and towards Baroque. **Bernini** played an essential role as both sculptor and architect. His works such as the *Ecstasy of St Theresa* in Santa Maria della Vittoria in Rome depict the movement of the garment, facial expressionism, and other theatrical, dramatic effects. In architecture, Sant'Andrea al Quinirale developed other features of Baroque art: an oval plan, an absence of interior axial chapels, the use of light, and a semicircular portico or a façade. Curved lines mark the work of architects **Pietro de Cortone** and **Borromini**.

D. Hée/MICHELIN

Palace of Versailles, France

French Classicism

Throughout the 17C, French art remained hostile to Roman Baroque. Bernini's design was rejected for the Louvre Palace.

Three architects, **Jacques Lemercier** (circa 1585-1654), **François Mansart** (1598-1666) and **Louis Le Vau** (1612-1670), played an essential role in defining the norms of Classical architecture in France. Lemercier built Cardinal Richelieu's mansion and the church of La Sorbonne in Paris. He relied on Italian influences, which predominated in the field of religious architecture: two-storey façades, a fore part with columns, and a crowning with a triangular pediment. François Mansart was more innovative, formulating the château plan of a central pavilion with a fore part. Mansart accentuated vertical and horizontal lines, the use of Doric, Ionic, and Corinthian orders. Le Vau was more attentive to the main examples of Italian Baroque in the cupola and concave wings of the Palais des Quatre Nations, today the Institute of France, in Paris. His château in Vaux-le-Vicomte, whose plan is similar to that of Balleroy in Normandy, foreshadowed Versailles.

Palais de Versailles/RMN

Coysevox: Bust of Louis XIV

Louis XIV and Versailles Classicism – Louis XIV and Colbert created the Academy and the Gobelins tapestry factory, leading to a triumph of French Classicism. In the Château de Versailles, Le Vau, **Jules Hardouin-Mansart** (1646-1708) and **Robert de Cotte** defined an architecture of pomp and splendour. Inside, **Le Brun** (1619-1690) and artists from his studio painted and sculpted decor to the

glory of the monarch. This art required perfection of draughtsmanship and used an allegorical language and references to antiquity. The Versailles park, designed by **Le Nôtre** (1613-1700), demonstrates the rigour and openness of a French garden. Geometrical plant compositions, wide avenues, fountains, backdrops of greenery, shrubbery and allegorical sculptures present an image of a perfectly mastered and orderly nature.
In painting, the return of **Simon Vouet** (1590-1649) to France in 1627 after a long period in Rome, followed by the creation of the Royal Academy of Painting and Sculpture in 1648 expanded the French School. Italian, Venetian (richness of colours) and Roman (dynamic composition) references mark the art of Vouet and his pupil **Eustache Le Sueur** (1616-1655). However, these French masters always tempered their emotion with a concern for order and clarity. Decoration with mythological subjects, religious subjects recommended by the Counter-Reformation and portraits formed the backbone of their work.
Landscape artists **Claude Gellée** known as Le Lorrain (1600-1682) and **Poussin** (1595-1665) spent their careers in Rome. Their Classical landscapes show an idealised nature. They often depicted heroic landscapes in episodes from Ancient History or the Bible.
In sculpture, the study of antiquity and the clarity of composition is epitomised by **François Girardon** (1628-1715) and **Antoine Coysevox** (1640-1720). The sculptor **Pierre Puget** (1620-1694), little appreciated during his lifetime, also proved sensitive to the dynamics of Baroque.

Seventeenth-Century art in Spain and the Netherlands

Spain – In the 17C, Spain reflected a large artistic autonomy. Religious art found its accomplishment in the decorative sumptuousness and the architectural complexity of the great Catholic altarpieces. The Churrigueresque style (from **Churriguera**, a dynasty of architects) shows a freedom and exuberance similar to Baroque. In painting, tenebrism identified the Spanish School with its dark tones, predilection and sometimes macabre realism. **Velasquez, Zurbaran** and **Murillo** were the most striking personalities of the period. Religious painting and archaic still life were the most popular styles.

The Netherlands – The Dutch attached particular importance to the town hall, a symbol of economic and political importance. **Jacob van Campen** built Amsterdam political headquarters after signing of the Treaty of Westphalia. **Elias Holl**'s Augsburg town hall combines the tradition of the medieval burgher's house and the Italian palazzo.
In painting, **Rembrandt** dominated the Dutch golden age. His genius covered both religious paintings and landscapes. **Frans Hals, Vermeer** and **Jacob van Ruysdael** also painted masterpieces. These geniuses were complemented by numerous painters with various talents. Pictorial art was intended to decorate the interiors of the wealthy middle class; the subjects provided a remarkable picture of everyday life.
In Catholic Flanders, large religious canvasses and portraits accounted for most of the paintings commissioned from **Rubens, Jordaens** and **Van Dyck**. Rubens was one of the most prized painters in the principal courts of Europe in the 17C. Verbose and Baroque, he worked for Marie de Medici in Luxembourg Palace in Paris, for Charles I on the ceiling of the Whitehall Banqueting Hall in London, and for Philippe IV of Spain decorating the hunting pavilion in the Torre de La Parada.

Musée du Louvre, Paris/RMN

Rubens: *Henri IV with the portrait of Marie de Medicis*, The Louvre, France

THE EIGHTEENTH CENTURY

In the 18C, Italy lost the supremacy it had enjoyed in the field of the arts during the two previous centuries. France, experiencing the Enlightenment, became widely imitated.

Rococo

Rococo and the Louis XV style in France – After Louis XIV's death, the Rococo style blossomed in reaction to the massive, didactic and academic character of official Versailles art. Outwardly, architecture changed little. Except in the abandonment of orders on the façade, **Jean Courtonne**'s Hôtel Matignon does not differ much from the 17C private mansions. The main courtyard, designed for the ceremonies and receptions of high society, became larger in town residences such as **Pierre Alexis Delamair**'s Hôtel de Soubise in Paris. But interior decoration was totally reformulated. Rococo woodwork was carved with arabesques, foliated scrolls, ivy and convolvulus. This decorative vocabulary drew inspiration from the plant, animal and aquatic worlds, particularly shells. The taste for complex, tortuous detail, S-shapes and coils, together with Chinese curios also characterised the Rococo style. Woodwork was frequently painted in canary yellow, sea green, or Pompadour blue, and the ornamental motifs were sometimes gilt on a cream or white background. Paintings were hung above the door or fireplace. The oval drawing room of the Hôtel de Soubise in Paris by **Germain Boffrand** represents a fine example of Rococo decor.

Watteau: *Pilgrimage to Cythera*, The Louvre, France

In painting, as in sculpture, the Rococo style drew inspiration from amorous tales in mythology, fables, bucolic or sentimental stories and pastoral plays and poems. Mundane pleasures and games dominate the work of **Watteau** (1684-1721), then **Fragonard** (1732-1806). **Boucher** (1703-1770) enjoyed a brilliant career as a decorator and painter of history. The light, dynamic character of his touch, his warm, pearly colours represent Rococo decorative taste. In sculpture, juvenile gods, children and nymphs became the preferred themes.

Alongside carefree, libertine high society, the simple middle class is depicted in its everyday activities by artists such as **Chardin** (1699-1779) and **Greuze** (1725-1805) with their well-mannered, sometimes even moralising works.

Germanic Rococo – In German-speaking regions, the Rococo language reached its full plenitude. **Jean-François de Cuvilliés**, the elder, who worked in France under Blondel became the enchanted master of Bavaria and court architect of the Elector Carl Albert. He executed numerous interior Rococo decors, such as the Room of Mirrors in the Amalienburg Pavilion in Nymphenburg Castle. The Kaisersaal in Wurzburg's Episcopal Palace, residence of the bishop princes, represents a brilliant example of the Rococo style. Johann Balthasar Neumann used the colossal composite order, polychrome marble and gilt stucco to decorate this masterpiece.

Pulpits and façades – Pulpits took on a decorative character. The Pulpit of Truth, sculpted in St-Bavon's in Gent, and that of the Wies Pilgrims' Church by the **Zimmermann** brothers, are beautiful examples. Façades were sometimes sculpted with great exuberance such as the portal of the palace of the Marquis of Dos Aguas in Valencia and the outside of the **Asam** brothers' house in Munich.

Decorative arts – In the field of furniture, soft S-shaped legs, parquetry with floral patterns, light-coloured exotic woods, and the use of porcelain on the surface reflect Rococo characteristics.

The ceramic arts blossomed, with several centres of creation in Europe. **Meissen** porcelain was highly prized by the European courts; the sculptor **Kändler** executed numerous animals. **Sèvres** porcelain in France and **Wedgwood** in England were the main rivals.

Italian Baroque – After Rome, Piedmont developed Baroque and sometimes Rococo art under the influence of **Guarini** in the 17C and later **Juvara** (1676-1736). In Apulia (particularly Lecce) and Sicily (Noto, Ragusa, Catania), buildings of sumptuous decorative extravagance appeared. Effects of movement, inverted perspective, scroll work and *trompe-l'œil* were also applied to painting.
In the 17C, Naples under Spanish yoke flourished with Mattia Preti, Ribera and **Luca Giordano**, who was also active in Florence. In the 18C, Venice took the lead with Piazzetta (1682-1754) and the great decorator **Giambattista Tiepolo** (1696-1770), who also worked in Würzburg and Spain.
At the same time, Venice produced serene, less ambitious painting, represented in the intimate middle class interiors of **Pietro Longhi**, the portraits of **Rosalba Carriera** and the urban landscapes of **Guardi** and **Canaletto** (1697-1768), who also painted scenes of London and Warsaw.

The neo-Classical reaction

The decorative freedom of Rococo art produced a backlash preaching sobriety, order, economy of plastic means, and meditation of models from Antiquity. Neo-Classicism defined the aesthetic order predominating in Europe in the late 1760s.

Neo-Classical architecture and sculpture – References to Greco-Roman art were paramount in defining this new architecture. Many architects produced almost complete reproductions of Greek and Roman buildings.
In England, the movement occurred early. Architect **Robert Adam** (Kenwood House, Hampstead, Home House) executed buildings based on simple geometrical volumes, sometimes variations on Roman baths. The town of Bath, partly designed by **John Wood the Younger**, is one of Europe's most beautiful neo-Classical cities.
In France, **Jacques-Ange Gabriel** produced mannered neo-Classicism with his Petit Trianon at Versailles. It breaks from the austere architecture proposed by **Soufflot** and **Ledoux.**
In Spain, **Juan de Villanueva** designed the Prado with Roman references. In Berlin, **Carl Gotthard Langhans** introduced the neo-Classical vocabulary with the Brandeburg Gate in Berlin.

Neo-Classicist painting and sculpture – In reaction to the style, iconography and ideology of Rococo, neo-Classical painters such as **Mengs**, **David** and **Koffmann** drew inspiration from Greek and Roman bas-reliefs. Their works preferred friezes, heroic subjects, order and the example of ancient virtue. In sculpture, the Venetian **Canova** created a pure, elegant statuary out of white marble.

D. Hée/MICHELIN

Louis XV Square, now Place de la Concorde, designed by Jacques-Ange Gabriel

NINETEENTH CENTURY

The main pictorial movements

Romanticism and Symbolism dominated 19C painting, but numerous avant-garde movements also developed throughout the century in opposition to the conservative teachings of the Academy of Fine Arts. Realism and Impressionism, the fruit of French artists, obtained often fashionable success.

Romanticism – Romanticism rose as a reaction to neo-Classicism. It drew on a renewal of individual and nationalistic values. A rejection of line drawing, academic conventions and idealism depicting the anatomy characterised by Romantic art. New themes led to iconographic research – numerous subjects referred to contemporary and medieval literature, legends, and national history.

Delacroix: *Liberty leading the People*, The Louvre, France

Musée du Louvre/R.M.N.

Romanticism developed earliest in the Germanic countries with the late-18C *Sturm und Drang*. The work of the **Nazarenes**, German artists established in Rome in 1810, created a considerable stir. Frescoes by Casa Batholdy, today in the National Gallery in Berlin, and by Casino Massino are their most famous works.
Romanticism also developed early in England. The works of the **Pre-Raphaelites Hunt, Millais,** and **Rossetti** led the movement. In France, **David**'s pupils, Baron **Gros, François Gérard** and **Anne-Louis Girodet-Trioson,** adopted Romanticism. So did **Ingres,** an exceptional draughtsman, and **Theodore Géricault** and **Eugène Delacroix.**
In Spain, **Francisco Goya** (1746-1828) dominated artistic life in the first three decades of the century. He began his career as an official painter and soon showed himself to be a portrait painter of great psychological truth. Subsequently, he pushed the boundaries of historical painting with bold, expressive treatment.
In England, apart from the visionary figure of **William Blake,** landscape painters influenced by the Dutch dominated the artistic scene. **Constable**, then **Turner** each sought to render the continual change of light while at the same time showing pre-Impressionist tendencies.

Symbolism – In the 1880s, the Symbolist movement took shape. It made reference to literary items and drew on a complex iconography with obscure or multiple meanings. The Symbolist language could be adapted to extremely varied styles, everything from neo-Impressionism to Academism. Symbolist artists exhibited their works together in Belgium, in the rooms of the group or the Free Aesthetics, or in Paris, at the Rose-Croix exhibitions. The main Symbolist artists were **Spillaert, Theo van Rysselberghe, Delville** and **Khnopff** in Belgium, **Gustave Moreau** and **Odilon Redon** in France, **Edvard Munch** in Norway, **Segantini** in Italy, and **Klimt** in Austria.

Neuschwanstein, Germany

FOTOGRAM – STONE

Impressionism – The name impressionism comes from **Monet**'s painting entitled *Impression, Rising Sun*. When exhibited in Paris in 1874, it caused a scandal and drew satiric jibes in the press. In reaction to the previous conventional dark tones, the Impressionists translated vibrations of light, colourful impressions. Light, its analysis and effects, dominated their thoughts, in sun-drenched gardens, snow, mist, and flesh tones. The movement took its first steps before the 1870 Franco-German war with **Manet** and **Fantin-Latour**. However, it reached its peak in 1877, with exhibitions by **Degas**, **Caillebotte**, **Pissarro' Sisley**, and **Renoir**.

Nineteenth-Century architecture

From neo-Gothic to Eclecticism – Up until the 1890s, architecture seemed stuck in the styles of the previous centuries. During the second half of the century, borrowings from medieval art were omnipresent. Historicism inspired many restorations such as Notre-Dame in Paris by Lassus and **Viollet-le-Duc.** Medieval re-creations or pastiches abounded such as London's Parliament Building by Barry and Pugin, and the completion of medieval buildings such as the Cathedral of Cologne under the direction of the architect **Zwirner**.

During the second half of the century, these references multiplied. Palatial Renaissance, medieval, Classical and even oriental art all provided the architects with inspiration – Eclecticism triumphed. **Poelaert** built a Court House in Brussels reminiscent of St Peter's in Rome. A Pantheon and Baroque cupolas mark the **Garnier** Opera House in Paris. The Maximilianeum in Munich by **Bürklein**, and Neuschwanstein Castle in Bavaria designed by the architects **Riedel, Van Dollmann** and **Hoffmann**, all display complex references to past centuries.

Art Nouveau at the end of the century

In the 1890s, certain architects, at odds with Eclecticism and the official architecture of the fine arts style, advocated sobriety of form, the absence of added ornamental sculpture, a concern for functionality and a greater correspondence between function and form.

This Art Nouveau was short-lived. Although a degenerated style persisted up until World War I, its creative inspiration died out around 1905.

Art Nouveau, from Glasgow to Vienna – In Glasgow, **Mackintosh** helped pioneer this new style with his regular participation in World Fairs and major international exhibitions. In France, **Guimard** was one of the most inventive architects – Castel Béranger in Paris showed a creative extravagance. Like virtually all the architects in the movement, Guimard also designed interior details and furniture, door handles, and wallpaper. Paris also owes the original design of the entrances to its Metro stations to Guimard. In Spain, **Antonio Gaudí** was one of the most eminent figures of the time – his Gueil house and gardens in Barcelona covered with fragments of polychrome ceramics display an originality. In Belgium, the functionalist theories of Viollet-le-Duc influenced Art Nouveau architects. **Paul Hankar** renewed the traditional middle class house by covering it with large glazed façades around a polygon-shaped floor plan. He also built numerous shops. **Van de Velde** and **Serrurier-Bovy** contributed equally to the success of this new art.

Horta Museum, Brussels: The Staircase

The Viennese School, the so-called Vienna **Secession movement**, was more geometrical and more austere. **Otto Wagner** became the leader of the new architecture with his Postparkasse. **Hoffmann**, another Viennese, drew up the plans for the Palais Stoclet in Brussels, whose interior decoration is by **Gustav Klimt**.

In the early 20C in Germany, the popularity of Art Nouveau or **Jugendstil** in terms of decoration reinforced the mass production of sturdy furniture.

Decorative arts – A revolution freed furniture and household items of Eclecticism and the taste for pastiche. The stained glass artist Emile Gallé in France and the cabinet designers **Paul Hankar** and **Victor Horta** in Belgium drew inspiration from the plant kingdom.

Furniture was subjected to new principles of geometrisation and functionalism. **Moser** in Vienna played an essential role. Japanese objects and **Mackintosh**'s models also help explain this evolution.

THE TWENTIETH CENTURY

Avant-Garde Painting at the beginning of the century

In the first decade of the 20C, numerous artists continued in the academic tradition, particularly for official commissions, but the **Fauves, Expressionists** and **Cubists** laid the foundations of modern art. They were influenced by primitive and Japanese art, and the works of the Post-Impressionists, **Cézanne, Van Gogh, Toulouse-Lautrec** and **Gauguin.**

Fauvism and Expressionism – When **Derain** and **Vlaminck** exhibited at the annual Salon d'Automne in Paris in 1906, the violence of the works inspired an art critic to dub the painters Fauves or Wild Beasts. The arbitrary use of colour, the simplification of forms and the two-dimensional representation of space shocked the public. After World War I, numerous Fauve artists returned to a certain classicism of form and colour. Only a few such as Dutch painter **Van Dongen**, remained Fauve throughout their career. The painter **Matisse**, after his Fauve debut, moved away towards a highly personal art which he claimed represented a synthesis of arabesque ornament and colour.
In Germany, Expressionist painters displayed affinities with the Fauves. The Die Brücke (The Bridge) group was formed in Dresden in 1905. **Kirchner, Heckel, Nolde** and **Schmidt-Rottluff** were the main representatives. For them, colour was the main mediator of expression, meaning and emotion. These Expressionists expressed much stronger social and political positions than the Fauves.
A second group of Expressionists developed in Munich, around **Kandinsky**. Born in Moscow, Kandinsky made several trips to Europe and settled in Murnau in 1908. He practised a figurative and Expressionist art. He founded a group called **Der Blaue Reiter** *(The Blue Rider)* in 1911. Other artists in the group, such as **Franz Marc** and **Mawslinski,** remained committed Expressionists, even as Kandinsky moved toward lyricism.
In Moscow, the painter **Larionov** created a movement called Rayonism close to Expressionism and Fauvism. Like **Gontcharova,** Larionov identified painting with colour. He was to play an important role in the beginnings of abstract art.
In Germany, architect **Walter Gropius** (1883-1969) founded in 1919 the **Bauhaus** School of Architecture and Art in Weimar. In 1925, the Bauhaus was transferred to Dessau. This school soon attracted a host of avant-garde painters and sculptors. They aimed to find unity between art and technique, not only in painting, but also in architecture, sculpture and design, which were considered complementary. The painters Paul Klee and Kandinsky began teaching there in 1921 and 1922.

Cubism and Futurism – Cubism arose from the experiments of **Braque** and **Picasso.** After going through a classical phase, strongly influenced by Iberian prehistoric art and Cézanne, Picasso rejected traditional conventions in the treatment of perspective and natural light. He gave a two-dimensional representation of volume, producing diagrammatic and geometric unfolded anatomies. *Les Demoiselles d'Avignon* (1907, MOMA, New York) was the first manifestation of cubism. This major work of 20C art was not exhibited until 1916, but a number of artists, including Braque, had already seen it. The landscapes Picasso painted in Estaque were compared to cubes by the critic Vauxelles; hence the term cubism. During the first decade of the 20C, **Braque** and **Picasso** also produced collages, adding various materials to the surface of the canvas. Other Cubists such as **Metzinger** and **Roger de La Fresnaye** kept their subjects legible.
Sculptors such as **Henry Laurens, Archinpenko**, of Russian origin, **Lipchitz**, from Lithuania, **Zatkine, Brancusi** and **Modigliani** broke down objects and simplified volumes. Most of these artists from Eastern Europe worked in Paris, where, along with the painters **Chagall** and **Soutine**, they formed the First School of Paris. In Italy, the Futurists also decomposed objects – **Balla** and **Russolo** expressed dynamism and decomposition of movement.

Georges Braque: *Estaque Landscape*

Since 1914

Abstract – **Malevich** initiated abstract art in Europe. After a Primitivist phase, in which his art, still figurative, was derived from icons and inspired by folklore, he painted *Black Square on White Background* in 1913 (now in Hermitage Museum, St Petersburg). This painting was created for the costume of a character in a contemporary opera which he directed. This work was the starting point of an art which he

Twentieth Century

Malborough / ARTEPHOT

Van Gogh: *Self-Portrait with Bandaged Ear*

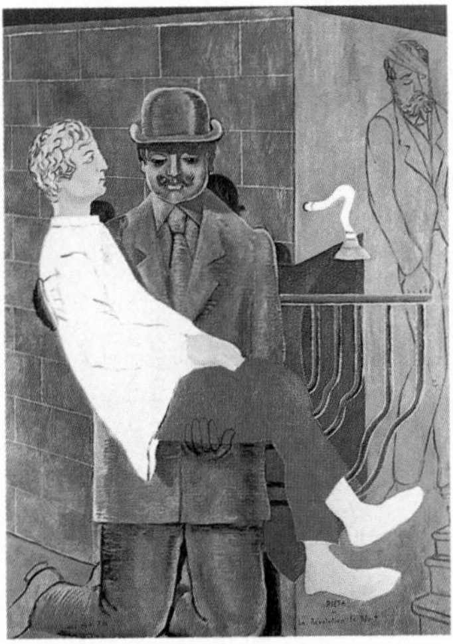

Coll. Penrose, London / GIRAUDON / © ADAGP SPADEM 1996

Max Ernst: *Pietà*

STAATLICHE KUNSTHALLE, Karlsruhe

Franz Marc: *Deer in the Forest*

Musée Picasso, Antibes / © ADAGP 1996

Picasso: *La joie de vivre* (detail)

Coll. NELLENS / LAUROS GIRAUDON

Dali: *Buste de femme rétrospectif*

Major movements and artists of the 20C

Shaded off colours indicate the origin and/or influence of a movement.

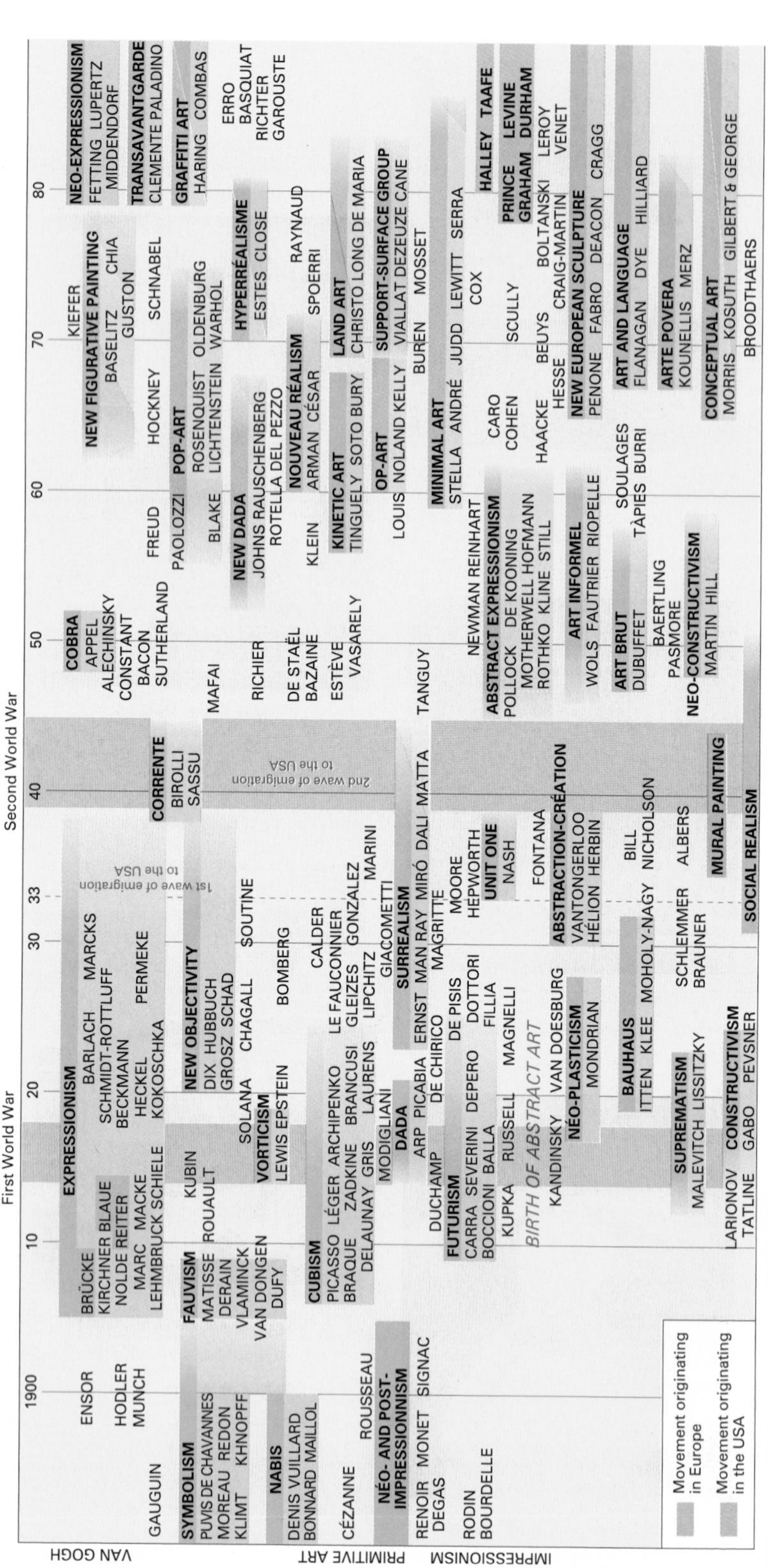

First World War
Second World War
1900
10
20
30
33
40
50
60
70
80
VAN GOGH
PRIMITIVE ART
IMPRESSIONISM
GAUGUIN
ENSOR
HODLER
MUNCH
BRÜCKE
KIRCHNER BLAUE
NOLDE REITER
MARC MACKE
LEHMBRUCK SCHIELE
EXPRESSIONISM
BARLACH MARCKS
SCHMIDT-ROTTLUFF
BECKMANN
HECKEL PERMEKE
KOKOSCHKA
1st wave of emigration to the USA
CORRENTE
BIROLLI
SASSU
COBRA
APPEL
ALECHINSKY
CONSTANT
BACON
SUTHERLAND
FREUD
NEW FIGURATIVE PAINTING
BASELITZ CHIA
GUSTON
HOCKNEY
SCHNABEL
KIEFER
NEO-EXPRESSIONISM
FETTING LUPERTZ
MIDDENDORF
TRANSAVANTGARDE
CLEMENTE PALADINO
SYMBOLISM
PUVIS DE CHAVANNES
MOREAU REDON
KLIMT KHNOPFF
FAUVISM
MATISSE ROUAULT
DERAIN
VLAMINCK
VAN DONGEN
DUFY
KUBIN
NEW OBJECTIVITY
DIX HUBBUCH
GROSZ SCHAD
SOLANA CHAGALL SOUTINE
MAFAI
PAOLOZZI
BLAKE
POP-ART
ROSENQUIST OLDENBURG
LICHTENSTEIN WARHOL
GRAFFITI ART
HARING COMBAS
ERRO
BASQUIAT
RICHTER
GAROUSTE
NABIS
DENIS VUILLARD
BONNARD MAILLOL
VORTICISM
LEWIS EPSTEIN
BOMBERG
RICHIER
NEW DADA
JOHNS RAUSCHENBERG
ROTELLA DEL PEZZO
HYPERRÉALISME
ESTES CLOSE
CÉZANNE
ROUSSEAU
CUBISM
PICASSO LÉGER ARCHIPENKO
BRAQUE ZADKINE BRANCUSI
DELAUNAY GRIS LAURENS
MODIGLIANI
LE FAUCONNIER
GLEIZES GONZALEZ
LIPCHITZ
CALDER
GIACOMETTI
MARINI
2nd wave of emigration to the USA
DE STAËL
BAZAINE
KLEIN
NOUVEAU RÉALISM
ARMAN CÉSAR
SPOERRI
RAYNAUD
ESTÈVE
VASARELY
KINETIC ART
TINGUELY SOTO BURY
LAND ART
CHRISTO LONG DE MARIA
NÉO- AND POST-IMPRESSIONISM
SIGNAC
DADA
ARP PICABIA
DUCHAMP
SURREALISM
ERNST MAN RAY MIRÓ DALI MATTA
DE CHIRICO MAGRITTE
TANGUY
LOUIS
OP-ART
NOLAND KELLY
SUPPORT-SURFACE GROUP
VIALLAT DEZEUZE CANE
BUREN MOSSET
RENOIR MONET
DEGAS
FUTURISM
CARRA SEVERINI DEPERO
BOCCIONI BALLA
DE PISIS
DOTTORI
FILLIA
MOORE
HEPWORTH
MINIMAL ART
STELLA ANDRÉ JUDD LEWITT SERRA
RODIN
BOURDELLE
KUPKA RUSSELL MAGNELLI
BIRTH OF ABSTRACT ART
UNIT ONE
NASH
NEWMAN REINHART
ABSTRACT EXPRESSIONISM
POLLOCK DE KOONING
MOTHERWELL HOFMANN
ROTHKO KLINE STILL
CARO
COHEN
COX
SCULLY
HALLEY TAAFE
PRINCE LEVINE
GRAHAM DURHAM
KANDINSKY VAN DOESBURG
FONTANA
HAACKE BEUYS BOLTANSKI LEROY
HESSE CRAIG-MARTIN VENET
NÉO-PLASTICISM
MONDRIAN
ABSTRACTION-CRÉATION
VANTONGERLOO
HÉLION HERBIN
ART INFORMEL
WOLS FAUTRIER RIOPELLE
NEW EUROPEAN SCULPTURE
PENONE FABRO DEACON CRAGG
BAUHAUS
ITTEN KLEE MOHOLY-NAGY NICHOLSON
BILL
ART BRUT
DUBUFFET
SOULAGES
TÀPIES BURRI
ART AND LANGUAGE
FLANAGAN DYE HILLIARD
SUPREMATISM
MALEVITCH LISSITZKY
SCHLEMMER
BRAUNER
ALBERS
BAERTLING
PASMORE
NEO-CONSTRUCTIVISM
MARTIN HILL
ARTE POVERA
KOUNELLIS MERZ
LARIONOV
TATLINE
CONSTRUCTIVISM
GABO PEVSNER
MURAL PAINTING
SOCIAL REALISM
CONCEPTUAL ART
MORRIS KOSUTH GILBERT & GEORGE
BROODTHAERS
Movement originating in Europe
Movement originating in the USA

Musée municipal de La Haye

Theo van Doesburg: *Counter-composition in Dissonance XVI*
Municipal Museum, The Hague, Netherlands

called Suprematism: a conceptual approach using economy of plastic means and pure abstraction. The painting only contained simple geometric shapes such as a square, a triangle, and a circle. In about 1920, architecture and town planning entered into his field of research. He made *planites* (mock-ups) whose basic component was the cube. During his trip to Berlin in 1927, Malevich met other European avant-garde artists.

The Dutch painter **Mondrian** also pioneered abstraction. The geometrical squares on his canvasses, black and white, or primary colours, defined neo-Plasticism which was soon to inspire painters such as **Theo van Doesburg** and sculptors such as Van Tongerloa. In France, the Circle and Square movement was founded by **A Herbin**. In the magazine *Esprit Nouveau*, **Le Corbusier** championed Purism. The Villa Savoye and the Cité Radieuse in Marseilles are among his most famous achievements.

Dadaism and Surrealism – Dada and Surrealist artists related creation to irrationalism, the unconscious mind, and games. The movement proved popular in France with **Arp**, **Tzara**, the Catalan **Salvador Dali**, in Belgium with **Magritte**, and in Germany with **Haussmann**, **Schwitters**, and **Max Ernst**. The Spanish painter **Miró** practised Surrealistic art in the 1920s.

Contemporary creation – Contemporary art extends aesthetic solutions discovered by the avant-garde artists at the beginning and in the middle of the century. Many new practices have been developed such as land art and optical art In architecture, functionalism predominated, followed by a return to Classicism at the end of the 1980s.

SUPERSTOCK/© ADAGP 1996

Magritte: *Le Chant d'amour*

THE DAWN OF THE TWENTY-FIRST CENTURY

After the Second World War, American prosperity favoured a large number of new artistic movements within the country. Today, Europe is asserting itself on an artistic scene structured around five ideas: an updating of our heritage, a break with the past, the influence of the environment and ecology, an aspiration to globalisation and new centres of cultural influence.

Artistic effervescence in the post-war period

Contemporary art was directly affected by the aftermath of the war and sought to express this in both Europe and the United States. It then translated the new values of the emerging mass consumer society before reflecting social unrest in the late 1960s. In the 1950s, abstract Expressionism took off in the United States, contributing to the country's artistic activity. Through this large-scale action painting, the best known proponents of the style, the American **Jackson Pollock** and Dutchman **Willem de Kooning**, expressed society's fears as it emerged from a period of crisis and war. In Europe, informal painting developed with the Frenchmen **Pierre Soulages** and **Jean Fautrier**, the German **Emil Schumacher**, the Russian **André Lanskoy**, the Italian **Emilio Vedova** and the Spaniards **Manolo Millares** and especially **Antoni Tapies**, an abstract and *matierist* painter. They expressed their feelings and emotions, and the trauma of the post-war period, through non-figurative painting based on the expression created by the unexpected assemblage of various materials.

In parallel with this, the **Obra** movement appeared in Northern Europe grouping poets and painters, especially the Belgian **Pierre Alechinsky**, the Dutchman **Karel Appel** and the Dane **Asger Jorn**. Through action painting, they translate a marvellous, poetical world inspired by Surrealism and Expressionism and are related to popular Scandinavian art by their naivety and spontaneity.

The consumer society and mass culture of the 1960s gave rise to three main trends. Pop art, which originated in England with **Richard Hamilton**, was followed in the United States and Europe by a number of artists, including the Englishman **David Hockney**, the Swede **Claes Oldenbourg**, and the Americans **Andy Warhol**, **Roy Lichtenstein** and **Jasper Johns**. Mass-produced everyday objects and publicity images were used directly in works of art or reproduced by technical means (collage, screen printing etc) without the artist's intervention. The now banal art object was seen as merchandise.

New Realism, a European artistic movement, placed value on urban reality, either by appropriating it like **César** with his compressions or by integrating characteristic every-day objects (posters, rubbish and industrial materials) like the Italian **Mimmo Rotella** and the Frenchman **Jacques Villeglé**.

In reaction to the consumer society, the Fluxus movement developed round the idea that everything is art. This appealed to many artists, especially the German **Joseph Beuys** and the Bulgarian **Christo**. They opposed the idea that art is merchandise and produced ephemeral works (called Performances) which escaped the art market. These included Christo's wrapping of the Berlin Reichstag in 1995.

Finally, **Francis Bacon**, an Irishman working in London, concentrated on the suffering of man living in an unsuitable, uncaring environment.

Alongside this, architecture underwent great upheavals with the disappearance of leading figures such as the Frenchman **Le Corbusier**, the German **Ludwig Mies van der Rohe** and the American **Richard Wright** Le Corbusier's cold, austere functionalism reached its zenith with the new value placed on anonymity, growing urbanisation, technological progress and economic development. This was the time of housing estates and tower blocks, including the Tour Maine-Montparnasse in Paris.

However, the 1960s ended in social tension. Large-scale council estates such as those at Nanterre on the outskirts of Paris sprang up everywhere and the outsize, uniform architecture of these soulless dormitory towns gave rise to boredom.

The mid-1970s saw the start of the present period, with architecture calling into question its very foundations. The aim was no longer to start from scratch but to fit in with the existing environment. Classicism came into fashion and old forms (columns, pilasters etc) were reinterpreted. With painters also looking to the past, the Postmodern trend was not confined to architecture.

By contrast, the Late-Modern or High Tech style which developed alongside it left the metal structure visible. The Centre Georges Pompidou by **Renzo Piano** and **Richard Rogers** was the forerunner of this type of architecture.

Updating our heritage

Some artists recognised and valued the past while reformulating it in terms of new needs and new aspirations.

Architecture saw a return to Classicism throughout Europe. In Milan, **Aldo Rossi** reorganised the Gallaratese district with colonnades and galleries. In London, the Englishman **James Stirling** enlarged the Tate Gallery with the addition of the Clore Gallery. The Spaniard **Ricardo Bofill** developed a monumental style in Paris and the Viennese **Hans Hollein**, designer of the Frankfurt Museum of Modern Art, which opened in 1991, also engaged in a return to the forms of the past. The Portuguese **Tomas Taveira** followed suit in building the Amoreiras (Mulberries) complex on the outskirts of Lisbon, while the Italian **Paolo Portoghesi** showed himself worthy of the great 17C Italian masters with the dome of the Mosque of Rome on the Aventine Hill.

Another architectural trend favoured the preservation of the old and its adaptation to contemporary needs.

When the Lyon Opera was renovated by **Jean Nouvel**, the external architecture was retained whereas the dome and enlarged basement tripled the original surface area. At the Nouvelle Bibliothèque Nationale François Mitterrand, the largest national library in the world, designed by **Dominique Perrault**, new media were added to France's literary heritage, with four monumental towers standing like four open books protecting an interior garden. In Berlin, **Norman Foster** was chosen to rebuild the Reichstag while preserving its exterior façade.

In painting, many artists engaged in a dialogue with art history. In Düsseldorf, **Markus Lüpertz** reinterpreted old themes, such as the legend of Parsifal. At the Musée National d'Art Moderne in Paris, **Gérard Garouste** rediscovered Dante's *Divine Comedy* and biblical subjects. In Italy, the **Trans-avant-garde** movement marked a return to Italian pictorial tradition based on the heritage of 20C masters, as well as legends. Its principal representatives were **Sandro Chia**, **Enzo Cucchi**, **Francesco Clemente** and **Mimmo Paladino**.

Other artists questioned the meaning of artistic creation and of language with works consisting of texts and quotations. The best-known European representatives of this Conceptual art were the Englishmen **Michael Baldwyn** and **Mel Ramsden** of the **Art and Language** group, with their monochrome paintings covering reproductions of historical pictures.

A break with the past

Other artists reacted against Europe's tragic recent history and its effects on national identity, and many examples of their desire to break with the past can be found throughout Europe.

In Germany, **Georg Baselitz**, the main representative of neo-Expressionism, illustrated the moral crisis of post-war Germany by means of naked, flayed figures painted upside down, and slashed, roughly painted woodcarvings. Also marked by the war, the work of the German **Anselm Kiefer** used a wide variety of materials, including sand, wood and straw, as well as words, to portray the horrors of Nazism. The fall of communism also allowed Russia to emerge from its cultural isolation, and formerly dissident artists such as **Erik Boulatov** and **Ilya Kabakov** were at last able to throw off the cloak of clandestinity and express themselves freely. The form of artistic expression they unveiled to the West was a parody of the ideological message of power and social realism of official Soviet art. In architecture, the break with history mainly took place in Berlin, the future capital of a reunited Germany in the throes of change, with the "zigzags" of the Museum of Jewish Art by the American architect **Daniel Libeskind** standing as a sign of this cultural openness. Such daring, provocative architecture continued the tradition of the Baroque architecture of the Berlin Museum. **Axel Schultes** renovation of the Spreebogen district of Berlin, with its East-West route through the historic and political symbol of the former Berlin Wall, is evidence of the cultural reunification building the new face of Germany at the dawn of the 21C.

The influence of the environment and ecology

Art also reflected on contemporary society, the urban landscape and its relations with the natural environment and engaged in a dialogue with nature.

English sculptors carved themselves a place on the artistic scene by developing a critique of consumer society. Working in Wuppertal in Germany, **Tony Cragg** explored the material world and presented various perceptions of objects and materials through his installations.

The Frenchmen **Robert Combas, Jean-Charles Blais** and **François Boisrond** drew their inspiration from contemporary popular culture, including comic strips and rock music, to create a humorous, figurative world using a very wide variety of supports such as cardboard and sheets.

Nature was also central to the artistic expression of Englishman **Richard Long**, a member of the land art movement, who made geometrically-shaped ephemeral sculptures from natural objects such as stones, wood and bark. In Italy, **Giuseppe Penone** used trees and prints as recurrent themes in his work, with human veins apparent on his marble sculptures. In Spain, **Eduardo Chillida**'s work developed around a dialogue between man and nature in monumental open-air works confronting matter and empty space.

The design for the entrance to the Grotte de Niaux in Ariège, France, by the Italian architect **Massimiliano Fuksas**, followed the natural forms of the environment and the unfinished appearance of his creations lends them a moving, dreamlike quality.

In Finland, **Juha Leiviskä** forged a link between nature, music and the architecture of the church and parish hall of Männistö in Kuopio.

J. L. Bohin/EXPLORER

Évry Cathedral

Global aspirations

While many European artists went abroad to seek artistic stimulation outside their traditional settings, some European organisations called on foreign artists.
Spain launched into grandiose creations, with the curves and steel of the Guggenheim Museum of Bilbao by the American **Franck Gehry** breathing new life into the Basque country. Similarly, in Barcelona, the white walls of the Museum of Contemporary Art by another American, **Richard Meier**, brightened up a traditionally working-class Catalonian district. In painting, **Miquel Barcelo** contributed to cultural renewal with his bestiary and African landscapes in shades of brown and blue mixed with earth.
In painting, sculpture and architecture, artists expressed themselves outside their countries of origin. The Frenchman **Jean-Pierre Raynaud** represented France at the Venice Biennial in 1993. His work was based on a reflection on solitude and death in hospital, with tiles translating the aseptic environment. His work *Le Grand Pot Doré*, reproduced on a monumental scale and covered in gold leaf, is now to be found in China's Forbidden City. The Swiss architect **Mario Botta** built Evry Cathedral in the Paris region and the Spaniard **Santiago Calatrava** designed the new high-speed railway station of Lyon-Satolas Airport in 1991.

New centres of cultural influence

At the dawn of the 21C, new centres of cultural influence are springing up.
With the boost given by the 1992 Olympic Games, **Barcelona** has continued to develop and increase its cultural influence, with **Ricardo Bofill** responsible for the design of the Mediterranean Cultural Centre.

The reconstruction of **Berlin** provides a great opportunity for contemporary architects. The renovation of all the city's districts will give it the appearance of a reunified international capital, reflecting economic, political and cultural changes.

London has rediscovered its Docklands, once home to industry then long abandoned. The new Tate Gallery housed in a former riverside electricity generating station will inject new life into the area. Its design was entrusted to the architects **Jacques Herzog** and **Pierre de Meuron**, who opted for radical simplicity.
In **Paris** too, designs such as the Cité de la Musique by the French architect **Christian de Portzamparc** have been built. Standing in the Parc de la Villette next to **Bernard Tschumi**'s Folies rouges architecturales (Red Architectural Follies) and opposite the Cité des Sciences, its plural, colourful, fragmented architecture groups the Musée National de la Musique and the National Academy of Music and Dance.

Rotterdam has also embarked on a programme of modernisation, including the Erasmus Bridge by Dutchman **Ben Van Berkel** and the architecture of **Rem Koolhaas**, in particular the brick-built Kunsthall. Rotterdam is taking up the challenge of Amsterdam, its eternal rival, to become a new Dutch centre of contemporary architecture.

Ph. Gajic/MICHELIN

Berlin – The Infobox provides information on all Berlin projects for the year 2000

Answers to the questions on p 59

1 Queen Sofia Art Centre in Madrid, Spain
2 The Louvre in Paris, France
3 Museum of Fine Arts in Bern, Switzerland
4 Rijksmuseum in Amsterdam, The Netherlands
5 The Hermitage in St Petersburg, Russia
6 Uffizzi Museum in Florence, Italy
7 Orsay Museum in Paris, France
8 Old Pinacotheque in Munich, Germany
9 Tate Gallery in London, Great Britain
10 Nasjonalgalleriet in Oslo, Norway
11 National Gallery in London, Great Britain
12 Antwerp Cathedral, Belgium
13 The Prado in Madrid, Spain
14 National Archeological Museum in Athens, Greece
15 The Belvedere (Upper Belvedere) in Vienna, Austria
16 The Prado in Madrid, Spain
17 Tretiakov Gallery in Moscow, Russia
18 Museum of Ancient Art in Lisbon, Portugal
19 Monastery of Jasna Góra, Czestochowa, Poland
20 Vatican Museums in Rome, Italy

planm. scheduled
verspätet delayed
Flugsteig Gate
Flug Flight
nach to
über via
AH 2931 ALGIER 1540
OK 731 PRAG 1540
LH 765 HAMBURG-ANNULLIERT 1545
AI 165 PARIS 1550
LH 964 MUENCHEN 1555
LH 766 HAMBURG 1600
LH 904 DUESSELDORF 1605
DW 115 MUENSTER-OSNABRUECK 1610
PA 646 BERLIN 1610
AF 745 PARIS 1615
LH 074 MANCHESTER 1615
LH 354 BUDAPEST 1615
erden nicht ausgerufen
will not be announced
Abflug
Departures
OFFERMANN
Sex-Shop

Next flight for?

Flug Flight
nach to
über via
planm. scheduled
verspätet delayed
Flugsteig Gate
LH 226 ZUERICH 1620 B
LH 366 ZAGREB 1620 B
TP 575 LISSABON 1620 B
LH 822 HANNOVER 1625 A
LH 965 MUENCHEN 1625 A
DW 105 HOF-BAYREUTH 1630 A
LH 298 VENEDIG 1630 A
OS 426 KLAGENFURT 1630 B
LH 034 LONDON 1635 A
LH 248 GENF 1635 B
LH 767 HAMBURG 1635 A
LH 966 MUENCHEN 1635 B
Abflug
Departures
Süßwaren
Tabakwaren
Juwelen, Uhren

Albania

Area: 28 748km² – 11 100sq mi – **Population:** 3.25 million – **Capital:** Tiranë (Tirana) – **Currency:** the "lek". Credit cards and travellers checks are not yet widely accepted so it is advisable to take cash. The American dollar and Italian lira are the most commonly used currencies. – **Time:** GMT + 1hr in winter, GMT + 2hr in summer.

Shqipëria

Albania is situated in the western part of the Balkan Peninsula. It is bordered to the north by Montenegro and Kosovo, to the east by Macedonia and to the south by Greece. Western Albania lies on the shores of the Adriatic and Ionian Seas. It has 350km/220mi of coastline with beaches of white sand. Inland, numerous lakes, Ohrid and Prespa in the east, and Shkodar (Scutari) in the north, break up the mountainous countryside. Albania enjoys a Mediterranean climate with hot dry summers, and mild wet winters on the plain. Harsh winters exist in the mountains.

IN BRIEF

Entry regulations – Valid passport. No visa required for citizens of the European Union, USA or Canada. Entry tax $5 and departure tax $10.

Specialities – Albanian cuisine is influenced by its Turkish and Greek neighbours. Traditional dishes include *fergese*, a dish of meat, eggs, cream cheese and garlic; *byrek*, a kind of flaky pastry stuffed with minced meat, vegetables, eggs or cheese; and *kukurec*, stuffed sheep's intestines. The fish from the lakes have a delicate flavour, especially the *koran*, a type of trout from Lake Ohrid and the carp from Lake Shkodar. *Raki* is a popular and strong alcoholic drink, often served as a sign of friendship.

Folklore – Folk dances vary depending on the region or even the village. Reels are the most popular, especially the *rrotullorja*. When dancing, Albanians dress in the traditional *guna* (cloak) or *xhublete* (tunic) costumes.

Souvenirs – Souvenir hunters will be tempted by a good choice of local craftwork, traditional *kilim* rugs with varied, brightly-coloured designs, silver filigree jewellery, woodcarvings (pipes, musical instruments) and the unusual jewellery boxes or cigarette cases decorated with coloured maize leaves.

TIRANË★

TIRANA – Population 350 000

Michelin map 970 N 8

The city lies more or less in the physical heart of the country. It was founded in 1614 by **Suleiman Baligjini**, who was a powerful nobleman. Tirana began to expand in the 18C and was officially declared capital of Albania in 1920 at the Lushnjë Congress.
Tirana serves as the country's political, administrative, cultural, scientific, commercial and industrial centre.
The city sits at the foot of **Mount Dajti**, 110m/361ft above sea level. With its mild sunny climate and predominant colours (green parks and gardens and yellow ochre buildings), it evokes a Mediterranean town.
Travellers arriving on the outskirts of Tirana are struck by the hundreds of individual mushroom-shaped bunkers. When the country was cut off from the outside world and feared a Soviet invasion, the bunkers were built to protect the city and its airport. Today, most serve as shelters for the goats. Some have been transformed into car washes.

Skanderbeg Square – The city's main avenues converge on this huge rectangular square dotted with fountains and gardens. In the centre of the square stands an equestrian statue of the national hero Skanderbeg, who symbolises the struggle against the Turks during the 15C. The monument was erected in 1968 to commemorate the 500th anniversary of the national hero's death. The capital's main historic buildings and administrative offices are found around this busy square filled with cars, bicycles and pedestrians.
The **Muzeu historik kombëtar**, the National History Museum, was built in 1981 and is decorated with a huge mosaic fresco entitled *Shqiperia* (Albania).
The **Cultural Centre** (Pallati i kultures) was constructed on the remains of the old bazaar in the late 1960s. It houses the National Library, the Opera and Ballet House and conference halls.
The **Haxhi Ethem Bey Mosque** (Xhamia e Haxhi Etem Beu) is an elegant rectangular building dating from the late 18C. It is topped with an octagonal dome, and a tall, slender minaret. Polychrome acanthus leaves decorate the arcades leading to the main part of the mosque. The building also includes the **Clock Tower** (Kulla e Sabatit) built in 1830 which stands 35m/115ft high and has a pointed red-tiled roof. The mosque is floodlit during Ramadan.

The main **Avenue Dëshmorët e Kombit** (National Martyrs), opposite Skanderbeg's statue, leads to the University. This is Tirana's elegant high street and an ideal place to stroll with the family or meet up with friends in the coolness of the evening after the stifling heat of summer afternoons. Numerous kiosks dot the **Youth Park** (Parku Rinia).

The **Dajti Residence**, an Italian legacy and a veritable historic building, stands on the left of the avenue leading towards the University.

Nearby, the **Art Gallery** (Galeri e arteve figurative) contains mostly paintings by Albanian artists along with a few Old Masters.

The **International Cultural Centre** (Quëndra ndërkombëtare e kultures) stands a little further on and is one of the city's landmarks. The huge white and green stone pyramid over 30m/97ft high was originally intended to be the mausoleum of the dictator President Enver Hoxha. It is now used for exhibitions and houses the American Cultural Centre. Children also amuse themselves here, sliding down the building's sloping sides.

Before reaching the University, the visitor can spot the **Conference Centre** (Pallati i Kongreseve), a modern steel and glass building, the **Archeology Museum** (Muzeu Arkeologjik) and, behind it, the main sports stadium. On the other side of the street lies the **National Academy** (Akadenia e Arteve te Bukura).

►► Varrezat e Deshmoreve te Kombit: National Martyrs Cemetery. Parku i Madh: Main Park. Kopshti Botanik: Botanical Gardens. Kopshti Zoologjik: Zoo.

EXCURSIONS

★★ **Kruje** – *50km/31mi north.* Kruje lies on a mountainside and is the former capital of Skanderbeg. It is now a tourist centre and holiday resort frequented by Tirana residents. Visitors should see the citadel, the Skanderbeg Museum or stroll through the narrow streets in the old medieval town.

★★ **Durrës** – *40km/25mi west.* Durrës, situated west of Tirana on the Adriatic Coast, is Albania's main port. Boats cross from here to the Italian ports of Ancona, Bari, Brindisi and Trieste. Durrës, one of the oldest towns in the country, was colonised by the Greeks in the 7C BC. Visitors should see the castle, the 2C Roman amphitheatre which could seat 15 000 spectators, the Roman baths, 3C and 4C mosaics in a Roman villa and the archeological museum. This holiday resort is popular with both Albanian and foreign tourists thanks to its fine white sandy beaches, clear shallow water, fragrant unspoiled pine forests and numerous bars, restaurants and night clubs.

Mount Dajti – *27km/17mi.* The mountain offers a fine **view**★ over the Tirana plain and the castles of Petrela and Preza.

To find the description of a sight, a historical event, a monument... consult the index at the end of the guide.

Austria

Österreich

Area: 84 000km^2/32 424 sq mi – **Population:** 7.5 million – **Capital:** Wien (Vienna) – **Currency:** Schilling (ATS) and Euro (13.7603 ATS) – **Time:** GMT + 1hr in winter, GMT + 2hr in summer.

Elongated Austria stretches through the heart of the Alps over 580km/360mi from Switzerland to the Hungarian border. Three mountain ranges, the North, South and Central Alps, cover more than two-thirds of its territory. The plateau in the north drains water off into the River Danube.

The country's nine provinces present enchanting scenery, from the snow-capped Tyrol Alps with lakes and rural villages to the Danube Valley dotted with old castles and vineyards. Beautiful towns and cities display artistic treasures. Both Vienna and Salzburg, Mozart's birthplace, exude prestige. Finally, folklore remains alive, with a deep crafts tradition and a reputation for hospitality.

Austria descends from an empire. The Sovereign in Vienna governed countries as diverse as Southern Italy and Galicia, Hungary and the Netherlands. Austria played an important role in Europe due to its historic past and geographical location.

IN BRIEF

Entry regulations – Passport.

Shopping – The shops are usually open from Mondays to Fridays between 8am and 6pm and on Saturdays from 8am to 12noon. On the first Saturday of each month, they remain open to 5pm.

Winter sports – Austria attracts an international clientele every year for winter sports. Brochures with panoramic maps can be obtained from tourist offices. The pleasures of the ski slopes can be enjoyed throughout the year on the glaciers in Mölltal (Carinthia), Kaprun (near Salzburg), Dachstein (Styria), Hintertux, Kaunertal, Stubal, Ötztal and Pitztal (Tyrol).

Wiesenhorfer/ÖSTERREICH WERBURG

Johann Strauß

Waltzes and operettas – Austria and particularly Vienna are associated with these waltzes and operettas. In 1820, the waltz, which originated from popular three-steps, met with triumphant success in Vienna. It had already been greeted with enormous enthusiasm during the Congress of Vienna (1814-1815) and was first copied in the inns and theatres in the suburbs. Its success led to an appearance at the Imperial Court. Two men, **Joseph Lanner** and **Johan Strauss the Elder**, contributed to the renown of the Viennese waltz.

The waltz has never aged. It is still danced at private functions or during prestigious events such as the debutantes' ball in Vienna. Countless couples have spun round the dance floor to the tunes of *Wienerblut, Tales from the Vienna Woods, Beautiful Blue Danube.*

In 1858, operettas became fashionable in Vienna thanks to Offenbach's *Le mariage aux lanternes,* first performed in the Carl Theatre. **Johann Strauss the Younger** followed Offenbach's example, composing successes such as *Die Fledermaus,* or *Der Zigeunerbaron.*

Keller, Gasthaüser or Weinhaüser – Cellars, cafés and wine bars play an important role in Austria and Vienna. The Keller's relaxed atmosphere resembles a German beer cellar. They often serve cold meals or a dish of the day with white wine or beer. At Gasthaüser or Weinhaüser, regional cuisine is offered at attractive prices. In Vienna, these establishments are known as **Beisel**. Austrians often have their own particular **Weinstuben**, charming taverns where people down a glass or two of white wine. The **Heurigen**, busy in the evening, are found mainly in wine-growing villages such as Grinzing, Nussdorf, Sievering, or Gumpoldskirchen on the outskirts of Vienna. They belong to vineyard owners who harvest their own grapes, produce their own wine and sell their own young vintage (Heuriger). They serve cold snacks and, in some cases, complete meals. Some Heurigen feature traditional **Schrammelmusik**, a band consisting of two violins, an accordion (or clarinet) and guitar. Otherwise, the unmistakably Viennese atmosphere is provided by a violin and an accordion.

The ARLBERG Region★★

Michelin map 970 K 6

The mountainous Arlberg region lies between the Rhine Valley's Alps and the narrow valley of the River Inn. The region is easily accessible in both summer and winter thanks to rail tunnels and two road tunnels stretching 14km/9mi. Downhill skiing began here in 1901.

★ARLBERG PASS

From Bludenz to Landeck *68km/42mi – about 5 hours*

Bludenz – This is one of the Vorarlberg's busiest towns, remarkably situated at the junction of five valleys.
Follow the old road through Innerbraz, Dalaas, Wald and Klösterle.
The road climbs up through the **Klostertal**, an austere rugged valley, to the **Arlbergpass**. On the Tyrolean side, the road runs down from St-Christoph to St-Anton, through majestic scenery. The mountain peak is the Patteriol.

St-Anton am Arlberg – This major winter sports resort is one of the stops on all the main international express rail routes. In the summer, the scenery is gracefully and restfully rustic.
Downhill, the delightful Stanzertal is full of limestone scarp slopes.
The bridge known as the **Trisannabrücke**★ crosses the tumbling mountain river amid romantic surroundings.

Pians in the Sanna Valley is picturesque.

Landeck – The massive fortress evokes the former strategic importance of this small industrial town. The Gothic parish church and delightful Tyrolean villages on the outskirts merit a visit.

★★MONTAFON AND THE SILVRETTA ROAD

From Bludenz to Landeck – *95km/59mi – one full day*
The Silvretta High Alpine Road (Silvretta-Hochalpenstrasse) connects the Ill and Trisanna Valleys via a pass across the Bielerhöhe that rises to 2036m/6617ft.

Blundenz – *See above.*

Montafon – It is a deep but attractive valley with a very high population density. Orchards, pastures, power stations and high-voltage power lines dot the landscape.

Schruns – The main town in Montafon and its twin town of **Tschagguns** are spread across a vast basin.
From Schruns to Partenen, the valley becomes narrower and more alpine. Onion domes and flower-decked hillside wooden chalets inject charm into the villages of St-Gallenkirch and Gortipohl. In the foreground, the pyramid outline of Vallüla Partenen marks the beginning of a 1000m/3250ft hairpin climb.

Vermunt-Stausee (Vermunt Lake) – From the dam, the **view**★ extends to the far off peaks of Gross Litzner and Grosses Seehorn.
The road then winds through a pass worn away by ancient glaciers.

Silvretta-Stausee (Silvretta Lake) – This manmade lake, located in the wide section of the **Bielerhöhe Pass**, is a magnificent beauty **spot**★★ with a number of luxury hotels. Woodlands cover the tall, straight Paznauntal Valley between Galtür and Ischgl. Terraces rise from the foot of the church in the pretty village of **Ischgl**. Houses perched on hilltops overlook the narrow but picturesque Trisanna Valley. The road runs alongside the mountain stream in the middle of thick woodland.

Trisannabrücke (Trisana Bridge) – *See above.*

Landeck – *See above.*

★THE FLEXENPASS

From Rauz to Warth *17km/11mi – about 30min*
The Flexen road breaks off from the Arlberg route at a sharp bend with a panoramic **view** of Stuben and the Klostertal. On the horizon, the jagged Zimba and the glacial Schesaplana dominate the Rätikon Range. After the **climb**★ up to the Flexenpass, the road arrives in Zürs.

★**Zürs** – This town full of hotels is a leading winter sports resort.

★★**Lech** – The resort, set amid grassy slopes, is particularly attractive in the winter. The church is all that remains of the village founded in the 14C. The adjacent resort of **Oberlech** is a collection of hotels. The summit of Biberkopf remains in view along the entire length of the route along the hillside to Warth in the upper Lech Valley.

BADGASTEIN★★

Population 5 600
Michelin map 970 L 6

Badgastein lies in a picturesque **setting★** on the north slope of the Tauern Range. It spreads out like a horseshoe on the wooded hillsides. The Gasteiner Ache tumbles down in a series of waterfalls into the town centre.

Winter sports – Chair-lifts carry skiers up the valley's east side into the Höllbrunn and Graukogel ranges. On the opposite side, the Stubnerkogel cable-car takes skiers to an altitude of 2 246m/7 300ft.
The adjacent resort of **Sportgastein** *(access by toll road)* sits on a vast plateau. A chair-lift and ski lift lead up to Kreuzkogel.

Taking the waters – Badgastein has a mineral water swimming pool complex with one of the pools dug out of the rock. The waters are beneficial because of the therapeutic effects of radon, a radioactive element. Another type of treatment is available in the Heilstollen, disused mine galleries above Böckstein. Rheumatism sufferers are taken here by a small gauge railway. They enjoy natural steam baths at temperatures of between 37.5° and 41.5° C/98° and 104° F.

Sightseeing – **Nikolauskirche**, a 15C church, and the Unterer Wasserfall, waterfall on the **Gasteiner Ache★**, are the main sites. The **Kaiser-Wilhelm-Promenade★** provides strollers with views of Bad Hofgastein. The **Kaiserin-Elisabeth-Promenade** links Badgastein to Böckstein, and the **Gasteiner Höhenweg** runs down the mountainside from Badgastein to Bad Hofgastein.

BREGENZ★★

Population 29 000
Michelin map 970 K 6

Bregenz is the Voralberg's administrative centre. It has become a major tourist centre owing to its geographical location on the shores of the Bodensee (Lake Constance), at the point where the Swabian Sea touches the mountain.

Innenstadt (Lower Town) – Commercial activity centres on the Lower Town at the foot of the old fortified town (Oberstadt).

Shores of the lake – The tree-lined lakeside promenade is decked with flowers. It forms the Seeanlagen and leads to the landing-stage. From the main breakwater, the **view★** extends as far as the island of Lindau with its two bell-towers.
The Strandweg to the west leads to the beach. Concerts and wonderful open-air theatre or operettas are put on here as part of the **festival**. Light shows also brighten up the lake.

★**Vorarlberger Landesmuseum** – The regional museum contains prehistoric and Roman collections, traditional costumes, works of popular art and religious art from the Romanesque and Gothic periods, and portraits by **Angelika Kauffmann** (1741-1807).

Oberstadt (Higher Town) and **church district** – This small walled town remains peaceful and restful when the season swings on the shores of the lake.

Martinsturm (St-Martin Tower) – This tower, built in the 13C but altered from 1599 to 1602, houses a chapel with a Flamboyant Gothic ciborium and a series of 14C murals. The dormer windows provide a number of attractive **glimpses★** of the town walls remnants, the old town rooftops, the lake with Lindau's bell-towers, and the Appenzell Alps.

Pfarrkirche St-Gallus (St Gall's Parish Church) – The parish church dedicated to St Gall is set on the edge of the Thalbach ravine. Its bell-tower porch dates from the 15C and the single aisle was built in the 18C. Walnut choir stalls are decorated with outstanding parquet dating from around 1740.

EXCURSION

★★**Climb to the Pfänder** – *11km/7mi then 1hr walk, there and back.* Leave Bregenz by the Lindau road along the lakeside promenade. Beyond **Lochau**, the village is dominated by the 16C Hofen Castle. The small Pfänder road provides several views of the lake and the island of Lindau. At the end of the road, a footpath climbs up past the tree-lined terrace of the Schwedenschanze to a television tower and on to the hill top. The **panoramic view** includes the vast stretch of water, along with an aerial view of Bregenz. Lower down, the Bergaus Pfänder has a viewing table and zoo. This southern panorama takes in the snow-capped Alps and the great Rhine Rift Valley.
A **cable-car** links Bregenz and the Pfänder.

GRAZ★★

Population 243 405
Michelin map 970 M6

Graz is the main town in Styria. It developed on the banks of the River Mur in a plain bordered to the west by the final Alpine outcrops. To the north and east lie the Styrian hills. The delightful setting and vast parks have sometimes won it the name of garden city.
Now Austria's second largest city, with its festival of modern art, the **Steirischer Herbst** (literally Styrian Autumn), Graz enjoys an international reputation.

Historical notes – Graz did not become a true town until the late 12C. In 1452, the Styrian prince, Frederick III Habsburg was crowned Holy Roman Emperor. He turned the city into an imperial capital.
Faced with threats from the Turks between the 13C and 17C, Graz became a bastion of the Christian world. The Styrian iron mountain **(Erzberg)** stored a gigantic amount of weapons and munitions.
When the Habsburgs partitioned the country in 1564, Graz became the capital of **Interior Austria**, including Styria, Carinthia, Görz, Carniole and Istria. The city enjoyed a period of great wealth and pomp in the days of Archduke Charles II who founded **Graz University** in 1585.
In 1619, however, Emperor Ferdinand II transferred the Court to Vienna. In the 18C, Joseph II took away Graz' final prerogatives. The Golden Age had come to an end.
In the 19C, Archduke **Johann von Habsburg** chose to live in Graz. He did much to modernise the city and the region.

★★OLD TOWN *3hr, not including a visit to the arsenal*

This is one of the largest old towns in a German-speaking country. In the shadow of the Schlossberg, the district is bordered to the west by the River Mur. Most house fronts were rebuilt in the 18C or 19C. Behind them, older houses grace silent, arcaded courtyards, some intimate and cosy, others austere.

★**Hauptplatz** – The main square forms the city's heart, always full of hustle and bustle. Behind the 17C, 18C and 19C coloured frontages, narrow medieval houses extend back a long way from the street. The **Luegg Houses** are covered in 17C stucco work. No 4 houses Graz's oldest pharmacy dating from 1535. In the square's centre, a **fountain** erected in 1878 is dedicated to **Archduke Johann**.
The Herrengasse is lined with elegant shops, including the **painted house** at no 3. This was the archdukes' residence until 1450 although the decoration dates from 1742.

★★**Landhaus** – This superb Renaissance mansion has an austere main façade contrasting sharply with the elegance of the courtyard's three tiers of arches. Adjacent to the Landhaus is the arsenal.

★★★**Zeughaus (Arsenal)** – It was built in 1642. In its day, it was the world's largest. Today, it is the only one to have retained its original layout. The depot contains more than 32 000 weapons, including suits of armour and breast plates. Many of the works are ornate and intricate.

H. Wiesenhofer/ÖSTERREICH WERBUNG

Roofs in Graz

Stadtpfarrkirche zum Heiligen Blut (Parish Church of Jesus' Precious Blood) – The church's Baroque wooden **bell-tower** is the city's most elegant. On the stained-glass windows in the chancel, created in 1953, are the profiles of Hitler and Mussolini *(left)*.
At no 7 Herrengasse, turn into Altstadtpassage leading through arched courtyards to the Mehlplatz, literally the Flour Square flanked by two impressive façades. The right one is Baroque; the left one Rococo. Turn right onto the Bell Square **Glockenspielplatz**, where a couple of automata dressed in Styrian costume dance on a pediment to old popular tunes at 11am and 6pm.
The narrow street called Abraham-a-Santa-Clara-Gasse leads to Burgergasse. An austere housefront **(no 1)** evokes a Roman palace; it has a Baroque Jesuit entrance. A flight of steps **(right)** leads to the mausoleum.

★★**Mausoleum** – This is Graz's most unusual monument, built by Italian architects from 1614. Its superb Baroque façade opens up into a richly decorated interior containing several tombs of princes.

★**Domkirche (Cathedral)** – The cathedral, built from 1438 to 1464, is decorated on the outside with fragments of the **painting of plagues** (1485). These frescos describe the ills that befell Graz. The interior has elegant reticular ribbed vaulting and two magnificent 15C **reliquaries**★★★ made of ebony, bone and ivory.
Outside the cathedral's north door, cross the entrance and courtyard of the 15C castle to visit the palace's sole surviving section – the **staircase tower**★★. Dating from 1499, it has been integrated into the modern *Landesregierung* buildings.

Freiheitsplatz (Freedom Square) – The square is dedicated to freedom. Its most outstanding features are the statue of Emperor Franz II and the woodwork on the former imperial bakery (Hofbäckerei).
Descend the winding, busy **Sporgasse** (literally Street of Spurs). No 22 holds a Gothic style arched courtyard and no 3 an Art Nouveau house.

Sackstrasse – This former cul-de-sac was known as the Lords' Cul-de-Sac because of its mansions built in the early 17C. A Renaissance **courtyard**, the Krebsenkeller, stands at no 12. The **Herberstein Palace** at no 16 has a grand staircase. The Khuenburg Palace at no 18 houses the **Stadtmuseum**, or Municipal Museum. Opposite stands the Baroque **façade**★★ of the early 18C **Attems Palace**, and adjacent, the **Dreifaltigkeitskirche**, the church dedicated to the Holy Trinity built in 1704. It has a harmonious and tranquil west front.

★**Medieval town** – This district, set between the Mur River and the town walls, included a cattle market in the Middle Ages. Hence its more usual name of Kälbernes Viertel (Calves District). Picturesque **narrow streets**★ such as Neue-Weltgasse and Franziskanergasse have retained their old-world charm.

Franziskanerkirche – The Franciscan church's interior has been modernised except for the Jakobskapelle, the chapel dedicated to St James built in 1330.

★★THE PARKS *2hr*

★**Schlossberg** – *Access by funicular railway* Schlossbergbahn. The upward journey is only from the northern end of Sackstrasse. A flight of steps also leads off Schlossbergplatz.
The hill rises to an altitude of 123m/400ft above the city. Although the fortress resisted attacks by French troops in 1809, the castle had to be demolished under the terms of the Treaty of Schönbrunn. Only the **Uhrturm** (clock tower) and **Glockenturm** (bell-tower) with the bell (Lisl) weighing 4.5t remain. The area has been turned into tree-lined gardens and terraces. From the terrace in the Herberstein Garden, several delightful **views**★ unfold of the city and the Mur Valley.
Paulustorgasse leads to the **Steirisches Volkskundemuseum**, a museum of popular arts and traditions illustrating Styrian folklore. Further on the 16C **Paulustor** (St Paul's Gate) was once part of the town's fortifications.

★★**Stadtpark** – This natural English-style park was laid out in the 19C with a wealth of different types of vegetation. In front of the building known as the Forum Stadtpark stands the **Stadtpark Brunnen**, a fountain cast by the Frenchman Antoine Durenne.

ADDITIONAL SIGHTS

★**Mariahilf-Kirche** – This church is dedicated to Our Lady of Assistance. Building work began between 1607 and 1611; the two towers were erected between 1742 and 1744. The church is admirable for its Baroque façade and the austere elegance of the late Baroque towers. In the adjacent cloisters, a 17C pavilion houses the Minoritensaal (Minor Brothers' Chamber) on the upper storey. The room was once the ceremonial refectory and it contains a charming walnut pulpit.

Alte Galerie of Landesmuseum Joanneum – The Ancient Art section of the Landesmuseum Joanneum displays outstanding exhibits on the ground and second floors. They include the medieval section with superb stained-glass windows, **sculptures** and **altarpieces**★, mainly by Austrian artists. The decorative objects *(Kunstgewerbe)* section also merits a look.

EXCURSIONS

★★ **Schloß Eggenburg** – *3·5km/2mi to the west.* The plan of the castle of the Princes of Eggenberg is somewhat reminiscent of the Escurial in Madrid *(see Spain)*. Its originality lies in the fact that it is an allegory of the universe down to the smallest details: the earth that bears it, the air around it, the water surrounding it and the fire of its red roofs. The four towers symbolise the four cardinal points and the 365 windows the days of the year. On the second floor, the sumptuous **ceremonial rooms**★★★ have seen illustrious guests such as Emperor Leopold I, who came here in 1673 to celebrate his marriage with Claude-Felicity of Tyrol. On the ground floor of the south wing, the **Styrian Antiquity Collection** (Abteilung für Vor- und Frügeschichte) contains an exceptional piece, the **Strettweg votive chariot**★★★. This unique work, delicately wrought in bronze, dates from the 7C BC and is a moving testimony to the Hallstatt period.

★Styria Wine Trail

Although the Wine Trail is off the usual tourist route, it provides an opportunity to discover the traditional face of Austria, unchanged in the heart of superb scenery. Traditions come alive in the happy atmosphere of the **Buschenschenken**, the country cafés where people meet for a glass of wine and a **Brettljause** cold meat platter or **Verackertbrot**, black bread with spiced bacon. Everyone listens to accordion music.

Almost all the Styrian vineyards produce white wine called Welschriesling. A dry white represents about a quarter of the vineyards.

The sweet, fruity Müller Thurgau white wine grows in about a fifth of the vineyards. The Weisser Burgunder, made from Pinot Blanc grapes, has a subtle bouquet and is produced on a tenth of wine-growing land. Although the Zweigelt is the most extensively-produced red wine, the Schilcher (rosé) is better-known and grows on Schilcher-producing territory to the southwest of Graz. The trail begins here.

Schilcher Trail – The southern-facing slopes of the Schilcher hills are covered with vines, sometimes on steep land.

At the exit from the motorway, the road climbs uphill. To the left are delightful **views**★★ of the plain around Graz. Mount Schöckl soars in the background. **Gundersdorf** marks the beginning of the wine-producing villages. The painted wooden farmhouses look like dolls' houses. In **Langegg**, an extensive **view**★★ unfolds of the Mur Valley and the hills in the Sausal. From Greisdorf to Marhof, the road runs through fields of corn. The crop is used to make a sort of local polenta called **Sterz**.

Stainz – At the northern end of the village, the 17C Augustinian abbey has been rechristened castle. It has two courtyards with arcaded galleries and a Baroque **church** with a superb high altar, as well as a **museum**★ exhibiting traditional farming practices and crafts in Styria. In particular, it contains some wonderful reconstructions of traditional rooms **(Stuben)**.

The region is attractive, with gently-rolling hills.

Bad Gams ob Frauental – The village takes the first word of its name from its Chalybeate springs. It is, however, also famous for its pottery workshops.

The road leaves the hills and runs down into the plain flanked on all sides by forests.

Deutschlandsberg – This large wine-growing town is the main centre of production for Schilder.

The town is also famous for its colourful Corpus Christi procession and the 12C keep in its reconstructed castle. It has a superb **view**★ of the plain.

Sausal hills – The hills rise to an altitude of 670m/2 178ft and are covered with vineyards producing **Rheinriesling**, a sparkling white wine with a pronounced bouquet. The road winds from one hill to the next.

★ **Kitzeck** – With an altitude of 564m/1 833ft, this is Europe's highest wine-producing village. The **view**★★ looks down over a sea of hilltops. The **Weinmuseum** (Wine Museum) is set out in a house built in 1726.

Cross Fresing and **Kleinklein** (see the storks' nests) and head for Grossklein. Then take the Eichberghof direction south. The winding road twists and turns through wild rugged country.

South Styria Road – In the town of **Leutschach**, surrounded by fields of hops, turn left in front of the church and follow the "Südsteirische Weinstrasse," the Southern Styria Wine Trail. The road runs through an area commonly known as **Styrian Tuscany**. Over a distance of several miles, it forms the border with Slovenia. The narrow picturesque road provides **views**★ of the vine-clad hillsides which produce Welschriesling and Sämling.

Ehrenhausen – The town's Baroque **church** has a Rococo interior. On a wooded rise stands a **castle** with an elegant Renaissance courtyard. There is also a strange **mausoleum**★ containing the tombs of Ruprech of Eggenberg, who distinguished himself as a general in the struggle with the Turks at the end of 16C.

GROSSGLOCKNER-HOCHALPENSTRASSE***

Michelin map 970 L 6

The mountainous region around the Grossglockner lies within the boundaries of the **Hohe Tauern National Park**, an area of 1 800km²/687 sq mi in which the flora and fauna are particularly well-protected.

J. Ducange/TOP, Paris

Großglockner

FROM ZELL AM SEE TO HEILIGENBLUT

75km/47mi – about 4hr

★**Zell am See** – The scenery around Zell am See combines the distant snows of the Hohe Tauern range, the rocks of the Steinernes Meer and the alpine pastures of the Grasberge. All these features are reflected in the still waters of the lake, **Zeller See.** Beyond Bruck, the road enters an austere murky valley called **Fuschertal**. Between Fusch and Ferleiten, one section of the road emerges from the valley and runs along a cliff face above a small wooded gorge **(Bärenschlucht)**. From here, the wonderful **Sonnenwelleck** and snow-capped Fuscherkarkopf come alive. From Ferleiten to Fuscher Törl, the road climbs 1 300m/4 225ft in a series of hairpin bends. Upstream from the Piffkar Ravine, the **views**★★ become magnificent. The road skirts the boulders known as the Witches' Kitchen *(Hexenküche)* and the succession of dips at Nassfeld before climbing to the **Edelweissspitze**★★, a peak that forms an observation platform. It then reaches the mountain pass.

★**Fuscher Törl Pass** – The road crosses the pass *(Törlein)* in a wide sweep producing a panoramic view of a sinister landscape full of rocks and trees.

Hochtor – This is the road's highest point, at 2 505m/8 141 ft.
The road then runs downhill amid alpine pastures. At the end of the Guttal ravine, take the **Gletscherstrasse**, the Glacier Road.

Schöneck – The superb view looks down over Heiligenblut.
A series of hairpin bends offers a magnificent **view**★★ over the Grossglockner, the Pasterze Glacier and the man-made Margaritze Lake.

★★★**Francis Josephs-Höhe** – The Glacier Road ends in a long terrace leading to the Freiwandeck Platform. At the foot of the Grossglockner, the highest peak in Austria soars to 3 797m/12 340ft, flanked by dazzling ice and sharp ridges. The magnificent iceflow forms the **Pasterze Glacier**. It covers a distance of 10km/6mi. *From Freiwandeck, it is possible to travel down to the glacier by funicular railway (Gletscherbahn).*

★★**Wasserfallwinkel** – *From Freiwandeck, a 1hr 30min walk.* Gamsgrubenweg, a path laid out above the Pasterze, leads to this spot with a superb view.

Go back along the same road and, at the Guttal junction, head downhill to Heiligenblut.

The final wooded step of rock is barred by a waterfall.

★**Kasereck** – This grassy spur provides views of the Grossglockner and the Heiligenblut basin.
Near the chalets are grain dryers in the form of grids. The final hairpin, above the Fleiss Valley, provides a view of the Sonnblock. Finally, the famous church in Heiligenblut comes into view like a stone spear erect in front of the distant Grossglockner.

★**Heiligenblut** – The village is mainly a mountaineering and skiing resort. The church stands in a picturesque **spot**★ and the building itself, dating from 1430 to 1483, is interesting.

INNSBRUCK★★ and the Tyrol

Population 116 000
Michelin map 970 K 6

Innsbruck, literally the bridge over the Inn, lies at the junction of the Inn Valley and Sill Gap. It is Tyrol's administrative capital and a traditional host city for the Winter Olympics thanks to its ever-improving sports facilities and its Alpine geographical location.

Historical notes – In the 14C, the Habsburgs captured the town. Innsbruck enjoyed a period of lavish expansion, especially from 1493 during the reign of Maximilian I. He married his second wife in the city. Maria Theresa and her successors also favoured the city.

A GLIMPSE OF THE CITY

Keep your eyes open while driving from the Brenner Pass along road no 182. From the bend at the hamlet of Sonnenburgerhof, a **general view**★ opens of Innsbruck.
In the city itself, Maria-Theresien-Strasse combines town planning and natural landscape. The **view**★★ is one of the best picture postcard scenes in Europe. Take a trip up the **Hungerburg**★ by car or funicular railway. From the terrace and observation platform, another **general view** unfolds of the city and the majestic pyramids formed by the Serles and Nockspitze mountains to the south.

★OLD TOWN *4hr*

Leave from the St Anne Column on Maria-Theresien-Strasse.

★★**Maria-Theresien-Strasse** – This street and square provides an impressive **view**★★ of the range of mountains rising to 2334m/7586ft, and the St Anne Column in the foreground.

Annasaüle (St Anne Column) – The monument was erected in 1706 to commemorate the defence of the city during the War of the Spanish Succession.

Stadtturm (Belfry) – A flight of steps inside the tower with its Renaissance top leads to a platform with a **panoramic view**★ of the city.

★**Goldenes Dachl (Little Golden Roof)** – This delightful building completed in 1500 adjoins the former ducal palace. The balustrade on the first floor is decorated with a frieze of coats of arms. The second floor resembles a loggia and is lavishly decorated with sculptures (the originals are in the Tyrolean Ferdinandeum). Inside the **Olympia-Museum** describes the 1964 and 1976 Winter Olympics held in Innsbruck.

★**Heiblinghaus** – This house was given a luxurious Rococo frontage in the 18C.
Further down on the left, notice the 16C Goldener Adler Hotel. *Come back to the Maria-Theresen Strasse and take the Pfarrgasse which leads to Domplatz.*

Dom zu St-Jakob – The Roman Catholic Cathedral Church of St James is the mother church of the Tyrol. It was rebuilt at the beginning of the 18C. The **Baroque interior**★ has three wide convex domes in the nave and a lantern-dome in the chancel, all of them skilfully decorated by artists from Munich.

The Little Golden Roof, Innsbruck

Around the cathedral, old houses with balconies form a colourful picture with sculptures in relief, stucco work and frescoes.

Return back by the same route. At the crossroads beside the Goldenes Dachl, go along Hofgasse, and after a vaulted passageway, turn into Rennweg which skirts the Hofburg.

★**Hofburg** – Maria Theresa built this palace, with its long yellow frontage flanked by two towers. It was completed in 1770. Inside, the most outstanding of all the State rooms is the **Riesensaal**★★, literally the Giants' Room, which is decorated with stucco work panels with a sheen of porcelain. It extends for 31.50m/102ft and includes a painted ceiling and portraits of the Habsburgs, the future Louis XVI and Marie-Antoinette.

Hofkirche – This 16C church has a nave containing three aisles of equal width built in the Gothic-Renaissance and Baroque styles. It houses the **Grabmal Kaiser Maximilians I**★, the tomb of Emperor Maximilian I. This is the largest existing piece of German Renaissance sculpture. It is surrounded by 28 impressive bronze and copper statues. The tomb itself is empty but encircled by **Alexandre Colin's** splendid Renaissance wrought-iron and sheet metal grille and sculptures. The church also has a Renaissance gallery, choir stalls dating from 1567, a 16C organ, and the tomb of the Tyrolean patriot, **Andreas Hofer**. The projecting Silver Chapel **(Silberne Kapelle**★★**)** contains tombs and a large silver statue of the Virgin Mary.

★★**Tiroler Volkskunstmuseum** – The Tyrolean Museum of Popular Arts and traditions contains collections of Christmas cribs, models of houses, a whole range of kitchen utensils, folk costumes, furniture, decorative objects relating to religion, and most importantly, reconstructed Stuben (rooms) in the decorative Gothic style (first floor) and Renaissance and Baroque style (second floor).

Take Angerzellgasse then Museumstrasse to the Ferdinandeum.

★**Tiroler Landesmuseum** or **Ferdinandeum** – The large collection of works in the Tyrolean Museum reflects the development of fine arts in the region, especially Tyrolean Gothic art.

ADDITIONAL SIGHTS

Town Centre

Hofgarten – This pleasant garden with ponds, basins and lakes stands in the shade of weeping willows.

Landhaus – In this Baroque mansion built in 1728, note the main staircase decorated with stucco work and statues of busts of ancient gods.

Triumphforte – The medallions and statues on this triumphal arch commemorate the sad and happy events in 1765 for the Habsburgs.

Riesenrundgemälde (panorama) von Bergisel – *Next to the Hungerburg funicular railway station.* This circular fresco runs 100m/325ft long and 10m/32ft high. It depicts the Battle of Bergisel *(see below)*.

Alpenzoo (Alpin Zoo) – This pleasant park set on a hillside overlooking the Inn Plain contains numerous species of alpine wild life.

Innsbruck-Witten, Bergisel and Ambras

Stiftskirche (Abbey Church) von Wilten – This 17C Baroque building with its red pebbledash walls was rebuilt after 1945. Note the entrance. Two painted wooden giants stand guard and, inside, the magnificent **grille**★ dates from 1707.

★**Basilika von Wilten** – The Rococo nave is decorated with superb stucco work and, on the vaulting, some excellent paintings.

Bergisel – *Access by the Brenner Pass road and Bergiselweg.* This wooded hillside crisscrossed by footpaths conceals a number of memorials to the Tyrolean uprising and the battles fought in 1809. The **Kaiserjäger-museum** (Imperial Hunters Museum) also commemorates the events. Its rooms show several different **views**★ of Innsbruck and the Nordkette, the mountain range barring the horizon.

Schloss (Castle) Ambras – From Innsbruck, follow the Olympiastrasse. Beyond the ice rink, pass under the motorway and turn left onto the Aldrans road.
This vast castle, modified since the end of the 16C, is divided into upper and lower castles. The upper castle contains an exhibition of portraits, furniture, frescoes and tapestries. The lower castle holds four **weapons rooms**★, the Kunst-und-Wunder-Kammer (Curios Room) and the Spanish chamber with its Renaissance ceiling.

EXCURSIONS

★★ Hafelekar – *Access by cable-car from Hungerburg – 3hr.* This magnificent observation platform overlooks the Inn Valley and the Stubaï Alps to the south, and the limestone Karwendel range to the north.

★ Stubaital – *44km/27mi to Mutterbergalm – about 2hr.* The peaceful Stubai Valley includes the tourist resorts of Mieders, Fulpmes and Neustift. The glacial core at the summit of **Hochstubai**, in the valley beyond Mutterbergalm, has been equipped as an all-year round ski resort.

KITZBÜHEL★★

Population 7 872
Michelin map 970 L6

Despite its increased popularity as a holiday resort, Kitzbühel has succeeded in retaining its traditional character as a small walled town in which the centre. Pedestrian precincts, the Vorderstadt and Hinterstadt, include stocky Bavarian-style houses.

Kitzbühler Alpen – The schist Alps rise to an altitude of 2362m/7,677ft at the Grosser Rettenstein and are known locally as Grasberge (lawn-clad mountains). A number of popular observation platforms unveil the colour contrasts in the landscapes of the surrounding ranges.

Winter sports – The interconnections between the different ski lifts provide pistes known as the Kitzbühel Ski Carousel — the Skizirkus. Famous ski competitions take place on the Streif piste running down the Hahnenkamm.

Pfarrkirche (Abbey Church) – The 15C Gothic parish church has retained its mountain-village character thanks to its huge enveloping shingle roof. A family of local artists named Faistenberger (17C – 18C) produced the decoration inside the church on the high altar and the chapel dedicated to St Rosa of Lima.

Liebfrauenkirche (Blessed Virgin Mary Church) – This church, dedicated to the Blessed Virgin Mary, has a massive square tower and, inside, a Coronation of the Virgin Mary (1739) painted on the vaulting. In front of the altar, a Rococo grille dates from 1778.

Heimatsmuseum – The local museum's collections give an insight into the origins of a town that was Bavarian for almost 1 000 years.

SIGHTS

★★ Kitzbühler Horn – *About 2hr there and back, including 35min by cable-car (two sections).*
A panoramic view unfolds of the jagged Kaisergebirge peaks and the glacial summits of the Grossglockner and Grossvenediger.

Schwarzsee (Black Lake) – *5km/3mi by the Kirchberg road and the track to the lakeside (right) which crosses the railway line.* However, the most attractive way of seeing the Black Lake, is to walk around via the Liebfrauenkirche and the path to Lebenberg. The lake, set against the background of the peaks of the Kaisergebirge, is suitable for swimming.

Pass Thurn – *20km/12mi south. Leave Kitzbühel by the Mittersill road.*
The **observation platform★** with the best parking facilities is 1 800m/1 950yds beyond the mountain pass on the Oberpinzgau slopes beside the Buffet Tauernblick. From there, the view extends over the Hollersbachtal leading south towards the highest summit in the Hohe Tauern range.

LINZ★ and the Danube Valley

Population 197 960
Michelin map 970 L5

Linz, the main city in Upper Austria, is built on the two banks of the Danube. The river has provided it with much of its economic development. In the Middle Ages, boats with timber and iron sailing the Danube made a major contribution to the city's expansion. Nowadays, Linz is the largest and best-equipped port on the middle reaches of the Danube.
The most characteristic **view★** of the city extends from the **Pöstlingberg** (hill).

★OLD TOWN

Hauptplatz – Historic buildings surround this large square. In the centre stands the Trinity Column erected in 1723 by the States of Upper Austria. It reminds future generations that the city had just survived the Black Death (1713), fire (1712), and an invasion by the Turks (1704).

Alter Dom St-Ignatus – The **former cathedral** is Linz's largest Baroque church. The austere west front forms a striking contrast with the ornate interior of stucco, pink marble columns, traceried pulpit and choir stalls.

Landhaus – This palace built in the second half of the 16C is the provincial government's seat. In the inner courtyard, seven figures represent the planets, a reminder that the great mathematician and astronomer, **Kepler**, taught in the provincial college from 1612 to 1626.

Schloss – The **castle** was the residence of Emperor Frederick III. It now houses the Oberösterreichisches Museum, the **provincial museum of Upper Austria★** covering the history of art, popular arts and crafts.

EXCURSIONS

★★**Danube Valley** – The Danube is Central Europe's longest river, stretching 2 826km/1 756mi. It only passes through Austria for a distance of 360km/224mi from Passau in Germany to Bratislava in Slovakia.
Over the centuries, the valley has acquired fortresses, graceful Renaissance residences, fortified churches, and abbeys built in a noble and elegant architectural style.
In the area between Linz and Vienna, the most picturesque part of the Danube Valley stretches from Grein to Krems. The river banks here were popular with the Romantics. This section of the valley was also used as the background for certain episodes in the **Ring Cycle**, a German epic poem composed around 1200 and inspired by Scandinavian and Germanic legends. It tells the story of Siegfried who captured the fabulous treasure belonging to a tribe of gnomes known as the Nibelungen. The name that was later to be given to the Burgundian warriors.

MELK★★

Michelin map 970 M5

Melk Abbey stands on top of a rocky rise overlooking the Danube and is the most accomplished example of Baroque architecture in Austria. In the late 11C, Leopold III of Babenberg gave the castle to the Benedictines and they turned it into a fortified abbey. Melk's spiritual and intellectual influence then spread throughout Lower Austria. The Reformation, Turkish invasion, and Napoleonic Wars-Napoleon used Melk as his headquarters in 1805 and 1809-put a halt to the abbey's development. But the city retains its artistic treasures.

Baumgartner/STIFT MELK

Melk Abbey

Tour – *1hr.* The outside gate leads into an initial courtyard. It is flanked by statues of St Leopold and St Colomn, the abbey's patron saints, and by two bastions dating from the 17C and 18C. The **Prälatehof**, or Prelates' courtyard, includes an admirable set of buildings whose walls are decorated with statues of the Prophets.

Kaisergang – The long **Emperor's Galery** led to the state chambers. It is now laid out as a museum reserved for high-ranking visitors.

Marmorsaal – The **Marble Chamber** is impressive for its lavish decoration and strict design, with a succession of reddish-brown stucco pilasters imitating marble.

Terrace – The terrace lies right at the tip of the spur of rock, providing a superb view of the Danube.

Library – More than 100 000 books and 2 000 manuscripts are stored. The wainscoting and gilding give it added brilliance.

★★★ **Stiftskirche (Abbey Church)** – The towers on the west front and the vast octagonal dome dominate the rest of the abbey. The lavish decoration in the interior includes frescoes, and golden or marble ornamentation. The amazing paintings on the vaulted roof are the work of Johann Michael Rottmayr. The paintings on the side and high altars are dazzlingly ornate.

MÖRBISCH★★

Population 2 360

Michelin map M⁶ southeast of Eisenstadt

Mörbisch is the last village on the west shores of the Lake Neusiedler before reaching the Hungarian border. It delights visitors because of its picturesque narrow streets. The houses are limewashed and almost all of them have a flight of steps in front leading up to a portico. The doors and shutters are painted in bright colours. Ears of corn are strung up along the walls, and the balconies and windows decked with flowers, giving added colour to the scene.
East of the village, a road leads through marshes and reedbeds to a holiday resort *(toll)* on the shores of Lake Neusiedler.

The Austrian Romantic Road follows the Danube Valley between Salzburg and Vienna.

SALZBURG★★★

Population 138 213

Michelin map 970 L 6

Salzburg, Mozart's birthplace, delights visitors with an undefinable charm. The Hohensalzburg, the fortress symbolising the prince-archbishops' power, stands high above the city crossed by the River Salzach. The geographical setting is outstanding, the palaces and churches suffused in soft lighting; the Salzkammergut attracts with its nearby natural delights, and the city celebrates with a prestigious festival. The squares are decorated with carved fountains, the architecture of the historic buildings is steeped in a sense of majesty, and the Mozart Museum is particularly moving. Everything about Salzburg creates unforgettable memories.

HISTORICAL NOTES

The Heritage of the Prince-Archbishops – The bishopric of Salzburg was founded shortly before 700 AD by St Rupert. In the following century, it was raised to an archbishopric. The archbishops were princes of the Holy Roman Empire from the 13C onwards and they exercised their temporal power as far away as Italy. They also gained immense wealth, mainly owing to the salt mines in Salzkammergut. Three of them in particular left their mark on the city through the buildings they commissioned – **Wolf Dietrich von Raitenau**, elected in 1587; **Marcus Sitticus**, his successor; and **Paris Lodron** (1619-1653) who made Salzburg an eminently musical city.

Wolfgang Amadeus Mozart (1756-1791) – Mozart was born in Salzburg on 27 January 1756. He was a naturally gifted child prodigy, and his talents were quickly recognised and exploited by his father, Leopold, himself a musician. He arranged a series of concerts for his son across Europe for four years starting in 1762. At the age of 14, Mozart was appointed concert master of the archbishop's orchestra in Salzburg. However, he soon began travelling again, especially in Italy. He had several arguments with the archbishop of the day, Colloredo, who finally withdrew his patronage.
In 1781, Mozart left Salzburg for Vienna. He married Constance Weber there in 1782. The Viennese public greeted his greatest lyric works with incomprehension, with the exception of *The Magic Flute*. The genius composer died at the age of 35 years and 10 months. His remains were buried in the paupers' grave in St Mark's Cemetery in Vienna and have never been identified.

Mozart's Music – The divine Mozart was at ease in every form of musical expression. His impressive creativity produced a listed 626 works. Hard work and lessons from his teacher **Haydn** added to his prodigious natural talent. His characteristic style and exquisitely pure melody lines support both profane and religious themes. Towards the end of his life, his music reflected the despair engendered by his lack of success in love, his illness and his abject poverty.

The Salzburg Festival – In 1842, Salzburg finally erected a statue in memory of Mozart and created the **Mozarteum** Academy of Music. In 1920, the city inaugurated the famous festival which, since then, has attracted all the greatest musicians and conductors including **Herbert von Karajan** who performed for more than 30 years. From the end of July to the end of August, daily performances of operas, concerts and ballets take place in different venues throughout the city, mainly in honour of Mozart but also in memory of other prestigious classical composers. The extraordinary puppets in the world-famous **Marionettentheater** *(Schwartzstrasse 24)* illustrate many of these works.

★★OBSERVATION PLATFORMS

For the best views of the city, climb to the top of the Mönchsberg or Hettwer Bastei.

★★**Mönchsberg** – *Access by lift from Gstättengasse (not on map).*
The terrace offers a superb **general view** of Salzburg and the nearby mountains.

★★**Hettwer Bastei** – Walk uphill to the Capuchins Church and on to the observation platform. The Hettwer Bastion on the southern edge of the Kapuzinerberg provides some outstanding **views** of the city's left bank, especially in the early morning. A succession of flights of steps leads back down to the narrow Steingasse. Turn left to the Steintor, a town gate dating from the 17C.

★★OLD TOWN *4hr*

Domplatz – The buildings on this wonderful square show great uniformity of architectural style. Three porticoes link the historic buildings around the cathedral and former archbishops' palaces. In the centre, a column in honour of the Virgin Mary was erected in 1771.

★**Dom** – The cathedral was built between 1614 and 1655. This vast building's Baroque style is discernible among the last few Italian Renaissance features.
The interior is striking for its sheer size and the richness of its marble, stucco work and paintings. Mozart was christened here, at the Romanesque font. The **crypt** has been refurbished; it contains the tombs of the prince-archbishops and a Romanesque crucifix. The **Dommuseum** holds the cathedral plate and the 17C archbishops' Kunst- und Wunderkammer, an art gallery and treasure.
Kapitelplatz is decorated with a monumental 17C fountain. Cross the square to the terminus where the **funicular railway** takes visitors up to Hohensalzburg.

★★**Hohensalzburg** – The former fortress of the prince-archbishops stands on a block of dolomite rock, some 120m/390ft above the River Salzach. Building work began on the fortress in 1077 and it was continually extended and refurbished until the late 15C. Inside, the **church** dedicated to St George is decorated with a red marble carving. To the right of the church, the terrace of the **Great Kuenburg bastion** provides a superb **view**★★ of the old town.

Salzburg

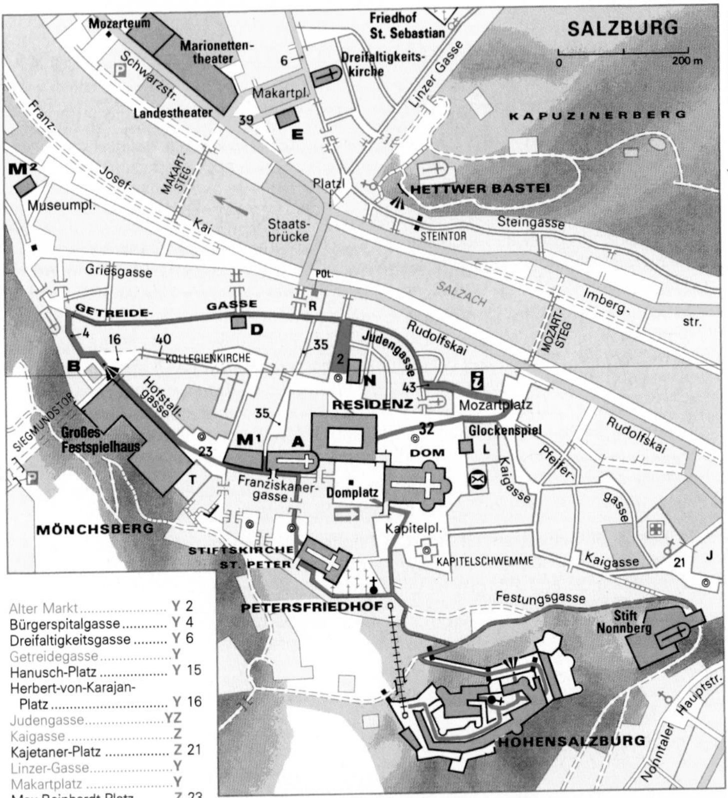

Alter Markt	Y 2
Bürgerspitalgasse	Y 4
Dreifaltigkeitsgasse	Y 6
Getreidegasse	Y
Hanusch-Platz	Y 15
Herbert-von-Karajan-Platz	Y 16
Judengasse	YZ
Kaigasse	Z
Kajetaner-Platz	Z 21
Linzer-Gasse	Y
Makartplatz	Y
Max-Reinhardt-Platz	Z 23
Reisidenzplatz	Z 32
Sigmund-Haffner-Gasse	YZ 35
Theatergasse	Y 39
Universitätsplatz	Y 40
Waagplatz	Z 43

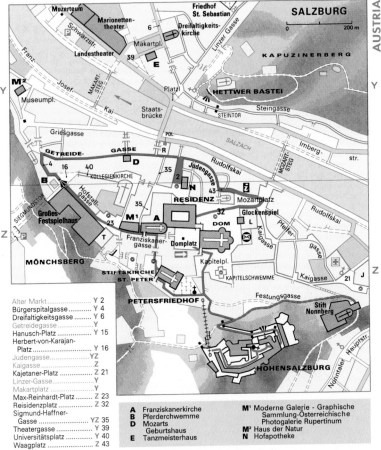

A Franziskanerkirche
B Pferderchwemme
D Mozarts Geburtshaus
E Tanzmeisterhaus
M¹ Moderne Galerie - Graphische Sammlung-Österreichische Photogalerie Rupertinum
M² Haus der Natur
N Hofapotheke

Castle and museum – From the watchtower (Reckturm), a **panoramic view★★** looks out to the south over the Tennengebirge and Salzburg Alps.
In the castle, visitors tour the State chambers and the **Burgmuseum★**. The most outstanding exhibits are collection of medieval art and weapons.

Stift Nonnberg (Nonnberg Abbey) – The abbey, founded around 714, is the oldest convent in German-speaking countries. The **building** in the middle of the graveyard was built in the Late Gothic style. The Romanesque tympanum was remounted in the main portal. Inside, a fine altarpiece rises behind the high altar. There is also a crypt with ogival vaulting and, in **St John's Chapel**, a Gothic altarpiece dating from 1498.

★★ **Petersfriedhof (St Peter's Cemetery)** – The cemetery backs onto the sheer rock face of the Mönchsberg. The catacombs here evoke the city's history. The 15C chapel dedicated to St Margaret displays Baroque arches.

★★ **Stiftskirche St-Peter** – The former Romanesque basilica church underwent alteration in the 17C and 18C. A superb gilded **wrought-iron grille★** dating from 1768 stands at the entrance to the three aisles decorated with rich Baroque ornamentation.

★ **Franziskanerkirche** (Z **A**) – The Franciscan church is interesting for the juxtaposition of the Romanesque nave and Gothic chancel. An admirable late 15C statue of the Virgin Mary graces the impressive high altar (1708).

Moderne Galerie, Graphische Sammlung, Österreichische Photogalerie (Z **M¹**) – This museum of contemporary graphic arts and photography is housed in a 17C palace.

Pferdeschwemme – The horse trough was built in 1695 and altered in 1732. It is a huge construction decorated with carvings and frescoes.

★ **Haus der Natur** (Y **M²**) – The 80-room Nature Centre *(tour: 2hr)* contains remarkable geological, mineralogical, zoological and ethnological collections. There is also an aquarium and a reptile house.

★ **Getreidegasse** – This narrow busy shopping street is lined with houses with carved window frames and the decorated fronts with wrought-iron shop signs. On the third floor of **Mozarts Geburtshaus** (Mozart's birthplace, *no 9*) are moving memorabilia, violins, spinet, and sheet music.

On Alter Markt, the former marketplace, a strange pharmacy, the **Hofapotheke**, still has its Rococo interior.

Judengasse – This narrow but picturesque street was the old Jewish quarter.

Residenzplatz – A fine 17C fountain decorates this square flanked on the south side by the cathedral, on the west by the Residence, and on the east by the **Glockenspiel**, a peal of 35 bells installed in 1702.

★★**Residenz (Residence Palace)** – This was once the residence of the prince-archbishops. It dates from 1585 although the northwest wing was built at the end of the 18C. The 15 State rooms **(Residenzgalerie)** are given added majesty by stucco work and 18C ceramic stoves. They contain extensive collections of 16C to 19C paintings.

★**Mirabellgarten** – These pleasant gardens were laid out in 1690. The castle, which was rebuilt in the 19C, now houses the Salzburg Council Chambers. All that remains of the former 17C building is an amazing **monumental staircase**★★ and the Marmorsaal or Marble Chamber lavishly decorated with gilding and stucco work.
In the former orangery, a delightful inner courtyard and a small Baroque museum **(Salzburger Barockmuseum)** exhibits 17C and 18C European works of art.

Tanzmeisterhaus (Y E) – *Makartplatz 8.* The Dancing Master's House was the Mozart family home. It was rebuilt after 1945 and has been turned into a museum specialising in memorabilia and historic 18C musical instruments.

Friedhof St-Sebastian (St Sebastian Cemetery) – Among the graves is that of the doctor and philosopher **Paracelsus**, the strange mausoleum of Wolf Dietrich covered with ceramics, and the graves of Mozart's father and wife.

Dreifaltigkeitskirche – Holy Trinity Church was built between 1694 and 1699. It has a Baroque interior and an oval dome decorated with frescoes.

Between Salzburg and Vienna, the Austrian Romantic Road follows part of the Danube Valley.

SALZKAMMERGUT★★★

Michelin map 970 L 6

Salt, the traditional symbol of health and a source of wealth, gave Salzkammergut its name and, until recent times, provided the area with an outstanding income. Nowadays, tourism, rather than salt, brings prosperity to this former saltpan area centred on Bad Ischl.
The 76 lakes, countless mountain peaks and huge ranges such as the **Dachstein** and **Totes Gebirge** are among the outstanding attractions of this justifiably famous region.

★★LAKE TOUR

Salzburg to Bad Ischl – *84km/52mi – one full day*

Mondsee – The main sights in this popular tourist town are the **Pfarrkirche** (parish church) dating from the late 15C but with a west front added on in 1740; the **Heimat und Pfahlbaumuseum** with exhibits from the Stone Age and other collections representing local traditions; the **Mondseer Rauchhaus**, literally the Smoking House but actually a 15C chalet; and the **Maria-Hilfkapelle**, a 15C chapel with Baroque features standing on a rise overlooking the lake.
Mondsee, though, is best-known for the nearby lake of the same name, the **Mondsee**★, shaped like a crescent moon. Its tree-lined shores overlook the **section**★ of motorway running above its north bank.

Burggrabenklamm – *5km/3mi from Au, then 30min on foot.* The rocks can be slippery in wet weather. The ravine leads to a waterfall.
Cross the small pass linking Scharfling and St-Gilgen for the **panoramic view**★★ from the detour above St-Gilgen. Beyond the village is Lake St-Wolfgang.

★**St-Gilgen** – The delightful village lies at one end of **Lake St-Wolfgang**★★. Some of Mozart's family lived here. On the lake, a **regular boat service** runs between nine jetties. The paddle steamer *Kaiser Francis Joseph*, built in 1873, can still be seen ploughing through the water.

Strobl – The centre of the village and lakeside promenade are elegant.

★★**St-Wolfgang** – It is preferable to come to this popular tourist village, famous for its **lake**★★, by boat. The setting was used for the operetta *White Horse Inn*, and the **Weisses Rössl** inn still stands beside the lake. The 15C **church** set on a spur of rock is part of an elegant 16C priory. An external walkway with arches completes the **beauty spot**★★ and provides views down the sheer sides of the rock to the lake. The church contains a masterpiece of Gothic art, the **altarpiece**★★, completed by **Michael Pacher** in 1481.

★**Bad Ischl** – This spa resort was the scene for some of Europe's most brilliant social life during the reign of Emperor Francis Joseph. It is set against a background of wooded mountains, in a meander formed by the Traun and Ischl rivers. **Auböckplatz** is the traditional centre. **Pfarrgasse** is the busiest shopping street, leading to the tree-lined **Esplanade** that runs along the banks of the Traun.
On the left bank of the Ischl, a magnificent landscaped park called the **Kaiser-park houses the Kaiservilla**★, the imperial residence where Francis Joseph lived with his wife, Elizabeth. The empress' favourite retreat also lies within the park. This **Marmorschlössel**, or Marble Castle, now houses a **museum of Photography**.

Mehlig/PIX

St-Wolfgang

From Bad Ischl to Gmunden

34km/22mi about 3hr. Downstream from Bad Ischl, the Traun Valley used to be one of Europe's main salt routes. The spectacular **cliff road**★ from Ebensee to Traunkirchen runs along the shores of the **Traunsee**★, the deepest lake in Austria (191m/621ft).

Traunkirchen – The **setting**★ on a promontory provides a wide range of views of the Traunsee. The **Corpus Christi Procession** is held on the lake. The **Pfarrkirche** parish church rebuilt in 1632 stands in the middle of a terraced graveyard. It contains some dazzling Baroque furnishings, in particular the **pulpit**★.
Near the end of the itinerary, the Greek Sleeper *(Schlafende Griechin)* refers to the jagged outline of the Erlakogel forming the face of a sleeping woman seen in profile. Beyond Altmünster is Ort Castle, a short distance from Gmunden.

★**Gmunden** – This colourful little town lies at the northern end of the Traunsee. It has one of Austria's best-equipped beaches, popular for its romantic setting and ceramics. Visitors usually take a stroll along the 2km/1mi lakeside **Esplanade**★ or go to **Ort Castle**★ which has a charming Renaissance courtyard lined with arcades. The **Kammerhofmuseum**★ gives an insight into the town and its region and has extensive collections of ceramics and memorabilia relating to the composer Johannes Brahms.

From Gmunden to Salzburg *117km/73mi one full day*

The route takes in three lakes (Traunsee, Attersee and Mondsee) and runs through rustic scenery in the upper Aurach Valley or wider, open spaces such as the Mondsee. Leave Gmunden by the Bad Ischl road to Altmünster then turn right.

★**Gmundnerberg** – The final stretch of road runs along the hilltops. **Views**★ extend over the entire Traunsee basin.
Return to Altmünster. The road enters an area of gently rolling hills dotted with dazzling white farmhouses and copses of enormous lime trees.
Beyond the Grossalm Pass, the road runs downhill, providing **panoramic views**★ down the mountainside to the Attersee. Beyond Steinbach am Attersee, the road forms an esplanade along the banks of the **Attersee**★ (or Kammersee), the largest lake in the Austrian Alps. An observation platform beside the Buchberg Chapel provides an attractive general view of the lake.

At the Attersee, follow the St-Georgen road then take the expressway to Salzburg.

The drive down to the Mondsee provides a **panoramic view** over the mountains flanking the lake.

Leave the expressway by the Mondsee exit.

Mondsee – *See above.*

★★THE DACHSTEIN TOUR

Round trip from Bad Ischl – *267km/166mi – one or two days.*

This round trip can also be made from the Salzach Valley (Golling) or Enns Valley (Radstadt, Schladming, and Steinach).

The road runs along the floor of the Traun Valley with its orchards. Beyond Steeg, it skirts the deep blue **Hallstatt Lake★★**. Near Hallstatt, a **view★** unfolds of the town and the Obertraun.

★★**Hallstatt** – This romantic village in an equally romantic setting clings to the outcrops of the Dachstein Range as it plunges down into the lake. The nearby **salt mines** have been worked since the Stone Age, the so-called **Hallstatt Period**. Tiers of **terraced observation platforms★** *(park the car)* overlook the village and surrounding countryside. Flights of steps lead up to the platforms. Among the sights worth visiting are the parish church for its **setting★★**, its 16C **altarpiece★**, **St Michael's Chapel** for its ossuary, and the picturesque **Heimatmuseum** where exhibits give an insight into local history and folklore.

★★**Krippenstein Climb** – *From Hallstatt, 4hr by cable-car and on foot.* The **Schönbergalpe** station on the cable-car run provides access to the **Dachstein Rieseneishöhle★**, an ice cavern, and the **Mammoth Cave**. The summit of the **Krippenstein★★** (2 109m/6 854ft), opens up a **general view** of the Upper Dachstein Plateau and several **breathtaking views★** down the mountainside over Lake Hallstatt.

From Gosaumühle, turn off towards the Gosausee (lake).

★★**Gosausee** – The shores of the **Lower Gosau Lake** offer a **panoramic view★★★** of the limestone peaks of the **Upper Dachstein** and its small glaciers.

Return the way you came and, in Gosau, take the road to Pass Gschütt.

Abtenau – A holiday resort at the foot of the enormous Kogel (rounded mountains with scarp slopes) form the Tennengebirge. The Gothic church and presbytery are interesting.

Return the way you came and turn right onto the Salzburg Dolomites road.

Radstadt – Built in the late 13C, this small town is surrounded by battlements. The surrounding countryside is dotted with manor houses.

★★**Hunerkogel** – *From Schladming, 16km/9mi via Ramsau and a toll road then about 1hr return including 10min by cable-car.* The upper terminus contains a **panoramic view★★** of the Tauern range and the Salzkammergut Alps.

Follow road no 146.

Trautenfels Castle – This castle built in the 17C now houses collections of regional exhibits.

At the Trautenfels junction, turn left onto road no 145.

Pürgg – Leave the car at the entrance to the village. The Johanneskapelle, a chapel dedicated to St John, is built on a rise. It has some interesting Romanesque frescoes. The old parish church is strangely constructed on the hillside.

The road leads into the Hinterberg Dip, facing the magnificent rocky slopes of the Grimming. Winter skiing takes place on the alpine pastures on the **Tauplitzalm**.

The road crosses Bad Mitterndorf and the Traun runs through a narrow gorge. Bad Aussee then comes into view.

★**Bad Aussee** – Set in a very busy mountainous area, Bad Aussee uses the brine and water from the Altaussee Mines which have a high sulphur and sodium content. The centre of the **Upper Town** is Chlumeckyplatz. The **Kammerhof** Palace decorated in the 17C now houses the local museum. The neighbouring Hoferhaus has some interesting 16C wall paintings.

★**Grundlsee and Toplitzsee** – *From Bad Aussee, 5km/3mi to Grundlsee then 10km/6mi to Gössl and 20min on foot.* From the Seeklausee jetty, a **view★★** unfolds of Lake Grundlsee in its basin. From the wild inaccessible shores of the **Toplitzsee★**, take a **boat** to the tiny **Kammersee** which seems to be totally enclosed by the walls of rock forming the Totes Gebirge.

The Pötschenhöhe road cuts across the great meander of the Traun which partially fills the lake at Hallstatt. The eastern side of the pass begins with a small panoramic **road running along the hilltop★★**.

On the other side, the road runs down through the delightful Bad Goisern basin. A final bend forms an **observation platform★** providing a view of the lake at Hallstatt.

In Bad Goisern, pick up the road you started from. Return to Bad Ischl.

★WÖRTHER SEE, Carinthi

This lake stretches from Velden to Klagenfurt, over a length of 17km/11mi. The mountain streams make the lake shallow, keeping the lake water warm in the summer, from 4-28°C/90-96°F. Holiday resorts such as Velden and Pörschach are located on the shores.

★THE SOUTH SHORE OF THE LAKE

From Villach to Klagenfurt – *76km/47mi – about 5hr*

Villach – This major railway junction is a tourist town. In the Schillerpark, a huge relief map of Carinthia is built to a scale of 1:10000.

Cross the Gail to the Maria Gail Church.

Maria Gail – The church contains an early 16C **altarpiece★★** depicting the Coronation of the Virgin Mary.
The road runs through the Villach basin to the delightful **Faakersee**.

Rosegg Wildpark – The Rosegg Wildlife Park contains lynxes, apes, wolves, and bison.

★★**Velden** – This resort is located at the western tip of the lake. The castle has a 17C entrance.

★**Maria Wörth** – The pilgrimage churches on their promontory contain 11C murals. Another displays an abundance of interior decoration from various periods.

Pyramidenkogel – From this 54m/176ft observation tower, a wide **panoramic view★★** opens.

Viktring – 12C Cistercian abbey was altered and extended in the 14C and 15C.

Take the road to the Loiblpass (no 91).

Hollenburg – This massive fortress overlooks the Drave Valley. The inner courtyard has arcades. There is a terrace and observation platform.

Klagenfurt – The walls of this former fortress town were demolished in 1809. It is the main city in Carinthia. The checkerboard streets cutting across each other at right angles date from the 16C. The Wörthersee to the west makes this a very pleasant place to stay. The **Landesmuseum★** has mineralogical, prehistoric and Roman collections as well as 15C and 16C **works of religious art★**. Around the building, a **Parkmuseum**, an open-air museum, displays statues and Roman remains.

WIEN★★★

VIENNA – Population 1 515 660
Michelin map 970 M5

Vienna was an imperial city for more than six centuries. The ruling Habsburgs left a definite mark on it. The vicissitudes of history have made it the seat of a republican government with jurisdiction over a much truncated state. But since 1955, Austria's neutrality has often been effective and Vienna has retained an incomparable level of prestige.
As the outpost of the Roman Empire and, later, a bastion of Christianity against which the Turks launched countless unsuccessful attacks, Vienna remained a bastion of the West. It continued in this role until the recent collapse of Marxist ideology and the Eastern Bloc. Since 1967, the city has been the permanent seat of OPEC, the organisation of oil-exporting countries. In 1979, the construction of the International Vienna Centre (UNO-City (BR) in the Donaupark brought together two UN bodies under one roof, the International Atomic Energy Agency and the Organisation for Industrial Development. Vienna is the United Nations' third permanent centre after New York and Geneva.

E. Streichan/PIX

Rathausplatz, Vienna

Historical notes – The main events in the history of the capital city were the **Black Death** in 1678; the **Turkish siege** in 1683; the reign of the great empress, **Maria Theresa** (1740-1780); the **Congress of Vienna** (1814-1815) which followed Napoleon's downfall and crowned with success Austrian diplomat **Metternich**; the **Vormärz** (literally Before March), a period of irresponsible enjoyment ending with the March 1848 revolution; and finally the long reign of **Francis Joseph** (1848-1916) which saw the construction of the ring roads, the **Ring** and the **Gürtel**. The **Augarten Porcelain Works** opened in 1717; they later became a national factory.

Vienna, a City of Music – Vienna was famous for its profane music in the 12C and it became a musical capital when Maximilian I transferred his chapel royal, the **Hofkapelle** here. Imperial music-lovers such as **Leopold I** were also accomplished composers or musicians.
The Baroque period of the 17C and 18C was marked by the triumph of operas, concerts and operettas. In the 18C and 19C, great Austrian musicians came to work in Vienna including **Haydn, Mozart, Schubert, Bruckner,** and **Mahler**. Germans such as **Beethoven, Gluck** and **Brahms** also contributed. At the beginning of the Vormärz Period, the **waltz** first appeared; its main exponents were **Joseph Lanner** and, more especially, **Johann Strauss** the Elder and Younger. In the first quarter of the 20C, the **New Viennese School** founded by **Arnold Schönberg** proclaimed a musical revolution.
Today, a number of prestigious establishments maintain Vienna's role as a leading musical centre. They include the **Staatsoper** (National Opera), the **Hofmusikkapelle** (the Chapel Royal), the Philharmonic Orchestra or **Musikverein**, The Symphonic Orchestra of **Konzerthaus**, the **Volksoper Wien** (the Comic Opera Company), and the **An der Wien** theatre which performs ballets and operas during the **Wiener Festwochen** (Vienna Festival). In addition, concerts are given throughout the city during the Summer Music Festival, **Musikalischer Sommer**.

Life in Vienna – Large department stores, elegant shops, pedestrian precincts, and the courtesy and kindness of locals delight tourists. **Coffee**, like croissants, the legacy of the Turkish siege in 1683, is served in the famed coffee shops. The best-known include the Café Central, Café Herrenhof, Café Museum, and Café Hawelka. Well known pastry shops include Demel, Lehmann, Heiner, and Sacher.
Local dishes owe much to influences from the former Habsburg Empire. They are eaten in **Keller** (cellar-grillrooms), **Beisel** (bistros), **Weinstuben** (wine bars) and, on the outskirts of Vienna, in the **Heurigen** (country pubs), often to the sound of typical bands known as **Schrammelmusik**.

DISCOVERING VIENNA

★★**Tour of the Ring** – *By car or tramway (circular routes 1 and 2) – about 1hr. Leave from Stubenring to the east, near the River Danube.*
This enjoyable drive by day or in the evening takes in the illuminated historic buildings. To right and left proceed:
– the early 20C **Savings Bank** built in the Art Nouveau style;
– the **Austrian Museum of Applied Arts**★★ in the Florentine Renaissance Style;
– the vast **Stadtpark**, the public park filled with statues of famous musicians;
– the elegant French Renaissance arches of the **Opera House**★★;
– the greenery and statues of the **Burggarten**, once the gardens of the Imperial Palace;
– the colonnade of the **Neue Burg** (New Imperial Palace), completed in 1913;
– **Maria-Theresien-Platz** with its monument erected in 1888 and its equestrian statues flanked by two symmetrical domed buildings housing the **Art Gallery**★★★ and the **Natural History Museum**★. The square extends to the Messepalast with its 18C façade;
– the popular gardens of the **Volksgarten**★ and its Temple of Theseus;
– the **Parliament** (1876-1883) whose frontage resembles a Greek temple;
– the **town hall** set at the end of pleasant gardens. It has a neo-Gothic façade and a central tower topped by the Rathausmann, a standard-bearer 3.40m/11ft high;
– the **Burgtheater**★, opposite the town hall, a 19C building in the Renaissance style;
– the **University**, built in the Renaissance neo-Gothic style, and the **votive church** with its two slender spires. Both come into view on the left after the last bend in the Ring.
The itinerary then leaves the **Stock Exchange** on the right-hand side and ends at Franz-Josephs-Kai.

Views of the city – Two hills to the northwest of the city, the **Kahlenberg**★ and **Leopoldsberg**★★, provide outstanding observation platforms. Other **striking views**★ extend from the **Donauturm**★★, or Danube Tower, in the Donauparkm, and from the **Riesenrad**, the ferris wheel in the Prater.

The Wien-Karte

This card, valid for 72hr and priced at 180 ATS allows unlimited travel on all public transport in zone 100. It must be filled in (with your name and the date) and punched the first time it is used. It also entitles you to reductions in a number of museums, for certain performances and in some shops and restaurants (see leaflet provided with card).

★★★HOFBURG, A TOWN WITHIN A TOWN (HJR)

The imperial palace accommodated the Habsburgs until 1918. It is a juxtaposition of very different styles, built from the 15C to 20C. It now contains the apartments of the President of the Republic, the national library, the winter manege for the horses of the Spanish Riding School and a number of museums.

Exterior

The façades, courtyards and monuments display an austere majestic style of architecture. The most outstanding features are the façade fronting **Michaelerplatz** which is decorated with gilded bronze grilles and two huge fountains, the so-called **Inder Burg** courtyard, the **Schweizerhof** (the Swiss Courtyard), the elegant **Josefsplatz** on which the pediments are topped with group sculptures, the early 18C **National Library** and finally the **Neue Burg** (new Imperial Palace) built from 1881 to 1913 in the Italian Renaissance style. The fan-shaped frontage faces Heldenplatz (Heroes' Square). This parade ground contains equestrian statues, a huge gateway (Ausseres Burgtor) and, since 1934, a war memorial (Heldendenkmal).

Interior: Memories of the Habsburgs

★★★**Schatzkammer** – The imperial treasure includes the **Crown Jewels**, a dazzling display of crowns and other dynastic insignia. It also displays the cradle used for the king of Rome, the **sacred treasure** including a number of works of art from the 12C to 19C, and most important, Holy Roman Empire treasures with the 9C Holy Lance and the famous **10C Imperial Crown★★★**.

★★**Kaiserappartements** – The 20-room imperial apartments contain luxurious furniture, 17C and 18C tapestries, and historical memorabilia.

★★**Schausammlung der ehemaligen Hofsilber und Tafelkammer** – The magnificent collection of court treasures includes 18C Chinese and Japanese porcelain, and gilded bronze tableware, silver gilt, gold and Sèvres porcelain dinner services, and glassware.

Hofburgkapelle – The Chapel Royal is a 15C Gothic building refurbished during the Baroque period. Sunday Mass is accompanied by the choir of the Chapel Royal.

Spanische Reitschule (Spanish School) – The winter manege, an 18C Baroque building, is used for training and **shows★★** by the famous school of equestrian art. The school was founded in the 16C. Next to it, the **Stallburg** houses on the ground floor, the school's Lippizaner horses and on the second floor the 19C European art gallery.

Österreichische Nationalbibliothek – The National Library dates from the early 18C. The **Great Hall★** in the Baroque style has **frescoes★★** by **Daniel Gran** in the dome.

★★**Kaisergruft (Capuchin Church)** – The crypt contains the tombs of 12 emperors, 17 empresses and more than 100 archdukes. Among the best-known are Marie-Louise (Napoleon's wife), Emperor Maximilian of Mexico, Archduke Rodolphe who died in Mayerling, and Emperor Francis Joseph. The church was built from 1619 to 1632.

Augustinerkirche – The 14C Augustinian church was used by the court. Inside, Canova carved the **tomb★** for Archduchess Marie-Christine. The **crypt** beneath the **Chapel of Our Lady of Loretta** holds 54 urns containing the hearts of the Habsburgs, including the heart of Napoleon's son.

★★**Albertina** – This remarkable collection of engravings, drawings, etchings and watercolours – more than one million in all including the ones from the **Dürer Bequest★** – illustrate the development of graphic arts from the 15C.

★★**Waffensammlung (Arms and Armour Collection)** – Hundreds of suits of armour, breast plates and harnesses, weapons of war and hunting, all of them magnificently worked by the greatest armourers of the time and all of them once belonging to the Habsburgs, are displayed next to the booty captured from the Turks at the end of the 17C.

★★**Sammlung alter Musikinstrumenten** – The collection of musical instruments provides a retrospective of wind, string, or percussion instruments from the 16C to 19C.

★★**Ephesos-Museum** – Among the many archeological exhibits on display at the Ephesus Museum are the **frieze of the Parthian monument★★** and the **Athlete of Ephesos★★**, a Roman copy of a Greek original from 340 to 330BC.

★**Museum für Völkerkunde** – The Ethnographic Museum has a section on African art, objects brought back from the voyages of Captain Cook, and a famous Mexican department containing **Montezuma's feather costume★★** (16C) as well as death masks, fabrics, an obsidian mirror, weapons etc.

WIEN

Street	Grid	No.
Babenbergerstr	HJS	
Bäckerstraße	KR	9
Bauernmarkt	KR	10
Bognergasse	JR	13
Bräunerstraße	JR	15
Dominikanerbastei	KR	22
Dorotheergasse	JR	25
Dr. Ignaz-Seipel-Pl.	KR	27
Falkerstraße	KLR	33
Friedrichstraße	JS	38
Georg-Coch-Pl.	LR	40
Getreidemarkt	HJS	42
Graben	JR	
Griechengasse	KR	46
Gutenberggasse	HS	51
Heiligenkreuzer Hof	KR	55
Himmelpfortgasse	KR	61
Judengasse	KR	66
Judenplatz	JR	67
Kärntner Straße	JRS	
Kettenbrückengasse	HS	69
Kohlmarkt	JR	70
Landstraßer Hauptstr	LR	73
Lichtensteg	KR	78
Löwelstraße	HR	79
Marc-Aurel-Str.	KPR	81
Mariahilfer Str.	HS	
Mölkerbastei	HP	84
Naglergasse	JR	85
Neuer Markt	JR	87
Neustiftgasse	HR	88
Oppolzergasse	HR	89
Philharmonikerstr.	JS	90
Plankengasse	JR	91
Renngasse	JPR	94
Rotenturmmstr.	KR	

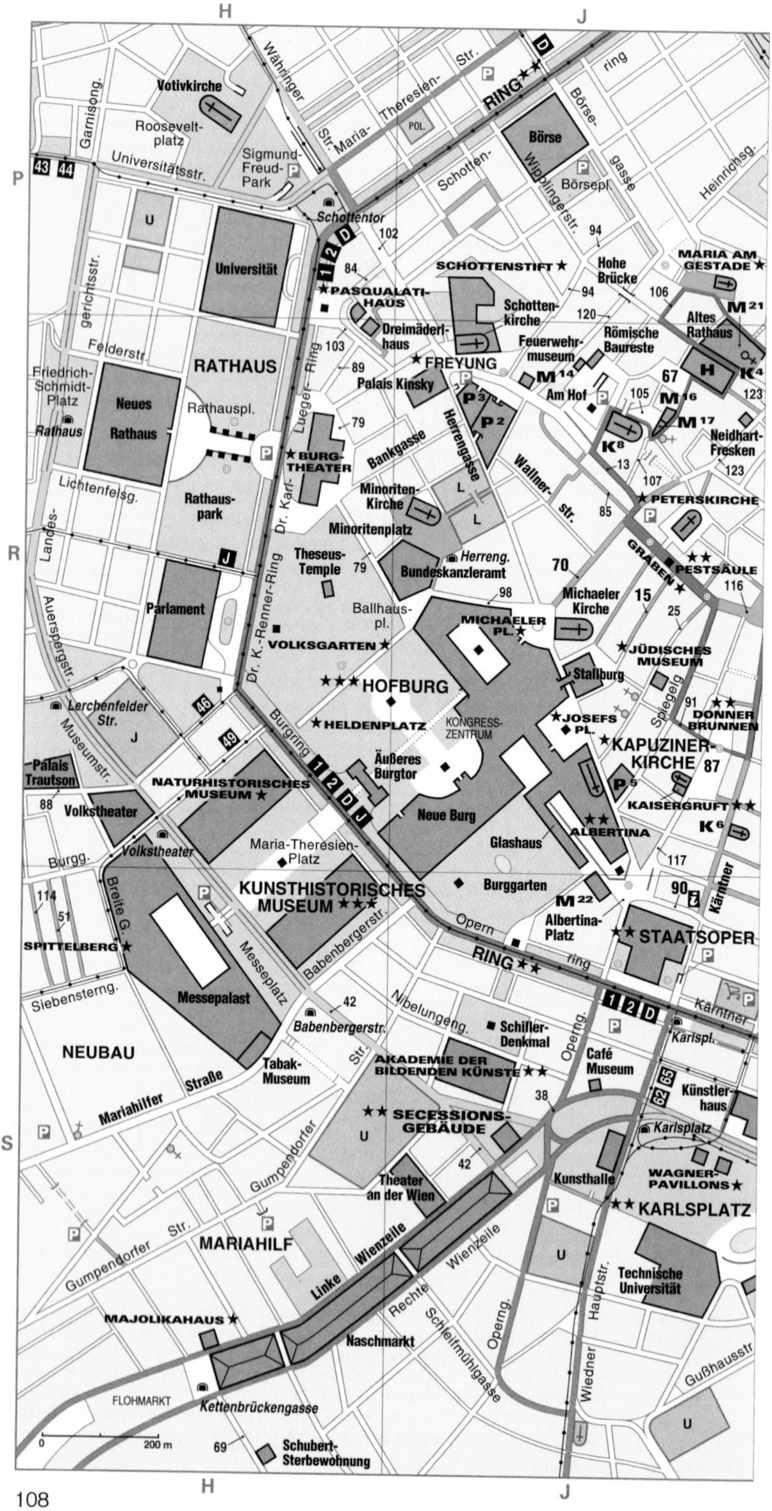

H Böhmische Hofkanzlei
K[4] Salvatorkapell
K[6] Malteserkirche
K[8] Kirche „Zu den neun Chören der Engel"
M[14] Kunstforum
M[15] Puppen-und Spielzeugmuseum
M[17] Uhrenmuseum der Stadt Wien★
M[18] Ursulinenkirche und Kloster
M[19] Dom-und Diözesanmuseum★
M[21] Ausstellung „der Österr. Freiheitskampf"
M[22] Gedenkräume des Österr. Theatemuseums
N Akademie der Wissenschaften
P[2] Palais Ferstel
P[3] Palais Harrach
P[5] Palais Lobkowitz

K L

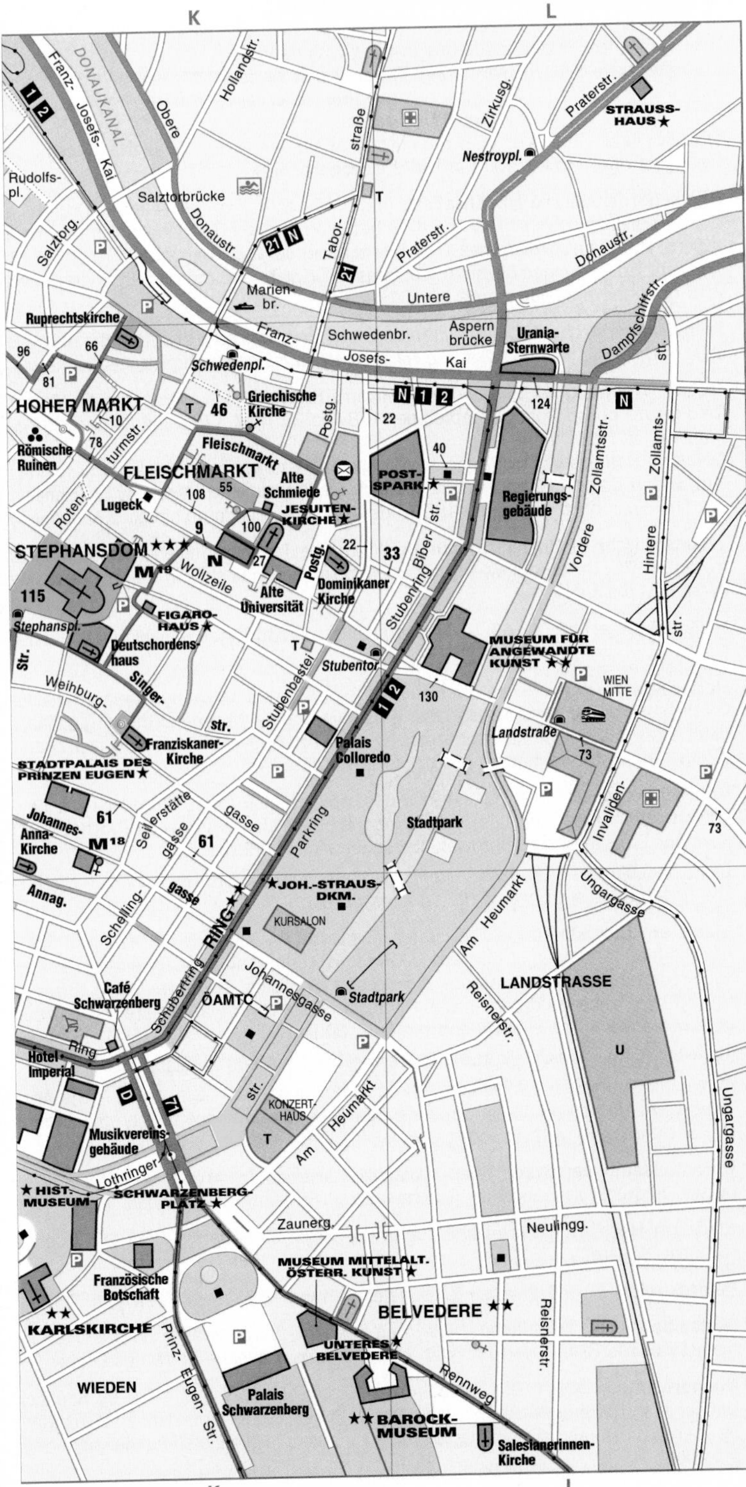

K L

★OLD TOWN *4hr not including museums*

The main heart of Vienna lies between the cathedral and the canal.

★★★**Stefansdom** (**St Stephen's Cathedral**) (**KR**) – Note the huge brightly-coloured roof of glazed tiles and the powerfully majestic south tower, the famous **Steffel** or **St Stephen's Tower**★★★. Its spire rises to a height of 137m/445ft. This impressive building was completed in 1433 and the north tower was given a Renaissance roof in 1579. It contains the **Pummerin**, a 21t tenor bell. The **Riesentor**★ (Portal of the Giants) is a late Romanesque design filled with statues.
The great nave is 107m/348ft long. The carved stone **pulpit**★★★ was made by Anton Pilgram in the early 16C and the **Wiener Neustadt altarpiece**★★ dates from the 15C. Frederick III's red marble **tomb**★★ by Nicolas de Leyde is a late 15C creation. The **catacombs** house the urns with the entrails of the emperors of Austria. A climb to the **top** of one of the towers provides a **panoramic view**.

Deutschordenskirche Hl.-Elisabeth (**KR**) – The church of the Teutonic Order is a Gothic building dating from the 14C but given a later Baroque finish. It has a superb 16C Flemish **altarpiece**★. The **Schatzkammer des Deutschen Ordens**★ (the Order's Treasure House-*Singerstrasse 7*), contains silver plate and coats of arms decorated with gold and precious stones.

Franziskanerkirche (**KR**) – The Franciscans' church was refurbished in the Baroque style in the 18C. The neighbouring **Franziskanerplatz** is lined with picturesque houses.

★**Mozart-Wohnung or Figaro-Haus** (**Mozart's House**) (**KR**) – *Domgasse 5.* Mozart lived in this house from 29 September 1784 to 23 April 1787 and composed *The Marriage of Figaro* here.
Go along Domgasse, Strobelgasse, Willzeile and Essiggasse to Bäckerstrasse lined with fine 16C and 17C houses. The **Akademie der Wissenschaften** (Academy of Sciences) (**KR N**) – was built in the mid-18C to designs by a French architect, J N Jadot.

★**Jesuitenkirche or Universitätskirche** (**KR**) – The Jesuit or University Church dates from the 17C. Its interior was refurbished in the Baroque style in the 18C. Lavishly decorated **pulpit**.

Heiligenkreuzerhof (**KR 55**) – This attractive courtyard stands behind 18C house fronts.

Hoher Markt (**KR**) – Recent digs have revealed some interesting Roman remains. On the square, the **Vermählungsbrunnen** (Fountain of the Marriage of the Virgin Mary) dates from 1732. The **Ankeruhr** at no 10 is an Art Nouveau clock with jack-o'the-clocks. The historical figures proceed past the face every day at noon.

Ruprechtskirche (**KR**) – This church, dedicated to St Rupert, is used by Vienna's French community. It is considered to be the oldest church in the city with its 11C nave and Romanesque bell-tower. Its appearance is unusual.

Climb the steps in Sterngasse and Fischersteige to Salvatorgasse: at no 5, there is the Renaissance entrance of the Salvatorkapelle.

★**Maria am Gestade** (**JP**) – The church dedicated to Our Lady of the River Bank has retained a number of interesting Gothic features. The west front is decorated with sculptures and the entrance is preceded by a dais. The seven-sided tower is topped by a traceried dome. Inside, the most outstanding features are the stained-glass windows in the chancel and the fine statues.

Take the Schwertgasse (**JP 106**)*: interesting Baroque entrance at no 3.*

In Wipplingerstrasse, two superb Baroque buildings face each other – the **Altes Rathaus**, the old town hall (**JR**), and the **Böhmische Hofkanzlei**, the former chancellery of Bohemia (**JR H**) with its impressive façade.

★**Uhrenmuseum der Stadt Wien** (**Clockmaking Museum**) (**JR M**[17]) – *Schulhof 2.* The outstanding collection includes Rustchmann's 18C astronomical clock.

Place am Hof (**JR**) – A bronze statue of the Virgin Mary dating from 1667 decorates this square.

★**Peterskirche** (**JR**) – The lavish Baroque church was built from 1702 to 1733.

★★**Pestsaüle** (**JR**) – This column, built in an awesome Baroque style, was erected in memory of the Black Death. It overlooks the elegant avenue known as Graben★.

★★**Donnerbrunnen** (**JR**) – This fountain made between 1737 and 1739 by Raphaël Donner is in the middle of the Neuer Markt. It represents Providence surrounded by cherubs, fish, and statues personifying the rivers in Vienna's four neighbouring provinces.

★★★KUNSTHISTORISCHES MUSEUM (HS)

The collections in this art gallery are among the largest in the world.

★★**Egyptian and near Eastern collections** – *Mezzanine.* Cult of the dead, sarcophagi, animal worship and daily life. Major exhibits are **papyrus-shaped columns**★ (18C dynasty), **Sebek-Em-Sauf**★★ (votive figure representing a spokesman of the city of Thebes, 13C dynasty) and **Funerary head**★★ (Ancient Empire, 4C dynasty).

★★**Greek, Etruscan and Roman antiquities** – *Mezzanine.* Greek and Roman sculptures: **Young Man of Magdalensberg**★ (16C copy), **Amazons' sarcophagus**★ (late 4C BC) and **portrait of Aristotle**★ (Roman copy). Roman cameos: **Gemma Augustea**★★★ (1C AD) glorifying the victories of the first Roman emperor enthroned in the upper register.

★★**Sculpture and decorative arts** – *Mezzanine.* Renaissance, Mannerism and German Baroque: **equestrian statue of Joseph I**★★ and **bust of Emperor Rudolph II**★★. Mannerism and French Baroque: **bust of Archduchess Marie-Antoinette**★. Renaissance and Italian Mannerism: **bust of Isabella of Aragon**★★ and **salt cellar**★★ (enamelled gold, by Benvenuto Cellini for François Ier). Middle Ages: aquamanile in the form of a gryphon★ (gilded bronze encrusted with silver and nielloed).

★★★**Picture gallery** – *First floor.*

Flemish, Dutch and German paintings – *Left wing.* Artists include Jan Van Eyck, Rogier Van der Weyden and Memling. An entire room is devoted to **Pieter Bruegel the Elder** (*Hunters in the Snow*★★★, an unquestionable masterpiece belonging to a series of 6 paintings), another to Van Dyck *(Nicolas Lantier★★)* and two more plus a study to **Rubens** *(The Little Pelisse★★* and *St Ildefonso altarpiece★★).* Of the 24 studies, one contains important works by **Albrecht Dürer** *(Adoration of the Holy Trinity★★),* the others works by **Martin Schongauer** *(Holy Family),* the **Danube School** (including works by Cranach and Altdorfer), Holbein the Younger *(Jane Seymour★),* Frans Hals, **Rembrandt** *(Large Self-Portrait★★)* and **Vermeer of Delft** *(Allegory of Painting★★★),* etc.

Italian, Spanish and French painting – *Right wing.* The collection includes works by **Parmigiano** *(*Self-Portrait*),* Corregio, **Raphael** *(Madonna of the Meadow★★),* Titian, Veronese, Tintoretto *(Suzanne and the Elders★★),* Caravaggio *(Madonna with Rosary★★),* Guido Reni, Mantegna, Giorgione *(The Three Philosophers★★),* **Velasquez** (portraits of infantes), Canaletto *(Vienna seen from the Belvedere★),* etc.

Coins and Medals – Coin collections from Antiquity onwards.

★★THE BELVEDERE

Built in the Baroque period for **Prince Eugene of Savoy**, who had defeated the Turks, the two Belvedere palaces were purchased by the Habsburgs on his death. The terraced gardens linking the palaces provide a **pleasant view**★ of Vienna.

★★**Oberes Belvedere** – The Upper Belvedere, built in 1723, houses the **Austrian Art Gallery**★ containing 19C and 20C works. It was in the great red marble hall on the first floor that the treaty putting an end to the Allied occupation of Austria was signed on 15 March 1955. In the East Wing are paintings by Waldmüller, Hans Makart, Anton Romako, and Emil Jakob Schindler. The second floor is given over to Austrian figuratives such as Gustav Klimt, Egon Schiele, Oskar Kokoschka, and Herbert Boetal structures.

★**Unteres Belvedere** – A Lower Belvedere from 1716 houses the **Museum of Baroque Art**★ with **sculptures**★ by **Raphaël Donner**, paintings by **Franz Anton Maulbertsch** such as the **Gilded Cabinet**★. There is also the **Museum of Austrian Medieval Art**★ dominated by Gothic art. The collection includes paintings by **Rueland Frueauf the Elder, Michael Pacher** and **Max Reichlich.**
Behind the Museum of Medieval Art are the former stables. They now house works designed to show the various trends and tendencies in European art in the 20C.

★★★SCHÖNBRUNN PALACE

Schönbrunn was built as the Habsburgs' summer residence, commissioned by Leopold I and built between 1695 and 1700 then altered during the reign of Maria Theresa between 1743 and 1749. It stands in an area of woodland once used for hunting, and crossed by a spring known as the Schöner Brunnen, or Beautiful Fountain. The palace and park have many links with history. Marie-Antoinette spent her childhood here, Mozart visited it, Napoleon stayed in 1805 and 1809 and his son, the Duke of Reichstadt was exiled to the palace. Emperor Francis Joseph was born and died, and it was here that Charles I, the last reigning Habsburg abdicated on November 11, 1918.

Tour – The main apartments run along a length of 180m/585ft, forming a yellow ochre façade with green window frames. From here, a superb **view**★★ looks out onto the park and the Gloriette.

★★★**Apartments** – Of the castle's 1 440 rooms, some 40 are open to the public. They provide a luxurious reminder of the 18C Rococo style. Beyond the **apartments of Emperor Francis Joseph and Empress Elizabeth** are the state rooms, with two Chinese studies, the Small Gallery and the Grand Chamber. The **Guest Apartments** include the Napoleon Bedchamber where his son died in 1832 at the age of 22. Another room has been turned into a memorial to Napoleon II. Diplomats who attended the Congress of Vienna in 1814-1815 used to dance in the Great Gallery. The castle's **Baroque theatre** was restored in 1980.

★★**Park** – This is a remarkable Baroque creation with arbours, bowers, flowerbeds, allegorical statues, fountains, ancient ruins, and a **zoological garden** set up in 1752.

★★**Gloriette** – This elegant arched observation platform celebrates the victory of Kolin won by Maria Theresa over Frederick II of Prussia.

★★**Wagenburg** – The Vehicles Room contains an extensive collection of carriages, sledges, and sedan chairs dating from the 17C to 19C. Among the most outstanding exhibits are the **King of Rome's phaeton** and Francis of Lorraine's **coronation coach**.

JUGENDSTIL BUILDINGS

These Viennese buildings are reminders of the Art Nouveau Jugdenstil movement which appeared in German-speaking countries at the end of the 19C.

★**Wagner Pavillons** (JS) – *Karlsplatz*. These old pavilions once marked the entrance to the subway. They stand opposite each other, built in an unusual style combining white marble, gilding and plant motifs, with the green of the metal structures.

★★**Secessionsgebäude** (JS) – This gem of Jugendstil architecture was designed to illustrate the Secession or breaking away from traditional arts. It is dominated by a sphere of gilded foliage. Cynics christened it the "golden cabbage". Inside, note the hallway and the **Beethoven Frieze**★★★ painted by Klimt.

Linke Wienzeile – The **Majolikhaus** *(no 40)* is decorated with floral motifs on glazed earthenware. The house at no 38 has gilded motifs.

★**Postsparkasse** (KLR) – The savings bank has marble plaques with gilded aluminium studs. It still has its original early 20C interior.

★★**Am Steinhof** – This was Vienna's first modern church, built in 1907. It has marble cladding on the outside. The inside is functional, with white and gold decoration.

MEMORIES OF MUSICIANS

★★**Staatsoper** (JS) – The National Opera House was inaugurated in 1869. Its **Vienna Philharmonic Orchestra** enjoys international fame. Note the **tea room**, the decoration of the **foyers** and the ultra-modern stage.

★**Schubert-Museum** – The museum is on the first floor of Schubert's birthplace.

★**Figarohaus** – *See Old Town.*

Dreimäderlhaus (HJR) – *Schreyvogelgasse 10*. Schubert supposedly courted three young girls from the same family in this elegant house dating from 1803.

Palais Lobkowitz (JR **P**[5]) – or Palais Dietrichstein. The palace was built between 1685 and 1687 and, at the beginning of the 18C, was given an attic flanked by statues. It houses the Austrian Museum of Theatre. Beethoven had his Eroica Symphony performed here.

Zentralfriedhof – In the musicians' square in the central cemetery (Gräbergruppe 32A) are the graves of Brahms, Gluck, Hugo Wolf, Johann Strauss the Elder and Younger, Joseph Strauss, Joseph Lanner, and Franz von Suppé.

St-Marxer Friedhof – Mozart has only a pathetic empty grave in this cemetery, topped by a weeping cherub.

ADDITIONAL SIGHTS

Inside the Ring

Herrengasse (JR) – This street lined with mansions now provides offices for major governmental ministries.

Michaelerkirche (JR) – The church dedicated to St Michael is built in a composite Romanesque, Gothic, and neo-Classical style. The interior is Baroque.

Minoritenkirche (JR) – The Minim Brothers' Church dates from the 14C but has a Baroque interior with three aisles and a vast mosaic. This copy of Leonardo da Vinci's *Last Supper* was made on Napoleon's orders.

Annakirche (KR) – The church dedicated to St Anne was altered and decorated in 1629.

Palais Kinsky (JR) – This is an outstanding example of 18C Baroque architecture.

Ursulinenkirche und Kloster (KR M[18]) – Convent and church built between 1665 and 1675 for the Ursulines of Liège. The museum of religious art houses a reconstruction of an old pharmacy (early 18C) and a collection of sacred art.

Outside the Ring

Karlskirche (KS) – The church dedicated to St Charles was built in a composite style from 1716 to 1737. Inside is a vast oval **dome**★★ decorated with frescoes. In the middle of the fountain opposite the church is a huge bronze sculpture.

★**Historisches Museum der Stadt Wien (Wien Historical Museum)** (KS) – *Karlsplatz*. Set out on three floors, a range of different collections illustrates the capital's historic past from Roman times to the present day, including architecture and town planning.

Österreichisches Museum für Volkskunde – This museum illustrates traditional home life, folklore and religion in Austria. In particular, it houses the largest collection of Christmas cribs in Austria.

★**Prater** – This vast famous park stretches between the two arms of the Danube. It was once popular for its cafés where people could sing and dance; now part of it is given over to sports and a fairground. Its famous Ferris wheel, the **Riesenrad**, has a diameter of 61m/198ft.

★★**Gemäldegalerie der Akademie der bildenden Künste** (JS) – The art gallery attached to the Academy of Fine Arts contains the extraordinary **Last Judgement Polyptych**★★ by **Hieronymus Bosch**, works by **Lucas Cranach the Elder**, Titian, **Ambroise Holbein** *(Dormition of the Virgin Mary)*, **Rubens** *(Borée enlève Orithye)*, Van Dyck, Rembrandt, and Francesco Guardi.

★★**Österreichisches Museum für angewandte Kunst** (LR) – The Museum of Applied Arts contains carpets and tapestries from the 15C and 16C, Limoges enamel (from the 13C–16C), gold and silver plate from the 15C to 19C. There are also various pieces of furniture by Riesener and Roentgen, Old Vienna porcelain, and Jugendstil objects.

★**Naturhistorisches Museum** (HR) – The Natural History Museum contains vast collections relating to zoology and botany. There is also a section on prehistory (Hallstatt).

Kurpark d'Oberlaa – The park is landscaped with flowerbeds and basins. Near the panoramic restaurant, there is a fine view of the surrounding countryside.

Palais Schwarzenberg (KS) – Built in the Baroque period from 1697 to 1723.

Naschmarkt (HJS) – This market has charming covered premises where the atmosphere is typical of Vienna. Beyond it, a **flea market** is held on Saturday mornings.

Piaristenkirche Basilika Maria Treu – This church has a fine Classical west front and two domes inside decorated with a fresco from 1752.

Salesianerinnenkirche (LS) – The Visitandines' Church was built between 1717 and 1730.

Hundertwasserhaus – This low-cost housing development was built in 1984 to designs by the cosmopolitan artist Friedensreich Hundertwasser. It is outstanding for the variety of the materials and architectural motifs, loggias, statues, and bulbs.

KunstHausWien – *Unter Weissgerberstrasse 13*. This building, also designed by Hundertwasser, contains a museum of his paintings, engravings, plans and models.

Museum Moderner Kunst – The Museum of Modern Art is housed in the former summer palace, built around 1700, of a prince of Liechtenstein. It still has its original **Baroque decoration** in the state room on the first floor. On the second floor are works by schools which marked the first few decades of this century.

Bundessammlung Alter Stilmöbel – The Federal Institute of Furniture was set up by Maria Theresa to preserve and maintain government furniture. The most outstanding of all the reconstructions of 18C and 19C apartments are the collections of **Biedermeier** furniture named after a bourgeois style contemporary with the Louis-Philippe style in France and the Early Victorian period in Britain.

EXCURSION

★**Grinzing** – *Tram38 : Grinzing* This village at the foot of vine-covered slopes is very lively in the evenings, when both Viennese and tourists come to dine in the typical Heurigen and drink new wine.

The Baltic States

ESTONIA

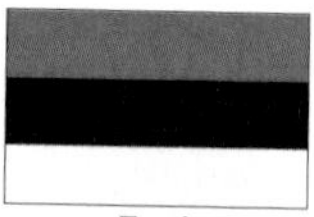

Eesti

Area: 45 200km² – 17 176sq mi – **Population:** 1.5 million – **Capital:** Tallinn – **Currency:** kroon – **Time:** GMT + 2hr in winter, GMT + 3hr in summer

LATVIA

Latvija

Area: 63,700km² – 24 206sq mi – **Population:** 2.7 million – **Capital:** Riga – **Currency:** lat – **Time:** GMT 2hr in winter, GMT + 3hr in summer

LITHUANIA

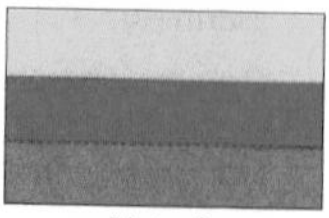

Lietuvà

Area: 65 200km² – 24 776sq mi – **Population:** 3.8 million – **Capital:** Vilnius – **Currency:** litas – **Time:** GMT + 2hr in winter, GMT + 3hr in summer

Since gaining independence in 1991 from the collapsing Soviet Union, Estonia, Latvia and Lithuania have emerged as a new tourist site for Northern Europe.
These three countries cover a total of 650km/403mi. They are bordered to the west by the Baltic Sea and to the north and south by Russia, Belorussia, Poland and the Russian enclave of Kaliningrad.
The land is flat (highest point reaching only 320m/1049ft) and covered primarily by lakes and forests (40 % of Estonia and Latvia, 25 % of Lithuania).
In addition to these charming landscapes, a rich architectural heritage includes magnificent castles and residences inherited from the powerful Hanseatic League as well as impressive Baroque churches. A vital folklore tradition persists.
Strong historical bonds unite the Baltic States – remember the long human chain connecting Tallin to Vilnius on 23 August 1989. All three demonstrate pride in recovering their sovereignty and showing off their rich natural resources and monuments to the West.

IN BRIEF

Entry Formalities – A passport and visa are required. However, a visa for one of the three Baltic countries allows entry into the other two.

RIGA★

LATVIA – Population 860 000

Michelin map 970 P2

This port is actually located 20km/13mi inland from the Baltic Sea on the River Daugava. Bishop Albert von Buxhoevden, originally from Bremen, founded the city in 1201. The following year, the bishop established the Order of Sword-Bearers who made Riga their fief. These German missionaries undertook the conquest of the Baltic territories to convert the northern pagans.
Thanks to the arrival of German colonists and merchants, Riga rapidly became the most important city in the German Baltic. In 1282, it joined the Hanseatic League. By the beginning of the 16C, the city was astonishingly prosperous. The Poles, Russians and Swedes, successively conquered the city. Under Peter the Great, the Russians returned and transformed Riga into the Empire's most important port.
Riga took on a new face at the beginning of the 20C. Foreign architects, followed by local artists, spurred a dazzling architectural renewal, constructing apartment houses and office buildings and transforming the Latvian city into a capital of Art Nouveau style *(see Alberta Street)*.

★VECRIGA (OLD TOWN)

The old town is surrounded by old ramparts and bordered to the west by the River Daugava. Kalku Street cuts the district into two, and continuing to the south, the October Bridge offers a fine **view**. Numerous cafés and restaurants make this the most animated part of the city. Most of the streets and alleys are reserved for pedestrians, who can discover a variety of architectural styles in the colourful façades. The **Swedish Gate** remains from the time of the Swedish domination.

★**Rigas Doms (Cathedral)** – This religious brick edifice presents a mixture of architectural styles. The oldest part dates to Roman times. The organ is considered as a masterpiece. Jakob Raab adorned the **organ case** with angels and garlands at the

General view of Riga

end of 16C. Latvian artist Tobias Heines sculpted the pulpit out of wood in 1641. Near the cathedral stands the **Riga History and Navigation Museum**. It presents the history of the city until the 18C and of navigation from the 10C.

Castle – The castle has undergone many transformations over the centuries. Originally, it was built in the 14C as a residence for the Livonian Order's Grand Master. At the end of the 14C and the beginning of the 15C, two round towers, the tower of the Holy Spirit and the Lead Tower, were added. During the first period of independence, it became the official presidential residence. Today the castle houses three museums: the **Museum of Latvian History** (history and folklore), the **Raīnis Museum of Literature and the Arts** (dedicated to the work of the Latvian poet Janis Raïnis and other writers) and the **Museum of Foreign Art** (temporary exhibits).

★**Trīs brāli (Three Brothers)** – This series of houses, located at nos 7, 19 and 21 along Mazä Pils Street, represents one of the city's most charming examples of traditional Hanseatic style. During the 15C, 17C and 18C, the houses belonged to rich cereal merchants.

Pulvertonis (Powder Magazine Tower) – Erected in the 14C, this is the only tower included in the walls surrounding the city. Through its long history, it has served as powder magazine, prison, and torture room, and, today, contains the **War Museum**.

★**Lielā Gilde (Grand Guild)** – All Hanseatic towns possessed guilds, which played an essential part in town administration. The Grand Guild, or Merchant House, was inspired by the English Tudor style. Banquets and receptions were held in the magnificent great hall, today the concert hall for the National Philharmonic Orchestra. Next door, the **Little Guild** was dedicated to craftsmen.

Pētera baznica (St Peter's Church) – This superb example of red brick Baltic Gothic style, with its soaring dome, is one of the city's familiar landmarks. The interior has been transformed into an exhibition hall. From the height of the steeple, there is a magnificent **panorama**★★.

►► Latvījas Brīvdabas muzejs★ (Ethnographic museum): This open-air museum, located on the banks of the Jugla Lake (bus no 1), evokes rural life in the past.

EXCURSION

★★**Rundale Castle** – *70km/42mi south.* Beautiful Baroque palace built by Rastrelli. This talented architect built several works during the 18C, like the Winter Palace in St Petersburg. Inside, the sumptuous Gold Room contains paintings of Baron Ernst Johan von Bühren (1690-1772), who built the palace. A walk in the park completes the visit.

For an excursion from Riga take one of the Baltic ferries to visit Stockholm, Helsinki, St Petersburg or Tallinn.

TALLINN★

ESTONIA – Population 495 000

Michelin map 970 P 2

Surmounted by the Toompea hill, Tallinn looks out onto the Gulf of Finland. The Estonian capital is located directly across from Helsinki. Boats regularly link the two cities.

After serving as a Danish fortress in the 13C, the city came under the control of the Teutonic Order in the 14C. Like many other Baltic cities, Tallinn continued to be coveted and occupied by many different nations.

A gracious city, Tallinn includes the old town (Vanalinn), divided into upper and lower sections, and a modern section dating primarily from the 19C and 20C. The city's ancient heart with its medieval walls, its churches, its tiny streets edged with small shops, is pleasant to explore on foot.

★VANALINN (OLD TOWN)

Toompea (Upper City)

Castle – Working from the Danish fortress built in 1219, knights of the Order of Sword-bearers reinforced the structure with four corner towers. Today only three remain. The national flag flies over the highest tower, **Pikk Hermann**. The castle today houses the Baroque Parliament building, which Empress Catherine II of Russia built for the governor of the province of Estonia.

St Alexander Nevsky Cathedral – Across from the Parliament building on Castle Square (Lossi plats) rises the imposing Orthodox cathedral built at the end of the 19C in the neo-Byzantine style.

Toomkirik (Church of the Dome) – Founded in the 13C, a fire destroyed the church in 1684. It was rebuilt in the Gothic style. In the 18C, a Baroque bell-tower was added. Numerous funerary monuments may be seen throughout the interior. Sculptures representing historical scenes often decorate these monuments. A particularly impressive one depicts the 16C siege of Narva in which the Swedish general, Pontus de la Gardie, shown in a life-size statue, met his end.

The visitor may then follow Kohtu Street which leads to an **observation platform** offering a superb view of the old town.

Lower City

★**Niguliste kirik (St Nicholas' Church)** – Dedicated to the patron saint of merchants and navigators, this church was built in the 13C by the city's merchants. It is famous for its works of art: an altarpiece in carved wood, and especially a fragment of the Dance Macabre, the work of Bernt Notke, a native of Lübeck.

Raekoja plats (Town Hall Square) – The town hall was constructed on the former market square. It commemorates Tallin's greatest days, when the city wielded unprecedented commercial power. A weathercock juts out at the summit of the tower in the form of a soldier from the Middle Ages, known locally as Old Thomas.

Pikk Street, with its old houses, formerly the property of guilds, confraternities, rich merchants and noblemen, begins at the Raekoja plats. This paved street, a much frequented promenade, was the main market thoroughfare during the Middle Ages. It connects the port to the town centre.

Grand Guild – Rich merchants congregated in this building with its huge doors in oak. The Estonian History Museum is now housed inside.

Oleviste kirik (St Olaf's Church) – Dedicated to Olaf II, King of Norway, this impressive religious edifice dominates the town with its 124m/406ft tower. Erected in the 16C, at the same time as the chapel adjoining the church, sailors used the steeple as a landmark until its destruction by lightning.

While walking up the street, the visitor may take a shortcut through Tolli Street to see a group of medieval houses known as the **Three Sisters**.

Pikk Street leads to the ramparts and the **Great Coast portal** to the port. Close by, a 16C tower, known locally as "Fat Margaret", houses the **Estonian Marine Museum**.

If they desire, visitors may return to Town hall Square by following Lai Street, which runs parallel to Pikk Street.

Read the chapter on art and architecture in the Introduction to best appreciate historic monuments described in this guide.

VILNIUS★

LITHUANIA – Population 590 000

Michelin map 970 P3

The Lithuanian capital is situated 300km/186mi from the sea, only some 30km/19mi from the Belorussian frontier. It is surrounded by hills.
According to legend, the Lithuanian Grand Duke Gediminas founded it around 1320 following a dream. He wished to create a powerful and impregnable city.
In the 16C, Lithuania and Poland formed a single State, and Vilnius became an important city. Magnificent buildings in the Gothic and Renaissance style were constructed, and Polish Jesuits founded the university in 1579. During the following century, with the support of the Jesuits, Baroque churches and monuments adorned the city.
At the beginning of the 19C, with a population of about 80 000 Jews, Vilnius became known as the "Lithuanian Jerusalem". During the 20C, Vilnius changed ownership several times.
In 1990, Lithuania declared independence, with Vytautas Landsbergis as the Republic's President. In 1991, Red Army troops attempted a bloody coup. Vilnius, an unfamiliar name for many, occupied the headlines of the world media. In 1993, Russia finally recognized the country's independence, and voters designated Algirdas Brazaukas as head of State.
A certain mildness prevails in Vilnius. Many monuments, witnesses to an eventful history, make the town a true architectural showcase.

Sights – On **Mount Gediminas**, the city's historic centre, a tower that was part of the fortress during the 14C, offers a superb **panorama**★★. A small museum on the castle is located inside. The section of the castle at the bottom of the hill served as a residence for the Grand Duke.

★OLD TOWN

South of Cathedral Square (Katedros aiksté), tiny streets with a large number of churches are perfect for wandering. Pilies gatvé (Castle Street), reserved for pedestrians, serves as the main thoroughfare.

Cathedral – Constructed on an ancient pagan site, the cathedral is dedicated to the God of Thunder and commemorates the Christianisation of the country. Originally in wood, the cathedral was reconstructed in the Gothic style, and remodeled in the 18C. The façade is characterised by a portico crowned by a triangular fronton.
Inside, the **chapel of St Casimir** merits its own visit. Dedicated to the patron saint of the country, Casimir IV, son of Ladislas Jagellon, Grand Duke of Lithuania and King of Poland, this feast of marble, granite, stucco and frescos depicts the life of the saint. Separate from the edifice, the octagonal, two-storey bell-tower possesses a carillon of 17 bells.

★**University** – Jesuits founded the university and remained in charge for two centuries. The visitor will find an impressive series of courtyards, which may be reached through the many passageways. In the court of honour, or Skarga Courtyard (named after the first rector), stands the **St John's Church** (Sv.-Jono). It presents a superb Baroque façade. In a neighbouring courtyard, a double dome, decorated with the signs of the zodiac, covers an **astronomical observatory** built in the Classical style.
The old **episcopal palace**, a sumptuous classical edifice, stands close to the University on Daukanto Square (Bishop's Square). Bishops, and later Russian dignitaries, used it as a residence. Napoleon is said to have lived there during the Russian campaign.

Mickiewicz Museum – Adam Mickiewicz, the best-known Polish Romantic poet, originally came from Lithuania. He lived in this flat in 1822. In his historical epic *Pan Tadeusz*, he forcefully proclaims his admiration for his country.
Near the museum, the **Sv-Mykolo** (St Michael Church), dating from the 16C and 17C, houses the Architecture Museum. The **Sv-Onos** (St-Anne) **Church**, entirely in brick, is considered the most beautiful example of Lithuanian Gothic art.

Artilerijos bastéja (Artillery Bastion) – This 17C defensive structure now houses a collection of weapons and armour.

Sv.-Kazimiero Church (St Casimir) – Vilnius' oldest Baroque church was inspired by Gesu Church in Rome. It signals the transition between Renaissance art and Baroque art, a period known for a long time as the "Jesuit style".

Nacionalinis Lietuvos valstybes Kulturos ir Istorijos muziejus (National Museum of Culture and History) – Rich archeological, historical and ethnographic collections explain the development of Lithuanian people and identity. Period interiors are reconstituted.

Belgium

Belgique, België

Area: 30 513km²/11 784sq mi – **Population:** 10 170 226 – **Capital:** Brussels – **Currency:** Belgian franc and Euro (40.3399 BEF). Bank notes issued in Luxembourg are also legal tender in Belgium, but are usually only accepted in shops in the Luxembourg Province – **Time:** GMT + 1hr in winter, GMT + 2hr in summer

Belgium stretches over a modest distance of 329km/204mi from the North Sea coast to the Ardennes forests. It enjoys varied scenery. The Ardennes consists of rolling hills rising to an altitude of 500m/1 625ft. Fertile plains ideal for crops and animal farming mark the middle of the country. Lakes, marshes and poulders dot the vast Campine Plain, which on the coast turns into rings of dunes and fine sandy beaches that draw crowds of summer holidaymakers. The Belgians have developed several major artistic trends and the country's cities are famous for their art, architecture and museums.
When it comes to cuisine, Belgium is much more than the stereotyped land of mussels and chips. Belgians enjoy and appreciate a well-garnished table. Whether in Flemish-speaking Flanders or French Wallonia, tourists are treated to a remarkable culinary tradition.

IN BRIEF

Formalities – Americans and Canadians require a valid passport. Nationals from other countries within the European Union need no identification papers. However, some means of identification always remains useful (Passport or identity card).

Shops – They are usually open from 8am to 7pm, but closed on Sundays.

Post Office – The post office (PTT) and telephone service (RTT) are not always in the same building.

Tourist Routes – Belgium maintains more than 60 tourist routes indicated with hexagonal signposts. They mark out picturesque roads linking a region's main places of interest. Brochures are available in bookshops or tourist offices.

Souvenirs – Pottery, glassware and lace make Belgian crafts famous. Belgian chocolates such as Léonidas and Jeff de Bruges need no introduction.

Beer – This is the national drink. Ale or stout, sweet or bitter, light or strong – Belgium produces beers to suit all tastes. Different fermentation processes produce three distinct types of beer. Low fermentation results in blond *pilsen* drinks. High-fermentation products are brewed in the great Cistercian abbeys such as Orval and Chimay. And finally, spontaneous fermentation without yeast produce *lambics* and *gueuzes*. *Gueuzes* are bottled in order to induce a second fermentation. Cherries macerated in *lambic* yield *krieks*, red in colour with a fruity flavour.

Folklore and Traditions – Folklore is important in Belgium, and very much alive. Almost every city houses a museum stuffed with reminders of centuries-old traditions. Carnivals, giants, bonfires, religious processions, historical pageants, military parades, games and theatrical events reflect the national character of a people who are happy, sociable, and loyal to the past.

Townscapes – The structure of Belgian towns, and especially Flemish ones, is a reflection of the autonomy they have enjoyed since the 13C. This is reflected by the imposing civic buildings the belfry, the town hall and the covered market. Towns are imbued with remarkable charm by the canals, the cheerful music of the chimes, the peacefulness of the beguine convents, the welcoming atmosphere of the cafés and *estaminets*.

Recchia/EUREKA SLIDE

Gilles

ANTWERPEN★★★

ANVERS – ANTWERP – Population 453 030

Michelin map 970 I 4

Antwerp, the second largest city in Belgium and one of the world's largest ports, lies on the banks of the River Schelde, 88km/55mi downriver from the North Sea.
The old town still evokes the delightful atmosphere of the long gone Flemish communities. Houses topped by gables and volutes or tall fronts with large numbers of windows crowd narrow streets and vast squares.

The Diamond Town – In 1476, Lodewijk Van Berchem from Bruges perfected the art of diamond-cutting. It soon became a veritable industry in Antwerp. In the 16C, several Jewish families arrived from Portugal and provided a new impetus. The craftsmen of Antwerp soon became famous for their excellence. These days, diamond-cutting remains the domain of local craftsmen. Indians, Zairians, and Lebanese share the trade with the original Jewish diamond merchants together with Jews who arrived in the second half of the 19C from Eastern Europe.
The **Provinciaal Diamantmuseum** (Provincial Diamond Museum) is located in the diamond district near the train station. It houses exhibits showing all the different aspects of the diamond trade.

Peter Paul Rubens – The painter was born in exile near Cologne on 28 June 1577. His father, a suspected heretic, had sought refuge in Germany. Rubens entered Antwerp for the first time at the age of 12 after the death of his father. He found a town that had been laid to waste. After spending some time in Italy, he returned to Antwerp in 1608. From that time, he enjoyed huge success. Rubens was a larger-than-life figure with a vast creative mind and he embodied the city's spirit of genius. His paintings combine Italian and traditional Flemish features. He died in Antwerp in 1640 and was buried in St-Jacobskerk, St Jacob's Church.

★★★AROUND GRAND-PLACE AND THE CATHEDRAL

A labyrinth of squares and narrow streets dominate this neighbourhood. Many of the niches contain statues of the Virgin Mary.

★**Grote Markt (Grand-Place)** – The **guildhalls** flanking the square represent fine examples of Flemish architecture from the 16C and 17C.
To the right of the town hall stand five superb late 16C houses, most of them in the Renaissance style. The Ange Blanc is appropriately capped by an angel. The Cooper's House contains a statue of St Matthew. An equestrian statue of St George tops the tall House of the Old Crossbow. The House of the Young Crossbowmen dates all the way from 1500 whereas the House of the Haberdashers is decorated with an eagle.

Stadhuis (Town Hall) – The 76m/247ft long façade combines features of Flemish architecture such as dormer windows and gables with the Italian Renaissance (loggia, pilasters between the windows and niches).
Behind the town hall, wonderful old houses line the narrow picturesque **Gildekamersstraat**.

Brabofontein – The fountain serves as a reminder of the story of Silvius Brabo, shown holding aloft the hand of Druon the Giant. According to a 16C legend, the Roman warrior Silvius Brabo cut off the hand of the giant Druon Antigon who was famous for pillaging boats sailing up the Schelde. He threw the hand into the river. This explains the presence of two hands (*handwerpen*: throw the hand) beside a castle *(Steen)* on Antwerp's coat of arms.

★**Vlaaikensgang** – This picturesque little street lies beyond the porch at no 16 **Oude Koormarkt**.

Handschoenmarkt – This triangular square was once the town's glove market and is lined with old houses. The well has a graceful wrought-iron crown said to have been designed by Quentin Massys, an ironsmith whose love of painting led him to become an artist.

★★★**Kathedraal (Cathedral)** – This is Belgium's largest public building. It covers an area of almost 1ha/2.5 acres. Building work began around 1352 and was not completed until 1521.

★★★**The Tower** – The ornate tower rises to a height of 123m/400ft. The magnificent bell-tower contains a peal of 47 bells.

★**Interior** – The cathedral is exceptionally large – 117m/380ft long and 65m/211ft wide at the transept with seven aisles and 125 pillars, all devoid of capitals. The nave's rich **pulpit** was carved by Michel van der Voort in 1713. Outstanding **works of art** offset some of the interior's cold majesty. Works by **Rubens** include the **Assumption** (high altar), the **Erection of the Cross** (north transept), the **Deposition** (south transept), and the **Resurrection** (*right*, in the second chapel in the ambulatory). The **Last Judgement** painted by De Backer (fourth chapel in the ambulatory) depicts the Plantin family on its side panels *(see Museum Plantin-Moretus)*.

★**Vleeshuis (Butchers' Hall)** – This impressive Gothic building with tall roof and dormer windows was built for the butchers guild from 1501 to 1504. One of the cathedral's architects designed it. Today, the hall houses a museum of local decorative arts, archeology and numismatics. There is an extensive collection of **musical instruments**★. Antwerp was famous for its harpsichords in the 17C.

MAIN MUSEUMS

City Centre

★★★**Museum Plantin-Moretus** – The museum is devoted to the Prince of Printers. It occupies 34 of the rooms in the house and printing shop that once belonged to Christophe Plantin, a man who came to Antwerp from his native Loire Valley in 1549 and became a printer in 1555. His finest piece of work was his **Biblia Regia** which was printed in 5 languages (Hebrew, Syriac, Greek, Latin and Aramaic).

★★**Museum Mayer van den Berg** – This neo-Gothic house contains a remarkable art collection put together by Fritz Mayer van den Bergh (1858-1901). It includes medieval sculptures, statue-columns from the cloisters of Notre-Dame-en-Vaux in Châlons-en-Champagne, Byzantine and Gothic ivories, and paintings by Bruegel the Elder such as **Mad Margot**, an apocalyptic vision of war.

★★**Rubenshuis (Rubens' House)** – Rubens purchased this luxurious townhouse in 1610, one year after his marriage to Isabella Brandt. The Flemish-style rooms are decorated with old tiles, gilded leather, 17C furniture, and paintings. The artist drew his inspiration from this lavish residence during a period of peace in the city's history.

Mad Margot (detail), by Bruegel the Elder

Outside the City Centre

★★★**Koninklijk Museum voor Schone Kunsten (Royal Museum of Fine Arts)** – This 19C building with its impressive Corinthian frontage exhibits an outstanding collection of paintings, especially by German Primitives and Rubens.
The Primitives include **Van Eyck's** *La Vierge à la fontaine*, **Van der Weyden's** *Triptyque des sept sacrements*, and **Memling's** *Portrait d'homme*.
Rubens' pupils and assistants are also present, including the **Brueghels, Van Dyck** and **Jordaens** with his *Le Concert de famille*.
Modern art is well represented with works from the Belgian School – **Henri de Braekeleer**'s *l'Homme à la chaise*, **James Ensor**, and the **Laethem-Saint-Martin Group**. Expressionists include **Permeke** *(Femme de pêcheur)*, the **de Smet** brothers, **van den Berghe, Servaes** and **van de Woestijne**. Surrealist works are by **Magritte** *(Seize septembre)* and **Delvaux**.

BOAT TRIPS

Scheldetocht (on the Schelde River) – A trip down the Schelde to Kallo offers a glimpse of the industrial development of Antwerp harbour.

Havenrondvaart (Harbour basins) – The busy harbour buzzes with activity during the week.

BINCHE★

Population 32 381

Binche lies in the heart of the Hainaut Province. The delightful quiet town is ringed by its original walls, consisting of 27 towers, dating from the 12C to the 14C. The town is famous for its **carnival** and its clowns, called *Gilles*.

★★★**The Carnival** – This tradition dates from the 14C. Special events are organised starting from January. On **Quinquagesima Sunday**, hundreds of people in disguise gather at 10am to the sound of the viola, hurdy-gurdy, accordion and drum. On **Mardi Gras**, the legendary *Gilles* dance on the main square at 10am. In the afternoon, they parade through the town wearing their magnificent hats with ostrich feathers. They take oranges out of a basket to throw to friends and acquaintances. In the evening, the Grand-Place is crowded for the **round dance**. The day ends with a superb fireworks display.

★**The Old Town** – The Gothic **town hall**, topped by an onion belfry, is located on the **Grand-Place**. The tower was named after St George. Nearby stands the most striking stretch of **town walls**. The **Collégiale St-Ursmer**, a collegiate church, the **town park** and the **Musée international du Carnaval et du Masque**★ represent the other main sites. This carnival museum is housed in the former Augustinian high school. Its displays focus on festivals both in Binche and other countries. It also displays an extensive collection of **masks**★★ from all over the world.

BRUGGE★★★

BRUGES – Population 115 000

Michelin map 970 I 4

Bruges seems to have stepped out of the Middle Ages. Passing centuries have smoothed its old houses and aristocratic mansions built of bricks. Its church bells peal almost on cue. All the buildings huddle together beside the dark waters of the canals, with swans swimming and gliding.

Every year on Ascension Day, the **Procession of the Precious Blood**★★★ carries through the streets the reliquary containing the Precious Blood. The clergy, dressed in costumes of the many religious brotherhoods, proceed the procession.

Bruges was **the birthplace of Flemish painting**. In the 15C, artists such as Jan van Eyck, Petrus Christus, van der Goes, Memling and Gerard David brought fame to the city.

★★★HISTORIC TOWN CENTRE

From early May to late September, visitors can enjoy a night-time tour of the floodlit canals and old town walls.

★★**Markt (Grand-Place)** – The market place lies in the heart of the town. Gabled houses, once the seats of craft guilds, line the square. In the centre stands a statue of Pieter de Coninck and Jan Breydel, heroes of a rebellion that occurred in 1302.

★★★**Belfort-Hallen (Belfry and Covered Market)** – The belfry and market form a magnificent set of brick buildings worn by the passing years.

The **belfry** represents the largest such construction in Belgium. The massive tower dates from the 13C, the corner towers from the 14C and the octagonal top from the late 15C. A climb to the second floor *(366 steps)* takes visitors to the **treasure room** and where they can see the **peal** of 47 bells that ring out every 15min. From the very top, a superb **view**★★ unfolds of the town and the surrounding area.

The **covered market** was built during the same period as the belfry. It consists of four buildings round an attractive courtyard. A flower market is located beneath the arches of the south wing.

★★**Burg** – The square was named after the castle *(Burg)* built by Baldwin I Iron-Arm.

★**Basiliek van het Heilig Bloed (Basilica Church of the Precious Blood)** – The church contains the relic of the Blood of Christ brought back from the Second Crusade to the Holy Land by the Count of Flanders, Thierry of Alsace. The **lower chapel**★, also known as Chapelle St-Basile from the 12C, retains its original appearance with massive cylindrical pillars. The small **museum** beside the **Chapel of the Precious Blood** contains 19C frescoes and the reliquary of the Precious Blood from 1671.

Stadhuis (Town hall) – It was built in the late 14C in the Flamboyant Gothic style and restored in the 19C. The most outstanding feature, the **Gothic Chamber** on the upper floor, has ogival vaulting and wainscoting.

Oude Griffie (Former Clerk of the Court's Office) – Now the Lower Court, it is notable for its Renaissance frontage.

Paleis van het Brugse Vrije (Palace of the Freemen of Bruges) – In the 14C, the Freemen of Bruges formed a council responsible for managing the area around the town. The palace houses the **Provincial Museum of the Freeman of Bruges** and contains the Renaissance **Freeman of Bruges fireplace**★ made of black marble and oak.

Rozewhoedkaai and the Belfry

Groene Rei (Green Quay) – Overlooking this leafy quayside is the Maison du Pélican, a low building with tall dormer windows decorated, appropriately enough, with the emblem of the pelican. At the end of the quay, a fine view appears of the canal, and the belfry and spire of the church dedicated to Our Lady.

Huidenvettersplaats (Tanners' Square) – A small column bearing two lions graces this delightful square.

Rozenhoedkaai (Rosary Quay) – Typical stunning **views**★★ of the city unfold from the canal quay. Near the basin stands the charming Tanners' House (Huidenvettershuis).

Dijver – From the end of the quay lined with lime trees, a delightful **view**★ is available of the tower and spire of Church of Our Lady.

★★★**Stedelijk Museum voor Schone Kunsten** – The first five rooms in this art gallery focus on Flemish Primitives from the Bruges School. Masterpieces include **van Eyck's** vividly-coloured *Vierge du chanoine van der Paele*, **van der Goes'** intensely dramatic *Mort de la Vierge*, **Memling's** *Moreel triptych* which is full of a feeling of meditation and inner peace, and **Gerard David's** splendidly coloured triptych depicting the *Baptism of Christ*.

★★★**Memlingmuseum** – This museum is housed in the former 12C Hôpital St-Jean. Memling is to Bruges what Rubens is to Antwerp. He produced a large number of works for the hospital, municipal magistrates or wealthy foreigners and the town has retained the most outstanding examples. The works of the Old Master are displayed in the church. They include the **Châsse de sainte Ursule**, the **Mariage mystique de sainte Catherine**, the **Adoration des Mages**, and the **triptyque de la Déploration**.

★★**Begijnhof** – The *Beguine Convent of the Vine* is a peaceful enclosure with flower beds and trees. It was founded in 1245 by Margaret of Constantinople, Countess of Flanders. The **Beguine House** (Begijnhuisje) is open to the public.
Further on, swans glide across the tranquil waters of the **Minnewater**, the famous "lake of love".

★★★**Boottocht (Boat trip on the canals)** – *Landing-stages (aanlegplaatsen): Rozenhoedkaai, Dijver*. For visitors with some free time, a boat trip represents one of the best ways of seeing the charming old town. Generally speaking, the boats sail to the Béguinage in the south and the **Spiegelrei**, with its statue of Van Eyck and Loge des Bourgeois at the Quai du Miroir to the north.

★EXCURSIONS

★★**Oostende (Ostend)** – *25km/16mi west by the N 9*. Ostend is a North Sea fishing harbour and the main ferry terminal for crossings to England. It also is a famed **seaside resort**. The resort area stretches from the Casino (Kursaal) to the Thermal Palace Hotel along the Albert Ier Promenade lining the beach surfing.

An unbroken line of restaurants stretch along the **Fishermen's Quay** (Visserskaai). From the quay, a view unfolds of the fishing harbour and the channel. Picturesque auctions are held at the **fish market**.
Further north lies the seaside resort of **Knokke-Heist**★★ which includes Heist, Duinbergen, Albert-Strand, Knokke and Le Zoute. The area is famed for its elegance and its amenities.

BRUXELLES/BRUSSEL★★★

BRUSSELS – Population 950 597

Michelin map 970 I5

Brussels is Belgium's capital, the official residence of the country's royal family, and the seat of European Union agencies and NATO. The bustling city exudes contrast. Languages and architectural styles mix, along with vast green parks and grey urban districts full of tall modern tower blocks. Commercial Brussels boasts a great variety of shops. **Rue Neuve** represents the main pedestrian precinct, and **Galeries St-Hubert★** houses luxury stores and elegant tea rooms beneath a neo-Classical glass roof. Brussels, placed under the patronage of Gambrinus the King of Beer, loves creature comforts and good food.
North of the city, the famous **Atomium★** serves as a reminder of the 1958 World Fair. It rises to a height of 102m/332ft above the Heysel Plateau. Nearby, **Mini-Europe** exhibits models of historic buildings from all the countries in the European Union.

Traditions – The people of Brussels have kept their traditional folk festivals. The aristocratic **Ommegang** procession is held every year in July. It re-enacts the ceremony which took place in 1549 in the presence of Emperor Charles V. Other festivals celebrate the May Tree *(Meyboom)* or Tree of Joy in August. Locals love their **open-air markets** – the bird market on Grand-Place, the antiques and book market on Place du Grand-Sablon, and the flea market on Place du Jeu-de-Balle.

J. Évrard

Carpet of flowers on Grand-Place

★★★GRAND-PLACE (JY)

This gigantic square is one of a kind. It comes alive in the morning when the flower market is in progress, on summer evenings when the floodlights pick out the flamboyant decorations on the buildings, and on Sunday mornings when the bird market is in full swing. In the month of August in even years, the Grand-Place's cobblestones disappear beneath a vast **Carpet of Flowers**.

Maisons des corporations – The fine Baroque façades of the guildhalls encircle the square. Most have tiers of three architectural orders – Ionic, Doric and Corinthian. At the top of the buildings, gables with swirls are decorated with carvings, gilded motifs and firepots.

Hôtel de ville (**H**) – The town hall was built in the purest of Gothic styles. It is dominated by an elegant tower on top of which stands a gilded copper statue of St Michael. Inside, a number of superb Brussels tapestries grace the walls.

Maison du Roi – Despite its name, no sovereign ever resided in the King's House. It is the former bread market. It now houses the **Musée de la Ville de Bruxelles**, a museum containing works of art and various collections recalling the city's history and its indigenous crafts industries.

★★LES SABLONS AND LE MONT DES ARTS

★★**Manneken Pis** (JZ) – For many, this statue, also known as Little Julian, symbolises Brussels. The tubby little boy demonstrates the city's self avowed mockery and rejection of all things prudish. In order to pay homage, Brussels' oldest citizen wears all different sorts of clothes. His wardrobe occupies an entire room in the Musée de la Ville de Bruxelles.

BRUXELLES BRUSSEL

Adolphe Max (Bd) .... JY 3
Albertine (Pl. de l') .... JZ 4
Anspach (Bd) .... JY
Assaut (R. d') .... JY 10
Baudet (R.) .... KZ 15
Beurre (Rue du) .... JY 19
Bortier (Galerie) .... JKZ 23
Bouchers
(Petite rue des) .... JY 24
Bouchers (R. des) .... JY 25
Bourse (Pl. de la) .... JY 27
Briques (Quai aux) .... JY 29
Chêne (R. du) .... JZ 39
Colonies (R. des) .... KY 43
Comédiens (R. des) .... KY 45
Commerce (R. du) .... KZ 46
Croix-de-Fer (R. de la) .... KY 52
Duquesnoy (Rue) .... JYZ 66
Ernest Allard (R.) .... JZ 87
Europe (Carr. de l') .... KY 90
Étuve (R. de l') .... JZ 88
Fossé-aux-Loups (R. du). JKY 99
Fripiers (R. des) .... JY 105
Grand sablon (Pl. du) .... KZ 112
Impératrice (Bd de l') ...... JKY 124
Ixelles (Chee d') .... KZ 129
Laeken (R. de) .... JY 151
Lebeau (R.) .... JZ 152
Louvain (R. de) .... KY 163
Marché-aux-Herbes (R. du) JY 168
Marché-aux-Poulets
(R. du) .... JY 169
Midi (R. du) .... JYZ
Mercier (R. du Card.) .... KY 172
Montagne (Rue de la) .... KY 178
Musée (Pl. du) .... KZ 179
Neuve (Rue) .... JY
Nord (Passage du) .... JY 182
Petit-Sablon (Pl. du) .... KZ 195
Presse (R. de la) .... KY 201
Princes (Galerie des) .... JY 205
Ravenstein (R.) .... KZ 207
Reine (Galerie de la) .... JY 210
Roi (Galerie du) .... KY 214
Rollebeek (R. de) .... JZ 217
Ruysbroeck (R. de) .... KZ 219
Ste-Catherine (Pl.) .... JY 221
Sainte-Gudule (Pl.) .... KY 222
Toison d'or (Av. de la) ...... KZ 238
Trône (R. du) .... KZ 241
Ursulines (R. des) .... JZ 243
Waterloo (Bd de) .... KZ 255
6 Jeunes Hommes (R. des) KZ 268

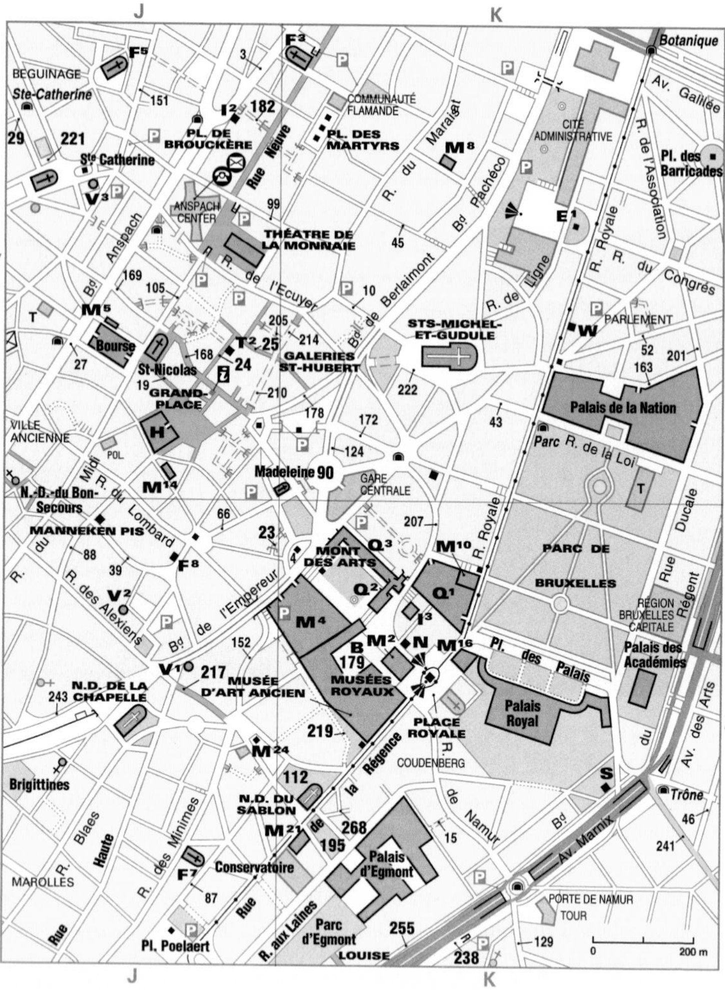

B	Appartements de Ch. de Lorraine
E¹	Colonne du Congrès
F²	Église N.-D.-du-Finistère
F⁵	Église St-Jean-Baptiste-au-Béguinage
F⁷	Église Sts-Jean-et-Étienne-aux-Minimes
F⁸	Fondation Brel
H	Hôtel de Ville
I²	Hôtel Métropole
I³	Hôtel Ravenstein
M²	Musée d'Art moderne
M⁴	Bibliothèque Royale de Belgique
M⁵	Musée Bruxelles 1238
M⁸	Musée Centre belge de la Bande dessinée
M¹⁰	Musée du Cinéma
M¹⁴	Musée du Costume et de la Dentelle
M¹⁶	Musée de la Dynastie (Hôtel Bellevue)
M²¹	Musée des Instruments de Musique
M²⁴	Musée des Postes et des Télécommunications
N	Old England
Q¹	Palais des Beaux-Arts
Q²	Palais des Congrès
Q³	Palais de la Dynastie
S	Statue équestre de Léopold II
T²	Théâtre de marionnettes de Toone
V¹	Tour d'Anneessens
V²	Tour de Villers
V³	Tour Noire
V⁴	Tour de l'ancienne église ste-Catherine
W	Vitrine de P. Hankar

Every two years for just a few days during the month of August, a carpet of flowers covers the cobblestones of the Grand-Place.

★**Place du Grand-Sablon** (KZ **112**) – This most elegant of all Brussels squares is lined with antique shops and chic restaurants.

★**Église Notre-Dame du Sablon** (KZ) – This fine Flamboyant Gothic building boasts an unusually tall chancel. Nearby stands the **burial chapel of the Thurn and Taxis**, a family of Austrian origin who founded the international postal service in 1516. The chapel is built of white and black marble.

★**Square du Petit-Sablon** – The columns around this square are topped by 48 charming bronze statuettes. They represent Brussels' craftsmen. In the middle stand statues of great 16C humanists including the counts of Egmont and Hornes. The **Palais d'Egmont**, located just to the southeast, is used for international functions.

★★**Musées royaux des Beaux-Arts de Belgique** (KZ) – This complex contains two museums – the Museum of Ancient Art and the Museum of Modern Art.

★★**Musée d'Art ancien** (KZ) – The museum is famous for its admirable Flemish Primitives and its works by Bruegel the Elder and Rubens.

15C – 16C: van der Weyden, Dirck Bouts, Hans Memling, Hieronymus Bosch, Gerard David, Quentin Massys, Bruegel the Elder.

17C – 18C: Rubens, Jordaens. **19C**: Fernand Khnopff, the Symbolist painter, and James Ensor, a crucial figure linking 19C and 20C art.

★★**Musée d'Art moderne** (KZ **M**[2]) – The permanent collections are displayed on eight floors below ground level. The descent to the various floors gives an insight into changes in artistic trends since Fauvism. Special pride is reserved for Belgian painters such as Rik Wouters, Léon Spilliaert, Delvaux, and Magritte.

★**Place Royale** (KZ) – The centre of this elegantly proportioned Louis XVI-style square offers a superb view of the Law Courts and the gardens in the Mont des Arts district.

★**Place des Palais** (KZ) – The square is dominated by the **Royal Palace**, with its semi-circular colonnade. If the flag is flying, it means that the sovereign is in residence. The palace was built during the reign of Leopold II. The **Throne Room**★ is a lavish chamber with large chandeliers. Two other palaces line the square. On the east side, the **Palais des Académies**★ once served as the residence of the Prince of Orange. On the west, the **Palais des Beaux-Arts** is used for major cultural events and houses the Musée du Cinéma.

LE CINQUANTENAIRE

Parc du Cinquantenaire – The park was created in 1880 for the exhibition marking the 50th anniversary of Belgian independence. It surrounds a huge palace consisting of two wings connected by a monumental archway.

★★★**Musée du Cinquantenaire** – In the south wing of the palace, extensive collections display objects from antiquity. Western Asia including Palestine, Cyprus, and Mesopotamia as well as Greece, Rome and Egypt are represented.
Examples of Belgian decorative arts include pre-Romanesque sculptures, gold and silverware, 12C ivories, and pewter. Tapestries from the 14C to the early 16C compete by the quality of their manufacture and the splendour of colours. Among the wooden altarpieces, the St-George Altarpiece by Jan Borman (1493) is striking for the lifelike intensity of its figures.

★★**Autoworld** – In the palace's south hall, most of the vehicles on show are part of the prestigious **Ghislain Mahy collection**. Born in Ghent in 1901, Mahy was passionate about cars. He collected more than 800 vehicles over a period of 40 years. Belgium is well represented with names like Belga Rise, FN, Fondu, and Hermes and, more particularly, through the famous **Minerva** brand that acquired a well-established reputation in the 1930s for the luxury and comfort of its automobiles. The oldest vehicle on display dates from 1910; it belonged to the Belgian Court during the reign of King Albert I.

►► Musée Horta★ *(south in the Saint-Gilles district)*: This outstanding reminder of Art Nouveau belonged to Victor Horta (1861-1947), one of the main creators of this distinctive architectural style.

EXCURSION

★**Waterloo** – *19km/12mi south via N 5.* The famous battle marking a turning point in the history of Europe took place here. On 18 June 1815, Dutch and British troops under the command of Wellington and Prussians led by Blücher, put an end to the Napoleonic epic.
Every five years, the Battle of Waterloo is re-enacted with more than 2000 soldiers dressed in period costumes.
The **battlefield** is dotted with historic buildings and memorials. The various phases of the battle are shown in a film and a model.

DINANT★★

Population 12 590
Michelin map 970 I 5

The town enjoys an outstanding **setting★** in the Meuse Valley. It forms a sea of blue-tinted roofs between the river and the rock. In French, Dinant has given its name to the Copperware trade *(dinanderie)*. The art of melting and beating copper or brass has been practised here since the 12C.
The strategic position in the Meuse Valley has caused much suffering and, over the centuries, numerous occupation forces have marched through its streets.

★**Citadel** – *Access by cable-car, by foot (408 steps), or by car via N 936 (Sorinnes road).* The citadel as visitors see it today dates from the days of the Dutch occupation (1818-1821). A **museum** gives an insight into the town's history. The top of its walls offers a delightful **view★★** of the town.

★**Grotte de "la Merveilleuse"** – *Left Bank of the Meuse, Philippeville road.* This cave is remarkable for the profusion and whiteness of its rock formations.

★**Rocher Bayard** – *1km/0.5mi south of the town (via N 95).* According to legend, Bayard the horse split this rock with a blow from his hoof when fleeing from Charlemagne *(see Namur, Excursions)*.

Boat trip – *Landing-stage opposite the town hall.*

GENT★★★

GAND/GHENT – Population 225 469
Michelin map 970 I 4

Ghent, built on numerous islands at the confluence of the Lys and Schelde rivers, represents Belgium's second largest port. The city is criss crossed by canals and waterways (**boat trips** available). The spiritual centre of Flanders was also the birthplace of Emperor **Charles V** (1500-1558).

★★★OLD TOWN

From the bridge known as **St-Michielsbrug** (St Michael's Bridge), there is an outstanding **view★★★** of the historic buildings and façades of the old town.
When the buildings are floodlit in the evening, it becomes a magnificent place for a stroll.

St-Baafskathedraal (St Bavo Cathedral) – The name of this collegiate church was chosen by Emperor Charles V himself in 1540 when he ordered the demolition of the Abbaye de St Bavon. From the top of the west tower, a panoramic **view** of the town and surrounding area unfolds. The cathedral is decorated with magnificent works of art including the extraordinary ***polyptique de l'Adoration de l'Agneau mystique*★★★**. This colossal work created mainly by **Jan van Eyck** includes no less than 248 figures, all lit by a single light source on the right-hand side. The **crypt★** houses a superb 15C **triptyque du Calvaire★**.

Ph. Gajic /MICHELIN

Graslei

★★★ **Belfort, Lakenhalle (Belfry, Cloth Market)** – The sturdy shape of the belfry beneath its gilded copper dragon symbolises the power of the guilds of Ghent during the Middle Ages. It stands adjacent to the **cloth market** and contains a peal of 52 bells.

★★ **Graslei (Grass Quay)** – A magnificent row of 12C to 17C house fronts line the quay. The scene is best admired from Korenlei (Corn Quay).

★★ **Gravensteen (Castle of the Counts of Flanders)** – The castle once belonged to the Counts of Flanders. It has curtain walls bristling with bartizans, lookout towers and merlons, and is reflected in the waters of the River Lieve. The architecture was inspired by the crusaders' fortresses in Syria. A wonderful **view**★ is available from the top of the keep.

★★ MAIN MUSEUMS

★★ **Museum voor Schone Kunsten (Fine Art Museum)** – The museum and art gallery are located on the edge of the Parc de la Citadelle. The park encircles the **Palais des Floralies** and contains extensive collections of ancient and modern art from the 15C to the 20C. Two works by **Hieronymus Bosch** stand out, *St Jerome*, and one of the artist's last paintings, *Bearing of the Cross*.

★★ **Bijloke Museum** – The old Cistercian abbey housing this museum of archeology and history is a remarkable set of brick buildings dating from the 14C to the 17C. The superb **refectory** soars with its great timber vaulting and frescoes.

►► Klein Begijnhof★: Joan of Constantinople founded this small Beguine convent in 1234.

LEUVEN★★

LOUVAIN – Population 87 789

Michelin map 970 I 5

Louvain lies on the banks of the River Dyle and possesses an internationally famous university. Reminders of its brilliant history include the town hall and superb religious buildings.

The **Louvain Catholic University (Université Catholique de Louvain – UCL)**, otherwise known as the Alma Mater, was founded in 1425 at the behest of Pope Martin V and Duke Jean IV of Brabant. It quickly became one of Europe's most prestigious universities. The names of Erasmus and Jansenius are linked forever with this institution. Since 1968, the university has been divided into the French-speaking UCL, in Louvain-la-Neuve and the Flemish-speaking Katholieke Universiteit Leuven (KUL) in Louvain itself.

The university's most famous guests or students include Dirck Bouts and Quentin Massys; the latter was born in Louvain in 1466.

★★★ **Stadhuis (Town Hall)** – The Flamboyant Gothic building was build in the mid 15C during the days of Duke Philip the Good of Burgundy. It was designed by **Mathieu de Layens**. The edifice resembles an elegantly carved stone reliquary, with gables topped by turrets and pinnacles, dormer windows and almost 300 niches filled with statues from the 19C.

The public can visit the **interior**. In the lobby, the Louis XVI Chamber with its painted ceiling served as a reception room. On the first floor, a number of Gothic chambers of varying sizes are decorated with oak ceilings and keystones carved with scenes from the Old and New Testaments.

The **cellars** (raadskelder) contain a café and a small Beer Museum.

★★ **Groot Begijnhof (Great Beguine Convent)** – The convent was founded in 1230. It covers an impressive area of 6ha/15 acres, and was the largest Beguine convent in Belgium. Since 1962, it has belonged to the university and now houses student residences. Behind the bulging brick walls stand a fine set of brick and white stone houses. Two arms of the River Dyle flow through the grounds.

The Gothic **church** is austere and has no tower, transept or ambulatory.

Naamsestraat – This street contains a large number of university colleges. It also includes the **St-Michielskerk**, a church dedicated to St Michael with a superb Baroque **façade**★. Equally outstanding are the Pauscollege founded by Pope Adrian II and the **university market** (Universiteitshalle), a cloth market dating back to the 14C.

★ **St-Pieterskerk** – This collegiate church dedicated to St Peter was built in the 15C in the Gothic style inherent to the Brabant region, on the site of an earlier Romanesque church. The pure Gothic **interior** includes a three-arched **choir screen**★ from 1499. It stands beneath a huge wooden statue of Christ; beyond is the chancel. In the north transept, a statue of the Madonna and Child dates from 1441. Our Lady is the patron saint of Louvain University.

★★ **Museum voor Religieuze Kunst (Museumof Religious Art)** – The ambulatory and chancel contain some of the church treasures and a number of magnificent paintings, including the **Last Supper** by Dirck Bouts from 1468. This masterpiece shines with warm light and of an admirable sense of understatement. Note, too, the 13C wooden **Head of Christ**★, called *of the Tortured Cross*. The chancel contains a superb **tabernacle**★, a tower made of Avernes stone.

LIÈGE★★

LUIK – Population 189 510
Michelin map 970 I 5

Liège is situated at the confluence of the Meuse and Ourthe rivers, in a basin surrounded by hills. It is a major river port and the third largest city in Belgium. Since it is near the Netherlands and Germany, it is also a major junction for road and rail traffic. Liège enjoys a reputation as a lively city. In the evening, numerous students from the Sart Tilman Campus meet in the cafés, bars and small restaurants in the *carré*, the area bounded by Rue du Pot-d'Or, Rue St-Adalbert, Rue St-Gilles and Boulevard de la Sauvenière.
During the day, the shopping areas around **Place St-Lambert** and between Feronstrée and the Meuse draw the crowds. The Sunday morning **La Batte Market** on Quai de Maastricht and Quai de la Batte is particularly attractive and animated.

Views – From the **Citadel** (access by road or by the 373 steps up the side of the Montagne de Bueren), enjoy a wonderful **view★★** of the town. Another fine **vantage point★** is from **Parc de Cointe**.

★★OLD TOWN

★**Palais des Princes-Évêques** – This palace was built around the year 1000 by Bishop Notget and entirely rebuilt on the orders of Prince-Bishop Everard de la Marck from 1526. The magnificent main **courtyard★★** incorporates galleries and 60 convex columns topped by richly decorated capitals.

★**The Perron** – The stepped column stands on the top of a huge fountain carved by Delcour. It is located on Place du Marché opposite the elegant 18C town hall. At the top, the Three Graces hold a pine cone and a Cross.

★★**Musée de la Vie wallonne** – The folk museum occupies a former monastery of the Order of Minor Friars, a magnificent building in the Mosan Renaissance style built in the 17C and elegantly combining brick and freestone.
Displays relate to life in days long gone, regional arts and crafts and popular beliefs. One room is devoted to sorcery. The second floor houses an exhibition of sundials and puppets. A **puppet theatre** opens at certain times of the year.

★**Musée d'Art religieux et d'Art mosan** – Religious art dating from the early Middle Ages from the diocese of Liège is exposed. Masterpieces of Mosan art include sculptures and gold or silverware – a Virgin Mary by Evegnée, a Crucifix by Rausa, a Virgin Mary with the Butterfly, and a Virgin Mary by Berselius.

EXCURSION

★★**Blégny-Trembleur** – *20km/12mi northeast in the direction of Aachen.* This was the last coal mine in the Liège Basin. The pit closed in 1980 but Blégny-Trembleur has been maintained as a reminder of the vanishing mining culture. Former miners serve as tour guides. The visit descends the **Marie** and **no 1 shafts**. Visitors go down the no 1 shaft to the **underground seams** where the *black faces* worked 8hr shifts in particularly difficult conditions.
Around the pit, in the tourist complex of **Le Trimbleu**, a **small-gauge railway** runs through the valleys and orchards of the Herve area to Mortoux. The **Musée de la vie régionale** offers insight into the craft techniques used to produce regional specialties such as pear and apple syrup, cheese and butter.

NAMUR★★

Population 105 243
Michelin map 970 I 5

Namur is a prosperous city in the heart of French-speaking Wallonia and because of its geographical location at the confluence of the Sambre and Moselle rivers, it used to be a vital military fortress. As such, it was besieged on many occasions. Its enormous citadel covers the hill known as Le Champeau, bearing witness to its warring past. Today the superb Jambes Bridge spans the two rivers.

Special Events – The **fêtes de Wallonie** are held every year on the third weekend in September; they provide an opportunity to see a number of traditional folk groups. The famous **stilt walkers** stage fights on stilts. The tradition originated in the 15C but the fighters dress in 17C costume.

Boat Trips on the Meuse – The landing-stage is located near the confluence of the Sambre and Meuse. Trips run to Dinant and Wépion.

★**The Citadel** – *Access via the Route Merveilleuse (1.5km/1mi) or by cable-car from the foot of the Citadel.* A tour of the fortress reveals a complex system of defence within each of the bastions both outside and inside. A guided visit passes through two underground passages. In a bend at the Northeast tip of the spur of rock, a terrace provides a magnificent **panoramic view★★** of the Sambre and Meuse valleys. The **Route des Panoramas** twists and turns its way downhill through the woods to the town centre.

★**Town Centre** – Numerous museums and religious buildings.

★**Musée des Arts anciens et du Namurois** – The museum is housed in the 17C Hôtel de Gaiffier d'Hestroy and contains some fine examples of regional art dating from the Middle Ages to the Renaissance. Numerous reliquaries are carved in the Mosan style.

★**Église St-Loup** – This remarkable Baroque building once served as the church for the Jesuit college. It now houses a high school, the Athénée Royal.

Cathédrale St-Aubain – Inside this Classical church surmounted by a dome are collected Baroque works of art, most from the region's churches and abbeys. Nearby, the **Musée diocésain★** contains the cathedral plate.

★**Musée de Croix** – This elegant 18C mansion built in the Louis XV style contains Rococo presses with tall cornices and additional decorative panels characteristic of the work of Namur's cabinetmakers. Interesting examples of regional art include paintings, sculptures, faience, glassware, and gold and silver plate.

EXCURSIONS

★★**The Meuse** – The River Meuse rises in France then flows through Belgium and the south of the Netherlands. It covers a distance of 950km/590mi before it reaches the North Sea. The stretch running through the province of Namur is its most picturesque part. Impressive walls of rock are very popular with climbers.
A number of the legendary exploits took place in the region. They are retold in Renaud de Montauban's famous *chanson de geste* about the four sons of Duke Aymon of Dordogne – Renaud, Alart, Guichard and Richard. Riding a magnificent horse, Bayard, the four fled from Charlemagne whose nephew had been killed by Renaud.
The two recommended routes, along the N 96 and N 92, show the different landscapes in the valley and the charms of the villages:

– **from Hastière-Lavaux to Namur★★**: *80km/50mi*. Walls of rock and ruined fortresses highlight the valley's former strategic importance. Villas, hostelries and cafés line the river banks.

– **from Namur to Andenne★**: *35km/22mi*. The Meuse widens out and the valley becomes larger, making the surrounding slopes gentler.

TOURNAI★★

DOORNIK – Population 67 891
Michelin map 970 I 5

This peaceful bourgeois town to the east of the River Schelde is located in the heart of a mainly agricultural region. Tournai is the oldest town in Belgium and it boasts a prestigious history. The kings of France always considered the city as the cradle of their monarchy. Clovis was born here in AD 465. Tournai was a major centre of the arts, particularly in the late Middle Ages. Its **tapestries** were popular throughout Europe and the industry flourished, especially from the 15C to the 18C.
Tournai maintains its folklore and traditions. The **Journées des quatre cortèges** mark the second weekend of June.

★★★**Cathédrale Notre-Dame** – *One of the best views of the cathedral is from Place P E Janson* – The building's sheer size and the massive outlines of its five famous towers never fail to impress.
The west front on Place de l'Evêché includes a **porch** containing three tiers of sculptures.

Interior – The nave has 10 spans and stands four storeys high, with arches including triple curves. Short pillars with fine carved capitals support the edifice. A **choir screen** with polychrome marble and lavish decoration by the sculptor Cornelis Floris de Vriendt II closes off the end of the nave. It is a magnificent piece of Renaissance work in the Antwerp style. A tall lantern tower stands above the majestic **transept** with its remains of frescoes and valuable stained-glass windows. The chapels in the ambulatory house works of art. *The Purgatory* by Rubens is located in the second side chapel on the right.
The **church plate★★** includes several fine examples of sacred art including the silver and gilded copper **Notre-Dame Reliquary** (1205).

Tournai Cathedral

★**Belfry** – This is Belgium's oldest belfry. The first storey offers an interesting **view** of the cathedral, and the belfry top provides a superb **view** of the town. At certain times of the year, bell **concerts** ring out using the church's 43 bells.
The belfry overlooks the triangular **Grand-Place.** Several fine houses have been rebuilt in the neighbourhood, including the old town hall which was once the cloth market. A short distance away, there is a wonderful brick-built mansion.

★**Pont des Trous** – The best **view**★ of the Pont des Trous is from the neighbouring bridge (Boulevard Delwart). Once part of the 13C walls, it formed a gateway defending the River Schelde. It was raised to facilitate river traffic.

Museums – Art Nouveau architect Victor Horta designed the **Musée des Beaux-Arts**★. It contains a fine collection of **old paintings**★, including works by Van der Weyden and Velvet Bruegel. The **Musée de la Tapisserie** overlooking Place Reine-Astrid recalls the finest hours of Tournai's tapestry industry. The **Musée du Folklore** in the Maison Tournaisienne features displays of popular arts and crafts from the town and the surrounding area. It serves as a reminder of everyday life around 1850.

For further details on Belgium, use the Michelin Green Guides Belgium – Grand Duchy of Luxembourg and Brussels.

When looking for a hotel or restaurant, use the Michelin Red Guide Benelux, updated annually.

Bosnia-Herzegovina

Bosna i Hercegovina

Because of the civil war that has raged through several of the countries in the former Yugoslavia, only a very brief description is provided of countries that were among Central Europe's most popular tourist venues.
Bosnia is a mountainous region – some of the peaks rise to altitudes of more than 2 000m/6 500ft – covered in forests. Herzegovina to the south, consists of limestone plateaux and a plain. Turks occupied the country from 1463 to 1873. Austro-Hungary then annexed it and Austria ruled until the end of the First World War.

SARAJEVO Michelin map 970 N 7

The name of the capital city sounds vaguely Turkish. In the 15C, the Turkish governor had his palace, or "*saraj*", built here.
On 28 June 1914, the assassination of Archduke Francis Ferdinand, heir to the throne of Austria, led to the First World War. In 1984, the city hosted the Winter Olympics. At present, the city is attempting to recover from Sarajevo's difficult years of fighting. The reconstruction is slow. Sarajevo's mosques, ancient Turkish marketplace (Bascarsija), houses, small shops and workshops give it an oriental atmosphere.

Bulgaria

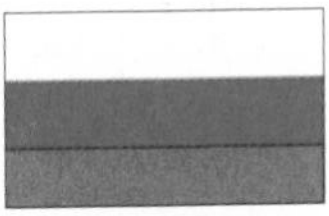

Bălgarija

Area: 110 912km²/42 146sq mi – **Population:** 8.5 million – **Capital:** Sofia – **Currency:** lev (plural *leva*) – **Time:** GMT + 2hr

Some 13 centuries ago, Bulgaria became a sovereign state. It occupies the centre of the Balkan Peninsula. To the north the River Danube separates Bulgaria from Romania. To the east, there is the Black Sea with a 380km/238mi coastline of superb sandy beaches. To the south, Turkey and Greece border the country, and to the west lie Macedonia and Serbia. The Balkan mountain chain, in Bulgarian *Stara Planina*, which means old mountain, extends from west to east, with an average altitude of 2 000m/6 560ft. Mountainous ridges separate the country into two equal parts.

IN BRIEF

Entry Formalities – A valid passport without a visa is required for all citizens of the European Union, Switzerland, Norway, Iceland and Liechtenstein for stays of up to 30 days. For French citizens not travelling by car, a passport or identity card is required.

Shopping – Shops are usually open from Monday to Saturday from 10am to 7pm. Large department stores open from 9am or 10am to 8pm.

Souvenirs – Eastern Europeans have preserved the art of copperware, and copper objects make excellent souvenirs. Wooden objects, icons, ceramics, woven products, and textiles represent other excellent purchases. A bottle of rose essence allows visitors to take home a memory from the Valley of the Roses.

A FEW HISTORICAL FACTS

686-1018 First Bulgarian State founded by Khan Asparukh, uniting the Slavs, who penetrated the Balkan Peninsula in the late 5C, and Bulgars, a Turkish-Tartar people from central Asia, who bring the Slavs the basis of their political organisation. For this reason, the new state is called the Bulgarian State despite a preponderance of Slavs.

803-814 Reign of Khan Krum. Following victorious wars, the Bulgarian territory stretches from the Danube to the Tisza, which separates it from the Magyars, in the west to Dniestr, which forms a natural frontier with the Pechenegs, in the east and the Rila and Rhodope mountains in the south.

816-831 Reign of Khan Omurtag, who concludes a 30 year peace treaty with Byzantium. The architecture and sculpture of the period have left remarkable monuments (Pliska, Madara).

852-889 Reign of Czar Boris I. Cyrillic alphabet invented in 855 by the brothers **Cyril** and **Methodius,** two monks from Salonika. In 865, Christianity is declared the official religion and Bulgaria becomes the centre of Slavic letters and culture.

893-927	Reign of Czar Symeon the Great. Golden age of Bulgarian literature. The First Bulgarian State reaches the zenith of its political power and greatest territorial expansion. It stretches as far as the Gallipoli Peninsula in Greece and encompasses Macedonia.
1018-1185	Byzantine occupation.
1187-1396	Second Bulgarian State.
1396-1878	Ottoman occupation. Political subjugation is aggravated by religious oppression. The Bulgarian patriarchate is abolished and the former Bulgarian Church is placed under the dependency of the Greek patriarchate. The monasteries, centres of culture, are sacked. In the middle of the 18C, the period known as the National Renaissance begins. A Bulgarian Church independent of the patriarchate of Constantinople is set up.
1876	The April insurrection seeks to throw off the Ottoman yoke. Stifled by massacres and pillage, it arouses heated indignation in Europe. Vassil Levski, the central figure of the liberation movement, is a Bulgarian national hero.
1877-1878	War of Liberation. Russia takes part in the war against Turkey. The Peace of San Stefano is signed on 3 March 1878 and leads to Bulgarian independence. Turkey loses a large part of its territory.
1879-1944	Third Bulgarian State. Parliamentary monarchy.
1885	Proclamation of the unification of the Principality of Bulgaria and Eastern Rumelia. Prince Alexander Battenberg, Prince Ferdinand of Saxe Cobourg-Gotha and Czar Boris III succeed one another on the throne.
1941	By the Vienna Pact, Bulgaria places its territory at the disposal of the German troops.
1944	The USSR makes war on Bulgaria. On 9 September, the monarchy is overthrown.
1946	Bulgaria becomes a People's Republic and satellite of the USSR.
1989	On 10 November, Todor Zhivkov, First Secretary of the Communist Party and Head of State for 30 years, is forced to resign.
1990	First free legislative elections.
1991	Parliamentary republic. Zhelju Zhelev is elected President of the Republic by universal suffrage.
1995-1997	Government by the Bulgarian Socialist Party, the former Communist Party. Grave social and economic crisis followed by early legislative elections giving the Coalition of Democratic Forces an absolute majority in Parliament. Ivan Kostov becomes Prime Minister.
1996	Peter Stoyanov, representing the Coalition of Democratic Forces, becomes President of the Republic.

The BLACK SEA

Michelin map 970 Q 7

The coastline, extending from the Romanian to Turkish borders, is the Bulgarian Riviera. Holidaymakers will enjoy the steep cliffs, rocky creeks and long sandy beaches.

North Coast – **Varna★** is Bulgaria's most important port and the country's major industrial centre. However, the city is most famous as a seaside resort, due to its attractive location in a bay surrounded by hills and fine beaches.
A seaside garden lies north of the harbour along the beach. Its cool shade is very welcome during the summer. Not far from this pleasant park stand the well-preserved 2C **Roman baths** and St Anastasia's Church.
North of the city, several seaside resorts have expanded in recent years. They include **Zlatni Pjasăci★★** (Golden Sands) and **Albena★**.

South Coast – **Burgas**, the second largest Bulgarian Black Sea port, lies near the famous seaside resort **Slăncěv Brjag★★**. This resort nestles at the back of a deep bay. Its sandy beach is several miles long. A wide variety of Greek and Byzantine souvenirs may be purchased at **Nesebăr★★**, a small peninsula of tiny winding streets lined with churches and picturesque old houses. During the summer, artists come to both the fishing port **Pomorie**, and the seaside resort **Sozopol★★**.

PLOVDIV★★★

Population 400 000
Michelin map 970 P 7

Plovdiv is located on the banks of the River Marica. It covers seven spectacularly beautiful hills. In 342 BC, Philip II of Macedonia entered the Thracian Plain and founded the town of Philippopolis. From that time, many different peoples have occupied the town. Romans, Byzantines, Bulgars, and Turks have all left visible traces of their culture all over the city. Plovdiv is rich in monuments, and has preserved a picturesque old quarter with steep, narrow paved streets lined with colourful houses concealing charming flowered courtyards.

Old Town – The old town covers three hills: Nébét Tépé (Watchtower Hill), Taksim Tépé (Reservoir Hill) and Djambaz Tépé (Acrobat Hill). The numerous cafés and restaurants are especially attractive. At the *Puldin*, visitors can enjoy vreteno, a local speciality made with veal and pork, crepes with preserves, and *baklavā*, a sweet pastry made with honey, almonds and pistachios. The *Thrakia Stan* offers folk-dancing performances, and the *Ritoria* is famous for its elegant setting.
The **Koyumdjioglu House**★★ *(2 Komarkov Street)*, a superb 19C residence, houses the Ethnographic Museum. Each year the museum welcomes an international chamber music festival. The **Lamartine House**★ *(Knyaz Tzeretelev Street)* is dedicated to the memory of the famous writer who lived there during his eastern travels in 1833.
The **antique theatre**★★ was built in the 2C under the reign of Marcus Aurelius.

City Centre – Vasil-Kolarov Street starts at Central Square, bordered in the west by Liberty Park (Park Na Svobodata). This busy street houses shops, art galleries and restaurants and leads north to Stambolijski Square with the imposing **Dzumaja Dzamija Mosque**★. In the same square, the superbly restored 2C **Roman amphitheatre**★★ is the setting for many concerts and other artistic performances. Further north towards the river in Saedinenie Square lies the **Archeological Museum**, which exhibits treasures from ancient Thrace and a collection of ancient coins.

EXCURSIONS

★★ **Bačkovo** – *30km/18mi to the southeast.* Founded in 1083 by two Georgian monks in the service of the Byzantine empire, the monastery is dedicated to the Virgin. It is Bulgaria's largest after the famed Rila Monastery and is renowned for its wall paintings and the **Icon of the Virgin**, which attracts the prayers of childless women. There are a number of churches to visit, including St Nicholas', which houses remarkable paintings of the **Last Judgement**, as well as kitchens, the refectory and a small museum of sacred art.

Pamporovo – *85km/53mi to the south.* The **Rhodope range** extends throughout the southern part of Bulgaria. Orpheus, Thracian prince, poet, musician and singer and a mythical hero, is said to have lived here. A land of poetry and legend, Rhodope was celebrated by many great poets of ancient times.
The ski resort of Pamporovo, known for its long winter season, lies in the midst of a pine forest at an altitude of 1 650m/5 412ft.

ROSOVA DOLINA★

Valley of the Roses
Michelin map 970 P 7

The Valley of the Roses is located in the Kazanlăk region, to the south of the Balkan mountain range. The picking season lasts from May to June. During this period, the area gives off a pleasant scent and is covered with multi-coloured flowers. Roses have been cultivated here for centuries. The extracts are used by perfumeries all over the world. The gathering process, traditionally a woman's task, requires great dexterity and patience. The flowers are carefully cut one by one and laid in willow-baskets, which are then sent to the distilleries.

Kazanlăk – Kazanlăk is the rose capital, with a research centre, experimental garden, museum, and distillery. Each year at the beginning of June the city hosts the Rose Festival. It includes folk-dancing and singing performances, a procession, and decorated wagons. Kazanlăk is also known for its Thracian tomb on a hill in the northeast part of the town. It dates from 4C BC and was discovered in 1944.

Kalofer – Kalofer is the birthplace of the revolutionary poet, Hristo Botev (1848-1876). The house where he was born can be visited. This national hero was killed 2 June 1876 during a battle with the Turks near Vratsa. Every year the entire country honours his memory on the anniversary of his death. This holiday also commemorates the memory of all war victims.

Karlovo – The town, with a charming old quarter of tiny winding streets, enjoys a pleasant location at the foot of the Balkan mountains. Vassil Levski (1837-1873), an ardent freedom fighter and founder of revolutionary parties, was born here. He organised the revolution in the country's interior, and was finally arrested by the Turks and later hanged in Sofia. Close to his house stands a small museum devoted to his memory. A former school houses the town's historical museum.

Sopot – The town is known as the birthplace of another writer, Ivan Vazov, who lived from 1850 to 1921. The statue of this poet and novelist stands in the central square. The house where he was born has been transformed into a museum. His writings express his strong patriotic sentiments and describe the resistance to the Turkish occupiers. The 1876 insurrection is very powerfully described in his novel *Under the Yoke.*

SOFIA★★★

Population 1 200 000
Michelin map 970 O 7

Comfortably nestled in the heart of the mountains, this former Roman fortress was originally known as Ulpia Serdica. The Czar Osvoboditel, Patriarch Evtimi and Vitosa Boulevards, and the Sveta Nedelja Square surround the town centre.

Boulevard Vitosa and Sveta Nedelja Square districts

Boulevard Vitocha – The pedestrian thoroughfare is lined with luxury shops, stores and car rental agencies. At no 2, not far from Sveta Nedelja Square, the **National History Museum★★★** occupies the former Law Courts. Treasures from the Thracian period, bas-reliefs from medieval capitals, ceramics and costumes, are exhibited. The **National Palace of Culture**, at the boulevard's south end, is an imposing modern building. Mount Vitosa can be seen in the distance.
Close by, a disaffected arsenal has been transformed into the **Museum of the People and their Country**. It houses a wide variety of minerals, crystals and precious stones.

Sveta Nedelja Church – This small church is located to the south of Sveta Nedelja Square. Of medieval origin, it was reconstructed following a bomb explosion in an assassination attempt on King Boris II.

★**St George's Church** – This Roman rotunda may have been a public bath before being transformed into a church and later a mosque under Ottoman occupation. It was restored to Christian worship after the Liberation. The frescoes depict 22 prophets.

★★**Archeological Museum** – The museum, installed in a former 15C mosque, houses an important collection of prehistoric and antique objects.

Largo – The town's ancient ramparts can be visited by following the underground passageways under the Largo esplanade. At the end of the esplanade, the small **Sveta Petka Samardzijska Church** (St Petka of the Harness-Makers) seems to rise out of the ground. The harness-makers corporation began construction in the late 14C and completed the work in the beginning of the 15C. The **National Gallery of Fine Arts★★** lies just opposite the esplanade. It contains icons and Bulgarian painting. The Ethnographic Museum stands nearby, as well as **St Nicholas'★**, a tiny Russian church whose golden domes and green tower look fairy tale like.

★**Banja Basi Mosque** – The baths are located in a fine building with a dome and slender minaret.

Cathedral district

★★★**St Alexander Nevski Cathedral** – The shining domes of the neo-Byzantine cathedral overlook this huge circular square. Russian architect Pomerantsev built it to commemorate the 1878 victory against the Turks. The cathedral is dedicated to Alexander Nevski, Grand Duke of Novgorod, who conquered the Swedes on the banks of the River Neva in 1240. The interior is richly decorated with marble, onyx, alabaster and wall paintings. The **crypt** houses an impressive collection of icons and merits a visit.

★**Sveta Sofija Basilica (Saint Sophia)** – The basilica rises on the other side of the square. In the 6C, the Byzantine princess, Sofia supposedly started construction. The city was later named after her in the 14C. The building forms a Latin cross with a cupola above the transept. Excavations under the basilica have uncovered vestiges, including mosaic fragments, of four earlier churches erected on the same site. The tomb of the poet and writer Ivan Vazov *(see Sopot under Rosova Dolina)* can be seen in the chancel. The tomb of the unknown soldier is also found nearby.

Narodno Sâbranie Square – The square is surrounded by several impressive buildings: the National Assembly, the Bulgarian Academy of Science and the Grand Hotel of Sofia. In the centre stands an equestrian statue of Czar Alexander II, liberator of Bulgaria. The University on Boulevard Ruski to the left is followed by the **Eagle Bridge★** (Orlov most), marking the city's former town gates.

ADDITIONAL SIGHTS

★★ **Mount Vitocha** – *By cable railway: 30min.* During the summer, the park makes an ideal spot for hiking and other leisure activities. The panorama is magnificent. Excellent skiing is possible during the winter. The highest summit is the Black Peak at 2290m/7511ft altitude.

EXCURSIONS

★★ **Bojana Church** – *20km/12mi to the southeast.* The church, dating from 1259, is built in the Greek cross design and stands in a lovely park. Inside, famed frescoes present an originality and beauty unparalleled in 13C religious art. They depict scenes from the life of Christ, flanked by portraits of donors.

★ **Koprivchtitza** – *110km/68mi to the east.* This peaceful little town, located in the Sredna Gora mountains, was a centre for crafts and trade with the Ottoman Empire during the 19C. The Bulgarian Renaissance style is visible in the wooden verandas, overhanging roofs and massive doors flanked by high stone walls. The first shot in the war against the Turks was fired here in 1876. Rich, cultured Bulgarians such as Kableshkov, Benkovski and Karavelov sacrificed their lives to free Bulgaria. Their residences, as well as that of the rich merchant Oslekov and the birthplace of the Romantic poet Debeljanov, have been transformed into museums.
Every five years, scheduled again in 2001, a Folk Festival is held in the cobblestone streets. Folk dancers dress in colourful costumes.

The SOUTHWEST

The southwest region rises steeply from the **Rila Mountain** to the peaks of **Mount Pusala** and **Mount Pirin.** At 2925m/9594ft, Mount Pusala is the highest summit in the Balkan peninsula except for Mount Olympus in Greece. A road follows the gorge dividing the mountain chains. It passes through several health resorts.

★ **Sandanski** – This spa has been famous since ancient times. Its hot springs reach 35°C. An exceptional climate adds to the spa's considerable reputation.

J.-P. Durand /DIAF

Rila Monastery

★★★**Rila Monastery** – This magnificent monastery, resembling a fortress, was founded by the Hermit Ivan Rilski, St John of Rila. Orthodox priests at the monastery have preserved a number of manuscripts which are now considered part of the national cultural heritage. Numerous icons and wall paintings have also been preserved. The frescoes painted on the church's outside walls depict scenes of religious fervour and clever satires. The monastery is a centre for Bulgarian spiritual life and was a respected pilgrimage site, even during the Turkish occupation. A series of remarkable icons are located in the Church of the Assumption, and a fine collection of icons and sacred art objects in the historical museum.

★**Bansko** – Lying at the foot of the Pirin range, Bansko leads to the Pirin National Park. Its architecture is characteristic of the 18C and 19C. Holy Trinity Church (1832-1835) is a fine example of the Bansko School of Art.

Melnik – In the past, Melnik served as the hub of the roads linking the coast of the Aegean Sea with Central Europe. Today this tiny town is best-known for its magnificent setting and its vineyards producing a much-appreciated, full-bodied wine.

★**Rojen Monastery** – The monastery, built in the 12C, contains 14C calligraphy and manuscripts, 16C wall paintings, 18C stained-glass windows, and a miraculously preserved icon depicting the Virgin and Child.

VELIKO TĂRNOVO★★★

Population 37 000
Michelin map 970 P 7

The town covers several hills situated along the winding course of the River Jantra. It served as the capital of the second Bulgarian kingdom that lasted from 1187 to 1398.

Tsavérets Hill – Vestiges of the ramparts surrounding this once strong medieval city remain visible. The famous **Baudouin Tower**★★ survived destruction by the Ottomans. After his victory over the crusaders in 1205 at Klokotnitsa, the Bulgarian Czar Kaloyan imprisoned Emperor Baudouin of Flanders in the citadel. When the Bulgarian queen fell in love with the prisoner, he was cast from the top of the tower into the ravine.
At the foot of the hill stands the **Church of the 40 Martyrs**★★, built in 1230 by Czar Ivan Assen II to commemorate the Turkish massacres. The Patriarch Evtimi, then head of the Church, led the prisoners to the block himself and was the first to be beheaded.

Old streets – **Samovodska Street**★★, located in the magnificently restored town centre, is lined with souvenir shops, bakers' and confectioners'. Follow Rakovski Street to **Monkey House**, known for the sculpture of a grimacing figurine. Continue to the **Hadji Nicoli Inn**★★, (1827) which houses the Ethnographic Museum. Include a stop in one of the cafés looking out over the river, to enjoy the remarkable views.

EXCURSIONS

★★**Gabrovo** – *50km/31mi to the south.* The town was nicknamed the Bulgarian Manchester and was the birthplace for many industries that arose in the 18C. The textile industry developed due to the hydraulic energy provided by the River Jantra. 10km/6mi upriver, a museum presents regional crafts and costumes.
Residents enjoy a reputation for creativity but also for frugality that borders on the miserly. This trait has exposed them to ridicule. In sheer self-defence they were obliged to invent jokes which make fun of themselves. As a result, Gabrovo is synonymous with a sense of humour. The town has built the **House of Satire and Humour** (inaugurated on 1 April) in a former leather factory, and hosts the bi-annual International Humour Festival which brings together comics and humorists from all over the world.
A statue of the town's founder, **Racho the Blacksmith**, has been installed in the middle of the river to save space!

★★★**Trjavna** – *20km/12mi to the east of Gabrovo.* In **Daskalova House**★★, the huge antechamber's ceiling is decorated with a magnificent carved wooden sun. It was finished after one month of non-stop work during a 19C competition.

Slavejkov House★ is the birthplace of the poets Petko and Penco Slavejkov, father and son. Petko, an ardent patriot, published a collection of Bulgarian proverbs and wise sayings during the 19C which marked the rebirth of the Bulgarian nation.

Croatia

Area: 56 638km²/21 775sq ft – **Population:** 4.6 million – **Capital:** Zagreb – **Currency:** kuna – **Time:** GMT + 1hr in winter, GMT + 2hr in summer – Formalities: passport for citizens of the European Union and Japan Visa for US, Canadian and Australian citizens.

Hrvatska

Most of the shoreline along the eastern Adriatic Sea is part of Croatia. The northern part of the country, which extends into the Pannonian Plain, is typically Central European, while the southern landscape is Mediterranean.

DALMATSKA KOTA **(ADRIATIC COAST)** Michelin map 970 M7

The indented shores of the Adriatic Coast are broken by many gulfs, creeks, promontories, and numerous islands are scattered along the coast. Among the most attractive to tourists are the Brijuni, Kornati, Mljet, Lokrum and Korcula islands.

★**Zadar** – A network of well laid out streets goes back to Roman times. The ancient **forum**★ displays vestiges of a capitol and temple. **St Donat Church**★★ shows a pre-Romanesque style. **Sv. Stosija Cathedral**★★ (St Anastasia) was built during the 12C and 13C on the site of an old Christian basilica. **Sv. Sime Church** (St Simon) contains the saint's **reliquary**★★ by an Italian goldsmith.

★**Šibenik** – The old town and **Sv. Jakov Cathedral**★★ (15C-16C) are interesting.

★★**Trogir** – The former Greek city of Tragurion has preserved a remarkable concentration of historic monuments. The streets still follow the pattern laid down in antiquity, but the buildings are from medieval times. The 13C **Sv. Lovre Cathedral**★★ (St Laurent) and the **chapel of Ivan the Blessed** are Croatia's most important Renaissance buildings.

★★★**Split** – The city grew up around the palace built by Emperor Diocletian from AD 295 to 305. During the 7C, the inhabitants of the Roman town of Salona took refuge in the palace. Today, this archeological site is a significant part of the world's cultural heritage.

★★★**Dubrovnik** – One of the architectural wonders of the Adriatic, Dubrovnik is surrounded by thick ramparts offering a splendid panorama. Damaged in the civil war following the break-up of the former Yugoslavia, this UNESCO world heritage city is gradually coming back to life and revealing its wonders to tourists. The tour of the old town is signposted from the 14C Pile gate, while the Placa (main street with 17C façades), Luza main square with its cafés, Gothic-Renaissance Sponza palace and 15C Pinceta fort on the north side of the ramparts are also worth visiting.

The islands

★★**Korcula Island** – This long (48km/30mi), narrow (8km/5mi) island bearing figs, almonds, olives and vines (from which highly-reputed wine is made) enjoys a mild climate. The main city is in a beautiful setting on a headland at the entrance to the Peljesac canal. The 12C - 16C cathedral, stately homes and Marco Polo's birthplace are worth visiting.
From Korcula, the small neighbouring island of Badija, with its Gothic Franciscan convent, can be reached.

★★**Hvar Island** – This mountainous island with Mediterranean vegetation was nicknamed the "Croatian Madeira" in view of its excellent climate. Needless to say, it attracts holiday-makers. The main locality, with the same name as the island, is a picturesque Venetian-style town with Renaissance loggias and wells and a part-Renaissance, part-Baroque cathedral.

★★ZAGREB and the Northwest Michelin map 970 M6

The centre of town is Gradec-Gornji, an elevated site dating back to prehistoric times. The old town, **Gornji grad**★★ has preserved its medieval layout. Around **Markov Trg.** are the Parliament buildings (Hrvatski sabor) and the Gothic Sv. Marko Church (St Mark). **Sv. Katarina Church**★★ (St Catherine) is a remarkable example of the Baroque style. Other interesting sights include the **Kaptol**★, the **Sv. Stjepan Cathedral** (St Stephen) quarter, the **Episcopal Palace** next to the cathedral, and the lower city (Donji grad).

Excursions – Many Baroque castles and numerous churches dot the rounded hills of a landscape that has inspired many painters. See **Sv. Marija Snjezna Church**★ (St Mary of the Snow) and **Varaždin**★, a Baroque city.

Czech Republic

Area: 78 864 km^2/30 449 sq mi – **Population:** 10 315 000 – **Capital:** Praha (Prague) – **Currency:** Crown – **Time:** GMT + 1 hr in winter, GMT + 2 hr in summer.

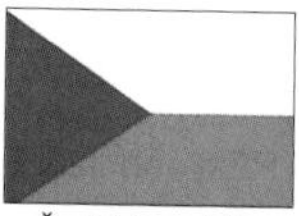
Česká Republika

The Czech Republic lies in the heart of Europe. It includes two historic provinces – Bohemia centering on Prague and Moravia-Silesia focusing on the industrial city of Brno.
The country has natural borders formed by mountain ranges. The wooded upper slopes rise to 1 603m/5 210ft at Snezka in the Krkonose Range (Giant mountains) on the Polish border. The rolling fields and woodlands in the interior are broken by magnificent river valleys. A dense network of footpaths and small roads makes the rural areas easy to reach. Numerous man-made lakes add beauty.
Visitors to the Czech Republic are particularly drawn to its capital. "Golden Prague" boasts an incomparable architectural heritage. Outside Prague, though, countless historic towns, remarkably well-preserved, merit a visit. They include Česky Krumlov with its majestic castle, České Budějovice and its huge square, and Olomouc, the second most popular tourist venue after Prague thanks to its impressive string of historic buildings.
Castles, large palaces and small manor houses dot the countryside. Monasteries, churches and chapels attract large numbers of pilgrimages.
The architectural and urban landscape has been greatly marked by the Baroque period. During this time, the Counter-Reformation (1630-1750) forcibly dragged Bohemia back into the Roman Catholic Church.
At the beginning of this century, an avant-garde movement gave rise to an architectural revival, producing distinguished Art Nouveau buildings.
The Czech lands were the richest and most industrialised part of the old Austro-Hungarian Empire. The scenery still bears the hallmarks of this past, especially in the north of Bohemia.

IN BRIEF

Entry regulations – Valid passport for British, US and Canadian citizens. Visa for Australians.

Souvenirs – Bohemian crystal is popular with tourists, as is Bohemian jewellery. Antique lovers will find much to satisfy them in Prague.

HISTORICAL NOTES

9C BC The earliest settlers are Celts known as Boii; they leave their name to Bohemia. Germanic tribes, the Marcomanni and Quadi, remove them in 1C BC.

2C Marcus Aurelius' Roman legions contain the German offensives on the Danube.

5C Slavonic tribes from Northeast Europe replace the Germans.

9C Great Moravia is formed, bringing together Bohemia, Slovakia and Moravia.

864 At Prince Rastislav's request, two missionary brothers named Cyril and Methodius spread the Byzantine form of worship and introduce the Cyrillic alphabet into the kingdom.

921 The Empire of Great Moravia comes under Magyar domination while further north the Slavonic tribe of Czechs settle permanently in the area around Prague.

Wenceslas is proclaimed king in 921. As an ardent defender of the faith, he opens his kingdom to Western influences.

929 Wenceslas is murdered by his brother and later becomes the country's patron saint.

950 Otto I defeats the Czechs in battle. When he is crowned Emperor in 962, Bohemia becomes part of the Holy Roman Empire.

1212 Emperor Frederick II grants the throne to Přemysl Ottokar I and makes it a hereditary title.

13C Bohemia enjoys a period of prosperity under the Premyslid dynasty. The monarchs encourage the immigration of a large number of German settlers who develop the mining industry and enhance the country's economic wealth.

1349 King Charles IV of Bohemia is recognised as the Holy Roman Emperor. He inaugurates a "Golden Age" and Prague becomes the capital of the Empire.

1415 Jan Hus, a preacher who fought for religious reformation and opposed increasing German influence, is burnt at the stake in Constance. His death leads to a rebellion which lasts until 1437.

1526 The crown of Bohemia passes to the Habsburgs as Ferdinand I accedes to the German throne after the death of his brother, Charles V. Bohemia remains part of the House of Austria until the end of the First World War.

1618 The Defenestration of Prague: three Roman Catholic representatives of the emperor are thrown from the castle windows. This leads to the Thirty Years' War as Protestant Bohemia rebels against Roman Catholic Austria.

1620 In the Battle of White Mountain, Bohemia's Protestant nobility is crushed and sent into exile. The country is returned to the Roman Catholic Church and the Czech language suppressed. Bohemia and Moravia become provinces within the Austrian monarchy.

1848 Czech nationalists organise a conference of Slavs in Prague. The movement is initially cultural in character but it takes on political overtones. The rebellions are crushed by the Austrian Army.

1918 Masaryk, the émigré Czech political leader, and émigré Slovak leaders sign the Pittsburgh Convention vowing to set up a State of Czechs and Slovaks.

1938 The Sudetenland is given to Nazi Germany.

1939-1945 The Czech territories of Bohemia and Moravia are annexed by the Third Reich and become a "German protectorate".

1945 American troops advance as far as Carlsbad and Pilsen but the Red Army liberates most of the country, including Prague on 9 May 1945.
More than three million Sudetenland Germans are expelled.

1948 The Prague Uprising: communists take control of the government.

1968 Warsaw Pact countries invade Czechoslovakia to crush the revolt known as the Prague Spring. Alexander Dubček loses power.

1989 The Velvet Revolution overthrows the Communist regime. Dissident writer Vaclav Havel is elected President of the Czechoslovak Republic.

1992 Elections reveal a deep split between the Czech and Slovak territories. Political leaders divide the country in two.

1993 The Czech Republic is born.

1999 The Czech Republic joins NATO.

BOHEMIA'S SPA RESORTS

Michelin map 970 L5

Few places in Europe were as fashionable as the three world-famous spa resorts in the "Bohemian Triangle" in the northwest tip of the country. Just before the First World War, when the resorts were at the height of fashion, they still bore their Austrian names – Franzenbad (now Františkovy Lázně), Marienbad (Mariánské Lázně), and the best-known of them all, Carlsbad (Karlovy Vary).

★★★KARLOVY VARY (CARLSBAD)

Karlovy Vary is not only famous for its hot spring water with a high sulphur content; it is also well known for the outstanding beauty of the surrounding countryside. In the deep wooded valley where shines the River Teplá, the splendid sight of this town is still steeped in a turn-of-the-century atmosphere.

The springs are said to have been discovered in 1348 by Emperor Charles IV when he was out on a hunting party. The water was initially used for baths but was later drunk; it is used to treat disorders of the digestive system. "Taking the waters" very soon became a social as much as a therapeutic event. Among the celebrities who flocked to the resort to see and be seen, was Goethe. The famed writer benefited greatly from his stays in Carlsbad and came no less than 13 times.

The luxury hotels and villas on the river bank or on the steep slopes above the town provide architectural charm. The **Grand Hotel Pupp** (badly named the Moskva for four decades) represents a typical example. It was founded by a pastry cook in 1793 and rebuilt in a luxuriously extravagant style during the 1870's. However, the most pretentious of all the buildings is the Imperial Hotel built in 1910.

Life in the resort centres on the impressive Classical colonnade dating from the late 19C, the **Mlýnská kolónadá**, where people drink the water from four springs, the most spectacular one being the **Vřídlo**. However, the town was not a purely 19C invention. Still standing are ruins of the castle tower, a column in memory of the 1776 plague epidemic and the splendid Baroque church dedicated to St Mary Magdalen.

The thermal sanatorium built in 1977 stands out like a sore thumb.

J.-P. Courau /EXPLORER

Gallery of the mineral springs

Visitors should take a walk along footpaths and enjoy the panoramic views which wind their way through the delightful forests covering the hilltops. A funicular railway reaches the forest.

★★★MARIÁNSKÉ LÁZNĚ (MARIENBAD)

This resort's reputation for elegance almost equals Carlsbad's. Yet Mariánské Lázně differs from its rival because it is set in a wide valley at an altitude of 600m/1603ft. It was founded later by the abbot of the nearby Tepla Monastery in 1812. The 39 cold water springs treat a wide range of disorders.
The superb covered gallery containing the **mineral springs★** is 120m/400ft long and is built of wrought iron. It dates from 1889 and represents an outstanding feat of technical prowess. Nearby, the elegant little pavilion in the Classical style contains the **Cross Spring** (Krizovy pramen) and a masterpiece of modern engineering, the singing fountain which is computer-controlled. Luxury hotels and other buildings from a bygone era embellish the scene. Roman Catholic, Russian Orthodox, and Anglican churches serve as a reminder of the various backgrounds of the people who came here to take the waters.

★FRANTIDŠKOVY LÁZNDĚ (FRANZENBAD)

The smallest of the three great spa resorts in Bohemia lies on a plateau surrounded by forests and marshland and is much more peaceful than its two rivals. It is reminiscent of the mid-19C garden cities, with a network of narrow streets leading to delightful woods. Founded in 1793, the town was named after Emperor Francis I; many of its neo-Classical buildings are still "Habsburg yellow" in colour. The 24 or more cold water springs are used for baths but the water is also drunk to treat cardiac disorders, rheumatism and gynecological problems.

★★CHEB

The medieval town of Cheb lies on the border with Bavaria and still has a decidedly German atmosphere owing to its houses with carved wooden roofs. The **Spalíÿcek**, a group of raised buildings, gives the main square a particularly picturesque air. The Flamboyant Gothic building overlooking the square is the house where General Albrecht von Wallenstein was assassinated in 1634; it has been turned into a museum.

★★LOKET

This tiny citadel-town was once considered as the "key to the kingdom of Bohemia." It is built on an outcrop of granite and almost totally encircled by a bend of the River Ohře. From the rugged 13C castle high above a deep wooded gorge, a breathtaking view unfolds. Most of the houses in the town and the distant market place have Baroque façades.

BRNO★★ and MORAVIA

Michelin map 970 M5

Brno, the main town in Moravia, is filled with the hustle and bustle of any large provincial city. Its superb churches, the Gothic church dedicated to St John and Baroque Minorities Church, bear witness to a long history. The rapid expansion of its textile industries in the 19C earned Brno the nickname "the Manchester of Austria". The city adapted rapidly to progress. During the inter-war years, it was a bastion of **modern architecture**. The Bata building and Avion Hotel in the town centre and the famous Tugendhat House designed by Mies van der Rohe in the suburbs rivalled developments in Prague. The circle of parks and gardens running along the ruins of the town walls provide delightful places for a stroll. The town centre is now a pedestrian precinct in which modern and ancient architecture live happily side by side.

SIGHTS

★**Zelnýtrh (Vegetable Market)** – In the centre of the sloping market place stands the stone-built Baroque Parnassus Fountain. On the north side, the former town hall contains the town's mascot, Brno the Dragon, which is actually a crocodile. From the tower, superb views unfold of the town.

Náměstí Svobody (Liberty Square) – This square, named in honour of liberty, is too large to be dominated by its memorial to plague victims. Around it stand buildings erected in various periods of history.

Dóm na Petrově (St Peter's Cathedral) – The Petrov Hill, which was once the site of a Slav fortress, marks the highest point in the old town. It is now topped by the Flamboyant Gothic outline of the cathedral dedicated to St Peter.

★**Moravská galérie (Moravian Gallery)** – This gallery has numerous rooms laid out in chronological order. It houses remarkable collections of applied arts, furniture, porcelain and glassware.

★**Špilberk** – Brno's citadel now looks down on peaceful woodland. For many years, though, it was one of the most infamous political prisons in Austria.

Moravské můzeum (Moravian Museum) – The greatest treasure in the regional Moravian museum is a terracotta statue 25 000 years old, known as the **Vestonice Venus**.

EXCURSIONS

★★**Telč** – *94km/58mi west*. This town includes an extraordinary row of perfectly preserved **old houses** around a narrow square. Arches support a succession of gables in the Baroque and Renaissance styles that are the only ones of their kind in the country. The long narrow plots of land laid out by the surveyors at the end of the medieval period run down to man-made lakes created out of the surrounding marshland. The top of the dam offers wonderful views of this most exquisite small town. The huge tower on the church dedicated to the Assumption of the Virgin Mary dominates the town's eastern end. On the west side, a collection of buildings merit attention: a Jesuit College and its church with a double bell-tower; St John's Church reached by a roofed passageway, and the **castle** commissioned by the Hradec family in the 14C. It was destroyed then enlarged in the 16C and is a charming sight because of its irregular design and its interior, full of fascinating Renaissance paintings and plaster work.

★★**Kroměřiž** – *67km/42mi east*. This attractive town lies in the heart of the fertile Hana region, and was chosen as the summer residence of the bishops of Olomouc in the early 13C. The main square is still dominated by the tower of their great palace.

The **Bishop's Palace** was rebuilt several times and now has an austere Baroque façade. The superb interior reflects the power and prosperity of the prelates. The vast luxurious Congress Chamber where the Austrian imperial suite met in 1848 is the most sumptuous of all the rooms. The **art collection** is one of the finest in the country. It includes works by Van Dyck, Titian, and Cranach. The vast park stretching from the north side of the palace to the River Morava was redesigned in the English style in the early 19C. Further on is another fine episcopal park, the Kvetna zahrada or Flower Garden which has retained its original Baroque character.

★★**Vranov Castle** – *85km/53mi southwest via Znojmo*. The rugged Dyje Valley adjacent to the Austrian border enjoys some of the finest scenery in southern Moravia. This ambitious castle was built in the 11C on a spur of rock high above the river. It is one of Central Europe's most superb fortresses. Originally it was built as a border castle, but it owes its present appearance to the preposterous vanity of the Althan family who, in the late 17C and early 18C, commissioned the greatest architects of the day to turn this medieval fortress into a luxurious palace. Strung out along the narrow promontory, a succession of courtyards encircle the castle with, at the very top, the impressive Ancestors' Chamber, an oval room paying homage to the family's fame.

★★**Olomouc** – *78km/48mi northeast.* Olomouc was crushed and pillaged by the people of the Sudetenland during the Thirty Years' War and lost its status as the main town in Moravia to Brno. By way of compensation, it was rebuilt in the Baroque style. Boulevards follow the line of the old town walls, and the town centre boasts a number of historic buildings second only to Prague. The city's many industries, university, theatres and symphony orchestra make for a lively place.

The extensive old town centre includes a large number of irregularly-shaped squares, all of them decorated with very fine fountains. On Horní náměstí, or **Upper Square**, stands the town hall. Its upper section was first raised in the 14C before being rebuilt several times. The mosaics and the original numerals on its astronomical clock were destroyed during the Second World War. The early 18C **Trinity Column**, 32m/105ft high, is decorated with a plethora of ornamentation that makes it one of the country's best-known sights. The square has two fountains – one representing Hercules and the other depicting Julius Caesar who is said to have founded Olomouc. To the north, the town's parish church is dedicated to St Maurice and, at the bottom of the slope to the south, another unusual square is decorated with several fountains.

The main thoroughfare in the town heads eastwards, skirting the large Baroque Jesuit Church and the large Tritons Fountain. It leads to the cathedral which was redesigned in the Gothic style. Not far away is Premyslid Palace.

★**Slavkov (Austerlitz)** – *20km/12mi east.* In the gently-rolling countryside to the east of Brno, Emperor Napoleon won brilliant victory over the Russian and Austrian armies on 2 December 1805. The setting is better known as Austerlitz.

The various stages in the battle and its cost in terms of human life are commemorated. The most moving memorial on this vast battlefield is the Mohyla miru, the **Peace Memorial**★ on the top of the hill above the village of Prace *(14km/7mi southeast of Brno).*

Czar Alexander and Emperor Francis I of Austria spent the evening before the battle in the **castle**★ overlooking the tiny town of Slakov *(20km/12mi east of Brno)*. A cease fire ending the battle was signed in the magnificent central reception room of this splendid Baroque palace.

The battle of Austerlitz and the Treaty of Presburg (in Bratislava) put an end to the third coalition.

★**Moravský kras (Moravian Karst)** – *75km/47mi northeast.* This limestone plateau, known as the Moravian Karst, is one of the most popular venues in the countryside around Brno. Water erosion has carved out amazing shapes and created countless caves with superb stalactites and stalagmites. A swallow hole plunges 139m/452ft deep. This **Macocha Abyss** contains some rare species of plants. To reach the abyss, visitors are taken on a boat trip along the subterranean River Punkva.

Zlín – *100km/62mi east.* The Tamas Bata shoe factory served as a prototype for 20C paternalistic businesses. The firm's head called in the most fashionable architects of the inter-war years to create an industrial dream in this small provincial town. Small but elegant houses were built in a rustic setting, along with the factory buildings and the community amenities provided for Bata workers. The result recalls the optimistic atmosphere of the First Czech Republic.

PRAHA★★★

PRAGUE – Population 1 200 000
Michelin map 970 L 5

The capital of the Czech Republic has been miraculously spared by the war and industrial development. Its extraordinarily rich architectural heritage covers every period in its long history. Four decades of communism kept commercial pressures at bay. No other city in Europe enjoys such a wealth of historic monuments blending so well into beautiful natural surroundings. Since the Velvet Revolution in 1989, Prague has recaptured its old vibrancy, combining ancient and modern.

Prague originally consisted of the Slav fortress of Hradcany, built high above a meander of the River Vltava. Three historic districts were then added onto this initial core. Malá Strana, the lower town, sits at the foot of the castle on the river's left bank. The magnificent Gothic-style Charles Bridge links it to the Staré Město or old town. The Nové Město, new town, is set further away on the right bank of the river. Medieval Prague was extensively rebuilt in the 17C and 18C, but behind the Baroque or Rococo façades, medieval structures remain recognisable. Superb architectural monuments, one of the characteristic features of Prague, also mark the appearance of new artistic movements linked to the Czech Secession movement. Some austere buildings represent Czech Cubism.

The city's historic heart is a very small area, easy to visit on foot. Public transport (underground, tramways and buses) is modern and well-integrated into the city landscape. Tickets are on sale in hotels and stations.

★★★ HRADČANY (CASTLE DISTRICT) (ABY)

Prague lies in the shadow of this fortress, the political and religious symbol of the country rising majestically from its spur of rock above the River Vltava. The castle's vast courtyard and the great curving Hradèany Square contrast with the nearby small streets cloaked in secrecy and swept by the wind.

★★★ **Prăzsky Hrad (Prague Royal Castle)** (ABY) – The castle windows in the long impressive south wall stare absentmindedly at the Malá Strana. When seen close-up in Castle Square (Hradcánské náměstí), the setting takes on a dramatic air. Statues of giants do battle with each other, making the guards in dazzling uniforms suddenly seem tiny.

At the end of the first courtyard, the Baroque Matthias Gate integrates into buildings dating from the reign of Maria Theresa. The combination of styles surprises practised eyes. Passageways lead into the second courtyard containing the Holy Cross Chapel and its richly ornate interior. In the third courtyard, the west front of the great Gothic cathedral rises vertiginously skywards.

★★★ **Katedrála sv.Vítá (St Vitus Cathedral)** (BY) – The twin spires and central bell-tower topped by an onion dome make St Vitus' Cathedral easy to recognise. Building began on the church in 1344. Later, two of the greatest Gothic architects in Europe, Matthieu of Arras and Peter Parlér, took over construction. Still, the cathedral was not completed until the late 19C and early 20C. The beautiful spacious interior houses treasures from every period of Bohemian art. Behind the altar, an extraordinary silver reliquary contains the remains of St John of Nepomuk. St Wenceslas' Chapel, a dazzling reminder of Gothic architecture, holds the saint's tomb and relics. Its walls are encrusted with semi-precious stones. The Bohemian Crown Jewels are kept in the treasure house above the chapel.

In front of the high altar, the vast white marble tomb contains the bodies of Emperor Ferdinand I of Habsburg, his wife, and his son, Maximilian II.

In the chancel and nave shine amazing stained-glass windows by Max Svabinsky and Mucha. These artists represent the "Czech Secession" movement.

★★ **Královský palác (Royal Palace)** (BY) – The royal palace served as the residence of the Lords of Bohemia from the 11C to the 16C. It reflects several periods of history. Above the Roman basement, Gothic rooms lead to one of the most surprising places in Prague – the **Vladislav Chamber**. Beneath the gigantic vaulted roof in the Flamboyant Gothic style, the austere early Renaissance windows are topped by amazing stone swirls seemingly defying the laws of gravity. The **equestrian staircase** enabled riders to reach the Vladislav Chamber where tournaments were held.

In 1618, two defenders of the Roman Catholic faith were thrown out of the windows of the Bohemian chancellery into the moat. Their defenestration marked the beginning of the Thirty Years' War.

★★ **Bazilika sv. Jiří (church of St George)** and **Jiřský klàster (convent)** (BY) – Behind the reddish Baroque west front of the Church of St-George lies one of the city's finest Romanesque sanctuary. Both church and convent were founded in the 10C. The church has been deconsecrated and is now used for chamber music concerts; the convent buildings around the cloisters have been ingeniously turned into the superb **National Gallery of Ancient Czech Art★★★**. Although works from the Renaissance, Mannerist and Baroque periods are also exhibited, the most outstanding pieces date from medieval times when Czech artists produced some of Europe's finest works of sacred art. Don't miss the Třeboń Altarpiece and works by the great masters, Vyšší Brod and Theodoric.

The three main courtyards in the castle were carefully repaved around 1920. Joze Plecnik, architect to President Masaryk, designed a majestic flight of steps running from the third courtyard down to vast **terraced gardens**.

Beyond St George's, the picturesque **Zlatá Ulička** (literally "Gold Alley") once housed the city's alchemists. The tiny houses are built into the castle walls.

★★ **Královský letohrádek (Belvedér)** (BX) – The walls and towers of the castle face north and are built high above a ravine called the "Stag's Moat". Further on, the great Baroque **Riding School** (Jízdárna) (ABY) is used for various exhibitions. Opposite stands the entrance to the **Royal Gardens** (Královská zahrada) (BXY). The well-maintained gardens contain some very rare species of plant. They run down a gentle slope to the elegant arches of the Belvedere, or royal summer palace. Building work began in 1532 on this castle, one of the first Renaissance constructions north of the Alps. In front, the famous "Singing Fountain" stands in the middle of a formal flower garden. The tiny waterfalls produce echoes in the basins.

★ **Hradčanske náměstí (Hradčany Square)** (ABY **37**) – This square in front of the castle faces west. Some of the city's largest mansions close off the sides. The elaborate "graffiti" paintings on which the frescoes are scratched in and daring gables make the **Schwarzenberg Palace★** (Schwarzenbersky palác) (AY **P**[4]) an amazing building. It now houses the Army's History Museum. Collections of weapons and other objects bear witness to the bitter fighting endured by Bohemia before the Christian era when it was the "outpost of Europe".

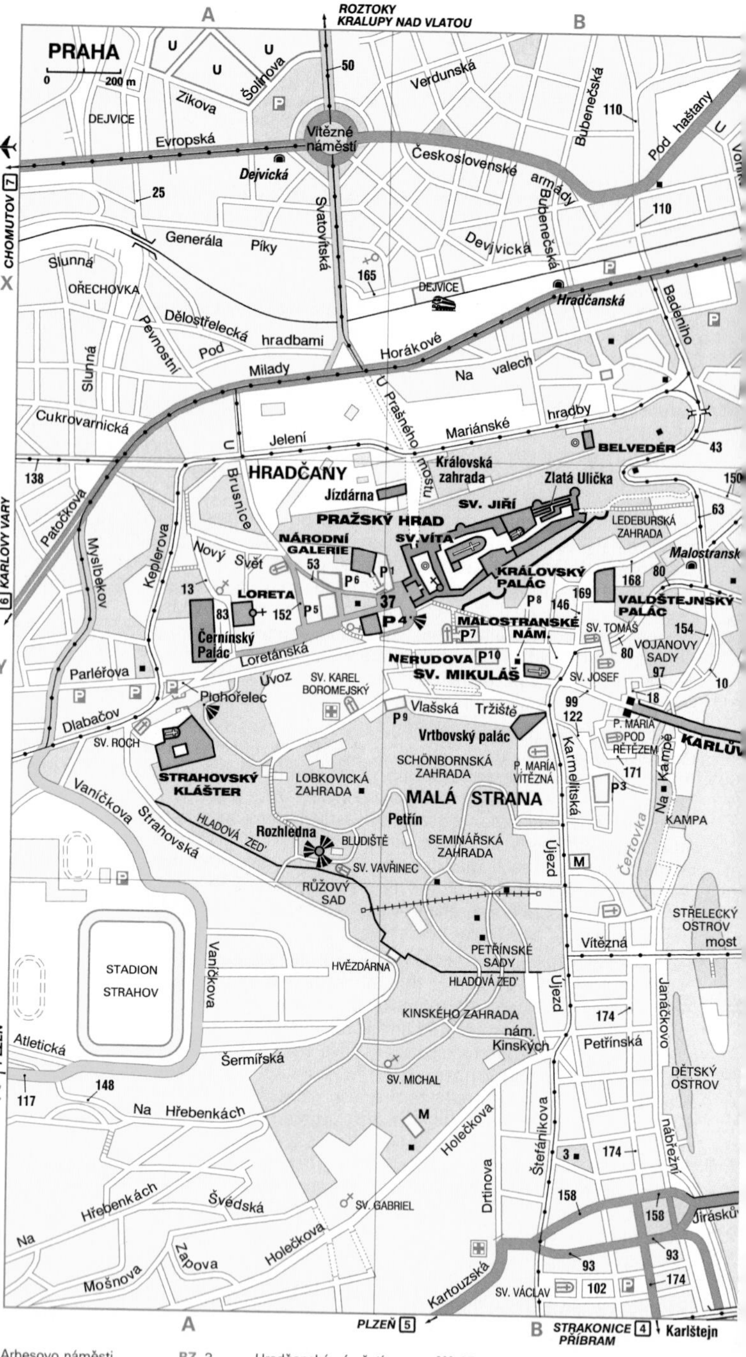

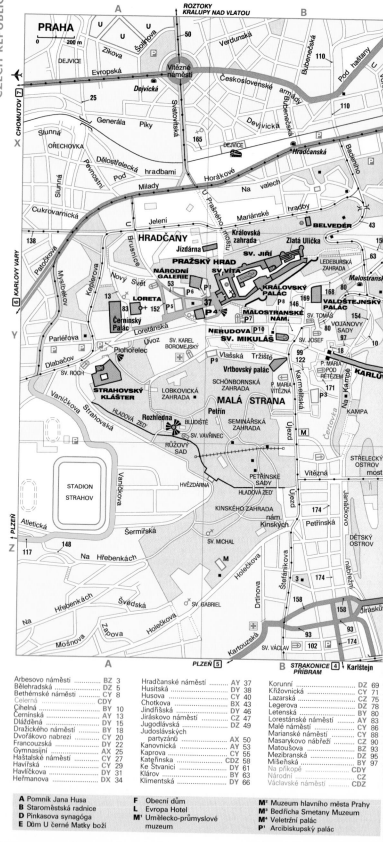

Arbesovo náměsti .... BZ 3
Bělehradská .... DZ 5
Bethémské náměsti .... CY 8
Celerná .... CDY
Cihelná .... BY 10
Černínská .... AY 13
Dlážděná .... DY 15
Dražického náměstí .... BY 18
Dvořákovo nabrezi .... CY 20
Francouzská .... DY 22
Gymnasijní .... AX 25
Haštalské náměstí .... CY 27
Havířská .... CY 29
Havlíčkova .... DY 31
Heřmanova .... DX 34

Hradčanské náměstí .... AY 37
Husitská .... DY 38
Husova .... CY 40
Chotkova .... BX 43
Jindřišská .... DY 46
Jiráskovo náměstí .... CZ 47
Jugodlávská .... DZ 49
Judoslávských partyzánů ..... AX 50
Kanovnická .... AY 53
Kaprova .... CY 55
Kateřinska .... CDZ 58
Ke Štvanici .... DY 61
Klárov .... BY 63
Klimentská .... DY 66

Korunní .... DZ 69
Křižovnická .... CY 71
Lazarská .... CZ 75
Legerova .... DZ 78
Letenská .... BY 80
Lorestánské náměstí .... AY 83
Malé náměstí .... CY 86
Marianské náměstí .... CY 88
Masarykovo nábřeží .... CZ 90
Matoušova .... BZ 93
Mezibranská .... DZ 95
Mišeňská .... BY 97
Na příkopě .... CDY
Národní .... CZ
Václavské náměstí .... CDZ

A Pomník Jana Husa
B Staroměstská radnice
D Pinkasova synagóga
E Dům U černé Matky boží
F Obecní dům
L Evropa Hotel
M¹ Umělecko-průmyslové muzeum
M² Muzeum hlavního města Prahy
M³ Bedřicha Smetany Muzeum
M⁴ Veletržní palác
P¹ Arcibiskupský palác

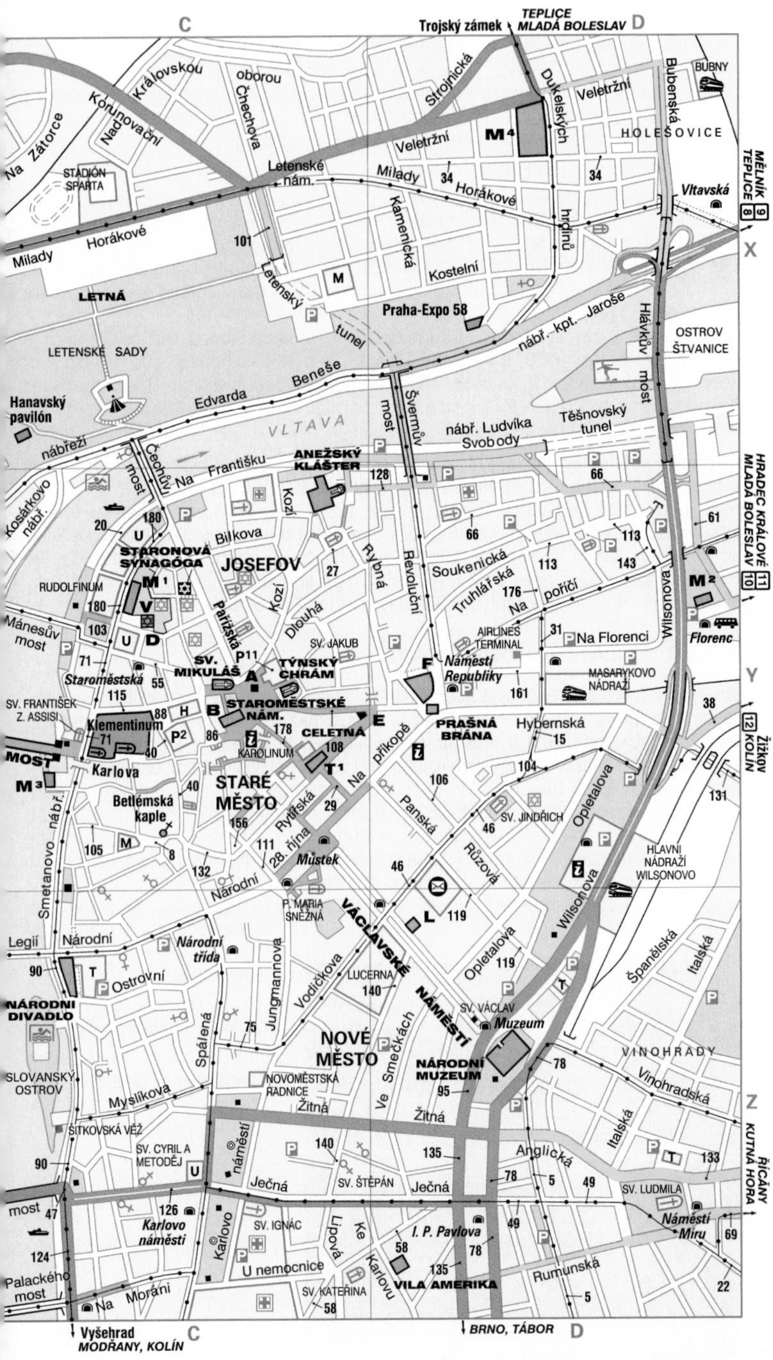

Mostecká	BY 99	Prokopská	BY 122	U lužického semináře	BY 154
Nad štolou	CX 101	Rašinovo nábřeží	CZ 124	Uhelný trh	CY 156
náměstí 14. října	BZ 102	Resslova	CZ 126	V botanice	BZ 158
náměstí Jana Palacha	CY 103	Řásnovka	DY 128	V celnici	DY 161
náměstí Maxima Gorkého	DY 104	Seifertova	DY 131	Václavkova	AX 165
Náprstkova	CY 105	Skořepka	CY 132	Valdštejnská	BY 168
Nekázanka	DY 106	Slezská	DZ 133	Valdštejnska náměstí	BY 169
Ovocný trh	CY 108	Sokolská	DZ 135	Velkopřevorské náměstí	BY 171
Pelléova	BX 110	Střešovická	AY 138	Zborovská	BZ 174
Perlová	CY 111	Štěpánská	DZ 140	Zlatnická	DY 176
Petrská	DY 113	Těšnov	DY 143	Zelezná	CY 178
Platnéřská	CY 115	Tomášská	BY 146	17 listopadu	CY 180
Pod Stadiony	AZ 117	Turistiká	AZ 148		
Politických vězňů	DZ 119	U Bruských Kasáren	BY 150		
		U kasáren	AY 152		

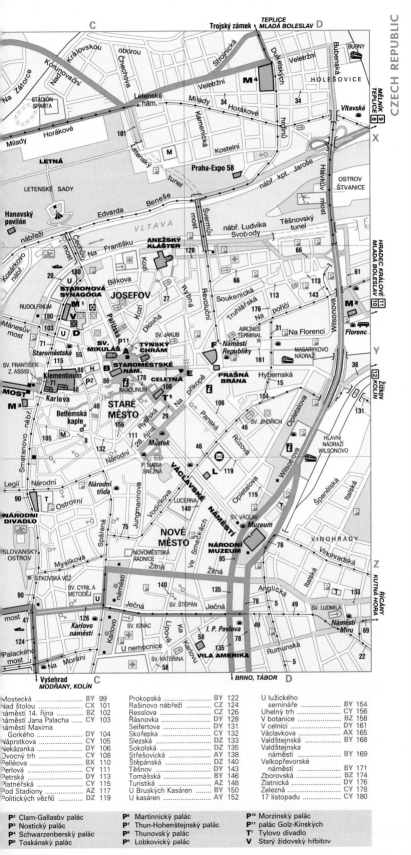

P² Clam-Gallasův palác
P³ Nostický palác
P⁴ Schwarzenberský palác
P⁵ Toskánský palác
P⁶ Martinnický palác
P⁷ Thun-Hohenštejnský palác
P⁸ Thunovský palác
P⁹ Lobkovický palác
P¹⁰ Morzinský palác
P¹¹ palác Golz-Kinských
T¹ Tylovo divadlo
V Starý židovský hřbitov

To the rear, the equally remarkable Archbishop's Palace houses the **National Gallery★★★** (Národní Galérie) (**AY**), with its admirable collection of European art. The Sternberg family once occupied the mansion. The gallery boasts works by masters such as Bruegel and Cranach, and French Impressionists and modern artists from Central Europe such as Klimt or Kokoschka.

★★**Loreta** (**AY**) – Prague's Loretta Church copies the Virgin Mary's House, a cowshed said to have been carried by angels from Palestine to the village of Loretto in Italy at the end of the 13C. The building demonstrates how the Virgin Mary was venerated during the rebirth of Roman Catholicism in Czech territories in the 17C.
The church of the Nativity of Jesus Christ is decorated in admirable Baroque style. The façade includes magnificent ciboria, among them the diamond-studded **Prague Sun** made in 1698.
Opposite the main bell-tower, Count Cerninsky commissioned the columns of a gigantic palace in 1669 (Cernínsky Palác) (**AY**). It has housed the Ministry of Foreign Affairs since 1920. After the Communist *coup d'état* in 1948, the third defenestration of Prague took place here. Foreign Minister Jan Masaryk fell to his death from his bathroom window.

★★**Strahovský Klášter (Strahov Monastery)** (**AY**) – The orchard-clad Petřín Hill rises steeply towards the austere buildings of this monastery. It has a double bell tower built in the 12C and reconstructed in the 17C. The monastery has been turned into a Literature Museum. The 18C library includes the outstanding **Philosophy Room** and **Theology Room**. At the top of the hill stands a replica of the Eiffel Tower (Rozhledna) (**AY**). It rises only 60m/195ft high and was built for the 1891 Fair, at the same time as the funicular railway to the Malá Strana.

★★★MALÁ STRANA (LOWER TOWN) (BY)

The lower town's streets and irregularly-shaped squares hemmed in between the castle and the river form one of the city's most picturesque districts. This used to be a market village until it was almost totally rebuilt after the Thirty Years' War. The Renaissance and Baroque mansions and town houses did not change the medieval structure; on the contrary. Instead, they blended into the complex network of narrow streets, giving each street corner an unexpected charm. Splendid churches include the ones dedicated to St Thomas, St Joseph, Our Lady under the Chain, and Our Lady of Victory. All stand around St Nicholas'. Secret gardens climb in terraces up towards the castle. Here, the city also has its closest connections with the river. The tree-lined streets seem protected by the foliage and, the Certovka (Devil's Stream) still works a waterwheel, forming an island in the Vltava.

Y. Travert/DIAF
Charles Bridge and Malá Strana

★★★**Karlů Most (Charles Bridge)** (**BCY**) – Until the 19C, the superb medieval Charles Bridge provided the only means of crossing the Vltava. Work began on Peter Parlér's 16 arches in 1357; they support a roadway some 500m/525yd long crossing the wide river from the tower in the old town to the tip of Kampa island into the heart of the Malá Strana. Baroque statues, some copies, decorate the bridge, making it much more than a mere roadway. The bridge has served as a market place, battlefield and execution site. It now symbolises the city of Prague, as well as being a meeting-place for the many tourists who have recently invaded the city.
At the entrance to the Charles Bridge *(right)* stands an **old mill** once part **of the Grand Priory**.

★★ **Malostranské náměstí** (BY) – On this square, named after the lower town, crowds wait for the red and yellow trams which creak and rattle their way up to the top of Karmelitska Street. An optical illusion gives the impression that the trams disappear inside the buildings next to St Thomas' Church. The townspeople join the flow of visitors who leave Charles Bridge behind them and climb to the castle overlooking the city. On the way, people stop to admire the aristocratic mansions high above the huge arches that line the sloping square. In its centre stands Central Europe's largest Baroque church, St Nicholas'.

★★★ **Sv. Mikuláš (St Nicholas Church)** (BY) – The austere architecture of the college buildings (now part of the university) highlights the ornate outside walls of the church dedicated to St Nicholas. The west front combines convex and concave planes. The great dome and adjacent bell-tower give the city its image. In the vast interior, statues and vaulting decorated with superb frescoes provide an ideal setting for concerts. St Nicholas' Church was the masterpiece of Kryštof Dienzenhofer and his son, Kilián Ignác.

A. Lorgnier/VISA

Interior of St-Nicholas Church

★★ **Nerudova** (BY) – This delightful street was named after Jan Neruda, A 19C chronicler who lived in the Lower Town. It climbs up to the castle, skirting magnificent Renaissance, Baroque and Rococo mansions. The Neruda House *(no 47)* is decorated with two suns. The Morzin Palace *(no 5)*, now the Romanian Embassy, has a splendid balcony supported by two Moors. The balcony on the Thun-Hohenstein Palace *(no 20)* is decorated with two eagles carved by Mr Braun.

★★ **Valdštejnsky palác (Wallenstein Palace)** (BY) – The palace was completed just before the assassination of its owner, General Wallenstein, in 1634. It remains one of Prague's most magnificent Renaissance palaces. On the ceiling of the main drawing room, a fresco represents Wallenstein as the god Mars leading the imperial armies. An impressive natural *sala terrena* looks down on the magnificent walled garden.

Vrtbovský palác, Vrtovská zahrada (Vrtba Palace and Gardens) (BY) – One of the most charming Baroque gardens in Prague lies on the other side of two courtyards in the Vrtba Palace. The sculptures were made in Braun's workshop.

★★★ STARÉ MĚSTO (OLD TOWN) (CY)

The Old Town used to be the trading centre of Prague during the Middle Ages. A network of winding streets covers the area between the River Vltava and the ring roads built by Narodni and Na Příkope along the line of the city walls. Narrow streets and amazing open spaces survived attempts by the city's leaders at the beginning of this century to restructure the glorious architectural confusion. Their Parisian-style boulevard, the Parizska, runs from the river bank to the old town main square, easing traffic travelling in a north-west direction. The same cannot be said of the east-west thoroughfare known as the Royal Road which was used for coronation processions in bygone days.

Betlémská kaple (CY), the **Bethlehem Chapel** where Jan Hus once preached, is lost in the maze of streets. Meanwhile, the splendidly renovated Tylovo divadlo (**CY T'**), an 18C **theatre**, stands proudly opposite the fruit market. Mozart gave his first performance here of *Don Giovanni* in 1787.

★★★ **Staroměstské náměstí (Old Town Square)** (CY) – Many of the most decisive events in Czech history have taken place in the town hall, the church of Our Lady of Týn and the houses and mansions flanking this central square. These days, the atmosphere is relaxed and happy. Young people meet around the great Pomník Jana husa or **Jan Hus monument** (CY **A**). Passers-by cast a glance at the goods offered by countless street vendors, while others stop for a drink at the pavement cafés. Every hour, a crowd gathers to admire the procession of Apostles and other allegorical figures on the famous **astronomical clock**★★ (Staromìstská radnice) (CY **B**). Above the clock stands the tower on the former town hall, offering one of the city's best **panoramic views**★★★. The view encompasses the dome and two bell-towers on the fine Baroque church of St Nicholas (CY) or **Sv. Mikuláš**★. On the square's east side, a delightful row of houses includes the Rococo Goltz-Kinsky palace, the Gothic Bell house and the Renaissance Týn School. The frontages seem luminous compared to the dark stonework, spires and steeples of the **church of Our Lady of Týn**★ (Tynsky chrám) (CY), built in the 14C.

Karlova (CY) – This busy thoroughfare and its neighbouring streets are dominated by souvenir shops and interesting glassware shops displaying fine pieces of Bohemian crystal.
The university of Prague is housed in the impressive building known as the **Klementinum** (CY). It contains a magnificent Baroque **library**★★ (early 18C).

★★ **Celetná** (CDY) – This is one of the most attractive streets in the city. The buildings are medieval in style but most of them have Baroque façades. The street runs westwards from the Praná brána (DY), the famous **Powder Tower**★, well restored in the 19C. Coronation processions set off from here. At the junction with the fruit market, another quite different landmark, the **Black Virgin's House**★ (Dům u černé Matky Bozí) (CDY **E**), represents a masterpiece of Czech Cubist architecture dating from 1911.

★★ **Obecní dům (Municipal House)** (DY **F**) – This extraordinary piece of architecture built between 1905 and 1911 is the town hall, a fine example of the exuberant Czech Secession movement. Beyond the sophisticated canopy above the main entrance, a complex interior combines staircases, galleries, restaurants and all sorts of public and semi-private areas including the prestigious Smetana Room. Many of the most fashionable artists of the day, such as Alfons Mucha, contributed to the decoration of the building, providing frescoes, stained-glass windows, and statues.

★ **Umělecko-průmyslové muzeum (Art Deco Museum)** (CY **M**¹) – The outstanding contribution made by artists and craftsmen from Czech territory to Europe's cultural heritage is evident in this museum's Art Deco collection. Space is at a premium here, restricting the number of exhibits on show. This explains why temporary exhibitions are sometimes organised in the neo-Renaissance Rudolfinium and Art College, both of which lie on the other side of the Nàmestí Jana Palacha. This square was named after the Czech student, Jan Palach, who set fire to himself in protest after the 1968 Soviet invasion.

★★ **Anežký klášter (St Agnes Convent)** (CXY) – The convent dedicated to St Agnes was renovated after being abandoned for 200 years. The 13C convent was named after its founding abbess, who was the sister of King Wenceslas I. She was canonised only a few days before the Velvet Revolution in 1989. The splendid St Saviour's Church and the Mary Magdalen Chapel are superb examples of early Gothic construction. St Francis' Church has been turned into a concert hall. The upper floors around the cloisters contain the **collection of 19C Czech paintings and sculptures**★ from the national gallery.

★★★ JOSEFOV (JEWISH QUARTER) (CY)

This maze of streets made up the oldest ghetto in Europe. It was cleaned up and redesigned in the late 19C. Old-fashioned buildings were demolished and replaced by wide streets like the Párizšká, the boulevard lined with luxurious apartment blocks built in an architectural style typical of Art Nouveau. The synagogues and cemetery were spared despite the zeal of the town planners. Later, the Nazis intended to integrate them into their "Museum of the Extinct Race". Despite the crowds of visitors, an almost tangible melancholy atmosphere reigns over this district. The hustle and bustle in the streets cannot conceal the emotion of seeing the early Gothic **Old-New Synagogue**★★ (Staronová synagóga) (CY). The tombstones in the **Old Jewish Cemetery**★★ (Starý Zidovský hrbitov) (CY), where the dead are buried on 12 levels because of the lack of space, are even more moving. This is the final resting place of Rabbi Loew, the great scholar and creator of the legendary Golem of Prague, as well as the mascot of certain Slav peoples who believe that the statue is capable of coming to life. Adjacent to the cemetery, the **Pinkas Synagogue** (Pinkasova synagóga) (CY **D**) lists the names on the walls of the 77297 Czech Jews exterminated by the Nazis.

★★★NOVÉ MĚSTO (NEW TOWN) (CDZ)

The New Town covers a much larger area than the other three "towns" in Prague. It was founded in the mid 14C by the imperial town planner, Emperor Charles IV, and rationally designed around three main market places, one of which has become the famous Wenceslas Square. In this spot, around the Gold Cross highlighting the square's junction with Na Prikope and 28 Rijna/Narodni lies the heart of the modern Prague. The Square is lined with department stores, shops, theatres and the busiest subway station in the city, Mustek. The expressway runs eastwards along the line of the old fortifications, intersecting with the great Secessionist-style railway station, the Opera House, and the National Museum, which looks tiny amid the traffic.

★★★**Václavské náměstí (Wenceslas Square)** (CDZ) – This tree-lined square resembles a boulevard. It faces southwest towards one of the most outstanding examples of late 19C Czech nationalist architecture, the **National Museum★** (Narodní muzeum) (DZ). The lavish interior contains countless collections of minerals, stuffed animals and finds resulting from archeological digs. The steps of the museum offer an unparalleled view of Prague. Below stands the great equestrian statue of the country's patron saint, Václav/Wenceslas I; the statue serves as a rendez-vous for locals. Not far away, the Jan Palach Memorial marks the spot where the martyr set fire to himself and committed suicide. Further on, the great boulevard has retained the atmosphere of the late 19C and early 20C. Its buildings are a perfect reflection of the architectural movements of the day. The delightful Secessionist façade of the **Europa Hotel** (DZ **L**) is undoubtedly the most remarkable of all the buildings. The sidewalks are crowded with people who enter shopping arcades through a labyrinth of covered passageways. In this secret "town within a town", the Lucerna Complex is watched over by the bust of its builder, Vaclav Havel's grandfather.

★★**Národni divadlo (National Theatre)** (CZ) – The National Theatre is located in one of the city's prime sites, at the junction where Narodní trída, or National Avenue, crosses the Vltava via the Legionnaires Bridge. The theatre is a monumental neo-Renaissance construction paid for by the Czech people to indicate their strong opposition to Germanic domination. It was completed in 1881 and almost immediately set on fire but money was rapidly found to pay for its reconstruction. Eminent artists who contributed to its ornate interior decoration grouped together under the name "National Theatre Generation". In the 1970s and 1980s new luxurious features were added to the highly controversial glass structure of the "New Stage" (Nova scena).

★**Muzeum hlavního města Prahy (City Museum)** (DY **M**²) – At no 24 of the busy eastbound shopping street called Na poříčí (DY), a remarkable building designed in the vigorous "national style" of the 1920s is decorated with sculptures in honour of the Czech legions during the First World War. Beyond the bridge on the ring road, a Classical building contains the city's history museum. The vast **model of Prague★★** represents a precise replica of the city as it was in 1834. It is a gem of archeological accuracy and is the museum's most outstanding exhibit.

►► Vila Amerika★ (DZ): The museum is devoted to the composer Antón Dvořák – Bedřicha Smetany Museum (CY **M**³): The museum is devoted to the composer Bedřich Smetana.

ADDITIONAL SIGHTS

★**Vyšehrad** – This fortress was built in the 11C on a rock upstream from the city. From it, a sheer drop plunges into the River Vltava. The myths and legends surrounding the fortress fed Romantic and nationalist feelings in the 19C. In the **national cemetery** here, the greatest representatives of the Czech nation are buried. Also in the fortress are St Martin's Rotunda and the impressive ruins of Baroque fortifications built by the Habsburgs. From the walls, there are superb views of the river and city. High above the valley stands the huge communist-built Palace of Culture (Palác kultury).

★**Žižkov** – The Žižkov Hill to the east of the city centre was the site chosen for the national memorial in 1920. It is still dominated by the gigantic equestrian statue of Jan Žižika, the proud one-eyed leader of the Hussite hordes.

★**Trojský zámek (Troja)** – The formal gardens around this Baroque palace look south to the Vltava as it flows towards the city centre. This holiday home of the Sternbergs was neglected for several decades before being enthusiastically restored. The interior is picturesque. The palace also has a splendid external flight of steps on which the carvings depict a battle between gods and giants. History has never revealed who won.

★**Letná** (CX) – From this plateau to the east of Hradcany, the city of Prague can be seen in all its splendour. Stop off at the Hanavsky Pavilion, a charming little café built in the Secessionist period, or at the restaurant in the Czechoslovak Pavilion built for the 1958 World Fair in Brussels and reconstructed (Praha-Expo 58).

When looking for a hotel or restaurant in Prague, use the Michelin Red Guide Europe, updated annually.

EXCURSIONS

★★**Hrad Karlštejn (Karlštejn Castle)** – *30km/19mi southwest.* This excursion in the winding wooded Berounka Valley is the most popular outing from Prague. Emperor Charles IV built this huge fortress to house the Crown Jewels, the imperial insignia and very valuable holy relics. Its current appearance results from over-enthusiastic restoration projects in the late 19C. Guided tours take tourists round the Imperial Palace and Mary Tower but visitors are no longer shown the greatest treasure in Karlstejn, the Holy Crucifix Chapel. Its walls encrusted with semi-precious stones and its paintings by the great master Theodoric proved to be too fragile to withstand the constant stream of visitors.

★★**Konopiště** – *40km/25mi southwest.* This early 14C Gothic fortress has been constantly enlarged over the centuries. It owes its present appearance to its last owner, Archduke Francis Ferdinand of Habsburg. He was the heir to the Austrian throne and gave the castle the Romantic medieval style fashionable at the time; he also added a very large collection of furniture. Ferdinand was so obsessed with hunting that the numerous trophies decorating the interior of the castle provide a Surrealist air. After leaving this fortress, the Archduke and his beloved wife, Sophie Chotek, began their last fatal trip to Sarajevo in the summer of 1914.

Zbraslav – *12km/7mi south.* This small town on the banks of the Vltava used to be very popular with visitors who came from Prague on a steamboat. Now, it is famous for its **collection of 19C and 20C Czech sculptures** brought here from **the National Gallery**★★. The collection is laid out in the buildings and park of **Zbraslav Abbey**. This majestic complex was designed by the original Baroque architect Santini in the early years of the 18C. It contains many works by the great 19C and 20C sculptors who did much to embellish Prague. The masterpieces from the 1920s and 1930s by artists such as Otto Gutfreund and Karel Dvořák highlight the originality of this relatively little-known school of sculpture.

★**Lidice** – *20km/12mi northwest.* In the spring of 1942, Czech parachutists assasinated the Third Reich's representative Heydrich. In reprisal, the Nazis wreaked vengeance on this innocent little mining village. The men were all murdered on the spot; the women and children were sent to the concentration camps. Like its population, Lidice seemed about to disappear for all time. But after the war, charming houses were rebuilt to the west of the old village where there is now a museum and a memorial park.

★**Terezín (Theresienstadt)** – *63km/39mi northwest.* The **Little Fortress** (Malá pevnost) stands alone and isolated. This sinister garrison town was built by the Habsburgs in the late 18C in order to keep watch over the northern approaches to Prague. For many years, the Little Fortress was used as a penitentiary – Princip, the Serbian assassin of Archduke Francis Ferdinand, was jailed here. Under the Nazis the entire town was turned into a concentration camp and all the Jews in Bohemia and Moravia were deported here. Guided tours of the town and the Little Fortress bring these years of martyrdom back to life; the most poignant site is the Muzeum Ghetta, the **Ghetto Museum**.

★★**Kutná Hora** – *69km/43mi to the east.* At the height of its glory, Kutná Hora, a mining town in which coins were minted in the late Middle Ages, was larger than London. The wealth of the town, like the wealth of the Bohemian monarchy, was based on its fabulous silver ore seams. Historic buildings serve as reminders of this period. They now stand sadly in the streets of what has become a peaceful provincial town. The largest building, at the end of the long wall of the Baroque-style Jesuit college, is **St Barbara's Cathedral**★★★, an extraordinary example of Flamboyant Gothic architecture bristling with flying buttresses and pinnacles. The recession in the mining industry in the middle of the 16C provided an abundant labour force to complete the building of the church. However, it was not until the arrival of Benedikt Ried that the nave was roofed with vaulting of which the ingenuity and elegance exceed his designs for the Vladislav Chamber in Prague.

This small hilltop town has many other sights – the Hradek Mining Museum, the medieval stone fountain, several magnificent mansions in the old town including the house with the great stone gable, the bell-tower on St John's Church and, best of all, the **Vlassky Dvur** or Italian Courtyard which was named after the Italian craftsmen who provided the know-how for the minting of Czech coinage.

In the suburb of **Sedlec**, a Gothic-Baroque chapel with a graveyard contains one of the most unusual sights in the country – a highly elaborate **ossuary** (kostnice) signed by its architect with bones.

★**Plzeň (Pilsen)** – *91km/57mi southwest.* Pilsen lies at the centre of western Bohemia and is now an industrial city. But the medieval checkerboard layout remains. On the vast Náměstí Republiky stands the tallest bell-tower (103m/335ft) in the country and a splendid Renaissance town hall decorated with paintings and frescoes. Pilsen is most famous for its beer which was developed in the middle of the 19C. Numerous brewers of "pils" have copied the original recipe, but the real Pilsner has never been equalled. The inevitable Beer Museum (Pivovarské muzeum) is worth a visit; it is housed in an old malting in the town centre. Another mandatory stop on any tour of the city is the Měštansky pivovar, the largest brewery in Pilsen, which has an entrance in the form of a triumphal arch, a popular restaurant and 9km/6mi of cellars.

SOUTHERN BOHEMIA

Michelin map 970 L 5

Upstream from Prague, dams across the River Vltava form a series of lakes mirroring the famous castles of **Orlik** and **Zvíkov**. The landscapes near the Austrian border represent the best of rural Bohemia, peaceful villages and "rural Baroque farmsteads", interspersed with castles and manor houses that once belonged to feudal lords. The region's historic towns are remarkably well-preserved.

★ČESKÝ KRUMLOV

Set in a meander of the River Vltava, this exquisite medieval town lies in the shadow of Schwarzenberg Castle, the Czech Republic's second largest fortress after the Hradcany in Prague.

A bridge crosses a narrow isthmus leading to picturesque cobbled streets and narrow alleyways. On the tiny main square, Náměstí Svornosti, a memorial marks homage to plague victims. The town hall is a good example of Renaissance architecture. The transept in the Flamboyant Gothic St Vitus' Church juts up above the river.

However, it is the huge castle on top of the north cliff that catches the eye. Building began in the 13C. During the Renaissance, it was enlarged to 300 rooms and the tower acquired its elegant upper section. In the 18C, a wonderful Baroque theatre and a ballroom decorated with *trompe-l'œil* paintings of merrymakers were added. A bridge, which is enclosed on several levels, spans a ravine, linking castle and gardens where statues and flower beds provide an atmosphere of a modern open-air theatre.

Throughout history, Krumlow has attracted a large number of conventional artists, but Viennese painter Egon Schiele best captured the spirit of the small ruined houses during his visits to the town before he died at an early age in 1918.

★★ČESKÉ BUDĚJOVICE

This is the main town in Southern Bohemia. Founded in 13C, it established royal authority in the border area and became one of the most elaborate urban communities in medieval Bohemia. It owed its rapid prosperity to trade with Austria, which lies only a short distance to the south. The town built one of the first passenger train links to Austria in 1827. The historic centre retains a checkerboard layout of streets around a spacious central square. The great Black Tower from the late 16C provides a good view of the town and the surrounding countryside.

ADDITIONAL SIGHTS

★**Hluboká Castle** – *10km/6mi northeast.* Hluboká Castle stands on an outcrop of rock high above the Vltava. The Schwarzenberg family rebuilt it in the mid 19C in a Bohemian interpretation of the English Tudor style. Beneath the towers, a museum contains some magnificent 19C furniture. The winter garden, made of wrought iron and glass, leads to byres that now house the Southern Bohemia Gallery with a superb collection of local medieval paintings and sculptures.

★★TÁBOR

Proud supporters of the martyr Jan Hus, led by their one-eyed General, Jan Žižká, founded this town-fortress on a hilltop in 1420. They gave it the biblical name of the Mount of the Transfiguration. Their love of warfare is evident in the collection of weapons and other objects in the museum located in the **former town hall**. The building's triple attics dominate the main square, Žižkovo náměstí. Beneath the square, a long network of underground passages were built for military purposes. The maze of well-preserved streets and narrow alleyways seem designed to confuse attackers. Extensive ruins of systems of defence can still be seen in Tábor. The round tower on Kostnov Castle dates from the 13C and is older than the town itself; next to it is the picturesque Bechyne Gate.

★★TŘEBOŇ

This tiny medieval town has an enchanting main square. In the centre stand a fountain and a memorial to plague victims. On the sides is an old brewery and a castle now housing a fishing museum. The Třeboň region has a great many rivers and streams. The water is drained off into a man-made lake used to breed carp for the traditional Czech Christmas meal. The 2km^2/1.25sq mi Svet Lake was created in 1571 on the outskirts of the town. Further North, the largest lake is Rozmberk, 7km^2/4.3sq mi.

Denmark

Area: 43 069km^2/16 366sq mi – **Population:** 5.1 million – **Capital:** København – **Currency:** Krone divided into 100 øre. **Time:** GMT + 1 hr in winter, GMT + 2 hr in summer.

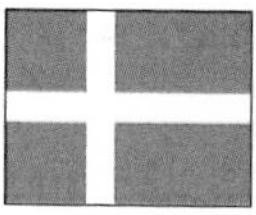

Danmark

Denmark is the smallest and most southerly Scandinavian country. It includes the Jutland peninsula and some 500 islands, although only 100 are inhabited. The two largest are Sjælland and Funen. The absence of mountains and the few hills makes Denmark an ideal setting for bicycle tours. Except for the western and northern parts of Jutland, the natural setting is both fertile and domesticated. Denmark's verdant landscapes and idyllic villages allow the attentive visitor to experience a pleasant lifestyle.
About one-fourth of the Danish population lives in the capital Copenhagen. This warm and friendly city reflects the open-hearted character of the Danish people. These "Nordic Latins" are gifted with a sense of humour that prevents them from taking themselves too seriously. Their innate appreciation of beauty combined with a strong dose of strong common sense has given the world the Danish style in the decorative arts, universally known as design.
The most famous Dane is no doubt Hans Christian Andersen, a brilliant storyteller. Other well-known Danes include philosopher Søren Kierkegaard, painters from the School of Skagen, the writer Karen Blixen, whose world-wide reputation was recently reinforced by the American film *Out of Africa*, the composer Carl Nielsen, and the painter Asger Jorn, founder of the Obra movement.

IN BRIEF

Entry Formalities – A passport is required for British, US, Canadian, Australian and Japanese citizens.

Shopping – Stores are generally open from 9.30am to 5.30pm.

Regional Cuisine: Smørrebrød – Slices of rye bread with herring and smoked meat, hard-boiled eggs and condiments.

KØBENHAVN★★★

COPENHAGEN – Population 622 000

Michelin map 970 L 3

Copenhagen covers the northeast coast of Sjælland Island. The medium-sized city is gracious and pleasant to the eye, with red-brick buildings and green copper roofs. The huge, busy harbour is a sign of the city's economic importance, but the visitor's first impression is that of a friendly, vital, and energetic city. Copenhagen carries its 800 years of history lightly, and the city's architectural heritage has been preserved with great care and acumen.

SLOTSHOLMEN *1 hr 30min*

Bishop Absalon, founder of Copenhagen, decided to build a fortress on this island, which, today, is surrounded by canals.

★**Christiansborg Slot** – This is the fifth castle built on the same site since 1167. Its austere granite facade, green copper roof and high square tower echo two earlier edifices. The Danish Parliament (Folketing), the Supreme Court and reception halls for the king are all housed here. There is a charming marble bridge in the Rococo style.

★**Marmorbroen** – This Rococo marble bridge leads to the vast courtyard of the Palace.

★★**Thorvaldsens Museum** – Located near the Palace chapel, the museum is dedicated to the memory of Denmark's most famous sculptor, Bertel Thordvaldsen (1770-1844).

★**Børsen (Stock Exchange)** – Christian IV, known as the Builder King, ordered the Børsen built in 1619. The stock exchange, which unfortunately cannot be visited, is a remarkable example of the Dutch Renaissance style. The tails of four dragons curl around the tall spire.

★STRØGET AND THE LATIN QUARTER *3hr*

★**Strøget** – The Strøget is the main shopping street of the capital, and is actually a series of 1.5km - 1 mile long pedestrian streets that cross the old town and connect Kongens Nytorv and Rådhuspladsen. Lined with interesting shops, attractive boutiques and café terraces, the Strøget is busy with street performances and parades by the Royal Guard. Two squares with fountains interrupt the lengthy avenue.

To the north of the Strøget is Copenhagen's **Latin Quarter★★**, reserved almost exclusively for pedestrians. The narrow streets are lined with small basement shops, a romantic square **Gråbrødretorv**, the **Round Tower★** (Rundetårn), an observatory built in 1642 by Christian IV, and the neo-Classical **cathedral** (Vor Frue Kirke) rebuilt following an English bombardment in 1807.

RÅDHUSPLADSEN AND TIVOLI *half a day*

The impressive red-brick **town hall** (Rådhuset) from the early 20C dominates the huge square (Rådhuspladsen). Inside, two rooms shelter Jens Olsen's **astronomical clock★** which shows local time everywhere in the world.
Some 200m/656ft further along the Vesterbrogade stands the entrance to **Tivoli★★**, one of the world's oldest and most prestigious amusement parks. More than 4 million visit each year. Tivoli offers imaginative and unique diversions. In the evening, 1000 Venetian lanterns suspended in the trees illuminate the gardens. The park is a favourite outing for Danish families.

MAIN MUSEUMS

★★★ **Nationalmuseet** – The National Museum, located not far from Rådhuspladsen, houses a collection tracing Denmark's history. The richest part of the collection dates from prehistoric times to AD 1000. The museum also includes antiquities from the Near East, Greece and Rome, an ethnographic collection and a collection of coins and medals.

★★★ **Ny Carlsberg Glyptotek** – This impressive building houses the collection of the brewer Carl Jacobsen. It was bequeathed to the state in 1897 and has since been enlarged with other works. The collection of French art from the 19C and 20C is especially impressive with a large selection of Impressionist and Post-Impressionist works, including many sculptures by Degas and Rodin.

★★ **Statens Museum for Kunst** – The Danish Fine Arts Museum contains the royal art collections. The museum is divided into two sections: foreign and Danish art. Of particular note is the magnificent collection of French 20C paintings, and several remarkable works by Edvard Munch.

★★★ROSENBORG SLOT *2hr*

This summer pavilion, located north of the University quarter, was built by Christian IV in 1633. It is considered a fine example of the Dutch Renaissance style with the characteristic red brick decorated with chalk. The pavilion served as a royal residence until 1710, when Frederick IV decided it was too small. Today it houses the personal collections of the royal family, open to the public since 1833.

KONGENS NYTORV AND THE NEW TOWN *2hr*

The new town, built in the late 17C and 18C along the sea shore, has become Copenhagen's most elegant neighbourhood.

★ **Kongens Nytorv** – The new royal square, completed in 1688, linked the overpopulated old town with the new town. It provided a impressive view of the newly constructed wide avenues.

★★ **Nyhavn** – The Nyhavn Canal was dug out in the 17C to allow ships to approach the royal square. Today Nyhavn is one of the most famous sites in Copenhagen. The picturesque canal, with its sailing ships and charming old-fashioned quays, is lined with narrow, brightly-painted houses and attractive cafés. In the summer, colourful crowds congregate around the canal.

★★ **Amalienborg** – Amalienburg, the heart of the new town, includes Queen Margaret's official residence, as well as the nearby square and **Marble Church★** (Marmorkirke). They all date from the 18C.

E. Baret

★KASTELLET AND THE LITTLE MERMAID *1 hr 30 min*

The **citadel** of Kastellet★, built in the 18C, stands in a vast park overlooking the sea. Nearby, the **Frihedmuseet** commemorates the Danish Resistance during World War II. The impressive three-tiered Gefion Fountain is located not far from the famous statue of the **Little Mermaid★** (Den Lille Havfrue). Her enigmatic form is perched on a rock at the water's edge; she gazes at the distant entrance of the huge harbour.

ADDITIONAL SIGHTS

Christianshavn – Christian IV's fortified town is crossed by a lengthy canal lined with trees and restored 18C houses. In the distance, the tall spire of the **Vor Frelsers Kirke** (Three Sisters) is visible. Thrill-seekers can climb the staircase that winds around the spire.

Frederiksberg – The famous **Royal Porcelain Factory of Copenhagen** (Kongelige Porcelænfabrik) is found to the north of Frederiksberg Park in Smallegade.

NORTH OF SJÆLLAND

Michelin map 970 L 3

North of Copenhagen, the island of Sjælland forms a vast peninsula. To the west lies the Roskilde fjord, to the north by the River Kattegat and to the east by the Øresund, the strait that separates Denmark from Sweden. Magnificent landscapes, a fertile natural terrain, impressive castles and rich museums make this region Denmark's prime tourist attraction.

E. Baret

Frederiksborg Castle

★★★FREDERIKSBORG SLOT (FREDERIKSBORG CASTLE) *2hr*

Located 35km/16mi north of the capital, this huge red brick castle stands in the middle of a lake. It represents a superb example of Renaissance architecture. By the 19C, the royal family had moved out. The castle was transformed into the National History Museum and opened to the public in 1882.
The Baroque castle of **Fredensborg**, 9km/5mi from Frederiksborg, is located on the shores of Lake Esrum. It is currently the royal family's summer residence.

THE DANISH RIVIERA

This flattering name refers to the coastal strip (45km/28mi) separating the capital from the small town of Helsingør, home of the famous Elsinore Castle. Leaving Copenhagen and driving north, many interesting sights tempt the tourist. Tiny idyllic ports and charming villas are surrounded by magnificent trees. The first stop, 10km/6mi from the capital, is the **Ordrupgård★★**, an impressive residence set in a landscaped park. The residence houses a superb collection of Danish and French paintings. The Impressionist and post-Impressionist periods are particularly well represented.
Some 15km/9mi further on is **Rungstedlund★**, birthplace of Africa adventurer and author Karen Blixen. Her home is located near a tiny port for pleasure-boats. Since her death, it has been transformed into a museum.
10km/6mi further north is one of Denmark's most interesting museums of modern art, **Louisiana★★**. In this extraordinary setting, the sculpture displayed takes on a new dimension.

The coastal road ends at Helsingør (Elsinore) with its austere castle overlooking the water. According to Shakespeare, the dark tragedy of Prince Hamlet took place here at **Kronborg Slot**★★★. The old quarters of Helsingør have been restored and make for a pleasant walk.

★★ROSKILDE

Roskilde was the capital of Denmark during the Viking period. It is located at the tip of a long, narrow fjord 30km/18mi from Copenhagen. For centuries, the magnificent red-brick **cathedral** topped with twin towers served as the final resting place of Danish kings. A modern museum of unusual design, the **Vikingeskibshallen**, contains the impressive remains of five Viking ships discovered in 1962 at the bottom of the fjord.

ROLD SKOV

Rold Skov, the largest Danish forest, is located in the heart of Jutland (Jylland). Its varied landscape, with heaths, marshes and vast stretches of forest with alternating patches of conifer and beech trees, attract nature lovers. The town of **Rebild**, 3km/2mi - west of Skørping, brings together Americans of Danish descent every 4 July. In 1912, a number of these descendants purchased the hills that surround the town and donated the land to the Danish government to create a national park. They were given permission to celebrate the American holiday Independence Day. **Lincoln blokhuset**, Lincoln's log cabin, houses a museum dedicated to Danish immigrants who settled in the United States.

For further details on Denmark, consult the Michelin Green Guide Scandinavia Finland.
When looking for a hotel or restaurant in Copenhagen, use the Michelin Red Guide Europe, updated annually.

The Vikings

The Vikings were strong warriors and fearless seamen. They played an enormous role in Northern Europe from the 8C to the 11C. For three centuries, Danes, Norwegians and Swedes pillaged the coasts of Western Europe. At the same time they traded as far as the Mediterranean Sea. The Vikings were also peaceful farmers and skilful crafstmen. Viking society was well organised, with a strong central authority. The Vikings converted to Christianity during the 10C.
Today, only vestiges of fortresses, wrecked ships, runic inscriptions on huge blocks of stone, and a few objects found buried in the ground, remain as testimony to this vibrant civilisation.

Finland

Area: 338 145km^2/128 495sq mi – **Population:** 4.9 million – **Capital:** Helsinki (Helsingfors) – **Currency:** markka (mark) divided into 100 penniä, and Euro (5,94573 FIM) – **Time:** GMT + 2 hr in winter, GMT + 3 hr in summer.

Suomi

For centuries Finland was controlled by its Swedish and Russian neighbours. Only recently has the country reaffirmed its identity and taken its rightful place among European nations. Geographically, Finland is part of Scandinavia. Its landscapes resemble the rest of the region. Immense forests surround innumerable lakes. A vast plain dominates the north. Small islands string along the Baltic coast.

Nevertheless, Finland remains the least Scandinavian of the Nordic countries. Finns did not descend from the Vikings. Their ancestors migrated from the East long before the Christian Era, and the Finnish language is related to Estonian and Hungarian.

The unique Finnish lifestyle centres around nature. This passionate love of the outdoors was superbly expressed by the composer **Jean Sibelius** (1865-1957) in his symphonic poem *Finlandia*. Architecture, especially the works of Eliel Saarinen (1873-1950) and Alvar Aalto (1898-1976), offers additional insights into Finnish culture.

IN BRIEF

Entry Formalities – A valid passport is required for British, US, Canadian and Japanese citizens.

Shopping – Stores are generally open Mondays through Saturdays from 9am to 6pm or 7pm. Typical souvenirs include porcelain, jewellery, glassware, furs and wooden objects.

Saunas – Nothing could be more natural than this typically Finnish ritual. Work up a good sweat and then plunge into icy water. In the country that invented the sauna, do not miss this unique experience.

HELSINKI/HELSINGFORS★★★

Population 491 177

Michelin map 970 P 1

Europe's most northern capital is located on a peninsula jutting out into the Baltic Sea. It has only been a capital since the Czar declared Finland a *Grand Duchy of Russia* in 1812. In less than two centuries, however Helsinki has acquired a varied and unusual architectural heritage and unique character different from other Nordic centres. The city is compact, and most sights are accessible on foot.

THE NEO-CLASSICAL QUARTER

The city centre was designed in the early 19C by the German architect Carl Ludvig Engel and his assistant Johan Albert Ehrenström. Two different squares dominate the neighbourhood, Senate Square and Market Square.

★★★ **Senaatintori** – This vast square, bordered with elegant buildings in the purest neo-Classical style, is crowned to the north by Carl Ludvig Engel's magnificent **Lutheran Cathedral★** (Tuomiokirkko). On other sides, various buildings in empire-yellow include the **University** and the **Senate**. A statue of Czar Alexander II stands in the square's centre.

At the end of Aleksanterinkatu, **Uspenskin katedraali**, the **Russian Orthodox cathedral★** soars with bulb-shaped domes. Icons decorate the interior.

★★ **Kauppatori** – Further west next to the port lies Market Square. Highly coloured stands of flowers, fruit and fresh fish create a colourful atmosphere. The **Presidentinlinna**, the presidential residence since 1919, the **Supreme Court**, and the **town hall** stand facing the sea.

★★ **Esplanadi** – This large avenue lined with elegant boutiques links the neo-Classical and modern neighbourhoods. To the north, the **Museum of Fine Arts**★★ (Ateneum) houses a rich collection of Finnish painting, including numerous works by Gallen-Kallela and Edelfelt. It also boasts a fine collection of international art, including paintings by Van Gogh, Gauguin, Chagall, and Munch.

THE 20C CENTURY CITY

Rautatieasema★★, the main train station, represents a superb example of Saarinen's Art Nouveau style. To the west, the long **Mannerheimintie** street leads to the city centre. The avenue is lined with buildings from the 20C. Towards the north-west stands firstly the **Kiasma** (Modern Art Museum), then the **Eduskuntatalo**★, the Parliament building, erected in 1931. Further on is the **Kansallismuseo**★★, the National Museum, a curious building in the Finnish version of the Romantic style. Then comes the **Finlandiatalo**★★, a concert hall built on the shores of Töölön Bay, a masterpiece by Alvar Aalto. On the other side of the Mannerheiminti, several streets lead to the **Temppeliaukion kirkko**★★, a circular church carved out of the rock and topped with a copper dome.
Further to the right stands the **Olympiastadion**★. The Olympic Stadium was built for the 1940 games but was actually used in 1952. Nearby to the left, **Sibelius Park** houses a **monument**★ to the composer. Eila Hiltunen created the design out of tubes of steel reminiscent of organ pipes.

THE ISLANDS

Among the countless islands that dot the coastline, Seurasaari and Suomenlinna are famous for their calm, peaceful atmosphere. **Seurasaari**★★, connected to Helsinki by a bridge, contains a charming open-air museum of 100 wooden houses from different regions dating from the 18C and 19C. **Suomenlinna**★★, can be reached by ferry starting from Kauppatori. It actually is a group of six islands. Among the islands stands a fortress, built in the 18C by the Swedes, which now shelters several museums.

EXCURSIONS

★★ **Hvitträsk** – *30km/18mi to the west by route no 51*. This house in the forest was built in the early 20C by three famous architects: Gesellius, Lindgren and Saarinen. The house served as a meeting place for many artists, including Sibelius, Gorki, Gallen-Kallela and Munch.

★★ **Porvoo/Borgå** – *50km/30mi to the east by E18*. From the town's rich medieval past, only the granite cathedral decorated with red brick has survived. Most of the wooden houses date from the late 18C and early 19C. Just beyond Market Square, admire a number of buildings in the Empire style by Carl Ludvig Engel.

C. Boisvieux

Porvoo/Borgå

JÄRVI-SUOMI★★

LAKE DISTRICT

Michelin map 985 J 24, 26 and K 20-26.

From the city of Tampere to the Russian border, southeast Finland is dotted with thousands of lakes. There are so many that the exact number remains unknown. The lakes were formed about 10 000 years ago after the retreat of the ice cap covering Finland. The lakes are often connected, and form a complex network of navigable waterways which, today, are reserved for pleasure-boating. The two most important networks are **Lake Päijänne** to the west and, **Lake Saimaa** to the east. Small tourist roads run through this exceptional environment of lakes, islands, and dense forests.

Savonlinna★★ is located on a group of islands that separate two lakes. The charming town contains a port, market square and medieval castle where the internationally renowned Opera Festival is held each summer.

To the east lies the former province of Karelia. The other half of the province was ceded to Russia in 1945. The towns of **Kuopio★** and **Joensuu** are living examples of the rich cultural heritage of this divided province.

LAPLAND★★★

Lapland **(Sápmi)** refers to the cold, empty region that covers the northern part of Scandinavia from Norway's northwest coast to the White Sea. Over the centuries, Laplanders have adapted to a hostile environment and a harsh climate. This nomadic people originated from the Lake Onega region in Russia. Today, they number about 70 000 scattered over a huge land area. The **Sami** live off hunting, fishing and the reindeer herds which they follow in seasonal migrations. This traditional lifestyle is threatened by modern civilisation. Fortunately, the Sami are aware of the danger and are attempting to preserve their language, music, brightly-coloured costumes and crafts.

★★**Rovaniemi** – Rovaniemi, the capital of Finnish Lapland, was destroyed during the Second World War and was rebuilt following a design by Alvar Aalto based on the shape of a reindeer antler. The **Cultural and Administrative Centre★★** is considered one of the famous architect's masterpieces.

★**Inari** – The village is located far to the north on the shores of a huge lake, Inarijärvi. It is an important centre of Sami culture, with a church and an **open-air museum★★** (Saamelaismuseo) illustrating the history of Lapland through traditional buildings.

For further details on Finland, consult the Michelin Green Guide Scandinavia Finland.

When looking for a hotel or restaurant in Helsinki, use the Michelin Red Guide Europe, updated annually.

France

France

Area: 551 602km^2 – 212 073sq mi – **Population:** 57 700 000 – **Capital:** Paris – **Currency:** French franc divided into 100 centimes, and Euro (6,55957 FRF) – **Time:** GMT + 1 hr in winter, GMT + 2 hr in summer

France is known as the "Hexagon" because of its shape. The country extends from the North plains to the Pyrenees in the south, from the jagged coast of Brittany to the Alpine glaciers, and from the sandy beaches of Bordeaux to the left bank of the Rhine. Its geographic position and history have turned it into a mosaic of distinct regions which have kept alive their customs and traditions.
France is known throughout the world for its luxury goods, its *haute couture* and perfumes and its gourmet food. Each region has its own specialities always accompanied by either a local wine of quality or by one of the fine wines for which France is justly famous. Alsace, Bordeaux, Burgundy, Champagne and the Loire Valley are names which not only evoke regions of picturesque beauty, but also the delights of Bacchus.

IN BRIEF

Entry formalities – Passports are required for American and Canadian citizens. Visas for Australian citizens.

Shopping – Department stores are usually open Mondays to Saturdays, 9am to 6.30pm or 7.30pm and hypermarkets until 9pm or 10pm. Small shops are often closed at lunchtime.

Souvenirs – France, and Paris in particular, is internationally reputed for its fashion, haute couture, jewellery, perfumes and leather goods. A country which loves good food and good living, France offers a marvellous range of regional specialities which make wonderful souvenirs. Each region proposes mouth-watering presentation boxes and baskets containing samples of local products. Handicrafts can be found throughout the country: fabrics, Christmas crib figures and pottery in Provence, articles made of olive-wood along the Mediterranean, earthenware in Quimper (Brittany), lace in Alençon, Argentan and Bayeux (Normandy), knives in Thiers (Auvergne) and Laguiole (Aveyron).

Cafés – These are one of the country's most charming features and often have their regulars. Whether they are small provincial bars or large open-air cafés, they are perfect for reading, writing and chatting or simply watching the world go by. In the capital, a bistro can mean anything from a small local *zinc* (or bar) to establishments offering elaborate meals. In Lyons, the *bouchon* is a must. These tiny restaurants serve a selection of cold cuts with St-Marcellin cheese and Beaujolais wine.

Outdoor Markets – Traditional markets, flower markets, flea markets – each town has its own picturesque rows of colourful stalls where people can meet and chat and visitors can soak in the local atmosphere. In Alsace, the Christmas markets, which go

A. Eil/MICHELIN

Paris – Terrace of the Deux Magots café

back to the Germanic Holy Roman Empire, are part of the festive tradition. Held on the Saturday between the 1st Sunday of Advent and December 24, they sell a wide variety of Christmas decorations, Christmas trees, crib figures, toys, and even turkeys and *foie gras*. The Christmas markets in Strasbourg and Kayersberg are among the oldest and most famous.

An Original Holiday – For those with a little time to spare, a river trip is an unusual holiday. France has the largest navigable network in Europe stretching about 8500km/5300mi. The slow speed of a river boat (no more than 6kph/3.5mph) is a perfect way to discover the country's many tourist attractions.
Because of the high demand, apply to the Syndicat national des loueurs de bateaux de plaisance, Port de Javel-Haut, 75015 Paris (telephone: 01 44 37 04 00). A licence is not required for boats with less than ten horsepower. GRAFOCARTE at 125, rue Jean-Jacques Rousseau, 92132 Issy-les-Moulineaux (telephone: 01 41 09 19 00) sells trilingual guides in French, English and German about cruising on French rivers and canals.

Five weeks of football or France triumphant

From 10 June to 12 July 1998, France thrilled to the rhythm of the 16th Football World Cup played in ten cities throughout France (Bordeaux, Toulouse, Montpellier, Marseilles, Lyon, St-Étienne, Nantes, Paris, St-Denis and Lens). For football fans and fanatics, it was a time of passionate involvement and celebration that left those with little interest in sport cold. By the end of the five weeks, however, a good many of the initially unenthusiastic had been caught up in the general excitement.
In the final between Brazil and France at the Stade de France in St-Denis, the French team swept to victory by 3 goals to 0 and received the much-coveted gold trophy from the hands of the French President, Jacques Chirac. It was a historic day celebrated in the capital and length and breadth of France by delirious crowds. Paris and the Champs-Élysées had seen nothing like it since the Liberation.
The next World Cup will be played in Japan and South Korea in 2002.

ALSACE and LORRAINE

In the east of France, the provinces of Alsace and Lorraine and the Vosges Mountains offer a wide variety of landscapes. They include mountain roads (Route des Crêtes) lined with numerous lakes, such as Gérardmer which lies at the foot of a winter ski resort/summer sports centre. Lorraine boasts a number of highly reputed spas including Vittel, Contrexéville and Bourbonne-les-Bains. Not far from the Rhine, the Route du Vin winds through vineyards from Marlenheim to Thann. The delightful little villages, their timber-frame houses brightly decorated with flowers, include Obernai, Andlau, Ribeauville, Riquewihr, and Eguisheim.
The food is original. Strasbourg sausages, sauerkraut, cockerel in Riesling, Munster cheese and *kugelhopf* cake with raisins and almonds have made the gastronomic reputation of Alsace. Quiche, a savoury tart containing eggs, cream and bacon pieces, is typical of Lorraine. Those with a sweet tooth will be tempted by madeleines in Commercy, *bergamots* in Nancy and almond sweets *(dragées)* in Verdun. The Alsatian vineyards are of high quality, with a wonderful selection of Riesling, Gewurtztraminer, Muscat, Pinot blanc, and Sylvaner. There are also Alsatian beers and fruit-flavoured liqueurs.

★★★COLMAR Population 63 498. Michelin map 970 J 5

The charm of Colmar lies in the Alsatian character of its streets. Attractive sculpted and decorated houses dominate both the Old Town and the **Little Venice★** quarter. The city's location along the Route du Vin and at the entrance to Munster Valley, makes it an excellent excursion centre.
In 1834, **Frédéric Bartholdi**, sculptor of the Statue of Liberty in New York, the statue of General Rapp and the Wine Grower's Fountain in Colmar and the Lion in Belfort, was born here. His birthplace has been converted into a museum (30, rue des Marchands).

★★★**Unterlinden Museum** – Housed in A 13C convent whose name means "under the linden trees," this museum contains the famous **Issenheim Altarpiece★★★**. Grünewald painted this 16C masterpiece to decorate the chapel of the Antonites' Monastery in Issenheim, a nursing home for people suffering from St Anthony's fire or epidemic gangrene. In the middle, a harrowing, dramatic Crucifixion offers a spiritual vision of suffering.

►► Church of the Dominicans (*Virgin in the Rose Bower*★★ by Schongauer, stained glass★) – Turckheim (6km/4mi west; night watchman every evening May to October).

★★MULHOUSE Population 108 357. Michelin map 970 J 6

Mulhouse, on the Ill River and the canal joining up the Rhône and the Rhine, is a prosperous industrial city with many technological museums, taverns and wine bars.

★★★**Musée national de l'Automobile (National Motor Museum) – Schlumpf Collection** – The fabulous collection of some 500 vintage cars collected by the Schlumpf brothers illustrates more than 100 years in the history of the motor vehicle – from the 1878 steam-powered Jacquot to the Citroën Xenia of the Year 2000. In between, there is Charlie Chaplin's Rolls-Royce Phaeton III limousine and a series of Bugattis, including two Royales.

★★★**Musée français du Chemin de fer (National Railway Museum)** – The museum exhibits rolling stock from the earliest days to the present. It features both steam and electric engines, including the BB 9004 which held the world train speed record in 1955 at 331kph/207mph.

★**Musée de l'impression sur étoffes (Printed Fabrics Museum)** – The first-ever printed fabrics factory was set up in Mulhouse in 1746. Three large rooms display collections of fabrics from France and around the world.

►► Musée historique★★ (History Museum) – Parc zoologique et botanique★★ (Zoo and Botanical Gardens) – Musée du Papier peint★ (Wallpaper Museum – in Rixheim – 6km/4mi east) – Écomusée d'Alsace★★ (Open-air Museum of Alsatian Crafts – in Ungersheim – 12km/7.5mi north).

★★★NANCY Population 99 351. Michelin map 970 J 5

Although Nancy was founded in the 11C, its history really began with the death of Charles the Bold, the last Duke of Burgundy on 5 January 1477, while the town was under siege. Charles the Bold coveted Lorraine because it lay between his Burgundian and Flemish possessions. But his body was found in an icy pond half-devoured by wolves.

The former capital of the Dukes of Lorraine owes its beautiful vistas and monuments to Louis XV's father-in-law, Stanislas Leszczyski. The dethroned king of Poland found himself on the throne of Nancy when the Duchy of Lorraine was exchanged for Tuscany in 1738.

★★★**Place Stanislas** – The square is the work of the architect Emmanuel Héré, who designed the city hall (Hôtel de Ville) and surrounding buildings. Jean Lamour, responsible for the gilded wrought-iron work. The result of this collaboration from 1751 to 1760 is perfect harmony of proportions, line and detail.

Between 1900 and 1910, the School of Nancy demonstrated such architectural vigour that the city became one of the European capitals of Art Nouveau, alongside Brussels and Vienna.

★★**Musée de l'École de Nancy (School of Nancy Museum)** – It offers a remarkable overview of furniture by Gallé and Majorelle; glass roofs by Gallé, Daum, Muller; stained glass by Gruber, along with posters and bound books.

►► Musée des Beaux-Arts★★ (Fine Arts Museum) – Palais ducal★★ (Ducal Palace) and Musée historique lorrain★★★ (Lorraine Historical Museum) – Place de la Carrière★ – Église et couvent des Cordeliers★ (Franciscan Church and Friary).

★★★STRASBOURG Population 252 338. Michelin map 970 J 5

Strasbourg, the intellectual and economic capital of Alsace, is, as its Germanic name indicates, the city of roads. A small town in the time of Julius Caesar, it rapidly became a prosperous city and a meeting point of different peoples. As a result, it was often pillaged, burnt to the ground and rebuilt. Since 1949, it has been the headquarters of the Council of Europe.

★★★**Cathédrale Notre-Dame** – Construction of this magnificent red Vosges sandstone building began in 1176; the **façade**★★★ was executed in 1284, and the 142m/466ft **spire**★★★, an architectural masterpiece, was built from 1399 to 1419. The tympanum on the central portal illustrates the Passion, while the parable of the Wise and the Foolish Virgins is told on the right portal, with the famous statue of the Seducer. Inside, in the south transept, near the **Pillar of the Angels** and the 13C **Last Judgement**★★, an astronomical clock attracts visitors every day at 12.30pm.

★**Palais Rohan** – Architect Robert de Cotte built this 18C palace for the Cardinal of Rohan. The apartments are among the most beautiful French interiors of the period. Several museums inside contain rich collections of ceramics, paintings and archeological exhibits.

★★ **La Petite France** – Once the home of fishermen, tanners and millers, this is one of best-conserved quarters of Old Strasbourg. Timber-framed houses reflect in the canal, and covered bridges and the Vauban Dam provide a magnificent **view**★★.

►► Église St-Thomas (mausoleum of Marshall de Saxe★★★) – Musée alsacien★★ (Alsatian Museum) – Boat trips on the Ill★ – Cruises on the Rhine.

VERDUN Population 20 753. Michelin map 970 I 5

The seat of a bishop and a fortress town, Verdun entered the mainstream of history with the treaty of 843 under which Charlemagne's grandsons shared his Empire among themselves. Its strategic position on the Meuse River made it the site of important military events. During the First World War, extraordinary acts of heroism and courage took place during some of the bloodiest fighting on the Western Front from 21 February 1916 to 20 August 1917. Nearly 400 000 French soldiers and as many Germans as well as thousands of American soldiers were killed. Several decades after this huge massacre, traces of battle still are visible in the sparse vegetation.

AUVERGNE

Auvergne, with its **volcanoes**★★★ of every age, shape and size, all extinct, has unique scenery for France. The Dôme and Dore Mountains and Puy Mary have produced a wide variety of lakes – Aydat, Chambon, Guéry and Pavin. The climb to the top of Puy de Sancy, the highest peak in Central France (1 885m/6 183ft), or Puy de Dôme, provides an extraordinary, singular sensation. In both cases, the view is breathtaking, particularly at sunset; a lunar landscape stretchs to the horizon.
Another characteristic feature of Auvergne is its wealth of mineral and thermal springs. Its **spas** at Vichy, Royat, Mont-Dore, and La Bourboule, attract thousands of people who come to take the waters every year. The region is also famous for its **Romanesque churches**★★. Outside, magnificently-stepped chevets are dominated by octagonal bell towers, Inside, barrel vaults are supported by imaginatively sculpted capitals. The most beautiful are Issoire, Orchival, St-Nectaire, St-Saturnin and Notre Dame du Port in Clermont-Ferrand. Gothic art has left its mark in the Abbey Church of La Chaise-Dieu.

J. Damase

Lake Chambon

★★LA CHAISE-DIEU Population 778

Solidly built of granite, **St Robert's Abbey Church**★★ (Église abbatiale de St-Robert) produces an impression of grandeur and severity. The **chancel**★★ is surrounded by beautiful 15C oak stalls. Admirable early 16C wool, linen and silk **tapestries**★★★ come from Arras and Brussels. Their subjects were taken from both the Old and New Testament.

★★CLERMONT-FERRAND Population 136 181. Michelin map 970 I 6

This site, in the heart of Auvergne, owes its originality to volcanic eruption. The black lava used to make the historical houses and cathedral in the old quarter produce an unusual townscape.
Clermont, an episcopal town, was rivalled by the feudal city of Montferrand and the judicial centre of Riom. In 1630, however, Clermont won the day. Montferrand was attached to its neighbour and the name of Clermont-Ferrand was adopted.

★★**Basilique de Notre-Dame du Port** – Built in about 1150, this Romanesque church is one of the finest in the Lower Auvergne. The raised **chancel**★★★ is surrounded by an ambulatory, in which the excellent lighting shows to advantage the lively, animated carvings on the **capitals**★★.

★★**Cathédrale Notre-Dame-de-l'Assomption (Cathedral Our Lady of the Assumption)** – The cathedral offers a striking contrast with the Basilica of Notre-Dame-du-Port. Its sombre colour is due to its construction from Volvic lava. The **stained glass medallions**★★ in the chancel illustrate the Life of Christ and the Saints. The **rose windows**★ in the transept are particularly striking.

►► Musée des Beaux-Arts★★ (Fine Arts Museum - inspired by the Guggenheim Museum in New York).

EXCURSIONS

★★**Brioude** – *60km/38mi southeast.* **St Julian's Basilica**★★ (Basilique St-Julien), the largest Romanesque church in Auvergne, is built on the spot where a Roman centurion is said to have suffered martyrdom in 304. In the **east end**★★, buttresses support the chapel. They are decorated with stone mosaics, while the cornices rest on modillions carved with monsters, human figures and foliage. Inside, the **capitals**★★ are elaborately sculpted.

★★**Issoire** – *28km/17.5mi southeast.* In the middle of fertile countryside, **St Austremoine Abbey**★★ (Ancienne Abbatiale) was built in the 12C. The east end is a fine example of Romanesque art; its carvings depict the signs of the zodiac. Inside, the historiated **capitals**★ illustrate the Last Supper, the Holy Women at the Tomb, and the Good Shepherd.

St-Nectaire – St-Nectaire-le-Bas is a spa. The old village of St-Nectaire-le-Haut is dominated by **St Nectaire Church**★★, a fine example of Auvergne Romanesque art. Magnificent **capitals**★ decorate the nave and chancel. The figures are treated with great vigour. Saint-Nectaire is also a well-known cheese, available in pasteurised and dairy versions.

★★**Orcival** – *20km/12.5mi southwest.* Founded by the La Chaise-Dieu monks, **Notre-Dame Basilica**★★ (Basilique) was probably built in the first half of the 12C, judging from its remarkable unity of style. Inside are slender pillars and behind the main altar, a highly venerated **Virgin Enthroned**★ with its original silver and gilt ornament. An important pilgrimage takes place on Ascension Thursday

★★★LE PUY-EN-VELAY Population 21 743

The **site**★★★ of Le Puy consists of enormous peaks of volcanic origin. A **Romanesque chapel**★★ sits atop the highest peak, St Michael's Rock (le Rocher St-Michel) or Mont d'Aiguilhe. The **cathedral quarter**★★★ and the statue of Notre-Dame-de-France crown the Corneille Rock.
The picturesque **Rue des Tables** leads to **Notre-Dame Cathedral**★★★. Its Romanesque style covered with cupolas is influenced by Byzantine art. The **cloisters**★★ adjoining the cathedral are decorated with historiated capitals and an allegorical frieze.

BOURGOGNE

BURGUNDY

For the art lover, Burgundy conjures up images of the Middle Ages and the Renaissance. It consists of several smaller regions – Puisaye, Morvan and Bresse – united in the 15C. Its "Grand Dukes of the West" were among the richest, most powerful princes in all of Christendom. From the ducal capital of Dijon, they ruled over a large part of Holland, Luxembourg, Flanders, Artois, Hainault, Picardy and the area between the Loire and the Jura. Burgundy, a land of imperial proportions, only joined the kingdom of France in the 17C.
A paradise for lovers of fine food, the region is reputed for its Charolais cattle, its trout and freshwater crayfish from the rivers of the Morvan Region and its world-famous snails. Culinary specialities abound – *andouillette* (chitterling sausage), *coq au vin*, eggs *meurette* (wine sauce) and gingerbread. Burgundy's wealth is linked to the 37 500 ha/92,600sq mi of vineyards considered to be amongst the finest in the world. South of the the Côte Dijonnaise, the Côtes de Nuits and Côtes de Beaune vineyards vie for celebrity – Gevrey-Chambertin, Vougeot, Vosne-Romanée, Aloxe-Corton, Meursault, Muligny-Montrachet. The Chablis region (Yonne) offers excellent dry, light white wines such as Mercurey and Pouilly-Fuissé.

★★AUTUN Population 17 906. Michelin map 970 I 6

At the beginning of the IC, Emperor Augustus founded Autun (Augustodunum) alongside the Roman road linking Lyon to Sens. The new town, which modelled itself on Rome, suffered from repeated invasions in the 3C. Today, all that remains of the fortified wall are two gates, the remains of a theatre and the Temple of Janus. During the Middle Ages, Autun enjoyed prosperity once again when Cardinal Rolin turned it into a major religious centre.

★★**Cathédrale St-Lazare (Cathedral of St Lazarus)** – It was built from 1120 to 1146 to create a centre of pilgrimage to rival Vézelay. The Burgundian Romanesque character inspired by Antiquity is visible inside. The cathedral's principal interest lies in the 12C sculpture by Master Gislebertus. The **tympanum**★★★ over the central doorway, executed between 1130 and 1135, depicts the Last Judgement. The mastery of its composition and varied attitude of the figures expressing in turn terror, anguish and expectation, make it far superior to all other contemporary work. The vivid biblical scenes on the **capitals**★★ in the nave and the chapter-house are carved with similar mastery.

Gash/CAMPAGNE CAMPAGNE

Gevrey-Chambertin

★★BEAUNE Population 21 289. Michelin map 970 I 6

A prestigious centre of wine-growing and an incomparable city of art, Beaune, fortified in 1368, was the residence of the Dukes of Burgundy before Dijon. Beaune stands in the heart of the Côte-d'Or region of fine wines. Its **Burgundy Wine Museum** (Musée du vin de Bourgogne) offers an excellent approach to discovering the Côtes de Nuits vineyards towards Dijon in the north, and the Côtes de Beaune vineyards to the south.

The Hospices – This charitable foundation was set up in the 15C by Nicolas Rolin, chancellor to Duke Philip the Good.

★★★**Hôtel-Dieu** (Hospital) – Founded in 1443, it served as a haven for the sick until 1971. Its original beauty is intact. The beauty of its architecture, the elegance of its decoration with gabled dormers, weathervanes, and ironwork, and the artistic arrangement of its glazed tiles are more suggestive of the luxury of a Gothic palace than the simplicity of a hospice. The **Polyptych of the Last Judgement**★★★ was commissioned by Rogier van de Weyden to go over the altar in the Great Hall. Its perfection of detail and the poignant expressions on all the figures makes it a major work of Gothic art.

★★ANCIENNE ABBAYE DE CLUNY (ABBEY OF CLUNY)

Founded in 909, the Abbey of Cluny was subject to one authority – the pope. It quickly gained huge prestige. By the early 12C, 1 184 monasteries throughout Europe came under its authority, including Paray-le-Monial, La Charité-sur-Loire, Autun, and Saulieu. Abbots Saint Odon, Saint Mayeul, Saint Hugues, and Peter the Venerable were great builders and royal advisors.

The **abbey church** was rebuilt three times. By 1130, it was one of the world's greatest, unrivalled until St Peter's was built in Rome. It spread 177m/580ft long with A 30m/98ft high vault. But the abbey was destroyed during the Wars of Religion and finally demolished from 1798 to 1823. All that remains of this marvel are the lower parts of two towers which once formed the narthex.

★★★DIJON Population 146 703. Michelin map 970 I 6

Surrounded by magnificent vineyards, the artistic city of Dijon straddles important communication routes linking up Paris, Germany, Switzerland and Italy.
In 1361, Philip the Bold was endowed with the Duchy of Bourgogne. In 1369, he married Marguerite of Flanders, the richest heiress in Europe. Later the title went to Philip the Good (1419-1467). On the day of his marriage to Isabel of Portugal, he founded the Order of the Golden Fleece, in honour of God, the Virgin Mary and Saint Andrew. The artistic patronage of his predecessors continued. Flemish artists such as Rogier van der Weyden and Van Eyck were engaged. At the same time, Chancellor Rolin founded the Hospices of Beaune. The last of the Dukes of Valois and perhaps the most famous of the Dukes of Burgundy, Charles the Bold waged war before meeting his death in the Nancy siege. Burgundy then passed to the House of the Hapsburgs.
Dijon's **historical quarter** have retained much of their original charm. Its streets, often pedestrian precincts, are lined with medieval timber – framed houses and Renaissance mansions. The most typical are **Rue des Forges**★, Place François-Rude and Rue Verrerie, which is full of antique shops.

★**Palais des ducs et des États de Bourgogne (Palace of the Dukes and States-General of Burgundy)** – The palace stands on the straight side of a vast semi-circle designed by the Versailles architect, Jules Hardouin-Mansart. Restored in the 17C, it now houses the Museum of Fine Arts (Musée des Beaux-Arts).

★★**Musée des Beaux-Arts (Museum of Fine Arts)** – The **Guard Room**★★★ contains two tombs which were housed in the chapel of the Champmol Charterhouse before it was destroyed during the Revolution. Philip the Bold commissioned the sculptor Jean de Marville to design the tomb. The marble was brought from Liège and the alabaster from Genoa. Claus Sluter executed the decoration consisting of alabaster arches above an extraordinary procession of mourners. The tomb of John the Fearless and Marguerite of Bavaria repeats the first tomb's pattern.

★**Chartreuse de Champmol (Champmol Charterhouse)** – *Entrance: 1, bd Chanoine-Kir.* Destroyed in 1793, the only element remaining from this sumptuous building executed by the finest artists of the time is **Le Puits de Moïse**★★. This pedestal of a polychrome calvary is decorated with six statues of Moses and the prophets David, Jeremy, Zechariah, Daniel and Isaiah. These strikingly realistic figures are the work of Claus Sluter, the prestigious Dijon sculptor, who also executed the **chapel doorway**★.

►► Cathédrale St Bégnine (crypt★) – Église Notre-Dame★ (Notre Dame Church: Jack-o'-the-clock – Église St Michel★ (St Michael's Church).

★★★Abbaye de FONTENAY (FONTENAY ABBEY) Michelin map 970 I 6

Saint Bernard (1091-1153) was one of the spiritual leaders of the Middle Ages – a writer, preacher, theologian and Statesman. In 1118, at the age of 27, he founded Fontenay. The abbey, nestled in a solitary valley, represents the architectural transcription of his ideas. It is the antithesis of Cluny. Cistercian abbeys such as Fontenay were built in desert-like areas far from pilgrim routes. The church is devoid of any ornamentation. No paint, sculpture and stained glass are visible. The east end is flat and the nave has a Gothic barrel vault. The same plan is found in nearly all the 700 Cistercian abbeys in Europe.

★★VÉZELAY Population 571. Michelin map 970 I 6

The site, the basilica, the historical houses and ramparts are one of the Burgundy's highlights.

★★★**Basilique Ste-Madeleine (Basilica of St Mary Magdalen)** – Founded in 878, the basilica was placed under the patronage of St Mary Magdalen in 1050. On March 31, 1146, Saint Bernard preached the Second Crusade here in the presence of the King of France, Louis VII. Vézelay was already a popular place of pilgrimage. After a huge fire in 1120 destroyed the building, it was immediately rebuilt. In the narthex, the **tympanum**★★★ above the central doorway depicts Christ blessing the 12 apostles before sending them out into the world. The virtuosity of the lines shows the influence of calligraphy. The 62m - 203ft long Romanesque nave is exceptionally well-lit. Its **capitals**★★★ with their learned compositions and vigorous subjects show a strong decorative sense.

BRETAGNE

BRITTANY

Brittany offers a wide variety of holiday spots – the untouched countryside of the Emerald Coast, the Pink Granite Coast, Crozon and the Quiberon Peninsulas, the popular beaches of La Baule and Carnac, the mysterious islands of Morbihan Gulf, and a unique historical and architectural heritage, from prehistoric times to the present. The last outpost of Celtic culture, Breton traditions remain strong.
The seafood – shells, crustaceans, fish – is excellent and so is the salt-pasture lamb raised near the coast. But when it comes to food, Brittany's real claim to fame are its thin pancakes or *crêpes* and its buckwheat *galettes* accompanied by a pungent cider.

★★★NANTES Population 244 995. Michelin map 970 G 6

The historical capital of the Dukes of Brittany, Nantes today is the capital of the Loire Valley region. It is both an artistic city and an active seaport. From 16C to 18C, Nantes grew rich on sugar imported from the West Indies, but it also owed its prosperity to the slave trade, discreetly known as the ebony trade. Rich ship-owners built mansions along Quai de la Fosse and on Feydeau Island.

M. Fouorou/AZIMUT

Pink granite coast

★★**Château des Ducs de Bretagne (Ducal Castle)** – This massive stronghold, protected by a moat which could be flooded if necessary, was host to Kings of France from Charles VIII to Louis XIV. In the courtyard, the **Golden Crown Tower★★** (Tour de la Couronne d'Or), with its Italian-type loggias, is connected to the Main Building (**Grand Logis**) with its massive dormer windows. This was the duke's residence. When rebuilt at the end of the 17C, it became the governor's residence. The **well★★** is surmounted by a remarkable wrought iron well-head incorporating the ducal crown.

Cathédrale St-Pierre et St-Paul (St Peter and St Paul Cathedral) – Although begun in 1434, the cathedral was not completed until 1893. The **interior★★**, with its white micaceous chalk facing and astonishing purity of line, is striking. In the south transept, the **tomb of François II★★** was commissioned by Duchess Anne for her father and her mother Marguerite de Foix. Michel Colombe executed this major Renaissance work in 1502.

►► Musée des Beaux-Arts★★ (Fine Arts Museum) – Boat trip on the Erdre.

★★QUIMPER Population 59 437. Michelin map 970 F 5

The former capital of Cornouaille has conserved both its architecture and its atmosphere. In July, the **Festival of Cornouaille★** is an important folklore event. The **old town★ (Rue Kéréon★)** is spread out round the Gothic style **St Corentin Cathedral★★**. Inside, the lack of alignment of the chancel is apparently due to re-use of the foundations of previous buildings. The 15C stained glass windows depict local lords accompanied by their patron saints.

►► Musée des Beaux-Arts★★ (Fine Arts Museum) – Musée de la Faïence★ (Pottery Museum) – Boat trip down the Odet Riviera★ to Bénodet – Raz Point★★★.

★★★ST-MALO Population 48 057. Michelin map 970 G 5

Behind its ramparts, St-Malo is built on an exceptional seaboard **site★★★** at the mouth of the Rance. The bay boasts the highest tide variations in Brittany. St-Malo was home to many famous navigators – Jacques Cartier, Duguay-Trouin, Surcouf – and Chateaubriand, author of *The Genius of Christianity*. The town first became

prosperous in the 16C when its fur trade was supplied by Canadian trappers and cod fishing developed in Newfoundland. But the town, fortified by Vauban, was destroyed in 1944 after the Germans turned it into an entrenched camp. The town has been carefully restored.
The walk around the **ramparts★★★** offers magnificent views of the walled city and bay. In the heart of the old town, **St Vincent's Cathedral** is covered with vaulting of the Angevin type. In the 12C, Brittany was a Plantagenet fiefdom. The cathedral is lit by brightly-coloured **stained-glass windows★** by Jean Le Moal.

★★**Rance Valley by boat** – Boats sail up the Rance estuary to **Dinan★★**, whose medieval town is enclosed by ramparts. The houses are most unusual, with their half-timbered triangular gables and stone footings on **Place des Merciers★** and **Rue du Jerzual★**. The top of the **Clock Tower** (Tour de l'Horloge) provides a **panoramic view★★**.

►► Côte d'Émeraude★★★ (Emerald Coast): Dinard★★★, St-Lunaire★★, Val-André★★ beaches; magnificent coastline: La Latte fort★★, Cape Fréhel★★★, Erquy Cape★.

★★VANNES Population 45 644. Michelin map 970 G 6

Vannes is built at the bottom of Morbihan Gulf (**boat trip★★★**). Eroding soil and a rise in the level of the ocean formed this original landscape which includes multitude of islands and a varied tidal flow. The **Old Town★**, enclosed by **ramparts★**, and clustered around **St Peter's Cathedral★** (Cathédrale St-Pierre), includes picturesque streets lined with beautiful shops.

►► Auraya (20km/12mi further: St-Goustan Quarter★) – Boat trips in the Morbihan Gulf★★ (Gavrinis★★, île aux Moines★)

CHAMPAGNE

Around Reims, the famous Champagne vineyards cover the steep, sometimes cliff-like slopes of the Côte de l'Île-de-France. The Champagne chalklands, a vast plain stretching from Châlons-en-Champagne to Troyes, are also known as the scene of many battles. Although champagne is referred to as "the wine of God" and "the wine of Kings", its vineyards account for only two percent of French vineyards in surface. Grown on the chalky slopes, champagne marks the northern limit of French wine-growing. Documents refer to the wine since antiquity. But Dom Pérignon (1638-1715) made it sparkle by employing a double fermentation process. Nearly one-third of the 220 million bottles produced per year are sold on the export market.

★★★REIMS Population 180 620. Michelin map 970 I 5

Reims, together with **Épernay**, is the champagne metropolis. The **cellars★★** of most of the main producers – Pommery, Taittinger, Veuve Clicquot-Ponsardin, Piper-Heidsieck, Ruinart, Mumm – are located in the Champs-de-Mars district. They are open to visitors. The city's animated centre, with many cafés, restaurants, hotels and cinemas, flows around Rue de Vesle and Place Drouet-d'Erlon.
After the Roman conquest, Reims expanded considerably. At a strategic crossroads, it was primarily a military fortress. Then on Christmas Day, 498, the baptism of Clovis by St Remigius (St-Rémi) sealed the union of the Franks and Christianity. In memory of this important event and, subsequently, of Louis the Pious's coronation in 816, the Kings of France were crowned in Reims from 1123 to 1825.

Roch-Cephas/TOP

★★★**Cathédrale Notre-Dame** – The High Gothic edifice offers more research in its tracery than even the masterpiece at Chartres. Although four architects worked on the building, it enjoys a great unity of style. The wonderful soaring lines and 13C statuary, including the **Smiling Angel** in a splay of the north portal, are among its finest features. On the façade's other side, the large rose window, 12m/40ft in diameter, stands above the triforium in the same shape as the arcades and the clerestory windows.

★★Tau Palace – The cathedral treasure housed here includes Charlemagne's Talisman, the coronation chalice, the reliquary of the Holy Ampula, and part of the original statuary. The former bishop's palace was built in 1690. It owes its name to its original T-shaped plan.

► ► Basilique★★ and musée St-Rémi★★ (local art, weapons, tapestries) – Chapelle Foujita★★.

★★★TROYES Population 59 255. Michelin map 970 I 5

Like Reims, Troyes is a capital of the Champagne region. But it faces southeast to Burgundy and the Langres plateau. The town developed in the Seine Valley on the great trade route between Italy and Flanders.
The outline of the **Old Troyes★★** evokes a Champagne cork; it includes the aristocratic centre of the Middle Ages and the surrounding village. Beautiful half-timbered houses are visible in Rue Champeaux and Ruelle des Chats; the infill is sometimes made of brick, with a local checkerboard pattern, rather than the usual cob or daub.

★★Cathédrale St-Pierre et St-Paul (St Peter and St Paul Cathedral) – The cathedral, begun in 1208, is one of the largest masterpieces of Gothic art. Its three-storeyed, open-work elevation gives an impression of amazing airiness. The 13C and 16C **stained glass windows★★** show this art's technical development.

★Église Ste-Madeleine (St Mary Magdalen's) – The famed Flamboyant **rood-screen★★** was made by a local artist in the early 16C. The **stained glass windows★** are of the Renaissance style.

★★Musée d'Art moderne (Museum of Modern Art) – Pierre and Denise Lévy, well-known Troyes hosiery manufacturers, donated this collection particularly rich in **works by the Fauves★★**.

CORSE

CORSICA

Sun-drenched Corsica stretches over 1 000km/625mi of jagged coastline. Its pine and sweet chestnut forests, its many peaks of over 2 000m/6 500ft, its nature reserve and its Agriates Desert, certainly merit the Greek name of Kalliste (Island of Beauty) bestowed 25 centuries ago. Corsica belonged to the Republic of Genoa from 1284 to 1768. It was handed over to France by the Treaty of Versailles the year before the birth of the future emperor, Napoleon Bonaparte (1769-1821).
Regional specialities include pork meats, *coppa* (a pork loin dish), *prisuttu* (salted raw ham), fish (mullet, bass, small fish), and Italian-type pasta. The famous cheeses include *brocciu*, a fresh ewe's or goat's cheese, and *niolo*, a dry, strong cheese. Chestnut flour is often used to make cakes and pastries. Cape Corsica produces excellent white wines.
There are regular air and sea links between France, Italy and Corsica. The island is ideal for rambling (GR 20), pony trekking, mountain climbing, nautical sports, yachting and diving.

★★AJACCIO Population 58 315. Michelin map 970 J 8

Ajaccio lies at the bottom of a magnificent gulf above the **Sanguinaires Islands★★**. The town continues to revere the memory of Napoleon, transforming the **birthplace★** into a museum, housing numerous souvenir shops and naming many streets after the emperor. Cours Napoléon, the main thoroughfare, leads to the Old Town built around the Renaissance cathedral.

Fesch Museum★★ houses the collections of Cardinal Fesch, Napoleon's uncle, in the college he founded in Ajaccio. It holds France's largest collection of Italian paintings, with works by Botticelli, Veronese, and Titian. French artists exhibited include Poussin and Subleyras.

★★★BONIFACIO Population 2 683. Michelin map 970 K 8

This medieval town forms a magnificent "land's end". A limestone plateau cut it off from the rest of the island. The town, perched on a rocky promontory 60m/200ft high, overlooks the sea. At the bottom of a rocky inlet, a marina, provides safe anchorage for pleasure boats. The **boat trip★★** to **Dragon's Cave★** (Grotte du Sdragonato) offers excellent views of the high, striated limestone cliffs, beaten by the wind and waves.

★★SARTÈNE Population 3 525

Sartène is built like an amphitheatre above the Bay of Valinco, 13km - 8 miles from its natural harbour and beaches at Propiano. "This most Corsican of Corsican towns" has kept much of its original character, with many historical houses and traditions. The **Catenacciu procession★★** on Good Friday fervently commemorates the way of the Cross. Above the town, a **Museum of Prehistory** (Musée de Préhistoire) is a reminder of the area's many megalithic monuments, including **Cauria★**, **Palaggiu★**, and Filitosa★★.

CÔTE ATLANTIQUE-AQUITAINE

ATLANTIC COAST-AQUITAINE

From the Loire to the Adour, vast sandy beaches and exceptionally sunny days contrasts with the varied lanscape of the interior. West of Niort lies the delightful Poitou marshlands. The Gironde, an estuary of the Garonne, runs along the cliff bearing the Romanesque church of Talmont. The many islands off the coast attract families and sailing enthusiasts – Noirmoutier, Yeu, Ré, and Oléron. Wonderful surfing beaches washed by the Bay of Biscay stand alongside the Landes pine forests and the Basque countryside. On the Spanish border, the Pyrenees offer a large number of spas and hot springs, including Dax, Eugénie-les-Bains, and Bagnères-de-Luchon.
Southwest France is reputed for its gourmet food which includes many regional specialities such as fish from the Gironde in the Bordeaux region, *foie gras, magret* or breast of duck, and *confit d'oie,* goose preserved in fat. There's also boiled chicken from Gascony and Béarn, and for the sweet tooth, Basque cake and macaroons from St-Jean-de-Luz.
The Bordeaux region is famous for its fine wines from the banks of the Garonne and Gironde Rivers. More than 8 000 "châteaux" produce about 75 percent red wines and 25 percent white wines. The reds – Médoc, Graves, Pomerol, Saint-Émilion, Fronsac – age remarkably well. The whites include fine Sauternes, noble-rotted sweet wines and white Graves. *(To visit the vineyards, apply to the Maison du Vin in Bordeaux.)*

★★ARCACHON Population 11 770. Michelin map 970 G 7

Arcachon consists of two distinct towns - the summer resort with its seafront casino, regattas and speedboat races, and the winter resort with its beautiful 19C holiday homes sheltered among the pines. The bay is reputed for its oysters.
To the south, the **Pilat Dune**★★ (Dune du Pilat) represents Europe's highest sand dune. It stretches about 2 700m/3 000yds long, 500m/1 600ft wide and 114m/374ft high. The top offers an excellent view of the Silver Coast (Côte d'Argent), an immense sandy beach which runs from the mouth of the Gironde to that of the Nivelle.

★★BAYONNE Population 40 051. Michelin map 970 G 7

Bayonne, 8km/5mi from the ocean front, is an estuary port on the Adour River. The town becomes particularly animated during the popular **summer festivals**★ with their bullfights, chistera and pelota matches, folklore dancing and rugby matches.

Rue du Port-Neuf retains its original arcades and high houses. Smells waft up from its pastry and confectionery shops. They suggest the importance of the town's cocoa industry begun back in the 17C.

►► Musée Bonnat★★ (Bonnat Museum - 14C to 19C paintings).

★★★BIARRITZ Population 28 742. Michelin map 970 G 7

The resort first became famous in the 19C when Napoleon III and his wife, the Empress Eugenia, built the Hôtel du Palais. Queen Victoria and later, King Edward VII, also spent long periods here. Biarritz is still home to cosmopolitan vacationers. Its fine sandy beaches, flanked by casinos and lined with promenade gardens and golf courses, have become an international mecca for surfing.

★★★BORDEAUX Population 210 336. Michelin map 970 G 7

"Take Versailles, add Antwerp, and you have Bordeaux". Victor Hugo, impressed by Bordeaux's 18C grandeur and splendid tidal river, thus described the city. As the centre of an internationally reputed wine-growing region, Bordeaux is both a dynamic regional metropolis hosting major international exhibitions, and an important link between Northern Europe and the Iberian Peninsula.
At the end of the reign of Louis IV, Bordeaux was a medieval walled city. Despite the objections of the populace, it soon became one of France's most beautiful cities. First, a vast terrace was built over the river. Then in 1735, the architect Gabriel constructed two business pavilions, one to house the customs offices and the other for the stockmarket. The Classical buildings are of gracious and elegant design, decorated with grotesque figures, keystones, trophies, flames and other ornaments. The main square – **Place de la Bourse** – became a strategic trading centre for foods from the colonies, the slave trade, and the export of wine. Trade with Northern Europe and America made Bordeaux the leading French port on the eve of the Revolution. The sovereign's statue was deposed in 1792 and replaced by a fountain. The vast terrace over the river disappeared in 1844.

Place de la Comédie – Along with Place Tourny and Place Gambetta, the square delimits the most prestigious quarters of Bordeaux. Luxury boutiques vie with famous cafés.

★★**Grand Theatre** – One of France's finiest theatres was built from 1773 to 1780 by the architect Victor Louis in the Louis XVI style. Its main feature is its Antique peristyle. A beautiful straight double staircase inspired Garnier when he designed the Opera House in Paris. It leads to a concert hall with perfect acoustics.

►► Musée des Beaux-Arts★★ (Fine Arts Museum) – Musée des Arts décoratifs★ (Decorative Arts Museum) – Cathédrale St-André★ (St Andrew's Cathedral) – Musée d'Aquitaine★★ (Aquitaine Museum) – Musée d'Art contemporain★ (Contemporary Art Museum).

J.-L. Barde/SCOPE

Bordeaux – Place de la Bourse

COGNAC Population 19 528

The brandy capital and birthplace of François I in 1494 lies in the heart of the Charentes region.
The historical quarter still has many 15C, 16C and 17C houses, while cognac storehouses line the Charente quays near the old castle.
Since the 16C, **cognac** has been produced by a two-stage distillation process in the "Charente" light white wine still. Nine litres of wine are needed to produce one litre of cognac. The fermenting brandy is stored in barrels made from Limoges oak whose fibres are conducive to the oxidation and produce an amber colour. Evaporation causes the liquid to lose 2.5% of its volume per year. This "angels' portion" totals about two million bottles a year, blackening nearby houses.

★★★LOURDES Population 16 300. Michelin map 970 G 7

On the banks of the Gave River, Lourdes is a religious town of universal fame. It comes alive in the summer months during the pilgrimage season, welcoming some 5 million visitors.
In 1858, Our Lady of the Immaculate Conception appeared to the young Bernadette Soubirous (1844-1879) in Massabielle Grotto for the first of 18 times. During one of these visions, the miraculous spring appeared. A sanctuary was built above the grotto and Lourdes became a cult centre for the Virgin Mary. Bernadette was canonised in 1933.
The **Grotto** *(appropriate dress essential)* consists of the Basilica of the Rosary (Basilique du Rosaire) built in 1889, the grotto of the miracles, the fountains and pools, the St Pius X Underground Basilica (Basilique souterraine St-Pie X) consecrated on the centenary of the visions, and the Stations of the Cross. During the summer, a film shown in the Pax Cinema retraces the life of St Bernadette.

★★POITIERS Population 78 894. Michelin map 970 H6

Two of the greatest battles in French history bear the name of Poitiers. In 732, Charles Martel saved Christianity by driving back the Arab invasion. In 1356, the Hundred Years War opposed Jean II le Bon (Good) and the Black Prince in a terrible battle. Poitiers fell to Charles V, who gave it to his brother, Duke Jean de Berry, a generous patron of art and letters. The influence of his university, founded in 1431, which still exists, turned the city into an important intellectual centre.

★★ **Église Notre-Dame-la-Grande** – The arcades of its richly decorated Romanesque west **front**★★★ depict scenes from the Incarnation. The interior vaults and arches are decorated with foliage and allegorical figures taken from the Book of Beasts. The nearby **Law Courts** (Palais de Justice) are famous for their 12C **Great Hall**★. The great gable wall, refurbished during the time of Duke Jean de Berry has three monumental fireplaces surmounted by a balcony, flamboyant windows and four monumental statues. In 1429, an ecclestical commission tried Joan of Arc.

★★ **Église St-Hilaire-le-Grand (St Hilary the Great Church)** – This major church of pilgrimage along the route to Santiago de Compostela was built in 1049. But when the wooden roof was destroyed by fire in the 12C, the architect reduced the width of the naves and added columns to take the stone vaulting.

► ► Cathédrale St-Pierre★ (St Peter's Cathedral – 13C stalls) – Baptistère St-Jean★ (St John's Baptistery) – Église Ste-Radegonde (St Radegund's Church) – Musée Ste-Croix★★ (Holy Cross Museum - archeological and painting collections).

Eight 8km/5mi north of Poitiers, the **Futuroscope**★★ or European Park of the Moving Image was designed by the French architect Denis Laming. It presents the latest advanced visual-image technology with dome, dynamic and circular cinema screens stretching 600m²/6666sq ft. The Magic Carpet with two screens makes viewers feel like they are flying.

★★ ST-JEAN-DE-LUZ Population 13 031. Michelin map 970 G 7

An elegant summer resort, St-Jean-de-Luz also is an animated historical town and fishing port. Louis XIV married the Spanish Infanta, Maria-Theresa, here on 9 June 1660.

★★ **Église St-Jean Baptiste (St John the Baptist's Church)** – This 15C building, its high walls pierced with narrow openings, has a forbidding appearance. The sumptuous interior mainly dates from the 17C. The nave is covered with a remarkable wood panelled ceiling, while the raised chancel has a resplendent gilt altarpiece.

CÔTE D'AZUR

The FRENCH RIVIERA

The French Riviera along the Mediterranean Coast from Toulon to Menton is reputed for its bewitching light, its deep blue sea and its abundant sunshine. The jagged coastline has beautiful beaches and excellent natural harbours in the Toulon area, two massifs, the Maures and Esterel, and wide bays from Cannes to Nice. Although famed for its mild winter, the French Riviera also has ski resorts such as Gréolières and Isola 1000. The Nice Carnival, the film festival in Cannes, the modern art museums in Antibes, Nice, Cagnes-sur-Mer, St-Tropez, the Monte-Carlo automobile rally and the Formula 1 Grand Prix in Monaco are all excellent pretexts for a visit. Animated outdoor markets and the production of original handicrafts such as glassware in Biot, ceramics and marionettes in Vallauris, and fabrics and olive wood carvings in Tourettes-sur-Loup, make excellent purchases.
Provençal cooking tastes strongly of garlic and olive oil. The region's most famous dish is *bouillabaisse*, a spicy rock fish soup. The most popular wines come from Bandol, Pierrefeu, Ollioules and Menton.

★★ ANTIBES Population 70 006

The town, famous for its international jazz festival in June, lies opposite Nice, on the other side of the Bay of Angels. The old streets inside the Vauban ramparts are lined with restaurants and cafés on Place Nationale as well as antique shops and attractive boutiques.
In the 4C BC, Greeks from Massalia (Marseilles) set up a series of trading posts along the coast, including Antibes. Bought by Henri V from the Grimaldi family, each reign saw its fortifications strengthened.
The Picasso Museum **(Musée Picasso)** is housed in the 12C **Grimaldi Castle** where the artist set up his studio in 1946.

Cap d'Antibes has hosted such famous guests as F Scott Fitzgerald. It is the site of sumptuous mansions and villas nestled among trees south of Antibes and Juan-les-Pins. The Garoupe plateau offers an excellent **panoramic view**★★.

★★★ CANNES Population 68 676. Michelin map 970 J 7

Cannes, a splendid natural harbour on the edge of Napoule Gulf is famous for its international regattas and meetings. It owes its popularity to the beauty of its **setting**★★ and its mild climate. It is one of the leading conference centres in France, and one of Europe's most prestigious tourist towns.

★★ **Boulevard de la Croisette** – This famous promenade, with its flower-filled gardens and tall palm trees, is lined with fine sandy beaches on one side and luxury hotels and exclusive boutiques on the other. On the port's eastern side, the Festival and

Conference Centre **(Palais des Festivals et des Congrès)**, houses the municipal casino. The International Film Festival, the town's most spectacular and prestigious event, takes place here in May every year.

Le Suquet – Cannes's Old Town overlooks the port. At the top, the château (Castre Museum) was built in the 11C and 12C by the Lérins monks. It houses archeological and ethnologic collections.

►► Massif de l'Esterel★★★ (Esterel Massif) – Iles de Lérins★★ (Lérins Islands).

★★GRASSE Population 41 388. Michelin map 970 J 7

The birthplace of Fragonard stands on the hilly slopes above Cannes. Grasse was known for its leather goods and glovemaking when perfumed gloves became fashionable in the 16C. The perfume industry bomed, with two crops predominating, rose and jasmine. Essences are obtained by distillation, enfleurage and extraction. They then are mixed in secret proportions by the perfume industry's great "noses". The International Perfume Museum (Musée international de la Parfumerie) retraces the history of perfume. It has its own perfume laboratory.

★★★PRINCIPAUTÉ DE MONACO Population 29 876. Michelin map 970 J 7

This sovereign state covers only 192 hectares – less than one square mile. Its history began when the Grimaldi family bought it from the Republic of Genoa in 1308. Recently, it has become an important conference centre, reputed for its orchestra, its car rallies and its golf and tennis championships.

★★**Le Rocher (The Rock)** – This terrace built on a peninsula 60m - 200ft above the sea, forms the administrative city. The changing of the guard takes place at 11.55am daily in front of the **Prince's Palace**★ (Palais du Prince). Other notable buildings include the **cathedral**, the **Tropical Gardens**★★ (Jardin Exotique) and the **Oceanographic Museum**★★ (Musée océanographique) with its splendid aquarium.

★★★**Monte-Carlo** – Europe's largest gambling centre was founded in 1856. High rise construction now has spread out onto reclaimed land. But the town, with its luxury hotels, select boutiques, sumptuous villas and flower-filled gardens, remains attractive. One of the villas, built by Charles Garnier, of Paris Opera House fame, houses the **Museum of Dolls and Mechanical Toys**★ (musée des Poupées et Automates).

★★★NICE Population 342 391 Michelin map 970 J 7

This Queen of the Riviera fronts onto the Bay of Angels, sheltered by the hills behind. It owes its success to its charming **setting**★★, its pleasant climate, its museums and its **carnival**★★★.

The fossil beach at Terra Amata has provided evidence of human occupation 4,000 centuries ago. Once a trading post for the Greeks from Marseille, Nice later became a Roman colony. Except for a few interruptions, it was owned by the Dukes of Savoy up until 1860, when it became part of France.

J. Sierpinski/SCOPE

Battle of the flowers

★★**Seafront** – The **Promenade des Anglais**★★ takes its name from the original seafront footpath established by the large English colony which started coming here in the 18C. It still has a certain grandeur with its many luxury hotels – Hôtel Méridien, Palais de la Méditerranée, the Négresco – and the Ruhl Casino. **Quai des États-Unis**, which runs off it, contains the **Raoul Dufy and Mossa Exhibition Galleries**.

★**Old Nice** – Wedged between the seafront, the castle, Place Garibaldi and Promenade du Paillon, this neighbourhood buzzes with intense activity all day long. The castle provides a sweeping **view**★ of the Bay of Angels and the Pre-Alps. The **Misericord Chapel**★ (Chapelle de la Miséricorde), a masterpiece of local Baroque, was built in 1740 according to the design of the Italian architect, Guarino Guarini.

★★**Cimiez** – Cimiez Hill is the aristocratic part of Nice. The statue of Queen Victoria is a reminder that Cimiez was once the home of royalty.
The **Marc Chagall Museum**★★ (Musée Marc-Chagall) exhibits the 17 paintings which form the artist's "Biblical Message" executed between 1954 and 1967.
The **Matisse Museum**★ (Musée Matisse) is housed in a 17C Italian building. It retraces the itinerary of the painter through the paintings, bronzes and drawings.

►► Musée des Beaux-Arts★★ (Fine Arts Museum) – Musée d'Art moderne et d'Art contemporain★★ (Museum of Modern and Contemporary Art) – Musée Masséna★★ – Phoenix Park★ – Eze★ (14km - 8.5 miles away, an intriguing village perched on top of a high rock overlooking the sea).

★★ROUTE NAPOLÉON

This route reproduces the Emperor's return journey after his escape from Elba Island. He disembarked at Golfe-Juan and travelled to Grenoble *(see Rhône-Alps)*. Commemorative plaques and monuments bearing the flying eagle symbol lie along the route, inspired by Napoleon's famous words, "The eagle will fly from steeple to steeple until it reaches the towers of Notre-Dame Cathedral". Between Golfe-Juan and Valferrière Pass, three passes offer magnificent views of the Esterel and Maures Massifs and the Bay of La Napoule.

★★ST-PAUL Population 2 903

Nestling amid the hills and vales, St-Paul is typical of the fortified towns along the Var border. In the 1920s, the village attracted many artists – Signac, Modigliani, Bonnard and Soutine. All met at the Colombe d'Or open-air café – joined later by film stars such as Greta Garbo, Sophia Loren and Burt Lancaster.
The houses with their coats of arms, arcades and loggias now contain art galleries and craft shops.

★★**Fondation Maeght** – In an attractive setting on Gardettes Hill, the Foundation exhibits contemporary art. Built in 1964 by the Catalan architect, José Luis Sert, it features an exemplary combination of white concrete and pink brick. The monumental works of Calder, Zadkine and Pol-Bury welcome visitors to the grounds. Inside the museum, paintings, sculptures and ceramics are exhibited. The collection includes works by Braque, Chagall, Kandinsky, Matisse, Hartung and Miró.

►► Vence★ (4km - 2.5 miles): Chapelle du Rosaire★ (Rosary Chapel – Matisse Chapel).

★★ST-TROPEZ Population 5 754. Michelin map 970 J 7

The little port of St-Tropez forms one of the most beautiful bays on the French Riviera opposite Ste-Maxime. It has become a popular resort for well-known show-business personalities.

★★**The port** – Superb yachts form a backdrop to St-Tropez's animated centre. Luxury boutiques, antique shops, restaurants and cafés crowd around the harbour. Another meeting place is **Place des Lices** which is a market in the morning and a hang-out for Harley Davidsons the rest of the time.

★★**Musée de l'Annonciade** – Housed in a chapel built in 1510, it contains paintings by Pointillist, Fauve and Nabi artists who came to St-Tropez in the late 19C, fascinated by the exceptional light. There also are works by Signac, Derain, Matisse, Bonnard, Vuillard, Rouault, Marquet.

★**Citadelle** – Overlooking the town to the east and providing a magnificent **panorama**★★, the keep now contains a **Naval Museum** (Musée naval).

►► Massif des Maures★★★ (Maures Massif) – Port-Grimaud★ (marina) – Ramatuelle★ (hill-top village).

LANGUEDOC-MIDI-PYRÉNÉES

The Roussillon plain, with its vast orchards, market gardens and vineyards forms the hinterland of the Côte Vermeille (Vermeil Coast). North of the Aude Valley, the Albigeois is rich farming country, whose produce mainly goes to Toulouse, the capital of Upper Languedoc. The region offers a wide variety of sporting and leisure activities – skiing in the winter resorts of Angles, Font-Romeu and Pas de la Cases (Andorra) and water sports in the Albi, Foix and Muret recreation parks. Sardana (Catalan) festivals brighten the village squares in summer, and music festivals light up Prades and Toulouse.

★★★ALBI Population 46 579. Michelin map 970 H 7

Old Albi★ owes the rosy hue of its brick monuments, houses and bridges to the clay dug from the Tarn riverbed.

★★★**Cathédrale Ste-Cécile (St Cecilia's Cathedral)** – The church's construction began in 1282, just after the Albigensian Crusade. It rises up like a fortress above the town. The 100m/330ft long, 30m/100ft high nave is supported by imposing buttresses. A Flamboyant Gothic **rood-screen★★★** closes off the chancel. The statues, above the stalls, mark the apotheosis of naturalism and realism in Gothic art. The **Last Judgement** was painted on the inside of the façade in the late 15C.

★**Palais de la Berbie** – A former bishop's residence, it now houses the **Toulouse-Lautrec Museum★★** and the artist's largest collection of works.

★★★CARCASSONNE Population 43 470

The walled town of Carcassonne provides an extraordinary vision of medieval military architecture. Today, it is an important business centre in the wine-producing district of Aude. The city consists of a fortified centre and an outer and inner curtain wall, part of which dates from the 6C. The outer wall was built by Saint Louis. However, after Roussillon was annexed by Louis XIV, Carcassonne lost its strategic importance and was abandoned. Viollet-le-Duc saved it from ruin in the 19C.

★★MONTPELLIER Population 207 996. Michelin map 970 I 7

Unlike its neighbours, Nîmes, Béziers and Narbonne, Montpellier only really entered the pages of history in the 10C. Its spice and dye merchants traded with the east and vaunted the therapeutic virtues of the products they sold, leading to the first "school" of medicine, which became a university in the 13C. When Provence joined France in 1481, however, Marseilles supplanted Montpellier. Louis XIV promoted the town to the rank of administrative capital of Lower Languedoc, causing an architectural boom which has continued up to the present day with the construction of contemporary architectural projects such as the Antigone quarter and the Polygone complex.

★★**Old Montpellier** – The old quarter with its narrow, winding streets dates back to medieval times. It extends from Place de la Comédie to the Peyrou Arc of Triumph, on either side of Rue Foch. The streets are lined with beautiful 17C and 18C mansions, such as **Hôtel des Trésoriers de la Bourse★**. *(The guided tours organised by the tourist office are highly recommended).*

★★**Promenade du Peyrou** – The esplanade was laid out in 1688 in the upper part of the town to accommodate a statue of Louis IV. Construction of an aqueduct in the 18C led to redevelopment of the site by Jean-Antoine Giral. He designed the **water tower** to look like a temple and added the terraces. The 17C **Arc of Triumph** is decorated with bas reliefs depicting the victories of the Sun King.

★★★TOULOUSE Population 358 688. Michelin map 970 H 7

Toulouse has been one of the main artistic centres of France since the late Middle Ages. A pleasant university town full of interesting walks, it has become a major industrial centre dominated by the aeronautical and other high-tech industries. Many cultural activities, concerts, theatre and museums make the metropolis live up to its name, the "Pink City".

★★★**Basilique St-Sernin (St Serninus' Basilica)** – This major Romanesque pilgrimage church, rich in relics and combining both stone and brick features several types of vaulting. The sculpted decoration shows a preoccupation with expression and movement, particularly on the Miégeville door.

★★**Eglise des Jacobins (Church of the Jacobeans)** – This first church of the Preaching Friars was founded by St-Dominic (1170-1220) in Fanjeaux in 1215. The marvellous ribbed vaulting and "palm tree" pillars in the chancel make for a graceful structure.

★★**Musée des Augustins (Augustinians' Museum)** – It is housed in a former southern French Gothic monastery. The **Romanesque sculptures**★★★, mainly carved from Pyrenees marble, come from various cloisters in Toulouse. There are admirable collections of 15C to 20C paintings, including a fine series by the French school.

►► Hôtel d'Assézat★ – Musée St-Raymond★★ (St Raymond Museum - archeology) – Capitol★ – Cathédrale St-Étienne (St Stephen's Cathedral) – Muséum d'histoire naturelle★★ (Natural History Museum).

The LOIRE Valley

The garden of France is reputed for its pleasant life style and beautiful châteaux. In the late 15C and throughout the 16C, the Kings of France, Charles VIII, Louis XII and François I, settled in the region, holding court amidst great pomp and splendour, and attracting artists such as Leonardo da Vinci. They set out to promote the Renaissance, which they had discovered during the wars in Italy. Their architects converted the Loire Valley into an immense construction site, producing masterpieces at Amboise, Blois, and Chambord. The great lords of the land imitated them and built ravishing châteaux in the countryside at Azay-le-Rideau, Chenonceaux, and Chaumont. *(Most of the châteaux feature Sound and Light shows).*
Residents here are considered to have the purest accent in France. The Valley is equally reputed for its high quality produce – delicious fruit, fresh vegetables, asparagus and mushrooms cultivated in chalk quarries. From Amboise to Tours, the slopes are covered with the white wine grapes of Vouvray and Montlouis.

★★Château D'AMBOISE

Amboise Château is built on a rocky spur overlooking the town. The Golden Age of Amboise came during the 15C when the château was extended and embellished by the Kings of France. Charles VIII, who was born here, continued the work begun by his father, Louis XI, but the Renaissance buildings disappeared after the fortress was partly demolished under Louis XIII. St Hubert's Chapel, built on the wall, is a gem of Flamboyant Gothic art. The right hand part of the lintel tells the legend of St Hubert. A keen hunter, Hubert followed a stag all day when it disappeared; suddenly the animal appeared to him with a luminous cross between his antlers.

Clos-Lucé★, a red brick manor was home to Leonardo da Vinci from 1516 until his death in 1519. During his stay in France, da Vinci organised numerous royal festivities and produced drawings for countless mechanical inventions, some of which are displayed in the basement in the form of scale models.

★★★ANGERS Population 141 404. Michelin map 970 G 6

The former capital of Anjou is built on the banks of the Maine River, 8km/5mi from the River Loire. The Old Town's pedestrian precincts and the Boulevard du Maréchal-Foch make this a busy city. In the 11C and 12C, Angers served as the capital of the Counts of Foulques. They wielded great power due to their remarkable political skill and an acute sense of matrimonial alliances. In 1128, Geoffrey Plantagenet married Mathilda, heir to the Norman and English thrones. He also governed Touraine and Maine. In 1152, their son Henry married Eleanor of Aquitaine, the divorced wife of Louis VII. This alliance extended the frontiers of their realm to Scotland and the Basque country. Philippe Auguste incorporated Anjou into the kingdom of France at the same time as Normandy, confiscating them from John Lackland, King of England.
The castle★★★, rebuilt by Saint Louis from 1228 to 1238, represents a fine specimen of feudal architecture. Its 17 round towers with their alternating courses of dark schist and white freestone cover more than 1km/0.5mi. They stand 40 to 50m/130 to 160ft high. Their former watch turrets disappeared during the Wars of Religion.

The **Apocalypse Tapestry**★★★ (Tenture de l'Apocalypse) is the oldest and most important tapestry surviving to the present day. Commissioned for the Duke of Anjou Louis I, it was probably executed between 1373 and 1383 in Paris and inspired by illuminations from a manuscript owned by King Charles V. The 76 extant scenes, impressive in their size and design, executed on panels with alternating red and blue backgrounds, illustrate the Apocalypse of St-John.

★★**Musée Jean-Lurçat et de la Tapisserie contemporaine (Jean-Lurçat Museum and Contemporary Tapestry)** – The old **St-John's Hospital**★ (Hôpital St-Jean) cared for the sick from 1174 to 1854. The ward contains a series of tapestries by Jean Lurçat (1892-1966) entitled **Le Chant du Monde**★★ (The Song of the World). They illustrate the joys and sorrows of man's existence and marking the revival of the art of tapestry in the 20C.

►► Cathédrale St-Maurice (stained glass★★) – Maison d'Adam★ – Galerie David d'Angers★ (sculptures) – La Doutre quarter★ (historical houses).

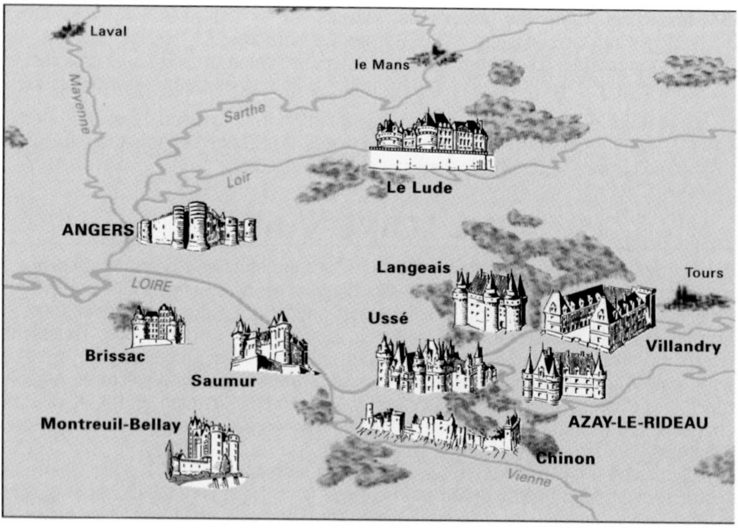

★★BLOIS Population 49 318. Michelin map 970 6

Blois, at the crossroads between Beauce and Sologne, still has its steeply sloping medieval streets and Renaissance houses built when Louis XII moved here from Amboise.
The **château**★★★ owes its round towers, spiral staircases, Foix Tower and Chamber of the States General to feudal times. The François I staircase represents a masterpiece of architecture and sculpture. Gaston d'Orléan's wing (Louis XIII's brother) belongs to the classical era. The château houses interesting archeological collections and a **Fine Arts Museum**★ (Musée des Beaux-Arts).

★★★Château DE CHAMBORD Michelin map 970 H 6

Chambord Château is a royal pleasure palace, which owes its beautiful sculptures and large openings to Italy. It stands on the edge of the Sologne Forest, a favorite royal hunting ground.in a park surrounded by a 32km/20mi long wall. When François I returned from Milan in 1519 after the victory of Marignan, he had a new castle built. It was still unfinished in 1559. The plan was of feudal inspiration with a central keep and four towers. The château has 440 rooms, 365 fireplaces, and 13 main staircases. The most famous is the double staircase with its two interlocking spirals leading up to the roof terrace from with unusual views of chimneys, lanterns, dormer windows and the immense park below.

★★★Château DE CHENONCEAU Michelin map 970 H 6

Chenonceau is a gem of Renaissance architecture, built from 1513 to 1521, for Thomas Bohier, François I's treasurer. The rectangular building decorated with corner-towers precedes a two-storey gallery spanning the River Cher. The six women who reigned over this elegant residence with its magnificent furniture included the wife of Thomas Bohier, Catherine Briçonnet. She was responsible for the innovative Italian staircase. Diane de Poitiers commissioned Philibert Delorme to landscape the gardens, and Catherine de Medici took Chenonceau from Diane de Poitiers and had the gallery built over the river.

★★TOURS Population 129 509. Michelin map 970 H 6

The centre of Touraine represents an excellent base for visiting the châteaux and vineyards of the Loire Valley. Tours has many attractions of its own. The Gallo-Roman metropolis's famous 4C bishop, Saint Martin was a great builder. His relics still attract large numbers of pilgrims each 11 November.

★★**Old Tours** – The historical quarter around **Place Plumereau**★ was brought back to life when the Arts Faculty moved to the banks of the Loire. Beautiful 15C and 16C stone and half-timbered mansions line the streets, often reserved for pedestrians, and containing many craft shops.

★★**Musée du Compagnonnage (Guilds Museum)** – In the St Julien quarter, it houses fine examples of the work of master craftsmen together with a description of their apprenticeship.

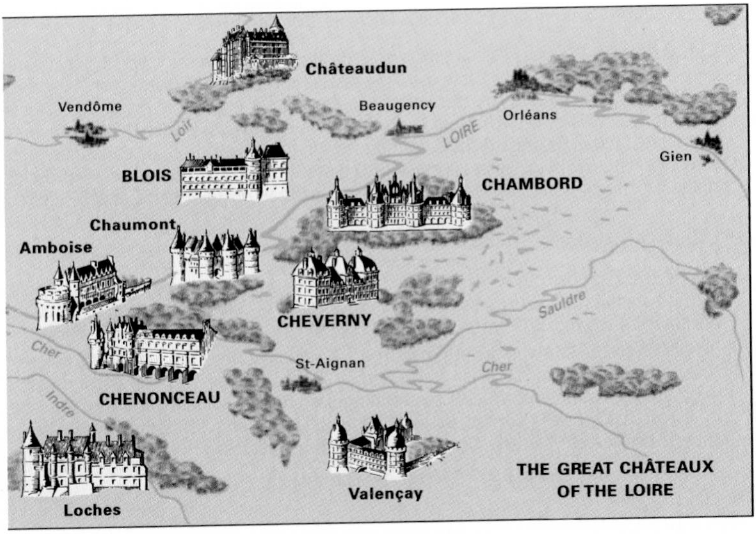

★★ **Cathédrale St Gatien** – The building illustrates the development of Gothic architecture from the 13C to the 16C, including a Flamboyant style west front and fine **stained glass windows**★★.

★★ **Musée des Beaux-Arts (Fine Arts Museum)** – Housed in the former 17C-18C bishop's palace, its collections include Italian Renaissance works (Mantegna) and 19C and 20C French paintings. The main courtyard contains a Lebanese cedar planted in 1804.

►► Hôtel Gouin★ – Jardins de Villandry★★★ (gardens) and château★★ *(15km/9.5mi southwest)*.

★★ CHATEAU D'USSÉ

Ussé Château projects a medieval character with its crenelated towers and watch-path. It is easy to imagine Sleeping Beauty lying within its walls. The Great Gallery contains a fine set of **Flemish tapestries**★.

NORD-PICARDIE

NORTHERN FRANCE and PICARDY

Picardy and Artois, with their vast chalk plateaux, are an extension of the Parisian Basin. The long coastline of Picardy with its vast expanses of fine, hard sand, is ideal for sand-yachting. The flat country of Flanders, with its many canals and windmills, continues into Belgium.
The people from the North France love to drink a beer in a warm, friendly atmosphere. Carnivals provide the occasion for them to dress up and organise processions of floats and giants.

★★★ AMIENS Population 131 872. Michelin map 970 H 5

Amiens is an important crossroads and the capital of Picardy. It has a superb cathedral, miraculously left unscathed in a modern city, 60% of which was destroyed during World War II.

★★★ **Cathédrale Notre-Dame** – Its architectural unity stems from its rapid construction, from 1220 to 1288. The decoration and sculpture are renowned – the noble figure of Christ known as the "Beau Dieu" (west front); the rose windows on the main façade and in the north and south transepts, and the 110 16C Flamboyant oak **stalls**★★★.

►► Musée de Picardie★★ (Picardy Museum - archaeology, painting) – Hortillonnages★★ (Riverside market gardens).

★★ ARRAS Population 38 983. Michelin map 970 H 5

The capital of Artois grew up during the Middle Ages around the Abbey of St Vaast. In the 15C, Artois passed into the hands of the Dukes of Burgundy, who were great patrons of the Arras tapestry industry.

Grand'Place and **Place des Héros**, connected by **Rue de la Taillerie**, form an exceptional architectural ensemble. The 17C and 18C Flemish baroque façades are varied and extremely harmonious.

★★BEAUVAIS Population 54 190. Michelin map 970 H 5

★★★**Cathédrale St-Pierre** – This architectural masterpiece defies the laws of gravity and equilibrium and is a remarkable example of the apotheosis of Gothic art. The walls are kept to a minimum, the clerestory windows leave practically no stone surfaces and the rear wall of the triforium is pierced with **stained glass windows**★★. These were the work of the Beauvais school founded by Ingrand Leprince. In particular, note the rose window by Nicolas Leprince in the south transept. The **astronomical clock**★, made on the same model as that of Strasbourg, has 90 000 parts and 52 dials.

★★LILLE Population 172 142. Michelin map 970 I 5

Lille is the regional metropolis of an urban community of nearly a million people. Flemish in the 11C, Burgundian in the 14C and 15C, and Spanish in the 16C, it became French in 1667 after which Vauban fortified it under Louis XIV (**citadel**★).

Old Lille★★ has fine, magnificently-restored 17C and 18C façades. The **Old Exchange**★★ (Vieille Bourse) from 1652 is composed of 24 houses of Flemish Baroque style with sloping roofs built around the rectangular court in which trading took place. In **Rue de la Monnaie**★, **Comtess Hospice**★ with its brick and sandstone walls, has a superb **timber roof**★★ in the Great Hall (Salle des malades).

►► Musée des Beaux-Arts★★ (French paintings).

NORMANDIE

NORMANDY

Normandy is known for its rural landscape, its small hedged fields, wooded hills, cool valleys and lush countryside, the white chalk cliffs of the Caux region and fine sandy beaches of Côte de Nacre. It is a farming region, with herds of cattle and horses and many orchards covering the countryside with their blossoms in April and May.
The region owes its name to the Normans or Norsemen, who arrived by sea from Scandinavia in the 9C. Ten centuries later, it became a meeting place for artists and the birthplace of Impressionism. Normandy is also a reminder of World War II. On **6 June 1944** – **D-Day** – two million allied soldiers landed on the Normandy coast on beaches which have been handed down to prosperity under their code names – Omaha, Utah, Gold, June, Sword. In Arromanches, Bayeux and Caen, museums commemorate the Battle of Normandy. Thousands of tombs are aligned in several military cemeteries – the Americans in Colleville, the British in Ranville and Bayeux, the Canadians in Reviers and the Germans in Huisnes.
Fresh cream is at the base of Norman cooking. Specialities include *tripe à la mode de Caen*, salt-pasture leg of lamb from Mont-St-Michel, *andouille* (chitterling sausage) from Vire, chicken from Auge Valley. Seafood lovers will find treats all along the coast. The cheeses are exceptionally fine: camembert, pont-l'évêque, livarot and soft, fresh cheese from Bray. Normandy is known for its apple cider from Auge Valley, its perry (pear cider) and calvados (cider brandy 50 to 55°).

★★BAYEUX Population 14 704

Bayeux, the birthplace of the Dukes of Normandy and capital of the Bessin district, was the first French town to be liberated on 7 June 1944.
The city owes its fame to the **Bayeux Tapestry**★★★ (Tapisserie de la Reine Mathilde) exhibited at the William the Conqueror Centre (Centre Guillaume-le-Conquérant). The 70m/330ft long piece of embroidery was probably made in England by Queen Mathilda in the 10C. It tells the story of the Norman Conquest with amazing insight. **Notre Dame Cathedral**★★★ is a beautiful example of Norman Gothic.

★★★CAEN Population 112 846. Michelin map 970 G 5

The capital of Lower Normandy is an attractive city with light cream-coloured Caen stone houses, its sail boats in the heart of the city and its Romanesque abbeys. The **castle**★ houses the **Fine Arts Museum**★★ (Musée des Beaux-Arts) with 15C to 20C paintings. The **Normandy Museum**★★ (Musée de Normandie) features local traditions.

★★**Église St-Étienne** – The Church of the Abbey for Men, founded by William the Conqueror, was built in the Romanesque style between 1066 and 1077. The strikingly sober west front is relieved by the soaring towers. In the 12C, the timber roof was replaced by sexpartite vaulting. The chancel was refurbished in the 13C.

★★**Abbaye aux Dames (Church of the Abbey for Women)** – Queen Mathilda founded the abbey in 1062 as the counterpart of the Abbey for Men. The vast nave is a beautiful example of Romanesque art. But the clerestory was altered in the 12C. The timber roof was replaced with sexpartite vaulting. The chancel was refurbished in the 13C.

★★ **Memorial** – This Peace Museum occupies the site of the command post of the German General Richter. On 6 June 1944, he resisted the Anglo-Canadian troops. The Memorial uses the aid of the latest audiovisual and scenographic techniques to recount contemporary history.

►► The D-Day beaches from Caen to Carentan.

★★★DEAUVILLE Population 4 261 Michelin map 970 H 5

Deauville owes its worldwide reputation to the luxury and refinement of its facilities – and the elegance of its social and sporting calendar. The season peaks in summer – with horse races, including the Grand Prix, regattas, international polo championships, the international yearling sales and the American Film Festival. The resort is famous for its seafront boardwalk, casino and port.

★LE HAVRE Population 195 854. Michelin map 970 H 5

This large seaport and industrial city is the last landmark in the magnificent Seine Valley, whose estuary lies more than 50m/165ft under the **Normandy Bridge**★★. Le Havre's vocation as a warehousing and transatlantic port began at the time of the American War of Independence. Ocean liners with such prestigious names as Franklin, Washington, Normandie, Ile-de-France, Liberté and France sailed between Le Havre and New York.

In 1945, however, Le Havre was rebuilt after the bombing and shelling of the Battle of Normandy.

The **André-Malraux Fine Arts Museum**★ (Musée des Beaux-Arts), a glass and metal construction, houses a large **collection**★ of works by Eugène Boudin and Raoul Dufy.

►► Étretat★★ (28 km/13mi north) is an elegant seaside resort in a magnificent setting of high chalk cliffs.

★★HONFLEUR Population 8 272

At the foot of **Côte de Grâce Hill**★★, this port is full of character. Its **Old Harbour**★★ (vieux bassin), its wooden **Church of St-Catherine**★, its historical streets and fishing harbour make for a colourful scene. Honfleur, bathed in the soft light of the Seine estuary, provided inspiration to numerous painters including Boudin, Lebourg, Corot,

Y. Arthus-Bertrand/ALTITUDE

Mont-St-Michel

Bonington and Jongkind, who used to meet at St Siméon Inn (auberge de St Siméon). Many famous navigators left Honfleur to discover the New World. Jean Denis explored the mouth of the River St Lawrence, Samuel de Champlain founded Quebec in 1608 and Cavelier de La Salle was the first to sail down the Mississippi and explore Louisiana in 1681.

★★★ MONT-ST-MICHEL Michelin map 970 H 5

Mont-St-Michel, with its highly original setting, its rich and influential history and its splendid architecture deserves to be called the Wonder of the Western World. In the 8C, the archangel St Michael is said to have appeared to Aubert, Bishop of Avranches on Mount Tombe. He founded an oratory, later replaced by an abbey, which still attracts numerous pilgrims. The mount is joined to the continent by a breakwater built across the bay, which has a very high tidal variation.
The **Abbey Church★★** *(église abbatiale)*, built from 1017-1144, is perched on the top of the rock. A striking contrast exists between the sober Romanesque nave and the light-filled Flamboyant Gothic chancel (1446-1526).

The Marvel★★★ (La Merveille) (1211-1128): these superb Gothic buildings occupy the north side of the mount. They consist of the **Guests' Hall★** *(salle des Hôtes)*, the **refectory★** *(réfectoire)*, the **Knights' Hall★** *(Salle des Chevaliers)* and the **cloisters★★★** *(cloître)*.

★★★ ROUEN Population 102 723. Michelin map 970 H 5

Since Roman times, Rouen has served as the first bridge over the Seine estuary. The Old Town's skyline of towers and spires demonstrate the city's historic wealth. The Norman Gothic buildings and many museums, make for a centre of great refinement. **Old Rouen★★★** has more than 700 timber-framed houses. They are concentrated next to **St Maclou Church★★** *(église St-Maclou)* and **St Maclou Cloisters★★** *(cloître St-Maclou)*. **Rue St-Romain★★**, **Rue Martainville★** and **Rue Gros-Horloge★★** form the bustling city centre. Joan of Arc was burnt at the stake on May 1431 on **Place du Vieux-Marché★**.

The Notre-Dame Cathedral★★★ is a magnificent 13C Gothic building embellished during the Renaissance with the sculpted **tombs★★** of the Cardinals of Amboise.
Three of the city's museums are reputed – **The Museum of Fine Arts★★** *(Beaux-Arts)*, the **Ceramics Museum★★** *(Céramique)* and **Le Secq des Tournelles Museum★★** featuring wrought ironwork.

► ► Tour of the Seine Valley★★★ abbeys★★★

PARIS★★★ and ILE-DE-FRANCE

Since the foundation of Lutetia on l'île de la Cité in the middle of the Seine 2000 years ago, ecclesiastics, royal sovereigns and heads of State have left their mark. They built churches, monuments and palaces, creating prestigious museums and tracing wide avenues affording marvellous vistas. Paris is the City of Light, reputed for its taste and elegance thanks to its fashion designers, perfumeries and jewellers. Its many festivities, concerts, and theatres, its famous cabarets and glittering reviews make for an exciting capital. The many bridges, river boats and tall monuments provide panoramic views.

THE LEFT BANK

Île de la Cité and its neighbour, l'île Saint-Louis, straddle the middle of the Seine River in the very heart of Paris. Both represent outstanding attractions. An extra treat for the ice-cream lover is a stop at Bertillon's in Rue-Saint-Louis-en-l'île. Around 200 BC, Gaulish fishermen from the Parisii tribe set up their huts on the largest of the islands in the Seine. Lutetia later specialised in river transport during Gallo-Roman times; a vessel is included in the city's coat of arms as a reminder of its beginnings. In 506, Clovis made the island his capital and named it La Cité. In the Middle Ages, famous schools developed. In the 19C, the centre of the island was demolished and enormous buildings erected – the Hôtel-Dieu hospital, an army barracks, now the police headquarters, and the Commercial Courts, with a flower market in their centre.

★★★ **Cathédrale Notre-Dame** – Construction began in 1163 under the direction of Bishop Maurice de Sully. The work was completed in about 1300. The last of the great gallery churches was one of the first to have flying buttresses. Its plan prefigures all the great Gothic churches. Three splendid rose windows decorate the main façade and the transept. On the right of the chancel, the old sacristy houses the Treasure with its precious relics. Square Jean-XXIII, at the east end, provides the best views of the cathedral.

★★★ **Sainte-Chapelle** – The architectural lightness and splendid stained glass windows make this tiny chapel one of the marvels of Gothic art. It was built for Saint Louis between 1240 and 1248 to house the relics of the Passion of Christ, including the Crown of Thorns, redeemed from the Emperor Baudouin II. The upper chapel resembles a shrine; its walls consist almost entirely of stained glass underlining the continuity between biblical royalty and the Capetian kings. The illustrations show the Life of Christ and of the two Saints John. They also depict the prophets and relate the discovery of the relics.

★★★ **Montagne Ste-Geneviève** – This Latin Quarter houses seven centuries of universities, colleges and libraries. The official language of learning was Latin until 1789. **Boulevard St-Michel**, or Boul'Mich, bustles with its cafés, clothing boutiques and book shops. **St Michael's Fountain** (Fontaine St-Michel), like Danton's statue at Odéon Metro Station, serves as a favourite meeting place. In the adjoining streets, cellars, cabarets, exotic restaurants, arts cinemas and regular cinemas open far into the night.

The **Sorbonne**, the most illustrious of all French universities, was originally a college of theology founded in 1253 by Robert de Sorbon. Chancellor Richelieu had extensive reconstruction carried out from 1624 to 1642. The **church**★ built in the Jesuit style, contains the **tomb of Cardinal Richelieu**★. This magnificent work as by Girardon. The dome prefigures those of Val-de-Grâce and Les Invalides.

The **Pantheon**★★ stands at the Left Bank's highest point. In 1744, Louis XV fell seriously ill. He vowed to build a new church to Saint Genevieve, Paris's patron saint, if he recovered. The architect Soufflot designed a monumental building, 110m/360ft long, 84m/276ft wide and 83m/272ft high. It stands in the form of a Greek cross surmounted by a **dome**★★.
Throughout its history, the Pantheon has served as a church dedicated to the great figures of history, a necropolis, and the headquarters of the Commune. The building, of Roman inspiration finally became a lay temple in 1885, when Victor Hugo's ashes were brought there.

Further on, **Rue Mouffetard**★ and **Place de la Contrescarpe**★ are among the Paris's most picturesque spots in Paris with grocery stores and exotic restaurants.

★★ **The Luxembourg Palace and Gardens** (Palais et jardin du Luxembourg) – They were built for Marie de Medici. She decided to leave the Louvre after the death of Henri IV in 1610, and wanted a palace to remind her of the Palazzo Pitti in Florence where she grew up. The work was carried out by Salomon de Brosse – the architect used rustication, ringed columns and Tuscan capitals to give a Florentine air to the palace with its French-style ground plan including a courtyard on one side and gardens on the other. Twenty-four huge paintings were commissioned from Rubens in 1621 for one of the galleries. They glorified Marie's reign and are now displayed in the Louvre. Today, the palace houses the Senate, the chamber elected by indirect suffrage. The garden is popular with students from the Latin Quarter and strollers looking for shade in the summer.

★ **St-Germain-des-Prés** – The oldest bell-tower in Paris watches over this favourite haunt of men of letters and artists. The famous cafés and bars along **Boulevard St-Germain**, Les Deux Magots, Le Flore, and Lipp, the jazz clubs in Rue St-Benoît and Rue Jacob, the pubs in Rue Guisarde and Rue des Canettes and bookshops stay open at night bringing alive St-Germain-des-Prés. Stylish boutiques, antique shops and art galleries give a Right Bank elegance to its narrow streets and picturesque intersections. The quaint **Rue de Furstemberg**★ with its shady little square and old-fashioned street lights is a popular place to stroll. Founded in the 7C, the **St-Germain-des-Prés Abbey**★★ soon became one of the most important Benedictine abbeys under Cluniac rule. The impressive bell-tower overlooking the square dates from the early 11C. The nave and chancel are more recent, mainly decorated in the 19C.

★★ **Montparnasse** – This neighbourhood was once the meeting place of early 20C artists – Modigliani, Soutine, Chagall, Stravinski, Satie, Cocteau, Hemingway and Picasso. A modern tower now dominates. The shops in Rue de Rennes, the theatres in Rue de la Gaîté, the crêpe restaurants in Rue d'Odessa, and the cinemas and restaurants along the boulevard create one of Paris's busiest regions. Many of the cafés which have gone down in the history of Paris are located here – La Closerie des Lilas, La Coupole, La Rotonde, Le Dôme, Le Select.
Construction of the **Maine-Montparnasse complex**★ began in 1961. The main building, completed in 1973, is the **tower**★★ *(tour)*, whose oblong silhouette soars 209m/688ft. The **view**★★★ from the 59th floor is extraordinary. A bar and panoramic restaurant offer visitors the possibility of appreciating the city's vistas in comfort.
Today, the adjoining train station has been refurbished to take the Atlantic TGV high-speed train. The main entrance, Porte Océane, is an immense glass hall in the form of an arch resembling a ship's sails. A concrete tile covers the rails and supports the largest suspended garden in Paris, the **Atlantic Garden** *(jardin Atlantique)*.

★★★ **Les Invalides** – This beautiful monumental group was founded in 1670 as a home for France's retired soldiers. The buildings, designed by the architect Libéral Bruant, were completed in 1674-1676. The majestic facade, nearly 200m/650ft long, precedes the main courtyard in front of the **St-Louis-des-Invalides Church**★ *(église)*. Also called the Soldiers' Church, its cold, functional architecture is softened by banners captured from the enemy. The **Army Museum**★★★ *(Musée de l'Armée)* is one of the world's richest museums of military art, technique and

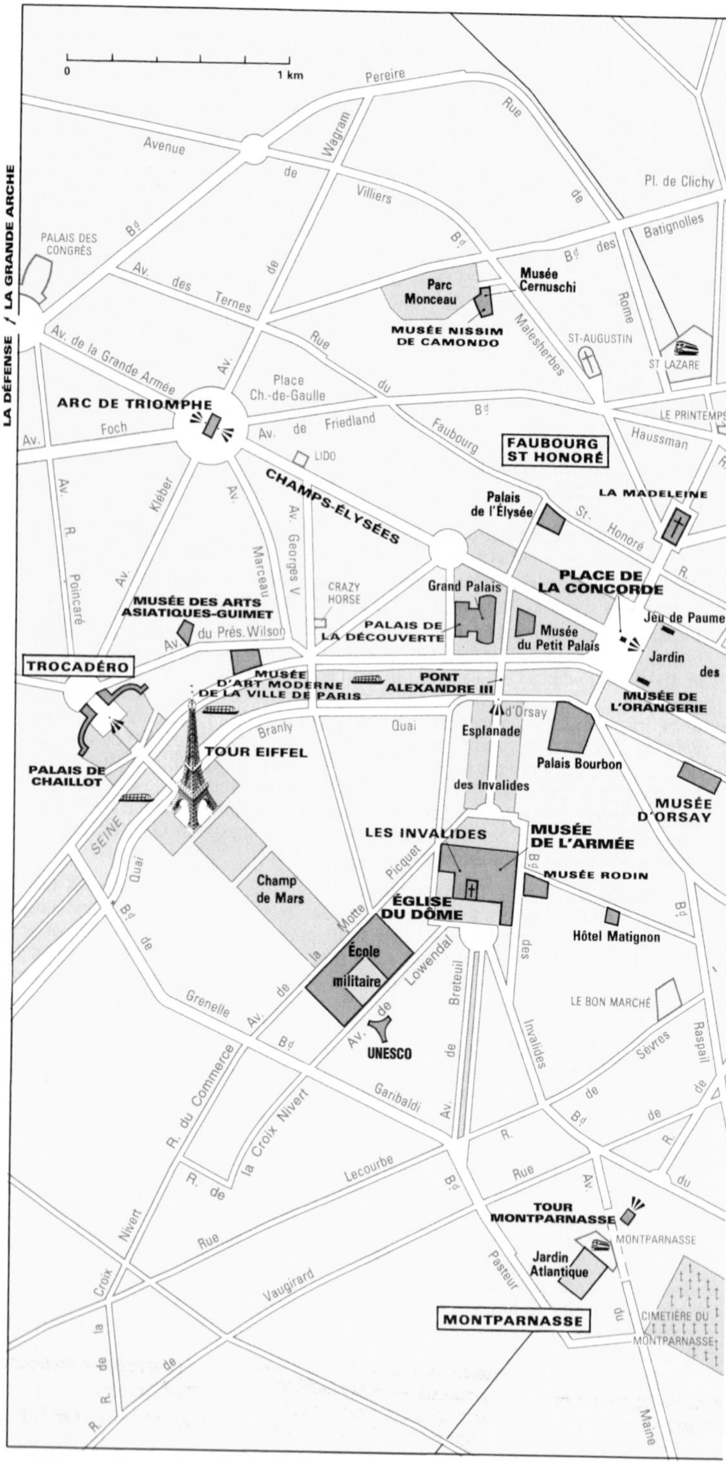

history. Place Vauban leads to the **Dome Church**★★★ (Église du Dôme), just behind the Soldiers' Church. Jules Hardouin-Mansart designed the church to glorify the reign of Louis XIV. The centrally-planned building is topped with a slender dome, whose design displays a prodigious knowledge of balance and proportion. In the crypt, **Napoleon's tomb** (tombeau) comprises a red porphyry sarcophagus resting on a base of green granite from the Vosges Mountains.

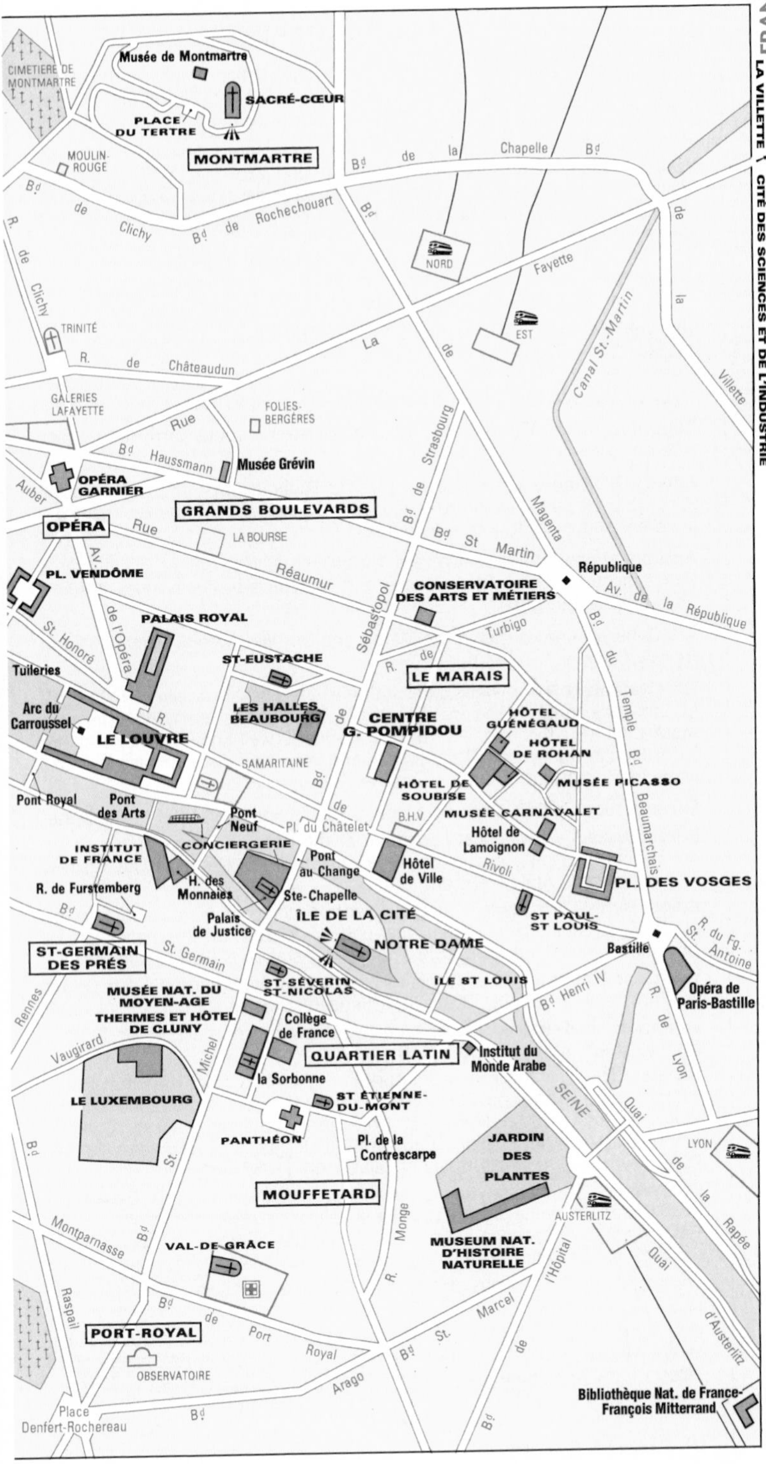

★★★**Tour Eiffel (Eiffel Tower)** – Paris' most famous monument took 26 months to build and was inaugurated in March 1889 during the World Fair. Despite its 7 000t frame, its 2.5 million rivets and 320.75m/1052ft height, the tower soars with lightness and boldness.

At night, the illuminated monument shines like a jewel. The **view**★★★ from the top floor sometimes stretches as far as 67km/42mi.

PRACTICAL PARIS

Information – The Paris Tourist and Conference Office is open to the public every day, 9am to 8pm, except 1 January, 1 May and 25 December. It is located at 127, Avenue des Champs-Élysées. ☎ (33) 01 49 52 53 54.

Public transport – The **Mobilis** card allows one day's unlimited travel by metro (underground), bus, RER (underground express) or SNCF (French Railways) train in the chosen zones. The **Ticket Jeunes** (Young People's Ticket for all holders of French or foreign Young People's Cards) allows one day's unlimited travel in the chosen zones on Saturdays, Sundays and holidays. The **Paris Visite** card allows unlimited travel by metro, bus, RER or SNCF train on any network in the chosen zones on 2, 3 or 5 consecutive days. Available from any metro, RER or SNCF station.

Bus tour of Paris – The best way to see all the famous places in Paris is by **Balabus.** This crosses Paris from East to West, from the Gare de Lyon to the Défense (stops are marked Balabus Bb). It only runs on Sundays and holidays from the last Sunday in April to the last Sunday in September, 12noon to 9pm.

Shopping – Department stores are concentrated on Boulevard Haussmann, Rue de Rivoli and Rue de Sèvres.

Luxury boutiques are found on Rue du Faubourg-St-Honoré, Rue de la Paix, Rue Royale, Avenue Montaigne and Place des Victoires. The main jewellery shops are in Place Vendôme.

Antique shops include Louvre des Antiquaires, Village Suisse (avenue de la Motte-Picquet), Carré Rive Gauche and Marché aux Puces (Flea Market, Porte de Clignancourt).

Art Galleries are located in the Marais and Bastille, Avenue Montaigne and Rue de Seine.

Entertainment – The week's programmes are published every Wednesday in *Pariscope* and *L'Officiel des Spectacles*. Paris boasts nearly 400 cinemas, more than 100 theatres, several opera houses, well-known reviews at the Lido, Moulin-Rouge and Crazy-Horse, and countless discotheques and jazz clubs in Montmartre and Montparnasse.

Paris by boat – The ideal way to see the sights on the banks of the Seine.

Bateaux-mouches – River boats boarding at the Pont de l'Alma landing stage on the right bank of the Seine, ☎ 01 42 25 96 10. The nearest metro station is Alma-Marceau.

Bateaux Parisiens Notre-Dame – Another river boat company with a landing stage at Quai de Montebello (from the end of March to the beginning of November), ☎ 01 43 26 92 55. The nearest station is RER C Saint-Michel.

Vedettes du Pont-Neuf – River launches boarding at the Square du Vert-Galant landing stage, ☎ 01 46 33 98 38. The nearest metro station is Pont-Neuf.

Vedettes de l'Île-de-France – River launches boarding at the Port de Suffren landing stage, ☎ 01 45 50 23 79.

Batobus – The river bus runs from April to September, from the Eiffel Tower to the Louvre, with 4 possible ports of call at the Port de Solférino (for the Musée d'Orsay), Quai Malaquais (for the Institut de France), Quai de Montebello (for Notre Dame Cathedral) and Quai de l'Hôtel-de-Ville (for Paris Town Hall). For information, call 01 44 11 33 44.

Canal cruises – Another way to discover the nostalgic side of Paris. Departures from the Bassin de La Villette, Quai de la Loire, nearest metro station Jaurès. From April to October, a shuttle runs from the Rotonde de La Villette to the Cité des Sciences et de l'Industrie in 15 minutes.

Canauxrama – Canal trips from 13, Quai de la Loire, 75019 Paris, ☎ 01 42 39 15 00.

Paris Canal – Canal trips from 19-21, Quai de la Loire, 75019 Paris, ☎ 01 42 40 96 97. "A la découverte du parc de La Villette" cruise of La Villette Park *(1hr 15min)*.

THE RIGHT BANK

★★**Colline de Chaillot (Chaillot Hill)** – Trocadéro with Chaillot Palace (palais) overlooks the Champs-de-Mars. Twin pavilions, linked by a portico, are extended by wings curving to frame the wide terrace lined with bronze statues. A magnificent **view**★★★ unfolds of the Left Bank. **Chaillot Palace**★★, inaugurated in 1937, houses the **Maritime Museum**★★ (Musée de la Marine), the **Museum of Mankind**★★ (Musée de l'Homme), the **Museum of French Monuments**★★ (Musée des Monuments français), the **Henri Langlois Cinema Museum**★ (Musée du Cinéma), and Chaillot National Theatre.

★★★**The Triumphal Way** – This majestic vista that extends from the Louvre, past the Tuileries Gardens and Place de la Concorde, and up the Avenue des Champs-Eélysées to the Arc de Triomphe.

★★★**Arc de Triomphe** – The monument stands in the middle of a huge circle of 12 radiating avenues. Napoleon commissioned the arch in 1806 in honour of the Great Army. The architect Chalgrin modelled it on the Arch of Titus in Rome. But the Paris monument's dimensions are colossal: 50m/164ft high and 45m/148ft wide with massive high reliefs by Etex, Cortot and Rude. The platform affords a magnificent view★★★.

★★★**The Champs-Élysées** – The popularity of this famous avenue dates from the Second Empire, when restaurants and entertainment halls became popular. Private mansions once rubbed shoulders with the Mabille Dance Hall. Today, the Païva mansion at no 25 is the only Belle Epoque survivor. But the Champs-Élysées remains a busy business, tourist and entertainment centre. Car showrooms, banks, airlines, shopping malls, drugstores, restaurants and cinemas line both sides. Nothing is more entertaining than to join the cosmopolitan crowd at night, take in a show at the **Lido**, or welcome in the dawn at a famous night club. From the Rond-Point des Champs-Élysées to the Place de la Concorde, landscaped gardens and rows of chestnut trees restore a calm grace to the avenue.

The **Petit Palais**★ and **Grand Palais**, like **Alexandre III Bridge**★, were built for the World Fair of 1900. Their stone and steel architecture, with glass roofs, typifies late 19C artistic taste. The **Petit Palais Museum**★ houses the paintings and decorative art collections owned by the City of Paris.

Élysée Palace (Palais de l'Élysée) *(not open to visitors)* has been the official residence of the French president since 1873. The building was erected in 1719 for the Count of Évreux. It has been home at various times to the Marquise de Pompadour, the Empress Josephine and Prince Louis-Napoleon Bonaparte before he became Napoleon III.

★★★**Place de la Concorde** – This vast 18C square was designed by Ange-Jacques Gabriel. The Seine stands on one side and a pair of colossal mansions on the other. The pavilion on the right, **Hôtel de la Marine**, now houses the Navy Headquarters, while the Automobile Club of France and the luxurious **Hôtel Crillon** occupy the opposite side of Rue Royale. The United States Embassy is located across the street from the Crillon in a corner of the square.

Eight allegorical statues of cities, the Marley Horses and the obelisk from Luxor in Egypt, complete the decor together with two fountains inspired by St-Peter's Square in Rome. Louis XVI was guillotined in the centre of the square on 21 January 1793.

Concorde Bridge was inaugurated in 1790 opposite the **Palais-Bourbon**★, now the Chamber of Deputies, whose columns are a reflection of those of the **Madeleine**★★, with its surprising resemblance to a Greek Temple. Begun in 1764, the church was only completed under Louis-Philippe, in 1842.

★★★**The Opera Quarter** – The **Opéra-Garnier**★★ symbolises Second Empire architecture. Today it is surrounded by theatres and the Printemps, Galeries Lafayette and the Marks & Spencer department stores.

The Opera was part of Haussmann's town planning project. Although Charles Garnier won the design competition held in 1860, the opera house was only inaugurated in 1875 by Marshal MacMahon. The building's sheer size, its juxtaposition of volumes, the taste for precious materials and the polychrome marbles still draw admiration. The magnificent ceremonial main staircase leads to the auditorium whose false ceiling was painted by Chagall in 1964.

E. Baret

View of Place de la Concorde, from rue Royale

★★**Place Vendôme** – This superb display of the majesty of French 17C architecture is the home of famous jewellers such as Van Cleef & Arpels and Boucheron, and a hotel of great prestige, the **Ritz**. In 1810, the equestrian statue of Louis XIV destroyed during the Revolution was replaced by the present column entwined with a bronze spiral. It was melted down from cannons taken from the enemy at the Battle of Austerlitz.

★**Hôtel de Ville** – This vast building serves as Paris's city hall. The first municipal government was set up here in the 13C. Under François I, the Pillared House (Maison aux Piliers) fell into ruin. A new building was constructed by Il Boccadoro and extended over the centuries. However, the building, with all its official registers, was burnt to the ground in 1871. Ballu and Deperthes rebuilt it, copying the façade of the previous building. The richly decorated interior exemplifies the official style at the beginning of the Third Republic.

★★★**The Marais** – The Marais quarter buzzes with in bars, fashion boutiques, antique shops and art galleries. Rue des Rosiers used to be the centre of Paris' Jewish Quarter.

★★★**Place des Vosges** – The square, entirely surrounded by arcades, owes its existence to Henri IV. In the early 17C, the great lords and courtiers of the day built splendid mansions decorated by famous artists around it. These represented the first examples of the French-style mansion, with a court at the front and a garden behind. The square has retained its original order. **Victor Hugo's house**★ occupies the former Hôtel de Rohan-Guéménée. Hugo lived here from 1832 to 1848.

★★★**Butte Montmartre** – The Butte as it is known locally, is full of contrasts: anonymous boulevards alternate with picturesque stone staircases and steeply-sloping streets; there is even a vineyard and a windmill. In the afternoon and evening, **Place du Tertre**★★ becomes a tourist centre drawing a cosmopolitan crowd. Numerous artists propose their paintings, charcoal portraits and cut-out silhouettes.
Since the 19C, Montmartre has attracted artists and men of letters; Toulouse-Lautrec drew La Goulue, Valentin le Désossé and Yvette Guilbert at the Moulin-Rouge, founded in 1889. Rue Cortor was home to Renoir, Dufy and Utrillo. The **Museum of Montmartre** (Musée de Montmartre) is rich in mementoes of the neighbourhood's Bohemian life.

★★**Basilique du Sacré-Cœur** (Sacred Heart Basilica) – The architect Abadie produced the winning design for this vast pilgrimage church in the Romanesque-Byzantine style. The work began in 1875 and was completed in 1914. The interior is decorated with mosaics illustrating the devotion of France to the Sacred Heart of Jesus. On a clear day, the terrace outside offers a splendid **panorama**★★★.

CONTEMPORARY ARCHITECTURE

Since the 1950s, Paris has experienced an architectural renewal. Modern monuments include the Maison de Radio-France, Unesco, the Palais du CNIT at La Défense, the Georges Pompidou Centre, the Forum des Halles, the City of Science and Industry (Cité des Sciences et de l'Industrie) and City of Music (Cité de la Musique) at La Villette, the Bastille Opera House, the Institute of the Arab World (Institut du Monde Arabe), the Louvre Pyramid, the Great Arch (Grande Arche de la Défense), the American Cultural Centre in Bercy and Le Ponant at Javel. Many modern sculptures also have been commissioned. Notable examples are *Le Défenseur du Temps*, a moving clock by Monestier near the Pompidou Centre, *Le Centaure* by César at Croix-Rouge Crossroads, the Open-Air Sculpture Museum (Musée de Sculpture en plein air) on Quai St-Bernard, La Défense's concrete podium, and the Stravinski Fountain (**Fontaine Stravinski**★) by Jean Tinguely and Niki de St-Phalle near St Merri.

Carte Musées et Monuments

This card valid 1 day (70 F), 3 days (140 F) or 5 consecutive days (200 F), allows unlimited entry to 70 museums and monuments in the Paris region.

On sale from the Paris Tourist Office, main metro stations, and museums and monuments.

MUSEUMS

★★★**The Louvre** – The former palace of the Kings of France now is a museum housing one of the world's greatest art collections. The renovated Grand Louvre is divided into three main sections: Sully, Denon and Richelieu. The collection of ancient art includes **The Victory of Samothrace** and **Venus of Milo.** Objets d'art are epitomised by the Regent's diamond. Paintings represent the various schools up until the 19C, with masterpieces by Leonardo da Vinci, including the famous **Mona Lisa**, Veronese, Rembrandt, Vermeer, Georges de La Tour, and Delacroix.

The History of Paris

Carnavalet Museum★★ retraces the city's history from its origins to 1789, in the Hôtel Carnavalet, and from 1789 to the present in the Hôtel Le-Peletier-de-St-Fargeau.
Hôtel de Cluny★★, the former 15C residence of the abbots of Cluny built over ancient Roman baths, has an interesting collection of objects from the Middle Ages including the **Lady and the Unicorn★★★** tapestries.

Oriental Art

The Guimet Museum★★ founded by the Lyons collector Émile Guimet provides an excellent overview of oriental art.

The Cernuschi Museum★ in the private mansion of the banker Henri Cernuschi is devoted to ancient China.

19C Art

The **Orsay Museum★★★** is housed in the first railway station built specifically for electrically driven trains and the former terminus for the Southwest France. Architect Gae Gaulenti has redesigned the interior. The museum is devoted to all forms of artistic expression in the 19C, above all Impressionist paintings and Art Nouveau.

The **Marmottan Museum★★** contains numerous paintings by Monet, most painted at the artist's home in Giverny in Normandy.

The **Rodin Museum★★** is housed in Hôtel Biron and its delightful garden, where Rodin lived at the end of his life. The artist's works, mainly in white marble and bronze, are extremely powerful.

20C Art

The **National Museum of Modern Art★★★** (Musée national d'Art moderne) in the **Pompidou Centre★★** (Centre Georges-Pompidou), built by Richard Rogers and Renzo Piano, retraces the development of art from Fauvism and Cubism to the most contemporary art forms. It contains more than 30 000 works.

The **Picasso Museum★★** is housed in the Hôtel Salé, built between 1655 and 1659. Restored to house the Picasso donation, the mansion has a beautiful **staircase★** with a wrought-iron banister. All the different stages in the artist's development and techniques are represented.

The **Orangery Museum★★** (Musée de l'Orangerie) contains Monet's **Nympheas★★★** and works by artists such as Cézanne, Renoir, Soutine, Modigliani, Matisse and Derain.

The **Museum of Modern Art of the City of Paris★★** (Musée d'Art moderne de la Ville de Paris) offers a retrospective of 20C art, with the famous *The Good Fairy Electricity*★ by Raoul Dufy and *Danse* by Matisse.

EXCURSIONS

★★★ **St Denis Basilica (Basilique)** – *Metro line 13 (direction Saint-Denis); RER B, La Plaine-Voyageurs; RER D, Saint-Denis SNCF station.*
While the Football World Cup and the final played at the Stade de France made St Denis a particularly lively place in June and July, 1998, it has always been a favourite destination of art lovers. Its magnificent basilica has a decisive place in the development of the Early Gothic style and it houses the **tombs★★★** of twelve centuries of kings of France from Dagobert to Louis XIV, together with those of queens and royal children. Their tombs form a veritable museum of medieval and Renaissance funerary sculpture. The Romanesque **crypt★★** is also worth visiting.

★★★ **Chartres** – *88km/55mi southwest.* Chartres is the capital of the Beauce region famous for its wheat fields. In ancient times, Druids worshipped here. Evidence also exists of the pagan cult of a holy spring and possibly of a mother-goddess. Crowds of pilgrims have converged on the city since the Middle Ages.

The Notre-Dame Cathedral★★★ (Cathédrale) was rebuilt in 25 years after the fire of 1194 which gutted the 11C building. The north and south porches were added 20 years later, giving the church a unity of style and decoration possessed by few other Gothic churches. The **Royal Doorway★★★** *(portail)*, a marvel of Romanesque art (1145-1170), depicts the life and triumph of Christ. The thin, elongated figures on either side of the doorway illustrates the kings and queens of the Bible. The chancel and transept were designed for large ceremonies and crowds of pilgrims. The **stained glass windows★★★** mainly date from the 12C and 13C. They are famous for the depth and clarity of their Chartres blue, which produces reflections of various shades of red. The best example is the marvellous Madonna Window (Notre-Dame-de-la-Belle-Verrière).

★★★ **Disneyland Paris** – *30km/19mi east.* The only attraction park of its kind in Europe is modelled after its American and Japanese counterparts: Disneyland in California, Magic Kingdom in Florida, Tokyo Disneyland in Japan. It is Walt Disney's dream come true, a little enchanted land in which children and adults can come and enjoy themselves.

The park covers 55ha/136sq mi and includes five fantasy lands: Main Street USA, Frontierland, Adventureland, Fantasyland and Discoveryland. The Hotels were designed by well-known architects such as Michael Graves, Robert Stern and Frank Gehry.

★★★ **Fontainebleau** – *65km/41mi south.* In the 12C, the Capetian kings built a hunting lodge in the middle of the game-filled **forest**★★★. But Fontainebleau's reputation really developed with the palace built by François I. A French architect Gilles Le Breton designed the building. But a team of Italian artists, Rosso, Primaticcio and Niccolo dell'Abbate, decorated it. They were searching for a dreamy elegance, and favoured elongated human bodies. Their decorative art was inspired by somewhat enigmatic allegories. The **Oval Court**★ (Cour Ovale), the **Golden Gate**★ (Porte Dorée), the **François I Gallery**★★ (Galerie) and the **Ballroom**★★★ (Salle de bal) also date from this time. Henri II, Catherine de' Medici and Charles IX carried on the work. Henri IV extended the palace further with a tennis court (Jeu de Paume), the Diana Gallery (Galerie de Diane) and finished enclosing the Oval Court (Cour Ovale). Napoleon bid farewell to his officers on 20 April 1814 from the **Farewell Court**★★ (Cour des Adieux).

★ **Giverny** – *76km/47mi west.* Claude Monet lived in this attractive little village in the Seine Valley from 1883 until his death in 1926. Subsequently dozens of American artists came here to set up their easel, forming an American colony in the village. There were 40 studios for 300 inhabitants.

Claude Monet's House★ (Maison) has been turned into a museum. Reproductions of his largest paintings are exhibited as well as his collection of Japanese prints. The garden designed by Monet has been restored, including the nymphea pool.

The **American Museum**★ (Musée Américain) was founded by two collectors, Judith and Daniel J. Terra. Housed in buildings converted by the architects Reichen and Robert, it has three adjoining galleries, containing about 100 paintings illustrating the work of the American artists who came here – Morse, Robinson, Sargent, and Mary Cassatt.

★★★ **Vaux-le-Vicomte** – *64km/40mi southeast.* Vaux-le-Vicomte castle was built by Nicolas Fouquet (1615-1680). Superintendent of Finances, Fouquet made his fortune by using state credit for his own purposes. In 1656, Fouquet called on three great artists to built a castle which would symbolise his success: Louis Le Vau, architect, Charles Le Brun, decorator and André Le Nôtre, landscape gardener. Some 18,000 people worked on the site. On 17 August 1661, Fouquet entertained Louis XIV with unparalleled extravagance. But the king, outraged by such luxury and refinement, which far exceeded that of the Court, had the superintendent thrown into prison 19 days later.

The **castle**★★, built on a piece of land surrounded by moats, overlooks the magnificent **gardens**★★★ landscaped by Le Nôtre. It is the first major example of the Louis IV style. The **Grand Salon**★ and the **King's Bedroom**★★ (Chambre du Roi) show the decorative talent of Le Brun.

★★★ **Versailles** – *20km/12.5mi southwest.* Versailles was created by the French Monarchy at the height of its glory. Apart from the Regency, it served as the seat of government and the political capital of France from 1682 to 1789. It deserves its reputation to the exceptional splendour of its palace, its gardens and the Trianons. The town, built to house all the people connected with life in the palace – dukes, ministers, officers, craftsmen – has retained its solemn appearance. The year 1661 marked the beginning of the personal reign of Louis X. The **chapel**★★★ with its harmonious white and gold decor, dedicated to Saint Louis, and begun by Mansart, was completed in 1710 by his brother-in-law Robert de Cotte. Interesting iconography covers the bas reliefs on the pillars and arcades.

The **State Apartments**★★★ (Grands Appartements) include the reception rooms, the Hall of Mirrors (Galerie des Glaces) and the King's and Queen's suites. The Hall of Mirrors, completed by Mansart in 1687, 75m/246ft long, 10m/33 ft wide and 12m/39ft high, is lit by large windows with corresponding mirrors to catch the sun's rays. They were the largest mirror panels technically possible at the time. Note the crystal chandeliers and the mouldings of the sculpted candelabra which lit the gallery in 1710 for the marriage of the Dauphin, the future Louis XVI, to Marie-Antoinette.

The **Royal Opera House**★★ (Opéra royal), begun by Gabriel in 1768, was inaugurated in 1770 for the festivities of the Dauphin's wedding. The first oval room in France, made entirely of wood, has exceptional acoustic qualities. The decoration sculpted by Pajou depicts two gods from Mount Olympus, zodiac signs and children. In the middle of the balcony, the king's private box has a removable gate.

The **Gardens**★★★, landscaped by Le Nôtre, are typical of the French or formal garden. During the Grands Eaux and evening festivities in the summer, fountains in the pools and copses embellish the park which is divided into two by the Tapis

J. L. Bohin/EXPLORER

The Chapel in the Palace of Versailles

Vert and Grand Canal stretching 1,650m/5,400ft. They provide an uninterrupted view of the horizon. Along the paths and in the copses, sculptures turn the gardens into an immense, open-air museum of classical statuary.
The **Grand Trianon**★★, or "Marble Trianon", was built in just six months by Mansart. The two main buildings, linked by a peristyle and covered with a flat roof, form a gracious ensemble. After the Revolution, Napoleon I refurbished the *Trianon*.
The **Petit Trianon**★★ stems from Louis XV's passion for botany and agronomy. The king had a "*ménagerie*" or experimental farm built, with a botanical garden and hothouses. The pavilion, with its pure lines, showcases the talent of the architect Gabriel.

PÉRIGORD-QUERCY

Périgord stretches from the Limousin to the valleys of Aquitaine. It consists of majestic valleys encircling low, wooded plateaux. Quercy, formed by a thick crust of limestone, is dissected by the valleys of the Dordogne, the Célé, the Lot and the Aveyron. The two regions are mostly farming country, with a wide variety of crops, including truffles, walnuts, strawberries and wine. It is reputed for its gourmet food – *foie gras, confit d'oie* (goose preserved in fat) and *magret de canard* (breast of duck). The area is also famed for its prehistoric sites and is known today as the French capital of prehistory.

★★CAHORS Population 19 735. Michelin map 970 H 7

Cahors, with its merchants and Lombard bankers, was a prosperous trading centre during the Middle Ages. It eventually became the most important banking centre in Europe. In 1332, Pope John XXII founded a university.

The **Valentré Bridge**★★ (Pont) was built from 1308 to 1378. Its three towers with their machicolations, crenelated parapets and Gothic arches made a formidable military construction, which kept back the English during the Hundred Years War.

St Stephen's Cathedral★ (Cathédrale St-Étienne) also resembles a fortress. It is one of the first domed churches in Aquitaine, standing 18m/59ft in diameter and 32m/105ft high. The Romanesque **North Door**★★, originally on the main façade, was moved in the 13C. Executed around 1135, the tympanum depicts the Ascension and episodes from the life of St Stephen.

★★LES EYZIES-DE-TAYAC Population 853

The village of Eyzies on the Vézère occupies a pleasant setting at the foot of cliffs topped with home oaks. The region teems with prehistoric sites, shelters and caves containing engravings and sculptures at Les Combarelles and La Mouthe, and caves with wall paintings at Font-de-Gaume★ and Lascaux★★★.

In the **National Museum of Prehistory**★ (Musée national de la Préhistoire), housed in a 13C fortress, exhibits use objects discovered in the region to retrace the activities of Cro-Magnon man 20 000 years ago.

★★★ SARLAT-LA-CANÉDA Population 9 909

At the heart of Périgord Noir (Black Périgord), Sarlat has kept its narrow medieval streets, Gothic and Renaissance mansions and Saturday market, where the produce of the season is bought and sold – poultry, cereals, walnuts, foie gras and truffles. The most typical mansions are **La Boétie's House★** (Maison de la Boétie) and the **Hôtel de Malleville★** near the cathedral, the **Hôtel Plamon★** near **Place des Oies★** and **Rue des Consuls★**.

► ► Rocamadour★★★ – Gouffre de Padirac★★★ (Padirac's Chasm).

Recapture the atmosphere, sights, sounds and gastronomic sensations of your French holiday with "France", a Michelin album packed with specially chosen photos.

PROVENCE

The lakes of Camargue, the mountain ranges of Le Ventoux and Le Luberon and the luminous banks of the rocky inlets of Cassis demonstrate the diversity of Provence. But the region also has a unity in its Mediterranean climate and flora. Antique monuments include Le Gard Bridge, Romanesque sanctuaries such as St-Trophime d'Arles, St-Gilles-du-Gard and Sénanque, and the works of artists fascinated by light – Van Gogh and Cézanne. Other attractions are the picturesque atmosphere of its markets, its pétanque games and traditional festivals.
Provençal cooking, like that of the French Riviera, smells of garlic and deep-frying oil. Marseille is famous for its *bouillabaisse*, Arles for its sausages and Aix for its almond paste sweets called *calissons*. Provence is also olive country. Wine-growing, practised since Antiquity, provides excellent local vintages such as Rosé de Provence.

★★ AIGUES-MORTES Population 4 999

The ramparts of Aigues-Mortes (dead waters) rise up in a landscape of marshland, lakes and salt-pans. In 1240, Saint Louis wanted to take a crusade to Palestine, but he needed a port on the Mediterranean. The solution was to buy land from a priory on which he rapidly built **Constance Tower★★** *(tour)*. A new town was constructed, on a regular plan surrounded by **ramparts★★**. In the 14C however, its waterways began to silt up and decline soon followed.

★★ AIX-EN-PROVENCE Population 123 842. Michelin map 970 I 7

The birthplace of Cézanne (1839-1906) has kept its 17C and 18C character. Its industrial, thermal and tourist activities, its cultural influence, particularly through its international festival of lyric art and music in July, ensure continuing popularity. And its almond-paste-based calisson sweets are delicious. During the Middle Ages, Aix expanded rapidly when the Counts of Provence made their domicile here. The Counts brought a love of literature and the arts. King René (1409-1480), Duke of Anjou and King of Naples, was a particularly great patron of the arts. He completed the cathedral and brought Flemish artists. After Provence was incorporated into France, the town was chosen as the seat of Parliament (sovereign court of justice) and its magistrates built themselves splendid mansions.

Old Aix★ owes its charm to the elegance of its mansions, squares, fountains and wide avenues built on the site of the old ramparts.

The **Cours Mirabeau★**, a delightful place to stroll with its shady plane trees, is lined with cafés – the most famous is Café des Deux Garçons – and shops. The avenue also displays beautiful sculpted doors and wrought-iron balconies.

The **Holy Saviour Cathedral★** (Cathédrale St-Sauveur) contains the **Triptych of the Burning Bush★★** (Triptych du buisson ardent). Nicolas Froment completed it around 1475. It depicts King René and Queen Joan kneeling on either side of the Virgin Mary. The portal has 16C carved walnut **leaves★**. The **cloisters★**, whose roof is supported by colonnettes, are elegant.

► ► Musée des Tapisseries★ (Tapestry Museum) – Musée Granet★ (archeology and fine arts) – Fondation Vasarely★ – Hôtel de Ville (town hall) – Fontaine des Quatre Dauphins★ (Fountain of the four Dolphins) – Montagne Ste-Victoire★★ (painted by Cézanne).

★★★ ARLES Population 52 058. Michelin map 970 I 7

Close to the Camargue plain, Arles first gained importance in Roman times and became a great religious centre in the Middle Ages. Its name is associated with Van Gogh, Daudet, Gounod and Bizet. The July festival includes folklore, dance and theatre events, as well as bull-fights in the Roman amphitheatre.

The **Amphitheatre★★** (Arènes), built in the first century, held up to 20 000 spectators. It was converted into a fortress in the Middle Ages, saving it from destruction.

The **Roman Theatre★★** (Théâtre Antique), constructed under Augustus in about 25 BC, was unfortunately quarried for stone to make churches. Only two columns from the stage wall still remain in a nostalgic setting.

The **Musée de l'Arles antique★★**, built on the edge of the Roman circus, houses behind its blue enamel walls the extensive Arles collection of ancient art (remarkable **sarcophagi★★**).

St Trophimus Church★ (Église St-Trophime) was rebuilt in the 11C, on the site of the original cathedral and dedicated to the first bishop of Arles. Its **porch★★**, whose sculpted decor compares in beauty to St-Gilles-du-Gard, boasts a triumphal arch of Roman inspiration. The 12C **cloisters★★** are renowned for their elegant sculpture.

The **Alyscamps★** was one of the most famous Western necropolises from Roman times to the end of the Middle Ages. Thousands of tombs and sarcophagi were brought here as early as the 4C.

►► Musée Réattu★ (modern and contemporary art, Picasso donation) – Museon Arlaten★ (Provençal culture and tradition).

★★★ AVIGNON Population 86 939. Michelin map 970 I 7

Avignon is an artistic and cultural centre surrounded by 14C ramparts. From 1309 to 1377 it housed the popes. The Papal Legates stayed until 1791. The city attracts cosmopolitan crowds during its annual **dramatic art festival** in July.

★★★ **Palais des Papes (Palace of the Popes)** – This fortress style building has walls flanked with high towers, some of which rise more than 50m - 164ft high. Pope Clement VI commissioned famous Italian artists such as Simone Martini and Matteo Giovanetti from Sienna to decorate the New Palace, the Consistory, the Wardrobe Room and the Stag Room.

★ **Petit Palais** – This former episcopal palace contains a magnificent collection of Italian Primitives, including a Madonna and Child by Botticelli.

★★ **Pont St-Bénézet (Bridge)** – This pedestrian and equestrian bridge is that of the famous French song, *Sur le Pont d'Avignon*. Built in 1177, rebuilt in the 13C, and restored in the 15C, Rhône floodwaters carried it away in the 17C.

►► Villeneuve-lès-Avignon★ on the Rhône's Right Bank is the cardinal city. It offers a splendid view of the Palace of the Popes. The Pierre-de-Luxembourg Municipal Museum contains a superb painting by Enguerrand Carton, *The Crowning of the Virgin*.

R. Mazin /TOP

Le Palais des Papes

EXCURSION

★★**Orange** – *30km/19mi north.* The gateway to Provence, Orange, is famous for its prestigious Roman monuments – the **Triumphal Arch**★★ (Arc de Triomphe) and the **Roman Theatre**★★★ (Théâtre antique). In July, the Theatre becomes one of the Meccas of European culture with high quality operas and symphonies.

★★★LES BAUX-DE-PROVENCE Michelin map 970 I 7

Les Baux stands 900m/3000ft long and 200m/650ft wide, silhouetted against the Alpilles with steep ravines on either side. The spectacular **site**★★★ alone merits a visit. The word "bauxite" came from the city. The arid rocky spur holds a ruined fortress and long-deserted houses. Numerous craftsmen have come to live in the village. The main attractions include the old Town Hall (Hôtel de Ville), now a Santon Museum with Christmas crib figures, **Place St-Vincent**★ with its Chapel of the White Penitents, St-Vincent's Church, in which a special **shepherds' celebration**★★ *(fête des bergers)* is held on Christmas Eve, and the citadel. An excellent **view**★★★ unfolds from the castle.

★★★MARSEILLE Population 800 550. Michelin map 970 I 7

The terraces of **Notre-Dame-de-la-Garde**, a pilgrim's basilica built in the 19C by Espérandieu, provide the best **view**★★★ of Marseille. The town began as a trading post set up by Greek mariners around 600 BC. They later set up other trading posts in Nice, Antibes and Arles. From 12C to 14C, Marseille rivalled with Genoa and Pisa for the Mediterranean shipping trade, particularly at the time of the crusades. In 1720, the town was devastated by bubonic plague killing some 100 000 people. Marseille has continued to grow and is now France's second city.

★★**Vieux Port (Old Port)** – All roads lead to the heart of Marseille, where a fish market, high in local colour, is held every morning. Restaurants along the quays sell mullet and traditional Bouillabaisse. The **Garden of Ruins** (Jardin des Vestiges) and the Museum of the History of Marseille (Musée d'Histoire de Marseille) include exhibits on the ancient Greek town and a 19m/62ft long merchant ship salvaged from the silt.

The **Old Charity Cultural Centre**★★ (Centre de la Vieille Charité), once a hospice and a workhouse for the poor, has been beautifully restored. The building, whose chapel is a Baroque masterpiece, was designed by Pierre and Jean Puget. The first floor contains a rich collection of **Oriental and Classical antiquities** and a Celt-Ligurian lapidary collection.

St Victor's Basilica★ (Basilique), on the Old Port's Left Bank, was built in the 11C and 12C on the site of a abbey. The **crypt**★★ contains a number of 4C sarcophagi.

►► Musée Cantini★ (contemporary art, Marseille earthenware) – Musée Grobet-Labadié★★ (decorative arts) – Corniche du président J F Kennedy★★ – Château d'If★★.

★★★NÎMES Population 128 471. Michelin map 970 I 7

At the foot of the limestone hills of the Garrigue, the medieval city of Nîmes owes its exceptional architectural heritage to Gallo-Roman Antiquity. Bull-fights and Camargue horse races take place in the ampitheatre.

The **amphitheatre**★★★ *(arènes)*, built slightly before the Christian era, dates from the reign of Caesar Augustus. It is exceptionally well-preserved and practically identical to that of Arles. The tiered seats are divided into four distinct areas, reflecting the social status of the spectators.

The **Maison Carrée**★★★, or Square House, is a magnificent Roman temple, built in the 5C AD. Its pure lines and careful execution, its harmonious proportions and the elegance of its fluted columns denote a Greek influence which can also be seen in the sculpted decoration of Corinthian capitals and foliated frieze.

★★★PONT DU GARD Michelin map 970 I 7

This wonder of the Ancient World is the most majestic part of an aqueduct which supplied spring water collected near Uzès to Nîmes. Built between 40 and 60 AD under the reign of the Emperor Claudius, it consists of three tiers of staggered arches. Its total height is 49m/160ft.

RHÔNE-ALPES

The Rhône Valley has always been a thoroughfare. Today, the motorway follows the river to the Mediterranean and branches into deep, wide Alpine valleys. The scenery in the Alps varies because of the different geological structures. The highest peak, Mont Blanc, rises to an altitude of 4807m/15767ft near the Swiss border. The Vanoise Massif, whose centre is covered by the Nature Park, now has the highest concentration of ski resorts in the French Alps, including Val d'Isère, Tignes, Courchevel, La Plagne, Méribel-les-Allues and Les Arcs. In the Vercors Regional Nature Park, the Autrans and Villard-de-Lans resorts are a paradise for cross-country skiers. Rambling, mountain climbing and nautical sports are popular in the summer. The recent development of the region has led to original contemporary architectural projects, such as the apartment buildings in Avoriaz, the church in Alpe-d'Huez and the Albertville Dome.
Lyon is reputed for its excellent food, supplied by rich herds of beef cattle from Bresse and Charolais, game from La Dombes, and fresh fruit and vegetables from the Rhône Valley. Specialities include *quenelles de brochet* (pike quenelles), *saucisson de Lyon* (sausage), *cervelas* (spicy saveloys containing truffles and pistachios), *cardons à la moelle* (cardoons with bone marrow) and, for those with a sweet tooth, *bugnes*. Wine comes from the Beaujolais and Côtes du Rhône vineyards.
Savoy specialises include fresh fish from its lakes, crayfish from its mountain streams, cheese from its Alpine pastures (Beaufort, Reblochon, tomme de Savoie, bleu de Sassenage) and blueberry tarts. The most well-known regional dish is the cheese fondue made with white wine. The region produces dry white wines – Abymes, Apremont or Chignin, and fruity reds such as Jongieux or Arbin. Gentian and absinthe liqueurs and marc de Savoie are a wonderful end to a meal.

★★ANNECY Population 49 644. Michelin map 970 J 6

The town of Annecy, built on the edge of a lake with fine beaches in a magnificent mountain setting, has been inhabited since prehistoric times. It was initially a lakeside settlement, then a township protected by a castle. The town became prosperous in the 16C supplanting Geneva. Annecy's main figure is Saint François de Sales (1567-1622), a bitter opponent of Calvinism. A favourite holiday place, Annecy and its surroundings are reputed for their gourmet food.

The mainly pedestrian **Old Town★★** is built on either side of the Thiou River. Its bridges offer attractive views of Mount Veyrier and the Palais de l'Île (a former prison). **Rue Ste-Claire★** has kept its 17C arcades and gable houses.

The **castle★**, constructed in the Middle Ages as a residence for the Counts of Geneva, houses an interesting regional museum and the Regional Observatory of Alpine Lakes. It contains exhibits from underwater archeological excavations.

►► Lake tour★★★ (39km/24mi by road or 1hr 30min by boat) – Talloires★★ – Crêt de Chatillon (Crest) (panoramic view★★★).

★★BRIANÇON Population 11 041. Michelin map 970 J 7

The highest town in Europe at 1321m/4333ft occupies a remarkable strategic site close to Montgenèvre Pass which leads into Italy. That explains the large number of fortresses – Dauphin Salettes, Randouillet, and Granon – surrounding the city. Briançon is near the **Serre-Chevalier★★★** ski resort, renowned for its exceptionally sunny weather of 300 days a year.

The **Upper Town★★** with its narrow, steeply-sloping streets, hasn't changed since the time of Louis XIV. It is dominated by fortifications designed by Vauban, and the citadel. The statue of France on the top is by Bourdelle. The main street **Grande Gargouille★** leads to Place d'Armes, where the façades are painted in warm colours and decorated with two sun dials.

The **Asfeld Bridge★** from the 18C boldly overlooks the Durance with its single arch spanning 40m/131ft.

★★CHAMBÉRY Population 54 120. Michelin map 970 I 6

In 1232, the Counts of Savoy chose their capital in the valley dividing the Chartreuse and Bauges massifs. Today, Chambéry is an important crossroads.

The old town is dominated by a castle. Its Flamboyant Gothic **chapel★** was built to house the Holy Shroud, which was removed to Turin when it became the capital of the House of Savoy. Chambery's most popular monument is the **Fountain of Elephants** (Fontaine des éléphants). It was errected in 1838 in memory of General de Boigne, one of the city's benefactors who made his fortune in India.

★★★CHAMONIX Population 9 700. Michelin map 970 J 6

The French capital of mountaineering lies at the widest point of the glacial Arve Valley in full view of the summit of Mont Blanc. It was climbed for the first time in 1786. Its needles and glaciers offer spectacular scenery. Chamonix hosted the first Winter Olympics in 1924. Since then, it has become a major ski resort with

a remarkable set of ski slopes covering several mountains. Experienced skiers adore the second section of the **Grands Montets★★★** and, especially, **White Valley★★★** (Vallée Blanche), a 20km/12.5mi run plunging 2800m/9200ft from Aiguille du Midi. The upper station of the **Aiguille du Midi★★★** ski lift rises to an altitude of 3800m/12500ft. The view encompasses the whole of the French side of Mont Blanc. The famous site of Montenvers lies at the foot of the **Mer de Glace★★★**, a 14km/9mi long glacier, and the formidable Dru Obelisk, with Grandes Jorasses in the background. *(For information on walks and competitions, apply to the Maison de la Montagne which is the headquarters of the Chamonix guides.)*
The **Mont-Blanc Tunnel**, built from 1959 to 1963, leads to Italy, putting Chamonix at less than 20km/12.5mi from Courmayeur. The journey takes about 25min.

★★GRENOBLE Population 150 758. Michelin map 970 I 6

Grenoble is a modern, fast-expanding city, the economic, intellectual and tourist capital of the Alps. The **site★★★** is exceptional - at the foot of the Chartreuse Massif, the rocky escarpments of Vercors and the Belledonne mountain chain. The best **view★★** is from Fort Bastille.

The **Grenoble Museum★★★** is one of France's most prestigious provincial museums with works from both the past and present, including *John the Baptist* by Champaigne, *St Jerome* by Georges de la Tour, *Interior with Aubergines* by Matisse and Picasso's *Woman Reading*.

The **Old Town** is centred around the busy **Place Grenette**, a favourite meeting place for the people of Grenoble who love to come here just to stroll.

►► Musée Dauphinois★ (Dauphiné Museum: contains exhibits on popular arts and traditions) – Palais de Justice★ (Law Courts).

★★★LYON Population 415 487. Michelin map 970 I 6

Lyon is France's second largest urban centre thanks to 20 centuries of history and an exceptional location at the junction of the Rhône and Saône Rivers. The TGV train links the city to Paris in two hours.
Chosen by Julius Caesar as a base camp, Lyon became the metropolis of the Roman Empire's Three Gauls under Augustus. Agrippa was responsible for choosing Lyon as the hub of the Roman road network linking it to Saintes, Orleans, Rouen, Geneva and Aoste. Christianity, which had reached Vienne, then Lyon, by the mid 2C, buried its first martyrs in the city. At the end of the Middle Ages, the creation of fairs and the development of the banking system attracted merchants from throughout Europe. In the 16C, silk-making turned Lyon into a major industrial city. The Croix-Rousse quarter is full of traboules or passageways designed to protect the silk from inclement weather.

The **Gallo-Roman Museum★★** (Musée de la Civilisation Gallo-Romaine) on Fourvière Hill, is at the heart of ancient Lagdunum. The architect Zehrfuss built the museum inside the hill. It overlooks the remains of a Roman amphitheatre. The museum's most striking exhibit is the bronze **Claudian Table★★★** engraved in 48 AD.

F. Barot

Place des Terreaux

Old Lyon★★, between the Saône and Fourvière Hill, forms an exceptional Gothic and Renaissance ensemble. To save space, the houses were built upwards and passageways or traboules used to connect the buildings. *(The tourist office organises guided tours.)*

The **Peninsula** (Presqu'île) contains the city centre around which both the classical and modern city have developed.
The main museums are found here: Musée de l'Imprimerie et de la Banque★★ (Printing and Banking); Musée des Beaux-Arts★★★ (Fine Arts); Musée Historique des Tissus★★★ (History of Fabrics); Musée des Arts Décoratifs★★ (Decorative Arts).

► ► Musée de la Marionette et Spectacle de Guignol (Puppet Museum) – Musée Guimet★★ (Asian art) – Musée Henri-Malartre★★ (Car Museum).

★★ROUTE NAPOLÉON

See also the section on the French Riviera. Napoleon passed through the Alps, from Valferrière Pass to Corps and from Corps to Grenoble. The route includes sites such as **Castellane★**, **Sisteron★★** and, in the last section, **Prairie de la Rencontre★**. Here the Emperor came face to face with the troops. He turned the situation to his advantage and made his triumphal entry into Grenoble. Up until Grenoble, I was an adventurer, he said. In Grenoble, I was a prince.

For further details on France, consult the Michelin Green Guide France and the Green Guides to the Regions

When looking for a hotel or restaurant, use the Michelin Red Guide France, updated annually.

Germany

Deutschland

Area: 356 500km² – 137 062sq mi – **Population:** 81 100 000 – **Capital:** Berlin – **Currency:** Deutschmark and Euro (1,95583 DEM) – **Time:** GMT + 1hr in winter, GMT + 2hr in summer

Germany, a country with no natural barriers to the west and east, is located in the heart of Europe. Neighbours have long enjoyed a large influence, helping explain the richness and diversity of German culture. Germany has varied landscapes, the lush plains bordering the River Rhine , the forested Harz mountains, the Baltic beaches, and the Luneburg Heath. Germans respect and protect this environment. The country's rich museums bear witness to a civilization deeply influenced by the arts. Tourists from around the world come to immerse themselves in this cradle of Romanticism.

IN BRIEF

Entry Formalities – A valid passport is required for British, US, Canadian, Australian and Japanese citizens.

Driving Regulations – In urban areas, drivers must not exceed 50kph/31mph, and on main roads, 100kph/81mph. No speed limit exists on the famed Autobahns, though drivers are advised not to exceed 130kph/81mph.

Shopping – Stores generally stay open from 9am to 6pm during the week, and Saturdays from 9am to 1pm. Chains proliferate throughout the country. Kaufhalle sells a complete range of moderately priced products. The department stores Karstadt, Hertie and Horten offer an extensive selection of articles.

Souvenirs – A vibrant crafts tradition remains alive. Each region and town still produces traditional objects. Examples include Christmas decorations from Nuremberg's famous Christkindlesmarkt, cuckoo clocks from the Black Forest, wooden toys from Seiffen, filigree work from Frise, Dirndl folk dresses from Miesbach and Berchtesgaden, and, of course, marzipan from Lübeck.

Biergarten and Beer Festivals – Germans quaff beer, their national drink. The country's 1200 breweries continue to respect the Reinheitsgebot decree regulating purity enacted in 1516. Hops, barley and pure water remain the basic ingredients. A wonderful afternoon consists of sitting in the early May sunlight in a Biergarten enjoying a beer. No German would think of abandoning this tradition. Munich's famous Oktoberfest brings out the German people's enjoyment of life.

Gastronomy – Although burdened with a mistaken reputation of being rich and monotonous, German cuisine serves all sorts of appetizing specialities. Excellent choices include Knödel, potato balls or soaked bread balls, and Hämchen, pig's feet with sauerkraut and mashed potatoes. However, perhaps the most successful German meal is the evening Abendessen, with its infinite variety of breads and an large number of different cheeses and cold meats.

Cherville/FOTOGRAM-STONE, Paris

Spas and Hydrotherapy – Germany boasts numerous hot springs. Resorts are found throughout the country, both medium-altitude health centres and seaside thermal establishments. Many tourists flock to the spas, often located near sites of astonishing natural beauty.

The Baroque – Many European artistic mouvements, from French Gothic to the Italian Renaissance, left their mark on Germany but the sumptuous decor of the Baroque churches stands out. The visitor should not miss the Bavarian abbeys of Ottobeuren, Wies and elsewhere which demonstrate the virtuosity of artists such as Johann Michael Fischer and Dominikus Zimmermann.

Deutsche ALPENSTRASSE★★★

GERMAN ALPINE ROAD

Michelin map 970 K 6

The German Alpine Road crosses the Allgäu and the Bavarian Alps through magnificent mountain landscapes. The traveller can also visit the famous castles of Louis II of Bavaria, stroll through the streets of pretty towns, and visit Baroque churches. This picturesque route begins at Lindau. It follows the banks of the Bodensee and leads to Berchtesgaden, in a succession of splendid sites. Some examples:

★★ **Lindau im Bodensee** – Lindau, an old imperial city, enjoys an island setting along the Bodensee (Lake Constance). Its famous old quarter is packed with gabled burgher houses bearing witness to the town's past as an important trading centre. A pleasant evening stroll lies between the port and the Maximilianstrasse, the town's main thoroughfare. Before the harbour stands the Mangturm, a fortified tower from the 12C. The visitor should proceed to the **Römerschanze**★ viewpoint and admire the Rhine Gap and the lake's Alpine surroundings.

★★★ **Königsschlösser (Bavaria's Royal castles)** – This name refers to Hohenschwangau and Neuschwanstein castles.

★ **Hohenschwangau** – Maximilian II of Bavaria built the castle in the neo-Gothic style on top of feudal ruins dating from the 12C. This architectural style was fashionable during the 1830s. In spite of a ponderous decor including vast wall paintings with medieval motifs, the Hohenschwangau preserves an intimate atmosphere. The visitor will appreciate the Biedermeier furniture in light-coloured wood, as well as a rich collection of objects attesting to the sovereign's admiration for Wagner, including the composer's correspondence and piano. Louis II's bedroom seems out of this world with its ceiling painted as the vault of heaven covered with stars that actually light up. From his window, the king could follow the progress of construction work on nearby Neuschwanstein.

★★ **Neuschwanstein** – Like the Hohenschwangau, a theatre designer, not an architect, designed this granite fortress studded with pinnacles and artificial turrets. That helps explain the unreal decor in gold and extravagant paintings. The false grotto with stalactites on the third floor remains a real highlight. It evokes the legend of Tannhäuser, a theme repeated many times throughout the castle. The swan, an etymological motif is also displayed in profusion in Neuschwanstein and Hohenschwangau. Louis II lived in Neuschwanstein for only 170 days.

★★ **Wies Church** – Dominikus Zimmermann (1685-1766) designed this church in the midst of meadows, forests and peat bogs. A sober exterior conceals the magnificent Rococo Baroque interior. Golden stucco, frescoes, columns and balustrades drown the choir. Light entering through many openings, typical of Zimmerman's style, bathes the entire church.

★ **Oberammergau** – Every 10 years in summer this small town of craftsmen becomes world famous by hosting a Passion Festival. After a plague epidemic in 1633 that was miraculously cut short, the inhabitants vowed to produce the festival. Painted façades mark certain houses in the town.

★★ **Linderhof Castle** – This small, luxurious palace is one of Prince Louis II of Bavaria's many commissions. The exotic **Maurischer Kiosk** (Moorish Pavilion), the Baroque castle and the gardens inspired by Italian Renaissance villas combine for an astonishing and charming site.

★★★ **Garmisch-Partenkirchen** – This famous international resort hosted the fourth Winter Olympic Games in 1936. Apart from a tour of the Olympic installations, visit the **Zugspitze**★★★, Germany's highest peak (2964m/9722ft). It offers a superb panorama. The ride up via a rack-railway climb takes 75 minutes.

★★ **Wendelstein** – Another ascent, the Wendelstein (1838/6029ft), starts from Brannenburg-Waching. The summit offers another panoramic view of the surrounding mountains with their jagged peaks and glacial crests.

★ **Chiemsee Lake** – Bavaria's largest lake, with a surface area of 82km²/31sq mi, is known as the Bavarian Sea . Surrounded by the Bavarian Alps, the lake contains two islands, one housing an unfinished copy of Versailles Palace, the other with an abbey.

Herreninsel – Ludwig II of Bavaria purchased this island in 1873 to build the sumptuous **Herrenchiemsee Castle**★★. His great admiration for Louis XIV inspired him to copy the entire Versailles palace, including the Mirror Gallery and the French style gardens. The King died after spending only one week in the castle and construction was stopped.

★★ **Berchtesgaden** – The town is located on a narrow stretch of land that extends across the German frontier into Austria, and is enclosed on three sides by the Watzmann, Steinernes Meer and Hagenbirge mountain chains. A starting point for

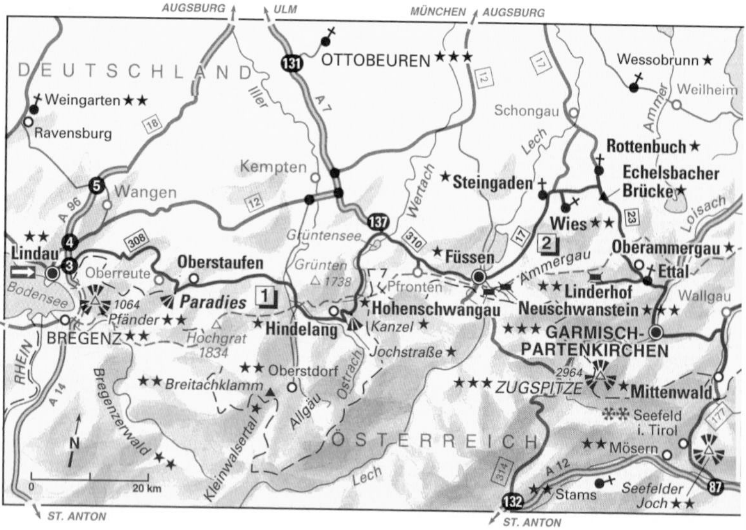

many excursions, tourists frequent it in the summer, especially for the train tour of its salt mines. The **Schloßplatz★**, at the old town's heart, is a triangular square with a gallery of arcades from the 16C on one side. A church and an old canon's priory dominate the other two sides.

Hitler chose Berchtesgaden as a holiday retreat. After the 1923 abortive putsch, he came to the nearby **Obersalzberg**, and after his seizure of power, the chalet Berghof was enlarged to host diplomatic receptions. An American bombing raid destroyed most of the buildings in April 1945.

Hitler built his Eagle's Nest in the mountainous landscape of **Kehlstein★★**. A bus climbs to the magnificent panorama on an impressive small **road★★★**. The **view★★** is magnificent.

★★ **Königsee** – The **St Bartholomä Chapel** stands at the edge of this beautiful lake nestled under steep mountains. A triple apse appears in the form of overlapping wedges. Further on, a small village lies hidden under leafy maple trees.

Two main festivals:

Bayreuth (end of July to end of August) Richard Wagner Festival.

Donaueschingen (third weekend in October) Festival of Contemporary Music.

BAYREUTH★

Population 72 000
Michelin map 970 K5

The Franconian town of Bayreuth served as the residence of the Margraves of Brandenburg-Bayreuth. In the 18C, it became the headquarters of Wilhelmina and Frederick of Brandenburg-Bayreuth. Later, lovers of **Wagner**'s great music turned it into a pilgrimage destination. Here the maestro lived and built his festival theatre, the Festspielhaus, inaugurated in 1876 by the Ring of the Nibelungs.

★ **Markgräfliches Opernhaus (Margrave Opera House)** – Margrave Princess, Wilhelmina built this Baroque court theatre in the mid-18C, and it remains one of Germany's best preserved. Exuberant wood ornamentation reveals the work of two brilliant decorators, Giuseppe and Carlo Galli-Bibiena, from Bologna, and makes the interior an astonishing sight.

★ **Haus Wahnfried** – Only the façade remains of the Wahnfried Villa, where Wagner lived from 1874. Nevertheless, the building has been transformed into a Wagnerian memorial including the maestro's furniture, manuscripts, and pianos.

EXCURSIONS

★ **Sanspareil** – This **rock garden★** *(Felsengarten)* dates from the 18C. It was created by Wilhemina and her husband, Frederick. The nearby **Morgenländische Bau** (Eastern House) demonstrates the purest Bayreuth Rococo style.

★★ **Luisenburg** – A path leads through this labyrinth of enormous granite boulders and eroded or superimposed rocks. Several viewpoints along the way give onto Fichtelgebirge.

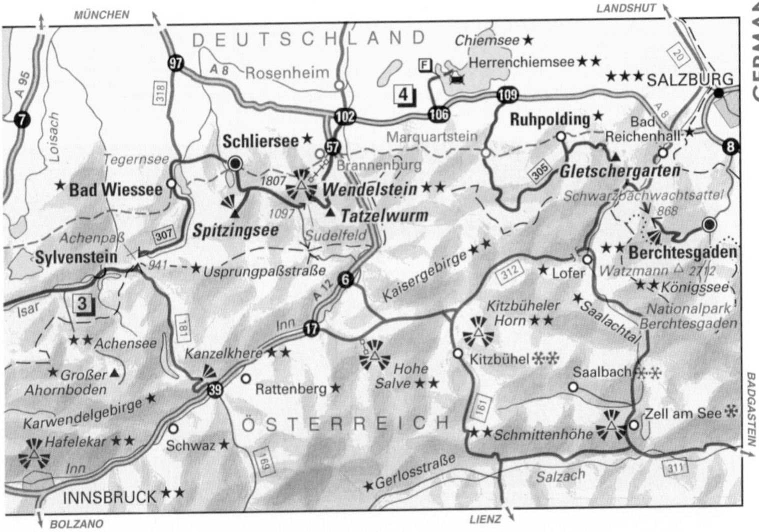

BERLIN★★★

Population 3 200 000
Michelin map 970 L 4

Berlin, the capital of reunited Germany, is one of Europe's most attractive large cities. It boasts a modern urban structure, and a dynamic cultural and economic life.

HISTORICAL NOTES

The Great Elector – After becoming the Hohenzollern dynasty's capital in the 15C, **Friedrich-Wilhelm** of Brandenburg (1640-1688) transformed Berlin into a clean, well-governed city. He welcomed Huguenots fleeing France from the Revocation of the Edict of Nantes, and during his rule, Berlin became a centre for trade and culture.
In the 18C, Frederick I built the Palace of Charlottenburg for his wife, Sophie-Charlotte. His successor, Friedrich-Wilhelm I (1713-1740), ordered construction of the town of Friedrichstadt, framed by three monumental squares. Frederick II the Great (1740-1786) built the famous Unter den Linden (literally Under the Lime Trees) and constructed the Forum Fredericianum.
Prussian Berlin entered the industrial era early in the 19C. The Reichstag was built, and new open spaces designed. In 1871, Berlin was named capital of the German Empire.

Grandeur and decadence – Berlin played a central role in the excitement of the roaring 1920s. In theatres, playwrights such as Max Reinhardt and Bertolt Brecht excelled, while in cinema, directors such as Ernst Lubitsch, Fritz Lang and Carl Mayer produced masterpieces. However, Hitler ended Berlin's artistic flowering by launching persecution of the Jews and repression of "degenerate art".
In February 1945 at the Yalta Conference, the major powers divided Berlin. From 21 April to 3 May, the final battles between the Red Army and the German Army devastated the city and its bridges. On 30 April, Hitler committed suicide. Germany surrendered in Berlin on 8 May, 1945, and Berlin was divided into American, French, English and Soviet sectors.

Division and Reunification – Soviet pressure isolated the Eastern sector beginning in 1948. Then, in 1949, the Eastern authorities proclaimed a Democratic Republic. On 13 August, 1961, they cut all communication between the two Berlins and build the infamous Wall.
The fall of the Berlin Wall on 9 November, 1989, restored free passage between the two parts of the city and signaled the opening of the East. In June 1991, the Bundestag declared Berlin once again capital of a reunited Germany.

LIFE IN BERLIN

Most of Berlin's houses and buildings were rebuilt following the war, giving the city a resolutely modern feel. Parks account for more than a third of the city's total area. The diversity and quality of theatre, concerts and exhibits make Berlin a cultural and artistic centre.
Many nationalities intermingle in Berlin; the visitor may choose between exotic Turkish cuisine to local choice Brandenburger cooking, complete with pig's feet and pea puree. Wash it all down with a *Berliner Weisse mit Schuss*, a dark beer with a dash of raspberry syrup.

★★HISTORIC CENTRE

★**Reichstag** (NY) – A fire destroyed this neo-Renaissance palace in 1933. Several times restored, it now houses reunited Germany's National Assembly.

Gregor /EXPLORER, Paris

Berlin's Brandebourg Gate

★★**Brandenburger Tor (Brandenburg Gate)** (NZ) – Before the Fall of Berlin's Wall, this monumental gate was located in no man's land and symbolised the city's division. Carl Gotthard Langhans' 1789 design incorporated six Doric columns inspired by the Propylae of the Parthenon. Gottfried Schadow's well-known 1793 Victory Quadraga crowns the frieze.

★★**Unter den Linden** (NOZ) – Starting at Friedrichstrasse, a series of monuments dating from the 17C to the 19C line this famous Under the Lime Trees Avenue.

★★**Gendarmenmarkt** (OZ)– Stables for King Friedrich-Wilhelm I's Men of Arms were first located in this square. Nowadays, the site is framed by the Schauspielhaus, a theatre built by Schinkel in 1821, the 18C Deutscher Dom (German Cathedral) and the 18C Französischer Dom (French Cathedral).

★**Alexanderplatz** (QY) – This huge esplanade designed in the 1960s was the heart of the socialist city. It is named after Czar Alexander I, who visited the city in November 1805. The nearby **Fernsehturm**, the head office of *Deutsche Telekom*, is 365m high. The view★★★ from the top is outstanding.

★**Nicolaiviertel (St Nicholas Quarter)** (PYZ)– The two bell-towers of St-Nicholas Church dominate this neighbourhood, located in the middle of the city. A tranquil provincial town atmosphere reigns with cobbled streets and taverns.

★★★MUSEUM ISLAND

This vast collection of buildings was erected in the beginning of the 19C to house the rich collections of the national museums of Berlin.

★★★**Pergamon-Museum (Pergamon Museum)** (OY) – The museum, which dates from the 1930s, is divided into five sections: the Antikensammlung (Antiquities Collection) including the Pergamon Altar, the Vorderasiatisches Museum (Middle East Museum) containing the remarkable ancient Babylon procession dating from 580 BC, the Islamisches Museum (Islamic Museum), the Far East Collection (Chinese and Japanese porcelain and ceramics), and the Museum für Volkskunde (Museum of Popular Art).

★★**Alte Nationalgalerie (National Gallery)** (PY **M**[20]) – This building (1867-1876) designed by Friedrich A Stüler contains 19C and early 20C paintings and sculptures from artists such as Adolph von Menzel, Max Liebermann, JG Schadow, and Franz Krüger.

★★**Bodemuseum (Bode Museum)** (OY) – The former Kaiser-Friedrich-Museum includes five sections: the Ägyptisches Museum (Egyptian Museum), the Museum für Spätanike und Byzantinische Kunst (Byzantine and pre-Christian Art), the Skulpturen Sammlung (Sculpture Collection), the Gemäldegalerie (paintings from the 13C to the 18C), and the Münzkabinett (Numismatic Exhibition).

★★**Altes Museum (Old Museum)** (PY **M**[18]) – Built by Schinkel, Berlin's first public museum is famed for its 87m-long neo-Classical colonnade and for hosting major exhibitions.

★★TIERGARTEN QUARTER (NZ)

Berlin's oldest park covers almost 3km/1.9mi. Architect PJ Lenné (1789-1866) transformed it into an elegant English-style park. Just to the north lies the Hanse residential quarter, rebuilt in 1957 by 14 world-famous architects, including Le Corbusier and Scharoun.

★★★**Zoologischer Garten (Zoological Garden)** – This is one of the largest zoos in the world, with more than 14 000 animals. The aquarium is also enormous. The first floor terrarium houses crocodiles.

★★**Kunstgewerbemuseum (Museum of the Decorative Arts)** – This museum surveys decorative arts from the Middle Ages through contemporary industrial design. A highlight is the **Guelph Treasure**★★★. This reliquary in the form of a Byzantine domed church was created in Cologne, around 1175. It supposedly holds the head of St Gregory. The Kupferstichkabinett und Sammlung of Zeichnungen und **Druckgraphik**★ (Print Collection) constitutes one of the world's most important collection of drawings and engravings, including works by Dürer, Bruegel the Elder, Rembrandt and Botticelli. Finally the Neue **Nationalgalerie**★★ (New National Gallery) houses paintings and sculptures from 19C and 20C artists such as Paul Klee, Max Ernst, and the Bauhaus School.

★★★**Philharmonic Hall** – Herbert von Karajan directed the Philharmonic Orchestra in this building. The architect Scharoun designed this asymmetrical edifice with an unusual interior, placing the orchestra in the centre of the concert hall, completely surrounded by tiered rows of seats.

►► **Musical Instruments Museum**★, in a nearby annex, contains many instruments, some dating back to the 16C.

★★CHARLOTTENBURG

Frederick I ordered the construction of this castle for his wife Sophie-Charlotte. Work began in 1695 and was finished in 1710 when a dome was built above the central building. Andreas Schlüter's 1703 **equestrian statue of the Great Elector**★★ stands majestically in the Court of Honor★.
The castle includes many remarkable rooms, especially the great apartments★★ (Historische Räume), the **Porcelain Room**★★ in the central building, the **Romantic Gallery**★ (Nationalgalerie) in the **Knobelsdorff wing**★★ housing an important collection of early 19C Romantic paintings, including works by Caspar David Friedrich and Schinkel, and lastly the **Golden Gallery**★★, a 42m-long gallery in the purest Prussian Rococo style, in shades of tender green and rose, with gilded stucco, intertwined scrolls, foliage, garlands and cornucopia. Of final note is the remarkable **French 18C painting**★★ collection assembled by Frederick II and displayed in the royal apartments.

►► **Ägyptisches Museum**★★★ (Egyptian Museum) includes a painted bust of **Nefertiti**★★★ (1350 BC). **Sammlung Berggreuen**★★ has works by Picasso and Paul Klee.

★★★DAHLEM MUSEUMS

★★★**Gemäldegalerie (Gallery of Painting)** – All schools from the 13C to the 18C are found here. The ground floor, reserved for 16C painting, includes fine paintings by Dürer and Hans Holbein the Younger as well as works by Dutch and Flemish Primitives, such as Brueghel the Elder and Jerome Bosch, and Italian painters such as Giotto and Botticelli. On the first floor, Rubens and Rembrandt represent the Dutch Golden Century, and Poussin and Claude Lorrain portray traditional French landscapes.

★★**Sculptures** – This fabulous collection includes Byzantine and Christian works from the 3C to the 19C. Medieval German statues include works of wood carvers from Swabia, Franconia and the Upper Rhine. Jean de Bologne's graceful terra-cotta virgins and small bronzes, and Donatello's Madone Pazzi are found in the Italian Renaissance collection.

★★★**Museum für Volkerkunde (Ethnographic Museum)** – The Central and South American collection attest to the complexity of Mayan culture. Sacred and profane Aztec sculptures are displayed. The **Gold Room**★★★ exhibits magnificent engraved jewellery and cult objects from the 7C to the 11C BC. The Oceania section presents sculpted wood and painted masks from New Guinea, while the Africa section houses Ife terracottas from Nigeria and bronzes from Benin.

►► **Museum für Deutsche Volkskunde**★ (German Folk Museum) presents various aspects of rural life, including furniture and costumes. It evokes agricultural and crafts traditions.

BERLIN HISTORIC CENTRE

Albrechtstraße .... OY 4
Alte Schönhauser Straße .... PX 9
Am Kupfergraben .... OY 13
Am Weidendamm .... OY 19
An der Spandauer Brücke .... PY 21
Bodestraße .... PY 36
Brüderstraße .... PZ 40
Bunsenstraße .... NY 46
Burgstraße .... PY 48
Charlottenstraße .... OYZ 52
Französische Straße .... OZ 69
Friedrichsgracht .... PZ 73
Friedrichstraße .... OYZ
Georgenstraße .... OY 79
Gertraudenbrücke .... PZ 81
Gertraudenstraße Große .... PZ 82
Hamburger Straße .... PX 100
Hackescher Markt .... PY 106
Holzmarktstraße .... QZ 124
Inselbrücke .... QZ 133
Inselstraße .... QZ 135
Jannowitzbrücke .... QZ 136

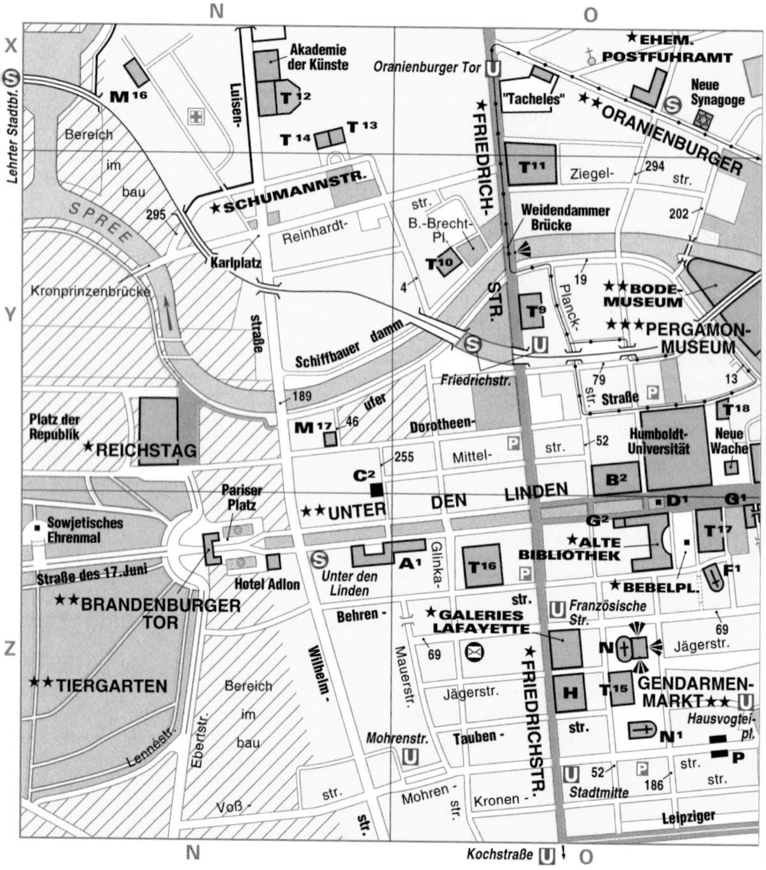

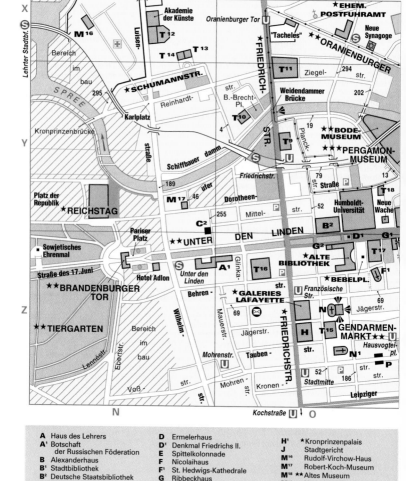

A Haus des Lehrers
A¹ Botschaft der Russischen Föderation
B Alexanderhaus
B¹ Stadtbibliothek
B² Deutsche Staatsbibliothek
C Berolinahaus
C¹ Heiliggeistkapelle
C² Schadowhaus
D Ermelerhaus
D¹ Denkmal Friedrichs II.
E Spittelkolonnade
F Nicolaihaus
F¹ St. Hedwigs-Kathedrale
G Ribbeckhaus
G¹ Prinzessinnenpalais
G² Gouverneurhaus
H „Quartier 206"
H¹ ★Kronprinzenpalais
J Stadtgericht
M¹⁶ Rudolf-Virchow-Haus
M¹⁷ Robert-Koch-Museum
M¹⁸ ★★Altes Museum
M¹⁹ Neues Museum
M²⁰ ★★Alte Nationalgalerie
M²¹ ★Knoblauchhaus

EXCURSIONS

★★ **Kloster Chorin (Chorin Abbey)** – *128km/58mi to the northeast.* Cistercian monks from Lehnin built this abbey, now in ruins, back in the 13C. The edifice is made of brick, with three naves, each preceded by a façade crowned with pediments. In spite of its poor condition, it represents a remarkable example of primitive Gothic architecture.

★ **Rheinsberg Castle** – *70km/32mi to the northwest.* In 1734, Friedrich-Wilhelm I purchased the Rheinsburg stronghold for his son, Friedrich II. Four years later, the latter entrusted the architect Johann Gottfried Kemmeter with the castle's transformation. Ensconced in his new Baroque castle, the young Friedrich began his correspondence with Voltaire.

The central building, designed by the Royal Prince, Georg Wenzeslaus von Knobelsdorff, includes an attic with four allegorical statues. The corner buildings were added at the end of the 18C by Georg Friedrich Boumann the Younger.

The **interior** includes magnificent ceilings painted by Antoine Pesne, especially in the mirror gallery and the Bacchus cabinet.

Jungfernbrücke	PZ	139	Mühlendammbrücke	PZ	205	Rungestraße	QZ	249
Klosterstraße	QY	150	Neue Roßstraße	QZ	210	Schadowstraße	NOY	255
Köpenicker Straße	QZ	154	Neue Schönhauser Straße	PX	211	Scharnhorststraße	NX	256
Krausnickstraße	PX	160	Niederwallstraße	PZ	214	Schillingstraße	QY	261
Liebknechtbrücke	PY	171	Oberwallstraße	PZ	216	Schloßbrücke	PYZ	264
Märkisches Ufer	QZ	177	Poststraße	PZ	226	Spandauer Damm	PY	280
Markgrafenstraße	OZ	186	Rathausbrücke	PZ	232	Unterbaumstraße	NY	295
Marschallbrücke	NY	189	Rathausstraße	PY	234	Waisenstraße	QZ	298
Memhardstraße	QXY	195	Roßstraßensbrücke	PZ	244	Weinmeisterstraße	PX	307
Monbijoustraße	OY	202				Werderstraße	PZ	309

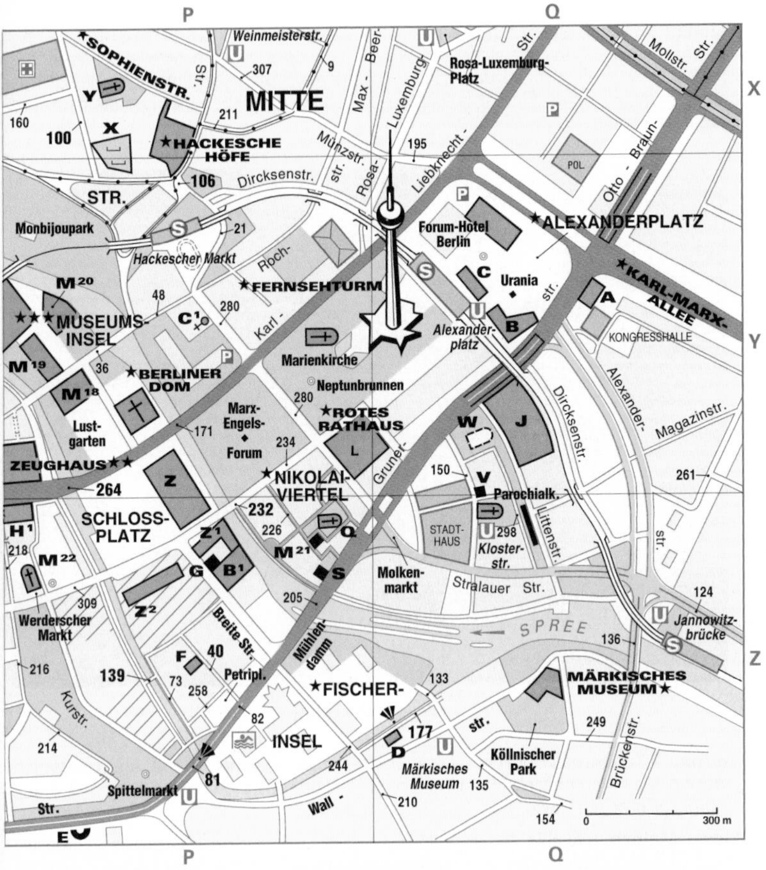

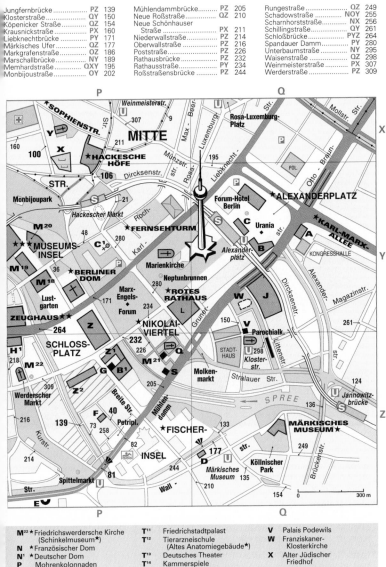

M²²	★Friedrichswerdersche Kirche (Schinkelmuseum★)	T¹¹	Friedrichstadtpalast	V	Palais Podewils
N	★Französischer Dom	T¹²	Tierarzneischule (Altes Anatomiegebäude★)	W	Franziskaner-Klosterkirche
N¹	★Deutscher Dom	T¹³	Deutsches Theater	X	Alter Jüdischer Friedhof
P	Mohrenkolonnaden	T¹⁴	Kammerspiele	Y	Sophienkirche
Q	★Nikolaikirche	T¹⁵	★★Schauspielhaus	Z	Palast der Republik
S	★Ephraim-Palais	T¹⁶	Komische Oper	Z¹	Neuer Marstall
T⁹	Metropol-Theater (ehem. Admiralspalast)	T¹⁷	★Deutsche Staatsoper	Z²	Staatsratsgebäude
T¹⁰	Berliner Ensemble	T¹⁸	Maxim-Gorki-Theater (ehem. Singakademie)		

The **park** was arranged following Frederick's strong taste for gardening; pleasure gardens lie next to vegetable gardens.

★★ **Spreewald** – *50km/23mi to the southeast.* This ancient swamp was painstakingly drained and cleared. Now it is crisscrossed by over 300 waterways. The Sorabians, a Slav people who migrated from Veneti, still live here.
From Lübbenau, **barge trips** *(Kahnfahrt)* take the visitor into the heart of delightful verdant countryside. The silence is absolute, broken only by occasional bird calls. The tiny lagoon village of **Lehde★** has an interesting open-air museum (Freilandmuseum Lehde).

To find the description of a sight, a historical event, a monument... consult the index at the end of the guide.

BODENSEE★★

Lake CONSTANCE

The Bodensee enjoys a remarkably mild climate, which Germans often compare to the Riviera. The lake extends from Bregenz to Radolfzell. Boat services offer cruises and excursions from Konstanz, Überlingen, Meersburg, Friedrichshafen, Lindau and Bregenz.

★★**Lindau im Bodensee** – Lindau adds the pleasant atmosphere of an island setting to the charm of its old streets. A visitor can take evening strolls between the harbour and Maximilianstrasse, savouring the retro charm and quality of life in this small Swabian town. Lindau is located on the edge of the lake, not far from the Austrian border.

B. Duke /SUPERBILD, München

Lindau

★**Birnau** – The Birnau Church, where pilgrims come to venerate the Virgin, is worth visiting for its architecture and Rococo decoration. In the choir, a flattened dome supports brackets decorated with Rococo scroll.

★★**Insel Mainau** – A mild climate allowed a vast park with exotic plants to flourish on this island. Baden's Grand Dukes and their heirs from the royal house of Sweden originally planted the garden. Romantic forested areas alternate with flower beds, hibiscus, orange trees and daturas.

★**Insel Reichenau** – Reichenau Island represented one of the West's most important monastic centres during the 10C and 11C. Today the St George Carolingian Church still stands. Its remarkable **wall paintings**★★ (executed c 1000) represent the miracles of Christ. In the town of Mittelzell, the **old abbey**★ (8C-12C) holds a Romanesque bell-tower with a decorative band in the Lombard style.

BREMEN★★

BREMEN – Population 530 000
Michelin map 970 J 4

Bremen is Germany's oldest maritime city. In 1358 the city joined the Hanseatic League, a maritime and trading league connecting cities throughout Northern Germany. In 1646, Bremen became a free Imperial city. As early as 1738, it established direct trading with the United States. Traditionally, the city traded cotton and coffee.

★★**Marktplatz** – The market square is found in the heart of old Bremen. It contains the city's oldest buildings such as the Schütting, the former merchant headquarters built in the Flemish style. A statue of Roland dating from 1404 stands in the square, covered by a Gothic canopy 10m/33ft high.

★**Rathaus (town hall)** – The building's main section is Gothic, with a three-floor façade. An arcade topped by a richly carved balustrade covers the first floor, where as the second supports Gothic statues of Charlemagne and the Seven Electors, and three gables embellish the top floor.

Inside, the impressive spiral **staircase★★** *(Treppe)* in carved wood dates from 1620. The **Güldenkammer** (Guildhall) still preserves the leather wall hangings enriched with gold.
When leaving, a bronze statue located at the corner of the west wing represents Bremen's animal musicians, a donkey, a cat and a cock standing in a pyramid. They come from the famous fairy tale by the Grimm brothers.

★**St.Petri-Dom (Cathedral)** – First built in the 11C, the cathedral was subsequently modified in the 16C and 19C. A lovely 16C **Virgin with child★** is found inside to the left of the raised chancel. The 11C crypt has Romanesque capitals and a splendid 13C bronze **baptismal font★★** *(Taufbecken)*.

★**Böttcherstrasse** – Roselius, a wealthy coffee merchant, built this narrow street connecting the Market Square to the River Weser from 1923 to 1933. The architecture mixes the local and Expressionist style inspired by the Jugendstil (Art Nouveau) mouvement. This unique street contains museums, theatres, bookstores, art galleries, and taverns.

★**The Schnoor** – This collection of small streets once housed fishermen. Its restored houses now contain restaurants, art galleries and shops. As one of the last vestiges of Old Bremen, the Schnoor remains lively in the evenings.

★★**Focke-Museum (Focke Regional Museum)** – This museum evokes Bremen's history. Rich art objects and statues, originally from the town hall façade, along Medieval and Renaissance furniture and tableware are all displayed. The first floor is devoted to the 17C and 18C art, with portraits of rich merchants, stained glass, and ceramics. The ground floor exhibits magnificent silverware from 19C Bremen. Another gallery details the city's seafaring economy from the Middle Ages through the 20C. In the park surrounding the museum, a traditional Lower Saxony thatched farmhouse, the Haus Mittelsbüren, can be visited.

BREMERHAVEN★

Population 133 300
Michelin map 970 J 4

Bremen's deep-sea port was constructed in 1827 at the mouth of the River Weser. In addition to this harbour for large cargo ships, Bremerhaven also possesses a shipping terminal **(Columbuskaje)** as well as a fishing port **(Fischereihafen)**. The famous fish auction can be visited from Monday to Friday starting at 7am in the Fischauktionshallen warehouses.

★★★**Deutsches Schiffahrtsmuseum (National Maritime Museum)** – This museum designed by the architect Scharoun presents the entire history of the German merchant marine and navy. Twentieth century passenger ships are exhibited in the basement. The large 18C and 19C sailing ships are on the ground floor, where as models of ancient ships from Europe are on the first floor. A basin filled with water and polyethylene glycol preserves a cog found in Bremen harbour in 1962. This type of ship was widely used during the Middle Ages.

DRESDEN★★★

DRESDEN – Population 500 000
Michelin map 970 L 4

Dresden was initially a Slavic town. The Margraves of Meissen germanized it in the 12C, and from 1485 to 1918, the city remained a possession of the Polish Albertine princes.
Dresden blossomed in the middle of the 18C under the reign of the Saxon electors Augustus II the Strong and Augustus III. They built splendid architecture and the amassed fabulous collections of objects and works of art.
Dresden became one of Europe's most prestigious artistic and cultural centres, known as the Florence of the Elba. Unfortunately the city was severely damaged by an air raid on the night of 13-14 February 1945, killing more than 100 000 people and destroying many monuments. Since that time, the historic patrimony has been rebuilt and the monuments restored.

HISTORIC CENTRE

★★★**Zwinger** – This magnificent Baroque ensemble, originally a greenhouse, was built by the architect Matthäus Daniel Pöppelmann (1662-1736). It includes a huge esplanade surrounded by galleries and pavilions. The architecture and carvings, a succession of windows with Romanesque arches, creates a harmonious rhythm.

The courtyard is flanked by the **Carillon Pavilion** and the **Rampart Pavilion★★** (Wallpavillon), with their decoration of atlantes drowned in a sea of vegetation. The **Bath of the Nymphs★★** (Nymphenbad) is a Baroque masterpiece of fountains and Rococo grottoes with gracefully sensual female statues.

★★ **Porzellansammlung (Porcelain Collection)** – Augustus the Strong collected porcelain pieces from Japan and China in the 18C and from the nearby Meissen factory. Kirchner and Kändler's giant animals are also displayed, as well as works by Böttger, the inventor of Saxon porcelain.

★★★ **Gemäldegalerie (Old Masters Gallery)** – Augustus the Strong and Augustus III amassed one of the richest 18C collections in the world. The quality of this collection can be appreciated through the works of many master artists. Rubens, Vermeer, Holbein, Cranach, and Dürer represent Dutch, Flemish and German painting. Italian painting includes works by Veronese, Tintoretto, Botticelli, Mantegna, and Raphael. The French painters include Claude Lorrain, Poussin and Watteau, and the Spanish School is represented by Velasquez, Murillo, El Greco and Zurbaran.

★★ **Rüstkammer (Arms Room)** – This room contains some fine weapons, especially tournament arms, muskets, rifles, and superb armours. King Eric XIV of Sweden's parade armour merits attention for its elaborately worked surface. Do not miss the collection of armour for children, the only one of its kind in the world.

Jogschies /EXPLORER, Paris

The Carillon Pavillon at the Zwinger

★★ **Mathematisch-Physikalischer Salon (Salon of Mathematics and Physics)** – In this pavilion, find instruments used for measurement, cartography and observation. On the first floor, a collection of clocks from the 16C is displayed.

★★ **Semper-Oper** – This opera house, which was built between 1871 and 1878, gets its name from its architect, Manfred Semper. It was inspired by the Italian Renaissance style and has two tiers of arches topped by a third tier set back from the main line of the building.

★★ **Ehemalige Katholische Hofkirche (Cathedral)** – Constructed in the Italian Baroque style in the mid 18C, this huge 5 000m²/53 820sq ft cathedral has a 85m/279ft bell-tower. It is decorated with many statues of the saints and apostles. Anton Raphael Mengs's magnificent 1750 painting on the main altar depicts the Ascension. Permoser executed the pulpit in 1722, while the organ (1750-1753) is master craftsman Gottfried Silbermann's last known work.

★★★ **Grünes Gewölbe (Green Vault Collection)** – The Saxon sovereigns assembled this veritable treasure-house of art. It includes a composition of more than 130 gilded and enamelled figurines depicting The Court of Delhi on the Birthday of the Grand Mogul.

★★★ **Gemäldegalerie Neue Meister (Gallery of 19C and 20C painting)** – Painters from various German schools are presented: the Romantic School (Caspar Friedrich David), the Biedermeier School (C Spitzweg), the Bourgeois Realists (A von Menzel), the Germans in Rome (A Böcklin), Jugendstil (Art Nouveau) painters (F von Uhde), Impressionists (M Liebermann), the Die Brücke mouvement (K Schmidt-Rottluf) and the period between the two world wars, including Otto Dix.

★ **Städtische Galerie im Lenbachhaus (Villa Lenbachhaus Collections)** – In this villa built in the Florentine style can be seen fine collections of 19C **Munich paintings**, especially Blaue Reiter works by Kandinski, F. Marc *(Cheval bleu)*, Klee and Macke.

EXCURSIONS

★**Schloß Moritzburg** – *14km/6.3mi to the northwest.* This castle originally was a hunting lodge from the Renaissance period. It was remodeled in the 18C by Pöppelmann as a Baroque-style castle. Four massive ochre and white towers rise at each corner of the building, and their domes reflect in the mirror of an artificial lake. Inside the Baroque Museum may be visited.

★**Schloß Pillnitz** – *15km/6.8mi to the east.* This castle upriver from Dresden was built from 1720-1724, and is yet another work by Pöppelmann. Baroque pavilions, covered by curved roofs in the Chinese style, house the Museum of Decorative Arts. The park on the banks of the River Elbe was transformed into an English-style garden in 1778.

★★★**Sächsische Schweiz (Swiss Saxony)** – The Swiss Saxony region is located between Dresden and the Czech border. The landscape is a succession of sandstone tables, long gorges cut out of the rock. The most spectacular rock carved out by the erratic passage of the water is the **Bastei Belvedere**★★★.

FRANKFURT AM MAIN★★

FRANKFURT ON THE MAIN – Population 627 500
Michelin map 970 J 5

Frankfurt is both the commercial capital of Germany and a centre for scientific research. Many cultural organisations, universities, museums and scientific research institutions are located in the city. Frankfurt's economic role is emphasized by its many huge trade shows, such as the famous Book Fair (Buchmesse). Daily life is vibrant, especially in and around the **Zeil**, the largest shopping street. A Handkäs mit Musik, a small yellow cheese served in onion sauce, may be tasted in the taverns located in the Alt-Sachsenhausen.
Frankfort acquired its status as an economic and political centre in the early 12C. Frederick Barbarossa engineered his election as Germanic emperor in 1152 here. The emperors of the Holy Roman Empire followed in his footsteps from 1563 to 1806. The financial market also grew in the 16C, 18C and 19C. The city became headquarters of prestigious banks, including Bethmann and Rothschild.
Last but not least, Frankfurt must be remembered as the birthplace of **Goethe** in 1749. The writer often mentions the city in his memoirs (*Aus meinem* Leben). He composed his novel *Werther* here in four short weeks.

OLD TOWN

Römer and Römerberg – The **Römer** is a hodge-podge of three reconstructed medieval burgher's houses. The complex owes its name to the **Zum Römer House**, the oldest and most luxurious merchant abode. Its imperial room can be visited. The three stepped Gothic gables, which have become the symbol for Frankfurt, look over the Römerberg. The **Fountain of Justice** stands in the middle of the square, surrounded by the charming half-timbered houses.

★**Dom (Cathedral)** – This hall-church was built between the 13C and the 15C. It includes a tall **West Tower**★★ (Westturm) from the 19C, topped by a dome and a lantern sitting on a neo-Gothic peristyle sheltering a strongly expressive Crucifixion (1509). The church itself is distinguished by three naves and a wide transept. The choir includes superb 14C **stalls**★ and mural paintings from 1427 depict the legend of St Bartholomew, the work of a master from Cologne. The **Altar of Mary Sleeping**, finished in 1434, can be found in the chapel to the left of the choir, while the **Descent from the Cross** of Anton van Dyck from 1627 hangs from the west wall of the north transept.

★**Goethe-Haus (Goethe's House)** and **Goethe-Museum (Goethe Museum)** – The house where Goethe was born still holds the furniture and memorabilia evoking the family atmosphere that surrounded the young poet when he was growing up. The nearby museum presents documents and manuscripts on his life and work.

LEFT BANK OF THE MAIN

The River Main's left bank is lined with an impressive series of museums known as Museum Row.

★★**Städelsches Museum und Städtische Galerie (Städel Museum and Municipal Gallery)** – An important collection of Flemish Primitives and 16C German masters, including works by Hans Memling, Van Eyck, Altdorfer, Brueghel the Younger, is displayed on the second floor. Flemish and French painting from the 17C is represented by

Rubens, Rembrandt, Chardin, Watteau and Poussin. Impressionism is dominated by Renoir and Monet, German Expressionism by Kirchner, Marc and Beckmann. Picasso, Braque and Matisse represent Cubism, and Dubuffet, Bacon and Tapiès highlight the contemporary art.

★**Museum für Kunsthandwerk (Museum of Applied Arts)** – New York architect Richard Meier designed this well-lit white building in 1985. The Museum houses a fine collection of 15C and 16C Venetian glass, a section devoted to Islamic art (faience, glassware, carpets, furniture), a Far-Eastern section (Tibetan and Chinese statues in bronze, porcelain from the Ming and Ch'ing period), and a collection of porcelain from the major European factories (Meissen, Vienna, Sèvres).

★**Deutsches Filmmuseum (German Cinema Museum)** – The many and varied inventions that heralded the birth of this new art form (stroboscopic discs, the praxinoscope, the kineto-scope) are exhibited in this museum. Old film studios have been faithfully reconstructed, and the secrets of special effects are revealed.

►► **Zoo**★★★ – The zoo, a centre for animal reproduction, contains more than 600 species and 5 000 animals. An immense aviary is home to many species of birds. The Grzimek-Haus is reserved for nocturnal animals.

EXCURSIONS

Offenbach – *7km/2.2mi to the east.* This town is the centre for the German leather industry. The **Leather Museum**★★ (Deutsches Ledermuseum) presents the fascinating history of the purse. It also contains a few rare objects such as Louis XV's toy elephant and a wallet belonging to Napoleon I. The same building houses the German Shoe Museum.

★**The Taunus** – A round trip tour of 62km/28mi explores this massif covered with magnificent forests and a number of hot springs. The **Großer Feldberg**★ (800m/2400ft high), is a telecommunication centre with an observation tower offering an immense **panorama**★★ of the surrounding tablelands and plains. The tiny resort of **Bad Homburg von der Höhe**★ was once one of Europe's gambling capitals. Today, the casino is closed and the **Spa Park**★ and the castle represent the main attractions.

HAMBURG★★★

Population 1 650 000
Michelin map 970 K 4

In 1189, Frederick Barbarossa conceded the right to free navigation on the lower Elba River to Hamburg. Since that time, Hamburg has become one of the world's busiest ports. The town's anniversary celebration generates much festivity each year on 7 May. When the small town of Hamburg joined the Hanseatic League in 1358, it soon entered a period of prosperity. Large amounts of traffic passed through the town between the Baltic and the North Sea. However, the discoveries of new sea routes soon forced the port to redirect its energies into warehousing and distribution. In the 19C, Hamburg began an extraordinary period of growth coinciding with the independence of the United States and the emergence of Latin America.

TOWN CENTRE

★★★**Außenalster** – This large body of water located in the middle of the city serves as a haven of peace and relaxation. Residents come to sail, canoe, and especially to take **boat tours**★★★ (*Alsterrundfarht*) which offer good vantage points of the city. Even a quick drive around the Alster permits visitors to admire Hamburg.

★**St-Michaelis-Kirche (St Michael's Church)** – This brick church is an excellent example of Northern German Baroque architecture. The giant space and luminous interior create a magnificent place of worship. Its famous tower (Turm der Michel) rises above the River Elbe, with a splendid **panorama**★ of the town and the river.

★★**Kunsthalle** – This recently reconstructed art museum is one of Germany's largest. From the Middle Ages, the visitor can admire Master Bertram's altarpiece, one of the most moving examples of the German primitive style. The 24 panels portray the story of the Redemption. Rembrandt, Ruysdael, Van Goyen and Jan Steen represent 17C Flemish painters. The marvelous 19C German painting section includes some fine works by CD Friedrich, Philipp Otto Runge, Feuerbach, Böcklin and Menzel. There are also paintings by Munch, Oskar Kokoschka as well as Nolde, Kirchner and Marc, artists of the Brücke and Blaue Reiter mouvements.

General view of Hamburg

★★THE PORT

The **boat visit** (Hafenrundfahrt) will acquaint the passenger with the port's huge dockyards, ship construction sites and the large amount of activity along the banks of the Elbe.

CITY OUTSKIRTS

★**Postmuseum (Postal Museum)** – This museum presents the history of mail transport from the 16C to the present. The museum also possesses a large collection of telegraphs, telephones, warning systems, fax machines and radio installations.

EXCURSIONS

★★**Norddeutsches Landsmuseum (Altona and North Germany Museum)** – Located in the town of **Altona**, the museum houses a collection of remarkable ship figureheads from the 18C and 19C. The principal traditional activities of the region are explained and illustrated.

HARZ★★

Michelin map 970 K 4

This wooded region with its many watercourses attracts hikers. They enjoy the pleasant trails that lead to beautiful sites such as Brocken, a windswept summit (altitude 1 142m/3 747ft). A railway drawn by old-style steam locomotives known as the Harzquerbahn connects Wernigerode and Nordhausen and leads the traveller into the heart of the natural beauty.

The witches of Brocken – During the first night of May, witches assemble on the summit of Brocken to celebrate their sabbath, made famous in a scene from Faust.

THE UPPER HARZ

★★**Goslar** – This town once owed its prosperity to silver and lead mines in the **Rammelsberg**. Today it has become part of UNESCO's world cultural heritage. The mines, which can be visited, have been worked for at least 1 000 years.
The **old town**★★★ lies in and around the **Marktplatz**★ (marketplace). It is surrounded by houses with façades clad with slate. The **Rathaus**★ (town hall), built in the 15C, contains a large ground floor hall, and a large **chamber of allegiance**★★ (Huldigungssaal) on the first floor. It can be appreciated for the rich decorations dating from 1510, including carved wood, statues of Roman emperors, and figures of the prophets and evangelists on the ceiling. The **Schuhhof** is surrounded by **timbered houses**★★ (Fachwerkhäuser), some of which stand on arcades. Further on, the Baker's Guild Hall (Bäckergildehaus) dates from the first half of the 16C.
To the south of Goslar, the **Upper Harz Mines Museum** in Zellerfeld and the **old silver mine**★ in St-Andreasberg evoke the area's mining history.

THE EASTERN HARZ

★★ **Bodetal (Bode Gorge)** – The River Bode flows sinuously through this valley. It makes its way through a tumble of rocks at the foot of immense cliffs. From the "**Roßtrappe**"★★ lookout point (the "Charger's Hoofmark") a giddy **view**★★ shows the river meandering along the base of craggy peaks and distant forests.

> **Snow White and the Seven Dwarfs**
>
> In this Grimm's fairy tale immortalized by Walt Disney's animated cartoon, the dwarfs' traditional costume is actually that of medieval miners.

HEIDELBERG★★

Population 132 000
Michelin map 970 J 5

During the Middle Ages, Heidelberg was the political centre of the Rhineland Palatinate. In 1386, the town founded a university. The Heidelberg Castle was reinforced and embellished in the 16C by the Palatinate elector or grand officers of the Holy Roman Empire. However, in 1685 the town was devastated and the castle destroyed by Louis XIV. The town was rebuilt in the Baroque style.
Today, Heidelberg is a lively city thanks to thousands of students and foreign tourists attracted by this centre of the Romantic movement.

★★★ **Schloß** – In the higher section of the town stand the ruins of the castle. It is surrounded by ramparts in red sandstone with five towers at the corners dating from the 14C and 16C. **Gardens**★ were laid out in terraces under the reign of Frederick II from 1616 to 1619.

The courtyard and buildings – To enter the courtyard, a fortified bridge guarded by the gate tower must be crossed. To the right stands the Gothic hall of the Well wing (Brunnenhalle), while the library (Bibliotheksbau), in the Gothic style, occupies the west wing. The Ottheinrichsbau (Othon-Henrich Wing) was built towards 1557 and evokes the fertile late Renaissance period in German architecture. But the best-conserved wing remains the **Friedrichsbau**★★ (Friedrich's Wing), restored in the early 20C. Its façade is divided by a superb sequence of Doric, Ionic and Corinthian columns from the end of the 16C. The incipient Baroque style is illustrated by the composition of the pilasters and cornices.

Interior – Two models suggest the appearance of the castle prior to its destruction in 1685.

★ **Großes Faß (Great Vat)** – This famous cask with a capacity of over 220 000l/ 48 780gal – dates from the 18C. It is covered by a platform for tasting wine or dancing. The dwarf jester Perkeo is the vat's guardian as he suddenly jumps out of a carved clock.

★ **Deutsches Apothekenmuseum (German Pharmaceutical Museum)** – This museum contains an important collection of pharmacist's utensils from the 18C and 19C and old pharmaceutical prescriptions.

ADDITIONAL SIGHTS

★ **Buchausstellung des Universität (University Library)** – The library of Germany's oldest university houses precious manuscripts, including the Manesse manuscript (Manessische Liederhandschrift), an anthology of songs by some 140 poets in old High German from the 14C. It is decorated with full-page delicate illuminations. The Mirror of the Saxons (Sachsenspiegel) from the 15C is the largest work on medieval law in the German language.

★ **Kurpfälzisches Museum (Electoral Palatinate Museum)** – The department devoted to German Primitives includes the **Altarpiece of the Twelve Apostles**★★ (1509) by Tilman Riemenschneider, and a collection of **works from the romantic period**★★ that mainly depict the castle and the town.

★ **Haus zum Ritter (The Knight's House)** – This magnificent burgher's house is adorned with a bust of St George in knightly armour resting on the pediment. This is the only house from the late Renaissance to have escaped the destruction of 1689 to1693.

KÖLN★★★

COLOGNE – Population 992 000

Michelin map 970 J 5

Cologne is the capital of Rhineland. The old town is squeezed between the Rhine and the Ring and was previously surrounded by 13C ramparts, of which only a few vestiges remain. Starting in the Middle Ages, Cologne was Germany's largest city, and to this day still holds some claim to that title. This busy town has many pedestrian streets and parks. The best views of the old town and the famous cathedral bell-towers are from the right bank.

Life in Cologne is friendly despite the big city bustle. The traditional quarters of the old town, the Veedeln, have preserved their special character. Crowds fill them day and night. In the Martinsviertel, locals gather in the many taverns where Kölsch, a regional beer served in large stemmed glasses, may be tasted.

Some history – Soon after its founding in 38 BC, Oppidum Ubiorum became a Roman colony. The town was surrounded with fortifications and renamed Colonia Claudia Ara Agrippinensium after Agrippa, the mother of Nero, who was born there.

After the wave of Great Invasions in the 5C, Cologne became a bishopric, and later a archbishopric. During the Middle Ages, it prospered. More than 150 churches were built.

The city remains today a Catholic centre hosting the Corpus Christi procession. In addition to its intense religious, intellectual and cultural life, Cologne stands out as a centre for trade, welcoming international fairs throughout the year. This is only natural: the city hosted its first trade fair all the way back in 1360.

During the Second World War, air raids destroyed almost the entire city. Rudolf Schwarz directed reconstruction. He built a modern city while simultaneously restoring the old town's architectural heritage.

Streichan /ZEFA, Paris

Cologne's Cathedral quarter, seen from the east bank of the Rhine

CATHEDRAL QUARTER

★★★ **Dom (Cathedral)** – This was the first Gothic church in the Rhineland. Most of it was built from 1248 to 1880 following the French cathedral model. The chancel was completed in 1320, but a three century long pause in construction left an empty space between it and the south tower. In 1842, building restarted and the cathedral was finally inaugurated in 1880.

The two towers of the west façade mark the high point of the flamboyant Gothic style. Decorative elements cover the entire height of the spires, which rise to 157m - 515ft. The apse facing the Rhine is an elegant ensemble of multiple turrets and pinnacles.

Entering by the west doors reveals a dramatic perspective rising 144m/472ft, 45m - 148ft wide, and 435m/143ft high. Five late Gothic **stained glass windows**★ (1507-1508) frame the north aisle. They depict the lives of the Virgin and St Peter. In a nearby chapel stands the **Cross of Gero**★ (Gerokreuz), an excellent example of Ottonian art. Behind the main altar, the marvelous **Reliquary of the Magi**★★★ (Dreikönigenschrein) contains relics of the three Magi of the Christmas story.

Nicolas de Verdun began in 1181 this huge reliquary, which measures 2.2m/7ft in diametre. He built it in the form of a basilica finely decorated with little figures. The masters of Cologne finished it only in 1220. The last chapel in the south ambulatory shelters the Stefan Lochner's **Adoration of the Magi Altarpiece★★★** (Dombild), painted around 1440. Finally, the chancel contains some fine large carved **choir stalls★**.

★★★Römisch-Germanisches Museum (Germano-Roman Museum) – Between the 1C and the 5C, Cologne enjoyed a period of considerable prosperity due to exchanges between Roman civilization and the Ubii Germanic culture. The museum has brought together objects evoking this fertile period. Among others, the **Dionysos Mosaic** is displayed exactly where it was discovered in 1941. In the past it decorated the dining room of a Roman villa. The **Mausoleum of Lucius Poblicius**, a Roman officer, occupies several floors measuring 14.5m/47ft high. A rich collection of glassware includes some fine pieces, such as the 4C diatreta cup and 2C bottles decorated with coils.

★★★Wallraf-Richartz-Museum and **Ludwig Museum** – This twin museum houses the Philharmonic orchestra and a number of cultural institutions, including a photography museum, an art cinema and library. This museum houses several paintings from the German, French, Dutch, Flemish and Italian Schools between the 14C and 19C: Durer, Franz Hals, Rembrandt, Titian, Boucher, and also Van Gogh, Renoir, CD Friedrich, Klinger, as well as masters of the School of Cologne, including Stefan Lochner and his contemporaries. The **Ludwig Museum** is reserved for 20C art. The Expressionists are well-represented by painters from the Brücke movement (Kirchner and Nolde), the Blaue Reiter movement (Macke, Marc, Kandinsky, Jawlensky), and the Expressionists Kokoschka and Beckmann. A large collection presents the Russian Avant-garde (1910-1930). The Surrealist section contains works by dadaists (the Dada movement was born in Cologne) such as Max Ernst, Schwitters and Arp, as well as paintings by Magritte, Miró and Dali. Painting after 1950 includes the Group Zero and Beuys, as well as American Pop Art.

OTHER MUSEUMS

★★Schnütgen Museum – Religious objects from the 6C to the 19C are assembled in the 12C Roman church of St Cecilia. They include a number of **madonnas carved in wood**, as well as a **Saint Heronymus with the lion** (1460-70), a masterpiece of flamboyant Gothic wooden sculpture. The museum also contains objects carved in ivory from Germany, France and the Byzantine Empire.

★★Museum für Ostasiatische Kunst (Museum of East Asian Art) – Founded in 1909, the Museum of East Asian Art is the oldest in Germany. The fine collection includes religious art objects from China, Japan and Korea. Other objects, such as painted Japanese screens and furniture from the Ming period round off the collection.

★ROMANESQUE CHURCHES

Many Romanesque churches were built between the 10C and the 13C. Today only a dozen remain, but these give an excellent idea of stylistic developments during these three centuries. Certain types of construction originated in Cologne, such as the trefoil chancel, which can be seen at **St-Aposteln** (Church of the Holy Apostles). The **St-Maria Lyskirschen** (St-Mary of the Lilies), contains sumptuous 13C **frescos★★**. St-Pantaleon's represents a fine example of Ottonian architecture (10C), and contains an ornate Gothic **roodscreen★**. The chancel of **St-Kunibert** (St Cunibert's) stands out for its **stained-glass windows★** (1230) painted in the courtly style.

LÜBECK★★★

Population 216 000
Michelin map 970 k 4

Lübeck, an oval-shaped city surrounded by water, has preserved its traditional Hanseatic character.

★★★OLD TOWN

★★Holstentor – Huge twin towers frame this imposing fortified gate built between 1469 and 1478. The prestigious edifice houses some fine ceramic frieze decorations.

★★Marienkirche (St Mary's Church) – This Gothic brick church is one of the loveliest in Germany. St Mary's was first built as a hall-style church in 1250, then later followed the inspiration of the French cathedral. The 125m/410ft tall spires were finished in

1350. Inside, the Flamboyant Gothic style can be admired in the elegant **Briefkapelle**. In the south tower, a 1942 air raid brought down the bells. They remain buried in the ground.

> **At the head of the League**
>
> In the 14C Lübeck became the capital of the Hanseatic League, a vast trading guild connecting towns throughout Northern Germany (Hamburg and Dantzig) and the Baltic Sea (Riga). Soon more than 200 towns were linked together in order to guarantee their own commercial prosperity.

★**Haus der Schiffergesellschaft (House of the Seamen's Guild)** – This Renaissance house, today transformed into a restaurant, preserves a traditional **interior**★★ typical of seafarer taverns. Copper lamps, lanterns and model ships are suspended from the beams.

★**Jacobikirche (St James' Church)** – This Gothic church is of interest for its two **organs**★★, constructed in the 16C and 17C. In a chapel on the south side, the altar known as Brömbse from the 15C includes two fine bas-reliefs.

MAGDEBURG★★

Population 287 000
Michelin map 970 K 4

Magdeburg owes its early prosperity to its location at the heart of the Germanic lands. The town was unfortunately destroyed twice, once in 1631 during the Thirty Years War, and later on 16 January, 1945.

★★★**Dom St-Mauritius und St-Katharina (St Maurice and St-Catherine's Cathedral)** – This cathedral represented the first attempt to import the Gothic style into Germany. Inspired by the cathedrals in the Paris region, it was begun in the 13C. The **Door of Paradise** is crowned by **statues**★★ of the Wise and Foolish Virgins. They are carved in Strasbourg style. Inside, other **statues**★★ are worth visiting, such as St Maurice from 1240 in painted sandstone. In a small chapel, statues represent Christ and the Church as well as Otto I and his wife Editha.

★★**Kloster Unser Lieben Frauen (Abbey of Our Lady)** – Founded in 1015 by Augustinian monks, this abbey typifies Romanesque style common in the second half of the 11C. Only the vaulting with its ribbed Gothic arches dates from 1230. The **cloister**★ is well preserved.

MOSELTAL★★★

MOSELLE Valley

The Moselle Valley curves around the Eifel and Hunsrück massifs. Vines producing dry white wines, particularly Riesling, surround the slopes. These wines give the valley its fame. A pleasant excursion from Treves to Koblenz passes through enchanting landscapes scattered with admirable monuments.

★★TRIER Population 99 000 Michelin map 970 J 5

Trier was considered the capital of the ancient Roman Empire in Germany. Today it remains active culturally and commercially. Constantine constructed high ramparts and magnificent buildings. The archbishopric of Trier, the oldest in Germany, was founded in 314. When Roman domination floundered, Trier fell into the hands of the Franks around 470.

★★**Porta Nigra** – The dark patina covering the stone walls gives this monumental gate its name. It was originally used for military purposes. In the 11C, the gate was transformed into a two-storeyed church.

★**Dreikönigenhaus (House of the Three Kings)** – The House represents early Gothic style with arched windows.

★**Hauptmarkt** – The **Market Cross**★ stands in the middle of a charming old square. It was erected in 958 to commemorate the town's acquisition of market rights.

★★**Rheinishes Landesmuseum (Rhineland Museum)** – The Prehistory section displays weapons from the Stone Age, ceramics from the Bronze Age and gold jewelry from the Iron Age. The Roman Antiquities section includes a selection of superb mosaics and sculptures.

★★**Kaiserthermen (Imperial Baths)** – These vast Roman baths date from the Constantine Era. They include a *caldarium* (hot baths), a *trepidarium* (warm baths), a *frigidarium* (cold baths) and a *gymnasium*.

★★**Schatzkammer der Stadtbibliothek (Municipal Library Treasure)** – The fine collection includes fine illuminations, precious manuscripts and the first illustrated Bibles.

★BERNKASTEL-KUES Population 7 200

These twin wine-producing towns are located on either side of the Moselle, at the entrance to a ravine. At the beginning of September each year, they organize a wine festival. During the festival, the famed Moselle wines are uncorked for tasting, including the fruity Bernkasteler Doktor wine. Smoked eel traditionally accompanies the wine.
From Bernkastel-Kues to Marienburg, the road passes through the typically Moselle villages of **Kröv, Enkirch, Starkenburg** (enjoy the fine **view★** from the platform) and **Pünderich**. While driving through the magnificent vineyards, note the many sundials set in the rocks.

MARIENBURG

Nestled on the narrowest stretch of the Zell, the old convent offers an exceptional **setting★★** with impressive **views★★** on the river and vineyards.

COCHEM

This is one of the Rhineland's most celebrated **sites★★**. The **castle** (Reichsburg) was restored in the 19C. Its turrets and pinnacles rise above the town.

★★ELTZ CASTLE

This romantic castle bristling with turrets enjoys an exceptional **setting★★**. Its interior contains fine furnishings and a treasure.

★KOBLENZ Population 107 000 Michelin map 970 J 5

Koblenz developed thanks to its position at the **Deutsches Eck★**, the meeting place for the Rhine and the Moselle rivers. Many **boat excursions** on both rivers leave from Koblenz. In the summer the town comes alive with open-air concerts and taverns in the town's wine village (Weindorf).
The old town (Altstadt) centres around the 13C Romanesque Church of Our Lady (Liefrauenkirche). A Gothic chancel was added in the 15C and a Baroque belltowers in the 17C.

MÜNCHEN★★★

MUNICH – Population 1 300 000
Michelin map 970 K 5

Munich is the capital of Bavaria and the centre of economic and cultural activity in southern Germany. Located a few kilometres from the Alps, its one of Germany's most attractive cities.

Some history – In the 9C, a town was founded near a Benedictine monastery and was named Muniche, meaning monk in Old High German. The city originally belonged to Duke Henry the Lion, before passing in 1180 into the hands of the Palatine count, Otto von Wittelsbach. In 1328, Louis the Bavarian of the Wittelsbach line was proclaimed King of Germany, then Emperor. Munich became the sole capital of the Bavarian Duchy. In the 17C, the city became a bastion of German Catholicism. Many churches were built, along with important public buildings including the Nymphenburg Castle and Residence Theatre. In the 19C, thanks to the influence of Maximilian I, King of Bavaria, and later to that of his son, Ludwig I (1825-1848), the city was transformed into an arts centre. The Pinakothek, Glyptothek and University were constructed. Ludwig II (1864-1896) also built three extravagant castles near Munich, the Neuschwnstein, Linderhof and Herrenschiemsee. The line of the kings of Bavaria came to an end with Ludwig III, who abdicated in the November 1918 revolution. In January 1919, Hitler announced the goals of the new German Worker's Party. After the failure of his 1923 popular uprising, the future dictator was imprisoned.

Life in Munich – Munich's various neighbourhoods enjoy their own particular attractions. Flea markets and antiquities may be found on the Ottostrasse. More elegant shops line the Maffeistrasse, while art galleries are located under the arcades of the Hofgartenstrasse. Schwabing, which was a meeting place for artists and intellectuals, still attracts visitors with its cafés, cabarets and shops.
Munich cannot be visited without tasting beer. Beer is found in brasseries and taverns, of course, but also in the gardens (Biergarten). During the **Oktoberfest** (October Festival), brasseries serve a special beer known as Wiesnbier which still is transported in the traditional way by horse-drawn wagons. At this time, more than seven million beer-lovers gather to taste the beer under canvas marquees on the **Theresenwiese**.

★★ ALTSTADT (OLD TOWN)

Wine Cup from the Palace Treasury

★ **Marienplatz** – The city is centered on the Marienplatz. To the north stands the new town hall built in the neo-Gothic style and possessing an animated carillon. Figurines in enameled copper emerge and act out the tournament that was held for the royal weddings in 1568. Nearby the old town hall, with its stepped gables, can be visited.

★ **Residenz** – Construction on the new palace for the Wittelsbach family began in 1385. The project grew larger and larger, ending up as a vast collection of buildings. The **Schatzkammer★★** (Treasury) includes precious objects such as the Hungarian Queen Gisela's 11C carved crucifix. Cuvilliés built the **Altes Residenz theatre★** (Residence Theatre) in the Rococo style between 1751 and 1753.

MUSEUMS

★★★ **Alte Pinakothek (Old Pinakothek)** – Leo von Klenze constructed this building between 1826 and 1836 in the Venetian Renaissance style. The collections on show include masterpieces of the 14C to the18C European painting.

★★★ **Neue Pinakothek (New Pinakothek)** – The New Pinakothek is something of a contrast to the Old with its post-modern architecture. It not only houses works from the 19C, which is its speciality, but also a wide range of painters, such as the Italian School (Botticelli, Ghirlandaio, Raphael, Mantegna and Tintoret), French (Claude Lorrain, Poussin, Boucher) and German painters (Stefan Lochner, Durer). The 19C exhibit is enriched by Romantic painters (Delacroix, Courbet), Impressionists (Cézanne, Manet, Degas) and Symbolists (Gustave Klimt).

★ **Glyptothek (Glyptothek)** – Architect Klenze designed this building with a porch supported by Ionic columns in the Classical style. It houses 1 000 years of Greek and Roman sculpture. The most interesting pieces are the *Tenea Apollo* with his mysterious smile, the *Barberini Faun* and the Aegina marbles, which are pediments from the Aphaia temple in Aegina.

★ **Staatliche Antikensammlungen (Collection of Antiquities)** – Entering by the porch supported by Corinthian columns (1838-1848) the visitor discovers a marvelous collection of Greek ceramics, including the famed vases with black figures on a red background. A series of Amphoras show the evolution of styles and techniques. In the basement, Etruscan jewelry testifies to the skill of the ancient artists.

★★★ **Deutsches Museum (German Museum)** – This is one of the world's most important science and technology museums. The founder, Oskar Von Miller, pioneered electrical power in Bavaria. He wanted to set up a teaching museum. Animated models and demonstrations explain various techniques such as the early types of electric or steam locomotion. The museum includes locomotives, airplanes and cars. A coal mine has been reconstructed in the basement. The first floor is devoted to the laws of physics. The second floor is dominated by glass and ceramic manufacture, and the third floor explains weights and measures. The last three floors are reserved for astronomy.

★★ **Bayerisches Nationalmuseum (National Bavarian Museum)** – Bavarian arts and crafts from the 5C to the 19C are displayed. The basement contains an interesting collection of Christmas cribs.

★★ NYMPHENBURG

The King of Bavaria's and Prince Elector's summer residence was enlarged over the centuries. Barelli erected the central pavilion in Italian style from 1664 to 1674. Two side pavilions connected by galleries, and later dependencies arranged in a half circle date from the end of the 18C.

★ **Palace** – The festival hall's Rococo decoration combines white, gold and pale green and is decorated with frescos by Zimmermann. The South Pavilion contains the famed **Gallery of Beauties of Ludwig I.**

★★ **Amalienburg** – Cuvilliés designed this small hunting lodge. The rich interior decor contrasts with the sober exterior.

★★ **Botanischer Garten (Botanical Garden)** – This fabulous garden includes a spring Garden, a Rosary, an alpine garden, a pine forest, and all sorts of tropical plants and marvelous orchids in the greenhouses.

ADDITIONAL SIGHTS

★ **Münchner Stadtmuseum (City Municipal Museum)** – Arms and armour bear witness to the city's history. The museum also possesses works of art, such as the **Moorish Dancers**★★ (Moriskentänzer), and 10 painted and gilded wooden figures by Erasmus Grasser dating from 1480.

★ **Tierpark Hellabrunn (Hellarunn Zoological Gardens)** – Created in 1911, this zoo is also a natural park. The elephant house, the large free-flight aviary and the monkey reserve make up the main attractions.

EXCURSIONS

★ **Schleißheim Castle** – *15km/6.8mi to the north.* This castle, built in the classical style, extends majestically over 330m - 1,083ft. It is surrounded by French-style gardens designed by Carbonet and Girard. The apartments have been converted into art galleries, holding paintings by the Flemish and Dutch masters of the 16C and 17C.

★ **Ammersee** – The lake, located at an altitude of 533m/1 749ft, serves as an active centre for sailing and swimming. On the western bank stands **Dießen's Baroque Church**★. The painted decorations on the dome are remarkable. The high altar is by Cuvilliés. A few kilometres away, a Benedictine **abbey church**★★ is found in **Andechs**. Originally Gothic, Zimmermann added frescos and stucco work in the Rococo style from 1680 to 1758. The painted panels in the gallery illustrate the abbey's history.

Dachau Concentration Camp – *19km/8.6mi to the northwest.* Nazi Germany's first concentration camp was opened in 1933. More than 32 000 Jews perished here in inhuman conditions. A Catholic expiatory chapel, a commemorative Protestant sanctuary and a Jewish memorial have been raised inside. Two barracks have been reconstructed.

MÜNSTER★★

Population 252 000
Michelin map 970 J 4

Münster, the historic capital of Westphalia, is one of Germany's most important university centres. Its many Gothic and Renaissance façades have been well restored, making the town a pleasant place.

★ **Dom (Cathedral)** – This edifice, with two towers, chancels and transepts, represents an excellent example of the Westphalian 13C transitional style. The central nave, covered by rounded vaulting, leads to an ambulatory. The **astronomical clock**★ from 1540 features moving figures which strike on the hour.

★★ **Domkammer (Treasure)** – Adjoining the cathedral cloisters, the treasure includes fourteen 15C reliquary busts of the prophets in embossed copper and silver, an 11C reliquary head of St Paul in embossed gold, and a **processional chapter cross**. The basement contains a rich collection of 17C and 18C liturgical vestments and a 12C portable altar, decorated with pearl embroidery.

★ **Westfälisches Landesmuseum für Kunst und Kulturgeschichte (Fine Arts Museum)** – Artworks from the city's monuments, including Gothic statues from the cathedral and stained-glass windows, and sculptures by Johann and Heinrich Brabender are displayed. A collection of **altarpieces**★★ by medieval Westphalian artists should not be missed. Luther and his wife, painted by Lucas Cranach, are among the exhibited paintings.

★ **Prinzipalmarkt** – The town's most historic street still serves as Münster's shopping centre. Burghers' houses with their Renaissance gables and arcades line the street. Shops and taverns are located under the arcades. Continuing down Bogenstrasse, the popular statue of a peddler with his basket *(Kiepenkerl)* stands in a small square.

Rathaus (Town Hall) – The gabled façade from the end of the 14C is typical of Gothic civic architecture. It is decorated with fine tracery and pinnacles. Inside, the **Peace Hall**★ has preserved its Gothic and Renaissance woodwork.

★ **Westfälisches Museum für Naturkunde (Westphalian Museum of Natural Sciences)** – The remarkable departments of mineralogy, geology, paleontology, botany and zoology (a collection of stuffed birds in natural positions) offer a vast panorama of environment and evolution. In the paleontology section, do not miss the largest **ammonite**★ fossil shells from the Mesozoic period ever discovered.

NÜRNBERG★★

NUREMBERG – Population 478 000

Michelin map 970 K 5

Until 1914, Nuremberg, with its half-timbered houses and historic gables, was Germany's loveliest medieval city. Unfortunately, the war destroyed them all and reconstruction efforts have not succeeded in restoring their past beauty.
The town reached its height in the 15C and 16C, attracting scientists such as the watch inventor Peter Henlein, and the two famous painters, Michael Wolgemut and Albrecht Dürer.
Hitler had declared the city the ideological capital of the Third Reich, so appropriately Nuremberg hosted the trials of Nazi war criminals from November 1945 to October 1946.

★★★ **Germanisches Nationalmuseum (German National Museum)** – Located in an old 14C convent, the museum has gathered together all the facets of German art and crafts. The first floor presents valuable pieces of sculpture from the 13C to the 16C, Gothic altars and virgins, by Adam Krafft and Tilman Riemenschneider. The ground floor presents paintings from the 14C and 15C, including works by Stephan Lochner and Dürer. The Crafts Museum holds the collections of the decorative arts such as ceramics and glassware. A remarkable collection of arms and old hunting pieces, as well as a department of ancient musical instruments, should not be missed. The Copper Print Gallery on the ground floor is also rich.

★ **Stadtbefestigung (Stronghold)** – Almost an exception in Nuremburg, these 15C fortifications have remained intact. The visitor can walk through the castle garden *(Burggarten)*. The defensive gallery and the ramparts offer an attractive view of the city skyline with its four huge 16C defensive towers.

★ **Sebalduskirche (St Sebald's Church)** – The church's sober Romanesque west façade from the 13C and 14C contrasts with the rich pinnacles and Gothic statues of the east chancel. Elsewhere, the Romanesque and 13C early Gothic central and side aisles contrast with the radiating High Gothic chancel in hall form and a 14C ambulatory. The many fine **works of art★★** include a richly decorated Gothic baptismal font in bronze from around 1430, the tomb of St Sebald covered with a profusion of small statuettes, and the east chancel's splendid 14C and 16C stained-glass windows.

★ **St-Lorenz-Kirche (St Laurence's Church)** – This Gothic Church from the 13C and 14C possesses a fine rose window on the west side. Inside, Veit Stoss (1517-1518) sculpted a wood **Annunciation★★** and A Krafft's **Gothic ciborium★★** rises up to the chancel vault.

OTTOBEUREN Abbey★★★

Michelin map 970 K 6

Founded in 764, the Benedictine abbey of Ottobeuren, architect Johann Michael Fischer transformed and created a Baroque masterpiece in the 18C. Zeillers contributed the frescoes, and Johann Michael Feuchtmayer completed the stucco work and statues.

CESA, Marburg

Interior view of the Ottobeuren abbey church

★★★**Klosterkirche (abbey church)** – This impressive church includes towers 82m/272ft high, a nave 90m/295ft long, and a transept 60m/200ft in length. The outside appearance gives little clue to the actual size. Inside, the play of light changes over the hours, due to an unusual north-south orientation. The diverse colours are harmonious, with rose, yellow and violet, in subdued hues perfectly complementing the warm colours of the frescoes on the vaulting.

The **transept crossing** (Vierung) gives an impression of extraordinary strength. A grandiose fresco depicting the Miracle of Pentecost decorates the flattened dome. The pulpit and the group representing Christ's baptism are visible. All around the dome are magnificent carved decorations.

The floor, designed by Johann Jakob Zeiller, uses cross, circle and star patterns.

The **chancel** (Chor) houses a small altar of the Holy Sacrament, above which stands a 12C Christ. The surrounding stars symbolise the sovereignty of the universe.

The walnut **choir stalls**★★ date to 1764. Joseph Christian's gilded bas-reliefs recounting stories from the Bible decorate their high backs. Karl Joseph Riepp constructed the **choir's**★★ richly decorated organ in 1766.

PASSAU★★

Michelin map 970 L 5

Passau enjoys a wonderful **setting**★★★ at the junction of the Danube, the Inn and the Ilz rivers. The old town is squeezed onto the narrow tongue of land between the Inn and the Danube. The bell-towers of Baroque churches rise above the ramparts.
Considerable river traffic has passed through the town as early as medieval times. Passau traders had the right of storage which was the basis of much trading with Bohemia.

Veste Oberhaus (Oberhaus Fortress) – The bishops of Passau used this imposing 13C edifice as a refuge from the constant rebellions of the burghers. A fortified road connects it to the **Niederhaus Fortress**. The **views**★★ are superb from the lookout point of the Danube and the city. A few ridged roofs, hidden by straight pediments, are visible. These are typical of the region.

Dom St. Stephan (St Steven's Cathedral) – A fire destroyed most of this late Gothic building in the 17C. Only the original east chancel and the transept remain. The rest was reconstructed in the Baroque style. As a result, the interior is over decorated with frescoes and stucco work. The pulpit dates from 1722 to 1726, and is a Viennese work richly adorned with statues. From the outside, the **chevet**★★ erected from 1407 to 1530 represents a magnificent example of high Gothic architecture. The transept's Baroque dome rises in the background.

★**Glasmuseum (Glass Museum)** – Bavarian, Bohemian and Austrian glass from the end of the 1700s to the 1930s, are displayed.

POTSDAM★★★

Population 50 000
Michelin map 970 L 4

Potsdam is located only a few kilometres from Berlin. In the 17C, it was chosen as the residence of the Bradenburg electors. Frederick II erected many prestigious monuments during his glorious reign from 1740 to 1786.

★SANS-SOUCI PALACE AND PARK

Peter Joseph Lenné, a famed Prussian landscape artist, designed the park. The various buildings were constructed between 1744 and 1860.

★**Bildergalerie (Painting Gallery)** – In its pompously decorated Rococo rooms, the oldest German museum exhibits paintings from Italy (Caravaggio, Tintoretto), France (Van Loo, Simon Vouet) and the Flemish lands (Van Dyck, Rubens).

★★★**Schloß Sanssouci (Sans-Souci Palace)** – Climb the great staircase bordering the tiered terraces to observe the majestic façade. A visit of the interior demonstrates the virtuosity of the artists who created a sumptuously rich Rococo decor. The **antechamber** is decorated in gray and golden tints, and the **concert hall** in rocaille ornamentation.

★★**Neues Palais (New Palace)** – Frederick II ordered construction of this edifice to demonstrate to the world the still-intact power of Prussia following the Seven Years War. Every element contributes to an overdone impression of grandeur. The building measures an enormous 213m/700ft wide and contains 400 rooms. The façade contains abundant sculptures and is decorated in Rococo style, far from the elegant simplicity of the Sans-Souci Palace. The **outbuildings**★ form an exuberantly festive scene. Among the many rooms, the **grotto** (decor of shells and minerals), the **Marble Room** (grey-blue marble enhanced with gold), the **Red Damask Room** (eight portraits of the royal family by Pesne) and the **theatre** (late German Rococo) merit visits.

The Potsdam Conference

The treaty defining the role of the victors in the occupation and future of Germany after the Second World War was signed here at Cecilienhof Palace on 2 August 1945 by the leaders of the allied powers (Churchill – subsequently Attlee – Roosevelt and Stalin).

★★**Chinesisches Teehaus (Chinese Tea House)** – In the 18C, Chinese culture was much in fashion, as this tea house testifies. At the entrance of the circular pavilion stand a group of gilded life-size Chinese statues.

RHEINTAL★★★

Rhine Valley
Michelin map 970 J 5

The River Rhine, an exceptional trading route since the Middle Ages, flows through Southwest Germany. This long winding river has inspired legends. Perched on a rock, the **Lorelei** bewitched boatmen with their melodious voices, drawing them to their doom. The treasure of the Nibelungen, which served as the basis of Wagner's well-known trilogy, still lies at the river bottom. The Rhine Valley enchants with castles and vineyards, providing an initiation into Germany's mythical past.

★★THE LORELEI from Rüdesheim to Koblenz

This bank is the valley's wildest and steepest section. The road winds past vineyards and ruined castles.

★**Rüdesheim** – The wine-producing city, located at the source of the romantic Rhine, charms with its tiny narrow streets and wine cellars serving the local Riesling.

★★★**Lorelei** – The legendary rock perched 132m/433ft above the river is a pilgrimage site for German romanticism. The view is splendid from the promontory. Many spurs with alternating vineyards and rocky outcrops offer other impressive **views**★★ on the heroic gorge.

★**Marksburg** – The castle (**setting**★★) is the only one still intact in the valley. Visit the giant medieval artillery, the medieval garden and the armour collection.

★★★THE RHINE CASTLES from Koblenz to Bingen

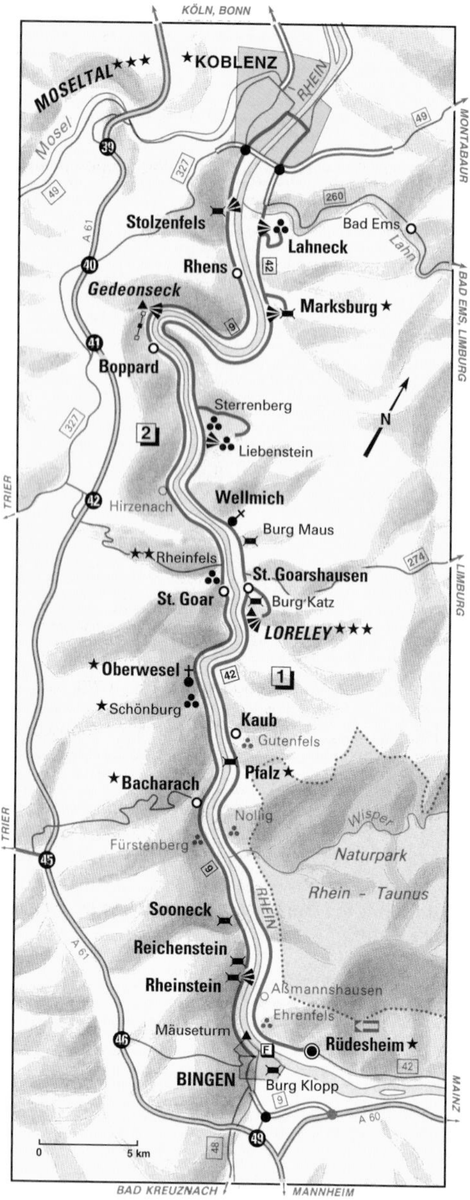

Stolzenfels – The castle was built in a neo-Gothic style reminiscent of an English manor house in 1842. The **interior★** is beautifully decorated.

St-Goar – The village nestles at the foot of the **Rheinfels Castle★★** (Burg Rheinfels), a fortress which offered an active defense against Louis XIV's troops. From the clock tower, the Cat and Mouse castles are visible on the other side of the river.

Oberwesel – The Gothic **Church of Our Lady★** (Liebfrauenkirche) shelters one of Germany's oldest high altars from the early 14C. From the **Schönburg Castle★** terrace, the fortified island of Pfalz is visible with its remarkable white stone nave.

★**Bacharach** – This pretty wine-producing town has preserved a few medieval houses on the Oberstrasse and on the Marktplatz. The Romanesque St Peter's Church (Peterskirche) already hints of the Gothic style to come, with its four-storey elevation of huge arcades, gallery, triforium and high windows.

Rheinstein – The castle built on a rock spur overlooks the river. A bird's-eye **view★★** is available from the foremost watchtower.

ROSTOCK★

Population 252 000
Michelin map 970 L 3

Rostock's reputation rests on its busy international harbour. Located on the banks of the River Warnow, Rostock joined the Hanseatic League as early as the 13C. The city is nicknamed the "Light of the North" because of the university that opened in 1419. Soon afterwards, Rostock attracted the attention of its powerful neighbours, the Danish and Swedish. During the Thirty Years War, the Swedes invaded. A few years later, the French arrived. They remained in possession of the city until 1813. Rostock's most interesting monument is the **Church of Our Lady★★** (Marienkirche), a hall-church from the 14C. The church was transformed into a basilica (in the shape of a cross) in the second half of the 15C. A **panorama★** can be enjoyed by climbing the 18C tower. The interior is impressively vertical. It shelters an **astronomic clock★★** from 1472 and delicately made bronze **baptismal fonts★** supported by statues of four men.

EXCURSIONS

Bad Doberan – *15km/6.8mi to the west.* The town arose around a 12C Cistercian convent. By 1800, it had become a fashionable resort town. Bad Doberan was also the summer residence of the Mecklemburg court, but the town still is best-known for the Cistercian convent's cathedral (**Münster★★**), one of the most remarkable examples of North German brick Gothic architecture. The cathedral was built according to the Flemish model, with a nave and ambulatory chancel ending in a chapel. The interior is richly decorated, concealing the brick surface in certain places. Of particular note, the **main altar★★** from 1310 illustrating scenes from the Old and New Testament, the **Triumphal Cross★** on the altar, and the late Gothic **tabernacle★** carved in oak.

ROTHENBURG OB DER TAUBER★★★

ROTHENBURG – Population 11 000

Michelin map 070 K 5

This charming town on the Romantic road overlooks the sinuous course of the River Tauber. Two 12C castles originally stood on the site overlooking the valley. In 1356, an earthquake destroyed the castles. From that time on, the town leaders preferred to build public monuments or burgher's houses, but the Thirty Years' War slowed growth. Rothenburg stagnated between the 17C and 18C. In the 19C, measures were taken to protect the monuments and houses, as well as the ramparts.

★★★ALSTADT (OLD TOWN)

★**Stadtmauer (Ramparts)** – The ramparts dating from the 13C and 14C, remain in perfect condition and open to the public. To the south, the **Hospital Gate★** (Spitaltor) defends the town. This powerful bastion dates from the 16C. Inside, the gate contains two oval towers.

★**Rathaus (Town Hall)** – Several periods of construction mark the town hall. The Gothic belfry, 60m/197ft high, dates from the 14C. The façade with its octagonal staircase tower, comes from the Renaissance, while the embossed portico was constructed in the 18C. The top of the bell-tower offers a superb view★ of the town's roofs and ramparts.

★**Spital (Hospital)** – This edifice lies in the shelter of an outgrowth of ramparts known as the "bonnet peak" (Kappenzipfel). It was built during the 16C and 17C. In the court stand the Gothic chapel and the Hegereiterhäuschen, a graceful pavilion with pointed roofs and a turret.

Herrngasse – This busy street is lined with the mansions built by the town's important citizens.

RÜGEN★

Michelin map 970 L 3

Rügen in the North Sea is Germany's largest island. It is connected to the mainland by a bridge that crosses the sea strait across from Strelasund. The west coast has irregular contours, creating small inland seas, while the east coast is more pleasant with sandy beaches and chalk cliffs.

★**Putbus** – The town in the south of the island is both a seaside resort and residential area. Prince Wilhelm Malte Putbus founded it in 1810, inspired by Bad Doberan. The circular square (**Circus★**) is surrounded by Classical-style white buildings. In the centre stands an obelisk built in 1845. Several streets form a star from the round square.

★**Jagdschloß Granitz** – Prince Wilhelm Malte I of Putpus built this neo-Gothic Tudor hunting palace in 1837. In the midst of a forest rise 14 square towers. A superb **spiral staircase** in wrought iron leads to a lookout platform high in the middle of the courtyard. The **view★** of Rügen Island is breathtaking.

★★**Stubbenkammer** – The coastline of chalk cliffs looks out over the sea from more than 100m/328ft. In good weather, the immaculate white rock can be seen against the blue of the sea, just like a postcard.

The length of time given in this guide

– for touring allows time to enjoy the views and the scenery;

– for sightseeing is the average time required for a visit.

Der SCHWARZWALD★★★

The BLACK FOREST

Michelin map 970 J 5

The Black Forest covers more than 170km/106mi between Karlsruhe and Basel. Most of the area is forested. Wood long has been the primary raw material and the basis for a strong crafts tradition. The region's west slopes are covered with vineyards and fruit trees. The Black Forest is a favourite holiday site with a reputation for a healthy climate.

★★★THE CREST ROAD

The Crest Road follows a route studded with lookout points at an average altitude of 1 000m/3 280ft.

★★**Baden-Baden** – This luxurious health resort has a long history. The Roman Emperor Caracalla spent some time here, and beginning in the 12C, the Baden Margraves. A casino and a theatre were added in the 19C. The **Lichtentaler Allee**★★ is shaded by 300 year old oak trees. In the past century, high society congregated in the resort town. Napoleon III and Eugénie, Queen Victoria and Bismarck all frequented the Allee.

J. Ducange /TOP, Paris

Black Forest landscape

★**Allerheiligen** – Only the porch, with its arches, transept walls and a many-sided Gothic chapel, remain of this 13C church.

★**Allerheiligen-Wasserfälle (Allerheiligen Waterfalls)** – A trail along the torrent passes between steep walls to the bottom of the falls.

★**Freudenstadt** – This 17C town, destroyed by fire in 1945, was reconstructed following a checkerboard plan centered on the arcaded **Marktplatz**★. The church has a fine 12C **lectern**★★.

★★CENTRAL BLACK FOREST

★**Alpirsbach** – The **abbey**★ church (Ehemaliges Kloster) dates from the 12C, making it the Black Forest's oldest Roman monument. Wall paintings in the apse's central niche decorate the interior.

Gutach – The Gutach Valley contains the **Black Forest Open-Air Museum**★★. Several farms give a good idea of the region's rural architecture.

★**Triberg** – This centre for clock manufacturing is also a famous health resort. The **Waterfall Walk**★ crosses a rocky, wooded landscape.

★**St-Peter** – The dukes of Zähringenn and other founders of Freiburg are buried in the **abbey's** Baroque church, which dates from 1727. The high altar's Rococo decoration contrasts with the **library's**★ delicate Baroque stucco work.

★**Kandel** – From here, a vast panoramic **view**★ unfolds of the Vosges, the Kaiserstuhl, the Feldberg and the Belchen.

★★ **Freiburg im Breisgau** – A peaceful town with a mild climate, Freiburg is considered one of the most pleasant towns in Germany. It came under Habsburg rule in 1388. Its **cathedral★** (Münster) is a fine example of the late Gothic style. The square-based **tower★★★** forms the basis of an octagonal bell-tower surmounted by a stone filigree spire.

★★★UPPER BLACK FOREST

This tour passes by the main summits and the two best-known lakes.

★★★ **Belchen** – On the summit of this dome-shaped mountain 1 414m/4 637ft high, a fine **panorama★★★** overlooks the Black Forest's many valleys. In good weather, the Rhine Valley and the rounded mountains of the upper Vosges and even part of the Alps are visible in the distance.

★ **Wasserfälle von Todtnau (Todtnau Falls)** – A narrow trail through the forest leads to the falls.

★★ **Feldberg** – From the summit of Seebuck (1 448m/4 750ft), a dramatic **view★** emerges of a small lake at the bottom of a glacial crater, the Feldsee. Another impressive **panorama★★** unfolds from the Feldberg summit at 1 493m/4 897ft.

★ **Schluchsee** – The lake, formed by a dam, is the Black Forest's largest.

★★ **Titisee** – This small mountain lake around Titisee-Neustadt and **Hinterzarten★**, an important tourist centre and health resort, serves as a starting point for numerous excursions.

WEIMAR★★

Population 10 500
Michelin map 970 K 5

Weimar, for many years a court capital, attracted not only courtiers and officials, but also some of Germany's best-known artists and writers. Cranach, Bach, Liszt, Schiller and especially Goethe all spent time in Weimar. A monument to Goethe and Schiller stands in the historic cemetery. In 1758, the Duchesse Anna Amalia provided an impetus for Weimar's development as an intellectual and cultural centre. Goethe wrote most of his work here, including *Faust*.

HISTORIC CENTRE

★★ **Goethehaus (Goethe's House)** – Goethe lived in this Baroque house from 1809 until his death in 1832. Since then, the house has remained unchanged. Goethe's work-room and library are open to the public.

★ **Schillerhaus (Schiller's House)** – Schiller established himself in Weimar in 1802 in order to be closer to his friend, Goethe. Part of his house also has been turned into a museum.

Stadkirche (St Peter's and St Paul's Church) – J G Herder, the great philosopher and theologian, pronounced famous sermons in this Gothic church dating from 1500. **Cranach's triptych★★** depicts scenes from the Old and New Testament.

Stadtschloß (Castle) – This 15C castle is decorated in classical fashion. It now houses the National Research Centre for Classical German Literature. The national art collection includes high Gothic altarpieces by Thuringe and many **works★★** by Cranach.

ILM PARK

This park is laid out in the English garden style. It lies along the banks of the River Ilm and includes several buildings devoted to the various artists who lived in Weimar.

★★ **Goethes Gardenhaus (Goethe Pavilion)** – Augustus the Strong offered this edifice to Goethe. The writer wrote a number of works there. Across the way is the Borkenhäuschen and the Roman House, a Classical building designed by Goethe for Carl August.

Franz-Liszt-Haus (Franz Liszt's House) – The musician lived in this old gardener's residence from 1869 to 1886.

Read the chapter on art and architecture in the Introduction to best appreciate historic monuments described in this guide.

WÜRZBURG★★

WURTZBURG – Population 124 000

Michelin map 970 K 5

Würzburg lies in the middle of vineyards. The town underwent a period of expansion between 1650 and 1750 thanks to three prince-bishops from the Schönborn family. The great Flamboyant Gothic Sculptor, Tilman Riemenschneider (1460-1531), was mayor of the town and some of his works can still be seen there.

★★RESIDENZ (PALACE)

This Baroque castle was built as a residence for the bishops between 1720 and 1744 following plans by Balthazar Neuman. A **grand staircase★** (Treppenhaus) and a gigantic **fresco★★** by the Venetian Tiepolo (1752-1753) adorn the entryway. Other Tiepolo frescos also decorate the first floor's **Imperial Hall★★**.

★★**Hofkirche (Church)** – This Baroque church is painted in rich, contrasting colours, including the warm colours of Rudolf Byss's frescos and marble columns veined with rose.

★**Museum Martin von Wagner** – The **painting gallery★** presents works from the 14C to the 19C. It includes altar paintings by the masters of Würzburg (14C-16C), Franconian sculpture, and Dutch and Italian painting (16C-18C). The **collection of antiquities** includes lovely **painted Greek vases★★** from the 6C and 4C BC.

ADDITIONAL SIGHTS

★**Festung Marienberg (Fortress of Marienberg)** – This fortress, perched on the heights of the left bank of the River Main, served as a residence for the prince-bishop from 1253 to 1719. The 13C castle was transformed into a Renaissance place around 1600. The round chapel of the Virgin (Marienkirche), dates from the 8C. It is crowned by a dome decorated with Baroque stuccoes.

★★**Mainfränkisches Museum (Franconian Museum of the Main)** – This museum, installed in a former arsenal, presents the region's arts and crafts. Sculptures by Tilman Riemenschneider proliferate, along with examples of religious silver pieces and Franconian folk art. In the ancient cellar, old wine presses are exhibited.

★**Mainbrücke (Old Bridge)** – Two monumental stone statues of saints decorate the bridge built in the 16C.

ZWIEFALTEN Church★★

Michelin map 970 K 5 southwest of Ulm

The church, built by J M Fischer between 1739 and 1753, is located in upper Swabia on a plateau of low hills bathed in light. The church typifies Baroque buildings; the exterior offers no hint of the sumptuous decorations inside. Painting, stucco, and statues cover every inch of surface. The vault paintings are devoted to the Virgin. The chancel, framed by superb grilles, dates from 1757. It houses richly carved stalls. Rococo exuberance is present even on the confessionals, decorated as grottos.

Lovers of Baroque art should tour the **Upper Swabian Baroque churches★★** (84km/52mi – 4hr) starting at Zwiefalten. The tour includes remarkable edifices decorated in pastel tints that project perfect harmony with the landscape. Not to be missed are Obermarchtal, **Steinhausen★**, Bad Schussenried, and **Weingarten★★**.

For further details on Germany, consult the Michelin Green Guides Germany, Rhineland and Berlin.

When looking for a hotel or restaurant, use the Michelin Red Guide Deutschland, updated annually.

The length of time given in this guide

– for touring allows time to enjoy the views and the scenery;

– for sightseeing is the average time required for a visit.

Great Britain

Great Britain

Area: 244 157km²/92 779sq mi – **Population:** 58 million – **Capital:** London – **Currency:** Pound sterling (£) – **Time:** GMT until the end of March; GMT + 1hr from the end of March to the end of October.

Great Britain is the largest of the British Isles. It comprises England (emblem: the rose), Wales (emblem: the leek) and Scotland (emblem: the thistle). Together with Northern Ireland, they form the United Kingdom. The countryside is dotted with castles, gardens, stately homes and peaceful villages along with majestic cathedrals and museums. Sporting events feature games of football (soccer), rugby and cricket. Traditional tourist attractions include concerts and the friendly ambiance in pubs. Everywhere, the British display consummate skills in the art of living.

IN BRIEF

Entry Formalities – Visitors must possess a passport or valid identity card.

Motoring – Driving on the left may cause some disorientation or anxiety. Basic rules include: drive at a moderate speed, remember that the idea of a right of way on your right does not exist, be especially careful at roundabouts and drive around them clockwise, pedestrians have priority.

Souvenirs – Shops generally open from 9am to 5.30pm. In London on Thursdays, shops in Oxford Street and Regent Street open until 8pm, on Wednesdays, shops in Knightsbridge and Kensington open until 7pm. During the Christmas period, from mid-November to Christmas, lights and decorations light up streets and shop windows.

What to buy – Clothes, knitwear, glass, china or pottery (Wedgwood), perfume (Yardley), also tea, ginger biscuits, confectionery and even CDs. From Scotland, tartans, tweed or mohair jackets, pullovers, travelling rugs, sheepskins, whisky (single malt is excellent) and smoked salmon.

Pubs – These meeting places in an old or traditional setting form part of the British psyche. Friends gather there in the evening for a pint of draught beer - everyone usually paying their round - and conversation is lively till closing time. In most public houses there are at least two bars: the public bar, simple and traditional, and the lounge bar, more comfortable with a quiet and relaxed ambiance of carpets and armchairs. Pubs also serve simple lunches: pies (pork pies or steak and kidney pies), ploughman's lunch (cheddar or stilton with salad, pickles, bread and butter), shepherd's pie (minced meat with carrots and mashed potatoes), jacket potatoes or the famous Lancashire hotpot (stewed meat).

Wine Bars – Food is served from a lavish buffet and wine sold by the glass or the bottle.

Tea – From 4pm, take the opportunity of sitting in a comfortable tearoom and enjoy a typical English tea. Mini-sandwiches and delicious pastries are served with a cup of tea mixed with a little cold milk.

Sport – Football (soccer) and rugby (Five Nations Cup) matches are quite an experience. The stadiums seethe with boisterous supporters brandishing the colours of their favourite teams and shouting and singing at the tops of their voices. Cricket is a very British game played from May to September on well-kept greens. To the layman, the games' complex rules can be disconcerting and need explanation. In June, fans of lawn tennis visit Wimbledon for the international tennis championships. Great Britain is also a horse country. Major race meetings include Epsom, Newmarket, Ascot and the Liverpool steeplechase. In polo, a typically British sport and Prince Charles's favourite, two teams play each other on horseback. The aim is for players to hit a wooden ball into the opposing camp using long-handled mallets.

EAST ANGLIA

Densely populated in medieval times, East Anglia has a wealth of ancient villages and small towns. Its dry climate and fertile soil have encouraged arable cultivation on much of its gently undulating farmland. East of Norwich, the regional capital, lie the Norfolk Broads, extensive shallow stretches of water formed by peat extraction. Building styles and windmills evoke past links with the Netherlands. Most of the drainage work was carried out by Dutch engineers who transformed the marshes and fens into arable land.

★★★CAMBRIDGE Population 87 111 Michelin map 970 H4

Cambridge is England's oldest university after Oxford. It established its academic reputation in the early 13C. Scholars from Paris and Oxford fled here. The first college, Peterhouse, was founded in 1284. Today the 31 colleges are independent self-governing bodies while the university undertakes all teaching and confers degrees.

★★★**The colleges** – *One day tour.* This architectural treasure is grouped on the east bank of the River Cam. Each college is linked by a bridge **The Backs**★★.The view is even better from a *punt*, one of the flat bottomed boats on hire at Silver Street Bridge. Towards the end of the afternoon, listen to the celebrated King's College choir.
The table below gives a summary of the principal sights in each college.

College and date of foundation		Principal sights
St John's College ★★★	1511	Tudor Court, neo-Gothic New Court, Bridge of Sighs.
Trinity College★★	1546	Great Court, founded by Henry VIII Gatehouse, Neville's Court (1612) with a library by Sir Christopher Wren.
King's College★★	1441	Founded by Henry VI William Wilkins' monumental neo-Gothic gatehouse, Gibb's Fellows Building.
King's College Chapel ★★★	1446-1515	Zenith of Gothic Perpendicular style
Queen's College★	1446 and 1515	Old Court (15C-16C), Cloister Court with President's Lodge and the Mathematical Bridge.

★★**Fitzwilliam Museum** – The university's renowned museum founded in 1816 possesses superb collections of classical antiquities and medieval art as well as a number of Old Masters, including Titian, Veronese, Van Ruisdael, Van Dyck, Gainsborough, Constable, Renoir and Vuillard. There is also an extensive collection of prints.

ELY Population 90 006

This little town rises 21m/68ft above the marshy flatlands of the Fens. In the 17C, the Dutch engineer Cornelius Vermuyden drained them. The town has been a place of worship since the 7C St Ethelreda. Sacked by the Danes in 870, it was here that Hereward the Wake made his last stand against the Normans.

★★**Cathedral** – Begun in 1033, it displays a whole range of architectural styles from the 11C to the 16C. Enter the nave and the Romanesque transepts to see the magnificent choir. The transept crossing reveals an exquisite Lady Chapel under an octagon topped by a wooden lantern.

★★NORWICH Population 169 814 Michelin map 970 H4

Norwich, the leading city in Norfolk county and East Anglia, has preserved a historic patrimony, including 32 medieval churches.

★★**Cathedral** – The Romanesque cathedral was begun in 1096. In the 15C its choir clerestory was rebuilt in Early English Gothic style and Perpendicular-style vaults were added. Constructed from Caen stone from Normandy, the massive Romanesque tower and 15C spire act as a foil to the long, low nave. The Prior's Door leads to the two-storey cloisters.

Castle – Dating from 1160, its **Museum and Art Gallery**★ displays antiques, arms and armour, landscape paintings from the Norwich School.

The Channel Tunnel provides a direct rail link between London (Waterloo Station), Paris (Gare du Nord) and Brussels (Belgium) and a road/rail (Le Shuttle) link between Folkestone (England) and Calais (France).

LONDON★★★

Population 7 566 620
Michelin map 970 H4

London, the capital of the United Kingdom and one of the world's great financial centres, is also a focus of fashion and entertainment. Only in London do these activities occur simultaneously. Before the Middle Ages, the **City of London** was already a busy commercial centre, while the palace and the abbey built by Edward the Confessor marked the start of the **City of Westminster**. The differences between them are still evident: the **City** is the hub of trade and finance, while the **West End** is renowned for its elegant shops, theatres, clubs, parks, the Houses of Parliament and Buckingham Palace.

Historical Notes – London grew from a wooden bridge which the Romans built across the Thames. Londinium became the centre of a road system and the city developed rapidly after AD 43. Later, in 1060, Edward the Confessor built the first royal palace. His successor, William the Conqueror settled there at his coronation in Westminster Abbey. It was not until the mid 12C however, that London became the official capital of England, replacing Winchester. The monarchs in Westminster, the City and its port gained considerable freedom and independence. One year after the plague of 1665, the City was destroyed by the Great Fire. Christopher Wren's plans were chosen to rebuild the City. It would have transformed London into an avant-garde urban centre. Although Wren's ambitious project was never carried out, he was commissioned to rebuild St Paul's Cathedral and 51 churches. The 18C was a period of contrasts. While the masses lived in appalling conditions, aristocrats constructed new districts around squares. John Nash (1752-1835) proposed to renovate the West End by opening up new perspectives.
Today, London covers an immense area of 1 580km²/600sq mi with more than 7 million inhabitants. The destruction caused by the Second World War is responsible for the rise of modern buildings in the City such as the Barbican and the South Bank Arts Centre, as well as the redevelopment of the obsolete docks.

Traditions – They play an important role in London life. They include the ceremonial mounting and changing of the guards at Buckingham Palace, the changing of the Horse Guards or the Tower of London, and the Lord Mayor's procession through the City in a golden state coach on the second Saturday in November.

Shopping – Regent Street – Burberry's, Liberty's, Hamleys (toys); New Bond Street – jewellers, antique shops, Sotheby's auction house; Oxford Street – Selfridges, Marks and Spencer; Piccadilly and Jermyn Street – luxury goods; Chelsea – avant-garde fashion.

SIGHTS

The principal sights are listed alphabetically.

★★★ **British Museum** (EX) – Sir Hans Sloane founded the museum by bequeathing his collection to the nation. Today, it comprises Egyptian antiquities such as the Rosetta Stone, Oriental antiquities, Greek and Roman antiquities including the Elgin marbles from the Parthenon, and the Roman Portland vase.

Ed Pritchard/Fotogram – STONE

Aerial view of the Thames and the City

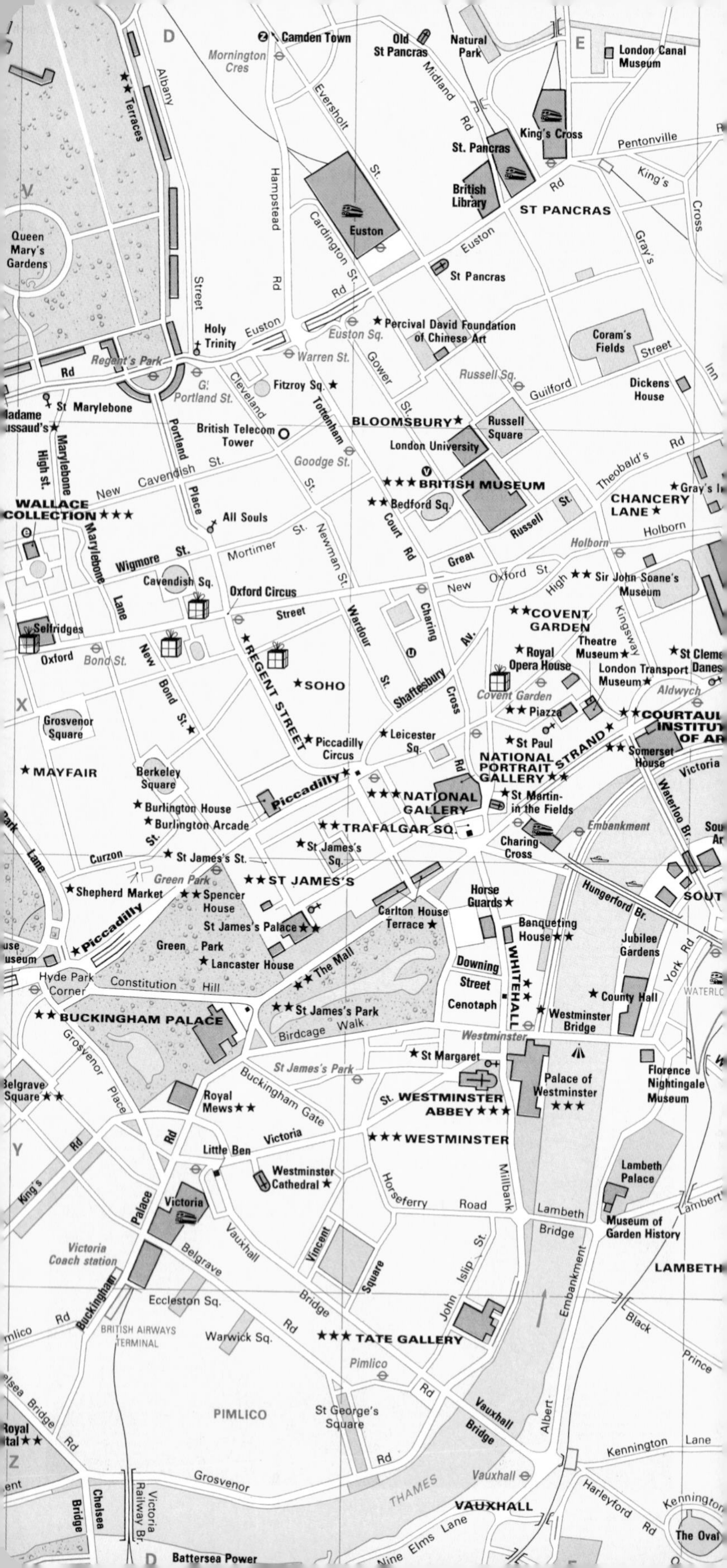
Camden Town
Old St Pancras
Natural Park
London Canal Museum
Mornington Cres
Terraces
Albany
Eversholt St.
Midland Rd
King's Cross
St. Pancras
Pentonville
King's
British Library
Hampstead Rd
Euston
ST PANCRAS
Cardington St.
Queen Mary's Gardens
Euston
St Pancras
Gray's
Cross
Street
Holy Trinity
Euston
Euston Sq.
Percival David Foundation of Chinese Art
Coram's Fields
Street
Regent's Park
Rd
Warren St.
Gower
Russell Sq.
Guilford
Dickens House
Inn
Gt Portland St.
Cleveland
Fitzroy Sq.
St Marylebone
Madame Tussaud's
BLOOMSBURY
Russell Square
British Telecom Tower
Tottenham
London University
Marylebone High St.
Portland Place
New Cavendish St.
Goodge St.
Theobald's Rd
BRITISH MUSEUM
Gray's Inn
WALLACE COLLECTION
All Souls
Bedford Sq.
Court Rd
St.
Russell
CHANCERY LANE
Holborn
Marylebone Lane
Mortimer St.
Newman St.
Wigmore St.
Great
Holborn
Cavendish Sq.
New Oxford St
High
Sir John Soane's Museum
Oxford Circus
Street
Charing
Kingsway
Selfridges
COVENT GARDEN
Oxford
Bond St.
New Bond St.
REGENT STREET
Wardour St.
Cross
Av.
Royal Opera House
Theatre Museum
St Clement Danes
SOHO
Shaftesbury
London Transport Museum
Aldwych
X
Grosvenor Square
Covent Garden
Piazza
COURTAULD INSTITUTE OF ART
Piccadilly Circus
Leicester Sq.
St Paul
Somerset House
Victoria
MAYFAIR
Berkeley Square
NATIONAL PORTRAIT GALLERY
STRAND
Waterloo Br.
Piccadilly
NATIONAL GALLERY
St Martin-in-the Fields
Burlington House
Burlington Arcade
TRAFALGAR SQ.
Embankment
Park Lane
St James's Sq.
Charing Cross
Curzon
St James's St.
Green Park
ST JAMES'S
Shepherd Market
Spencer House
Horse Guards
Hungerford Br.
Carlton House Terrace
Piccadilly
St James's Palace
Banqueting House
Jubilee Gardens
Green Park
WHITEHALL
York Rd
Lancaster House
The Mall
Downing Street
Hyde Park Corner
Constitution Hill
County Hall
Cenotaph
WATERLOO
BUCKINGHAM PALACE
St James's Park
Westminster Bridge
Birdcage Walk
Westminster
St Margaret
Grosvenor Place
St James's Park
Florence Nightingale Museum
Palace of Westminster
Belgrave Square
Royal Mews
Buckingham Gate
St. WESTMINSTER ABBEY
Victoria
WESTMINSTER
Y
King's Rd
Rd
Little Ben
Westminster Cathedral
Millbank
Lambeth Palace
Horseferry Road
Palace
Victoria
Lambeth
Lambeth Bridge
Museum of Garden History
Victoria Coach station
Vauxhall
Vincent
Islip St.
Belgrave
Square
Embankment
LAMBETH
Buckingham
Eccleston Sq.
Bridge
John
Black
Pimlico Rd
BRITISH AIRWAYS TERMINAL
Warwick Sq.
Rd
TATE GALLERY
Prince
Pimlico
Chelsea Bridge
PIMLICO
St George's Square
Rd
Vauxhall Bridge
Albert
Royal Hospital
Rd
Kennington Lane
Z
Grosvenor
Rd
Vauxhall
Victoria Railway Br.
THAMES
Harleyford Rd
Kennington
Chelsea Bridge
VAUXHALL
Nine Elms Lane
The Oval
Battersea Power

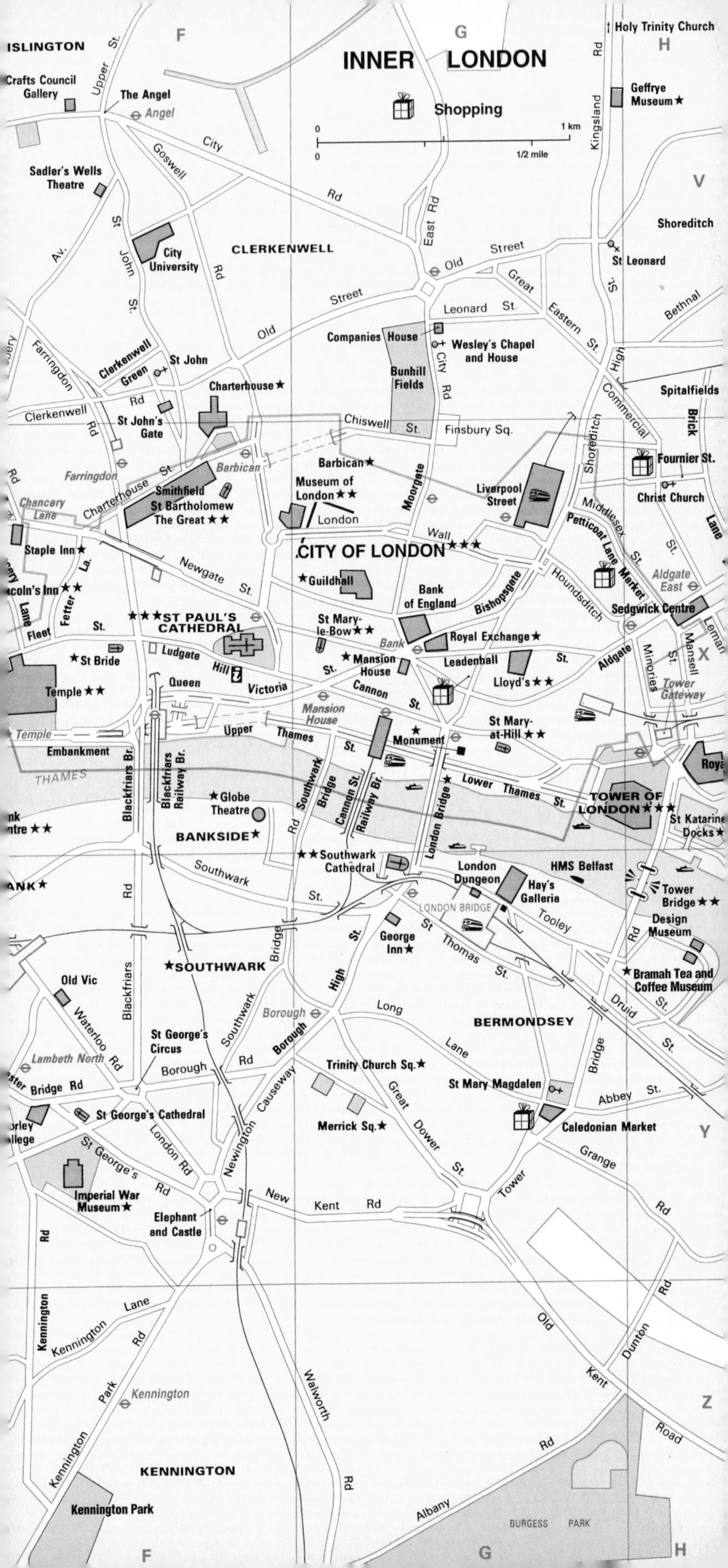

INNER LONDON
Shopping
0
1 km
0
1/2 mile
F
G
H
V
X
Y
Z
Holy Trinity Church
ISLINGTON
Crafts Council Gallery
The Angel
Angel
Upper St.
City
Rd
Goswell
Sadler's Wells Theatre
Geffrye Museum ★
Kingsland Rd
East Rd
Shoreditch
St Leonard
City University
CLERKENWELL
St John St.
Rd
Av.
Old Street
Great Eastern St.
Leonard St.
Bethnal
Companies House
Wesley's Chapel and House
Bunhill Fields
City Rd
Farringdon
Clerkenwell Green
St John
Charterhouse ★
Clerkenwell Rd
St John's Gate
Chiswell St.
Finsbury Sq.
High St.
Commercial
Spitalfields
Brick
Lane
Farringdon
Barbican
Barbican ★
Museum of London ★★
Moorgate
Liverpool Street
Shoreditch
Fournier St.
Christ Church
Chancery Lane
Charterhouse St.
Smithfield
St Bartholomew The Great ★★
London Wall ★★★
Middlesex St.
Petticoat Lane Market
Staple Inn ★
Fetter La.
Lincoln's Inn ★★
Lane
CITY OF LONDON
Newgate St.
Guildhall
Bank of England
Bishopsgate
Houndsditch
Aldgate East
Sedgwick Centre
Fleet St.
★★★ ST PAUL'S CATHEDRAL
St Mary-le-Bow ★★
Bank
Royal Exchange ★
Leman
Mansell St.
Minories
★ St Bride
Ludgate Hill
★ Mansion House
Leadenhall St.
Aldgate
Queen Victoria St.
Cannon St.
Lloyd's ★★
Tower Gateway
Temple ★★
Mansion House
Temple
Upper Thames St.
Monument
St Mary-at-Hill ★★
Embankment
THAMES
Blackfriars Br.
Blackfriars Railway Br.
Southwark Bridge
Cannon St. Railway Br.
London Bridge
Lower Thames St.
TOWER OF LONDON ★★★
Roya
★ Globe Theatre
BANKSIDE ★
Rd
St Katharine Docks ★
★★ Southwark Cathedral
London Dungeon
HMS Belfast
Hay's Galleria
Tower Bridge ★★
Southwark St.
LONDON BRIDGE
Tooley
Design Museum
Rd
St Thomas St.
George Inn ★
High St.
★ SOUTHWARK
★ Bramah Tea and Coffee Museum
Old Vic
Waterloo Rd
Blackfriars Rd
Southwark Bridge Rd
Borough
Long Lane
BERMONDSEY
Druid St.
Lambeth North
St George's Circus
Borough Rd
Borough High St.
Trinity Church Sq. ★
Bridge
St Mary Magdalen
Abbey St.
Bridge Rd
St George's Cathedral
Great Dover St.
Caledonian Market
Merrick Sq. ★
London Rd
Newington Causeway
Grange
St George's Rd
Imperial War Museum ★
Elephant and Castle
New Kent Rd
Tower Bridge
Rd
Rd
Kennington Lane
Kennington Rd
Old Kent Rd
Dunton
Kennington
Park Rd
Walworth Rd
Kennington
KENNINGTON
Kennington Park
Albany Rd
Road
BURGESS PARK
F
G
H

★★**Buckingham Palace** (DY) – The royal residence is visible in **St James's Park**★★, London's oldest royal park established in 1532. In 1703, the Duke of Buckingham built a house of brick for himself at the edge of the park. It remained virtually unchanged until the time of George IV, when his architect, John Nash, clad its walls in Bath stone. Under Queen Victoria, the east façade was constructed and the wings linked to enclose the front court with the balcony. The **Changing of the Guard**★★ takes place in this front court. When the Queen is in residence, the Royal Standard flies over the palace.

★★★**St Paul's Cathedral** (FX) – On Ludgate Hill, St Paul's Cathedral and its massive dome tower above the City. After the Great Fire destroyed Old St Paul's, Sir Christopher Wren submitted plans for a new cathedral. The foundation stone was laid on 21 June 1675. Thirty-three years later, Wren saw his son set the final stone in place, the topmost in the lantern. When Wren died, he was buried within the walls of the cathedral. Traditionally, it is the setting for the funerals of war leaders such as Nelson, Wellington, and, in 1965, Winston Churchill.
The south esplanade offers a spectacular view. Unlike St Peter's dome in Rome, which influenced Wren, St Paul's **dome** is not a true hemisphere. The drum is in two tiers; and the lantern in the typical restrained English Baroque style. The west face displays a Corinthian portico and a pediment surmounted by the figure of St Paul. On either side rise Wren's most Baroque spires. The Whispering Gallery in the dome is noted for the accoustic effect which has given it its name. The views from the Golden Gallery at the top of the dome extend over London and the Thames.

★★**Kensington Palace** – Since its purchase in 1689 by William III, this house has become a residence for members of the Royal Family. Wren was its principal architect. The State Apartments decorated by Colen Campbell and William Kent are open to the public. On the ground floor, the Court Dress Collection exhibits date back to 1750.

★★**Hyde Park** – This park extends east of the Serpentine. Pitt called it the lungs of London. Orators may debate anything at **Speakers' Corner**. To the north, **Marble Arch**, a marble triumphal arch, was designed by John Nash as a grand entrance to Buckingham Palace. It commemorates the battles of Trafalgar and Waterloo.

★**Piccadilly Circus** (DEX) – The circus, adorned with the statue of Eros, is one of London's symbols. In the evening, it glitters with a thousand sparkling lights from the illuminated signs. It constitutes one of the capital's nerve centres. Coventry Street leads to Leicester Square and its cinemas. Charing Cross Road is lined with theatres. To the north, Shaftesbury Avenue runs into **Soho**, famed for its night-life and restaurants of every nationality.

★**Regent Street** (DX) was designed in the early 19C by the architect John Nash as a triumphal avenue to link Carlton House, the Regent's Palace, with Regent's Park where the prince planned to build a country residence.

South Kensington – After the 1851 Great Exhibition, Prince Albert used the profit to buy land in South Kensington to build the Royal College of Art, the Royal Geographical Society, the Royal College of Music and several museums.
The **Victoria and Albert Museum**★★★ displays treasures from the Middle Ages to the Renaissance. They include tapestries depicting the Trojan War and a series of Triumphs after Petrarch; the Raphael cartoons for the tapestries of the Acts of the Apostles; a collection of musical instruments; an exceptional collection of 18C French furniture, and British works from 1500 to the 20C.
The **Science Museum**★★★ exhibits all kinds of scientific activity with practical applications.

★★★**Tate Gallery** (EZ) – The gallery developed from the collection donated to the nation by Henry Tate in 1891. A grocer's assistant, he made a fortune as a sugar refiner, and assembled a collection of paintings of the British School, including Gainsborough, Turner *(The Burning of the Houses of Parliament)*, William Blake, landscape artists such as Constable, and Stubbs specialising in animals. The Pre-Raphaelites, including Rossetti and Millais, are all well represented. From the post-Victorian Era, Sargent's portraits stand out. A major collection of 20C work rounds out the museum.

★★★**Tower of London** (GHX) – The tower, full of grim historical associations, is situated on the north bank of the River Thames. A Yeomen of the Guard in Tudor costume guard its treasures which include the Crown Jewels.
When William the Conqueror settled in London, he strengthened the fortifications by adding three towers, one made of wood. In 1078, he built a stone tower to discourage Londoners from rioting. The vantage point beside the river gave a good view of any hostile force coming up the Thames.

From 1300 to 1810, the tower housed the Royal Mint and because of its defences it became the Royal Jewel House and served as a prison. Many of its prisoners were famous individuals and some were executed; among these were the King of France, John the Good, the poet Charles of Orléans, Geoffrey Chaucer, the author of the *Canterbury Tales*, Henry VI, the founder of Eton, the children of Edward IV, the chancellor Thomas More, Anne Boleyn and Jane Grey.
William I commissioned the White Tower or keep in 1078. The stone walls 31m/101ft high form an uneven quadrilateral. It houses the Armoury. The 13C Beauchamp Tower served as a prison. The **Crown Jewels★★★** are kept in the **Jewel House**, most of them used for coronations. They incorporate fabulous gems, diamonds, rubies, and sapphires.

★★**Tower Bridge** (HY) – These Gothic towers are open to the public. The museum explains the mechanism of the hydraulic system which, until 1976, raised the bascules.

★★**Trafalgar Square** (EX) – The square was designed by Nash in 1820. Nelson's column was erected in 1842. The monument, 56m/183ft high, commemorates the memory of Admiral Nelson who died at the battle of Trafalgar (1805).

★★★**National Gallery** (EX) – The nucleus of the gallery was formed by the collection of Sir John Julius Angerstein (1735-1823). Additional donations came from Beaumont and Carr, as well as purchases made by the government. Today, the National Gallery is the proud possessor of works by Giotto, Uccello, Botticelli, Raphael, Leonardo, Michelangelo, Caravaggio, Velasquez, Poussin, Watteau, Chardin, Constable, Gainsborough, Vermeer and Rembrandt. It is one of the world's finest collections.

★★**Whitehall** (EY) – This wide street leading from Trafalgar Square to Parliament Square is lined with government offices. The **Banqueting Hall★★** was begun by Inigo Jones for James I in 1619.

★★★**Westminster Abbey** (EY) – The abbey, the burial place of British monarchs, is a masterpiece of Gothic architecture. For centuries, it has served as the setting for great state occasions. Edward the Confessor built it first in the Romanesque style. The Plantagenet Henry III reconstructed it in 1220. Inspired by Amiens and Reims cathedrals, the king's rebuilding began with the Lady Chapel. Work continued for two centuries. Then, in the early 16C, the Lady Chapel was replaced by a larger one. The Dissolution of the monasteries in 1540 precipitated the confiscation of the abbey's treasure, the loss of its lands and the dispersal of the Benedictine community. A century later, Queen Elizabeth granted Westminster a charter establishing a Collegiate with a royally appointed chapter of 12 canons.
The interior is dominated by the six-part vaulting soaring to 31m/101ft, but the perspective to the nave is broken by the choir screen. The Henry VII Chapel has a superb fan vaulted roof. The Coronation Chair is found in the chapel of Edward the Confessor. The Chapter-house displays harmonious lierne and tierceron vaulting springing from a central pillar.

★★★**Palace of Westminster** (EY) – This palace, where Parliament meets, was rebuilt in the Gothic style after a fire in 1834 on a site occupied by British monarchs since 1060. The term Parliament was first used in 1240 to designate the assembly of knights and members of the court meeting for discussions. During this early period, Westminster Hall hosted royal banquets and medieval jousts; the wood ceiling is an extraordinary example of a hammerbeam roof. The 19C reconstruction of the palace was entrusted to Charles Barry and Augustus Pugin, who created a masterpiece of Victorian Gothic architecture. Its most famous feature, the clock tower **Big Ben★** was completed in 1859.

►► Boat trip on the Thames – Excursions: **Greenwich★★★** (a royal residence since King Alfred's time), **Hampton Court★★★** (a Tudor palace), **Kew Gardens★★★** (Royal Botanic Gardens).

The Dome, or the Third Millenium

On 31 December 1999, the last day of the present millenium, Greenwich, famous for its meridian, will celebrate the dawn of the new millenium with the opening of the Dome, a gigantic structure 320m/1 048ft in diameter and 50m/164ft high covering an area of 80 425m²/865 244sq ft (twice Wembley Stadium). The Dome is as high as Nelson's Column and large enough to cover Trafalgar Square and part of the surrounding buildings. A futuristic building, it seeks to predict what life will be like in the 21C, with all the drastic changes involved.
Until 31 December 2000, visitors will be treated to a multimedia show on the theme of time with many special effects.

The MIDLANDS

The centre of England is firmly defined to the north and west by the Pennine hills and the mountains of Wales. To the south and east, a less precise boundary is formed by a series of broad vales watered by slow rivers. The most prominent is the belt of oolitic limestone at its widest in the Cotswolds. The regular pattern of ancient county towns such as Gloucester, Northampton, and Lincoln was often swept over by the Industrial Revolution. At this time, Birmingham became a huge metropolis.

★BIRMINGHAM Population 1 013 995 Michelin map 970 G 4

The second largest city of the United Kingdom was one of the centres of the 19C Industrial Revolution. The excellent position of this city, well served by transport links, its rich coalfields, and its ever increasing population made the Birmingham area a powerhouse for the development of numerous techniques and inventions.

James Watt (1736-1819) invented the double-action steam engine and **William Murdock** (1754-1839) discovered coal-gas lighting. The factory of **Matthew Boulton** (1728-1809) was the first ever lit by gas.
Grim conditions caused by the city's phenomenal growth bred both public and private reformers. Joseph Chamberlain (1869-1940), the long-time mayor and father of Prime Minister Neville Chamberlain, advocated radical municipal action. Philanthropist George Cadbury (1839-1922), the cocoa manufacturer, was responsible for one of the world's first garden suburbs, Bournville.

A tourist could plan an interesting visit in Birmingham organised around the theme of the Industrial Revolution. Such a visit could include: the Museum of Science and Industry, the canals, Gas Street Basin, and the Art Gallery. These, combined with a visit to the Black Country Museum and Ironbridge, would form the highlight of a stay in England for those interested in industrial history.

The **Museum of Science and Industry★** records Birmingham's technological and industrial progress. Locomotive Hall is particularly noteworthy with its imposing steam engine *City of Birmingham* (no.46235) in its gold and green livery. The James Watt Building houses an educational account of Watt's steam engine and the machine built by Boulton and Watt in 1779 at Smethwick. *(Demonstration on the first and third Wednesdays of each month).* Watt's life and work is described up to his meeting with Boulton. Other sections display further examples of Birmingham's engineering achievement.

After leaving the museum, the tour of Birmingham's industrial past may be extended by walking along the canal adjoining the museum towards Gas Street Basin. This walk of 1km/0.5mi – goes past the locks, iron bridges and various structures spawned by the city's industrial growth in the last century.

Gas Street Basin is surrounded by both new and restored 18C and 19C buildings, including Matthew Boulton's factory, **the Brasshouse,** on Broad Street. It has now been refurbished and transformed into a restaurant and pub. The gaily-painted narrow boats, moored along the quay, evoke the craft which once plied the Midlands' canal network.

►► Birmingham **Museum and Art Gallery★★** contains an outstanding collection of Pre-Raphaelite paintings. The **Barber Institute of Fine Arts★★** holds European paintings from Bellini to Van Gogh.

EXCURSIONS

★★**Ironbridge Gorge Museum** – *58km/36 miles to the northwest.* This important industrial museum extends over several sites along the densely-wooded, mineral-rich Severn Gorge, the birthplace of the Industrial Revolution. In the autumn of 1708, British ironmaster Abraham Darby (1678-1717) settled in Coalbrookdale. In 1709, he was the first to use coke as a fuel for smelting iron instead of the traditional charcoal. His experiments made possible the use of iron in transport (wheels, rails), engineering (steam engines, locomotives, ships) and construction (buildings and bridges, including the famous Iron Bridge).

★**Black Country Museum** – *Dudley, 15km/9 miles to the northwest.* It consists of a number of buildings representing the heritage of the old coal industry: a pit head, an impressive underground display and an industrial village.

★★CHESTER Population 80 154 Michelin map 970 G 4

This fortified garrison town was built on a sandstone ridge in a loop of the River Dee. It was one of the largest in Roman times. Its walls were rebuilt in the early 9C. The title of Earl of Chester reverted to the Crown in 1237. Ever since Henry III gave it to his son, later Edward I, it has remained one of the titles of the monarch's eldest son.

Chester is the only city in England to have preserved its complete ramparts. Parts of the Roman walls can be seen between King Charles' Tower and the North Gate. The width of the Roman fortress becomes evident from the East Gate. The Rodee, on the site of a former Roman port, became a race course in 1540, when the city's founding fathers forbade football matches, because of spectator hooliganism.
The **cathedral★** is a red sandstone edifice built between 1250 and 1540 and much restored since the 19C; but many of the original abbey buildings, such as the Refectory and the chapter-house are still standing around the 12C cloisters. The carved choir stalls, comparable to those at Lincoln and Beverley, are remarkable for their fine craftsmanship. The **town hall** is a Gothic-style building of red and grey sandstone. It stands on the way to the 14C **Rows★★**, a set of attractive shopping arcades.

NOTTINGHAM Population 273 000 Michelin map 970 G 4

Nottingham is famed for its sheriff and Robin Hood, whose legendary exploits first took shape in the 15C. It also was the birthplace of **David Herbert Lawrence** (1885-1930), author of *Lady Chatterley's Lover.*
The city defended the River Trent and was the gateway to the north. During the Middle Ages, it grew in importance and became a Danish burg, like Derby, Leicester, Lincoln and Stamford. From 1350 to 1530, Nottingham was the home of a school of alabaster carvers specialising in panels illustrating the New Testament. It soon industrialised and is still a base for well-known firms such as Boots pharmaceuticals, Players' cigarettes and Raleigh cycles.
Nothing is left of the original Romanesque castle built by William the Conqueror. Supporters of King John surrendered there to Richard the Lionheart in 1194. Mortimer and Queen Isabella were imprisoned here after murdering Edward II. In 1485, Richard III emerged from the castle to lead his troops to defeat and death at Bosworth Field. The **Castle Museum★** traces the history of Nottingham.

★★★ OXFORD Population 113 847 Michelin map 970 G 4

England's oldest university developed in Saxon times around a nunnery, now Christchurch Cathedral. The university was founded around 1200. During the Reformation, it became secular and provided martyrs for both sides – Latimer, Ridley, Cranmer and Campion. The Royalists used it as a headquarters during the Civil War, and Charles I took shelter there. Despite reforms and innovations, particularly in the development of scientific research, Oxford remains a traditional place, producing generations of intellectuals. This university possesses one of the world's greatest libraries, the Bodleian, which was founded in the 14C and today contains almost 5 million books.

Many colleges are not open to the public until the afternoon.

The most important sights in each college are listed below.

College and foundation date		Sights
All Souls College	1438	Perpendicular style Chapel.
Christ Church ★★	1525	**Tom Quad★★** and **Tom Tower★** by Wren. The **Tudor Hall★★** with a remarkable collection of portraits.
Christ Church Cathedral★		15C choir **roof★**.
Merton College	1264	Mob Quad Chapel.
Queen's College	1340	Front Quadrangle hall and chapel.
Magdalen College	1456	Perpendicular style cloisters and bell-tower.
St John's College★	1555	Canterbury Quadrangle.

★★ **Ashmolean Museum** – This museum possesses a substantial art collection of Greek and Roman sculpture and Italian paintings. Note the Pre-Raphaelite section.

EXCURSIONS

★★★ **Blenheim Palace** – *6.5km/4mi northwest.* Blenheim Palace is one of the finest examples of the English Baroque. Saxon kings once hunted on the estate. Queen Anne gave it to John Churchill, Duke of Marlborough (1650-1722) as a reward for vanquishing Louis XIV's troops at Blenheim (Bavaria) in 1704. Seemingly limitless funds were made available and leading architects and craftsmen employed. Sir John Vanbrugh, one of England's most original architects, and his associate Hawksmoor, took the lead in the design. Unfortunately, court intrigues precipitated Marlborough's downfall and construction came to a halt. The project was completed after the duke's death. A century and a half later, on 30 November 1874, his direct descendant Winston Churchill was born here.

The palace was inspired both by the works of Palladio and by Versailles. Its towers are built on an impressively grandiose scale. Symbols of military prowess and patriotism abound. The interior boasts a series of splendidly decorated rooms, including portraits by Reynolds, Romney, and Van Dyck. Note also the magnificent stucco ceiling in the library and the Winston Churchill memorabilia.
The **park★★★** was planned in the early 18C, but later redesigned by Lancelot Capability Brown, one of the great English landscape gardeners. Sweeping grassy slopes, impressive groves of trees, and the lake's contours create a magnificent setting.

★★**Waddesdon Manor** – *40km/24mi northeast.* The manor was built in the 19C for Baron Ferdinand de Rothschild in French Renaissance style. It contains Dutch, Flemish and French paintings, French royal furniture and Sèvres porcelain.

★★**Thames Valley** – The River Thames flows through a typically English countryside of low hills, woods, meadows, and attractive country houses. In summer, many riverside villages offer boat trips. Most avoid the mishaps described in Jerome K Jerome's *Three Men in a Boat*.
From Oxford to Windsor, the itinerary *(114km/70mi)* passes through Iffley (**Romanesque Church★**), **Abingdon★** (17C **County Hall★**), **Basildon Park★** (Palladian villa of Bath stone), **Mapledurham★** (Elizabethan manor house), Henley (Royal Regatta first week in July), and **Eton College★★**, founded in 1440. Note there the college **chapel★** built in the Perpendicular style and decorated with 15C wall paintings.

STOKE-ON-TRENT Population 272 446 Michelin map 970 G 4

Potteries existed here long before the time of England's most distinguished creator **Josiah Wedgwood** (1730-1795). Kilns dating from about 1300 have been found at Sneyd Green and potters named Wedgwood and Adams worked here in the 1600s. The opening of the Etruria factory in 1769, the exploitation of the Staffordshire coalfields and the digging of the Trent-Mersey canal created a national industry noted for its art. Most of the great brick bottle kilns have now disappeared. A few remain, particularly in Longton. There, the Gladstone Pottery retains its original workshops. Demonstrations of the potter's traditional skills are offered.
The Hanley **Museum and Art Gallery★** houses one the area's finest ceramics collection. The **Wedgwood Visitor Centre★** at Barlaston displays a superb collection of Wedgwood products. Also exhibited are portraits of Josiah Wedgwood by Stubbs, Reynolds, Lawrence and Wright of Derby.

★STRATFORD-UPON-AVON Population 20 941 Michelin map 970 G 4

Stratford, an attractive town with half-timbered houses, is famous as the native town of **William Shakespeare** (1564-1616). Little is known about the playwright except that he left his wife, Anne Hathaway, and his home town to go to London. Success arrived at the Globe Theatre. Shakespeare later bought a house in Stratford where he spent the last years of his life. His work, which includes poems, consists primarily of plays, including such masterpieces as *Othello, Macbeth* and *Romeo and Juliet.*

Shakespeare's Birthplace – In the half-timbered house where Shakespeare was born, some of his original editions are displayed. The adjoining Shakespeare Centre shows off an exhibition of costumes from the BBC Shakespeare series.

William Shakespeare by Coblitz

Royal Shakespeare Theatre – It opened in 1932 and is now the headquarters of the Royal Shakespeare Company, which also plays in London at the Barbican and at the Pit Theatre. The museum contains paintings, sculpture and historical theatre material.

Holy Trinity Church – In the Gothic-style Holy Trinity contains the tomb of the great dramatist.

►► **Hidcote Manor Garden★★** *(16km/10mi on the Chipping Camden Road)* displays splendid 20C gardens.

The NORTH of ENGLAND and the LAKE DISTRICT

The Pennine chain dominates the region, flanked by extensive lowlands. To the west extend the Cheshire and Lancashire plains and to the east, the densely populated Yorkshire coalfields. Three National Parks are located in the Pennines, including the Lake District National Park with England's highest peaks. Further north, Christianity established early roots in the moorland region of Northumbria.

★★★ CHATSWORTH Michelin map 970 G 4

In the Peak District National Park, Chatsworth House was once described as a second Versailles. Its vast collection of works of art were assembled by the dukes of Devonshire.

Chatsworth House – The original palace was built in 1551 by Sir William Cavendish and Bess of Hardwick, an indomitable woman who married four times, increasing her wealth with each marriage. She first indulged her passion for building at Chatsworth. However, on deciding that her third husband, the Earl of Shrewsbury, was a knave, fool and beast because he had an affair with his prisoner, Mary Queen of Scots, she returned to her property Hardwick, and built a new house.
Among the riches of Chatsworth are ceilings and walls painted by Laguerre and Verrio, Louis XIV furniture, tapestries based on Raphael, paintings by Poussin, Bruegel the Elder, Tintoretto, Veronese, the 28m/91ft long library and the Sculpture Gallery housing the works of Canova.

★★★ **Park** – The park designed by Capability Brown (1716-1783) possesses an unusually majestic feature, the Cascade designed by Grillet, a pupil of Louis XIV's Versailles gardener Le Nôtre. A maze now covers the ground plan of a conservatory built by Paxton.

►► **Hardwick Hall**★★ *(24km-14mi east)* is a fine example of A 16C mansion – **Haddon Hall**★★ *(5km/3mi south)* is a charming 17C manor – **Bolsover Castle**★ *(26km-16mi east)* represents a folly by the architect Robert Smythson.

★★★ DURHAM Population 38 105 Michelin map 970 G 3

The cathedral is perched on the summit of a rocky slope. Below, the peaceful River Wear flows between grassy banks. The medieval city has remained compact, physically unaffected by the once intense industrial activity.
In 875 the monks of Lindisfarne fled south from a Danish attack, taking with them the body of St Cuthbert. They reached this rocky landscape, where the Normans built a castle and took advantage of the site's natural assets. In 1093 the cathedral's foundation stone was laid.

★★ **Cathedral** – This masterpiece of Romanesque architecture was constructed between 1095 and 1133. Its imposing structure dominates the **Palace Green Gardens** and the university buildings. Inside, the **nave**★★★ gives an impression of overwhelming power. Massive columns with geometric decoration alternate with piers to support the intersecting ribs of the vault. The choir contains fine stalls. Beyond the 14C choir screen stands the reliquary of St Cuthbert. The chapel of the Nine Altars, in an early Gothic style, displays extravagantly tall lancet windows.

★ **Castle** – The only one in the region never taken by the Scots, is now part of Durham University. The courtyard is overlooked by the keep. The 15C kitchens, the Great Hall and the **Norman Chapel**★ are open to the public.

★★★ LAKE DISTRICT Michelin map 970 F 3

England's largest national park covers an area of 2280km²/866sq mi. The magnificent stretches of water give the region its name. Rocks, steep cliffs and precipices surround the lakes. Among the many famous peaks is the stony desert of **Scafell Pike**. It rises to 977m/3204ft. To the south, the commanding figure of The **Old Man** looms over Coniston Water. To the west, near the the summit of Wasdale lies the the most austere of the lakes, Wastwater.
The peaks are often wreathed in cloud and the slopes shrouded in mist. The air is mild and the changing light plays subtly upon the rich harmonious range of colours of the rocks and vegetation of heather, rowan, birch, dark pine, oak and sycamore. The little villages form part of the mountain landscape. Above all, the Lake District is a rambler's paradise. The region offers many options, appealing both to walkers and mountaineers.

Lakeland Poets' Tour – This tour *(48km/29mi)* around the Lake District's central section evokes the memory of the poets Wordsworth, Coleridge and Southey who were inspired by the landscape. Ambleside and Windermere are two convenient excursion centres.

★**Lake Windermere** – Wooded slopes and bare fells frame this lake stretching for 16km/9mi. The district's liveliest lake is visited for sailing, water-skiing and boat trips, which pass close to the unspoilt west bank, and the many islets, including Belle Isle.

Bowness-on-Windermere – This pretty village is known for its promenade along the bay. From its pier, boat trips head north to Waterhead and south to Lake Side.

Hill Top – The home of **Beatrix Potter** and her kingdom of Peter Rabbit, Benjamin Bunny and Jemima Puddle-Duck has remained unchanged since the author's death in 1943. Each year, thousands of visitors come seeking to recapture their childhood. In Miss Potter's 17C house, her watercolours and dolls' houses are displayed.

★**Hawkshead** – Flower-decked cottages line the narrow slate-walled lanes and paths of this traditional Lakeland village.
From the top of the crest, a view looks out onto the lake and the surrounding fells. The **Old Man**, 801m/2627ft tall, dominates.

A. Williams

Lake Windermere

★**Coniston Water** – Donald Campbell died here in 1967 trying to beat the world water speed record.

★**Brantwood** – On the east shore of Coniston Water is the former home of **John Ruskin**, one of the greatest figures of the Victorian age. Its walls are covered by his own exquisite watercolours and some by the Pre-Raphaelite contemporaries he championed. His study, in a turret, provides a splendid **view**★ of Coniston and its attractive lakeside setting. Ruskin (1819-1900) author, artist and social reformer is buried in Coniston churchyard. The Ruskin Museum in the village displays examples of his many talents.

★**Dove Cottage** – This early 17C converted inn *(The Dove and Olive Branch)* was the home of **William Wordsworth** (1770-1850) and his sister Dorothy from 1799 to 1808. It became a magnet for the early 19C romantic writers, Coleridge, Southey and De Quincey. The adjacent museum contains manuscripts, memorabilia and Lakeland paintings.

Rydal Mount – This cottage, dating from about 1574 and extended in the 18C into a farmhouse, was the home of William Wordsworth. The poet moved here in 1813, the date when he officially became a revolutionary poet. He stayed until his death in 1850. Inside, his library now forms part of the drawing room and the study ceiling is still painted with the Renaissance designs he copied during a visit to Italy.

★LIVERPOOL Population 535 809 Michelin map 970 F 4

Like Birmingham and Manchester, the Beatles' home town marks a highly interesting stop to learn about the Industrial Revolution in Britain. Liverpool was once a hive of commercial activity. In the 19C, it served as the home port of the Cunard and White Star liners. Today, the city, with its glorious architecture and fine civic buildings, displays great cultural dynamism particularly in leisure developments such as the **Albert Dock**★.

The **Merseyside Maritime Museum★** recounts Liverpool's past involvement with the sea, its shipbuilding prowess and its port's role in slavery.
The **Tate Gallery★** displays part of the national collection of 20C art. Fans of the **Beatles** will discover the story of their idols in the Britannia Pavillion.
The **Walker Art Gallery★★** houses a large collection of British paintings.
The **Liverpool Anglican Cathedral★★** is the world's largest Anglican church. The **Lady Chapel★** has a remarkable altar piece and A 15C Madonna by Giovanni della Robbia.
The Roman Catholic cathedral, **Metropolitan Cathedral of Christ the King★★** on Brownlow Hill was constructed relatively recently. The exterior, an extraordinary circular structure in concrete, is unique.

★MANCHESTER Population 437 612 Michelin map 970 G 4

In the 16C an active linen and wool industry already existed in the Manchester area. But the appearance of cotton around 1600 ensured the city's wealth. In the 19C, British cotton was sold throughout the world and the Manchester cotton exchange became the centre of this industry. Today, after the long decline, bomb damage of the last war and a series of economic crises, Manchester still remains a major provincial city. Offices, banks, insurance companies, export-import businesses give the city a major financial role. Manchester also remains a centre of artistic and intellectual endeavour.

★**Museum of Science and Industry** – *Liverpool Road.* The station, first opened in 1830, was the world's oldest passenger station. The comprehensive museum gives an excellent view of Manchester's industrial heritage.
The **Lower Byrom Street Warehouse** has exhibitions on printing, textiles, and machine tools. **Xperiment** is a hands-on science centre. In the **Power Hall**, the locomotives take pride of place. The building along Liverpool Road houses an exhibition on the history of the city. Inside Liverpool Road Station, there also is a reconstruction of a first-class booking hall, as well as a display on the Liverpool and Manchester Railway. Finally, the **Air and Space Gallery** occupies the former city exhibition hall, beyond Lower Byrom Street. It shows the history of flight from the exploits of the first flying machines to the space age. The enormous four-engined Avro Schackleton reconnaissance aeroplane is only one of the many aircraft manufactured by the famous Manchester aircraft company, Avro.

★**City Art Gallery** – This museum displays an interesting Pre-Raphaelite collection with works by Millais, Hunt, Rossetti and Ford Madox Brown. Brown's Work depicts the various classes in a developing industrial society. There are also paintings by Stubbs, Turner and Constable. The northern industrial landscape is conveyed sensitively by LS Lowry (1887-1976). His studio has been reconstructed on the ground floor.

Royal Exchange – The former Cotton Exchange lies behind the 19C town hall. Today this immense hall is partly occupied by the 700-seat Royal Exchange Theatre. The prices of cotton on the day the market last traded are still shown on the board.

►► **Cathedral★** – The choir screen and stalls depict humorous scenes from medieval life.

★NEWCASTLE-UPON-TYNE Population 199 064 Michelin map 970 G 3

The city's spectacular **site★★**, its rich history and the population's distinctive Geordie dialect have created a strong identity.
The easily defended bridging point was exploited by the Roman founders of Pons Aelius. It served as a post along Hadrian's Wall. Later the Normans built a castle dating from 1080. Abundant mineral resources, particularly coal, stimulated trade and manufacture. In the 19C, Tyneside became one of the great industrial centres, dominated by figures like Lord William Armstrong (1810-1900) whose engineering and armament works helped to equip the navies of the world.
The approach from the south reveals an astonishing urban panorama. The city spread from the quayside up steeply sloping streets and precipitous stairways to the flatter lands in the north. The dramatic appearance is enhanced by the monumental piers of the **Tyne Bridge**, built in 1928. From the quay, the six bridges come into view successively, forming an outstanding vista.
The city is named after the New Castle built by William the Conqueror's son, Robert Curthose. The keep is all that remains. In 1848 the railway was built straight through the castle precincts.

EXCURSIONS

★★**Hadrian's Wall** – In AD 122, the Roman emperor, Hadrian, who enjoyed foreign travel, visited Britain. To ensure peace, he ordered the building of a defensive wall across the northernmost boundary of the empire. It extended 117km/72mi from Wallsend on the Tyne to Bowness on the Solway Firth.

The wall was built by legionaries in stone and turf with forts and turrets at regular intervals along its length. A ditch on the north side and a military road on the south defined the military zone. Hadrian's Wall follows the best strategic and geographical line and, at places like Cawfields or Walltown Crags, commands splendid views.

Corstopitum★, west of Corbridge, was occupied longer than any other site. The museum of the Roman camp displays granaries, a fountain and temples.
At **Chesters**★, a fort, bridge remains, and the foundations of the four gateways and vestiges of the bath house are visible.
Near Carawburgh, the **Temple of Mithras**, is an unexpected find in these moorlands. Inside the lobby stands the statue of the mother goddess. Three alters are placed beyond the benches for worshippers.

H. Phillips/The National Trust

Hadrian's Wall

Housesteads★★ a fort, perched high on the ridge, is the most complete example of such constructions on the wall. Still visible are the foundations of the commandant's house, the granaries, barracks, hospital, and the latrine block.
At Carvoran, the **Roman Army Museum**★ with its audio-visual presentation and examples of Roman armour and costumes, gives a lively picture of the wall and its garrison.

★★ **North of England Open-Air Museum (Beamish)** – *Beamish, 16km/10mi.* This important and popular open-air museum recreates life in the north of England at the turn of the century. Period tramcars take visitors through the site.

PEAK DISTRICT Michelin map 970 G 4

The national park covers 1 400km²/532sq mi from Holmfirth in the north to Ashbourne in the south and from Sheffield in the east to Macclesfield in the west. A thick layer of gridstone extends to the level of the moors in the north and the precipitous outcrops of Dark Peak. It culminates in **Kinder Scout** which rises to 636m/2 086ft. In the south, the lighter stone forms the base of the more pastoral White Peak, a plateau divided by drystone walls and deeply sunken vales.
A mass trespass by ramblers was organised on Kinder Scout on 24 April 1932. They were anxious to establish right of access to these wild spots. Five trespassers were arrested but their demonstration for freedom of access to privately owned land eventually led to the establishment of National Parks.
The annual Well Dressing is a local tradition. This ancient pagan thanksgiving to local water spirits takes place from May to August in about 20 villages, including Eyam, Youlgreave, Wirksworth and Monyash.

Arbor Low – This well-known prehistoric monument consists of a circle of stones in the shape of a clock within a surrounding bank and a ditch.

Buxton – The mineral waters of this small spa town were first discovered by the Romans. Its chief attractions are the Crescent, built in 1780, and the Opera House.

Castleton Caves – The nearest cave is Peak Cavern. To the west, Speedwell Cavern is reached by boat along an underground canal. **Blue John Cavern**★ is the source of a purplish-blue form of fluorspar known as Blue John, a semi-precious stone which has been worked into jewellery.

★ **Dovedale** – This dramatic 3km/2mi gorge runs through the Derbyshire Hills.

★★★ YORK Population 123 126 Michelin map 970 G 4

Today York is famous for its cathedral but it was already a prosperous trading centre during the Viking Age (9C-10C) when it was known as Jorvik. The **Jorvik Viking Centre**★ brings to life this period and the annual **Jorvik Viking Festival** produces a splash of colour and gaiety in February with its longship races, feasting and fireworks. Prior to the Wars of the Roses (1453-1487) between the Yorkists and the

Lancastrians medieval York, its prosperity based on wool, was the richest city in the country after London. **The Walls**★★ (3mi/5km long) encircle the whole of medieval York and the **Shambles**★ with overhanging timber-framed houses is the most visited of York's many picturesque streets.

★★★ **York Minster** – The Minster is the largest Gothic church north of the Alps and its architecture a review of the three main Gothic phases: Early English in the transepts, decorated in the nave and chapter-house, and Perpendicular in the chancel. The 15C **choir screen**★★ is flanked by statues of English kings from William the Conqueror. The Minster contains the largest single collection of **medieval stained glass**★★★ to have survived in England. Take particular note of the East Window in the Lady Chapel, the Five Sisters Window with their tall lancets in the north transept, the Pilgrimage and Bellfounders Windows in the north aisle. The **Chapter-house**★★, octagonal with a magnificent wooden ceiling, can be dated to just before 1300.

★★★ **National Railway Museum** – This magnificent collection presents the history of railways in the country of their invention. The great hall houses an array of locomotives from the earliest crudely engineered Agenoria of 1829 to a mock-up of a Channel Tunnel locomotive.

SCOTLAND

Although Scotland has been united with England since 1707, the Scots have kept an independent identity, which goes deeper than the kilt and the bagpipes. Scotland teems with castles and historic towns. Ghosts supposedly haunt the castles of Glamis, Fyvie, Barnbogle, and the Isle of Skye. Scotland is also a paradise for salmon fishing, golf and the savouring of whisky in the the Spey Valley distilleries.
This territory covers the north of Great Britain. Although it displays features similar to those of the English countryside, fields, hedges, and parks, the Scottish landscape is wilder and the climate distinctly harsher.
Scotland can be divided into three main regions. The Southern Uplands; the Central Lowlands, densely populated, with some minerals and prosperous agriculture, are the focus of urban and industrial life; and the magnificent Highlands include the Shetland Isles and the Orkney Islands.
Here water abounds. Freshwater lakes hide the mysterious sea lochs, while the sea, particularly in the west, defines an extraordinary jagged coastline and provides a refuge for numerous sea birds. A particular specialty are puffins recognizable by their parrot beaks. There are also grey and common seals.
Scottish culinary specialities include Aberdeen Angus beef, spring lamb, game, as well as salmon, trout, halibut and tasty shrimps. *Haggis*, the national dish, consists of offal, oatmeal and seasonings boiled in a skin made of lamb's stomach. Raspberries and loganberries, *Dundee Cake* and *shortbread* will delight the gourmet.

LARA PESSINA

★★ **ABERDEEN** Population 186 757 Michelin map 970 G 2

Set on the banks of the Dee and the Don, Aberdeen grew up from two North Sea fishing villages. One was an episcopal city, while the other developed around the King's Castle and became an active commercial centre. It prospered thanks to the Baltic trade, the construction of whaling boats and the importation of China tea. More recently, this flower-decked city has become Scotland's leading fishing port and Europe's off-shore oil capital. It provides an excellent base to visit the nearby castles.

★★ **Old Aberdeen** – The town extends from **King's College Chapel**★ renowned for is **Renaissance spire**★★★ to St Machar's Cathedral, famous for its twin spires. The renowned interior contains A 16C heraldic oak ceiling depicting key figures of the time: Pope Leo X, the Kings of France, Spain and Scotland, all preceding the king of England!
The early 14C **Brig o'Balgownie**★ has a defensive crenel at the south end.

In 1801, following the example of Edinburgh and Perth, Aberdeen expanded its town centre, lining Union Street and King Street with impressive buildings made of granite. Not far from Marischal College, the **Art Gallery**★★ has a strong emphasis on contemporary art and the **Macdonald Collection**★★ consists of portraits by 19C British artists.

►► Excursions on the banks of the **River Dee**★★ lead to the castles of Drum, Crathes, Craigievar and Balmoral. The latter is the Royal Family's summer residence but it is not open to the public. Braemar is the most important venue for the September Highland Games. Other castles include Fraser, Haddo House, Fyvie and Duff House. Note also the Dunnottar ruins near Stonehaven. **Pitmedden Gardens**★★ *(23km/14mi north)* are best seen in July and August.

★★★EDINBURGH Population 408 222 Michelin map 970 F 3

Edinburgh, the capital of Scotland, is set on a series of volcanic hills. The best-known is probably Arthur's Seat rising 251m/823ft over Holyrood Park. The city is rich in history and becomes especially lively every August during the international festival, featuring the **military tattoo**, jazz and film festivals, and avant-garde theatre. A royal residence since the 11C, Edinburgh became the seat of government and the capital of Scotland under the Stuarts. With the Union of the Crowns in 1603 and the departure of James VI of Scotland to London, Edinburgh lost much of its pageantry, but towards the end of the 18C, projects for a new town centre led to the creation of the Georgian New Town.

★★**The Castle** – The impressive silhouette of the castle and its rock overlooks the city. The most popular event of the summer festival, the military tattoo, takes place on the 18C esplanade parade ground. At the heart of the castle in the Crown Room, the Scottish crown jewels, called the **Honours of Scotland**, are on display. Another building houses the Royal Scot Regimental Museum. From the terrace in front of St Margaret's Chapel, a view extends over the north of the city.
St Giles' Cathedral★★ with its **spire**★★★ decorated with gables was finished in 1495. Nearby, Lady Stair's House features an exhibition of Scotland's most famous writers, Robert Burns (1759-1796), Sir Walter Scott (1771-1832) and Robert Louis Stevenson (1850-1894).

STR/STILL MOVING

Military Tattoo

★★**Abbey and Palace of Holyrood House** – The palace stands at the east end of the Royal Mile, amid the green slopes of Holyrood Park. It is the official residence of the monarch in Scotland. The abbey was founded in 1128 by David I. The roofless nave is all that remains of the once great abbey. James IV transformed the guest-house into a palace, and Charles II commissioned his architect **Sir William Bruce** to draw up the designs. Influenced perhaps by the work of Inigo Jones at Whitehall, Bruce created a magnificent building in the Palladian style *(see Vicenza, Italy)*. The buildings of the inner court are a fine example of Renaissance work. The decoration of the State Apartments is lavish, particularly the **plasterwork ceilings**★★★.

★★**The New Town** – The architect James Craig designed the new town according to a geometric plan. He erected the North Bridge, but it was Robert Adam who built the new town's finest square, **Charlotte Square**★★★ in 1791. Its elegant façades surround the equestrian statue of Prince Albert.

At the foot of **Princes Street Gardens**, the **Walter Scott Monument**★ faces Princes Street, Edinburgh's main thoroughfare. The nearby **National Gallery of Scotland**★★★ was built in the 1850s. Its galleries display paintings by Raphael, Titian, Tintoretto, Velasquez, and Rubens. English 18C portrait painters such as Gainsborough, Reynolds and Romney are featured as well as some French Impressionists.
Victoria Street and the Grassmarket are attractive shopping streets.
In the northern part of Edinburgh are the world famous **Royal Botanic Gardens**★★★ dating from the 17C. The **rhododendrons** are a major attraction.
The lively port of **Leith** is lined with restaurants, pubs and wine bars.

EXCURSIONS

★★ **Forth Bridges** – *15km/9mi by A 90. Best viewed from the esplanade at South Queensferry.* The construction of the Forth Bridge, an intrepid endeavour, was begun in 1883 and completed in 1890. The road bridge, a slim-line bridge with an amazing curve, was built between 1958 and 1964.

★★★ **Culross** – *30km/18mi west by the bridge over the Forth.* On the north bank of the Firth of Forth, this little village boasts 16C and 17C houses (the Study★).

★★★ **St Andrews** – This Fife seaside resort possesses an imposing ruined 12C cathedral, a relic of what was once Scotland's ecclesiastical capital. Founded in 1754, the Society of St Andrew's Golfers is today recognised as the sport's ruling body. The **British Golf Museum** traces 500 years of golfing history.

★★★ GLASGOW Population 754 586 Michelin map 970 F 3

Glasgow, Scotland's most populous city, is a prime industrial centre and port. Renowned for its museums and concerts, it has now won a City of Culture award. In the 6C St Mungo set up his wooden church on the banks of the Molendinar Burn. In the 17C Glasgow became the centre of the Protestant cause. During the next century the city grew rich from trade in textiles, sugar and tobacco. Banking, shipbuilding and heavy industry added to its prosperity.
At the same time, the arts flourished. The **Glasgow Boys** with MacGregor, Guthrie, George Henry and John Lavery led the city into an Romantic Era. Architect and designer Charles Mackintosh (1869-1928), built the renowned Glasgow School of Art and became a leader of the Art Nouveau movement.

★★★ **Cathedral** – The 13C to 15C Gothic cathedral was erected on the site of St Mungo's original building. The interior reveals one church superimposed on another. The lower building is a Gothic delight covering the tomb of Glasgow's patron saint. The upper church, beyond the 15C stone screen, includes the choir.

University District – The collection of William Hunter (1718-1783) represented the main highlight. The museum contains displays on geology, archeology, and ethnography. The **Hunterian Art Gallery**★★ houses works by Whistler and the reconstruction of Charles Rennie Mackintosh's home. The Kelvingrove Art Gallery contains donations by local captains of industry. They include Flemish and Dutch paintings: Jordaens, Rubens, Rembrandt; 19C French and 20C works; including a comprehensive British section. The **Transport Museum**★★ displays trams and trolleybuses, fire engines, and bicycles.

★★★ **The Burrell Collection** – *5km/3mi southwest in Pollok Park.* This collection was donated to the city by the shipowner Sir William Burrell (1861-1958). One gallery includes exhibits on ancient civilization, oriental art, medieval and post-medieval art, paintings, drawings and bronzes. Nearby the 18C **Pollok House**★ holds a fine collection of **Spanish paintings**★★, including works by El Greco, Goya, and Murillo.

★ GREAT GLEN

The geological fault of the Great Glen cuts across the Highlands, linking the Atlantic Ocean with the North Sea through a series of narrow lochs joined together by Thomas Telford's Caledonian Canal (1803-1822). The canal is now mainly used for pleasure craft. *(From Fort William to Inverness, 105km/65mi)*

★ **Fort William** – This town lies on the banks of Loch Linnhe at the foot of Britain's highest mountain, Ben Nevis. It rises 1 344m/4 408ft.

★★ **Loch Ness** – The dark waters of this 230m/754ft deep loch are renowned throughout the world as the home of the mysterious Nessie, first seen by a local monk in the 8C. Despite numerous expeditions equipped with sonars and other modern technology, Loch Ness has failed to reveal the identity of the monster. In the village of Drumnadrochit, the official Loch Ness Monster Exhibition provides information on this enigma.

★**Inverness** – This traditional capital of the Scottish Highlands has played an important strategic role since the time of the Picts; St Columba visited King Brude here, and King Duncan, murdered in his castle by Macbeth in the 11C. Few historic buildings remain, however, because so many battles were fought in the city.

►► *Northeast of Inverness*: **Cawdor Castle**★ *(21km-13mi)*. In Shakespeare's *Macbeth*, Duncan's murder took place in this 14C and 17C castle. **Fort George**★ *(22km/13 mi)* represents an impressive 18C fortress. Nairn *(25km/15mi)* is a pleasant seaside resort.

★★ ORKNEY Islands Population 19 040 Michelin map 970 F G 2

Of the 67 islands comprising the Orkney Archipelago, only about 20 are inhabited. Prehistoric remains can be seen on several of the islands. In the late 8C, the Vikings landed on the Orkneys, sweeping away the Pict civilization. Orkney's culture still has Scandinavian elements.

Kirkwall★★ the capital, since Viking times, is a suitable base for an interesting excursion to Western Mainland.

★ SHETLAND Islands Population 27 271 Michelin map 970 G 1, 2

Unlike the Orkneys, the Shetland's 100 islands contain few tracts of flat land. Visitors will enjoy the wild beauty of empty spaces. On the last Tuesday of January, Shetland celebrates its past with a torch-lit festival, **Up Helly Aa**. It implores the Norse gods for the return of the sun in spring. The highlight of the festival is the burning of a Viking ship called a *drakkar.*

★★ STIRLING Population 36 640

Strategically important from time immemorial, Stirling was the setting for the famous battles of Stirling Bridge in 1297 and Bannockburn in 1314.

★★**Stirling Castle** – The castle, a former royal residence, is situated on an impregnable peak, overlooking the medieval town. It was several times captured then lost by the English. Between 1370 and 1603, it became the Stuarts' residence. Mary Stuart, Queen of Scotland, was crowned here. Begun by James IV in 1496, the present castle was completed in 1546. A masterpiece of Renaissance architecture, it displays elaborate exterior elevations, best viewed from Upper Square.

Old Town – Its narrow streets wind downhill from the castle. Examples abound of the Scottish Renaissance style. **Argyll's Lodging**★ is a superb mansion built in 1632 by Sir William Alexander.

★★ TWEED VALLEY

The Tweed, Scotland's third longest river, flows through the Borders in majestic curves. The valley is lined with castles, mansions and abbeys. Its prosperity comes from the traditional woollen and knitwear industries. *(From Moffat to Berwick-upon-Tweed: 210km/130mi).*

★★**Grey Mare's Trail** – A spectacular 60m/196ft waterfall.

Peebles – This is a good centre to explore the countryside or fish for salmon. The writer **Robert Louis Stevenson** lived here. William Chambers, publisher of the famous dictionary, also was born here.

★★**Traquair House** – This house, typical of the region, was transformed into a fortified tower house during the Wars of Independence. A part of its collections contain personal belongings of Mary Queen of Scots.

★★**Abbotsford** – This fantasy in stone reflects the taste of Sir Walter Scott (1171-1832). The celebrated poet and writer, fascinated by Scottish legends, popularised Scotland and give it a romantic aura in his books such as *Ivanhoe* and *Quentin Durward.*

★**Melrose** – Unlike most Cistercian buildings, the ruins of the Cistercian abbey★★ are decorated with a profusion of sculpture. They were restored in 1820 at the suggestion of Sir Walter Scott. The abbey was founded in 1136 and built in the Gothic Perpendicular style.

★★**Scott's View** – This viewpoint 181m/593ft high provides a view over the winding Tweed to the three conical peaks of the Eildons.

★★**Dryburg Abbey** – Like Melrose, this abbey was founded by David I in 1150. The English attacked in the 1300s. The conventual buildings are well preserved.

★★**Berwick-upon-Tweed** – In the 16C, the surrounding walls★ were replaced by ramparts and bastions. Ruins are all that remain of the castle, where Edward I heard the petitions of the 13 contenders for the throne of Scotland. The Old Bridge dates from 1611.

The SOUTH and SOUTHEAST

The chalklands centred on Salisbury Plain composed the heart of prehistoric England. Innumerable earthworks form the setting for imposing monuments such as Stonehenge. Later, populations settled in the river valleys, and in the ports and coastal resorts off the Isle of Wight. The island's great seawater estuaries sheltered from the Channel are a yachtsman's paradise. Wessex has been celebrated by Thomas Hardy who set his novels there. To the east, the Downs reveal the dense oakwoods of the Weald before emerging towards impressive chalk cliffs.

★BATTLE Population 4 662

On this hilltop stand the remains of the commemorative abbey built by William the Conqueror to mark the Normans' famous victory over King Harold's English army at the Battle of Hastings, on 14 October 1066. The small village, at the foot of the hill, which grew up to serve the abbey, was named after the battle.

★**Battlefield** – From the terrace walk, the whole site of England's most decisive battle can be seen. Harold deployed his men on this ridge after their exhausting forced march from York. On the far side of the swampy valley their Norman adversaries were ranged with their French and Breton allies, fresh from their recent landing near Hastings. The day-long battle was fierce and bloody.

★★BRIGHTON Population 200 168 Michelin map 970 G 5

Brighton is the queen of English seaside resorts. Its south-facing beach is punctuated by piers and backed by a wide promenade. The Georgian, Regency and Victorian architecture is elegant and the labyrinthine lanes of the old fishing town contrast with lavishly planted open spaces and parkways.
The city began to grow in the 18C when Dr Richard Russell promoted the healthy effect of drinking and bathing in seawater. In the 1840s, the railway brought ever-increasing numbers of holidaymakers of all classes to Brighton. The city then truly became London-by-the-Sea.

★★★**Royal Pavilion** – The Royal Pavilion is an incredible oriental confection in stucco and stone. It reflects the personality of George Augustus Frederick, Prince of Wales (1762-1811), later King George IV. A year after his clandestine marriage in 1785 to the young and attractive Catholic commoner Mrs Fitzherbert, Prinny rented Brighton House. After a series of extensions and alterations, he created, in association with the architect John Nash and several interior designers a unique setting for the extravagant festivities of his seaside court. It became a symbol of the Regency period.
The Pavilion's extraordinary silhouette with its bulbous domes is a free interpretation of Hindu architecture. Inside, chinoiserie represents the dominant style, particularly in the music room, lit by lotus-shaped gasoliers. Here painted serpents and dragons writhe beneath the gilded scales of the dome. Equally sumptuous is the banqueting room; from the centre of the 14m/45ft high dome hangs a 1t crystal chandelier; at its apex a huge winged silver dragon is outlined against enormous *trompe-l'œil* leaves.

★★**Seafront** – The promenade built on massive brick vaults descends by ramps and staircases to sea level. Details ranging from decorative ironwork to little kiosks set the holiday mood. The **Palace Pier** is a lively place of fun and refreshment. The electric **Volks Railway**, one of the first of its kind, was built in 1883. It leads to the **marina** which with 2 000 moorings is one of Europe's largest sailing centres.
The seafront is lined with notable groups of buildings. **Brunswick Square** (1825-1827) boasts its stucco, bow windows and elegant wrought ironwork. The **Royal Crescent** (1798-1807 has black geometrically arranged tiles. Most grandiose of all is **Lewes Crescent** at the eastern end. The richly decorated Grand and Metropole Hotels represent good examples of Victorian architecture, where elegance vies with the panache typical of that era.

★**The Lanes** – In the old town, a maze of animated alleyways are lined with countless shops and antique dealers.

►► Near Eastbourne *(37km/22mi east)*, visit the extraordinary site of **Beachy Head★★★**.

EXCURSIONS

★**Lewes** – *11km/6mi east.* The site's strategic value was appreciated by William of Warenne who built his castle here soon after the Norman Conquest. In 1264, Simon de Montfort's rebellion against Henry III led to the defeat of the royal forces at the battle of Lewes. It was fought on nearby Mount Harry.
Apart from the splendour of its architecture, the town is famous for its **celebrations** on 5 November: torchlit processions, tar-barrel rolling, fireworks and giant bonfires. These commemorate not just Guy Fawkes and the Gunpowder Plot, but also the burning at the stake of 17 Protestant martyrs in the mid 16C.

In the town there are delightful streets such as **High Street★** and **Keere Street★**. In **Southover High Street is Anne of Cleves' House**, now a museum of local history.
Entry to the **castle** ruins is via Barbican House, a fine 16C timber-framed building with a late-Georgian façade. The keep is perched on top of a mound rising well above the rooftops. From one of its towers, there are fine views of the town and the gracefully rounded outlines of the surrounding chalk hills.
East of Lewis, beyond the chalk massif of Caburn looming over the town is the famous country house Glyndebourne. Since 1934 the **Glyndebourne Festival** takes place annually from May to early August. John Christie (died in 1962) and his wife, the soprano Audrey Mildmay, originally concentrated on the works of Mozart, but the festival has extended its repertoire, now ranging from Monteverdi to Stravinski.

★★★ CANTERBURY Population 34 546 Michelin map 970 H4

The ecclesiastical capital of England, rich in medieval atmosphere, is dominated by its renowned cathedral. Long open to influences from the Continent, the city lies on Watling Street, the great Roman thoroughfare linking London to the port of Dover. Today, Canterbury exerts as strong an attraction on the modern tourist as on the pilgrims of the Middle Ages.
Canterbury's recorded history begins with Emperor Claudius' invasion of AD 43. In 597, St Augustine was sent there by Rome to convert the pagan population to Christianity. The impact of his mission was decisive; the city became the centre of the English Church and St Augustine was consecrated as its first archbishop.

★★★ **Cathedral** – The original cathedral was destroyed in a fire in 1067 and replaced by a large edifice built by the first Norman Archbishop, **Lanfranc**. In 1170, another Archbishop, **Thomas Becket**, was cruelly murdered in the north transept of the cathedral by four of Henry II's knights who had taken all too literally their sovereign's desire to be rid of this turbulent priest. Thomas was canonised two years later and his shrine immediately attracted countless pilgrims, many of whose stories are related in **Chaucer's** *Canterbury Tales*.
Lanfranc reconstructed the cathedral destroyed in 1067. Work was completed in seven years. An equally enterprising archbishop, Anselm, replaced the choir built by his predecessor by a more ambitious choir which was longer than the nave. After its consecration in 1130, the building was again destroyed by fire in 1174, though the crypt and nave were spared. The cathedral became the most important centre of pilgrimage in Northern Europe, and the opportunity was seized to rebuild it in a manner worthy of Thomas Becket, the martyr. The choir and its extension eastwards were constructed in an early Gothic English style. The nave and the cloisters were rebuilt in Perpendicular style in the 14C. The transept and towers, including **Bell Harry Tower** crowning the entire building, were completed in the 15C.

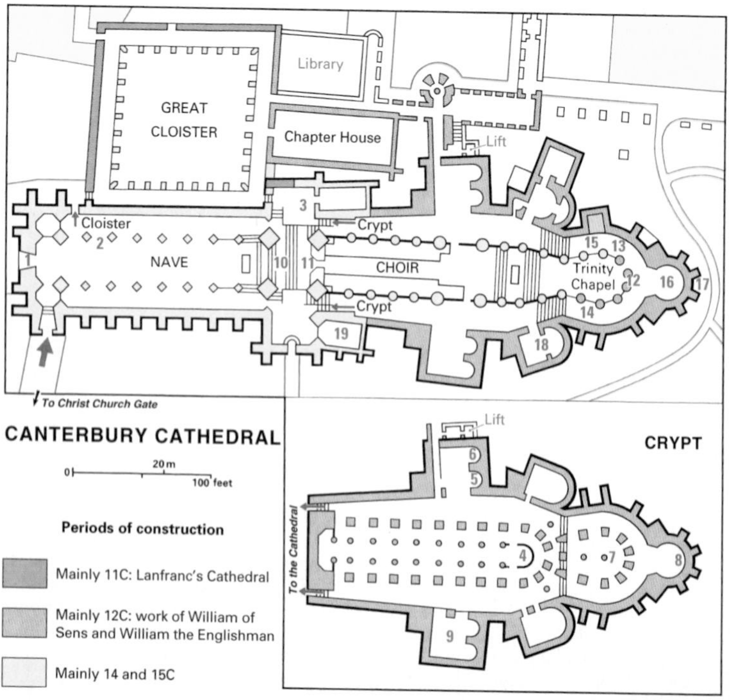

Principal sights:

1. The nave built between 1391 and 1404 by Henry Yevele. The great west window displays 12C stained glass.
2. A 17C classical marble baptismal font. Access to the Great Cloister rebuilt in Perpendicular style c.1400.
3. Site of Becket's martyrdom.
4. Chapel of Our Lady Undercroft.
5. and 6. Altars of St Nicholas and St Mary Magdalene.
7. Site where the body of St Thomas Becket was entombed until 1220.
8. Jesus Chapel.
9. Black Prince's Chantry.
10. Transept crossing; fan vaulting under the Bell Harry Tower.
11. Choir screen decorated with statues of kings (mid 15C)
12. Marble seat known as St Augustine's Chair (13C)
13. Trinity Chapel; medieval stained glass depicting miracles wrought by St Thomas.
14. Tomb of the Black Prince
15. Alabaster tomb of Henry IV, the only English king to have been buried in the cathedral.
16. A circular chapel known as the Corona (Becket's Crown) because it was said to have housed St Thomas' skull.
17. Early 13C redemption windows.
18. Chapel of St Anselm, in the Romanesque style.
19. Chapel of St Michael.

The city – The surrounding walls provide a circular tour and a fine overall view. Overlooking the River Stour, a group of picturesque Tudor houses forms the **Canterbury Weavers** district named after the Huguenot weavers who settled there.

★PORTSMOUTH Population 174 218 Michelin map 970 G 5

Britain's premier naval base is set on Portsea Island between two almost land-locked harbours, Portsmouth and Langstone. The port developed in the early 15C and expanded rapidly under Charles I. In the 18C, when France was Britain's major enemy, the fortifications were strengthened making it an ideal naval base. After heavy bombing during the Second World War, the city was reconstructed.

★★★**HMS Victory** – The splendid three-masted flagship is moored in the port. Admiral Nelson led the victorious attack off Cape Trafalgar in Spain on 21 October 1805. After being in dry dock for 150 years, HMS Victory continues to serve as the flagship of the Commander in Chief of the Royal Navy.

★★**The Mary Rose** – On 19 July 1545, the four-masted Mary Rose sank while preparing to meet a French attack. The wreck was found on the seabed, amazingly well preserved in the silt, and was raised in 1982. The exhibition conveys a vivid impression of life at sea in the 16C.

►► **Royal Naval Museum**★ – **St Thomas Cathedral**★ (12C–18C) – Southsea and the seafront.

★★SALISBURY Population 36 890 Michelin map 970 G 4

The town came into existence with the new cathedral. In 1227 it was granted a charter and was controlled by the bishops until 1611.

★★★**Cathedral** – The cathedral is architecturally uniform. The main structure was erected between 1220 and 1265. The famous spire was built later between 1285 and 1320. This spire, the most spectacular feature of this Early English edifice, creates a genuine harmony with the rest of the cathedral. The 70m/229ft long nave is bordered by grey pillars girded with black shafts. The bishops' tombs and the chain-mailed effigy of William Longsword are located between the arcade pillars.

Cloisters and Chapter-house – Work began on the cloisters and chapter-house in 1263. The vaulted arcades display keystones depicting dragons, mermaids and human figures. The magnificent fan-vaulted roof of the chapter-house rises from a slim central column.

Medieval Streets – Between the cathedral and Market Square, gabled half-timbered houses dating from the 14C to the 17C line an extensive network of medieval streets. The names of the alleys indicate the trades which once flourished there – Fish Row, Butcher Row and so on.

★★★STONEHENGE Michelin map 970 G 4

Britain's most celebrated prehistoric site dates from c 2000 BC. It was built in the early Bronze Age on a communal necropolis. The monoliths are aligned over a distance of 230km/142mi. Some believe it served as a sanctuary for a sun-worshipping cult. Although many of the stones have fallen or disappeared, on Midsummer Day, the circle's centre still permits the sun to rise over the entrance's Head Stone.

BMV Picturebank, London

Stonehenge

Around 2800 BC, a ditch with an inner bank of chalk rubble was dug. Along with a ring of 56 holes, these Aubrey Holes are named after the 17C pioneer of field archeology John Aubrey (1626-1697). They enclose an area 91m/298ft in diameter. To the northeast, the bank and ditch were cut to form an entrance. Inside, four sandstone blocks were set up at the cardinal points of the compass.
Around 1900 BC, a double ring of undressed bluestones was erected towards the centre. These stones, weighing up to 4t each were transported 386km/239mi, mainly by water, from the Presely Hills in southwest Wales.
Around 1650 BC, the bluestone rings were replaced by a circle of tall trilithons. These standing stones were tapered at one end and tenoned at the top to secure the curving mortised lintels. Inside the circle, five separate giant trilithons rose in a horseshoe, opening towards the Heel Stone.
Finally, around 1500 BC, the dressed bluestones were re-introduced and reset in the present horseshoe.

*** STOURHEAD *36km/22mi west of Stonehenge*

Stourhead is one of the finest examples of English landscape gardening. When the banker Henry Hoare II (1705-1785) designed the **garden**, he was inspired by the landscapes he saw on his travels and by the paintings of Claude Lorrain and Nicholas Poussin.
He first made the triangular lake. Then he planted deciduous trees and conifers, ranged in large masses as the shades in a painting. His architect, Henry Flitcroft, built gems of garden architecture such as the Temple of Hercules, Watch Cottage, the grotto, Pantheon, and Temple of Apollo. Hoare's successors maintained the variety of his plantings, adding exotic specimens. There is something to admire all year round.

*** ISLE OF WIGHT Population 118 594 Michelin map 970 G 5

The 380km²/144sq mi island has been a holiday destination ever since Queen Victoria chose Osborne for her country retreat. It is renowned for its mild sunny climate, its varied scenery, the fine sandy beaches of resorts such as Sandown, Shanklin and Ventnor, and the celebrated regattas at Cowes.

****Carisbrooke Castle** – The castle was built in 1100 by Richard de Redvers on the site of a Roman stronghold. In the 14C and later in the 16C, the fortifications were strengthened. Until 1944, the castle was the residence of the Crown-appointed Governors.

****Osborne House** – This Palladian villa overlooking the Solent was built between 1845 and 1851 for Queen Victoria and Prince Albert by the architect Thomas Cubitt. The Prince Consort chose this style, because, with its view of the sea, the site reminded him of the Bay of Naples. After Albert's death in 1861, Queen

Victoria spent much of her 40 years of her widowhood there. The only significant alteration made after Albert's death was the addition in 1890 of the Durbar Wing. This work of Bhai Ram Singh and John Lockwood Kipling reflects the Queen's pride in her Indian possessions. It has been open to the public since the Queen's death and gives a remarkable insight into the life of the royal family in the 19C.

★★WINCHESTER Population 34 127 Michelin map 970 G 4

This ancient cathedral city was the capital of England from the 9C to about 1166. At the time of the Norman Conquest, the city was already of such importance that William I was crowned there as well as in London.
However, after the 12C, Winchester yielded to London as the preferred royal residence. During the Civil War, the Norman castle was largely destroyed, the cathedral damaged and the town looted by Parliamentary troops. In 1682, Charles II commissioned Wren to design a great palace, but work stopped on the King's death in 1685.

★★★**Cathedral** – The longest Gothic cathedral in Europe was begun in 1079 under William I and not completed until 1528. Built largely of stone from the Isle of Wight, the cathedral's Romanesque exterior is impressive. The Norman pillars in the 12-bay nave have been reinforced to support the Perpendicular arches. The 12C baptismal font is made of black Tournai marble. In the choir, the canopied stalls are decorated with remarkable misericords, displaying smiling faces. The 13C retro-choir represents a magnificent example of Early English Gothic style.

►► **Winchester College**★ – Bishop William of Wykeham founded this college in 1832 – **St Cross Hospital**★★ is the oldest charitable institution in England.

For further details on Great Britain, consult the Michelin Green Guides Great Britain, London, Wales, The West Country, Scotland.

The SOUTHWEST

A granite backbone covered by rugged moorland runs through Devon and Cornwall. In the north, the Exmoor National Park is clothed in bracken and heather. The patchwork pattern of the fields, so typical of the English landscape, is frequently seen in Devon. In the harsher climate of Cornwall, small plots of land bounded by stone walls replace it. The long magnificent coastline of the peninsula extending over Devon and Somerset is surrounded by the Bristol Channel, the Atlantic Ocean and the English Channel. This was the land of King Arthur and the Knights of the Round Table.

★★★BATH Population 84 283 Michelin map 970 G 4

A jewel of architecture, Bath epitomises the grace and elegance of the 18C. Its hot springs were already well known before the arrival of the Romans in the 1C, who made it into England's first spa resort. Bath provides a good base to visit Wells, Longleat, Stonehenge and Salisbury.
In 1668, Samuel Pepys visited the city but expressed some doubt about the hygiene of the baths. This did not prevent more trusting people from following the royal example and going to Bath. By the early 18C, it had become a fashionable city, though dull and disorganised. In 1704, John Nash followed the fashion and came to Bath. As Master of Ceremonies, he then launched a programme for the entertainment of polite society, ranging from baths in the morning to evening assemblies. He opened the first Pump Room for taking the waters. He organised concerts, balls, gambling and drew up regulations. Bath prospered – as did Nash. While Nash restructured Bath society, Allen and Wood transformed its architecture and urban plan into a masterpiece. Allen (1694-1764) settled in Bath in 1710 and made his fortune by creating an efficient postal service for the entire region. He then bought quarries in Claverton and Combe Down to erect a new city using the fine local honey-coloured stone. Wood the Elder (1700-1754) came to Bath in 1728. He and his son, John Wood (1728-1781), built in the Palladian style using Combe Down stone, now known as Bath Stone.

★★**Roman Baths** – These are fed by a spring which pours out approximately 1 250 000l/280 000gal per day at a temperature of 46.5°C/116°F. The Roman complex comprised the Great Bath, a large warm swimming pool, now open to the sky, and two other baths of decreasing heat. The *frigidarium*, *tepidarium* and *caldarium* were added later.

★**Bath Abbey** – The abbey was built in 1499 by Bishop King in a pure late Perpendicular style on the site of a Romanesque church. Inside, the nave, chancel and transepts soar towards the fan vaulting. Robert and William Vertue, designers of the fan vaulting in the Henry VII Chapel, Westminster Abbey, repeated their genius here.

★★★**Royal Crescent** – An emblem of Bath, the Royal Crescent is curved into an arc of 30 terrace houses with monumental façades, punctuated by 114 Ionic columns. This was the great achievement of John Wood the Younger (1767-1774). **No 1 Royal Crescent** houses a magnificent collection of Chippendale, Sheraton and Hepplewhite furniture, and 18C porcelain and glass.

Brock Street links the Crescent to the Circus.

★★★**The Circus** – Built in 1754, this circle of identical houses is pierced by three equidistant roads. The houses of pale Bath stone, decorated with twinned columns, rise three floors to a frieze and acorn-topped balustrade.

★**Assembly Rooms** – These elegant rooms (1769-1771) were constructed for the evening assemblies. People met to dance, play cards, drink tea and to gossip. The Tea Room has a rich interior with a splendid two-tiered screen at its west end. The **Museum of Costume**★★★ displays an extensive collection ranging from the 16C to the present day.

★**Pulteney Bridge** – The bridge (1769-1774) built by Robert Adam is lined with small shops and domed pavilions.

► ► **Corsham Court**★★ *(18km/11mi northeast)*. This Elizabethan manor house built in 1582 exhibits the extensive Methuen collection. It includes works by Fra Filippo Lippi, Michelangelo, and Caravaggio.

The American Museum★★★ *(Claverton, 3km/1.4mi east)* features furnished rooms displaying 200 years of life styles.

★★BRISTOL Population 413861 Michelin map 970 G 4

Bristol has been a commercial city since medieval times. In the 17C, it became a prosperous port trading with America, the West Indies and even Africa. In 1497, the explorer John Cabot set sail and discovered Newfoundland off the Canadian coast. In the 19C, the city benefited from the genius of the visionary engineer Isambard Kingdom Brunel (1806-1859), designer of the Clifton Suspension Bridge and the steamship Great Britain. He was also the architect of the broad-gauge Great Western Railway in 1841, which reached its terminus in Bristol at Station Building.

★★**The Floating Harbour Area** – In the port, the ship *SS Great Britain*, launched in 1843, rests in its original dry dock. Built of metal and propeller-driven, it was the first ship of its kind to cross the Atlantic. Within its massive hull (98m x 16m/321ft x 52ft), it contains a museum describing Brunel's innovations. Near the port, on King Street, the Llandoger Trow Inn inspired Stevenson when he wrote *Treasure Island*.

G. Paxton/COSMOS/ASPECT

Clifton Suspension Bridge

★★**St Mary Redcliffe** – This late 13C church represents a fine example of Perpendicular style. The exterior displays carved pinnacles, finialled flying buttresses and exquisite statues of saints. Inside, the nave's pillars soar to the vaulting. Every one of the keystones – 1 200 in all – is different. The armour of Admiral Sir William Penn (died 1670) can be seen in the nave.

★★**Clifton Suspension Bridge** – Brunel (1829-1831) designed one of England's finest early suspension bridges. Unfortunatly the project to build it was underbudgeted. Brunel died in 1859, five years before the completition of his 214m/702ft long structure. Close by, on the cliff stands an Observatory Tower, built in 1729. It contains an 18C camera obscura, where the landscape for miles around may be viewed.

★★★CORNISH COAST Michelin map 970 F 5

Wild solitude is a major attraction of the Cornish Peninsula. A coast path winds sinuously for 430km/266mi above sheer cliffs and indented coves. The southern coastline contains two types of contrasting landscape, rocky, jagged headlands eroded by the sea alternating with the estuaries of the Tamar, Fowey, Fal and Helford rivers and vast bays. In these sheltered creeks, many gardens exhibit a flourishing sub-tropical vegetation.

The South Coast

On the road out of Plymouth, the following sites are worth visiting.

★★**Fowey** – This small town on the hillside overlooks an excellent natural harbour. Take a boat trip around the harbour and coast edged with steep cliffs, or up the river among wooded hills.

★★**Mevagissey** – The charm of this old fishing village lies in its ancient boathouses and maze of winding alleys and stairways.

★★**St Just-in-Roseland** – The 13C church, adjoining a remarkably steep churchyard, stands so close to the creek that at high tide it is reflected in the water.

★**St Mawes** – The cloverleaf-shaped castle was built by Henry VIII between 1539 and 1543.

★★**Trelissick Gardens** – There are three gardens at Trelissick – Valley Garden, East Lawn Garden and Flower Garden. In early summer, they bloom. Performances of Shakespeare's plays take place in mid-August.

★★**Glendurgan Garden** – This richly planted garden contains an outstanding maze.

★**Lizard Peninsula** – This peninsula, much frequented by sailors, lies at England's southernmost tip. The Gweek Seal Sanctuary, **Coverack**★ village and the magnificent **Kynance**★★ and **Mullion**★★ creeks are all worth visiting.

★★**St Michael's Mount** – A legend tells how fishermen once saw the archangel Michael standing on a granite rock. The island became a place of pilgrimage. Around 1150 Abbot Bernard of Mont-Saint-Michel in Normandy built a Benedictine monastery there, which is now a hybrid of 14C to 19C styles.

★★**Penwith** – This headland possesses a unique bleak beauty derived from its granite foundation, the wind, the blue of the ocean, its small granite churches and Celtic wayside crosses.

★**Land's End** – The surging Atlantic buffets this westermost tip of England. Come early in the morning or at sunset to see this extraordinary **craggy landscape**★★★ washed over by continuous waves.

North Coast

This long stretch of land exposed to the wild Atlantic benefits from the warm Gulf Stream. The combination of warm water and sandy beaches makes Cornwall popular with holidaymakers and surfers.

★**Geevor Tin Mine** – This mine, near Pendeen Lighthouse, is open to the public. It is one of the three mines operating in the area.

★★**St Ives** – This attractive fishing harbour is dominated by narrow winding lanes. Barbara Hepworth's former studio has been converted into a **museum**★★.

★★**St Agnes Beacon** – This natural promontory offers a panoramic view of the coast.

Newquay – The fashionable resort is also Britain's surfing capital.

★**Padstow** – The town grew around the harbour, enclosed on three sides by attractive houses. A network of narrow streets ends at St Petroc's Church and Prideaux Place, an Elizabethan manor house still in the Prideaux family.

Morwenstow – Morwenstow parish, rising from its spectacular 133m/436ft **cliffs**★★, possesses a fine **church**★.

★★PLYMOUTH Population 238 583 Michelin map 970 F 5

Situated at the mouth of the Plym, the fishing port developed with the growth of trade with France during the Plantagenet Era. From the 13C, Plymouth played a major role as a naval and military port. Explorers such as Drake, Raleigh and Cook sailed from here. During the Second World War the city suffered serious bomb damage.
The promontory is an ideal point from which to view the maritime traffic on the Sound. The Royal Citadel here was reinforced by Drake in the late 16C, then rebuilt by Charles II.
The **Barbican** is the oldest district in Plymouth. On the pier, a plaque commemorates the voyage of the Pilgrim Fathers in the *Mayflower* in 1620. In New Street, the **Elizabethan House** (no 32) and its neighbour were built of sandstone in the 16C.

►► **Saltram House**★★ is the work of Robert Adam, Thomas Chippendale and Joshua Reynolds – **Buckland Abbey**★★ *(15km/9mi north)*.

★★WELLS Population 9 252 Michelin map 970 G 4

The calm of the cathedral within its precinct contrasts with the bustle of the market square in England's smallest cathedral city.

★★★**Cathedral** – Wells was the first cathedral in the Early English style. It took more than three centuries to build, from 1175 to 1508. Gates from the 15C lead from the city streets to the Close. Fine views open from here to the cathedral. On the south side, the Bishop's Palace Gardens contains the welling springs after which the city is named. Despite damage caused by the Puritans, the west front has one of England's richest arrays of 13C sculpture. The interior is notable for the stained glass-window depicting the Tree of Jesse; in the retro-choir and the Lady Chapel, the columns form a forest of ribs. In the north transept, **the** astronomic **clock** (1390) displays a knights' tournament every 15min.

►► **Glastonbury Abbey**★★ *(9km/5mi south)* – This famous abbey supposedly shelter the tombs of King Arthur and Queen Guinevere. The Abbot's Kitchen dates from the 14C.

WALES

Wales is approached via the English **Marchlands**. To the south, the River Wye's luxuriantly wooded gorge cuts through the Royal Forest of Dean. In the north, the narrow coastal plain dotted with seaside resorts leads to the Isle of Anglesey and the Lleyn Peninsula. The **mountains of Snowdonia**, near the coast, form a grandiose highland region contrasting with the gentle curves of the sheep-grazed uplands of Mid-Wales. Beyond the steep red sandstone bastion of **Brecon Beacons**, the immense coalfield of South Wales form a high plateau deeply cut by valleys filled with mining settlements. These surround Cardiff, the capital and other former coastal coal ports. To the west, the landscape is again rural, winding towards the cliffs and rocks of the **Pembrokeshire** Coast National Park.
Wales abounds in castles. Four fortified castles are particularly noteworthy: Beaumaris, Caernarfon, Conwy and Harlech. They were built by **King Edward I** (1272-1307). Their exceptional importance was officially recognised as world heritage sites.
In the Statute of Rhuddlan of 1284, Edward I acknowledged Welsh as an official and legal language. After the battle of Bosworth which brought to an end the wars of the Roses, Welsh nobles followed the Tudors to London. But Henry VIII decreed that "no person shall hold office within the Realme unless they exercise the English speech". Nonetheless, bards and music and poetry contests have preserved the tradition of literature in the Welsh language.

After leaving Chester, a good itinerary includes Flint, Rhuddlan, Conwy, Beaumaris, Caernarfon, Harlech and Aberystwyth castles.

★★ISLE OF ANGLESEY Michelin map 970 F 4

Anglesey means Mother of Wales. The isle has a landscape of low hills unlike anywhere else in the region. Anglesey and the strait offer walkers and yachtsmen marvellous opportunities to practise their favourite sport.
Beaumaris Castle was built in 1295. Though never completed, it represents the finest example of a concentric castle. It is surrounded by a moat. The fortified dock is capable of taking ships up to 40t.

Llanfairpwllgwyngyllgogerychwyrndrobwllllantysiliogogogoch – This is the translation of the village name, Llanfair PG for short. It was almost certainly strung together in the 19C to amuse and baffle English tourists. On a hill, 34m/111ft high, overlooking the village, a column and statue commemorates William Henry Paget, first Marquess of Anglesey (1768-1854), and one of the Duke of Wellington's most trusted commanders.

★★**Plas Newydd** – This late 18C mansion was home of the Marquess of Anglesey. It stands on a magnificent site overlooking the strait and the Snowdonia mountains. In 1936, the artist Rex Whistler was commissioned to decorate the dining room in *trompe-l'œil* style.

★★CAERNARFON Michelin map 970 F 4

The town bristles with towers and turrets. These walls have guarded the strait ever since the Romans built the nearby fort of Segontium. Caernarfon today is a centre for visitors to Snowdonia and for yachtsmen.
In the 13C, two great princes, Llywelyn the Great (1173-1240) and his grandson Llywelyn ap Gruffydd (died in 1282) established a united principality of Wales. But Edward I launched his military campaigns and a programme of castle building to consolidate his power. The major castles were the work of Master James of St George (c 1235-1308). Most were constructed to be supplied from the sea and all, excepting Harlech, were connected to a town built to a geometric plan, similar to the bastides of Southwest France. Round towers, less vulnerable than square ones, made their first appearance.

★★★**Caernarfon Castle** – Work on this castle was started in 1283 under James of St George. The walls were decorated with bands of coloured stone and polygonal towers evoking Byzantine architecture. The castle was designed to serve as the seat of the English government in the principality. Despite ferocious local opposition, it was restored and renovated in the 1840s by Sir Llewelyn Turner (1823-1903).
Three turrets crown the **Eagle Tower**, each crested by an eagle as in Constantinople. In April 1284, the first English Prince of Wales was born here. Edward of Caernarfon later became Edward II. Since 1301, the title of Prince of Wales is bestowed on the British sovereign's eldest son.
In 1911, when the title passed to another Edward, an investiture ceremony was organised at Caernarfon. Charles, Prince of Wales, greeted his subjects in **Castle Square**. Facing the balcony is the statue of David Lloyd George (1863-1945). He served as Liberal MP for Caernarfon for 55 years and Prime Minister from 1916 to 1922.

Segontium Roman Fort – The museum traces the Roman conquest and occupation of Wales and gives an account of Roman military organisation. It also displays selected finds excavated on the site, which throw a new light on daily life in this distant Roman outpost.

A. Williams

Caernarfon Castle

★★★CARDIFF Population 262 313 Michelin map 970 F 4

The capital of Wales grew up around the Roman fort guarding the crossing of the Taff between Caerleon and Carmarthen. It was the world's principal coal port in the early 20C and much of its appearance today can be attributed to this period. Rugby, the national sport of Wales, has its headquarters in the National Stadium, Cardiff Arms Park.

★**Cardiff Castle** – The castle was built after the battle of Hastings in 1066. William the Conqueror gave Robert FitzHamon free rein in the southern Marches. Within the ruins of the Roman fort, a castle was built with a courtyard and wooden ramparts. The stone keep dates from the 12C.
The third Marquis of Bute (1847-1900), reputedly the richest man in England, commissioned an extraordinary series of **exotic interiors**★ from the architect William Burgess. They are now open to the public.

★**National Museum of Wales** – It has displays of archeology, silver, 18C porcelain, and French Impressionist and Post-Impressionist as well as Welsh paintings.

★★Welsh Folk Museum – St Fagans, on the western outskirts of Cardiff. This Museum of Art and Folklore houses one of the finest collection of vernacular buildings in Britain. It includes cottages, farms, a chapel, bakehouse, school, corn mill, woollen mill and a cockpit. Craftsmen demonstrate their skills in their workshops.

►► Caerphilly Castle★★ *(11km/6mi north)* – Pembrokeshire Coast★★ *(west)*

★CONWY Population 3 649

Conwy Castle★★ is set in a breathtaking location against a backdrop of mountains. It was built between 1283 and 1287 under James of St George. Eight massive drum towers with pinnacled battlements protect the castle's two wards. The inner ward was reached by water. The town, which was constructed at the same time, is protected by its town walls. In the High Street, at the corner of Crown Lane stands Plas Mawr, a 16C Elizabethan manor house.
The **town** is enclosed by its 13C **town walls★★**. They provide a pleasant walk between Upper Church Gate and Berry Street.

★★HARLECH CASTLE

Harlech Castle was built between 1283 and 1289. It rises 60m - 196ft above the sea. Its entrance lies on the massive front with a gatehouse and solid drum towers. Traceried windows give ample light to the apartments. This is a fine example of fortified domestic architecture.

Since Edward I, the title of Prince of Wales has been given to the heir apparent to the British throne.

★★SNOWDONIA Michelin map 970 F 4

Snowdonia National Park displays the Gwynedd mountains' scenic landscape. The National Park Visitor Centre is housed in the stables of the hotel at Betws-y-Coed. The easiest ascent to the summit of **Snowdon** (1 085m/3 558ft) can be from the town of Llanberis, overlooking Llyn Padarn. The steam train has been running since 1896. On a fine day, the panorama★★★ extends over the whole of Anglesey, the Isle of Man and the Wicklow mountains in Ireland.

Ph. Gajic /MICHELIN

London pub

Greece

Elláda

Area: 131 944km²/50 944sq mi – **Population:** 10.5 million – **Capital:** Athína (Athens) – **Currency:** the drachma (dr) – **Time:** GMT + 2 hr in winter, GMT + 3 hr in summer.

Greece, land of the sun god Apollo and sea god Poseidon, stands at the tip of the Balkan Peninsula. The mountainous country enjoys a jagged coastline. Its highest point is Mount Olympus at an altitude of 2 917m/9 571ft. Another of Greece's notable features is its large number of islands – 427 in all, 134 inhabited.
As the cradle of European civilization, Greece has an intensely rich history. Its philosophers Plato, Socrates and Aristotle, theorists of the city, analysed royalty, democracy, and tyranny, and its scientists Thales, Pythagoras, Euclid, Archimedes and Hippocrates invented the physical sciences, geometry, mathematics and medicine.

IN BRIEF

Entry regulations – A valid passport is required for British, US, Canadian, Australian and Japanese citizens.

Shopping – Department stores and supermarkets are open daily from 9am to 8pm, and 3.30pm on Saturdays. Other shops are open from 9am to 3pm on Mondays, Wednesdays and Saturdays and from 9am to 2pm and 5pm to 8pm on Tuesdays, Thursdays and Fridays.

Souvenirs – Pottery and ceramics, handmade rugs and fabrics, embroidered garments, lace, shag-pile rugs (from Thessalía), gold and silver jewellery, woodwork or carvings, marble or onyx sculptures, leather sandals or bags. The famous *Komboloï*, worry beads still used today, are on sale in shops everywhere.
Visitors can also bring back culinary specialities such as honey, jams, and *amigdalotá* (a type of macaroon), *kourabiédes* (almond cookies), *Aegina* (pistachio nuts), *hálva* (sesame paste sometimes filled with pistachio), retsina, aperitif wine (muscadel from Samos, Mavrodaphni) and *oúzo, raki* (spirits).
Purchases of antiques, icons or other works of art require authorisation. Contact 13 Polignotou Street in Athens.

Kiosks ***(períptera)*** – These sell newspapers, cigarettes, postage stamps, post cards, sweets, sunglasses, sun cream and aspirin. They almost always have a telephone available. Some have a meter so that users can make intercity or international calls.

Post Offices – Post office signs and letterboxes are yellow. Post offices are generally open Mondays to Fridays from 7.30am to 2pm. They will exchange currency, but do not have phone boxes.

Telephone (OTE) – This public service is separate from the postal service. Offices are generally open all day including Saturdays (except in certain small towns) and close late in the evening, especially in the major cities (10pm or midnight).
Phone cards are available from the OTE or kiosks.

Local Customs – Gestures are significant. Never stretch out the palm of the hand towards the person to whom you are speaking. This gesture is considered to be a grave insult. The Greeks often express a no without opening their mouth but rather by tipping their head back almost imperceptibly while lowering their eyelids slightly.
Water can be in short supply, particularly in the Cyclades, so it should not be wasted. It may be cut off at certain times of the day.
Please dress decently if visiting religious buildings. Men in shorts and women in shorts, miniskirts, trousers or low-cut tops are not admitted to monasteries.

In Greece the religious festivals from Lent to Whitsun are fixed according to the Gregorian calendar and may be from one to four weeks later than in western Europe.

Musée de l'Acropole, Athènes/Ministère de la Culture, ATHÈNES

Kore

ATHENS and ATTICA

Michelin map 970 O 9

Attica is the heartland of Greece. It spreads out over small mountain ranges and plains planted with vines and olive trees. The city is bounded by mounts Parnís and Imittós (Hymettus) and sprawls northeast towards Eleusis Bay. During the summer, the nearby islands of the Saronic Gulf provide a respite from the pollution that chokes the city.

★★★ATHÍNA (ATHENS) Population 772 072

Athens forms a huge conurbation with a total population of more than three million. It is a lively cosmopolitan city with a wealth of ancient buildings and museums. It has also preserved many reminders of the Roman, Byzantine and neo-Classical eras. Some of its districts such as the former Monastiráki Bazaar or Omónia with its central market place are steeped in an air of oriental charm.

The elegant Síndagma Square is a popular tourist attraction to watch the changing of the guard *(evzone)* in front of the Parliament building. Nearby, Ermou Street is lined with off-the-peg clothes shops. The Pláka district is the centre of Athens' night-life and filled with souvenir shops and tavernas. To the north of S'ndagma, the high-class shopping districts of Kolonáki and Panepistimiou house antique shops, haute couture houses, jewellers' shops, elegant restaurants and luxury hotels.

The Herodes Atticus Odeum hosts music and drama performances in the summer, while folk dancing can be seen at the Philopappos Theatre and Lycabettos. There is also the Acropolis *son et lumière* show on Pnyx Hill.

According to mythology, the sea god Poseidon and Athena, goddess of wisdom, performed miracles during a quarrel over the patronage of the first inhabitants of the Acropolis. Poseidon brought a spring and a horse up out of the ground; Athena created an olive tree, symbol of peace and harmony. Later, Theseus, son of Aegeus *(see Crete)*, made Athens the capital of Attica and organised lavish processions known as Panathenaea in honour of Athena.

In the 6C and 5C BC, following major town planning operations commissioned first by Solon and later by Pisistratus and his sons, Athens expanded. Civil engineering work was undertaken in the lower town to provide water supplies, sewers and roads. The first coins were minted, bearing the head of Athena. After the destruction waged by the Persians in 479 BC, Pericles undertook the reconstruction of Athens. A general plan was drawn up for the Acropolis where the temples were built. The agora, the centre of public life, was extended. The city maintained its cultural precedence after the Roman conquest. Emperor Hadrian even undertook improvement work in his turn. When the Roman Empire was divided up in 395, Athens was allotted to Constantinople.

After the Frankish occupation in the Middle Ages, the town fell under Ottoman rule. The fortified Acropolis became the centre of the Turkish keep. The Parthenon was turned into a mosque and then a powder magazine; it was blown up during the bombardment of the town by the Venetians and Königsmark.

During the 19C, Athens underwent a period of revival amid the War of Independence. A major development policy was implemented and a number of neo-Classical buildings constructed. After the Second World War, the capital continued to expand bringing with it a serious disadvantage – pollution.

★★★**Likavitós** – From Mount **Lycabettos** (Wolves' Hill), there is a **panoramic view** of the city built on eight hills.

★★★**Akrópoli** – The **Acropolis**, meaning upper town, epitomises Greek civilization. It stands on top of a steep rock and measures 270m/886ft in length and 156m/512ft in width. It covers an area of 4ha/10 acres.

The **Propylaea**★ or monumental entrance consists of five gates. The wings of the building were used as a palace in the Middle Ages.

The **Parthenon**★★★, a Doric temple, was built during the reign of Pericles by the architect Ictinus under the directions of Phidias. It was dedicated to Athena whose chryselephantine statue by Phidias once decorated the sanctuary. The temple is surrounded by a peristyle with 46 fluted columns standing 10.43m/34ft high. The columns lean slightly inwards to offset an optical illusion which made the distance between them appear greater at the top than on ground level. The pediments were decorated with polychrome sculptures which stood out against a blue background. The Doric frieze contains the usual triglyphs and 92 carved metopes on a red background depict among other things the battles of the Giants and the gods of Mount Olympus.

The **Erechtheum**★★★ is a small elegant temple completed in 407 BC. It was built to a complicated layout owing to the sloping ground. The famous *korai* porch, also known as the **Caryatid Porch**, bears six statues of young girls (2m/6.5ft high), poised in serenely noble attitudes and dressed in tunics with parallel pleats like the fluting of the columns they are designed to replace.

The **Acropolis Museum★★★** contains a remarkable collection of Archaic works, including the statue of Moscophoros bearing a sacrificial calf. The sculpture marks the beginning of an artistic movement around 570 BC. A number of *korai*, figures of young girls, are dressed in long tunics. The relief of **Mourning Athena** heralds the early Classical style. Finally, do not miss Victory removing her sandal. The sculpture dates from around 42 BC and was made for the frieze of the temple of Athena Nike. It displays remarkable harmony.
The **Temple of Athena Nike★★★** projects from the front of the Propylaea. Legend recounts that the elderly Aegeus, father of Theseus, threw himself into the sea from the top of the rock on which the temple is built. He thought his son was dead after seeing a black sail hoisted by mistake on the mast of the ship bringing home the man who had defeated the Minotaur. The Ionic temple was reconstructed by the Bavarian archeologists of King Otto.

►► **Theatre of Dionysus★★** – **Theseum★** and **Agora★★**.

Old Athens – The old town lies on the northern slopes of the Acropolis, within the districts of Pláka and Monastiráki.

★★**Pláka** – In the upper part of the Pláka dictrict, a network of narrow streets and peaceful little squares contain small Byzantine churches alternating with rows of houses with roofs covered in round tiles. The neighbourhood comes to life at night with tavernas and bars serving Greek specialities to the sound of the *bouzouki*.
From Síndagma Square, Mitropoleos Street leads to the Greek Orthodox cathedral and the **Small Metropolitan★★**, a charming 12C Byzantine church laid out in the shape of a Greek cross and topped with a dome. Its small proportions give an idea of the size of medieval housing in Athens. The walls are embellished with older decorative features re-utilised here, including an Antique frieze depicting the Months and the signs of the Zodiac.
Go down Erehtehos Street and Kiristou Street to the **Tower of the Winds★**, a white marble octagonal building constructed in the 1C BC. The building gets its name from the winged figures carved on the sides of the tower. They symbolise the prevailing winds in Athens. The tower was designed to house a hydraulic clock. Water was channelled from the Clepsydra Spring. This name later was given to water-clocks.
There is a fine **view★★** from the top of the Anafitika District, especially in the evening.
The **Olympeum★★**, or Temple of Olympian Zeus, was one of the largest Greek temples. In the 6C BC, the sons of Pisistratus began building on this spot. The work was abandoned but was resumed in the 2C BC. It was not completed until 132 during the reign of Emperor Hadrian. Although demolished in the Middle Ages, the 15 marble Corinthian columns of impressive proportions have survived.

★★★**Ethnikó Arheologikó Moussío** – The national archeological museum contains the major works from Greece's main archeological sites. The ground floor houses an exhibition of sculptures. The first floor has a collection of ceramics and the top floor displays frescoes and ceramics from Santorini.
From the Mycenaean Age there is the **gold mask of Agamemnon** and two gold goblets. Exhibits from the Classical Era include the bronze statue of **Artemisium Poseidon**, its arm open wide and the admirable solemn **Eleusinian Relief**. Here Demeter, the goddess of Agriculture, accompanied by her daughter Persephone, is shown giving an ear of corn to Triptolemus, son of the King of Eleusis. Finally, the **Jockey of Artemisium**, a Hellenistic bronze statue from the 2C BC was recovered from the sea. Like the figure of Poseidon, it displays a vigourous style.

►► **Moussío Benáki★★** (the Benaki Museum houses Ancient Greek and, Byzantine art and costumes) – **Vizandinó Moussío★★** (the Byzantine Museum contains an extensive collection of icons) – **Museum of Cycladic and Ancient Greek Art★★** (this attractive display of a private collection provides a full insight into the development of Greek art).

★**Piréas** – Piraeus is Greece's largest port and industrial centre. It stands in an outstanding spot on the coastline. It also serves as the point of departure for the islands. Piraeus is a colourful modern town with a boisterous local population, tavernas serving fish and seafood and popular bars attracting seamen from all four corners of the world.

EXCURSIONS

★★★**Akrí Soúnio (Cape Sounion)** – *70km/43mi southeast*. The headland at the entrance to the Saronic Gulf lies in a superb coastal setting, enhanced by the ruins of the Temple of Poseidon the sea god, who is portrayed with a trident, or three-pronged harpoon. Tours of the island are traditionally made in the late afternoon so that visitors can duplicate the experience of Romantic authors such as Byron, Chateaubriand or Lamartine, who watched the sunset over the Aegean Sea. The marble temple, built between 444 and 440 BC on the orders of Pericles, is a Classical Doric building with a peristyle; it is constructed of tufa. The 16 remaining columns have a tall slender appearance although they stand only 6.10m/20ft high.

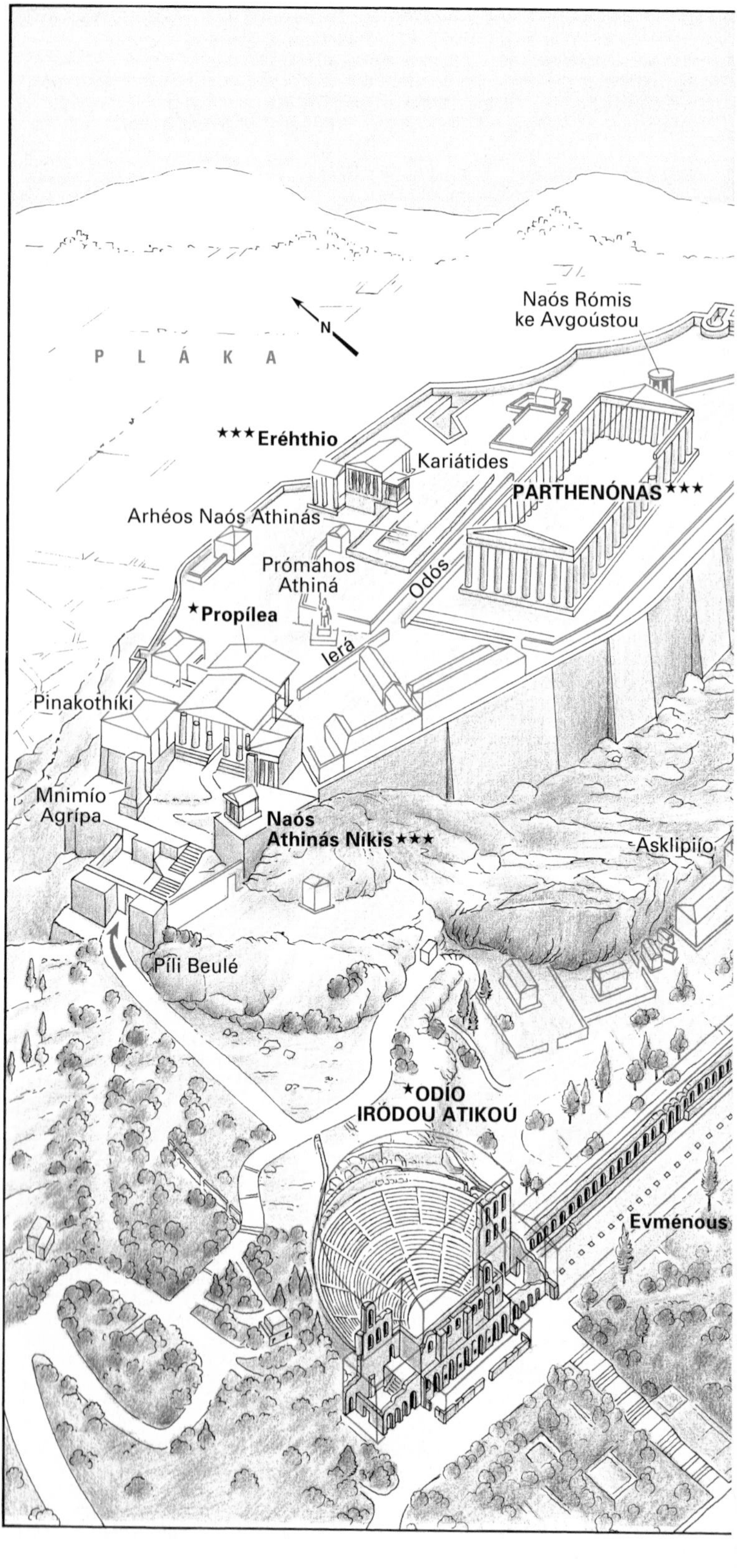

In summer it is better to avoid the middle of the day for visiting archaeological situs owing to the heat and glare.

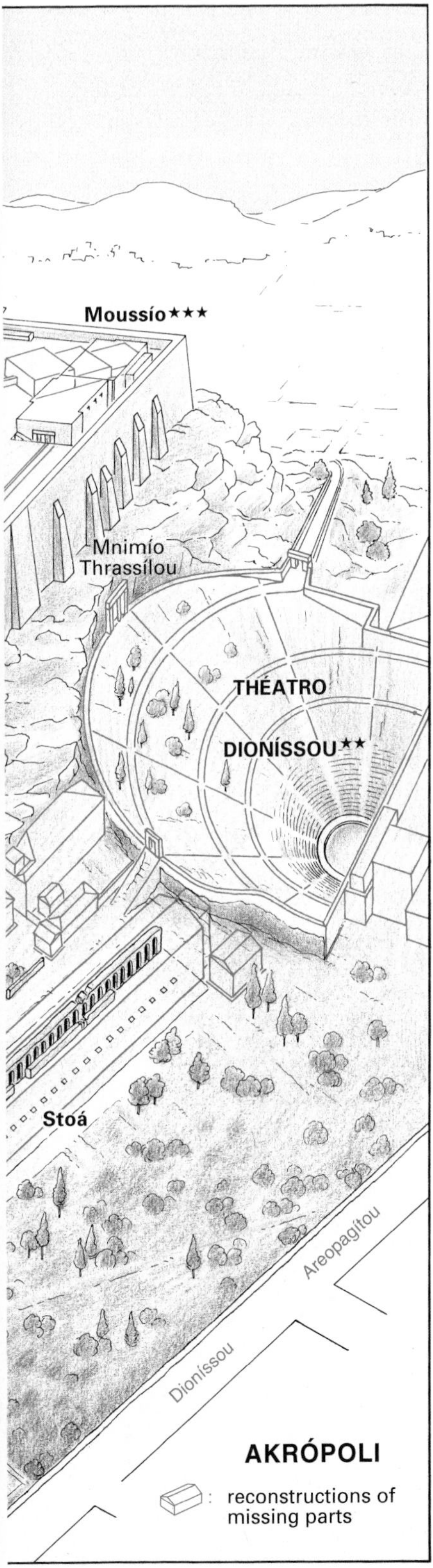

The Saronic Gulf Islands – *By boat from Piraeus.*

★**Égina (Aegina)** – This is the largest of the islands in the gulf. Caïques and low white and pink houses line the harbour. Shops sell the island's speciality, pistachio nuts.

In the Archaic period, Aegina's strategic location between the Peloponnese and Attica made a powerful seafaring nation. It minted its own money and exported its ceramics and bronzeware. However rivalry with Athens during the Peloponnesian War (431-404 BC) brought about its downfall. The island enjoyed a new period of glory when Kapod'strias (Capo d'Istria) (1776-1831) set up the first modern Greek government there from 1827 to 1829.

The **Temple of Aphaea**★★ *(14km/8mi east on the Agía Marina road)* stands on a magnificent spot at the top of a pine forest overlooking the bay and coastline. This Doric temple was built in the early 5C BC in honour of the local divinity, Aphaea. The pediments depicted Athena watching over battles between Greeks and Trojans. These Aegina Marbles were bought by Prince Ludwig of Bavaria in 1812 and are now exhibited in the Glyptothek in Munich.

★★**Idra (Hydra)** – The island of Hydra south of Argolis forms an impressive spine of bare rock. Its pine forests were stripped by shipowners. From the 18C, its huge vessels plied the whole of the Mediterranean and sailed as far as America. The Hydriotes played an active role in the War of Independence, turning their vessels into warships.

The harbour is tucked away in a cove and crowded with yachts in the summer season. The quays are lively, lined with craft shops, cafés, tavernas and cake shops selling delicious almond cookies called *amidalotá*. In the more peaceful upper part of town, the shipowners' houses date from the early 19C. They were built in the style of Venetian *palazzi* with loggias and interior courtyards and still have their period furniture. The monasteries at the top of the hill offer a fine view.

★★**Póros** – The lush green island of Póros is a delightful holiday resort. It can be reached from both Piraeus and Hydra. The harbour provides excellent moorings overlooking Galatás and its lemon groves. Its white cube-shaped houses adorned with trellises and flower-decked yards cover the slopes of the headland. From the top, there is a wonderful **view**★★. To the east, the fishermen's district is full of cafés and fish restaurants decorated with naive paintings. A road leads into a cool valley to the Panagía Zoodóhos Pigí Monastery and the ruins of the Poseidon's sanctuary. Here the great Athenian orator Demosthenes reportedly committed suicide in 322 BC after Greece's defeat at the hands of Macedonia.

IONIAN Islands

Michelin map 970 N 8

The string of islands off the west coast in the Ionian Sea take their name from the nymph Io. Zeus turned her into a heifer. The seven islands include Kérika (Corfu), Paxoí (Paxos), Levkás (Leucas), Kefallinía (Cephalonia), Itháki (Ithaca), Zákinthos (Zacynthus or Zante) and Kíthira (Cythera). They enjoy a temperate climate. Their geographical location is close to Italy and this makes their scenery and atmosphere as much Latin as Greek.

★★★KÉRKIRA (CORFU)

Corfu is the most attractive of the Ionian islands and also the easiest to access with good flights and ferry services. The variety of beaches, luxuriant gardens planted with magnolias, palm trees, jujubes, and myrtle, the mild climate and friendly locals make Corfu a popular holiday destination throughout the year.

The island has an abundance of fruit and olive trees. It has its own traditional specialities such as *sofritó* (beef or veal cooked in a garlic, vinegar and black pepper sauce), spiny lobster, fish, *graviéra* (cheese), *dzinzerbíra* (ginger beer) and Paloumbi white wine.

In the Odyssey, Homer tells how Odysseus was heading for Ithaca when a storm drove him onto the island of Scheria, identified as present-day Corfu. He was found there by the gracious Nausicaä who was playing ball with her companions while waiting for the washing to dry. The young girl took him to her father Alcinous, King of the Phaeacians, whose palace had wonderful gardens. A banquet was organized. The wise son of Laërtes told of his adventures and a ship was fitted out to carry him back to his homeland.

Corfu was a Corinthian colony during the Archaic period and has often been invaded. In the Middle Ages, the Angevin kings of Naples attacked, one of the kings, Robert Guiscard, who died in Cephalonia in 1085. Later, in 1500, the Venetians captured the island and held it until 1797. Under Venetian rule, the island became an arsenal and storehouse and the shortage of oil in Venice led the authorities to offer the local people one sequin for each new olive tree planted. Finally the French invaded Corfu during the Napoleonic Wars. In 1808, the English undertook major town planning works. Corfu **was returned to Greece in 1864.**

★★**Kérkira (Corfu town)** – Corfu has retained a Greco-Venetian atmosphere in its old districts while the Esplanade bears the hallmark of British dignity. This busy promenade and former parade ground now includes a cricket pitch with matches every evening during the summer. On the west side, the "Liston" consists of arcaded houses which are now restaurants, tearooms and bookshops. The architecture takes its inspiration from Rue de Rivoli in Paris and was designed by Matthieu de Lesseps, the father of the famous designer of the Suez Canal.

Not far from the town hall, the 16C **Agios Spiridónas** (St Spyridon's Church) is recognisable by its tall bell-tower. The church is dedicated to a 4C Cypriot bishop, St Spyridon, whose relics were brought back from Constantinople in 1456. Spyridon became the patron saint of Corfu and is still revered today during major festivities held on 11 August.

The **Archeological Museum**★ near the seafront on the island's south side contains a Gorgon pediment from the Archaic period. A carving of Medusa with her hair of snakes covers it. This mythological monster turned to stone anybody who dared look. But Perseus succeeded in killing the monster by using his shield as a mirror.

EXCURSIONS

★★**Kanóni** – *4km/2.5mi south.* The promenade at Kanóni skirts Garítsa Bay. Halfway along stands the church of St Jason and St Sosipater containing some fine 17C icons. A magnificent **view**★★ unfolds of the Vlacherna Islands (Virgin of the Seafarers) and Pondikoníssi (Mouse Island).

★★**Ahílio** – Beyond Gatsoúri stands the **Achilleion**, the villa of Empress Elizabeth of Austria (1837-1898). It is now a casino. The rooms decorated in Antique style display memorabilia relating to the Empress. The Italianate gardens are adorned with statues including a victorious Achilles placed there by the German Emperor Wilhelm II.

►► Fine beaches: Agios Geórgios, Mirtiótissa and Glifada. Seaside resorts: Sidári, Ipsos and Kassíopi and Paleokastrítsa.

KIKLÁDES★★★

Cyclades

Michelin map 970 P 9

The 39 Cyclades islands are classed in three groups. Western islands include Sífnos and Mílos, Central islands, Síros, Páros, Náxos, and los, and northern islands, Tínos, Míkonos, and Dílos. The Ancient Greeks named them this way because they formed a sort of halo *(kyklos)* around the sacred island of Dílos (Delos). The Cyclades islands are a colourful sight with white houses, limpid blue sea and bright sunshine. But the land is arid and fresh water scarce. Náxos, Thíra (Santorini) and Mílos produce white wines that are served with squid, red mullet or grilled sardines. In summer the north wind blows in strong gusts, occasionally whipping up the waves of the Aegean and forming white horses.

The archipelago has been inhabited since the third millenium BC. A brilliant civilization flourished before being wiped out by the cataclysm which devastated the Aegean Sea around 1500 BC. Cycladic idols bearing witness to this period have survived to the present day. These small polished stone sculptures have amazing stylised faces devoid of features except for the bridge of the nose. In the 8C BC, the Cyclades came under Athenian control. During the fourth Crusade of the early 13C the Venetians settled in the Cyclades and placed them under the rule of the dukes of Náxos. The Cyclades became a port of call on the sea route to Constantinople, a busy economic centre despite the pirate raids which made it essential to build towns inland.

★★★DÍLOS (ISLAND OF DELOS)

The island of Apollo acquired major religious and commercial importance during Antiquity. Its sanctuary attracted pilgrims and wealth. The town's population rose to 25 000. *(The site is only open in the mornings and closed on Mondays).*
According to mythology, Leto was seduced and abandoned by Zeus. She proceeded to wander the world pursued by the wrath of Hera, who had forbidden all lands to provide shelter for the unfortunate goddess. When she was due to give birth, she found only one island, Ortygia, which offered her refuge. Here she bore the twins Apollo and Artemis. Ortygia then became Delos the Brilliant. Its Sanctuary of Apollo ranks with Delphi as the most important temple in the Greek world.
The **Processional Way**★ leads to the remains of the temples of Apollo, and to the Lion district built during the Hellenistic Era. The famous Archaic lions stand in a line overlooking the Sacred Lake. They were gifts from the people of Náxos. The **museum**★★ on the way to Mount Cynthos (superb **panoramic view**★★★) contains an outstanding series of nude male figures known as *kouroi* and clothed females known as *korai*. Archaic hieratic statues mimic Egyptian works. The road runs through the residential district including the theatre which dates back to the 2C BC. It includes houses in which the rooms with mosaic pavements were once laid out around a courtyard. Note especially the **House of Masks**★★, a large dwelling with an upper floor.

The best time of the year for visiting the Cyclades is May and June.

C. Friend/PIX

General view of Míkonos

KIKLÁDES

★★MÍKONOS

Míkonos is one of the most typical Cyclades' islands with its white box-shaped houses, mills and chapels, bright light and wild windswept shores. It is also a fashionable holiday resort with a lively night-life. Board here for crossings to Delos.

Míkonos-the-White, the main town, is a maze of narrow streets. These originally were designed to act as wind breaks, and as a means of confusing pirates! The lively picturesque harbour is the perfect place for a stroll. Visitors may occasionally come across the island's mascot, the pelican Petros. While wandering through the small flower-decked squares, vaulted passageways and footpaths, small donkeys pass by loaded with fruit and vegetables. Leondiou Boni Street leads to the 16C Boni Mill and a magnificent **view★★★**. Just opposite to the west, the famous windmills stand on the hill above the picturesque **Little Venice** district. Finally, near the delightful Tría Pigádia (Square of the Three Wells), the Aegean Maritime Museum contains scale models of boats, maps and navigational instruments.

★★★THÍRA (THERA OR SANTORINI)

Santorini★★★ is one of the most spectacular beauty spots in the Mediterranean. The volcano crater extends 10km/6mi in diameter and is engulfed by the waves. It can be visited by boat, providing visitors with a close-up view of volcanic phenomena such as gas bubbles. Take a dip in the water tinged red by the mud.
Around 2000 BC, a sophisticated civilization similar to that of Minoan Crete developed on Santorini, but an earthquake about 1500 BC followed by a volcanic eruption buried its towns beneath ash and scoria. The history of the island has been punctuated by earth tremors, the most recent on 9 July 1956. The Venetians named the island Santorini after a church dedicated to St Irene of Salonika who died here in 304.

Thíra town★★ stands 300m/984ft above the road that plunges deep down like an abyss. The cliff is made up of layers of volcanic debris including black lava, reddish scoria, grey-purple ash, pozzolana and a light strip of pumice which is commercially quarried.
Take the coast road to reach the more peaceful town of **Ia★★**, attractively rebuilt after the 1956 earthquake. Visit in the late afternoon to enjoy the sunset.
The **Akrotiri★★** archeological site at the island's southwestern tip includes a large shed in which visitors can see the town buried beneath the debris from the volcanic eruption. Although the paintings which decorated the houses are now kept in the National Museum in Athens, this remains a fascinating site. You can walk through the streets in front of the houses which, since no bodies were found there, must have been abandoned before disaster struck.

KRÍTI

CRETE

Michelin map 970 P 10

Despite the tourist boom on the north coast, the island of the gods has retained the wild splendour of its landscapes. The inhabitants still display their traditional qualities of pride, honesty and hospitality.
Crete is a mountainous island. Its three ranges reaching an altitude of almost 2,400m/7,875ft. The remarkable Gorge of Samaria is a highlight. Goats and sheep live in the mountains while the coastal plains are planted with wheat, rice, citrus fruit trees, banana plantations and vines.
Cretan culinary specialities include tasty dishes such as lamb with artichokes *(arnáki me angináres)*, fish such as swordfish *(ksifiós)*, gray and red mullet, cheeses *(féta, graviéra, manoúri)* and a honey yoghurt. The wines, Minos, Lato, Gortys and Angelo, are full-bodied with a heady bouquet, but the most typical are sold in carafes in the country inns. Those who are partial to liqueurs will want to try *rakí* and *tsikoudía*, a strong and fruity marc.
Crete, the cradle of the **Minoan civilization** (2800-1100 BC), has a mythological origin. According to Homer, Zeus was born in Crete. He fell in love with the Phoenician princess, Europa, who bore him three sons, Minos, Rhadamanthus and Sarpedon. Minos became a powerful king and founded the civilization which bears his name.
In 1204 after the forth Crusade, Venice occupied Crete and used the island as a base to control the Eastern maritime trade routes. After Constantinople was captured by the Turks in 1453, artists and scholars flooded into Crete. The churches and monasteries were decorated with frescoes by painters from the Cretan School. Its leading practitioner was the famous Doménikos Theotokópoulos, better known as **El Greco** (1541-1614).
Crete was occupied by the Turks from 1699 to 1878. There were several uprisings during the 19C, which are described by the Cretan writers Kazantzakis and Prevelakis.

★IRÁKLIO (HERAKLION) Population 101 634. Michelin map 970 P 10

Heraklion, formerly known as Candia under Venetian rule, is Crete's capital and main port of Crete. It has retained its 16C and 17C walls. Inside, Liberty Square (Platia Eleftherias) and El Venizelou Square buzz night and day with cafés and bookshops. Dedalou Street is lined with craft shops, restaurants and taverns.
Not far from the Venetian **old harbour★** (Paleó Limáni), the **Archeological Museum★★★** (Arheologikó Moussio) displays objects found during digs at the main archeological sites of Knossós, Phaestos, Mália and Zákros. It also contains scale models of the palaces. Masterpieces include the earthenware statuettes of snake goddesses, the bull's head steatite vase, an ivory acrobat, the Harvesters vase, the chieftain's goblet, gold jewellery found in Mália, the Agía Triáda fresco-deocrated sarcophagus, and the famous Parisienne from Knossós.

St Catherine's Church (Agía Ekateríni) contains six remarkable **icons★★** by Damaskinos who, after his stay in Venice (1574-1582), combined the relaxed poses with the conventional Byzantine tradition.

★★★KNOSSÓS Michelin map 970 P 10

This palace was supposedly built at the request of Minos by the architect Daedalus as a prison for the Minotaur, a monster with the body of a man and the head of a bull. The strange creature was the offspring of Minos' wife Pasiphae and a bull. Athenians offer human sacrifices to the Minotaur, but Theseus, son of the King of Athens, seduced Minos' daughter, entered the palace with its labyrinth of rooms and corridors, killed the Minotaur and returned to the entrance by following the thread given to him by Ariadne. Minos avenged himself by imprisoning Daedalus and his son Icarus in the labyrinth. The prisoners escaped by making themselves wings with birds' feathers stuck together with wax. However, Icarus plunged into the sea after flying too close to the sun and causing the wax to melt. Daedalus succeeded in reaching Cumae in Italy.
Knossós, like Mycenae, was discovered by Schliemann in the late 19C. The archeological digs and reconstructions were completed by the British archeologist Sir Arthur Evans (1851-1941).
The **palace** covers an area of 22 000m²/236 720sq ft. Its complex plan gives a semblance of truth to the legend. Just beyond the entrance, a propylaeum leads to the "Processional Corridor" from which the paintings have been removed; they are now stored in the museum in Heraklion. The central courtyard (60m x 29m/197ft x 95ft) is surrounded by the **sanctuary★★**, royal apartments and outbuildings including the craft workshops.

★RÉTHIMNO Population 17 736. Michelin map 970 P 10

This town has retained its old character. Its Venetian fortress, old narrow streets, former Nerandzé mosque and quays lined with fish restaurants make for a perfect stroll. The town hosts a famous wine festival in July.

► ► **Farángi Samariás★★★** (Samaria Gorge: 5-6hr walk) – **Festós★★** (Phaestos Palace) – **Ruins of Mália★★** – Sea resorts: Ágios Nikólaosa, Eloúnd

MAINLAND GREECE

Phocis extends from the Parnassus mountains, now a major ski resort. The bauxite mines here have given rise to the large Andikíra aluminium complex. The region is best-known for the sanctuary in Delphi. To the north, Lamía serves as a busy trading centre and an important rail and road junction. The Thermopílai (Thermopylae) Pass where Leonidas won fame during the second Median war in 480 BC leads to the seaside resort of Kaména Voúrla overlooking Évvoia (Euboea). Thessalía (Thessaly) is linked to Ipiros (Epirus) and Ioánnina by the highest mountain road in Greece, the Métsovo Pass (alt 1 705m/5 594ft). To the west, the approaches to the Pindhos Óros (Pindus Mountains) are marked by strangely eroded rocks, the Metéora.

★★★DELFÍ (DELPHI) Michelin map 970 O 9

In the days of the Ancient Greeks, the sanctuary of Apollo attracted crowds of pilgrims fascinated by the oracle. Delphi is still steeped in mystery. It lies above a famous olive grove, known as the sea of olives, which carpets the hillsides of the Pleistos Valley. It contains some 400 000 olive trees; the fruit is harvested in September.

Legend and history – According to legend, Zeus founded Delphi. He wanted to find the centre of the world over which he reigned and sent two eagles on a reconnaissance mission. The birds met above Parnassus where they spotted the "omphalos." Thus, Delphi became the navel of the Universe.

From the 2nd millenium BC, the site contained a place of worship dedicated to the Earth goddess Ge or Gaea. The goddess, guarded by her son, the snake Python, hid at the bottom of one of the chasms. An oracle already translated the goddess' murmurings. One day, Apollo the son of Zeus came to Delphi and shot Python dead with his arrows. This battle symbolises the struggle between the light of Apollo and the darkness of Python. When the Athenians controlled central Greece in the early 6C BC, they upheld the tradition of the Pythian Games held every four years and added sporting competitions. Delphi became a Panhellenic sanctuary, gaining immense wealth from donations and the taxes levied on those who came to consult the Pythia who were chosen from among the local virgins and who received answers from Apollo to requests from pilgrims. After drinking water from the fountain near the temple which was believed to bestow the gift of prophecy, she entered the temple crypt and placed herself on a sort of tripod cauldron near the famous omphalos. The pilgrims were allowed into the room next to the crypt. They presented their questions to the priests who passed them on to the Pythia. She would plunge into a trance and the sounds she uttered were recorded and cryptically written down by her acolytes. The replies, which resembled advice rather than predictions, were finally returned to the questioners.

★★★ **Sanctuary of Apollo** – The Sacred Way leads up to the temple of Apollo. It is lined with small temple-like buildings which are in fact treasures offered by different nations. The treasury of Sicyon and the wall of the treasury of Siphnus were built around 525 BC. They are followed by the treasury of Thebes.

★ **Athenian Treasury** – Reconstructed using the process of anastylosis, it is a Doric edifice in white Parian marble dating from 490 to 480 BC. It was built using part of the booty captured from the Medes in Marathon. The sculptures depict the Athenians' favourite subjects, the battle between the Greeks and the Amazons and the legends of Theseus and Heracles.

The 83m/272ft long polygonal wall supports the terrace of the temple of Apollo. It dates from the 6C to the 5C BC and is built in heavy limestone ashlar. More than 800 edicts from Hellenistic and Roman times granting freedom to slaves are engraved in the wall.

★★ **Temple of Apollo** – The remains come from the temple built in the 4C BC after an earthquake. This temple replaced a structure two centuries older which had been built with the financial backing of Croesus. The later edifice is a Doric monument with a peristyle stretching 60.3m x 23.8m/198ft x 78ft with 12m/39ft high tufa columns faced with stucco. The porch contains a statue of Homer and inscriptions recalling the precepts of the Greek sages such as "know thyself", "bear and abstain", and "all things in moderation". The columns of the temple stand out against the backdrop of the Pleistos Valley planted with olive trees, while further uphill on the other side are the perfect outlines of the theatre.

★★ **Theatre** – The theatre dates from the 4C BC but was altered two centuries later by the Romans. The 35 tiers of seats once accommodated 5 000 spectators who came to watch the religious recitals. Note the seats reserved for the priests and dignitaries in the front row.

The theatre passageway extends west into a footpath winding its way up to the stadium in a series of hairpin bends. Fine views open onto Delphi.

MICHELIN

Thólos, Delphi

★ **Stadium** – The stadium surrounded by conifers was built in the 3C BC. During the next century tiers of stone seats and a monumental gate were added. The stadium could accommodate about 6500 people. The track has retained its starting and finishing lines which lie 178m/195yd apart. Plays are performed in the stadium in the summer.

★★ **Museum** – The museum displays the works of art uncovered on the site. They include a Parian marble frieze with some original colouring from the Treasury of Siphnus, metopes from the Athenian Treasury illustrating the legends of Heracles and Theseus, and the Delphic **Auriga**★★★, one of the finest Greek statues from the late Archaic period. It dates from 478 BC and was discovered near the theatre in 1896. The charioteer (*auriga* in Latin) was part of a bronze ex-voto depicting the winning quadriga at the Olympic Games in 474 BC. Note the nobility in the attitude of the life-size figure, 1.8m/5ft 11ins tall, gripping his horses' reins. He wears the victor's wreath around his beautifully modelled head. The original eyes of enamel and coloured stones remain. The marble statue of Antinous from the 2C AD is one of the finest representations of this man who was one of Emperor Hadrian's favourites. Antinous was deified after his death.

★★ **Marmaria** – Downhill, the sanctuary of Athena Pronaia contains one of the most elegant monuments in Delphi, the **tholos**★★. The fluted shafts of three raised Doric columns topped by an entablature give a picturesque suggestion of the elegant marble rotunda with peristyle, built in the 4C BC.

EXCURSIONS

★★ **Óssios Loukás** – *36km/22mi southeast.* St Luke's monastery lies in a peaceful beauty spot. It was founded by the hermit Loukás the Styriot, who died in 953. Occupied by Cistercians in the 13C and 14C, Orthodox Greek monks now live here. The huge **church of Óssios Loukás**★★ (St Luke's) is a place of pilgrimage built in the 11C with typical Greek bonding consisting of stonework with brick courses. The square church forms the shape of a Greek cross with a central dome. The interior decor, mostly from the 11C, includes some splendid mosaics on a gold background, a masterpiece of Byzantine art. The compositions depict Christ Teaching, the Crucifixion, the Resurrection, Madonna and Archangels, the Washing of Christ's Feet and the Disbelief of St Thomas. All show a great clarity of style. The mosaics damaged by an earthquake in the 16C have been replaced by frescoes, notably the Christ Pantocrator on the dome.

METÉORA★★★

Michelin map 970 O 8

Above the town of Kalambáka, jagged rocks form weird and wonderful shapes on sheer cliffs. At their summit are the famous Cenobitic monasteries. They are known as the Metéora, meaning hanging in mid air.
The water running down from the Pindus mountains has carried away the limestone and left behind banks of sandstone and harder tertiary conglomerates which rise almost 300m/1 000ft above the surrounding countryside.
As early as the 11C, anchorites sought solitude in the caves. In the 14C, the hermitages became monasteries. During this time St Athanasius from Mount Athos founded the Great Meteoron. In the 15C and 16C, there were as many as 24 monasteries. They were decorated with frescoes and icons by great artists such as the monk Theophanes the Cretan. Only five monasteries are occupied today. Until recently, they could only be reached by removable ladders or by baskets attached to ropes hauled up with a winch. Now steps have been built and a road runs to the main monasteries.

★★ **Mégalo Metéoro** – The Great Meteoron houses a collection of manuscripts, icons and liturgical objects in the refectory. The frescoes in the 16C church contain austere portrayals of the Christ Pantocrator and faces of saints.

★★ **Varlaám** – The church in 16C Varlaám Monastery is decorated with some remarkable **frescoes**★★ depicting the Last Judgement and the life of St John the Baptist. The undercroft houses a huge 12 000l/2 640gal barrel and a press. The treasury is housed in the refectory.

Cornet/PIX

Roussánou Monastery, Metéora

The PELOPONNESE

Michelin map 970 O 9

The Peloponnese is a mountainous peninsula linked to Attica by the Isthmus of Corinth. To the east, the ruins of Mycenae overlook Argolís, a fertile plain of market gardens, fruit trees and cereal crops. To the north are Korinthía and Akhaia (Achaea) with Greece's third largest city Pátrai (Patras). This area produces wine, oranges and raisins. The south is divided into three headlands. The largest, Máni (Maina) is a wild timeless region extending into the Taíyetos (Taygetus mountains). To the west, local canning factories process the produce of small market gardens.

★★★ARHÉA EPÍDAVROS (EPIDAURUS)

In a peaceful setting among pine trees and oleanders lie the remains of the Sanctuary of Asclepius. Oracles brought people here from all over Ancient Greece. People still come to Epidaurus to admire the perfect design of its theatre and attend performances of Ancient Greek plays and concerts in summer.

Asclepius, son of Apollo and a Boeotian princess, was nursed by a goat and brought up by the centaur Chiron. This half-man, half-horse taught him surgery and the art of healing using plants. Asclepius became so knowledgeable that he succeeded in raising the dead. This earned him the hatred of Hades and Zeus. As a result, Zeus killed Asclepius by sending down a bolt of lightning. Asclepius' body supposedly was buried in Epidaurus. He became worshipped as a god and was depicted resting on the staff of omens accompanied by the magic snake, features which later appeared in the caduceus, the emblem of the medical profession.

★★★**Theatre** – The theatre lies at a slight distance from the sanctuary. It is probably the most accomplished piece of building in the Ancient world owing to its scenic surroundings, majestic lines and perfect proportions. The architect Polyclitus the Younger designed the building in the 4C BC on a hillside. Hence the excellent acoustics. The sound rises perfectly to the back row 22.50m/74ft above the stage. Fourteen thousand spectators could be seated around the circular stage, or orchestra. Behind lie the foundations of the stage. The seats reserved for magistrates and priests were built with backs found in the first few rows.

★★★ARHÉA OLIMBÍA (OLYMPIA)

The sanctuary of Zeus, the symbol of the unity of Ancient Greece, is tucked away behind the trees near the River Alfiós (Alpheus). Mount Krónion (Hill of Cronus) looks down on the building. The serenity of this spot contrasts with the tragic grandeur of Delphi's Panhellenic Sanctuary.

Two myths are connected with Olympia. Oenomaus, the regional king, was warned by an oracle that his son-in-law would oust him from the throne. He therefore ordered all the suitors of his daughter, Hippodamia, to take part in a chariot race in which the loser was put to death. Oenomaus, however, owned a team of invincible horses. Pelops fell in love with Hippodamia. Together they bribed the driver of the royal chariot and replaced the bronze axle pins with wax which melted during the race. Oenomaus was killed after being dragged by his horses. Pelops then married Hippodamia and ruled over the Peloponnese to which he gave his name. He was the father of Atreus *(see Mycenae)*.

Another legend tells how Heracles, the son of Zeus, built the sacred Altis Wall after cleaning the stables of Augeas with the waters of the Alpheus. The wall surrounds the sanctuaries in honour of Pelops, Zeus and Hera. Heracles introduced gymnastics and athletics competitions in honour of the hero who vanquished Oenomaus.

The Olympic Games date back to the 8C BC. The Greek people gathered during a sacred month-long truce, which was renewed every four years. The festivities lasted for seven days, five of which were devoted to athletics competitions. The stadium hosted running, wrestling, pugilism (a type of boxing), the pancratium (boxing and wrestling combined) and the pentathlon (combination of five events, ie running, jumping, discus, javelin and wrestling). The hippodrome hosted horse and chariot races. For each of the specialist events, the winner was crowned with an olive wreath made from branches cut from the sacred olive tree with a golden sickle.

During the reign of Emperor Theodosius, pagan religions were outlawed and the Games took place for the last time in 393. The Frenchman Baron Pierre de Coubertin (1863-1937) and the Greek Ghéorghios Avyheris (1818-1899) were responsible for reviving the Games in 1896 in Athens. Ever since then, they have been held every four years. Near the archeological site, the altar of the Olympic flame bears five circles symbolising the union of the five continents. At the start of each Olympiad, the sacred flame is carried to the place where the Games will be held.

★★**The Ruins** – Near the entrance, the **palaestra**★ or sports hall is recognisable for its double colonnade. Beyond, the numerous temples, votive monuments and altars form the sanctuary, evidence of the religious fervour behind the Games. The 5C

BC **Temple of Zeus**★★ built in local shell-filled limestone was razed to the ground by an earthquake in the 6C. The huge drums and Doric capitals piled up on the terrace create a striking effect. The cella contains a statue of Olympian Zeus by the sculptor Phidias (430-420 BC). It was considered to be one of the Seven Wonders of the World. This impressive chryselephantine gold-and-ivory 13.50m/44ft high statue represented Zeus seated on an ebony and ivory throne.
Beyond the sanctuary, the **stadium**★ accommodated up to 20 000 spectators. The starting and finishing lines lie 192m/210yd apart and can still be seen.
The **museum**★★ houses the carved Parian marble decoration from the pediments of the Temple of Zeus, the metopes depicting the Labours of Hercules, and a magnificent statue of Hermes by the 4C BC sculptor Praxiteles. Hermes, the messenger of the gods, carries the infant Dionysus. He is taking the child to the nymphs to protect him from the jealousy of Hera, as Dionysus was the son of Zeus and Semele. Note the perfect modelling and well-balanced proportions.

►► **Olympic Games Museum**★ (in Olympia town) – **Vassés**★★ (Temple of Bassae, *68km/42mi south*).

★★KÓRINTHOS (CORINTH)

Corinth lies at the junction of land and sea routes linking Attica and the Peloponnese, or the Ionian and Aegean seas. The town controlled passage across the isthmus from an acropolis.
According to legend, Corinth was founded by Corinthos, grandson of the sun god Helios and was ruled by King Sisyphus who was the most cunning of mortals. The exasperated and jealous Zeus condemned him to heave a rock uphill in the Underworld, but the rock constantly rolled back down again.
From the Archaic period, the town reaped huge income from the goods carried across the isthmus. Its storehouses were stocked with wheat from Sicily, papyrus from Egypt, ivory from Libya, incense from Arabia and rugs from Carthage. Furthermore, Corinth used the clay from the coast to make vases, especially perfume bottles. These were exported throughout the Mediterranean. Opulence led the Corinthians to a life of luxury and pleasure-seeking. The entire Ancient World knew about the courtesans who indulged in sacred prostitution within the walls of the Temple of Aphrodite, goddess of Love and Beauty. Diogenes the Cynic lived here in a barrel and, later, St Paul the Apostle decried the shamelessness of its people. After Corinth was pillaged and burnt by the Roman legions in 146 BC, a new town was founded by Julius Caesar. Corinth became the capital of Roman Greece in 44 BC. In the Middle Ages, the town retained its importance as an agricultural market and its name became associated with currants, formerly known as raisins of corauns.

★★**Ancient Corinth** – The ancient town lies to the southwest of the modern city. On the top of the hill stand seven monolithic Doric columns from the 6C Temple of Apollo. The spot offers a spectacular view of the gulf and the citadel, the Acrocorinth. Excavations have revealed the agora, the centre of public life, which was once covered with statues, as well as a theatre, odeum, and the arcades of the Peirene fountain.

L. Y. Loirat/EXPLORER

Pereine Fountain

★★★ **Acrocorinth** – The original Greek acropolis became a Roman and Byzantine citadel. The Franks captured it in 1210. It subsequently belonged to the Palaeologi of Mistras, the knights of Rhodes and the Turks. Today the ruins which rise 574m/1 883ft above the gulf, blend in with the surrounding countryside.

EXCURSIONS

★★ **Isthmus of Corinth and Corinth Canal** – After Nero's attempt to break through the isthmus in AD 67, the project was shelved until 1882, when a French company resurrected it. The work was interrupted in 1889 after the company went bankrupt but was finally completed by the Greeks in 1893. The canal is 6343m/3.9mi long, 24.60m/81ft wide and has walls reaching a height of 79.50m/261ft.

★★ MIKÍNES (MYCENAE)

According to mythology, Mycenae was founded by Perseus, the son of Zeus and Danaë. He supposedly built the citadel wall with the help of the Cyclops, giant builders who had only one eye in the middle of their foreheads. The town then fell into the hands of the Atridae who were cursed by the gods. An account of their complex history was given by Homer in the *Iliad*. The best-known members of this family include: Menelaus, son of Atreus and King of Sparta, whose wife Helen was seduced by Paris, the son of King Priam of Troy, thereby causing the Trojan War; Agamemnon was brother of Menelaus, King of Mycenae and husband of Clytemnestra, Helen's sister. This king of kings led the Achaeans during the Trojan expedition, and ordered his daughter Iphigeneia to be sacrificed on Aulis in order to obtain favourable winds.

In 1876, the German Heinrich Schliemann (1822-1890), who was fascinated by Homer's text, followed it and arrived at Mycenae where he discovered royal tombs containing 19 bodies. The men had gold masks over their faces and the women wore gold jewellery.

Mycenae was the richest and most powerful State in the Mediterranean world from the 16C to the 12C BC. It had links with Crete and Egypt. The civilization bearing its name died out after the arrival of the Dorians. The proud ruins stand in a wild setting on a rocky hill. The entrance is via the famous **Lioness Gate**★★★ which derives its name from the carvings of the animals in relief on the monolithic tympanum. They measure almost 4m/13ft at its base for a height of 3.30m/10ft 9in. Note on the city outskirts, the three different styles of tombs: the graves, the sepulchres hewn into the rock and the domes covering a circular chamber *(tholos)* reached via a corridor *(dromos)*. A splendid example of a tholos is Agamemnon's tomb. The sophisticated elegance of the objects discovered here reveal the astonishing wealth of the princes who were buried here.

★★★ MISTRÁS (RUINS OF MISTRA)

Mistrás lies in an outstanding setting at the foot of the Taygetus mountains, overlooking the modern town of Sparta. Its churches and Byzantine monasteries, palaces and ruined houses bear witness to the splendour of the former capital of the Despotate of Morea.

Mistrás dates back to the 13C when the fort was built by Guillaume de Villehardouin of Champagne on A 621m/2 038ft high hilltop. In the following centuries, the citadel fell to the emperors from the Cantacuzenus and Palaeologus dynasties. They made Mistrás the centre of a Hellenic political and cultural revival, presiding over the construction of churches combining a cruciform layout and a five-domed roof. The painstakingly executed decoration is evident in the frescoes which superseded the use of marble and mosaic. During the Turkish occupation from 1460, the churches were turned into mosques. By the 17C, the town and its silk industry prospered with a population of 42 000. The Venetians then occupied it. In 1779, Russians under Count Orlov followed by Albanian mercenaries put residents to death by fire and sword. The town was abandoned and was later saved by the restoration work undertaken by the French Archeological School.

The old town includes three sectors bounded by their respective walls. They are the Villehardouins' castle *(kástro)*, the aristocratic upper town with the palace of the despots, and the middle-class and religious lower town, which still has a number of religious buildings decorated with murals remarkable for the harmonious colours, flowing lines and expressive faces. Examples can be seen in the monasteries of Vrontohión, Pandánassa and Perívleptos.

★★ NÁFPLIO (NAUPLIA)

The charming old town of Nauplia overlooked by the Acronauplia Citadel and the Venetian Fortress of Palamedes lies on a picturesque rocky peninsula in the Argolis Gulf.

Palamedes, grandson of the sea god Poseidon, was considered as the king of inventors by the Ancient Greeks. They credited him with the invention of lighthouses, money, weights and measures, and military tactics. He is also said to have invented the games of dice and chess to entertain the besieged citizens of Troy.

★★Seafront – The **Philhellines Monument** beside the harbour recalls Nauplia's role in the forefront of the war against the Turks during the 1821 Revolution. French, English and Russian naval forces gathered there before attacking the Ottoman fleet in Navarin. On 7 January 1828, Kapod'strias arrived in Nauplia. It became the official capital of Greece the following year, losing this status to Athens in 1834. The neo-Classical buildings which give the town its aristocratic air date from this period.

★★Old town – The old town is laid out like a simple checkerboard. In the centre, Sindagma Square served as a political forum during the revolution. The 18C Venetian building at the end now houses the Archeological Museum which exhib-its objects found during excavations in Argolis. They include a remarkable collection of idols and a 15C BC bronze breast plate discovered in Mycenae.

★★Palamídi – *Visit recommended in the morning.* The Palamedes Fort stands on top of A 216m/709ft hill. The fortress, built by the French architect Lasalle, dates back to the Venetian occupation of the town between 1686 and 1715. It is a mighty complex of eight forts or bastions linked by systems of defence, vaults, corridors and secret passages and dotted with watchtowers. There are some magnificent views from the parapet walk.

★Akronafplía – *Visit recommended in the evening.* The Acronauplia Citadel stands at the end of a narrow street above the Frankish church. This Greek, Frankish then Venetian fortress comprises a number of walls with gates bearing the lion emblem of St Mark.

RHODES and the DODECANESE

Michelin map 970 Q 9

As its name suggests, the Dodecanese Archipelago in the East Aeageanis represents a group of 12 islands. The main islands are Rhodes and Kos (Cos). Others include Pátmos, St John's island Léros, and the sponge fisherman's Kálimnos. Sími and Kastelórizo are the most beautiful. These picturesque mountainous islands played an important role during the Middle Ages against the threat from Turkey. They came under Italian rule in 1912 and were reunified with Greece in 1948.

★★★RÓDOS (ISLAND OF RHODES)

The island of roses is renowned for its mild climate, flower gardens, vineyards, scenic beauty and wonderful beaches. The island is 77km/48mi long, 37km/23mi wide. Its highest point is Mount Atáviros which rises to 1,215m/3 986ft.

In the 7C BC, the cities of Ialissós, Líndos and Kámiros were already trading with the entire Middle East, spreading colonies along the coast of Asia Minor and even in Italy. Production of gold jewellery and ceramics decorated in oriental style with plants and stylised animals were developed. In 408 BC the three towns joined force to form Rhodes, and the new city soon superseded them. The development of its naval fleet and the minting of its own money confirmed the island's role as a powerful force in the eastern Mediterranean. At the same time, a school of sculp-ture was producing works still famous today, such as the Colossus (265 BC), the Victory of Samothrace (Paris, Louvre Museum) and the Laocoon (Vatican).

The arrival of the Knights Hospitaller of St John of Jerusalem in 1306 marked the beginning of a turbulent period which ended in 1522. The island became a last bastion of Christianity in the face of the Turkish threat. The knights built walls, the town and harbour of Rhodes, citadels in Monólithos and Líndos, monasteries and churches. The island then fell into the hands of the Turks, the Italians in 1912, the Germans from 1943 to 1945 and the English before finally being reunited with Greece on 7 March 1948.

★★Rhodes town – The former Knights Hospitaller's city, now an internationally renowned resort, spreads out from its two harbours at the northeast end of the island. It is also a modern city offering such tourist attractions as hotels, beaches, nightclubs and shops selling jewellery, silverware and ceramics. In the evening a *son et lumière* show is held in the gardens of the Palace Boulevard, while folk dancing can be seen in the old town.

★★★The walled town – The **citadel★★** (Collachium) houses the remarkable **Palace of the Grand Masters★** and the knights' residences are concentrated along **Odós Ipotón★★** (Knight Street). This medieval cobbled street is lined with Gothic buildings. The knights once lived grouped according to their tongue. They are known as the hostels of Provence, Spain, France, Italy and England.

The **Nossokomio Ipotón**★ (Knights' Hospital), on which building work began in 1440, still has the Main Ward upstairs. It contained 32 beds totally lacking in privacy. Beside it stand the refectory and kitchen. The hospital now houses the Archeological Museum. Its most outstanding exhibit is the Aphrodite of Rhodes, a masterpiece dating from the 1C BC.

In the **town**★, Sokratous Street was the bazar's main thoroughfare. It leads to the picturesque narrow streets of the **Turkish district**★. The mosques and luxurious Turkish baths recently were restored.

EXCURSION

★★ **Líndos** – On the east coast, the white houses of the old village and dark walls of the medieval citadel perched on a spur of rock contrast with the blue sea. They combine to make Líndos a truly spectacular spot serving as a reminder of three civilizations – Ancient Greek, Byzantine and medieval.

The rock rises to a dizzy height of 116m/381ft above the sea. It is topped by the remains of antique and medieval buildings. Building work began on the citadel under Grand Master Fulvian (1421-1437) and was completed under Pierre d'Aubusson (1476-1503). A long flight of steps beside the governor's palace leads up to the barbican topped by a bartizan.

Enjoy a pleasant stroll through the narrow lanes of the village and past the houses with patios. The finest date from the 16C and 17C and were built for rich ship-owners or sea captains. They still have their pointed arched windows and flattened mouldings of roses, plants, birds and tracery in a composite style showing both Gothic and Oriental influences.

For further details on Greece, consult the Michelin Green Guide Greece.

When looking for a hotel or restaurant in Athens, use the Michelin Red Guide Europe, updated annually.

Hungary

Area: 93 000km²/35 907sq mi – **Population:** 10.6 million – **Capital:** Budapest – **Currency:** the forint (Ft) – **Time:** GMT + 1 hr in winter, GMT + 2 hr in summer

Magyarország

Hungary is situated in the heart of Central Europe, bordered by seven countries. The land, cut in two by the River Danube, composes various geographical regions with differing landscapes. West of the Danube lies Lower Transdanubia covered with forest and pasture land. East of the Danube, another lowland region, the Great Plain or Puszta, forms a huge prairie dominated by agriculture and livestock farming. Mountains dominate the northeast and north. The highest peak, Mount Kékes, rises to an altitude of just over 1 000m/3 250ft.

Hungary is the land of Romany gypsies, Baroque architecture and hot springs; it offers visitors a wealth of historic buildings and a strong folk tradition expressed through its music and dance.

R. Bacon

IN BRIEF

Entry Formalities – Valid passport for British, US, Canadian citizens. Visa for Australian and Japanese citizens. Identity card acceptable for French citizens.

Tourist information – From Tourinform or Ibusz (main travel agent) offices. Information and organised tours or excursions are available in most hotels.

Specialities – Many dishes are flavoured with paprika. Typical fare includes *halászlé* (fish stew), *gulyás* (soup with pieces of meat and potatoes) and *pörkölt* (stew).
Red wine: Bikavér (Bull's Blood); white wines: Badacsony szürkebarát, Mori Ezerjo and Tokaj.
Aperitif: *bárackpálinka* (apricot brandy).

HISTORICAL NOTES

1-4C AD	The Romans found the province of Pannonia in the western part of modern-day Hungary. Later, the Romans establish a military camp of Aquincum in present-day Obuda, near Budapest. A civilian town expands around the camp and Aquincum soon became a flourishing community, the main town in lower Pannonia during the days of Emperor Trajan.
5C	The Huns under Attila capture Aquincum. Various Barbarian invasions follow, driving out the last remaining Romans.
896	The Magyars led by Prince Arpád, cross the Carpathians and settle in the region.
1000	Stephen I is crowned King of Hungary.
1241	Buda and Pest are laid to waste by the Mongol invasions.
1458-1490	Matthias Corvinus accedes to the throne. This cultured man demonstrates enormous skill in the art of politics. During his reign, Hungary enjoys a dazzling period marked by the development of the arts and letters and the founding of the Corvinä Library.
1526	Suleiman the Magnificent's troops defeat Hungary in Mohács.
1541	The Turks capture Buda and occupy most of the country.
1686	The Habsburgs liberate Hungary which soon comes under Austrian rule.
1848-49	A revolution, led first by the lawyer and journalist Lajos Kossuth, then by the poet Sandor Petőfi, fails.
1867	The Austro-Hungarian Compromise is struck. The Dual Monarchy. Emperor Francis Joseph and Empress Elizabeth become King and Queen of Hungary.
1919	After the defeat of Germany and its allies, the Treaty of Saint-Germain-en-Laye separates Austria and Hungary.
1941	Hungary, governed by Admiral Horthy, sides with Hitler.
1945	The Red Army liberates the country transforming it into a satellite State of the USSR.

1949 The People's Socialist Republic of Hungary is proclaimed.

1956 On 23 October, a popular uprising sweeps Budapest. In November the reformer **Imre Nagy** becomes Prime Minister. Soviet tanks crush the rebellion. János Kádár takes over the country's leadership.

1988 Kádár steps down from power.

1989 On 23 October, the People's Socialist Republic of Hungary discards communism and becomes the Hungarian Republic.

1990 Árpád Göncz is elected President of the Republic.

1999 Hungary joins NATO.

BALATON★★

Michelin map 970 M6

Balaton is known as the Hungarian Sea. It is central Europe's largest lake, stretching for a distance of 70km/45mi with a width of 14km/8.5mi at its widest point. The hotels, holiday flats, guest houses, camp sites and man-made beaches attract hordes in the summer, especially Germans. Signs of Zimmer Frei are found almost everywhere. Swimming and water sports are available. Enthusiastic sailors or wind surfers do not have to worry about motor boats. Walkers may enjoy the numerous beauty spots along the shores. The vines clinging to the north shore yield a reasonably good white wine.

Balatonfüred – This spa is a main holiday resort.

Tihany – A ferry service runs from the end of the peninsula, the narrowest point of the lake, to Szánföd. The quay is lined with restaurants, souvenir shops and street vendors selling Russian dolls, wickerwork, and leather goods.
The hillside village of Tihany attracts large numbers of visitors in the summer. In addition to souvenir shops and restaurants, it houses a Baroque church with two towers. Inside, there is a fine pulpit and altar. Just below to the left, an observation platform offers telescopes with an unspoilt view of the lake.

Badacsony – From the top of an extinct volcano *(fairly difficult climb)*, the **view★** extends over the vineyards and lake.

Sziglilet – The ruins of a citadel on a hill are visible from the road. A number of viewpoints have been provided along the walls. They are reached by flights of wooden steps. From the highest point, a splendid **panoramic view★★** unfolds over the shores of the lake and the hinterland. The village contains picturesque houses with thatched roofs.

Keszthely – The Baroque **mansion** of the Festetic family is set in delightful grounds with well-kept lawns and superb flower beds. It consists of a main section and two wings set at right angles. The mansion now houses a museum mainly concerning 18C to 19C aristocratic life.

Héviz – The town's lake, Europe's largest, produces mineral water. The water temperature varies between 25°C/77°F and 35°C/95°F depending on the season.

BUDAPEST★★★

Population 2 172 000
Michelin map 970 M7

The Hungarian capital lies along the two banks of the River Danube. It was formed in 1872 by the merger of the three towns of Óbuda, whose Roman remains (the army camp amphitheatre, Villa Hercules and ruins of **Aquincum★**) are still visible, Buda and Pest.
Budapest, situated right in the heart of Europe, is a lively, friendly city with a continental climate – summers can be very hot. It has succeeded in adapting to the modern world while preserving its rich historic past. The city offers a wealth of entertainment and cultural activities, museums, concerts, theatres, opera, and musicals as well as elegant shops and good food. An excellent inexpensive public transport system of buses, trolley buses, trams and three underground lines coloured blue, red and yellow covers the city.
Buda and Pest are linked by a number of bridges, the most famous being the **Chain Bridge★★** (Széchenyi lánchíd) (AZ **64**) guarded by huge stone lions and the **Freedom Bridge★** (Szabadág híd) (AZ **62**), a fine metal structure built at the end of the 19C.
A hydrofoil service provides regular links with the Austrian capital, Vienna, (boarding at Belgrád rakpart, between Vigadó tér and Elizabeth Bridge) and the Slovakian capital, Bratislava.

P. Somelet/DIAF
Széchenyi Baths

Spa Town – The public baths, open from 6am, represent a Budapest institution. For city dwellers, they are a traditional ritual and for tourists a unique experience in surroundings belonging to another time and another world. Budapest boasts some 100 thermal springs supplying every day around 70 million litres (1.5 million gal) of hot water. The Romans used these healing waters. But under Turkish rule the **baths★★** *(fürdö)* gained their real importance.

Gellért Baths (AZ **F**[1]) – The baths in the Gellért Hotel were opened in 1918. The pool built in the former greenhouse is renowned for its splendid mosaics, columns and flower-decked balconies.

Széchenyi Baths (BY **F**[2]) – A huge neo-Classical building with domes, pediments and statues. The interior is late 19C. In the open-air pool, chess players indulge in their favourite game around floating boards.

Rudach Baths (AY **F**[3]) – Four small pools steam around a central octagonal section called the Green-Column Pool. The structure's domed roof with tiny windows let in rays of light. The water temperature varies in each pool.

Király Baths (AY **F**[4]) – These historic baths were built under Turkish rule.

Budapest Kártya, Budapest Card

This card, valid for 2 days (2 450 forints) or 3 days (2 950 forints) allows free, unlimited travel on all public transport in the city, as well as free entry to a very large number of museums. It also entitles you to reductions in shops, bars and restaurants, for various performances, baths, the airport minibus, bus rides and boat trips. On sale at Tourinform (tourist office), Sütö utca 2, Pest, or at the airport.

BUDA

Buda is the old historic town rising on several hills. Its castle majestically overlooks the left bank of the Danube on which the modern town of Pest has spread and developed.

★★ **Budavári palota (Royal Castle)** (AZ) – *Right bank. Take the funicular railway just beyond Chain Bridge.* The former residence of the Hungarian royalty stands on Várhegy, Castle Hill. This limestone plateau 1.5km/1mi long rises 60m/197ft above the river. Reconstructed in the Classical and Baroque styles, the impressive dome is flanked by two symmetrical wings decorated with colonnades.
In front of the main building stands the equestrian statue of Prince **Eugene of Savoy**, hero of the war of liberation against the Turks in the 17C.
The terrace offers a fine **view★** over the Danube and Pest including *(left to right)* Margaret Island, the Parliament building, Chain Bridge, the old town church, and Elizabeth Bridge. On the same bank as the castle rises Gellért Hill with the Liberation Monument.
In the 14C, the Hungarian king, Sigismund of Luxembourg erected his residence on the foundations of a small fortress. In the 15C, Matthias Corvinus, a highly-cultured man (see the King Matthias Fountain in the west courtyard, depicting the sovereign at a hunt), undertook major extension and refurbishment work. The castle then enjoyed some of its finest hours. It came under siege in 1686 during the war against the Turks and was badly damaged. In the 18C, it was rebuilt in the Classical then Baroque styles and was used as the residence for the representatives of the Habsburgs.

★★**Magyar Nemzeti Galéria (Hungarian National Gallery)** (AZ **M**[4])– This museum is devoted to Hungarian art with medieval sculpture, late Gothic altarpieces (former throne room) and above all, 19C and 20C paintings and sculptures. Artists represented include Mihály Munkácsy *(The Condemned Man's Last Day)*, Impressionists such as Pál Szinyei Merse *(Lunch on the Grass)* or Károly Ferencsy *(October)* and contemporary artists, notably Béla Kondor *(The Genius of the Flying Machine)*.

★**Budapesti Történeti Múzeum (Budapest History Museum)** (AZ **M**[2]) – The museum explains the development of the Hungarian capital from the Magyar period. In the maze of underground passages, an interesting section on the Middle Ages displays fine sculptures. The passage leads to the Gothic chapel.

BUDAPEST

Árpád Fejedelem útja .... AY 3
Erzsébet Híd .... AZ 9
Erzsébet Krt. .... BZ 10
Fehérvári út .... AZ 11
Ferenc Krt. .... BZ 14
Irinyi József u. .... AZ 27
Karinthy Frigyes út .... AZ 31
Karolina út .... AZ 32
Lajos u. .... AY 40
Moszkva Tér .... AZ 45
Nagyszölös u. .... AZ 47
Pacsirtamezö u. .... AY 52
Schönherz Zoltán u. .... AZ 61
Szabadság Híd .... AZ 62
Széchenyi Lánchíd .... AZ 64
Szentendrei út .... AY 65
Szt. István Krt. .... AY 67
Váci u. .... AZ 72
Vörösvári út .... AY 75

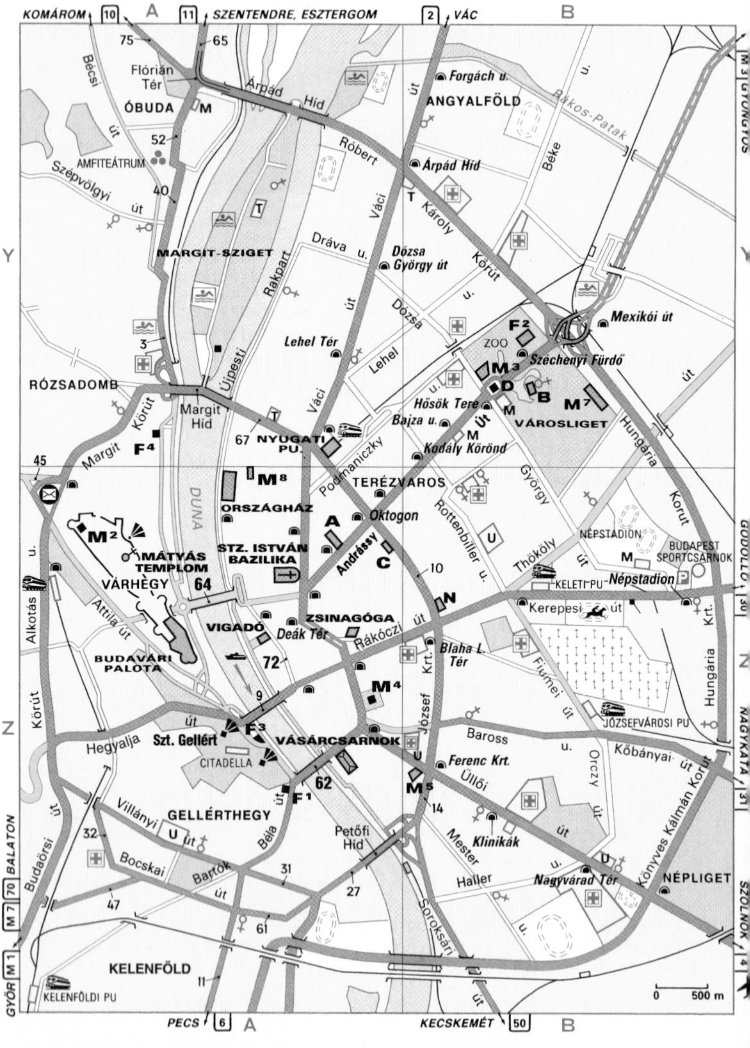

A Magyar Allami Operaház
B Vajdahunyad vára
C Liszt Ferenc Zeneművészeti Föiskola
D Millenniumi emlékmű
F[1] Gellért Gyógyfürdö
F[2] Széchenyi fürdö
F[3] Rudas fürdö
F[4] Király fürdö
M[2] Budapesti Történeti Múzeum
M[3] Szépművészeti Múzeum
M[4] Magyar Nemzeti Múzeum
M[5] Iparművészeti Múzeum
M[7] Magyar Közlekedési Múzeum
M[8] Néprajzi Múzeum
N Hungária Ettermek

★★ **Várhegy (Castle District)** (AZ) – Take time out for a stroll in this historic centre. In addition to charming streets lined with bright coloured houses and small interior courtyards, interesting historic buildings represent reminders of the town's past. In summer, horse-drawn carriages drive through the streets while the souvenir shops, cafés, restaurants and inns are filled with music, song and people.

Szentháromság tér (Holy Trinity Square) – A marble column in the centre commemorates victims of the 18C plague epidemic.
On the corner of Szentháromság utca, an austere white house has a lantern tower. This former town hall was built in the Baroque style by the Italian architect Ceresola. Beneath a loggia, a statue of the town's protector, Pallas Athena, bears Buda's coat of arms.

★★ **Mátyás templom (Matthias Church)** (AZ) – This Gothic church dates from the 13C. During Turkish rule, it was turned into a mosque. Its fine stone tracery and tiles glazed in different colours make it a unique building. The south doorway or St Mary's Door is decorated with a 14C bas-relief sculpture depicting the Dormition of the Virgin. Emperor Francis Joseph and his consort Elizabeth were crowned King and Queen of Hungary here in 1867.

A short step away is the **equestrian statue of Stephen I**, Hungary's first Catholic king.

Halászbástya (Fishermen's Bastion) – This unusual group of towers linked by a parapet wall overlooks the Danube. It resembles a medieval castle and Romanesque cloisters. Its name plays homage to the fishermen who, in the Middle Ages, defended this fortified part of the town. A superb **view**★★ overlooks the two riverbanks.

★★ **Picturesque streets** – Táncsis Mihály utca, Uri utca and Fortuna utca have retained splendid examples of medieval houses and Baroque mansions. The walls conceal a wealth of tales or historical facts.

►► Hilton Hotel is built on the remains of a Gothic church and cloisters. Magyar Kereskedelmi és Vendéglátóipari Múzeum (Hungarian Museum of Commerce and the Hotel Trade) has a display of early 20C Budapest's fashionable hotels, restaurants and cafés. Vienna Gate★ (where the market used to be held on Saturdays) bears a plaque commemorating the liberation of Buda in 1686 and is surrounded by some fine examples of old houses. Hadtörténeti Intézet és Múzeum★ (Military History Museum) has an exhibition of swords and knives, firearms, and weapons from the 1956 revolution.

Gellérthegy (Gellért Hill) (AZ) - *No 27 bus.* This dolomite hill was named after Bishop Gerald (Gellért), a much-loved figure in Hungary; he was martyred in 1046. Halfway up, in line with Elizabeth Bridge, stands a monumental statue of the saint in front of a 12-column peristyle. From the foot of the monument, a magnificent **view**★★★ overlooks the Danube and Pest plain.
The **Liberation Monument**, erected in 1947, stands on the top of the hill beside by A 19C Austrian citadel. The monument symbolises the liberation of Hungary. From the terrace, another splendid **view**★★★ of the town unfolds.

Budai-hegység (Buda Hills) – An interesting way to discover the hills of Buda, where lovely villas can be seen nestling in the foliage, is to take an excursion on the **Children's Train**★ (Gyermekvasú) or Pioneers' Train. First, take the rack train near the Hotel Budapest (a tall cylindrical tower in Szilágyi Erzsébet Fasor). The train's upper station is at the top of Mount Széchenyi. From there, it is an easy walk to the small Children's Train station. The ticket sellers and inspectors are boys and girls in uniform who salute each train as it arrives and leaves. The whole 12km/7mi trip is a very pleasant one running mainly through woods. The little train makes several stops, in particular at **Janós-hegy** Station, where a path leads to a viewing tower with a magnificent **panorama**★★.

►► Bartók Béla Emékház (Csalán út 29) – Béla Bartok lived in this house, now a museum and concert venue, from 1932 to 1940 before leaving for the United States.

PEST

This busy commercial part of the city swarms with cars and people. The area includes the offices of various official bodies, museums and the university.

Shops and souvenirs – Popular areas for shoppers or souvenir hunters include **Váci utca**★ (AZ **72**), a pedestrian street lined with fashion boutiques, indoor and pavement cafés, jewellers shops, bookstores, shops of every description and street vendors. Another prime shopping area, the **Párizsi udvar**★ (Paris Arcade), is also worth seeing for its architecture.
Váci utca leads to **Vörösmarty tér**, named after the writer Mihály Vörösmarty. A marble statue was erected in the centre in his honour. Portrait artists, musicians and souvenir sellers crowd the square. The famous cake shop and tearoom **Gerbeaud** is steeped in an air of late 19C nostalgia and elegance.

★**Vigadó (The Redoubt)** (AZ) – *Vigadó tér.* This fine example of 19C Hungarian Romanticism was originally designed as a venue for concerts. Franz Liszt played here. The façade overlooking the Danube is decorated with allegorical figures representing music and dance.
In the summer season, the square becomes a hive of activity with groups of musicians and souvenir sellers. The avenue lined with pavement cafés running alongside the Danube (formerly called *corso*) is a favourite place for a stroll and provides a fine view over Buda Castle and Chain Bridge. On warm summer days and evenings, crowds of strollers pass between rows of little wooden booths selling souvenirs and craft objects or, a little further on, lace and doll sellers.

★★★**Országház (Parliament Building)** (AZ) - *No 2 tram line from Vigadó tér.* The central part of this highly eclectic building stands on the banks of the Danube. It evokes the Houses of Parliament in London and symbolises the city. A combination of pinnacle turrets, arcades and flying buttresses make it look like a cathedral, topped with a central dome. The entrance in Kossuth Lajos tér is particularly impressive with its monumental staircase and two bronze lions. *Party tours only.*
On either side of the square, memorials have been erected to **Lajos Kossuth** and **Ferenc Rákóczi**. The latter was Prince of Hungary in 1705 and fervent defender of Hungarian independence. After the failure of his movement he was forced to seek exile in Turkey, where he died in 1735.

★★**Néprajzi Múzeum (Ethnography Museum)** (AZ **M**[8]) – Rural life is examined in the various regions of Hungary in the 19C and early 20C.

★**Szent István-Bazilika (St Stephen's Basilica)** (AZ) – This immense building with A 96m/315ft high dome is dedicated to the first king of Hungary, Stephen I, who was canonised in 1083.

★**Nyugati pályaudvar (West Station)** (AY) – A metal and glass construction built in the 1870s bears the unmistakable hallmark of Gustave Eiffel.

Andrássy út (ABYZ) – Andrássy Avenue was designed in 1872 by Miklós Ybl. It recalls the heyday of the old middle classes, stretching almost 3km/2mi. Trees, apartments, mansions and town houses line the avenue. At Heroes' Square, it crosses the City Park. Two roundabouts, the **oktogon** (an octagonal square formerly the 7 November Square) (AZ) and **Kodály körönd** (circular square) (BY), divide it into almost equal sections. Cutting below the avenue runs Europe's first subway line, the yellow line M[1]. King Francis Joseph II opened it in the late 19C. The **Subway Museum** (Földatti Vasúti Múzeum) is housed in a tunnel at Deák tér Station.

G. Durand/DIAF

Parliament Building

★**Magyar Allami Operaház (Opera House)** (AZ **A**) – The building designed by Miklos Ybl was inspired by the Vienna Opera House. On the main façade, a projecting loggia, forms a porch. A niche on either side contains statues of the great Hungarian composers, Ferenc Erkel (who composed the national anthem) *(left)* and Franz Liszt *(right)*. Statues of famous composers top the first floor balustrade. The luxurious interior contains a grand marble staircase and a foyer richly decorated with bronze statues, gilding and magnificent chandeliers.

★★ **Hősök tere** – *On foot, walk along Andrássy Avenue. By underground, take the M[1] yellow line in the direction of Mexikói út and get off at Hősök tere station.*
On the vast **Heroes' Square** skirting the City Park stands the **Millennium Monument**★ (Millénniumi emlékmu) (BY **D**). A 38m/125ft column crowned by the archangel Gabriel symbolising 1 000 years of Hungarian history. Around its base, a number of statues of horsemen represent Prince Aárpád accompanied by the chieftains of Magyar tribes. Soldiers in arms stand guard before the tomb of the unknown soldier. Behind the monument, two semicircular colonnades each bear seven famous historical figures and beneath each is a scene from that person's life. Included among these national heroes are St Stephen (Szent István), King Béla IV, King Matthias (Mátyás) and Ferenc Rákóczi *(see above)*.

★★ **Szépművészeti Múzeum (National Museum of Fine Arts)** (BY **M[3]**) – A remarkable drawing and print room contains works by Leonardo da Vinci, Veronese, Rembrandt, Rubens, Poussin and Picasso, but the old masters gallery is the museum's main showpiece. Its collections include Italian paintings with works by Gentile Bellini *(Portrait of Caterina Cornaro, Queen of Cyprus)*, Filippo Lippi *(St Jerome)*, and Giorgione *(Portrait of a Man)*, the Dutch School with works by Pieter Bruegel the Elder *(The Preaching of John the Baptist)*, Van Goyen *(Seascape with Fishermen)* and the Spanish School represented by El Greco, Velásquez and Goya.
The **Art Gallery** on the other side of the square houses temporary exhibitions.

★ **Városliget (City Park)** (BYZ) – *Metro: yellow line M[1], Széchenyi fürdö station.* On summer days, when the blazing sun becomes too hot to bear, Hungarians seek the shade of the trees or cool off by the lake. A zoo, circus and amusement park are situated nearby.

★ **Vajdahunyad vára** (BY **B**) – This castle, which combines different styles from the Romanesque to the Baroque, looks as though it has been made from children's building blocks or come straight out of a fairy tale.
Opposite the entrance, in the grounds, note the statue of a monk sitting on a bench with his hood covering his head and his face hidden. This fine bronze by the sculptor Miklos Ligeti is called *Anonymus*. It represents the anonymous 12C historian and author of Hungary's first chronicles.
Inside the Baroque part of the castle, the **Mezögazdasági Múzeum** (Farming Museum) contains interesting collections on livestock farming, forestry, fishing, hunting, work in the fields and wheat growing.

★★ **Magyar Nemzeti Múzeum (Hungarian National Museum)** (AZ **M[4]**) – A portico with eight Corinthian columns marks the entrance. The tympanum contains an allegory depicting Pannonia enthroned, surrounded by Science and Art. The museum is housed on three floors; it describes the country's history from Prehistoric times through the Roman Era, the Magyar conquest, the war of independence and the 1848 revolution. There is also a natural history section. The **crown jewels**★★ represent one of the museum's prize exhibits. They include the crown of the kings of Hungary encrusted with gemstones, enamels and pearls, the sword, the sceptre in the shape of a mace and the golden orb. The silk coronation robe embroidered in gold and silver thread is displayed in another glass case.

★ **Vásárcsarnok (Central Market)** (AZ) – The façade of the city's largest covered market is worth taking a look at, while the interior is characterised by its metal architecture. The fruit and vegetable stalls are a riot of colour. In the upper gallery running round the building, you can admire or even buy embroidered tablecloths, napkins and craft objects and try a glass of a local wine such as the celebrated Tokaj that Louis XIV called the king of wines and wine of kings.

►► **Iparművészeti Múzeum**★★ (BZ **M[5]**) – Housed in an Art Nouveau building, the Museum of Applied Arts contains a reconstruction of Hungarian and European interiors. **À Dohány utcai Zsinagóga**★★ (AZ) – The Great Synagogue has a Byzantine-Moorish flavour with very beautiful interior decoration. The Museum of Jewish Art is nearby. **Café New York**★ or **Hungária Ettermek**★ (Erzsébet Krt.) (BZ **N**) – This famous café and restaurant was the favourite haunt of writers and artists at the turn-of-the-century. Its Baroque interior is a riot of marble and gold. Liszt Ferenc Zeneművészeti Föiskola (AZ **C**) – **The hall**★ of the Franz Liszt Music Academy is worth a visit for its decoration. **Magyar Közlekedési Múzeum**★ (BY **M[7]**) – The Transport Museum recounts the history of road, rail, sea, and air transport with an interesting exhibition of old machinery. A special section on railways includes a Mohács-Pécs line coach dating from 1887. Liszt Ferenc Emlékmúzeum (Vörösmarty utca 35) – Franz (Ferenc) Liszt's apartment has been turned into a museum.

★MARGIT-SZIGET (MARGARET ISLAND) (AY)

Take no 2 or 2A tram from Vigadó tér to the terminus, then walk across Margit Hid (Margaret Bridge), or trams 4 or 6 which run along the Grand Boulevard and stop on Margit híd (Margaret Bridge).

A narrow-gauge railway runs around the island. Bike hire available.

This tiny green island stretches more than 2.5km/1.5mi. It serves as an ideal spot to relax and enjoy a number of leisure activities, away from the traffic. Walks, play areas, sports grounds, swimming pools, pump rooms and hotels have been laid out between the lawns, flower beds and trees, creating a recreation park.
The island was named after Béla IV's daughter. She lived in the Dominican convent, of which a few ruins remain.
At the island's entrance, a bronze monument soars towards the sky. The sculpture by István Kiss was unveiled in 1973 to commemorate Budapest's centenary.

CRUISES ON THE DANUBE

★**The city** – *Embark at Belgrad rakpart, between Vigadó tér and Elizabeth Bridge.* A number of companies organise Danube cruises by motor boat or waterbus during the day or in the evening. All offer recorded commentary in several languages. These trips *(1 hr-1 hr 30min)* represent an excellent way to take in the city's main sights, many of which are floodlit in the evening.

★★**The Danube Bend** – *Embark as above.*
Between Budapest and Esztergom, the Danube winds its way between the Pilis hills to the west and Börzsöm to the east. This cruise reveals the scenic landscape along the river banks and the charms of villages and towns such as Szentendre, Vác, Visegrád or Esztergom *(see below)*.

EXCURSIONS

★★**Szentendre** – *20km/12mi north on road no 11* (AY). *By train: take the HÉV line to Batthyany tér. By bus: departure from Engels tér. By boat: departure from Belgrad rakpart.*

This charming village lies on the right bank of the Danube. Its sloping narrow cobbled streets are lined with brightly-coloured houses. The main Fötér Square is decorated with a column bearing an 18C cast-iron cross. Many artists have lived here. Nowadays, the town attracts crowds of visitors.
In addition to a number of churches of different denominations (the Catholic Parish Church, Greek Orthodox Blagovestanska Church, and Serbian Orthodox Church of the Annunciation), Szentendre houses some noteworthy art museums. The Ferenczy Károly Museum shows works by the artist and members of his family. The Kmetty Museum concentrates on an artist from Szentendre. The Margit Kovács Museum displays ceramic sculptures inspired by Hungarian folklore. A number of art galleries are also located in the town.
A few miles from Szentendre in the direction of Skanzen is the **Hungarian Open-air Museum**★ *(Open 1 April to 31 October 9am to 5pm, except Mondays. Admission: 60 forints)*. A group of hamlets include farmhouses with their outbuildings, farm buildings, mills and churches. They recall rural life and traditional architecture from the 18C and 19C. The tastefully and elegantly furnished white Kisalföld houses reflect the high social standing of this fertile region in the northwest.

★**The Danube Bend** – *By car, leave Budapest by the left bank, then follow road no 11.*

★★**Szentendre** – *See above.*

Vác – The city's triumphal arch was built to mark Empress Maria Theresa of Austria's visit in 1764. Vác still has a number of Baroque buildings around March 15 Square.

Visegrád – The village has been coveted throughout the centuries owing to its strategic location. Situated in a picturesque setting on a bend in the river, it is now one of the Danube's top sightseeing attractions. The citadel perched on top of the hill was built after the Mongol invasions during the reign of King Béla IV. A tour of the ruins reveals some fine military architecture. A magnificent **view**★★ overlooks the Danube Bend.

Esztergom – The city is dominated by a huge basilica with a dome supported by a set of pillars. Esztergom was founded by the Magyars and for many years was the residence of Hungary's sovereigns. On the other side of the river lies Slovakia *(reached by ferry)*.

PÉCS★

Population 180 000
Michelin map 970 N 6

Pécs is situated in the south of Hungary in Transdanubia not far from the Croatian border. It is a town of major historical importance.
The Romans, probably attracted by its mild climate, fertile soil and geographical location protected by the Mecsek hills, settled here and founded Sopianae. In 1009, King Stephen ordered the country's first cathedral to be built here.
Pécs was the birthplace of two great artists, **Tivadar Csontváry Kosztka** (1853-1919) and **Victor Vasarely** (b 1908). *(Káptaclan utca 3)*. Both have museums dedicated to them containing a large selection of works (*Janus Pannonius utca 11* and *Káptalan utca 3* respectively).

★**Széchenyi tér** – Pécs' main square once held markets. It is lined with Baroque buildings as well as the town's largest historic building dating from the Turkish occupation. The former **Ghazi Kassim Pacha Mosque**★, topped with an oriental dome, is now a church and symbol of the town.

★**Dom St Peter** – St Peter's Cathedral is a Romanesque building with four towers; it stands majestically on the higher area of Dom tér (Cathedral Square). To the left is the bishop's palace. Inside, note the fine red marble Renaissance altar in the Corpus Christi Chapel.

The **catacombs** beneath the square in front of the cathedral are open to the public. To the west and north of Cathedral Square, a few stretches of the medieval town walls remain. They were built after the Mongol invasion. The **barbican**, a round stone-built bastion, has been turned into a pleasant place for a stroll.

Zsolnai Museum – Corner of Káptalan and Hunyadi u. The museum tells the story of the Zsolnay Porcelain Factory, opened in Pécs in 1851.

EXCURSIONS

Szigetvár – *36km/22mi west*. The fortress houses a museum recounting the siege of the town in 1566. For more than a month, 2500 men under the leadership of Miklós Zrínyi fiercely resisted the 100000 Turkish soldiers of Sultan Suleiman II.

Harkány – This famous spa contains the country's most sulphurous springs which gush at a temperature of more than 60°C/140°F.

On the cover of Michelin Green Guides, the coloured band on top indicates the language:
blue for French
pink for English
yellow for German
orange for Spanish
green for Italian, etc.

Iceland

Ísland

Area: 102 828km^2/39 701sq m – **Population:** 260 000 – **Capital:** Reykjavík – **Currency:** krona – **Time:** GMT

Iceland is the second largest island in Europe after Great Britain. Its geographical location near the Arctic Circle in the North Atlantic makes it Europe's northernmost island. The country is a geologist's paradise, with extraordinary volcanic activity. The last eruption, by the volcano Hekla, dates back to only 1991.
Iceland enjoys landscapes unlike anywhere else in the world. It boasts spectacular mountains, volcanoes, glaciers, hot springs, fjords, waterfalls, lakes and rugged coastlines, all weathered by the elements. Iceland's full splendour comes most alive in the summer when it never gets dark, even after nightfall.
Norway ruled the territory from 1262 to 1264. After 1380, the Danes dominated. Iceland became an independent republic on 17 June 1944. The president serves a four-year term. Vigdis Finnbogadottir, a woman, was elected Head of State in 1984, 1988 and 1992.

IN BRIEF

Entry Formalities – Valid passport for British, US, Canadian, Australian and Japanese citizens.

Souvenirs – Woollen sweaters and scarves are widely available. Smoked salmon, tinned fish and vodka also make good holiday souvenirs.

MÝVATN★★

The region east of Lake Mývatn has experienced major volcanic upheavals. In Hverfjall, one of the region's many craters, the first American astronauts underwent training. The lake stretches over 37km^2/14sq mi and is noted for its shallow waters. It was formed during the second Ice Age.

Skutustaóir – Enjoy a fine **view★** of the lake. The pseudo-craters dotted around it appeared 2 000 years ago. A myriad of colours and a wide variety of flora and fauna brighten the scenery.

Dimmuborgir – This veritable maze of volcanic formations dates back 2 500 years. Huge rocks take on weird shapes to form a strange eerie landscape. One of the few caves has become the Kirkjan Church.

Namafjall – East of Reykjahlid, the road runs past a diatomite plant and skirts an orange-yellow mountain with plumes of smoke rising from its fumaroles. At the foot of the mountain, the much-visited **Namarskad★★** is famed for its solfatara, potholes of boiling mud that spew out a mixture of clay and gas and give off clouds of sulphurous steam. As if by magic, the ground is turned into an artist's palette of colours, with ochre and grey-blue the dominant hues.

Viti – This route passes the geothermal plant which looks almost unreal with its shafts and tentacle-like pipelines running down the slopes.
The crater of the Viti volcano contains a lake of crystal clear water. In the distance stands the still active **Krafla** volcano.

REYKJAVÍK★

Population 87 000

Reykjavík is Iceland's biggest town, accounting with its outskirts for one-half of the island's population. The city is washed by the warm Gulf Stream. It was founded by the exiled Norseman, Ingólfur Amarson, who gave the town its name in AD 874 after seeing the clouds of steam billowing from the hot springs. The founder's statue stands on Arnahöll Hill. However, the town only began to flourish in the 18C under Danish sovereignty and the leadership of Skúli Magnússon.
Reykjavik covers a surprisingly large area. It is a fishing and commercial port and a university town. The university was founded in 1911. Yet the city still feels like a quiet, peaceful provincial town. There are no traffic jams, cars drive with dipped headlights even in summer and pedestrians enjoy wide leeway. Although the outskirts bristle with modern tower blocks, the centre has retained a touch of Scandinavian charm with low brightly coloured wooden houses.
In October 1986, Reykjavík jumped into world attention, hosting the East-West summit between the Soviet and American leaders Mikhaïl Gorbachev and Ronald Reagan. The meeting marked an important step in the ending of the Cold War. It was held in **Höfdhi House**. This white wooden single-storey house lies in Borgartun on the sea front.

Town Centre – The centre is busy during shopping hours but empties fast in the evening. In summer, tourists wander through the shopping streets in search of typical Icelandic goods and souvenirs such as the famous woollen sweaters. Sometimes they just enjoy browsing. At the weekend the streets again attract the crowds when trendy youngsters and older people alike come to enjoy an evening out and take advantage of the late closing times of pubs and cafés. On Friday and Saturday evenings, they are open until 3am.
The old town lies between **Lake Tjörnin** and the harbour. Take a stroll around the lake especially along the Tjarnargardar, the gardens. To the north of the lake stands the town hall, with the tourist information office. Its modern architecture contrasts sharply with the surrounding buildings.

Austurvöllur – This small square represents one of the town's busiest areas. In summer, tempting street cafés fill it. A statue of the national hero Jan Sigurdhsson, the defender of Icelandic independence, stands in the centre. The square is ringed by the Lutheran cathedral, the **Parliament building**, called the Althingi, built in 1881 of rusticated volcanic rock and decorated with coats of arms, and the high-class Borg Hotel which has hosted a great number of famous people.

Posthusstr leads into **Austurstræti**, one of the town's main shopping streets, with two successive roads off to the right, **Bankastræti** and **Laugavegur**. On the corner of Bankastraeti and Laekjargata is one of the town's oldest wooden houses, **Lækjarbrekka**. It now is a famous restaurant. On the other side overlooking Laekjargata is the white building of **Government House**, fronted by statues of King Christian IX of Denmark (1863-1906) and Hannes Hafstein, a poet who was also the first prime minister (1904-1905).

Hallsgrimskirka – Iceland's largest church dominates the town. Its 73m/240ft tower juts into the sky like water spurting from a geyser. The architect intended this unusual construction to symbolise the Icelandic landscape of columnar basalt and glaciers. The church was built in memory of the minister and great hymn writer Hallgrimur Pétursson (1614-1674). The interior is bare and austere. The pipes on the main organ rise to a height of 15m/49ft. This remarkable instrument consists of four keyboards and pedals, 72 stops and 5 275 pipes. From the top of the tower *(admission fee for lift)*, a magnificent **view**★★ unfolds of the town and the majestic Mount Esja to the northeast. To the south on Öskjuhlid Hill is an unusual construction known as **Pearlan** (The Pearl). It houses the town's hot water tanks beneath a glass dome and was created for architectural effect. Inside is a revolving restaurant. The platform offers a splendid **view**★★ of the town *(no 1 bus to the Loftleidir Hotel)*.
In front of the church stands a statue of Leifur Eriksson by Alexander Calder, a gift from the United States in honour of the first man to discover what was later to become known as the New World.

A Few Museums – The most famous is the **National Museum**★★ *(Sudurgata 41)*. It shows superb collections concerning the country's history, art and folklore. A remarkable 13C carved wooden door remains from Valthjofsstadur Church. In Frikirkjuvegur which skirts Lake Tjörnin, the **National Gallery**★ specialises in Icelandic modern art from 1930 to 1944. It includes portraits, landscapes, and historical subjects. The **Einar-Jonsson Museum** *(in Njardargata)* and **Asmundur-Sveinsson Museum** *(in Sigtun)* exhibit works by these two great sculptors, some of whose statues can be seen in the town. The **Municipal Art Gallery** *(in Miklatun)*, also known as the Kjarval Gallery after the artist Johannes Kjarval, houses a contemporary art collection. The **Arbaer Museum** *(no 10 bus departing from Hlemmur)* is an outdoor museum with a group of several wooden houses in a reconstruction of 19C and 20C Icelandic life. It exhibits a doctor's house, a middle-class home, rural houses, small church and old trades.
The Volcano Show *(Hellusundi 6 A)* consists of three films on the formation of Surtsey, the eruption on Heimaey and a general look at Iceland. It provides a good introduction to the country. The show lasts about 2hr 15min.

EXCURSIONS

Cars may be rented at the airport, hotels, and from agencies, but the condition of the roads come as something of a surprise since there is no tarmacadam. Only road no 1 which runs round the island is properly surfaced. For venturing far afield, hire a four-wheel drive such as a Subaru.
A number of travel agencies, with offices in hotels, organise excursions departing from the capital to the island's main beauty spots. The excursions vary in length and some may take the better part of a day especially if the journey is by plane.

★★★**The Golden Circle** – This name covers several of Iceland's most characteristic sights.

Skálholt – This major historic and religious landmark became the seat of the first bishopric in 1056. It soon evolved into an important intellectual centre. Iceland's last Catholic bishop was beheaded here in 1550, and a memorial marks the execution.

The tiny white church surrounded by well-kept lawns stands on a hill in the midst of desolate countryside. Visitors should see the stained-glass windows, and in the crypt, a tiny museum of sacred art. Concerts are held during the summer.

Geyser – Visitors are treated to one of the world's most astonishing natural phenomena. Several basins or craters contain boiling water whose liquid spurts up into the air at intervals. The **Strokkur** is the most typical geyser, discharging an impressive jet of water and steam about every 5min. In volcanic regions, underground water is heated to boiling point. The magma and gases then push it up through a vent to the surface where it cools before being violently expelled into the air under high pressure.

J.-C. Saturnin/MICHELIN

Geyser

Gulfoss – This splendid two-tier waterfall roars furiously down into a narrow ravine lined with columnar basalt. For a good overall view, take the flight of wooden steps from the car park. A footpath along the ravine allows visitors to approach the waterfalls.

Thingvellir – This spot, marked by an Icelandic flag, summarises Iceland's entire history. The first Icelandic Parliament, the Althing, met here in 930, and the Republic was proclaimed here on 17 June 1944. From a geological point of view, Thingvellir is of major importance because it reveals the **Almannagjá**, the fault separating the American and Eurasian continents. The fissure widens by 2cm/1in every year. A superb **view★★** is available from the vantage point above the Valhöll Hotel. The plain unfolds in a wonderful carpet of colour strewn with sheets of water and bordered in the distance by mountains, while the church and white houses below form a delightful, picturesque scene.

Blaa Lonid (The Blue Lagoon) – *40km/25mi southwest of Reykjavík. Follow the signs to Keflavík then Grindavík.* The plumes of steam that can be seen from a distance seemingly escaping from lava fields actually come from the Svartsengi geothermal plant which supplies hot water to central heating systems in the surrounding area. Nearby, a lake has been created so that people can swim at any time of the year. The blue-tinged water is salty, rich in minerals and hot, or very hot. This is a pleasant place to stop especially on cold or rainy days.

The SOUTH

The route from Reykjavík to Höfn offers scenery ranging from lush green fertile countryside where flocks of sheep and horses roam – the Icelandic horse is typically short with a thick mane – to austere bare landscapes with dark sinister expanses of wilderness.

Krísuvik – This fine example of hot springs gives off a pungent smell of sulphur. There are potholes of boiling mud and fumeroles set in a desolate landscape.

Skógar – This tiny village houses a **regional museum**, which exhibits fishing, old trades and the reconstruction of rural houses. A 60m/197ft waterfall is also located here, called **Skógafoss**.

★**Dyrhóley** – This site on the southernmost tip of Iceland can be reached by the unsurfaced road no 218. Its main feature is its sheer cliffs. On the other side of the lighthouse, the **view** encompasses a huge basalt arch which attracts large colonies of nesting seabirds. There is a long beach of black sand *(right)*.

Vík – The strange **Reynisdrangar** needles, thrashed by the waves, jut up from the ocean waters.

★★★**Jökulsárlón** – A visit to Iceland would not be complete without a boat trip on this glacial lake with its magical polar landscape. The boats sail between the icebergs which have broken away from the Vatnajökull Glacier. The icebergs take on ghostly shapes and changing colours, some appearing as iridescent blue and others shimmering black. A remarkable contrast exists between the long beach of black sand and the gigantic blocks of stranded ice.

★★★**Vatnajökull** – Europe's largest glacier covering an area of 8400km²/3243sq mi, is one of the island's most breathtaking landscapes. The road up to the chalet requires four-wheel drive vehicles. A trip over the glacier includes a impressive ride on a snowmobile. The views are remarkable: a few bare peaks rise above from this huge expanse of white and, weather permitting, the view extends as far as the Atlantic.
In autumn 1996, a huge volcano erupted from the glacier, destroying the natural environment of the whole area and cutting off the only route to the capital in the west of the island.

Höfn – A small fishing harbour.

VESTMANNAEYJAR★★

VESTMANN ISLANDS

The Vestmann Archipelago consists of a dozen islands, all formed as a result of volcanic eruptions which have occurred over the past 10000 years. The largest and only inhabited island is Heimaey. The youngest of them, **Surtsey**, emerged from the sea in 1963 after an underwater eruption. It covers an area of 2.5km²/1sq mi and rises to a height of 150m/492ft above sea level. A large number of geologists keep it under permanent observation.

Heimaey – *Access by car ferry from Thorlákshöfn (2hr 30min)* or by plane from Reykjavík – domestic flights airport *(20min)*.
In January 1973 a terrible volcanic eruption led to the evacuation of the eastern part of the island. The houses there were either burnt down or buried. In the months that followed, the inhabitants lived through a period of great anxiety.
However the fight against the wrath of the elements ended in victory for man. The lava flow which was even threatening to block the harbour entrance, was held back and stopped after thousands of tons of water were pumped over it from the sea. Bulldozers worked non-stop to erect barrages.

J.-C. Saturnin/MICHELIN

Heimaey

Heimaey was miraculously saved, although its appearance was strangely altered. Its area increased by $3km^2$/1sq mi and a new volcano, Eldfell, came into being. Steam still escapes from its slopes and the ground is still warm. A striking contrast exists between the new part of the island with its dark, sinister, apocalyptic landscape dominated by the eerie Eldfell and the rest of the island where the green, peaceful countryside lies in the shadow of the old dormant Helgafell volcano. Walking through this barren landscape with its extraordinary jumble of shapes and colours is an unforgettable experience.

Heimaey's economy is based on fishing. Its fleet moors in the well-sheltered harbour are surrounded by impressive steeply-sloping rocks. The boats supply a large share of the country's exports. There are fish processing plants near the harbour and a distinctive odour lingers in the air, enveloping the whole village.

In the village itself, rows of small white houses stretch as far as the solidified lava flow. Two museums are open to visitors, the **Local History Museum** near the town hall (fishing, puffin hunting, the 1973 volcano eruption) and the **Natural History Museum** in Heidarvegur (birds, aquarium).

A **boat trip★★** is a perfect way to complete a visit to Heimaey. The boat sails round the island and approaches the small neighbouring islands. Thousands of sea birds, mostly guillemots and puffins, come to nest on the sheer cliff faces or in the sea caves. The **puffin**, which is skilled in the art of diving and catching fish, is recognizable by its parrot beak. It is hunted for food using large nets attached to a long handle. Lengths of knotted rope hang down the sides of the cliffs. The boldest of the islanders, often children, hang onto the rope to get eggs out of the nests, practically a national sport.

D'après photo Baranger/JACANA

A puffin

Ireland

This land of legends offers dramatic scenery – towering cliffs and great sand beaches, soaring mountains, peat bogs and quiet lakes, forest parks and luxuriant gardens. Its many ruined castles are witness to a troubled past, interspersed with rebellions, particularly after the arrival of the Normans in the 12C. Ireland is also an art of living with its elegant Georgian terraces and cottage industries.
The island has been divided into two entities since 1921: the **Republic of Ireland** or Eire (whose emblem is the shamrock) and **Northern Ireland** or Ulster, which is part of the United Kingdom.

IN BRIEF

Entry Formalities – Valid passport.

Shopping – In the larger towns, the shops are open Mondays to Saturdays, 9am to 5.30pm, and 8pm on Thursdays. Shops also close earlier, or completely, on Mondays, Wednesdays or Thursdays.

Souvenirs – Tweed from Donegal, woollen sweaters from the Aran Islands, lace from Limerick and Carrickmacross, linen tablecloths and clothing, porcelain from Belleek, pottery from Arlow, glasses from Waterford, jewellery made out of peat and other handicrafts.

Pubs – The local drinking houses are warm and convivial, with a friendly welcome and boisterous conversation.
In the evening, the pubs become particularly animated and usually feature live musicians. They serve beer (thick, brown Guinness), Black Velvet (a cocktail of beer and champagne) whiskey (more than 13 types produced by two distilleries, Bushlills in County Antrim and Midleton in County Cork), and the world-famous **Irish Coffee** (a measure of whiskey, brown sugar and very hot black coffee, topped with a layer of fresh cream).

1 FINGAL **2** SOUTH DUBLIN **3** DUN LAOGHAIRE-RATHDOWN

REPUBLIC OF IRELAND

Michelin map 970 E4

Area: 70 282km²/27 136sq mi – **Population:** 3.6 million – **Capital:** Dublin – **Currency:** Irish Punt, and Euro (0,787564 IEP) – **Time:** GMT + 1hr in summer, GMT in winter.

Ireland

★★★CASHEL (CAISEAL MUMHAN) Michelin map 970 E 4

Visible from afar, the outcrop of limestone rises 61m/200ft from the Tipperary Plain. Striking ecclesiastical ruins top it.
The seat of the kings of Munster from 370 onwards, the Rock was visited by St Patrick in 450 when he baptised King Aengus. In 1101 the site was given to the ecclesiastical authorities. They consecrated Cormac Chapel in 1134 and founded the first cathedral 30 years later. However, the arrival of Henry II in Ireland marked the beginning of a long period of unrest: the cathedral was burnt down in 1494 by Gerald Mor, Great Earl of Kildare. The greatest act of desecration came in 1647, under Cromwell, when Lord Inchiquin set fire to the cathedral – the 3 000 people who had sought refuge within its walls perished.

Tour – At the site's entrance, the renovated Hall of the Vicars Choral, served as the clergy residence. The main room contains an enormous 17C stone fireplace and medieval-style furniture. The kitchen has been restored to its original state. The museum displays articles associated with the history of the Rock.

Cormac's Chapel★★, an ornate Romanesque style building flanked by twin towers, was built by MacCarthy, king and bishop of Cashel, in 1127. Almost every stone inside is adorned with carvings.
At the end of the cathedral's transept, the **round tower★** is made of irregularly-coursed sandstone. The upper floors were connected by ladders. It served as a bell-tower and as a place of safe keeping for treasures – the doorway is 3.50m/11.5ft from the ground.

★Cashel Palace Gardens – The **gardens** lead to the Rock of Cashel. They contain a mulberry tree from 1702. The hop plants are descendants of those used in 1759 to brew the first Guinness dark beer invented by Richard Guinis. His son Arthur founded the world-famous brewery in Dublin.

★GPA Bolton Library – The library houses an exceptional collection of 12 000 books, including an encyclopaedia dating from 1168, two leaves from Chaucer's *The Book of Fame* printed in 1483 and pieces of ecclesiastical silver.

►► **Caher Castle★★** *(66km/41.5mi southwest of Kilkenny)*, Ronald Reagan Centre in Balyporeen *(84km/52.5mi southwest of Kilkenny)* contains souvenirs of President Reagan's visit in 1984.

★★★CONNEMARA Michelin map 970 D 4

In northwest County Galway, Connemara is a wild region of mountains, lakes, bogs, moors and unspoilt beaches. **Cong★**, once the seat of the kings of Connaught, is where John Ford filmed *The Quiet Man* in 1951. It represents an excellent point of departure to explore this area where Gaelic is still spoken and numerous weavers, potters and jewellery makers still practise their craft.

D. H. Davison

Lough Inagh

In the middle of Connemara, the **Twelve Ben Mountain Chain** culminates in Benbaun at 728m/2 388ft. The region can be visited in a day. The many lakes and ponds will delight trout fishermen. A steep and narrow passage, **Sky Road★★★**, climbs along the cliffs north of Clifden. John D'Arcy, descendant of an Anglo-Norman family, founded this town in 1815. The road leads to **Pairc Naisiunta Chonamara★★** a 2 000ha/4 940 acre park, home to red deer and Connemara ponies. To the north, the **Benedictine Abbey of Kylemore** is housed in a neo-Gothic castle built around 1860 for Mitchell Henry and his wife Margaret Vaughan.
South of **Clifden**, Roundstone Bog runs along the very jagged coastline. In **Derryginlagh Bog**, Alcock and Brown landed after the first non-stop trans-Atlantic flight in 1919. Marconi established the first trans-Atlantic wireless telegraph station at **Ballyconneely. Cashel★** is an attractive little resort with excellent shooting and angling.

★★CORK (CORCAIGH) Population 127 253. Michelin map 970 E 4

A major commercial centre, this attractive city is easy to reach from holiday resorts such as Kinsale, Crosshaven and Cobh. The city is famed for Bishop George Berkeley (1684-1753) after whom the university and town of Berkeley in California were named. Irish emigrants set sail for America from Ballycotton, and Youghal. A few miles to the east, in **Midleton**, the Jameson whiskey **distillery** was established in the 1800s.
In the 12C Cork began exporting hides and cloth and importing wine from Bordeaux. In the 18C the city controlled its secular trade in butter with England, continental Europe and America, but this activity disappeared after the First World War. In 1917 the Ford car company set up its first overseas factory in Cork. Founder, Henry Ford (1863-1947) was born in the area, in Ballinascarty.
In the city centre, the main business street **Grand Parade★** contains some handsome late-18C buildings. **St Patrick's Street★** is also lively. To the south, **Cork Public Museum★★** is housed in a mansion in Fitzgerald Park. The exhibits trace life in the region since prehistoric times.
St Fin Barre's Cathedral★★ an Anglican church was designed in an early pointed French Gothic style in 1865 by William Burges.
To the north is Cork's most famous attraction, **Shandon Bells★**, a carillon of eight bells hung in 1752 in the church tower of St Anne's Anglican Church.

EXCURSIONS

★★ **Blarney Castle** – *7km/4.5mi to the north.* The castle consists of a 15C fortified tower. In the 16C the Earl of Leicester was commanded by Queen Elisabeth I to take the castle from the head of the McCarthy clan, but his mission failed and he sent back numerous progress reports which so irritated the Queen that she referred to them as all Blarney, now a popular expression. Alongside, **Blarney Castle House** demonstrates the Scottish baronial style. It dates from the end of the 19C.

★★ **Kinsale** – *25km/16mi to the south.* Kinsale, on the Bandon estuary, is a small, typical Irish village, with narrow lanes and slate-hung houses. Kinsale is known for its fine food, and holds a gourmet festival in October. It is also popular for its deep sea fishing and yachting. A room in the **regional museum★** is devoted to the torpedoing of the Lusitania, on 7 May 1915, which resulted in the death of 1 500 people and brought the United States into the First World War sooner than expected.

SLIDE FILE
High Cross

★DROGHEDA Population 23 848. Michelin map 970 E 4

This major port on the Boyne estuary benefits from the vast beaches of Bettystown and many historical places.

EXCURSIONS

★ **Monasterboice** – *13km/8mi to the north.* Three **high crosses** mark the site of a monastery founded by St Buithe (Boethius) in the 6C. The crosses are richly decorated. A shrine stands on the top. The carvings form historiated panels illustrating bible stories. The main New Testament themes described are the Crucifixion, Christ with St Peter and Paul, Doubting Thomas, the Arrest of Christ, the Resurrection and the Last Judgement; and from the Old Testament, the Fall of Man, Cain slaying Abel, Moses striking the Rock, the Golden Calf, the Sacrifice of Isaac, and David and Goliath.

★★★ **Newgrange** – *13km/8mi to the west.* Boyne Valley was a main thoroughfare in prehistoric times. In about 3000 BC, a community of farmers and herdsmen built one of the most beautiful examples of passage graves in Western Europe.
The mound, about 80m/260ft in diameter and 11m/36ft high consists of a cairn of medium-sized stones, enclosed within a circle of 97 kerb stones, some of which are decorated. Above the entrance, originally closed by a vertical slab, is the roof box, a unique structure with a finely decorated lintel. Rays of the rising sun penetrate to the inner chamber at the winter solstice on 21 December. The passage leads into a corbelled chamber which held the bones of the dead and funeral offerings.

★★★ DUBLIN (BAILE ATHA CLIATH) Population 525 822. Michelin map 970 E 4

Ireland's capital spreads out on either side of the River Liffey. Dublin has preserved its Neoclassical monuments and elegant Georgian terraces from a prosperous 18C, particularly around St Stephen's Green and Merrion Square. Alongside, though, are neighbourhoods of great poverty. A city of parks and museums, Dublin is the birthplace of now famous writers, such as Swift, Wilde, Shaw, Yeats, Synge, O'Casey and Joyce. Many have their own museum. Haendel gave the first performance of the *Messiah* here in 1742.
Dublin, home of the **Guinness Brewery**, is proud of having the oldest pub in the country – the Brazen Head in Bridge Street. Beer goes well with Dublin's culinary specialities such as coddle (pork and potato stew), Irish (mutton) stew and oysters. The visitor will enjoy shopping in Grafton Street and Temple Bar or wandering through the Moore Street Market.
Dublin is also famous for its greyhound racing at the Shelbourne Park and for the horse races at Harold's Cross racing tracks. The Kerrygold Dublin Horse Show in August is the main event.
After settlement by the Vikings in the 9C, and the Anglo-Norman invasion in the late 17C, Dublin was granted by Henri II to the port of Bristol as a trading post. The city became the seat of Parliament and the centre of government. In the 18C, relative peace and flourishing trade resulted in the construction of new buildings, development of the docks and the construction of bridges over the Liffey. During the Easter Uprising in 1916, columns of Volunteers marched into the town and took possession of various strong-points, including the General Post Office. They declared Ireland a republic.

★★ **Dublin Castle** – The castle represented British rule in Ireland for seven centuries until 1922. Built in 1204 on the orders of King John, the medieval fortress was modernised in the 16C as the vice-regal residence. In 1684, much of the medieval castle was destroyed by fire; most of the rooms go back to the 18C and contain Sheraton and Regency style furniture.

★★ **Christ Church Cathedral** – The building combines the Romanesque and early English Gothic styles. The seat of the Anglican bishop of Dublin was built of wood in 1038 and replaced by a stone construction soon after 1170. Until 1871, it was also the State church where the officers of the Crown were instituted.

The Board of TRINITY COLLEGE
Portrait of John in the Book of Kells

★★ **St Patrick's Cathedral** – The early English Gothic style cathedral was dedicated in 1254. The Lady Chapel was added about 1270; destroyed by fire in the 14C, and restored by the Guinness family during the last century. Inside, a bronze plaque indicates the tomb of **Jonathan Swift**, the dean of St Patrick's from 1713 to 1745; articles belonging to him are displayed in the north arm of the transept.
The arches along **St Patrick's Park** form a literary parade of Dublin-born writers, three of whom won a Nobel Prize for Literature: WB Yeats in 1923, GB Shaw in 1925 and Samuel Beckett in 1969.

★★★ **Trinity College** – Founded in 1592 by Elisabeth I, the college developed according to the tradition of the Oxford and Cambridge colleges. Since 1801, a copy of every book published in Ireland has been sent to the **Old Library★★★**, an austere 18C building designed by Thomas Burgh. The most precious manuscripts, produced in the scriptoria of Irish monasteries in the late 7C and early 8C, are displayed in the **Treasury★★★** Gallery. The illuminated manuscripts include the library's greatest treasure, the **Book of Kells**. Its meticulous ornamentation and full-page, somewhat abstract illuminations make it a true work of art.

★★ **National Museum** – The museum houses unique collections of antiquities and Irish historical material, including a 1C BC model boat in gold, the 8C Ardagh Chalice, various collections of glassware, ceramics, silverware and musical instruments.

★★ **National Gallery** – It contains European paintings, including works from the French (Chardin, Géricault, Sisley) and British schools (Reynolds and Yeats).

★★ **Merrion Square** – The square behind the museums was laid out in 1762. Commemorative plaques show that the houses were once the homes of famous people.

★★★ **Chester Beatty Library** – Southwest of the city centre. The library houses Islamic and Far Eastern works of art of outstanding quality, and precious prints by Dürer, Holbein and Piranesi.

►► **Rotunda Hospital Chapel★★** (Rococo decor) – **Hugh Lane Municipal Gallery of Art★** (19C and 20C works) – **Phoenix Park★★★** (zoo in attractive grounds) – **Guinness Museum★** (film and free glass of Guinness ale).

EXCURSIONS

★★ **Castletown House** – *17km/11mi to the south.* The house commissioned by William Connolly was the first Palladian mansion built in Ireland. The central block was designed by the Florentine architect Alessandro Galilei (1691-1737). The inside still has its original 18C decor and Rococo plasterwork.

★★ **Powerscourt** – *22km/14mi to the south.* The estate takes its name from Eustache Le Poer, a Norman knight. The gardens with their southern aspect are famous for their roses, flowering shrubs and eucalyptus trees. The 18C house, however, was destroyed by fire in 1974.

★★★ **Russborough** - *37km/23mi southwest.* This magnificent Palladian mansion, built at the foot of Wicklow mountains, was designed by Richard Cassels in the 1740s and 1750s. The drawing rooms are richly decorated with stuccoes by the Lafranchini brothers and the Beit Collection of paintings from the Dutch, Flemish and Spanish Schools.

★★★ **Tully** – *51km/32mi west.* Near Kildare, this little village in an extensive plain is the centre of horse breeding in Ireland. The **stud★★** founded by Lord Wavertree was handed over to the Irish government in 1943. A museum traces the history of horses, horse racing and steeple-chasing. The splendid **Japanese Gardens★★★** in the vicinity were created at the beginning of the century by the Japanese gardener Eida for the same Lord Wavertree, a wealthy Scotsman from a brewery family.

★★★ GLENDALOUGH (GLEANN DA LOCHA) Michelin map 970 E 4

At the foot of **Wicklow mountains**, this group of monastic ruins is one of the largest historical sites in Ireland.
St Kevin lived as a hermit in the 6C in this lake valley, but disciples joined him and forced him to found a monastery. This first abbot attracted thousands of students from Ireland, Brittany and throughout Europe. However, Danish Vikings plundered the abbey in the 9C and 10C; the monastery was then revived before its final destruction by the English forces in 1398. The site was restored in 1875 to 1876.

Tour – In the Visitor Centre, an audio-visual show retraces the monastic history of Ireland. Near the Lower Lake, ruins occupy most of the site – the **cathedral★★** consists of a nave and chancel. Like most Irish churches, it is relatively small, only 14.5/47.5ft x 9m/29.5ft. The 33m/108ft high **round tower★** was built in the 11C or 12C. The tower summoned the monks to prayer. It also provided a refuge, which is why the door is more than 3.50m/11.5ft above the ground. **St Kevin's★** has a stone barrel vault, a rare occurrence. **St Kevin's Cross★** is one of the site's best preserved. Other beautiful crosses, which originally marked the boundary of the monastic site, can be seen near the **Upper Lake★**.

★★ KILKENNY (CILL CHAINNIGH)

This county town, also an outstanding medieval city dominated by its castle and cathedral, owes its reputation to its pubs, its antique dealers, its bookshops and its Design Centre.
In the 2C Kilkenny became the capital of the Gaelic kingdom of Ossory. After the Anglo-Norman invasion, in the 12C, the city confirmed its strategic and political role – it became the seat of the Anglo-Irish Parliament, but after its defeat by Cromwell, in 1650, Kilkenny lost its political importance.

St Canice's Cathedral★★ was built in 13C, in the early English Gothic style. Inside, among the best-known tombs are those of the Earl of Ormond and Ossory, Piers Butler (d 1539) and his wife, Margaret Fitzgerald. A wooden staircase leads to the top of the round tower and a beautiful panoramic view.

The **castle★★** is on one of the most imposing sites on the River Nore. Built in about 1200, it was the home of the Butler family, the earls and then dukes of Ormond, until 1967. The neo-Gothic style galleries house collections of paintings and tapestries collected by the Butlers since the 16C, as well as a collection of 19C and 20C Irish art.

Smithwick's Brewery, founded in 1170, now belongs to the Guinness group. A video presentation, followed by a complimentary drink, describes the brewing process. In the grounds, the ruined tower and chancel of a Franciscan abbey were destroyed by Cromwell in 1650. The monks brewed a light ale as early as the 14C.

EXCURSIONS

★**Dunmore Cave** – *11km/7mil north.* The cave contains stalagmites and stalactites. Its sinister reputation stems from the Viking massacre of 1 000 people in 928.

★★**Jerpoint Abbey** – *19km/12mi south.* This 12C abbey, initially Benedictine, later became an annex of the Cistercian monastery of Baltinglass, near Carlow. The Romanesque church has the effigies of two bishops in the chancel and, on the north wall, the remains of a 15C to 16C wall painting showing heraldic shields. The cloisters from the 14C and 15C bear remarkable carvings of animals, saints and secular figures.

Kennedy Homestead – Near New Ross *(41km/26mi south)* in **Dunganstown**, is the birthplace of the great-grandfather of John F Kennedy, president of the United States from 1961 to 1963. Photographs and mementoes of Kennedy's visit to County Wexford are exhibited. An **arboretum★** 6.5km/4mi south, was inaugurated in 1968 in the President's memory.

★★KILLARNEY (CILL AIRNE) Michelin map 970 D 4

The village, destroyed during the Cromwellian wars, was laid out by Thomas Browne (1726-1795). The fourth viscount of Kenmare created a neat town of slated houses and shops. Today, Killarney is an ideal touring centre for the Ring of Kerry and Killarney National Park, reputed for its exceptionally beautiful lakes and two golf courses. In the evening, bands play and sing traditional tunes in many of the pubs.

Behind the cathedral, at **Knockreer Demesne★**, the park's flora and fauna are presented in the thatched cottage called Deenagh Lodge near the Lower Lake.

The **National Museum of Irish Transport** presents a collection of veteran cars, bicycles and motors.

EXCURSIONS

★★★**Iveragh Peninsula** – Leave Killarney in the direction of Kenmare where the road joins the coast.

Iveragh Peninsula, west of Killarney, and particularly the **Ring of Kerry★★★**, presents a succession of spectacular land and seascapes throughout the tour *(203km/126mi)*, which can be continued by a tour of Dingle Peninsula.

The attractive village of **Sneem★** has an Anglican church decorated with a salmon-shaped weathercock. **Staigue Fort★** is a drystone construction about 2 000 years old, reached by a narrow path.

The coast has beautiful beaches, particularly **Ballinskelligs**, and tiny creeks. The **Derrynane National Historic Park★★** was the property of Daniel O'Connell (1775-1847), the Great Liberator of the Irish people.

The little resort of **Waterville** once had a famous guest, Charlie Chaplin. His photographs are exhibited at the Butler Arms Hotel.

Opposite Portmagee, a bridge leads to **Valencia Island**, where an audio-visual presentation in the Visitor Centre describes the life of the first Irish Christians, the history of the lighthouse, and the flora and fauna of the Skellig Islands.

After **Lough Caragh★** Lake, the road to Killarney passes through Killorglin, a village famous for its Puck Fair in early August.

★**Muckross Abbey** – *6.5km/4mi south.* The Franciscan abbey of Muckross goes back to the 15C. In the choir, the tombs of abbots and Gaelic poets can still be seen. Further along the same path, **Muckross House★★** is an Elizabethan-style mansion built about 1840. The beautiful gardens are planted with azaleas and rhododendrons, extending down to the lakeside. Traditional regional crafts are recalled in working displays. On the first floor, dolls from the end of the last century are housed in the nursery. The path continues on to **Torc Waterfall★★** (18m/60ft high) and **Ladies View★★**.

★LIMERICK (LUIMNEACH) Population 76 557. Michelin map 970 E 4

Set astride the River Shannon, Limerick still has a historic centre, the English town, with many examples of medieval architecture. The 18C Irish town lies on the south bank. During the last century, Limerick flourished as a result of bacon curing and grain milling. After heavy emigration, it took off again with the opening of Shannon Airport and the arrival of new industries such as computer manufacturing and electronic engineering. After the Battle of the Boyne on 12 July 1690 between the Catholic army of James II and the Protestant troops of William III of Orange, the Irish army retreated to Limerick and surrendered. The Treaty of Limerick guaranteed Catholic religious rights and land. In the early 20C, the town and its county provided three leaders for the 1916 Easter Rising, including the future president of the Republic, Eamon de Valera (1882-1975).

Limerick Museum★★ depicts the history of the city. It has the brass-topped limestone Nail from the Old Exchange on which commercial transactions were settled. Paying on the nail was a common feature of English trading centres. An extensive collection of silverware and lace recalls the city's traditional crafts.

The **Limerick City Gallery of Art** houses a collection of leading Irish painters, including Sean Keating, Jack B Yeats and Evie Hone.

►► Bunratty Castle *(14.5km/9mi northeast)* – Foynes Flying Boat Museum *(37.5km/23.5mi west)* served as an operational base for flying boats: the museum retraces the conquest of the Atlantic Ocean.

NORTHERN IRELAND

Area: 14 153km²/5 462sq mi – **Population:** 1.4 million – **Regional capital:** Belfast – **Currency:** Pound Sterling – **Time:** GMT + 1hr in summer, GMT in winter.

★★★ANTRIM GLENS

North of Belfast, the coast offers a wide variety of scenery and a sense of expectancy at each approaching headland.
From Larne to Ballycastle *(110km/70mi)*, several sights are worth visiting, including:

Glenarm Village – This attractive village of glens is set in a narrow valley created by tumbling mountain streams.

Carnlough – Its large sandy bay makes it an attractive resort.

★★**Glenariff Forest Park** – The forest contains a superb waterfall known as Ess na Larach (1hr on foot from the car park).

★★★**Murlough Bay** – This beautiful bay on the Antrim coast is sheltered from the wind at the foot of steep and towering cliffs. One of its many waymarked paths leads from the upper car park to Fair Head which provides wide views of Rathlin Island and the Mull of Kintyre.

Bonamargy Friary – The ruins of this Franciscan friary are now in the middle of Ballycastle Golf Course. The church was once lit by an impressive east window.

Ballycastle – At the foot of Knocklayd Mountain, Ballycastle is a holiday resort with an admirable view of the bay. In August, Ould Lammas Fair combines livestock sales with street stalls selling sweet meats such as yellowman, a sort of toffee, and dulse, a dried edible seaweed.

★BELFAST Population 329 958. Michelin map 970 F 3

The regional capital of Northern Ireland since 1920, Belfast owes its rapid expansion in the 18C and 19C to the textile, engineering and shipbuilding industries. Today it is still an important shopping centre for linen and woollen goods, glassware and pottery.
The town has a lively cultural life, with four theatres, an Arts Festival each November, and an opera season. Owing to the predominance of the Presbyterian Church and its cultural links with Scotland it was a centre of intense intellectual activity and dissidence.
Belfast takes its name from the ford by the sandbank (*bealfeirste* in Irish) on which John de Courcy built a castle when he invaded Ulster in 1177. The castle was destroyed by Edward Bruce in 1315 and the town was held by the O'Neill clan until their possessions were forfeited in 1603. Belfast then passed to Sir Arthur Chichester and remained in the family until his descendant, the Marquis of Donegall, went bankrupt in the 1840s. The development of the port began in the 17C. Shipbuilding is still a significant element of the local economy. The linen industry benefited from the new methods introduced by French Huguenot refugees. It grew steadily in importance, along with cotton spinning.

In the university district, the **Ulster Museum★★** houses a collection of British and continental painting before 1900, including works by Turner, Reynolds and Stubbs. Irish furniture and objets d'art, glassware, ceramics, jewellery and costumes, are also presented. In the Antiquities section artefacts, extracted from archeological sites are exhibited, including the **Spanish Armada Treasure★★**. This extraordinary fleet, arrived from Spain in 1588 with some 130 vessels and nearly 30 000 men to dethrone Elisabeth I. It was wrecked off the coast between Antrim and Kerry. A gallery displays various species of dinosaurs and fossil formations.
In the **Botanic Gardens, Palm House★** is a beautiful cast-iron and curvilinear glass structure designed by Charles Lanyon and built by Richard Turner in 1840, who jointly collaborated on the construction of the Great Palm House at Kew.

City Centre

★**City Hall** – The city hall was built in the late 18C out of Portland stone by Brumwell Thomas in the Renaissance style. It has a a great copper-covered dome capped by a stone lantern. Inside, the decor, enriched with Greek and Italian marble, depicts the history of the Belfast Corporation.

★**Donegall Square** – This vast rectangle of grass and flower beds is the hub of the city. It stands on the edge of the pedestrian shopping precinct. In the gardens, a group commemorates the Titanic, which was built in Belfast by Harland and Wolff and sank after colliding with an iceberg on her maiden voyage in 1912.

★**Crown Liquor Saloon** – The Victorian interior is richly decorated with coloured glass and brightly coloured and moulded tiles, reflected in the arcaded mirrors. Patrick Flanagan built the public house as a railway hotel in 1885.

★**St Anne's Cathedral** – Belfast's Anglican cathedral is built of white stone on the basilical plan in an adapted Romanesque style designed by Sir Thomas Drew and Sir Charles Nicolson.

★**Sinclair Seamen's Church** – Located near the docks, this church is reserved for Belfast's maritime community. The tower containing the stairs to the gallery is linked to the church by a half bridge resembling the Bridge of Sighs in Venice. All the furniture is inspired by ships: model life-boats instead of pole boxes, reading desk shaped like the prow of a ship, pulpit and organ adorned with port and starboard lights.

EXCURSIONS

★★**Carrickefergus Castle** – *15km/9.5mi northeast.* It is the largest and best preserved Norman castle in Ireland. Built at the end of the 12C by the Anglo-Norman Jean de Courcy on a basalt promontory, it was extended twice in the 13C. The oldest part consists of a keep which provided living accommodation for the lord of the castle. Medieval banquets are held in this beautiful example of defensive architecture.

Boneybefore is the site of the Jackson family's homestead. The **American Connection** traces the Ulster-American connection, in particular the life of Andrew Jackson, who was elected seventh President of the USA in 1829 and served two terms of office.

★★CAUSEWAY COAST

Go west along the north coast from Balleycastle. It begins as dramatic cliffs and ends in a long sand dune extending into Lough Foyle. In between, superb sites await the visitor: the Giant's Causeway *(see below)*, seaside resorts and sandy beaches at Portballintrae, Portstewart and Castlerock.

★★★**Carrick-a-rede Rope Bridge** – Near Barry Lane Bay, the 20m/66ft long rope bridge can be crossed by foot (not recommended during strong winds). The water lies 25m/80ft below. The rope bridge is put up every spring for the fishermen who operate the island salmon fishery.

★★**Dunluce Castle** – The jagged silhouette of the ruins of Dunluce Castle rises from the cliff edge above the sea for 30m/100ft. The Scottish MacDonnells captured it from the MacQuillans in the 16C. The building was badly damaged by the English Lord Deputy, but repaired and strengthened by James MacDonnell. The lower yard offers a superb view of the Giant's Causeway.

★**Downhill** – The buildings on the cliff top at Downhill were erected by Frederick Harvey, Bishop of Derry. On the edge of cliffs, the Classical rotunda was based on the Temple of Vesta at Tivoli. It was built in 1785. The castle was designed in 1772 by Michael Shanahan to house the large collection of sculpture and paintings which the Bishop had collected during his travels on the Continent. Most of the art collection was destroyed in a fire in 1851.

★★★GIANT'S CAUSEWAY Michelin map No 970 E 3

The **Giant's Causeway** is the most spectacular of a series of similar geological features to be found all along the North Antrim coast. They were caused by a volcanic eruption which took place some 60 million years ago and affected not only Northeast Ireland but also Western Scotland, the Faroes, Iceland and Greenland. Several flows of lava flowed from fissures in the chalk and solidified into layers of hard basalt. As they contracted, they formed masses of adjoining columns; the majority are hexagonal in shape although some have four, five, seven, eight and even nine sides. *(Sturdy shoes are required)*.

The **Visitors' Centre** contains a restaurant, a shop, an excellent video, and an exhibition about the Causeway Coast: geological formation, flora and fauna, mining and kelping.

The **Causeway** proper extends from the foot of the cliffs into the sea like a sloping pavement. It consists of about 40000 prism-like columns, split horizontally, forming concave and convex surfaces. According to legend, the giant Finn McCool built it so that the Scottish giant could accept his invitation to Ireland for a trial of strength. When the latter returned home defeated, the causeway sank beneath the sea.

The headland, Aird Snout, provides an excellent view of the causeway. The walk to Benbane Head includes many of the different volcanic formations.

The Giant's Causeway painted *c*1740 by Susanna Drury

SPERRIN MOUNTAINS

A region of moorland and forests, these mountains are an angler's paradise. The highest point is Sawel Mountain, rising to 678m/2224ft.

In the 17C, some of the area was granted to the London city livery companies – drapers, skinners, grocers and fishmongers. They brought in new settlers, mainly from Scotland. In the 19C, model farms were established to promote modern methods. Roads and bridges, churches, schools and dispensaries were built.

★★**Ulster-American Folk Park** – The theme of the park is the 18C emigration to America of 250000 Ulster Scots – known in the USA as Scotch Irish. The Mellon family of Pittsburg, Pennsylvania, who come from the area, helped with the finance. The **Outdoor Exhibition** contains a replica of part of an emigration ship. The New World section shows the way of life the emigrants adopted on their arrival in America. A Conestoga Wagon is a sort of covered wagon in which the pioneers trekked into the Wild West. In the workshops and cottages, local people in period costume demonstrate the old crafts.

Wilson Ancestral Home, Dergalt – In Dergalt, the home of James Wilson, Woodrow Wilson's grandfather (US president from 1913 to 1921) is open to visitors. The thatched cottage contains some of the original furniture.

Strabane – In the 18C, the town of Strabane was a lively centre of printing. Two apprentices from the area gained fame in the US. John Dunlap (1747-1812) printed the US Declaration of Independence in his newspaper, the **Pennsylvania Packet**, and James Wilson became editor of a Philadelphian newspaper.

For further details on Ireland, consult the Michelin Green Guide Ireland.
When looking for a hotel or restaurant, use the Michelin Red Guide Ireland, updated annually.

Italy

Area: 301 262km²/117 492sq mi – **Population:** 57 460 977 inhabitants – **Capital:** Roma (Rome) – **Currency:** Italian lira and Euro (1936.27 ITL) – **Time:** GMT + 1hr in winter, GMT + 2hr in summer.

Italia

The charm of Italy is such that most visitors fall in love with it at first sight. It stretches over 1 300km/808mi from north to south, its familiar boot-shape wading into the Mediterranean sea. Added to its extraordinary variety of climates and landscapes is a unique architectural heritage reflecting centuries of history in the course of which the Etruscans, Ancient Romans, Popes and artists of the Renaissance endowed Italy with an enduring, infinitely rich heritage. Rome, Venice and Florence dazzle the visitor with a thousand splendours, while humbler towns disclose a modern, beautiful Italy exuding a welcoming tranquillity. Those who love art, the sea and the mountains will be eager to return. Italy is also a gourmet's paradise with its wide choice of delicious regional specialities, accompanied by exquisite wines such as the famous Chianti.

IN BRIEF

Entry formalities – Valid passport for British, Irish, US, Canadian, Australian and Japanese citizens.

Sightseeing by car – In Italy, tourist sights are indicated by road signs with a yellow background.

Shopping – In the centre of large towns, shops usually remain open during lunchtime. Others are generally open between 9am and noon and between 3.30pm and 7.30pm. In seaside resorts, many shops do not close until late in the evening.

Good buys – The reputation of Italian shoes and leather articles needs hardly be repeated here. Apart from the well-known names, it is worth trying out the smaller shops in town centres, which offer a wide range of items at bargain prices. There is a wide range of high quality regional handicrafts: glassware and embroidery from Venice, ceramics from Tuscany and Umbria, traditional Christmas crib figures from Naples... and excellent locally produced foodstuffs.

Pasta – The most common are: **cannelloni**, large rolls stuffed with minced meat (ground meat), cheese or spinach; **farfalle**, in the shape of butterflies; **fettuccine**, the Roman version of tagliatelle, but slightly narrower; **fusilli**, twisted into small spirals; **lasagne**, large sheets of pasta baked in alternating layers of minced meat and tomato sauce, and topped with Parmesan cheese; **maccheroni**, shaped into narrow tubes; **ravioli**, small envelopes filled with minced meat or spinach; long thin **spaghetti**, the great classic; **tagliatelle**, long narrow ribbons; **tortellini**, tiny pasta triangles rolled into rings, filled with minced meat or cheese and served in a clear broth.

G. del Magro/SIPA PRESS

Ice creams – **Gelati**, Italy's world-famous ice creams and sherbets, are part of the pleasures of vacations. Among the lesser known flavours outside the country are **stracciatella**, an ice cream streaked with chocolate chips; **gianduia**, named after the small oblong hazelnut milk chocolates from Turin; **bacio** is a milk chocolate and hazelnut ice cream; **fior di latte** (or the similar *fior di panna*), an ice cream made with full cream, and last but not least **cassata**, garnished with candied fruit, and **crema**, a yellow vanilla-flavoured ice cream.

Coffee – Coffee, the great Italian favourite, is drunk at all times. The most common is **espresso**, a very strong coffee barely covering the bottom of the cup. If this is too strong, there is the weaker, watered down **caffé lungo**. **Caffé corretto** is coffee which has been corrected with brandy or some other spirit. A **caffé latte** is coffee with hot milk, while a **macchiato** is merely stained with a drop of milk and served in a small cup. **Cappuccino** is topped with milk which is frothy and sprinkled with cocoa to taste. As a general rule, in bars you first pay at the cashier's where you are given a receipt, and then go to the counter to place your order with the barman who does not handle money.

Telephones – Telecom is responsible for telephone communications. Telephone booths are available in its agencies where you can pay for your call at a cashier's. There are also public telephone booths operated by cash or cards (cards of 5 000 to 10 000 lire may be obtained from Telecom agencies or tobacconists displaying a white T sign on a black background). Before using a telephone card for the first time, tear off the corner as indicated.

The ALPS and DOLOMITES

The Alps sweep across the north of Italy, from the French and Swiss borders up to Austria. These mountains offer scenic attractions and numerous possibilities for walks in natural parks (Gran Paradiso, Stelvio, Dolomites) or skiing and mountaineering at Sestriere, Courmayeur, Breuil-Cervinia, Bormio, Madonna di Campiglio and Cortina d'Ampezzo.
To the west, the **Valle d'Aosta** is dominated by the towering peaks of the French and Swiss Alps: Mont-Blanc, Matterhorn, Monte Rosa, Gran Paradiso... The protected nature of secluded valleys, the castles in the central valley (Sarre, Fénis, Verrès), the village houses with their typical flat-stoned roofs and wooden balconies, the traditional lifestyle which still lingers on, the breathtaking routes leading to the foot of glaciers have transformed the Aosta Valley into an enchanting land.
To the east, *Trentino-Alto-Adige* has inherited a language and culture that is partially Germanic. It consists mainly of the deeply embedded Adige Valley, basking in frequent sunshine at the opening of the Brenner, and the limestone Dolomite massif with its jagged outline sculpted by erosion and sparkling with a kaleidoscope of colours that change with the light. Here, the traveller will find very good roads, clearly marked paths, dramatic views and excellent hotel accommodation.

★AOSTA Population 33 184. Michelin map 970 J 6

The old city still has the geometric plan of a Roman castrum (military camp) and a few monuments going back to the time of Emperor Augustus (gateway, arch, bridge and theatre). After the Mont-Blanc tunnel was completed in 1965, it became an important crossroads leading to the Grand St Bernard Pass and to Switzerland.

★★**Gran Paradiso National Park** – This park spreads over 70 000ha/270sq mi and is the refuge of the last European ibex. It is also home to other wild animals such as the chamois, marmot and ermine, as well as rare birds, including the royal eagle. The Gran Paradiso range is a patchwork of glaciers, gigantic peaks, waterfalls and pine woods. Its most beautiful valleys are undoubtedly the Val di Cogne and Valsavarenche.

★★★THE DOLOMITES (DOLIMITI) Michelin map 970 K 6

The massif is formed mainly of limestone rocks named Dolomites after the French geologist Dolomieu who was the first to study their formation at the end of the 18C.

From Bolzano to Cortina – *210km/131mi, allow 2 days.* The road, an engineering masterpiece, follows the central depression of the massif and winds its way through varied and majestic landscapes. It was used as far back as the Renaissance by merchants travelling from Venice to Germany. Below are some of the major sites.

★**Bolzano** – The urban architecture of the capital of Alto Adige, on the Brenner transalpine route, still shows traces of the Tyrolean and Austrian influences prevalent between the 16C and 1918.

★★**Canazei** – This is the starting point for excursions and challenging climbs in the **Marmolada**★★★ mountains; the highest point of the massif reaches 3 342m/10 965ft.

★★★**Val Gardena** – This northern valley owes its reputation to its spectacular scenery and excellent winter sports facilities. The slopes are covered with forests, waterfalls and typical mountain chalets. The valley's inhabitants are highly skilled wood craftsmen.

★★★**Passo Pordoi** – The Pordoi Pass, at an altitude of 2 239m/7 346ft, is the highest pass in the Dolomites, an impressive site cutting through enormous sheer rock-faces and truncated pinnacles.

★★★**Cortina d'Ampezzo** – Cortina, capital of the Dolomites and 1956 Olympic village, occupies a stunning setting at an altitude of 1 210m/3 970ft in the heart of the massif. It is an elegant and well-equipped ski resort and also an ideal starting point for mountain treks.

BOLOGNA and EMILIA ROMAGNA

The plain bordering the Apennines derives its name from the Via Emilia, an old Roman road which crosses it from Rimini to Piacenza; to the south and east, this plain is called Romagna. Its soil is considered to be the best in Italy for growing wheat and beet. Many interesting towns are to be found along this historical road: **Bologna** of gastronomic fame; **Ferrara** in the Comacchio valleys, a region dotted with lagoons from which eels are fished; **Ravenna**, the ancient capital of the Western Roman Empire, which has come to life again thanks to its port and oil refinery; **Rimini**, a seaside resort with a sweeping beach of fine sand.

This region is home to some of Italy's great gastronomic specialities: *prosciutto di Parma* (ham), *salami* and *mortadella* (a spicy pork sausage from Bologna); *spaghetti Alla Bolognese* with meat and tomato sauce; and Parmesan, a sharp yet delicate cheese. Emilia also produces Lambrusco, a sparkling and fruity red wine.

★★BOLOGNA Population 403 397. Michelin map 970 K 7

Located in the extreme south of the Po Plain, the regional capital of Emilia-Romagna is not only an elegant and intellectual town but also a thriving industrial and commercial centre hosting numerous international trade fairs and exhibitions. Since the town follows the rhythm of academic life, it can give the impression of being almost deserted in July and August.

Led by an independent communal government in the Middle Ages, the town expanded in the 13C, adding ramparts and towers for protection, palaces and churches for prestige. Its fame spread largely due to its university, one of the oldest in Europe. In the 15C, at the end of violent struggles among rival families, Bologna fell into the hands of the Bentivoglio who in turn were overthrown by Pope Julius II. It remained under papal authority until the arrival of Napoleon.

★★★**The historical centre** – Two adjacent squares form the heart of the town: **Piazza Maggiore** and **Piazza del Nettuno**★★★. The latter is enhanced by the **Neptune fountain**★★, the work of a Flemish sculptor, Giovanni da Bologna or Giambologna (16C). This double square contains several noteworthy monuments:

The **Palazzo Comunale**★ (town hall) features an interesting 16C portal surmounted by a statue of Pope Gregory XIII, inventor of the Gregorian calendar (1582). At the end of the courtyard, a superb flight of steps (once climbed on horseback) leads to the richly decorated rooms displaying the city's collections.

The **Palazzo del Podestà**★ (Governor's Palace), with its Renaissance façade, stands next to **King Enzo's Palace** which was built in the 13C. This has a beautiful inner courtyard and magnificent staircase.

On the other side of the square is the **Basilica of San Petronio**★★ (St Petronius). Although work on it began as early as 1390, it was only roofed in the 17C. The central **portal**★★ is the masterpiece of the Sienese sculptor Jacopo della Quercia (15C). The vast interior contains frescoes by Giovanni da Modena, a Madonna by Lorenzo Costa, and one of the oldest organs in Italy (15C).

★★**Leaning Towers** – Dominating the Piazza di Porta Ravegnana are two towers, the remaining symbols of medieval rivalries between the Guelphs (who were partisans of the city's independence) and the Ghibellines (who supported the Emperor). The top of the **Torre degli Asinelli**, which dates back to 1109 and stands nearly 100m/328ft high, affords a beautiful **view**★★. The shorter **Torre Garisenda** is 50m/164ft high and has a tilt of over 3m/10ft.

★★**Pinacoteca Nazionale** – The National Picture Gallery in Via Zamboni houses a rich collection from the Bologna School of miniaturists which flourished from the 13C onwards (illuminated manuscripts proliferated under the impetus of Bologna University). In the 17C, the Carracci founded a painting academy. Their pure tones and vigorous decorative schemes exerted a strong influence over other artists and heralded Baroque art. They had many talented disciples, including Albani, Guercino, Domenichino and Guido Reni who often worked together as a team.

►► **Museo Civico Archeologico**★★ (Municipal Archeological Museum)

★★FERRARA Population 143 736. Michelin map 970 K 7

From 1208 to 1598, the Este Dukes, despite their bloody feuds, commissioned many elegant buildings for the town and were patrons of artists such as Ariosto and Tasso, the two greatest writers of the Italian Renaissance. From this period, the town still has its rectilinear streets lined with red-brick houses, austere palaces and the vast empty squares which inspired the painter De Chirico.

Town centre – In the heart of the town, not far from the **cathedral**★★ built in the Lombard Romanesque-Gothic style with a magnificent marble façade (12C to 16C), stands the **Schifanoia Palace**★ (the carefree palace), where the Este family resided when in Ferrara. The room of the Months contains **frescoes**★★ painted by artists of the Ferrara School (15C). Next to it is the **Castello Estensea** (Este Castle), an imposing edifice surrounded by moats and protected by four fortified gates with drawbridges. On the Corso Ercole I d'Este stands the **Palazzo dei Diamanti★★** (Palace of Diamonds) which takes its name from the 12500 diamond-shaped marble blocks covering it. This building houses the **Pinacoteca Nazionale★** (National Picture Gallery) exhibiting collections of works by Costa, Cosimo Tura, Dosso Dossi and Garofalo, fine examples of the pronouncedly realistic style so typical of the Ferrara School.

★★★RAVENNA Population 135 807. Michelin map 970 L 7

The heart of this town, on the Adriatic, retains the sober architecture and precious treasures accumulated during the period when it was the capital of the Western Roman Empire (404-476), and then seat of the Exarchate of Byzantium (584-751).

★★★The Mosaics – Covering the walls of ecclesiastical buildings they are considered to be the most impressive in Europe because of their brilliant colours, opulent decor and powerful symbolism expressing a profound spirituality.

The **Tomb of Placidia Galla★★★** (5C) takes the form of a small building entirely covered with mosaics on a dark blue background. Above the door can be seen the Good Shepherd seated among His flock in an idyllic landscape. The southern lunette depicts St Lawrence carrying the cross on his way to the grille on which he was martyred by being roasted alive.

Nearby, **San Vitale★★** (St Vitalis Church), consecrated in 547, features a rich decor of precious marbles, carved capitals, frescoes and brilliant **mosaics.** On the vault of the apse note **Christ the King** between St Vitalis and Bishop Ecclesius, founder of the church. The choir is decorated with scenes illustrating the Old Testament, while on the side walls of the church, two processional panels depicting Theodora and Justinian, accompanied by the clergy and court dignitaries, stand out as genuine portraits.

GIRAUDON

Church of St Vitalis: Empress Theodora

5km/3mi south of the town, the 6C **Basilica of Sant'Apollinare★★** (St Apollinaris in Classe) boasts a majestic triple-nave, and a triumphal arch and choir decorated with mosaics symbolizing the Transfiguration.

►► **Battistero Neoniano★** (Neonian Baptistery) – Battistero degli Ariani (Arian Baptistery) – **Sant'Apollinare Nuovo★** (Basilica of St Apollinaris the New).

★★RIMINI Population 127 884. Michelin map 970 L 7

The internationally popular seaside resort of Rimini, birthplace of the great film-maker Federico Fellini (1920-1993), is a good starting point for exploring the town of Urbino, the San Marino Republic and the southeastern coast. The old town centre of Rimini contains a number of monuments worth visiting, such as the **Tempio Malatestiano★** (Malatesta Temple). Although unfinished, the temple, which was altered from 1447 onwards by Leon Battista Alberti, inaugurated a new type of façade for religious buildings with its antique decoration, where as the interior has retained its delicately wrought allegorical sculpted decoration.

LIGURIA and the EASTERN RIVIERA

Liguria, which is furrowed by deep narrow valleys, has always been a thriving maritime region thanks to its small deep-water ports and the relatively good fishing off its rocky coast. The Riviera coast stretches from Ventimiglia to La Spezia, a naval base, and is well-sheltered from winds, forming a semicircle with Genoa in the centre. The western Riviera di Ponente is more exposed to the sun than the eastern Riviera di Levante, which is more rugged with denser vegetation. Like the French Côte d'Azur, the seaside resorts are a paradise for holidaymakers (**Bordighera★★**, **San Remo★★**, **Rapallo★★**, **Lerici★**); the best season is spring.

★★CINQUE TERRE

Cinque Terre, situated to the northwest of La Spezia Bay, is still rather difficult to get to. Fishing villages which have kept their traditions almost intact dot the steep-sloped coast covered in vineyards. **Vernazza★★** is the most attractive with its tall colourful houses huddled around a cove.

★★GENOVA (GENOA) Population 676 062. Michelin map 970 J 7

Genoa the Superb, Italy's leading port and home of Christopher Columbus (1451-1506), owes its expansion and prestige to a fleet which from the 11C onwards made its presence felt all the way up to the Black Sea. It competed with Venice, for a long time, for the monopoly of Mediterranean trade. In the 16C and 17C, the arts flourished, churches and palaces were erected, and the city attracted foreign painters, mainly Flemish masters, including Rubens and Van Dyck. In 1684, Louis XIV had the port destroyed to divert shipping to Atlantic ports and in 1768 the city ceded Corsica to France.
The **old town★★** stretches east of the old **port★★** and climbs up through picturesque alleys to Via Garibaldi★, lined with splendid palaces. The **Palazzo Bianco** (White Palace) and **Palazzo Rosso** (Red Palace), as well as the **Spinola Palace★** a little further away, all house fine collections of paintings. **Piazza San Matteo★** is borded by palaces which belonged to the Doria family.

★★★PROMONTORIO DI PORTOFINO (PORTOFINO PENINSULA)

Part of the rocky Portofino Peninsula has been turned into a nature reserve with pleasant footpaths, one leading to the San Fruttuoso Monastery tucked into a narrow cove, another to the **Chiappa Point★★★**. Portofino can be reached from the elegant seaside resort of **Santa Margherita Ligure★★★** *(5km/3mi)* along a coast road lined with chestnut trees and oleanders. This small fishing village of pretty, colourful houses, tucked away at the end of an inlet, has now become a favourite haunt of visitors from many different countries. *(Admission fee for all beaches in the area).*

Marmounier /CEDRI

Portofino

MILAN and LOMBARDY

Lombardy, the busiest region in Italy, spreads across the fertile Po plain between the Ticino and the Mincio which, together with the Adda, feed the Maggiore, Como and Garda lakes. During the Middle Ages, the towns scattered over its countryside were the seat of intensive banking and commerce: Como, Brescia, Bergamo, Mantua, Cremona and Pavia. Milan, the economic capital of all of Italy, now has the highest population and business density. Like Bologna, Milan has given its name to several favourite Italian dishes: *minestrone* (vegetable soup), *scaloppina* (breaded veal escallop) and *ossobuco* (veal shank with bone marrow). The best-known cheese of the region is Gorgonzola. *Panettone* (a Christmas speciality) is a light cake filled with raisins and candied lemon peel.

★★★THE LAKE DISTRICT

These long narrow lakes lying at the foot of the Alps are of glacial origin. Local vegetation is luxuriant thanks to the very mild climate. The shores of the lakes are dotted with villas surrounded by grandiose neo-Classical gardens. The little ports where one can eat excellent fish are one of the charms of the area.

★★★**Lake Maggiore** – This enormous lake, of legendary beauty, is best admired from a boat. The resort of **Angera★** is dominated by a fortress, the Rocca Borromeo, which still houses a law court decorated with 14C **frescoes★★** and also contains a Doll Museum. The **Borromean Islands★★★** (Isole Borromee) can be easily reached from **Stresa★★**, **Baveno★** and **Pallanza★★**. Like much of the lake region, the islands belonged to the princely Borromeo family. The **Isola Bella★★★** is named after Isabella, wife of Charles III. The island is home to a baroque palace and gardens laid out with statues and fragrant plants (pomegranate and orange trees, camellias and roses). The **Isola dei Pescatori★★** shelters a fishing village whereas the **Isola Madre★★★** is enhanced by a botanical garden.

★★★**Lake Como** – This lake was a great favourite among 19C Romantics because of its captivating landscape. Its scenery is the most varied of all the lakes. The intersection of Lake Como's three branches forming the **Bellagio★★★** promontory is the most attractive part. This holiday resort is appreciated for its beautiful setting and the opulent lakeside **gardens★★** of **the Villas Serbelloni** and **Melzi**. The prettiest resorts are on the western shore: **Como★**, an important silk production centre, with a fine cathedral (ornate façade, magnificent tapestries, paintings by B Luini), **Cernobbio★★**, an elegant holiday resort, **Cadenabbia★★** opposite Bellagio, **Menaggio★★** and **Tremezzo★★★**, known for the **Villa Carlotta★★★** with its fine sculpture collection and wonderful gardens.

★★★**Lake Garda** – The largest Italian lake was named the beneficent lake in ancient times because of its gentle climate. Among the breathtaking landscapes and picturesque villages on its shores, mention should be made of **Sirmione★★**, a spa with houses clustered around the castle of the Scaligers of Verona; the remains of a villa belonging to the Roman poet Catullus at the tip of the headland; **Gardone Riviera★★** where D'Annunzio used to stay; **Limone sul Garda★** named after its groves of lemon trees and, on the other side, **Malcesine★**, dominated by a 13C fortified castle and **Mount Baldo** offering one of the best **panoramas★★★**.

★★★MILANO **(MILAN)** Population 1 367 733. Michelin map 970 K 6

This dynamic capital of Lombardy is the second largest city in Italy in terms of population, as well as political, cultural and artistic influence, and it is the leader in commerce, industry and banking. Two ring roads encircle it, one demarcating its medieval heart by following the original 14C ramparts, the other outlining the larger Renaissance town.

Historical notes – Seat of the Western Roman Empire from the end of the 3C, it was here that Constantine issued the **Edict of Milan** granting Christians freedom of worship in the year 313. In 375, St Ambrose, a Church doctor, became its bishop and founded the basilica which bears his name (magnificent gold **altar front★★**). In the Middle Ages, the Visconti, Ghibellines and leaders of the aristocracy, seized power. The most famous of them, Gian Galeazzo, was responsible for having the Duomo and the Pavia Charter house built. His daughter Valentine married Louis, Duke of Orleans, the grandfather of Louis XII, King of France: it was these family ties which started the wars of Italy. The Sforza family succeeded the Visconti. One of them, Ludovic il Moro, turned Milan into the new Athens by attracting the geniuses of the period, Leonardo da Vinci and Bramante. Louis XII proclaimed himself heir to the Duchy of Milan and set out to conquer it in 1500. Francis I renewed the offensive; after a victory at Marignano (1515), he was defeated at Pavia by Emperor Charles V (1525). Milan then became a Spanish possession. Under Napoleon, the town became the capital of the Cisalpine Republic, and later of the Kingdom of Italy (1805).

Life in Milan – Milan is certainly the most European of Italian cities. Nonetheless, almost everything closes down during the month of August. It has a good public transport system, including three subway lines. Despite its ultra-modern architecture, the heart of the city is full of historical monuments and interesting museums. The starting point for visiting the city is Piazza del Duomo leading to the **Galleria Vittorio Emanuele★**, centre of political and social life where the Milanese love to meet for lively discussions or to read their local newspaper, the *Corriere della Sera*.

La Scala★★, built in the 18C, puts on a prestigious opera season which opens in December, while the equally famous **Piccolo Teatro** also offers an interesting cultural programme.

S. Chirol

Galleria Vittoria Emmanuelle

The leading dress designers (Armani, Ferragamo, Ferre, Gucci, Valentino) and the fashionable shops are found behind the Duomo, along Corso Vittorio Emanuele II, Piazza San Babila, Via Borgospesso, Via della Spiga and Via Monte Napoleone.
The Brera district, with its proliferation of artists' studios and art galleries, comes to life in the evening.
Old Milan, dotted with cafés and antique shops, is situated around Corso Magenta and Sant'Ambrogio.

★★★ **Duomo** – Bristling with belfries, pinnacles, gables and a multitude of statues, the cathedral marks the height of the Flamboyant Gothic style. It is particularly beautiful in the late-afternoon light. The construction of the cathedral was started in 1386 and continued up to the 16C. In sharp contrast to its opulent exterior, the inside is austere and plain, an atmosphere accentuated by the dim light. There is a superb view of the statues and spires from the **Rooftop Promenade★★★** *(admission fee)*.

★★★ **Pinacoteca di Brera (Brera Picture Gallery)** – The Brera Gallery is housed in a 17C palace. Its collection of paintings, one of the richest in Italy, includes masterpieces from the Venetian School (Mantegna, Dead Christ; G Bellini, Pietà), the Lombardy School (B Luini, Madonna of the Rose Garden), and the Central Italian School (Piero della Francesca, Virgin Mary in Majesty; Raphael, Marriage of the Virgin; Caravaggio, Supper at Emmaus), and works by Ribera, Van Dyck, Rubens, Reynolds...

★★★ **Castello Sforzesco (Castle of the Sforza)** – The Sforza castle at the end of Via Dante was once the residence of the dukes of Milan. Today it contains a **Sculpture Museum★★**, including the **Rondandini Pietà★★★** by Michelangelo, a **Picture Gallery★**, an **Archeological Museum**, as well as a large collection of **musical instruments★**.

★ **Santa Maria delle Grazie (Church of St Mary of Grace)** – The famous **Last Supper★★★** by Leonardo da Vinci, a mural commissioned by Ludovic il Moro, adorns the old convent refectory (cenacolo). This learned work on the theme of the Eucharist has a central and dramatic perspective and constitutes a masterful study of physiognomy. Since it was severely damaged, it had to undergo a lengthy restoration process at the end of the 1970s.

►► **Biblioteca Ambrosiana★★** (Ambrosian Library) – **Poldo Pezzoli Museum★★** – **Bagatti Valsecchi Palace★★** – **Sant'Ambrogio★★** (Basilica of St Ambrose) – **San Maurizio★★** (Church of St Maurice) – Modern Art Gallery (Impressionists, Futurists and works by Marino Marini).

★★★ CERTOSA DI PAVIA (Carthusian Monastery of PAVIA) Michelin map 970 K 6

Founded by Gian Galeazzo Visconti to serve as a mausoleum for his family, the Carthusian monastery was built mainly during the 15C and 16C. Although the façade is unfinished, it is remarkable for its carefully designed and ornate decor: polychrome sculptures, copies of ancient medallions, alcoves containing statues of saints and an endless variety of ornamental motifs. The interior is Gothic in style; the recumbent statues of Ludovic il Moro and Beatrice d'Este and the tomb of the founder lie in the transept. There is an interesting view of the roofs from the first cloister; the second cloister is surrounded by the cells of the Carthusian monks.

NAPLES and CAMPANIA

The fertile land of Campania encircles the Bay of Naples, guarded by the familiar silhouette of Vesuvius. This beautiful bay fascinated the Ancients who believed it to be the entrance to the Underworld. The immense gulf, its deep blue waters bathed in bright sunshine, embraces the famous Islands of Capri, Ischia and Procida, all linked by boat. Even though its coast has been spoiled by over-development, there are still some enchanting spots such as the Sorrento Peninsula or the interesting archaeological site of Pompeii.

★★★ISOLA DI CAPRI (Island of CAPRI) Population 7 074. Michelin map 970 L 8

This small island attracts tourists of all nationalities because of its beautiful rugged landscape, mild climate, lush and varied vegetation; Capri's excellent restaurants and attractive boutiques have also added to its reputation.
Boats from Naples or Sorrento arrive at **Marina Grande★** from where a funicular leads up to the centre of **Capri town★★★**. This resembles a Moorish-style stage setting for an operetta, with its small squares, tiny houses and narrow village alleys. **Via Le Botteghe★** leads to **Villa Jovis★★** (Jupiter's Villa) *(30min by foot)*, once the residence of Emperor Tiberius. During the reign of Augustus, Capri became part of the imperial domain, and Tiberius took up residence here from AD 27 to 37. He governed Rome from this villa perched on top of the island's eastern promontory which drops vertically into the sea. A scenic coast road winds its way up to **Anacapri★★★** where the Swedish doctor Axel Munthe built his **Villa San Michele★** at the end of the 19C. A chair-lift gives access to **Mount Solaro summit★★★**, the highest point of the island which offers visitors an unforgettable panorama.
Boat rides are the best way to **tour the island★★★** or visit the **Grotta Azzurra★★** (Blue Grotto); the magical colours are due to the light filtering through its one tiny entrance at the foot of a very steep slope.

★CASERTA Population 68 869.

The **Reggia Palace★★** is the Versailles of the kingdom of Naples. In 1752, the Bourbon king, Charles III, commissioned the architect Vanvitelli to build this vast palace (249 x 190m/273 x 208yd). In the **park★**, a succession of fountains and ornamental lakes decorated with statues lead to the great waterfall cascading down (78m/256ft).

★★★COSTIERA AMALFITANA (AMALFI Coast) Michelin map 970 L 8

From Sorrento to Salerno *(70km/43mi)*, the road follows the most beautiful coastline in Italy, punctuated by deep gorges (the Furore Valley), sheer rocks plunging straight down to the sea, marine caves (**Grotta dello Smeraldo★★** – Emerald Cave), picturesque fishing villages and popular seaside resorts (Amalfi, Positano, Praiano), against a background of magnificent vineyards and groves of orange, lemon and almond trees, overlooking a sea of the deepest blue.

★★**Sorrento** – This is a pleasant holiday resort with lovely gardens enclosing hotels and villas. Local craftsmen produce lace and objects in inlaid wood. A narrow serpentine road winds around the **peninsula★★** *(itinerary: 33km/21mi)*, offering wonderful views.

★★★**Ravello** – This village lies suspended between the sky and sea, with alleys clinging to the steep slopes of Dragon Hill. Near the cathedral (fine mosaic-covered pulpit), the 13C **Villa Rufolo★★★** was used as the residence of the Supreme Pontiff; later, in 880, Wagner was one of its distinguished guests. There are some breathtaking views from belvederes, such as the one at **Villa Cimbrone★★★**, which is surrounded by superb gardens.

★★**Amalfi** – This ancient Italian Maritime Republic (9C) gave its name to the oldest maritime code in the world, the Amalfi Navigation Tables. In the Middle Ages, Amalfi had a busy arsenal where many galleys were built, mainly to carry crusaders to the Levant. Today, this small Spanish-style town has become a famous tourist resort because of its idyllic setting★★★.

★**Salerno** – A flourishing commercial centre in the Middle Ages, the city's intellectual fame spread thanks to the university and medical school. The **cathedral★★**, built by the Norman, Robert Guiscard, contains a crypt in which reposes the body of St Matthew.

★★★NAPOLI (NAPLES) Population 1 068 927. Michelin map 970 L 8

Naples, one of the most colourful cities in Italy, has been praised by generations of travellers for its beauty and surprises. Its bay, dominated by Vesuvius and embraced on both sides by the Posillipo and Sorrento peninsulas and various islands, is one of the most spectacular in the world. Its reputation has been enhanced by a pleasant climate as well as the Neapolitan combination of imagination and seriousness, vivacity and fatalism. However the alleys littered with garbage, the rundown buildings damaged by the 1980 earthquake, and the heavy traffic may disappoint visitors.

Since Naples is the land of Bel Canto, it is not surprising that the San Carlo theatre organises an excellent opera season. There are also many other kinds of events ranging from football matches to religious feasts. Unfortunately, traffic brings the town's arteries to a standstill at certain times of the day.

The hub of public life is centred around Piazza del Plebiscito and the Galleria Umberto I. Via Santa Lucia is the street for jewellers and sellers of coral objects. As for antiquarians, they are to be found on Via Santa Maria di Costantinopoli.

Naples is the best place for eating *spaghetti alle vongole* (clams). Trattorias and pizzerias serve mozzarella, a buffalo milk cheese, fresh as a starter accompanied by tomatoes, or melted over pizzas. The wines of the volcano – white Lacryma Christi and red Gragnano – have a slight taste of sulphur.

An eventful history – The town began as a Greek colony called Neapolis and was conquered by the Romans in the 4C BC. The rich inhabitants of Rome – Virgil, Augustus and Tiberius among others – spent the winter months here.

Since the 12C, seven families have reigned over Naples: the Normans, Hohenstaufens, Angevins, Spanish, Aragonese and Bourbons. At the beginning of the 19C, the French kings, Joseph Bonaparte and Joachim Murat introduced far-reaching reforms.

Under the princes of Anjou, Naples was endowed with many religious buildings designed in the French Gothic style. The arrival in 1606 of Caravaggio, who revolutionized Italian painting, led to the establishment of a local school well represented by Artemisia Gentileschi, Ribera, Mattia Preti and Salvatore Rosa. Many architects, such as Ferdinande Sanfelice and Luigi Vanvitelli, embellished Naples with fine Baroque buildings.

The town

★★**Castel Nuovo** – The so-called new castle, surrounded by deep moats, was built in 1282 by the French architects of Charles I of Anjou, on a model of the castle at Angers. The **triumphal arch**★, designed by Francesco Laurana, was erected in 1467 to commemorate the entry of Alphonso I of Aragon into Naples.

★**Piazza del Plebiscito** – This square, laid out under Murat, is bounded on one side by the Royal Palace designed by Domenico Fontana and built at the beginning of the 17C, and on the other side by the **Church of San Francesco di Paola** (St Francis of Paola), constructed on the model of the Roman Pantheon. Equestrian statues of two Bourbons, Ferdinand I and Charles III, stand in the centre of the square.

★★★**Museo Archeologico Nazionale (National Archeological Museum)** – At the end of Via Toledo, the museum occupies 16C buildings which were once used for the royal cavalry. The collections include works that belonged to the Farnese family. The museum also possesses treasures found at Herculaneum and Pompeii, thus making it one of the best Greek and Roman antiquity museums in the world.

★★**Certosa di San Martino (Carthusian Monastery of St Martin)** – This occupies a beautiful site on the Comero Hill which can be reached by cable-car. Highlights include an ornate Baroque church and a museum containing a unique collection of **Neapolitan cribs**★★.

★★**Palazzo e Galleria Nazionale di Capodimonte (Capodimonte Palace and National Gallery)** – This former royal estate, was built in the 18C on the hills above Naples. The palace houses a **Pinacotec**★★★ (Picture Gallery) displaying works by the Primitives and by Renaissance artists (Botticelli, Filippino Lippi, Raphael, Mantegna, Giovanni Bellini), as well as later paintings by Correggio, Parmigianino, Titian, El Greco, Caravaggio and his followers.

★★**Spaccanapoli and the Decumanus Maximus** – Many churches line the main axis of old Naples, formed by Via Benedetto Croce and Via S. Biagio dei Librai, which follows the course of the Roman Decumanus Maximus. This axis is nicknamed Spacca Napoli (from the Italian word *spaccare* meaning to split), as it cuts Naples into two.

Santa Chiara★ (St Clare's), built in a Provençal Gothic style, contains the mausoleum of the Angevin dynasty (**tomb**★★ of Robert the Wise) and features an attractive **cloister**★. The exuberantly Baroque **Sansevero Chapel** houses some unusual marble **sculptures**★. The Duomo is not far away; its Baroque chapel dedicated to St Januarius (San Gennaro is the patron saint of Naples) is the repository for two phials of the holy man's blood. Frescoes by Lanfranco adorn the dome. Nearby, the Pio Monte della Misericordia is home to Caravaggio's **Seven Works of Mercy**★★★.

When visiting the older areas like Spacca Napoli, visitors are advised to avoid attracting undue attention to themselves by either behaviour or dress, to refrain from night-time strolls, to leave nothing of value in the car and to be on the alert at all times.

The Bay of Naples

★★ **Ercolano (HERCULANEUM)** – *10km/6mi to the south.* Like Pompeii, this small Roman town was buried after the eruption of Vesuvius in AD 79. It was inhabited by many artisans, while patricians used it as a place for relaxation. Its population had just enough time to flee, but the torrent of mud which swept over the town filled every little corner, thus preserving all the wooden structures. In addition to the public **baths**★★★, still intact, Herculaneum has a wide variety of houses: the **Trellis House**★★, the **Samnite House**★★ with an atrium, the **Neptune and Amphitrite House**★★ containing a shop, and the **House of the Stags**★★, a once luxurious residence consisting of several apartments.

★★★ **Vesuvio (Vesuvius)** – *20km/12mi to the southeast.* Vesuvius is a double-peaked active volcano: to the north lies Mount Somma (1 132m/3 714ft) and to the south Vesuvius itself (1 277m/4 190ft). Its lower fertile slopes are now covered with orchards and vineyards. From Herculaneum – with a detour possible on the way back via Torre del Greco (known for its locally made objects in coral or lava stone) – a road goes up to the middle of the lava flows, followed by a path hugging the side of the volcano (wear sturdy shoes). From the summit there is an extensive **panorama**★★★ over the Bay of Naples.

B. Morandi /DIAF

Bay of Naples

★★★ **Pompeii** – *28km/17mi to the south.* In AD 79, when Vesuvius violently erupted, Pompeii was a prosperous village with a population of about 25 000. In two days, the city was covered by a layer of ash 6m/20ft – 7m/23ft deep. Systematic excavations only began in the 18C. The discovery of the site made a tremendous impact all over Europe, revealing Pompeii's wide diversity of building materials and techniques, and its many different types of houses. Most of the decorative wall paintings have been removed and can now be seen in the Naples Archeological Museum.

★★★ PAESTUM Michelin map 970 L 8

This important archeological site was discovered by chance in 1750. A number of monuments from the ancient Greek Poseidonia founded in 600 BC are still standing: the **Basilica**★★, a temple from the 6C BC consisting of a peristyle with 50 archaic columns, the perfectly preserved **Temple of Neptune**★★★ (Tempio di Nettuno) from the 5C BC, in a Doric style of incredible purity, the **Forum (foro)**, the heart of the city surrounded by porticos and shops, the **Roman Amphitheatre**, and the **Tempio di Cerere**★★ (Temple of Ceres) near the sacrificial altar. The **Museum**★★ contains the **metopes**★★ (Doric bas-reliefs originally decorating the temples), as well as the famous **Tomba del Tuffatore**★★ (Tomb of the Diver) adorned with paintings.

In this guide town plans show the main streets and the way to the sights; local maps show the main roads and the roads o the recommended tour.

PIEDMONT

A large part of Piedmont consists of an immense plain, the valley of the Po, lying at the foot of mountains, between the Alps and Apennines. The plain is crisscrossed by lines of poplars dividing grasslands, wheat fields and rice paddies. The hills of Montferrat, southeast of Turin, produce the famous Asti wines. Piedmont has its own culinary specialities: *cardi in bagna cauda* (cardoons in a piquant sauce), *tartufi bianchi* (white truffles), and all kinds of sweets, the most popular being *torrone piemontese* (nougat) and *gianduiotti* (praline chocolates).

★★TORINO (TURIN) Population 961 512. Michelin map 970 J 6

This dynamic city is the capital of the region and has attracted the fashion and car industries (it is the headquarters of Fiat and Lancia).
From the 11C onwards, Turin's destiny was linked to the House of Savoy which reigned over Savoy and Piedmont, then over Sardinia and Italy. The kings of the House of Savoy ruled Italy from 1861 to 1946. At the beginning of the 18C, Charles Emmanuel II and Victor Amadeus II commissioned the architects Guarini and Juvara to build monuments and fine residences for the city and its outskirts. After the fall of Napoleon, Turin became the bastion of opposition to Austria and the centre of the movement to unify Italy.

The city

Most of Turin's layout goes back to the 17C and 18C: it has a regular plan cut by wide roads, featuring large squares and numerous green areas. **Piazza San Carlo**★★ and Via Roma are lined with elegant shop windows. The **Palazzo dell'Accademia delle Scienze** (Science Academy) not far from San Carlo Square houses two museums of great interest, the Egyptian Museum★★ and the Sabauda Gallery★★ (painting collection). The **Palazzo Reale**★ (Royal Palace) and its magnificent armory, residence of the Savoy princes until 1865, is just beyond **Palazzo Madama**★ in Piazza Castello. **Duomo San Giovanni**★ (St John's Cathedral) adjoining the palace, includes a chapel designed by the architect Guarini in the 17C to enshrine the famous **Holy Shroud**★★★ (Santa Sindone).

★**Museo dell'Automobile Carlo Biscaretti di Ruffia (Motor Museum)** – *4km/2mi to the south.* This automobile museum boasts an extensive collection of cars: there is also a room devoted to the evolution of research and technology related to car tyre manufacture.

EXCURSIONS

★★**Superga Basilica** – *10km/6mi to the east.* The Superga Basilica, built between 1717 and 1731, is the work of the architect Filippo Juvara (1678-1736). It has a circular plan surmounted by a dome, and a crypt containing the tombs of many of the Savoy princes.

★**Palazzina di caccia di Stupinigi (Stupinigi Palace)** – *11km/17mi to the southwest.* The Stupinigi Palace is in fact a hunting lodge, built by Juvara for Victor Amadeus of Savoy. It contains a rich interior decor, mainly by Carle Van Loo.

ROME and LATIUM

Latium, the cradle of Roman civilization, lies between the Tyrrhenian Sea and the Apennines, from Maremma in Tuscany to Gaeta. The region has a sandy coast whose ancient ports, such as Ostia at the mouth of the Tiber, have been silted up. Today, Civitavecchia is the only modern port along this stretch of coast. Rome, the capital of Italy and Christianity, lies at the centre of Latium, and is mainly a residential city crowded with officials, clergymen and tourists.
To the east and north, volcanic hills whose craters now cradle solitary lakes, overlook the Roman Campagna, once a malaria-infested area which was drained during the Fascist régime (especially the Pontine marshes).

★★★ROMA (ROME) Population 2 773 889. Michelin map 970 L 8

As a symbol of Christianity and centre of influence for artistic movements, Rome, the capital of Italy since 1870, offers many pleasant surprises to art lovers and visitors fascinated by this country. At least three days are needed to visit the city. The origin of Rome lies in mythology; the twins Romulus and Remus, born of a union between the god Mars and a Vestal Virgin, were thrown into the Tiber and landed on the banks below the Palatine where they were nourished by a she-wolf. Romulus later drew a furrow around this spot where the city was to be built.

Rome subsequently became a republic but it was eventually split by political rivalries.
Julius Caesar (101-44 BC) emerged as a leader, overthrew his adversaries and conquered Gaul in 51 BC. He was nominated consul and dictator for life but was murdered in March 44 BC. He was succeeded by his nephew Octavian to whom the Senate granted the title Augustus. He became the first Roman emperor and extended Rome's domination throughout the Mediterranean basin. After his death, he was followed by a long line of emperors. Some of his successors, particularly Caligula, Nero and Domitian, were notorious for their acts of folly and cruelty, while others like Vespasian, Titus, Trajan and Hadrian made great contributions to civilization.
Christianity became organized at the end of the 1C, but it was not until the Edict of Milan in 313 that there was freedom of worship and that churches could be built. The popes shaped Rome into the Eternal City. During the Renaissance, many erudite sovereign pontiffs were patrons of the arts and attracted to their court the greatest artists of that period such as Raphael and Michelangelo. Among the patrons were Sixtus IV, who commissioned the Sistine Chapel, Julius II, Leo X, Sixtus V, a great builder, and Paul III, responsible for the Farnese Palace.
The best views of this great city, which sprawls over seven hills, are from the belvederes of the Janiculum (Gianicolo), Aventine or Pincio. Luxury shops are clustered around **Piazza del Popolo, Via del Corso** and **Piazza di Spagna.** The **Via Veneto** is lined with plush hotels and café terraces, a favourite meeting place of tourists from all over the world. **Via dei Coronari** is the domain of antiquarians and secondhand dealers. Buses are convenient for getting around *(tickets can be bought from tobacconists)* but the best way to discover the city is on foot.

★★★Ancient Rome

Colosseo (Coliseum) (CY) – The Coliseum is also known as the Flavian Amphitheatre, after Vespasian, the first of the Flavian emperors, who had it built over the gardens of Nero's Golden House. It was inaugurated in AD 80 and could hold 50 000 spectators who came to watch duels, gladiators wrestling against lions, chariot races and even naval battles.

Close by is **Arco di Constantino**★★★ (Constantine's Arch), the largest Roman arch. It was erected in AD 315 to commemorate Constantine's victory over Maxentius at the battle of the Milvian Bridge. Most of the bas-reliefs come from 2C monuments.

★★★**Foro Romano (Roman Forum)** (CY) – The Forum, once the religious, political and trade centre of Ancient Rome, was built in a valley between the Capitol and the Palatine. It reflects the 12 centuries of history which have forged Roman civilization. The best views of the ruins are from the Capitol's terrace or the Farnese gardens on the Palatine.

Roman Forum

ROMA

A[1] CY S. Maria d'Aracoeli
A[2] BX S. Maria della Pace
B[1] BX S. Maria Sopra Minerva
B[2] CY Tempio di Venere e di Roma
C[1] BV S. Maria del Popolo
C[2] CZ Piramide di Caio Cestio
D[1] BX S. Agnese in Agone
D[2] CY Tempio della Fortuna Virile
E[1] CY Palazzo Venezia
E[2] BX Ara Pacis Augustae
F[1] BX S. Luigi dei Francesi
F[2] CY Tempio di Vesta
G BX Chiesa Nuova
H CY Palazzo Senatorio
K[1] CX S. Andrea al Quirinale
K[2] BX Mausoleo di Augusto
L BX S. Agostino
M[1] CY Palazzo dei Conservatori
M[2] CY Palazzo Nuovo
M[3] CX Palazzo Barberini

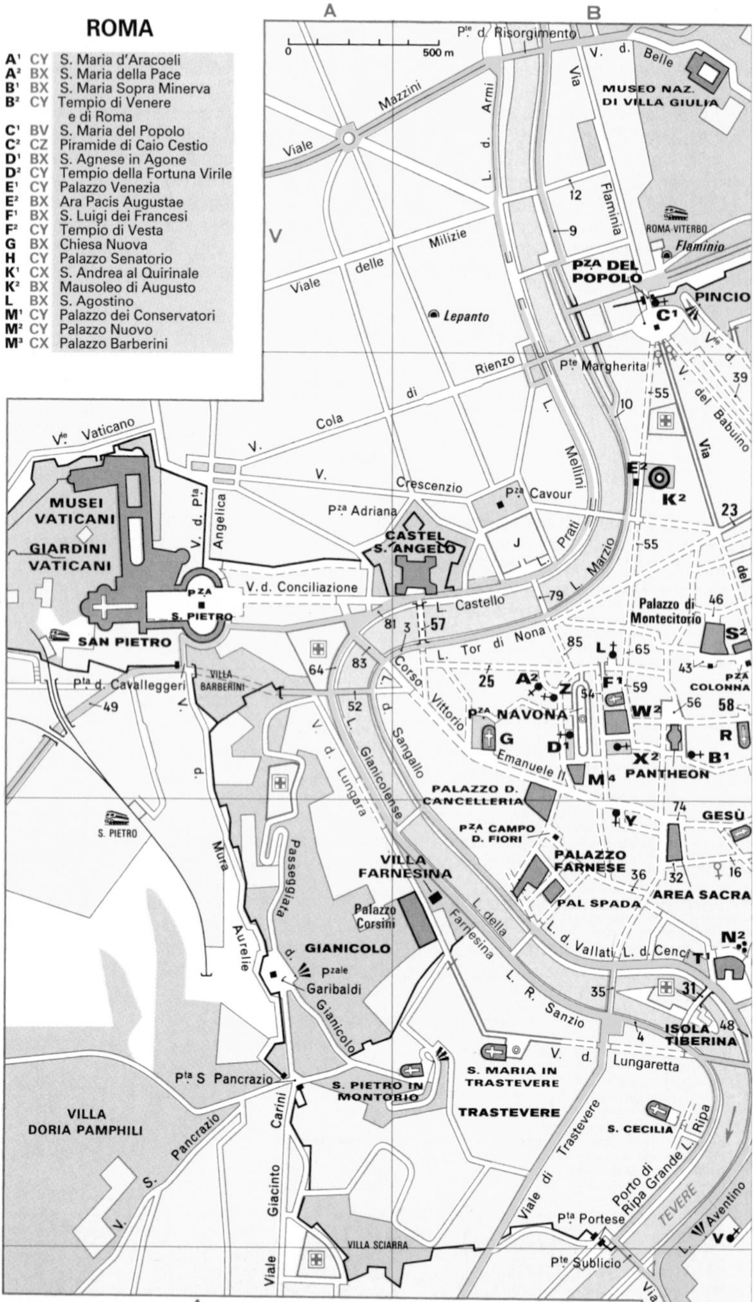

Alessandra (Via) .... CY 2	Emmanuelle Filiberto (Via) .... DY 30	S. Marco (Pza di) .... CY 60
Alvoti (L. degli) .... BX 3	Fabricio (Ponte) .... BY 31	S. Silvestro (Pza) .... CX 63
Anguillara (L. degli) .... BY 4	Florida (V.) .... BY 32	Sassia (L. in) .... AX 64
Annibaldi (V. degli) ...... CY 6	Frattina (Via) .... BCX 33	Savoia Aosta (Ponte) JAX 52
Aracœeli (Pza e V.) ..... CY 7	Garibaldi (Ponte) .... BY 35	Scrofa (V. della) .... BX 65
Arnaldo da Brescia (L.). BV 9	Guibonnari (Via dei) .... BY 36	Sistina (Via) .... CX 68
Augusta (L. in) .... BX 10	Margutta (Via) .... BX 39	Spagna (Piazza di)........ CX
Azuni (Via D.A.) .... BV 12	Mercede (Via della) .... CX 41	Stamperia (V. della) .... CX 69
Babuino (Via del) .... BX	Montecitorio (Pza di) .. BX 43	Teatro di Marcello (V. del) ...... CY 73
Battisti (Via C.) .... CXY 14	Navicella (Via della) .... DY 44	Torre Argentina (Largo di) .... BY 74
Bocca della Verità (Pza della) ... CY 15	Nomentana (Via) .... DV 45	Traforo (V. del) .... CX 75
Botteghe Oscure .... BY 16	Parlemento (Pza del) .. BX 46	Tritone (Via del) CX
Campidoglio (Pza del) CY 17	Petroselli (Via L.) .... CY 47	Tulliano (V. del) .... CY 77
Campidoglio (L. del) ... CY 19	Pierleoni (L. dei) .... BY 48	Umberto I (Ponte) .... BX 79
Carlo Alberto (V.) .... DY 20	Pta Cavalleggeri (V. di) AX 49	Umiltà (Via) .... CX 80
Collegio Romano (Pza del) .... CX 22	Pta S. Giovanni (Pza) .. DY 51	Vaticano (L.) .... ABX 81
Condotti (Via dei) .... BCX 23	Principe Amedeo	Vittorio Emmanuelle (Ponte) AX 83
Coronari (V. del) .... BX 25	Ramni (V. dei) .... DX 53	Vittorio Veneto CX
Corso (Via del) .... BCX	Rinascimento (Cso d.) BX 54	Zanardello (Via) .... BX 85
Dataria (V. della) .... CX 26	Ripetta (V. di) .... BX 55	4-Novembre (Via) ..... CXY 87
Depretis (V. A.) .... CX 27	Rotonda (Pza d.) .... BX 56	24-Maggio (Via) .... CX 88
Due Macelli (Via) .... CX 28	S. Angelo (Ponte) .... BX 57	
Einaudi (Viale Luigi) .... DX 29	S. Ignazio .... BX 58	
	S. Luigi dei Francesi (Pza) .... BX 59	

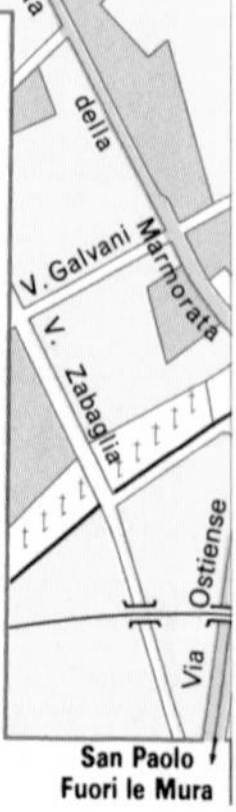

M[4]	BX	Palazzo Braschi
M[5]	CX	Palazzo Doria Pamphili
N[1]	CX	S. Carlo alle Quattro Fontane
N[2]	BY	Tempio di Apollo Sosiano
R	BX	S. Ignazio
S[1]	DX	S. Maria degli Angeli
S[2]	BX	Palazzo Chigi
T[1]	CY	Teatro di Marcello
V	BY	S. Sabina
W[1]	CX	S. Susanna
W[2]	BX	Palazzo Madama
X[1]	CY	SS. Cosma e Damiano
X[2]	BX	Palazzo della Sapienza
Y	BY	S. Andrea della Valle
Z	BX	S. Maria dell'Anima

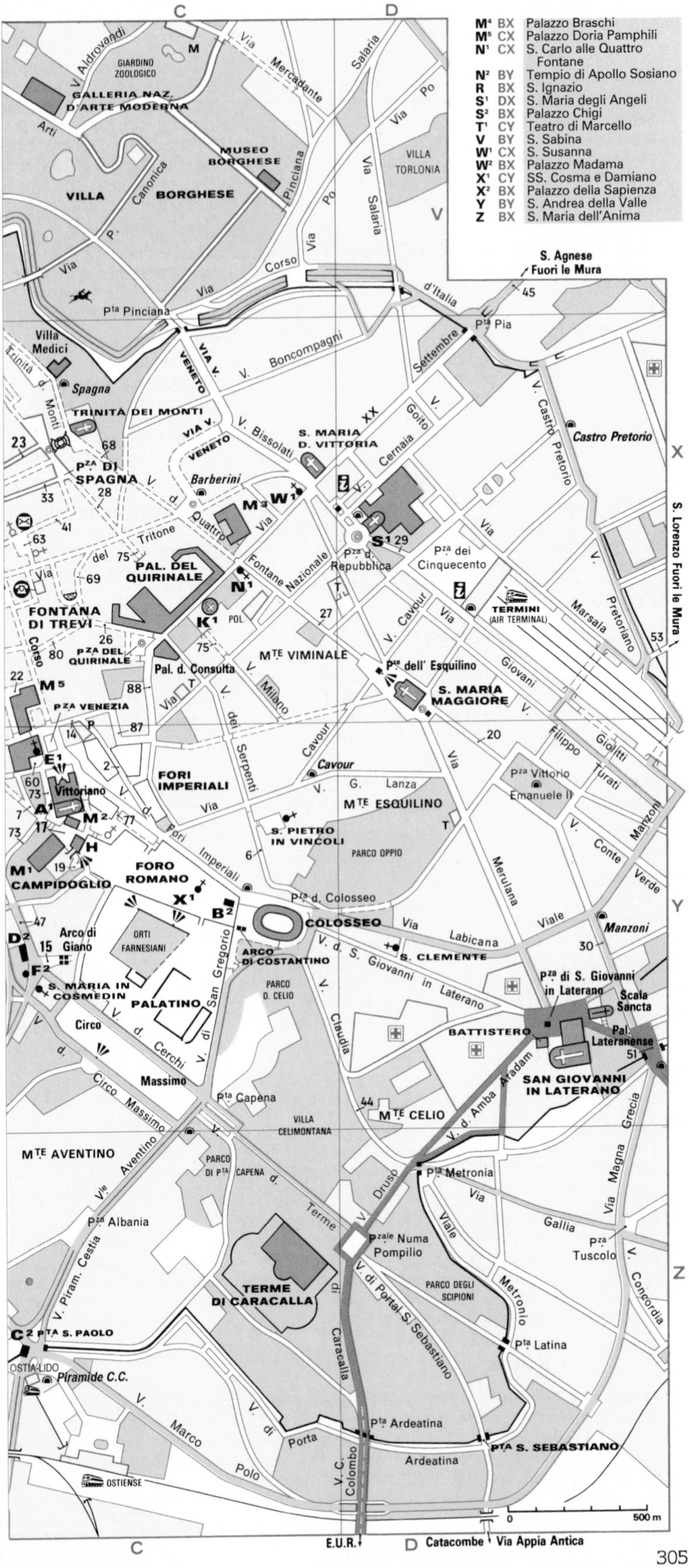

The **Via Sacra★** (Sacred Way), along which victorious generals marched in triumph, leads to the **Curia★★**, reconstructed in brick by Diocletian in the 3C. Senate meetings were held in this building. The elaborately decorated **Triumphal Arch of Septimus Severus★★** was erected in AD 203 following the Emperor's victories over the Parthians. A number of temples had been erected at the foot of the Capitol: some of their columns are still standing, including those of the **Tempio di Castore e Polluce★★★** (Temple of Castor and Pollux) with their Corinthian capitals. The **Arco di Tito★★** (Triumphal Arch of Titus) was built in AD 81 to commemorate the capture of Jerusalem in AD 70.

★★★ **Palatino (Palatine)** (CY) – The Palatine hill is both of great archeological interest and a very pleasant place for walks. This is where Emperor Domitian built his official palace, the **Domus Flavia★** and his private residence, the **Domus Augustana★★**. Augustus is believed to have lived in **Livia's House★★**. The **Farnese Gardens** were built during the Renaissance on the site of the palace of Tiberius.

★★★ **Pantheon** (BX) – The well preserved Pantheon (a temple dedicated to planetary divinities) was built by Agrippa in 27 BC, reconstructed by Emperor Hadrian (117-125) and finally converted into a church in the 7C. The imposing porch is supported by ancient granite columns. The interior is dominated by the **antique dome★★★**, the diameter of which is equal to its height (43.40m/139ft). This enormous central opening creates a striking effect. The chapels contain the tombs of the Italian kings as well as that of the painter Raphael.

★★★ **Castel Sant'Angelo** (BX) – The fortress was built in AD 135 as a mausoleum for Emperor Hadrian and his family. During the Middle Ages, it was used as a fortress against barbarian invasions and imperial expeditions. Pope Clement VII took refuge here when Rome was sacked in 1527. However, the fortified castle was mainly used as a prison. There is a magnificent **view★★★** of the city from the terrace. The entrance to Castel Sant'Angelo is through an elegant spiral ramp, dating from Antiquity.

★★★ **Terme di Caracalla (Caracalla's Baths)** (CZ) – The baths were built in AD 212 over an area of more than 11ha/27 acres and could hold 1 600 bathers at a time. In the days of Ancient Rome, the baths were public and free: they were places to bathe and practise *palaestra* (wrestling), but also to have discussions, to read and do business. The buildings, decorated with marble, mosaics and statues, were heated by a complex system of underground heaters *(hypocausts)* which circulated hot air under the floor tiles and along the walls.

★★★ **Museo Nazionale di Villa Giulia (Villa Giulia National Museum)** (BV) – This national museum displays an outstanding collection devoted to the Etruscan civilization.

★★★ **Campidoglio (Capitol)** (CY) – The Capitol has been the seat of government in Rome since Antiquity.

★★★ **The Square** – The trapeze-shaped Capitol Square was designed by Michelangelo in 1536. It is framed by an exceptional architectural ensemble of three palaces and a balustrade, dominated by statues of the Dioscuri (Twin Heroes), Castor and Pollux. The **Palazzo dei Conservatori★★★** (**M**[1]) houses a **museum★★★** of works from Antiquity, including the **She-Wolf★★★** (6C to 5C BC), **Boy Extracting a Thorn★★** and a bust of **Junius Brutus★★** (3C BC). The **Picture Gallery★** exhibits paintings from the 14C to the 17C. The **Palazzo Nuovo★★★** (New Palace) (**M**[2]) was built in 1655 by Rainaldi. It is now the home of the Capitoline Museum★★; its treasures include the **equestrian statue of Marcus Aurelius★★** which used to stand in the middle of the Capitol Square, and the **Dying Gaul★★★**.
The 12C **Palazzo Senatorio★★★** (the Senate) (H) is the town hall of Rome.
Two visits at the foot of the Capitol should not be missed:

★★ **Church of Santa Maria in Cosmedin** (CY) – This is considered to be one of the most charming medieval churches in Rome. It features a 12C **bell-tower★** *(campanile)* and, under its porch, the **Bocca della Verità** (Mouth of Truth) which according to legend bites off the hands of liars; in reality this is just an ancient decorative drainage stone.

★ **Piazza Venezia** (CXY) – Rome's main square lies at the foot of the Victor Emmanuel II monument, nicknamed the typewriter. It was erected in 1885 in honour of the first king of a unified Italy. Its sheer size and blinding white colour overshadow the other monuments in the vicinity. **Palazzo Venezia★** was built by Pope Paul II in the 15C; more recently, it was used as a residence by Mussolini, and it now houses a museum of medieval art.

Baroque Rome

★★★ **Fontana di Trevi** (CX) – The Trevi Fountain is the most well known of all Roman Baroque monuments. It was designed in 1762, on the request of Pope Clement XIII, by Nicola Salvi who set it against the entire width of a palace façade. The allegorical figure of the Ocean springs out of the central niche riding a chariot drawn by two sea horses and two tritons. According to tradition, any tourist who throws two coins over his shoulder into the basin is sure to return to Rome and to have a wish come true.

★★★ **Chiesa del Gesù (Gesu Church)** (BY) – The mother-church of the Jesuits in Rome was built by Vignola in 1568, thanks to the generosity of Cardinal Alexander Farnese. It served as a model for other Counter-Reformation churches. On the outside, the engaged pillars replace the flat pilasters of the Renaissance, with light and shade effects and recesses. The spacious interior was designed to draw large crowds to the sermons, and the Baroque decor to amaze the onlooker: the **frescoes by Baciccia**★★ on the dome illustrate the *Triumph of the Name of Jesus*. The **Chapel of Sant'Ignazio**★★★ (St Ignatius), the work (1696-1700) of the Jesuit Andrea Pozzo is very ornate. This church had an enormous artistic impact when the Company of Jesus started to expand.

★★★ **Piazza Navona** (BX) – This delightful square was built on the site of Domitian's circus and has retained its original shape. It is a pleasant and lively meeting place reserved for pedestrians. The centre is adorned by the **Fountain of the Four Rivers**★★★, Bernini's Baroque masterpiece, completed in 1651. The statues symbolize four rivers – the Danube, the Ganges, the Rio de la Plata and the Nile – representing the four corners of the world. Surrounding churches and palaces include **Sant'Agnese in Agone**★★ (**D**[1]), with a Greek-cross plan and a façade designed by Borromini, and the 17C **Pamphili Palace**.

★★★ **Piazza di Spagna** (CX) – The square acquired its name when the Spanish embassy moved into the Palazzo di Spagna in the 17C. It is dominated by the majestic **Spanish Steps**★★★ (Scala della Trinité dei Monti) built in the 18C. The piazza has an irregular ground plan, formed by two triangles, their points meeting in the centre at the **Fontana della Barcaccia**★ (Boat Fountain) designed by Pietro Bernini. One of the most elegant streets in Rome, **Via dei Condotti**, connects this square with Via del Corso. The famous Caffé Greco at no 86 was frequented by artists and writers in the 19C.

★★★ **Piazza del Popolo** (BV) – The Renaissance **Church of Santa Maria del Popolo**★★ (**C**[1]) on this square contains **frescoes**★ by Pinturicchio, two tombs by Sansovino and two magnificent **Caravaggio paintings**★★★: *The Crucifixion of St Peter* and *The Conversion of St Paul.*

The Major Basilicas

★★★ **San Giovanni in Laterano** (DY) – St John Lateran is the cathedral of Rome. Constantine built the first Lateran basilica before St Peter's in the Vatican. During the Middle Ages, this basilica was the symbol of the papacy. As the building fell into ruins, it was rebuilt by Borromini, a master of Baroque architecture; the main façade dates from the 18C. **Statues of the Apostles**★ by Bernini's pupils decorate the vast solemn interior.

★★★ **Santa Maria Maggiore (Basilica of St Mary Major)** (DX) – Santa Maria Maggiore was founded by Pope Liberius. According to legend, the Virgin Mary indicated the site for the basilica by a miraculous snowfall in the middle of August. The church was built in the 5C. Its majestic interior is adorned with some remarkable **mosaics**★★★, among the oldest in Rome (5C), illustrating scenes from the Old Testament. During the Counter-Reformation, two large **chapels** were added and the façade was remodelled in the middle of the 18C by Fuga.

★★ **San Paolo Fuori le Mura (Basilica of St Paul Without the Walls)** (BZ) – The basilica was built over the tomb of St Paul by Constantine in the 4C. When it was reconstructed in the 19C after being destroyed by a fire, it retained the original basilical plan of the early Christian churches. The sheer size of the grandiose **interior**★★★ is overwhelming. A Gothic **ciborium**★★★ made by Arnolfo di Cambio stands on the altar. The **cloister**★ is decorated with marble inlay.

★★★ The Catacombs (DZ)

These underground cemeteries were located outside Rome, along the major roads, as Roman legislation did not allow burials within the city walls. The network around the city is estimated to extend over several hundred miles.
The catacombs consist of galleries, *hypogea* (burial chambers), connecting passages and smaller rooms also used as tombs. These catacombs are decorated with paintings of symbolic motifs, considered to be the first examples of Christian art. Among the most interesting catacombs are those of **San Callisto**★★★ (St Callistus), **San Sebastiano**★★★ (St Sebastian) and **Domitilla**★★★.

★★★ Vaticano (AX)

The Vatican City is bounded by a wall overlooking Viale Vaticano and by the colonnade around St Peter's Square. This is the largest part of the Vatican, established as a sovereign State in 1929 by the Lateran Treaty. It is the smallest State in the world, now reduced to 44ha/109 acres and less than 1 000 inhabitants. The Vatican originates from the Church States which emerged in the 8C and disappeared in 1870 when Italy was unified and Rome became its capital. The Vatican,

headed by the Pope, has its own flag, strikes its own money and issues its own stamps. All that is left of the army are the Swiss Guards wearing colourful uniforms which might have been designed by Michelangelo himself.
The **Pope** is not only the Chief of State but also the supreme head of the Universal Church, and from this very small State, the spiritual influence of the Church radiates throughout the world through the person of the sovereign pontiff. When he is in Rome, the Holy Father grants public audiences. At midday on Easter Sunday, he gives his famous blessing Urbi et Orbi (to the City and the World) from a balcony overlooking St Peter's Square. Christmas and Easter, Good Friday and 28 and 29 June are important religious festivals in Rome.

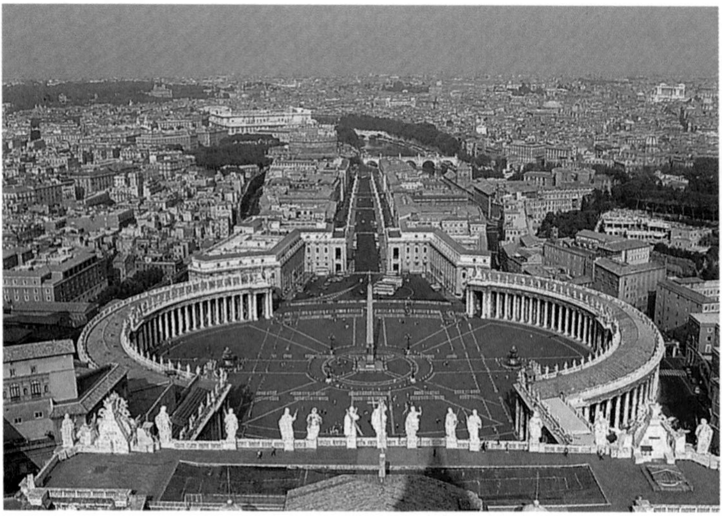
Gould/SCOPE

St Peter's Square, Rome

★★★ **Piazza San Pietro** – St Peter's Square, embraced by two semicircular colonnades, was begun in 1656 by Bernini. The centre is marked by an obelisk from the 1C BC, transported to Rome from Heliopolis in Egypt, on the orders of Caligula.

★★★ **Basilica di San Pietro** – St Peter's Basilica was built in AD 324 on the orders of the first Christian emperor, Constantine, on the spot where Peter the Apostle was buried after being martyred in Nero's circus. In the 15C, it proved necessary to rebuild the church, and reconstruction work lasted for over a century. The Greek-cross plan surmounted by a dome, designed by Bramante and continued by Michelangelo, was transformed into a Latin cross in 1606 when Carlo Maderna added two bays and a façade 115m/377ft wide and 45m/151ft high.
At the entrance, a porphyry disk indicates the spot where Charlemagne and later emperors were crowned by the Pope. Urban VIII entrusted Bernini with the task of decorating the basilica. The first chapel on the right contains the **Pietà**★★★ by Michelangelo, an extraordinary work executed during his youth, combining mastery of technique, creative power and profound spiritual feeling.
Above St Peter's tomb, Bernini created a gigantic bronze **Baldaquin**★★★ (29m/95ft high), standing on spiralling columns. He carved out alcoves in the supporting pillars of the dome to hold statues symbolizing the holy relics: St Longinus carrying the lance, St Andrew with his own oblique cross, St Veronica holding her veil, St Helen with the Holy Cross. Most of the paintings (Domenichino, Lanfranco and Poussin) were also commissioned during the Pontificate of Urban VIII. Finally, between 1657 and 1666, Bernini installed the huge bronze Cathedra Petri, the symbolic **St Peter's Throne**★★★ encasing the alleged chair of the apostle, supported by statues of the Church fathers.
Despite its enormous size, the basilica is so perfectly proportioned that visitors are not astonished by the fonts at the entrance which are held by larger-than-life statues of children. The dimensions of the largest Christian churches are marked in bronze letters on the floor of the central nave.
There is a magnificent **view**★★★ from the top of the **dome**★★★ designed by Michelangelo.

★★★ **Musei Vaticani (Vatican Museums)** – The museums *(open most of the year but only in the mornings)* occupy part of the palaces built by the popes from the 13C onwards.

The **Pio-Clementino Museum★★★** on the first floor has a collection of Greek and Roman masterpieces: the **Belvedere Torso★★★**, the **Venus of Cnidus★★**, the **Laocoon Group★★★**, the **Apollo Belvedere★★★**, **Hermes★★★**, and the **Apoxyomenos★★★**.
The **Etruscan Museum★** is on the second floor; among its notable objects are a gold 7C BC **fibula** and the **Mars** of Todi, a rare example of a bronze statue from the 5C BC.
The **Raphael Rooms★★★** (Stanze di Rafaello) used to be the apartments of Pope Julius II. As soon as he arrived in Rome, Raphael (1483-1520) was given this important commission; he was assisted in this large-scale task by his pupils. The subjects of the frescoes are the Borgo Fire, the School of Athens, Parnassus, the Expulsion of Heliodorus from the Temple, the Mass at Bolsena, and St Peter Delivered from Prison.
The **Cappella Sistina★★★** (Sistine Chapel) owes its name to Pope Sixtus IV who commissioned it for conclave meetings and as a papal chapel. The paintings on the side walls illustrate themes from the Old and New Testaments. After negotiations with Pope Julius II, Michelangelo (1475-1564) painted his vision of the Creation on the ceiling, from 1508 to 1512. Then in 1533, Pope Clement VII asked Michelangelo to decorate the wall behind the altar with a huge painting of the Last Judgement. This was completed in 1541.
The **Pinacoteca★★★** (Picture Gallery) exhibits works by Fra Angelico, Raphael, Leonardo da Vinci, Caravaggio and others.

★★CASTELLI ROMANI

Round tour of 122km/76mi to the southeast starting from Rome – allow a whole day

These fortified castles, built during the Middle Ages by noble families who fled Rome in search of safety, occupied strategic positions on the rim of a huge crater. Modern Romans are fond of spending the summer season in this area.

Castel Gandolfo★ is the summer residence of the Pope. **Albano Laziale** boasts attractive gardens (Villa Communale). **Velletri** nestles in the heart of a wine-growing region. **Nemi** is a charming village on the shores of the lake. There is a beautiful **view★** of the region from **Mount Cavo** (altitude: 949m/3 124ft). **Rocca di Papa** faces the lakes. **Grottaferrata** is known for its 11C **abbey★**. **Frascati★** is famous for its wines and is home to some fine 16C and 17C villas. The Cinecittà studios, Italy's Hollywood, can be seen on the way back to Rome.

★★Abbazia di MONTECASSINO

(MONTE CASSINO Abbey) Michelin map 970 L 8

This is one of the most important Roman Catholic monasteries. St Benedict of Nursia retired here in 529 after he left Subiaco. The patron saint of Europe drew up the rules of his order, adding intellectual study and manual labor to the virtues of chastity, poverty and obedience.
The abbey was destroyed several times, more recently at the **Battle of Cassino** (October 1943 to May 1944). The Germans had used the town as their key stronghold on the road to Rome. After the Allied assaults on this bastion of resistance failed, heavy American air bombardments reduced the place to rubble, causing numerous deaths on both sides. The abbey has been rebuilt according to the original plans. It is preceded by a succession of four cloisters. The **interior★★** is richly decorated with marble, stucco and mosaics. The tombs of St Benedict and his sister St Scholastica are placed under the altar in the choir. The **Museum★★** contains a collection of art objects which survived the 1944 bombing.

★★OSTIA ANTICA **(OSTIA)** Michelin map 970 L 8

The port of Ostia, situated at the mouth of the Tiber, followed the same destiny as that of Rome. It was founded in the 4C BC and served first as a military port, then a commercial one, before becoming a town in its own right, built entirely in brick. Sulla had it protected by ramparts in 79 BC. At that time, Ostia had up to 100 000 inhabitants. The town was abandoned after the fall of the empire and disappeared under layers of alluvium deposits, but it was rediscovered at the beginning of this century.
The **Decumanus Maximus** is the main east-west axis. On the right: are the **Terme di Nettuno** (Neptune Baths) with **mosaics★★** depicting the marriage of Neptune and Amphitrite; and the **Piazza delle Corporazioni★★★** where 70 guilds which traded with the known world had their establishments, each one with mosaics portraying the emblems of their trade. On the left is the **Thermopolium★★**, a bar which served hot drinks. The **Forum★★**, opposite the **Capitol★★**, was the largest temple in Ostia. On the right stands the 4C **Casa di Amore e Psiche★★** (House of Cupid and Psyche) with mosaic floors and a lovely nymphaeum.

The Decumanus Maximus can be reached by continuing through the **Terme dei Sette Sapienti★** (Baths of the Seven Sages), then a cluster of houses *(turn left into the Decumanus Maximus to return to the entrance)*. The **Schola del Traiano★★** on the right, an impressive 2C to 3C building, used to be the seat of a guild of merchants.

★★★TIVOLI Michelin map 970 L 8

Tivoli is perched on the slopes of the Apennines and has been a holiday resort since ancient Roman times.

★★★**Villa d'Este** – In 1550 Cardinal Ippolito d'Este retired to Tivoli where he built a villa. He entrusted the plans to a Neapolitan architect, Pirro Ligorio, who embellished the villa with elaborate gardens, adding waterfalls, **fountains★★★** and statues to create a typically Mannierist decor. The gardens are illuminated in the evenings during the summer months.

★★★**Villa Adriana (Hadrian's Villa)** – After touring the Empire, Emperor Hadrian (76-138), who had a great passion for art and architecture, decided to recreate some of the monuments and sites he had seen. Unfortunately, the villa was stripped of its art works between the 15C and 19C. All that remains are the imposing ruins of the buildings: the **Pecile★★**, resembling an Athenian portico, the **Teatro Marittimo★★★** (Maritime Theatre), the **Terme★★** (Baths), a remarkable reconstitution of the Egyptian town of **Canopus★★★**, the **Piazza d'Oro★★** and the **Doric Pillared Hall★★**.

SARDINIA

Sardinia (Sardegna) covers an area of 24 089km²/9 300sq mi and is the second largest island in the Mediterranean, after Sicily. It is situated about 250km/155mi to the west of Rome and only 12km/8mi south of Corsica and is worth a visit of at least three days. The landscape is rugged, featuring magnificent jagged coasts and miles of soft sandy beaches. Its scrub vegetation consists mainly of holm oaks and aromatic plants. Its economy is essentially based on stock-raising, with more than half of the island suitable for grazing. Ewe's milk is used for making the Sardinian cheese, *Pecorino*. A favourite meal of Sardinians is lamb or suckling pig *(porceddu)* cooked on a spit.
In the second millenium BC, the Nuraghi civilization left over 7 000 conical structures made of enormous blocks of stone assembled without mortar. The Giants' Tombs in the Olbia region are also from this period; these are collective graves consisting of a circle of standing stones and a burial chamber. The island was subsequently occupied by the Phoenicians, the Carthaginians, the Byzantines and, later, the Spanish.

East Coast

Two magnificent **roads★★★** run from the island's capital, **Cagliari** (**Archeological Museum★** and the medieval quarter) to Muravera, and from Arbatax to Dorgali, passing through impressive gorges and Nuraghi sites. Nuoro has kept its traditional folklore. To the northeast, Olbia is the entry point to the Costa Smeralda★★ (Emerald Coast), a holiday area known for its breathtaking views which attracts a wealthy international clientele. Garibaldi, hero of the expedition of the thousand, is buried in the Maddalena Archipelago.

West Coast

Sassari still has a medieval quarter where traditional festivals are held (Calvacata Sarda, the Feast of the Candles). Near **Alghero★**, a charming port which still looks like a Catalan town and is known for its coral fishing, are **Grotta di Nettuno★★★** (Neptune's Cave), which is accessible by boat or a stairway cut into the cliff, the superb headland **Capo Caccia★★** and the **Palmavera Nuraghe★**. To the south, near Barumini, is the **Nuraghe Su Nuraxi★★**, a huge Nuraghic settlement.

SICILY

The largest island in the Mediterranean with the most beautiful beaches (Mondello, Mazzaro, Marina di Ragusa...) can be visited in about eight days. It is separated from the Italian "boot" by the Messina Straits, barely 3km/2mi wide. The Ancients believed the Straits were home to the sea monsters, Scylla and Charybdis, who terrorized the sailors of Ulysses. The island's highest point is Mount Etna at an altitude of 3 340m/10 958ft. Sicily is mainly an agricultural region: citrus fruit, vineyards and olive trees grow along the coast on the Catania and Palermo plains while cereals are cultivated in the grandiose but desolate land of the interior. It has a wonderful climate with an average of 2 200 hours of sunshine a year.

Sicily, whose capital is Palermo, now has a population of nearly 5 million. The Mafia, the fearsome secret society, exerts a strong political influence by resorting to the law of silence *(omertà)*.

Throughout its history, Sicily has always been coveted because of its strategic position in the Mediterranean: the Greeks settled in the 8C BC and covered the island with theatres (Taormina, Syracuse) and Doric temples which are still very well preserved (Agrigento, Segesta, Selinus); in the 12C, the Normans imposed years of political power and cultural influence, constructing churches and palaces in a mixture of Moorish, Byzantine and Norman styles (Palermo, Monreale, Cefalù, Messina). After the 1693 earthquake, the Baroque style came into its own when the towns of Catania, Noto and Ragusa had to be reconstructed.

Like its history, Sicilian cooking is a combination of influences: pasta, couscous, different varieties of fish (swordfish, tuna, red mullet) and desserts such as *cassata siciliana* and *cannoli* stuffed with sweetened Ricotta cheese. The most well-known wines are Marsala and Malvasia.

★★★ AGRIGENTO Population 56 273. Michelin map 970 L 9

Founded in 580 BC by people who originated from Rhodes, this old Greek city built on a hillside facing the sea consists of a charming medieval city and an impressive site of ancient monuments, the **Valle dei Templi★★★**. (Valley of the Temples). Of the 10 Doric temples built in the 5C BC, nine are still partially visible along the Sacred Way: the Doric **Tempio della Concordia★★★** (Temple of Concord) is the best preserved, with a peristyle of 34 columns; the **Tempio di Giunone★★** (Temple of Juno) still has a sacrificial altar. Finally, there is the **Tempio di Jove★** (Temple of Jupiter) which would have been enormous (113 x 56m/371 x 184ft) had it been completed.

★ CATANIA Population 333 485. Michelin map 970 M9

Catania is a busy port and industrial town. Nevertheless, it has a number of Baroque monuments along wide avenues, especially on **Via Etnea★** (luxury shops) and **Piazza del Duomo★** (where a highly picturesque fish market is held every morning, except Sundays). A famous native of the town is Vincenzo Bellini (1801-1835), composer of the opera *Norma*.

★★ CEFALU Population 13 873. Michelin map 970

This charming fishing port is on a magnificent **site★★**, between the sea and a rocky headland. It has a splendid Romanesque **Cathedral★★** which was built between 1131 and 1240, following a vow made by the Norman king, Roger II during a violent storm. The cathedral has Norman features (façade framed by square towers, high apse flanked by apsidioles, timber ceiling over two of the three naves and the transept galleries). Inside, the columns have fine **capitals★★** while the Byzantine-style **mosaics★★** on a gold background in the apse depict Christ Pantocrator (the Almighty Ruler), the Virgin Mary, four archangels and the Apostles.

★★★ Isole EOLIE o LIPARI (AEOLIAN or LIPARI Islands) Michelin map 970 L 9

The Ancients believed that these islands were inhabited by Aeolus, the god of the Winds, hence their name Aeolian. Situated to the north of Milazzo, the islands of this archipelago are of great interest because of their volcanic nature and climate. The sea is crystal-clear and warm, with an unusual marine fauna of swordfish, flying fish, sea horses and turtles which makes it particularly attractive for skin divers.

★★ **Lipari** – This is the largest island of the archipelago. Two bays frame the town of **Lipari★**, dominated by a castle which was rebuilt by the Spanish in the 16C (**Museum★★**). The **Quattrocchi** belvedere offers one of the most breathtaking **views★★★** of the archipelago.

★★★ **Vulcano** – This island is named after Vulcan, the god of Fire, who according to legend installed his forges in this volcano. It is still an active volcano, emanating smoke and gas, spouting out steam jets and sending hot sulphurous mud-flows down to the beach of **Porto Levante**. About 5hr are needed to ascend and descend the **Great Crater★★★**.

★★★ **Stromboli** – The island of Stromboli is capped by an ominous-looking volcano. The crater forms a cone of 924m/3 032ft and is still very active, exploding noisily with eruptions of lava. At night, the spectacle of the *sciara del fuoco* (incandescent flows of smoke and lava) is quite awesome. Seven hours of difficult walking are needed to reach the crater; you should be accompanied by a guide.

★★★ETNA Michelin map 970 I 9

Mount Etna is one of the most well-known volcanoes in Europe. It is still very active and erupts frequently. The worst disaster occurred in 1669 when lava rushed down to the sea, devastating part of Catania, but there was also a serious eruption in 1910 after the formation of 23 new craters and, more recently, in 1987 and 1991. The volcano can be climbed from the southern slope, leaving from Catania, or from the northeastern slope, leaving from Taormina. *Wear warm clothes and walking shoes.*

★★★MONREALE Population 26 466. Michelin map 970 L 9

The town overlooks the Palermo plain known as the Conca d'Oro (Golden Conch Shell), and grew around the Benedictine abbey founded in the 12C by the Norman king, William II.

★★★**The Cathedral** – The decoration of the cathedral's chevet is a mixture of Moorish and Norman influences. The interior has a basilical plan and a dazzling ornamentation of marble, paintings and, above all, an exceptional cycle of **mosaics**★★★ from the 12C and 13C, illustrating the Old and New Testaments. In the **cloister**★★★, arcaded galleries are supported by slender twinned columns and capitals carved in an amazingly free style.

★★★PALERMO Population 698 141. Michelin map 970 L 9

Palermo, now the main port and capital of Sicily, was built at the end of a wide bay. Behind it stretches a very fertile plain bounded by hills, the Conca d'Oro, where citrus fruit trees grow in profusion. Palermo is a city of sharp contrasts, full of monuments built in different styles. However, it was seriously damaged during the last war and many of its old districts have not been restored.
Three squares form the lively centre of the city: the **Quattro Canti**★ (the square of the four corners) with Baroque façades; **Piazza Pretoria**★★ embellished with a **fountain**★★ surmounted by numerous marble statues by a 16C Florentine sculptor; and **Piazza Bellini**★ with both Moorish and Norman features, on which stands the **Church of La Martorana**★★ decorated with superb Byzantine **mosaics**★★.
All that remains of the **Palazzo dei Normanni**★★ (Palace of the Normans) is the 12C **Palatine Chapel**★★★, a superb example of the sophistication which characterized the reign of Roger II. It is magnificently decorated in the Moorish-Norman style, with horseshoe arches, mosaics★★★, a ceiling honeycombed with stalactite carvings, and marble paving. Mosaics depicting hunting scenes can be seen in **King Roger's Room**★★ on the second floor of the palace.
Palermo is also known for the strange **Catacombi dei Cappuccini**★★ (Capuchin Catacombs) where some 8 000 mummies in fine clothing have been lying since the 17C.

►► **Galleria Regionale della Sicilia**★★ (Regional Gallery of Sicily) – **Museo Archeologico**★ (National Archeological Museum).

★★★Villa romana di PIAZZA ARMERINA Michelin Map 970 L 9

The Roman Villa of Casale probably belonged to an important individual. Most of the floor is covered with mosaics, over an area of 3 500m²/37 760sq ft, dating from the 3C or 4C AD. Figures from mythology, hunting scenes, sports and animals are depicted in a picturesque way, using a wide palette of colours.

★★★SIRACUSA (SYRACUSE) Population 125 972. Michelin map 970 M 9

Syracuse, the great rival of Athens in Antiquity, is ideally located in the shelter of a bay. It was colonized in the 8C BC by Corinthians who occupied the island of Ortygia. The city then fell into the hands of tyrants and prospered. During the 5C and 4C BC, it had nearly 300 000 inhabitants: one of them, the mathematician and physicist Archimedes, helped defend the city against Rome by inventing catapults and setting enemy boats on fire through a system of giant lenses.

★★**Città Vecchia (old town)** – This is situated on the island of Ortygia. Its roads are lined with medieval and Baroque palaces. The **Piazza del Duomo** is a very harmonious architectural ensemble of palaces with elegant balconies and a **cathedral**★, built over the site of a Doric temple devoted to Athena, with some of the original massive columns still standing.

★★★**Archeological site** – This area includes a **Greek Theatre**★★★ with tiered seats cut out of the rock (5C BC). The **Ear of Denis**★★★ nearby is an artificial grotto with incredible acoustics. On the other side is a very well preserved **Roman amphitheatre**★.

★★Museo archeologico regionale Paolo Orsi – This archeological museum in the grounds of the **Villa Landolina** conjures up the history of Sicily from prehistoric times to the Syracuse colonies (7C BC).

★★★TAORMINA Population 10 115. Michelin map 970 M 9

Taormina has become a holiday resort with a worldwide reputation because of its spectacular **setting★★★** facing the sea and Mount Etna, overlooking picturesque creeks. The lush vegetation of its gardens makes it even more charming.
The 3C BC **Greek theatre★★★** was remodelled by the Romans who added the stage wall. Concerts are now held here in summer.

HELBIG /ZEFA

The theatre and Mount Etna, Taormina

TUSCANY

The Tuscan scenery makes it particularly appealing: small low hills with wide views and terraced gardens surrounding Renaissance villas. Olive groves, vineyards and cypress trees form a natural architecture under a subtle golden light. Florence is in the heart of the Arno basin while further south, set in the midst of hills is Siena, another city of art. Tuscany also has its own archipelago, including the island of Elba, and a coast with seaside resorts, such as Viareggio not far from the villa where Puccini composed *La Bohème, Madame Butterfly* and *Tosca.*
Italian cuisine was born in Tuscany, at the Medici court. Florence has many specialities alla fiorentina: *baccalà* (cod) dressed in oil, garlic and pepper; *bistecca* or *costata*, a very thick steak grilled with oil, salt and pepper; *fagioli*, beans in oil flavoured with garlic and onion. And of course, the famous Chianti wines from vineyards in the south of Tuscany.

★★AREZZO Population 91 578. Michelin map 970 K 7

Arezzo is an old Etruscan city which was annexed by Florence in 1384, following a long struggle. It was the birthplace of the humanist poet Petrarch (1304-1374) and Giorgio Vasari (1511-1574), known for his book on the life of the artists of his time. **Piazza Grande★**, surrounded by medieval houses and Renaissance palaces, is the venue for a historical event, the **Saracen's Tournament** *(held on the last Sunday of August or first Sunday of September).*

San Francesco (Church of St Francis) – This Gothic church dedicated to St Francis was built by Franciscan monks, guardians of the Sacred Sites, who venerated the Holy Cross. They commissioned Piero della Francesca to decorate the choir of their church. The **frescoes★★★**, executed between 1452 and 1466, relate the story of the Holy Cross. These paintings are outstanding for their gay colours. The intense blues of the sky, shades of green and pink, browns and whites create an effect of perfect serenity and everlasting peace. The extraordinary modelling and anatomical realism of the figures, who almost seem to reflect the architectural background, is the work of a genius. The night scene of Constantine's Dream is particularly remarkable.

★★★ FIRENZE (FLORENCE) Population 402 211. Michelin map 970 K 7

Florence, capital of the arts, is without a doubt the city where the Italian genius flourished at its best. From the 13C to the 16C, it was the cradle of an exceptional artistic output by the most creative minds. It is the birthplace of Dante (1265-1321), Machiavelli (1469-1527) and Michelangelo. Florentine art is characterized by a constant search for clarity and harmony.

It was founded by Julius Caesar but only became prosperous under the influence of its merchants in the 12C, when it acquired some fine buildings such as San Miniato or the baptistery. During the 13C, the wool and silk crafts employed one third of the population and craftsmen, who backed by Florentine bankers, were able to export their products all over Europe.

Despite its wealth, Florence did not escape the internal strife that raged between the Ghibellines who were partisans of the emperor, and the Guelphs who supported the Pope. The 1348 plague decimated half the population but brought the struggles to an end. The Medici, who were wealthy bankers, exerted great financial power and artistic influence. They attracted artists and craftsmen to their court, studding the surrounding countryside with villas and beautiful gardens (the Villas of La Petraia, Castello, Poggio a Caiano). They ruled Florence until the 18C.

Since the monuments are close to each other, sightseeing is best done on foot.

Florence is famous for articles in leather (Leather School in the Santa Croce Monastery), silk or straw, for its marbled paper (Piazza dei Pitti) and of course for the jewellers on Ponte Vecchio. Antique shops can be found in Borgo Ognissanti, Via dei Fossi and Via Maggio, while the dress designers are in Via Tornabuoni.

★★★ **Piazza del Duomo** (Y) – The cathedral, bell-tower and baptistery, in white, green and pink marble, form the heart of the city and show how Florentine art developed from the Middle Ages to the Renaissance.

★★★ **Duomo** – **The Cathedral of Santa Maria del Fiore** has an exceptionally beautiful dome and is one of the largest churches of the Christian world. The Sienese architect Arnolfo di Cambio started work on it in 1296, and it was consecrated in 1436. Brunelleschi was commissioned to design the **dome**★★★, the first to be built since Antiquity. He invented an ingenious method to counteract excessive lateral thrust by constructing two round domes linked by invisible struts. The façade was completed at the end of the 19C. Its bare interior is in sharp contrast to the opulent exterior.

★★★ **Campanile** (**B**) – This tall slender bell-tower (82m/269ft), with its geometric decoration emphasising straight, mainly horizontal lines, counterbalances the curves of the dome. Giotto drew up the plans and construction started in 1334, but it was not finished until the end of the 14C.

★★★ **Baptistery** (**A**) – It was built in the 4C or 5C and was encased in marble between the 11C and 13C. Its famous **bronze doors**★★★ are the work of Andrea Pisano (1330) who portrayed the life of St John the Baptist on the south door, and of Lorenzo Ghiberti (1403-1424) who illustrated scenes from the life of Christ on the north door. Opposite the cathedral, the east door, described as the **Gate to Paradise** by

S. Chirol

View of Florence

FIRENZE

Agli (Via degli) .... Y 3
Antinori (Piazza degli).......... Y 10
Archibusieri (Lungarno)....... Z 12
Avelli (Via degli).................. Y 16
Brunelleschi (Via de') .... YZ 22
Calimala (Via) ....Z 24
Calzaiuoli (Via dei)............ YZ
Canto de' Nelli
(Via dei)............................ Y 27
Castellani (Via de')............... Z 31
Dante Alighieri (Via)............ Z 42
Davanzati (Piazza)................ Z 43
Fiordaliso (Via del).............. Z 52
Gondi (Via dei)..................... Z 61
Lambertesca (Via)................ Z 69
Leoni (Via dei)...................... Z 70
Madonna degli Aldobrandini
(Piazza di)......................... Y 75
Magazzini (Via dei) .... Z 76
Melarancio (Via del) .... Y 85
Mornalda (Via) .... Z 88
Orsanmichele (Via).............. Z 99
Parte Guelfa
(Piazza di)......................... Z 106
Pellicceria (Via) .... Z 109
Pescioni (Via de') .... YZ 111
Por S. Maria (Via)................ Z 126
Porta Rossa (Via)................ Z
Roma (Via)........................ YZ
Rondinelli (Via de') .... Y 138
S. Giovanni (Piazza) .... Y 150
S. Jacopo (Borgo)................ Z .
S. Trinita (Piazza) .... Z 163
Sassetti (Via de').................. Z 171
Spada (Via della).................. Z 173
Spieziali (Via degli) .... Z 174
Strozzi (Piazza)..................... Z 177
Strozzi (Via degli)................ Z
Tavolini (Via dei)................... Z 180
Terme (Via delle) .... Z 181
Tornabuoni (Via) .... Z
Trebbio (Via del) .... Y 187
Uffizi (Piazzale degli)............. Z 188
Vacchereccia (Via) .... Z 189
Vecchio (Ponte).................... Z
Vigna Nuova (Via della)......... Z 193

Battistero.......................... Y A
Campanile .... Y B
Loggia dei Rucellai........... Z F
Loggia del Bigallo .... Y G
Loggia della Signoria....... Z K
Loggia di S. Paolo............ Y L
Mercato Nuovo .... Z N
Museo dell'Antica
casa fiorentina.............. Z M4
Museo dell'Opera
del Duomo .... Y M5
Museo di Storia
della Scienza .... Z M6
Museo Marino Marini ...... Z M7
Orsanmichele.................... Z R
Palazzo di Parte Guelfa .... Z S1
Palazzo Vecchio .... Z H
Torre della Castagna........ Z Z

Traffic restricted in town centre

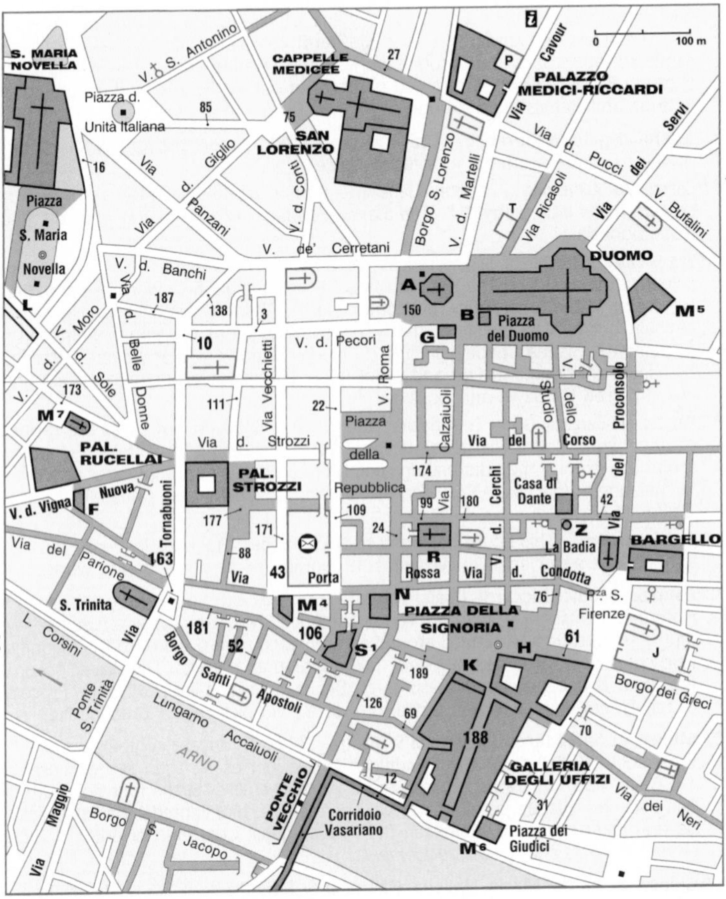

Michelangelo, was also sculpted by Ghiberti from 1425 to 1452 on themes taken from the Old Testament. Inside, the wide dome has a diameter of 25m (82ft) and is decorated with 13C **mosaics**★★★ of the Last Judgement, on each side of Christ the King.

★★ **Piazza della Signoria** (Z) – This square, the political centre of Florence, is virtually an open-air museum against the backcloth of **Palazzo Vecchio**★★★ (**H**), a 14C Gothic fortress which used to be the city's seat of government. In the middle of the Renaissance **courtyard**★ is a fountain with a winged spirit carrying a dolphin. The **Loggia della Signoria**★★ (**K**), in front of the palace, served as an assembly hall for the Lansquenets (foot soldiers) of Cosimo I. It contains Renaissance statues, including the *Rape of a Sabine* and *Hercules and Nessus* by Giovanni da Bologna and **Perseus Holding the Head of Medusa**★★★ by Benvenuto Cellini.

★★★ **Galleria degli Uffizi** (Z) – The Uffizi museum was built by Vasari in the 16C. It is one of the finest painting galleries in the world, thanks to the works collected by the Medici which trace the development of Italian and European painting from the

13C to the 18C. Among the numerous masterpieces belonging to the museum, mention should be made of the following: *The Annunciation* by Simone Martini, *Battle of San Romano* by Paolo Uccello, **several works by Botticelli★★★** *(Birth of Venus, Spring...)*, the famous *Portinari Triptych* by the Flemish Hugo Van der Goes, *The Annunciation* by Leonardo da Vinci, *Adoration of the Magi* by Dürer, *The Holy Family* by Michelangelo, *Madonna with a Goldfinch* by Raphael, *Bacchus as a Youth* by Caravaggio.

★★**Ponte Vecchio** (Z) – This old bridge goes back to the 14C. It is one of the very few medieval bridges which still has shops on it, as in the Middle Ages. Jewellers have been established on this bridge since the 16C. The covered passageway over it connects the Palazzo Vecchio with the Palazzo Pitti.

★★**Palazzo Pitti** – The Pitti Palace is an austere and imposing Renaissance building, with a massive rusticated base and numerous windows. The Pitti family, rivals of the Medici, built it on plans by Brunelleschi. Today, it houses several museums, including the **Galleria palatina★★★** (Palatine Gallery) with a sumptuous **painting collection★★★** (Raphael, Titian, Van Dyck, Rubens, Caravaggio, Veronese and Velasquez) and the **Museo degli Argenti★★** (Silver Museum) containing antique vases, objects in semi-precious stones and Baroque works. A nice way of ending this visit is to stroll through **Boboli Gardens★**, a terraced garden laid out in the 16C and decorated with antique and Renaissance statues.

Michelangelo in Florence – The works executed by the artist for the Medici family or the town are scattered all over Florence.

★★**Galleria dell'Accademia** (Academy Gallery) – Michelangelo's sculptures are well presented in the **main gallery★★★**: *The Slaves, St Matthew* and the *David* of the Piazza della Signoria.

★★**San Lorenzo** (Church of St Lawrence) (Y) – San Lorenzo served as the family mausoleum of the Medici. The **New Sacristy** is Michelangelo's first work as an architect. He designed the funerary chapel containing the **Medici tombs★★★** which he sculpted himself, but he was unable to finish this commission as the Pope summoned him to paint the Sistine Chapel. Giulano de Medici is portrayed as Action, surrounded by allegorical figures of Day and Night while Lorenzo II is portrayed as a Thinker, accompanied by Dawn and Dusk.

★★★**Palazzo del Bargello** (Z) – This palace, built in the 13C and 14C, was the residence of the chief of police *(bargello)*. It now houses a **museum★★★** of Italian Renaissance sculpture. Among the outstanding sculptures on display are a number of works by Michelangelo *(Bacchus; Pitti Tondo)*, Benvenuto Cellini and Donatello (a bronze *David; St Georges*).

★**Casa Buonarroti** – This house belonged to Michelangelo Buonarotti (hence the name) although he never actually lived in it. It contains some of his earlier works.

★★**Palazzo Medici-Riccardi (Medici Palace)** (Y) – This building is very typical of the Florentine Renaissance style with its mathematical layout and massive rusticated walls on the ground floor, arranged around an arched courtyard. Lorenzo the Magnificent held court here, attended by poets, philosophers and artists. The **chapel★★★** on the first floor is decorated with frescoes by Benozzo Gozzoli illustrating the Procession of the Three Kings, which in fact also gives a vivid picture of Florentine life.

★★**Museo di San Marco (Museum of St Mark)** – This old convent contains **works★★★** by Fra Angelico. He joined the Dominican Order in Fiesole, then settled here from 1438 to 1455, where he covered the walls of the cells on the first floor with edifying scenes. His art is full of mystical gentleness, highlighted by refined colours. Several paintings are exhibited in the former guest quarters, including a *Descent from the Cross* and a *Last Judgement*.

★★**Chiesa di Santa Maria Novella (Church of St Mary the New)** (Y) – The church and adjacent convent were founded by the Dominicans in the 13C. The 15C façade in white and green marble is the work of Alberti. The choir of this enormous church (100m - 328ft long) is decorated with **frescoes★★★** by Ghirlandaio, describing the lives of the Virgin and of St John the Baptist. The cloister also has frescoes by Paolo Uccello illustrating scenes from the Old Testament.

►► **Santa Maria del Carmine★★** (frescoes by Masaccio in the Brancacci Chapel) – **Santa Croce★★** (pantheon to the glory of Italy) – **San Miniato al Monte★★** – **Fiesole★** *(8km/5mi to the north)*: **view★★★** of Florence.

★★★LUCCA Population 87 577. Michelin map 970 K 7

Protected by a green belt, Lucca has retained the plan of a Roman camp structured around two main roads to which were added a complicated network of alleys and unusually-shaped squares during the Middle Ages. The city flourished as a result of trading and silk manufacture. It is the home town of the composers Luigi Boccherini (1743-1805) and Giacomo Puccini (1858-1924) and in spring and summer two music festivals are organized in their honour.

★★**Duomo** – Lucca's cathedral is dedicated to St Martin. The white and green marble **façade**★★ gives an impression of strength and balance despite its asymmetry. The Romanesque reliefs in the porch illustrate the Works of the Months and the life of St Martin. On the west wall is an unusual Romanesque sculpture of **St Martin Dividing his Cloak**★. The sacristy contains a masterpiece of funerary sculpture created in 1406 by the Sienese sculptor Jacopo della Quercia, the **Tomb of Ilaria del Carretto**★★, wife of Paolo Guinigi, Lord of Lucca at the beginning of the 15C.

►► **San Michele in Foro**★★ (St Michael's Church) – **San Frediano**★ (St Frigidian's Church).

★★★PISA Population 98 810. Michelin map 970 K 7

Pisa was an ancient Roman naval base. It soon equalled Genoa and Venice, and contributed to protecting the Mediterranean from Muslim domination. But in 1284, its fleet was destroyed by the Genoese at the battle of Meloria. By 1406 it was under Florentine rule.

★★★Piazza dei Miracoli

The famous Square of the Miracles, also known as Piazza del Duomo, forms one of the finest architectural ensembles in the world. The best way to approach it is through Porta Santa Maria, where the view of the leaning tower is at its most spectacular.

★★★**Torre Pendente (Leaning Tower)** – This white marble tower is a fine example of the pure Romanesque style. It is (58m/189ft) high and served both as a bell-tower for the cathedral and as a belfry. Construction started in 1173 but from 1178 onwards, the tower slowly began to lean because of the unstable alluvial ground on which it was built. The situation has become so serious over the last few years that in 1993 the base had to be reinforced by a concrete sheath. It was from the top of this tower that Galileo (1564-1642) carried out his experiments which enabled him to establish the laws of falling bodies.

★★**Duomo** – The cathedral, which was started in 1063, has a graceful **façade**★★★ with four tiers of galleries on small slender columns. The **bronze doors**★ of the main entrance were cast in the 16C to designs by Giovanni Bologna, while the door **panels**★★ of the right transept are from the Romanesque period. The imposing interior is 100m/328ft long. The **pulpit**★★★ by Giovanni Pisano is from the early 14C and illustrates the life of Christ; the dramatic expressions of the figures are quite exceptional for the period.

★★★**Battistero (Baptistery)** – Work began on the baptistery in 1153. It is another typical example of the Romanesque Pisan style, although the gables and pinnacles over the arcades on the first floor are Gothic. It is surmounted by a dome in the shape of a truncated pyramid. The **pulpit**★★, sculpted by Nicola Pisano in 1260, is simpler than the one in the cathedral and seems to be inspired by Roman sarcophagi.

★★**Camposanto** – This cemetery is bounded by Gothic arcades forming graceful bays. Unfortunately, a fire caused by artillery shelling in 1944, damaged the frescoes on the walls. A few of them were saved, including the **Triumph of Death**★★★, painted by an artist in 1360 who was obviously influenced by the great plague of 1348. The fresco sketches can be seen in the **Museo delle Sinopie**★ (Sinopia Museum).

►► **Museo dell'Opera del Duomo**★★ (Cathedral Museum) containing works relating to the Piazza dei Miracoli monuments – **Museo Nazionale**★★ di San Matteo (National Museum) – **Santa Maria della Spina**★★ (Church of St Mary of the Thorn).

★★★SAN GIMIGNANO Population 6 945. Michelin map 970 K 7

This imposing fortress stands at the top of a hill, its picturesque medieval towers soaring into the sky. They are symbols of the power of noble families and testify to the glorious economic past of the city which was once an important textile centre.

Piazza della Cisterna★★, paved with bricks laid edgewise in a herring-bone pattern, is named after the well *(cisterna)* in the middle.

Piazza del Duomo★★ is surrounded by the **Collegiate Church**★, decorated with interesting 14C and 15C frescoes, and the **Palazzo del Popolo**★ (Palace of the People) with Lippo Memmi's **Maestà (Madonna and Child Enthroned in Majesty)**★ in the Council Chamber. There is a fine **view**★★ from the top of the tower.
The **Church of Sant'Agostino** (St Augustine) has a cycle of 17 **frescoes**★★ by Benozzo Gozzoli.

S. Chirol

Piazza del Campo

*** SIENA Population 58 842. Michelin map 970 K 7

Siena, which gave its name to the colour burnt sienna, is built on three red clay hills. It is a city of the arts, with a serpentine plan protected by impressive ramparts. It is also a mystical city for St Catherine was born here in 1347. She joined the Dominican order and in 1377 played an important role in bringing back to Rome the papal court, which had moved to Avignon in 1309. The Sienese are also very devoted to St Bernardino who spent much time preaching all over Italy.
The wealth of Siena dates from the 13C and 14C, during which the independent republic flourished thanks to its dynamic merchants and bankers. For a long time, it opposed Florence, its powerful neighbour. Yet it was during this troubled period that it built its most prestigious monuments and gave birth to the Sienese School of Painting. The city began to decline after the Black Death decimated its population in 1348.

*** **Piazza del Campo** – This is one of the most beautiful squares in the world. It is fan-shaped, slightly inclined, paved with bricks, and encircled in a ring of stone slabs. Eight white lines radiate from the town hall (Palazzo Pubblico), dividing the Campo into nine parts, each representing one of the Sienese governments in the Middle Ages. This is where the famous **Palio delle Contrade** is held every year, on 2 July and 16 August. During this festival, which goes back to the Renaissance, a very colourful costumed procession is followed by a bare-back horse race between the different parishes (contrade) of the town. The winner receives the *palio*, a banner bearing the effigy of the Virgin who protects the city.

*** **Palazzo Pubblico** (town hall) – This unusually elegant Gothic building contains some famous frescoes, including the **Allegories of Good and Bad Government** by Ambrogio Lorenzetti in the **Peace Room**★★ (Sala della Pace) or the equestrian portrait of Giudoriccio da **Fogliano**★★, by Simone Martini. There is a superb **view**★★ from the top of the tower (88m/288ft).

*** **Duomo** – The façade of the cathedral has alternating bands of light and dark marble like that of Orvieto. Inside, the marble **paving**★★★ consists of 56 panels portraying figures or biblical scenes. The **pulpit**★★★ by Nicola Pisano (13C) is carved with powerfully dramatic reliefs. A doorway in the north aisle leads to the **Libreria Piccolomini** (**frescoes**★★ painted between 1502 and 1509 by Pinturicchio).

*** **Pinacoteca (Picture Gallery)** – A rich collection of art, in particular works by the Sienese Primitives, is housed in the 15C **Palazzo Buonsignori**★. Among the paintings on display are a Madonna of the Franciscans by Duccio, a Madonna and Child by Simone Martini, and works by the Lorenzetti brothers.

►► **Museo dell'Opera Metropolitana**★★ (Cathedral Museum) – **Battistero San Giovanni**★ (Baptistery of St John).

On all town plans north is at the top of the page.

UMBRIA

Umbria is the peaceful land of St Francis of Assisi, a region of gently rolling hills, sinuous valleys, rivers, and poplars outlined against a very luminous sky. The region deserves its reputation as the green heart of Italy. The medieval cities and art centres which succeeded the Etruscan settlements overlook the hollows and valleys of the countryside: austere Gubbio, haughty Perugia, capital of the region, holy Assisi, Orvieto and Spoleto.

★★★ ASSISI Population 24 567. Michelin map 970 J 4

The terraced town on the slopes of Mount Subasio has hardly changed since the Middle Ages. It is permeated with the memory of St Francis (1182-1226), founder of the Franciscan Order, and attracts large crowds of pilgrims.

★★★ **Basilica di San Francesco (Basilica of St Francis)** – At the end of the 14C, master builders from Rome and Florence worked on the site of this Basilica.
The sober Lower Basilica is entirely covered with 13C to 14C **frescoes**★★★. In the first chapel on the left, paintings by Simone Martini illustrating the life of St Martin are remarkable for their delicate lines and harmonious composition. The **frescoes**★★ in the left transept depict the Passion with a wealth of narrative details. The *Madonna with Four Angels and St Francis*, a majestic composition by Cimabue, is placed in the right transept. Steps lead down to the saint's tomb.
The Upper Basilica, tall and slender, is bathed in light filtering through the high windows. A cycle of 28 **frescoes**★★★ on the life of St Francis was executed by Giotto and his assistants. The scenes, with their clear airy composition and obvious search for realism, led the way to Renaissance art.

The town has other monuments recalling the life of the saint: the **Church of Santa Chiara**★★ (St Clare), the **cathedral**★ (Duomo San Rufino), and in the outskirts the **Monastery of San Damiano**★ (St Damian) and the **Carceri Hermitage**★★ (Eremo delle Carceri).

★★ GUBBIO Population 30 758. Michelin map 970 L 7

Gubbio is firmly rooted in its medieval origins. The steep little streets are lined with ochre-coloured houses with Roman-tile roofs, noble palaces and towers, and shops selling pottery, a local craft which began in the Middle Ages.
Every year, a spectacular festival is held on 15 May: the **Candle Race** (Ceri), in which men carrying three enormous wooden candles weighing 300kg/660lb and topped by statutes of saints race up to Mount St Ubald over a 5km/3mi route.
In the **old town**★, some of the house fronts have a second, narrower door through which coffins were carried out. The **Palazzo dei Consoli**★★ (Consuls' Palace), a 15C Gothic building with a majestic façade, is the main feature of Piazza della Signoria. The **Palazzo Ducale**★ (Ducal Palace) near the Duomo was built for Federico de Montefeltro, the Duke of Urbino. The reception rooms are decorated with frescoes.

★★ ORVIETO Population 21 378. Michelin map 970 L 7

Orvieto was once a major Etruscan settlement and has now become a pleasant city, full of monuments, set in a particularly scenic **site**★★★.

★★★ **Duomo** – This cathedral, a perfect example of the transitional Romanesque-Gothic style, was built in tufa at the end of the 13C. The sumptuous decor of its **façade**★★★ makes it the boldest and most colourful of all Italian Gothic constructions. Sculptures cover the lower part, while the upper part is decorated with polychrome marble and mosaics, surmounted by gables and spires. Inside, the **Corporal Chapel** enshrines the relics of the Bolsena miracle; during the celebration of a mass, a host dripped blood on the white altar cloth, the **corporale**, now kept in a magnificent **reliquary**★★, the brilliant masterpiece of medieval goldsmiths (1338).

► ► **Pozzo di San Patrizio**★★ (St Patrick's Well), composed of two spiral staircases designed by Sangallo the Younger.

★★ PERUGIA Population 150 576. Michelin map 970 L 7

Despite Etruscan remains, medieval monuments and the solid artistic reputation of its Renaissance Painting School, Perugia has remained a young town because of the thousands of foreign students studying at its university.
The **Galleria Nazionale dell'Umbria**★★ (National Gallery of Umbria) is housed in the Priors' Palace. Its collections trace the development of Umbrian art from the 13C to the 18C, with works by Piero della Francesca, Perugino who was Raphael's master, Pinturicchio, Pietro da Cortona and Orazio Gentileschi.

URBINO and the MARCHES

The Marches derive their name from the fact that they were once frontier provinces. The region, situated between San Marino and Ascoli Piceno, is cut up by the parallel secondary ranges of the Apennines which slope down towards the Adriatic and form a succession of deep narrow valleys. There are numerous beaches along the flat straight stretch of coast. Apart from the busy port of Ancona, the capital, most of the older towns are on high ground; Urbino and Loreto (well known for the House of Mary) are on particularly attractive sites.

★★URBINO Population 15 111

This charming town built of rose-coloured brick and surrounded by ramparts is spread over two hills. It used to be one of the greatest artistic centres of the Renaissance. From the 12C onwards, it was ruled by the Montefeltro family, and the town reached the height of its glory under the reign of **Duke Federico da Montefeltro** (1444-1482), a skillful Condottiere (leader), man of letters, collector and patron of the arts. A portrait of him by Piero della Francesca can be seen in the Uffizi Gallery in Florence.

★★★**Palazzo Ducale (Ducal Place)** – The Ducal Palace was built between 1444 and 1472 for Duke Federico by the Dalmatian architect Luciano Laurana. It was designed to make the most of the splendid view. On the valley side, the high façade of the palace is decorated with an unusual and elegant pattern of superimposed loggias framed by two high round towers. The pure lines and architectural rhythm of the inner courtyard is a perfect example of Renaissance harmony.

★★**Galleria Nazionale delle Marche** (National Gallery of the Marches) – The palace houses a gallery exhibiting a number of masterpieces by Paolo Uccello, Piero della Francesca, Laurana, Raphael, and the Duke of Montefeltro's **Library**★★★ decorated with *trompe-l'œil* inlaid wood panels.

VENETIA

Venetia is composed mainly of the alluvial Po plain, overlooked in the north by the Pre-Alps, and even further north by the Dolomites. Although this region is basically agricultural, there is no lack of industry: oil refineries and chemical plants are concentrated in Mestre-Marghera. Two small volcanic ranges give an unexpected touch to the landscape: the Berici mountains south of Vicenza and the Euganean hills near Padua, their fertile vine-covered slopes bubbling with hot springs. The coastline is formed by lagoons separated from the sea by an offshore bar (lido). Venice is built on piles in one of these lagoons.
Here, as in the rest of the Po plain, the favourite dishes are *polenta*, a cake of salted cornmeal, *risi e bisi* (rice and peas), *fegato alla veneziana* (calf liver fried with onions). The Verona region produces the best wines: Valpolicella and Bardolino, both rosé and red.

★★Riviera del Brenta (BRENTA Riviera)

A number of magnificent **villas**★ in the classic Palladian style are strung along about 30km/19mi of the Brenta Canal. The Venetian nobility used to come here in summer and give sumptuous banquets at night, entertaining guests with firework displays and music by Vivaldi, Pergolese and Cimarosa. This area can be visited by boat *(from May to October)*, leaving from Venice or Padua, or by a road which runs by the side of the canal and crosses Strà, Dolo, Mira and Malcontenta.

Strà – The 18C **Villa Pisani**★ contains luxurious **apartments**★ decorated by G Tiepolo, F Zuccarelli, S Ricci and J Amigoni, and is set in a garden with a beautiful vista. Many distinguished guests have stayed at this villa: the Grand Dukes of Russia, Maximilian of Hapsburg and Napoleon. A famous 18C labyrinth can be seen in the park.

Malcontenta – **Villa Foscari**★, built in 1574 by Palladio, is named after a lady from the Foscari family who was highly displeased (malcontenta) about having to live there. It is the first villa Palladio designed with a temple façade.

MAROSTICA

This medieval town is very close to **Bassano del Grappa**★ (famous for its grappa brandy and pottery). Its **main square**★ is laid out like a giant chessboard for a highly original chess game, **Partita a Scacchi**, in which people dressed in historical costumes move as instructed by the players *(first Sunday in September)*.

★★PADOVA (PADUA) Population 215 017. Michelin map 970 K 6

In the Middle Ages, Padua was a busy town and place of pilgrimage. It was also the second largest university town after Bologna *(see the 1594 Anatomy Theatre in the university)*. Galileo taught here. The vast **Piazza dei Signori** in the centre is worth visiting to see the **Palazzo del Capitano**, former residence of the Venetian governors, and the **Torre dell'Orologio**★ (clock tower) which gives the time but also indicates the movements of the planets and stars.

St Anthony the Hermit – Although he was born in Lisbon, he spent much of his life in the region of Padua. This Franciscan monk and Church doctor was an eloquent preacher. He is usually portrayed holding a book and lily branch, and is venerated as the patron saint of lost objects. The **Basilica del Santo**★★ (St's Basilica) dedicated to him is surmounted by Byzantine domes, like St Mark in Venice. The **high altar**★★ is decorated with bronze panels by Donatello.

Art in Padua – In 1304, **Giotto** arrived in Padua from Florence to decorate the Scrovegni Chapel with a cycle of **frescoes**★★★, one of the greatest masterpieces of Italian painting. This cycle reveals the powerful modelling of figures, masterful handling of perspective, keen sense of dramatic narrative (lives of Anna and Joachim, the Virgin and Christ, allegories of the Vices and Virtues) and rich colour palette of his later works.
In the 15C, the Renaissance in Padua was marked by another Florentine, the sculptor **Donatello**, who worked there from 1444 to 1453 on the first equestrian statue since Antiquity (in front of St Anthony's Basilica), portraying **Gattamelata**★★, a Venetian Condottiere who died in Padua in 1443. Finally, art in Padua also flourished thanks to the work of **Mantegna** (1431-1506), a Paduan painter of great originality and an innovative master of perspective, who was fascinated by anatomy and archeology, as can be seen in his **frescoes**★★ inside the **Church degli Eremitani** (of the Hermits) which were unfortunately damaged by bombing in 1944.

★★★VENEZIA (VENICE) Population 309 041. Michelin map 970 L 6

"This is the town which has inspired amazement in everyone... he who does not contemplate it is unworthy of light, he who does not admire it is unworthy of the mind... he who has not seen it will not believe what he is told, while he who has seen it will hardly believes his eyes. He who has heard of its glory will not rest until he has seen it, and he who has seen it will not rest until he has seen it again...." This is how a Doge described La Serenissima in 1570.

Historical notes – Venice was founded in 811, and in 828 was placed under the protection of St Mark whose body was brought from Alexandria. Venice then became a republic ruled by a Doge, a word derived from the Latin dux (leader), assisted by several councillors. Until the 13C, the city was able to take advantage of its favourable position between East and West. In 1204, thanks to the skill and cunning of Doge Dandolo, it conquered Constantinople with the help of the Crusaders. Plundered treasures flowed into Venice while trade in precious commodities flourished. Marco Polo (1254-1324) returned from China with fabulous riches and dazzled Europe with his travel accounts written in French. The long-standing rivalry with Genoa, jealous of its supremacy over the seas, ended in victory for the Venetian Republic. Venetian power reached its peak in the first half of the 15C. In Italy, the Venetians seized Verona, Vicenza, Padua, Udine, Brescia and Bergamo. The Adriatic became the Venetian Sea from Corfu to the Po. However, the capture of Constantinople by the Turks in 1453 started the decline of Venice, while the discovery of America opened up new trading routes. In 1797, the Most Serene Republic came to an end. Napoleon entered Venice and abolished the old constitution under which it had been governed for 10 centuries. Under the Treaty of Campoformio, he ceded the town to Austria. Venice was finally united with Italy in 1866.

The best seasons – The best seasons to visit Venice are spring and autumn, even though there are some exciting events in summer (Feast of the Redeemer on the third Saturday of July; traditional regatta on the first Sunday of September). Then there is the Film Festival in September, Biennial Modern Art Show and the winter Carnival. In the 18C, the latter used to last for three months and Venetians wore their masks for more than six months!

Aspects of Venice – The Serenissima is built on 177 islands linked by an intricate network of some 150 canals. It is this unique position which now threatens Venice: the nature of the ground on which it was built is causing it to sink, while the water level is constantly rising. Whether one arrives by train, plane or car, visitors can only explore Venice on foot or by water bus. The best way to get to know the city is by using the little steamer (**vaporetto** – *line 1*) which goes down the Grand Canal to the centre of public life: Piazza San Marco where both tourists and Venetians enjoy sitting on the terraces of the Florian and Quadri cafés to listen to music, daydream and admire the mosaics of St Mark's Basilica, dropping in later at the popular

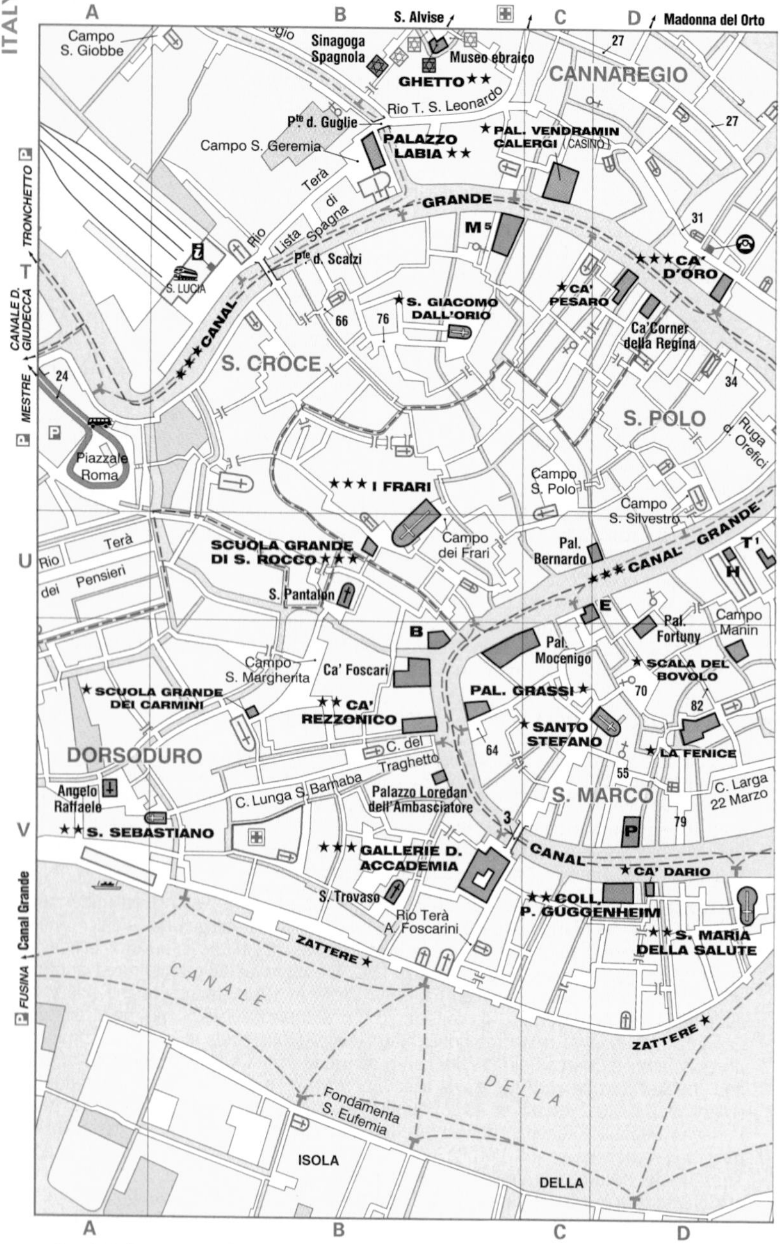

Accademia Ponte dell' .... BV 3
Bandera e Moro (Campo) .. FV 6
Capello (Ramo) .... FT 10
Gallina, Giacinco
(Calle Larga) .... FT 18
Leoncini (Plazetta dei) .... EV 21
Libertà (Ponte della) .... AT 24
Misericordia
(Fondamenta della) .... DT 27

Nuova (Strada) .... ET 28
Orologio
(Merceria dell') .... EV 31
Pescaria
(Campo della) .... DT 34
San Bartolomeo
(Campo) .... ET 39
San Giovanni
Crisostomo (Salizzada) .... ET 43

San Lorenzo (Calle Larga) ... FT 46
San Marco (Calle Larga) ..... EV 49
San Marco (Piazzetta) .... EV 52
S. Maurizio (Campo) .... DV 55
San Moisé (Salizzada) .... EV 58
San Salvador (Merceria) ..... EU 61
San Samuelle (Campo) ...... BV 64
San Simeon Profeta
(Campo) .... BT 66

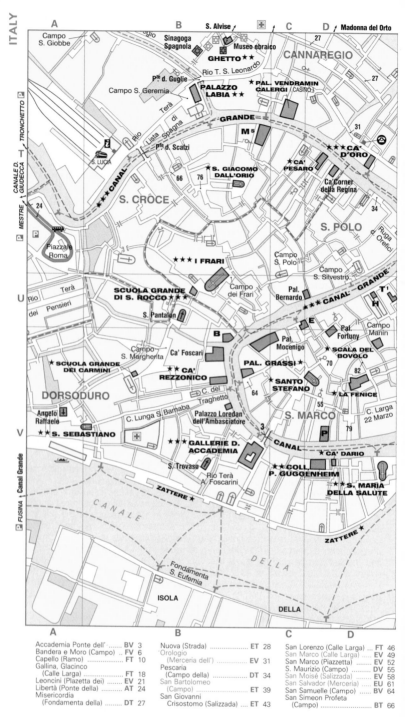

Harry's Bar *(near the San Marco landing-stage)* for a cocktail. The shops on this square have attractive windows shimmering with displays of lace, jewellery, masks, mirrors and Murano crystal. Beyond are the mercerie, shopping streets which lead to the Rialto. On the other side of this bridge are the crowded stalls of greengrocers and fishmongers supplied by numerous cargo boats. Monuments and directions are indicated at all street corners on signposts with a yellow background.

Gondolas are virtually the symbol of Venice. Gondoliers, dressed in sailors' sweaters and wearing a straw hat with a coloured ribbon, murmur the words gondola, gondola, singing as they steer their craft with a single oar. Meals at the local *trattorie* are one of the great pleasures of life in Venice; their specialities are based on fish and sea food.

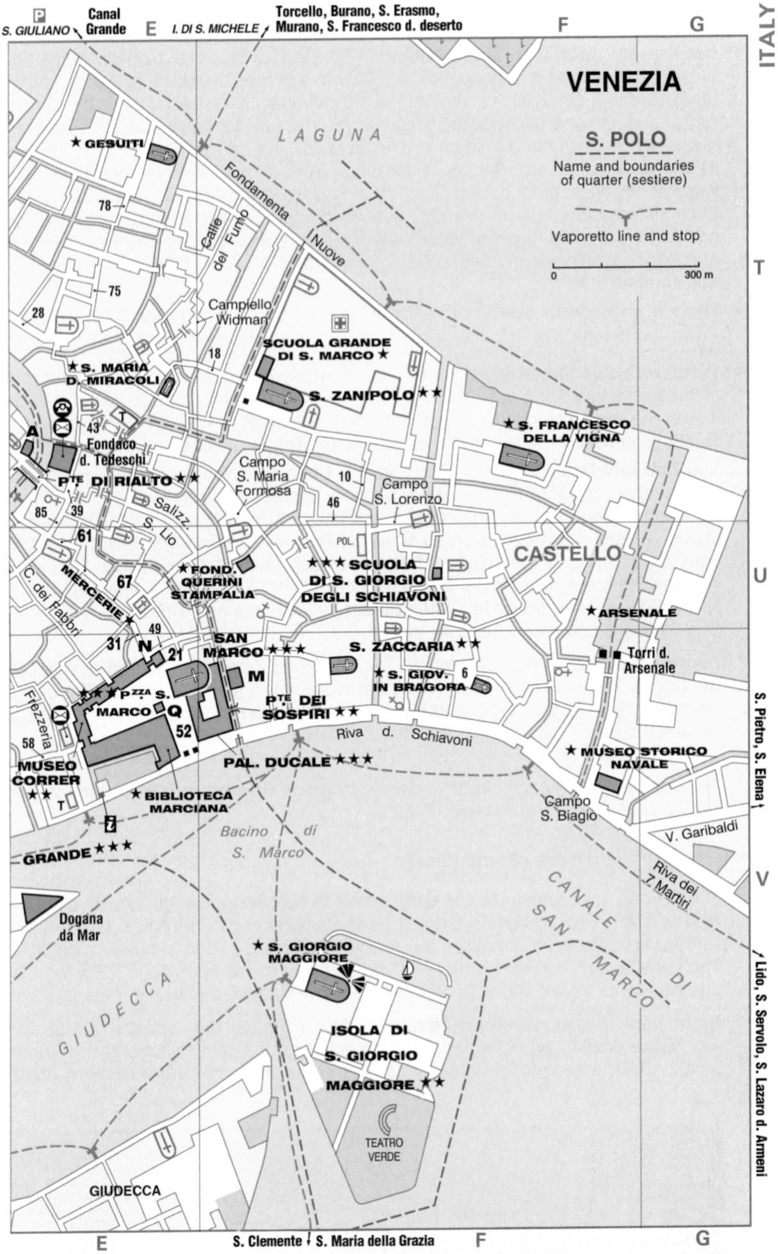

San Zulian (Merceria) .... EU 67
Sant'Angelo (Campo) .... DV 70
Santi Apostoli
(Rio Terà dei) .... ET 75
Sauro Nazario (Campo) .... BT 76
Seriman (Salizzada) .... ET 78
Traghetto (Campo dei) .... DV 79
Verona (Calle della) .... DV 82
2 Aprille (Via) .... ET 85

A Palazzo dei Camerlenghi
B Palazzo Balbi (Pal. della Regione)
E Palazzo Lando Corner Spinelli
H Palazzo Loredan (Municipio)
M Museo diocesano di arte sadra
M⁵ Fondaco dei Turchi (Museo di storia naturale)
N Torre dell'Orologio
P Pal. Corner della Ca' Granda (Prefettura)
Q Campanile
T¹ Teatro Goldoni

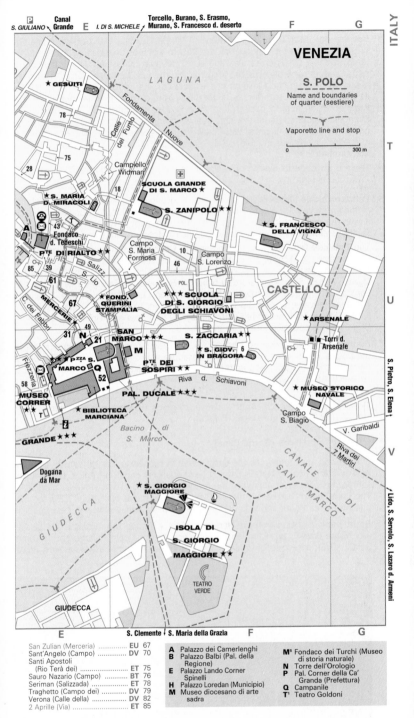

★★★ Piazza San Marco (St Mark's Square) (EV) *a half day*

St Mark's Square is like an enormous roofless marble reception room. All around it, the covered galleries of the procuratorships (procuratie) shelter cafés and luxury boutiques. The **Torre dell'Orologio** (clock tower), from the end of the 15C, has a fine dial with the signs of the zodiac; the famous bronze Moors have been striking the hours for 500 years. Three flag-poles stand in front of the basilica, symbolizing the Venetian kingdoms of Cyprus, Candia (Crete) and Morea. The square opens onto the Grand Canal through the delightful Piazzetta. The two granite columns surmounted by St Mark's Lion and a statue of St Theodore slaying a crocodile were brought from Constantinople.

★★★**Basilica San Marco (St Mark's Basilica)** – The Basilica is a blend of Byzantine and Western influences. It was built from 1063 to 1073 as a repository for St Mark's tomb. It has a Greek-cross plan and is surmounted by domes. Above the central portal and its superbly sculpted archivolt are the famous **Bronze Horses**★★ (the originals are kept in the Museum of the Basilica). Its interior, which is in perfect harmony with the exterior, is a dazzling sight of rare marble, porphyry, and **mosaics**★★★ on a gold background. The floor has remarkable 12C decor. The Evangelist is buried under the high altar over which is a green marble canopy supported by alabaster columns with finely sculpted gospel scenes; the **Pala d'Oro**★★★, marvellous altarpiece in gold, silver, enamel and precious stones, was made in Constantinople in the 10C.

There is a wonderful **view**★★ of Venice from the top of the **bell-tower**★★ (campanile) (99m/325ft high).

★★★**Palazzo Ducale (Doges' Palace)** (FV) – The 4C group of Tetrarchs in porphyry stands at the entrance on the left. The palace symbolizes the glory and power of Venice; it was the residence of the Doges, seat of government, law court and prison. The façade is enhanced by an attractive geometric decor in white and pink marble.

The **Porta della Carta**★★ (Door of the Papers), the main entrance in the Flamboyant-Gothic style (1442), is so named because decrees were posted on it. On its tympanum, Doge Foscari is portrayed kneeling before St Mark's Lion. The **Scala dei Giganti** (Giants' Staircase), starting from the Renaissance Courtyard, is guarded by Sansovino's gigantic statues of Mars and Neptune. The renowned **Scala d'Oro** (Golden Staircase) leads from the first floor gallery to the Doges' apartments and to the College Hall, decorated with **paintings** by Veronese and Tintoretto, where the Doge and his councillors used to meet.

★★**Ponte dei Sospiri (Bridge of Sighs)** (FV) – This world–famous small bridge connects the Doges' Palace to the prison where Casanova was once incarcerated. The bridge owes its name to the sighs of the prisoners being led away from their prison to be executed.

The inside of the Arch, built in Istria stone, is divided into two narrow corridors that lead to the Doges Palace.

★★★Canal Grande (Grand Canal)

The Grand Canal, known as the finest street in the world, curves its way from the railway station to St Mark's basin. It is the largest canal in Venice, bordered by sumptuous palaces of all styles, the former residences of the Venetian patricians. The **Rialto Bridge**★★ crosses it more or less halfway; it was built from 1588 to 1592 by Antonio da Ponte and was designed to allow an armed galley to pass under it.

Right bank *(starting from St Mark's Square)* – Among the most famous palaces are **Palazzo Grassi**★, used for large international exhibitions; Palazzo Lando **Corner-Spinelli** (CUE), easily recognizable by its bays in the shape of basket handles; **Palazzo**

Ch. Boisvieux

Rialto Bridge

Grimani, Sanmicheli's late Renaissance masterpiece; the **Ca'd'Oro**★★★ (the Golden House), so named because it was once gilded all over, has a fine collection of paintings (Mantegna, Carpaccio, Titian, Guardi); **Palazzo Vendramin-Calergi**★ where Wagner died in 1883.

Left Bank *(just like the right bank, it starts from St Mark's Square)* – This side is lined with the 17C **Church of Santa Maria della Salute**★★ (St Mary of Salvation); the Renaissance **Palazzo Dario**★; the **Academy of Fine Arts**★★★ (Gallerie dell'Accademia) *(see below)*; **Palazzo Rezzonico**★★, a large Baroque building which houses a museum of 18C Venetian art (**frescoes** by Gian Domenico Tiepolo); **Palazzo Giustiniano**, comprising magnificent twin buildings; **Ca'Foscari**, which together with **Palazzo Bernardo**, is one of the finest examples of the Gothic Flamboyant style; **Ca'Pesaro**★, now a Museum of Modern Art.

★★★ **Galleria dell'Accademia** (Academy of Fine Arts) – The Accademia provides an extensive panorama of the Venetian School of Painting from the 14C to the 18C, with the Renaissance represented by Giovanni Bellini, Carpaccio, Mantegna and Hans Memling. One of the jewels of this picture gallery is Giorgone's **Tempest**. Other major works are **Portrait of a Gentleman** by Lorenzo Lotto, **Meal in the House of Levi** by Veronese and the paintings by Tintoretto. The following rooms exhibit works by Tiepolo, Canaletto, Guardi and Piazzetta. The picture gallery also contains the famous cycles of paintings by Gentile Bellini **(Miracles of the Holy Cross)** and Carpaccio **(Legend of St Ursula)**, as well as Titian's moving masterpiece **Presentation of the Virgin at the Temple**.

Scuole (Schools)

A *scuola* was a building where persons exercising the same profession and devoted to the same saint, a kind of brotherhood, could meet to organize their social activities.

★★★ **Scuola di San Rocco** (BU) – This was established in a Renaissance building with an elegant façade. It contains an outstanding series of 56 **paintings by Tintoretto** on which he worked for 18 years.

★★★ **Scuola di San Giorgio degli Schiavoni** (FU) – The oratory on the ground floor is decorated with exquisite **works by Carpaccio**, relating the *Legend of St Georges, Miracle of St Tryphonius* and *Story of St Jerome*; there is also a remarkable *St Augustine in his Cell*.

Churches

★★★ **Santa Maria Gloriosa dei Frari (Church of St Mary)** (BTU) – This Franciscan Gothic church contains many **tombs**, **works by Titian**, and in the sacristy a **Tryptich of a Madonna and Saints** by Giovanni Bellini.

★★ **Santa Maria della Salute (Church of St Mary of Salvation)** (DV) – Longhena built this Baroque church in the 17C to give thanks to the Virgin Mary for ending the devastating plague epidemic of 1630. Tintoretto painted the **Marriage at Cana** in warm and luminous colours for the sacristy (1561), while Titian depicted **St Mark's Altarpiece** on the ceiling.

★ **San Giorgio Maggiore (St George Major)** (FV) – Palladio began this church which stands on an island opposite St Mark's Square. Two **paintings by Tintoretto**★ in the choir show the artist's skillful handling of dramatic contrasts of light and shade (chiaroscuro). There is a **panorama**★★★ of Venice and the lagoon from the terrace of the campanile.

★★ **SS Giovanni e Paolo** o **San Zanipolo (Church of St John and St Paul)** (FT) – This Gothic church was built by the Dominicans at the end of a spacious square in which stands a powerful Renaissance **equestrian statue**★★ of Condottiere Bartolomeo Colleoni by Verrochio (1480). Inside, there are many **tombs** of doges and some fine paintings (**Polyptych of St Vincent Ferrier** by Bellini); the **ceiling** of the Rosary Chapel is the work of Veronese.

► ► **Peggy Guggenheim** Collections★★ (principal art movements of the 20C).

The Lagoon

The boat ride across the lagoon to the **Lido**★★ is very enjoyable. This resort has one of the few casinos in Italy and some attractive beaches. Other places worth visiting are **Murano**★★, a famous glass-making centre since 1292 which now has a **Glass Museum**★★; **Burano**★★, an island with a fishing village known for its brightly painted houses and lace-making; and **Torcello**★★ which used to be the seat of a bishopric. Its cathedral, **Santa Maria Assunta**, houses a magnificent iconostasis adorned with Byzantine bas reliefs and some superb **mosaics**★★, the most remarkable of which is the one representing the Last Judgement (12C-13C) on the west wall.

★★★VERONA Population 255 313. Michelin map 970 K 6

Verona, the most beautiful art city in Venetia after Venice, nestles in a meander of the Adige, on a hilly site planted with cypresses. The fashionable **Piazza Bra** is joined to the old centre by Via Mazzini. In summer, Verona is host to a prestigious opera festival which attracts large crowds to the splendid **Roman Amphitheatre★★**.
The city reached its zenith under the **Scaliger** princes (1260 to 1387) who governed on behalf of the emperor. Later, it was ruled by the Visconti of Milan, before becoming part of the Venetian Republic in 1405. Verona was immortalized by Shakespeare's **Romeo and Juliet** (1595), a tragedy about the hopeless love between two young people from rival families. The drama took place in 1302 when the city was still in the grips of internal struggles between the Guelphs to which the Montagues (Romeo's family) belonged, and the Ghibellines, the party of the Capulets (Juliet's family).

★★Piazza delle Erbe (Square of Herbs) – This is an enchanting square lined with picturesque old houses which is full of life on market days. It is built on the former site of the Roman forum. St Mark's column bearing the Lion of Venice stands in the middle. Via Cappello is just off this square; no 23 is **Juliet's House** (Casa di Giulietta), a Gothic palace which is said to have belonged to the Capulets.

★★Piazza dei Signori – The elegant Square of the Lords is framed by the 12C **Palazzo del Comune** (town hall), dominated by the **Lamberti Tower** and the **Loggia del Consiglio** (Council Lodge), a fine Venetian Renaissance building. An arch leads to the **Arche Scaligere★★** (Scaliger Tombs) which the family had erected between their palace and church. The tombs are marked with their coat of arms, recognizable by a symbolic ladder *(scala)*.

★★Castelvecchio e Ponte Scaliger (Old Castle and Scaliger Bridge) – This magnificent fortified ensemble was built in 1354. The castle houses an **Art Museum★★**, a wonderful example of modern museum architecture. It includes an interesting section on Italian painting.

★★San Zeno Maggiore (St Zeno Major) – The church has an interesting façade patterned with Lombard bands and arcatures. The porch, resting on two lions, has two **bronze doors★★** with illustrations from the Bible. A splendid **Triptych★★** by Mantegna stands on the high altar.

►► **Sant'Anastasia★** (Church of St Anastasia) containing Pisanello's frescoes of **St George Delivering the Princess of Trezibond★★**, painted in 1436.

★★VICENZA Population 107 318. Michelin map 970 K 6

Vicenza lies at the foot of the Berici mountains, at the crossroads linking Venetia and Trentino. This commercial and industrial centre has a fine reputation for its gold and silver work.
In the 15C, the community came under the protection of Venice and as a result acquired an impressive number of palaces. But the Venice on *terra firma* owes its fame mainly to one artist who lived there for a long time: **Andrea Palladio**. He was born in Padua in 1508 and died in Vicenza in 1580. He was the first great Renaissance architect who achieved the height of architectural harmony by adapting ancient precepts to modern preoccupations. His style is characterized by a rigorous plan, in which simple and symmetrical lines predominate, and façades perfectly balanced by pediments and porticoes.

The Palladian City – Apart from **Corso Palladio★** (the main street) on which many private palaces have been built on the plans of the artist and his pupils, there is **Piazza dei Signori★★** with the **Loggia del Capitano★** (unfinished), once the Governor's residence, and the **Basilica★★** (a meeting place for notables in the ancient meaning of the word), with two superimposed galleries displaying an exquisite rhythmic simplicity.
The **Olympic Theatre★★** (Teatro Olimpico), an extraordinary building in wood and stucco, was designed by Palladio in the year he died; he based his plan on models of antiquity for the hemicycle of tiered seats. The **stage★★★**, on the other hand, is modern and has amazing *trompe l'œil* perspectives, niches, columns and statues. Opposite the theatre is the grandiose **Palazzo Chiericati** (1551), also by Palladio, now housing a **Picture Gallery★** (Pinacoteca) of Venetian and Flemish paintings, including a **Crucifixion★★** by Hans Memling.

Villas in the Region – *2km/1mi towards the east.* The **Villa Valmarana ai Nani★★** was decorated with **frescoes★★★** depicting Carnival by Gian Domenico Tiepolo. Nearby, the **Rotonda★** is the most famous of Palladio's creations; it was imitated in England in the 17C by Inigo Jones and in the United States in the 18C by Jefferson. This is where Joseph Losey shot his film Don Giovanni.

For further details on Italy, consult the Michelin Green Guides Italy, Rome, Tuscany, Venice.

When looking for a hotel or restaurant, use the Michelin Red Guide Italia, updated annually.

Grand Duchy of Luxembourg

Luxembourg

Area: 2 586km²/998sq mi – **Population:** 384 062 – **Capital:** Luxembourg – **Currency:** Belgian or Luxembourg franc, and Euro (40.3399 BEF) – **Time:** GMT + 1hr in winter, GMT + 2hr in summer – **Entry Formalities:** See Belgium.

Two distinct geographical regions mark this tiny country often associated with neighbouring Belgium. Oesling in the north suffers from a harsh climate. Yet its physical beauty attracts many tourists. Gutland in the south enjoys a milder climate and contains most of the country's farmland and industry.

ECHTERNACH*

Population 4 360
Michelin map 970 J 5

This famous tourist centre serves as the capital of Luxembourgís Little Switzerland – La Petite Suisse. The **abbey*** dominates the city. During the Middle Ages, the abbey enjoyed a huge cultural influence because of its scriptorium. The charming **Place du Marché***, containing the former law courts or **Denzelt**, is flanked by traditional houses with flower-decked balconies.

***LUXEMBOURG'S PETITE SUISSE

A one-day round trip beginning in Echternach provides a chance to discover a scenic region with lush green rugged landscape. One of the area's most picturesque spots is the **Mullerthal*****, the name given to the Ernz Noire Valley with its waterfalls and piles of sandstone rock.

LUXEMBOURG**

Population 74 400
Michelin map 970 J 5

The capital represents both a major financial centre and the seat of European institutions. It occupies a **superb setting**** on top of a sandstone rock, skirted by the Alzette and Pétrusse rivers.

**OLD TOWN

Place d'Armes – This shady square is the bustling heart of the town.

Place de la Constitution – From this square, remarkable **views**** unfold of the gardens in the Pétrusse Ravine and the Adolphe Bridge.

****Chemin de la Corniche** – This cliff road has earned the title of Europe's most beautiful vantage point because of the magnificent **views****.

Le Bock – Little except the **blockhouses**** remains of the fortifications built by the Austrians in 1745. The blockhouses formed part of a network of corridors used during the SecondWorld War. They are open to visitors.

Musée national d'Histoire et d'Art** – The Art and History Museum has an outstanding section on **Life in Luxembourg*.

***Palais Grand-Ducal** – Elegant turrets flank the façade of the Grand Ducal Palace, which is decorated with low-relief geometrically designed sculptures. The **Salon des Rois**, the Kings' Drawing Room, contains the portraits of successive grand dukes.

***Cathédrale Notre-Dame** – In this former Jesuit church, the doorway is decorated with Renaissance and Baroque motifs.

The KIRSCHBERG

The European institutions are located here. The bold red **Grande-Duchesse Charlotte Bridge*** symbolizes the ECSC. It spans the River Alzette with a length of 300m/984ft.

In 1354, the county of Luxembourg was raised to the status of duchy.

SÛRE Valley★★

The River Sûre begins in Belgium and flows through the Grand Duchy as far as the River Moselle and the German border.
The stretch along the **upper valley**★★ from Hochfels to Erpeldange is spectacular, with the river cutting deeply into the Oesling Uplands. **Esch-sur-Sûre**★ slate-roofed houses attract visitors. From the top of an impressive escarpment, the **vantage point**★★ at **Grenglay** offers a fine view of the **Château de Bourscheid**★. The castle is perched on a long headland skirted by a meandering arm of the River Sûre. The **lower valley**★ from Erpeldange to Wasserbillig offers less dramatic but more pastoral landscape.

Ph. Gajic /MICHELIN

Esch-sur-Sûre

VIANDEN★★

Population 1 460

The old houses in this charming little town cling to sheer hillsides tumbling down from the castle to the River Our. The hills overlooking the town from the west have fine **views**★★ of this **picturesque setting**★ and can be reached from the St Nicholas Mountain road.

★★ **Château** – The castle's romantic outline dominates the town. Tours include visits to the 13C Petit Palais, the Grand Palais with its Knights' Hall, and the Romanesque chapel.
The parapet and gardens offer **views**★ of the Our Valley and the town.

For further details on Luxembourg, consult the Michelin Green Guides Belgium Grand Duchy of Luxembourg, Brussels.

When looking for a hotel or restaurant, use the Michelin Red Guide Benelux, updated annually.

Macedonia

Makedonija

Area: 25 713km^2/9771sq mi – **Population:** 2 million – **Capital:** Skopje – **Currency:** denar – **Entry Formalities:** a passport is required for British citizens, a visa for US, Canadian, Australian and Japanese citizens.

This Balkan country, once part of former Yugoslavia, possesses a varied landscape of mountains, forests and fertile plains. Macedonia shares its borders with Bulgaria, Yugoslavia, Albania and southern Greece. Although not officially recognised by the European Union and the United States, Macedonia has nevertheless been admitted to the United Nations as Arym. A brief description of the country's major sights follows.

BITOLA Michelin map 970 O 8

The town has been strongly influenced by Turkish culture. The Ajdar-Gazi and Evi mosques from the 15C and 16C respectively are of interest, as well as the covered market, or bazaar (bezistan).

★★★OHRID Michelin map 970 N 8

Located on the eastern banks of the 30km/18mi-long **Ohrid Lake**, the city is overlooked by a citadel, built on the site of the former acropolis in the ancient Greek city Lychnidos. Ohrid has preserved several important monuments that illustrate its chequered history. The old town is very attractive with houses made of wood and brick. The 11C **St Sofia Cathedral★★★** has some interesting frescoes.

SKOPJE Michelin map 970 O 8

For over a century, from 1282 to 1392, Skopje was under Serbian occupation, and was later transformed into a stronghold by the Turks. On 26 July, 1963 at 5.17am, Skopje was flattened by a powerful earthquake. The train station's clock, which stopped at the time of the disaster, has been left standing in memory of that time.
The fortress (Kale) and the **old town★**, with many sites preserved from the time of the Turkish occupation (mosques, a charming market place), are worth a visit.
Outside the city, the **church★★** of the Sv. Pantelejmon monastery shelters remarkable Byzantine frescoes.

Malta

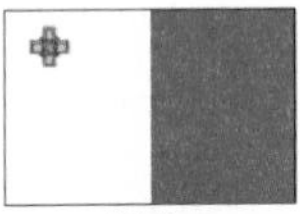

Malta

Area: 316km^2/122sq mi – **Population:** 350 000 – **Capital:** Valletta – **Currency:** Maltese pound (LM) – **Time:** GMT + 2hr in summer, GMT + 1hr in winter – **Entry Formalities:** a passport is required for British, US, Canadian, Australian and Japanese citizens.

The Maltese archipelago sits at the heart of the Mediterranean, 93km - 58 miles from Sicily and 230km/144mil from Tunisia. It includes several islands: Malta, Gozo, Comino, Cominetto and Filfola, the last two are uninhabited.
On Malta, the main island, the indented coast is lined with ports, bays, creeks and rocky coves. For holidaymakers and particularly deep-sea divers, the island is a paradise. The climate is Mediterranean. In summer, balmy sea breezes keep the heat bearable.
Throughout the ages, geographical position has made Malta a much-coveted strategic site. Many different peoples have occupied the archipelago. The Phoenicians, Greeks, Carthaginians, Romans, Arabs, Byzantines, Knights of St John of Jerusalem, French and English all have left traces, not only in the palaces, churches and ramparts, but also in the place names and life style.

The Order of Malta

The Order of Malta, derived from the Order of the Hospital of St John of Jerusalem (the Knights Hospitallers), was founded in 1099 to provide aid to sick pilgrims and Christians. It became a military order in 1113. After Acre, Cyprus and Rhodes, the Hospitallers settled in Malta in 1530 and left in 1798 when Bonaparte captured the island. Today, the Order's headquarters are in Rome. The organisation devoted to medical aid owns numerous hospitals throughout the world.

Malta was British for 174 years, from 1800 to 1974, when it was proclaimed a Republic. The visitor will not be surprised to see that people drive on the left – the number of carefully preserved vintage cars and buses is astonishing. English is the second official language after Maltese, which originated in Phoenician and Carthaginian times. This unusual mix – predominantly British, but with Oriental and Italian overtones – makes Malta a charming, somewhat underrated Mediterranean curiosity.

***VALLETTA Population 9 500. Michelin map 970 L 10

A street in Valletta

J. Gabanou /DIAF

The capital was founded by Jean Parisot de la Valette, Grand Master of the Order. At the price of enormous losses, he drove back the Turkish armies of Suleiman the Magnificent during the Ottoman Siege of 1565.

The town owes its geometrical plan to the Italian architect Francesco Laparelli. Surrounded by hilly landscape and a thick belt of ramparts and strongholds, the walled city is spread out over a peninsula. Fort St Elmo's War Museum lies at the promontory edge and picturesque streets run in steep steps down to the sea. The outlying district of **Sliema** has become a modern seaside resort, with a large number of hotels and shops.

Republic Street, the main pedestrian precinct, is animated and lined with numerous souvenir shops.

Main Sights – **St John's Co-cathedral**, with its austere façade, has a richly decorated **interior★★★**. The 400 or so different-coloured marble tombstones beneath which lie the Knights represent the whole of 17C and 18C European history. The paintings illustrating the life of St John the Baptist decorating the vault are Mattia Preti's masterpiece. The **co-cathedral museum★** contains many other treasures, including Caravaggio's famous painting, the *Decollation of St John*, as well as a magnificent set of Flemish tapestries. Also worth a visit are the **National Museum of the Fine Arts★** containing 14C-16C Italian paintings, works by Mattia Preti and 17C furniture, and the **National Archeological Museum★** housed in the Auberge de Provence, a majestic 16C building containing interesting prehistoric remains from various sites on the island, including the famous Venus of Malta and Sleeping Goddess found in Hal Saflieni hypogeum. The 16C **Grand Master's Palace★★** is worth seeing for its sumptuous interior, including a splendid weapons and armour collection and Gobelins tapestries.

Most tourist activity is concentrated on the other side of the bay, especially in the evening, in the seaside resorts of **Sliema** and **St Julians**, which have a large number of hotels, boutiques and restaurants.

EXCURSIONS

★★★**Prehistoric remains** – These include **Hal Saflieni** hypogeum, **Ghar Dalam** cave, and the **Tarxien** and **Hagar Qim** temples.

★★**M'dina and Rabat** – Inside the ramparts of **M'dina**, Baroque churches and palaces dominate. The **cathedral of St Peter and St Paul★★** is a magnificent example of the period, with frescoes illustrating the life of St Paul and a carved oak sacristy door. The **Cathedral Museum★★** next door contains some fine sacred art objects and works by Dürer and Rembrandt. See, too, the **catacombs★★** of St Paul and St Agatha containing 15C frescoes. At **Rabat**, there are remains of the Roman Era and catacombs.

★**Marsaxlokk** – This fishing village's typical, brightly coloured boats have eyes painted on the bow to ward off ill-fortune.

Gozo Island – See **Victoria**, the main town, with its **cathedral★** and **citadel★**, Calypso's Cave, the temples of **Ggantija★★★** (prehistoric remains), the **azure window★★** (an arch hollowed out of the rock by the waves) at Dwejra Point in the south of the island, **Xlendi★** and Xlendi Bay.

The Netherlands

Nederland

Area: 41 863km^2/16 163sq mi, of which 33 937km^2/12 896sq mi above sea level – **Population:** 15 million – **Capital:** Amsterdam – **Currency:** guilder and Euro (2,2037 NLG) – **Time:** GMT + 1hr in winter, GMT + 2hr in summer

Wedged between sea and land, the Dutch have fought since 500 BC to keep their land above water. The polder technique, adopted in the Middle Ages, has reclaimed thousands of acres. The name Netherlands or Lowlands is apt, as one-third of the surface area lies above sea level. The Dutch, whether the great navigators of yesteryear or the businessmen of today, have always made the most of its seaboard location and countless inland river routes. Under the cloudy skies, so often depicted by the 17C masters, the Dutch lead a peaceful life, halfway between town and country, alongside canals and tulip fields.

IN BRIEF

Entry Formalities – A passport for British, US, Canadian, Australian and Japanese citizens.

Banks and shops – Shops usually open from 9am to 6pm with early closing on Saturdays. They close on Sunday and Monday mornings. Banks open from 9am to 4pm every day except Saturdays and Sundays.

Cycling – The Netherlands are best visited by bicycle. There are about 11.7 million bicycles, two for every three inhabitants. Roads and streets are busy, particularly during rush hour. However, the country has a remarkable network of cycle paths. Bicycles can be hired in all the railway stations in all larger towns.

Polders – Polders represent the most typical Dutch scenery. In the 14C, man's continual struggle against the sea led to the construction of dikes, the draining of marshland, and the drying out of lakes using windmills. Naturally, most of the polders lie along the Dutch coast, particularly in the Delta at the mouth of the Rhine, Meuse and Escaut rivers. The Zuiderzee was converted into IJsselmeer Lake by the construction of a barrier dam, the Afsluitdijk, in the 1930s. Since the 13C, some 7,050km^2/2 720sq mi have been reclaimed from the sea.

Windmills – Windmills tower above the horizon of this flattest of lands. Painted green with white frames, they once pumped water from the polders. Today, carefully preserved, the greatest concentration of windmills is found in Kinderdijk.

/MICROGRAFX

Cheese – Cheese is the staple ingredient of breakfast and cold meals. Creamy when fresh *(jonge)*, it becomes dry and pungent when ripe *(oude)*: cylindrical, flat **Gouda** and spherical **Edam**, both are found on the picturesque market of Alkmaar *(see Haarlem, Excursion)*. **Leyden** cheese (Leidse kaas) contains caraway seeds, while that of **Friesland** (Friese kaas) is flavoured with cloves.

Flowers – The Netherlands are an important flower-producing country. In the spring, the visitor will be entranced with the colourful checkerboards of tulips, daffodils, hyacinths and other bulbs in the fields between Haarlem and Leyden and around Alkmaar. Floral float processions are organised in April and September at Haarlem-Noordwijk, Alsmeer-Amsterdam and Zundert.

Dutch Masters – The great masters made the country famous. In the 15C, Hieronymus Bosch distinguished himself with his fantastic pictorial subjects. Art peaked in the 17C with Frans Hals, Rembrandt, Ruysdael and Vermeer. In the late 19C, Van Gogh went into exile in France, while Piet Mondrian and Theo van Doesburg contributed to the birth of Constructivism.

A few proverbs relating to windmills:

Hij heeft een klap van de molen gehad: *he was struck by a mill (he is a bit mad).*
Hij loopt met molentjes: *he functions with small mills (he is little simple-minded).*
Dat is koren op zijn molen: *it is grain for his mill (it brings water to his mill).*

AMSTERDAM★★★

Population 702 444
Michelin map 970 I 4

Amsterdam is built on the banks of the IJ and Amstel rivers. Along the canals dividing the city into different quarters, tall, narrow brick houses rise their stepped façades. The beautiful city's many museums make it a cultural centre.

Historical Notes – Amsterdam began as a village of herring fishermen. It was awarded a city charter in about 1300 and annexed to the province of Holland. In 1428, the town passed into the hands of the Duke of Burgundy, Philip the Good. In 1555, Charles V left the Netherlands to his son Philip II, who was soon to be crowned King of Spain. Amsterdam, however, was freed from Spanish dominance in 1579 by the Union of Utrecht. It then became a prosperous city, mainly due to the diamond trade. Its wealth was reinforced by the arrival of the Marranos, Jews from Spain and Portugal converted by force to Catholicism.

The Golden Age – The 17C marked the height of Amsterdam and Dutch artistic and commercial glory. Navigators left to conquer the Far East. The East India Company (Verenigde Oostindische Compagnie or VOC), then the West India Company, were founded in 1602 and 1621. The Bank of Amsterdam, one of the first European credit establishments, opened for business in 1609. Construction of the three main canals, Herengracht, Keizersgracht and Prinsengracht began in 1610.
In 1648, with the Treaty of Munster, the independence of the United Provinces vis-à-vis Philip IV of Spain, was officially recognised. The Revocation of the Edict of Nantes brought about the immigration of a large number of Huguenots who joined in the town's commercial activities.
In 1806, the French occupied Amsterdam. Napoleon made his brother Louis Bonaparte King of Holland. Amsterdam became the capital of the country. After Dutch trade had been ruined by the Continental System, the population revolted in 1813 and recognised the Prince of Orange as sovereign of the United Provinces. Amsterdam's shipping trade took off again after 1876 with the inauguration of the new canal linking the capital to the North Sea (Noordzeekanaal). The diamond industry rapidly recovered.

Town Planning in the 20C – The city changed its face with the construction of new quarters after the First World War. The Amsterdam School of Architecture, of which Michel de Klerk was one of the central figures, advocated asymmetrical forms and built a large amount of local authority housing on the periphery of the town centre. Today, new urban districts continue to be built, though many prefer to live on one of the 2 400 house-boats mooring along the 36km/22mi of quays.

P. van Riel /EXPLORER

Amsterdam in winter

★OLD AMSTERDAM

★★★ **Grachten** – The **canals** in the town centre are lined with beautiful town houses built by wealthy merchants in the 17C and 18C. All have brick façades with gables of various shapes and decoration, surmounted by carved pediments. Some have a small sculptured stone which was the owner's emblem or the symbol of his trade. To the north, near the port, warehouses display characteristic wooden shutters.

Boat trips★ (Rondvaart) leave from the **Dam**, Amsterdam's main square. They give an excellent overview of the canals, providing attractive views of the city and its inhabitants.
On returning to the Dam, the visitor should tour **Koninklijk Paleis★** (Royal Palace) (**KX**), the former town hall redesigned in 1808 by Louis Bonaparte, and **Nieuwe Kerk★** (New Church) (**KX**), in which the Dutch sovereigns are still enthroned.

★★ Begijnhof (Beguinage) (KX) – Founded in the 14C, the former church of the Beguines appears a haven of peace in the middle of a green meadow. Around it, lovely sculptured 17C and 18C stone façades are visible. This is one of the rare church enclosures still existing in the Netherlands.

★ Bloemenmarkt (Flower Market) (KY) – Many flower stalls crowd Amsterdam, but the most picturesque are the open-air stalls, whose multi-coloured flowers are supplied by barges operating up and down the Singel. Some of the stalls are actually on barges.

PRINCIPAL MUSEUMS

★★★ Rijksmuseum (KZ) – This national museum, founded by Louis Bonaparte in 1808, is known for its exceptional collection of 15C to 17C paintings. It also contains a sculpture and decorative arts section, a historical department, a print collection, and an Asian arts section.

Schilderkunst 15de-17de eeuw (15C-17C paintings) – The first rooms feature Primitives (Geert-gen tot Sint-Jans), and Renaissance painters such as Lucas van Leyden. Then comes the Golden Age. In this vast section, the visitor can admire the portraits of Frans Hals, the astonishing light of Rembrandt's composition *(The Night Watch)*, the famous skies of Ruysdael and the masterpieces of Vermeer. A few works by Goya and Rubens dominate the foreign painting collection.

Beeldhouwkunst en Kunstnijverheid (Sculpture and Decorative Arts) – The rooms are richly furnished and decorated with sculptures, paintings, gold and silver ware, glassware, tapestries and furniture dating from 1400 to 1900.

Aziatische Kunst (Asian Art) – The rooms house a beautiful collection of Chinese porcelain, Japanese ceramics and lacquerwork and a few works of art from India and Indonesia.

★★★ Van Gogh Museum (JZ)– More than 200 paintings and 600 drawings by Vincent Van Gogh (1853-1890) show the artist's development, from the dark landscapes of his early period to the violent colours of his mature works. Dutch and Provençal landscapes, a series of peasant portraits, views of Paris and numerous self-portraits are exhibited.

★★ Stedelijk Museum (Municipal Museum) (JZ)– This modern art museum houses works of art from 1850 to the present day. There are paintings by Cézanne, Monet, Picasso, Léger, Malevitch, Chagall, Mondrian and Van Doesburg as well as others showing the most recent trends in European and American Art.

★★ Nederlands Scheepvaart Museum (Netherlands Historical Maritime Museum) (MX)– The museum is housed in a large 17C maritime warehouse. It has interesting exhibits on navigation in Holland, including the replica of an 18C merchant ship owned by the Dutch East India Company and moored along the quays.

ADDITIONAL SIGHTS

★ Magere Brug (Thin Bridge) (LY) – This fragile 18C bridge built across the wide Amstel Canal evokes the bridges so dear to Van Gogh. From beside the bridge, several bell-towers can be seen, including that of the Zuiderkerk, the first church built in Amsterdam after the Reformation, between 1603 and 1611.

★ Museum Het Rembrandthuis (Rembrandt House) (LX) – The house, which is situated in the main street of the old quarter, where the Jews of Amsterdam had congregated, contains a collection of the master's drawings.

★★ Anne Frank Huis (Anne Frank's House) (KX) – At the rear of a narrow 17C building, Anne Frank and her family hid before being deported to the Auschwitz concentration camp in 1944. A secret passage camouflaged behind a revolving bookcase leads to the bare rooms where the Frank family lived underground. Here Anne Frank wrote her moving diary. Today, numerous documents concerning the Second World War and anti-Semitism are on display.

★ Westerkerk (KX) – Extensive renovation has restored the original colours to the brick and stone façade of this beautiful church built between 1619 and 1631. Its 85m/280ft bell-tower has a remarkable carillon topped by an Imperial Crown commemorating Maximilian of Austria. The central nave is covered with beautiful wooden vaulting.

★★ Artis (MY)– Amsterdam's zoological garden is named after the company which founded it in 1838, the Natura Artis Magistra (Nature, the Mistress of Art). The large park contains more than 6 000 animals. The Zeiss Planetarium offers a fabulous planet show using ultra-modern audio-visual equipment and a 630m²/6,780sq ft. screen.

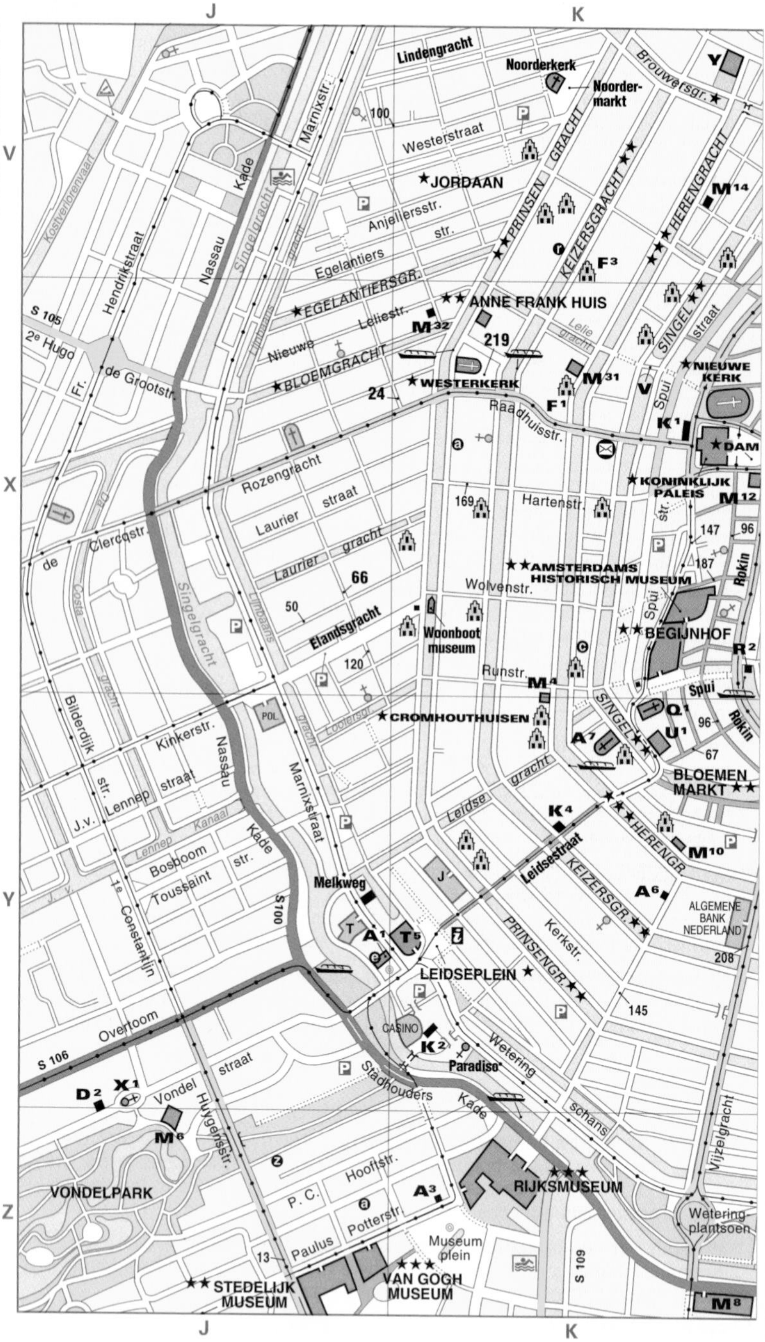

Amstelveld .... LY 9	's-Gravelandseveer .... LY 58	Kattengat .... LV 105
Van Baerlestr .... JZ 13	Hazenstr .... JY 66	Kinkerstr. .... JY
Beursplein .... LX 19	Heiligeweg .... KY 67	Langebrugsteeg .... LX 115
Binnenkant .... MX 22	Hekelved .... LV 69	Looiersdwarsstr. (1e) .... JX 120
Bloemdwarsstr. (1e) .... JX 24	Jodenbreestr. .... LX 88	Martelaarsgracht .... LV 126
Damrak LX	Kadijksplein .... MX 93	Nieuwe Amstelstr. .... LY 139
Damstr. .... LY 40	Kalverstr. .... KXY 96	Nieuwe Doelenstr. .... LY 141
Elandsgracht .... JX 50	Karthuizersstr. .... JKV 100	Nieuwe Hoogstr. .... LX 142

American Hotel .... JY **A1**	Huis Leeuwenburg .... LX **F2**	Hash Marihuana Museum . LX **M7**
Coster Diamonds .... KZ **A3**	Huis met de Hoofden* ..... KVX **F3**	Heinekenbrouwerij .... KZ **M8**
De Appel .... KY **A6**	Huis met de Kolommen ...... LY **F4**	Kattenkabinet .... KY **M10**
De Krijtberg .... KY **A7**	Magna Plaza .... KX **K1**	Koffie- en Theemuseum ..... LX **M11**
Dokwerker .... MY **B1**	Max Euwe Centrum .... KY **K2**	Madame Tussaud Scenerama KX **M12**
Groenburgwal .... LX **B2**	Metz & Co .... KY **K4**	Multatuli-Museum .... KV **M14**
Holland Experience .... LX **D1**	Mozes- en Aäronkerk .... LY **L2**	Nationaal Vakbonds Museum .... MY **M19**
Hollandse Manege .... JY **D2**	**Museums**	Sexmuseum Amsterdam
Hollandse Shouwburg .... MY **D3**	Bijbels Museum .... KY **M4**	Venustempel .... LV **M28**
Huis Bartolotti* .... KX **F1**	Filmmuseum .... JZ **M6**	

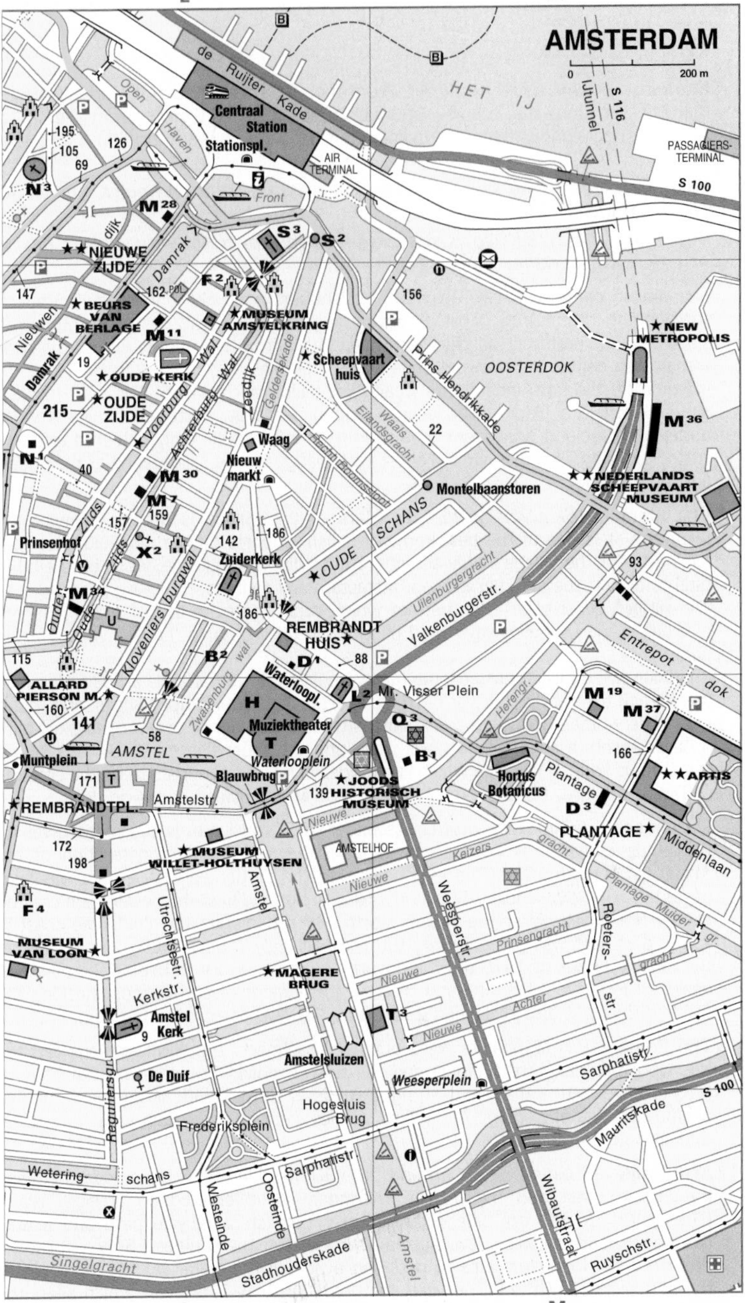

Nieuwe Spiegelstr. .... KY 145
Nieuwendijk LVX
Nieuwezijds Voorburgwal . KLX 147
Oosterdokskade .... MX 156
Oude Doelenstr. .... LX 157
Oude Hoogstr. .... LX 159
Oude Turfmarkt .... LY 160
Oudebrugsteeg .... LX 162

P.C. Hooftstr. .... JKZ
Plantage Kerklaan .... MY 166
Resstraat .... KX 169
Reguliersbreestr. .... LY 171
Reguliersdwarsstr. .... LY 172
Rozengracht .... JX
Sint Antoniesbreestr. .... LX 186
Sint Luciënsteeg .... KX 187

Spui .... KXY
Stromarkt .... LV 195
Thorbeckeplein .... LY 198
Utrechtsestr. .... LY
Vijzelstr. .... KY 208
Warmoesstr. .... LX 215
Westermarkt .... KX 219

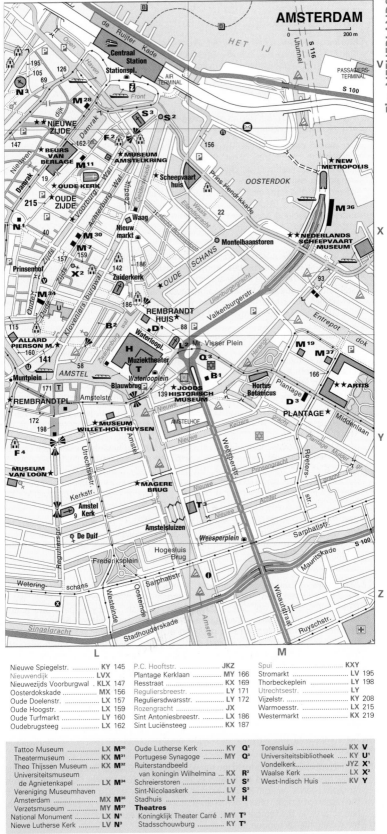

Tattoo Museum .... LX M^{30}
Theatermuseum .... KX M^{31}
Theo Thijssen Museum ..... KX M^{32}
Universiteitsmuseum
de Agnietenkapel .... LX M^{34}
Vereniging Museumhaven
Amsterdam .... MX M^{36}
Verzetsmuseum .... MY M^{37}
National Monument .... LX N^{1}
Niewe Lutherse Kerk .... LV N^{3}

Oude Lutherse Kerk .... KY Q^{1}
Portugese Synagoge .... MY Q^{3}
Ruiterstandbeeld
van koningin Wilhelmina ... KX R^{2}
Schreierstoren .... LV S^{2}
Sint-Nicolaaskerk .... LV S^{3}
Stadhuis .... LY H

Theatres

Koningklijk Theater Carré . MY T^{3}
Stadsschouwburg .... KY T^{5}

Torensluis .... KX V
Universiteitsbibliotheek ..... KY U^{1}
Vondelkerk.......................... JYZ X^{1}
Waalse Kerk .... LX X^{2}
West-Indisch Huis .... KV Y

EXCURSIONS

★**Marken** – *20km/12.5mi northeast.* From the 13C through 1957, Marken was an island in the Gouwzee, a small land-locked sea 2.5km/1.5 miles from the shore. Although now connected to the mainland, it has kept its island traditions and folklore.

Taxi-boats, maximum seven passengers, are a pleasant and quick way to get around the city.

The hiring of bicycles allows you to choose your own itinerary without having to cope with parking.

The **village**★ consists of two quarters, Havenbuurt, near the port, and Kerkbuurt, surrounding the church. Most of the dark green timber houses are grouped on small mounds and built on piles to protect them from high tides. Inside, the beds are alcoves containing drawers once used as cradles.
In summer, the local inhabitants wear their **traditional costumes**★. The women wear a full skirt and a black apron over a striped petticoat. A striped blouse is worn under a corset and print front. The headdress is a simple, gaily coloured lace and cotton skullcap. The men wear a short vest, baggy trousers tightened at the knees, and black socks.

★**Volendam** – *15km/9mi north.* Like Marken, this village is on the edge of the Gouwzee. It is one of the best-known eel fishing ports on the old Zuiderzee, but fishing is not the village's only activity. The traditional costume, worn by the inhabitants during the summer season, attracts many tourists.
The **village**★ consists of a long street which runs along the top of a dike. Behind and below, narrow alleyways wind past delightful little brick houses with wooden gables.
The **traditional costume**★ has become the symbol of the Netherlands abroad. The men wear black trousers with silver buttons, short jackets over striped shirts, and round caps. The women dress in a black skirt with a striped apron or a striped skirt with a black apron, a shirt with a floral front under a short-sleeved black blouse, and the famous winged lace cap which is considered by many tourists to be the epitome of Dutch folklore. Both the men and women wear buckled shoes or clogs.

IJsselmeer – *60km/37mi north.* IJsselmeer, or IJssel Lake, is the name given to the Zuiderzee after it was separated from the sea by the construction of the Afsluitdijk Dam in 1932. The idea of closing the Zuiderzee with a dike was suggested in 1667 by Hendrick Stevin, in order to fight against the devastation created by the North Sea. After the violent storm which damaged the Zuiderzee coast in 1825, a project was presented by the engineer Lely (1854-1929). But only after the terrible floods of 1916 did the government order work to begin. The dike was designed to prevent flooding and create a fresh water reservoir, thus checking the soil's saltiness. It also reclaimed 225 000ha/49 400 acres of fertile land.

The Polders – Four polders were built at IJsselmeer: the **Wieringermeerpolder**, the Noordoostpolder (North Polder) and the two **Flevoland**★ Polders. This flat country criss-crossed with canals and straight roads is dotted with large farms hidden behind curtains of poplars. Many bird species can be found such as golden pheasant and green plovers.

★★**Afsluitdijk** – 30km/10.5mi long and 90m/300ft wide. This barrier dam between the Frisian coast and the former Wieringen Island created an artificial island (Breezand). On the sea side, a breakwater protects a bicycle path and a dual carriageway. **Stevin Locks** (Slevinsluizen), named after the engineer, Stevin, form the first group of locks for ships to pass and evacuate the water. At the point where the two sections of the barrier dam met in 1932 there is a tower which bears the inscription: "A living nation builds for its future". The top of the monument offers a panoramic view of IJsselmeer.

ARNHEM

Population 131 703

Arnhem, capital of the province of Guelderland, is famed for its *Arnhemse jeisjes*, or small puff-pastry biscuits.

★★**Het Nederlands Openluchtmuseum (Netherlands Open-Air Museum)** – This vast 44ha/109 acre wooded park land contains some 100 typical Dutch farmhouses, cottages, barns, windmills and workshops. Each building, furnished according to the region of origin, offers demonstrations on such activities as bread-making and handicrafts. In the temporary exhibition centre, models in traditional costume illustrate daily life of bygone days.

DELFT★★

Population 89 365
Michelin map 970 I 4

Delft's shady, old canals, museums and monuments, coupled with the world-wide reputation of its Delftware factories, enjoys a unique charm. **Boat trips★** leave from the landing-stage on Wijnhaven 6.

Vermeer (1632-1675) was born and died here. He applied an extraordinary science of composition and his incomparable mastery of light effects in his painting.
Delft conjures up the tin-glazed **earthenware** with its translucent coating known as Delftware, best-known for its monochrome blue on a white background. In the late 17C, however, polychrome appeared in the copies of Chinese and Japanese porcelain patterns which were fashionable in Europe. Today, the tradition continues in several local factories.

★**Nieuwe Kerk (New Church)** – This Gothic church from 1381 has a brick bell-tower with a carillon by Hemony. The church itself contains the crypt of the princes of the House of Orange, whose entrance is indicated by a large emblazoned slab. The **mausoleum of William the Silent★**, Prince of Orange and Stathouder (governor) of the provinces of Holland, Zealand and Utrecht in 1559, stands in the chancel.

★**Oude Delft (Old Canal)** – A walk along the lime-tree shaded canal offers attractive views of delightful humpbacked bridges and elegant façades. No 39 houses the Dutch East India Company and is surmounted by a weather vane in the shape of a ship.

★**Prinsenhof** – In 1572, this former convent became the residence of William the Silent. He was assassinated here in 1584. Today, the Flamboyant Gothic style palace houses a museum concerning the House of Orange-Nassau.

V.C.L./PIX

Decorating Delftware

Den HAAG★★

The HAGUE
Population 444 242 – Michelin map 970 I 4

Although Amsterdam is the capital of the Netherlands, the elegant, worldly city of The Hague is its seat of government.
Up until 13C, The Hague was a hunting lodge for Count Floris IV of Holland. A castle was built in 1250. The town grew steadily throughout the centuries and, in the 17C, became the seat of the States General of the United Provinces, then of the government. Amsterdam became the capital of the Netherlands in 1806, but The Hague has kept its status as a diplomatic centre through the present day.

★★★**Mauritshuis** – The Royal Picture Gallery is one of the most prestigious in the world. It contains a large number of masterpieces including works by Holbein the Younger (16C), Rubens, David Téniers, Rembrandt (*The Anatomy Lesson of Doctor Tulp*, the first canvas which brought him recognition), Vermeer and the famous *View of Delft* so dear to the French writer, Proust.

★★**Haags Gemeentemuseum (Municipal Museum)** – Built in 1935 by Berlage, this municipal museum is devoted to the decorative arts and 19C and 20C sculpture and painting. It includes a large collection of works by Piet Mondrian and artists from the De Stijl movement.

★★**Scheveningen** – An elegant seaside resort with a very crowded beach. The Strandweg boulevard runs alongside the long, wide stretch of fine sand for 3km/2 mi before continuing as a footpath in the east.
Beyond the lighthouse in the west, the fishing port is still very busy. Full-day North Sea fishing trips for tourists are organised *(departing from Dr. Lelykade)*.

HAARLEM★★

Population 149 474
Michelin map 970 I 4

This historical capital of the Holland earldom is also the birthplace of Frans Hals and the centre of a large bulb-growing area.
Haarlem was founded around the 10C and used as a fortified residence for the earls of Holland. The town was the site of a bloody siege during the uprising against the Spanish in 1572-73. Haarlem only sided with the States General in 1577. In the 17C, Haarlem became wealthy through its linen industry, producing cloth and unbleached linen.

★**Grote of St Bavokerk** – On the Grote Markt or **Great Square**★, the 15C Great Church or Church of St Bavon has a superb lead-roofed lantern tower surmounting the transept crossing. Inside, Haendel and Mozart supposedly played on the beautiful 16C **choir screen**★ and an **organ**★ built in 1738.

★★★**Frans Halsmuseum** – The museum in a former 17C almshouse for old men consists of eight paintings of civil guards and regents by Frans Hals, the great master of vividly coloured portraits.

EXCURSION

★**Alkmaar** – *30km/19mi north*. This historical town laid out inside a moat owes its present-day reputation to its picturesque **cheese market**★★. The Kaarsmarkt is held on the Waagplein (Public Weights Square) each Friday morning from mid-April to mid-September. The market, known since the early 17C, is an excellent opportunity to discover the famous cheese porters *(kaasdragers)*, wearing the traditional white clothes and straw hats of the past.

Rijksmuseum Paleis HET LOO★★★

HET LOO Palace and National Museum

Opened in 1984, the former royal palace of Het Loo and its gardens are set in an exceptional park. William III, Prince of Orange, bought Het Oude Loo castle in 1684. A short distance away, his wife, Mary Stuart, commissioned the architect Jacob Roman to build Het Loo Palace. The interior decoration and landscaping were executed by Daniel Marot. When William III was proclaimed King of England, Het Loo became a royal palace and was enlarged.

★★★**Apartments** – The palace contains a large number of beautiful rooms. During the visit, note the remarkable **new dining room**★★★ by Daniel Marot, in which white columns with pilasters decorated with gold bands reach right up to the ceiling. The furniture includes admirable 17C Dutch chairs with high backs of finely carved wood. On the first floor, the **Queen's Antechamber**★★★ has a lacquer cabinet (1690) and fine pieces of Delftware and Chinese porcelain. The tour ends on the ground floor with **Queen Wilhelmina's Drawing Room** and **Office**★, which she occupied until her death in 1962. The small kitchen covered with Delft tiles in which Queen Mary made jam, leads out to the gardens.

★★★**The gardens** – The superb gilded **wrought-iron gate**★★★ designed by Marot once opened out onto the terrace, affording a fine view of the gardens. There are four gardens. The lower garden consists of four flower beds with embroidery-like patterns and four English-style flower beds decorated with statues. The upper garden, enclosed by colonnades, contains large trees and the king's fountain. The king's garden is blue and orange, while the more intimate queen's garden has pastel coloured flowers and fruit trees.

Nationaal Park de HOGE VELUWE★★★

DE HOGE VELUWE National Park

★★★**Park** – Heath, sand dunes and lakes are interspersed with beech, oak, pine and birch trees. This peaceful spot is a perfect habitat for numerous woodland animals which can be observed from life observation towers. Cycling and walking are also popular.

★★★**Rijksmuseum Kröller-Müller** – Henry van de Velde inaugurated this contemporary art museum in 1938. It contains a large collection of paintings, sculptures and drawings. The early 20C is represented by works by Mondrian, the Constructivists (Strzeminsky), Futurists (Ballà, Severini) and Cubists (Picasso, Braque, Juan Gris and Fernand Léger). Around the patio several works by Van Gogh include the famous *Sunflowers* (1887). French Impressionists, Cézanne, Renoir and Monet are also represented. In the new wing, contemporary sculptures illustrate various movements such as Minimal Art, the Zero Group and Arte Povera.

★★ **Beeldenpark (Sculpture Garden)** – In the shade of this 10ha/25 acre park, more than 90 contemporary sculptures are displayed including works by Permeke, Bourdelle and Maillol. There is also Giacometti's *Walking Man* (1960), Lucio Fontana's *5 Spheres* (1965) and Dubuffet's *Enamel Garden* (1975), an enormous white honeycomb-like structure.

KEUKENHOF★★★

BULBFIELDS

This landscape garden, which welcomes more than 900 000 visitors every spring, contains the country's most beautiful varieties of bulbs. Tulips, hyacinths and narcissus create a patchwork of colours against a green background of lawns criss-crossed with winding canals and ponds. Hot-houses contain the most fragile species.
Keukenhof is in the vicinity of the bulb fields which stretch from Leyden to Haarlem. Their perfect geometry can be admired from the footbridge at the Keukenhof windmill.

ROTTERDAM★★

Population 582 266
Michelin map 970 I 4

The city has been improving its port facilities since it was first developed in the late 16C. From 1866 to 1872, the Nieuwe Waterweg (New Waterway) leading to the sea, was excavated. Several man-made harbours were built in the late 19C. The port and town were badly bombed during the last war, but immediately rebuilt. Today, Rotterdam is the world's largest port.
It is also the birthplace of the great humanist, Erasmus, after whom the city's university is named.

The CENTRE

★★★ **Museum Boymans-van Beuningen** – The Fine Arts Museum houses a rich collection of antique exhibits, modern and contemporary works of art, engravings and a decorative arts section with 17C glassware and earthenware.
The collection of Primitives includes admirable paintings by Van Eyck, Hieronymus Bosch and Bruegel the Elder. The 17C works include masterpieces by Frans Hals, Rembrandt, Jacob van Ruysdael and Rubens.
The new wing contains paintings by the Impressionists Monet, Sisley, Pissarro, Signac, Van Gogh, Mondrian, and Kandinsky. Degas' *A Dancer at the Age of Fourteen* is a highlight. Surrealist artists include Dali and Magritte.

★★THE PORT

A boat trip can be taken down the Nieuwe Mass on the River Meuse to Eemhaven or Botlek. On the other side, various harbours, docks and quays feature attractive rectilinear buildings. The vast facilities of the **Europoort** (Europe Gate) and the **Maasvlakte** (Meuse Plain) are visible.

E. Luider /RAPHO

Kinderdijk on a winter's day

EXCURSIONS

★★Kinderdijk Windmills – This series of 19 windmills lies along the canals amid-meadows and reeds. The windmills were used to drain the Alblasserwaard up until 1950. Today, they are a tourist attraction, particularly during Windmill Days *(in July and August, on Saturday afternoons)*.
The first set of windmills built in 1738 lies along the canal and consists of eight tall truncated brick polder mills with rotating caps. A little further on is a smaller hollow post mill, of the wipmolen type, called De Blokker, whose base is wider than the top, and is inhabited. On the other bank are eight other windmills built in the 1740s. They are octagonal in shape and thatched. Further on, several large thatched farmhouses and hall-farmhouses have a safety exit a little above ground level. It leads to the living room and is used during floods.

★★★Stormvloedkering Oosterschelde (Eastern Escaut River Dam) – Inaugurated in 1986, this storm surge barrier is unique in the world. 3km/2mi long, it is built on two artificial islands and consists of 65 piers and 62 sliding steel gates. During stormy weather, the gates can be closed in just one hour. The barrier controls the tidal flow and protects the oyster and mussel beds. The Ir. Topshuis building houses the barrier's central control room and the **Delta Expo** explains development of the Delta. The film *Delta Finale* recounts the various stages in the barrier's development.
In summer, **boat trips** and a tour of oyster beds are organised.

UTRECHT★★

Population 231 231

Utrecht is both a religious city – home of the Catholic primate of the Netherlands – and a commercial centre with a world famous international trade fair founded in 1916. Intellectual Utrecht is home to the country's largest University. Cultural Utrecht hosts the Holland Festival of Ancient Music each year in late August/early September. All year round, the city's many museums, often housed in old convents and churches, attract attention.
Utrecht was founded at the beginning of the Christian era. In the 7C, it was chosen as the seat of the Friesland Missions. The town received its charter in 1122 and was surrounded by ramparts. Under Spanish dominion, Utrecht became an archbishopric. The Union of Utrecht, in 1569, combined the seven Dutch Protestant provinces and rejected Spanish rule. In the 17C, Utrecht was an important fortified town; today, a ring of canals has replaced the old fortifications. In 1712, the Peace of Utrecht brought an end to the Spanish War of Succession.
The once-famous Utrecht velvet, woven with linen, goat's hair and cotton, and used as a wall covering, is no longer made in the area. Today, the town has spread out, with a gigantic shopping centre, Hoog Catherijne, and to the west, the Kanaleneiland (island of canals) district.

★★OLD TOWN

★Oudegracht (Old Canal) – This canal runs right through the town. It has a series of upper quays and lower quays lined with shops and restaurants. Several attractive little bridges span the canal, one of which, the Bakkerbrug, becomes a flower market on Saturdays.

★Nationaal Museum van Speelklok tot Pierement – Today, the old Buurkerk hall-church houses an interesting museum containing 18C to 20C mechanical musical instruments: clocks, music boxes, superb barrel organs and *orchestrions*, a type of organ imitating orchestral instruments.

★★Domtoren – The highest campanile in the province was built from 1321 to 1382 in the Gothic style used for many of the country's bell-towers. From the top, 112m/367ft high, a panoramic **view★★** unfolds of the town and province.

★Domkerk – The chancel and transept of the old cathedral (1254-1517) are Gothic. The five chapels radiating around an ambulatory were inspired by the cathedral of Tournai in Belgium. The chapels contain some beautiful **funerary monuments**.

ADDITIONAL SIGHTS

★★Centraal Museum – Housed in an old convent, the museum has a rich collection of paintings and decorative arts. The first floor is given over to Utrecht painters, from Jan van Scorel to Hendrick Terbrugghen, and fashion from 18C to the present day. The Van Baaren collection on the mezzanine includes paintings by J B Jongkind, Van Gogh, Fantin-Latour, and members of the De Stijl movement. The basement contains the Utrecht Boat (1100) discovered in 1930.

★★ **Rijksmuseum Het Catharijneconvent** – The former monastery contains collections of sacred art from throughout the Netherlands. Altar pieces, liturgical vestments, manuscripts, miniatures and paintings illustrate the history of the Catholic and Protestant churches from the beginnings of Christianity to modern times.

★★ **Rietveld Schröder Huis** – Architect Rietveld (1888-1964), a member of the De Stijl movement, built this house where Mrs Schröder lived. It consists of various elements placed at right angles and painted in neutral tones for the large surfaces and primary colours for the linear details.

EXCURSION

★★ **Loosdrechtse Plassen (Loosdrecht Ponds)** *–70km/44mi allow a day for the round trip. Leave Utrecht by way of Sartreweg in the north-west.*
The ponds cover 2 500ha/6 200 acres - of beautiful, wild and peaceful countryside. They stand on the site of former peat bogs and are dotted with a large number of marinas.

For further details on the Netherlands, consult the Michelin Green Guide Netherlands.

When looking for a hotel or restaurant, use the Michelin Red Guide Benelux, updated annually.

Norway

Area: 323 878km²/123 074sq mi. – **Population:** 4.3 million – **Capital:** Oslo – **Currency:** Krone (crown), divided into 100 ore – **Time:** GMT + 1hr in winter, GMT + 2hr in summer

Norge

Norway is dominated by fjords and mountains, stretching more than 2 000km/1 240mi from north to south. Sparsely populated, many regions are almost completely isolated, especially in the winter. The wild landscapes are awe-inspiring. In summer, the invigorating midnight sun burns, and in winter, the vast reaches of snow are wrapped in silence. More reserved than the Danish, Norwegians are a courageous people who have mastered a sometimes hostile environment by building numerous tunnels and daring bridges. They are famous for their very efficient network of ferries, which includes the famous Coastal Express (Hurtigruten). Skiing was invented in the Telemark county, and this sport is as essential to the Norwegian people as cycling is to the Danes. The great explorers Nansen, Amundsen and Heyerdahl have maintained the tradition of their dashing forebears, the Vikings, who set out across the ocean to discover new lands. In the arts, the independent, reserved yet passionate and sensitive Norwegian character has been reflected by playwright Henrik Ibsen, composer Edvard Grieg, and painter Edvard Munch.

E. Baret

IN BRIEF

Entry Formalities – A valid passport is needed for British, US, Canadian, Australian and Japanese citizens.

Wooden Churches (Stavkirker) – In Scandinavia, these churches are found mainly in Norway and are considered an important part of the national cultural heritage. The first wooden churches were built in the 12C. The roof rises by stages, which gives them a unique and unusual appearance. They are often decorated with real and mythical animals in the mythical tradition. The churches are found mainly in the southern mountainous regions. Heddal is one of the most famous.

BERGEN★★★ and the FJORDS

Michelin map 970 I 1

Bergen is known as the "Wooden City" and the "Portal to the Fjords." It was a trading centre for the Hanseatic League, controlling commerce between the North Sea and the Baltic. Until the 19C, it was Norway's largest city. The North Sea oil industry has provided a new lease on life, enabling the city to preserve its unique architecture, part of the UNESCO's world cultural heritage.

★★★ **Bryggen** – Bryggen was once the centre of the medieval city. This remarkable collection of wooden buildings painted in brick-red or ochre and topped by pointed gables looks onto the old, still busy harbour. In the past, the houses here served as lodgings, warehouses and workshops. **Det Hanseatisk Museum** (Hanseatic Museum) displays the Spartan lifestyle of a League merchant and his employees. In a neighbouring street stands the Schøtstuene, a building that served as a refectory and meeting place. Nearby, the **Bryggens Museum** is located in a modern building built around the vestiges of 12C constructions. Nearby, **Mariakirken★★**, a superb 12C Romanesque church, served as the parish for Hanseatic merchants for more than three centuries.

★★ **Mount Fløyen** – *Access via cable-railway (Fløibanen)* – Time: 8min. The top of the mountain (320m/1 050ft) offers a magnificent view of the town and surrounding islands.

★ **Troldhaugen** – *8km/5mi to the south.* Enthusiasts of the greatest Norwegian composer, **Edvard Grieg** (1843-1907) come on pilgrimage here. The composer worked in peace in the wooden shack in the gardens.

Fjords

During the last Ice Age, Norway was covered by ice relatively thin along the edge, but much thicker towards the centre. The ice's great weight widened and deepened the existing valleys. When the ice finally retreated, the sea advanced and filled the valleys. Thus, fjords were created. Their depth varies a great deal. Shallow near the coast, inland they sometimes reach a depth of more than 1 300m/4 264ft. The longest fjords extends more than 100km/62mi into the heart of the country, dividing into several arms. The most spectacular are located along the western coast between Bergen and Ålesund.

★★★ GEIRANGERFJORD

Geirangerfjord is best appreciated by boat. The fjord is enclosed in a magnificent mountain landscape. The sheer cliffs and peaks are covered with snow all year round. Only one road passes through the village nestled at the end of the fjord. It crosses the mountains to connect Geiranger to the outside world, and is known as the "**Golden Road**" for the superb views along the way.
To the south, an ascent of the **Dalsnibba**★★★ (1,495m - 5,681ft) provides a view of the fjord and its small village. To the north, the last turn of **Eagle Road** (Ørnevegen) reveals the fjord winding through the valley. To reach Åndalsnes, follow Trollstigveien, which crosses one of Norway's most desolate regions.

★★ HARDANGERFJORD

Hardangerfjord is easily reached from Bergen. Its many arms extend 179km - 111 miles inland. A series of roads show off the variety of landscapes. The tour follows the fjord from Skånevik, a charming small ferry harbour northeast of Haugesund to Norheimsund to the east of Bergen. In addition to boat trips on the fjord, many opportunities exist for hiking in the valleys or mountains. Admire the waterfalls and the attractive villages such as Kinsarvik, Eidfjord, Ulvik and Ålvik.

★★★ NORDFJORD

Nordfjord is considered one of the finest fjords, winding inland to the foot of the country's largest glacier Jostedalsbreen. The Coastal Express makes a daily stop at Måløy at the fjord's entrance. From there, the northern shores lead to the villages of **Loen** and **Olden**. These villages are calm, pleasant places to stay. Magnificent excursions begin here. Climb by car and later by foot into the Olden Valley (Oldendalen) to the edge of the **Briksdalsbreen** Glacier★★.

★★★ SOGNEFJORD

Sognefjord is Norway's longest and most impressive fjord. Its arms extend right up to the Jotunheimen massif. At mid-point, the fjord reaches its maximum depth of 1 308m/4 290ft. Awe-inspiring, enigmatic, wild and luminous in turn, the fjord is at its best in late spring, when fruit trees are blossoming against the idyllic background of snow-covered peaks. Sognefjord is easily reached by road, but also by aeroplane from Oslo or by boat starting from Bergen. There are many sights and excursions to enjoy. **Vik** and **Kaupanger** are famous for their 12C wooden churches, **Balestrand** for a remarkable setting, **Fjærland** for its Glacier Museum. One of the oldest and most beautiful wooden churches, **Urnes Stavkirke**★★, stands alone on the banks of the Lustrafjord. The church is part of the UNESCO's world heritage.

FINNMARK, The NORWEGIAN LAPLAND

In spite of a surface area of 48 000km²/18 240sq mi, Finnmark has a population of only 75,000. The extremely harsh climate reaches -50°C/-58°F in winter and climbs to 32°C/90°F in summer. Still, increasing numbers of visitors are attracted to the Arctic light, the midnight sun and the aurora borealis, as well as by the culture and way of life of the Sami Laplanders. Karasjok and Kautokeino, each with a population of 3,000, are the only urban areas in Finnmark's high desert plateau. *See FINLAND and SWEDEN.*

HURTIGRUTEN★★

COASTAL EXPRESS

The Coastal Express is considered the king of the Norwegian ferries. For more than a century, it has linked Bergen to Kirkenes, a distance of more than 2 500km/1 550mi. The Gulf Stream makes possible regular boat travel so far north. Half of the ferry's journey is above the polar circle, and life at the ports along Norway's northwestern coast is organised around the Coastal Express's schedule. A round trip lasts 11 days. But the traveller can disembark at any port, with or without a car. A reservation is nevertheless recommended. The ships follow the coastline and navigate between the islands, revealing extraordinary sights such as **Runde**, a bird sanctuary near Ålesund. The boats stop long enough to allow their passengers to come ashore, and excursions are organised to coincide with the schedule of the Coastal Express. The old city of **Trondheim**, Norway's third largest city, represents an important stop. The next port is the famous **Lofoten Wall**, which looms over huge Vestfjorden. Do not miss Tromsø, bathed in a strange ethereal light. Another final must is an excursion to the **North Cap** from the fishing port of Honningsvåg.

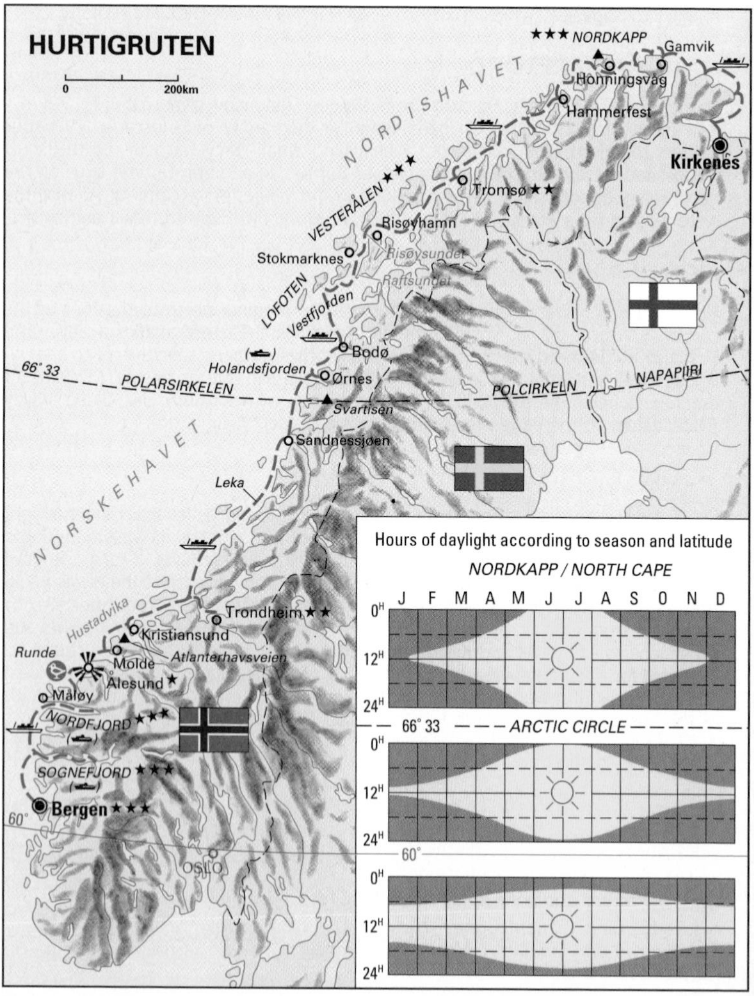

NORDKAPP★★★

NORTH CAPE

Michelin map 985 A 22

This impressive promontory located at a latitude of 71°10'21 north, occupies the northernmost part of the European continent. Fog often covers the plateau. But sometimes the mists lift to reveal the immense, empty stretch of ocean from Nordkapp to the North Pole. The rocky slopes of the steep 307m/1 007ft cliff plunge into the sea. A transparent globe of the planet earth set near the cliff's edge reflects the rays of the midnight sun. The **North Cape Experimental Centre (Nordkapphallen)**, hidden in the side of the cliff, offers visitors instructive exhibits and a pleasant reception area to wait – in summer – for the magical hour when the midnight sun pauses briefly on the horizon before rising again to begin a new day.

OSLO★★★

Population 467 000

Michelin map 970 K 2

Oslo lies in a remarkable setting at the end of the only large fjord on the southern coast of Norway. The city is surrounded by forested hills and steep slopes. It is a lively, modern place with a provincial air.

The capital's busiest district is Aker Brygge and Karl Johans Gate lying on the banks of the fjord. The quays have been invaded by a plethora of café terraces and restaurants, overwhelmed by customers starting at 6pm. Karl Johan Gate crosses the centre of town from the Central Station to the Royal Palace. It passes near the restored cathedral, and then in front of the Parliament and the University Gardens.

★★NASJONALGALLERIET and the MUNCH Museum

The **National Gallery**, located behind the University, houses Norway's most important collection of Norwegian and international art. Apart from a collection of French painting from the 19C and 20C, the two rooms devoted to the work of Edvard Munch (1863-1944) should not be missed. The visitor can then explore the **Munch Museum** with some 1 100 paintings displayed in rotating exhibitions.

BYGDØY

The peninsula of Bygdøy can be reached by car by going to the west around the port. Ferries also travel there from Rådhusbryggae at the back of the old port. After leaving the dock, the ferry passes in front of **Akershus Festning★**, a Renaissance castle that replaced the earlier medieval fortress.

Bygdøy is a pleasant residential quarter with five remarkable museums. The **Norsk Folkemuseum★★★** is an open-air folk art museum illustrating the wooden architecture from various regions, especially the south. The **Viking Ship Museum★★★** (Vikingskiphuset) shelters three boats and their contents used for a funeral ceremony and discovered near Oslo Fjord. The **Fram Museum★★** is devoted to the polar vessel *Fram* used by the Norwegian explorers Fridtjof Nansen (1861-1930) and Roald Amundsen (1872-1928). The **Kon-Tiki Museum★★** illustrates the voyages of Thor Heyerdahl, who attempted to discover the routes followed by ancient civilisations in their migrations. Finally, the **Norsk Sjøfartsmuseum★★** organises its naval collection by theme.

The **Vigeland Park★** (Videlandsanlegget) is the only one of its kind in the world. It contains 200 monumental sculptures by Gustav Vigeland (1869-1943) who worked there for more than 20 years. The artist expresses his personal vision of life with strength and realism.

For further details on Norway, consult the Michelin Green Guide Denmark Norway Sweden Finland.

When looking for a hotel or restaurant in Oslo, use the Michelin Red Guide Europe, updated annually.

Poland

Area: 312 683km²/120 727sq mi – **Population:** 38.5 million – **Capital:** Warszawa (Warsaw) – **Currency:** Zloty – **Time:** GMT + 1hr in winter, GMT + 2hr in summer.

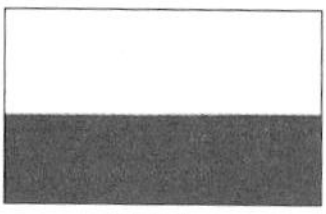

Polska

This Central European nation is bordered to the north by the Baltic Sea beaches and to the south by the Sudety, Carpathian, and Tatra mountains. Lakes, picturesque hills and magnificent forests dot the North Polish regions of Pomerania and Mazuria. This attractive country boasts a wealth of artistic and architectural heritage, a sign of several centuries of dense, eventful history.

IN BRIEF

Entry Formalities – Valid passport for British and US citizens; visa for Canadian, Australian and Japanese citizens.

Shopping – Large stores open Mondays to Saturdays from 9am to 8pm. In major cities, shops open from 11am to 7pm. Food stores open earlier, at 6am, but also close at 7pm.

Souvenirs – Cepelia shops sell woodcarvings, tapestries, embroidery, striped woollen fabrics known as *pasiak* used to make skirts and aprons, painting on glass, and pottery. Amber, the gold of the north, is found in yellow, russet or brown. The mineral, transparent as crystal, is used to make necklaces, earrings, and a wide range of statues; sometimes it is mounted in silver jewellery. The Delia stores also have a good selection of works of art and antiques.

GDAŃSK**

Population 480 000
Michelin map 970 N 3

Gdańsk, formerly known in German as Danzig, lies on the Baltic Sea. For more than a century in the Middle Ages, the Teutonic Knights dominated, creating a prosperous town. In the 14C, Gdańsk was one of the Hanseatic League's large wealthy trading posts. As the largest Baltic harbour, it attracted merchants from every corner of the globe.

Like many Polish cities, Gdańsk was occupied on numerous occasions. Its historic old town was almost totally destroyed during the Second World War. Nowadays, the city has risen from its ashes like Warsaw and its architecture bears some resemblance to Flemish buildings.

During the 1980s, Gdańsk soared into the international headlines as the birthplace of the trade union Solidarity. The protest movement started in the city shipyards. A little-known electrician named Lech Walesa led the workers against the government. Walesa was awarded the Nobel Peace Prize in 1983 and was elected President of the Polish Republic in 1990.

**GŁÓWNE MIASTO (MAIN TOWN)

Brama Wyżynna (Upper Gate) – This gate, designed in the 16C by the Flemish architect Willem van den Blocke and remodelled at the end of the 19C, marked the main entrance to the town. It is decorated with the coats of arms of Gdańsk (lions), Prussia (unicorns) and Poland. Behind, the group of buildings make up the 14C Foregate (Przedbramie). The Prison Tower and torture chamber are clearly visible.

Brama Złota (Golden Gate) – This gate was built in the 17C by the son of architect Brama Wyzynna. It consists of a triumphal arch with two tiers of columns and a balustrade topped with allegorical statues representing Peace, Liberty, Glory, and Fortune. This marks the start of the Royal Way (Ulica Dluga and Dlugi Targ) which extends to the quays beside the River Motlawa.

Ulica Długa – The name means Long Street, and Ulica Dluga is one of the city's most attractive thoroughfares. The pedestrian precinct is animated, especially on market days and during the tourist season. Gabled houses flank the street with lavishly decorated frontages in several different architectural styles (nos 12, 28, 35 and 45).

Ratsz Glownego Miasta (town hall of the main town) – The town hall combines Gothic and Renaissance styles. At the top of the belfry, the gilded statue of King Sigismund Augustus looks down over the city. The interior houses the Gdańsk History Museum, along with numerous state rooms.

Długi Targ (Long Market) – City life long centred on the Long Market Square. Major markets, important ceremonies, popular events, and entertainment took place here. The houses, rebuilt after the war, evoke typical local architecture, with flights of steps over cellars.
In the centre stands the popular 17C **Neptune Fountain**. The bronze statue was made by Peter Husen, a Flemish artist. Next to it, the **Artus House** (Dwór arusa) was used by the city's traders as a meetingplace. The adjacent **Golden House** (Złota Kamienica) is ornately decorated with bas-reliefs depicting scenes from the history of Rome and busts of famous people such as Brutus, Horace and two Polish kings Casimir, Jagiellonian and Sigismund III Vasa.

Brama Zielona (Green Gate) – The Green Gate marks the end of the Royal Way. It was built in the Flemish Renaissance style and intended for use as a royal residence by Polish sovereigns passing through the town. The rustic ground floor has four porches decorated with the coats of arms of the city, Poland and Prussia.

J.-P. Garcin /DIAF

On the banks of the Motlawe, Gdańsk

The Quaysides – From Most Zielony **(Green Bridge)**, the **view★** encompasses the picturesque Dlugie Pobrzeze, called the Long Quay. This was Gdańsk's former harbour. Ships tied up alongside a wooden jetty. On the other side of the bridge is Loft Island.
Żuraw, the **Crane Gate★**, on Long Quay, is one of the city's symbols. It was built in the mid 15C and doubled as a gate and as a crane. Men moved two huge wheels by walking around inside. The crane hoisted loads weighing up to 2t. It also lifted ships' masts into place. Inside the gate, the maritime museum (Muzeum Morskie) depicts the history of Gdańsk harbour and river traffic on the River Vistula.

Ulica Mariacka (Notre-Dame Street) – The picturesque housefronts, flights of steps, gutters and gargoyles express the best of Gdańsk's old town.

Kaplica Królewska (Royal Chapel) – This chapel was built in the Baroque style by King John III Sobieski.

Kósciól Mariacki (Notre-Dame Church) – Building work began on the church dedicated to the Virgin Mary in 1343 and was completed in 1502. The vast red brick church symbolised the power of the town's wealthy middle classes. The impressive high altar has a triptych with a central panel depicting the Coronation of the Virgin Mary. Note the **astronomic clock**, 14m/46ft high, designed in 1460 by Hans Düringer.

EXCURSIONS

★Oliwa – This suburb of Gdańsk includes the remains of a Cistercian abbey. Oliwa is famous for its cathedral whose two tall octagonal brick towers overlook a superb park. The interior is mainly Baroque. The 18C organ is one of the cathedral's finest features. Organ concerts are held in the summer.

★**Sopot** – This busy seaside resort is famed for its beaches. Its wooden pier, stretching 516m/1 677ft, is said to be the longest on the Baltic coast. The open-air theatre puts on yearly shows.

★**Malbork** – *51km/32 mi southeast.* Malbork Castle was built by the Teutonic Knights. These sworn enemies of Poland were finally defeated at the Battle of Grunwald in 1410. Formerly known as Marienburg, it is a splendid example of a medieval fortress. The Order had its headquarters here for 150 years. The castle is a huge red-brick construction divided into three sections – the Upper Castle consisting of superb rooms housing the grand masters and knights, the Middle Castle with an amber, porcelain and weaponry exhibition, and the Lower Castle.
For a good view, go to the other bank of the Nogat. The sight is amazing at sunset.

KRAKÓW★★★

CRACOW – Population 745 000
Michelin map 970 N 5

Although Warsaw has been the administrative capital of Poland since 1596, Krakow remains the country's historic centre, dear to the hearts of the Polish people. The River Vistula flows through the city. Krakow was miraculously spared during the Second World War and its famous medieval town offers an outstanding wealth of architectural heritage.
From the 14C, Polish kings were crowned and buried in Krakow. The city flourished during the reign of Casimir the Great. In the first half of the 16C, the Italian Renaissance made major contributions. Artists and craftsmen of great genius embellished historic buildings and luxurious works of art.
Krakow is now a hospitable and delightful city, proud of its heritage, careful to show it off. In 1994, Krakow inaugurated the ultra-modern **Centre of Japanese Art and Technology** designed by the architect Arata Isozaki.
This major cultural city houses a prestigious ancient university. Nicholas Copernicus lived here. The equally famous seminary included among its students Karol Wojtyla who, after being appointed Archbishop of Krakow, was elected Pope John Paul II in 1978.

★★★WAWEL

The Wawel Hill, Poland's historic heartland, stands proudly between two bends in the Vistula flowing majestically past its foot. On the river bank, the legendary dragon forms part of the city's history. It stands erect at the entrance to its cave, spitting fire. The bronze sculpture is by Bronislaw Chromy.
Along the access ramp, an equestrian statue of Tadeus Kosciuszko graces a terrace in front of the gateway.

★★★**Cathedral** – The cathedral remains the timeless witness of Poland's history. The country's monarchs were crowned and buried here. Dedicated to St Stanislas and St Wenceslas, this is the third church built on this site, this time in the Gothic style. At the transept crossing, an impressive black marble monument is decorated with gilded bronzes; it is known as the **St Stanislas Confession**. The bishop-martyr's mausoleum was built between 1626 and 1629 to plans by Giovanni Trevano. The silver coffin, topped by a huge canopy, is carried on the shoulders of four angels. From close up, the profusion of sculptures is visible. Between the pillars separating the nave from the south aisle is **King Wladyslaw II Jagiello's Tomb** made of red marble and topped by a canopy. It is a veritable masterpiece. The coats of arms of Poland and Lithuania serve as a reminder of the alliance between the two countries in their struggle to defeat the Teutonic Knights.
Coronation services were held in the chancel with its Baroque choir stalls and high altar. In the south aisle, backing onto the chancel and roofed with a dome, Italian artists created the finest example of Renaissance architecture in Poland, **Sigismund Chapel**. The last two kings of the Jagiellonian dynasty are buried here – Sigismund I the Elder, and his son Sigismund-Augustus.
Near the main door, Gothic vaulting marks the **Holy Cross Chapel**. The paintings represent scenes from the Gospels and were created by artists from the Pskow School (Russia, 1470). The sarcophagus of King Casimir Jagiellonian (1492) was made by Wit Stwosz who also carved the altarpiece in the Church of Our Lady.
The maze of crypts contains the **royal tombs** of John III Sobieski, Sigismund III Vasa and others, as well as the tombs of national heroes such as Prince Joseph Poniatowski and Tadeusz Kościuszko and poets such as Adam Mickiewicz and Juliusz Slowacki.
From the sacristy, visitors can climb the Sigismund Tower (**view**★ of the city) containing the largest bell in Poland. Cast in 1520 for King Sigismund I the Elder, it weighs 11t and measures 2.60m/8ft in diameter.

►► Cathedral Museum: Treasury.

The esplanade provides is a superb view of the south side of the cathedral and the gilded dome. On the west side, the Baszta Zlodziejska, **Thieves' Tower** overlooks the river. A path runs down and through, the Smocza Jama, the **Dragon's Lair**, and out onto the banks of the Vistula.

★★★ **Zamek Królewski (Royal Palace)** – This palace has a vast courtyard flanked by two tiers of arches; it was once used for jousting tournaments. The palace was built in the Renaissance style to designs by two Florentine architects for King Sigismund I. The Austrians turned it into barracks around 1850. At the beginning of the 20C, and again after the Second World War, the Polish people worked to give it back its original splendour.

On the ground floor, the Gothic section shines with superb vaulted rooms housing the crown jewels and a collection of weaponry. Among the main items on display are the 13C Szczerbiec (the sword of state), the shoes worn at his coronation by 10-year old King Sigismund-Augustus, delicately worked swords and scabbards, an 18C Polish flag bearing the eagle that was once the country's emblem, a ceremonial cloak, and arms dating from the 15C to the 17C.

The first floor contains a collection of 16C and 17C portraits that once belonged to royal and noble families. On the second floor, the **royal apartments**★★★ consist of vast luxurious chambers summarising several centuries of art and history. Huge magnificent hangings taken to Canada for safety during the Second World War decorate the walls in several of the rooms. In the audience chamber, the ceiling's coffers are decorated with carved heads. On the walls, tapestries depict biblical scenes. In the Senators' or Ceremonial Chamber, the tapestries illustrate the Old Testament and the Cordovan leather.

★★★ STARE MIASTO (OLD TOWN)

The historic city centre lies within a green belt, the **Planty Park**. It was laid out in the 19C on the site of the old town walls. The park is full of trees and is a pleasant spot for a stroll. The footpaths cover a distance of some 4km/2.5 mi and provide views of the remaining town walls. The park also contains statues representing scenes from Polish history.

★ **Ulica Kanonicza** – This street is one of the city's oldest. It has retained its medieval character with a fine set of houses with decorated façades. Inside, arcades flank the courtyards. The most outstanding houses are at nos 23-25; at no 21, the entrance is decorated with geometric motifs; no 24 shows off a sacerdotal emblem, no 22 has a statue; no 19 a window with balustrades, and no 3 windows with geometric designs.

Ulica Grodzka – This street, part of the Royal Way, is a hive of activity. It includes two interesting churches, one dedicated to **St Andrew** (Kościól Św. Andrzejza) with a Romanesque exterior and Baroque interior and one to **St Peter and St Paul** (Kosciól Św. Piotra i Pawla). The latter was commissioned by Sigismund III Wasa and is topped by a lantern dome. Its design was inspired by the Gesù Church in Rome. Statues of the twelve Apostles stand at the entrance.

►► Kościól Dominikanów: This red-brick Gothic church was built for the Dominican Order.

★★★ **Rynek Główny (Marketplace)** – The vast market place square spans 200m/650ft in length along each side. It evokes many historic events. Today it is lined with superb mansions, cafés and shops. The square is always full of people. The terraces of cafés and restaurants are crowded and bright with multi-coloured parasols. Groups gather when bands begin to play jazz or traditional music. Folk musicians are usually in traditional costume. Artists, portraitists and flower sellers expose their wares while flocks of pigeons peck at the crumbs thrown to them. Horse-drawn omnibuses, carriages and even rickshaws take tourists through the streets of the old town.

In the centre of the square beside the church, a **monument** is dedicated to the poet Adam Mickiewicz. For many locals, this spot serves as an ideal rendez-vous point. Every hour on the hour, trumpets ring out from one of the towers of the Church of Our Lady. But the piece of music is never completed. This *hejnal* commemorates the capture of Kraków by the Tatars in the 13C. From the top of the tower, the lookout indicated the arrival of the invaders by sounding a horn and a trumpet when he was shot in the throat by an arrow. His call came to an abrupt end. Today, the trumpet sounds from the four points of the compass, perpetuating the memory of this dramatic historical event.

★★★ **Sukiennice (Cloth Hall)** – The 14C Cloth Hall is an amazing and dazzling building with a yellow ochre frontage. It is lined with arcaded galleries supported on columns with carved capitals. An attic was added to the building in the 16C. Further renovations took place during the 19C. The combination of Gothic, Renaissance and Baroque features and the wealth of decorative elements make this a highly unusual construction.

F. Jalain /EXPLORER

Altarpiece (detail)

Inside, stalls sell souvenirs and popular arts and crafts. They stretch in a continuous line from one end of the building to the other. Outside, beside the church, is the entrance to the **Gallery of 19C Polish Art and Sculpture**. The ticket office and cloakroom are on the first floor. On the second floor, a collection of Romantic works features paintings of horses. Among the representative artists are Jan Matejko whose huge works draw inspiration from history *(Kosciusko in Raclawice, L'hommage de la Prusse)*; Piotr Michalowski and his portraits *(Napoleon)*; Wladyslaw Podkowinski *(Champ de lupins, Frénésie)* and Józef Chelmónski *(Le quadrige)*. Near the Cloth Hall stands the clock tower, all that remains of the old **town hall**. The steps inside are steep and narrow. The tower houses temporary exhibitions and a collection of photographs of Krakow during the first half of the 20C.

★★**Kościól Mariacki (Church of Our Lady)** – The Church of Our Lady is an impressive red-brick Gothic building with a pentagonal porch flanked by two square towers. The left tower's crown contains a bell and is topped by a spire. The trumpet is sounded every hour here.

The ornate interior with three aisles but no transept reveals a combination of styles and colours. The main point of interest, though, is undoubtedly the extraordinary, monumental **altarpiece**★★★. Every day at noon, soft music can be heard and the panels of the altarpiece open at the back of the chancel. This masterpiece, which is made of lime wood, was created between 1477 and 1489 by one of the greatest of all medieval sculptors, Wit Śtwosz. He came here from Nuremberg and produced his masterpiece at the request of the wealthy burghers of Kraków. On the central panel, note the striking realism in the facial expressions of the figures. In the south aisle, the same artist produced a stone figure of Christ, remarkable for its aura of pathos.

Outside the church *(left)*, a small square called **Plac Mariacki** has a fountain decorated with a bronze figure of a young boy. Small groups of tourists gather every hour. Here the trumpet player finishes his piece and gives the amused onlookers a friendly wave. Take the narrow **Sienna Street** to the delightful little rectangular square called **Maly Rynek**.

★**Ulica Floriánska (St Florian Street)** – The street named after St Florian is Krakow's busiest thoroughfare. It is also part of the Royal Road. Street artists, portrait artists, caricaturists, ice cream sellers, and vendors selling drinks, cigarettes and cakes can all be found here.

The so-called Negroes' House *(no 1)* is outstanding for its sculptures. The **birthplace of Jan Matejko** *(no 41)*, a Romantic painter who lived from 1830 to 1893, has been turned into a museum featuring furniture, paintings, and personal effects.

The street leads to the **Bramy Florianskie Gate** which is integrated into the old town walls. It includes a square tower with slit windows and a bas-relief of St Florian.

Amateur artists display their work along the wall in **Ulica Pijarska**. Turn right and find the **Julius Slowacki Theatre**★ (Teatr im Juliusza Slowackiego) built in 1893 to designs inspired by the Garnier Opera House in Paris.

Beyond St Florian's Gate, the **Barbakan**, a strange circular building was part of the town's system of defence. It was built of red brick with slit windows in 1498. The seven turrets were originally linked to the Florian Gate by a gallery above the moat.

To the other side of the avenue on Plac Matejski, the impressive Battle of Grunwald Memorial commemorates the victory of the Polish and Lithuanian troops over the Teutonic Knights in 1410. The tomb of the unknown soldier stands in front of this monument.

★★**Czartoryski Museum** – The museum was set up by Countess Czartoryski. It houses an extensive collection of 16C to 19C European paintings, porcelain, glassware, tapestries, weapons and coats of armour. The most famous work of art in the museum is Leonardo da Vinci's ***Lady with an Ermine***★★★ which he painted in 1485 at the Court of Milan. The artist was attracted by the gentleness of Cecilia Gallerani, the young mistress of Ludovico Sforza the Moor. Another major work in the gallery is Rembrandt's ***Landscape with the Good Samartine***.

Ulica Św. Jana, a street lined with art galleries and craft shops, leads to the market place.

★★Collegius Maius – *Entrance at 15 Ulica Jagiellonska*. This is the oldest Gothic building at the Jagellonian University. The brick frontage includes three tiers of pediments. The courtyard is flanked on all sides by ogive arching supporting a balustrade gallery protected by an awning. It has a coffer roof and the stone round about gives it a great deal of charm. The library opens onto the gallery; the doorway is surrounded by gilding. A tour of the **University Museum** includes visits to superb rooms with an old-fashioned atmosphere, some still used, including the Libraria Magna, Stuba Communis, the staff common room with a carved Gdańsk Staircase dating from 1700, Aula, a ceremonial chamber with coffer ceiling and portraits of past rectors. Among the items on display, a late-15C rector's mace and astronomical instruments recall Copernicus.

Collegium Novum and Collegium Witkowskiego – These colleges also form part of the Jagellonian University. They were built in the 19C in the neo-Gothic style. In front of the second of the colleges stands a statue of Nicholas Copernicus.

★KAZIMIERZ

Access by foot or tramway, nos 8, 13 or 43.

Casimir the Great founded this district in 1335; hence the name of Kazimierz. In former times, it was an independent town encircled by walls and distinct from Kraków with its own charter and laws. In 1494, King John Albert ordered the Jews of Krakow to move to the eastern part of the town and Kazimierz quickly became a major Jewish cultural centre. Its population rose rapidly because of the massive influx of Jews fleeing persecution throughout Europe. Their numbers increased to 70 000 by the outbreak of the Second World War. Only a few hundred survived.

★Stara Synagoga (Old Synagogue) – Ulica Szeroka, in the heart of the old Jewish quarter.
The Old Synagogue was built in the second half of the 15C when Jewish culture was in its heyday. It was destroyed by fire in 1557 and rebuilt in Renaissance style in 1570 by an Italian architect, Matteo Gucci. The Nazis ransacked it then turned it into a store. From 1956 to 1959, it underwent extensive restoration.
Nowadays the old synagogue houses an interesting **museum** dedicated to Jewish culture. It includes items for worship, religious cloth embroidered in silver and gold, and an exhibition relating the martyrdom of the Jews of Krakow.
At the other end of the street stands the 16C **Remu'h Synagogue**. *Visitors are expected to give a tip.* Next door, the **Jewish Cemetery** still has carved Renaissance and Baroque tombs. Note, in particular, the small piles of stones heaped up in homage to the deceased. Rabbi Moses Isserles, alias Remu'h, who gave his name to the synagogue, is buried here under a tree; his grave is surrounded by wrought-iron railings.

►► **Muzeum Etnograficzne★** (in the former town hall on Plac Wolnica): reconstructions of the interiors of rural cottages, old crafts, headdresses and costumes, religious festivals, and popular sacred art.
Kościól Bozego Ciala *(Plac Wolnica)*: this church dedicated to Corpus Christi was the first church in Kazimierz, built in 1340. The interior is furnished in the Baroque style with choir stalls and a boat-shaped pulpit.
Kościól Sw. Katarzyny *(Ulica Augustianska)*: this massive red-brick church dedicated to St Catherine has a Gothic porch, a 17C high altar and cloisters.

ADDITIONAL SIGHTS

Kościuszko Hill – *(Buses nos 103, 119, 164 and 173)*. This cone-shaped mound was built in 1820 in honour of **Tadeusz Kościuszko** (1746-1817) who was considered as a national hero. He served in the American War of Independence as George Washington's aide-de-camp. When he returned to his homeland, he fought valiantly against the Russians and Prussians before being defeated by the Russians at the Battle of Maciejowice in 1794. He was taken prisoner but released two years later on the orders of Czar Paul I. He settled first in France then in Switzerland while continuing the struggle for his country's independence. He died in Soleure.
A spiral path leads up to the top of the mound and a magnificent **panoramic view★★** of the Vistula, the Wawel Hill, the tower on the old town hall, and Our Lady Church. In the distance, the chimneys of the Nowa Huta steel-making plant are visible. At the foot of the hill, a former Austrian fortress has been turned into a hotel called Pod Kopcem.

EXCURSIONS

★★★ **Wieliczka Salt Mines** – *13km/8mi southeast by road no 4 (E40) to Tarnów.* The Wieliczka rock salt mine, still in operation, is part of a vast salt-producing area. The salt was deposited some 15 to 25 million years ago when the sea that covered this region evaporated. The immense salt deposit was first mined around 1290. The mine includes some 330km/205mi of galleries on nine levels. The tour takes visitors around the first three levels; the working mine lies deeper. In order to reach the lowest levels open to the public 135m/439ft below the surface, visitors go down flights of steps. They come back up by elevator. A number of illustrious visitors have come here, from Goethe, Chopin, Emperor Francis Joseph, Maréchal Foch, to Pope John Paul II. The first two levels of chambers and chapels – decorated with sculptures carved in the salt, underground lakes and surprise, astonish and amaze. The Chapel of the Blessed King – the legend of the patron saint of Wieliczka's miners is illustrated in one of the chambers – represents an outstanding sights. In addition to its impressive size, the carvings, statues, bas-reliefs, and altars form a fairy tale scene thanks to the skilful use of lighting. The vast Warszawa Chamber can be used as a tennis court, theatre or ballroom, and St Barbara, the universal patron saint of miners, is celebrated here every year. The third level even includes a sanatorium. It shows the work in the mine and the mining activity in the region as a whole. The tour ends in the geology museum.

Częstochowa – *110km/68mi northeast by road no 4 (E40) to Dabrowa Górnicza then turn right onto road no 1 (E75).* This pilgrimage town is famed for the **Jasna Góra Monastery★★★**, a centre of Polish Catholic spirituality. The Pauline monastery or convent stands on a hill surrounded by walls, beneath the tall tower topping its basilica church. Visitors can climb to the top of the tower for a **view** of the city. Wladyslaw, Duke of Opole, founded the monastery in 1382. It was fortified in the 17C. Swedes attacked the community several times but in vain. Visitors enter by the Lubomirski Gate – note the impressive bells to the left – and by three triumphal gateways. The basilica was refurbished in the Baroque style and filled with gold leaf, marble and stucco work.
The Lady Chapel in the chancel contains an exceptional item, which people worship, even venerate. This **Black Virgin Icon** depicts a Madonna and Child. The Madonna's face is scarred but she seems to be able to provide protection and work miracles, and she is resplendent in gold and precious stones. The icon's origin is unknown. Although legend says that St Luke painted it, experts believe the icon is a 14C work created by an Italian artist with a talent akin to genius.
Inside the walls, visitors can also visit the armoury with paintings and weapons. The monastery's museum holds dresses for the Black Virgin, monastery treasure of liturgical vestments, musical instruments, and even Lech Walesa's 1983 Nobel Peace Prize.

►► Between Częstochowa and Krakow, the Jurassian countryside is dotted with ruined castles. These **eagle's nests** were built by Casimir the Great (See **Olsztyn★** and **Ogrodzieniec★★**).

★ **Ojców National Park** – *Northwest by road no 4 (E40) then turn right to Ojców.* The road crosses a wooded area of valleys gouged out by the Pradnik. The countryside bristles with rocks carved out of a high limestone plateau. Underground rivers have formed caves; the best-known is the **Lokietek Cave** (Jaskinia Lokietka). The flora and fauna delight walkers.

★★ **Pieskowa Skala Castle** – The mighty outline of this castle stands in a picturesque setting on a rocky promontory high above the Pradnik Valley. It was built in the 14C by Casimir the Great and belonged for several centuries to the influential Szafraniec family. It underwent alterations over the years and now combines a fortified castle with bastions and lookout towers and a country house with Gothic and Renaissance features. A gateway in a curtain wall leads to the outer courtyard then, at the end, the great carriage entrance opens onto the inner courtyard with arches, an old wooden well, and two storeys of galleries. Several of the rooms are open to the public, showing reconstructed interiors from the Middle Ages to the 19C with wonderful furniture, porcelain, silverware, paintings and tapestries.
On the roadside at the bottom of the hill, a huge rock seems to defy the laws of gravity. Its shape has won it the nickname **Hercules' Mace.**

Óświecim (Auschwitz) – *55km/34mi west by A 4 highway to Katowice. Turn left off highway after about 35km/22mi at the signpost marked Chrzanów and Óświecim.*
A visit to the Auschwitz concentration camp is alarming. The horrific extermination of millions of human beings is relived. The camp itself is now a State-owned museum. When the camp was liberated some Russian troops made a film which

serves as an introduction. Its pictures are harrowing. The camp was opened in 1940, originally for Polish political prisoners, but it later received deportees from all over Europe and symbolises the Nazi attempt to wipe out all Jews and gypsies. An opening in the barbed wire forms the main gate. The terrifying mott, which, translated into English, proclaims Freedom through Work tops the entry. Visitors follow a precise route through the camp. Several of the barracks are open to the public. Exhibitions include information panels, objects and clothes belonging to deportees, women's hair used to make fabrics, drawings done by prisoners, and photos. All illustrate the living conditions, experiments, and executions. Several barracks deal with specific countries, and special exhibitions concern the Second World War, Occupation, Resistance and Liberation. Barrack no 27 reveals the martyrdom and struggle of the Jews. Bouquets of flowers are placed in various spots by anonymous visitors. The tour ends at the gas chambers and crematorium. Nearby is the stake at which Rudolf Höss, the camp's commandant, was executed on 16 April 1947. Höss was arrested in 1946 under the false name of Franz Lang and sentenced to death by the Supreme Court in Warsaw.
The **Birkenau Camp** (Brzezinka) or Auschwitz II lies 3km/2mi from Auschwitz I. This extermination complex was built in 1941. In August 1944, some 100 000 men, women and children were imprisoned here. Its sinister gate, through which convoys crowded with prisoners entered the camp, is featured on many photographs. The camp's scale is best appreciated from the platform at the top of the former SS watchtower. The view is desolate. To the right stands the seemingly endless railroad and few wooden barracks, originally stables; to the left, brick barracks, their chimneys indicating the location of the demolished barracks. A signpost leads past and into the huts, to the ruins of the crematoria and gas chambers. At the end of the railroad is the International Monument to the Victims of Fascism. Visitors can continue the tour beyond this point if they wish to do so.

★★**Cruise down the Dunajec** – *3 hr.* Boatmen propel a raft with long poles. Passengers embark at Katy and the cruise ends in Szczawnica, a spa town near the Slovak border. Leave your car in Szczawnica and take the bus back to the point of departure, or vice versa. The river's current is smooth in some places and quite rough in others. The banks consist of sheer limestone cliffs that are part of the Pieniny Range. In places, they rise to a height of 300m/975ft.

★**Zakopane and the Tatras** – *100km/62mi south, via roads nos 7 and 77.* This well-known winter sports resort sits at the foot of the Tatras range, an alpine section of the Carpathians and the point of departure for mountain walks. Zakopane became fashionable in the second half of the 19C, attracting large numbers of artists because of the delightful setting. Its timber houses in the Zakopane style typify the area's alpine architecture. Tourists crowd the main street, **Krupówski**, with its shops, cafés, and restaurants. The **Tatras Museum** (no 10) covers ethnography, history and geography. For **views**★★ of the area, take the funicular railway up Mount Gubalówka or the cable-car on Mount Kasprowy Wierch.

WARSZAWA★★★

WARSAW – Population 1 650 000

Michelin map 970 O 4

The capital of Poland lies in the Mazovian Lowland around the River Vistular. The city, systematically razed to the ground during the Second World War, rose miraculously from the ashes thanks to the determination and obstinacy of the local people. Today it has become a lively bustling metropolis on both banks of the river.
Warsaw's name derives from a legend about a mermaid asking two young lovers, Wars and Zawa, to found a town and call it Warszawa. The mermaid now is the city's emblem.
In actual fact, the town was founded in the 10C and 11C when large villages spread out along each side of the Vistula. It became a capital in 1596 during the reign of Sigismund III, after a terrible fire had destroyed the royal castle in Krakow.

Warsaw's Child Prodigy – **Frédéric Chopin** was born on 14 March, 1810 in the village of Zelazowa Wola to a French father and Polish mother, both of whom were in the service of Count Skarbek. His musical gifts, especially his talents as a pianist, became apparent early on in his life. Young Chopin attended the Central Academy of Music from 1826 to 1829. Already, he composed works that drew a great deal of attention – *Waltzes in A flat major, Polonaise in D major*, and *Nocturne in E minor*.
He left Poland in 1830 and settled in Paris. After a rough start in France, he met Heine, Liszt and Berlioz and began to frequent Parisian high society. Chopin was a much sought-after teacher and a talented composer. In 1837, he met George Sand who had

Chopin

attracted public attention through her first novel, *Indiana*, published in 1832. The idyllic love affair of these two tormented Romantics lasted for 10 creative years. During this time, Chopin composed a large number of outstanding works.
He was ill for several years and died of tuberculosis in Paris on 17 October,1849 at 12 Place Vendôme. He is buried in the Père-Lachaise Cemetery *(see Michelin Green Guide on Paris)*. Chopin left a wide range of different works representing every facet of his sensitive nature – waltzes, some dazzling, others melancholic; polonaises in which he expresses his revolt against oppression and his sense of liberty; mazurkas which are a translation of the Polish soul; intimate nocturnes; études which show his full virtuosity; and of course, ballads, impromptus and scherzos.

★★★STARE MIASTO (OLD TOWN) (BX)

After the war, the old town was rebuilt as an almost exact copy of its former self, using old documents. It lies within the medieval walls. From this core, the city expanded over the centuries.

★**Plac Zamkowy (Castle Square)** (BX **64**) – This square stands in front of the castle. The **Sigismund Column** (BX **B**), a tall column on a stepped base, makes it visible from some distance away. It was erected in 1644 by Wladyslaw IV in honour of his father, King Sigismund III Vasa. The monarch is represented at the top, dressed in armour and wearing his coronation cloak. He leans on a cross and brandishes a sabre.
A Gothic bridge spans the moat to the left. Further on, is the **statue of the cobbler**, J Kilinski, who, with the help of Kosciuszko, played a major role in the 1794 uprising against the Russians.
A row of colourful houses lines the square's left side facing the royal castle's pink façade. Just in front of the castle, downhill and to the right, is the **Palac Pod Blacha**, literally, the castle beneath the sheet metal. Its four-sided sheet metal roof was built in the 18C and integrated into the castle by King Stanislas-Augustus Poniatowski. Previous owners included Prince Joseph Poniatowski and Czar Alexander I.
Carriage rides and a miniature train leave from the square in front of the castle.

★★**Zamek Królewski (Royal Palace)** (BX) – At the end of the 13C, the dukes of Mazovia built a wooden castle near the town, on the Vistula's high bank. In the early 15C, a stone-built Gothic residence was added, with a round tower containing a staircase. The royal castle was further extended in the early 17C, a few years after Warsaw had become a capital. It took on a pentagonal shape with a large inner courtyard and forecourt. King Stanislas-Augustus Poniatowski made additional renovations, paying particular attention to the interior decoration. He also added on new apartments for members of the royal family or leading statesmen. The castle was rebuilt between 1971 and 1984. The onion towers highlight the façade's stark austerity. The castle flanks one entire side of the square.
The interior has been carefully and elegantly reconstructed, recreating the luxury of the 17C and 18C. The main part of the visit takes place in the Court Chambers, the Diet Chambers and the **royal apartments**. Of particular interest, note the Senators' Room, where the 1791 constitution was voted, the Marble Room with a portrait of King Stanislas Augustus, the Knights' Chamber with paintings illustrating Polish history by Marcello Bacciarelli, the Throne Room, the State Chamber with allegorical statues and Marcello Bacciarelli's painting on the ceiling, and the Senators' Lobby or Canaletto Room. The paintings created by the famous Venitian artist Giovanni Antonio Canal, alias Canaletto, at the request of King Stanislas Augustus consist of accurate and detailed views of Warsaw.

Ulica Piwna (BX) – Beer Street is the old town's longest thoroughfare. Shop signs and old street lights make for a picturesque sight.

Ulica Świetojanska (BX **57**) – This busy shopping street leads to the old town market place.

★**Katedra Św. Jana (St John's Cathedral)** (BX) – The cathedral church, dedicated to St John, has a brick façade topped by a crow-stepped gable. The bronze door opens onto an austere Gothic interior. In the south aisle, stained-glass windows depict major figures from Polish history. In the crypt are the tombs of the dukes of Mazovia, the archbishops of Warsaw, the first President of the Polish Republic, Gabriel Narutowicz (he was assassinated in 1922), and Henryk Sienkiewicz, the author of Quo Vadis, the winner of the Nobel Prize for Literature in 1905.

Dziekania Street (BX **13**) runs along the right-hand side of the cathedral. Note the fragment of caterpillar track from a German Goliath tank embedded in the wall. It leads to the peaceful **Kanonia Street** (BX **19**), named after the cathedral canons. Beyond, a small triangular square called Placyk Kanonia has a bell in the middle and is lined with houses built in the Hanseatic style. Note the narrowest house in the city at the end of the square on the right side.
Beside the cathedral, another church, the Kosciól Sw. Matki Dzienkczynnej, is dedicated to **Our Holy Mother of Grace**, the city's patron saint. Also known as the Kosciól Jezuitów, the **Jesuit Church**, it was founded by King Sigismund Vasa III.

A. Towy /EXPLORER

Old Town Market place

★★★**Rynek Starego Miasta (Old Town Market place)** (BX **54**) – This is Warsaw's most popular venue. Street cafés, restaurants, vendors of paintings, souvenirs, drinks and ice cream, all add to the hustle and bustle of the tourist season. Carriage rides start from the square.
Until the end of the 18C, this was the city's heart, used for markets and fairs, ceremonies, shows and public executions or other forms of punishment. In the early 19C, it lost its popularity when poorer people began to move into the houses. The square is flanked on all four sides by bourgeois homes representing several centuries of architectural style. Some façades are austere, others richly decorated with friezes and sculptures. Overall, the spot bursts out in colour.

★**Muzeum Historyczne Warszawy (Warsaw History Museum)** (BX **M**¹) – The museum shows a film on the destruction and reconstruction of Warsaw entitled *Warsaw Nevertheless*. Enquire about the times of the English version. It represents an excellent introduction to the local history museum.
The city's past is illustrated on four floors – political and religious life, trade, art, the struggle against occupation, and Warsaw today.

►► Muzeum Mickiewicz (BX **M**²): This museum depicts the life and works of the great writer, Adam Mickiewicz.

Barbakan (BX **A**) – This red-brick construction at the end of the old town served as part of the city's system of defence. Follow the town walls *(right)* to the **Statue of the Little Mermaid** (Syrena), the capital's emblem. The **view** overlooks the new town. In the other direction *(left)*, the **Monument to the Young Rebel** commemorates the role played by children during the 1944 uprising, many of whom used the city's sewers to move from one area to another.

★NOWE MIASTO (NEW TOWN) (ABX)

Enter the new town by **Nowomiejska Street** (BX **37**). On the left stands the **Church of the Holy Spirit** (Sw Ducha) (BX), a Baroque building with two towers. Further on is the **Church of St Hyacinth** (Sw Jacka) (BX). At 16 **Freta Street**, the **Muzeum Marie Sklodowska-Curie** (BX **M**³), is the birthplace of the winner of the Nobel Prize for Physics (1903) and Chemistry (1911).

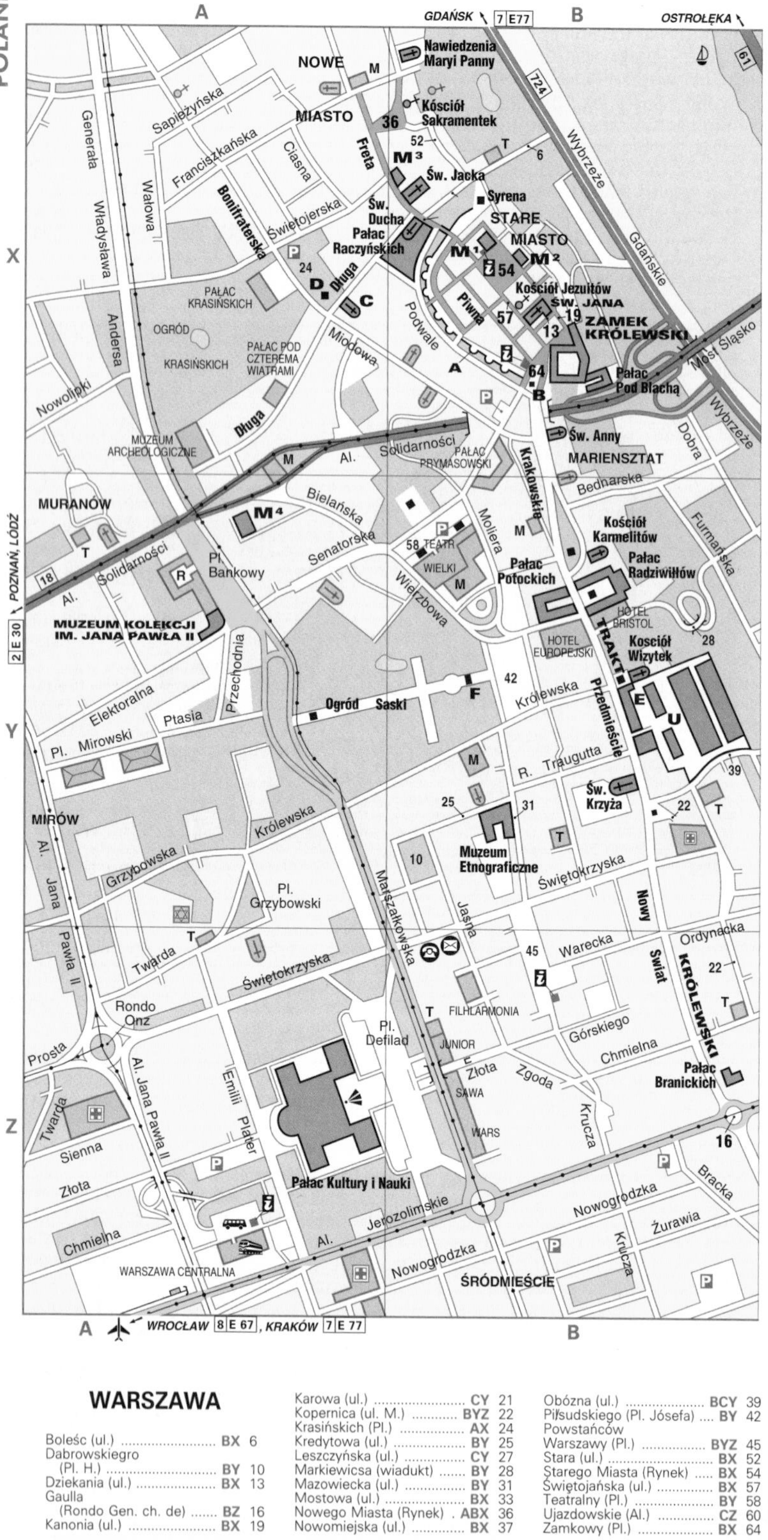

WARSZAWA

Boleśc (ul.) .... BX 6
Dabrowskiegro (Pl. H.) .... BY 10
Dziekania (ul.) .... BX 13
Gaulla (Rondo Gen. ch. de) .... BZ 16
Kanonia (ul.) .... BX 19
Karowa (ul.) .... CY 21
Kopernica (ul. M.) .... BYZ 22
Krasińskich (Pl.) .... AX 24
Kredytowa (ul.) .... BY 25
Leszczyńska (ul.) .... CY 27
Markiewicsa (wiadukt) .... BY 28
Mazowiecka (ul.) .... BY 31
Mostowa (ul.) .... BX 33
Nowego Miasta (Rynek) . ABX 36
Nowomiejska (ul.) .... BX 37
Obózna (ul.) .... BCY 39
Piłsudskiego (Pl. Józefa) .... BY 42
Powstańców Warszawy (Pl.) .... BYZ 45
Stara (ul.) .... BX 52
Starego Miasta (Rynek) ..... BX 54
Świętojańska (ul.) .... BX 57
Teatralny (Pl.) .... BY 58
Ujazdowskie (Al.) .... CZ 60
Zamkowy (Pl.) .... BX 64

A Barbakan
B Kolumna Zygmunta III Wazy
C Katedra Wojska Polskiego
D Pomnik Powstania Warszawskiego
E Pałac Tyszkiewiczów/Potockich
F Grob Nieznanego Zołnierza
M¹ Muzeum Historyczne
M² Muzeum Mickiewicz
M³ Muzeum Skłodowskiej-Curie
M⁴ Muzeum Żydowskiego Instytutu Historyeznego w Polsce
U Uniwersytet Warszawski

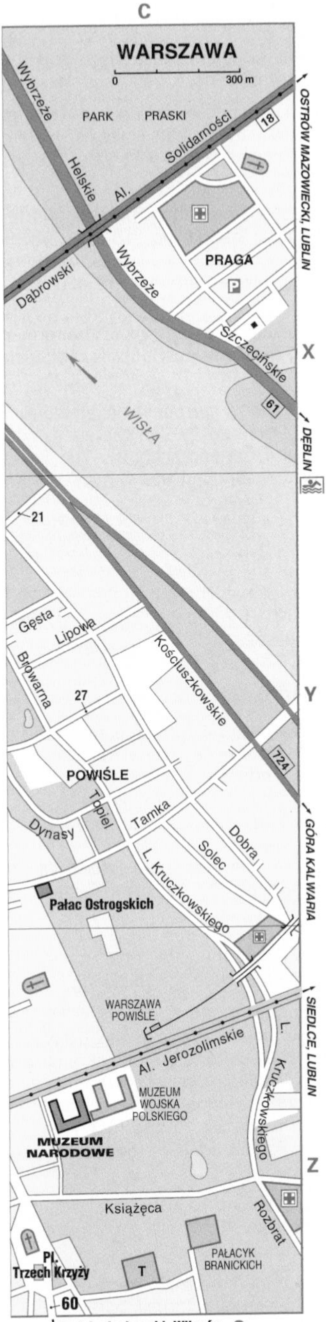

Rynek Nowego Miasta (Market place of the New Town) (**ABX 36**) – The marketplace has a well decorated with a Madonna and Unicorn, the emblem of the new town.
Nearby, the **Kosciól Sakramentek**, a Baroque Sacramentarian Church is laid out in the shape of a Greek Cross and roofed with a lantern dome. Queen Maria Casimira gave it as a gift after the victory of Polish King John III Sobieski over the Turks in Vienna in 1683. The interior is plain with white walls.

Kosciol Nawiedzenia Maryi Panny (**BX**), the red-brick church of Our Lady of the Visitation, has a separate campanile with a crow-stepped gable.

Return by Freta Street.

Ulica Dluga (**ABX**) – Long Street, as this thoroughfare is called, runs alongside the 18C **Palac Raczynskich** and the **Polish Army Cathedral Church** (Katedra Wojska Polskiego) (**AX C**). It is dedicated to the Virgin Mary, Poland's patron saint. At the corner of Bonifraterska Street, an impressive **Memorial to the Warsaw Uprising** (Pomnik Powstania Warszawskiego) (**AX D**) commemorates the 1944 revolt. It was unveiled on 1 August 1989, the uprising's 41st anniversary. During this tragic period, the sewers played a crucial role, as shown by sculpture and a plaque against the wall of a building.
To the northwest lies the **former Warsaw ghetto**. A memorial is located on Avenue Gen. Wladyslawa Andersa. The **Jewish History Museum** *(3-5 ulica Tlomackie)* (**AY M**[4]) tells the story of the martyrdom of the Jews.

★TRAKT KRÓLEWSKI (ROYAL WAY)

The king used to proceed along this long street – hence its name – linking the castle to the summer residence in the Lazienski Park. It dicovers a distance of some 4km/2.5mi and is divided into several streets lined with historic buildings, elegant residences and mansions containing several centuries of history. Further south, it leads to the Wilanów Palace.

Krakowskie Przedmiescie (Krakow's District Street) (**BXY**) – This was once part of the road between Warsaw and Krakow. In the 19C, it became the centre of the city's chic residential district.
Near the square in front of the castle, a church is dedicated to St Anne (Św. Anny) (**BX**). Princess Anne of Mazovia commissioned the Classical west front in 1454. The interior is Baroque with a single aisle and vaulting in the form of crystals. Adjacent to the church are the former Bernardines' cloisters. Several palaces, mansions and memorials line both sides of the street including: the **Statue of Adam Mickiewicz** in a small square; the former **Carmelite church** (Karmelitów) (**BY**); the **Palac Radzíwillów** (Radzivill Palace: Council of Ministers); the **equestrian statue of Prince Jósef Poniatowski** in the guise of the Roman emperor, Marcus Aurelius (**BY**); opposite, the Baroque **Palac Potocki** (**BY**) followed by the neo-Renaissance Bristol and Europejski hotels. The Bristol has been magnificently restored. Continuing, the stroller passes the **statue of Cardinal Stefan Wyszynski**, primate of Poland from 1951 to 1981 and the Visitandines Church **(Wizytek)** (**BY**) next to the **Palac Tyszkiewicz/Potocki** (**BY E**). See the statue of Atlas supporting the balcony.
Finally, a Polish eagle tops the **university** entrance (**BY U**); and the Chopin's family apartment is found no 410 near the Palac Krasinski (a commemorative plaque: *entrance in the courtyard, 2nd floor*). This has been reconstructed in accordance with a watercolour and was Chopin's last home before he left Poland at the age of 20. The apartment contains family memorabilia, drawings by Frédéric himself, three pianos, and copies of his compositions.

The 18C **Św. Krzyza** (BY) is dedicated to the Holy Cross. A statue of Christ carrying the Cross stands in front. Inside, an urn contains Chopin's heart. Note also the **memorial to Nicholas Copernicus** in front of the Palac Staszic.

►► Palac Ostrogskich *(Ulica Tamka)* (CY): This palace houses the Chopin Museum describing Chopin's life in Poland, his family, studies and illnesses, his life abroad, his concerts, the piano on which he played, and a portrait of George Sand.

Nowy Swiat (New World Street) (BYZ) – This street, named after the New World, contains palaces and fine mansions such as the **Palac Branicki** (nos 18-20) (BZ). It is one of the busiest shopping streets in the city with numerous stores, galleries, cafés and the famous **Blikle** bakery, with an old-fashioned atmosphere and wonderful cakes.

Rondo General Charles de Gaulle (BZ **16**): This roundabout stands in front of the former Communist Party headquarters, a vast austere building that now houses the Stock Exchange.

★★ **Muzeum Narodowe (National Museum)** (CZ) – The national museum covers medieval Polish art, Polish painting (16C-20C, *Battle of Grunwald* by Jan Matejko), and foreign artists (Flemish, Dutch, French, Italian and German schools). The Faras gallery contains frescoes discovered in the Coptic cathedral in Faras (Egypt) during the construction of the Aswan Dam.

KANTOR: follow this sign to change cash.

Nowy Swiat ends at **Plac Trzech Krzyzy**, the Square of the Three Crosses. The 19C church dedicated to St Alexander imitates the Roman Pantheon. Beyond it, **Aleje Ujazdowskie** (CZ **60**) is lined with a number of embassies.

★★★ PARK ŁAZIENKOWSKI (LAZIENKI PARK)

In 1766 King Stanislas Augustus Poniatowski purchased a former game reserve and turned it into a park in which he could have his summer residence built.
This superb estate with lakes, flower beds, lawns, and trees is a popular place for a stroll. Tame squirrels approach visitors, much to the delight of children.
On Aleje Ujazdowkise, Warsaw University's **botanical gardens** contain an arboretum, medicinal plants, and a rose garden.
On the same avenue but set back within the park, the impressive **Frédéric Chopin Memorial** was unveiled in 1926. The artist is shown playing the piano beneath a willow tree which symbolises his hand.
In summer, free concerts are given near the memorial.
Numerous buildings and sculptures scattered throughout the park serve as reminders of several different reigns. The most outstanding include the following.

Stara Pomaranczarnia (Former Orangery) – The former orangery was built by the Italian architect Merlini between 1784 and 1788. It houses the royal theatre which can cater for an audience of up to 200 people. The auditorium looks like marble and is similar in this respect to Versailles. In fact, the walls are panelled with painted wood in order to improve the acoustics. Around the edge of the ceiling, the *trompe-l'œil* painting depicts Apollo the King on a chariot. At the four corners, medallions represent world famous playwrights: Racine, Molière, Sophocles and Shakespeare.

Bialy Dom (White House) – The White House, King Stanislas Augustus' first summer residence, is built in a square with four identical façades. Above is a square lantern. A balustrade surrounds the house.

★★ **Palac na Wodzie (Palace-on-the-Water)** – This palace was the third royal residence designed by Merlini. It stands on a tiny island, the site of a former bathing pavilion. Two colonnades span the lake to the small pavilions. The harmonious building is modest in size, with only one upper storey. A balustrade decorated with Classical statues runs along the south side. The interior includes some superb furnished and decorated rooms, the Bacchus Room with Delft tiles, the ballroom, the Solomon Chamber, the picture gallery with paintings from the property of King Stanislas Augustus, the sunny study overlooking the lake, the King's Bedchamber with tester bed, portraits of the monarch's parents on each side, weapons and personal effects, and the dining room where VIPs were invited each Thursday.

Palac Myślewicki – This second summer residence was built in the form of arc of a circle after the White House. It was also designed by Merlini.

Teatr na Wyspie (Theatre on the Island) – The amphitheatre in the theatre on the island is decorated with statues of famous dramatists and stands on the edge of the lake; the stage imitates the Temple of Jupiter in Baalbeck and is set on a tiny island.

Belweder (Belvedere Palace) – The Polish flag flies over the Belvedere, the official residence of the President of the Republic. A portico with four columns marks the entrance to this austere neo-Classical white building.
The Belvedere was built in the 18C but underwent alteration over the years, changing its appearance, and its occupant. Stanislas Augustus set up a glazed earthenware and porcelain works here.

★★★ WILANÓW

About 10km/6mi from the castle. Drive along the Royal Way. By bus, take the no 122 along the Royal Way to the terminus.

Before reaching the estate, note the 18C St Anne's Church and the mausoleum of Stanislas Kostka Potocki and his wife, Alexandra, the founders of the Wilanów Museum.
Nicknamed Mini-Versailles, the Baroque palace in Wilanów was the residence of King John III Sobieski who defeated the Turks at the Battle of Vienna in 1683.
It consists of a central section flanked by two corner pavilions highlighting the two wings set at right angles to the main building. Vases and statues decorate the balustrade on top of the building and, seen from the courtyard, the palace gives an impression of great luxury.

Interior – A series of rooms *(entrance in right wing)* contain a large number of Polish portraits, including 17C and 18C funeral portraits which were painted post humonsly, fixed onto the coffin and removed after the burial service, ceramics and frescoes. Beyond are the **apartments** of Queen Maria Casimira and the king, lavishly furnished and elegantly decorated. Several rooms have particularly fine ceilings, some of which are decorated on the theme of the seasons of the year: Autumn is shown in the queen's antechamber with 17C furniture, Spring in the queen's bedchamber with Baroque fabrics, Winter in the king's antechamber, and Summer in the king's bedchamber. Completing the visit are the apartments used by Maréchale Lubomirska. She was the daughter of the Czartoryskis, and wife of a Grand Marshal of the Crown, who lived in and refurbished the palace in the late 18C.

Park – The park is worth a visit. It consists of a Baroque garden with decorative flower beds laid out in the shape of circles, palmettos and fleurs-de-lys, statues of Classical gods, and fountain. There is also an English-style garden and an Anglo-Chinese garden on the edge of the lake.

►► Muzeum Plakatu: The Poster Museum shows works publicising events in aviation, sports, shoes, matches, theatre and tourism.

ADDITIONAL SIGHTS

City Centre

★★ **Muzeum Kolekcji im. Jana Pawla II (John Paul II Collection)** (AY) – *1 Plac Bankowy.* The former Stock Exchange, easily recognisable because it is shaped like a rotunda and topped by a dome, now houses the John Paul II Collection, a collection of outstanding European paintings bequeathed by a couple of patrons of the arts, Janina and Zbigniew Carroll-Porczynski, to the city of Warsaw. The collection was named after the Holy Father and includes some 400 paintings illustrating six centuries of art, everything from religious subjects, landscapes, mythology, portraits, to Impressionists. There are works by Cranach, Rubens, Jordaens, Poussin, Velasquez, Goya and Renoir.

Palac Kultury i Nauki (Palace of Culture and Science) (AZ) – The gigantic Palace of Culture and Science was a "gift" from the ex-USSR; it typifies Stalinist architecture in the 1950's. The spire rises to a height of 234m/761ft. Its vast portico with 10 Corinthian columns is flanked by statues of the famous Russian writer Aleksandr Pushkin *(right)* and the well-known Polish poet Adam Mickiewicz *(left)*. Inside, the more than 3 000 rooms include a shopping centre, restaurant, theatres, conference halls, and exhibition halls.
On the 30th floor, a panoramic gallery provides a breathtaking **view**★★ of the city and the surrounding area. On the east side are modern apartment blocks topped with advertising signs. They mark out the Avenue Marszalkowska, one of the city's main shopping streets with the Wars, Sawa and Junior stores. Further away on Vistula's other bank in the Praga district is the huge circular stadium. To the south rise the tall towers of the Marriott and Forum hotels, jutting up from the urban landscape. The two hotels dominate the Aleje Jerozolimskie, a major shopping street cut at right angles by the Avenue Marszalkowska. To the north lies the Jewish ghetto. Further right are the old town walls.
A particularly lively market is held outside the Palace of Culture every day. Stands sell caviar, clothing, footwear, disks and drinks.

Muzeum Etnograficzne (**BY**) – *1 ul Kredytowa*. The ethnographic museum has exhibits pertaining to old trades, headdresses and costume, sacred art and traditional festivals.

Grób Nieznanego Zolnierza (Tomb of Unknown Soldier) (**BY F**) – The tomb of the unknown soldier lies on the edge of the Park Ogród Saski (**ABY**) and Plac Józefa Pilsudskiego (**BY 42**). John Paul II celebrated Mass in this vast square when he made his official visit to Poland in 1979, which is lined on the north side by the rear of the main theatre and on the south side by the Victoria Intercontinental Hotel. Two sentries stand guard over the tomb at all times. The changing of the guard takes place every hour in front of a triple triumphal arch, once part of an old palace, and the flame of remembrance.

EXCURSIONS

★★ **Zelazowa Wola** – *51km/32mi west by road no 2 (E30) in the Poznan direction.* Frédéric Chopin was born on 22 February, 1810 in this peaceful village in Mazovia. A superb avenue lined with trees and flowers leads to his **birthplace**, a white manor house nestling amid the trees. Memories of the great composer are everywhere. His music accompanies visitors as they pass through the various furnished rooms recalling the life of the Chopin family. The music room hosts concerts. Other sights include the dining room, the alcove where he was born, and the bedrooms, one of which contains an amazing vertical piano known as a "giraffe".
The **park** contains statues of the composer. It merits a leisurely stroll because of its palette of colours. The wide varieties of trees, shady paths, flowers and river spanned by a small bridge evoke a Romantic painting.

★★ **Palac Nieborów** – *90km/56mi southwest by road No 8 (E 67) in the Wroclaw direction. Turn right after about 50km/31mi onto road no 70 to Skierniewice and cross this town to get to Łowicz.*
This fine mansion, inspired by the Italian Baroque, was designed by Tylman van Gameren, the royal architect. It was built between 1695 and 1697 for Cardinal Michal Stefan Radziejowski, Primate of Poland. His portrait hangs in the library. The estate belonged to the Radziwills, a famous Lithuanian-Polish family, from 1774 to 1945 before becoming the property of the National Museum of Warsaw. The main building, flanked by two square towers, is decorated in the centre with a projecting pediment bearing the Polish eagle.
The main staircase bears a portrait of King Stanislas Augustus Poniatowski. Its walls and ceiling are covered with thousands of Delft tiles, each of them different. The yellow study, bedchamber, green study, library, and red drawing room contain superb furniture, tapestries and paintings, serving as reminders of a refined way of life amid various decorative styles.
The **formal gardens** are defined by a central path lined with lime trees. On the right, an L-shaped canal borders the gardens. They are separated from a lake by a dike. An **English-style park** lies within this L. The lake is home to a number of graceful water fowl, and sculptures are scattered through the park.

Arkadia – *3km/2mi on the Łowicz road.* This English-style park was commissioned by Helena, the wife of Michal Hieronim Radziwill. In the second half of the 18C, influenced by the fashion for a return to the days of Antiquity, she took as her theme for this park Arcadia, the land of happiness in Ancient Greece. The park includes replicas of Classical monuments such as the Temple of Diana and Sybil's Cave.

When looking for a hotel or restaurant in Warsaw, use the Michelin Red Guide Europe, updated annually.

Portugal

Portugal

Area: 88944km^2/34341sq mi – **Population:** – 10.5 million – **Capital:** Lisboa (Lisbon) – **Currency:** Escudo and Euro (200,482 PTE) – **Time:** GMT + 1hr in winter, GMT + 2hr in summer.

Portugal lies on the western side of the Iberian Peninsula facing the Atlantic Ocean. The birthplace of countless great explorers offers vornate historic buildings, fishing harbours with vividly-coloured smacks, seemingly endless beaches, picturesque markets, and towns with a somewhat old-fashioned charm. One of the great attractions is the friendliness of the Portuguese. The famous *sausade*, a sort of nostalgic melancholy, creates an austere façade, but behind this, the people are full of life and fun.

IN BRIEF

Entry Formalities – Passport for British, US, Canadian, Australian and Japanese citizens.

Shopping – Most shops are open from 9am to 1pm and from 3pm to 7pm. They usually close on Saturday afternoons and Sundays.

Souvenirs – A wide range of craft products including ceramics and pottery, lace, embroidery, filigree jewellery, wickerwork, rugs, woodwork and objects made of cork. The weekly markets in the small towns provide a good choice.

The fado – This singing style is of Moorish or Afro-Brazilian origin. It first appeared in Portugal in the late 18C in the form of a nostalgic sea shanty. It developed in the early 19C during a period of strife marked by the Napoleonic Wars and the independence of Brazil. It gets its name from the Latin word *fatum* meaning fate or destiny. The *fado* describes changes in personal destiny.
The singer *(fadista)* is often a woman dressed in black. She is accompanied by one or two Spanish guitars. Emotions run high during a *fado*. The performance is often very moving and enthralling.
In Lisbon, the *fado* heard in the old town's small restaurants is pure and is closer to the original style than the *fado* heard in Coimbra.

The azulejos – The etymology of the word *azulejo* varies. Some believe it comes from the word *azul* meaning "blue". In fact it comes from the Arabic word *azzulay* or *al zuleich* meaning a piece of smooth soil.

B. Brillon/MICHELIN

Azulejos, Palácio dos Marquêses de Fronteira, Lisbon

The tourada – Unlike the Spanish *corrida*, the *tourada* is a bullfight fought partly on horseback and the bull is not killed. To the Portuguese, this is first and foremost a show of skill, elegance and courage. The *tourada*, like the *corrida*, begins with the ceremonial entrance of the bullfighters set to music. A traditional *tourada* includes three horsemen *(cavaleiros)* and several *toureiros* on foot. The *cavaleiro* is dressed in a Louis XV style costume wih a gold-embroidered silk or velvet tunic, feathered tricorn, patent leather boots, and silver spurs. The *toureiros* wear a costume embroidered with sequins and spangles and they flourish yellow and pink capes.
In Portugal, the bullfighting season runs from Easter to October, with bullfights generally taking place twice a week on Thursdays and Sundays. The most prestigious are staged in the arenas *(praças de touros)* of Lisbon, Santarém and Vila Franca de Xira.

Port – The vineyards in the valleys of the Upper Douru and its tributaries produce wines left to age. Most are exported from the harbour in Oporto. The town which has given its name to the distinctive wine. Port is usually 20% proof. **White port** or **Branco** and **Blended** red ports are made with a skilful combination of different wines from different vintages. The blending and ageing differ depending on the required quality of the port finally produced. Ports include Tinto, or Red, Tinto-Alourado or Ruby, Alourado or Tawny, and Alourado-Claro or Light Tawny. **Full** or **Vintage** port is obtained from grapes of outstanding quality.
The least expensive ports are the whites, followed by the Tinto-Alourado then the Tawny. The most expensive are the Vintage and LBVs (Late Bottled Vintage).

ALCOBAÇA★★

Population 5 383
Michelin map 970 E 8

In the heart of this small town is one of the finest Cistercian abbeys to have survived since the Middle Ages.
Alcobaça lies in an agricultural area at the confluence of the Alcoa and Baça rivers. It specialises in the sale of fruit, the production of wine and the distilling of a cherry liqueur known as *ginginha*.
It is also a busy shopping town, famous for its local pottery. The vases, water fountains and platters of all shapes and sizes are predominantly blue, with traditional patterns. They can be found on street stalls around the vast square in front of the monastery.

★★SANTA MARIA Monastery *Tour about 45 min*

From outside the walls, the 18C buildings give no hint of the splendours of the Cistercian architecture.
Little remains of the original west front except the portal and rose window. It was altered in the 17C and 18C. The façade was rebuilt in the 17C and 18C in the Baroque style. The statues decorating it represent, from bottom to top, St Benedict and St Bernard, the four cardinal virtues, Strength, Prudence, Justice and Temperance, and, in a niche, Our Lady of Alcobaça.

★★**Church and abbey buildings** – The restored church has regained the nobility and bareness characteristic of Cistercian buildings. It is one of the largest and tallest churches in this style.

The Nave – The nave is unusually wide. The intersecting ribs of its vaulting are supported on transverse ribs resting on huge pillars strengthened by engaged columns. The transept contains two 14C tombs carved out of soft limestone in the Flamboyant Gothic style.

★★**Tomb of Inés de Castro** – *Left arm of the transept.* The recumbent figure is supported by six angels. The four sides of the tomb are topped by a frieze decorated with the arms of Portugal and the de Castro family.

★★**Tomb of Peter I** – *Right arm of the transept.* The recumbent figure looks particularly severe. On the sides of the tomb are scenes from the life of St Bartholomew, the king's patron saint.

Cloisters of Silence – The Cloisters of Silence were built in the early 14C. They are attractive for the simplicity of their design. Between piers, slender gemel colonnettes elegantly support three arches topped by a rose. The upper floor was added in the 16C by Diogo and João de Castilho.

Chapter House – *Opens onto the east gallery in the cloisters.* The archivolts are supported on graceful colonnettes. The ribs in the vaulting splay out from central pillars and brackets.

Monks' Dormitory – This vast Gothic chamber is striking for its sheer size, more than 60m/195ft. in length. Three aisles are separated by two rows of columns topped with capitals.

Kings' Chamber – 18C. A frieze of *azulejos* illustrates the founding of the monastery. Statues made by the monks represent the kings of Portugal up to Joseph I. There is a fine Gothic statue of the Madonna and Child.

The ALGARVE★

Michelin map 970 E 9

The Algarve covers the entire southern region of Portugal. Its name comes from the Arabic word *El-Gharb* meaning West. Its climate is mild throughout the year and this, along with the scenery, forms a good introduction to North Africa. The vegetation makes it a true garden. White houses with ornate chimney stacks are surrounded by fig, orange and carob trees, bougainvilleas, geraniums and oleanders.
The beaches have attracted large numbers of holidaymakers since the 1970s. This has led to major redevelopment programmes, some of which have unfortunately disfigured coastal areas.
The coastline is very different from east to west.

The Almond Trees of the Algarve

Although the Algarve is famous for its beaches, its countryside has a certain charm, with orchards full of fig, orange and almond trees. Legend has it that a Moorish Emir married a Scandinavian princess who was pining for the snows of the distant north. To bring a smile back to the lips of his wife, the Emir ordered a vast field of almond trees planted. One morning in January, the princess gave a cry of joy when she awoke to see the landscape covered with a myriad of almond blossoms as dazzlingly white as any snowflakes.

★FARO Population 28 622

The main town in the Algarve stands on the southern headland in Portugal, at the end of a plain flanked by rolling hillsides backing onto the Serra do Caldeirao. Faro's economy is based on the salt gathered in the saltpans, tunny and sardine fishing, cork and marble, food-processing, plastics and building.
The international airport has turned the city into the gateway of the Algarve. A network of roads links it with the seaside resorts. Faro's vast sandy beach lies on an island and attracts large numbers of tourists.

Seafront – The tourist attractions are concentrated on the harbour **(doca)**. A 15m - 49ft **obelisk** stands in the centre of the Square Dom Francisco Gomes. The palm trees, the wide Avenue de la République and the Manuel Bivar Gardens give this modern urban district its charm.

★**Old Town** – The old town lies to the south of the Manuel Bivar Gardens. It forms a quiet district within the circle of rampart-like houses.

Arco da Vila – This is the finest of the town gates. Note the Italianate pilasters and, in a niche, the white marble statue of St Thomas Aquinas.

Sé – The cathedral has a heavy porch with a bell-tower to one side. The church was rebuilt in the 18C and is decorated with 17C *azulejos*, especially in the Rosary Chapel. It has retained the Gothic bell-tower from the earlier cathedral. From the top, there are some fine views of the town and coast.

Municipal Museum – This museum is housed in the former Nossa Senhora de Assuncão convent built in the 16C and recently restored. It contains an archeological collection, a 1C Roman sepulchre, a 15C sarcophagus and sculptures and paintings since the 18C.

★LAGOS Population 10 504

Although Lagos has become a popular holiday resort, it has retained character and charm, with its fortress, town walls and old streets. The city was Algarve's capital from 1576 to 1756. It was a major harbour during the days of the great voyages of discovery; most of the African expeditions set off from here.
Visitors arriving in Lagos from the north (no 120 road) or from Vila do Bispo to the west (No 125 road) enjoy a superb **view**★. The resort is expanding as the bay to the north by the Serra de Monchique becomes full of silt.
This seaside destination is also a major sailing centre. International regattas are held here. The fishing harbour is sheltered by the Ponta da Piedale headland.

★**Santo António** – The plain west front on this church gives no indication of the exuberance and genius of the interior **Baroque decoration**★. The most admirable features are the *trompe-l'œil* ceiling, the symbols of the Eucharist and gilded wooden statues in the chancel, and the walls and ceiling in the gallery.

EXCURSIONS

★★**Ponta da Piedade** – *3km/2mi.* Ponta da Piedade is a **beauty spot**★★ which gives this headland its own very special charm. The reddish coloured cliffs worn away into tormented shapes by the waves of the ocean conceal sea caves and form a spectacular contrast to the limpid green waters below. The sea caves can be visited by boat.
From behind the lighthouse, the **view**★ extends from Cape St Vincent in the west to Cape Carvoeiro in the east. Take the narrow road to the left of the lighthouse and, from the observation platform, enjoy the breathtaking view down over the rocks to the delightful seaside resort of **Praia de Dona Ana**★.

★**Bravura Dam** – *14km/9mi northeast.* The "vaulted" dam closes off the Odiáxere Valley. To the west, a pressure pipe collects the water for the downstream electrical power station. The dam irrigates 1800 ha/4500 acres of fields between Lagos and Portimão.

★★PONTA DE SAGRES AND CABO DE SAO VICENTE

This windswept cape at Europe's south-western tip plunges into the waves. This is a place steeped in history and emotion.
Prince Henry the Navigator came here in the 15C facing the Atlantic and the immense stretch of unknown territory of the Mother Ocean. He set up the Sagres School which was to pave the way for the great discoveries.

The Sagres School – After the capture of Ceuta in 1415, the heir apparent retired to Sagres, called upon Arab astronomers, cartographers from Majorca and the most famous seafarers of the day and established his school of navigation. The results of the research were subjected to constant experiment and deployed during expeditions that took explorers further and further afield.
The demands of the expeditions led the Portuguese to develop a new type of ship which revolutionised navigation – the **caravel**.

★★Ponta de Sagres – The headlands fortress was built in the 16C and badly damaged by the earthquake in 1755. Beyond the entrance is a vast courtyard decorated with a huge compass motif measuring 43m/140ft in diameter. The buildings are said to be the former school of navigation and the Prince's House. But in fact all the original buildings were destroyed by Sir Francis Drake's men in 1587.
Around the cape's edge, flanked by impressive scarp slopes, **views★** spread out of the bay and of Cape St Vincent to the west, and of the coast around Lagos to the east. Two sea caves filled with the roaring tumult of the waves add to the spot's wild untamed beauty.

★★Cabo de São Vicente – Cape St Vincent forms the south-western tip of Europe. It stands 75m/244ft above the waves. It has always been considered as a sacred spot; the Romans called it the "Promontarium sacrum."
A legend is behind the present name. The ship containing the body of St Vincent, who died a martyr's death in Valencia in the 4C, was grounded on this spot. Two crows kept watch over the vessel and she stayed there for several centuries until setting sail again for Lisbon where she arrived in 1173.
The old fortress on the headland has been turned into a lighthouse. The **views★★** are impressive, especially at sunset; they encompass the cliffs stretching endlessly into the distance in the north and over the Sagres headland to the east.

★★PRAIA DA ROCHA

Praia da Rocha was made famous by a group of English writers and intellectuals who settled here between 1930 and 1950. Since then, the village has become one of the Algarve's largest and most frequented seaside resorts, even in winter. It owes its reputation to its climate, the outstanding hours of sunshine, and the vast beach. Sand extends into a series of **creeks★★** of turquoise blue water curving between red and yellow ochre cliffs dotted with caves.

★Miradouri (Observation Platform) – To the west of the resort near the Castelos creek, a headland offers a general view of the coast with the long gently-sloping beach backed by the resort's white apartment blocks. In the other direction, the view encompasses a succession of creeks sheltered by the cliff.

B. Brillon/MICHELIN

The beach at Praia da Rocha

When looking for a hotel or restaurant, use the Michelin Red Guide Portugal, updated annually.

Mosteiro da BATALHA★★★

Michelin map 970 E 8

The Batalha Monastery is set in the depths of a lush green valley, unfortunately crossed by the N 1 road. It contains a plethora of gables, pinnacles, piers, bellcotes and colonnettes. This golden pink gem is considered as one of the masterpieces of Gothic Manueline architecture.

The Building of the Monastery – Work began under the Portuguese architect Afonso Domingues and was taken up again by Master Huguet. From 1402 to 1438, he constructed the founder's chapel containing the tombs of Dom João I, his wife Philippa of Lancaster and his sons, in the Flamboyant Gothic style. Death prevented him from completing the octagonal pantheon for King Duarte I (unfinished chapels).
During the reign of Dom Afonso V (1438-1481), the Portuguese architect Fernão de Evora built the so-called Afonso V cloisters in an austere style. Mateus Fernandes the Elder, one of the masters of Manueline art, completed the tracery for the arches in the royal cloisters. He worked with the famous Boytac, continuing to build the chapels in the octagon. King João III (1521-1557), however, showed little interest in Batalha, preferring instead Lisbon's Jerónimos Monastery. Because of this, the chapels in the octagon remained unfinished.

Tour – *1hr.* In accordance with the Rule of St Dominic, the monastery has no bell-tower but an impressive number of pinnacles, flying buttresses, and traceried balustrades highlighted by Gothic and Flamboyant windows. Over the years, the building constructed of fine limestone has taken on an attractive yellow ochre tinge.

★★ **Church** – The vast church is striking for its austerity and for the height of the vaulting. The chancel has **stained-glass windows**★ dating from the 16C Manueline period. They depict scenes from the lives of the Virgin Mary and Christ.

★ **Capela do Fundador** (Founder's Chapel) – This square chamber, measuring 20m/65ft along each side, is lit from Flamboyant Gothic windows and is topped by an octagonal lantern. Above, a star-studded dome is perched. Tierce-point arches link the huge pillars supporting the lantern.

★★★ **Claustro Real** (Royal Cloisters) – The combination of Gothic and Manueline styles is particularly successful. The Manueline additions have not detracted from the simplicity of the original Gothic design. Instead, the balustrade with fleurs-de-lys and the pinnacles decorated with flowers blend with the Manueline tracery in the arches. The tracery is carved in marble and as intricate as a piece of embroidery. The colonnettes supporting the tracery are decorated with twists, pearls and scales.

★★ **Sala do Capitulo** (Chapter House) – The chapter house contains the tomb of the Unknown Soldier. In fact, the grave contains the bodies of two Portuguese soldiers, one of whom died in France and the other in Africa, during the Great War. The **vaulting**★★★ is unusually daring in design. After two unsuccessful attempts, Master Huguet managed to construct a square vault almost 20m - 65ft in length without any intermediate support. The work was so dangerous that it reportedly was completed by men awaiting capital punishment. After removing the last of the scaffolding, Huguet spent an entire night beneath his audacious construction.
The window letting light into the room is decorated with attractive **stained glass**★ dating from the early 16C. It represents scenes from the Passion of Christ.

★ **Claustro de D. Alfonso V** (Alfonso V's Cloisters) – In this fine Gothic construction, the keystones are decorated with the coats of arms of Dom Duarte I and Dom Afonso V.

★★ **Capelas Imperfeitas** (Unfinished Chapels) – Dom Duarte dreamed of a vast pantheon for himself and his descendants. He is the only monarch buried here in an unfinished building open to the sky. Later, Dom Manuel added a vast porch in the transitional Gothic-Renaissance style. He also linked the church's chevet to the entrance to the octagon. The original Gothic **portal**★★ was decorated in the 16C with unusually exuberant Manueline ornamentation. It opens beneath a reinforced multifoil arch and, on the church side, by a concave arch. The festoons and the meticulous decoration in the coving and columns are particularly admirable.

Respect the natural environment:
Beautiful sites and pleasant drives are best kept clean.
Dispose of your litter (plastic bottles and bags, cans, papers, etc) in a bin or carry it with you until you find one.

COIMBRA★★

Population 79 799
Michelin map 970 E 8

Coimbra clings to a hillside crossed by the River Mondego in the shadow of the tall tower of its old university. Many a poet has been inspired by this romantic **spot★**. Portugal's original capital, it has long been a town of arts and letters. Coimbra is best seen from the Santa Clara Bridge or the observation platform in Vale do Inferno. Although the town has expanded greatly over the past few decades and is now surrounded by modern districts, the traditional upper town (A Alta) and university district, including the bishop's palace, continue to dominate. The lower town (A Baia) houses the main shops.
Many shops are clustered around the **Praça do Comércio** in picturesque pedestrian streets.

★OLD TOWN and UNIVERSITY *Time: 3hr*

The old town climbs up Alcáçova Hill. A network of picturesque narrow streets, some broken up by flights of steps, have colourful names such as Quebra-Costas (rib-breaker).

Porte d'Almedina – This town gate with its Arabic name (in Arabic *medina* means town) is topped by a tower and decorated with a statue of the Madonna and Child between two shields. It represents one of the last traces of the medieval walls.

Palais de Sobre-Ribas – This mansion was built in the early 16C in the Manueline style. The street passes under one wing of the Casa de Arco.

Torre de Anto – This tower, once part of the medieval town walls, houses the Coimbra region craft centre.

★★**Sé Velha** – The former cathedral church was commissioned by the king, Afonso Henriques, in the days when Coimbra was the capital of Portugal and stood on the border between the Christian and Moslem worlds. This explains the fortress-like appearance and the pyramidal merlons on top. It was the first cathedral in the country, built between 1140 and 1175 by two Frenchmen, Bernard and Robert. It bears certain resemblances to the Romanesque churches in Auvergne and to the churches built in the Cluniac style.
The west front is austere, contrasting with the north portal added around 1530. The portal, one of the earliest examples of Renaissance architecture in Portugal, is attributed to Jean de Rouen but is unfortunately badly damaged.
Above the aisles, a wide gallery opens onto the nave by an elegant triforium with Byzantine capitals of oriental inspiration.

G. Sioën /TOP

Library of the Old University

★★ **Machado de Castro National Museum** – This museum has an exceptionally large collection of sculptures. It is housed in the former bishop's palace which was altered in the 16C. It was named after the sculptor Machado de Castro who was born in Coimbra in 1731. The Renaissance porch opens onto a courtyard-patio. On the west side. a loggia designed by Filippo Terzi provides a delightful view of the top of the former cathedral, the Lower Town and the River Mondego.

★★ **Velha Universidade** – The old university is housed in the former royal palace. The **library**★★, built by King Jão V in 1724, has three huge chambers in which the furniture, made of precious wood, is highlighted by lavish gilded wood Baroque decoration.

EXCURSIONS

★★ **Buçaco Forest** – *18km/11mi north.* Near the spa town of Luso, the Buçaco Forest Park *(Mata)*, is set within a stone wall that includes a number of gates. It lies at the northernmost tip of the Serra do Buçaco. In the centre of the forest and the many different varieties of trees, a Belle Epoque palace hotel built in a vast clearing resembles something out of a fairy tale.
The 105ha/259 acres of the Buçaco Forest include more than 400 indigenous varieties of trees, including eucalyptus and mastic trees, and 300 tropical varieties, including Maidenhairs, Chilean pines, cedars, Himalayan firs, arbor vitae, oriental larch, palms, arbutus, redwoods, and Japanese camphor laurel. Between the trees are tree ferns, hydrangeas, mimosas, camelias, magnolias, philarias and even lily-of-the-valley.
A number of footpaths pass through the Buçaco Forest dotted with hermitages built by monks in the 17C. There are also interesting Stations of the Cross *(Via Sacra*★*)*. From the *Cruz Alta*★★, there are panoramic views of the forest.

★ **Conimbriga** – *10km/6mi south.* The **Roman ruins**, situated on a triangular spur of rock between two steep-sided valleys, are considered to be some of the finest in the Iberian Peninsula. They are the ruins of a Roman villa founded in the 1C on each side of a major road linking Lisbon and Braga. The villa enjoyed a long period of prosperity.

ÉVORA★★★

Population 35 117
Michelin map 970 E 9

Évora has been surrounded by walls since Roman times. Its narrow streets interspersed with archways evoke a Moorish character, along with its dazzling white houses with flower-decked terraces, traceried balconies and paved patios.
Évora has a number of reminders of its eventful past in its medieval and Renaissance mansions which make the town a museum of Portuguese architecture. They are best seen at night-time when they stand out against the star-studded sky. During the summer season they are floodlit from 9pm to midnight.
Évora is the main town in the Alentejo area and a major agricultural market town. It also has the head offices of several industrial firms and small or medium enterprises based on farming and small scale industry, cork, wool rugs, hides and painted furniture.

HISTORICAL NOTES

Évora flourished during the Roman period and fell into decline during the reign of the Visigoths. In AD 715, the Muslims occupied the city. Under their control, the town became a major agricultural and trading community centered on its castle and mosque.

A Centre of Humanism – At the end of the 12C, the Portuguese monarchy chose Évora as its capital. The city enjoyed another brilliant period in the 15C and 16C. A succession of artists and scientists accompanied the royal court. They included humanists Garcia and Andre de Resende, the chronicler Duarte Galvão, the creator of Portuguese theatre Gil Vicente, the sculptor Nicolas Chanterene, and the artists Cristovão de Figueiredo and Gregorio Lopes. Large numbers of palaces and convents were built in the Manueline and Renaissance styles. Moslem decorative arts came back in a few buildings and a hybrid style known as the Luso-Moorish emerged. A Jesuit university was founded in 1559 with the backing of a patron of the arts, Cardinal Dom Henrique.
In 1580, however, after the disaster of El-Ksar-El-Kebir, Spain annexed Portugal and Évora fell into decline. Despite the revolt that broke out in 1637 and led to the restoration of Portuguese independence, the town did not regain its past splendour. In 1759, the Marquis de Pombal put the Jesuits to flight and closed down the university, dealing a death blow to Évora. The city plunged into a deep-seated lethargy lasting several centuries.

OLD TOWN *Tour 3hr*

★★**Sé** – The cathedral was built in the late 12C and 13C in the transitional Gothic style. Although it includes a few Romanesque features, Gothic designs dominated the latter stages of construction.

Exterior – The austere pink granite west front is flanked by two massive towers topped with conical spires. They were added in the 16C. The spire on the right consists of several bell-cotes similar to the ones on the Saintonge-style Romanesque lanterntower.

★**Interior** – The nave has ribbed barrel vaulting and an elegant triforium. It surprises by its size. A Baroque altar *(left)* contains a 15C polychrome stone statue of the Virgin Mary with child. Opposite, the 16C gilded wooden statue is attributed to Olivier de Gand. It represents the Archangel Gabriel.
Above the transept crossing, a superb octagonal **cupola**★ on squinches hangs above a chandelier. The transept includes two Gothic rose windows – the morning star *(left)* and the mystic rose *(right)*.

★**Choir Stalls** – The oak choir stalls in the gallery were carved during the Renaissance period by artists from Antwerp. They are decorated with holy and profane motifs. On the lower panels, note the scenes from everyday country life such as grape harvesting, sticking a pig and sheep shearing.
The great Renaissance organ is considered the oldest such instrument in Europe.

★**Museum** – The museum contains vestments and a large collection of church plate including a fine ivory **statue of the Virgin Mary**★★ made in France in the 13C. The 17C reliquary Cross of Santo Lenho is composed of gilded silver and polychrome enamel work and decorated with 1 426 precious stones.

★**Cloisters** – The Gothic cloisters were built between 1322 and 1340. Their heavy appearance is emphasised by the use of granite, though round bays with radiating tracery add a touch of elegance. Each corner is decorated with a statue of one of the Evangelists.

★**Museu de Évora** – The museum of ancient art is housed in the former archbishop's palace dating from the 16C and 17C.
The ground floor has Roman, medieval, Manueline and Luso-Moorish sculptures. A fragment of a marble **bas-relief**★ represents the body of a vestal virgin. But the face has disappeared. Outstanding exhibits include a 14C marble **Annunciation**★ and a 16C statue of the Holy Trinity made of stone from Ança.
The first floor contains Portuguese furniture and interesting collections of paintings by Primitives.

★**Roman Temple** – The Corinthian-type temple was built in the 2C and probably dedicated to Diana. The capitals and bases are made of Estremoz marble where as the shafts of the columns are made of granite.
The temple is reasonably well-preserved because it was used as a fortress in the Middle Ages. It was only rediscovered during the last century.

★**Dos Lóis Convent** – This convent, named after St Ely and dedicated to St John the Baptist, was founded in the 15C.
The west front of the **church**★ was altered after the 1755 earthquake. Only the porch includes an original Flamboyant Gothic doorway. Beneath a canopy is the coat of arms of the Melos family. Counts of Olivença are buried in the church.
The nave has lierne and tierceron vaulting and is decorated with fine *azulejos* made by Antonio de Oliveira Bernardes in 1711. They illustrate the life of St Lawrence Justinian, patriarch of Venice, whose writing influenced the congregation occupying the convent. Two trap doors in the pavement can be opened to reveal the water tank for the old castle *(left)* and an ossuary *(right)*.

For further details on Portugal, consult the Michelin Green Guide Portugal.

LISBOA★★★

LISBON – Population 681 000

Michelin map 970 D 9

Portugal's capital is set midway between the north and south of the country. Its conurbation counts a total population of almost two million people.
The old town was built on the right bank of the Straw Sea. This nickname was given to a bulge in the River Tagus because of its golden reflections before it flows into a wide channel and out into the Atlantic Ocean. The jumble of buildings cover seven hills. Numerous observation platforms provide a range of different views. The city is striking for the quality of the light, for its colours (pale pinks, yellow ochres, blues, and greens), and for its streets and squares surfaced with a mosaic of tiny white and black limestone and basalt cobblestones *(empedrados)*. The city has retained picturesque aspects of past centuries and avoided an invasion of modern buildings with the exception of the strange Amoreiras Towers. The old quarters are a labyrinth of narrow streets. But wide avenues provide fine views, the harbour is full of activity, and tropical gardens are hidden away amid the urban landscape. In short, charming Lisbon is a patchwork to be enjoyed on foot or on the old-fashioned tramways.
The town of the *fado*, pronounced Lishboa in Portuguese, is the main heroine of these songs steeped in the famous nostalgia, or *saudade*.
The city comes alive in June when it celebrates its saints. On the night of the Feast of St Anthony, the patron saint of Lisbon, groups of young people in fancy dress *(marchas populares)* parade to musical accompaniment down the Avenida da Liberdade.
The city may be marked by its past but it has also been resolutely casting an eye to the future since Portugal became a member of the European Union. Business districts are growing up around Campo Pequeno and Campo Grande. The new Belém Arts Centre, which opened in 1992, has given the district another monument. The resolutely modern **Amoreiras** towers erected by the architect Tomás Taveira, to which may be added other towers in the Campo Pequeno district, as well as the head offices of BNU banks and Caixa Geral de Depósitos, have become city landmarks.

EXPO'98

The last universal exhibition of the century, held from 22 May to 30 September 1998 along the Tage at Doca dos Olivais coincided with the 500th anniversary of Vasco da Gama's journey to India and allowed Lisbon to recall its history and culture. With 1998 having been declared International Ocean Year, EXPO' 98's main theme was the importance of the oceans for the human race and the urgent need to preserve them. The **Oceanarium, designed by the American**, Peter Chermayeff, **remains open to the public**. It includes a huge central pool and four secondary pools with animals and plant-life typical of Arctic, Pacific and Atlantic coastlines.

HISTORICAL NOTES

Legend has it that the town was founded by Ulysses. Historians claim it was set up in 1200 BC by the Phoenicians who nicknamed it Serene Roadstead. The town quickly became a port of call for the people of Mediterranean countries trading with Northen Europe. It was conquered by the Greeks and Carthaginians before becoming a Roman settlement in 205 BC.
After the barbarian invasions, Lisbon fell into Arab hands in 714 and the Moors retained power for 400 years, renaming the town Lissabona. The period of Arab ascendancy ended on 25 October, 1147 when the king, Dom Afonso Henriques, captured the town with the assistance of a fleet of ships on their way to the Second Crusade.
In 1255, Dom Afonso III chose Lisbon as his capital in place of Coimbra.

The Age of Voyages of Discovery – Lisbon took advantage of the wealth amassed after the voyages of Vasco da Gama to the Indies and the discovery of Brazil by Pedro Alvares Cabral.
New trade routes were introduced to the detriment of Venice and Genoa. Merchants came instead to Lisbon and shops dealt in gold, spices, silver, ivory, fabrics, jewellery and precious wood.
The town acquired historic buildings such as the Jerónimos Monastery and Belém Tower. Its decorative style, based on maritime subject and named after the king, Dom Manuel, became known as the Manueline style. The harbour, where caravels came to drop anchor, is filled with constant traffic.

LIFE IN LISBON

The Urban Districts – Lisbon must be seen from the River Tagus. In the foreground, the 18C town with the Praça do Comércio and the checkerboard layout of the **Baixa** (lower town) extends into the Rossio and Praça dos Restauradores. On the hill to the right, the castle São Jorge is surrounded by the medieval districts of **Alfama** and **Mouraria**. On the hill to the left stands the shopping district, **Chiado**, the working-class areas of **Bairro Alto** and **Madragoa** and, beyond them, the elegant residential districts of **Lapa, Alcántara** and **Belém**. The modern districts around the Eduardo VII Park and beyond are marked out by a network of wide avenues such as Fontes Pereira de Melo, Republica, Roma, and Berna. The city is undergoing constant development, swallowing up districts such as **Restelo** or **Benfica**. Commuter towns cover the surrounding hillsides, separated by rural landscapes filled with market gardens. The centre has retained its old-fashioned appearance with pastel-fronted mansions and apartment blocks covered with *azulejos*. Lisbon is also a harbour and a large industrial city. The main industrial districts lie on the south bank of the River Tagus near Barreiro.

★★POMBAL'S BAIXA

A tragic earthquake and tidal wave devastated this part of the city on 1 November, 1755. Pombal rebuilt the city's main shopping area. Pedestrian streets are lined with stores. All the streets between the Rossio and the Praça do Comércio are named after trade and craft guilds such as Correrios (saddlers), Sapateiros (shoemakers), and the three main streets – Rua do Ouro (gold), Rua da Prata (silver), and finally the wide **Rua Augusta**.

★**Rossio** (KX) – Praça Dom Pedro IV, the main square in the lower town, has existed since the 13C. Three sides of 18C and 19C apartment blocks line the square. The upper floor consists of cafés, including the famous *Nicola* with its Art Deco façade. Small shops have kept their turn-of-the-century interior. See the tobacconist's shop near *Nicola*, decorated with *azulejos* and the shop where people drink the famous cherry liqueur called ginginha at the corner of the Largo de S. Domingos. The **Dona Maria National Theater** (**T**[3]) closes off the north side of the square.

★★**Praça do Comércio (or Terreiro do Paço)** (KZ) – The royal palace used to stand here until the earthquake demolished it. In memory, the people of Lisbon still call this square, which is the city's most beautiful open space, Terreiro do Paço (Palace Terrace). It runs 192m/625ft long and 177m/575ft wide. On three sides Classical buildings house government ministries. Seen as a whole, this is an excellent example of Pombal's designs.
A 19C triumphal arch in the Baroque style provides the background to the equestrian statue of Dom José I by Machado de Castro.

★★ALFAMA

This quarter, with its labyrinth of winding streets, and alleyways *(becos)* crossed by staircases and arches, is similat to certain districts in North Africa towns not simply because of its Arabic name *al-hama* (hot waters), which evokes the thermal fountains of the Lago das Alcaçarias.

★★**Sé** (LY) – Like the cathedrals in Oporto, Coimbra and Evora, this was used as a fortress, a fact obvious from the two towers on its west front and its crenellations. It was built in the Romanesque style in the late 12C shortly after the town was captured by Afonso Henriques with the assistance of the Crusaders. The architects are said to be the French craftsmen Robert and Bernard, who also designed the cathedral in Coimbra. Here, though, the cathedral has been altered on many occasions, especially after earthquakes.

★★**Castelo de São Jorge** (LX) – The building of this castle paved the way for the city's development. It stands in a superb strategic position on a hilltop. The Visigoths built it in the 5C, the Moors extended it in the 9C and Dom Afonso Henriques altered it. The Castelo is now a pleasant flower garden.
After crossing the outer wall providing shelter for the old medieval Santa Cruz district, visitors arrive on the parade ground. A magnificent **view**★★ opens up of the Straw Sea, the districts on the left bank of the river, the suspension bridge, the lower town and the Monsanto Park. This is a delightful place for a stroll.

MODERN LISBON

The long **Avenida da Liberdade**★ (JV) runs from Praça dos Restauradores to the Eduardo VII Park and is the most majestic avenue in Lisbon. Beyond the park, the **Praça Marquês de Pombal**, serves the city's nerve centre on which all the main avenues converge. The **Eduardo VII Park**★ is an elegant formal garden with a superb **view**★ of the lower town and River Tagus.

★★★**Museu Calouste Gulbenkian** – This museum has vast, airy rooms overlooking the gardens and was designed especially for the collections of Calouste Gulbenkian, a great art lover. Particularly rich in Oriental and European art, the works are beautifully enhanced by the building. The section on European art begins with medieval religious art, including marvellously intricate **ivories**★, a number of illuminated manuscripts and books of hours. Paintings by Thierry Bouts, Rembrandt, Rubens, Quentin de la Tour, Gainsborough, Degas, Manet and many others illustrate painting from the 15C to the 19C.

★★THE MANUELINE WEST END: BELÉM

Ships set sail across the Atlantic to explore the globe and discover unknown continents from Belém. In Portuguese, the name means Bethlehem.

★★★**Mosteiro dos Jerónimos** – Henry the Navigator first founded a hermitage on the site. Then Dom Manuel decided in 1502 to built this magnificent monastery for the Hieronymites. It is considered as the most consummate example of Manueline architecture.

★★★**Santa Maria** – The **South Portal** designed by Boytac and Joao de Castilho bristles with gables, pinnacles and niches containing statues. To each side of the portal, admirable windows are decorated with moulding. The West Portal beneath the 19C porch leading into the cloisters was designed by Nicolas Chanterene. It is decorated with fine statues.
The interior surprises for the audaciousness of the **vaulting**★★ which withstood the 1755 earthquake despite the slender pillars. The nave and aisles are of the same height, forming a Hallenkirche type of building.

R. Mazin/TOP

Cloisters, Moisteiro dos Jerónimos

★★★**Cloisters** – This masterpiece of Manueline architecture contains a dazzling wealth of sculptures. In the late afternoon, the stone takes on a warm golden glow. The cloisters form a quadrilateral 55m/179ft in length and have two floors. The lower floor has wide arches with tracery supported by slender colonnettes. The decoration is inspired by the style fashionable at the end of the Gothic period and by the Renaissance. The upper floor was built with less exuberance. A staircase leads to the coro alto, the gallery providing another view of the vaulting.

★★**Torre de Belém** – This elegant Manueline tower was constructed between 1515 and 1519 in the middle of the Tagus. It defended the mouth of the river and the Hieronymites Monastery. The 1755 earthquake, however, changed the course of the river and the tower now stands on the edge of a beach. It represents an architectural gem. The Romanesque and Gothic construction is decorated with Venetian-style loggias and domes reminiscent of Morocco, a country well-known to its architect, Francisco de Arruda. Next to the square tower laid out for use by artillery is a platform with crenellations decorated with shields and bearing the Cross of the Order of Christ.
The terrace overlooks the sea and contains a fine statue of Our Lady of Success. The tower itself has five floors and ends in a terrace. On the ground floor, the openings in the flagstones through which prisoners were thrown into the dungeons inevitably cause a shudder. The dungeons were often flooded. On the third floor, elegant balconies with gemel windows and a magnificent Renaissance loggia are topped by the arms of the Dom Manuel and two armillary spheres. This softens the building's original severity.

★★**Museu nacional dos Coches** – Belém Palace's former royal *manege* is now the official residence of the President of the Republic. The museum contains a magnificent collection of coaches, carriages, berlins and litters. The oldest exhibit is the painted coach which Philippe II of Spain brought from his home country in the late 16C.

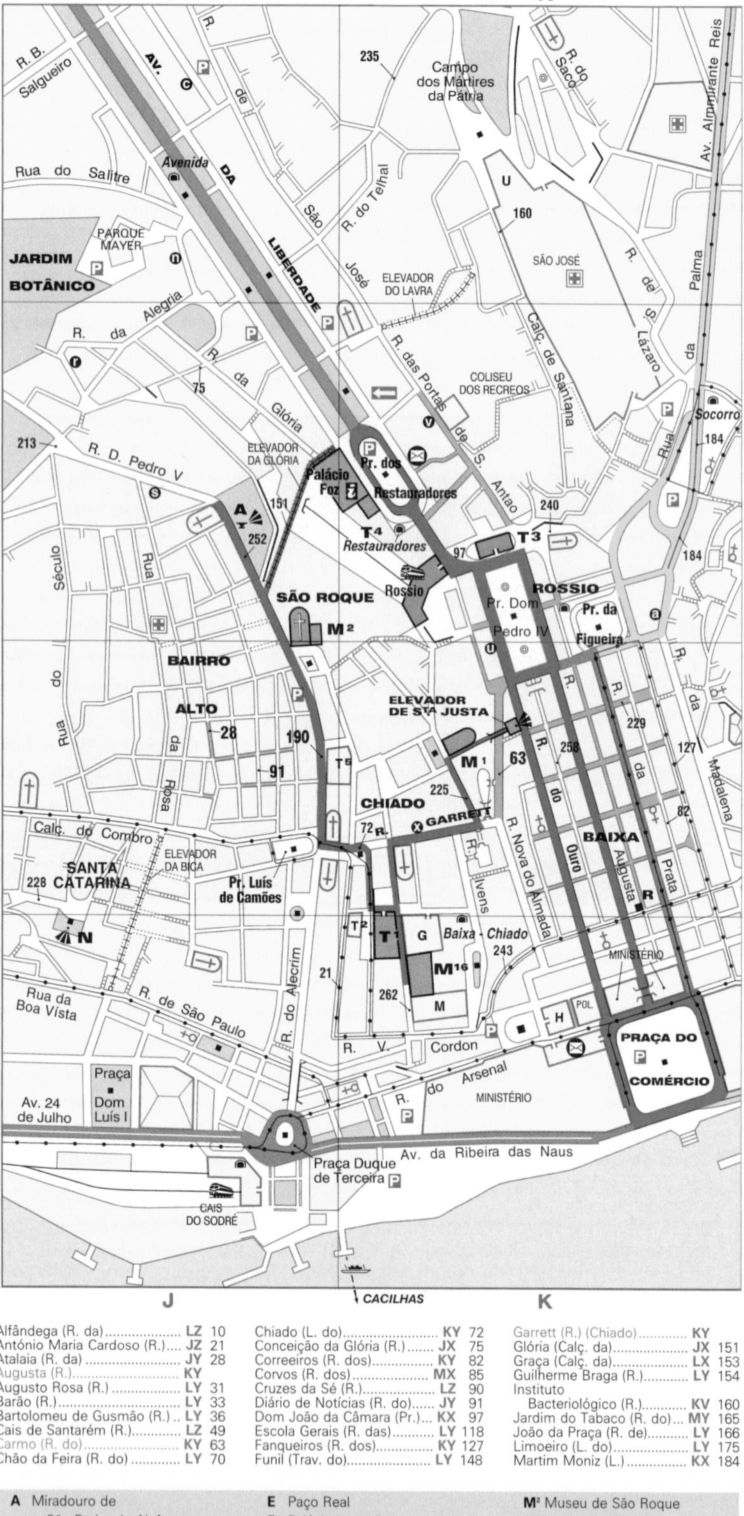

Alfândega (R. da) .... LZ 10	Chiado (L. do) .... KY 72	Garrett (R.) (Chiado) .... KY
António Maria Cardoso (R.) .... JZ 21	Conceição da Glória (R.) .... JX 75	Glória (Calç. da) .... JX 151
Atalaia (R. da) .... JY 28	Correeiros (R. dos) .... KY 82	Graça (Calç. da) .... LX 153
Augusta (R.) .... KY	Corvos (R. dos) .... MX 85	Guilherme Braga (R.) .... LY 154
Augusto Rosa (R.) .... LY 31	Cruzes da Sé (R.) .... LZ 90	Instituto Bacteriológico (R.) .... KV 160
Barão (R.) .... LY 33	Diário de Notícias (R. do) ...... JY 91	Jardim do Tabaco (R. do) ... MY 165
Bartolomeu de Gusmão (R.) .. LY 36	Dom João da Câmara (Pr.) ... KX 97	João da Praça (R. de) .... LY 166
Cais de Santarém (R.) .... LZ 49	Escola Gerais (R. das) .... LY 118	Limoeiro (L. do) .... LY 175
Carmo (R. do) .... KY 63	Fanqueiros (R. dos) .... KY 127	Martim Moniz (L.) .... KX 184
Chão da Feira (R. do) .... LY 70	Funil (Trav. do) .... LY 148	

A Miradouro de São Pedro de Alcântara	**E** Paço Real	**M²** Museu de São Roque
B Igreja Santo António da Sé	**F** Palácio Lavradio	**M³** Fundação Ricardo do Espírito Sto Silva
C Miradouro de Santa Luzia	**L** Jardim Boto Machado	**M¹⁰** Museu Militar
	M¹ Igreja do Carmo	

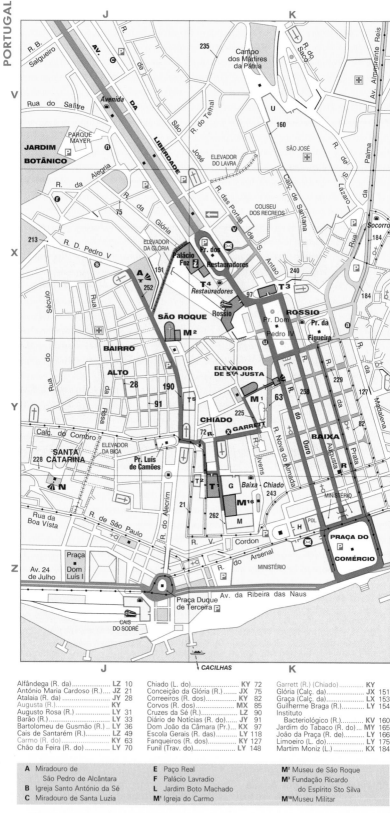

Trams (eléctricos): special tourist tram routes are set up in summer (enquire at the Tourist Information Centre).

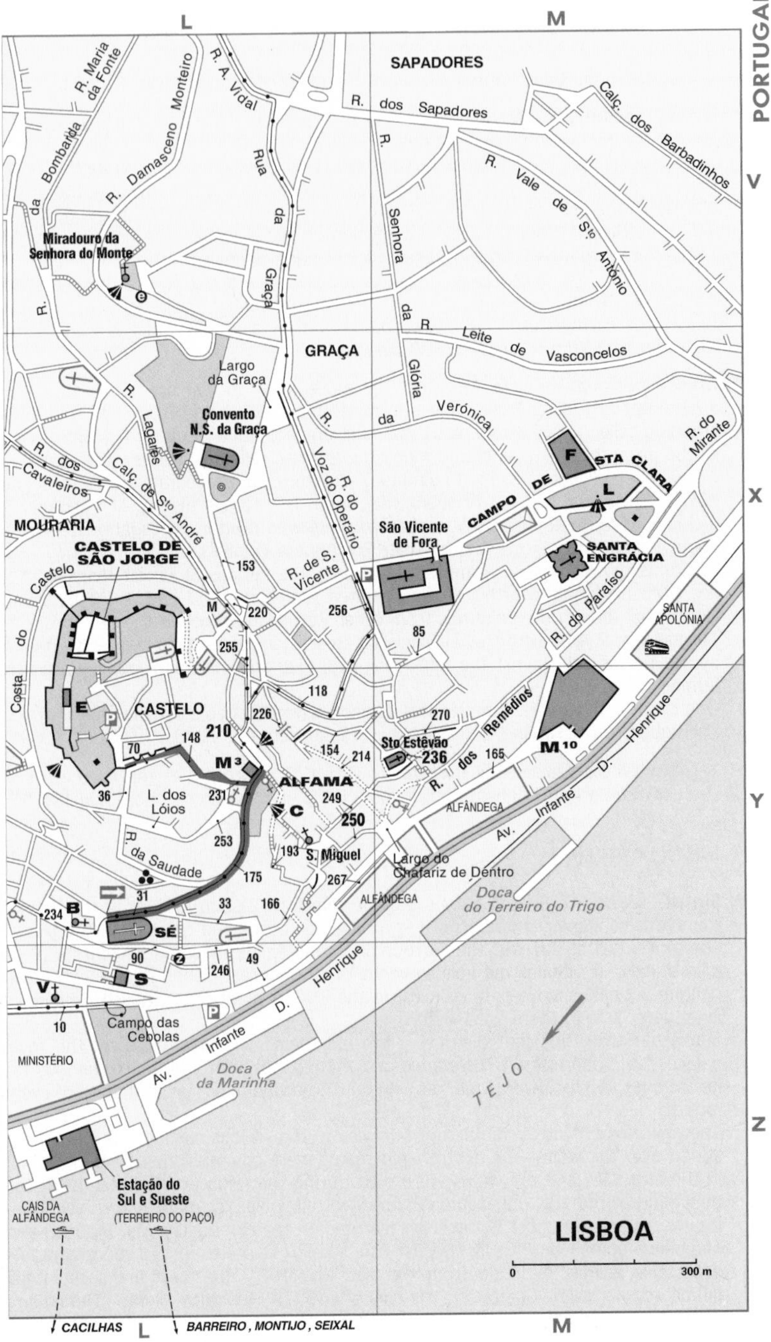

Misericórdia (R. da) .... JY 190	Santa Justa (R. de)........ KY 229	S. Pedro (R. de)........ LY 250
Norberto de Araújo (R.)........ LY 193	Santa Luzia (Trav. de)........ LY 231	S. Pedro de Alcântara (R. de)........ JX 252
Ouro (R. do) .... KY	Santo António da Sé (L.)........ LY 234	S. Tiago (R. de) .... LY 253
Portas do Sol (L. das)........ LY 210	Santo António dos Capuchos (R.)........ KV 235	S. Tomé (R. de)........ LX 255
Prata (R. da) .... KY	Santo Estêvão (Escadinhas de)........ MY 236	S. Vicente (Calç. de) .... LX 256
Príncipe Real (Pr. do) .... JX 213	S. Domingos (L. de)........ KX 240	Sapateiros (R. dos) .... KY 258
Regueira (R. da)........ LY 214	S. Francisco (Calç. de) .... KZ 243	Serpa Pinto (R.)........ KZ 262
Rodrigues de Freitas (L.) .... LX 220	S. João da Praça (R.)........ LZ 246	Terreiro do Trigo (R. do)........ LY 267
Sacramento (Calç. do) .... KY 225	S. Miguel (R. de)........ LY 249	Vigário (R. do)........ MY 270
Salvador (R. do)........ LY 226		
Santa Catarina (R. de) .... JY 228		

M[16] Museu do Chiado	S Casa dos Bicos	T[3] Teatro Nacional D. Maria II
N Alto de Santa Catarina	T[1] Teatro Nacional de São Carlos (Opera)	T[4] Éden Teatro
R Nùcleo Arqueológico da Rua dos Correeiros	T[2] Teatro São Luis	T[5] Teatro da Trindade
		V Igreja da Conceição Velha

Entertainment: a good source for practical information is the weekly Sete magazine which comes out on Wednesdays.

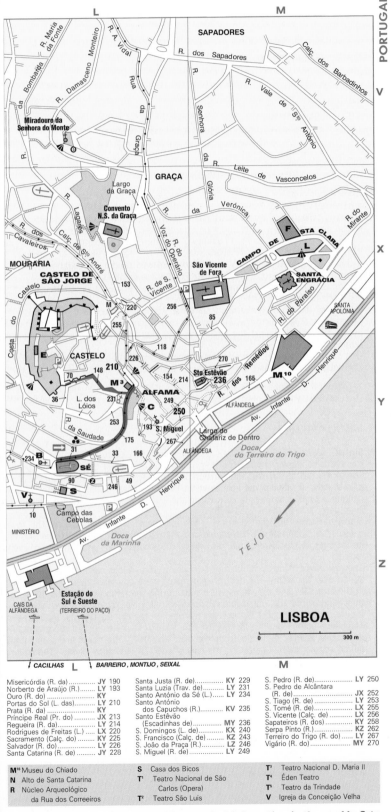

THE PORT AND THE TAGUS

A **boat ride on the Tagus★** offers a view of the city and a good idea of port traffic.

★★**Museu nacional do Azulejo** – The story of *azulejos* from the Hispanic-Moorish tiles of the 15C to modern creations is housed in the buildings of the **Madre de Deus convent,** which was rebuilt following the terrible earthquake of 1755. Note the handsome Manueline portal in the church's street-facing façade. Around the great cloister, there are fine exemples of azulejos imported from Seville in the 15C and 16C. The **church★★** has a dazzling profusion of gilded wood. The first floor has a display of magnificent azulejo panels representing animals, battles and scenes of everyday life. The **chapter house★** overlooking the nave has a fine painted coffered ceiling. In the great cloister, stop to look at the famous **panoramic view of Lisbon** before the earthquake. This lovely composition in blue and white is 23m/75ft -long and made up of nearly 1 300 *azulejos.*

★★★**Museu nacional de Arte Antiga** – The museum of ancient art is housed in the 17C Count of Alvor's Palace and in a modern annexe dating from 1940. Its outstanding collection of works of art was built up partly as a result of the confiscation of the property of convents and monasteries when religious orders were closed in 1833. The collections include paintings, sculptures, and decorative arts from the 12C to the early 19C, all of them with some link to the history of Portugal. It includes Portuguese artists, European painters who lived in Portugal or knew the country well, and objects from former Portuguese colonies.
Paintings by Portuguese Primitives, especially the famous **St Vincent Altarpiece★★★**, are particularly noteworthy. It was painted between 1460 and 1470 by Nuno Gonçalvez. Among the paintings from other European schools is the extraordinary **Temptation of St Anthony★★★** by Hieronymus Bosch, one of his later works filled with hybrid beings set against the background of Hell and including fauna, flora and human faces.
One room is filled with the priceless **Japanese screens★★** depicting the arrival of the Portuguese on the island of Tanegasha (Tanegayima) in 1543.

► ► **Palacio dos Marqueses de Fronteira★★**: This 17C palace lies at the northern end of the park in Benfica. It contains a particularly fine collection of **azulejos★★**.

EXCURSIONS

★★**Sintra** – *28km/17mi west.* Sintra, only 30 min from Lisbon, nestles at the foot of the southern slopes of its Serra. It is a haven of peace and quiet amid the trees. For six centuries, this was the surrounding countryside monarch's favourite place of residence. It remains the holiday venue of all the great Lisbon families who own delightful *quintas* or elegant palaces. In the 19C, a number of English Romantics lived here, among them Lord Byron.
Sintra has three adjacent districts – the old town *(Vila Velha)* around the royal palace, the modern town *(Estefania)* and the old village of São Pedro, famous for its antiques and bric-à-brac market held on the second and fourth Sundays of every month.
The **royal palace★★** owes its mixture of styles to the various elements and buildings added over the years. The central apartments were commissioned by Dom João I in the late 14C, and the wings were built during the reign of Dom Manuel at the beginning of the 16C. In addition to the two tall conical chimney stacks overlooking the palace, the most noteworthy features on the exterior are the Moorish and Manueline gemel windows *(ajimeces)*. The interior is interesting for its remarkable decorative **azulejos★★** dating from the 15C and 16C. The finest are seen in the dining room (Arabs' Chamber), the chapel and the Mermaids' Room. The square Armory has a domed **ceiling★★** supported on corner squinches. It consists of coffers painted with the coats of arms of 16C Portuguese noblemen.

★★**Serra de Sintra** – The Sintra mountains south of the town are formed by a granite range. The highest peak is Cruz Alta, 529m/1 719ft. Rain condenses here after coming in off the ocean. The humidity and the impermeability of the rock have produced dense vegetation covering the entire range and partially concealing the granite outcrops. There is a wide range of plant life – oaks, cedars, tropical and sub-tropical trees, tree ferns and camelias.
From Sintra to Cruz Alta, the road runs through the **Pena Park★★** and provides a number of interesting views.

To find the description of a sight, a historical event, a monument ... consult the index at the end of the guide.

PORTO★★

OPORTO – Population 302 535
Michelin map 970 E 8

Portugal's second largest city is the main urban centre in the north. Counting its suburbs, Oporto has a population of more than one million. It has a reputation as a dark, austere industrial city yet in the sunshine the city shines with light, colour and people.
Oporto lies on a scarp slope, apparently indifferent to the difficulties of its geographical **location★★**. Its houses cling onto the slopes overlooking the Douro, the mythical river that ends its long course through Spain and Portugal here. By giving its name to the famous wines, the city has gained a global reputation.
The best **view★** extends from the parvis of the former convent called Nossa Senhora da Serra do Pilar.

Urban Districts – The traditional shopping centre radiates out from Praça la Liberdade and the railway station (São Bento). During the day, men and women crowd round the windows of often old-fashioned shops in Rua Santa Catarina, Rua Formosa, Rua Sa da Bandeira, or Rua Fernades Tomas. They also stop in one of the many cake shops, joining the students who wear black gowns.
The working-class districts of **Ribeira** and **Miragaia** near the River Douro have been subjected to renovation and urban improvement over the past few years. As a result, the Ribeira has become the centre of the city's night-life with a number of fashionable restaurants. On the other bank, **Vila Nova de Gaia** has the warehouses where port wines are stored to age.
The economic centre is tending to move westwards and now focusses on the Avenue de Boavista between Oporto and Foz. Leading banks, businessmen's hotels, and shopping centres are all housed in modern tower blocks.

The Bridges – The banks of the Douro are linked by three bridges, each of them a feat of technical prowess.
The **Maria Pia Railway Bridge★** is the furthest upstream and the most elegant with its single 350m/1 138ft span. French engineer, Gustave Eiffel designed the structure built entirely of metal in 1877.
The **Luis I Road Bridge★★** is the most spectacular with its two-tiered roadway running simultaneously to the upper and lower districts on each river bank. It symbolises Oporto. The span of 172m/559ft was built in 1886 by the Belgian de Willebroeck company using a technique similar to the one developed by Eiffel.
The **Arrábida Road Bridge** is furthest downstream. It carries the expressway and was built in 1963. Using a particularly daring technique, it crosses the Douro in a single reinforced concrete span almost 270m/878ft in length.
Both road bridges provide some interesting views of the city and river.

Oporto, Capital of Port Wine – The **wine cellars★** *(las caves)* stand in Vila Nova da Gaia on the left bank of the Douro River. They cover several hectares. More than 58 port-producing companies have premises here. Almost 20 cellars are open to the public, including those owned by Porto Cálem, Sandeman, Ramos Pinto and Ferreira.

★★ **Oporto Old Town** – The old town stretches from Terreiro da Sé, the square in front of the cathedral, to the **cais da Ribera★**, a picturesque quay in the shadow of the Luis I Bridge high above. The most outstanding sights are the **cathedral★**, **Rua das Flores**, the **Stock Exchange** and **Sao Francisco★★**.

J.-P. Lescourret/EXPLORER

Luís I Road Bridge

Romania

România

Area: 238 891km²/92 236sq mi – **Population:** 22.6 million – **Capital:** Bucuresti (Bucharest) – **Currency:** Leu – **Time:** GMT + 2hr.

Romania is situated an equal distance from the Atlantic Ocean and the Ural mountains. It borders the Black Sea and is crossed by the Danube and the Carpathian mountains.
Its territory corresponds to the ancient Dacia colonised by the Romans.
The beauty and diversity of the natural environment, which includes mountains, plateaux, hills and plains, the large number of well-established spas, the well-preserved folklore and the generous hospitality of its people make Romania an ideal tourist venue.

IN BRIEF

Entry formalities – Passport required for British, US, Canadian, Australian and Japanese citizens.

Souvenirs – Among the many objects you can bring back are icons painted on glass or wood, black ceramics, pottery, hand-woven carpets *(olteneşti)*, carved wooden objects and traditional costumes.

Holidays – 1 and 2 January, Easter Day, 1 May, 1 December (national holiday) and Christmas.

A FEW HISTORICAL FACTS

101-106	Dacia becomes a province of the Roman Empire after wars waged by Emperor Trajan. The Trajan Column is erected in Rome to commemorate the victory.
271-275	Under the reign of Aurelian, the Romans withdraw south in the face of Barbarian invasions.
5C-10C	Great migrations. Strong links with Orthodox Byzantium.
14C	Formation of the states *(voivodinas)* of Wallachia and Moldavia. First resistance to Ottoman attack.
1599-1600	Union of Wallachia and Transylvania due to Voivod Mihai Vizeazul (Michael the Brave).
1848-1849	National insurrection put down by the troops of Czar Nicolas I, together with Ottoman and Austrian troops.
1859	Union of Wallachia and Moldavia under the reign of Prince Ion Couza (Alexandru Ioan Cuza).
1861	The union leads to the name Romania.
1877-1878	War of independence. With Russian aid, Romania struggles against the Ottomans. The independence of Romania is recognised by the Treaty of Berlin.
1881	Charles of Hohenzollern, a prince of German origin, becomes King of Romania under the name of Carol I.
1912-1913	Balkan War. Allied to Greece and Bulgaria, Romania enters the war against Turkey.
1917	During the First World War, Romania sides with the Entente (France, Great Britain and Russia).
1 December 1918	Romania, Transylvania, Bucovina and Bessarabia form Greater Romania.
June 1940	Threatened with an ultimatum by the USSR and Nazi Germany, Romania loses a third of its territory and population. She is obliged to cede Transylvania to Hungary, and Bessarabia and Bucovina to the USSR.
June 1941	Romania allies herself to Germany and Italy in an attempt to recover her former territories.
August 1944	A *coup d'état* reverses the situation. Romania passes over to the Allies.
February 1947	The Treaty of Paris returns Transylvania to Romania but Bessarabia and Northern Bucovina remain in the hands of the USSR.
December 1947	Under pressure from the USSR, the monarchy is abolished, King Michael is forced to abdicate and the country becomes a people's democracy.
1955	Romania joins the Warsaw Pact.
1968	Despite its membership of the Warsaw Pact, Romania decides not to take part in the Prague Spring.

December 1989	Revolution leading to the fall and execution of the Communist dictator Ceaucescu and his wife, masters of the country since 1965.
May 1990	Ion Iliescu is elected president of the Republic.
November 1996	Emil Constantinescu becomes the second elected president.

SOME FAMOUS ROMANIANS

Constantin Brancusi (1876-1957, Paris) – Sculptor influenced by Rodin.

Georges Enesco (1881-1955, Paris) – Composer and violonist. Taught Yehudi Menuhin. Created the opera *Œdipus* in 1936.

Anna de Noailles (1876-1933, Paris) – Princess Brancovan, Countess of Noailles, was a talented poet. Had literary friendships with Anatole France and Maurice Barrès.

Panaït Istrati (1884-1935, Bucharest) – Writer in love with adventure and travel. Friend of Romain Rolland.

Eugène Ionesco (1909-1994, Paris)

Mircea Eliade (1907-1985, Chicago) – Novelist and religious historian. Left his country after the Second World War.

Emil Cioran (1911-1991, Paris) – Writer, essayist and moralist.

Elvire Popesco (1894-1991, Paris) – Actress and member of the Comédie française.

Tristan Tzara (1896-1963, Paris) – One of the founders of the avant-garde Dada movement. Born in Zurich in the Cabaret Voltaire in 1916.

Nadia Comaneci (1961) – Gymnast and revelation of the 1976 Montreal Olympics.

Angela Gheorghiu (1965) – Lyric soprano.

ARAD

Population 182 980

Michelin map 970 O 6

Situated 47km/29mi from the Hungarian frontier, Arad lies on one of the main routes from Romania to Hungary. In Roman times, this Transylvanian town was a Dacian settlement known as Ziridava.

The city is crossed by one of the largest rivers in Romania, the **Mures**. The **Palace of Culture★**, built in 1913, houses museums of history, archeology, ethnography, and art. Other interesting sights include the 19C **town hall★** (Palatul Prefecturii) (1876) and the 18C Vauban-type **citadel**.

Cheile BICAZULUI★

BICAZ Gorge

The Bicaz Gorge lies on the 55km/34mi long DN 12c road linking Bicaz in Moldavia and Gheorghieni in Transylvania. The gorge is the most spectacular natural beauty spot in the eastern Carpathians.

Sightseeing includes the man-made dam at **Lake Izvorul Muntelui★★** near Bicaz, the natural dam and holiday resort at **Lake Rosu**, the **monasteries★★** in **Agapia** and **Varatec** near Targu Neamt, and the **monastery of Neamt**, also near the town of Tîrgu Neamt.

★★IASI

This city, founded in the 14C, served as Moldavia's capital from 1565 to 1862. It lies on seven hills (like Rome) and is now Moldavia's largest city. It also is the main town in the district of the same name and one of Romania's most important cultural, industrial and university cities.

★★ **Palatul Culturii (Palace of Culture)** – The impressive neo-Gothic arts centre was built between 1906 and 1925 on the site of a former prince's palace. It contains several museums specialising in fine arts, history, ethnography, and technology. The last includes an unusual section on sound recording.

★★★ **Trei Ierarhi Church (Church of the Three Hierarchs)** – This 17C building was restored in 1890 by the Frenchman Lecomte de Nouy. It is famous for the richness and beauty of its sculpted exterior decorations. The former ruling princes of Moldavia – Vasili Lupu, Dimitri Cantemir and Alexandru Ioan Cuza – are buried here

★★ **Muzeul de Istorie naturala (Natural History Museum)** – Founded in 1834, the museum is housed in the 18C Ruset Residence.

★★**Teatral national** (**National Theatre**) – An impressive neo-Baroque building completed in 1896, the theatre has one of the finest auditoriums in Romania.

★**Palatul** (**Palace**) – The former residence of Prince Alexandru Ioan Cuza was built in the Empire style in 1806 and now houses the Union Museum.

★**Copou Park** – This large park famous for its Eminescu lime was named after the greatest of all Romanian poets, who was born in Moldavia and used to come and sit in its shade.

★**Sfantul Gheorghe Church** – Built in 1761, St George's church was for many years the seat of Moldavia's metropolitan. It contains the relics of St Paraskéva, which are famous throughout the country.

BLACK SEA COAST★★★

Michelin map 970 Q7

From north to south, spanning 245km/152mi, the Romanian part of the Black Sea provides access to seas and oceans.
The southern part consists of one long fine sandy beach with eleven seaside resorts. It covers a distance of approximately 60km/37mi from Constanta to the Bulgarian border. This is Romania's largest tourist area.
The main advantages of the Romanian coast are its long hours of sunshine, 14hr a day in summer, the gently-sloping beaches, the low salt levels in the water, the pleasant water temperature averaging 25°C/77°F, the absence of tides, and the proximity of fresh or salt water lakes, forests, vineyards and orchards.
Numerous natural springs used in the treatment of disease or for spa therapy make the Romanian Riviera unique in Europe.

★★**Mamaia** – The region's largest resort stretches 7km/4mil to the north of Constanta.

★★**Eforie** – The oldest and best-known resort lies 15km/9mi south of Constanta on the DN 39.

Techirghiol – This resort is located on the banks of a lake with the same name. Mud with healing properties is used to cure rheumatism here.

★★**Costineşti** – The young people's resort lies 32km/20mi south of Constanta.

★★★**Olimp-Neptun** – These twin resorts contain luxury hotels.

★**Jupiter, Aurora, Venus and Saturn** – These large modern developments are situated 2.6km/2mi north of Mangalia.

★★**Mangalia** – This highly-acclaimed resort is what remains of the ancient town of Callatis, founded by the Greeks of Heracleea Pontica in the 6C BC.

BRAŞOV★★★

Population 324 100
Michelin map 970 P 6

Braşov was founded in the 12C by Saxon settlers. It is now one of Transylvania's largest and most attractive cities, with a strong influence of the once large German minority.
The city lies in the centre of the **Barsa** district (Tara Bârsei), at the junction of several major road and rail links.

★★★**Biserica Neagra** (**Black Church**) – This Gothic building, which owes its name to a fire, was originally built from 1384 to 1477. It includes, among other things, a superb collection of 17C Persian-style carpets. The church also is used for organ recitals.

★★**Primaria Veche** (**Former Town Hall**) – This building (1420) set in the middle of the city's main square now houses an interesting **Museum of History of Medieval Guilds** (Muzuel Breslelor).

★**Old Romanian Quarter** (**Shei**) – This district, centring on the 16C Orthodox Church of St Nicholas of Schei, includes a magnificent set of buildings. The **Museum of Old Romanian Books** is housed in a 16C school.

Turnul Tesatorilor (**Weavers' Bastion**) – Tourists come here to visit the Braşov Citadel Museum and fortifications. The 16C Drapers' Bastion, Blacksmiths' Bastion, White Tower and Black Tower represent the largest sections of the fortifications.

EXCURSIONS

★★Tampa Hill – *Access by cable-car.* Belvedere.

★Poïana Braşov – *13km/9mi south.* This is one of Romania's largest winter sports resorts. It includes 12 chairlifts, two cable-cars, paths for high-altitude hiking and climbing, and comfortable chalets.

★★Castelui Bran – *69km/43mi south-west via DN 73 and Rasnov.* The magnificent 14C Bran Castle once belonged to Prince Vlad Tepes the Impaler, who provided Bram Stoker with the inspiration for Dracula.

Prejmer Church – *17km/11mi north-east via DN 10.* This fortified church, completed more than 500 years ago, was built by knights of the Teutonic Order.

A few dates

1859 ***The independent principalities of Moldavia and Walachia elected Prince Alexandru Cuza to the united Romania.***

1862 ***Official Union of the two former principalities to form the State of Romania.***

1877 ***Russo-Turkish War: Romanians struggle to gain independence from the Ottomans.***

1989 ***Uprising against Ceausescu (leader since 1967) and the communist regime.***

BUCOVINA★★★

Michelin map 970 P 6

Bucovina lies to the north of the Romanian part of Moldavia. Since 1940, it has been separated from Ukrainian Bucovina by the border. This beautiful, quiet region set with hills and pastures conceals famous churches with external frescoes that constitute a real poor man's Bible, the only one of its kind in the world, which figures on UNESCO's World Heritage list.

These jewels of 15C and 16C Romanian civilisation and havens of peace, prayer and beauty bear witness to the personality of the reigning prince, **Stephen the Great (1457-1504)**, whom a Pope dubbed Christ's Athlete. He won fame as a military chief fighting the Ottoman invaders and at the same time became the spiritual father of Moldavia, building a great many monasteries, churches and citadels in his country – one for each victorious battle.

His successor, **Petru Rares (1530-1547)**, continued this remarkable work. The main feature of the Moldavian style, specific to the days of Stephen the Great, is the harmonious blend of indigenious Moldavian artistic traditions with a number of Byzantine and Gothic influences brought into the country from Russia, Poland and Serbia. Fresco work, described by Michelangelo as the most difficult and most audacious manner of painting, has existed in Bucovina for almost 500 years.

J.-P. Courau/EXPLORER

Moldovita Monastery

★★★ **Suceviţa (1596)** – A thick wall flanked by massive towers with pepper pot roofs protects this monastery. Within the walls stand the church and the prince's residence, transformed into a religious museum.
The frescoes inside and out repeat a large number of theological themes. The setting is magnificent.

★★★ **Voroneţ (1547)** – The church is decorated on both the outside and inside with beautiful frescoes. *Voronet Blue* is as famous as *Veronese green* or *Titian red*. The famous *Last Judgement* covers the entire west front of the church. The masterpiece of religious painting is well preserved, a reason why the church was nicknamed the Jewel of Bucovina and the Sixtine Chapel of the Orient.

★★★ **Moldoviţa (1532)** – Like Sucevita, this fortified monastery exhibits superb frescoes. The prince's residence houses a religious museum.

★★ **Humor (1530)** – In front of the church, a bell-tower served as part of the system of defence. The frescoes inside and out are remarkable and well-preserved.

★★ **Arbore (1503)** – This nobleman's church has superb frescoes on the outside and no tower. Only the west front is well preserved. Green is the predominant colour.

★★★ **Putna (1466)** – The fortified monastery was founded by Stephen the Great who is buried here with his whole family. The monastery attracts huge crowds and is revered by both Romanians and Moldavians who make pilgrimages from the Republic of Moldavia. It includes a Museum of Sacred Medieval Art.

★★ **Suceava** – This town lies at the gateway to Romanian Bucovina. It was the capital of Moldavia from 1388 to 1566 and is now the main industrial centre and town in the Moldavian district.
See also the ruins of the former prince's residence, **Cetatea de Scaun**★, and the **Museum of Popular Art**★, which contains black ceramics, weaving, carpets and costumes.

★ **Radauţi** – This busy little town contains the oldest stone-built church in Moldavia, the **Bogdana Church**★ built in 1359. An interesting **Ethnographic Museum** displays collections of pottery, painted eggs, icons on glass, and embroidered clothing.

BUCUREŞTI★★

BUCHAREST – Population 2 066 700
Michelin map 970 P 7

Romania's capital straddles the middle of the Wallachian Plain. It lies on the banks of the River Dambovita, 60km/37mil north of the River Danube and 100km/62mi south of the Carpathian mountains.
The city was founded in 1459, in the time of Vlad the Impaler, reigning prince of Wallachia. It was Wallachia's capital before becoming the capital of the entire country in 1862.
From the end of the 19C, French architects such as Galleron, Gassien-Bernard, Gottereau and a large number of French-trained Romanian architects designed a Parisian style of building. Hence Bucharest's nickname – Little Paris or the Paris of the Balkans.
During the past 40 years, and particularly after the major earthquake of 1977, the city has undergone considerable change. Many older buildings have been razed to the ground to make way for high-rise apartment blocks. During the 1980's, an entire city-centre district was cleared to allow the building of the gigantic Parliament Palace and Fountain Avenue.

OLD BUCHAREST

In Romanian, **Bucuresti** comes from the name of a shepherd, Bucur who used to bring his sheep to graze on the banks of the Dambovita River in the 15C. Bucurie means joy. The tiny **Bucur Church** built in the 17C keeps his name alive.
Near the huge Unirii Square, the **Curtea Veche Museum** is set out around the remains of the former prince's palaces dating from the 16C to the 19C. The 13C walls of Bucharest's citadel and the 17C **Curtea Veche Church** date back to the beginnings of the city.
On a hillside in the vicinity of the square are the 17C **Patriarch's Church**★ and **Palace**. The celebration of Orthodox Easter here has a very special charm. The palace also houses the relics of St Dumitru, the city's patron saint, whose feast-day is celebrated with great pomp every year on 26 October. Close to the Stavropoleos Church, **Carul cu Bere** (the Beer Waggon), one of the most popular restaurants in the city, has remarkable decor. **Hanul lui Manuc** (Manouk's Inn), a former caravanserai (1808) and starting-place of the Romanian revolution of 1848, is nowadays a picturesque restaurant.
The **Casa Melic House** at 22, Spatarului Street is Bucharest's oldest secular building (1760).

CALEA VICTORIEI

Victory Street, named in memory of the 1877 War of Independence, epitomises all of Bucharest's architectural styles. It has the city's largest number of sights and tourist attractions. The old buildings house offices, restaurants, cafés and stores.

★★★ **Ateneul Român (Romanian Atheneum)** – This magnificent building inaugurated in 1888 was designed by the French architect Albert Galleron. A number of Romanian architects assisted him. The Athenaeu now symbolises the city of Bucharest. Inside, an enormous fresco runs around a superb circular room. The fresco summarises the history of Romania. The room is used regularly for recitals and classical music concerts. Nearby, the Hotel Athénée Palace was designed in 1912 by the French architect Théophile Bradeau.

★★ **Muzeul Naţional de Artă (National Art Gallery)** – The art gallery is located in one wing of the former royal palace built in 1937; it contains extensive collections of paintings as well as Romanian, European and Asian objets d'art.

★★ **Muzeul Colecţiilor de Artà (Museum of Art Collections)** – The museum's fine collections are housed in an early-19C building.

★★ **Muzeul Naţional de Istorie a României (National Museum of Romanian History)** – This museum is located in the former post office, constructed in 1900. Its huge collections offer insights into the development of Romanian society.

★★ **St Stavropoleos Church** – In this typical example of the Brancovan style built in 1724, visitors are treated to a fine presbytery, a delightful set of cloisters, and an archeology museum.

★★ **Palatul CEC (Savings Bank)** – This building was designed by the architect Paul Gottereau in 1896 and inaugurated in 1907. It bears some resemblance to the Grand Palais in Paris.

★★ **Muzeul Ceramicii şi Sticlei (Museum of Ceramics and Glass)** – The museum, housed in the 19C ceremonial palace of Prince Barbu Stirbei. It has some wonderful faience, porcelain and glassware.

★★ **Muzeul muzicii George Enescu (Museum of Romanian Music)** – The architecture of the former Cantacuzino (or Cantacuzene) Palace is outstanding. The museum honours Georges Enesco, the greatest of all Romanian composers, whose grave is in the Père Lachaise Cemetery in Paris.

★ **Piaţa Revoluţiei (Revolution Square)** – The square is lined with impressive buildings including the **Central University Library** (Biblioteca Centrala Universitara), designed by Paul Gottereau in 1914, the Royal Palace and the 18C **Cretulescu Church**. The palace of the former Central Committee of the Romanian Communist Party now lodges the offices of several ministries.

Palatul Telefoanelor (Telephone Palace) – This American-style skyscraper built in 1933 once housed Bucharest's first telephone exchange.

★★ **Palatul Parlamentului (Parliament Palace)** – This gigantic building, now the seat of Parliament, is the second largest in the world after the American Pentagon. It has around 6000 rooms.

G. Durand /DIAF

Parliament Palace

The BOULEVARDS

The boulevards Ipātescu, Magheru, Balcescu, and Bratianu serve as arteries north to south, while Carol I, Républicii, Kogālniceanu runs east to west. Always busy, they are lined with luxury hotels, airline offices, foreign tourist offices, theatres, and the best restaurants and casinos.

★**Piaţa Universitatii (University Square)** – The boulevards meet at this square, flanked by the main university buildings erected in 1869 to plans by a Romanian architect, Alexandru Orāscu. The National Theatre, built in 1975, with its museum, the Hotel Intercontinental, the tallest tower in Bucharest, and the **Bucharest Museum of History and Art**★ all are located here.

★★**Cotroceni National Museum** – This museum, housed in the Cotroceni Palace, a former royal residence and present seat of the Romanian presidency, retraces three centuries of Romanian history, art and architecture.

★★**Muzeul Naţional Militar (National Military Museum)** – Collection of weapons and documents.

★★**Gradina Cismigiu (Cismigiu Gardens)** – This 1.7 ha/4.2 acre garden was laid out in 1860 and spreads itself around Lake Cismigiu opposite the town hall in the city centre.

►► **Gradina Botanicā**★ (Botanical garden) – This 10 hectare - 25 acre garden laid out in 1860 contains around 10 000 species of plants.

North of BUCHAREST

★★★**Muzeul Satului (Village Museum)** – This museum near Lake Herāstrāu covers an area of 15 ha/37 acres and boasts nearly 300 houses, churches and other rural buildings from all the Romanian regions. Craft objects, including icons, ceramics and carpets, are on sale.

★★**Vila-muzeul Nicolae Minovici** – This museum of popular art housed in a fine building has extensive ethnographic collections dating from the beginning of the century.

★★**Muzeul Ţāranului Român** – The **Museum of Romanian Peasantry** is devoted to folklore and popular art.

★★**Muzeul Grigore Antipa** – The Natural History Museum inaugurated in 1906 contains more than 600 000 exhibits.

★★**Arcul de Triumf (Triumphal Arch)** – Bucharest's Arc de Triomphe, standing 27m/88ft high, was built in 1936.

★**Casa Presei Libere (Free Press Centre)** – This building constructed in a traditional Stalinist style in 1956 houses the main Romanian newspapers and most important publishing houses.

★★**Herāstrāu Park** – Lakes, footpaths and beaches grace this green area.

EXCURSIONS

★★**Snagov** – *35km/22mi by DN 1 road.* The lake spreads over more than 10km/6mil in the middle of the forest. The monastery, with a church dating from 1517 situated on a small island, is a popular tourist venue. Tomb of Vlad Tepes (the Impaler).

★★**Mogoşoaia** – *15km/10mi northwest via DN 1a.* The lake and fine Brancovan palace from 1702 now attract large numbers of visitors to its museum.

★**Băneasa Woods** – *10km/6mi to the north via DN 1a.* This spot is popular with the people of Bucharest.

Michelin's famous star ratings are allocated for various categories: regions of scenic beauty with dramatic natural features cities with on exceptional cultural heritage elegant resorts and charming villages ancient monuments and fine architecture museums and galleries.

The CARPATHIAN MOUNTAINS★★★

The Carpathians are the most human of all mountains, said Emmanuel de Martonne. In Romania, the Carpathians form a range almost 900km/559mi in length. They stretch like the arc of a circle from one of the country's borders to the other. The mountains are carpeted in thick age-old forests, and dotted with superb alpine lakes. They rise to an altitude of 2543m/8265ft. Some of the slopes are gentle and covered in alpine pastures; others are spectacularly rugged.

– Holiday and winter sports resorts include **Poïana Braşov**★★, **Sinaia**★★★, **Predeal**★★, **Buşteni**★, **Păltiniş**★, Durau, and Borsa.

– High-altitude hiking and climbing is found on the peaks called **Fagaras**★★, **Retezat**★★★, **Piatra Craiului**★★, **Bucegi**★★, **Ceahlău**★ and Rodeni. Access roads and marked footpaths show the route from one chalet to the next. There are also cable-cars, chair-lifts, and ski lifts.

– Seaside and health resorts number more than 160, including **Herculane**★★, **Felix**★★, **Sovata**★, **Calimăneşti-Căciulata**★, **Covasna**★, Tusnad, Olanesti, Buzias, Vatra Dornei, and Slanic Moldova. More than one-third of all Europe's mineral springs rise in Romania. Even the Romans and Emperor Napoleon III used these waters to treat their ailments!

– Hunters can track brown bears, Carpathian stags, wild boar, roe deer, fallow deer, chamois, moufflon, pheasants and wolves here.

★★★**Porţile de Fier (Iron Gate)** – The Danube flows through this narrow gorge from Cazanele to the border with Serbia.
It can be reached by boat from Orsova to Moldova Noua or by car along the DN 57 (same trip, 114km/71mi).

★★**Cheile Nerei (Nera Gorge)** – This gorge is located in the Anina Mountains near Oraviţa, between the villages of Sasca Montana and Sopotu Nou.

★★**Pe tera Ur ilor (Bear Caves)** – The caves are found on DN 76 from Chişcău near Beiuş.

CLUJ-NAPOCA★★

Population 321,850
Michelin map 970 O 6

This ancient city was once a Daco-Roman settlement called Napoca. In the 12C the Saxons colonised it. Cluj now is Romania's fifth largest city after Bucharest, Constanta, Lasi and Timisoara. It is also the largest city in Transylvania and a leading industrial and university town.

★★**Muzeul Etnografic al Transilvaniei (Transylvanian Ethnography Museum)** – The museum was founded in 1922. It illustrates life in Transylvanian villages. The collection includes more than 65000 objects, woodcarvings, pottery, weaving, festive costumes, Christmas or carnival masks, and local musical instruments. An open-air section in the Hoia Forest displays wooden houses.

★★**Muzeul de Artă (Art Gallery)** – The gallery is housed in the former **Banffy Palace**★★, a wonderful Baroque building erected in 1780. The gallery has collections of paintings, sculptures and objets d'art by great masters from Romania, Hungary, Italy, Flanders, the Netherlands, Germany and Russia.

★★**Muzeul de Istorie (Transylvanian History Museum)** – This is one of the province's most prestigious museums, both for the size of its collections and for their value. They offer insights into life in Transylvania from the days of antiquity.

★★★**Gradina botanica (Botanical Gardens)** – The gardens were laid out in 1920 and now provide a superb natural setting for more than 10000 varieties of plants.

★**Roman Catholic Church of St Michael** – The 14C German Gothic style building stands on the city's main square named in honour of Liberty, near the **equestrian statue**★ of Matthias Corvinus, King of Hungary from 1458 to 1490.

★**Muzeul Istorei Farmaciei (History of Pharmacy Museum)** – The museum is housed in a building which, in 1573, contained the town's first apothecary's shop. It has collections of old furniture, instruments, jars and documents.

EXCURSION

★★**Cheile Turzii (Turda Gorge)** – *31km/19mi south.* This impressive ravine is gouged out of sheer walls of limestone rock.

CONSTANŢA★★

Population 350 000

Michelin map 970 Q 7

This is the second largest city in Romania and capital of the administative area of the same name. It used to lie within the old region of **Dobrogea/Dobroudja**, which was founded by Greek settlers from Miletus in the 6C BC. At that time, it was known as **Tomis**. Nowadays, this is the largest port on the Black Sea, as well as an important university town and tourist centre.

★★ **Muzeul de Arheologie (Archeology Museum)** – Numerous Greek, Scythian and Roman objects are exhibited. The museum includes an open-air section.

★★ **Building with mosaics** – During an archaeological dig in 1959, the gigantic mosaic from a Roman building was uncovered. Some 800m²/8 608 sq. ft of the original 2 000m²/21 520sq ft mosaic are displayed. The decoration consists of geometric and floral motifs.

★★ **Muzeul Marinei (Romanian Navy Museum)** – The museum contains a large collection of historical model ships, both commercial vessels and warships.

★ **Faleza (Seafront)** – The famous promenade takes visitors past a Rococo **casino**★, an old **Genoese lighthouse** rebuilt in 1860, an **Orthodox cathedral** dating from 1885, and the **Aquarium**.

★ **Muzeul de Artă populară** (Dobroudja Museum of Popular Art) – This museum is mainly concerned with regional weaving, costume, jewellery and folklore.

EXCURSIONS

★★★ **Histria Archaeological Site** – *65km/40mi north via DN 22 road and a local road.* Greek settlers founded an ancient Pontic city and trading post in the 7C BC. Well-preserved walls, towers and bastions circle the site. Visitors can see houses, baths, stores, and a basilica.

★★★ **Seaside resorts** – (see Black Sea Coast) *stretching over a distance of 55km/34mi to the south along the DN 39 road to the Bulgarian border.*

★ **Agigea** – *6km - almost four miles south via DN 39 road* – A canal cruise is recommended here at the mouth of the **Danube – Black Sea Canal**.

CURTEA DE ARGEŞ★★

Since this small town long housed the residence of the Walachian Voivodes, it also served as the capital of Walachia. It lies in a delightful area of hills in the valley of the river Argeş.

★★ **Biserica domnească (Prince's Church)** – This impressive austere building was commissioned in the 14C by Prince Basarab the Great. The well-preserved church represents a fine example of the austere but harmonious style of Walachian architecture. Beside the church stand the foundations of the **prince's former palace** and a small museum.

★★ **Biserica episcopala (Episcopal Church)** – The church is richly decorated inside and out. The external decorations in shades of blue, green and gold are based on Muslim and Byzantine motifs. They fascinate visitors as much as the legend surrounding the church's construction. In order to complete construction work, the prime contractor **Manole** reportedly walled up his wife, "Anne his darling, flower of the meadows". The church was built in the 16C but has undergone restoration on several occasions, most recently in the 19C by the French architect Leconte de Nouy. The tombs of the first two kings of Romania and their wives inside are considered masterpieces of Romanian architecture.

DUNARII Delta★★★

DANUBE Delta

Michelin map 970 Q 6

The Danube Delta lies at the point where the Danube flows into the Black Sea. The "youngest" land in Europe, it forms the largest area of marshland, covering 5 165km²/1 994sq mi. This represents an area five times larger than the Camargue in Southern France. Four-fifths of the marshland is located in Romania, the remainder in Ukraine. In 1992, a twinning agreement was signed by the Danube and Rhône Delta administrations under the aegis of the Council of Europe. Thanks to the efforts of Jacques-Yves Cousteau, a quarter of the delta has also been designated a "biosphere reserve" by UNESCO.
The Danube is Europe's second longest river after the Volga. It flows through eight countries and three capital cities over its course of some 2 880km/1 780 mi. About 1 075km/668mil of the Danube are located within Romania. About 80km/50mi from the river mouth, the Danube splits into three main arms forming a triangle:

– Chilia meanders to the north forming part of the border with Ukraine.
– Sulina in the centre, 79km/49mi long, was excavated and calibrated in 1888 in order to make the waterway navigable by large ships.
– St George in the south runs for 113km/70mi.
Although the Danube Delta looks homogeneous, it includes a wide variety of environments and landscapes. Organic matter carried along the long river's passage has built up this natural wonderland. The Danube Delta includes more than 25 ecosystems, providing a habitat for numerous species of plant life, birds, fish and shellfish. Approximately 15 000 people live in the Danube Delta, in small villages. Sulina, the largest centre, is also a free port. The only way of moving around the area is via natural and man-made canals.
The town of **Tulcea★**, with approximately 80 000 inhabitants, serves as the launching area for cruises lasting one to seven days. Greeks founded Tulcea in the 7C BC. The **cruises★★** take both private individuals and groups. Visitors can hire boats to fish and hunt, or attend traditional events in August (international festival) and December. The region's fish soup and caviar should not be missed.

MARAMUREŞ★★

Population 544 000
Michelin map 970 O 6

This area lies in the north of Transylvania near the northern stretches of the Carpathians. It includes the districts of Maramureş and Satu Mare and is a sprawling piece of varied countryside.
This land of lumberjacks and miners is dotted here and there by rivers, streams, fields of crops, pastures, and orchards. Wood is omnipresent. Log houses built to age-old traditions dominate the villages. They huddle round a church, also built of wood.
The **Maramureş Dip★★** in the heart of this area is bordered by the rivers Iza, Viseu, Mara and Cosau. This austere area is lightened by the beauty of the oak country houses with shingled roofs, magnificent gateways and traditional carved verandas. The wooden churches are small; they date from the 14C to the18C.
The villagers have always earned their living from forestry and sheep farming and they still wear their beautiful traditional costumes. From time to time, folk festivals offer visitors an insight into the country's traditions.

★**Sighetul Marmaţiei** – This small town, the main urban centre in the **Oaş Area**, houses the interesting **Maramureş Museum★** containing woodwork, embroidered waistcoats, and winter festival masks.

EXCURSIONS

★★**From Sighetul Marmaţiei to Campulung Moldovenesc** – *190km/118mi by DN 18 linking the Maramures District to Bucovina.* This route takes tourists past a number of typical villages, over the Prislop *(Pasul)* Pass at an altitude of 1 413m/4 592ft and, more particularly, through picturesque scenery.

Săpînţa – The village is famous for its **gaily-decorated cemetery★★** *(cimitirul vesel)*, a gem of naive Romanian art. The wooden crosses, painted bright colours and bearing portraits of the deceased, have amusing inscriptions.

J. Gabanou/DIAF

ORADEA★

Population 221 600

The largest city in the district of Bihor lies 12km/7mi from the main crossing point on the Hungarian border on the E 15 trans-European expressway.
For many visitors, this popular stopover is their first sight of Romania and Transylvania. Documents date the existence of this city on the banks of Crisul Repede from the 12C.

★★**Muzeul Ţării Crisurilor (Cris District Museum)** – An Austrian architect designed this former Baroque-style bishop's palace in the 18C. The museum has extensive outstanding collections relating to archeology, history, ethnography, natural sciences, and the arts. A magnificent collection of 14000 **painted eggs** is one of its kind in Romania. The nearby park is superb.

★★**Roman Catholic Cathedral** – Romania's largest Baroque church was built in the 18C by an Italian architect.

★**Cetatea Oradiei (Oradea Citadel)** – The citadel was constructed in the 15C but altered in French style in the 18C. This is the largest Renaissance construction in Transylvania.

★**Şirul Canonicilor (Canons' Corridor)** – A fine row of 10 Baroque houses with 25 arches built for the seminarists.

★**Biserica cu lună (To the Moon Church)** – The church was built in the 18C using a mixture of Baroque and neo-Classical architecture. Its main tower, 3m/10ft in diameter, is fitted with a mechanism showing the phases of the moon.
Also worth a visit is Ady Endre's house. He was a famous Hungarian poet who lived in this town.

VALEA PRAHOVEI★★

PRAHOVA Valley
Michelin map 970 P 6

The valley lies on the DN 1 road 20km - 12 miles south of Brasov and 110km - 68 miles north of Bucharest. Along with the Timis Valley and Predeal Pass (alt 1,060m - 3,445ft), this represents the main route through the southern part of the Carpathians, linking Walachia and Transylvania. It is also the main tourist route.

★★★**Sinaia** – This town, the Romanian capital of mountaineering and hill walking, is known as the "pearl of the Bucegi". It is most famous for the **Peleş Castle**★★★, built from 1873-1883. An art gallery now occupies the former royal family's summer residence. The 18C **monastery**★★ also is remarkable.
Walking on the Plateau in the Bucegi Mountains. A cable car ride leads to Hotel Cota at 1400m/4550ft. Chalets are found at Piatra Arsa, 2000m/6500ft, Babele, 2200m/7150ft, Omul, 2507m/8148ft and Poïana Stânii. The **panoramic view**★★ alone merits a visit.

★★**Predeal** – This winter sports resort serves as point of departure for walkers.

★**Pârâul Rece** – Trei Brazi chalet.

★**Buşteni** – This well-known holiday resort rises from 800m/2600- to 900m/2925ft. The Pic Babele cable-car offers a **panoramic view**★★.

SIBIU★★

Population 168 620
Michelin map 970 P6

This Transylvanian town lies in the heart of Romania. A former Daco-Roman settlement, German Saxons and Mosellans colonised it in the 12C. The town has a large number of German and Austro-Hungarian features, including the medieval layout, Gothic houses from the 14C to 16C, bastions and towers, churches, mansions, Baroque residences and palaces.

★★**Muzeul Bruckenthal** – This museum of painting and popular art is housed in a building in the Austrian Baroque style erected in the 18C by Baron Samuel Bruckenthal, former Governor of Transylvania. In 1817, it became a museum, the oldest of its type in the country. Next door, the **evangelical church** was built in the Gothic style.

★★**Muzeul civilizaţiei populare tradiţionale Astra (Museum of Popular Technology)** – This open-air museum in the Dumbrava Sibiului Park deals with aspects of country life. A lake and zoo is located nearby.

★★ **Oraşul Vechi (Old Town)** – Numerous houses decorated with Gothic or Baroque gables and arcades mark this medieval neighbourhood. See the Steps, the Pharmacy Museum, and the Council Tower, which houses a local history museum and observation platform.

★ **Medieval citadel** – Little remains of the four successive walls except the Carpenters, Potters, and Arquebusiers towers, all dating from the 14C, and the 16C Haller and 17C Soldisch bastions.
The Weaponry and Hunting Trophy Museum and the 15C Ursuline Church merit a visit.

EXCURSIONS

★ **Păltiniş** – *34km/21mi south-west.* This holiday and winter sports resort stands at 1 400m/4 550ft. It serves as a point of departure for walkers wishing to explore the mountains.

SIGHIŞOARA★★

Michelin map 970 P 6

Saxons colonised this former Roman fort around 1260. It was the birthplace of Vlad Tepes the Impaler, reigning prince of 16C Walachia, who provided Bram Stoker with inspiration for the famous Dracula legend.

★★ **Cetatea** – The medieval **citadel** in the upper town represents the most typical and best-preserved of all the Transylvanian fortresses. It includes the 13C clock tower with its observation platform, the Tailors' Bastion, the History Museum, and numerous redoubts and the bastions. Vlad the Impaler's birthplace is also open to the public.

TIMIŞOARA★

Population 334 115
Michelin map 970 O 6

Timisoara, fourth largest city in Romania and birthplace of the December 1989 revolution, is the main town in the district of Timis and the region of Banat. It was founded in the 13C and, owing to its geographical location near the Hungarian and Serbian borders, serves as a major overnight stop for travellers.

★ **Castelul Huniazilor** – The **castle museum** is housed in the 15C Huniade Castle. It deals with regional history, natural sciences, ethnography, and fine arts.

★ **Roman Catholic Cathedral** – It dates from the 18C and has a superb Baroque entrance.
Also worth a visit are the **Orthodox cathedral**, the **Iron Tree House** and the former Baroque **City Hall.**

Russia

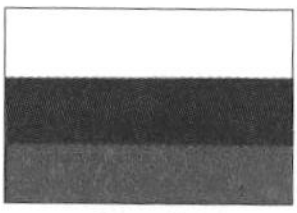

Rossija

Area: 17 075 400km²/6 592 812sq mi – **Population:** 150 million – **Capital:** Moskva (Moscow) – **Currency:** Rouble – **Time:** in Moscow and St Petersburg GMT + 3hr in winter, GMT + 4hr in summer

Russia, officially the Russian Federation, is the largest state in the Commonwealth of Independent States (CIS) founded on December 21, 1991. It stretches about 9 000km - 5 600 miles from east to west and 4 000km - 2 500 miles from north to south. Russia has vast expanses of wilderness, huge rivers and harsh winters as well as an impressive architectural heritage.
A brief description is offered of the main sights in Moscow and St Petersburg. No visit to this unique country would be complete without seeing these two major cities. Elsewhere, independent travellers may find touring difficult.

IN BRIEF

Entry Formalities – Passport and visa (a lodging certificate or hotel reservation is obligatory).

Souvenirs – Since the break-up of the Soviet Union's, traditional Russian dolls or *matrioshkas* include effigies of past and present politicians. The lacquered painted boxes and *samovars*, elaborate tea-making kettles, are often splendidly decorated. Fur hats or *shapkas* can be bought in the street or on the stalls along Moscow's Arbat Street. Caviar or vodka outside the official shops is subject to caution.

Street vendors – Street vendors are a familiar part of the Russian urban landscape. **Icecream vendors:** the Russians are great icecream eaters (even though the weather is hardly appropriate) and people can be seen queueing in the streets and avenues by the icecream vendor's outmoded cart or steaming boxes. Usually only one flavour is available – vanilla, wrapped in coarse paper. **Drinks vendors** may be found manning small stalls, booths or even just cardboard boxes. Depending on their location and supplies, they sell local and imported beers, mineral water, sodas, Coca Cola, Pepsi and vodka. Some also sell *kvass*, a refreshing fermented beverage. Coca Cola kiosks shaped like metal cans are currently springing up everywhere. **Flower sellers** are also a familiar part of the street scene.

S. Viron/EXPLORER

MOSKVA★★★

MOSCOW – Population 9 000 000
Michelin map 970 T 3

Moscow is a huge city on the banks of the River Moskova. It is composed of long avenues, grand squares, tall 1950s Stalinist-style skyscrapers, such as the Ministry of Foreign Affairs, and an impressive number of historic buildings and churches with statues and golden domes.
It is circumscribed by a number of concentric rings, each a highway – the Bulvarnoje Koltso (Boulevard Ring), Sadovoja Kolsto (Garden Ring) and finally, about 15km/10mi from the centre, an expressway forming an urban ring road. The city's other main streets run across the various circles and converge on the city centre.

★★ **City Vistas** – The gigantic Stalinist Lomonosov University skyscraper tops the Lenin Hills *(Leninskie Gory Metro Station)*. The esplanade offers a splendid view of the city and River Moskova. In the foreground stand the stadium and sports facilities built for the 1980 Olympics.
An impressive view also unfolds from the Ostankino Television Tower *(VDNKH Metro Station)*.

★★★KREML' (THE KREMLIN) (BY) *half a day*

The word Kremlin is steeped in mystery. It describes the seat of Russian (or ex-Soviet) power. In a literal sense, it refers to the fortified triangular enclosure bristling with towers – some topped with the red star. The complex is built on rocky escarpment overlooking the River Moskova, and constitutes the heart of the city. The Kremlin's red crenellated walls blend harmoniously with the yellow ochre and white tones of the palaces and religious buildings with their golden domes inside. The ensemble forms a beautiful picture worth seeing in the evening from Red Square or the banks of the Moskova.
The Kremlin was originally a log fortress designed to protect the residence of the grand prince. Later it was rebuilt of stone. Its architectural splendour peaked in the late 15C under the supervision of the Italian masters commissioned by Grand Prince Ivan III.
Along the west wall lies **Aleksandrovskij Sad**, the shady flower-decked Alexander Gardens harbouring the Tomb of the Unknown Soldier and the Flame of Remembrance (**BY**).

Entrance via Koutafia Tower. Tickets are on sale at the foot of the tower in Alexander Gardens. Leave bags and bulky objects at the left-luggage office.

Across the stone-built Trinity Bridge, the Kremlin can be entered via **Troiakaja** (Trinity) Tower. On the right, the modern **Dvorec s'jezdov** (Palace of Congresses) is open during shows or exhibitions. On the left, a row of cannon captured from the Napoleon's army stands beside the wall of the former armaments depot. Beyond, a group of red official buildings are not open to the public.

Patriaršij Dvorec, Cerkov' Dvenadcati apostolov (Church of the Twelve Apostles) – Five onion domes distinguish this tiny church. It was built above the two arches of the Patriarch's Palace, which now houses the Museum of 17C crafts. Furniture, crockery, manuscripts, church vestments, embroidery, firearms and cutting and thrusting weapons all are exhibited. The huge pillarless vaulted Cross Room was once used as a State room.
On the church's left, the **Czar Pouchka** (Caŕ-Puska) or Czar Cannon was cast in 1586. This bronze monster weighs 40t, measures more than 5m/16ft – in length and has an 890mm/35in calibre. But it never has been fired. Its elegant carvings make it a work of art.
Along the same side of the street past the Ivan the Great bell-tower, the **Czar Kolokol** (Caŕ-Kolokol) or "Emperor Bell" is probably the world's largest bell. It weighs 200t, with a height and diameter of over 6m/19ft. Cast between 1733 and 1735, it has never rung. The 11.5t piece lying beside it fell away during the fire of 1737. Water poured into the bell's pit and caused a sudden change of temperature that broke off the piece. The bell is exquisitely carved with religious characters and the portraits of Czar Alexis Mikhaylovich (1645-1676) and Czarina Anna Ivanovna (1730-1740).

★★**Sobornaja ploščad' (Cathedral Square)** – The square dates back to the 14C. Many grandiose religious ceremonies have been held on the stone pavement. The square's sheer size, its majestic religious buildings and ornate palaces, create a breathtaking sight.

★**Kolokoln'a Ivana Velikogo (Ivan the Great Bell-Tower)** – The white stone Ivan the Great Bell Tower is topped by a golden dome. Beneath the cupola, an inscription indicates 1600 as the date of fabrication during the reign of Czar Boris Godunov. In fact, the tower was built between 1505 and 1508; its height was merely increased during Boris Godunov's reign. The tower conveys an impression of lightness despite its succession of octagonal tiers. It served as a watch tower, offering a view of 30km/20mi. Beside it stands the campanile from 1532 to 1543.

★★★**Uspenskij sobor (Cathedral of the Dormition or Assumption)** – Between 1475 and 1479 Grand Prince Ivan III commisioned Italian master Aristote Fioravanti to design this building of fine architectural proportions. Five apses of Italian influence are topped by five golden domes. Fioravanti sought inspiration for his design in Vladimir Cathedral. Czars were crowned in the cathedral for 400 years; it served as the burial place of the metropolitans and patriarchs. Gilt bronze chandeliers illuminate the interior and its splendid 14C–17C frescoes. To the right in front of the iconostasis stands the canopied Monomakh's Throne otherwise known as the throne of Ivan the Terrible. It is a remarkable example of 16C wood carving. Thrones of the patriarchs and Czarinas are set against the pillars.

Teremnoj dvorec (Térem Palace) – *Closed to the public.* From Cathedral Square, the group of golden onion domes mark the former private chapels of the Terem Palace.

Cerkov' Rizpolozenija (Church of the Virgin Gown's Deposition) – The wood carvings date from the 15C to 18C. The frescoes and iconostasis are from the 17C.

Granovitaja palata (Palace of Facets) – *Closed to the public.* Italian architects built the palace in the late 15C. The façade contains diamond-pointed rusticated stonework.

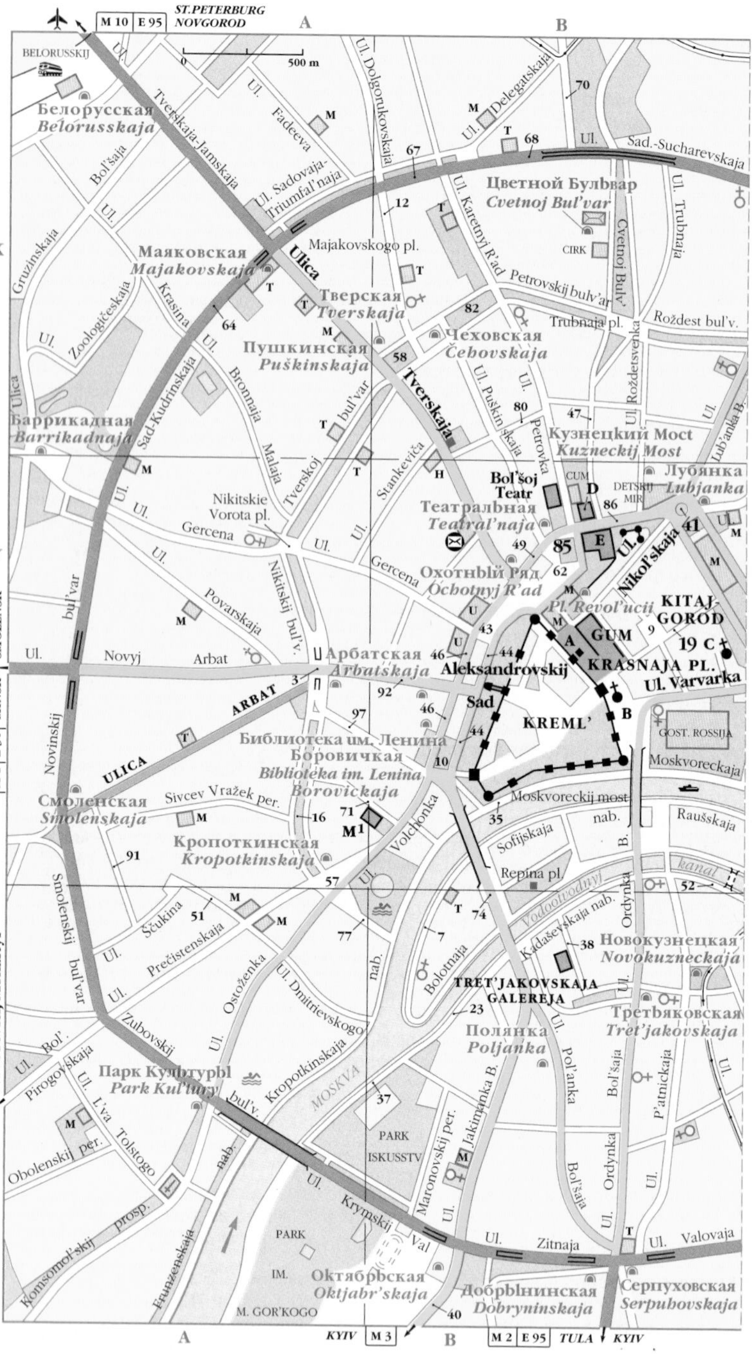

★★Archangel' skij sobor (Cathedral Church of St Michael the Archangel) – The façades of this church are decorated with shell-shaped tympana. The 16C church replaced a 14C structure of the same name. It honours the patron saint of the princes of Moscow. In addition to the splendid frescoes decorating the walls and pillars, the interior contains an icon depicting St Michael, the Archangel. The master Andrei Rublyov, or an artist from his school, painted the work. The central picture, highlighted by brilliant colouring on a gold background, is surrounded by several scenes retracing the archangel's life. The cathedral was the burial place of the princes of Moscow and the Czar: Ivan Kalita, Ivan the Terrible, his sons, and Peter II all are buried here.

★Blagoveščenskij sobor (Cathedral Church of the Annunciation) – This former private chapel of the grand princes and Czars is now the Cathedral Church of the Annunciation. The nine golden domes make it easily recognisable. Beautiful frescoes depicting the Apocalypse grace the interior.

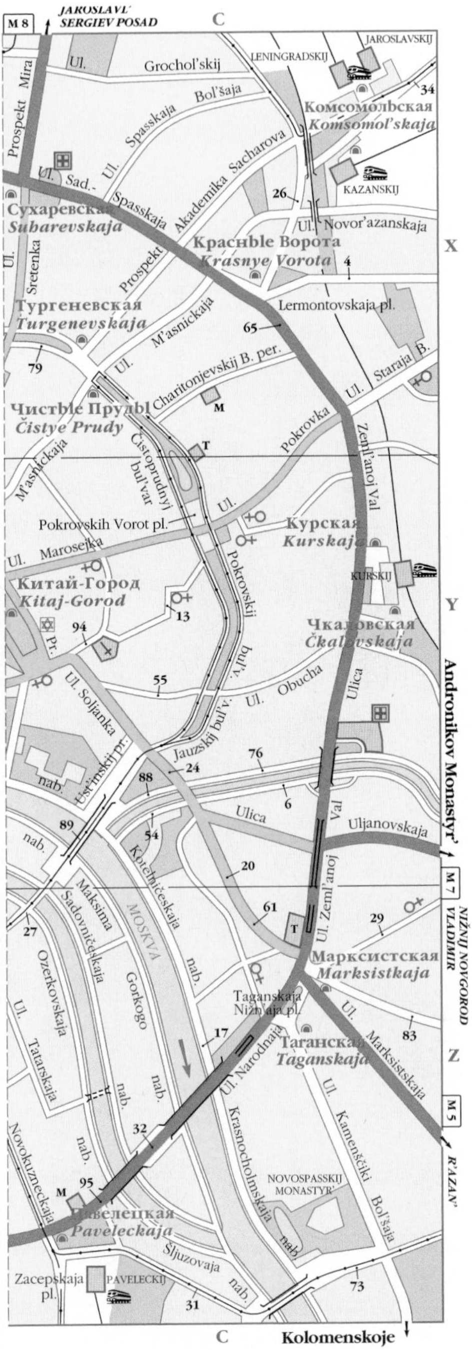

MOSKVA

Arbatskaja pl. .... AY 3
Basmannaja Novaja ul. .... CX 4
Bernikovskaya nab. .... CY 6
Bersenevskaja nab. .... BYZ 7
Birževaja pl. .... BY 9
Borovickaja pl. .... BY 10
Čechova ul. .... BX 12
Chochlovskij per. .... CY 13
Gogolevskij bul'v .... AY 16
Gončarnaja nab. .... CZ 17
Iljinka ul. .... BY 19
Internacional'naja ul. .... CY 20
Jakimanskaja nab. .... BZ 23
Jauzskaja ul. .... CY 24
Kalančevskaja ul. .... CX 26
Komissariatskij most .... CYZ 27
Kommunističeskaja Bol' ul. ... CZ 29
Koževničeskaja ul. .... CZ 31
Krasnocholmskaja Niž. ul. ...... CZ 32
Krasnoprudnaja ul. .... CX 34
Kremlevskaja .... BY 35
Krymskaja nab. .... ABZ 37
Lavrušinskij per. .... BZ 38
Leninskij prosp. .... BY 40
Lub'anskaja pl. .... BY 41
Manežnaja pl. .... BY 43
Manežnaja ul. .... BY 44
Mochovaja ul. .... BY 46
Neglinnaja ul. .... BX 47
Ochotnyj R'ad ul. .... BY 49
Ostrovskogo N. A. ul. .... AYZ 51
Ovčinnikovskaja nab. .... BCY 52
Podgorskaja nab. .... CY 54
Podkolokol'nyj per. .... CY 55
Prečistenskie Vorota .... AY 57
Puškinskaja pl. .... BX 58
Radiščevskaja Verhnjaja ul. ... CZ 61
Revol'ucii pl. .... BY 62
Sadovaja-Bol'šaja ul. .... AX 64
Sadovaja-Cernogrjazskaja ul. CX 65
Sadovaja-Karetnaja ul. .... BX 67
Sadovaja-Samotěčnaja ul. ..... BX 68
Samotěčnaja ul. .... BX 70
Šapošnikova Maršala ul. ..... ABY 71
Sarinskij pr. .... CZ 73
Serafimoviča ul. .... BYZ 74
Serebrjaničeskaja nab. .... CY 76
Sojmonovskij pr. .... ABZ 77
Sretenskij bul'v .... CX 79
Stolešnikov per. .... BX 80
Strastnoj bul'v .... BX 82
Taganskaja ul. .... CZ 83
Teatral'naja pl. .... BY 85
Teatral'nyj pr. .... BY 86
Ust'inskaja nab. .... CY 88
Ust'inskij most .... CY 89
Vesnina ul. .... AYZ 91
Vozdvizenka ul. .... BY 92
Zabelina ul. .... CY 94
Zacepskij Val ul. .... CZ 95
Znamenka ul. .... ABY 97

A Mavzolej Lenina
B Sobor Vasilija Blažennogo
C Cerkov'Troicy v Nikitnikach
D Malyj Teatr
E Gostinica Metropol'
M' Muzej izobrazitel' nych iskusstv im. Puškina

The **Kremlin Great Palace** (Bol'oj Kreml'ovskij dvorec) *(closed to the public)*, was formerly the residence of the Czars and now serves as the Russian Federation's official residence of thePresident. Official ceremonies are held here. The main façade's alternating yellow and white paint is set with three tiers of windows overlooking the River Moskova. The **White House** occupied by the Parliament is situated further west on the banks of the Moskova opposite the Oukraïna Hotel.

★★★ **Oružejnaja palata (Armour Palace)** – *Tours only. Contact the tourist office in each hotel.* The museum contains a vast collection illustrating several centuries of Russian history. The priceless treasures include Catherine the Great's coronation robe and summer carriage designed to resemble a gondola, Ivan the Terrible's ivory throne and dazzling jewel-encrusted crown, Boris Godunov's gemstones and state carriage with panels painted by Boucher, and Peter the Great's two-seat throne. Upstairs,

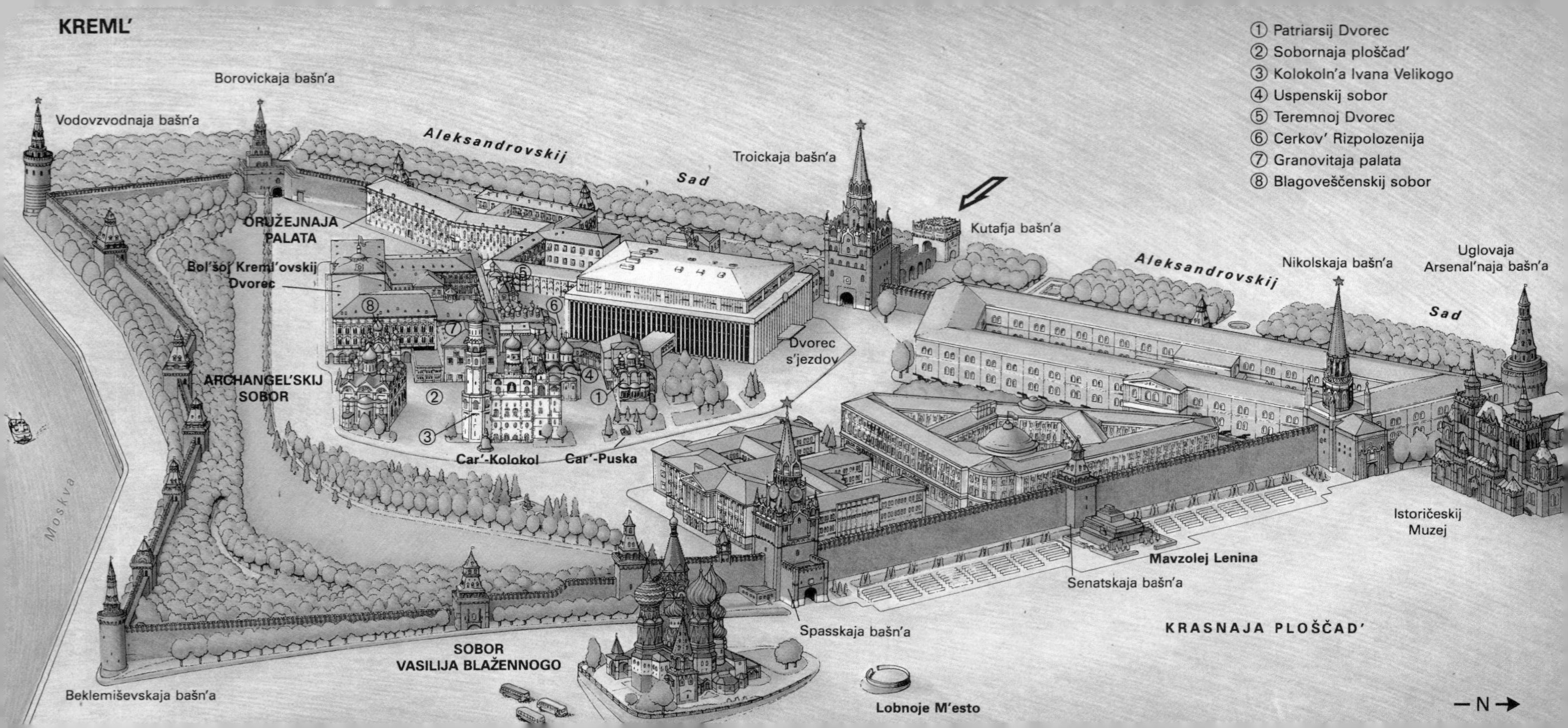
KREMĽ
① Patriarsij Dvorec
② Sobornaja ploščad'
③ Kolokoln'a Ivana Velikogo
④ Uspenskij sobor
⑤ Teremnoj Dvorec
⑥ Cerkov' Rizpolozenija
⑦ Granovitaja palata
⑧ Blagoveščenskij sobor
Vodovzvodnaja bašn'a
Borovickaja bašn'a
Aleksandrovskij
Sad
Troickaja bašn'a
Kutafja bašn'a
Aleksandrovskij
Nikolskaja bašn'a
Uglovaja
Arsenal'naja bašn'a
Sad
ORUŽEJNAJA
PALATA
Boľšoj Kremľovskij
Dvorec
ARCHANGEL'SKIJ
SOBOR
Dvorec
s'jezdov
Car'-Kolokol
Car'-Puska
Moskva
Istoričeskij
Muzej
Mavzolej Lenina
Senatskaja bašn'a
Spasskaja bašn'a
KRASNAJA PLOŠČAD'
SOBOR
VASILIJA BLAŽENNOGO
Beklemiševskaja bašn'a
Lobnoje M'esto
N

fine collections of weapons and armour are on display alongside Russian and European gold and silverware. The ambassadors' gift room contains the 150-piece Sèvres porcelain service given by Napoleon to Czar Alexander I after the signing of the Treaty of Tilsit on 7 July, 1807.

★★ **Almaznyj fond (Diamond Fund)** – *Same admission conditions as the Armour Palace.* The Diamond Fund houses a number of unique gems including the Shah and Orlov diamonds, the tiara belonging to Alexander I's consort Elizabeth, and Catherine II's brilliant-encrusted silver coronation crown, insignia of Russian orders. The gold nuggets have acquired delightful names such as the Camel, Mephistopheles, and the Elephant after their shapes. The world's largest platinum nugget, christened the Ural Giant, weighs 7.8kg/7.2lb. Russia's largest gold nugget, the Great Triangle, comes in at 36kg/79lb.

★★★ KRASNAJA PLOŠČAD' (RED SQUARE) (BY)

Red Square flanks the east wall of the Kremlin. This unique, solemn, grandiose landmark recalls the impressive military parades commemorating the October Revolution. The turreted red brick History Museum *(closed)* and the Cathedral of St Basil the Blessed stand at opposite end of the square. Across from the Kremlin walls is the GOUM department store.
Red Square began as a market place in the 15C. It took its present name, *kras-naïa* meaning both red and beautiful, in the 17C.
The square also merits a visit at night when floodlit.

Mavzolej Lenina (Lenin Mausoleum) (**BY A**) – Two armed sentries stand guard at all times in front of the Lenin Mausoleum. The monument, originally built of wood, is intentionally plain and designed in the form of a stepped pyramid over a base. Marble, porphyry, granite and labradorite were used in its construction. Lenin's name is carved in red Cyrillic letters against a black labradorite background above the doorway. The leader of the Revolution's embalmed body lies in the centre of the burial chamber beneath a glass cover.
A number of other major Soviet figures, Andropov, Brezhnev, Stalin, Kalinin, Kirov and Dzerzhinsky, are buried at the rear of the mausoleum. Stone busts make them recognisable. Also buried here are cosmonaut Yuri Gagarin (a sculpture of the space hero sits atop an impressive tall titanium monument on Gagarin Square), Russian writer Maxim Gorky, and American writer John Reed (1887-1920). Reed wrote *Ten Days That Shook the World* based on the October Revolution. He became one of the leaders of the Communist International and lived in Moscow at the end of his life.
Set within the Kremlin Walls, urns contain the ashes of heroes of the Communist Workers' Movement.
In front of the cathedral *(left)*, Czars and patriarchs once addressed the people from the **Lobnoje M'esto**, a round stone rostrum.

★★★ **Sobor Vasilja Blažennogo (Cathedral of St Basil the Blessed)** (**BY B**) – In front of the cathedral, the bronze Minim and Pojarsky Monument honours the two Russian heroes, leaders of the popular militia who drove the Polish invaders from Moscow in 1612.
The cathedral originally was dedicated to the Intercession of the Virgin. It was built as a memorial by Ivan the Terrible in the 16C to commemorate the defeat of the Tatars in 1552. The present name dates back to the 17C when a chapel was built over the grave of a simpleton named Basil. The remarkable combination of shapes and colours makes it the most unusual example of Russian religious architecture. A central church

J.-P. Garcin/DIAF

Cathedral of St Basil the Blessed

topped by a pyramid-shaped tower is surrounded by eight smaller churches each with a painted onion dome topped with a golden cross. The interior, now a museum, forms a type of maze leading to the various churches. It contains outstanding frescoes and iconostasis, along with an exhibition on the history of the cathedral.

★**GUM** (BY) – The largest store in Russia was built in the late 19C. It merits a visit for its architecture and atmosphere. Some 100 shops line several tiers of colourful arcades linked by footbridges beneath an immense glass roof with metal framework. The complex has a distinctive Art Nouveau style and is decorated with fountains and clocks.

★KITAJ-GOROD (BY)

This district begins behind GOUM. It lies between Nikol'skaja Street, formerly 25 Oktiabria Street, and the River Moskova and the huge Rossia Hotel behind the Cathedral of St Basil the Blessed. Kitaj-Gorod was once a small walled town. Remains of the fortifications have survived to the present day. In the 15C and 16C, it was a bustling trading centre.
Today, busy streets such as **Nikol'skaja** and **Iljinka** (formerly oulitsa Kouibicheva) (BY **19**) are lined with shops and market stalls.

★**Ulica Varvarka (formerly oulitsa Razina)** (BY) – This picturesque street with tiny churches and rows of rooftops from a bygone era flanks the Rossia Hotel. It contains the homes of dignitaries and was part of the Zaradié district bounded by the Moskova.
The former House of the English, recognisable by its white walls and timber roof, once provided accommodation and a meetingplace for English traders and diplomats passing through the Russian capital.
At no 4, a small **craft museum** has been set up in the former St Maximus' Church. Exhibits include wood carvings, Russian dolls, and lacquered boxes. Embroidery and costumes are found in the basement. At no 10, the **House of the Romanov Boyars**★ provides an insight into the life of a family of 16C and 17C boyars. The cellar and rooms with low vaulted ceilings show off furniture and other household objects. At no 12, the former **St George's Church** with four star-studded blue domes and one golden dome has been turned into an exhibition centre.

►► **Cer kov' Troicy v Nikitnikach**★ (Church of the Holy Trinity of Nikitniki) (BY **C**, *Nikitnikov Alley*): it contains lavish 17C decoration.

MAIN MUSEUMS

★★★**Tret'jakovskaja galereja (Tretiakov Art Gallery)** (BZ) – This gallery is housed in a huge red brick-building. Its collections focus on Russian art from the Middle Ages. Artists represented include Pavel Fedotov (genre scenes: *The Major's Marriage Proposal*), Kiprensky *(Portrait of Aleksandr Pushkin)*, Vasily Perov *(Portrait of Dostoyevsky)*, Nikolay Gay (the pathos-filled *Golgotha*), Ivan Kramskoy *(Portrait of Tolstoy)*, Isaac Levitan (great landscape painter) and Ilya Repin (historic scenes). The museum is also famous for its valuable icons. The most outstanding exhibits include a 12C Byzantine icon called *The Madonna of Vladmir*, and master Andrei Rublyov's *Trinity* from the Zagorsk Monastery.

★★**Muzej izobrazitel'nykch iskusstv im. Puskina (Pushkin Museum of Fine Arts)** (ABY **M**[1]) – This neo-Classical museum named after the famous poet and novelist Aleksander Pushkin houses extensive collections of Western art. Notable works from the second half of the 19C include Monet's *Déjeuner sur l'herbe*. Picasso's *Family of Saltimbanques* and *Girl on a Ball* are highlights from the 20C.

★★NOVODEVIČIJ MONASTYR' (NOVODEVICHY CONVENT)

1 Novodevichy Projezd. Sportivnaya Metro Station.

The nearby lake offers a fine **view**★ of the convent.
Vasily III founded his splendid group of monastic buildings surrounded by red-brick walls and flanked by 12 towers to celebrate the capture of Smolensk from Poland and its annexation to Russia. The five domed **Collegiate Church of Our Lady of Smolensk** contains fine **frescoes** depicting scenes from the Old and New Testaments. The **iconostasis** consists of five rows of magnificent icons. Princess Sophia, the sister of Peter the Great, commissioned it. A tiny museum houses the church plate. Flanking the east wall, a golden dome tops the Baroque bell-tower.
On the convent's south side, a **cemetery** evokes Père-Lachaise in Paris. Famous figures buried here include the film-maker Eisenstein, the writers Gogol, Chekov and Mayakovsky, the composer Prokofiev and the politicians Molotov, Krushchev and Gromyko.

Icons

The word icon comes from the Greek *eikona* and is used to describe a religious picture painted on a wooden panel (lime, pine, cypress or poplar). The icon, which is of Byzantine origin, spread to Russia in the 10C during the country's conversion to Christianity, and is an expression of popular piety and Orthodox faith. In most cases, icons depict a religious scene or portrait (the Virgin Mary, much worshipped in the Orthodox religion, Christ and the saints). From the 7C onwards, icons were produced using the *a tempera* technique in which colours were thinned in a mixture of water and egg yolk. For each topic or subject, a preliminary sketch was made prior to the painting itself. Icons were occasionally given a silver or silver gilt coating forming a background or frame.
The oldest Russian School was probably the one in Kiev. In the 14C, the arrival of Theophanes the Greek, who came to Novgorod from Constantinople and later went on to Moscow, had a profound influence on icon painting. At the beginning of the next century, Theophanes' pupil, the monk Andrey Rublyov, became the undisputed master of the Moscow School. He moved away from the dramatic intensity and austerity of earlier works and introduced free, flowing lines and subtle colours, creating compositions of greater sweetness, delicacy and harmony.

ADDITIONAL SIGHTS

★**Ulica Arbat (Arbat Street)** (AY) – *Arbatskaja Metro Station.* During the day, shoppers crowd this street, along with street musicians, portrait artists and tumblers. The famous Praga restaurant at the start of the thoroughfare has a yellow façade in the shape of a ship's bow. Market stalls sell a wide variety of goods including traditional Russian dolls called *matriochkas* and more humourous modern versions of Yeltsin, Gorbachev, Lenin and Brezhnev. Lacquered boxes, military items or badges, souvenirs, watercolours and T-shirts – including one inscribed McLenin's! – also are offered.
At no 53, the first floor of a fine 18C town house contains the **Pushkin Apartment Museum.** On exhibit are memorabilia of the writer who came to live here in 1831 after his marriage.

★★**The Subway** – The Moscow subway claims to be the world's fastest and deepest underground system. Countless escalators carry throngs of passengers down into the bowels of the earth. The stations are often far apart, which means that trains can reach speeds of up to 90 kph/56 mph. Stations are announced in each carriage. The stations themselves constitute an underground museum. Stalin wanted to make the subway "a people's palace", and the abundant, lavish decorations include marble, stucco, huge crystal chandeliers, mosaics, stained glass windows and monumental statues. Representative stations include Komsomolskaja, Belorusskaja, Majakovskaja, Revol'ucii, Kievskaja and Arbatskaja.

Teatral'naja ploščad (Theatre Square) (BY **85**) – A number of impressive buildings flank this square. The **Bol'soj Teatr**★ (Grand Theatre) (BY) is famous the world over for the Bolshoi ballet. A pediment with the four-horsed chariot of Apollo, protector of the Arts, stands over the impressive Classical building. The entrance consists of an eight-columned porch.
To the Bolshoi's right, the **Malyj Teatr** (Little Theatre) (BY **D**) specialises in classical repertory. A memorial to the dramatist Aleksandr Ostrovsky stands at the entrance. The **TSOUM** department store (CUM) is set back from the theatre. On the other side of Ochotnyj R'ad Avenue stands the luxury **Metropol Hotel** (BY **E**).
At no 2 Ochotnyj R'ad, **Destskij Mir** offers the city's largest selection of toys.

Lub'anskaja ploščad (BY **41**) is overlooked by the tall Federal Security Services building, formerly the KGB headquarters. In the square's centre, an Orthodox cross has replaced the infamous statue of Feliks Dzerzhinsky. Dzerzhinsky founded the Cheka, the forerunner of the KGB.

Tverskaja oulitsa (formerly Gorky Street) (ABX) – One of the capital's longest streets, this is a busy shopping street thanks to the nearby Moskva, National and Intourist hotels. Some Western companies have also opened premises here including Yves Rocher, Pizza Hut, and Christian Dior. Near the top of the street *(right)*, stands the equestrian statue of the city's founder, Yuri Dolgoruky. Further along is the bustling Puskinskaja Ploščad or Pushkin Square with the memorial to the great writer. Tverskaja Street runs across Ploščad Majakovskogo before crossing the ring of gardens. On Mayakovski Square, see the memorial to the poet.

Andronikov Monastyr' (Andronikov Monastery) – *10 Ploščad Prymikova. Pl. Ilyicha Metro Station.* The monk Andronik founded the monastery in 1359. One of the greatest icon and fresco painters of medieval times, Andrei Rublyov (1360-1430), spent the last years of his life and was buried here. A museum dedicated to him contains a collection of magnificent **works**★★.

★**Kolomenskoje** – *10km/6mi southeast. Metro: Kolomenskaja Station. Then about 15min walk beyond the Orbita cinema and a complex of apartment blocks. The blue domes and white walls are visible from some distance.*
The village of Kolomenskoje is an exhilarating open-air museum. From the 15C, the grand princes and Czars built their summer residences here. This rustic spot overlooking the river is a haven of peace. Amateur artists set up their easels and Muscovites come for family outings. The blue star-studded domes of the **Church of Our Lady of Kazan** were built here in the 17C. On each side of the front door, the rooms of a **museum** illustrate the history of the estate through remains of the wooden palace, wood carvings, icons, wrought and cast-iron objects, and everyday objects. The **Church of the Ascension** overlooking the Moskova was built in 1532 by Grand Prince Vasily II to celebrate the birth of his son, the future Ivan the Terrible. Its distinctive tall pyramid-shaped tower soars upwards. A **view** of the Moskova opens up from the left of the church beside a row of cannons. Interesting buildings are dotted throughout the park, including the 16C St George bell-tower, the Sokolinaja Tower and the church-refectory. Fine examples of wooden architecture from a number of regions are reconstructed. They include the door from St Nicholas' monastery, the watch tower of Bratsk Prison and Peter I's *izba* (log cabin).

EXCURSIONS

The scenic **Golden Ring** to the northeast takes in old towns with a rich architectural heritage. Golden onion domes dot the countryside at Sergyev Posad, Pereslavl-Zalesski, Rostov, Yaroslavl, Vladimir, Suzdal and Ivanovo. The three towns described below can be visited on day trips from Moscow. Contact the tourist office in each hotel or negotiate a price for a shared taxi ride.

★★★**Sergiev Posad (Zagorsk)** – *70km/44mi north.* Zagorsk recently changed its name back to Sergiev Porad. The spiritual centre of the Russian Orthodox Church owes its fame to the **Trinity St Sergius laura**, a shrine of Orthodox faith. The monastery has massive walls with loopholes and towers and constitutes a fortress. Built from the 15C to 18C, it represents one of Russia's most prestigious architectural achievements. Enter via the **Dormition Gate**. The **Cathedral of the Assumption**, with its four blue star-studded domes around a central golden dome, stands out above white walls. Work began on the building during the reign of Ivan the Terrible. The design is based on the cathedral of the same name situated within the Kremlin in Moscow. Inside, splendid copper chandeliers reveal 17C frescoes and an 18C carved wooden iconostasis. By the south door are the tombs of Boris Godunov, his wife and their children. On the north side is the chapel built over the Holy Spring. Its waters supposedly have miraculous properties.
The long 17C **church-refectory** is striking for the profusion of decorative features –walls embellished with multicoloured motifs laid out in a checkerboard pattern and topped by friezes of tiles, and half-columns decorated with bunches of grapes. Next to the Church of the Holy Spirit, a cylindrical drum and onion dome top the austere cube-shaped 15C **Trinity Cathedral**. It contains a fine iconostasis; master Andrei Rublyov and his school painted some of the icons. On the right, a silver canopied reliquary holds the relics of the monk **Sergius of Radonezh**, the founder of the monastery and an ardent defender of the united Russia stand against the 14C Mongol invaders. A short distance from the cathedral stands the majestic 18C **bell-tower**; it is composed of five tiers of twin columns set closer and closer together.

★★**Vladimir** – The town is famed for its 12C Golden Gate and two major religious buildings. The 12C **Cathedral of the Dormition** is recognisable by its five golden domes. It contains some remarkable frescoes by Andrei Rublyov (note in particular the Last Judgement above the chancel). The **Cathedral of St Dimitry**, also dating from the 12C, is built of limestone. The doorway has intricately carved arch moulding. The building's upper section is covered in carvings depicting various motifs, animals, plants, religious and hunting scenes.

★★**Souzdal** – This medieval town is famous for its **Kremlin**. Inside the walls, a superbly beautiful monastery sits in the shade of the 13C **Cathedral of the Nativity of Our Lady**. Five blue domes studded with golden stars top this majestic building with white walls. Ornaments and motifs engraved on sheets of gilded copper decorate the doors. Inside are fragments of frescoes and a 15C iconostasis. The **bishop's apartments** have been turned into a museum.
Not far from Souzdal, the village of Glotovo houses a **Museum of Wooden Architecture** with *izbas*, churches and rural residences.

Credit cards (American Express, Visa) are generally accepted in most hotels and restaurants while travellers cheques must be cashed at a bank: they are not accepted as payment. When taking dollars to exchange against the official rouble, make sure you have banknotes of small denomination to avoid great wads of roubles.

ST.PETERBURG★★★

ST PETERSBURG – Population 5 000 000

Michelin map 970 R 2

Peter the Great founded St Petersburg in an effort to open the country up to Europe. The strategic setting also provided protection against the Swedish. In 1712, the city became the capital of the Russian Empire. It evokes the Czarist Russia of lavish ceremonies and majestic palaces. Most of the magnificent residences were designed by talented Italian architects, Bartolomeo Rastrelli, and Carlo Ross, invited to Russia by the reigning sovereigns.
In 1914 St Petersburg became Petrograd, literally Peter's Town. In 1924, the Bolsheviks renamed it Leningrad, Lenin's town. In the wake of *perestroika*, the city changed back to its original name again in 1991.
St Petersburg has a population of almost five million and includes over 40 islands criss-crossed by canals and bridges. Each night, the bridges are raised for several hours to allow boats to pass. It has earned the nickname of the Venice of the North.
The historic core is signalled by the golden spire of the Admiralty building. Several main avenues converge on this landmark. Along the banks of the river, Baroque and Classical style palaces display a palette of colours. They form a particularly spectacular showcase of the major trends in Western and Russian architecture. Beyond the river banks, the city is much less attractive.
Like Venice, water poses a constant threat. In 1824 and 1924 devastating floods hit. A dike was built across the Gulf of Finland in 1966 to protect the city from the River Neva. On Vassilevski Island, the Neva splits off into two branches, the Bol'sajaa Neva (Great Neva) and the Malaja Neva (Little Neva).
St Petersburg has numerous parks and gardens that provide a pleasant stroll.
As a Baltic Sea port, St Petersburg receives a large number of cargo ships and liners.

The City at a Glance – Visitors arriving from Poulkovo Airport immediately get an idea of the city's vastness. The unending Moskovskij Prospekt (Moscow Avenue) runs past austere post-war apartment blocks and a number of historic monuments of impressive proportions. Ploščad Pobiedy, Victory Square, is dominated by a monument to the heroes who defended Leningrad during the Second World War. Ploščad Moskovskaja, Moscow Square, has a statue of Lenin. Ploščad Moskovskje Vorota, Moscow Gate Square, shows off a triumphal cast-iron gate with double colonnade commemorating the victory over the Turks in 1829.
The best way to see the sights is to take a **coach tour**.
Contact the tourist office in the hotels for details. **Boat trips★★** on the River Neva provide another good introduction. Board near the Hermitage Museum on Dvorcovaja Nab. A **trip along the canals★★** is equally interesting. Board near Anichkov Bridge on Nevskij Prospekt.
During the **White Nights Festival** in late June, St Petersburg becomes unforgettable. Nightfall and sunrise merge into one. The city, bathed in a strange light, buzzes with entertainment and merrymaking.

★★★HISTORIC CENTRE

★**Admiraltejstvo (Admiralty)** (AY) – The Admiralty is the city's emblem. Its tall spire topped by a carvel-shaped weather vane serves as a reminder of St Petersburg's maritime tradition. The Classical building is divided into three sections with an arch in the centre. A golden spire juts up from a square tower, reaching a height of 72.5m - 238ft. Carved figures of nymphs and high-relief sculptures provide decoration.

★★**Isaakievskij sobor (St Isaac's Cathedral)** (AY) – This huge domed red granite and grey marble church stands on Isaakievskaja Ploščad near the equestrian statue of Nicholas I. French architect Auguste Ricard de Montferrand built the building between 1818 and 1858. Massive Corinthian porticoes, the pediments decorated with bronze highreliefs, dominate all four sides. In the centre a column drum supports a golden dome topped by an octagonal lantern turret and surrounded by four bell towers with cupolas. The giant interior can accommodate 14 000 people. Although excessively ornate, the church is full of sumptuous decoration. Different coloured marble, granite, bronze, shale, malachite, lapis lazuli, precious and semi-precious stones embellish the walls, columns and capitals creating a dazzling polychrome effect. The central dome contains a painting by Karl Brullov depicting the Virgin Mary surrounded by saints. The main white marble iconostasis contains mosaics of the saints.
Since 1931, the church has been a museum. A remarkable **panoramic view★★** unfolds from the top of the dome.

Senatskaja ploščad (Senate Square) (AY) – Across from St Isaac's Cathedral on the Neva banks, the Admiralty and former Senate and Synod flank the former Decembrists' Square. Carlo Rossi designed the Senate and Synod's yellow and white façades. The two symmetrical buildings are linked by an arcade. In Senate Square on 14 December, 1825, some 3 000 soldiers led by officers from the nobility refused to swear allegiance to Czar Nicholas I in protest against absolutism and

serfdom. The uprising supported by Pushkin was crushed immediately and ended in a bloodbath. The leaders were executed and followers deported. To commemorate this tragedy, Senate Square was named Decembrists' Square in 1925.
In the centre, the **Bronze Horseman**★★, an equestrian statue of Peter I the Great, was mainly the work of the French sculptor Etienne Falconet. Catherine II the Great commissioned it. On the sculpture's base, an inscription in Latin and Russian honours the sovereign.

★★ **Ploščad' Dvorcovaja (Palace Square)** (AY) – The huge semicircular Palace Square surrounded by impressive buildings is the venue for parades, processions and events. The pink granite Alexander Column, erected in 1834 by Auguste de Montferrand commemorates the victory of the Russians over Napoleon's troops in 1812. Tsar Alexander I is represented at the top as an angel bearing a cross, crushing the snake symbolising Napoleon's *Grande Armée*. Bas-reliefs on the bronze pedestal depict allegories of the war against the French.
Carlo Rossi's straw-coloured **former General Staff Building** in Classical style forms a semicircle along one side of the square. A monumental arch showing the chariot of Victory drawn by six horses leads to Nevsky Avenue. The Classical Staff Building contrasts with the Baroque façade and Italianate style and colours of the czar's **Winter Palace**★★★. Architect Bartolomeo Rastrelli constructed the palace between 1754 and 1762 during the reign of Empress Elizabeth, the daughter of Peter the Great. It contains most of the collections from the famous Hermitage Museum. Architect Alexander Brullov's **former Guards Headquarters**, a building of more modest dimensions, borders the square's east side.

►► **Dom Puškina**★ (Pushkin's House) (BY) *(12 nab. reki Moyki)*: the great writer died here at the age of 37 after fighting a duel with the Frenchman Georges d'Anthès. The suite of rooms contains period furniture, memorabilia of his wife Natalya, numerous documents, and a library study containing more than 4000 volumes, a desk, a mechanised armchair, and personal effects.

★★NEVSKIJ PROSPEKT (NEVSKY AVENUE) (ABY)

Nevsky Avenue, formerly the Grand Avenue, was commissioned by Peter the Great. Tower blocks and prestigious mansions have replaced the tree-lined walks. Stores, cafés, restaurants, banks, cinemas and theatres line both sides of the avenue.
The city's most lively shopping street stretches for 4.5km/3mi between the Admiralty and Alexander Nevsky Monastery. Although relatively little traffic passes, the pavements are constantly crowded. City dwellers and tourists wander past vendors selling icecream, *kvass*, books, newspapers, postcards, rolls of film, tee-shirts, soap, toothpaste, beer, Coca Cola, cigarettes, shoes and clothing. Crowds of people debate politics and sign petitions. Often the debates become heated or even violent. Painters, jazz bands, seamen and soldiers on leave, and individuals offer in English to "change" money on the black market. At road junctions, the subway passages and steps leading down into them serve as blackmarket selling points. Locals make a few roubles or dollars on the side selling anything that can be sold.

Y. Travert/DIAF

Winter Palace

★**Kazanskij sobor (Cathedral of Our Lady of Kazan)** (**BY L**) – This colossal religious building heralded by two huge semicircular Corinthian colonnades surrounds a central porch. Voronikhin built it for Czar Paul I. He based his design on St Peter's Basilica in Rome. Tall red granite Corinthian columns and marble floor grace the interior. The church now houses the **Museum of the History of Religion and Atheism.** Exhibits include documents, scale models, and the tomb of Marshal Kutuzov with trophies captured from the enemy.
Opposite the cathedral, **Dom Knigi** or the House of Books, is the city's largest book store.
The square outside the church displays statues of Kutuzov and Barclay de Tolly, commanders-in-chief of the Russian army against Napoleon.
From the next bridge spanning the Griboyedov Canal, a view opens up of the **Church of the Resurrection of Christ**★★ (Chram Voskressenia Christova) (**BY C**). The brightly-coloured domes evoke the Church of St Basil the Blessed in Moscow. Czar Alexander III commissioned this church, built on the very spot where his father Czar Alexander II was assassinated by members of the Narodnaya Volya Movement (Will of the People).
On the corner of Mikhajlovskaja Street, the **Grand Europe Hotel** (Jevropejskaja) (**BY G**), is a splendidly restored luxury hotel. It was first opened in 1824.

►► Ploščad' Iskusstv (Arts Square) (**BY**) was designed by Carlo Rossi. It includes gardens and a statue of Aleksander Pushkin, all surrounded by museums and theatres.

★**Gostinyj Dvor** (**BY**) – The city's largest store is designed in the form of a trapezium. It gets its name from the word *gosti*, once used to describe the peddlers who came to this spot to sell their wares. This huge shopping arcade was built in the 18C by Vallin de la Mothe and restored in the 19C and around 1950. It consists of two floors of various shops, not all of them as well-stocked as others. The stores line central walkways.
On the other side of the avenue, the large 19C **Passaz** gallery shelters a number of clothes shops under its glass roof.
Nearby on the same side of the road, the food store **Elisseiev** merits a visit. It sells Russian and imported produce in a sumptuous Art Nouveau decor.

Ploščad' Ostrovskogo (Ostrovsky Square) (**BY**) – Designed by the architect Carlo Rossi, this square originally was known as Alexandra Square after the consort of Nicholas I. It was renamed Ostrovsky in 1923 in honour of the dramatist Aleksander Ostrovsky (1823-1886). In the centre, the monument built in 1873 commemorates Catherine II the Great. The sovereign is dressed in an ermine cloak and enthroned with a sceptre in her hand. All round the pedestal are statues of her favourites. On the square's west side, the National Saltykov-Shchedrin Library represents the oldest institution of its kind in the country.

★**Teatr Puškina (Puskhin Theatre)** (**BY T'**) – The Pushkin Theatre was formerly known as the Alexandra Theatre. Its elegant building includes a loggia of six Corinthian columns, topped by an attic and quadriga.
Behind the theatre, the elegant perfectly-proportioned **Architect Rossi Street** (ulica Zodèego Rossi) (**BY Z**) is a fine example of town planning and extends 220m/240yd long, 22m/24yd wide, and 22m/72ft high.

★**Aničkov most (Anichkov Bridge)** (**BY**) – This fine stone construction is flanked by four bronze statues entitled the *Horse Tamers*. The bridge was built in the late 18C. It replaced a wooden footbridge constructed during Peter the Great's reigns by the troops of Colonel Mikhail Anichkov. At the time, the Fontanka marked the city's boundary.

★★**Aleksandro-Nevskaja Lavra (Alexander Nevsky Laura)** (**CZ**) – The monastery was built during Peter the Great's reign in honour of the Prince of Novgorod Aleksandr Yaroslavich. This prince conquered the Swedish army on the banks of the Neva in 1240. He was canonised in 1263 under the name of Alexander Nevsky. Like Zagorsk, Kiev and Pochayev, it became a residence of the metropolitans. The monastery is surrounded by walls.
Inside, a dozen churches and four cemeteries make up the vast complex. The **Cemetery of Our Lady of Tikhvin,** right of the entrance, is the final restingplace of composers Mussorgsky, Borodin, Rimski-Korsakov, Tchaikovsky and Glinka and the writer Dostoyevsky. On the left **St Lazarus' Cemetery** holds the tombs of architects Ivan Starov, Vasily Stassov and Carlo Rossi, Pushkin's widow Countess Lanskaya and scientist Mikhail Lomonossov.

The Trinity Cathedral (Trojtski sobor) designed by Starov and built during the reign of Catherine II dominates the entire estate. It is a fine example of Russian Classical architecture. The colonnaded entrance leads into a sumptuous interior with marble decor, containing a white marble iconostasis decorated with copies of works by Rubens, Van Dyck and Guido Reni. The *Annunciation* is by Raffael Mengs.

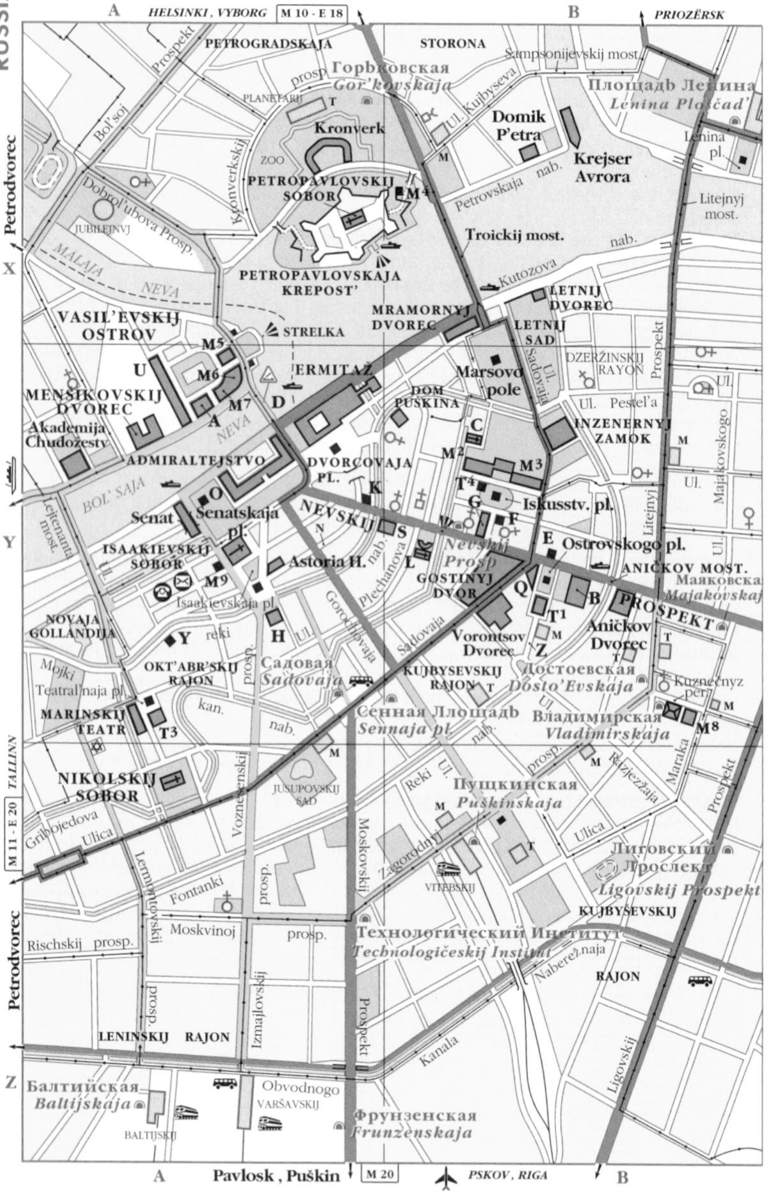

★VASIL'EVSKIJ OSTROV (VASILEVSKY ISLAND) (AXY)

Vasilevsky Island is reached by the Palace Bridge over the Neva (**AY D**). Majestic façades line the University Quay (Universitetskaja nabereznaja). The former **Curio Room** (Kunstkamera) (**AY M**[7]) is an example of Russian Baroque architecture. It consists of a pair of two-floor buildings linked by a stepped tower. Today, it houses several museums. The more austere **Academy of Science** (Akademija Nauk) (**AY A**) was built in Classical style by Giacomo Quareghi. An eight-column portico topped by a pediment dominates its entrance. The Academy was founded in 1724 by Peter the Great. At no 15, the **Menshikov Palace**★★ (Mensikovskij dvorec) (**AY**), represents the city's first luxury residence built for St Petersburg's first governor, Aleksandr Menshikov. Its yellow façade is marked out with white pilasters. Splendid furnishings and a magnificent reception room attract visitors inside. Further along the quay, the **Academy of Fine Arts** (Akademijachudozestv) (**AY**) was founded in 1757 by Elizabeth I.

Strelka (**AXY**) – This is the island's headland. The park in Pushkin Square offers a superb **view**★★ of the two banks of the Neva with the Winter Palace and its Hermitage Museum on the right and the Peter and Paul Fortress on the left. The two **rostral columns** decorated with ships' bows were built in honour of the Russian fleet. At the foot of the columns are allegorical figures symbolising the great rivers Volga, Dnepr, Neva and Volkhov.

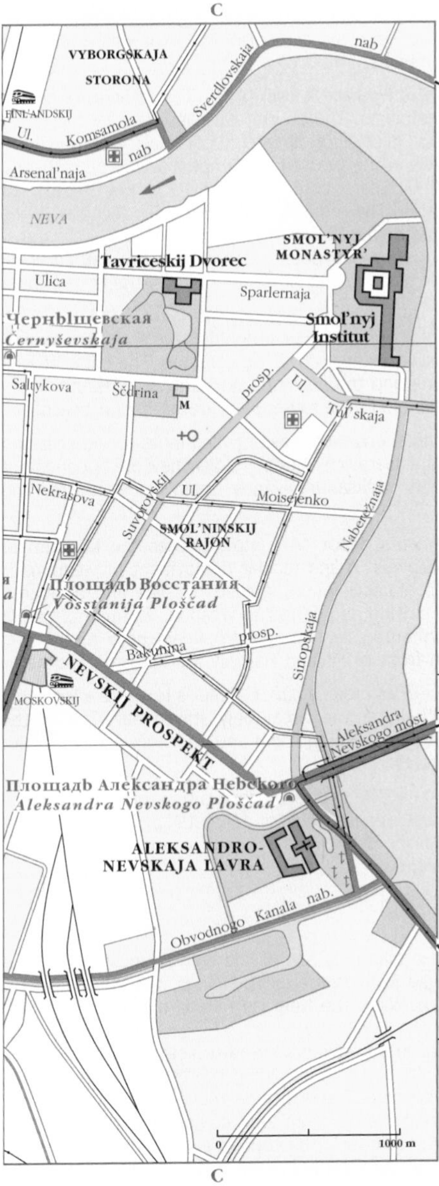

ST. PETERBURG

Admiraltejstvo ... AY
Akademija Chudozestv ... AY
Aleksandro-Nevskaja lavra ... CZ
Anickov dvorec ... BY
Anickov most ... BY
Astoria Hotel ... AY
Dom Puskina ... BY
Domik P'etra ... BX
Dvorcovaja pl. ... AY
Ermitaz (Zimniy dvorec) ... AY
Gostinyj Dvor ... BY
Inzenernyj Zamok ... BY
Issaakievskij sobor ... AY
Iskusstv pl. ... BY
Krejser Avrora ... BX
Kronverk ... AX
Kuznecnyz Market ... BY
Letnij dvorec - Letnij sad ... BXY
Mariinskij Teatr ... AY
Marsovo pole ... BY
Mensikovskij dvorec ... AY
Mramornyj dvorec ... BY
Nevskij Prospekt ... ABY
Nikolskij sobor ... AZ
Ostrovskogo pl. ... BY
Petropavlovskaja krepost ... ABX
Petropavlovskij sobor ... AX
Senat ... AY
Senatskaja (Dekabristov) pl. ... AY
Sinagoga ... AYZ
Smol'nyj Institut ... CX
Smol'nyj monastyr' ... CX
Strelka ... AXY
Tavriceskij dvorec ... CX
Teatral'naja pl. ... AY
Troickij most ... BX
Vasii'evskij ostrov ... AXY
Vorontsvov dvorec ... BY
Zimniy dvorec (Ermitaz) ... AY

Akademija Nauk ... AY **A**
Beloselsky-Belozersky dvorec .. BY **B**
Centralnyj Voenno-Morskoj muzej ... AXY **M5**
Chram Voskressenia Christova ... BY **C**
Dvorcovyj most ... AY **D**
Elisseiev Magazin ... BY **E**
Filarmonija ... BY **F**
Gosudarstvennyj muzej étnografi ... BY **M3**
Grand Hotel Europe ... BY **G**
Kafe Literaturnoe ... AY **K**
Kazanskij sobor ... BY **L**
Konservatoija ... AY **T3**
Kunstkamera ... AY **M7**
Malaya Morskaja ul. ... AY **N**
Mariinskij dvorec ... AY **H**
Medny vsardnik ... AY **O**
Muzej Gasodinamicekoj laboratorii kosmonavtiki ... BX **M4**
Muzej-kvartira Dostojevskogo . BY **M8**
Muzej-svjazi ... AY **M9**
Nacional'naja biblioteka ... BY **Q**
Russkij Muzej ... BY **M2**
Stroganovevsvkij dvorec ... BY **S**
Teatr opery i baleta im Musorgskogo ... BY **T4**
Teatr Puskina ... BY **T1**
Universitet ... AX **U**
Yusupovskij dvorec ... AY **Y**
Zodčego Rossi ul. ... BY **Z**
Zoologiceskij muzej ... AY **M6**

►► **Central'nyj Voenno-Morskoj muzej★** (Naval Museum) (**AXY M5**): Housed in the former Stock Exchange (Birja), the Classical building resembles a Greek temple. Extensive collections illustrate the history of the imperial and Soviet fleets.

★★ PETROPAVLOVSKAJA KREPOST' (PETER AND PAUL FORTRESS) (ABX)

The Peter and Paul Fortress represents a fine example of a fortified enclosure. Shaped like an irregular hexagon, it includes six bastions and six curtain walls. Peter the Great built it to defend the outlet to the Baltic and prevent any attack from Swedish troops, but the fortress soon lost its strategic role and became a prison. The Czar's own son, the Czarevich Alexis was even imprisoned there after being accused of plotting against his father.
Today, the fortress' golden spire forms the city's historic centre.

Entrance on the east side via the bridge and St John's Gate. The main entrance or **St Peter's Gate** is a triumphal arch topped by the imperial coat of arms and the two-headed eagle. The central shield portrays St George slaying the dragon. It was the former coat of arms of Moscow. Visitors pass the Engineers' Building and the Guardroom and Officers' Residence to reach Cathedral Square. Near the cathedral entrance, the Boat House, a small Baroque building was designed to house the boat in which the future Peter the Great learned to sail as a child. The boat is now on show in the Naval Museum. Opposite the cathedral, the Mint was established in 1724; it still mints coins and medals.

★★ **Petropavlovskij sobor (Cathedral of St Peter and St Paul)** (AX) – The cathedral's golden spire is one of the city's other emblems. The church was designed by the architect Domenico Trezzini. Its interior decoration is worthy of a palace and includes a gilded carved wooden iconostasis in the form of a triumphal arch. The cathedral contains the tombs of the Romanov Czars, beginning with Peter the Great, most of them are of white Carrara marble. The remains of the last Czar, Nicholas II, the Czarina and their children, executed by the Bolsheviks on 17 July 1918, were transferred from Ekaterinburg (where they had been exhumed) to the cathedral on 17 July 1998. The funerals took place in the presence of the Russian president Boris Yeltsin.

Neva Gate – This gate leads to the landing-stage overlooking the river. Its Classical portico with a pediment is set on two rows of double columns. The gate offers a fine **view**★★ of the other river bank and the headland on Vasilyevsky Island.
In summer, the banks of the Neva along the town walls are used as a beach.

Trubetskoy Bastion – Many political prisoners lived or died in its sordid cells and dungeons. Among them were the tsarevich Alexis, Radishchev an opponent of Catherine II, the writer Dostoyevsky, Aleksandr Ulyanov, Lenin's elder brother and Maxim Gorky.

►► Kronwerk, a former armaments depot (AX), now houses the Museum of Artillery, Engineering and Signals. A spectacular deployment of weapons is exhibited. The courtyard contains cannon, guided missiles and armoured vehicles. A whole range of cutting and thrusting weapons to huge pieces of artillery are visible. The armoured car from which Lenin gave his historic speech on 3 April, 1917 in front of Finland Railway Station is parked here.

Domik P'etra (Peter's House) (BX) – *P'etrovskaja nab. 6.* Peter's House is a log cabin built in three days in May 1703. Peter the Great only stayed here during the summer that year. It comprises a study, dining room and bedroom complete with period furniture and personal effects.

★ **Krejser Avrora (Cruiser Aurora)** (BX) – The Cruiser Aurora is now part of the Naval Museum. It took part in the Russo-Japanese War of 1904-1905. On 25 October, 1917, at 9.45pm, a gunshot was fired giving the signal to attack the Summer Palace, then the seat of government.

MAIN MUSEUMS

★★★ **Ermitaž (Hermitage)** (AY) – The Hermitage is one of the world's most prestigious museums. Collections are displayed in five different buildings, the Winter Palace, the Little Hermitage, the Old Hermitage, the New Hermitage and the Hermitage Theatre.
In the Winter Palace, the main Carrara marble double-return staircase is known as the **Ambassadors' or Jordan Staircase**. Its stucco and gilding represent an introduction to the splendour of the rooms beyond. These include the Peter the Great Hall, designed by Montferrand, the great throne room with its splendid parquet flooring and white marble columns, the ballroom, the concert hall containing the solid silver reliquary of Alexander Nevsky and the malachite hall, a remarkable combination of gold chandeliers and green columns.
The collections cover art from all over the world from prehistoric times to the 20C. Western European art is especially well-represented, particularly the Italian School, with Leonardo da Vinci *(Benois Madonna* and *Litta Madonna)*, the Impressionists, with Monet, Cézanne, Degas, Renoir, and Van Gogh *(Les Arènes d'Arles)*, Matisse *(Music and Dance)*, and the Dutch School, with several works by Rembrandt (including the *Holy Family, Portrait of an Old Man in Red* and *The Return of the Prodigal Son*).

★★★ **Russkij Muzej (Russian Museum)** (BY M²) – This museum is housed in the former Michael Palace, a majestic Classical building with Corinthian portico designed by Carlo Rossi. The museum was set up by Czar Alexander III to counterbalance Moscow's Tretyakov Gallery. A remarkable **collection of icons** spans the 12C to the 17C with works from Novgorod, Pskov, Tver and Moscow. The Wanderers movement founded in 1870 as a reaction against traditional painting is well-represented by Vasily Perov, Nikolay Gay and Ivan Kramskoy. Their works highlighted social injustice and the abject poverty of the Russian masses.

★★ **Gosudarstvennyj muzej étnografii** (BY M³) – The National Ethnographic Museum includes reconstruction of traditional houses. It gives an insight into the extreme diversity of peoples, cultures and languages which once made up the former USSR.

ADDITIONAL SIGHTS

★★**Smol'nyj monastyr'** (CX) – The Smolny Monastery is a fine group of Baroque buildings designed by Rastrelli. The majestic Cathedral of the Resurrection has a brilliant blue façade which blends harmoniously with the white and gold columns, pilasters and onion domes. The interior is stark. The corners of the outbuildings are topped by lantern towers. The **Smolny Institute** next to the monastery was founded by Catherine II for young ladies of the nobility.

★**Nikol'skij morskoj sobor** (AZ) – The Church of St Nicholas, patron saint of seafarers can be seen from considerable distance. Its five golden domes soar above the blue and white bell-towers. It lies in the former mariners' district and was named after the patron saint of seafarers. Chevakinski, one of Rastrelli's pupils, built it at the request of Elizabeth Petrovna, Peter the Great's daughter. The church bears a distinct resemblance to Smolny Cathedral. It contains a splendid carved wooden iconostasis laden with gold decoration.

★**Letnij sad, letnij dvorec (Summer Palace and Gardens)** (BXY) – The gardens on the banks of the Neva opposite the Peter and Paul Fortress have a fine wrought-iron gate. Peter the Great had the gardens laid out in 1704 in the Versailles style. The modest Summer Palace contains the apartments of the Czar on the ground floor and those of his consort Catherine upstairs.

Marsovo pole (Field of Mars) (BY) – Military parades and reviews were once held on this vast Field of Mars. The monument's eternal flame commemorates those who fought in the Revolution. On the left towards the Neva stands the luxurious **Marble Palace**★ (Mramornyj dvorec) (BX), an annex of the Russian Museum.

Muzej-kvartira Dostojevskogo (Dostoyevsky Apartment Museum) (BY **M**[8]) – The great writer lived here from October 1878 until his death on 28 January, 1881. He wrote *The Brothers Karamazov* here.
A Kolkhoz covered market is held nearby.

EXCURSIONS

International hotels all have tourist offices selling tickets for day trips and guided tours.

★★★**Petrodvorec (Petrodvorets)** – *29km/18mi west. Access by train, departing from the Baltic Station (Baltiskij Voksal), and from May to September by hydrofoil, boarding in front of the Hermitage.*
In 1713, Peter the Great began work on the Fortress of Cronstadt on the Island of Kotlin. It was designed to protect the new city of St Petersburg. In order to keep track of the work, he had a small wooden house built on the Gulf of Finland. This formed the first modest core of the sumptuous imperial residence of Peterhof, renamed Petrovodrets (Stone Palace) in 1944. Inspired by Versailles, the residence consists of a large palace and a series of secondary buildings surrounded by a vast park decorated with ingenious waterfalls and fountains. J-B Leblond and Rastrelli, among others, worked on the Great Palace, with its richly-decorated rooms and galleries (including the throne room, Chinese study and Partridge Chamber). Behind the palace, decorated with numerous sculptures and fountains, is the grand **cascade**★★ (which Peter the Great himself helped to build). In the central basin stands a group of sculptures representing Sampson and the Dragon, commemorating Peter the Great's defeat of the Swedes at Poltava (symbolised by the dragon) on 27 June 1709, St Sampson's Day. At the foot of the grand cascade is the start of the maritime canal which opens into the Gulf of Finland.
To the right of the palace, **Monplaisir** shows the Czar's appreciation of the Dutch style. This pretty little country house served as a private residence. From his study, the Czar could gaze at the sea. The park reveals a little-known side of the Czar's personality, his love of jokes, and it is a good idea not to go too near some of the **fountains**★. The Czar must really have enjoyed seeing his courtiers showered with water.

★★★**Puškin (Tsarskoye Selo)** – *25km/15mi south. By train from Vitebs station (Vitebskij Voksal).*
The estate of Tsarkoïe Selo (Czar's Village), attributed to Peter the Great's wife, Catherine I in 1710, was a source of particular delight to his daughter Elizabeth and later Catherine II, the Great Catherine, both of whom contributed considerably to its splendour. However, the estate's name is mainly associated with the imperial high school, where Alexandr Pushkin was a pupil from 1812 to 1817, and it was renamed Pushkin in his honour in 1937. He loved the place so much that he returned to live there in 1831. Memorabilia of the famous writer can be seen in his datcha. The main body of the residence is the Catherine Palace, a masterpiece by Rastrelli (1752-1757), which has a richly decorated monumental façade 300m/984ft in length. The blue walls are interspersed with white columns and

Petrodvorets

pilasters topped with golden capitals. The interior is luxurious, with a grand staircase, ceremonial dining room with laid table and gilded walls, amber room and Alexander I's reception room. Towards the end of the 18C, the magnificent Rococo lines of the Cameron Gallery, Agatha Pavilion and frigidarium were remodelled by Charles Cameron in a more severe neo-Classical form.

The grounds, with their gardens, large lake and pavilions, are worth a visit.

★★ **Pavlosk** – *30km/18mi south.*

The last of the imperial residences stands on hunting grounds given by Catherine II to her son Pavel, later Paul I. With his wife, Maria Feodorovna, he made it his summer residence when he became Czar. A grand esplanade (Paul I liked military parades and his statue shows him in Prussian uniform) stands in front of the Great Palace designed by Charles Cameron and remodelled several times with the assistance of Carlo Rossi. The central building on a square plan is flanked on either side by arc-shaped colonnades surmounted by galleries. A tour of the interior reveals richly-decorated rooms, including the tapestry room, ceremonial library, and throne room.

The River Slavyanka flows through the landscaped gardens dotted with bridges, statues and pavilions.

★ **Novgorod** – *190km - 118 miles southeast.* The thousand-year-old town of Novgorod on the shores of Ilmen Lake is a major centre of Russian culture. Its main attraction is **St Sophia's Cathedral**★ set within the kremlin wall running along one bank of the River Volkhov. Like Kiev Cathedral, St Sophia's was inspired by the Byzantine Church in Constantinople. The west doorway or **Sigtuna Door** was brought back as a trophy from a Swedish fortress in 1187. It is one of the building's masterpieces. The oak panels are covered with bronze plaques depicting scenes from the Old and New Testaments.

To the south of St Sophia's, the huge **Russian Millennium Monument**' colossal statues recount centuries of Russian history.

Slovakia

Area: 49 035km²/1 893sq mi – **Population:** 5 310 000 – **Capital:** Bratislava – **Currency:** Slovak koruna – **Time:** GMT + 1hr in winter, GMT + 2hr in summer.

Slovensko

Slovakia is a mountainous land covered in forests. The great shield of the Carpathians reaches its highest peak in the country's High Tatra mountains (Gerlachovský štít 2 655m/8 711ft). In the west, cliffs overlook the Danube. The river plain is fertile and the sunny hillsides of the upper slopes covered in vines. Tributaries of the Danube cut large valleys through the mountains, facilitating road and rail communications. The country's population is concentrated along these routes. Heavy industry, a legacy of Communism, has transformed the formerly rural agricultural nation.

Slovakia's huge potential as a tourist destination is not fully exploited. The High Tatras and other mountain ranges offer countless possibilities for summer and winter holidays while the splendid woods and forests hide various wild animals. The spring waters wash down in numerous spa resorts.

The country's long history has left a remarkable architectural heritage. Slovakia has some of Europe's best preserved medieval towns such as Levoča and Bardejov. The manor houses of the old Hungarian nobility contrast with the picturesque medieval fortresses of Spišký hrad, Orava or Strečno. East Slovakia is one of Europe's most isolated regions, though its small capital Košice is busy and interesting Roman Orthodox wooden churches dot the countryside.

IN BRIEF

Entry Formalities – Valid passport for British and US citizens; visa for Canadian, Australian and Japanese citizens.

Souvenirs – Local embroidery, crystal and wooden items all are famous.

HISTORICAL NOTES

1C-3C Germanic tribes from West Slovakia threaten the Roman Empire. In AD 179-180, the legions advance northwards to **Trenčín** on the River Váh. An inscription engraved in the rock marks the spot where the fortress was built.

9C The short-lived **State of Great Moravia** brings together Slovaks and Czechs. Slovakia prospers. Meanwhile the missionaries **Cyril and Methodius**, two brothers called upon by Prince Rastilav, convert the region to Christianity. They introduce the Cyrillic alphabet and establish Slavic script.

906 The Magyars invade Moravia. After being separated from the Czechs, Slovakia remains under Hungarian rule for almost 1 000 years until 1918.

1240-41 The Tartar invasion lays waste to Hungary. In order to repopulate the country, the Hungarian rulers encourage the immigration of Germans. The German colony develops the mining industry and founds new towns.

1526 After the Turkish victory in **Mohacs** over Louis II of Hungary, Slovakia becomes the final outpost of Christianity in Europe. The Hungarian Court is established in Bratislava.

1792 A Bernolak founds the Slovak Society of Sciences in Trnava. Later patriots such as **L Stur** attempt to impose the Slovak language.

1848 The Hungarian government rejects demands of the new Slovak nationalist movement, quashing the 1848 revolution. Hungarian is confirmed as the official language. The Slovaks side in vain with Austria under the Habsburgs.

1867 The Hungarian government introduces Magyarisation. Extreme poverty leads to mass emigration to America.

1918 Czech leader Masaryk and emigré Slovak leaders sign the Pittsburgh Convention pledging to create one State uniting Czechs and Slovaks.

The first **Republic of Czechoslovakia** is proclaimed in Prague on 28 October 1918.

1939-45 A Slovak State places itself under the "protection of the (German) Reich".

1945 The Red Army liberates the country. A provisional Czechoslovakian government is formed in Kosice in East Slovakia. The Slovak State is overturned and Czechoslovakia restored.

1948 The communists seize power in Prague.

1968 Slovak **Alexander Dubček's** attempt to introduce socialism with a human face in the Prague Spring fails.

1989 The Slovak movement against violence joins forces with the Czech Civil Forum to overturn Communism. Dubček becomes President of the Czechoslovakian Parliament.

1992 Elections reveal major differences of opinion between the Czech and Slovak territories.

1993 Slovakia proclaims its sovereignty.

BRATISLAVA★★

Population 500 000
Michelin map 970 M5

Three major landmarks dominate Bratislava, formerly known as Pressburg: a **castle** with four towers high upon a rock, a **futurist bridge** commemorating the **Slovak National Uprising** (SNP) jutting upwards from its single leaning tower and **St Martin's Cathedral** on the Old Town's edge.

Bratislava's charm is found in the old town, easily visited on foot. This historic centre is interesting for its splendid Baroque palaces, its churches attracting large congregations and delightful squares built along the former city walls. Elsewhere, faceless suburbs and industrial regions spread along the two banks of the River Danube.

Bratislava has a current population of almost half a million people. Its political and cultural institutions make the city the undisputed capital of the new independent Slovakia.

★★**Hrad** – The **castle** stands on top of the final outcrop of the Carpathians overlooking the wide River Danube. Although rebuilt several times, its rectangular structure dates back to medieval times. The Baroque decoration was commissioned by Empress Maria Theresa in the second half of the 18C. Fire destroyed the castle in 1811, and it was only restored a few years ago to house the **National Museum's** historical collections.

The castle's ramparts, like the terraces and gardens surrounding the nearby **Parliament building**, offer brilliant **views**★★ of the city, the Danube and the surrounding plains. They also take in the futuristic SNP Bridge and the modern buildings of the suburb of Petrzalka on the river's right bank.

★★**Hlavné námestie** – Bratislava's former medieval market place with its Renaissance-style **Roland Fountain** now bears the hallmark of the 18C and 19C. The **café** at no 5 represents a masterpiece of Art Deco design. The most impressive building remains the old Town Hall with its huge tower. Its numerous architectural styles evoke the city's long history.

Opposite the town hall stands the Rococo-style **Kutcherfeld Palace** which now houses the French Embassy and Cultural Centre.

To the north lies **Františkánske námestie** (Franciscan Square). Its trees provide an almost rustic setting for the Jesuit Church. Not far away, the Rococo **Mirbach Palace**★ is a fine building. Two **rooms**★ are unusually decorated with more than 200 coloured engravings from the 17C and 18C. A narrow street runs alongside the Mestké múzeum (City Museum), leading from Hlavné Square to Primacialné Square. The **primate's palace** with its delightful **façade**★ is even more beautiful when floodlit at night. The Peace of Pressburg was signed here by Emperor Napoleon I and Emperor Francis I of Austria after the Battle of Austerlitz in December, 1805.

★**Michalská brána (St Michael's Gate)** – The last surviving gate from the city's old fortifications consists of a Gothic tower rebuilt in its Baroque style. On top stands a statue of St Michael 51m/167ft above the ground. Nearby, the Museum of Pharmacy is fascinating. South on Michalska Street then Venturska Street, delightful Baroque and Renaissance houses and palaces surround the miniature Gothic St Catherine's Chapel.

★**Dom sv. Martina (St Martin's Cathedral)** – Bratislava's Gothic Cathedral, dedicated to St Martin, dominates the south-west corner of the old town. It is separated from the hill up to the castle by the road that leads to the SNP Bridge. The architects of Vienna's St Stephen's Cathedral were involved in its design. up to 1830, the cathedral was used for the coronations of Hungarian monarchs.

★**U Dobrého Pastiera (Good Shepherd's House)** – This delightful Rococo house of the Good Shepherd, now the Clock Museum, sits at the foot of the steep hill leading up to the castle. It evokes the picturesque Jewish quarter which once lay between the castle and the cathedral. The charming, if dirty, neighbourhood was demolished to make way for the highway.

Hviezdoslavovo námestie – Many of the city's cultural institutions were built between the Old Town walls and the banks of the Danube. The National Theatre dating from 1886 stands at the eastern end of the tree-lined **Hviezdoslav Square**. This was one of the countless buildings constructed during the days of the Austro-Hungarian Empire by the Viennese architects Fellner and Helmer. Nearer the river, the neo-Classical **Reduta** was built in 1919. It houses the Slovak Philharmonic Orchestra. On the banks of the Danube, the **National Gallery★★** features works dating from the Middle Ages and the inter-war years of the first Republic of Czechoslovakia. Examples of this latter period include the bold brightly-coloured paintings depicting scenes of everyday life by Ludovit Fulla and Martin Benka.

EXCURSIONS

★**Devín** – *11km/7mi west.* The former Devín fortress perched on a rock overlooks the spot at which the River Morava flows into the Danube. This medieval fortress, a legacy of Celtic, Roman and Moravian strongholds, was even more impressive than Bratislava Castle. However Napoleon's troops reduced it to a pile of Romantic ruins in 1809.

★**The Little Carpathians** – Rows of vineyards stretch from the outskirts of Bratislava to the foot of the mountains. To the northeast, a string of wine-producing villages and small towns include **Sv. Jur** with its famous early Renaissance **altarpiece**, **Pezinok** with its delightful Museum of the Little Carpathians, and **Modrá**, famous for its pottery and wines.

★**Piešt'any** – *80km/48mi north.* On the way, take time out to visit **Trnava★**, the residence of the Hungarian primates during the years of the Turkish occupation. Piest'any lies on the banks of the River Váh. It is the wealthy rival of the Czech Republic's Western Bohemian spa resorts. Like those spas, Piest'any was at the peak of its popularity in the late 19C and early 20C. The **colonnaded bridge** adorned with a famous statue of a patient gleefully discarding his crutches leads to a large island. Most of the spa facilities are concentrated here.

Day-trip to Vienna – Hydrofoil services link Bratislava and Vienna in about 2hr 30 min. The trip takes in the sights along the banks of the Danube and the impressive **Fredenau Locks**. It also provides an opportunity to spend a day in the capital of the former Austro-Hungarian Empire.

CENTRAL SLOVAKIA

Michelin map 970 N 5

From the Danube's wide river plain, valleys of its major tributaries push northwards into a vast region of splendid plateaux and wooded mountains. This is the heart of Slovakia. People here preserved their language and identity despite one thousand 1 000 years of Hungarian rule. They speak pure Slovak. Castles stand proudly along the river valleys. A cluster of old towns made their fortune from the extraction of precious metals during the Middle Ages.

★**Banská Bystrica** – Silver and copper were mined from the early 13C. This wealth led to the construction of splendid middle-class houses lining the market square overlooking the River Hron. One of these houses with a magnificent Renaissance **sgraffito** façade is now the regional museum. At the square's northeast end beyond the large **clock tower**, the castle walls contain two churches and a row of towers.
Banská Bystrica became the nerve centre of the national Slovak uprising in August 1944. The nationalists staged attacks from the mountains within easy reach of the town. The Germans crushed the uprising after fierce fighting in late October. The highly original **SNP Memorial building** commemorates this heroic chapter of Slovakia's history.

★★**Banská Stiavnica** – Set against a delightful mountain backdrop far from the main road and rail routes, this is Slovakia's most fascinating old mining town. Copper, lead, silver and gold were mined using primitive techniques long before Germans arrived with new methods in the 13C. By the 18C, Banská Stiavnica had become the third largest city in the Hungarian Kingdom. The first powder guns were developed here at the world's first mining academy. Empress Maria Theresa granted the institution the status of university in 1770.
When the mining seams were worked out in the 19C, decline set in, but the town's steep streets and squares and fine middle-class dwellings have retained some of their Gothic and Romanesque walls. Banská Stiavnica also boasts both an **Old Castle** (Starý zámok) and a **New Castle** (Nový zámok). The latter served as an advanced position to ward off Turkish attacks. It now houses a museum retelling the story of this turbulent period. On another hilltop, the **Calvary Church** has a double bell-tower. The most interesting museum describing the town's mining history is the **Open-Air Museum** just outside the town.

★**Kremnica** – Like the other Slovak mining towns, Kremnica made its fortune out of gold and silver. The Royal Hungarian Mint was located here, guarded by a large castle. Today, Kremnica is no more than a large village. The sloping square is one of Slovakia's most beautiful. Its large memorial column honours victims of the plague. A restored Gothic manor houses the **Mint and Medal Museum**.

★ **Martin** – Martin is located in the middle of the wide fertile Turiec Valley. The River Turiec flows across the ski slopes and footpaths of the Great and Little Fatra mountains. For many years, Martin served as a stronghold of Slovak nationalism. Slovaks proclaimed independence from Hungary here in October 1918. The town was even considered as a potential capital for Slovakia, competing with Bratislava. Although the town is best-known today for its tank factory, it remains the home of the main Slovak cultural organisation, Matica Slovenská. Martin has a **National Museum** housing major collections of folk art and an **Open-Air Museum** representing a typical Slovak village.

Downstream, the River Váh has gouged out a deep wooded gorge through the Little Fatra Mountains. The site, overlooked by the romantic ruins of the two medieval castles **Stary Hrad** and **Strecno**★, was the scene of fierce fighting during the 1944 uprising.

The HIGH TATRAS

The **High Tatras** rise sharply from the valley floor up toward the highest peak in the Carpathians, Gerlachovský štít 2655m/8711ft. This is one of Europe's most picturesque mountain landscapes.

The High Tatras' granite ridge extends barely 26km/15.5 mi long. To the west stand the Western Tatras' rounded summits and to the east, the limestone peaks of the **White Tatras**. Almost one-fifth of the mountain range lies in Poland.

Splendid spruce forests cover the foot of the slopes. Higher, an occasional fir tree twisted by the wind dots the alpine pastures; further up, bare rock covers the mountain tops. Glaciers existed here during the Ice Age. They gouged out deep valleys now filled with lakes described as the eyes of the sea. Chamois, marmots, wolves and wild boar still are found in addition to a few bears and lynx.

In the early 19C, these mountains became the symbol of the Slovak nation. The national anthem begins with the words *Nad Tatrou sa blyska* – "Light comes from the Tatras." Tourism began to develop around 1870 when the great east-west railway was opened running through the old town of **Poprad**. The villas and hotels from this period convey the atmosphere of idle luxury characteristic of the turn of the century. The splendid scenic **road 537**★ links Podbanské and Stary Smokovec and runs through the national park. The area offers many opportunities for hiking.

Tourist facilities are concentrated in three main resorts, each offering excellent footpaths of varying length and difficulty. The westernmost and most modern resort is **Štrbské pleso**, built alongside a 20ha lake. World skiing championships are held here. To the east, the largest mountain resort **Starý Smokovec** has mineral springs which have been working since the late 18C. **Tatranská Lomnica** includes the **National Park Museum**. Its

J.-P. Courau/EXPLORER

Štrbské Pleso

cable cars carry visitors to **Skalnate pleso★★** and across a chasm to the summit of **Lomnickrý štít**, the second highest peak in the Tatras, at an altitude of 2 632m/8 636ft. A narrow-gauge railway runs between the resorts.
Most of the White Tatras has been turned into a nature reserve closed to the public. Beyond lies the village of **Ždiar**. With its old wooden farmhouses, this is Slovakia's best-preserved rural village. It is also one of the few to have resisted communist collectivisation and retain its traditional farm fields laid out in strips.

SPIS Region

Michelin map 970 O 5

Just east of the Tatras lies the Spis. German farmers and miners colonised this region in the 12C and 13C. They came at the invitation of the kings of Hungary. At one point, one-half of the towns were sold to Poland. But the region retained its Saxon character until the start of Magyarisation in the late 19C. Most of the (German-speaking) population was expelled at the end of the Second World War.
The region is teeming with fascinating reminders of the past. The town of **Levoča** is well preserved. **Spišsky hrad** was one of Europe's largest castles. **Spišská Nová Ves**'s long market street merits attention. So does **St Ladislas's Church** on the outskirts of **Spišsky Štvrtok. Poprad**, Gateway to the Tatras, has a lively main street, and St George's Church near **Spišská Sobota** contains an altarpiece engraved by the great Flamboyant Gothic sculptor, **Master Pavol**, a native of the region.

★★**Spišský hrad** – This immense ruin on a spur of limestone rock stands 200m/656ft above the road. It was built in the 12C and withstood the Tartar invasion. For many years the castle served as the Spis region's administrative centre. It was extended over the centuries before being abandoned in the 18C.
Near the castle lies the small fortified town of **Spišská Kapitula**. Its restored Romanesque cathedral was once the region's spiritual centre.

★★**Levoča** – Encircled by its walls, this is one of Slovakia's most attractive medieval towns. The maze of streets were laid out with no attempt at town planning. In 1271, the population chose it as the Spis regional capital. Levoca peaked in prosperity in the early 16C before a fire marked the start of a long period of decline. The main square bears the name of the town's most famous figure, the sculptor **Master Pavol** (or Paul), famous for his remarkable wood engravings. His high altar in St. James' Church, built between 1508 and 1517, is one of the world's largest. It portrays saints and disciples filled with grace, humanity and cheerfulness. Near the church in the centre of the square stands the splendid **Town Hall**. Originally Gothic, it was rebuilt in an exuberant Renaissance style after the fire of 1550. The square is surrounded by fine middle-class dwellings, one of which bears the name of Master Pavol. Another building is **Thurzo House**, a small Renaissance mansion created from the combination of two Gothic residences.
On the hilltop to the north of Levoča stands a 20C church which hosts one of Slovakia's largest pilgrimages in July.

★**Kežmarok** – This former German town (*Käsmark* meaning cheese market) sits at the foot of the Eastern Tatras. Its old walls and historic buildings are well preserved.
The two main streets cut across each other in front of the 18C town hall. Nearby, the **Church of the True Cross** has magnificent vaulting, wood engravings by Master Pavol, and a separate campanile with splendid sgraffito decoration. In the late 16C, the castle was transformed into a fine Renaissance residence by the Hungarian Count Thököly. Count Imre, a descendant of the Thököly dynasty, led a failed revolt against the Habsburg regime. He died in exile in Turkey in 1705. His remains were buried outside the old town in the remarkable neo-Byzantine **Lutheran Church**. Hungarian patriots still make pilgrimages here today. Nearby stands the early 18C **Evangelical Church** built entirely of wood by the Protestants who were forbidden to use stone or build within the city walls. The church now houses a museum.

Slovenia

Slovenija

Area: 20 226km²/7 686sq mi. – **Population:** 1.9 million – **Capital:** Ljubljana – **Currency:** tolar – **Time:** GMT + 1hr in winter, GMT + 2hr in summer – **Formalities:** valid passport.

Slovenia is a typical Central European country resembling Austria. Only along the coast can one detect an Italian, especially Venetian, influence. The country's many styles of European architecture fit well into the magnificent natural surroundings. The Catholic influence gave rise to numerous churches, including two Gothic Cistercian abbeys, **Sticna**★ and **Kostanjevica**★. The Baroque style, which was once a symbol of the resistance to the Protestant influence, has left a large legacy. Many charming villages evoke the past. Historic cities include **Celje, Skofja Loka, Kranj, Ptuj** and **Novo Mesto**, all surrounded by Alpine forests. By way of contrast, the coastal cities of Piran and Koper are Mediterranean. The churches and palaces in the historic town centres show a strong Venetian influence.

The JULIAN ALPS

Triglav marks the highest part of the Julian Alps at 2 863m/9 390ft. Snow covers the peaks of the mountainous Alpine geography all year round. A small glacier tops the summit of Triglav, a national park. Seven lakes vary in altitudes between 1 340m/4 395ft to 1 805m/5 920ft. Chamois and eagles are the only inhabitants of the high peaks, while the mountainsides are covered by conifer forests. The ski resort of **Kranjska gora** is located here.

★★BLEJSKO JEZERO (BLED LAKE) Michelin map 970 L 6

The 2 130m - 6 986ft long glacial lake sits on a plateau at 475m - 1 558ft. A castle built in the 11C on a rock overlooks the lake. The German emperor gave it to the Brixen archdiocese. The castle was rebuilt many times,it is now open to the public. An island in the middle of the lake houses the Baroque church **Sveta Marija na Jezeru** (Our Lady of the Lake) and a 11C Slavic necropolis. Above the deep forests surrounding the lake, the snowy peaks of the Alps pierce the clouds. The resorts played host to last century's aristocratic elite. They still do not interfere with the natural beauty of the landscape.

★★BOHINJSKO JEZERO (BOHINJ LAKE)

A glacier carved out this 4.1km - 2.5 mile long, 1.2km - 0.7 mile wide lake. It lies in a depression at the heart of the Julian Alps. In certain areas, the mountain slopes seem to plunge right into the water. In the west, the small River Savica reappears at the other side under a different name, Sava Bohinjka. This rare phenomenon accounts for the lake water's freshness and transparency. Hotel construction has been limited in order to avoid destroying the lake's magnificent mountain panorama.

The KARST Region

The countryside at the back of the Trieste Gulf has become part of the geological terminology. Karstic reliefs are thick calcareous formations resulting from water erosion, often underground. The landscape is almost completely treeless, riddled with hundreds of caverns and crevasses, as well as an underground network of galleries and lakes.

★★SKOCJAN JAME (SKOCJAN Caverns)

The Skocjan Caverns (along the road connecting Ljubljana to Koper), are listed as part of UNESCO's world heritage. Underground streams from the River Reka have gouged out a gallery and formed stalactites and stalagmites. Rushing through narrow gorges and cataracts, the foaming waters finally plunge into subterranean chasms. This universe served as a refuge for prehistoric man. Scientists have discovered a network of caves and chasms, some of which are several hundred meters deep.

★★★POSTOJNSKA JAMA (POSTOJNA Caverns)

The Postojna Caverns (45km/27mi southeast of Ljubljana) are among Europe's most fascinating geological formations. Their subterranean cavities were formed by the River Pivka, which continues through a third underground gorge. The deep gallery stretches more than 23km/14mi, with several enormous caves along the

way. Only 8km/5mi are open to visitors. A large hall 120m/393ft long, known as the Great Dome, is covered with stalagmites and stalactites whose fantastic shapes range from massive columns to lacy calcareous formations. An indigenous species of animal known as Proteus Anguineus lives in the darkness of the underground water.
At **Predjamski grad★**, a medieval castle, firmly anchored in the rock facing the cavern entrance, today houses a collection of prehistoric objects.

S. Marmounier/VISA

Medieval castle in Predjamski grad

LIPICA

This little village near Trieste in Italy formerly known as Lipizza owes its fame to its 400-year-old **stud farm★★**, which was the origin of the prestigious Lipizzaner breed of horses. In 1580, Archduke Charles of Austria decided to found a stud farm at Lipizza to be responsible for the breeding and rearing of the famous horses of the Spanish Riding School of Vienna. These magnificent white horses are born grey, bay or chestnut and only get the brilliant white coats for which they are famous when they are between four and ten years of age *(see Michelin Green Guide Vienna)*. Characterised by intelligence, grace, agility and robustness, they are considered the best saddle and parade horses in the world and are given special care.

LJUBLJANA★★

Population 250 000
Michelin map 970 L 6

The Slovenian capital resembles a typical Central European city, with well-planned streets, elegant buildings in the Baroque style, and an aristocratic atmosphere. The Romans founded the colony of Emona here in 34 BC due to a geographical position at the crossroads of several natural routes, especially the route that linked Pannonia to the Alps. The layout of the medieval town followed the curve of the River Ljubljancica. The counts of Carniola constructed their castle on the river's rocky spur. Other houses were built at the foot of the castle and along the river banks. In the 18C, the town ramparts were destroyed as Ljubljana expanded.

Right Bank

★**Ljubljanski grad** – First built in the 12C and formerly the town stronghold, Ljubljana Castle has been rebuilt many times over the centuries. A fine **panorama** of the city unfolds from the castle.

★**Sveti Jakob** – St Jacob's church stands at the foot of the castle. Once the parish Church of the oldest quarter in the town, it later belonged to the Jesuits. The interior is richly decorated, with a marble altar, stucco, and remarkable paintings in *trompe-l'œil*.
The church stands at the beginning of a street, formerly a trade route, that widens into the funnel-shaped Mestni Trg Square.

★★ **Mestni Trg** – This square, lined with Baroque and neo-Classical town houses, dominates the city centre.
Several buildings and monuments evoke interest. The 15C **Magistrat**★ (Corporation Palace) was remodelled in the Baroque style by the architect Georg Macek. He designed the porch and arcades of the inner courtyard. Italian sculptor Francesco Robba completed the **Carniola Rivers Fountain**★★. His works can be seen throughout Slovenia and in Croatia. Painter and architect Andrea Pozzo built the **Sv. Nikola Cathedral**★★★ (St Nicholas) in 1701 in the Baroque style. Giulio Giulio's wall paintings decorate the rich interior with its magnificent organs. Not far away stand the **Episcopal Palace**★ and **Seminary**★. The latter's Baroque portal leads to a library sumptuously decorated with 18C mural paintings.

Left Bank

Starting in the Middle Ages, the city expanded to the other side of the River Ljubljanica. Today several bridges connect the two parts of the town.

Churches – **St Francis' Church**★ (Franciskanska cerkev) was built in 1660 and boasts a Baroque façade in the typically Jesuit style. The façade and interior of the **Church of the Ursulines**★ date from 1726 and were designed following the best examples of the Classical style. The **Krisanke**★★, a charming Baroque church of the Crusades order, was erected in 1707 in a circular shape, designed by the Venetian architect Domenico Rossi.

★ **National Museum** – The museum houses a rich archeological collection as well as other exhibits of anthropology and natural history. A visit to the **National Gallery**★ provides a complete history of Slovenian art, which produced a very interesting variation on European Impressionism.

Spain

Area: 505 000km^2/191 900sq mi – **Population:** 39 million – **Capital:** Madrid – **Currency:** peseta and Euro (166 386 ESP) – **Time:** GMT + 1hr in winter, GMT + 2hr in summer

España

Spain sits on the extreme southern tip of Europe. The country projects a strong personality with varied landscapes: the turquoise waters of rocky inlets along the Costa Brava, vast stretches of land scorched by the sun of Castile, the green hills of Asturia, the desert of Almeria, the snows of the Pyrenees and the Sierra Nevada. The same diversity characterises the culture, the gastronomy, the folklore and the rich artistic and architectural heritage. With its southern shores less than 15km-9.3 miles from North Africa, Spain enjoys a unique position in Europe.

IN BRIEF

Entry Formalities – Valid passport for British, US, Canadian, Australian and Japanese citizens.

Shopping – Stores are generally open from 9.30am or 10.30am to 1.30pm and from 4.30 to 8.00pm. More and more businesses are remaining open at midday, and even on Saturday afternoons. Most are closed on Sundays. In summer, it is not unusual to find shops in tourist areas open until 10pm or 1am.

Daily schedules – Generally speaking, morning *(mañana)* lasts until 2pm, time for lunch *(almuerzo or comida)*. After eating, it is siesta time. The real afternoon *(tarde)* begins around 5pm. Toward 8pm, cocktails mark the start of evening *(noche)* festivities. Dinner *(cena)* is served from 9pm, and can last well into the night.

Bars – An aperitif *(chateo)*, is a well-established tradition that includes a glass of wine *(vino)* and a variety of tapas, small dishes to nibble on such as olives, squid, or potato crisps with mayonnaise. Beer *(cerveza)* may be found on draught *(caña)* or in bottles *(botella)*. *Sangría*, a red wine-based punch with macerated fruit, is also drunk with tapas.

Detendia/IMAGES PHOTOTHÈQUE

Bullfights – Love them or hate them, the *corrida* is a fact of life in Spanish culture.
Tauromachy, or bullfighting, was on horseback from the Middle Ages to the 18C, only later did it become a popular spectacle performed on foot. Today's rules for bullfighting were established during the 18C and 19C.
Fighting bulls are reared in almost total freedom on vast properties in Andalucia and Castile. They are tested for their fighting ability in *tientas*, tests of bravery, at the age of two.
The corrida begins at 5pm and consists of six kills by three *matadores* (the verb *matar* means to kill). The programme opens to the strains of a paso doble with the *paseo*, or grand entry of the toreros led by two *alguaziles* (servants of the president of the corrida) on horseback and in 17C costume. Each of the three *matadores* in glittering costume marches in front of his *cuadrilla* (team). The combat *(lidia)* has three acts *(tercios)*, heralded by trumpets.
Act One is for observing the bull. The famous swirling figures with red capes appear and the *picadores* on their caparisoned horses await the bull's charge to thrust a lance into its withers, the knotted muscles above the shoulder bones. During Act Two, the *banderilleros* plant their *banderillas* (beribboned sticks with a harpoon-like tip) to arouse the animal. The kill is reserved for Act Three, a true ceremonial which begins with skilful use of the *muleta*, a length of scarlet serge bound to a stick. The *estocada* marks the final moment when the matador thrusts his sword between the bull's shoulder blades. If he has fought with valour, he may be rewarded with one ear, perhaps even two, and sometimes the tail of the bull.

Religious Festivals – Each region has its own traditions. All are high in colour. Those celebrated throughout Spain are Epiphany, Corpus Christi and Holy Week. In Sevilla, this major occasion features a long procession of penitents.

Local Folklore – From the gypsy and Arab-inspired flamenco in Andalucia, the *jota* in Aragon, the *sardana* in the Catalonia and Levante regions to the *seguidilla* in Castile, each part of Spain is coloured by the dances and music.

ISLAS BALEARES

Balearic Islands

Michelin map 971 H 9

The Balearic Archipelago covers an area of 5 000 km²/1 900sq mi. It includes three major islands – Majorca, Minorca and Ibiza – two smaller ones – Formentera and Cabrera – and a number of little islets. The Balearic Autonomous Community is one of the 50 Spanish provinces, with its administrative capital in Palma de Mallorca.

★★★MALLORCA (Island of MAJORCA)

Area 3 640km²/1 383sq mi – Population 602 074

Majorca is the largest of the Balearic islands. Its magnificent landscapes, mild climate and considerable hotel capacity place it among the favoured European tourist destinations.

★★Palma de Mallorca

The traveller arriving in Palma by boat discovers the city spread out around a wide bay. Its proud cathedral watches over a city whose glorious maritime history is reflected in many of its ancient monuments.

Sheltered by the Puig Major chain from the north and west winds, the bay of Palma enjoys a delightfully mild climate year-round.

When it was liberated after the battle of 31 December 1229, the city was known as **ciutat de Mallorca**. It soon experienced prosperity, maintaining constant relations with Barcelona, Valencia, Africa and Northern Europe. A Jewish colony was set up, and the Genoese had their own stock exchange. James II (Jaime II) and his successors graced the city with its most beautiful Gothic buildings.

Today, Palma is home to over half the inhabitants of Majorca. Travellers are more numerous than anywhere else in Spain. Most of the tourist activity is centred around the Terreno, in the western part of the city, and the Cala Major. The real heart of Palma is nonetheless the Passeig des Born.

Ch. Bowman/SCOPE

The cathedral, Palma de Mallorca

★★**Cathedral** – The strikingly elegant forms of the cathedral rise majestically above the seafront, its high buttresses surmounted by pinnacles. The Santany limestone used in its construction lends vivid colours varying with the time of day: ochre, golden and pink.

Begun early in the 14C on the site of a former mosque, the cathedral is one of the major achievements in the late Gothic style.

★★★The Rocky coast

The west coast of Majorca is dominated by the Tramuntana limestone barrier whose highest peak, Puig Major, rises to 1 436m/4 710ft. The wild mountainous landscapes, softened only by tender green pine forests, drop dramatically into the turquoise depths of the sea below.

From Palma to Sóller – Beautiful beaches are punctuated by seaside resorts. From Andratx to Sóller, the **cliff road★★★** offers amazing viewpoints, as does the **mirador Ricardo Roca★★** and **Ses Animes★★**.

From Sóller to Alcúdia – The most impressive stretch is the **Sa Calobra road★★★**. Descending a dizzying 900m/2 952ft in only 14km/8.5mi, the spectacular road sweeps down toward the Mediterranean amid a maze of jagged rocks chiselled by time into strange forms. The desolate landscape is dominated by Puig Major. **Sa Calobra★** is a tiny seaside village on the rocky coastline visited by pleasure boats from Puerto de Soller. Before reaching **Cap Formentor★**, the northernmost tip of the island, stop at the **belvedere Es Colomer★★★** and enjoy a view of the rocky promontories plunging into the sea.

★★The East coast and its caves

This part of the island is known for its caves (*coves* or *cuevas* in Castilian). They make popular destinations for excursions out of Palma.

★★★**Coves del Drach** – This cavern was explored in 1896 by the speleologist Edouard Martel. Four chambers with translucent pools reflecting their abundant concretions stretch over 2km/1.2mi. The amazing vaulted roofs are hung with a multitude of needle-like icicles. The Martel lake chamber has been converted into an amphitheatre for a final musical interlude.

★★★**Coves d'Arta** – Largely carved in large part by the sea into the cape closing Canyamel Bay, this magnificently situated cave can be reached by a cliff road. The monumental mouth overlooks the sea 35m/115ft below. It is remarkable for its vast vaulted chambers.

★★MENORCA (ISLAND OF MINORCA)

Area 668km²/254sq mi – Population 65 109

Minorca is the most northerly and second largest of the Balearic islands. Its 189km/117mi of coastline have largely been protected from excessive development. The island remains a stranger to the major tourist flows. Yet this windswept plateau, with its landscapes that seem shaped by the mists of the Atlantic, has a melancholy charm. Its vegetation is typically Mediterranean. The pine forests and wild olive trees, their tormented lines betraying harsh treatment by the north wind, are punctuated by bushes of lentiscus, rosemary, heather, camomile and thyme.
Ciutadella★, once the capital of the island, has a special charm due to its peaceful lifestyle, pure air and the atmosphere of the old town and port.

★IBIZA Area 572km²/217sq mi – Population 74 001

The White Island of Ibiza lies 45 nautical miles southwest of Majorca and 52 miles from the peninsula.
Its shining white stucco walls, roof terraces, winding narrow streets and the feeling of a Greek island create an atmosphere quite unlike any other in the Balearics.

★EIVISSA (IBIZA)

Discover the luminous beauty of the town of Ibiza and its **site★★** from the sea. Otherwise, the road of Talamanca *(3km/1.8mi to the northeast)* offers a lovely view. The city sits on a hill that drops to the sea; explore the old walled quarter and the marina near the port, the most animated part of town.
The **upper town★**, reached by way of the Puerta de las Tablas, is surrounded by 16C walls built under Emperor Charles V. It was the heart of the old city, and still retains a charming rustic, medieval character.

The chapter on Practical Information at the end of the guide lists:
festivals and other seasonal events,
official tourist offices,
tips on getting around Europe,
advice for panning seaside or mountain holidays,
useful addresses for travellers,
eating habits in different countries,
suggested reading.

BARCELONA★★★

Population 1 681 132
Michelin map 970 H 8

Capital of Catalonia and the second-largest city in Spain, Barcelona stretches along the shores of the Mediterranean between the hills of Monjuïc, Vallvidrera and Tibidabo. One of its principal attractions is its rich architectural heritage.

The early City – The Phocaeans founded the city. It grew during the Roman era and was known during the 1C BC as Barcino. The Romans settled on Mount Taber, where the cathedral now stands, and, beginning in the 3C, built fortified walls. In the 12C, Barcelona controlled most of the former Catalan earldoms, becoming the capital of Catalonia and seat of the Catalonia-Aragon confederation, as well as a major trade centre. Its influence extended to a great part of the Mediterranean. This was the apogee of Catalan Gothic and the city spilled out beyond its walls.
At the time of the Spanish War of Succession (1701-1714), Catalonia took the side of the Archduke of Austria. Following the triumph of the Bourbons (11 September 1714), Barcelona lost its municipal government and its time-honoured freedoms. Montjuïc Hill was fortified and a citadel, La Ciutadella, constructed. The people of Barcelona were forbidden to build within 2km/1.2mi around the walls, a radius corresponding to cannon range. The city therefore grew upward inside the ramparts, with the population becoming incredibly dense. The building ban was only lifted in the 19C. The decision was then taken to urbanize the no man's land around the old city. In just 30 years, Barcelona expanded and engulfed neighbouring villages such as Gràcia, Sants, Horta, Sarrià, and Pedralbes. With the industrial revolution, it became one of the most active cities in Europe, hosting two universal expositions, one in 1888 (on the site of the Ciutadella) and the other in 1929 on Monjuïc. Modernist architecture flourished.

Barcelona Today and Tomorrow – More dynamic than ever, Barcelona is a major industrial centre with a busy port as well as a university campus, the seat of the Generalitat de Catalonia and a large cultural complex with a number of museums, theatres, opera houses and concert halls.
The 1992 Olympic Games provided an occasion for large-scale urbanisation projects. One part of the seafront, formerly a warehouse area, was reconstructed next to the Olympic village. A ring road was constructed around the city and a pleasure-boat harbour replaced the industrial fishing port.

LIVING IN BARCELONA

For a real taste of the unique atmosphere of Barcelona, begin with a stroll on the Ramblas and the Passeig de Gràcia, the most typical avenues, and wander through the maze of narrow streets in the Gothic district.

Cafés and Restaurants – For the best restaurants, consult the Michelin Red Guide España Portugal. Eixample has a great number of restaurants and cafés, some of which are decorated in the modernist style, while others are avant-garde. In the Gothic quarter and near the port, restaurants are more traditional. Unpretentious little restaurants in Barceloneta serve paella and seafood and have become popular due to their proximity to the sea.

Shopping – The most elegant fashion, furniture design and antique shops are found on and around the Passeig de Gràcia, Rambla de Catalunya and the Diagonal on both sides of Plaça Joan Carles I. Another major shopping area lies beyond the Plaça de Catalunya, with the Corte Inglés department store. Avenida Portal de l'Angel houses another department store, Galerias Preciados. The Ramblas also has good shopping.

Entertainment – Barcelona boasts a famous concert hall, the Palau de la Mùsica Catalana (**MV**), as well as many theatres and cinemas. The **Liceu** (**LY**), specialised in operas, is to be rebuild after the fire that destroyed it in January 1994. To find out what's on, consult the *Guía de Ocio*, on sale at all newstands.

Amusement Parks – The city has two well-known amusement parks, one on **Montjuïc** hill, reached by cable-car from the port, and the other on **Tibidabo**, offering a vast **panoramic view**★★ from its altitude of 532m/1 745ft, over Barcelona, the Mediterranean and the interior. It is accessible by road, and by a funicular served by trams and buses.

Transportation – Yellow and black taxis abound, but those who like public transport will appreciate the four subway lines which serve most city districts. Passes are available for 10 trips. The city also has an extensive bus network.

Catalan Identity – Barcelona is a Catalan city: this means that Catalan is considered an official language alongside Castilian Spanish. Franco forbade the use of Catalan. Today, a short stroll will reveal the extent to which street names and signs are written in Catalan, and a look into bookshop windows will show the same revival of its literature.
Barcelona has always been a thriving centre for artists. Among them are: the painters Picasso, Miró, Dali, Tàpies, the sculptor Suborachs, and the architects Gaudí, Josep Lluis Sert, Bofill and Bohigas.

★★BARRI GOTIC (THE GOTHIC QUARTER)

Though rich in monuments of the 13C and the 15C, this area is actually much older. Vestiges remain of the Roman city as well as of the great walls built in the 4C after a Barbarian invasion.

Plaça Nova (**MX 128**) – This is the heart of the Gothic quarter. Two towers flanking the western gate are all that remain of the 9m/30ft – high rectangular fortifications built by the Romans. As the city expanded in the Middle Ages, the gateway was converted into a residence and covered with additions that served no defensive purpose.
Opposite the cathedral, notice the modern façade of the college of architects. It stands out singularly among the much older buildings and is decorated with a concrete band engraved by Picasso.

★★**Cathedral** – The present cathedral, dedicated to St Eulalia and the Holy Cross, was built on the site of a Romanesque church. Begun at the end of the 13C, it was only completed in 1450. The façade and spire are from the 19C.
The interior is in the Catalan Gothic style, and has a sense of great elevation due to the delicate, slender pillars.

★★**Plaça del Rei** (**MX 149**) – The royal palace here includes the Talaia, or **mirador del Rei Marti** (**K**), a tall five-storey tower and the **salon del Tinell** (**C**) (credence chamber), a former refectory whose six Roman arches support a wooden ceiling with a span of 17m/56ft. The **Chapel of St Agatha** (**F**) or Agueda exemplifies the purest Catalan Gothic style. It houses the reredos of the Constable or of the Epiphany, by Jaime Guguet. On the square's other side stands the palace of the viceroys of Catalonia. This Renaissance construction contains the regional archives, and the Padellàs house, a museum on the history of the city.

★**Museu Frederic Marès** (**MVX M²**) – This museum is a gift to the city from the sculptor Frederic Marès. Its collections are especially well endowed in polychrome wood statues, and provide an excellent illustration of the diversity in Spanish art. They are found on three levels:

Crypt: stone sculpture, Romanesque and Gothic capitals, Romanesque portals, including an unusual primitive doorway from the 12C Tubilla del Agua monastery.

Ground floor: Impressive **collection**★ of crucifixes and calvaries in polychrome wood (12C-13C)

First floor: Note the 16C **Entombment**★, composed of six separate figures, and the **Vocation of St Peter**★, a 12C marble by the master Cabestany.
The second section of the museum or **museu sentimental** has more than 50 collections of everyday objects.

★LA RAMBLA

The best-known and most lively street in Barcelona borders the Gothic quarter, and follows an old river bed. It runs between the Plaça Portal de la Pau near the port, with its monument to Christopher Columbus, and Plaça de Catalunya, which separates Eixample from the old quarter.

★★**Drassanes** (**MY**) –The old naval shipyards (*atarazanas* in Castilian, or *drassanes* in Catalan) are close to the **Christopher Columbus monument** erected in 1886. They consist of 10 sections. Seven date from the 14C and the three on the Rambla side from the 17C. Together they form a series of arches supporting the long roof and provide an ideal setting for a maritime museum.

★**Museu Marítim** – The history of the Catalan navy, with a collection of figureheads and miniature ships.

★★**Plaça Reial** (**MY**) – This vast pedestrian square surrounded by neo-Classical buildings dates from 1848 to 1859. It is beautifully shaded by palm trees and bordered by cafés. The fountain in the centre is flanked by lamp posts designed by Gaudi.

BARCELONA

Bacardi (Pas) .... MY 4
Banys Nous .... MX 7
Bergara .... LV 10
Bisbe Irurita .... MX 15
Bòria .... MV 18
Born (Pas. del) .... NX 20
Boters .... MX 23
Canaletes (Rambla de) .... LV 27
Canonge Colom (Pl.) .... LY 28
Canvis Vells .... NX 32
Caputxins
(Rambla dels) .... MY 35
Cardenal Casañas .... LX 36
Catalunya (Pl. de) LV
Catedral (Av. de la) .... MV 40
Ciutat .... MX 43
Comercial (Pl.) .... NV 45
Cucurulla .... LX 55
Doctor Joaquim Pou .... MV 61
Escudellers .... MY
Estudis (Rambla dels) LX
Francesc Cambó (Av.) .... MV 79
Garriga i Bach .... MX 81
Isabel II (Pas d') .... NX 98
Montcada .... NV 122
Montjuïc del Bisbe .... MX 123
Nou de Sant Francesc .... MY 126
Nova (Pl.) .... MX 128
Paradis .... MX 133
Pi (Pl. del) .... LX 137
Pintor Fortuny .... LX 140
Portal de Santa
Madrona .... MX 142
Ramon Berenguer
el Gran (Pl. de) .... MX 147
Rei (Plaça del) .... MX 149
Sant Felip Neri (Pl.) .... MX 163
Sant Josep (Rambla de) .... LX 168
Sant Miquel (Pl. de) .... MX 173
Sant Sever .... MX 181
Santa Anna .... LV 182
Santa Maria (Pl.) .... NX 189
Santa Mònica
(Rambla de) .... MY
Seu (Pl. de la) .... MX 192
Tapineria .... MX 193
Universitat
(Ronda de la) .... LV 199

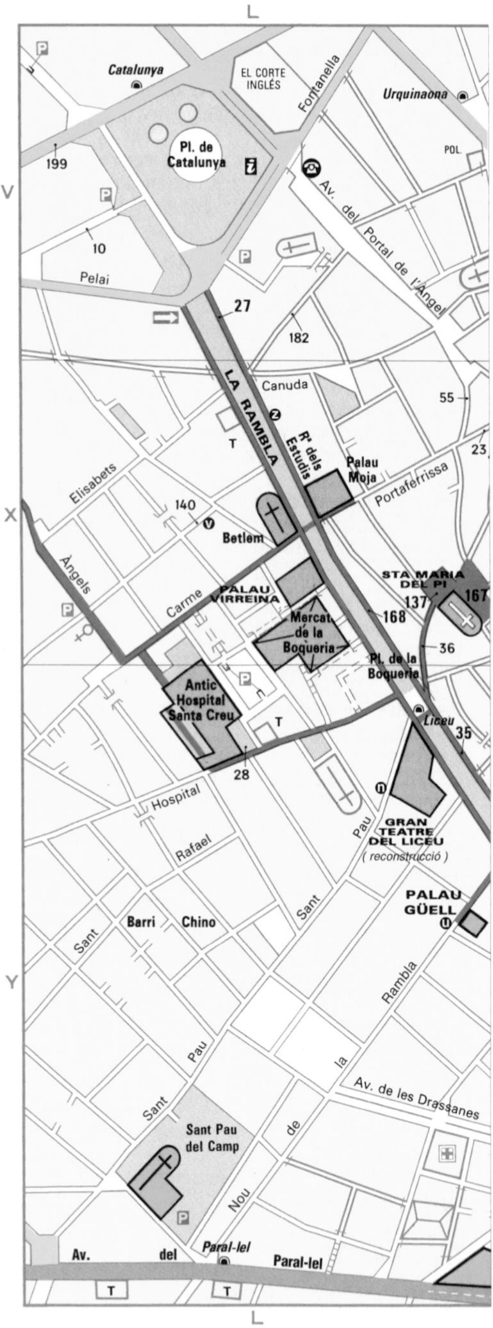

A Casa de l'Ardiaca
B Casa dels Canonges
C Saló del Tinell
E Palau del Lloctinent
F Capella Sta-Agueda
G Duana Nova
H Ajuntament
K Mirador del Rey Marti
L Col. legi d'Arquitectes
M1 Museu d'História de la Ciutat
M2 Museu Frederic Marès
M3 Museu de Cera
M7 Castell dels tres Dragons, Museu Zoologia
M12 Museu Barbier-Mueller d'art precolombí
M13 Museu Geologia
M16 Palau del Marquès de Liò (Museu Textil i de la Indumentária)
M17 Museu del Calçat
M20 Convento de Santa Mònica
N Casa Pia Almoina
S Palau Marc
V Casa de la Canonja

On the other side of La Rambla is the **Barrio chino** (LY), famous for its bars frequented by dubious characters and now in the process of renovation. Some of the streets are still to be avoided.

★★ **Museu d'Art Contemporáni de Barcelona** – This monumental building forms part of the Barri Chino development. Designed by the American architect Richard Meyer, its large white rooms make a perfect setting for the permanent **collection**★ illustrating the artistic movements of the last 50 years with particular emphasis on the Catalan contribution and foreign trends which have most influenced artistic expression in Catalonia.

The **Palau Güell**★★ (LY) (1888) in the Carrer Nou de Rambla is a theatre museum, and a Gaudi construction, interesting for its interior architecture and furnishings. Going further up the Rambla, on the left is the façade of the **Gran Teatre del Liceu**★ opera house (LY) (1845). Before the fire of 1994 it was reputed to be one of Europe's finest concert halls. Its reconstruction is a matter of priority.

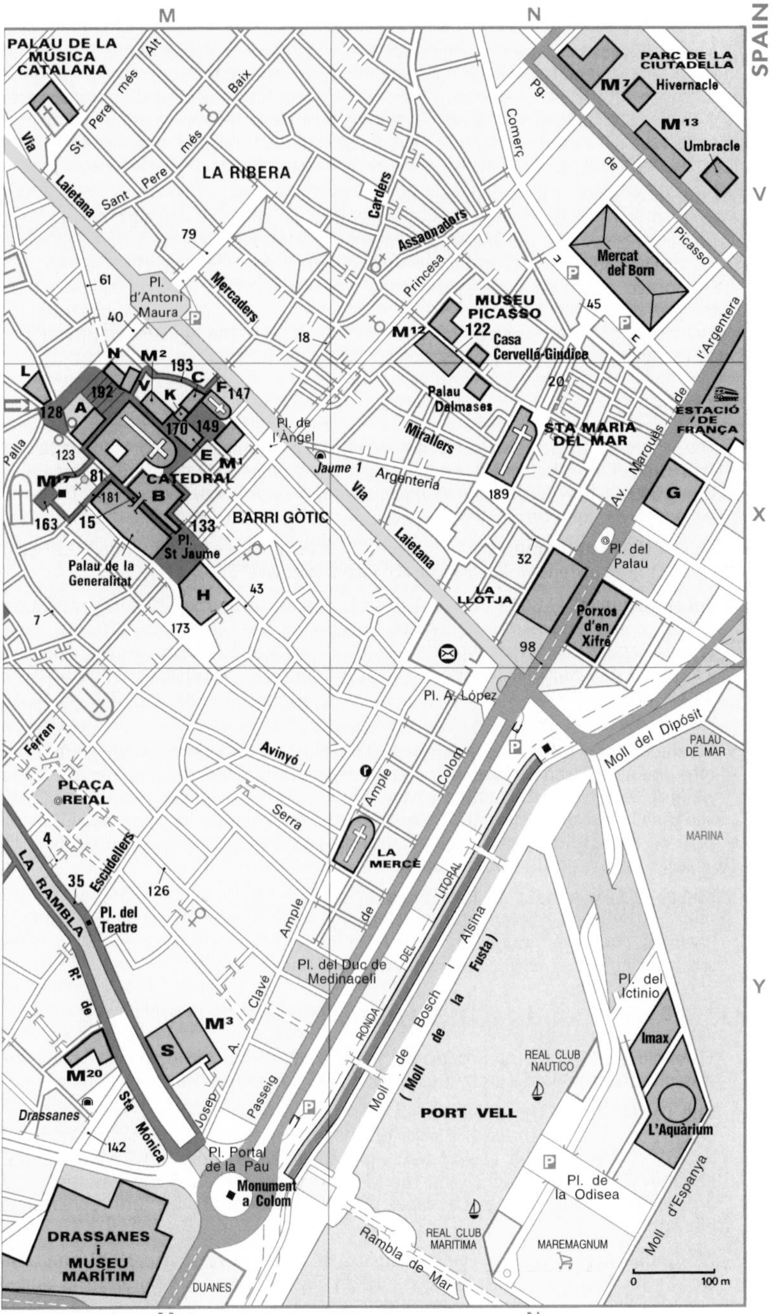

★★CARRER DE MONTCADA (NV 122)

East of the Gothic quarter, this street in the Ribera district owes its name to the powerful Montcada family, and is bordered by Gothic homes once reserved for the aristocracy and later, the wealthy bourgeoisie. Some of the mansions are open to the public. Behind their smooth façades, narrow patios keep with the pure lines characteristic of medieval Catalan architecture. On one side, a single flight of stairs supported by a rising arch leads to the first floor which, in many homes, is graced by a gallery of delicate arches.

Among these little palaces with their lovely patios, note in particular that of 15C Berenguer de Aguilar, now housing the Picasso Museum, the 14C Palau des Marqués de Llio which holds the Museum of Textiles and Costumes, the 17C Palau Dalmases at no 20 and the 16C Cervello House at no 25 with a beautiful stairway, now home to the Maeght Gallery.

★**Museu Picasso** (NV) – The museum is set in the magnificent Gothic palaces of Berenguer de Aguilar and the Baron de Castellet. Most of Picasso's works are dedicated to his friend Sabartès. They include several portraits. His remarkable engravings of bullfights and his ceramic work, a series of vases, dishes and plates date from the 1950s. Jacqueline Picasso donated them. Note the ***Las Meninas***★ series of 58 oil paintings, 44 of which were inspired by the work of Velázquez.

★★**Church of Santa María del Mar** (NX) – This church is one of the most beautiful examples of Catalan Gothic. Sailors from the neighbourhood built it in the 14C. Despite their modest means, they wanted to rival the bourgeois financing the building of the cathedral. The result was this elegant yet simple church. The walls are unadorned, in the Catalan style, and the façade is enlivened only by the gable over the portal and two buttresses framing the great 15C Flemish Gothic **rose window**★. The **interior**★★★ lends a sense of great harmony due to the high nave and the side aisles separated from it only by slender octagonal pillars.

★MONTJUÏC

The Mountain of the Jews lies south of the city, overlooking the port from a height of 213m/699ft. Barcelona's residents built a fort when they rebelled against Philip V in 1640. It now houses a military museum. A superb **view** looks down from the terraces over the port.

★★★**Museu d'Art de Catalunya** – The former National Palace built for the 1929 exhibition houses extensive **Romanesque and Gothic collections**★★★.

★**Poble Espanyol** – Built for the 1929 exposition, this large village reconstitutes typical streets and plazas of various Spanish regions. One passes from a small Castilian square to the all-white street of an Andalusian village resplendent with geraniums or a Mudéjar tower of Aragon. Restaurants, old pharmacy and perfume shops, and traditional craftsmen complete this miniature vision of a most picturesque Spain.

★★★**Fondació Joan Miró** – Joan Miró (1893-1983) left an indelible mark on the city through his personal style, a blend of light-hearted humour and airy, elegant whims. He left this foundation to the city in 1971. It was inaugurated in 1976. See the video films about Miró's life and art. The supreme Barcelona artist's work is to be found throughout the city, including ceramic frescoes at the airport and mosaics on the ground of La Rambla.

★**Museu d'Arqueológia de Catalunya** – This outstanding presentation of megalithic civilizations in Spain displays dolmens from Antequera, *talayots* from the Balearics, and Punic burial art from Ibiza. The Roman and Hellenistic collections are from Ampurias, ancient Barcino, and Badalona.

★★EIXAMPLE and MODERNIST ARCHITECTURE

Eixample (in Catalan) or Ensanche (in Castilian) means enlargement. This name was given to the modern city built in the 19C according to the Cerdà plan.

The Cerdà plan – The 1859 map laid out a geometric pattern of streets parallel or perpendicular to the sea. Blocks of houses, known as manzanas or apples in Spanish, were octagonal in shape. All right angles were eliminated. Two broad diagonal avenues, the Diagonal and the Méridiana, cut the district in half and meet on the Plaça de les Glòries Catalanes. The rich modern architecture represents a highlight.

Modernist Architecture – The style flourished between 1890 and 1920, and coincided with Art Nouveau in France, Modern Style in Great Britain and the United States, Sezession in Austria and Judendstil in Germany. Modernist architecture combined new industrial materials with modern techniques. It employed decorative elements such as sinuous curves, asymmetrical forms, stained glass, ceramics and metal. It reached its apogee in Catalonia at a time when large fortunes were being made thanks to industrialisation. The most representative architects are Antoni Gaudi, Domènech i Montaner, Puig i Cadafalch and Jufol. The parallel movement in literature was known as the Renaixanca.

★★★**Sagrada Familia** – The Sagrada Familia remains unfinished and might disappoint the inadvised visitor, but the eastern spire commands a view over the entire building site and Barcelona.
The project was undertaken in 1882 by Francisco de P Villar, and resumed in 1883 by Gaudi. The original plan called for a Latin cross with five naves and a transept with three naves. Outside, four high spires would represent the 12 apostles. Above, a central spire flanked by four other spires would carry the transept crossing. They would represent Christ and the Evangelists. The nave would resemble a forest of columns.

Only the crypt, the apse and the façade of the Nativity were completed during Gaudi's lifetime. After his death, work resumed in 1940. Today, we can admire eight spires and the Passion façade, completed in 1981.

J.-L. Bohin/EXPLORER

Gaudi's Casa Battló, Barcelona

★★**Passeig de Gràcia** – Pere Falqués decorated this splendid avenue with elegant wrought-iron lamp posts in 1906. It contains the most beautiful examples of modernist architecture. The **manzana de la discordia**★★, or apple of discord, shows off the different styles of the three most famous architects. Domènech i Montaner built **Casa Lleó Morera**★ in 1905 at no 35. Puig i Cadafalch completed **Casa Amatller**★ in 1900 at no 41. Gaudi designed **Casa Batlló**★ at no 43 in 1905. It displays a remarkable mosaic façade and an undulating roof covered with scales. On the corner of Carrer d'Arago, Domènech i Montaner's Casa Montaner i Simo houses the **Fondació Antoni Tàpies**★★. A little further on to the right, Gaudi's **Pedrera**★, or Casa Mila, resembles an underwater cliff face. A visit to the rooftop leaves a strange impression. Chimneys and ventilation funnels rise on all sides like a phantasmagorical army.

Diagonal – On the right stands the **Casa Quadras** by Josep Puig i Cadafalch housing the **Museum of Music** with its remarkable collection of instruments from the four corners of the world. A little further on the left, the Flemish style influenced the same architect's **Casa Terrades**★, better known as the **Casa de las Punxes**.

★**Parc Güell** – This is Gaudi's most famous undertaking. The architect was allowed to give free rein to his imagination. He created an enchanted world of mushroom-like villas, stairways inhabited by a mosaic dragon and undulating benches. The paths seem intended for rites of initiation, suddenly opening into grottoes and alcoves surmounted by cacti.

EXCURSIONS

★★**Sierra de Montserrat** – The Montserrat chain of hard Eocene conglomerate stands in vivid relief to the surrounding rock eroded by wind and water. The impressive **site**★★★ inspired Wagner in designing the settings for *Parsifal.*
The blocks of stone piled on top of sharp cliffs and crowned by jagged toothing gave it the name of saw mountain. Pilgrims flock to this holy mountain to worship Mary. It represents the main religious and cultural centre of Catalonia.

Access – Approach the chain from the west. The road by the monastery offers beautiful **vistas**★★ over the rocks. In order to reach the Montserrat cable car, follow the road from Barcelona to Manresa and park near Monistrol de Montserrat.

★**La Moreneta** – This is the Catalan name for the black Virgin. The polychrome wood statue dates approximately from the 12C, but the child on the Virgin's knees was restored in the 19C. According to legend, she was discovered by shepherds in a mountain cave. The statue now stands above the main altar.

Hermitages and Belvederes – Mountain roads or any one of a number of cable-cars and funiculars lead to these isolated spots.
Prior to the occupation by Napoleon's army, hermits inhabited 13 hermitages. Today all are abandoned, however they make pleasant destinations for an afternoon walk. Some of the best-known are Sant Jeroni, Santa Cecilia, Santa Cova, Sant Miquel, and Sant Joan.

The star ratings are allocated for various categories:
– regions of scenic beauty with dramatic natural features
– cities with a cultural heritage
– elegant resorts and charming villages
– ancient monuments and fine architecture, museum and picture galleries.

BURGOS★★

Population 169 111
Michelin map 970 F 7

Burgos, the cradle of Castile, stands on the banks of the River Alarzon. It shows off the slender lacy spires of its celebrated cathedral. The isolated position on the 900m/295ft high plateau leaves the city exposed to the rigours of the cold, sweeping winds.

History – Diego Rodrigues Burgos founded the city in 884. It was chosen to be the capital of the united kingdom of Castile and Leon in 1037. But Vallodolid took the title in 1492 at the time of the fall of Granada. Though politically forgotten, Burgos experienced a commercial and artistic boom. Wool produced by the major mesta growers was transformed and commercialized here. Architects and sculptors, particularly from the north, transformed the city in the fashionable Gothic style. Burgos became the Gothic capital of Spain, with outstanding monuments such as the cathedral, the royal monastery of Las Huelgas and the charterhouse of Miraflores. The end of the 16C saw the decline of the mesta and the end of Burgos' prosperity.
Between 1936 and 1938, Burgos was the seat of the Franco government.

★★★CATHEDRAL

This is the third-largest cathedral in Spain after those of Seville and Toledo. The remarkable Gothic edifice blends the flowery style imported from France and Germany with the natural exuberance of Spanish decorative arts. The many works of art found inside make this a magnificent showcase of European Gothic sculpture.
After Ferdinand II laid the first stone in 1221, the cathedral was built in two major phases. Local architects completed the naves and portals during the 13C. They followed plans brought back by Bishop Don Mauricio after a trip through France. In the 15C, the spires, the constable's chapel and the decoration of the aisle chapels were constructed.

Interior

★**Transept crossing, choir stalls and chancel** – The superb star-ribbed lantern rises 54m/177ft above the transept crossing. Below are the funerary slabs of El Cid and Ximena. The imposing set of 103 walnut choir stalls was sculpted by Felipe Bigarny from 1507 to 1512.

★**Ambulatory** – The back of the high altar holds an amazingly expressive scene of the Ascent to Calvary. Felipe Bigarny was the main sculptor.

★**Constable's Chapel** – The Isabelline chapel founded by the Castilian Constable Hernandez de Velasco and built by Simon of Cologne is lit by a lantern surmounted by an elegant star-ribbed cupola. Each of the major sculptors of the early Renaissance contributed to the exuberant decoration of the walls and the reredos.

★★REAL MONASTERIO DE LAS HUELGAS (ROYAL CONVENT)

1.5km/0.9mi west of the city, reached by Avenida del Monasterio de las Huelgas.

Founded in 1180 by Alphonse VII and his wife Eleanor of England, this gilded convent was reserved for high-born Cistercian nuns. It was built on the site of a royal residence *(las huelgas)*. During the 13C, the convent's spiritual and temporal influence spread to more than 50 towns. Members of the royal family of Castile made this a retreat, and even their pantheon.

CARTUJA DE MIRAFLORES (CHARTER HOUSE OF MIRAFLORES)

4 km east of Burgos

This former royal foundation was donated to the Carthusian monks in 1442. Then Juan II chose it as a pantheon for himself and his wife Isabella of Portugal. The church was completed in 1498, at the apogee of the Isabelline Gothic period.

★**The Church** – The façade's austerity, lightened only by the pinnacles of the buttresses and the two coats of arms of the founders, does not suggest the resplendent interior, the single elegantly-vaulted nave with gilded keystones and, above all, the apse's exceptional sculptures.

★★★**Absidal Sculptures** – The late-5C ensemble by Gil de Siloé of Flanders consists in the reredos, the royal mausoleum and a recessed tomb.
The polychrome wood reredos, for which Gil de Siloé was helped by Diego de la Cruz, is unique. Scenes generally found in rectangular compartments are set instead in circles.
The white-marble royal mausoleum forms an elegant eight-branch star. It contains the recumbent statues of Juan II and his queen, the parents of Isabella the Catholic. The four Evangelists dominate the tomb with its flamboyant decor of foliage, canopies, pinnacles, cupids and coats of arms.

CÓRDOBA★★★

Population 310 488
Michelin map 970 F 9

Córdoba stands on the right bank of the River Guadalquivir, halfway between the La Campina plain of wheat fields and olive groves to the south, and the Sierra de Córdoba farmland to the north. Its legacy stems from the brilliant civilizations which, twice in its history, made it their capital. Although the city could just live off its past, Cordoba developed industry on the outskirts and encouraged traditional craftsmanship (filigree and tooled leather) and folklore.
Mid-May is the season for decorating crosses, patios, windows, narrow streets and squares with abundant flowers. The *feria* at the end of the month marks an occasion for balls in Andalusian costume and flamenco dancing.
Between Montilla and Lucena, a wine-growing region lies some 50km/31mi south of Cordoba. It produces a full range of wine and liqueurs under the brand name of Montilla-Moriles.

Córdoba under the Caliphs – The emirs under the Caliph of Damascus established themselves in Cordoba in 719. Abd al-Rahman I arrived in 756. He was the sole survivor of the Damascus Umayyads massacred by the Abbasids. Under the al-Rahman dynasty, Cordoba entered an era of prosperity. As early as the 10C, it boasted a famous university. A spirit of open-mindedness and tolerance made it possible for the Christian, Jewish and Muslim cultures to not only live together but also enrich each other. When the **Hicham II** took power in 976, his minister **Al-Mansour** (The Victor) maintained an iron hand. But rising discord led to the break-up of Al-Andalus into tiny kingdoms, the *reinos de taifas*. In 1070, Cordoba was incorporated into Seville. Political decadence did not affect the city's intellectual vitality. The Moor Averroès (1126-1198) was a physicist, astrologer, mathematician, physician and philosopher. Although his theories were disavowed and he was obliged to give up teaching, it is nonetheless thanks to him that Aristotle became known to the Western Christian world. During the same period, the celebrated Jewish doctor, theologian and philosopher Maimonides (1135-1204), fled persecution to Morocco and Egypt.
After the Christians conquered Córdoba in 1236, the city dwindled in prosperity. Good times returned in the 16C and 17C thanks to the famous tooled leatherwork with polychrome motifs. It decorates walls and furniture.

★★★THE MOSQUE AND THE JUDÉRIA

Cordoba's three civilisations are represented in this single neighbourhood. The remarkable Islamic *mezquita*, the Christian cathedral curiously incorporated into the mosque, and the Jewish synagogue all coexist.

★★★**Mezquita-Catedral (Mosque-Cathedral)** – The eclectic construction can be divided into several parts.

The Mosque – The classic overall plan consists of a crenellated rectangular enclosure, the Orange Tree Courtyard bordered by galleries, the large Al-Mansour basin for ritual ablutions, a prayer hall, and finally a minaret.
The mosque was built in several stages. When the first Muslims settled in Cordoba, they shared half of the Visigothic Church of St Vincent with the Christians. Quickly, however, this became inadequate. Abd al-Rahman I (758-788) bought the Christian part of the church, razed it and, in one year, built a splendid mosque with 11 aisles, all opening onto the Orange Tree Court. Marble and stone columns from Roman and Visigothic edifices were used in the construction.
The architectural innovation superposing two tiers of arches made the mosque famous. It lent greater height and lightened the building's overall effect. Abd al-Rahman II first enlarged the mosque in 848, lengthening it to the spot where the Villaviciosa chapel now stands. In 961, El-Hakam II built the Mihrab. Finally in 987, Al-Mansour added eight aisles parallel to the first. The red-brick paving stones distinguish this work.
The interior is a veritable forest of columns, numbering around 850. The horseshoe arches are formed of alternating white stone and red brick. Walk toward the Puerta de las Palmas. The wide aisle leading from the doorway is decorated with a fine *artesonado* ceiling. This was the central aisle of the original mosque and led to the **mirhab**★★★. The faithful would kneel to pray, under the imam's direction. The niche has been enlarged into a real room, sumptuously decorated. A triple **maksourah** proceeds it. The enclosure is reserved for the caliph, with three ribbed domes covered with mosaics on a gold background and resting on a remarkable series of interweaving multifoil arches. The architecture's richness is underscored by the decoration: arabesques and palm leaves cover the chiselled alabaster plaques, and the stucco and mosaics are often framed in Cufic script.
Christian rite in the 13C brought further changes. Most of the aisles giving onto the courtyard were walled off. Eliminating columns and adding pointed Gothic arches created a cathedral without destroying the original mosque. Alphonse X built the chancel in the **Villaviciosa Chapel**, or Lucernario. He also constructed the13C **Royal Chapel**★, decorated with Mudéjar stucco.

F. Gouverneur/MICHELIN

Tower of the Mezquita – Cathedral

The Cathedral – In the 16C the canons of the cathedral desired a more sumptuous sanctuary. They broke through the roofs in the centre of the mosque to raise lofty vaulted ceilings. Despite the architectural talent of the Hernan Ruiz family, Emperor Charles V was disappointed. "You have destroyed something that existed nowhere else, to build something that exists everywhere", he declared. In any other location, the cathedral would have been a marvel. The architecture of an entire century was fused into a single quest for supreme grandeur: in the transept and the apse (1523-1547). The vault of the apse from 1560 bears busts in Renaissance medallions. The nave from 1598 contains luxuriant stucco decor peopled with cherubim. The coffered cupolas of the transept from 1600 are in the Italianate style. Pedro Duque Cornejo's beautiful Baroque **choir stalls★★** were sculpted around 1750. Two **pulpits**, with marble and jasper enriching the mahogany, complete the decor.

Outside, the **minaret** was enveloped in the 17C by a Baroque tower. The view from the top is excellent. Below, the 14C Mudéjar Pardon Doorway is covered with decorated bronze plaques. Nearby, the small chapel of the Virgin of the Lanterns is a venerated place of prayer in Córdoba.

★★ **Judería (former Jewish quarter)** – The old Jewish quarter is a maze of narrow streets. White walls are decked in brilliant flowers. Doors open onto cool-looking patios, elegant grill-work – a labyrinth punctuated by colourful street stalls and bars. Inside, Cordobans often burst into song, to the accompaniment of a guitar and the sound of sharply clapping hands.

Synagogue – This is one of the rare synagogues remaining in modern Spain, together with that of Toledo. It dates from the 14C, and consists of a small square room opening onto a balcony. Women prayed here. The wall's upper parts are covered in Mudéjar stucco.

Nearby, the **Zoco** bazaar crowds crafts shops around a patio. In summer, it is used for flamenco music and dancing.

COSTA BRAVA★★

Michelin map 970 I 8

The Costa Brava extends the length of Girona's entire shore. It owes its name to its wild coastline tormented by wind and sea. The ancient rocks of the Catalan cordillera form a line of cliffs that plunge straight to the sea. The coast is famed for its beautiful rocky inlets, limpid waters, picturesque ports and tiny villages.

★★THE ALBERES COASTLINE

From Port-bou to Roses *66km/41mi – about 4hr*

The last foothills of the Alberes chain form vast, closed-in bays such as Port-bou and El Port de la Selva. The road winds upward along towering cliffs, particularly from Port-bou to Colera.

★★ **Sant Pere de Rodes** – *7km/4.4mi from El Port de la Selva, followed by a 15 min walk.* The ruins of the monastery rise in the middle of a magnificent site at the foot of San Salvador Mountain. It overlooks the entire coastline from Cerbère (France) to Cap Creus. The 10C Benedictine construction is protected by high walls and surmounted by two tall towers. It was abandoned and pillaged in the 18C. The church remains the best preserved element. Its interior architecture is most unusual, featuring two tiers of columns reminiscent of ancient temples supporting the nave's vaulting. Splendid **capitals** sculpted with interlacing and acanthus leaves show the influence of Cordoban and Byzantine art.

★★ **Cadaqués** – In the 19C, this was a fishing village. It became fashionable with the arrival of a number of contemporary writers and painters. Salvador Dali built his house on the inlet of Portlligat. Yet Cadaquès has kept intact the charm of its white houses with their picturesque arches. The old quarter invites a rest in the welcome shade at the foot of the church. Its sober exterior contrasts vividly with the rich Baroque reredos inside.

★ THE EMPORDÀ PLAIN

From Roses to Begur *65km/40mi – about 3hr*

The fertile plain of Empordà stretches out between the Fluvia and Ter rivers. The Gulf of Roses forms a jagged, though flat **coastline**★ perfect for water sports.

★ **Empuriabrava** – A luxury marina built in 1973 where pleasure boats are moored to the doors of the houses. Long sandy beach.

★ **Castelló d'Empúries** – Village standing on a promontory. **Santa Maria Church**★ (14C-15C) is worth seeing for its **portal**★★, a fine example of the Catalan Gothic style, and alabaster high **altarpiece**★ (15C).

★★ **Empúries** – Built on a remarkable coastal **site**★★, the Greco-Roman town of Ampurias (Emporion being the Greek word for market) has three centres: Palaiapolis, or old town, Neapolis, or new town, and the Roman town.
In the mid-6C BC, the Phocaeans were already settled in Marseille. They founded the trading port of Palaiapolis on an island near the coast. Today, it is connected to the land and occupied by the village of Sant Marti d'Ampuries. A few years later, Neapolis emerged on the shore facing the island. A Roman expeditionary force under the command of Scipio Africanus occupied it in 218 BC. In 100 BC, the Roman city came into existence to the west. When Augustus granted Roman citizenship to the Greeks, the two independent settlements merged. In the 3C, barbarians sacked the city. It nonetheless became the seat of a bishopric. But the city's importance waned with the arrival of the Arabs in the 8C.

Museum – Among its collections are a cross-section of Neapolis, scale models of temples and objects unearthed during archeological digs. A Greek mosaic dating from the 2C or 1C BC illustrates the sacrifice of Iphigenia.

★ **Pals** – This medieval village of rosy stone houses has been restored. The vestiges of its ramparts stand over old houses and sinuous streets passing beneath covered walkways.

★★ THE CORNICHE

From Begur to Blanes *98km/61mi – about 4 hours*

Sometimes flat, sometimes hilly, the coastline is a series of long beaches and little coves or pine-edged inlets.
The Costa Brava's most beautiful, best preserved inlets are found around Begur: the most popular of these lovely coves is Tamariu. **Aiguafreda** and **Aiguablava** represent tiny pieces of paradise. Sumptuous villas and luxury hotels rise from amidst the pine trees.

★ **Cap Roig Botanical Gardens** – A road south of Calella leads to the picturesque farm where the gardens are located. Terraces grip the rocks overhanging the sea. They are filled with beautifully arranged rare plants and Mediterranean shrubs. The **vistas**★★ spread out over Calella and the coastline.

★ **S'Agaro** – This elegant resort of luxury villas is set in a pine forest. A walk provides lovely **views**★ of the sea and the coast.
Between the two popular resorts of **Sant Feliu de Guixols**★ and **Tossa de Mar**★, a number of belevederes provide opportunities to appreciate the admirable **corniche**★★ road. Its sheer cliff face plunges to the rocky **inlets**★ with clusters of houses.
The **cliff road**★★ continues between Tossa de Mar and Blanes as far as Playa Canyelles. It then descends between the hills to long stretches of beach.

★ **Mar i Murtra Botanical Gardens** – More than 4 000 varieties of plants from the five continents have been attractively grouped in this garden on a promontory plunging into the sea. At every turn, the twisting paths reveal beautiful **views**★★ of the coastline.

COSTA DEL SOL★

Michelin map 970 F 9

The famous "Sunshine Coast" stretches along Andalucia's Mediterranean shore from Tarifa to Cap de Gata, east of Almeria. Sheltered from the extreme continental climate, the Costa del Sol enjoys mild winters averaging (12°C/54°F), warm summers (26°C/79°F) and sufficiently abundant rain in winter and spring for exotic crops.

★THE WEST COAST

From Estepona to Málaga *139km/86mi – allow half-a day*

The coast is nestled between sea and mountain. A succession of seaside resorts, hotels, large residential buildings and tourist complexes are built around pleasure boat harbours, golf courses and tennis courts.

Estepona – Fishing port and pleasure boat harbour.

Casares – This lovely white inland village enjoys an outstanding **site★** atop a rocky peak.

★**Marbella** – The Costa del Sol's pioneering town is situated on a bay sheltered by the Sierra Blanca.
Luxury hotels and elegant residential buildings have sprung up among the pine forests and flower-filled gardens, together with golf courses. They attract celebrities from the over world.
The town has preserved an attractive old quarter. Its maze of narrow streets edged by white-walled houses leads to a bustling little square shaded by orange trees. The city also boasts several beaches and a pleasure boat harbour.

★**Mijas** – This village's beautiful white homes are decorated with grill-work. Many have been renovated as restaurants or cafés. The village offers a variety of Andalusian handicrafts such as pottery, baskets, and woven goods. The higher terraces provide a lovely view of the shore.

Torremolinos – In the 1950s, this was a quiet little fishing port. Today it has become a helter-skelter complex of high-rise buildings, famous for its boutiques, nightclubs, and beautiful sandy beach.

★**Málaga** – The sprawling all-white city is situated at the mouth of the Guadalmedina. The Gibralfaro, lighthouse hill, crowned by 14C walls, commands a **view★★** over the city, the harbour and the region.
The Phoenician port of Málaga became a major Roman colony. Under the Arabs, it served as the principal port of the kingdom of Granada.
Today Málaga bustles with activity as the capital of the Costa del Sol. It has regular ferry links with Africa (Mellila).
Some parts of the city have preserved their unique style. **Caleta** to the east is filled with old houses surrounded by gardens. **El Palo**, 7km/4.4mi to the east, is a former fishing district known for its seafood restaurants.

Málaga is a sweet aperitif and dessert wine with great body. It is produced in the vineyards on the hills above the city. as sales have been uneven in recent years, the growers have begun to develop their produce in the form of currants.

★★THE EAST COAST

From Málaga to Almeria *209km/130mi– allow half-a day*

This often beautiful coast is marked by Moorish towers built after the Reconquest to guard the sea and protect against attack by Barbary pirates.

Nerja – Its palm-shaded terrace promenade bears the curious name of Balcony of Europe. Attractive inlets provide shelter on all sides.

★★**Cueva (cave) de Nerja** – This gigantic natural cavity contains vestiges of paintings, weapons, jewels and bones from Paleolithic times.
The Cascade chamber is used for a music and dance festival.

★**From Nerja to Herradura** – The road follows the mountainside rich in russet and mauve vegetation. It offers astonishing **viewpoints★** over the deep cuts in the coastline.

★**From Calahonda to Castell de Ferro** – The road along the rocky coast commands fine views of both sea and mountain.

From Aguadulce to Almería – Aguadulce was the pioneering beach along the Almeria coast. From the cliff road, a panoramic view unfolds of Almeria, the bay, the sheltered harbour and the fortress.

Estrecho de GIBRALTAR

Strait of GIBRALTAR

Michelin map 970 F 9

The **strait** across the Mediterranean, only 14km/8.7mi wide, has always played an important strategic role.

Algeciras – Its Moorish name was Al-Djezirah, meaning island. The Arabs occupied the area from 711 to 1344. Regular sea links are provided with Tangiers in Morocco and Ceuta, a Spanish enclave on Moroccan territory. The spot is famous for its **views**★★ of the Rock of Gibraltar.

Gibraltar – *British territory.* The massive rock stretches 4.5km/2.8mi along the sea and pushes inland for 1.4km/0.9mi. *The summit can be reached by cable-car or by car from Main Street; follow the signs to the Upper Rock.* Breathtaking **views**★★ look down from the top.

Tarifa – The castle on this southernmost tip of Spain commands an excellent **view**★ of the straits and Moroccan coast 13·5km/8·5mi away.

GIRONA★★

Population 70 409

Michelin map 970 H 8

Girona sits on a promontory at the confluence of the Ter and Onyar rivers. Its eventful history has bequeathed it the nickname of city of a thousand sieges. Iberians built its first ramparts, followed by the Romans and medieval inhabitants.

Girona and Judaism – The Jewish community of Girona, settled in the old town on either side of the **Calle de la Força**. It was known for its prestigious Cabalistic School.

★★FORÇA VELLA (OLD CITY)

Footbridges over the River Onyar offer picturesque views of the long lines of ochre and orange façades, the spire of San Feliu, and the cathedral tower.
Walk to the cathedral through the narrow streets and up the vast **Pera Staircase** with its 90 steps. To the right, the 14C **house of Pia Almonia** represents an elegant example of Gothic architecture.

★**Cathedral** – Except for the Baroque façade, the construction is Gothic. The chancel, surrounded by an ambulatory and chapels, was begun in 1312. At the beginning of the 15C the bold decision was taken to add a single **nave**★★. Its breadth is the greatest in all Gothic architecture. The same powerful yet sober style is broken only by the chapel arches, the niches of the triforium and the tall windows.
Beneath the chancel's silver canopy symbolizing the sky, the 14C silver **reredos**★ trace the life of Christ.

★★**Treasure** – This rich and exceptional collection contains one of the most beautiful versions of the **Beatus**★, the 8C commentary on the Apocalypse by St John. The miniatures by the monk Emerteri and the nun Eude date from 975. Their brilliant colour and the vigorous expressionism illustrate imaginary animals. They betray the clear influence of Caliphate art and contain vestiges of the Visigothic decorative style. In the same room is the 12C *Virgin of the Cathedral.* Superb church pieces are found in the following rooms, including an enamelled 14C cross. The Hixem embossed silver coffer represents a fine example of Caliphate art. The last room holds the famous 12C **Tapestry of the Creation**★★★, outstanding for its delicacy and unaltered colours. This unique piece – in fact a work of embroidery – consists of a majestic Christ surrounded by the phases in the Creation. The angles are occupied by the four winds.

EXCURSION

Figueres – *37km/23mi to the north.* Figueres, capital of Alt Empordà, is above all a trade centre, lying at the crossroads of French and Spanish Catalonia. Its name is often associated with the most famous of its sons: **Salvador Dalí** (1905-1989).

★★**Teatre-Museu Dalí** – The Dalí Museum, located in a former 19C municipal theatre, is a hymn to madness, to the fool who either charms or annoys, but fully in the image of the artist, it never leaves one indifferent. "This museum cannot be considered to be a museum", Dalí himself said. "It is a gigantic surrealist object in which everything is coherent, nothing is beyond my understanding".

GRANADA★★★

Population 280 592
Michelin map 970 F 9

Granada is a wonder of prestigious Moorish monuments. They are bathed in a luminous sky and imbued with the enchantment of a verdant **site★★**. The city stands in the middle of a great plain called the Vega The snow-topped Sierra Nevada rises on the horizon. Grenada is built on three hills: Albaicin, Sacromonte and the Alhambra. Each offers new perspectives. From Albaicin, the view over the red walls of the Alhambra is magnificent.

The celebrations of Holy Week and Corpus Christi are the occasion for brilliant festivities. The International Festival of Music and Dance takes place in June and July.

Grenada is the capital of an essentially agricultural province producing cereals, beets, fruit trees and raising cattle. It also is the seat of an archbishopric and a famous university. Tourism is its prime resource.

The city is most surprising for the contrast between its tranquil old town on the hills of the Alhambra and Albaicin and the lower town, noisy and busy, crossed by the major arteries of Gran via de Colon and Los Reyes Catolicos. A vast network of shopping streets and a pedestrian area lie around the cathedral. Restaurants in the centre of the city feature the speciality of Granada, beans with ham *(habas)*.

F. Gouverneur/MICHELIN

The Alhambra, Granada with the Sierra Nevada in the distance

★★★THE ALHAMBRA AND THE GÉNÉRALIFE *time: a half day*

The Art of Granada – The Grenada style represents the supreme culmination of Muslim art in Spain. The Nasrid princes gave no thought to building for posterity. Beneath the fabulous decoration are the simplest of materials, ill-adjusted bricks and plaster. Each successive sovereign razed the construction of his predecessor to build a palace to suit him, always around the same central feature, the patio.

Decoration featured wall hangings and rugs. Little furniture remains but sculptures still line the walls and the ceilings are unparalleled in beauty. Stuccowork is omnipresent, both outside and inside, finely sculpted and sometimes pierced, worked in fine planes with just enough relief to catch the light. Often, behind a maze of polygons appear one or two superimposed arabesque motifs, repeated over an entire panel. Another technique was to hollow out stalactites called *mocarabes* These become capitals, mouldings, arches, pendentives, and sometimes entire cupolas. Such chiselled plaster was then totally painted and sometimes gilded.

Ceramic tiles cover wall panels in geometric designs. *Alicatados* form a colourful marquetry with arabesques shaping star patterns. Colours are isolated on the *azulejos* by a thin raised filament or by a black line. Calligraphic decoration makes great use of the particularly elegant Andalusian cursive. More ornamental, complex Cufic was reserved for religious aphorisms.

★★★ALHAMBRA

The Calat Alhambra, or Red Castle, is built on a long platform at the summit of a wooded hill. It is one of the most remarkable fortresses ever conceived by man. The views over the city, toward the austere heights of Sacromonte and the hills drenched in magnificent gardens, add even greater pleasure to the visit.

The entrance is through the Puerta de las Granadas, built under Charles V. The paved path rises through **shrub groves★** to the imposing **Gate of Justice★**, whose tower is incorporated in the ramparts that support and protect the palace terrace.

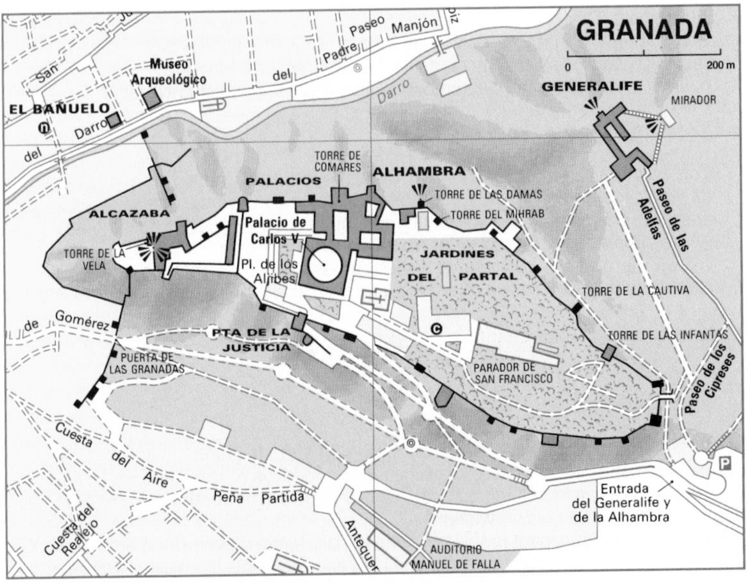

★★★ **Palacios Nazaríes (Nasrid Palace)** – The 14C Nasrid Palace was built around the Myrtle Court and the Lion Court. The stalactite-covered vaulted ceilings, cupolas, etched stucco and courtyards surrounded by elegant arcades are all architectural gems making optimum use of the play of light on water.

The visit begins with the **Mexuar**. This part of the first palace was reserved for the government and judicial administration. The chamber was transformed into a chapel after the Reconquest. It opens onto the Mexuar Court whose southern wall's admirable sculpted wood cornice is framed by panels covered with endless variations in stucco and ceramic. The chamber provides a lovely **view**★ of the Albaicin Hill. Enter next the **Myrte Court** (de los Arrayanes). The pool stretches the length of the court bordered by a hedge of myrtle. It reflects the massive Comares Tower with its crenellated walls. This forms a strange contrast with the elegantly delicate porticoes leading to the **Barca Chamber** (Barakha means benediction).

The **Hall of the Ambassadors** is Alhambra's masterpiece. It served as the audience chamber for the emirs. Below its magnificent cedar dome, its large bay windows command a glorious **view**★★ over Granada. The decoration consists of *azulejos* and stucco work bearing Koranic inscriptions and praising the princes.

After leaving the Myrtle Court, proceed to the second palace, the residence of the royal family. Its celebrated **Lion Court** was constructed under Mohammed V. A graceful gallery of arches gives onto the main reception rooms. The ancient fountain is decorated with 12 rough-stone lions resembling aquamaniles.

The Abencerrages Chamber has beautiful stalactite-covered vaulting crowned by a superb star-shaped lanterncupola. After Boabdil executed the Abencerrages, their heads supposedly were piled one on the other in the great basin in the centre of the room. The back of the King's chamber is lined with alcoves with painted vaulting. This decoration is so different from its surroundings that experts believe the sultan may have commissioned a Christian artist.

The **Hall of the Two Sisters**, crowned by a great honeycomb cupola, owes its name to two large identical marble slabs in its pavement. At the back is the door to the Ajimeces Chamber and the Mirador de Daraxa, also superbly decorated. Pass through the Partal Gardens to reach the cool, hushed Daraxa Garden, from which a gallery leads to the **Window Grille Court**. From here, descend to the royal baths with their ornate polychrome decoration. The hammam is lit by little star-shaped openings.

★★ **Gardens and Perimeter Towers** – The Partal Gardens extend to the east of the royal palaces. They slope in terraces toward the **Lady Tower** (de las Damas) with its lovely portico. This early-14C building is elegantly decorated and commands an excellent view over Albaicin and the Sacromonte Hills.

The Mihrab Tower to the right is a former Nasrid Oratory, a rarity as these princes were not known for their piety. Nearby, the Captive Tower (de la Cautiva) and Infanta Tower (de las Infantas) also boast abundantly decorated chambers.

★ **Palacio de Carlos V (Palace of Emperor Charles V)** – The vast court with its double tier of galleries is one of the finest Renaissance achievements in Spain. The palace contains two museums, the Hispano-Moorish Museum and the Fine Arts Museum.

★**Alcazaba** – This is Alhambra's oldest section, dating from the 9C. The two towers dominating the Plaza de los Aljibes (Cistern Court) were erected in the 13C. From the tall Watch Tower (Torre de la Vela), a superb **panorama**★★ opens over the palaces, the Generalife, Sacromonte, Granada and the Sierra Nevada.

★★THE GENERALIFE

This country palace of the kings of Granada was built in the 14C and is known for its terraced gardens. The Cypress (los Cipreses) and Oleander (de las Adelfas) pathways become breathtaking in July and August. They lead to the modest palace which consists only in a long, narrow **Canal Court** (patio de la Acequia), bordered by roses. The graceful pavilions at either end are linked on the left by a gallery and on the right by the palace apartments. The mirador offers a fine **view** over Albaicin.

MADRID★★★

Population 3 084 673
Michelin map 970

Madrid is Europeís highest capital at 646m/2 119ft. It stands in the centre of the Iberian peninsula and the Meseta, nestled in the foothills of the Sierra de Guadarrama. The warm, welcoming, luminous city enjoys with a dry continental climate, hot in summer, sunny and cold in winter.
Madrid became the capital in the 16C when Spain reigned over a vast empire. Its principal monuments date from the 17C and19C, and are in the Classical or Baroque style. Collections bequeathed by the Habsburgs and the Bourbons have made world leaders out of Prado Museum, the Academy San Fernando, the Lazaro Galdiano Museum. Recently, the city gained the magnificent Thyssen-Bornemisza Collection.
Cosmopolitan Madrid has grown remarkably in the past few decades. Today, it is striking for its bustling activity and the ceaseless traffic on its wide avenues.

Madrid Yesterday – Madrid was an unimportant village until the time of the Moorish invasion. It owes its name to the Alcazar (fortress) of Majerit, built by Mohammed I in the 9C on the banks of the River Manzanares. Alphonse I conquered the fortress in 1083. According to legend, he found a statue of the Virgin near an almudin (grain warehouse) at the entrance to the city. So when the mosque was transformed into a church, Alphonse dedicated it to the Virgin de la Almudena. She now is the city's patron. After the 14C, the kings of Castile came more and more frequently to the city. Charles V rebuilt the Moorish Alcazar, and in 1561, Philip II transferred the royal court from Toledo to Madrid. The medieval city, whose narrow winding streets can still be discerned around the Plaza Mayor, suddenly boomed and the population tripled. More expansion came during the Habsburg reign of Spain's golden age. Under Philip III, Juan Gomez de Mora undertook a series of reforms. Plaza Mayor became the heart of the city. A map by Pedro Texeira in 1656 gives a good idea of Philip IV's Madrid with innumerable convents and churches. The royal art-lover protected many artists, including Velasquez and Murillo, and men of letters such as Lope de Vega, Quevado, Calderon, and Tirso de Molina.
Under the Bourbons in the 18C, the city underwent more important changes. Philip V ordered the construction of the royal palace, while Charles III, much influenced by ideas from other European courts, endowed Madrid with unprecedented splendour. Together, the Prado and the Alcala Gate represent a magnificent example of neo-Classical urban design. The nobility too yearned for palaces set amid gardens, and built Liria (**KV**) and Buenavista (**MX**).
The 19C began with the French occupation. In the second half of the century, Madrid underwent considerable further urban renewal. In 1857, the remains of the ramparts were demolished and a vast plan for enlarging the city *(ensanche)* was undertaken. The Chamberi, Salamanca and Argüelles neighbourhoods emerged. At the end of the century, Arturo Soria designed the Ciudad Lineal, a revolutionary plan for a residential district for 30 000 inhabitants around today's Avenida Arturo Soria. The beginning of the 20C was heavily influenced by the French style, seen in the Ritz (**NY**) and Palace (**MY**) hotels. The neo-Mudéjar style also came into fashion and the brick façades so characteristic of Madrid went up on all sides **(Plaza de Toros de la Ventas)**. The Gran Via was inaugurated in 1910. This major artery cut through the city centre, linking up the newly built districts.

Madrid Today – Madrid dominates Spain in terms of banking, insurance, universities, government administration and political institutions. Its suburbs have become major industrial centres. The business district around the Puerta de Alcala and Paseo de la Castellana were radically changed in the 1950s and 1960s. Classical palaces were razed to make way for modern buildings. The **Azca** area, one of the more revolutionary projects in modern-day Madrid, fulfils residential, commercial and administrative functions. It is the site of the most modern skyscrapers such as the avant-garde Bank of Bilbao-Viscaya and the Picasso Tower.

LIFE IN MADRID

Madrid is a cosmopolitan city of museums, exhibitions, entertainment and concerts. *(For details, consult the weekly Guia del Ocio.)* An almost infinite range of choices exists for drinks, the so-called ir de copas. The jet set crowd frequents elegant modern cafés in Chamberi and Salamanca. More traditional cafés in the centre such as the Gijon or Oriente, opposite the Royal Palace, are institutions, while modest, neighbourhood bars dot Malasana (LV) and Chueca (MV). The Moncloa district is well worth a visit for its university atmosphere. The most typical taverns and bistros are concentrated around the Plaza Major and Glorieta de Bilbao (LV). The choice of restaurants is particularly rich in the old town, the Salamanca district and in Castellana-Orense.
In summer, sidewalk cafés with their colourful terraces lend a festive feel to the capital, especially on Paseos de la Castellana (NV), Recoletos (NV) and del Pintor Rosales and around the Las Vistillas Gardens.

Shopping – Downtown Madrid (Puerta del Sol, Callao, Preciados etc) is a popular, animated shopping area with everything from traditional shops selling fans and lace to modern boutiques and large department stores.
The luxury and high fashion boutiques are found in Salamanca, around Serrano, Ortega y Gasset, Lagasca and Goya streets. This area is fine for making classic purchases of jewellery, home decoration, perfumes and cosmetics.
The more modern shops are found on Calle Almirante (MNV) and the nearby streets. Argüelles is another bustling shopping district.
Each of the two major department stores, El Corte Inglés and Las Galerias Preciados, has branches in Preciados, Carmen, Goya, Serrano, Arapiles, Raimundo Fernandez Villaverde and Princesa streets. A good shopping mall is La Vaguada in the north with cinemas, a supermarket, brasseries and cafeterias. Another more luxurious version is the Galeria del Prado opposite the museum.
Antique-lovers will enjoy Calle del Prado (MY), the Cortes district (MY), and the Puerta de Toledo market. On Sundays morning, the famous Rastro flea-market offers an incredible variety of articles. Cuesta de Claudio Moyano (NZ) and Calle Libreros are favourite streets for finding good books.

Art Galleries – Many are located in the Salamanca area near Puerta de Alcala and on Paseo de la Castellana near Calle Génova. In recent years, new galleries have opened in the Atocha district.

Entertainment – Madrid is full of cinemas and has some 20 theatres in addition to its casino and concert halls. The **National Auditorium** inaugurated in 1988 offers various programmes of classical music. The **Teatro de la Zarzuela** (MY) presents a seasonal programme of zarzuelas and ballets. The **Royal Theatre** or 19C Opera is the setting for the opera season. During its annual autumn festival, Madrid organises a rich programme of cultural events.

Parks – The **Buen Retiro park** is particularly lively on Sunday mornings with open-air concerts and improvised shows. Regular concerts by the municipal orchestra from the park bandstand are a Madrid tradition.
Parque del Oeste is a quiet English-style garden. Casa del Campo is Madrid's largest garden, with a wooded, country-style atmosphere. Campo del Moro, the Botanical Gardens (NZ) and Parque de la Fuente del Berro are other local favourites.

Environs – From December to March, the snow-capped peaks of Sierra de Guadarrama draw sports enthusiasts to their fine ski slopes only an hour from Madrid.
In summer, locals flee the heat to enjoy a cool swim in nearby reservoirs such as San Juan and Mar de Castilla.

★OLD MADRID *time: 2 hr 30 min*

★★**Plaza Mayor** (KY) – Built by Juan Gomez de Mora under Philip III (1619), this is the architectural centre of the Habsburgs' Madrid. The 17C equestrian statue of Philip II in the centre is the work of Jean de Bologne and Pietro Tacca.
The square was the site of auto-da-fés and mounted bullfights. Philip V, Ferdinand VI and Charles IV were proclaimed king here.
Every Sunday morning under the arcades, a stamp and coin market takes place. At Christmas, stands are set up to sell Christmas decorations. The surrounding shops, including many hat-makers, have maintained the same appearance for years. Pass beneath the **Arch of Cuchilleros** to reach the street with its high façades of old houses. Little restaurants *(mesones)* and bistros *(tavernas)*. crowd here and in the neighbouring street, **Cava de San Miguel** which received its name cava because long ditches once ran along it.

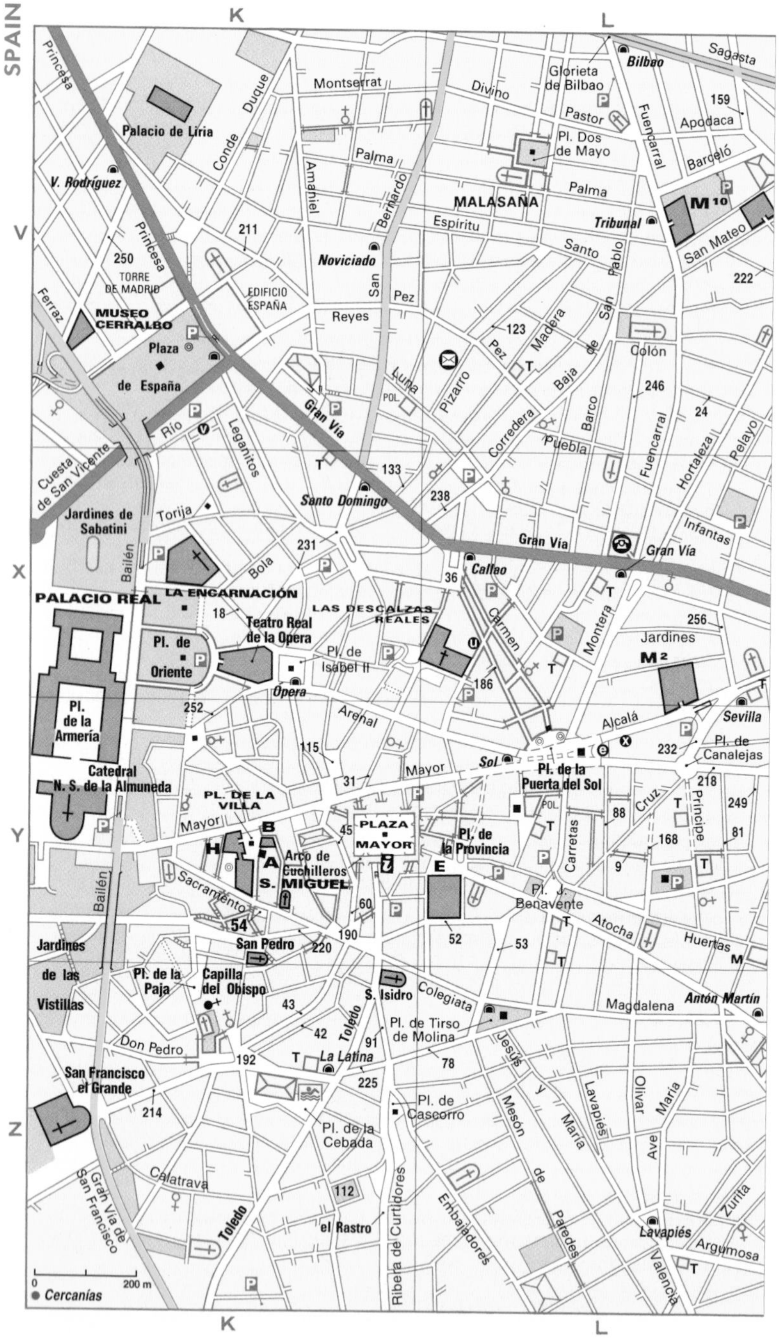

Basilica of San Miguel (KY) – This work of Bonavia is one of the rare churches in Spain inspired by 18C Italian Baroque. The convex façade forms an elaborate play of curves and counter-curves. Fine statues cover it. Above the door, a bas relief shows Saints Justus and Pastor, to whom the church was formerly dedicated. The interior is graceful and elegant, with an oval cupola, intersecting ribbed vaulting, softly rounded cornices and a great deal of stucco decoration.

★**Plaza de la Villa** (KY) – Benlliure's 1888 statue of Alvaro de Bazan, hero of the 16C Battle of Lepanto, dominates this quiet pedestrian square. Many of the surrounding buildings are famous. The town hall, or **Ayuntamiento** (H), was built by Gomez de Mora in 1617. In the **Torre de los Lujanes**, French king François I was held prisoner after the battle of Pavia. It is one of the rare examples of 15C non-religious architecture still standing in Madrid. Beside it, the former **Hemeroteca** contains the two beautiful Renaissance tombs of Beatriz Galindo and her husband.

MADRID

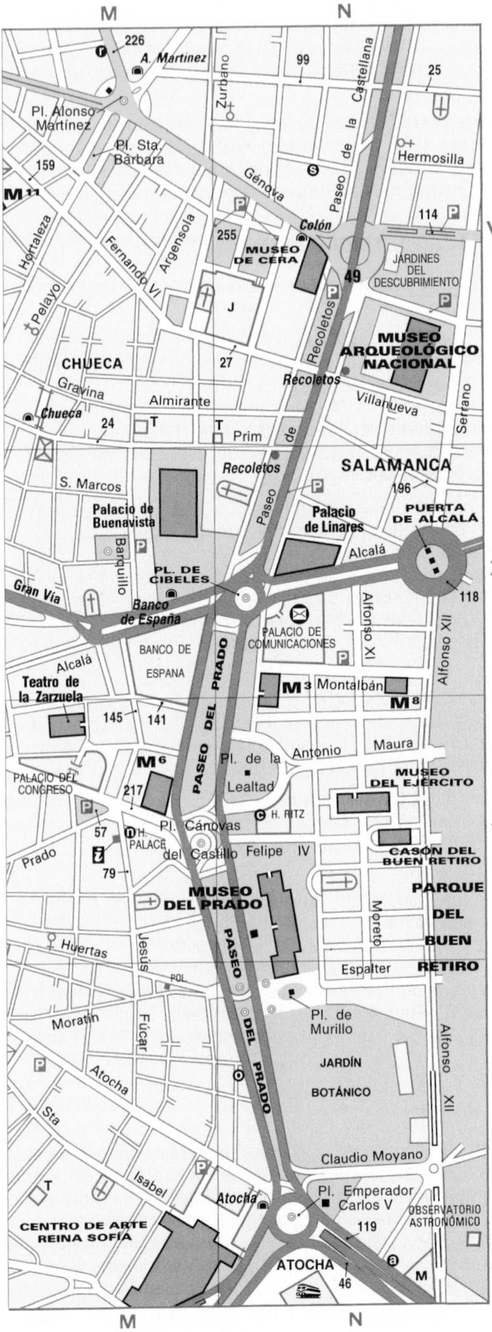

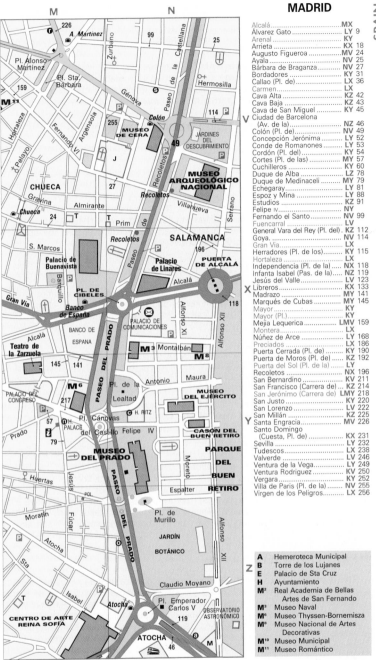

- **A** Hemeroteca Municipal
- **B** Torre de los Lujanes
- **E** Palacio de Sta Cruz
- **H** Ayuntamiento
- **M²** Real Academia de Bellas Artes de San Fernando
- **M³** Museo Naval
- **M⁶** Museo Thyssen-Bornemisza
- **M⁸** Museo Nacional de Artes Decorativas
- **M¹⁰** Museo Municipal
- **M¹¹** Museo Romántico

Finally, an arch connects **Casa de Cisneros**, built several years after the death of the Cardinal of the same name, with the town hall. Nothing remains of the original 16C house except a lovely window overlooking **Plazuela del Cordon**.

San Francisco el Grande Church (KZ) – The impressive neo-Classical façade is the work of Sabatini, but the building itself, circular in layout with six chapels radiating outwards and a giant 33m/108ft dome, is by Francisco Cabezas. In St Bernardin's Chapel, note the *Sermon of St Bernardin of Sienna to the King of Aragon* (1781) painted by the young Goya. Some of the chancel's plateresque choir **stalls★** come from the Monastery of El Parral (Segovia). The 16C **stalls★** in the sacristy and the chapter house are from the Carthusian Monastery of El Paular.

Calle de Toledo (KZ) – This is one of old Madrid's busiest streets. Every Sunday morning and on holidays, the **Rastro** sets up here and in Ribera de Curtidores.

Plaza Provincia (LY) – Note particularly the façade of the 17C **Palacio de Santa Cruz** (**E**). This former court prison where Lope de Vega was held, today houses the Ministry of Foreign Affairs.

Puerta del Sol (LY) – This is Madrid's most popular, lively square, the site of historic events. Its present design dates from the 19C. Many of the streets that lead to Puerta del Sol are filled with small traditional shops with picturesque wood storefronts. They offer everything from fans and mantillas to delicatessen fare.

★★BARRIO DE ORIENTE (EASTERN QUARTER) *A full day*

The visit provides an opportunity to admire both monumental buildings and vast panoramic views.

★★**Palacio Real** (KX) – The best view of this royal palace is from Paseo de Extremadura and the Campo del Moro Gardens. The imposing edifice was built by the Bourbons. It remained the official royal residence up to 1931. Today it belongs to Spain's National Trust, and is used by the king for official receptions.
The **Sabatini** and **Campo del Moro Gardens** were designed to hide the difference in levels between the north and west façades. The west façade overlooks the **Plaza de la Armería** and the east façade, **Plaza de Oriente**.

★**Palace** – Take the monumental staircase and admire the ceiling painted by Giaquinto. It leads to the **Column Room**, where the treaty joining Spain to the European Community was signed on 12 June, 1985.
The **Throne Room**★ is hung with crimson velvet, underscoring the magnificent ceiling painted by Tiepolo in 1764. The consoles and mirrors were designed by Ventura Rodrigues, and the gilded bronze lions are the work of the Italian Benicelli in 1621. Adjoining rooms present the musical instruments collection which includes several Stradivarius violins.

★★**Royal Armoury** – This outstanding collection of armour and weapons was put together by the Catholic kings Charles V and Philip II. The core of the collection is the personal armour of Emperor Charles V, Philip II and Philip III. The basement's vaulted hall presents an excellent collection of hunting rifles that belonged to the Bourbons.

★**Museo de Carruajes Reales (Royal Carriage Museum)** – This pavilion built in 1967 in the centre of the **Campo del Moro**★ Winter Garden contains former royal carriages. Most date from the reign of Charles IV in the late 18C.

★★**Monasterio de las Descalzas Reales** (LX) – Although this convent lies in the heart of busy Madrid, the visitor enters and finds himself transported back to the 16C. Note the splendour of the main **staircase**★, decorated with frescoes. In the cloister's Upper Gallery, each chapel outdoes its neighbour in magnificence. In particular, pay attention to the 16C *Recumbent Figure of Christ* by Gaspar Becerra.
Ten 17C **tapestries**★★ are displayed in the former convent dormitory. They were inspired by sketches by Rubens. The reliquary room contains many rare, finely chiselled chalices and coffers, and the painting rooms have works by Titian, Bruegel the Elder and Rubens.

★★★PRADO MUSEUM (NY) *3hr*

This is probably the world's finest museum of classical painting. The neo-Classical building was designed by Juan de Villanueva to house the Academy of Natural Science. After the War of Independence, Ferdinand VII changed the original project and decided to house collections of Spanish art put together by the Habsburg and Bourbon kings. The paintings reflect the evolution in artistic taste among the kings of Spain. The Prado also has excellent collections of Flemish works and a number of examples from the Italian School, a favourite of Charles V and Philip II.

The Spanish School★★★ (15C-18C) holds pride of place. Some artists were inspired by foreign influences. **Yañez de la Almedina** studied the style and technique of Leonardo da Vinci in his *St Catherine*. Macip and his son **Juan de Juanes** adopted Raphael's style. A *Virgin and Child* by **Morales** illustrates the artist's favourite theme. The Prado is home to Velasquez's greatest masterpieces and much of **Goya**'s work. The ground floor holds an exceptional collection of 15C-17C **Flemish paintings**★★★, thanks to the close relations between Spain and Holland. The first floor is devoted to the 15C-17C **Italian School**★★.

★★BOURBON MADRID *3hr*

This elegant residential section with its tree-lined streets and avenues is graced by luxurious buildings, once private mansions and palaces, and now museums. Tourists and local residents alike enjoy strolling here between a visit to the Prado and a walk in the Retiro Garden. The best-known sites are **Plaza de las Cibeles**★ (MNX) and **Paseo del Prado**★ (MNXZ **S**).

Detail of *The Family of Charles IV* by Goya (in the Prado, Madrid)

★★★ **Museo Thyssen-Bornemisza** (MV M[6]) – The former Villahermosa Palace, a fine example of neo-Classical architecture of the late 18C and early 19C, was redesigned by the architect Rafael Moneo to house part of the remarkable collection of paintings. The collection, first exhibited at Villa Favorita in Lugano (Switzerland), contains more than 800 works presented in chronological order on three levels, with the oldest on the top floor.
The European schools are well represented, together with fine collections of modern works. French Impressionists include Monet, Manet and Degas, and post-Impressionists Cézanne, Van Gogh, Toulouse-Lautrec and Gauguin. From the 20C are Matisse, Braque, Picasso, Kandinsky, Klee, Mondrian, Magritte, Ernst, Chagall, Miró and Hopper.

Centro de Arte Reina Sofia (MZ) – This art centre is devoted to Spanish works from 1900 up to the 1970s. It also contains some more recent Spanish and foreign art, and above all, Picasso's stupendous **Guernica**★★★.

EXCURSIONS

★★★ **Monasterio de El Escorial** – *55km/34mi north-west of Madrid.* The impressive monastery of San Lorenzo el Real, the Escurial, is set at an altitude of 1 065m/3 493ft on the southern flank of the Sierra de Guadarrama, at the foot of Mount Abantos.
The **Seat of Philip II** (Silla de Felipe II) offers a fine panoramic **view**★ of the monastery. On 10 August, the feast of San Lorenzo, patron saint of the village and the monastery, is celebrated. On that day in 1557, Philip II conquered the French in the memorable battle of St Quentin. To commemorate, he decided to build a monastery in honour of the saint, entrusting it to the care of the Hieronymites. The result was also a palace and royal pantheon.

★★ **Palacios** (Royal apartments) – The building's northwest quarter is occupied by the Bourbon palace, while the part around the apse of the church and the Mascaroon cloister was home to Philip II. The Bourbon palace has high Pompeian ceilings and lovely **tapestries**★, some from the Royal Tapestry Works in Madrid, and others from Flanders. Those based on Goya's drawings illustrate picturesque popular themes: Neptune is part of a series on Telemachus and comes from the Netherlands. The last room contains works by Teniers in a vivid lifelike style.

★★ **Pantheons** – A marble and jasper staircase leads to the **Royal Pantheon**★★★ beneath the church chancel. It contains the tombs of all the kings of Spain since Charles V, with the exception of Philip V, Ferdinand VI and Amédée de Savoie.

★★ **Library** – *Second floor.* The 54m/177ft room is magnificently decorated. Philip II filled this library with more than 10 000 volumes, but many were destroyed in a fire in 1671 and during the Napoleonic Wars. Today it has become public library with more than 40 000 books and some 2 700 manuscripts dating from the 5C to 18C.
The central display cases, on marble tables, hold a few rare manuscripts, including Arabic manuscripts, books by Saint Teresa, the *Cantigas de Santa Maria*, a poetic work by Alphonse the Wise with beautiful illuminations, and an 11C Beatus.

New Museums – **The Art Museum** contains an interesting collection of religious art. In the vaulted cellars, the **Architecture Museum** recalls the building of the monastery. The ground floor houses a section featuring El Greco's *Martyrdom of Saint Maurice* *and the Theban Legion*★. Philip II commissioned the work but when he saw the unusual composition and the acid colours, he rejected it. By pushing the legion's martyrdom into the background, the dominant theme becomes the crucial moment in which St Maurice attempts to convince his companions to submit to execution.

★★**Valle de los Caídos** – This gigantic monument in memory of those killed in the Civil War dead (1936-1939) was erected between 1940 and 1958 in the heart of the Sierra de Guaderrama. The Valle de Cuelgamuros, rebaptized Valle de la Caidos (Valley of the Fallen), offers a grandiose and dramatic **setting**★★ of giant blocks of granite and soft pine forests. The road leads to the esplanade in front of the **basilica**★★, hollowed out of the mountain and dominated by the **monumental Cross**★.

SALAMANCA★★★

Population 186 322
Michelin map 970 F 8

The narrow streets edged by façades in golden stone, the splendour of its monuments and a brilliant intellectual life make Salamanca a vibrant modern city evocative of a rich past. It is famous for its **university**, founded like that of Paris in 1215. **Miguel de Unamuno** (1864-1936), one of the great Spanish humanists, was a professor of Greek and later become the rector.

★★★HISTORICAL CENTRE

★★★**Plaza Major** – Built under Philip V between 1729 and 1755 to thank the city for its loyalty during the War of Succession, this is one of Spain's most beautiful squares. Its homogeneous style is largely the work of the Churriguera brothers. On the ground level, four galleries of rounded arcades are decorated with a series of medallions representing the kings of Spain from Alphonse XI to Ferdinand VI, or famous personalities such as Cervantes, El Cid, Christopher Columbus and Cortes. Pediment façades of the town hall and the Royal Pavilion bearing a bust of Philip V dominate the other two sides. An elegant balustrade crowns the three floors' high arcades.

San Martín Church – This Romanesque church has preserved its north portal with indented archivolts in the Zamora style.

★**Casa de la Conchas (House of Shells)** – The austere walls of this 15C house are softened by some 400 scallop shells and a row of Isabelline windows. The bottom of the bay windows is protected by superb wrought-iron grill-work. The patio of delicate mixtilineal arcades is graced with lovely openwork balustrades, lions' heads and coats of arms.

Clerecía – This Jesuit college, the building of which was started in 1617 is both impressive and majestic. The Baroque towers were completed by Andrés Garcia de Quinones in 1755. Beside the church stands a Baroque cloister.

★★**Patio de las Escuelas** – The small square off the old Calle Libreros is surrounded by the most characteristic monuments in Salamanca. In the centre stands a bronze statue of Fray Luis de Leon.

University – The ornate **portal**★★★ dating from 1534, is covered with delicate sculptures and composed like a work of art. Basket-handle arches stand above the double door. The relief of each successive tier of sculptures is accentuated to compensate for the increasing distance from the viewer.
Lecture rooms give directly onto a **patio**. The **Great Hall** (Paraninfo) hung with 17C Brussels tapestries, served as the setting for official ceremonies. It contains a portrait of Charles IV by Goya. The hall *(aula)* of **Maestro Salinas**, a professor of music who lived from 1513 to 1590, contains a 15C music portfolio. Fray Luis de Leon taught theology in a hall furnished in the 16C. His professor's desk with its sounding board presides over the rough-hewn benches, a luxury in those days when students generally sat on the ground. Luis de Leon's ashes are buried in the chapel. Beneath the grand staircase's high star-vaulting, the ramp is sculpted with foliage and imaginary scenes; sculptures on the third flight represent a mounted bullfight. The first floor gallery still has a richly decorated coffered ceiling with stalactite ornamentation, underlined by a fine bas-relief frieze on the wall. A Gothic doorway with beautiful 16C grillwork leads to the 18C library with 40,000 volumes dating from the 16C to 18C. Some of the rare manuscripts are much older, from the 11C.

★★**Catedral Nueva (New Cathedral)** – Construction began in 1513 on the large cathedral. It was only completed in 1560. Further additions were made up to the 18C, hence the great diversity: Gothic, Renaissance and Baroque.

★★**Catedral Vieja (Old Cathedral)** – The powerful pillars of this beautiful Romanesque cathedral support a ribbed vault which was an innovation at the time. The lantern-tower (Torre del Gallo) with two tiers of windows and ribbing is one of the most beautiful of the period. High beneath the vaulted ceiling, sculpted capitals represent scenes of tournaments and imaginary animals.

The **reredos★★** in the central apse are attributed to Nicolas of Florence, in 1445. The 53 compartments are painted in amazingly fresh colours with delightful detail illustrating the architecture and dress of the period. In the centre, the 12C Virgin de la Vega is of wood covered in enamelled gilt bronze.
Recesses in the right transept contain 13C recumbent figures and frescos influenced by the French style.
At the back of the nave, the St Martin's Chapel is covered with 13C frescoes by Anton Sanchez de Segovia, and others dating from the 14C.

Cloister – The Romanesque arcades were destroyed in the Lisbon earthquake of 1755. Only a few capitals remain standing out curiously in the plateresque decor. The ancient Mozarabic rite was celebrated in the Talavera Chapel, with its Mudéjar dome rising from sculpted ribbing and altarpiece of the School of Pedro Berruguete. University examinations took place in the St Barbara Chapel. The Diocesan Museum, which is in the chapter-house, contains several works by Fernando Gallego and his brother Francisco. Others by Juan de Flandres (St Michael reredos) are found on the first floor.
Note the beautiful 15C **tomb★★** in the Anaya Chapel by Diego de Anaya, Archbishop of Salamanca and later of Seville. The sides of the alabaster tomb are decorated with saints and their emblems; around it runs a beautifully worked plateresque grille. The chapel also contains a 15C organ and 16C recumbent figures by Gutierre.
From the Patio Chico, note the apse of the old cathedral and the shell-design roof of the Torre del Gallo, reminiscent of St Front's in Périgueux (France).

★**Convento de San Esteban** – This 16C to 17C convent is striking for its mix of Gothic and Renaissance styles. While the pinnacles of the lateral buttresses are typical Gothic, the imposing **façade★** is a remarkable example of plateresque. The bas-relief illustrates the lapidation of St Stephen. It was done by Juan Antonio Ceroni in 1610. In the cloisters, note the prophets' heads in **medallions★** and the grand staircase (1553).

Convento de las Dueñas – The capitals of the Renaissance **cloister★★** bear a profusion of small, yet astonishingly powerful sculptures: symbolic animals, bodies in tortuous positions, medallions containing majestic heads of old men or charming feminine faces.

DONOSTIA/SAN SEBASTIÁN★★

Population 176 019
Michelin map 970 G7

The lovely **site★★★** of San Sebastian stretches around a shell-shaped bay, **Concha**, which gave it its name of "pearl of Cantabria."
The celebrated seaside resort boasts a dazzling line of elegant, deluxe residences, beautiful promenades and gardens that edge its two, gloriously curving sandy beaches: Concha, and, beyond the promontory, the stylish **Ondarreta**. San Sebastian has been a famed resort since the 19C when Queen Maria Christina of Habsburg chose it as her summer residence.

Panoramic Views – From **Monte Igueldo★★★** *(access by car or by cable-car)* and from **Monte Urgul★★**.

SANTIAGO DE COMPOSTELA★★★

Population 105 851
Michelin map 970 E 7

Santiago de Compostela is the world's third most important place of pilgrimage after Jerusalem and Rome. From the Middle Ages, pilgrims have flocked here from the four corners of Europe. Today, it remains one of the most remarkable cities in Spain. The **Old Town's★★** numerous churches and convents lend a pervasive atmosphere of mysticism. Surprisingly, Romanesque art does not prevail but rather Baroque and neo-Classical monuments. The old streets are still lively today, thanks to the some 32 000 students at the University.

Legend and History – The Apostle James, known as the Son of Thunder for his fiery temper, is said to have crossed the ocean to convert Spain to Christianity. His small boat was wrecked at the mouth of the Ulla River. For seven years, he crisscrossed the country before returning to the Holy Land. Herod Agrippa forced him to flee Palestine, and his disciples brought his body to Spain. They buried it near the coast where their boat was cast ashore, on the spot where he had landed a few years earlier. Barbarians and later the Moors invaded Spain erasing even the memory of the location of his tomb.

According to legend, a star revealed to shepherds the resting place of St James at the beginning of the 9C. thus, Compostella or Campus Stellae, field of the star. Another theory is that the name comes from the Low Latin *compostela* or cemetery.

★★★PLAZA DEL OBRADOIRO

This worthy setting for the cathedral is remarkable due to the size and number of its monuments.

★★★**Cathedral** – The first basilica was built over the Apostle's tomb shortly after it was discovered. Alphonse III built another church on the site, but Al-Mansour destroyed it in a raid in 997. The present structure looks Baroque, but it was built between the 11C and the early 13C.

★★★**Obradoiro Façade** – Fernando Casas y Novoa's Baroque masterpiece – the name means work of gold – has graced the entrance to the cathedral since 1750. The richly sculpted centre with its elegant play of line and curve rises to form a slender triangle. Two high towers, sumptuously decorated and slightly in retreat, flank the central spire and accentuate its upward lines.

★★★**Portico de la Gloria** – In the narthex, the statuary of this beautiful triple portico is unusually harmonious yet extremely varied in expression, detail, style and colour. Mateo fashioned the masterpiece in the late 12C, later than the rest of the Romanesque cathedral. It already seems to announce the Gothic style. Mateo, a master-builder of bridges, reinforced the crypt beneath to support its massive weight. The central portal is dedicated to the Christian church: on the tympanum, the Saviour is surrounded by the four Evangelists, while the 24 Old Men of the Apocalypse are found on the archivolt.

Treasure and Reliquary Chapel – This Gothic chapel on the nave's right side holds a silver and gold custodial by Antonio de Arfe (1539-1566). The head of St James the Minor is preserved in the plateresque Reliquary chapel, designed by Juan de Alava.

Museum – The ground floor library contains the *botafumeiros*, and the chapter house hung with 17C Flemish tapestries together with three woven in Madrid in the 18C. The **Tapestry Museum** on the first floor has works after Téniers, Goya and Bayeu. The basement is devoted to archeology. Some pieces come from digs beneath the nave and the south transept.

★**Cloister** – The simple yet majestic cloister with its expansive galleries was built in 1521; it is crowned by an openwork balustrade and pinnacles.

Lower Church – The 11C crypt lies at the foot of the grand staircase preceding the Obradoiro Façade. The style is beautifully Romanesque, with sculpted capitals and columns.

★★**Puerta de las Platerias** (Goldsmiths' Doorway) – This Romanesque door with its double arch is entirely sculpted with bas-relief scenes. They date from the 11C and show a French influence. Most famous are the scenes of Adam and Eve being driven out of Paradise and, in the right-hand corner of the tympanum on the left, the Adulteress. The clock tower to the right was built at the end of the 17C; to the left is the tower of the treasure.

Palacio Gelmírez – This archbishop's palace stands to the left of the cathedral. A few rooms date from the 12C and the Gothic period, including the vast **Synod Hall**★. It extends more than 30m/98ft in length, with sculptured ribbed vaulting. Scenes of Alphonse IX de Leon's wedding banquet are carved in high relief.

★**Hostal de los Reyes Catolicos** – The Hostelry of the Catholic Kings is now a *parador*. It was founded by Ferdinand of Aragon and Isabella of Castile to serve as an inn and hospital for the pilgrims. The imposing **façade**★ is highlighted by a superb plateresque portal. Its layout resembles all hospitals of the period: a cross within a square, forming four elegant plateresque patios.

City Hall – The former Palacio de Raxoy faces the cathedral. Its Classical façade was designed in the 18C by the French artist Charles Lemaur. It serves as both City Hall and seat of the presidency of the Xunta de Galicia.

San Jeronimo College – On the square's south side, this 17C edifice has preserved its 15C portal, with a heavy Romanesque influence.

SEGOVIA★★★

Population 55 496
Michelin map 970 F 8

In the Middle Ages, this noble Castilian city served as the residence of Alphonse X the Wise and Henry IV. It was a major economic and political hub that played a decisive role in the history of Castile. The **site★★** is most unusual – the centre of the city, enclosed by ramparts, stands perched at 1 000m/3 280ft atop a triangular rock. To the left is the Roman aqueduct, to the right are the cathedral domes and further right still, at the tip of the triangle, the Alcázar, 100m-328ft above the confluence of the Eresma and the Clamores rivers. For a good view, approach on the road via Cuesta de los Hoyos and Paseo de Santo Domingo de Guzman.
In Roman times, Segovia was an important military post. The Arabs introduced wool working and made it an industrial centre in the Middle Ages. The Golden Age of Segovia was the 15C, when it boasted 60 000 inhabitants.
Inside the walls, most of the picturesque streets are edged by Castilian doorways framed with 15C and 16C *alfiz* and façades decorated with interlacing Mudéjar geometric designs. These *esgrafiados* are carved into the plaster. Segovia's greatest richness, however, comes from its Romanesque churches.

The Romanesque Churches – Built of golden stone, all present the same features: a pronounced rounded apse, often a square tower rising beside the chevet, and a covered gallery running along one wall for meetings of the weavers' and tradesmen's guilds.

Segovia Today – Essentially a tourist city, Segovia is popular for its many monuments as well as for its gastronomic specialities, including the exquisite suckling pig *(cochinillo asado)* roasted over an open fire.

★★★ROMAN AQUEDUCT

The simple, elegant architecture makes this one of the most beautiful of Roman aqueducts. It is still in service today, stretching in 728m/2 388 ft and rising in two tiers of arches 28m/92ft above the ground. It was built in the time of Trajan (1C) to convey water from Rio Acebada, in the Sierra de Fuenfria.

★★OLD CITY *4hr*

Plaza Major – This favourite meeting place is dominated by the cathedral's towering silhouette. Locals gather on the café terraces beneath the arcades. Prominent buildings include the City Hall and the Juan Bravo Theatre.

★★**Cathedral** – The soft golden stone, the tiered chevet topped by pinnacles and balustrades and the high tower lend definite grace to the cathedral's massive forms. It was built under Charles V after the destruction of the previous cathedral during an uprising in 1511. The style is Gothic even though the Renaissance already had begun. The broad naves, linear pillars and ribbed vaulting render it luminous and elegant. Note the beautiful grilles and a reredos by Juan de Juni just right of the entrance.
The choir stalls in the late-15C Flamboyant Gothic style come from the earlier cathedral.

★**Cloister** – It dates from the 15C and was transported stone by stone from the earlier cathedral near the Alcazar.
Beautiful 17C Brussels **tapestries★** in the chapter-house illustrate the story of Queen Zenobia. The museum contains a church plate and the Corpus Christi custodial.

★**Plaza de San Martín** – Segovia's history seems most alive on this square in the heart of the former aristocratic quarter. A statue of Juan Bravo stands in the centre. Note the **15C house** with a gallery beneath the roof. It is known as the Juan Bravo house. The 14C tower of the **House of the Lozoyas** bears witness to the family's great influence. The façade of the **Solier House**, or Casa de Correos, is notable for its richly decorated doorways. The 12C **Church of San Martín★** is surrounded on three sides by a covered gallery with capitals carved with network and animals.
The 17C **old prison** has a lovely Baroque pediment.

Casa del Conde de Alpuente – This beautiful 15C Gothic home has a façade decorated with graceful *esgrafiados*.

Casa de los Picos – The most unusual 15C residence in Segovia is known for its diamond-point stones.

SEVILLA★★★

SEVILLE – Population 668 256
Michelin map 970 F 9

Spain's fourth-largest city and the capital of Andalucia lies on Guadalquivir Plain. It boasts all the characteristics of a bustling metropolis. Take time to explore the old quarters with their narrow streets and to ride slowly through the peaceful gardens and parks by horse-drawn carriage.
Seville comes vibrantly alive on the occasion of its brilliant festivals. **Holy Week** features a succession of pasos processions in which districts and guilds rival each other in opulence and fervour. The *pasos* are great litters laden with flowers and bearing polychrome wood statues. Groups of 25 to 60 men carry them. They are saluted along the way by the *Saeta*, a poignant improvised song. Lines of penitents, hidden and anonymous, follow under their tall pointed hoods.
Yet another Seville reveals itself during the April **Feria**. Beautiful Andalusian women swirl in their flounced dresses and the proud cavaliers sit astride their horses. Superb horse-drawn carriages deposit their passengers in front of canvas pavilions, to dance the *sevillanas*. Seville is the home of the flamenco. It is also famed for its *tablaos*, little cafés to drink *copas* and savour *tapas*.

C. et J. Lenars/EXPLORER

Penitents' procession

★★★ THE GIRALDA AND THE CATHEDRAL *1hr 30 min*

★★★ **La Giralda** – The Weather Vane rises 98m/321ft. It is a former minaret and owes its name to the bronze statue of Faith which sits on its top and turns with the wind. When La Giralda was built in the 12C, it looked much like its Moroccan sisters, the Koutoubia in Marrakech and the Hassan Tower in Rabat. The upper story and Renaissance lantern were added in the 16C. Its delicate decoration typifies Almohades' style. These religious purists who abhorred ostentation created monumental art in harmony with their ideal of simplicity. A gentle ramp, broken by a number of platforms, leads to the top of the 70m/230ft tower which commands a beautiful **view**★★ over the city.
The **Orange Court** (Patio de los Naranjos) also remains from the mosque, while the north side's Pardon Doorway of 1552 (viewed from the street) represents a fine example of the Mudéjar style.

★★★ **Cathedral** – "Let us build a cathedral so grand that those who see it will take us for madmen", decided the cathedral chapter in 1401. And indeed, Sevilla's cathedral is Europe's third-largest, after St Peter's in Rome and Saint Paul's in London. The massive exterior is one of the last Gothic cathedral constructions. Some early Renaissance influences are visible. The main portals are modern, yet fully in keeping with the overall style. Framing the west portal, the doors of the Nativity *(on the right)* and the Baptism *(on the left)*, bear beautiful sculptures by Mercadante de Bretagne from around 1460. The chevet, on either side of the rounded Royal Chapel (1575) and the Gothic Los Palos and Las Campanillas doors are surprising for their Renaissance tympana which give full play to perspective. They are the work of Miguel Perrin from around 1520.
Inside, the giant columns supporting great arches appear thin and delicate. At the transept crossing, magnificent Flamboyant vaulting rises 56m/184ft above the paving stones.
The colossal tomb of Christopher Columbus dates from the 19C. It is found in the south transept and represents his coffin borne by four kings, symbolizing the four kingdoms of Leon, Castile, Navarra and Aragon.

Capilla Mayor (Chancel) – Superb plateresque grilles carved from 1518 to 1533 protect the immense Flemish **reredos**★★ blazing with gold and sculpted with profusion and delicacy. They represent scenes in the life of Christ.

★★ **Capilla Real** (Royal Chapel) – This typical Renaissance building is covered by an elegant dome richly decorated with cells containing sculpted busts.

★★★ THE ALCÁZAR AND THE SANTA CRUZ DISTRICT *2hr 30min*

★★★ **Alcázar (Reales Alcazares)** – All that remains of the original Almohade Alcazar are the Patio de Yeso and a piece of wall separating the Monteria and Lion courts. The rest dates from Christian times. The palace was built in 1362 by King Peter the Cruel (1350-1369), 78 years after the departure of the Moors from Seville.
The decoration systematically is based on that of the Alhambra. Arab architects probably contributed to the construction.

★★★ **Palace of Peter the Cruel** – The narrow façade sheltered by a sculpted wood overhang shows the strong influence of the Mexuar Court in Granada.
Inside, the **Court of the Maidens** (Patio de la Doncellas) is admirable in proportion and in decoration, despite the upper storey added in the 16C. Wonderful rooms surround it, abundant in stuccowork, multicoloured *azulejos* and *artesonados*. The Hall of the Ambassadors is surmounted by a remarkable half-orange 15C cedar **dome**★★. The adjoining Philip II chamber leads to the graceful **Dolls' Court** (Patio de la Munecas), named for its diminutive scale. The bedroom of Isabella the Catholic, the Princes' chamber and that of the Moorish kings, with lovely blue stucco work are nearby.

ADDITIONAL SIGHTS

★★ **Museo de Bellas Artes (Fine Arts Museum)** – The museum is housed in the former 17C and 18C La Merced Convent . Its cool cloisters, it provides an outstanding perspective of Sevilla's paintings from the Golden Age. The best represented artists are Murillo and Zurbaran.

★★ **Casa de Pilatos (House of Pilate)** – The palace is said to be inspired by the house of Pontius Pilate in Jerusalem.
It was built in the late 15C and completed at the beginning of the 16C by Don Fabrique, first Marquis of Tarifa. The architecture is a blend of Mudéjar, Renaissance and Flamboyant Gothic. The Mudéjar style dominates the first floor, evoking an elegant Moorish palace with finely carved stucco work and remarkable shimmering **azulejos**★★. The building is filled with statues, some from ancient times and others from the 16C.

J.-L. Barde/SCOPE

Casa de Pilatos

TARRAGONA★★★

Population 112 801
Michelin map 970 H 8

The venerable city of Tarragona is both a showcase rich in vestiges of ancient and medieval times and a modern town offering delightful walks. The flower-covered seafront rises in a series of terraces up along a cliff overlooking the Mediterranean. It skirts the old town, circles the palace of Augustus and follows the walls behind the silhouette of the cathedral.

★★ROMAN TARRAGONA

The best preserved monuments are outside the town, the **Centcelles Mausoleum**★ and Las **Ferreres Aqueduct**★, the Scipion Tower and Bera Triumphal arch.

★★ **Passeig Arqueològic** – The 3C BC walls were erected on a Herculean base of giant boulders laid on top of each other, held in place by their sheer weight, and pierced by a few doorways. For a long time they were thought to pre-date the Roman Era, seeming so barbarian in their massive size. They were extensively transformed and raised in the Middle Ages and redesigned in the 18C. A walk along their base leads through delightful gardens.
The outer perimeter was raised in 1707 during the War of Succession by the English, allies of Charles of Hapsburg.

★★**Museu Nacional Arqueológic** – The pieces on display were found in Tarragona and the immediate environs. Most date from the Roman era. They include beautiful mosaics, such as a **head of Medusa**★★ with piercing eyes, statues from monuments and public squares, friezes, cornices and sculpted medallions from the Temples of Jupiter (where the cathedral now stands) and Augustus. The nearby **praetorium** houses the city history museum.

MEDIEVAL TOWN

Inside the ramparts is a maze of narrow old streets. A broad staircase leads to the cathedral.

★★**Cathedral** – The 12C apse is Romanesque in style, but most of the church is Gothic. In the adjoining chapels, the magnificence of the Flamboyant Gothic, plateresque and Baroque decoration is overwhelming.
The many works of art include, in the central apse, the **reredos of St Thecla**★★★, patron saint of the city.

★★**Cloister** – The cloister surprises by its dimensions (45m/148ft on one side) and its originality. Built in the 12C and 13C, the arches and geometric decoration are Romanesque. But the vaulted ceiling is Gothic, as are the great relieving arches.

EXCURSIONS

★★★**Monasterio de Poblet** – *46km/28.5mi to the north west.*
This monastery lies at the foot of hills covered in oak and almond trees. It is one of the largest and best preserved of the Cistercian order. Poblet owes its existence to the Reconquest. Having recovered Catalonia from the Moors, Ramon Berenguer IV wished to thank God. In 1150, he brought 12 Cistercian monks from the Abbey of Fontfroide, near Narbonne in France. They constructed the buildings, cleared the surrounding land and prepared it for cultivation.
The ample **cloister**★★ with its pure, sober lines, the **church**★★ and the dormitory may be visited.

TOLEDO★★★

Population 68 831
Michelin map 970 F 8

Toledo rises into the luminous blue Castilian sky like an incredible stage decor at the summit of a granite hill. The green waters of the River Tagus circle it at the bottom of a steep ravine. Inside the ramparts, a multitude of monuments and a labyrinth of narrow winding streets provide a magnificent setting for the **Corpus Christi** procession. History is omnipresent. Each stone of Toledo speaks of its past and the artistic treasures reflect the fusion, as in Cordoba, of the Christian, Jewish and Moorish cultures. Toledo is renowned for all its damascene ware, burnished steel inlaid with threads of gold, silver and copper. Its culinary specialities include braised partridge and marzipan.

F. Gouverneur/MICHELIN

General view of Toledo

The incomparable **site★★★** can best be admired from the *circunvalacion* road from the Alcantara Bridge to San Martin. This follows the 3.5km/2.2mi loop formed by the river. The sun-scorched hills are covered with *cigarrales*, vast olive plantations dotted with white residences. Lookout points include the terrace of the Parador above the *circunvalacion*. At sunset or at night, the spectacle is equally memorable.

★★★OLD TOLEDO *A full day*

The maze of narrow streets rises in steps to churches and ancient palaces.

★★★ **Cathedral** – Construction began under Ferdinand III (St Ferdinand) in 1227. Unlike other churches in the town, it adopted the French Gothic style. Building continued to the end of the 15C, leaving traces of each phase in the evolution of Spanish Gothic. The richly sculpted decoration and innumerable works of art make this an excellent museum of religious art.

Exterior – The 13C Clock Doorway (Puerta del Reloj) on the left flank is the oldest. But it was modified in the 19C.
The main façade is composed of three tall 15C portals. The upper part was completed in the 16C and 17C. In the centre, the Pardon Doorway (Puerta del Perdon) is covered with statues and crowned by a tympanum.
The harmonious tower is 15C. The dome replacing the second tower was built in the 17C by El Greco's son. On the south façade, the 15C Lion Portal was by Hennequin of Brussels and Juan Aleman. In 1800, it was flanked by a neo-Classical portal.

Interior – Superb stained glass-windows (1418-1561) adorn the many bays. The chancel, choir and most of the chapels are enclosed by beautiful grill-work.

Chancel – This most sumptuous part of the cathedral was enlarged by Cardinal Cisneros in the 16C. The gigantic sculpted polychrome **reredos★★** in the flamboyant Gothic style are admirable and imposing.

Coro – A series of 14C high reliefs and wrought-iron enclosed chapels compose the coro protected behind an elegant grille dating from 1574. It contains magnificent 15C and 16C **choir stalls★★★**. The lower part in wood, by Rodrigo Aleman, retraces 54 scenes of the conquest of the province of Granada. The 16C alabaster upper part, represents figures from the Old Testament. The left-hand side is by Berruguete, and the right side by Philip of Burgundy (Felipe Bigarny). The central bas-relief of the Transfiguration is also by Berruguete. His style projects a sense of movement, as opposed to Bigarny's more rigid composition.

★ **Casa y Museo del Greco** – El Greco moved to Toledo in 1585. His house is a charming example of the 16C home. The museum contains several of his works. **The Burial of Count Orgaz★★★** is found in the **Iglesia Santo Tomé**, for which it was painted in 1586.

VALENCIA★★

Population 777 427
Michelin map 970 G 8

Valencia, Spain's third-largest city, has all the atmosphere of a major Mediterranean metropolis. It is blessed with a mild climate and a beautiful quality of light. Its broad avenues (Grandes Vias), shaded by palms and fig trees, circle the old quarter with its fortified gates, churches and narrow streets of old-fashioned shops and Gothic homes. The city lies on the banks of the River Turia in the heart of very fertile land, the **huerta**. Tourism in Valencia has flourished due to its location on the Costa del Azahar. This poetic name, meaning orange blossom coast, evokes the broad band of sand stretching from the north to the south of the city. The sun-drenched coastline, sheltered by the sierras from the winds off the Meseta, has become one of Spain's major summer tourism centres. The seaside resorts of **Benicasim, Oropesa, Peñiscola, Benicarló** and **Vinarós** to the north, and **Saler, Culléra, Gandía** and **Oliva** to the south, have high rise buildings forming a strange urban forest between the long sandy beaches and orange groves.

★THE OLD CITY *time: 2 hours*

★ **Cathedral** – It stands on the site of a former mosque. Construction began in 1262 but most of the cathedral dates from the 14-15C. At the end of the 18C, a neo-Classical renovation completely masked the earlier Gothic architecture: today, the original lines have been restored.

★ **The Miguelete** – This octagonal tower adjoining the façade was known to the Valencians as El Micalet. It owes its name to the large clock baptized on the feast of St Michael. From the top, an excellent view looks over the cathedral roofs and the city's innumerable church domes shining with glazed tiles.

Exterior – The 18C main façade was designed by a German architect to imitate Italian Baroque. The Assumption on the pediment is by Ignacio Vergara and Estève. The south portal (Puerta del Palau) is Romanesque; the doorway of the Apostles on the north, Gothic.

Interior – The elegant **lantern-tower** is a fine example of Flamboyant Gothic.
The reredos on the main altar, painted at the beginning of the 16C by Fernando de Llanos and Yanez de la Almedina, represents the life of Christ and the Virgin in a style reminiscent of Da Vinci.
In the ambulatory back of the main altar, a 1510 alabaster relief of the Resurrection is found beneath a lovely balustrade. Opposite is the 15C Virgen del Coro in polychrome alabaster, and a Christ of Good Death in a nearby chapel.

★**Palacio de la Generalidad** – This beautiful 15C Gothic palace was until 1707 the seat of the Valencia Cortes, responsible for collecting taxes. A tower was added in the 17C, and an identical one in the 20C.
The elegant Gothic patio shows off a sculpture by Benlliure, Dante's Inferno (1900). The gilded chamber's gilt and polychrome **artesonado ceiling★** is outstanding. One large painting is of the Water Tribunal. On the first floor, the Kings' Hall contains portraits of the kings of Valencia. It leads to an oratory with 16C reredos by the Valencia artist Juan Sarinena. The great hall of the Cortes is decorated with an *azulejos* frieze and a coffered ceiling dating from the 16C. Several of the 16C paintings are of members of the Cortes.

For further details on Spain, consult the Michelin Green Guides Spain, Barcelona and Catalonia.

When looking for a hotel or restaurant, use the Michelin Red Guide España Portugal, updated annually.

Sweden

Sverige

Area: 450 000km^2/173 700sq mi – **Population:** 8.5 million – **Capital:** Stockholm – **Currency:** Swedish crown (krona) divided into 100 öre – **Time:** GMT + 1hr in winter, GMT + 2hr in summer

Sweden is admired by most of Europe as a symbol of neutrality, tolerance and efficiency. The country is first and foremost Scandinavian sharing much with its neighbours. Lakes, forests and hills dominate the countryside. Although the landscape varies little, it gives a definite impression of space. Swedes love their rugged, grandiose natural environment and take great pleasure in outdoor activities.
The sophistication of Swedish society also allows this hard-working, highly organised, responsible people to live with ease and comfort. No doubt, the most significant Swedish contribution to international culture is the Nobel Prize, attributed yearly since 1895 by Stockholm's literary and scientific academies. Novelist Selma Lagerlöf was the first woman to obtain this coveted prize. Another well-known Swedish name is Anders Celsius who, during the 18C, created the centigrade temperature scale.

IN BRIEF

Entry Formalities – Valid passport for British, US, Canadian, Australian and Japanese citizens.

Shopping – The stores are generally open from 9am to 6pm, Mondays to Fridays. On Saturdays, most close at 1pm.

The Smörgåsbord – This perfect solution to a quick lunch consists of a large buffet with a wide choice of meat, fish, hot dishes, cold cuts and vegetables.

GÖTEBORG and the SOUTHWEST

Denmark's long occupation and proximity has shaped the region's character.

★★GÖTEBORG (GOTHENBURG) Michelin map 970 K2

The maritime importance of Sweden's second largest city has never ceased to grow since the 17C, in spite of the ups and downs of international politics. Today Gothenburg is Scandinavia's biggest port housing the country's largest shipyards as well as prestigious industries such as Volvo.
Gothenburg's canals and architecture reflect the influence of the Dutch builders called in by King Gustavus Adolphus II. The quays are lined with 17C and 18C buildings. A floating museum, **Göteborgs Maritima Centrum**, is docked. From here, many emigrants sailed in search of the American dream *(see VÄXJÖ)*.
The historical centre is organised around **Gustaf Adolfs Torg**, a large square on Stora Hamn kanalen. Further south, the city's cultural life is centred on **Götaplatsen**. In the middle of the square stands Carl Mille's **Fontaine de Poséidon**★, a symbol of Gothenburg's maritime vocation. The **Konstmuseet**★, also on the square, houses rich collections of Scandinavian art. **Kungsportavenyn**★ connects Götaplatsen to the old city. It is Gothenburg's most animated avenue – as well as one of the greenest, with numerous parks.
Two immense lakes, Vänern and Vättern, lie northeast of Gothenburg. A long canal called the **Göta Kanal**★★ joins the two bodies of water, part of a larger link between the North Sea and the Baltic. Cruises are organised from Gothenburg and Stockholm.
South of Gothenburg, beautiful beaches and pleasant seaside resorts string along the coast.
Further south beyond Helsingborg, the Scania (Skåne) region only threw off Danish rule during the second half of the 17C. Several beautiful castles, enhanced by the beauty of the green countryside and the fertile plains, remain from this period of unending conflict.

★MALMÖ Michelin map 970 L3

Malmö acts as the gateway to Sweden and the capital of the country's south. It is an old city set amid canals and parks. **Stortorget**★, the large market square, is lined with interesting buildings such as the town hall, **Rådhuset**. Built in the 16C, it was later remodelled. Behind the Rådhuset stands **Sankt Petri Kyrka**★, a beautiful Gothic church of German inspiration. On the other side of Stortorget stands an attractive little cobblestone square lined with half-timbered houses, **Lilla Torg**★★.

To the west, a fortified red-brick castle, **Malmöhus★**, towers over the city centre. This former residence of Danish kings now houses several museums, including the **Museum of Fine Arts★★** (Konstmuseet), which displays Nordic art from the 1920s and 1930s.

★★LUND Michelin map 970 L3

The Danish king founded this old university city almost a 1 000 years ago. It is located less then 30km/19mi northeast of Malmö. Consecrated in 1145, the cathedral, **Domkyrkan★★★** represents one of Sweden's most beautiful examples of Romanesque architecture. Its 14C astronomical clock puts on a delightful display of automatons every day at noon and 3pm.

★YSTAD Michelin map 970 L3

Along its winding cobblestone streets, this charming medieval town still has a large number of half-timbered houses. The imposing **Sankta Maria Kyrka**, remodelled several times since the 14C, overlooks Stortorget. Its fine Renaissance **pulpit★★** is worth seeing. **Lilla Västergatan**, the former high street, is lined with attractive 17C and 18C houses. Sladdergatan leads to **Sankt Petrikyrkan** church (13C), the remains of a Franciscan monastery. The municipal museum is housed in the cloister.
Along Scania's East Coast, Kristianstad stands out as an interesting Renaissance town. The avid builder Christian IV of Denmark founded the city.

The LAKE DISTRICT

Michelin map 970 L, M[1]

The region of idyllic landscapes surrounding Lake Siljan is known as Dalarna. The local population has used imagination to keep alive ancestral rural traditions. Summer chalets which in the past provided summer pastures for local herds today welcome tourists. Handicraft production is encouraged, and villagers dress up in their colourful costumes for local festivities. Throughout the summer, music and folklore dance festivals, rowing races and other festivities are held.
On the southern end of Lake Siljan, a church, its silhouette crowned with an onion-shaped dome, marks the charming village of **Leksand★★**. The **Leksands Kulturhus** (Cultural Centre) houses a museum of regional culture and traditions.
At the lake's other end, **Mora★★** is famous for the **Vasaloppet**, its annual 90km/55mi cross-country ski race. More than 14 000 participants commemorate the exploit of the future king Gustav Vasa who fled on skis from Mora to Sälen in 1519 to escape the Danes (a museum retraces the history of the race from its origins to the present day). The home of the painter **Anders Zorn** and the museum housing his works are also open to visitors.
Near Orsa, some 30km/19mi north of Mora, lies **Grönklitts Björnpark**, a bear reserve where the animals live in a natural forest environment. Visitors are welcome.
Between Leksand and Mora, in the heart of Dalarna, the small town of **Rättvik★★** is particularly attached to its regional culture. It organises an **international folklore festival**. As in Leksand, the church has an attractive lakeside location.

C. Boisvieux

Midsummer procession

The key on page 4 explains the abbreviations and symbols used in the text or on the maps.

SWEDISH LAPLAND★★★

Lapland occupies almost one-fourth of Sweden's land area, but remains sparsely populated. Although it shares much with Norwegian Lapland *(see Norway)* and Finnish Lapland *(see Finland)*, Swedish Lapland lies further to the south, making it less arid. Reindeer herds set up their winter quarters in the thick forests.
Close to the Norwegian border, an ideal tourist resort for nature lovers, **Abisko**, occupies a scenic mountain setting.
Sami culture centres in **Arvidsjaur★**, to the west of Luleå. The village dates from the 18C, when Arvidsjaur was an important winter market.
Tärnaby, the birthplace of the downhill ski champion, Ingemar Stenmark, enjoys an interesting ski museum. Not far away, Samegården has a small Sami folk museum.
Another Sami museum lies just north of the Polar Circle in **Jokkmokk★**. An important winter market is located here.
The mining town of **Kiruna** has exported iron ore from the port of Narvik for almost a century. During the summer, part of the mine is opened to visitors. The church is shaped like a Lapp tent. The city also has a Sami cultural centre.

Emancipation of Scandinavian women

Finnish women were the first in the world to obtain the vote in 1906 followed by the Norwegians in 1913, the Danes in 1915 and the Swedes in 1920. British women over 30 were given the right to vote in 1918, American women in 1920 and the French followed in 1945.

SMÅLAND

Michelin map 970 I3, M3

This southeastern region of Sweden, covered with thick forests, encountered serious economic difficulties during the 19C. Only a flourishing glass industry saved it from bankruptcy.

★**Kalmar** – This ancient walled city played an essential role during the Middle Ages, not only for Sweden but also for Norway and Denmark. Within its walls, the **Kalmar Union** was signed in 1397. The treaty expresses the wish that the three Scandinavian countries be united under the authority of a single monarch. That it was never a success can be seen in the never-ending wars that followed. It is not certain that the union treaty was actually signed in the imposing fortress of **Kalmar Slott★★★** built opposite the island of Öland, but it is indeed one of the most beautiful castles in Sweden. Built during the 12C and 13C, it was entirely remodelled in the Renaissance style during the 16C.

Växjö – In the mid 19C, farming conditions became more and more difficult. Year after year, the harvests were insufficient to nourish the rural population. Industry could not offer work to those leaving the land. So an unprecedented wave of emigration swept over Europe. Several generations of country folk crossed the Atlantic Ocean, dazzled by the American dream. All in all, a quarter of the Swedish population emigrated before the mass exodus stopped in 1925. Many emigrants came from the province of Småland. **Utvandrarnas Hus★★**, the House of Emigrants, tells their story and how they settled on the virgin lands of North America. Founded in 1965, the institute holds the most important European records on emigration, a database and a library of 25 000 books. The names of most of the emigrants are documented and numerous Americans come to trace their ancestors.

STOCKHOLM★★★

Population 674 459
Michelin map 970 N 2

Stockholm is built on a group of islands linked by bridges and is surrounded on all sides by water. Lake Mälaren joins the Baltic Sea and the coast breaks up with countless islands, each more scenic than the last. Parks and gardens add to the undeniable beauty of this exceptional setting. Enthusiastic admirers say that the Swedish capital is the most beautiful city in the world!
Stockholm is modern and efficient as well as attractive. If necessary, the city does not hesitate to break with tradition. Like inhabitants in Oslo and Copenhagen, Stockholmers live outdoors during the summer, making for animated streets and the park. Activity peaks during the second week of August when the internationally renowned **Stockholm Water Festival** is held.
In 1998, Stockholm was made the **cultural capital of Europe.**

STOCKHOLM

Biblioteksgatan	CY	2
Birger Jarlsgatan	CXY	3
Brunkebergstorg	CY	5
Brunnsgränd	AZ	6
Bryggargatan	BY	7
Brända Tomten	AZ	8
Djurgårsbron	DY	9
Drottninggatan	BX CY	10
Evert Taubes terrass	AZ	13
Gallerian	CY	14
Grev Turegatan	CY	18
Gustav Adolfs torg	CY	16
Hamngatan	CY	
Herkulesgatan	CY	19
Hötorget	CY	20
Järntorget	AZ	21
Järntorgsgatan	AZ	23
Kindstugatan	AZ	24
Klarabergsgatan	CY	25
Klarabergsviadukten	BY	27
Kornhamnstorg	AZ	28
Kungsgatan	BCY	
Kungsträdgårdsgatan	CY	32
Köpmangatan	AZ	35
Lilla Nygatan	AZ	36
Mosebacke Torg	CZ	39
Munkbrogatan	AZ	40
Mäster Mikaels gata	DZ	42
Myntgatan	AZ	41
Norrbro	CY	43
Norrlandsgatan	CY	44
Nybroplan	CY	45
Olof Palmes Gata	BY	47
Prästgatan	AZ	48
Riddarhusgrand	AZ	49
Riddarhustorget	AZ	50
Rådhusgränd	AZ	52
Sergelgatan	CY	53
Sergels Torg	CY	54
Sista Styverns trappor	DZ	55
Slottskajen	AZ	56
Slussplan	AZ	57
Stallgatan	CY	59
Stigbergsgatan	DZ	60
Storkyrkobrinken	AZ	61
Strömbron	CY	62
Strömgatan	CY	63
Södermalmstorg	CZ	64
Södra Blasieholmshammen	CY	66
Tegelbacken	CY	67
Tegnerlunden	BX	69
Triewaldsgränd	AZ	70
Tyska Brinken	AZ	73
Urvädersgränd	CZ	74
Västerlånggatan	AZ	
Österlånggatan	AZ	
Östermalmstorg	DY	76
Östra Järnvägsgatan	BY	78

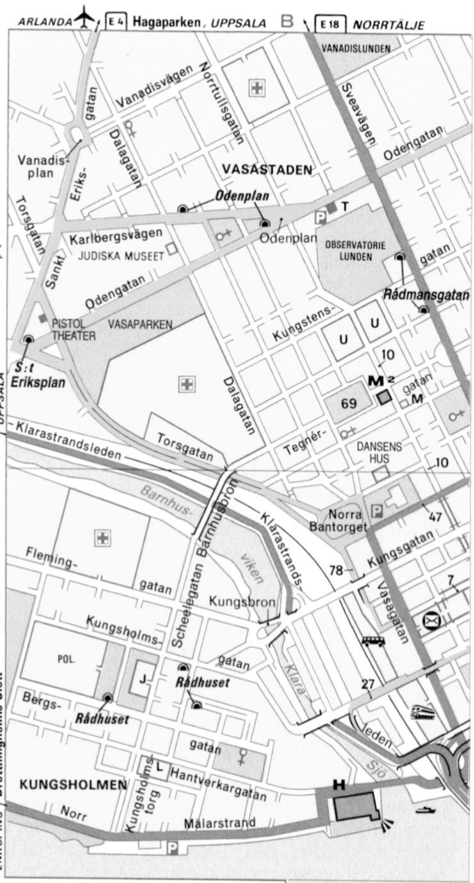

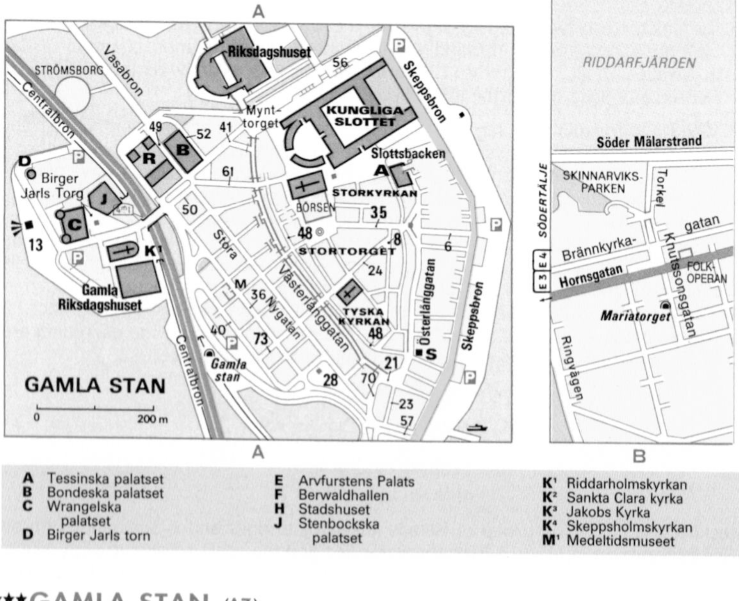

A Tessinska palatset		**E** Arvfurstens Palats		**K¹** Riddarholmskyrkan	
B Bondeska palatset		**F** Berwaldhallen		**K²** Sankta Clara kyrka	
C Wrangelska palatset		**H** Stadshuset		**K³** Jakobs Kyrka	
D Birger Jarls torn		**J** Stenbockska palatset		**K⁴** Skeppsholmskyrkan	
				M¹ Medeltidsmuseet	

★★★GAMLA STAN (AZ)

Stockholm's historical heart consists of a maze of narrow streets, with a 17C architectural cohesiveness and several prestigious buildings erected on three islands (Stadsholmen, Riddarholmen and Helgeandsholmen).

★★**Kungliga Slottet** (AZ) – The royal castle was rebuilt in the Baroque style after being destroyed by fire. It is only used for official receptions, and houses several museums.

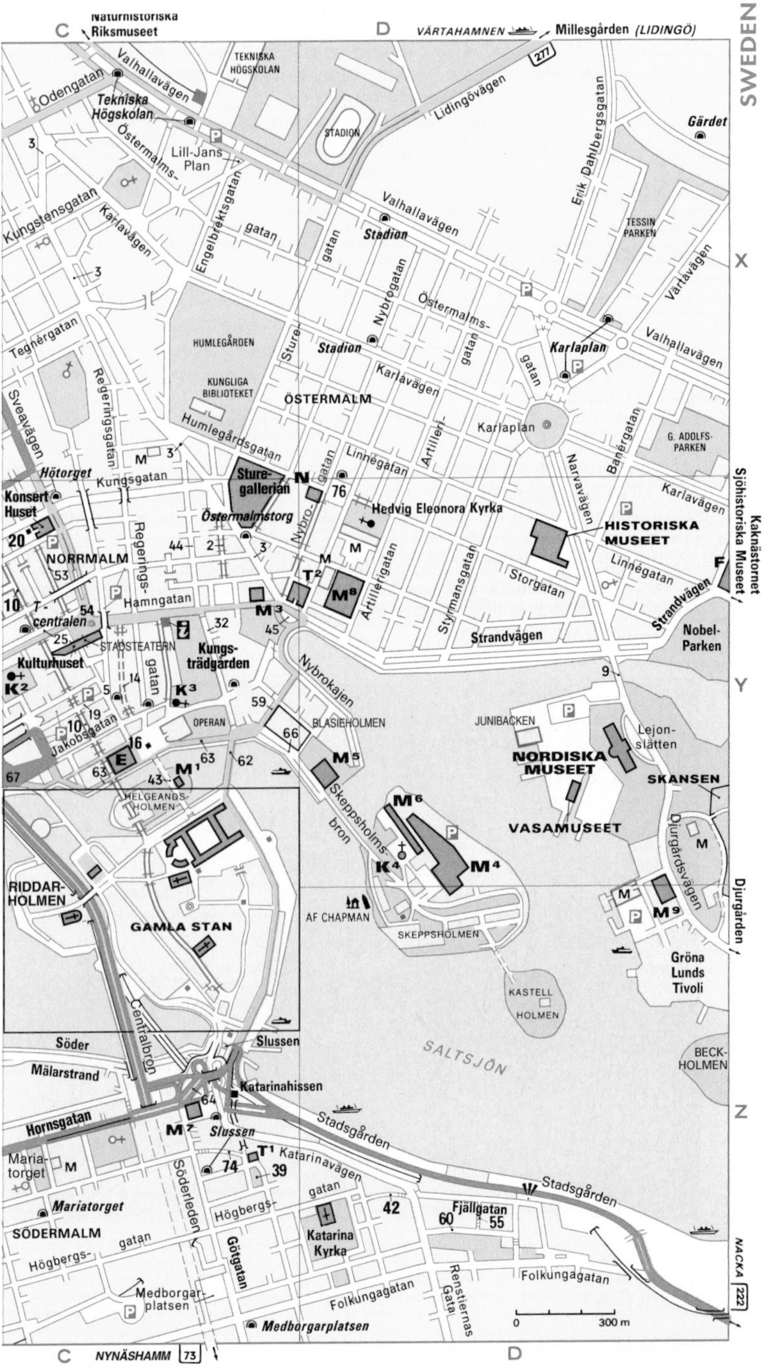

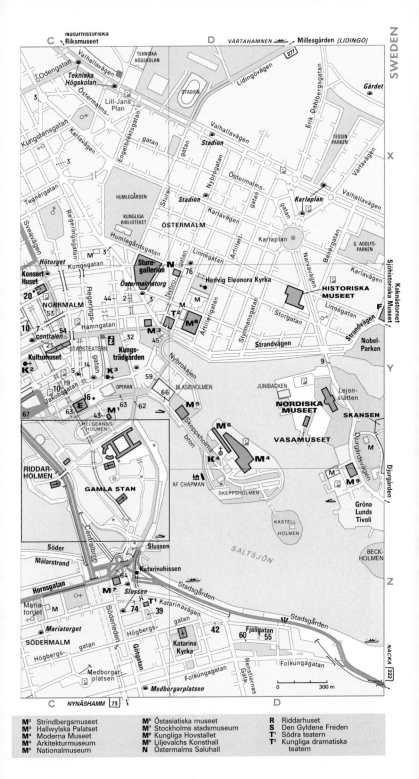

M² Strindbergsmuseet
M³ Hallwylska Palatset
M⁴ Moderna Museet
M⁴ Arkitekturmuseum
M⁵ Nationalmuseum
M⁶ Östasiatiska museet
M⁷ Stockholms stadsmuseum
M⁸ Kungliga Hovstallet
M⁹ Liljevalchs Konsthall
N Östermalms Saluhall
R Riddarhuset
S Den Gyldene Freden
T¹ Södra teatern
T² Kungliga dramatiska teatern

★**Storkyrkan** (AZ) – The cathedral was consecrated in 1306 and later refurbished. It boasts a magnificent wooden 15C sculpture depicting St George and the Dragon, by Bernt Notke from Lübeck.

Stortorget, the old town's main square, houses a Rococo-style building from the late 18C. The former **Börsen** (Stock Exchange) today is the home of the Royal Academy. It is from here that the winner of the Nobel Prize for literature is announced to the international press.

★**Riddarholmskyrkan** (AZ **K**[1]) – Situated on the small island of Riddarholmen, this is one of the capital's most ancient churches which now houses a museum. It contains the tombs of the Swedish monarchs.
Leaving the old town and heading northward lies Riksdagshuset (Parliament House). Steps lead down to an underground museum, **Medeltidsmuseet**★★ (CY **M**[1]) where visitors can see the capital's medieval ruins, discovered when building an underground car park.

NORRMALM (CY)

North of the old town, this modern, functional city consists of wide, straight streets. Offices and shops are clustered around Sergels Torg.
Kungsträdgården, once the king's vegetable garden, is now an elegant pleasure garden and a favourite meeting place with a wide selection of entertainment such as chess and boules.
Not far away, the **Nationalmuseum**★★ (DY **M**[5]) is Sweden's most important museum of fine arts.
Cross the bridge to the island of Skeppsholmen to visit the **Moderna Museet** (Museum of Modern Art) and **Arkitekturmuseum** (Museum of Architecture). The two museums share a new building designed by the Spanish architect José Rafael Moneo that fits in perfectly with the environment.
On the other side of the central train station, the island of Kungsholmen is home to the familiar outline of **Stadshuset**★★ (Town Hall) (BY **H**). The building, completed in 1923, represents a fine example of National Romantic style. The view from the top of the tower is striking.

C. Boisvieux

General view of Stockholm

DJURGÅRDEN (DY)

This former hunting ground, now a vast park, attracts picnic lovers, ramblers, horse riders and other outdoor enthusiasts. The island also has three interesting museums.

★★★**Skansen** – Founded in 1891, this was the world's first **open-air museum**. It contains 150 houses from different regions of Sweden, the interiors of which have all been reconstructed.

★★★**Vasamuseet** – This museum represents a highlight for both its historical interest and originality. It houses the Vasa warship which sank in the Stockholm harbour in 1628, and was salvaged and restored in 1961.

★★**Nordiska Museet** – Not far from Vasamuseet, this museum retraces the cultural history of Sweden. It contains a particularly interesting section devoted to the Lapps.

EXCURSIONS

★★★ **Drottningholm Slott** – *1hr boat ride from City Hall.* Built during the second half of the 17C in the Baroque style, this royal castle is the king's official residence. Do not miss the monumental staircase and the Court Theatre as well as the formal gardens, the French gardens and the English park.

★★★ **The Archipelago** – It consists of 24000 islands and reefs. Mini cruises go to individual islands, where swimming is possible. Many Stockholm residents have summer houses and chalets on the islands.

★★ **Millesgården** – In a magnificent setting on the island of Lidingö, the residence of the sculptor Carl Milles (1875-1955) has been converted into a museum dedicated to the artist's memory and work.

For further details on Sweden, consult the Michelin Green Guide Scandinavia Finland.

When looking for a hotel or restaurant in Göthenburg and Stockholm, use the Michelin Red Guide Europe, updated annually.

Switzerland

Schweiz, Suisse, Svizzera

Area: 41 300km²/15 694sq mi – **Population:** 6.9 million – **Capital:** Bern (Berne) – **Currency:** Swiss Franc – **Time:** GMT + 1hr in winter, GMT + 2hr in summer

Switzerland, the Helvetic Confederation, is an attractive country made up of 23 cantons. Many contrasts – even paradoxes – stem from the diversity of its inhabitants, languages and religions. The Alps occupy three-fifths of the territory. The highest point, the Dufour peak in the Monte Rosa massif reaches 4634m/15 200ft. The snow-capped summits of the Vaud, Valais, Grisons and Ticino Alps and the romantic lakes at Geneva, Lucerne and Interlaken with their picturesque paddle-steamers, have long attracted poets, musicians and other travellers. All seek to rediscover the calmness and purity of nature. Switzerland is a country of little trains, some electric and others running on rack-rails. They climb the steep mountain slopes and provide exceptional panoramas for passengers travelling along their routes.

IN BRIEF

Formalities – A valid passport is required for British, US, Canadian, Australian and Japanese citizens.

Shopping – Shops are generally open Mondays to Fridays from 8am to 6.30pm. On Sundays, they close early at either 4pm or 5 pm.

Souvenirs – Swiss-made products enjoy an unrivalled reputation, particularly for watches and clocks. Milk, dark and white varieties of delicious chocolate are sold in tablet form, or as Neapolitans (miniature tablets), sweets and figurines.

Urban Architecture – Several Swiss towns have admirably designed groups of buildings or contain some remnants of their medieval architecture. The **fountains**, which are invariably decorated with flowers, make for welcoming streets and squares. The central columns of these fountains are painted and decorated with great care, often depicting an animal or an allegorical subject: a warrior, a legendary hero or, in many cases, a banneret, a man-at-arms carrying a banner with the arms of the town. **Arcades** became popular in regions north of the Alps from the 14C. They bear witness to the dominating influence of Berne. **Covered bridges** are found widely in German linguistic regions of Switzerland. Numerous examples of **oriel** windows, corbelled loggias – sometimes spanning two floors – are to be found in the northeast towns such as St-Gallen, Stein-am-Rhein and Rorschach. Sculptures and paintings adorn these masterpieces.

Unusual Sports – Traditional rustic sports include wrestling on grass with the contenders wearing short breeches made of jute cloth, stone throwing, flag games and hornuss, a popular game which consists of using a racket to return a hard ball thrown with a kind of crossbow. These customs persist in areas of mountain pasture or can be seen at some village feasts in German-speaking Switzerland. It also is possible to hear the hollow tones of the **alpenhorn** or the vocal performances of yodellers.

Musée International d'Horlogerie, La Chaux-de-Fonds

Post Buses – These famous vehicles *(post-auto)*, identified by their bright yellow colour and disk with the Swiss horn symbol, are a common sight on country roads. They leave from railway stations or post offices and are the ideal way for visiting more isolated villages.

Tourist Trains, Small Railways and Steamers – Several comfortable **tourist trains** serve as a means of discovering the enchanting scenery. The William Tell Express connects Central Switzerland with the canton of Ticino (Tessin), the Glacier Express links Zermatt with St Moritz or Davos, the Bernina Express runs between Chur (Coire) and Tirano in Italy, the Golden-Pass Express between Montreux and Zweisimmen, the Palm Express from Domosdossola in Italy to Brig (Brigue) and Zermatt, and, finally, the Montreux-Bernese Oberland line (MOB).

During the tourist season, small **steam trains** return to service with their characteristic plumes of smoke and nostalgic whistles. These include the Rive-Bleue Express from Bouveret to Évian in France, the Blonay-Chamby line, the Interlaken-Brienz or **Grindelwald line**, and the Montreux-Caux-Rochers de Naye line. **Paddle steamers** proudly flying the national flag – a white cross on a red background – have become a familiar sight on the Swiss scene. During the tourist season, cruises are organized on almost all the Swiss lakes.

BASEL★★★

BASEL – Population 175 510
Michelin map 970 J 6

Switzerland's second largest city, Basle, is situated on the banks of the River Rhine at the junction of the Swiss, French and German frontiers.
The city owes its origin to a Roman colony founded by Augusta Raurica in 44 BC. It came into the Swiss Confederation at a late stage in 1501. During the 15C, the activity of leading printers contributed to the intellectual reputation of Basle University. The **St Alban District** (St Alban-Tal) has several mills which evoke the city's paper industry.
Basle is an important commercial and industrial centre owing to its geographical location. Nowadays, the prosperity of the city is based on its port, banking organisations, insurance companies and chemical industries.
Every year, the famous **carnival** attracts vast crowds. Its origins date back to the Catholicism of the Middle Ages. It is the only carnival to have survived in Protestant Europe after the Reformation. Gangs of masked revellers in costume wander through the streets, following large lanterns and accompanied by the sound of fifes and drums.

M. Frugier /SCOPE
Basle Carnival

★THE OLD CITY

The **Oberer Rheinweg**, a promenade along the banks of the Rhine, provides an attractive **overview** of the city, particularly from the **Wettsteinbrücke**.

★★★ **Kunstmuseum (Fine Arts Museum)** – The museum exhibits incomparable works by Swiss and German artists of the 15C and 16C. A rich collection of modern paintings ranges from the Impressionists to the present day. The exhibits are renewed on a regular basis, so it is never possible to see the entire collection.
A highlight among the 15C and 16C masters is Grünewald, the most famous Germanic painter of the late Middle Ages. His *Christ on the Cross*, demonstrates frightening realism. Other remarkable works are by Hans Baldung Grien, illustrator of grotesque art *(Death and the Young Girl* and *Death and the Woman)*, and Niklaus Manuel Deutch *(The Judgement of Paris)*. Hans Holbein the Younger epitomises Renaissance Art in *Christ in the Tomb* and *Portrait of Eramus as an Old Man*.
Work from the 20C is well represented, with paintings by Picasso (*Seated Harlequin*), Braque, Chagall, Henri Rousseau (known as le Douanier), Rouault, Soutine and the Flemish artist Constant Permeke, as well as Fernand Leger, Dali, Max Ernst and many others.

★★ **Münster (Cathedral)** – This vast edifice of red sandstone was built in the 12C. Its two Gothic towers offer a beautiful **view** of the city. The lower part of the chevet is Romanesque and comprises a frieze with delightful modillions. It faces the Pfalz terrace, the former Bishop's Palace. An attractive **panorama** overlooks the Rhine, the city, the Black Forest and the Vosges.
Inside the cathedral, the sculptures decorating the recessed arches are worth seeing. The **crypt** beneath the chancel is Romanesque in origin, comprising an ambulatory with Gothic arches and containing some fine mural paintings.

★ **Old streets** – **Spalenberg:** this small steep street offers a large choice of antique and craft shops. **Gemsberg:** an attractive alley leads to a square surrounded with 13C and 14C houses displaying bright and light-coloured façades. The Chamois Fountain adds further charm.

Heuberg is notable for its medieval houses.

Marktplatz (Market-Square) – This square, lined by corbelled houses, comes to life every morning with a market held in front of the Guildhall Arcade, near the Coopers' House (1578).

★**Rathaus (Town Hall)** – Built between 1504 and 1514 in Late Gothic style, the Guildhall was enlarged and restored from 1898 to 1902. The façade is decorated with frescoes and flanked by a modern belfry ornamented with pinnacles.
A statue of the city's founder, Muniatus Plancus, graces the inner courtyard. The rich wood carvings in the State Council Chamber merit a visit.

Fischmarkt (Fish Market) – The market is located in a busy part of the commercial district of Basle decorated by the **Fish Market fountain**★ (Fischmarktbrunnen), a Gothic column carrying a statue of the Virgin and two saints. The original by Jacob Sarbach dating back to 1390 is on show at the History Museum.

OTHER SIGHTS

★★★**Zoologischer Garten (Zoological Garden)** – This internationally famous zoo was founded in 1874. It covers 13ha/32 acres and contains more than 5600 animals from all continents. It specialises in the breeding and rearing of species in danger of extinction, including Asian rhinoceros, gorillas, and spectacled bears. Children are allowed to touch certain young or new-born animals in the childrens' zoo. They can also take rides on poneys and elephants.
A trip to the zoo finishes with a visit to the prestigous vivarium. The pool's display window features the penguins as a star attraction.

★**Museum Jean Tinguely** – Designed by Mario Botta, an architect from the Ticino, this museum on the banks of the Rhine is dedicated to Jean Tinguely of Freiburg, father of the strange machines.

EXCURSIONS

★★**Roman Remains at Augst (Augusta Raurica)** – *11km/6.8mi east of Basle.*
The oldest Roman settlement on the Rhine – *colonia raurica* – was founded here from 44 to 43 BC.
About 20 monuments have been restored, including the **theatre** which was built to accomodate 8000 spectators and is now used for open-air events and concerts. The **forum** served as a market but also for certain official festivities. In addition, a Roman house can be visited. A typical dwelling is reconstructed. The **Roman Museum**★ (Römermuseum) exhibits the **Silver Treasure**★★ (Silberschatz). This treasure, which was discovered in 1962 at the foot of the ancient walls of Kaiseraugst, comprises in particular a sumptuous 68-piece dinner set.

★★**Fondation Beyeler** – *Located in Riehen. Take the no 6 tram to Weilstrasse.* This museum was the work of the Genoese architect Renzo Piano (well known for designing the Centre Georges-Pompidou in Paris with Richard Rogers). It houses a rich collection of paintings and sculptures mainly illustrating the period from post-Impressionism to Cubism.

BERN★★★

BERN – Population 130 069
Michelin map 970 J 6

Berne is the seat of the Helvetic government and crossing-point between French and German-speaking Switzerland. It lies on an incised meander of the Aare facing the Alps. An attractive **view**★ of the old city can be obtained from the Rose Garden (Rosengarten). From the terrace of the Federal Palace (Bundeshaus) there is a fine **panorama** of the River Aare and the city. The Bernese Alps are visible in the distance.

★★OLD BERN

From Easter to the end of October, the principal monuments are floodlit until midnight.

The old city has preserved its picturesque medieval charm. It is best visited on foot. The historic towers offer a pleasant perspective. Yellowish-green sandstone buildings are decked abundantly with flags and flanked by arcades. A fair number of streets are embellished by **fountains**, each decorated by flowers. The central column of these fountains is painted and decorated with great care, often portraying an animal or an allegorical subject: a warrior, a legendary hero or, notably, an armed knight carrying a banner with the arms of the town called a banneret.

Typical streets start with the **Spitalgasse** a bustling passageway lined with arcades and boasting the Piper Fountain at its centre. The elegant **Marktgasse★** is lined with luxury goods shops and numerous florist stalls. See the Anna Seiler Fountain, the Marksman Fountain and, on the Kornhausplatz, the Ogre Fountain. The **Kramgasse★** has rows of old houses with oriel windows and corner turrets. The physicist Albert Einstein lived at no 49 from 1902 to 1909 *(visit possible)*.

Ferdinand Hodler

Born in 1853, Hodler is considered as the greatest Swiss artist of his epoch. His principal movements demonstrate Realism, Symbolism and Art Nouveau. His major compositions on allegorical subjects reveal the influence of his preoccupation with death. *Night, Day,* and *Disillusioned Souls* take their place alongside his landscapes, based on the principles of symmetry and parallelism. As in *Lake Thun*, they often reflect an inner state of mind. The portrait paintings display a strong dramatic intensity in the facial expressions.

★**Zytgloggeturm (Clock Tower)** – This was the city's west gate from 1191 to 1250. Its famous chimes start pealing at 4min to the hour. This picture-postcard scene is Berne's most popular souvenir thanks to its 16C jack and its painted figures. Note especially the delightful little bear cubs filing past to the sound of the fool's hand bells.

★**Bärengraben (Bear Pit)** – These favourite mascots, who also figure on the city's coat of arms, are fond of tit-bits and may take to playing pranks on the amused visitors.

★**Münster (Cathedral of St Vincent)** – Above its main portal, this collegiate Gothic church possesses a remarkable **tympanum★★** illustrating the Last Judgement. Inside, the visitor's attention is drawn to the great 15C stained-glass windows on the chancel. The **panorama★★** from the top of the tower extends over the city's reddish-brown tiled roofs.

MUSEUMS

★★**Kunstmuseum (Fine Arts Museum)** – The native-born Ferdinand Hodler has been given a choice spot alongside **Paul Klee.** Although Klee was of German origin, this major figure in abstract painting died in Berne in 1940. The artist's development is traced through a series of rooms displaying his drawings, oils and watercolours.

★★**Bernisches Historisches Museum (Bernese Historical Museum)** – Varied collections of historical, archeological and ethnographic interest are exposed. The museum includes fine tapestries that belonged to Charles the Bold.

★★**Schweizerisches Alpines Museum (Swiss Alpine Museum)** – This museum provides a good understanding of the Alps, their geological composition and conquest by mankind. It also explores the fascination for the mountains of painters such as Ferdinand Hodler. Everyday life, traditional customs, and Alpine lore are discussed.

EXCURSIONS

★★**Murten (Murat)** – *18km/11mi to the west of Bern by the motorway N 1 or road No 1.* A former fortified city with picturesque charm, Murten looks over the eastern shores of the lake bearing its name (Murtensee). This peaceful rectangular body of water is rich in fish. Murten also has a harbour for small craft which attracts visitors. Inside the **town walls** (Stadtmauer), the **High Street** (Hauptgasse) displays a remarkable degree of unity with its arcaded houses, overhanging roofs covered in brown tiles, fountains and the Berne gate surmounted by a graceful pinnacle. From the **castle's inner court**, a fine view extends over Lake Murten and the Jura mountains.

★★**Fribourg** – *27km/18mi to the southwest of Berne by the motorway N 12 or road no 12.* Fribourg, the native city of the sculptor **Jean Tinguely** (1925-1991), is situated at the boundary

The introduction of chocolate to Europe

The Swiss chocolate-makers of today enjoy an enviable reputation. However it was not until the mid 19C that they started making chocolate bars. Chocolate was one of the foodstuffs that the New World contributed to the Old World in the 17C. Initially introduced as a drink, it was popular in the 17C coffee houses of Oxford, Marseilles and Vienna. James Baker opened the first chocolate factory in New England and by 1876 the Swiss MD Peter was making milk chocolate on a commercial scale.

between the German and French linguistic areas. The city occupies a remarkable **site**★★ on a rocky spur hemmed in by a bend of the River Sarine. From the Gottéron Bridge, enjoy a fine **view**★★ over the old roofs of Fribourg.
The **Old Quarters**★ extend from the Sarine to the **upper town**★. They bristle with church towers and monasteries, and are dotted with sculpted **fountains**★ many being the masterpieces of artists such as Hans Geiler, Hans Gieng and Stephan Ammann. In the upper town, see the Cathedral of St Nicholas with its **tympanum**★★ and the **Art and History Museum**★.

BERNER OBERLAND★★★

BERNESE OBERLAND

Michelin map 970 J 6

This massif is set in Switzerland's heart. It is bounded to the north by the Thun and Brienz lakes, to the east by the Grison mountains, to the south by the Upper Valais and to the west by the Vaud and Fribourg Alps. It abounds in natural and man-made attractions of international renown. The natural sights include the Jungfrau and Eiger, the Rhône Glacier, the Trümmelbach Falls, and Lake Thun. A number of major resorts such as Interlaken and Grindelwald, as well as the highest rack railway in Europe, the Jungfraujoch, are all situated within the Bernese Oberland.
A grandiose natural barrier is formed by the mountains that rise proudly to the south and southeast, separating the Bernese Oberland from the Upper Valais. Some of these dazzling white snowy peaks are among the most famous summits in the Alps – the Eiger, Jungfrau, Mönch, Finsteraahorn, Wetterhon, and the Blümlisalp.
The Bernese Oberland has become a foremost natural holiday attraction in Europe as well as an international centre for mountaineering.

RECOMMENDED ITINERARIES

★★★**Jungfrau** – *See INTERLAKEN: EXCURSIONS.*

★★★**Round tour of the Three Passes (Grimsel, Furka and Suten)** – Start from Interlaken and enjoy the breathtaking views.

GENÈVE★★★

GENEVA – Population 170 189

Michelin map 970 J 6

Favoured by an exceptional location, Geneva is the second seat of the United Nations after New York and the headquarters of numerous international organisations. The waterfront of Lake Geneva – with its harbour and giant water jet – enjoys incomparable views set against a backdrop of woods, mountains and opulent mansions.
Geneva is also the city of **Calvin**, a bastion of the Reformation which has earnt its name as the Rome of the Protestants.
The **Reformation Monument**★ (**FZ D**) is found on the Promenade des Bastions. The four Genevese reformers Farel, Calvin, Beza and Knox evoke the history of the Reformed Church in Europe and the persecutions suffered by its followers.
Jean-Jacques Rousseau was born in Geneva in 1712. Voltaire made frequent stays in the city from 1755 to 1765. His main residence, Les Délices, has become a centre for research. The **Voltaire Institute and Museum**★ is devoted to the life and times of its famous guest.

★★HARBOUR AND LAKE SHORES

No one leaves Geneva without seeing the famous harbour and its majestic **Jet d'Eau**, the world's highest fountain shooting up 145m/476ft.

North Bank

Walk along the north lake shore from the Pont du Mont-Blanch. The Île Jean-Jacques Rousseau, with its statue of the writer, lies just downstream from the bridge. Paddle-steamers pass and the surrounding **mountains**★★ are visible in the distance. The Quai du Mont-Blanc and its continuation, the Quai Wilson, are much frequented by local residents and tourists. All enjoy strolling along the waterfront and visiting the cafés and souvenir stalls.

★★**Parks of Mon Repos, Perle du Lac and Villa Burton** (**GWX**) – These three parks are connected, forming the finest landscaped area within the city of Geneva. The Bartholoni Villa, situated in the Perle du Lac park, houses the **History of Science Museum.**

South Bank

Lawns planted with trees and decorated with flower beds grace the embankment. From the **English Garden**, a panorama takes in the harbour and the Jura mountains.

P. Wysocki /EXPLORER

MUSEUMS OF THE SOUTH BANK

★★ **Petit Palais – Museum of Modern Art** (GZ) – The 19C private residence is regarded as the mecca of both French and European avant-garde painting. The collection concentrates on the era from 1880 to 1930, incorporating works by Manet, Cézanne, Degas, Vallotton, Picasso, and Chagal.

★★ **Art and History Museum** (GZ) – The collections present an outline of the history of civilisation from prehistoric times up to the mid 20C. The largest sections are devoted to archeology and painting.

►► The Horology and Enamels Museum (GZ) exhibits sundials, clocks and watches.

★THE OLD TOWN

Wander through the small streets lined with old houses and private residences.

Picturesque streets (FZ) – **Grand'Rue**. This well preserved street offers a wide choice of antique shops, bookstores and art galleries. No 40 is the birthplace of Jean-Jacques Rousseau. The **Rue des Granges (65)** contains several aristocratic residences built in the 18C French style. Albert Gallatin (1761-1849), who contributed to the drawing up the Constitution of the United States of America, was born in the house at no 7.

Place du Bourg-de-Four (FZ 14) – This attractive square, located in the heart of Old Geneva, is surrounded by many buildings with their original inn signs. Antique shops, art galleries, cafés and restaurants surround the square's flower-decked fountain.

★ **St Peter's Cathedral** (FZ) – This great building was given a surprising Neo-Grecian façade and Corinthian peristyle in the 18C. The interior is plain but impressive. Calvin preached here between 1536 and 1564. The top of the tower commands a superb **panorama**★★ of Geneva, the lake, the Jura and the Alps.
Under the Cathedral lies an **archeological site**★ with remains of 2 000 years of history.

City Hall (FZ H) – In the **Alabama Room**, the first convention of the Red Cross – known as the Geneva Convention – was signed on 22 August 22 1864.

★ **Maison Tavel** (FZ) – This elegant residence is the oldest house in Geneva. It now accomodates a museum devoted to the history of the city from the 14C to the 19C.

THE INTERNATIONAL DISTRICT

★★ **Palais des Nations** (FW) – The palace, set in the beautiful garden, was the League of Nations, headquarters. Since 1946, it has served as the second centre of the United Nations Organisation. A visit shows the **Salle des Pas Perdus**, the great **Assembly Room** and the **Council Chamber**.

★★ **Ariana Museum** (FW) – Founded by the Genevese patron Gustave Revilliod, this museum provides an illustration of nearly ten centuries of the history of ceramics in Europe, the Near East and Asia. Several rooms are devoted to Swiss manufacturers: Winterthur, Genève, Nyon and Zürich.

GENÈVE

Bel-Air (Pl.)	FY	10
Bergues (Quai des)	FY	12
Bourg-de-Four (Pl. du)	FZ	14
Candolle (R. de)	FZ	21
Chantepoulet (R. de)	FY	28
Cirque (Pl. du)	FZ	37
Confédération (R. de la)	FY	42
Cornavin (Pl. de)	FY	43
Corraterie (R. de la)	FY	45
Coulouvrenière (Pont de la)	FY	48
Croix-d'Or (R. de la)	FY	49
Eaux-Vives (Pl. des)	GZ	52
Fort-Barreau (R. du)	FX	58
Frontenex (Av. du)	GZ	61
Granges (R. des)	FZ	65
Italie (R. d')	GZ	72
Jeunes (Rte des)	EZ	75
Longemalle (Pl.)	FY	76
Malagnou (Rte de)	GZ	79
Marché (R. du)	FY	81
Molard (Pl. du)	FY	84
Mont-Blanc (R. du)	FY	85
Monthoux (R. de)	FXY	87
Pépinière (R. de la)	FY	90
Pictet de Rochemont (Av.)	GZ	93
Pierre Fatio (R.)	GYZ	94
Rhône (R. du)	FGY	
Rive (Rond-Point de)	GZ	105
Rive (R. de)	FGZ	
St-Georges (Pont de)	EZ	114
St-Léger (R.)	FZ	118
Temple (R. du)	FY	120
Terrassière (R. de la)	GZ	121
Terreaux-du-Temple (R. des)	FY	123
Théâtre (Bd du)	FZ	124
Tour (Bd de la)	FZ	126
Turrettini (Quai)	FY	127
Versonnex (R.)	GY	133
Villereuse (R. de)	GZ	139
22-Cantons (Pl. des)	FY	142

B Mausolée du duc de Brunswick
D Monument de la Réformation
E Porte de la Treille
H Hôtel de ville
K Église St-Germain
M² Musée Barbier-Mueller
N Église orthodoxe Ste-Croix

The Geneva Escalade

This traditional festival commemorates the successful defense of the town against the Savoyards who attempted to scale the walls (l'escalade). The celebrations include a torchlight procession with the Genevese in period costume through the narrow streets of the town and along the banks of the Rhône. The procession makes a number of halts along the way when a herald on horseback reads out the official proclamation claiming victory over Savoy. To celebrate the anniversary the local confectioners make chocolate cauldrons, thus symbolising the heroic deeds of the "Motherland" who vanquished the enemy by pouring the boiling contents of a cauldron over their heads. A religious service in St Peter's Cathedral, fireworks and bangers complete the day's festivities.

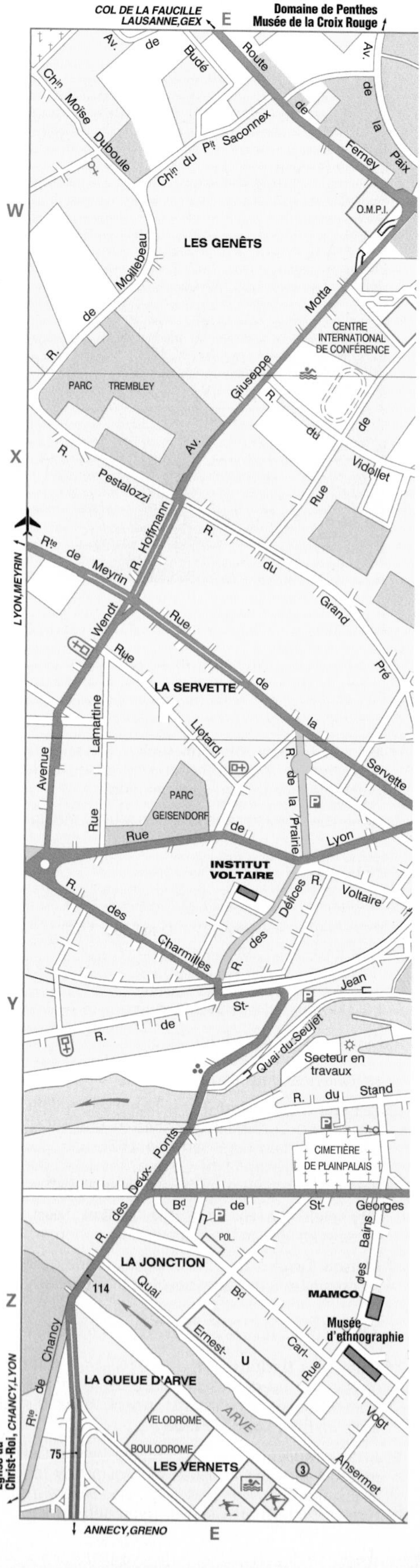

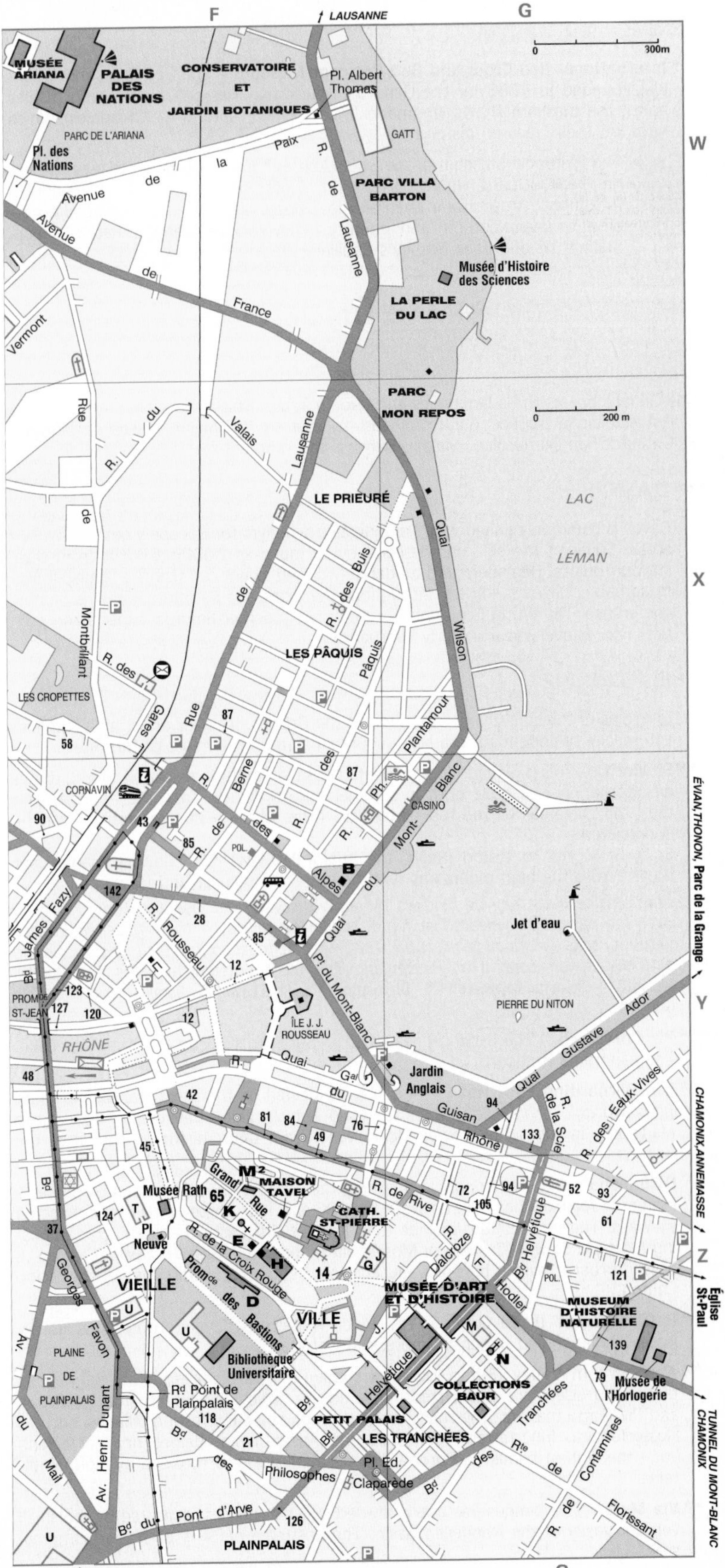
LAUSANNE
F
G
W
X
Y
Z
0
300m
200 m
MUSÉE ARIANA
PALAIS DES NATIONS
CONSERVATOIRE ET JARDIN BOTANIQUES
Pl. Albert Thomas
GATT
PARC DE L'ARIANA
Pl. des Nations
Avenue de la Paix
Avenue de France
R. de Lausanne
PARC VILLA BARTON
Musée d'Histoire des Sciences
LA PERLE DU LAC
PARC MON REPOS
Vermont
Rue du Valais
R. de Montbrillant
Rue de Lausanne
LE PRIEURÉ
Quai Wilson
LAC LÉMAN
R. des Buis
LES PÂQUIS
R. des Pâquis
R. des Gares
LES CROPETTES
Rue de Berne
R. des Alpes
R. Ph. Plantamour
Quai du Mont-Blanc
CASINO
CORNAVIN
POL.
B
Jet d'eau
R. Rousseau
Bd James Fazy
PROMDE ST-JEAN
ÎLE J. J. ROUSSEAU
Pt du Mont-Blanc
PIERRE DU NITON
Quai Gustave Ador
RHÔNE
Quai Gal Guisan
Jardin Anglais
R. du Rhône
R. de la Scie
R. des Eaux-Vives
Grand Rue
M2 MAISON TAVEL
Musée Rath
R. de Rive
CATH. ST-PIERRE
Pl. Neuve
K
E
H
G
J
R. de la Croix Rouge
Promde des Bastions
D
VIEILLE VILLE
R. Dalcroze
R. F. Hodler
Bd Helvétique
MUSÉE D'ART ET D'HISTOIRE
M
N
MUSEUM D'HISTOIRE NATURELLE
Musée de l'Horlogerie
Bd Georges Favon
Av. du Mail
Av. Henri Dunant
PLAINE DE PLAINPALAIS
U
Bibliothèque Universitaire
Rd Point de Plainpalais
COLLECTIONS BAUR
PETIT PALAIS
LES TRANCHÉES
Bd des Tranchées
Bd des Philosophes
Pl. Ed. Claparède
Rte de Florissant
R. de Contamines
Bd du Pont d'Arve
PLAINPALAIS
Carouge
ÉVIAN, THONON, Parc de la Grange
CHAMONIX, ANNEMASSE
Église St-Paul
TUNNEL DU MONT-BLANC CHAMONIX
58
87
90
43
85
142
28
12
123
127
120
48
42
81
84
49
76
94
133
45
65
72
105
52
93
61
124
37
14
121
139
79
118
21
126

★**International Red Cross and Red Crescent Museum** – The Red Cross movement was founded in 1863 by the Geneva businessman Henri Dunant. Using display areas, the museum shows landmarks events (wars, natural catastrophies) which have left their trace on history.

►► The Historical Museum of the Swiss Abroad★ in the Penthes Château focuses on Papal Guard, mercenaries and Swiss celebrities. The International Automobile Museum★ in the Palexpo exposes 400 vehicules, arranged according to manufacturer and country. They include General Patton's jeep, Stalin's Zis and Elvis Presley's Cadillac.

GRAUBÜNDEN★★★

GRISONS

Michelin map 970 K 6

The Grisons boasts three languages and two churches. This large Alpine terrain forms a vast semicircle marked out from west to east by the major passes of Oberalp, St Gothard, San Bernardino, Maloja, Bernina and Umbrail.

★★★DAVOS

Davos is commonly linked with Parsenn as a synonym for Europe's best-known ski areas. Some of the ski runs descend by as much as 2000m/6000ft from their starting points. Beginners and moderately-skilled skiers can use the Strela slopes. In addition, Davos is known throughout the world for its international economic conference. The World Economic Forum brings together financial experts and political figures every year in early February.

★★★ENGADINE

Engadine is the star tourist attraction of the Grisons. Its clear skies, high summits and glacial splendour form a little mountain state in the midst of the Alps.

★★★**St Moritz** – This is Switzerland's most famous high-altitude resort. St Moritz draws an international clientele both in summer and in winter. Take the funicular and then the cable-car to the top of **Piz Nair**, from where a fine **panorama**★★ can be appreciated.

From St Moritz to Tirano (Italy), the **Bernina Pass Road**★★★ follows a magnificent route across the high mountains with breathtaking scenery and view-points.

The Bernina Pass may be blocked by snow between October and May. The road over the pass is not cleared at night, while the railway – the highest in Europe without racks – runs all year round. The Swiss customs control is at Campocologno and the Italian control at Piattamala. The most noteworthy sites are **Muottas Muragl**★★, **Chünetta Belvedere**★★★, **Diavolezza**★★★, **Piz Lagalb**★★, **Bernina Pass**★★ and **Alp Grü**★★★.

★★★**Piz Corvatsch** – The cable-car leaves from Surlej to the east of Silvaplana Lake. The panorama is superb.

★★**San Bernardino Pass Road** – This pass is located on the great transalpine route *(impracticable from November to May)* which links Bellinzona (near Lake Maggiore) in the sunny Lower Ticino valley with Chur, historical capital of the Grisons.

Bellinzona – Once a stronghold guarding the Ticino Valley, Bellinzona possesses a system of fortifications built between the 13C and 15C. Three castles are connected by walls. The fortifications include the Castle of Uri (Castello Grande), the imposing **fortress of Schwyz** (Castello di Montebello), and the **Unterwalden Castle** (Castello di Sasso Corbaro), which houses a museum of costumes and traditions of the Ticino Canton.

★**Rofflaschlucht (Roffla Gorge)** – The River Hinterhein flows through this gorge. Access galleries end under an impressive waterfall.

★★**Averserrhein Valley (Ferrera Valley, Avers Valley)** – This picturesque valley, wide in places and elsewhere constricted into a gorge, carves its way into the Piz Grisch and Piz Platta massifs. The road passes through some interesting villages, such as Ausserferrera, Innerferrera, Campsut, and Avers-Cresta, before finally reaching Juf – the highest hamlet in Europe. The desolate site is surrounded by high mountains.

★★**Via Mala** – This famous passage is divided into two gorges separated by the small verdant valley of the Rongellen Basin. The upstream defile is particularly impressive.

INTERLAKEN★★★

Population 5 176
Michelin map 970 J 6

This well-known resort, the tourist centre of the Bernese Oberland, grew up between the lakes of Thun and Brienz. Its famous avenue, the **Höheweg★★**, is lined by trees, lawns and flower beds. It is always busy. Interlaken functions as the starting point for excursions to some exceptional sites and mountain summits. Among the nearby belvederes reached by funicular or on foot, **Schynige Platte★★★**, **Harderkulm★★** and **Heimwehfluh★** stand out.

EXCURSIONS

By rail, car or cable-car

★★★ **Jungfraujoch** – This excursion is subject to weather conditions. Choose a cloudless day and equip yourself with warm clothing, sun-glasses and stout boots.
This high mountain resort, 3 475m/11 401ft high, is the highest installation in Europe served by a **railway**. It offers a grandiose spectacle. A great choice of attractions include dog sledge rides and the Ice Palace (Eispalast).

★★★ **Lauterbrunnen Valley** – *18km/11mi to the south of Interlaken.* Excursions by car and by cable-car.

– **The Staubbach Waterfall★★** – Byron compared this waterfall to "the tail of the pale horse ridden by Death in the Apocalypse."

– **Trümmelbach Falls★★★** (Trümmelbachfälle);

– **Mürren★★**, a village of chalets perched on a shelf of Alpine pasture forms a balcony over the steep cleft of the Lauterbrünnen Valley,

– **The Schilthorn★★★**, in a desolate landscape of torrents and scree, offers an exceptional panorama from the top over the Jungfrau Massif.

★★★ **Grindelwald** – *20km/14mi to the southeast of Interlaken.* Located in an unforgettable setting, the glacier village of Grindelwald is the only major high-altitude resort in the Jungfrau area reached by motor car. Viewed from left to right, the Wetterhorn Alps gives way to the Mettenberg and the Lower Grindelwald Glacier. At the end of a long rocky barrier stands the pyramidal Eiger peak.

Boat Trips

During the tourist season, steamer and motor-cruiser services run on Lake Thun from the Thunersee landing-stage at the Interlaken-West railway station and on Lake Brienz from the Brienzersee landing-stage at the rear of the Interlaken-Ost or Böningen railway station. The trips stop off at scenic places such as the **Giessbach Falls★★**, the main attraction on the shores of Lake Brienz. Evening cruises are also offered *(in July and August only).*

LAUSANNE★★

Population 117 571
Michelin map 970 J 6

The old town is built on uneven ground, rising in tiers on three hills. A number of old, steep, narrow streets lead to the cathedral. After being confined to the promontory for several centuries, Lausanne then spread as far as Ouchy, a former fisherman's hamlet on the shores of Lake Geneva.
Lausanne has acquired a worldwide reputation thanks to the famous ballet troupe directed by Maurice Béjart and the classical music concerts performed by the French Swiss Orchestra and the Lausanne Chamber Orchestra. As world capital of the Olympic movement, Lausanne in the headquarters of the International Olympic Committee (**IOC**), founded in 1894 by Baron Pierre de Coubertin. The city houses an Olympic Museum.

★OUCHY

A famous hotel resort and popular spot for strollers, Ouchy has become the Lausanne waterfront. It is also one of Lake Geneva's busiest leisure cruise and small craft harbours with a vast yachting marina opposite the Place de la Navigation. This square has been redeveloped and converted into a pedestrian area where passers-by can enjoy the fountains and giant chessboards.
The shaded lakeside frontage extends over more than 1km/0.6mi – and offers a charming route with lovely **views★★** of the harbour, Lake Geneva and the Chablais mountains.

The Olympic Games

The first games took place at Olympus (Greece) in 776 BC. Dedicated in honour of Zeus, these games allowed athletes from all social classes to compete provided only that they were Greek. Ten months of training in the athlete's native city would be followed by a month's intensive preparation at Olympus. A single winner was nominated. He received a prize composed of a laurel wreath and ribbons awarded by Nike, the goddess of victory. The Games were held every four years and became a great popular success. Between 150 000 and 200 000 spectators attended the events. Apart from athletic competitions, the Olympics included cultural ceremonies and a great fair. The Roman emperor Theodosus abolished the Games in AD 393.
In 1898, the Games were reborn in Athens due to the impetus of Baron Pierre de Coubertin. The first Winter Olympics were organized in Chamonix (France), heralding the start of a new epoch in winter sports.

★★ **Olympic Museum** – A modern building inspired by Greek temple architecture serves as the setting for some interesting exhibits on the Olympic movement and the history of the Games since their origin in Ancient Greece.

OLD QUARTERS OF THE CITY

Place de la Palud – The square is lined by old houses and by the Renaissance façade of the Guild Hall with the arms of the City. The charming 16C-18C Fountain of Justice stands in the middle. The picturesque covered staircases behind the fountain lead through to the Cathedral Square.

★★ **Cathedral** – This is considered to be the finest Gothic building in Switzerland. Its construction started during the 12C, the church being consecrated in 1275. A complete restoration was undertaken by Viollet-le-Duc during the 19C. The lantern-tower at the crossing of the transept – along with the bell-tower – evokes Anglo-Norman architecture, marking the transition between Romanesque and Gothic styles. The south door, or Apostle's Porch, is decorated with a fine group of 13C sculptures. The interior is plain and exhibits certain Burgundian features such as the narthex, with no side chapels as well as other influences derived from the English Gothic style such as the gallery running below the clerestory windows. From the top of the tower, a fine **view**★ unfolds over the city, Lake Geneva and the Alps.

Palais de Rumine (Rumine Palace) – Built in the early 20C in the Italian Renaissance style, this imposing edifice houses five museums, including the Fine Arts Museum. It focuses on works of Swiss artists, notably Vallotton who was born in the region.

Lac LÉMAN★★

Lake GENEVA

Michelin map 970 J 6

The Swiss shore of Lake Geneva traces out a harmonious semicircle fringed with vineyards on the lower slopes of the Jura. Further east, it abuts into the ridges of the Swiss Plateau and the foothills of the Vaud Alps. The lake is crescent-shaped, 72km/49mi long and 13km/9mi across at its widest point. The Little Lake between Geneva and Yvoire is usually considered separately from the Great Lake.

The lake by boat – Steamers of the Compagnie Générale de Navigation call regularly on the Swiss and French shores, offering many different types of excursions. The afternoon tour of the Little Lake starts from Geneva. The tour of the Upper Lake begins in Lausanne-Ouchy. A round trip of the whole lake takes between 11 and 12hr.

The vineyards★ from Geneva to Lausanne are characterised by an almost continuous carpet of vines which climb the south-facing slopes of the Jura. This itinerary has added charm during the grape harvest.
The Vaud Riviera has several summer resorts of international reputation.

★NYON Population 14 650

Julius Caesar founded Nyon under the name of Colonia Julia Equestris. The **Roman Museum** evokes this epoch. The arcaded houses on the Place du Marché (Market Square) display architecture from the period of Bernese domination in the 16C. The castle contains the **History and Porcelain Museum**.
The **Lake Geneva Museum** is housed in an 18C hospital in the Rive quarter overlooking the lake. Many different aspects of the lake are presented: its flora, fauna, boats and human activities.

★VEVEY

Population 15371

Jaeger/PIX

Already capital of the Lavaux vineyards, Vevey became the cradle of the Swiss dairy and chocolate products industry in the 19C. The powerful Nestlé Group has its headquarters in Vevey. The town is also linked to the great film-maker and actor Charlie Chaplin, who died here in 1977. A statue in his honour can be seen on the lakeside.

The picturesque traditional markets on Sunday mornings are worth seeing. In addition, visit the **Swiss Museum of Cameras** and the **Alimentarium**.

★★MONTREUX Population 21362

Montreux is the most visited resort on Lake Geneva thanks to its beautiful site and pleasant surroundings. The town stretches along the shores of a large bay and is lined with sumptuous palaces and hotels from the Edwardian epoch reminiscent of the French Riviera. Every year from the end of August to the end of September, the classical music festival draws a faithful public. Go up through Old Montreux as far as the terrace of the parish church to obtain the best overall impression of the city and the lake.

★★CHILLON CASTLE

Chillon Castle is built on a rocky islet, its towers reflected in the waters of Lake Geneva. This picturesque site lies in an incomparable setting framed by the lake and the Alps. The castle has its origins in the 9C, and its dungeons have served on several occasions as a state prison. When visiting Chillon in 1816 on a pilgrimage to Jean-Jacques Rousseau's home region, the English poet Byron commemorated the captivity of the castle's most famous prisoner – De Bonivard – who, on account of his support for the Reformation, had been imprisoned here by the Duke of Savoy. Byron's poem is an outpouring of romantic lyricism. The poet cut his name on the third pillar of De Bonivard's cell.

LOCARNO★★

Population 14 099
Michelin map 970 K 6

Locarno, in the hollow of a sunny bay bordering **Lake Maggiore**, enjoys an exceptional climate. Visitors will find pleasant walks among the gardens, along the shores of the lake, on the vine-covered slopes of Orselina dotted with villas, and in the Cardada Hills. The **Piazza Grande** in the heart of the old town always attracts tourists with its shop-lined arcades, cafés and restaurants.

★**Madonna del Sasso** – *(access possible by funicular)*. This sanctuary, which stands at the summit of a wooded spur, is also a place of pilgrimage. It offers a good view of the town and the lake.

★★**Cimetta** – The funicular to Madonna del Sasso is continued by a cable-car which climbs the Cardada Alp. From Cardada, a chairlift goes to the top of the Cimetta (alt 1672m/5482ft). Below, a stunning panorama of Lake Maggiore and the Alps.

EXCURSIONS

★★**Ascona** – *3km/2mi west.* Ascona's lovely lakeside setting makes it a popular holiday resort. New Orleans jazz festival in July. The boat trip to the **Brissago islands**★ is a classic.

LUGANO★★

Population 25 130
Michelin map 970 K 6

Lugano is an ideal health and tourist resort, lying at the end of a beautiful bay framed between Mount Bré and Mount San Salvatore. It benefits from numerous leisure facilities and entertainments. Lugano is also a convenient excursion centre for touring by car, mountain railway (**Monte Generoso★★★**), or by boat on lakes Maggiore, Lugano and Como.
Visit the Piazza di Riforma and stroll under the arcades of the Via Nassa and down the shady promenade along the lake shore.
Most of the **lake★★**, called Lago Ceresio in Italian, is in Swiss territory. It is set among the steep slopes of the Prealpine chain and attains a maximum length of 33km/21mi. A visit to the **old town★** with its pedestrian streets and shops is a must for all tourists. See the Via Nassa, Piazza della Riforma, Via Pelissa, Piazza Cioccaro and Via Catedrale.

★★**Parco Civico (Municipal Park)** – This delightful garden stands on the shores of the lake.

★★★**Monte San Salvatore** – Alt 912m/2 996ft. *About 45min there and back, including 20min by funicular starting from the Paradiso district.* The summit offers an incomparable view of Lugano, the lake, as well as the Bernese and Valais Alps.

★★**Villa Favorita** – *Located in Castagnola. Take the no 1 bus from Piazza Manzoni.* This fine residence in a lovely lakeside setting houses a collection of works illustrating European and American painting of the 19C and 20C. The fine-quality pictures are part of the art collection belonging to the Thyssen-Bornemisza family, the famous dynasty of German steel industrialists.

★★**Monte Bré** – Alt 925m/3 051ft. *About 1hr there and back, including 30min by funicular, starting from Cassarate.* The summit has a fine view and numerous walks.

EXCURSIONS

★★**Morcote** – *11km/7mi south or by boat from Lugano.* A very picturesque village by the side of a lake known as the Pearl of Ceresio.

★**Monte Tamaro** – Alt 1 960m/6 430ft. *15km/9.30mi northwest. 20min by cable-car from Rivera.* There is a fine, plunging **view★**. **Santa Maria degli Angeli church** is by Mario Botta, the famous architect from Ticino.

LUZERN★★★

LUCERNE – Population 59 976
Michelin map 970 J 6

The town occupies a remarkable site at the northwestern end of Lake Lucerne, where the River Reuss resumes its flow. The fame of Lucerne as a tourist resort is kept up by the international music weeks held every year from mid-August to early September.

★★THE OLD TOWN

The old town, whose access was guarded by covered wooden bridges, abuts against the flank of a mountain and seven large square towers connected by walls, remains of the town's fortifications.

★**Kapellbrücke** – This wooden covered bridge – the symbol of Lucerne – crosses the Reuss at the point where the river flows out of the lake. The bridge is flanked by an octagonal tower, roofed by tiles, called the **Wasserturm** (Water Tower). An identical replica was rebuilt after a fire on the night of 17-18 August 1993. The bridge is adorned with about 100 paintings on wood set in the triangles formed by the roof beams. These paintings depict the history of Lucerne and of Switzerland, evoking St Leger and Maurice, patron saints of the town.

★**Altes Rathaus (Old Town Hall)** – This fine Renaissance building is flanked by a tall square tower and overlooks the Kornmarkt (Grain Market).

Picasso Sammlung (Picasso Collection) – Numerous photographs illustrate the artist's career and family life. Paintings and drawings are exhibited.

★**Weinmarkt (Wine Market)** – On this pretty square in the heart of the old town, old houses are covered with paintings and decorated with signs and flags. In medieval days, the buildings served as the seats of the various guilds. Note the house at no 7, the Scales' Mansion, no 20 with a façade depicting the Mariage Feast at Canaan and the Wine Market Pharmacy (Weinmarktapotheke) built in 1530. The Gothic fountain in the centre of the square portrays warriors and St Maurice, patron saint of soldiers.

Tony Adena/EXPLORER

Altes Rathaus on the banks of the Reuss

Spreuerbrücke – This covered bridge – known as Mills Bridge – is decorated with wooden panels depicting the *Dance of Death*. They were executed by Kaspar Meglinger in the 17C.

Jesuitenkirche (Jesuits' Church) – The first church in Switzerland to be built in the Jesuit style is dedicated to St Francis Xavier. The plain façade is framed between two tall towers surmounted by domed belfries. Inside are frescoes and a high altar embellished with a huge pink marble stucco altarpiece.

LAKE SHORE

The lakeside quays, planted with trees and flanked by mansions serving as hotels, offer **views**★★ of the town site and Lake Lucerne, as well as the Alps. **Cruises** on comfortable steamers provide an unforgettable experience. The **Richard Wagner Museum** at Tribschen is accessible by boat in just a few minutes.

★★★ **Verkehrhaus (Swiss Transport Museum)** – The museum offers a fascinating voyage through the past, present and future. The different sections devoted to railways, shipping, and aviation are spread over a dozen buildings separated by play areas, refreshment facilities and gardens.

EXCURSIONS

★★★ **Pilatus** – *15km/9mi to the south of Lucerne. At Alpnachstad, take the rack-railway.* There is an exceptional view from the summit (alt 2 212m/6 957ft).

★★★ **Rigi-Kulm** – *24km/15mi to the east of Lucerne.* Take the mountain railway from Arth-Goldau to the terminus. A magnificent panorama can be appreciated from the summit.

★★★ **Vierwaldstättersee (Lake Lucerne)** – The country around Lake Lucerne offers a perspective of hills and mountains, small towns with old-fashioned charm and innumerable belvedere-summits.
From Lucerne to Altdorf, the road along the north shore *(see itinerary no 2 on the map)* provides an approach to historical sites such as the Rütli *(accessible by boat leaving from Brunnen)* or Tell's Chapel (Tellskapelelle).
The Field of **Rütli** (or Grütli), over which the national flag proudly flies, symbolises the foundation of the Swiss Confederation. On 1 August 1291, Walter Fürst, Werner Stauffacher and Arnold von Melchtal representing the three valleys of Uri, Schwyz and Underwalden met to seal the alliance. According to local tradition, this meeting took place in the presence of William Tell. **Tell's Chapel** commemorates one of the most dramatic episodes on the story of **William Tell** – a legendary hero of the struggle for Swiss independence – made famous by the play written by Schiller in 1804.

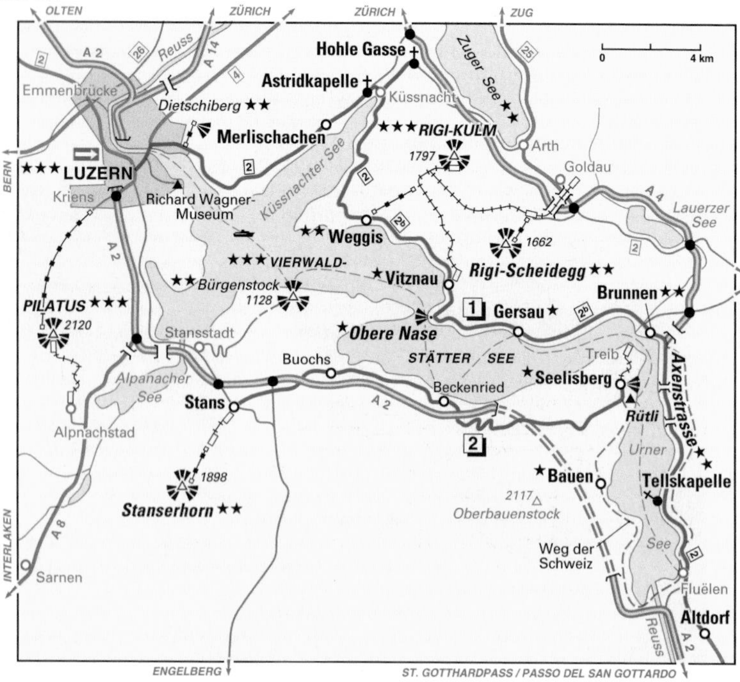

Lake Cruises – Take a boat trip around the lake, and climb to one of the surrounding summits. With its fleet of steamers and pleasure boats, the Lake Lucerne Navigation Company runs services all year round linking Lucerne with the famous lakeside resorts of Weggis, Vitznau, and Gersau. Commented tours are also available of the most treasured historical sights, as well as night cruises with music and dancing. It is possible to make connections or combine the boat trip with all the funiculars and cable-cars in the region. In addition, boat-train connections are ensured with the William Tell Express, which links central Switzerland with the Ticino canton via the St Gothard line. A first-class ticket on this Alpine tourist train includes the paddle steamer journey from Lucerne to Flüelen and onwards by rail to Lugano/Locarno.

Town plans indicate useful information, including car parks, tourist offices, post offices, etc.

NEUCHÂTEL★★★

Population 31 684
Michelin map 970 J 6

Neuchâtel enjoys a charming site between its lake of the same name and Chaumont Hill. With its quarters ranged in tiers of pale ochre houses made of Hauterive stone, the town is set in the midst of vineyards. Neuchâtel wines are produced in the area extending between the lake and the Jura mountains. Walk along the flowery lakeside quays, which afford superb views of the lake with the Alps in the background (Osterwald Quay: **view**★★).

★**Old Town (Ville Ancienne)** – The picturesque quarter includes Rue du Château, Rue du Trésor, Rue du Pommier, and Rue des Moulins. Old houses, 16C and 17C fountains and defensive towers, extends between the town hall, built in 1788, and the buildings formed by the collegiate church and the castle.

★**Collegiate Church and Castle** – The **church** with multi-coloured glazed tile contains the 14C cenotaph of the counts of Neuchâtel. The stone composition represents a striking example of medieval sculpture. The **Castle**, formerly the residence of the Neuchâtel lords, is nowadays the seat of the cantonal government. The interior may be visited.

★**Art and History Museum (Musée d'Art et d'Histoire)** – The three **automata**★★, the Musician, the Writer and the Daughtsman, are marvels of ingenuity constructed by 18C master watchmakers.

EXCURSIONS

Clock and watchmaking, the centrepiece of Swiss craftsmanship

La Chaux-de-Fonds – *25km/17mi to the north-west of Neuchâtel.* This town, situated in the Jura, is the largest watch and clock-making centre in Switzerland. It is also the birthplace of the great architect Le Corbusier, whose real name was Charles Edouard Jeanneret (1887-1965). The **International Museum of Horology★★** is housed in underground rooms. It illustrates the history of measuring time from Antiquity to the present with more than 3 000 exhibits from all over the world.

Collection Musée intèrnational d'horlogerie

Le Locle – *8km/5mi from Chaux-de-Fonds.* The Château des Monts, an elegant 18C mansion, contains the **Museum of Horology★** (Musée d'Horlogerie). The collection of clocks, timepieces, jewellery and automata exhibited complete the museum in Chaux-de-Fonds.

VALAIS WALLIS★★

Michelin map 970 J 6

This canton is one of the Alp's most isolated districts. It reaches the Upper Rhône Valley from the Furka Pass to Lake Geneva. Although this wide furrow is almost completely cut off from the economic centres of German-speaking Switzerland, it is nevertheless kept busy by the intense international traffic through the Great St Bernard and Simplon passes. This region rewards with some unforgettable sights of high mountain peaks including the Matterhorn (Mont Cervin in French) and the Monte Rosa, as well as its landscape dotted with chalets and *raccards* or *mazots*, small barns perched on piles and used as granaries or store houses. The Valais also contains wayside calvaries composed of wooden crosses bearing the Instruments of the Passion. The Valais is also well known for its white wines (Fendant, Johannisberg) and red wines (Dôle).

MARTIGNY Population 13 795

The urban district of Martigny is an international road junction of prime importance. The town is situated on a bend in the River Rhône, just where the River Drance joins the main stream. Traffic on the Simplon and Great St Bernard routes converge with traffic from the Forclaz Pass road.

★★ **Pierre Gianadda Foundation** – In addition to its permanent collections, the foundation holds temporary exhibitions of a high standard showing works by such renowned artists as Goya, Renoir, Modigliani, Picasso, Klee, Braque, Botero and Degas.

EXCURSION

★ **Great St Bernard Pass Road** – The road linking the Drance and Dora Baltea valleys provides one of the most historic transalpine routes. Napoleon crossed the Alps here in the winter of 1800 with 40 000 of his soldiers, even though the route was covered with snow. The French took the Austrians by surprise at Marengo.
The Great St Bernard hospice stands in a rocky gulley, almost continuously swept by icy winds. The lake is frozen, on average, for 265 days in the year. Winter here lasts for more than eight months. The refuge perpetuates the admirable Christian tradition of help and hospitality. A museum recalls the history of the pass.

★★ SAAS-FEE Population 1 567

Nicknamed the Pearl of the Alps, Saas-Fee, was formerly an unsophisticated Valais mountain village. It is now an attractive resort enjoying a magnificent setting. Motor traffic is forbidden, and electric vehicles transport visitors and their luggage. A funicular called the **Métro Alpin** runs up to Mittelallin at 3 500m/11 483ft. It follows an underground passage cut in the mountainside. Saas-Fee is a well-known mountaineering centre and has become the finishing point for the famous **High Route** (Haute Route) starting at Chamonix, or more usually Verbier.

★★★ ZERMATT Population 4 896

In earlier times, Zermatt was a simple mountain village at the bottom of the Nikolaital Valley. Today, it has become an internationally famous resort. Zermatt can only be reached by rail either from Brig or Visp (Vièg). From the railway station to the parish church, the town is a thoroughfare of hotels and shops. Beyond the church, **Old Zermatt** is composed of Valais-style chalets and toast-coloured mazots. The presence of numerous snowfields spread at different altitudes makes summer skiing easy in Zermatt.

The Matterhorn (Mont Cervin) – Alt 4078m/13 380ft. From the middle of the resort, the hooked and inclined summit pyramid comes majestically into view. In the 1860s, the young British illustrator William Whymper travelled extensively in the Valais Alps. Keen on Zermatt, he decided in 1865 to attack the Matterhorn along its northeast ridge, which is the part of the mountain facing Zermatt. On 13 July, the roped climbing party set off. It reached the summit on 14 July. On the descent, a terrible accident caused the death of four of the climbers.

★★★ **Gornergrat** – Alt 3 135m/10 272ft. *2hr return journey.* This railway – the highest open-air railway in Europe – provides a panorama of Monte Rosa (highest point: Pointe Dufour, alt 4 634m/15 203ft) and its glaciers.

★★★ **Klein Matterhorn (Petit Cervin)** – Alt 3 886m/12 684ft. *Access by four successive cable-cars.* The trip provides spectacular scenery of rocky screes on Théodule Glacier. From Frugg, another cable-car climbs the **Schwarzee** (Lac Noir). A reflection of the Matterhorn is visible in the lake.

★★ **Rothorn** – Alt 3 103m/10 180ft. Access by funicular, cable-cabin and cable-car. Several views are obtained of the Matterhorn before arriving at the flat rocky summit of the Rothorn.

ZÜRICH★★★

Population 345 235

Michelin map 970 J 6

As an important financial, industrial and commercial centre, Zurich is the most populous city of Switzerland. It is also a major venue for international conferences. The city is built between the wooded slopes of the Uetliberg and the Zürichberg at the point where the Limmat, flowing out of Lake Zurich, meets the River Sihl. **Boat trips** leave from the landing-stage at Bürkliplatz.

A pretty **view** of the city, particularly the old quarters, is visible from the **Lindenhof**, a tree-shaded esplanade on the crest of a hill overlooking the Limmat. Stop at the **Bar Jules Verne** – a Lipp breweries house – to appreciate the fine panorama.

WEST BANK

Bahnhofstrasse – Switzerland's commercial activity is concentrated here on the busiest and most elegant street in Zurich. Extending from the central station to the lake, this avenue planted with lime trees is lined with luxury goods shops such as Globus, Vilan, and Jelmoli. Banks have sumptuous premises on the Paradeplatz. Many pastry shops, cafés and restaurants also are located here.

★★ **Schweizerisches Landesmuseum (Swiss National Museum)** – The rich collections are being reorganised. The museum illustrates all aspects of Swiss civilization, including prehistoric and religious art, paintings, and clock and watch-making.

Fraumünster – Built in the 12C and 15C, this church is above all famous for its beautiful **stained-glass windows** by Marc Chagall.

Weinplatz – The pretty fountain on this small square is topped by a wine grower carrying a basket on his back. The view over the quays on the opposite shore is dominated by the towers of the Grossmünster (Cathedral), and the town hall (Rathaus), a graceful building built in the Italian Renaissance style. Some fine houses with oriel windows are found on **Augustinergasse**, a street leading back to the Bahnhofstrasse.

EAST BANK

The old section of Zurich is crossed by several pedestrian streets. It is particularly busy in summer when the fine weather allows strollers to stay late into the evening at pavement cafés, restaurants or musical entertainments. A plaque recalls the **Cabaret Voltaire**, situated at no 1 Spiegelgasse. In 1916, this house became the meeting place of avant-garde artists, Hugo Ball, Emmy Jennings, Tristan Tzara, Marcel Janco, Jean Arp, Richard Hueulsenbeck, and Sophie Taeuber. Together, they launched the Dada movement.

★**Grossmünster (Cathedral)** – The cathedral symbolises the Reformation for the German-speaking Swiss. It is an impressive building erected between the 11C and 13C. The façade is flanked by a pair of three-storeyed towers surmounted by wooden domes faced with metal plates. The South Tower is crowned by a colossal statue of Charlemagne seated with a sword across his knees.

★★**Kunsthaus (Fine Art Museum)** – Important collections of sculptures from the French and German early Middle Ages and paintings by 15C Swiss and German Primitives are housed here. The museum also has some of the most representative canvases of Ferdinand Hodler, who was considered the leader of the Swiss School of the beginning of the century, as well as works by the Norwegian painter Edvard Munch (1863-1944).

★★**Sammlung Bührle (EG Bührle Foundation)** – *No 172 Zollikerstrasse, access via the Zeltweg.* The sculptures and paintings collected by Emil Bührle between 1934 and 1956 are housed in a villa set in the lovely southeast suburbs of Zurich. This German industrialist was a great admirer of Claude Monet. He came to live in Zurich in 1924 and assembled a remarkable collection of Impressionist and Post-Impressionist masters. These include works by Renoir (the lovely portrait of *Little Irene*), Monet (*Poppies near Vétheuil*, in which the figures represented by rapid brush strokes appear to blend into the landscape), Van Gogh (*The Sower*), Cézanne (with his famous *Boy in the Red Waistcoat*, who strikes a melancholic pose) and Sisley (*The Luminous Summer at Bougival*).
Those with a special interest in Impressionism and Post-Impressionism may make a visit to the Villa Flora at Winterthur and the Langmatt Foundation at Baden. Taken together, these three museums provide a unique display of painting and sculpture covering art from the 1870s up to about 1910.

EXCURSIONS

★★**Uetliberg** – *Access by rail from the central station. About 2hr return journey, including 50min by train.* The train journey is mainly through woods. From the arrival station, a footpath leads to the summit at 871m/2857ft. From the top of the belvedere tower, a sweeping panorama opens out to the whole Zurich district, the Limmat Valley, Lake Zurich and the Alps.

Impressionism and Post-Impressionism – *See also EG Bührle Foundation.*

★★**Villa Flora** – *At Wintherthur, 28km/17mi northeast of Zurich. No 44 Tösstalstrasse.* Between 1907 and 1932, Arthur and Hedy Hahnloser-Bühler brought together a valuable collection of Post-Impressionist works. The Nabi School, formed as a reaction against Impressionism – and composed of painters born between 1860 and 1870 – makes up the core of the collection. On display are works by Valloton *(The Cart)*, Vuillard *(The Game of Draughts)* and Bonnard *(The Provençal Carafe)*. The Fauves are represented by their uncontested master Matisse *(Standing Odalesque)*, as well as by some works by Marquet. *The Sower* by Van Gogh can also be seen and compared with the same subject exhibited at the Bührle Foundation.

★**Langmatt Foundation (Sidney and Jenny Brown)** – *At Baden, 24km/15mi to the northwest of Zurich.* This former residence of the industrialist Sidney Brown and his wife Jenny now houses a collection mainly devoted to small-format Impressionist paintings. Pride of place is given to works by Renoir, Cézanne, Degas *(Nude)*, Boudin *(Fishing Boats Returning to Trouville)* and Monet *(Ice Breaking up on the Seine/Seine in Flood)*.

For further details on Switzerland, consult the Michelin Green Guide Switzerland.

When looking for a hotel or restaurant, use the Michelin Red Guide Suisse Schweiz Svizzera, updated annually.

The star ratings are allocated for various categories:
– regions of scenic beauty with dramatic natural features
– cities with a cultural heritage
– elegant resorts and charming villages
– ancient monuments and fine architecture, museum and picture galleries.

Turkey

Türkyje

Area: 779 452km²/296 191sq mi – **Population:** 58 million – **Capital:** Ankara – **Currency:** Turkish lira – **Time:** GMT + 2hr in winter, GMT + 3hr in summer

Turkey is divided into two parts, European Eastern Thrace on the Balkan Peninsula including Istanbul, and Asian Anotolia, formerly Asia Minor, with the capital city of Ankara. The two regions are separated by the Sea of Marmara which connects with the Aegean Sea through the Strait of the Dardanelles, and the Black Sea through the Bosphorus.
Below is a brief overview of the major high points of Istanbul, a European metropolis once the capital of the Ottoman Empire.

IN BRIEF

Entry Formalities – For British and US citizens a visa must be obtained on arrival. For Canadian, Australian and Japanese citizens only a passport is needed.

Shopping – Shops generally open Mondays to Saturdays from 9am to 1pm and from 2pm to 7pm.

Souvenirs – A handmade *hali* or machine-made *kilim* rug makes by far the favourite tourist souvenir. For expensive, large rugs, convenient payment and shipping are offered. Leather clothing is also popular. Other classics include jewellery, wooden objects, ceramics and some food items: spices, tea (apple-flavoured), *raki* (a white alcohol), and of course the famous, fragrantly sweet Turkish Delight.

ISTANBUL★★★

Population 7 million
Michelin map 970 Q8

Greek Byzantium, Roman Constantinople, and Ottoman Istanbul have succeeded one another on this unique site with a foot in both Europe and Asia. The mere sound of these names evokes a rich panoply of images: the city of 1 000 domes and minarets, with its vast bazaars and superb mosaics resplendent with gold. East and West come together in curious, unexpected ways. In the narrow streets, shoe-shiners, water vendors and veiled women mingle with grey-suited businessmen and elegant women in the latest European fashions. Daily life follows the rhythms of the ships winding their way between the two shores of the Bosphorus, their sirens wailing on the wind. Amid the urban tangle and ceaseless bustling, the courtyards of mosques and the grass-filled cemeteries provide welcome havens of peace.

From Byzantium to Istanbul – In the 7C BC, a Greek colony was founded by Byzas, hence the name of **Byzantium**. The small city's destiny was irreversibly transformed in AD 324 when the Roman Emperor Constantine made it his capital, rebaptising it six years later as **Constantinople**. Emperor Constantine filled the city with magnificent monuments: the hippodrome, the Roman baths, the forum and the palace. He created a New Rome, the hub of the Eastern Empire stretching from one end of the Mediterranean to the other and encompassing a large part of Europe. In the 6C, Constantinople boasted close to 400 000 inhabitants; citizenship required only that one be able to speak Greek and belong to the Orthodox Church.
In 867, Basil I founded the Macedonian Empire and the Byzantines succeeded the Romans. At the time, the Empire consisted only in southern Italy, Greece and Turkey. In 1204, the leaders of the fourth Crusade set up an ephemeral Eastern Latin Empire and plundered its many treasures (including the famous horses on St Mark Square in Venice). The population fled the city. Greek Michael VIII Paleologue recovered Constantinople in 1261, encouraging an artistic rebirth of which St Savior in Chora (Kariye Camii) represents the most shining example. The Paleologues retained their hold on this capital without an empire until it fell to the troops of the Ottoman Sultan Mehmet II, on 29 May, 1453.
The Ottomans gave the city its new name of **Istanbul**, gracing it with their mosques and the Topkapı Palace. By the beginning of the 16C, the Ottoman Empire once again encompassed almost the entire Mediterranean basin and the Balkans. It reached its pinnacle under Suleiman the Magnificent (1520-1566). This period of glory, featuring the remarkable edifices of the great architect Sinan, lasted until 1571 when the Ottoman fleet was vanquished in the battle of Lepanto. Istanbul remained unchanged until the 19C when Mahmut II undertook its modernisation. After the First World War, the humiliation of the Allied occupation and the break-up of the Ottoman Empire led the great general Mustafa Kemal (Atatürk) to launch

a war of independence. In 1923, the Republic was born, with Atatürk, its first president, founding his capital in Ankara. Istanbul's glorious reign was ended, though it remains even today the major city of Turkey.

Districts – Istanbul is divided into three major sections. The historic **old district** lies between the Golden Horn (Haliç), the Sea of Marmara (Marmara Denizi) and the wall of Theodosius, encompassing Topkapı, St Sophia, the Blue Mosque, the Grand Bazaar and Sülemaniye Mosque. It extends beyond the Golden Horn into the **Eyüp** district, famed for its mosque, the cemetery and the Pierre Loti café. The **European City** stands opposite the Golden Horn, beyond new Galata bridge. Home from the Middle Ages to the Franks, the Genoese and the Venetians, it grew during the 19C with the arrival of consulates, churches and modern shops, particularly in the quarter of **Beyoglü**. Behind it rise the skyscrapers of the business district and the elegant boutiques of **Sisli**.
The third part of the city, on the Asian continent, is best-known for **Üküdar**, with its vast cemetery, beautiful fountains and many mosques. Sunset is the perfect time for a stroll here along the promenade that edges the Bosphorus (Boğaziçi) and offers romantic vistas over the historic section's domes and minarets.
The restaurant districts come alive at night: **Kumkapi** on the shore of the Sea of Marmara, Itiklal Avenue and the **Ortaköy** neighbourhood beside the Bosphorus.
Surrounding the city are the poor **gegekondu** suburbs, inhabited primarily by Anotolian and Kurdish immigrants.

A brief glossary to help you understand Istanbul

Bazaar: covered market
Caddesi: avenue
Camii: mosque
Hammam: steam baths, the modern-day version of the Roman baths
Han: caravansary
Imam: the leader of prayers in the mosque
Madrasa: institution of religious teaching
Mirhab: the niche in which the Imam stands to lead prayers
Parraclesion: a funeral chapel in a Byzantine church
Turbe: a mausoleum, a funeral monument for important personages

THE HISTORIC DISTRICT

★★★ **Topkapı** (CZ) – *Allow at least half a day. For lunch, try the cafeteria or restaurant in the fourth court.*
Topkapı was built on the site of the Byzantine Acropolis, barely 10 years after Mehmet II captured Constantinople in 1457. Its name stands for Gate of the Cannon. The stupendous site protrudes as a promontory advancing like a ship's prow into the Bosphorus, with the mouth of the Golden Horn to port and the Sea of Marmara to starboard.
The visitor enters a series of four garden-filled courts containing a strange mixture of buildings of different periods. For four centuries, the seraglio (the Turkish term for the palace) served as seat of the government and residence for the sultans. The palace is more famous for the sumptuous decor and the treasures it contains than for its architecture. The sultans abandoned Topkapı in 1839.

Visit – **The Imperial Gate** in the outer wall opens onto a vast court bordered by buildings which housed government services. To the left stands the ancient Byzantine church of **St Irene**, contemporary with St Sophia. The **Middle Gate** leads to the second court, where official services were held. The *Kubbe alti chamber* houses a magnificent collection of armour and weapons.
South of this court is a row of monumental **kitchens** designed by the architect Sinan. More than 20 000 meals could be prepared at once. A remarkable porcelain collection is exhibited beneath the impressive vaulted ceiling and the domed fireplaces. On the other side of the court lies the entrance to the **harem**★★ restricted to women. Only the sultan and the eunuchs had the right to enter. Concubines and slaves lived in this gilded cage consisting of an eclectic series of chambers, corridors, narrow courtyards and baths. Intrigue reigned; only four women held the rank of concubine and could aspire one day to become the Valide Sultan, the mother of the sultan, the sole enviable position in this female world. Official unions remained rare, though Suleiman the Magnificent did marry Roxelane, a Circassian.

ISTANBUL

Ak. Ağalar Cad. .... CX 2
Alemdar Cad. .... CZ 3
Ayvansaray Cad. .... AX 4
Babı Ali Cad. .... BZ 7
Beşiktaş Cad. .... BX 8
Boğaz Kesen Cad. .... CY 10
Cumhuriyet Meydani .... CXY 12
Darüşşafaka Cad. .... AY 13
Divan Yolu .... BZ 14
Dolmabahçe
Gazhanezi Sok .... CX 15
Elmadağ Cad. .... CX 16
Evliya Çelebi Cad. .... BY 18
Hacı Hüsrev Cad. .... BX 19
Hakimiyet-i Milliye Cad. ..... DY 21
Hayriye Tüccarı Cad. .... AZ 22
İtfaiye Cad. .... AYZ 23
Kadırga Limanı Cad. .... BZ 25
Kemer Altı Cad. .... CY 27
Küçük Ayasofya Cad. .... BZ 28
Macar Kardeşler Cad. .... AZ 30
Muradiye Cad. .... CZ 31
Namık Kemal Cad. .... AZ 32
Oğuzhan Cad. .... AZ 35
Okçu Musa Cad. .... BY 36
Ord. Prof. Cemil Bilsel Cad BZ 37

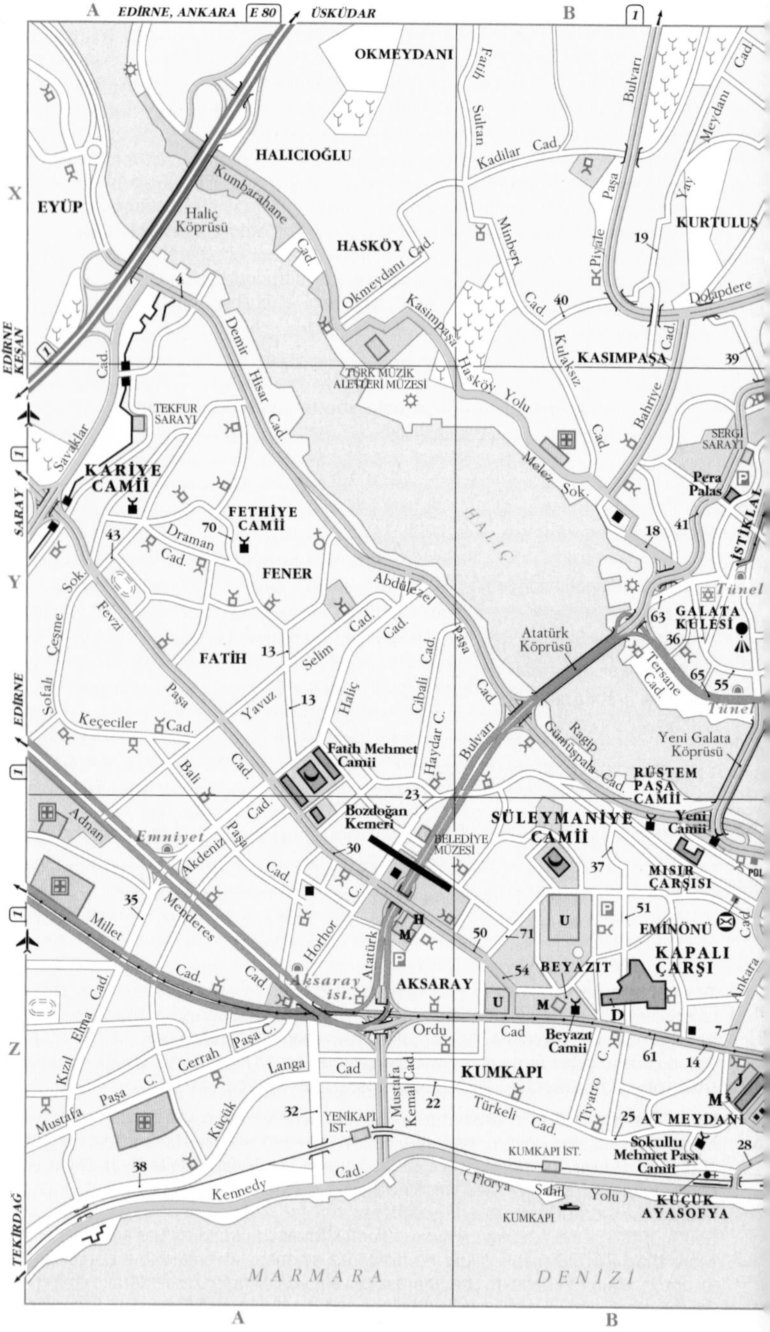

Discover the suggested Touring Programmes at the beginning of the guide
Plan a trip with the help of the Map of Principal Sights.

B Yerebatan Sarayı
D Sahaflar Çarşısı
M¹ Eski Sark Eserleri Müzesi
M² Çinili Köskü
M³ Türk ve Islam Eserleri Müzesi

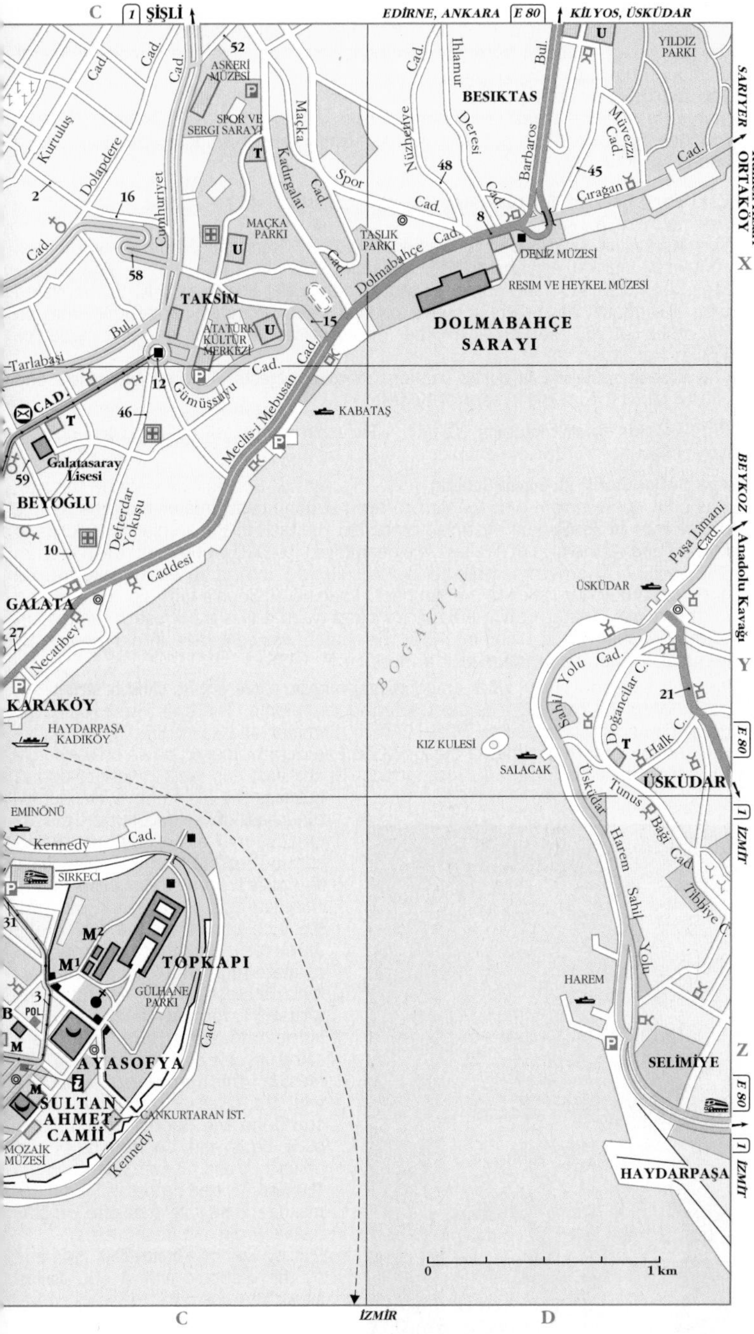

Michelin Maps are updated constantly.
Always travel with the latest edition.

Amid the amazing labyrinth of tiny rooms, a few opulent chambers intended for the Valide and the sultan stand out: the library and dining room of Ahmet I, the dining room of Ahmet III and the chamber of Murat III.
The **Gate of Felicity** leads to the third court: it opens onto the audience chamber where the sultan received foreign ambassadors. Beyond, the section of the seraglio was reserved for the sultan alone. It contains several separate pavilions which house: to the left, sacred relics, including the cloak and saber of the Prophet; straight ahead, miniatures and portraits and to the right, the treasure.
The **treasure★★★** is a splendour to behold, due to the fabulous amount of gold and precious stones that glitter on all sides: the emerald-encrusted Topkapı dagger, the throne of Ahmet I with its shimmering canopy, and the famous 86-carat diamond known as Kasikçi elmasi.
The fourth court stretches toward Saray Burnu, the nose of the seraglio. It is a marvel in miniature, with enchanting kiosks dating from the 17C and 18C surrounded by flower-filled gardens. A magnificent view extends over Galata Bridge and the Hill of Pera.

★★★**Eski Şark Eserleri Müzesi (Archeological Museums)** (CZ **M**[1]) – *Access by way of the first court of Topkapı.*
The **Museum of Antiquities★★★**, well-endowed in Greek and Roman antiquities, contains remarkable **sarcophagi★★★** found in Sidon in 1887: admire that of the Mourners (350 BC), and above all that of Alexander the Great (4C BC), covered with exceptional bas-reliefs showing on one side Alexander lion-hunting, and on the other battling the Persians. Other masterpieces not to be missed include the Tralles Ephebus.
The **Museum of Oriental Antiquities** contains statues, objects, Assyrian bas-reliefs and Hittite tablets from the Treaty of Kadesh.

★**Çinili köşkü (Ceramic Museum)** (CZ **M**[2]) – This charming kiosk built in 1466 holds a rich collection of Turkish ceramics.

★★★**Aya Sofya Camii (St Sophia Basilika)** (CZ) – Today's St Sophia, the third on the site, was built by Justinian, who wanted to raise a monument greater than the temple of Solomon in Jerusalem. Justinian entrusted the task to the architects Isidorus of Miletus and Anthemius of Tralles. They employed 10 000 workers on the site from 532 to 537. The overly-ambitious dome collapsed during an earthquake in 559 and was rebuilt by Isidorus the Younger. Imagine St Sophia with no minaret and no buttresses. That is how the basilica looked when it was the greatest monument of the Christian world. Then in 1453, the church was converted into a mosque by Mehmet II. Atatürk proclaimed it a museum in 1935.
Visit – The narrow entry, with a magnificent mosaic representing **Christ in Majesty★★**, opens onto the basilica. It is astounding in its volume. The eyes rise toward the great dome which measures 31m/101ft in diameter and soars 56m/183ft above the ground. In former times, a gigantic God Pantocrator looked down on the faithful instead of today's Koranic inscriptions. To the east and west, two half-domes buttress the main dome. The sumptuousness of the decor rivals the architectural achievement. Polychrome marble plaques cover walls and pillars; light stone capitals more chiselled than sculpted top the dark stone columns. Pass the Wish Stone (Dilek tasi), thought to be propitious to maternity, and through the narthex, to reach a ramp leading to the **tribunes★★**, formerly reserved for religious students. Here, one has a close-up view of the remarkable 12C mosaics: the fragment of a **Deisis★★** with the faces of the Virgin, Christ and John the Baptist and, further back, Christ with Constantine IX Monomachist and his wife Zoe, then the **Théotokos★★** (the Emperor John II Comenus and his wife Irene offering gifts to the Virgin and Infant Jesus).
Exit by way of a **bronze door** (9C) and by the vestibule with a 10C **donors' mosaic★★** (look back to see it) representing the Virgin and Child with Constantine carrying a scale model of Constantinople and Justinian presenting a scale model of St Sophia. Walk around St Sophia toward Topkapı to admire the beautiful **Fountain of Sultan Ahmet II**.

D. Hée /MICHELIN
Head of Medusa

Y.Travert /DIAF

Blue Mosque

★★**Yerebatan Sarayi (Sunken Palace)** (**CZ B**) – This cistern, whose name signifies sunken palace, is contemporary with St Sophia, having been built under Justinian in 532. The Valens aqueduct supplied it. A walkway just above water level allows the visitor to view the 336 columns in 12 rows stretching a full 140m/ 459ft. The forest of illuminated stone is reflected in the water; great **heads of Medusa**, green with age, support the columns at the base, lending an eerie impression of mystery.

At Meydani (Hippodrome) (**BZ**) – This old hippodrome built in 203 by Septimius Severus, served as the major axis of Byzantine Constantinople. Constantine lengthened it to 400m/1312ft. Stables, wild animal cages and a giant market, were located below. Trophies taken from conquered countries decorated the Spina, around which the chariots raced. **The Serpentine Column** still stands. Formed of three entwined bronze serpents, it was raised in Delphi in 479 BC and brought from Greece by Constantine. **Theodosius' Obelisk** comes from the temple of Karnak in Egypt (16C BC). Its base is decorated with Byzantine **bas-reliefs**★ showing Theodosius I with his family.

★★★**Sultan Ahmet Camii (Blue Mosque)** (**CZ**) – The Blue Mosque is renowned for its magnificent azure hues. Officially, it bears the name of its creator, Sultan Ahmet, who sponsored its construction from 1609 to 1616 by the architect Mehmet Aga, a student of the great Sinan. From the outside, its extraordinary elegance lies in the terraced series of domes. The six minarets came close to causing a break with Mecca, which prided itself on its own six. The addition of a seventh minaret to the Kaaba saved its honor. The mosque lies beyond a rectangular courtyard surrounded by porticoes. Inside, there is a vast **prayer room**★★ whose floor is covered with a multitude of carpets. The **central dome**, broadened by four half-domes, rests on gigantic **pillars**★. A multitude of windows illuminate the interior with light that is tinged blue by the **Iznik faience tiles**★ and azure, turquoise and red-on-white paintings. The soft blue tones and the hushed steps of bare feet on the thick rugs transport the visitor into a universe of tranquillity that invites prayer and meditation.

Turbe of Sultan Ahmet I – The mausoleum of Sultan Ahmet dates from two years after his death.

★**Türk ve Islam Eserleri Müzesi (Turkish and Islamic Arts Museum)** (**BZ M**[3]) – The museum is located in the ancient palace, now beautifully restored, of Ibrahim Paça. Small rooms with fireplaces create a fine setting for collections of Islamic decorative arts: calligraphy, painting, architecture and, above all, faience. The reception rooms hold the collection of Seljouk prayer rugs. An ethnographic section reconstitutes various traditional styles of homes.

★★**Kapali Carşi (Grand Bazaar)** (**BZ**) – The Grand Bazaar forms a city within a city, a labyrinth of broad vaulted streets bordered by more than 4000 shops selling jewelry, ceramics, rugs, leather products and all other sorts of goods. The Sultan created it in 1461, though today's bazaar dates only from 1898. The exit on **Sahaflar Çarüşisi** (**D**), the book market, gives out on **Beyazit Square**★ (**BZ**). This square is dominated on one side by the entrance to the university and on the other, by **Beyazit Camii** (Bajazet Mosque).

Egyptian Bazaar

★★★**Süleymaniye Camii** (BZ) – Suleiman the Magnificent's mosque, with its adjoining buildings topped by more than 400 domes *(madrasas, hospices, caravansaries, hammams)*, forms a vast complex overlooking the Golden Horn. The architect Sinan built it between 1550 and 1557.
The portal gives onto the courtyard, decorated with porphyry tiles. The ancient columns supporting the portal come from the hippodrome. Two pairs of minarets of equal height surround the courtyard.
The interior is amazingly spacious. On the *qibla* wall, the *mirhab* and the *minbar* are built on the same giant scale as the mosque itself. Admire also the stained-glass windows by the master glassworker Sarkos Ibrahim, the Iznik faience panels and the glorious calligraphy of Hasa Celevi.
Outside to the east, rise the *turbes* of **Suleiman** and his wife **Roxelane**.
The esplanade offers a superb view of the Golden Horn.

★**Rüstem Paşa Camii (Rüstem Paşa Mosque)** (BYZ) – Sinan built this mosque for the Vizier Rustem Paça and it is justly famous for its splendid tile work★★.

★**Misir Çarşisi (Egyptian Bazaar)** (BZ) – Opposite the Eminönü Embarcadero, the Genoese and Venetians set up this celebrated spice market. It occupies an elegant U-shaped building rebuilt in 1943. Buy turkish delight and pistachios and lunch in the picturesque Pandeli restaurant.
Beside the Egyptian bazaar rises the great **Yeni Camii Mosque** (New Mosque, 1597-1663).

★**Küçük Ayasofya Camii (Little St Sophia Mosque)** (BZ) – The church built in 527 under Justinian was known as the Church of St Sergius and St Bacchus. Its architecture prefigures that of St Sophia, hence the name given when it became a mosque at the end of the 15C.

Sokullu Mehmet Paça Camii (BZ) – Sinan built this tiny mosque, full of beautiful ceramics, in 1571 for the vizier whose name it bears.

THE WESTERN SECTIONS

Begin your walk at the brick and stone wall of Theodosius, restored by UNESCO.

★★★**Kariye Camii (St Savior in Chora)** (AY) – The mosaics make Kariye Camii glorious. After a period of decadence, the Paleologues came to power in the 13C paving the way for a new renaissance in Byzantium. St Savior in Chora Church, rebaptized Kariye Camii when it became a mosque, represents the period jewel. It is located outside the walls *(in chora)* near the palace of Constantine Porphyrogenetus and served as the emperor's chapel. Only the cruciform nave and the wide shallow dome survive from this period, together with two mosaics, Christ Pantocrator and the Virgin with Emperor Isaac Comenus.
Under Andronic II Paleologue (1282-1328), the logothete (Minister of Finance) Theodore Metochite modified the design of the church, adding the interior narthex on the west and a long gallery on the southern side, the *parraclesion*, or funeral chapel. **Frescoes**★★★ and **mosaics**★★★ illustrate major theological themes. In the choir and the nave, the images are of salvation, while in the narthex, the emphasis is on prefiguration of salvation, represented in one dome by the Virgin surrounded by the 16 kings of Israel and in the other, by Christ surrounded by the patriarchs and the 12 tribes of Israel. Note the remarkable fresco in the *parraclesion*, showing scenes of the Last Judgement.

★**Fethiye Camii** (AY) – A 14C Byzantine church.

Fâtih Mehmet Camii (AY) – Mehmet the Conqueror's mosque has become the favoured place of prayer of today's most Orthodox Muslims. In the cemetery, visitors can admire the very fine turbe of **Mehmet Fatih**★.

Bozdoğan Kemeri (Valens Aqueduct) (AZ) – This aqueduct dating from the 4C is composed of two flights of arches. It supplied water to the innumerable baths and cisterns of Istanbul.

EUROPEAN DISTRICTS

On the hill of Pera, across the Golden Horn, lie **Galata** and **Beyoğlü**. Pass first through **Karaköy** and its *hans* (formerly caravansaries, today filled with craftsmen's workshops), to reach Galata Tower.

★**Galata Kulesi (Galata Tower)** (**BY**) – This Byzantine tower restored by the Genoese has become justly famous for the incredible **panorama**★★★ it provides of the city.

★**Istiklai Caddesi** (**BCY**) – Independence Avenue, created at the end of the 19C, now is a pedestrian street served by a rickety tramway. The buildings on both sides represent good examples of Art Nouveau; some have Victorian passageways like **Çiçek pasaji**, the Flower Passageway whose colourful restaurants serve the same fish you can buy from the vendors on the neighbouring street. Along Istiklai stretches the famous **Galatasaray High School**, whose students speak French as well as Turkish, and the **Dervishes' Tekke**, now a museum. Not far away, the **Pera Palas Hotel**★ merits a detour for a glimpse of the great days when prestigious travellers on the Orient Express such as Agatha Christie made it a favourite haunt. Just before reaching **Taksim Square**, see on the left the **Institute of French Studies**.

★★**Dolmabahçe Sarayi (Dolmabahçe Palace)** (**DX**) – The long white façade with its multitude of windows is reflected elegantly in the Bosphorus. Built by Sultan Abdul Mecit between 1842 and 1856, its half-oriental, half-occidental architecture designed by the Armenian Baylan is fully in the spirit of the Istanbul of the period. The 285 rooms, six hammams, and gigantic reception rooms, including the luxurious **Great Reception Hall of the Ambassadors**★★, the **baths**★★ made entirely of marble and the impressive **throne room**★ give an idea of the size of the palace where the sultans lived from 1856 to 1876. Atatürk died in the palace on 10 November 1938.

A CRUISE ON THE BOSPHORUS

The cruise lasts a day. Boats depart from Eminonü Embarcadero (**CZ**).

Boğaziçi (The Bosphorus) – This strait between Europe and Asia is the only outlet from the Black Sea; from the outset, it has played a key strategic role. Rich inhabitants of Istanbul have long loved its shores, building lovely wooden palaces known as **yalis**.

A trip up the Bosphorus by boat provides a view of the elegant sections of Istanbul, with the endless façade of Dolmabahçe Palace and the elegantly Baroque Ortaköy Mosque under the bridge built over the Bosphorus in 1973. The boat zigzags from one bank to the other, as houses become more and more sparse and large buildings yield to yalis and small fishing ports. To the left lies, **Rumeli Hisar** Castle★, built by Mehmet II one year before the fall of Constantinople. Further on, **Mehmet Fatih's gigantic bridge**★, the second suspended bridge spanning the straits, was built by the Japanese in 1988. As you walk towards the Black Sea, pause several times on the Asian shore before completing the walk to **Anadolu Kavaÿği**★, a village overshadowed by the massive walls of a **Genoese castle** (1350), with a marvellous **view**★★ of the surrounding countryside.

Ukraine

Area: 603 700km^2/229 406sq mi – **Population:** 51.9 million – **Capital:** Kyív (Kiev) – **Currency:** gryvna – **Time:** GMT + 2hr in winter, GMT +3hr in summer – **Formalities:** passport and visa (a lodging certificat or hotel reservation is obligatory).

Ukraïna

On 24 August 1991, Ukraine became an independent member of the Community of Independent States. The former bread-basket of the URSS, is bordered to the south by the Black Sea and inland by Russia, Belorussia, Poland, Slovakia, Hungary, Romania and Moldavia.
We give here a simple overview of the principal sights of the capital, Kiev, which is worth a visit of a day or two.

KYÏV★★

KIEV – Population 2 580 000
Michelin map 970 R 5

While still a part of the former USSR, Kiev was known as the mother of Russian cities because of its ancient past. Like many other much-coveted cities, it has experienced an eventful history. Kiev was under Viking rule before St Vladimir and his son Iaroslav the Wise took it over for the Russians. It became a great religious centre with the construction of the church of St Sophia, and an important centre for trade. Kiev reaped the rewards of its position on the amber route that connected the Baltic coast with the Black Sea. However, during the 12C, following unification of much of Russia, dynastic conflicts resulted in the country's decline. The Mongol invasion during the 13C accelerated the process which ended in ruin and the destruction of the capital.
Many centuries of foreign occupation by Lithuania and Poland ensued. The national hero Bogdan Khmelnitski finally freed the city from foreign domination and re-established Kiev as part of Muscovite Russia. His statue can be seen on the square next to St Sophia Cathedral.
Of the original building constructed by Iaroslav the Wise, only the famous **Golden Door** remains. It has become the main entrance to the town. An exhibit presents the fortifications and the reconstruction of the door.
The city lies on the banks of the River Dniepr. Its many parks, gardens and ancient monuments bear witness to its glorious past.

Krechtchatik is the 2km-long main street. It connects Bessarabskaja Square with Leninskogo Komsomola Square. In Bessarabskaja Square, a statue of Lenin still stands near an interesting covered Kolkhoz market. A modern building is devoted to temporary exhibits. The tree-lined street is a busy town centre with many shops, large department stores and open-air stands selling drinks, pastries, magazines and newspapers, and souvenirs.

Tarass Chevtchenko (1814-1861) – Both a poet and a painter, Tarass Chevtchenko has the same importance in Ukraine Alexander Pushkin as in Russia. The son of a serf, he was freed in 1938 and devoted his life to the defence of freedom and Ukrainian language and culture. His fight against despotism has made him a true national hero. A boulevard, the university, a garden and the opera all bear his name. He has his own museum, and his house can also be visited at no 8 per Sevcenko.

THE HOLY CITY

★★ **St Sophia's Cathedral** – This magnificent Byzantine sanctuary was originally built by Iaroslav the Wise in the 11C, and restored in the Baroque style in the 17C. It is one of old Russia's most ancient religious edifices.
The cathedral, surrounded by trees, can be entered through the Baroque bell-tower capped by a golden dome. The white-walled building has 13 domes that symbolise Christ and the apostles. The richness and profusion of the interior decoration is dazzling. A magnificent icon in gilded carved wood immediately strikes the eye upon entering the cathedral. St Sophia's has preserved a number of **mosaics and frescoes★★★** of extraordinary beauty. Some of the most remarkable mosaics include the Pantocrater surrounded by four archangels. It decorates the inside of the central dome. The Virgin Praying in the central apse and the Annunciation in the transept also merit attention. The frescoes illustrate historical subjects such as the family of Iaroslav the Wise, religious events, and everyday pastimes such as hunting scenes.
To the left of the choir, the sarcophagus of Iaroslav the Wise is sculpted with marble reliefs.

★★ **Kievo-Petcherska Lavra** – The monastery of the Kiev catacombs is a remarkable group of churches and monastic buildings, with a history of sheltering pilgrims and victims of war or illness.

D. Thierry /DIAF

St Sophia's Cathedral

The upper monastery, the nearby catacombs and the distant catacombs are built on two hills separated by a small valley.
The monastery can be entered through the 12C Church of the Trinity. An 18C belfry stands in front of the ruins of the cathedral of the Dormition of the Blessed Virgin. This three-storied octagonal tower is covered with a gilded copper dome. From the summit, a superb **panoramic view**★★ extends along the river from the monument to the mother country all the way to the Podol district. Many churches and museums are worth a visit. They include the All Saints Church with its five Baroque towers. The **Museum of Ukrainian Historical Treasures**★ houses sacred art, jewellery, and art works. The church-refectory stands under a huge dome, four corner domes, and wall paintings. The Museum of Folk Art and Tradition exhibits costumes, painted eggs, objects used in daily life, and glassware. Finally, the Microscopic Museum's powerful microscopes reveal the smallest book in the world – 0.6mm^2/0.02sq in with 12 pages, and a chess game on the head of a pin.

The Catacombs – A visit is recommended. *Purchase a candle before making the descent.* During the 11C, St Anthony, a Russian monk, led a hermit's life in a cave. Faithfully following his example, many disciples inhabited neighbouring caves. An important hermitage started consisting of cave-cells. Later a group of monks decided to abandon the hermetic rule and founded a monastery. By the end of the 11C, the hermits' cells were used as burial places for the monastery's monks. In the nearby catacombs a series of galleries lead to cells containing the monks' remarkably well-preserved, mummified bodies.

St Vladimir's Cathedral – The cathedral was built in the late 19C in the Byzantine style. The interior is covered with wall paintings. Today, the building is used as a place of worship.

ADDITIONAL SIGHTS

The Central Park for Culture and Relaxation – Located in the Petchersk district, the huge park with its many statues is actually made up of several parks lying one above the other on the side of a hill overlooking the River Dniepr. The **Museum of Ukrainian Art,** recognised by its imposing Doric porch, is located in the park. It exhibits a superb collection of icons. At the park's southern end stands the gracious **Maria Palace**. Maria was the name of the wife of Alexander II. Rastrelli completed the palace in 1755.

Podol – A steep road, Andreyevsky spusk, leads from the Baroque **St Andrew's Collegiate Church** near the History Museum to the lower town. The paved street is picturesque with old, one-storey coloured houses and wooden houses called *isbas*. Amateur artists exhibit their works here. Podol is a square-shaped business quarter extending along the river banks to the river dock.

Monument to the Reunification of Ukraine and Russia – A huge half-circle arc in metal with groups of monumental sculpture. The **view**★ overlooks the River Dniepr. Below stands a statue of St Vladimir.

J.-C. Saturnin /MICHELIN

City Centre

Monument to the Mother Country – This group of monumental sculptures was erected in honour of the soldiers who fought in the Second World War. A colossal statue (102m/334ft) holding a sword and shield stands on a huge pedestal. It contains a memorial museum. On the wide esplanade stand impressive groups of sculptures of soldiers of many different armies. The **view★** looks out onto the Dniepr.

Fomine University Botanical Garden – The garden is named after Alexander Fomine, a famous botanist from the 1920s. It offers a pleasant walk through a wide variety of plants and trees.

EXCURSIONS

★**Open-Air Museum of Folk Architecture and Ukrainian Life** – *15km/9mi south of the city, Odessa route.* These reconstituted villages illustrate rural life in the 18C and 19C in many Ukrainian regions. Fine examples of wooden architecture are exhibited.

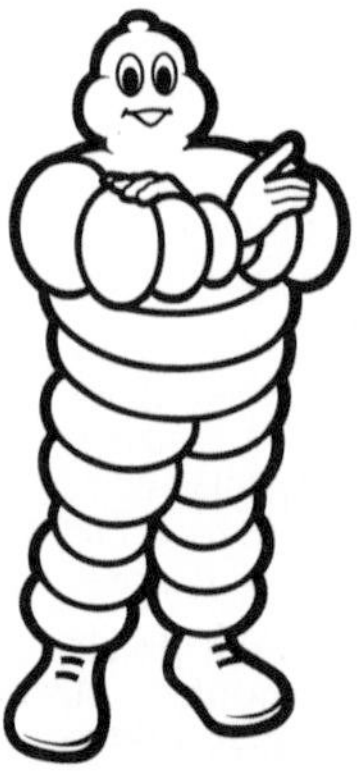

Yugoslavia

Jugoslavija

Area: 102 198km^2/38 835sq mi – **Population:** 10.6 million – **Capital:** Beograd (Belgrad) – **Currency:** dinar – **Time:** GMT + 1hr in winter, GMT + 2hr in summer – **Formalities:** passport and visa for British, US, Canadian and Australian visitors. Passport only for Japanese citizens.

Yugoslavia, constituted on 27 April 1992 as the Federal Republic of Yugoslavia, now includes the republics of Serbia and Montenegro. The current situation in Balkan countries has led us to give only a brief description of the most important tourist sites in this country.

MONTENEGRO

Montenegro (Crna Gora) is mountainous and sparsely populated in the northern part. In contrast, the south of the region, lying along the Adriatic coastline, is crowded and urban.

BAR Michelin map 970 N 7

The **Old Town★** is perched on a hill in a charming setting, along with the remains of a Turkish fortress from the 15C. Bar is also an important trading port.

★BUDVA Michelin map 970 N 7

A small town located on a peninsula, fortified during the 15C by the Venetians. Of interest is the Cathedral of St John the Baptist.

★CETINJE Michelin map 970 N 7

The former capital of the kingdom of Montenegro. See the monastery and the castle of the last sovereign, Nicholas I (museum).

★★KOTOR Michelin map 970 N 7

The ancient city, surrounded by ramparts, nestles at the back of the Kotor Gulf at the foot of the Lovcen mountain. The 12C cathedral is worth a visit.
The region is famous for its natural setting, the **Mouths of Kotor★★★**. These form a series of bays separated by straits in a mountain setting with typically Mediterranean vegetation. The view from the Lovcen is remarkable.

PODGORICA Population 118 000 – Michelin map 970 N 7

Formerly known as Titograd, the Montenegrin capital has recently taken back its original name, which dates from the 14C. The town was named Titograd after reconstruction following the Second World War in honour of Marshal Tito. Vestiges of the Roman town of **Doclea★** can be visited a few kilometres outside the city.

★ULCINJ Michelin map 970 N 8

Once a trading centre for pirates and a hold-out for slavers until the 19C, today Ulcinj is a coastal town much appreciated for its long beach. Take a stroll down the small streets, and visit the mosque and the ruins of a Turkish fortress.

This Europe guide, like all other Michelin guides, will be updated every two years. More detailed information on the countries of Eastern Europe will be provided as their tourist facilities and highway infrastructure improve.

SERBIA

★BEOGRAD (BELGRADE) Population 1 136 800 – Michelin map 970 N 7

Located at the junction of the Danube and Save rivers, Belgrade is a spacious modern city, with Terazije and Republike squares at the city's busy centre. Visitors can stroll through **Skadarlija**, the artists' quarter and Montmartre of Belgrade, and stop at a typical little restaurant.

★★ **Kalemegdan** – The park is surrounded by ramparts that overlook the urban area and provide a fine view of the city. A monument by Mestrovic (1930), Gratitude to France, stands in the park. Inside the 18C fortress, a military museum exhibits weapons and uniforms.

★★ **National Museum** – The museum houses a series of rich archeological collections from prehistoric and ancient times, as well as numerous paintings by Serbian artists. There are also works by Gauguin and Kandinsky.

EXCURSIONS

Monasteries – To the south of Belgrade are many monasteries of considerable interest for their setting and artistic legacy. The following sights, in alphabetic order, are of interest: **Gradac**★★, a church built in the 13C by Queen Helen of Savoy as a mausoleum, in a mixture of Gothic and Byzantine styles; **Kalenic**★★ from the 15C, isolated, with frescoes in the Byzantine style; **Manisija**★★, a 15C fortified monastery. The church and its cupolas house frescoes painted a background of gold and lapis-lazuli; **Milesevo**★★ from the 13C with splendid wall paintings; **Ravanica**★★ (a five-cupola church from the end of the 14C; **Sopocani**★★ from the 13C, with frescoes dating from the 13C and 14C; and last but not least **Studenica**★★, three 12C churches in a mountain setting that shelter a series of admirable frescoes.

★★ **Smederovo** – *40km/24mi to the east.* This large stronghold was standing on the plain above the Danube, built in 1430 in a triangular plan.

*Life in America is in most ways pleasanter,
easier, simpler than in Europe. It floats
in a sense of happiness like that
of a radiant summer morning.
But life in one of the great European centers
is capable of an intensity, a richness
blended of many elements which has
not yet been reached in America. There are
more problems in Europe calling for
a solution; there is more passion in the
struggles that rage round them; the past
more frequently kindles the present
in a glow of imaginative light.
In whichever country of Europe one dwells,
one feels that the other countries are
near, that the fortunes of their
people are bound up with the fortunes
of one's own, that ideas are shooting
to and fro between them.*

James Bryce, The American Commonwealth, 1888

HUNDERT
DEUTSCHE
MARK
BUNDESBANK 1962
G.162
100
100
DEUTSCHE
BUNDESBANK
100
FÜNFZIG
DEUTSCHE MARK
50
DEUTSCHE
BUNDESBANK
Frankfurt am Main
2. Januar 1980
50
FÜNFZIG
DEUTSCHE
MARK
S0086253
0086253

Practical information

Incentives for a visit

From January to December, life in Europe follows the rhythm of its festivals, giving visitors countless opportunities to discover its countries in a totally different way: spend a week-end or take a few daysí break, to get to know the countryís customs.

Carnival-time – Carnivals are celebrated all over Europe, generally in February and March. This is a great opportunity to discover the diversity of each country's traditions: Cadiz (Spain), Nice (France), Venice (Italy), Paturai (Greece), Breda (the Netherlands), Binche (Belgium), Cologne and Rottweil (Germany), Basle (Switzerland), Mohacs (Hungary).

Springtime – Traditionally celebrated for the return of fine weather especially in countries where the winter is long: Farewell to Russian Winter (snow and ice festivals and folk dancing); Valborgsmässoafton (Evening of the Walpurgis Mass) in Scandinavia; the national flower show in Keukenhof (the Netherlands); the giant May tree in Stockholm.

Religious festivals and pilgrimages – Holy Week in Braga (Portugal) and in Seville (Spain); the Catenacciu in Sartène (Corsica); Miracle of St Januarius in Naples; Procession of the Holy Blood in Bruges; the feasts of St Lucy (Sweden) and St John (fireworks and making of floral crowns) all over Europe and in particular in Scandinavia; Seker Bayrami (sugar festival) and Kurban Bayrami (sheep festival) in Turkey.
Europe is also an important place of pilgrimage such as Fátima (Portugal), Lourdes (France), Assisi (Italy) and Częstochowa (Poland).

R. Mattes/EXPLORER

Venice Carnival

Wine and beer festivals – Most European countries produce wine and celebrate the vines when the grapes are harvested in Burgenland (Austria), Logroño (Spain), Gravenmacher (Luxembourg), Bad Dürkheim and Neustadt-an-der-Weinstrasse (Germany), Ribeauvillé and Riquewihr in Alsace, during the Trifon Zarezan (Bulgaria) and at the international food festival in Dijon, etc.
Munich celebrates beer (Oktoberfest), when Bavarians get together in spirited, good humour in big marquees.

Major traditional events – Bullfighting and bull-running are more predominant in southern Europe: *touradas* in Portugal; *corridas* at the Festival of Seville and bull-running (Sanfermines) of Pamplona (Spain). The Pallo della Contrade in Siena (Italy) is a famous horse race which takes place every year.
Folk dancing and music bring the smallest European village to life (information about these festivals to be found locally). Here are one or two of the most famous traditional events: Feis na nGleann Festival in Antrim (Ireland); Festival de Cornouaille in Quimper (France); Festival of the Cordovan Patios and the National Flamenco Dancing Competition in Cordoba (Spain); Spring in Kiev (Ukraine); Baltic Festival, Festival of Folklore of Straznica (Czech Republic); National Folklore Festival in Gjiro Kastêr (Albania); Festival of Roses (Bulgaria).

Music and theatre – For music lovers, Europe is one big concert hall. There are many world famous festivals especially in summer: Montreux International Jazz Festival (Switzerland); Copenhagen Jazz Festival (Denmark); World Jazz Festival of Juan-les-Pins (France); Krakow Jazz Festival (Poland); Roskilde Rock Festival (Denmark); Holland Festival (the Netherlands); Florentine May Music Festival (Italy); Fiddle Stone Festival in Belleck (Ireland); the Edinburgh Military Tattoo (Scotland); Richard Wagner Festival in Bayreuth (Germany); Savonlinna Opera Festival (Finland); Glyndebourne Annual Opera and Music Festival (Great Britain); Aix-en-Provence International Festival of Opera and Music (France); Chorégies in Orange (France); Bergen International Music Festival (Norway); Festival of Vienna, Festival of Salzburg (Austria); White Nights of St Petersburg (Russia); Autumn in Warsaw (Poland), etc. The theatre is a must: in Avignon (France); during the Festival dei Due Mondi in Spoleta (Italy). For dancing in particular the eastern countries: Russian Winter in Moscow; Stars of Moscow, and for circus-lovers, there is the world famous Moscow Circus.

S. Viron/DIAF

Moscow Circus

There are also international film festivals, the main ones in Cannes (France), Venice (Italy) and Berlin (Germany).

Christmas in Europe – Spending Christmas in Europe will without a doubt be a memorable experience whether you go to the Christmas markets in Nuremberg (Germany), Salzburg (Austria), Freiburg (Switzerland), Strasbourg (France) or go to the Feast of St Nicholas in Amsterdam (the Netherlands), Bad Mitterndorf (Austria), listen to carol singing in London (Great Britain) and Koledouvane (Bulgaria), or even admire the Christmas Lights in London.

Land of the midnight sun – From May to September, the sight of the midnight sun at the North Cape is an unforgettable experience.

This is a quick outline of the many festivals that bring Europe alive all year round. There are many other festivals to be discovered, the smaller ones being of interest as well. For more information go to the local tourist office.

The cultural capitals of Europe

1985	Athens (Greece)	**1995**	Luxembourg (Grand Duchy of Luxembourg
1986	Florence (Italy)	**1996**	Copenhague (Denmark)
1987	Amsterdam (Netherlands)	**1997**	Thessalonika (Greece)
1988	Berlin (Germany)	**1998**	Stockholm (Sweden)
1989	Paris (France)	**1999**	Weimar (Germany)
1900	Glasgow (Great Britain)	**2000**	Avignon (France), Bergen (Norway), Bologna (Italy), Brussels (Belgium), Krakow (Poland), Helsinki (Finland), Prague (Czech Republic), Reykjavik (Iceland), Santiago de Compostela (Spain)
1991	Dublin (Ireland)		
1992	Madrid (Spain)		
1993	Anvers (Belgium)		
1994	Lisbon (Portugal)		

Planning your trip

Michelin publications and services

The Michelin map of Europe 970 at a scale of 1:3 000 000 indicates motorways, international and national highways, local roads, and distances between major towns and cities. There is an index to help you locate the main place-names on the map.
The **Michelin Road Atlas Europe** lists the main highway codes by country, with details of speed limits, wearing of safety belts, maximum blood-alcohol levels, required documents, minimum driving age, etc., under the heading "Driving in Europe". The atlas also contains a European weather chart, a map of major tourist routes, an insert of western Europe at a scale of 1:1 000 000, of Greece at 1:700 000, of Scandinavia at 1:1 500 000 and of eastern Europe at 1:300 000, maps of major towns and cities and the Channel Tunnel terminals of Calais and Folkestone, an index and a table of distances.

In France use 3615 MICHELIN Minitel Service

Minitel is a French Telecom videotex service offering a wide variety of information *(fee charged)*. Public terminals are to be found in most post offices, some petrol stations and hotels.

36 15 MICHELIN: access code to connect with the service. This user-friendly travel service is available round the clock.

Route planning: give your point of departure and destination, stipulate your preference for motorways or local roads, indicate the sights to see along the way, and it will do the rest (also available by fax on 36 17 MICHELIN, or by high-speed Minitel and fax on 36 23 MICHELIN).

Lunchtime or overnight stops: now look for that special restaurant, secluded country hotel or pleasant campsite along the chosen route.

Access for users outside France: foreign subscribers can access French Telecom videotex services; consult your documentation.

Field of operation: this outstanding European and road data covers most European countries.

Listed below are some of the telematic services offered:

36 14 ED	Directory inquiries in English
36 15 TCAMP	Camping information
36 15 METEO	Weather report
36 15 HORAV	General airline information and flights schedules from and to Paris or 36 16 HORAV
36 15 BBC	BBC news

Internet: http://www.michelin-travel.com – Route planning, hotels, restaurants, campsites (in France) and tourist attractions.

Tourist offices

For more information, brochures, maps and assistance in planning a trip to Europe, apply to the official tourist offices.
The **Michelin Red Guides** Europe, Benelux, Deutschland, España Portugal, France, Great Britain and Ireland, Italia, London, Paris and environs, Portugal, and Suisse give the addresses and telephone numbers of the Tourist Information Centres to be found in most large towns and many tourist resorts.
We give below some addresses of tourist offices in Great Britain, Ireland, North America, Australia and New Zealand.

Austria

Website http://www.austria-tourism.at

Austrian National Tourist Offices

Great Britain: PO Box 2363, London W1A 2QB, ☎ (44 171) 629 04 61, fax (44 171) 499 60 38, email oewlon@easynet.co.uk.

USA: PO Box 1142, New York, N.Y. 10108-1142, ☎ (1 212) 944 6880, fax (1 212) 730 45 68, email antonyc@ibm.net, website http://www.anto.com.

Canada: 2 Bloor Street East, Suite 3330, Toronto, Ontario M4W 1A 8, ☎ (1 416) 967 33 81, fax (1 416) 967 41 01, email anto-tor@sympatico.ca.

Australia: 1st Floor, 36 Carrington Street, Sydney NSW 2000, ☎ (61 2) 92 99 36 21, fax (61 2) 92 99 38 08, email oewsyd@world.net.

Belgium

Website http://www.visitbelgium.com

Belgian Tourist Offices

Great Britain: Tourism Flanders – Brussels, 31 Pepperstreet, London E 14 9RW, ☏ (44 171) 458 00 44, fax (44 171) 458 00 45.

USA: 780 3rd Ave., Suite 1501, New York, NY 10017, ☏ (1 212) 758 81 30, fax (1 212) 355 7675, email trade@visitbelgium.com.

Canada: PO Box 760, NDG, Montreal, QUE HA4 3S2, ☏ (1 514) 484 35 94, fax (1 514) 489 89 65.

Bulgaria

Great Britain: Commercial Section of Bulgaria, 186-188 Queen's Gate, London SW7 5 HL, ☏ (44 171) 584 94 00, fax (44 171) 589 48 75.

USA: Balkan Holidays, 317 Madison Ave., Suite 508, New York, NY 10017, ☏ (1 212) 573 55 30, fax (1 212) 573 65 38.

Croatia

Great Britain: Embassy of the Republic of Croatia, Tourist Information Department, 2 Belgrave Street, London SW1 5 BJ, ☏ (44 171) 235 69 91, fax (44 171) 434 29 53.

USA: Embassy of the Republic of Croatia, 2343 Massachusetts Ave., N.W., Washington DC 20008, ☏ (1 202) 588 58 99, fax (1 202) 588 89 38.

Czech Republic

Great Britain: Czech Centre, 95 Great Portland Street, London W1N 5RA, ☏ (44 171) 291 99 20, fax (44 171) 436 83 00.

USA: 1109 11 11 Madison Avenue, New York, NY 10028, ☏ (1 212) 288 08 30, fax (1 212) 288 09 71.

Canada: PO Box 198, Exchange Tower, 2 1st Canadian Place, Toronto, Ontario, M5X 1A6, ☏ (1 416) 3 67 34 32, fax (1 416) 3 67 33 92.

Denmark

Website http://www.dt.dk

Danish Tourist Board

Great Britain: 55 Sloane Street, PO Box 2LT, London W1X 9SY, ☏ (44 171) 259 59 59, fax (44 171) 259 59 55.

USA: 655 3rd Ave., 18th Floor, New York, NY 10017, ☏ (1 212) 885 9700, fax (1 212) 885 97, 983 52 60.

Estonia

Website http://www.vm.ee

Great Britain: Estonian Embassy, 16 Hyde Park Gate, London SW7 5DG, ☏ (44 171) 589 3428, fax (0171) 589 3430.

USA: Consulate General of Estonia, Tourist Information, 630 Fifth Ave., Suite 2415, New York, NY 10111, ☏ (1 212) 247 76 34, fax (1 212) 262 08 93.

Finland

Great Britain: Finnish Tourist Board, 3rd Floor, 30-35 Pall Mall, London, SW1Y 5LP, ☏ (44 171) 839 40 48, fax (44 171) 321 06 96, email mek.lon@mek.fi.

USA: Finnish Tourist Board, Grand Central Station, New York, NY 10163-4649, ☏ (1 212) 885 9700, fax (1 212) 885 9710, email mek@usa.fi.

France

Website http://www.franceguide.com

French Government Tourist Offices

Great Britain: 178 Picadilly, London W1V 0AL, ☏ 0171 499 6911 (24-hour answering service with recorded message and information) or (44 171) 399 35 00, fax (44 171) 493 65 94.

USA: 444 Madison Avenue, New York, N-Y 10022, ☏ (1 212) 838 78 00, fax (1 212) 838 78 55; France On Call Hotline, ☏ (900) 990-0040 (US$ 0.50/min.) for information on hotels, restaurants and transportation.

Canada: 1981 av. Mac Gill College, suite 490, Montreal, QUE H3A 2W9, ☎ (1 514) 845 48 68; 30 St Patrick's St, Suite 700, Toronto, ONT M5T 3A 3, ☎ (1 416) 593 47 23.

Ireland: 10 Suffolk Street, Dublin (2), ☎ (353 1) 679 08 13, fax (353 1) 679 08 14.

Australia: 25 Bligh Street, level 22, Sydney NSW 2000, ☎ (61 292) 31 52 44, fax (61 292) 21 86 82.

Germany

Website http://www.germany-tourism.de

German National Tourist Offices

Great Britain: PO Box 2695, London W1A 3TN, ☎ (44 171) 3 17 09 08, fax (44 171) 4 95 61 29, email 106167.3216@compuserve.com.

USA: 122 East 42nd Street, Chanin Bldg., 52nd Floor, New York, N-Y 101 68 - 00 72, ☎ (1 212) 6 61 72 00, fax (1 212) 6 61 71 74, email gntony@aol.com.

Canada: 175 Bloor Street East, North Tower, 6th floor, suite 604, Toronto, Ontario, M4W 3R8, ☎ (1 416) 968 15 70, fax (1 416) 968 19 86, email germanto@idirect.com.

Australia: PO Box A 980, Sydney South NSW 1235, ☎ (61 2) 92 67 81 48, fax (61 2) 92 67 90 35.

Great Britain

Website http://www.visitbritain.com

USA: British Tourist Authority, 561 Fifth Ave., Suite 701, New York, NY 10179, ☎ (1 212) 986 22 66, fax (1 212) 986 1188.

Canada: 111 Avenue Road, Suite 450, Toronto, Ontario, M5R 3J8, ☎ (416) 961 8124, fax (416) 961 2175.

Ireland: 123 Lower Baggot Street, Dublin 2, (353 1) 661 4273, fax (353 1) 678 5280.

Australia: 210 Clarence Street, Sydney, NSW 2000, (61 2) 267 4666, (61 2) 267 4442.

New Zealand: Suite 305, 3rd Floor, Dilworth Building, Cnr Custom & Queens Streets, Auckland 1, ☎ (10 649) 303 14 46, fax (10 649) 377 69 65.

Greece

Website http://www.travelling.org

Greek National Tourist Offices

Great Britain: Greek National Tourist Organisation, 4 Conduit Street, London W1R ODJ, ☎ (0171) 49 94 976, fax (0171) 287 13 69.

USA: Greek National Tourist Office, 611 W. 6th St., Suite 2198, Los Angeles, CA 90017, ☎ (1 213) 62 66 696, fax (1 213) 489 97 44.

Canada: 1300 Bay Street, Toronto, Ontario, M5R 3K8, ☎ (1 416) 968 65 22.

Australia: 51-57 Pitt Street, Sydney, NSW 2000, ☎ (61 2) 924 11 663, fax (61 2) 923 52 174.

New Zealand: contact the Greek National Tourist Office in Sydney (Australia).

Hungary

Hungarian National Tourist Offices

Great Britain: 46 Eaton Place, London SW1X 8AL, ☎ (44 171) 823 1032, fax (44 171) 823 14 59.

USA: 150 East 58th St., 33rd Floor, New York, NY 10155, ☎ (212) 355 02 40, fax (212) 207 41 03, email huntour@idt.net.

Iceland

Website http://www.goiceland.org

Great Britain: Icelandic Tourist Information, 172 Tottenham Court Road, London W19 OLY, ☎ (44 171) 388 5346.

USA: Scandinavian Tourist Board, 655 3rd Ave., New York, NY 10017, ☎ (1 212) 885 97 00.

Republic of Ireland

Irish Tourist Boards

Great Britain: 150 New Bound Street, London W1Y OAQ, ☎ (44 171) 518 0800, fax (44 171) 493 9065.

USA: 345 Park Avenue, New York, NY 10154, ☎ (1 212) 418 08 00, fax (1 212) 371 90 52.

Canada: contact the Irish Tourist Board in New York (USA).

Australia: 5th Level, 36 Carrington Street, Sydney 2000, New South Wales, ☎ (61 2) 92 99 61 77, fax (61 2) 92 99 63 23.

New Zealand: 2nd Floor, Dingwall Building, 87 Queens Street, Auckland, ☎ (64 9) 379 87 20, fax (64 9) 302 24 20.

Italy

Italian Government Tourist Boards

Great Britain: 1 Princess Street, London W1R 8AY, ☎ (44 171) 408 12 54 or (44 171) 355 14 38, fax (44 171) 493 6695.

USA: 630 5 th. Avenue, Suite 1566, New York, NY 10111, ☎ (1 212) 24 55 095, fax (1 212) 58 69 249 ; 12400 Wilshire Blvd., Suite 550, Los Angeles, CA 90025, ☎ (1 310) 820 18 98 or 820 19 59, fax (1 310) 820 6357.

Canada: 1 place Ville Marie, Suite 1914, Montréal H3B 2C3, ☎ (1 514) 866 1669, fax (1 514) 392 14 29.

Latvia

Great Britain: Embassy of Latvia, information Office, 45 Nottingham Place, London W1M 3FE, ☎ (44 171) 312 00 40, fax (44 171) 312 00 42, email latvia-embassy@magmacom.com.

USA: Latvian Embassy, 4325 17th St., N.W., Washington DC 20011, ☎ (1 202) 726 82 13, fax (1 202) 726-6785 http://www.seas.gwu.edu/guest/latvia/.

Canada: 112 Kent Street, Place de la Ville, Tower B, Suite 208, Ottawa, Ontario K1P 5P2, email latvia-embassy@magmacom.com, website http://www2.magmacom/~latemb/.

Ireland: contact the Embassy of Latvia in London (Great Britain).

Lithuania

Great Britain: Embassy of Republic of Lithuania, Tourist Information Department, 84 Gloucester Place, London W1H 3HN, ☎ (44 171) 486 6401, fax (44 171) 486 6403.

USA: Honorary Consulate of Lithuania, Tourist Information, 3238 N. Sawlcoth Court, Westlake Village, CA 91362, ☎ (1 805) 496 53 24, fax (1 805) 496 74 35.

Luxembourg

Luxembourg National Tourist Offices

Great Britain: 122 Regent Street, London W1R 5FE, ☎ (44 171) 434 28 00, fax (44 171) 734 12 05, website www.luxembourg.co.uk.

USA: 17 Beekman Place, New York, NY 10022, ☎ (212) 935-8888, fax (212) 935-5896.

Malta

Website http://www.tourism.org.mt

Malta National Tourist Offices

Great Britain: 36-38 Piccadilly, London W1 V0PP, ☎ (44 171) 292 49 00, fax (44 171) 734 18 80, email office.uk@tourism.org.mt.

USA: Empire State Building, 350 Fifth Ave., Suite 4412, New York, NY 10118, ☎ (212) 695 95 20, fax (212) 695 82 29, email office.us@tourism.org.mt.

Canada: contact Maltese Tourist Office in New York (USA)

Ireland: contact Maltese Tourist Office in London (Great Britain)

The Netherlands

Website http://www.goholland.com

Netherlands Boards of Tourism

Great Britain: PO Box 523, London SW1^{E} 6NT, ☎ (44 891) 71 77 77, fax (44 171) 828 79 41.

USA: 355 Lexington Avenue, 21st Floor, New York, NY, ☎ (1 212) 37 07 360, fax (1 212) 37 09 507.

Canada: 25 Adelaide Street East, Suite 710, Toronto, Ontario M5C 1Y2, ☎ (1 416) 363 1577, fax (1 416) 363 14 70.

Ireland: contact the Netherlands Board of Tourism in London (Great Britain).

Norway

Website http://www.tourist.no

Great Britain: Norwegian Tourist Board, 5-11 (Lower) Regent Street, London SW1Y 4LR, ☎ (44 171) 839 62 55, fax (44 171) 839 60 14.

USA: 655 3rd Ave., 18th Floor, New York, NY 10017, ☎ (1 212) 885 9700, fax (1 212) 885 97 10.

Ireland: contact the Norwegian Tourism Board in London (Great Britain).

Australia: contact the Norwegian Tourism Board in New York (USA).

Poland

Polish National Tourist Offices

Great Britain: 1st Floor, Remo House, 310-312 Regents Street, London W1R 5AJ, ☎ (44 171) 580 88 11, fax (44 171) 580 88 66.

USA: 215 Madison Ave., Suite 1711, New York, NY 10016, ☎ (1 212) 338 94 12, fax (1 212) 338 92 83, email pnto@dial.pitex.com.

Portugal

Website http://www.portugalinsite.pt

Portuguese National Tourist Offices

Great Britain: 22/25a Sackville Street, 4th Floor, London W1X 1DE, ☎ (44 171) 494 1441, fax (44 171) 494 18 68, email iceplond@dircon.co.uk.

USA: 590 Fifth Avenue, 4th Floor, New York, NY 10036-4785, ☎ (1 212) 719 3985 or (1 212) 40 491, fax (1 212) 764-6137, email jfcosta@portugal.org.

Canada: 60 Bloor Street West, Suite 1005, Toronto, Ontario M4W 3B8, ☎ (1 416) 921 73 76, fax (1 416) 13 53, email iceptor@direct.com.

Ireland: 54 Dawson Street, Dublin 2, ☎ (353 1) 670 91 33, fax (353 1) 670 91 41, email info@icep.ie.

Romania

Romanian National Tourist Offices

Great Britain: 83A Marylebone High Street, London W1M 3DE, ☎ (44 171) 224 3692, fax (44 171) 935 64 35.

USA: 14 East, 38th Street, 12th Floor, New York, NY 10016, ☎ (1 212) 545 84 84, fax (1 212) 251 04 29.

Russia

To get tourist informations about Russia, contact Inexco Voyages, 29 rue Tronchet, 75008 Paris, France, (33 1) 47 42 25 80, fax (33 1) 47 42 25 81, email paris@inexco-travel.fr, or Inexco Main Board in Moscow (7 095) 921 82 50, or 928 40 68, fax (7 095) 921 81 87, Moscow.

Slovakia

Great Britain: Embassy of Slovakia, 25 Kensington Palace Gardens, London W8 4QY, ☎ (44 171) 243 0803, fax (44 171) 727 58 24.

USA: Slovak Information Center, 406 E. 67th ST. New York, NY 10021, ☎ (212) 737-3971, fax (212) 737-3454 ; Embassy of Slovakia, Wisconsin Avenue, NV Washington, (1 202) 96 55 161, fax (1 202) 96 55 166, email svkemb@concentric.net.

Canada: Embassy of Slovakia, 50 Rideau Terrace, Ottawa, Ontario, ☎ (1 613) 749 44 42, fax (1 613) 749 49 89.

Australia: Embassy of Slovakia, 47 Culgoa, Circuit O'Malley, Camberra, ACT 2606, ☎ (61 6) 290 15 16, fax (61 6) 290 17 55.

Slovenia

Slovenian Tourist Offices

Great Britain: 49 Conduit Street, London W1R 9FB, ☎ (44 171) 287 71 33, fax (44 171) 28 75 476.

USA: 345 East 42nd Street, New York, NY 10003, ☎ (1 212) 358 96 86, fax (1 212) 358 90 25, email slotouristboard@soveniatravel.com.

Spain

Spanish National Tourist Offices

Great Britain: 22-23 Manchester Square, London W1M 5AP, ☎ (44 171) 486 80 77, fax (44 171) 486 80 34, email buzon.oficial@londres.oet.mox.es.

USA: 666 Fifth Avenue, New York, NY 10103, (1 212) 265 88 22, fax (1 212) 265 88 64, email buzon.oficial@nuevayork.oet.mox.es; 8383 Wilshire Blvd., Suite 960, Beverly Hills, CA 90211, ☎ (1 213) 658-7188, fax (1 213) 658-1061, email buzon.oficial@losangeles.oet.mox.es.

Canada: 2 Bloor Street West, 34th Floor, Toronto, Ontario M4W 3E2, ☎ (1 416) 961 3131, fax (1 416) 961 1992, spainto@globalserve.net.

Sweden

Website http://www.visit-sweden.com

Great Britain: 11 Montagu Place, London W1H 2AL, ☎ (44 171) 870 56 00, fax (44 171) 724 58 72, email info@swetourism.org.uk.

USA: PO Box 4649, Grand Central Station, New York, NY 10163-4649, ☎ (1 212) 885 97 00, fax (1 212) 885 97 64, info@gosweden.org.

Switzerland

Website http://www.switzerlandtourism.com

Switzerland Tourism

Great Britain: Swiss Centre, Swiss Court, London W1V 8EE, ☎ (44 171) 734 19 21, fax (44 171) 437 45 77, email urseberhard@stlondon.com.

USA: 608 Fifth Avenue, New York, NY 10020-2303, (1 212) 757 5944, fax (1 212) 262 6116, email stnewyork@switzerlandtourism.com; 222 N. Sepulveda Blvd., Suite 1570, El Segundo, CA 90245, ☎ (1 310) 414-8484, fax (1 310) 414-8490.

Canada: 926 The East Mall, Etobicoke, Ontario M9B 6K1, ☎ (1 416) 695-2090, fax (1 416) 695-2774.

Australia: Swissair, 33 Pitt Street, Level 8, NSW 2000 Sydney, (61 2) 92 31 37 44, fax (61 2) 92 51 65 31, email swissair@tiasnet.com.au

Turkey

Website http://www.turkey.org/turkey

Turkish Tourist Offices

Great Britain: 170-173 Piccadilly, London W1V 9DD, ☎ (44 171) 629 7771, fax (44 171) 491 07 73, email eb25@cityscape.co.uk.

USA: 821 United Nations Plaza, New York, NY 10017, ☎ (1 212) 687 2194 or (1 212) 687 21 95, fax (212) 599 75 68.

Canada: Constitution Square, 360 Albert Street, Suite 801, Ottawa, Ontario, K1R 7X7, (1 613) 230 86 54, fax (1 613) 230 36 83.

Australia: Suite 101, 280 George Street, Sydney, NSW 2000, (61 2) 92 23 30 55, fax (61 2) 92 23 32 04, email turkish@ozemail.com.

Ukraine

Great Britain: Ukraine Embassy, 78 Kensington Park Road, London W11 2PL, fax (44 171) 792 17 08.

USA: Kobasnjuk Travel, 157 2nd Ave., New York, NY 10017, ☎ (1 212) 254 87 79, fax (1 212) 254 40 05.

Yugoslavia **(Serbia and Montenegro)**

Great Britain: Tourist Information Department, Yugoslav Embassy, 5 Lexham Gardens, London W8 5JJ, ☎ (44 171) 370 61 05.

USA: Embassy of the Federal Republic of Yugoslavia, 2410 California St., N.W., Washington DC 20008, ☎ (1 202) 462 65 66, fax (1 202) 797 96 63.

Getting around Europe

At the beginning of this guide, the map of **European transport** indicates the major highways, the main international airports, regular sea links, the main rail connections as well as high speed or luxury trains (Spanish Talgo, French TGV, German ICE, Venice Simplon-Orient Express).

Europe by air

Europe's capital cities and many main towns are linked by national airlines providing regular flights: Lufthansa (Germany); Austrian Airlines (Austria); Sabena Belgian World Airlines (Belgium); Scandinavian Airlines (Denmark, Norway and Sweden); Iberia Airlines (Spain); Finnair (Finland); Air France, Air Inter Europe (France); British Airways, British Midland (Great Britain); Olympic Airways (Greece); Malèv Hungarian Airlines (Hungary); Aer Lingus (Ireland); Icelandair (Iceland); Alitalia (Italy); Air Malta (Malta); KLM Dutch Royal Airlines (the Netherlands); LOT Polish Airlines (Poland); TAP Air Portugal (Portugal); Tarom Romanian Airlines (Romania); Swissair (Switzerland); Czechoslovak Airlines (Czech Republic and the Slovak Republic); THY Turkish Airlines (Turkey). There are sometimes reduced rates for young people (under 25s or students) available from these larger airlines. Further information can be obtained from travel agencies or airline offices in main towns or airports.
Airlines flying regularly to Europe from the United States are: American Airlines, Continental Airlines, Delta Airlines, Northwest Airlines, TWA and United Airlines; from Canada: Air Canada and Canadian International Airlines.
Competitively priced flights to capital cities throughout the world and main European cities are also available from many charter companies. Further information can be obtained from travel agencies, airlines and airports.

Some boat trips

The Michelin map 970 indicates the car ferry links between various European countries. It is easy to get from one country to the next by sea whether it be the Mediterranean (Spain, the Balearics, France, Corsica, Sardinia, Italy, Greece, Yugoslavia, the Canary Islands, Crete and Turkey); the Channel (France, Belgium, the Netherlands, and Great Britain), the Irish Sea (Ireland and Great Britain); the North Sea (Denmark, Sweden, Norway, and Great Britain) or the Baltic Sea (Germany, Sweden, Poland, Iceland, Finland, Lithuania, Estonia, Latvia, and Russia). These short crossings are often just like going on a mini-cruise.

Europe by coach

Travelling by coach can be an economical way to explore Europe. There are many coach companies providing connections between towns and cities and even between countries. Highways are generally good and coaches nowadays are comfortable and quick, and have the added advantage of being able to take travellers to places where the plane or train cannot go. In some countries, such as Greece and Turkey, coaches are quicker and more reliable than trains. For information about coach companies, ask in the respective country's tourist offices.

P. Diot/VISA

Hurtigruten – Coastal Steamer, Norway

Special rates are offered by some travel agencies: transport, board, accommodation and guided tours of towns and the sights being included in the price of the vacation. Regular coach connections from London to European capitals and main cities are provided by the following companies: National Express, Citysprint and Eurolines. These companies operate and depart from the Victoria Coach Station. In Paris, Eurolines also has regular departures from the "Paris-Galliéni" international coach station, avenue du Général-de-Gaulle, 93 Bagnolet, ☎ 01 49 72 51 51.

Europe by train

Europe is well serviced by trains allowing quick, comfortable and relatively cheap travel between towns and cities. Timetables are available in mainline stations. It is wise to reserve a seat for a long journey, particularly in peak travel periods, such as vacations and national holidays.

Travel cards – These are passes giving reductions, with special rates available for children, the under-26s and the over-26s (regardless of nationality, resident of a member country of the European Union for at least 6 months). The Inter Rail Pass allows unlimited travel in countries in the chosen zone or zones. Europe is divided into 7 zones: zone A (Great Britain, Northern Ireland and Republic of Ireland), zone B (Sweden, Norway and Finland), zone C (Denmark, Germany, Switzerland and Austria), zone D (Poland, Czech Republic, Slovakia, Hungary and Croatia), zone E (Belgium, the Netherlands, Luxembourg and France), zone F (Spain, Portugal and Morocco) and zone G (Italy, Slovenia and Turkey, and boats between Italy and Greece). There are four different types of Inter Rail Pass offering unlimited travel to choose from: 1 zone valid 22 days, 2 zones valid 1 month, 3 zones valid 1 month, and all zones valid 1 month. Prices vary according to the number of zones. French railways give A 50% reduction on a return ticket from the station of departure to the national border. Likewise, if the zones chosen are not adjacent, 50% reduction is given for the countries of transit. Special rates are also given for certain sea links, highways and private railways within the chosen zone. The **Eurodomino** Pass can be used in the same way as the Inter Rail Pass and gives A 25% reduction in the price of journeys from the station of departure to the station in the chosen country. It is valid 3, 5 or 10 days per country, according to choice, and one month in all. The Inter Rail and Eurodomino Passes are available from many stations on presentation of a passport.
For **European non-residents, the Eurailpass and Europass** offer unlimited travel for a certain number of days in the following countries: Austria, Belgium, Denmark, Finland, France, Germany, Greece, Hungary, Ireland, Italy, Luxembourg, Norway, the Netherlands, Portugal, Spain, Sweden and Switzerland. **Purchase before departure as these cards are not sold in Europe.** Prices vary according to the number of days validity (15 or 21 days, 1, 2, or 3 months). For the under 26s, the **Eurorail Youthpass** offers unlimited travel for 15 days valid for 2 months. These cards also give reductions on certain boat, ferry or coach lines. For groups of three or more travelling together (two or more from October to March), the **Eurorail Saverpass** offers unlimited travel in 1st class for 15 days. The **Eurorail Flexipass** offers 1st class travel for 5 days within 15 days, 9 days within 21 days and 14 days within 1 month. For the under-26s the **Eurorail Youth Flexipass** can be used for 15 days within 2 months. The **Europass** valid for 5 or 15 days within 2 months offers unlimited travel in three of the five following countries: Germany, Spain, France, Italy and Switzerland.
Several countries have cards offering unlimited travel within their borders, with prices varying according to class and the number of days validity: **BahnCard**, **Twenticket**, **Mitfahrer-Fahrpreis**, **Sparpreis** and **ICE Sparpreis** (Germany), **Billet Puzzle**, **Bon Kilométrique** and **Billet Touristique** (Austria), **Inter Rail** (Austria, Czech Republic, Hungary and Poland), **Benelux Tourrail** (Belgium, Luxembourg and the Netherlands), **Scanrail Pass** for trains and ferries (Denmark, Finland, Norway and Sweden), **Carte Touristique** (Spain), **Finnrail** (Finland), **Carte Jeune** for the under-26s (France), **Britrail Pass and Scotrail Pass** (Great Britain), **Rambler Pass and Emerald Isle Card** for train and bus travel (Ireland), **Italy Rail Card** (Italy), **Kundekort** (Norway), **Meerman's Kaart, Tourtime, Rail Runner, Rail Idée and Treintaxi** (the Netherlands), **Tourist Pass** (Portugal), and **Swiss Pass, Swiss Flexipass, Swiss Card** and **Swiss Regional Pass** (Switzerland). These passes can only be purchased by non-residents of the countries in question and are available from the latter's mainline stations.

The Channel Tunnel – This undersea tunnel is the realisation of dreams of linking Britain to mainland Europe which date back over two hundred years. The Channel link consists of two single-track tunnels (7.60m - 24ft in diameter) for passenger and freight transport, and one service tunnel (4.80m - 15ft in diameter) for safety and ventilation. The tunnels are 50.5km - 31 miles long, 37km - 23 miles of which are under the Channel. Most of the tunnel is 40m - 13ft beneath the seabed, in a layer of blue chalk. **Le Shuttle** trains (800m - 2,624ft long) have two levels for passengers and cars (capacity 118 cars per shuttle) and one level for coaches and caravans. Journey time is 35 minutes, 28 of which are in the tunnel at a maximum speed of 130km - 80 miles per hour.
For information, contact Le Shuttle passenger enquiries ☎ 01 303 271 271100.

Eurostar – A high-speed French (SNCF), Belgian (SNCB) and British Rail train carries passenger (without cars) from London (Waterloo station) to Paris (gare du Nord) or Brussels (Midi) in 3 1/2 hours.

DISTANCES IN EUROPE

Distances are calculated from centres and along the best roads from a motoring point of view - not necessarily the shortest.

Luxembourg-Warszawa : **1321 km**

	Amsterdam	Athína	Barcelona	Beograd	Berlin	Bratislava	Brussel	Bucuresti	Budapest	Dublin	Frankfurt a. Main	Genève	Helsinki	Istanbul	Kyïv	København	Lisboa	Ljubljana	London	Luxembourg	Madrid	Milano	Moskva	München	Nice	Oslo	Paris	Praha	Roma	St. Peterburg	Sofia	Stockholm	Thessaloníki	Warszawa	Wien	Zagreb
Athína	2836																																			
Barcelona	1551	3090																																		
Beograd	1718	1118	1972																																	
Berlin	665	2584	1864	1466																																
Bratislava	1213	1771	1843	588	663																															
Brussel	207	2792	1360	1674	774	1172																														
Bucuresti	2221	1238	2611	639	1711	1053	2177																													
Budapest	1384	1510	1994	392	857	196	1343	828																												
Dublin	953	3586	1927	2468	1528	1974	794	912	2145																											
Frankfurt a. Main	441	2396	1331	1278	538	780	399	602	951	1201																										
Genève	901	2446	762	1328	1074	1093	711	503	1262	1334	588																									
Helsinki	1204	2540	2388	1422	505	2246	1316	1858	1030	2153	1101	1656																								
Istanbul	2665	1171	2919	947	2413	1538	2621	692	1339	3415	2225	2275	2369																							
Kyïv	2017	2311	3114	1336	1383	1712	2129	1073	1162	2966	1914	2339	1146	489																						
København	778	2938	2096	1820	392	1058	897	1249	1253	1677	799	1381	795	2767	318																					
Lisboa	2276	4320	1237	3202	2826	3064	2088	1765	3216	2655	2346	1984	3423	4149	2804	2992																				
Ljubljana	1246	1708	1460	525	1001	427	1157	1249	578	1967	813	804	2235	1475	2015	1362	2681																			
London	479	3252	1453	2134	1055	1500	321	438	1671	468	727	860	1819	3081	1033	1195	2182	1492																		
Luxembourg	384	2637	1156	1519	768	997	214	382	1167	1002	237	506	1302	2466	740	927	2127	941	528																	
Madrid	1772	3760	616	2642	2323	2444	1585	1262	2595	2152	1842	1364	2913	3589	2301	2489	621	2061	1678	1622																
Milano	1085	2128	980	1010	1034	877	885	849	1029	1610	674	317	1575	1957	1085	1426	2202	499	1137	679	1581															
Moskva	2463	3169	3630	2194	1829	2013	2575	1931	1918	3412	2360	2898	1127	1347	858	2211	4682	2372	3078	2561	4172	2817														
München	831	2063	1378	945	586	461	730	849	632	1539	398	594	1120	1892	637	947	2600	411	1065	514	1980	498	2362													
Nice	1389	2434	663	1316	1350	1181	1199	934	1333	1810	988	457	1890	2263	1401	1741	1884	799	1337	994	1264	319	3132	812												
Oslo	1047	3521	2365	2403	970	1636	1166	1518	1861	1000	1079	1662	690	3350	896	556	3262	1940	454	1197	2759	1707	1817	1525	2022											
Paris	496	2912	1048	1794	1047	1298	309	2297	1469	876	577	501	1604	2741	1025	1213	1777	1250	402	357	1274	847	2863	823	932	1482										
Praha	849	2154	1706	1036	348	315	872	1051	509	1674	498	915	859	1983	448	744	2795	573	1200	724	2307	855	1860	367	1171	1322	1025									
Roma	1653	2389	1351	1271	1476	1131	1453	1404	1282	2178	1242	871	2040	2218	1527	1837	2572	748	1705	1247	1952	564	3074	886	690	2415	1401	1256								
St. Peterburg	1637	2973	2821	1855	938	2504	1749	2625	1463	2588	1534	2089	433	2041	1552	1228	3856	2493	2252	1735	3346	2008	694	1553	2323	1123	2037	1292	2473							
Sofia	2104	818	2358	386	1852	974	2060	420	778	2854	1664	1714	1808	561	1493	2206	3588	911	2520	1905	3028	1396	2351	1331	1702	2789	2180	1422	1657	2241						
Stockholm	1387	3568	2705	2450	1001	1667	1505	1857	1861	1056	1407	1990	165	3397	927	586	3601	1970	616	1536	3098	2034	1292	1556	2350	534	1822	1352	2445	598	2836					
Thessaloníki	2350	511	2604	632	2098	1260	2306	727	1024	3100	1910	1960	2054	660	1800	2452	3834	1197	2766	2151	3274	1642	2658	1577	1948	3035	2426	1668	1903	2487	307	3082				
Warszawa	1223	2188	2390	1070	589	1130	1335	1506	678	2172	1120	1658	352	2017	794	971	3442	1119	1838	1321	2932	1577	1240	1122	1892	1554	1623	620	1834	785	1456	1601	1702			
Wien	1146	1862	1787	744	634	68	1105	1256	239	1907	713	1024	924	1691	733	1029	3009	381	1433	929	2388	822	1965	394	1126	1607	1231	286	1075	1357	1130	1638	1376	725		
Zagreb	1337	1499	1591	381	1085	416	1293	1020	350	2087	897	947	1287	1328	1512	1439	2821	138	1753	1138	2261	629	2268	564	935	2022	1413	655	890	1720	767	2069	1013	1028	363	
Zürich	803	2416	1048	1298	832	825	629	602	994	1355	392	286	1387	2245	883	1169	2269	663	882	424	1649	280	2629	313	594	1450	593	674	848	1820	1684	1777	1930	1389	758	917

Europe by car

Documents – For all countries, a driving licence, vehicle registration document, insurance certificate and national identity plate (F, B, CH, etc.) are required. For non-European Union residents, an **international driver's licence** may also be required. Further information should be obtained before leaving.

Driving – Drive on the right hand side of the road, except in Great Britain, Ireland, the Channel Islands and Malta.

Headlights – In Denmark, Finland, Hungary (outside built-up areas), Ireland, Iceland, Norway, Poland, Sweden and Yugoslavia, cars must be driven with dipped headlights, even in daytime.

Alcohol – "If you drink, don't drive." There is zero alcohol tolerance in Bulgaria, the Czech Republic, Estonia, Hungary, Latvia, Lithuania, Norway, Poland, Romania, Russia, Slovakia, Sweden and Yugoslavia. Frequent checks are made, even for foreigners, and offenders risk on-the-spot fines.

Car rental – The main car rental companies (Avis, Hertz, Europcar, InterRent, Budget etc.) are well represented in the majority of countries, at airports, mainline stations and big international hotels. For further information and addresses abroad, make inquiries at car rental companies before leaving your country.
In Europe, cars with automatic transmission are less common. Be sure to find out from the agencies and specify if you wish to rent this type of vehicle, likewise for air conditioning.

What you need to know before renting a car:

- You must have a credit card such as Visa, American Express or MasterCard/Eurocard as it acts as a deposit.
- Vehicles are rented on a daily, weekly or monthly basis. Mileage is often unlimited.
- Prices vary from one company to the other, so find out before renting.
- It is sometimes possible to rent an car in one city and return it to a city in a different country. You will have to pay a repatriation fee.
- Find out whether the insurance is included in the cost of rental. Take out supplementary insurance if necessary.
- When signing the contract, make sure to specify the people authorised to drive the vehicle.

To find out the distances between the major European cities, refer to the table of distances in Europe.

DISTANCES IN EUROPE

Distances are counted between town or city centres and by the most practical route, i.e. the one which offers the best ride but which may not be the shortest.

Europe made to measure

For all those who wish to discover Europe in a different way, travel agencies now offer thematic trips and tours, some as complete packages, and others made to measure or for each particular client's choice of visits, hotels or excursions. The agency looks after the reservation of rooms, supplies the plane, train or coach tickets, contacts car rental agencies etc. It is better to choose a tour operator who will look after everything from A to Z (transport, accommodation, car hire, guides etc.) if time is running short for you to organise a vacation or if you want to leave without the worries of making reservations. This solution often works out cheaper than a vacation made to measure. Certain precautions should, however, be taken if you don't want to have some unpleasant surprises during the trip: find out about the suggested hotels, the costs not included (taxes, tips, airport transfers, excursions etc.).
Below, there are a few ideas for vacations, listed under the headings: Geography, History, Art, Religion, Traditions, Nature and Health. It is then up to the individual to take notes and to organise the trip around his or her own interests.

Geography

Europe by river – This can be done as a cruise or more simply by following roads which run along the river bank: the Danube (Passau, Vienna, Bratislava, Budapest); Volga (from St Petersburg to Moscow); Rhine (Rotterdam, Cologne, Bonn, Mainz, Heidelberg, Strasbourg and Basle) and Elbe (Hamburg, Madgeburg and Dresden).

Europe by sea – There are two possible solutions, either use the ferry or boat links which provide daily crossings or choose the "cruise" option organised by travel agencies.
There are regular services that could be made into a sea cruise: the Atlantic Ocean from Santander in Spain to Plymouth in Great Britain; the Mediterranean (from Valencia or Barcelona to the Balearics, from Genoa in Italy to the Balearics, Sardinia or Palermo in Italy, from Marseille to Corsica in France, etc.); the Adriatic, (from Piraeus in Greece to Ancona in Italy, to Dubrovnik in Yugoslavia); the Aegean (from Thessalonika to Crete or to the Cyclades in Greece, from Atalya in Turkey to Venice in Italy); the Baltic (from Stockholm in Sweden to St Petersburg in Russia, Helsinki in Finland to Tallinn in Estonia, from Gdánsk in Poland to Helsinki, etc.); the North Sea (from Bergen in Norway to Aberdeen and Newcastle in Great Britain, from Kingston-upon-Hull in Great Britain to Rotterdam in the Netherlands and Zeebrugge in Belgium), the Norwegian Coast by the Hurtigruten Coastal Express Ferry.
For organised cruises (private or accompanied), every option is available by organising stop-overs in ports of interest on the European seas listed above, not forgetting the Black Sea.

Cruises in the Mediterranean or trips exploring the Norwegian fjords and the Arctic are the most popular. Thematic cruises are often organised (theatre, opera, history etc.), with stop-overs taking in live performances in famous and unforgettable locations. Thematic cruises are often accompanied by entertainers.
From mid-April to mid-December, the cruise liner *Queen Elizabeth 2* of the Cunard Line goes regularly back and forth between the United States (New York) and Europe (Southampton in England). The vessel also stops in Cherbourg (France) three times a year. The crossing takes five days. It is an unforgettable experience aboard this magnificent floating city where the maximum is done to assure the passenger's well-being (comfort, good food, sporting activities, swimming pool, shows, casino, dancing, beauty salons, massage parlours, shops, library etc.).
For the rest of the year, the QE2 operates cruises to the North Cape, Iceland and the Norwegian fjords, Scandinavia, the Mediterranean, Spain and Portugal etc. For all information: Cunard Line, 555 5th Avenue, New York, NY 10017, ☎ (800) 458 9000. Cunard Line, Canute Road, Southampton, SO14 3NR, ☎ (01703) 716603.

Celtic Countries – Cornwall, Ireland, Scotland, Wales, (Great Britain), Brittany (France) and Galicia (Spain) all share a strong identity, beautiful countryside and a fascinating culture.

Mountains of Europe – In Europe, the mountains often form the border between several countries. They are well serviced by modern roads and have numerous hotels whether it be in mountain villages or the winter skiing resorts. The Alps are, without a doubt, the most international mountain range, as you can be in France, in Switzerland, in Austria, in Italy and even in Slovenia. The Carpathians are shared between Slovakia, Ukraine, and Romania. Last but not least, the Pyrenees form a natural border between France and Spain.
The Sierra Nevada, Cantabrian Mountains of which the highest are the Picos de Europa (Spain) and the Scandinavian mountains are also well developed skiing areas.
These high mountains are well equipped with chair lifts and rack and pinion railways giving access to the highest summits.

The rooftops of Europe:

Jungfraujoch★★★ (3 475m - 11 259ft) – Swiss Alps.
The highest resort accessed by a rack and pinion railway.
Depart from Lauterbrunnen or Grindelwald.

Grossglockner★★★ – Austrian Alps.
Depart from Zell am See or Heiligenblut, the road leads as far as Franz-Josephs-Höhe (2 369m - 7 770ft), at the foot of Grossglockner, the highest point of Austria at 3 797m - 12 454ft in altitude.

Petit Cervin★★★ (Klein Matterhorn) – Swiss Alps.
Departing from Zermatt the highest resort in Europe (3 820m - 12 530ft) can be reached using a series of chair lifts.

The Aiguille du Midi★★★ (3 842m - 12 602ft) – Pointe Helbronner (3 462m -11 355ft) – French Alps.
From Chamonix, chair lifts, elevators and cable cars give access to the whole of the Mont Blanc mountain range from Chamonix to La Palud. Return to Chamonix by the tunnel through the Mont Blanc for a thoroughly unforgettable day.

Zugspitze★★★ (2 964m - 9 722ft) – German Alps.
Accessible from Garmish-Partenkirschen in Germany.
Not all mountain ranges are on the same scale as the Alps. Many ranges are much lower in altitude where resorts can be found with a reputation for their fresh air, tranquillity and cross country skiing in winter.

Some lower mountain ranges:

Amongst mountains drawing visitors in search of unspoilt countryside are: the Vosges (France) with their summits rounded by erosion, the Ballons; the other side of the Rhine there is the romantic Black Forest (Germany) which is wonderfully adapted for tourism; the Harz (Germany) with all its legends; Romanian Carpathians for great walking; Snowdonia (Wales); the windswept moors of Scotland or the Belgian Ardennes and Jura (France) and Slovak Tatry which are both more undulating.

Volcanoes – Volcanoes are still active and there are earthquakes in the Azores, Iceland (Hekla) and in the south of Italy (Vesuvius, Stromboli, Vulcano and Etna in Sicily).
In central France, the vast Massif Central is made up of the Monts Dômes, Monts Dore and the Cantal volcano, offering the most comprehensive volcanic landscape imaginable.

The Norwegian Fjords – The best way to admire this spectacular landscape is a cruise on board one of the magnificent floating palaces departing from Stavanger or Bergen. For those wanting a more down to earth trip, the Hurtigruten Coastal Express Ferry links all the ports of the Norwegian coast right up to the North Cape.

The Arctic – The famous highway E6 goes from Trondheim to Hammerfest, one of the towns situated at the most northerly point in Europe. Just north of MO 1 Rana you cross the Arctic Circle.
(Be careful as the road is long and often difficult when towing a caravan).
In Lapland you will discover great silence, long winters and its long-preserved traditions. You can return via Finland or Sweden.

Touring the lakes – The most beautiful lakes are to be found at the foot of the great Alpine valleys: Lake Geneva, Lake Vierwaldstättersee (Switzerland); Lake Maggiore, Lake Lugano, Lake Como and Lake Garda (Italy); Lake Annecy and Lake Bourget (France).
There are often roads running along the lake shore, but fortunately, there is still a way to discover these beautiful lakes by taking a tranquil cruise on one of the magnificent paddle steamers, remnants of the Belle Epoque.
Famous authors and composers stayed on these romantic lakes of unparalleled beauty: Lord Byron at Chillon (Lake Geneva), Tchaïkovsky at Clarens, G. de Staël at Coppet (Lake Geneva), Annuzio at Gardone (Lake Garda). The life of William Tell is told around Lake Vierwaldstättersee.
The great Swedish lakes, the Scottish lochs, or the great lakes of the central European plain, Lake Balaton (Hungary), Lake Constance (between Switzerland and Germany), Lake Ohrid (Macedonia) also have plenty to offer the visitor: typical fauna and flora and a special kind of silence so beautifully described by the famous French author JJ Rousseau in *Rêveries.*
Secretively hidden away and yet more romantic than the Swiss lakes are the stretches of water in the Lake District (Great Britain), one of the most beautiful landscapes in the world.

History

Greek Antiquity – Testimonies to Greek Antiquity can be found in Greece (Delphi, Athens, Epidaurus, Olympia etc.); as well as in Turkey (Istanbul, Ancient Byzantium); Sicily (Agrigento, Syracusa, Taormine); Macedonia (Ohrid); in Crete (Chossos, Heraklion), Italy (Taranto, Crotone) and even in Bulgaria (Nesebar) and Romania (Histria).

Roman times – Not only did the Romans colonise the whole of the Mediterranean as did the Greeks, they also set up colonies a long way further north and north-east of their native land. In fact, Roman legions, the guardians of the Empire, set up camp in the far reaches of England, in Dacia (Romania) and in the present Bulgaria, in order to contain the Barbarians.

P. Ancenay/PIX

Pont du Gard, France

In other words, most cities in Europe still have remnants of Roman times. Those fascinated by Roman history can go far beyond Italy and the Mediterranean (Segovia and Tarragona in Spain, Arles, Nîmes, the Pont du Gard, Vaison-la-Romaine and Lyons in France, and Split and Zadar in Croatia), all the way to England to follow Hadrian's Wall, the Augst ruins near Basle (Switzerland) and Plovdiv (Bugaria).

The great Italian Renaissance courts and their patrons – In the 15C, central and northern Italy were economically and culturally dominated by several cities, which in turn were controlled by these influential families: Milan by the Visconti and Sforza families, Florence by the Medicis, Urbino by the Montefeltres; Ferrara by the Estes, Mantoua by the Gonzagues and Rome by the popes.
Riches of the Renaissance period and discoveries made in this new age were spear-headed by such universal geniuses as Leonardo da Vinci, Michael Angelo and Raphaël.

Europe and the Habsburg empire – For centuries, in the heart of Europe, the Hapsburg empire played a leading role in the history of continental Europe. It was heavily involved in the Counter-Reformation and alongside this, the development of Baroque art. Remnants of this empire can not only be found in Vienna, Prague and Budapest, but also in numerous small villages, abbeys and village churches.

Battlefields – Europe has endured many wars from Antiquity right up to the 20C. There are places recalling these glorious yet bloody battles (memorials, museums etc.): Marathon in Greece (victory of the Athenians against the Persians in 490 BC); The Battle of Hastings in Great Britain (won by the Normans against the English in 1066); Agincourt in the north of France (victory of the English against the French in 1415); Portsmouth in England where Admiral Nelson's three-master The Victory was sunk, he also defeated the French and Spanish fleets in the Battle of Trafalgar (Spain); Austerlitz in the Czech Republic (victory of Napoleon's troops against the Russians and Austrians in 1805). Borodino, west of Moscow in Russia (victory of Napoleon's troops against the Russians in 1812); Waterloo in Belgium (victory of the English, Dutch and Prussians against Napoleon's troops in 1815); Solferino in Italy (victory of the French and Piedmontese armies against the Austrians in 1859); Verdun in the east of France (from 1916-1917 between the French and Germans) and the D-day landings on the beaches of Normandy on 6 June 1944.

Art

No other continent contains such a wealth of artistic riches as Europe, so there is no lack of ideas for trips on this theme.

Byzantine Europe – Take a trip to Byzantine monuments and buildings in the gate-ways to the East: Ravenna and Venice (Italy); Thessalonika (Greece); Crete; Nesebar, Backovo and Sofia (Bulgaria); Constantinople (now Istanbul); and monasteries in Northern Bucovina (Romania).

Cathedrals in Europe – Évora in Portugal; Burgos, Barcelona, Seville and Santiago de Compostella in Spain; Durham, Canterbury, Salisbury, Lincoln and Wells in Great Britain; Anvers in Belgium; Chartres, Paris, Amiens, Bourges, Reims and Strasbourg in France; Lübeck, Cologne and Ulm in Germany; Milan, Assisi and Orvieto in Italy; Prague in the Czech Republic and Krakow in Poland are all gems of 13-15C Gothic art.

Baroque and Rococo Europe – Baroque and Rococo were all over Europe in the 17C and 18C. It would be impossible to do a tour of Europe without visiting showcase monuments from this rich period. Several towns in Germany, Austria and Bohemia are entirely Baroque in style. Madrid and Valencia (Spain), Rome and Palermo (Italy); Malta; Versailles (France); Noto (Sicily), Nymphenburg in Munich, Würzburg, Zwiefalten, Dresden, Bayreuth, Ottobeuren, Wies and Postdam (Germany); Salzburg, Vienna and Melk (Austria); Drottningholm near Stockholm (Sweden); Prague (Czech Republic); Bratislava (Slovakia); Warsaw (Poland); St Petersburg (Russia); Oradea and Bras,ov (Romania); Ljubljana (Slovenia) and Zagreb (Croatia) are to mention but a few examples amidst a wealth of others.

Art Nouveau in Europe – At the end of the 19C and beginning of the 20C, Europe was discovering a new art form called Art Nouveau. Stylised representations of nature appeared in architecture and on decorative ornaments. Some cities in Europe witnessed the birth of Art Nouveau's great theorists: Mackintosh in Glasgow (Great Britain); Guimard in Paris and Emile Gallé in Nancy (France); Gaudí in Barcelona (Spain); Paul Hankar and Van de Velde in Brussels (Belgium) and Otto Wagner and artists of the Secession in Vienna (Austria). There are also beautiful Art Nouveau monuments in Riga (Lithuania) and Helsinki (Finland).

Religion

Pilgrimage of Santiago de Compostella – Since the Middle Ages, pilgrims have come to Compostella in droves: routes they have always taken from Paris, Vézelay, Le Puy and Marseille (France) and Barcelona (Spain), still exist.

Religion in Russia – Gold of the Czars shines in St Petersburg, Moscow and Zagorsk.

Traditions

The art and craft markets of Europe – In Europe, there is a strong craft tradition that has been handed down over the centuries. You can admire and buy beautiful wares (china, rugs, glassware, jewellery, etc.) in colourful markets in Spain, Portugal, Great Britain, France, Hungary, Romania, Greece and Turkey.

Nature and Health

Unusual European countryside – The Scandinavian fjords, geysers (Iceland), the Giant's Causeway (Ireland), the Highlands (Scotland), the polders (the Netherlands), Pilat Dune (France), the Sierra Nevada (Spain), the Dolomites (Italy), Meteoras (Greece) and the Danube Delta (Romania).

The sports scene – For all sports-lovers and those seeking adventure or a challenge, the European countryside can be explored on foot, by bicycle, on horseback, in a 4-wheel drive etc.

Great sporting events can also be made into the feature of a vacation in Europe: tennis tournaments of Wimbledon (Great Britain) and Roland-Garros (France), Five Nations rugby tournament; Grand Prix car racing in Monza (Italy) and Monaco; 24-hours of Le Mans car rally (France); Monte Carlo Car Rally (Principality of Monaco), Tour de France bicycle race; Vasaloppet, A 54-mile ski race (Sweden).

As for fishing enthusiasts they can go off and fish for salmon in the North Sea (off the coast of Scotland and Norway).

The quieter waters of lakes and rivers welcome thousands of fishermen to their banks. Be careful, as the regulations are sometimes different from one country to the next. Find out before indulging in your favourite sport.

Europe's spa resorts – The spa resorts were frequented by the rich and famous in the Belle Epoque: Vichy (France); Baden-Baden and Wiesbaden (Germany); Carlsbad and Marienbad (Czech Republic), Budapest (Hungary).

The above suggestions are only a quick insight into the amazing vacations that you can have in Europe.

Whether you are a sports lover, an art enthusiast, keen historian, whether you are used to package tours or an expert in arranging a trip to suit yourself, the time has come to study the maps and... to dream away!

Sun and snow in Europe

In Europe, the diversity of the countryside's physical relief and climate offers tourists a wide range of places to stay for either winter sports or for enjoying the beach. The map of the main tourist routes at the beginning of this guide, indicates the main beach and skiing resorts. Some of them are so well-known that it is not unusual to find Europeans from all countries, as well as tourists from much further afield. Resorts have an international feel, so for those who prefer peace and quiet and a more authentic feel, there are a host of less well-known resorts which offer all the comforts and activities that you need.

Nothing but sunshine

In Europe, the **Mediterranean coast** attracts the majority of holiday-makers, especially northern Europeans in the search of sunshine. Beaches are usually very long, some sandy and others pebbly. Countless little inlets are paradise for bathers, fishermen and naturists. As there is virtually no tide, you can bathe and go out on boat trips the whole day long, except in bad weather. Picturesque ports in the Mediterranean are an attraction in themselves, especially for early-birds (unloading of the first catch of fish is a colourful sight). Beach resorts are usually well-equipped with lifeguard stations, activities for children, games and sailing clubs, stores, hotels, camp-grounds, restaurants etc. Let's take a quick look at some of the most attractive ones to visit: in Spain, Marbella and Torremolinos (Costa del Sol), Benidorm (Costa Blanca) and Tossa del Mar (Costa Brava); beaches on the islands of Ibiza and Majorca (the Balearics); in France, St Tropez, Cannes, Juan-les-Pins, Nice (Côte d'Azur); Monte Carlo (Principality of Monaco); in Italy, San Remo (Riviera de Pentente), Viareggio (Riviera de Levante), beaches of the islands of Capri, Ischia and Positano (Costiera Amalfitana), Rimini, the Lido (Venice); Opadja in Croatia; Kerkira (island of Corfu) in Greece; Nauplion and the beaches of Mikinos; Sliema (island of Malta), and Kusadsi in Turkey.

The **Atlantic coast** has a wet maritime climate, milder in the south, colder in the north. The coastline is generally rocky in Galicia, on the Basque coast (Spain), in Brittany (France), in Cornwall and Ireland (Great Britain). Sandy beaches are therefore quite rare (notable exceptions are the French Atlantic coast and beaches in the Channel). The Atlantic Ocean is often rougher than the Mediterranean and has good waves which are ideal for surfing (on the oceanic side), and favourable winds for pleasure cruising. There are well-equipped resorts, the most popular being: in Portugal, Faro (the Algarve), Estoril (Costa de Lisboa) and Nazaré (Costa de Prata); in Spain, Santander and San Sebastiano (Costa Basca); in France, Biarritz, and Arcachon (Côte d'Argent), Royan (Côte de Beauté), Sables-d'Olonne, (Côte de Lumière), La Baule (Côte Sauvage), Perros-Guirec (Côte de Granit Rose), Dinard (Côte d'Emeraude), Deauville (Côte Fleurie), and Le Touquet (Côte d'Opale) and in Great Britain, there are some particularly pleasant, sunny resorts such as Torquay, Bournemouth, Brighton and Eastbourne (the Channel coast), Newquay (Cornwall) and Blackpool (Irish Sea).

The **North and Baltic seas** are colder, but it is still possible to swim in these waters in summer, particularly in bays protected from the weather. The most popular in the North Sea are Ostend and Knokke-Heist (Belgium); Scheveningen and Zandvoort (the Netherlands); Westerland (island of Sylt in Germany); Angelholm, Bøstad Strömstad (Sweden); Krager, Risør and Mandal (Norway); Marielyst and resorts on the island of Bornholm (Denmark).

Popular resorts on the Baltic Sea are Travemünde and Warnemünde (Germany), Swinoujscie and Sopot (Poland), Hanko, Ingå and Naantali (Finland).

The shores of the **Black Sea** are renowned for their superb weather. These resorts and their beautiful beaches attract more and more tourists, for example: Slănčev Brjag and Zlatni Pjasăci (Bulgaria) and Eforie, Mamaia and Olimp-Neptun (Romania).

Last but not least, we must mention some lake-shore resorts, as they are also popular during the summer months, whether it be by the great Swedish lakes, around Lake Bodensee (Lindau in Germany and Bregenz in Austria) or around the Swiss lakes (Montreux, and Evian, Lake Geneva, Lugano, Locarno or on the shores of Lake Maggiore).

Snow-blanketed Europe

The mountains and heavy snowfalls in certain regions of Europe have encouraged the development of winter sports that have in some cases been popular for centuries: skiing which is a speciality in Scandinavia, skating in the Netherlands and troïka (sleigh) racing in Russia. All over Europe, the passion for winter sports is continually on the increase and resorts all over Europe now boast sophisticated equipment. There are other activities available besides skiing: sleigh rides, walking in snow-shoes, snow-scooter rides, paragliding, hang-gliding and climbing. Some of these activities are available in winter as well as summer, so you can visit these resorts in both seasons.

Down-hill skiing is popular in the Alps: in Chamonix, Courchevel, Megève and Val d'Isère in the French Alps; Courmayeur, Breuil-Cervinia (Val d'Aoste) and Cortina d'Ampezzo in the Italian Dolomites; St Moritz, Zermatt, Davos, Crans-Montana and Saas-Fee in the Swiss Alps; Kitzbühel and Innsbruck in the Austrian Tyrol; Garmisch-Partenkirchen in the German Alps and Kranjska Gora in the Julian Alps (Slovenia). Many European resorts have now become extremely fashionable, having gained a reputation for their beauty and extensive network of ski runs (all levels). These resorts have a distinctive character and you will find plenty of things to keep you occupied. Other mountains in Europe offer good down-hill skiing, for example the Pyrenees, with resorts such as Font-Romeau (also popular for its cross-country skiing) in France and La Molina and Baqueira Beret (Spain). You can also ski in the Carpathians, in Zakopane (Poland), in Sinaia and Poiana Bra,sov (Romania).

Ascher/PIX

Kitzbühel, Austria

Nordic skiing was invented in the Scandinavian countries: it was the easiest way for inhabitants to get around in the snow. It has now become a sport in its own right, including tests in cross-country skiing and also ski-jumping (an activity reserved for experts). There are many popular skiing resorts in Scandinavia. The most well-known in Finland are, without any doubt, the international skiing resorts of Koli and Tahko. In Sweden, you can go to Åre, Mora (this is the town where the famous Vasaloppet cross-country ski race finishes), Idre and Riskgränsen (popular for summer skiing). In Norway, the most frequented resorts are the popular resorts of Geilo, Oppdal, Voss and of course, Lillehammer, which hosted the 1994 winter Olympics.

Plan ahead!
To plan your route, the sights to see, to select a hotel or a restaurant, Internet users can log in at www.michelin-travel.com.

A practical guide to Europe

See also "In brief", the heading for each country.

Electricity

British citizens must purchase an adapter, as most sockets in the majority of countries are different to the ones in Great Britain. In Europe the voltage is 220 volts. In North America it is 110 volts, so Americans and Canadians must purchase an adapter and a transformer.

Medical treatment

For members of the European Union, it is recommended that you take a E111 form to avoid paying medical expenses in the event of sickness or accident in any one of the member countries. It is, however, always advisable to take out a supplementary insurance (Europ Assistance, Elvia etc.), which cover, for example, urgent medical repatriation from any non-member country.
American citizens must take out medical insurance which covers them outside the United States, or take out a travel insurance that covers loss of luggage, sickness, accident, cancellation of vacation etc. Find out from your own insurance company or Access America, Carefree Travel Insurance etc.

Money

The local currencies of each country are mentioned in the general information section which precedes the description of unusual sights in different countries. Main credit cards (American Express, Visa, MasterCard, Diners Club etc.) are accepted in most countries and, certainly in western Europe, can be used to draw out money from most automatic distributors. In eastern Europe, use of credit cards is becoming more and more common in hotels, restaurants, stores or car rental agencies.
There are places to change money in airports, mainline stations, banks and international hotels.
In eastern European countries, money changing is done on the black market, in the street, at extremely tempting rates. This is not at all advisable. In these countries, the American dollar and the German mark are often currencies that are highly sought after: these currencies can be changed in the respective countries or even sometimes used instead of the local currency.
Travellers cheques can be changed in banks. For countries with weak currencies such as Russia, take currency in small denominations or travellers cheques in small sums so as to avoid being handed back an enormous amount of bank notes in change. Usually, bureaux de change only accept currency in bank notes.
Be careful, as some currencies cannot be exchanged, so upon your return you cannot change these currencies back. The main ones are the Polish zloty, Hungarian forint, Czech and Slovak crowns, Russian rouble and the currencies of Romania, Bulgaria and the Baltic countries.

The Euro

On 1 January 1999, eleven European Union countries (Austria, Belgium, Finland, France, Germany, Ireland, Italy, the Grand Duchy of Luxembourg, the Netherlands, Portugal and Spain) adopted the Euro as their single currency and prices are now shown in the national currencies and in Euros in these countries.

1 Euro	*Austria*	*13,7603 ATS*	*Italy*	*1936,27 ITL*
1 Euro	*Belgium*	*40,3399 BEF*	*Luxembourg*	*40,3399 BEF*
1 Euro	*Finland*	*5,94573 FIM*	*The Nederlands*	*2,20371 ATS*
1 Euro	*France*	*6,55957 FRF*	*Portugal*	*200,482 PTE*
1 Euro	*Germany*	*1,95583 DEM*	*Spain*	*166,386 PTE*
1 Euro	*Ireland*	*0,787564 IEP*		

On 1 January 2002, coins and notes in Euros will be introduced. These will replace the national currencies in the short term and the latter will gradually be withdrawn from circulation. Each coin and note will have one side identifying its country of origin, while the other will be common to the European Union. The Euro will be divided into 100 cents.

Coins: 1, 2, 5, 10, 20 and 50 cents; 1 and 2 Euros.

Notes: 5, 10, 20, 50, 100, 200 and 500 Euros.

VAT (Value-added tax) refunds

In member countries of the European Union, and for those residents of non-member countries, you can get this tax refunded over a certain amount of money spent in the same store. This applies to all products and the percentage varies from one country to the next. In stores or department stores who advertise this facility, the salesperson must fill in an exportation sales voucher and list each purchase and its price. Get this document stamped by customs at the airport before getting your refund (with a small service charge) at the tax refund desk.

National holidays

On national holidays, stores, banks and museums are generally closed. The main holidays are the following: New Year's Day, Easter, 15 August, All Saints Day and Christmas. Confirm specific dates with tourist offices in the respective country.

Telephone

Several countries, especially in western Europe, have phone booths where you can call abroad. If you do this, be sure to have large quantities of change. In some countries, international telephone cards are on sale in, for example, post offices and tobacco stores. Avoid calling from hotels because you have to pay a lot of money for the convenience.
American citizens, can of course call the United States via AT&T, MCI, Sprint using an access code given for each country.

International dialling codes:

from / to	B	CH	F	GB	J	USA
ALBANIA	0032	0041	0033	0044	0081	001
AUSTRIA	«	05	«	«	«	«
BELGIUM	–	0041	«	«	«	«
BULGARIA	«	«	«	«	«	«
CZECH Republic	«	«	«	«	«	«
GERMANY	«	«	«	«	«	«
GREAT BRITAIN	«	«	«	–	«	«
GREECE	«	«	«	«	«	«
HUNGARY	«	«	«	«	«	«
ICELAND	«	«	«	«	«	«
IRELAND	«	«	«	«	«	«
ITALY	«	«	«	«	«	«
LUXEMBOURG	«	«	«	«	«	«
MALTA	«	«	«	«	«	«
NETHERLANDS	«	«	«	«	«	«
POLAND	«	«	«	«	«	«
PORTUGAL	«	«	«	«	«	«
ROMANIA	«	«	«	«	«	«
SLOVAKIA	«	«	«	«	«	«
SWITZERLAND	«	–	«	«	«	«
TURKEY	«	«	«	«	«	«
BOSNIA-HERZEGOVINA	9932	9941	9933	9944	9981	991
CROATIA	«	«	«	«	«	«
MACEDONIA	«	«	«	«	«	«
SLOVENIA	«	«	«	81044	81081	8101
YUGOSLAVIA	«	«	«	9944	9981	991
DENMARK	00932	00941	00933	00944	00981	0091
SWEDEN	«	«	«	«	«	«
SPAIN	0732	0741	0733	0744	0781	071
ESTONIA	81032	81041	81033	81044	81081	8101
LATVIA	«	«	«	«	«	«
LITUANIA	«	«	«	«	«	«
RUSSIE	«	«	«	«	«	«
UKRAINE	«	«	«	«	«	«
FINLAND	99032	99041	99033	99044	99081	9901
FRANCE	0032	0041	–	0044	0081	001
NORWAY	09532	09541	09533	09544	09581	0951

EMBASSIES

Albania

GB: Rruga Skenderberg 12, Tirana, ☎ (355 42) 34 973.

USA: Rruga E. Labinoti 103, Tirana, ☎ (355 42) 32 875, fax (355 42) 32 222.

Canada: c/o Canadian Embassy in Budapest (Hungary), Budakeszi utca 32, Budapest (XII), Hungary, ☎ (36 1) 275 1200, fax (36 1) 275 1210, email bpest@bpest01.x400.gc.ca.

Ireland: c/o Irish Embassy in Athens (Greece), 7 Leoforos Vasileos Konstantinou, Athin, ☎ (30 1) 723 27 71, fax (30 1) 724 02 17.

Australia: c/o Australian Embassy in Rome (Italy), Via Alessandria 215, Roma, Italia ☎ (39 6) 85 27 21, fax (39 6) 85 27 23 00, website agora.stm.it\market\ausembassy.

Austria

GB: Jauresgasse 12, Vienna, ☎ (43 1) 71630, fax (43 1) 71613 2999, email britem@netway.at.

USA: Boltzmanngasse 16, Vienna, ☎ (43 1) 313 39, fax (43 1) 3100 682, website http://www.usembassy-vienna.at/.

Canada: Laurenzerberg 2, Vienna, ☎ (43 1) 531 38 3000, fax: (43 1) 531 38 3321, email: vienn@vienn01.x400.gc.ca.

Ireland: Hilton Centre, Landstrasse Haupstrasse 2A, Vienna, ☎ (43 1) 715 42 46, fax (431) 713 60 04.

Australia: Mattiellistrasse 2, Vienna, ☎ (43 1) 512 85 80, fax (43 1) 513 16 56, email austemb@xpoint.at..

New Zealand: Springsiedelgasse 28, Vienna, ☎ (43 1) 318 85 05, fax (43 1) 318 67 17, email bbolt@cso.at.

Belgium

GB: 85 rue d'Arlon, Brussels, ☎ (32 2) 287 62 11, fax (32 2) 287 63 55, website http//www.british-embassy.be.

Conversion tables

Weights and measures

1 kilogram (kg)	2.2 pounds (lb)	2.2 pounds
1 metric ton (tn)	1.1 tons	1.1 tons

to convert kilograms to pounds, multiply by 2.2

1 litre (l)	2.1 pints (pt)	1.8 pints
1 litre	0.3 gallon (gal)	0.2 gallon

to convert litres to gallons, multiply by 0.26 (US) or 0.22 (UK)

1 hectare (ha)	2.5 acres	2.5 acres
1 square kilometre (km^2)	0.4 square miles (sq mi)	0.4 square miles

to convert hectares to acres, multiply by 2.4

1centimetre (cm)	0.4 inches (in)	0.4 inches
1 metre (m)	3.3 feet (ft) - 39.4 inches - 1.1 yards (yd)	
1 kilometre (km)	0.6 miles (mi)	0.6 miles

to convert metres to feet, multiply by 3.28. kilometres to miles, multiply by 0.6

Clothing

Women			
	35	4	2½
	36	5	3½
	37	6	4½
Shoes	38	7	5½
	39	8	6½
	40	9	7½
	41	10	8½
	36	4	8
	38	6	10
Dresses & Suits	40	8	12
	42	12	14
	44	14	16
	46	16	18
	36	08	30
	38	10	32
Blouses & sweaters	40	12	14
	42	14	36
	44	16	38
	46	18	40

			Men
40	7½	7	
41	8½	8	
42	9½	9	
43	10½	10	**Shoes**
44	11½	11	
45	12½	12	
46	13½	13	
46	36	36	
48	38	38	
50	40	40	**Suits**
52	42	42	
54	44	44	
56	46	48	
37	14½	14,5	
38	15	15	
39	15½	15½	**Shirts**
40	15¾	15¾	
41	16	16	
42	16½	16½	

Sizes often vary depending on the designer. These equivalents are given for guidance only.

Speed

kph	10	30	50	70	80	90	100	110	120	130
mph	6	19	31	43	50	56	62	68	75	81

Temperature

Celsius (°C)	0°	5°	10°	15°	20°	25°	30°	40°	60°	80°	100°
Fahrenheit (°F)	32°	41°	50°	59°	68°	77°	86°	104°	140°	176°	212°

To convert Celsius into Fahrenheit, multiply °C by 9, divide by 5, and add 32.
To convert Fahrenheit into Celsius, subtract 32 from °F, multiply by 5, and divide by 9.

USA: 27 boulevard du Régent, Brussels, ☎ (32 2) 508 2111, fax (32 2) 511 27 25, website http://www.usinfo.be/.

Canada: 2 avenue de Tervuren, Brussels, ☎ (32 2) 741 0611, fax (32 2) 741 0643, email bru@bru02.x400.gc.ca.

Ireland: 89-93 rue Froissart, Brussels, ☎ (32 2) 230 53 37, fax (32 2) 230 53 12.

Australia: Guimard Centre, 6-8 rue Guimard, Brussels, ☎ (32 2) 286 05 00, fax (32 22 30 68 02, websitehttp://ourworld.compuserve.com/homepages/Australian Embassy Brussels.

New Zealand: 47-48 boulevard du Régent, Brussels, ☎ (32 2) 512 1040, fax (32 2) 513 48 56, email nzembbru@compuserve.com.

Bosnia Herzegovina

GB: 8 Tina Ujevica, Sarajevo, ☎ (387 71) 444 429, fax (387 71) 666 131, email britainba@bih.net.ba.

USA: 42 ul. Dure Dakovica, Sarajevo, ☎ (387 71) 445 700, fax (387 71) 659 722, website http://www.usis.com.ba/.

Canada: Logavina 7, Sarajevo, ☎ (387 71) 447 900, fax: (387 71) 447 901.

Ireland: c/o Irish Embassy in Berne (Switzlerand), Kirchenfeldstrasse 68, Berne, Switzlerand, ☎ (41 31) 352 14 42, fax (41 31) 352 14 55.

Australia: c/o Australian Embassy in Belgrade (Yugoslavia), 13 Cika Ljubina, Belgrade, Yugoslavia, ☎ (381 11) 624 655, fax (381 11) 624 029, email austemba@eunet.yu, website www.australia.org.yu.

New Zealand: c/o New Zealander Embassy in Rome (Italy), Via Zara 28, Roma, Italia, ☎ (39 6) 441 7171, fax (39 6) 440 29 84, email nzemb.rom@agora.stm.it.

Bulgaria

GB: 38 Vassil Levski blvd., Sofia, ☎ (359) 2980 1220, fax (359) 2980 1229, email britembsof@mbox.cit.bg.

USA: 1 Saborna St., Sofia, ☎ (359 2) 980 524 1, fax (359 2) 981 8977, website http://www.usis.bg/.

Canada: c/o Canadian Embassy in Bucharest (Romania), 36 Nicolae Iorga, Bucharest, Romania, ☎ (40 1) 222 9845, fax (40 1) 312 9680, email bucst@bucst01.x400.gc.ca.

Ireland: c/o Irish Embassy in Budapest (Hungary), Szabadsag ter 7-9, Budapest, ☎ (36 1) 302 9600, fax (36 1) 302 9599.

Australia: 3 Iantra Street, 1124 Sofia, ☎ and fax (359 2) 44 3468.

New Zealand: contact the British Embassy.

Croatia

GB: Vlaska 121, 3rd Floor, Zagreb, ☎ (385 1) 455 53 10, fax (385 1) 455 16 85, email british-embassy@zg.tel.hr.

USA: Andrije Hebranga 2, Zagreb, ☎ (385 1) 455 55 00, fax (385 1) 455 85 85, website http://www.usembassy.hr/.

Canada: Hotel Esplanade, Mihanoviceva 1, Zagreb, ☎ (385 1) 457 32 23, fax (385 1) 457 79 13, email zagrb@dfait.x400.gc.ca.

Ireland: c/o Irish Embassy in Berne (Switzlerand), Kirchenfeldstrasse 68, Berne, Switzlerand, ☎ (41 31) 352 14 42, fax (41 31) 352 14 55.

Australia: Hotel Esplanade, Mihanoviceva 1, Zagreb, ☎ (385 1) 457 74 33, fax (385 1) 457 7907, email australian.consulate@zg.tel.hr.

New Zealand: c/o New Zealander Embassy in Rome (Italy), Via Zara 28, Roma, Italia, ☎ (39 6) 441 7171, fax (39 6) 440 29 84, email nzemb.rom@agora.stm.it.

Czech Republic

GB: Thunovská 14, Mála Strana, Praha, ☎ (420 2) 24 51 04 39, fax (420 2) 57 32 10 23, email: info@britain.cz. , website: http://www.britain.cz.

USA: Trziste 15, Praha, ☎ (420 2) 24 51 0847, fax (420 2) 24 51 1001, website http://www.usis.cz/.

Canada: Mickiewiczova 6, Praha 6, ☎ (420 2) 431 1108, fax (420 2) 43 10 294, email prgue@prgue01.x400.gc.ca, website http://www.dfait-maeci.gc.ca/~prague/.

Ireland: Velvyslanectve Irska, Trziste 13, Praha, ☎ (420 2) 57 53 00 61, fax (420 2) 57 31 14 92.

Australia: Na Orechovce 38, Prague (6), ☎ (42 02) 24 31 07 43, fax (42 02) 31 19 531.

New Zealand: c/o New Zealander Embassy in Bonn (Germany), Bundeskanzlerpl. 2-10, Bonn, Germany, ☎ (49 228) 22 80 70, fax (49 228) 22 16 87, email nzemb.bon@.T-online.de.

Denmark

GB: Kastelsvej 36-40, Kobenhavn, ☎ (45) 35 44 52 00, fax (45) 35 44 52 93, email brit-emb@post6.tele.dk, website http://www.britishembassy.dk.

USA: Dag Hammarksjölds Alle 24, København, ☎ (45) 31 42 31 44, fax (45 31) 42 72 73, website http://www.usis.dk/.

Canada: Kristen Bernikowsgade 1, København, ☎ (45) 33 12 22 99, fax (45 33) 14 05 85, email copen@copen01.x400.gc.ca, web http://www.canada.dk
Ireland: Ostbanegade 21, København, ☎ (45) 31 42 32 33, fax (45) 35 43 18 58.

Australia: c/o Australian Embassy in Stockholm (Sweden), Sergels Torg 12, Stockholm, Sweden, ☎(46 8) 613 29 00, fax (46 8) 24 74 14, email info@austemb.se.: c/o New Zealander Embassy in Brussels (Belgium), 47-48 boulevard du Régent, Brussels, Belgium,☎ (32 2) 512 1040, fax (32 2) 513 48 56, email nzembbru@compuserve.com.

Estonia

GB: Kentmanni 20, Tallinn, ☎ (372 6) 313 353, fax (372 6) 313 354.

USA: Kentmanni 20, Tallin, ☎ (372 6) 312 021, fax (372 6) 312 025, website http://www.estnet.ee/usislib/mission.html.

Canada: Toomkooli 13, 2nd Floor, Talinn, ☎ (372) 631 3570, fax (372) 631 3573.

Ireland: c/o Irish Embassy in Helsinki (Finland), Erottajankatu 7 A, Helsinki, Finland, ☎ (358 9) 64 60 06, fax (358 9) 64 60 22.

Australia: Kopli 25, Tallinn, ☎ (372 6) 509 308, fax (372 6) 541 333, email mati@standard.ee.

New Zealand: c/o New Zealander Embassy in Moscow (Russia), 44 Ulitsa Povarskaya (formerly Voroskovo), Moscow, Russia, ☎ (7 095) 956 35 79, fax (7 095) 956 35 83, email nzembmos@glasnet.ru.

Finland

GB: Itäinen Puistotie 14, Helsinki, ☎ (358 9) 22 86 51 00, fax (358) 9 2286 5284, email info@ukembassy.fi, website http://www.ukembassy.fi/.

USA: Itainen Puistotie 14A, Helsinki, ☎ (358 9) 171 931, fax (358 9) 174 681, website http://www.usembassy.fi/.

Canada: P. Esplanadi 25B, Helsinki, ☎ (358 9) 17 11 41, fax (358 9) 60 10 60. Website http://www.canada.fi.

Ireland: c/o Irish Embassy in Helsinki (Finland), Erottajankatu 7 A, Helsinki, ☎ (358 9) 64 60 06, fax (358 9) 64 60 22.

Australia: Museokatu 25B, Helsinki, ☎ (358 9) 44 72 33, fax (358 9) 44 09 16, email stephen.kemppainen@auscon.inet.fi.

New Zealand: Matkatoimisto Finlandia, Kruunuvuorenkatu 5A, Helsinki, ☎ (358 9) 065 91 00, fax (358 9) 064 13 55.

France

GB: 35 rue du Faubourg St-Honoré, Paris (VIII), ☎ (33 1) 44 51 31 00, fax (01) 47 05 77 02, website http://www.amb-grandebretagne.fr.

USA: 2 avenue Gabriel, Paris (8e), ☎ (33 1) 43 12 22 22, fax (33 1) 42 66 97 83, website http://www.amb-usa.fr.

Canada: 35-37 avenue Montaigne, Paris (8e), ☎ (33 1) 44 43 29 00, fax (33 1) 44 43 29 99, email paris@paris02.x400.gc.ca, website http://www.dfait-maeci.gc.ca/~paris/.

Ireland: 12 avenue Foch, Paris (XVI), ☎ (33 1) 44 17 67 00, fax (33 1) 44 17 67 60.

Australia: 4, rue Jean Rey, Paris (XV), ☎(33 1) 40 59 33 00, fax (33 1) 40 59 33 10, www.austgov.fr.

New Zealand: 7 ter rue Léonard de Vinci, Paris (XVI), ☎ (33 1) 45 00 24 11, (33 1) 45 01 26 39, email nzembpar@compuserve.com ou nzembassy.paris@wanadoo.fr.

Germany

GB: Unter den Linden 32-34, Berlin, ☎ (49 030) 20 18 40, fax (49 030) 20 18 41 58, website http://www.britbot.de/ and http://www.british-dgtip.de/

USA: U.S. Citizens Service, Clayallee 170, Berlin, ☎ (49 030) 832 92 33, fax (49 030) 831 49 26, website http://www.usembassy.de/e0.htm and http://www.usembassy.de/hamburg/.

Canada: Friedrich Strasse 95, Berlin, ☎ (49 30) 261 11 61, fax (49 30) 262 92 06; Friedrich-Wilhelm Strasse 18, Bonn,☎ (49 228) 968 0, fax (49 228) 96 83 904, email bonn@02.x400.gc.ca, website http://www.dfait-maeci.gc.ca/~bonn/.

Ireland: Ernst-Reuter Pl. 10, Berlin, ☎ (49 30) 34 80 08 22, fax (49 30) 34 80 08 63.

Australia: Kempinski Plaza, Uhlandstrasse 181-183, Berlin, ☎ (49 30) 880 08 80, fax (49 30) 88 00 88 99.

New Zealand: Bundeskanzlerpl. 2-10, Bonn, ☎ (49 228) 22 80 70, fax (49 228) 22 16 87, email nzemb.bon@.T-online.de.

Great Britain

USA: 24/31 Grosvenor Square, London, ☎ (44 171) 49 99 000, fax (44 171) 409 16 37, website http://www.usembassy.org.uk/ukaddres.html#amemb.

Canada: Canadian High Commission, MacDonald House, 1 Grosvenor Square, London, ☎ (44 171) 258 66 00, fax (44 171) 258 633, email 1dn@1dn01.x400.gc.ca, website http://www. dfait-maeci.gc.ca/~/london/.

Ireland: 17 Grosvenor Place, London, ☎ (44 171) 235 21 71, fax (44 171) 245 69 61.

Australia: Australia House, The Strand, London, ☎ (44 171) 379 43 34, fax (44 171) 465 8210.

New Zealand: New Zealand House, The Haymarket, London, ☎ (44 171) 973 03 63, fax (44 171) 839 89 29, website http://www.newzealandhc.org.uk.

Greece

GB: Ploutarchou 1, Athin, ☎ (30 1) 723 6211, fax (30 1) 724 1872, email britania@hol.gr, website: http://www.british-embassy.gr.

USA: Vasilissis Sofias blvd 91, Athin, ☎ (30 1) 721 2951, fax (30 1) 645 6282, website http://www.usisathens.gr/usisathens/amembloc.html.

Canada: I. Gennadiou 4, Athin, ☎ (30 1) 727 3400, fax (30 1) 727 3480, email athns@athns01.x400.gc.ca.

Ireland: 7 Leoforos Vasileos Konstantinou, Athin, ☎ (30 1) 723 27 71, fax (30 1) 724 02 17.

Australia: 37 Dimitriou Soutsou Street, Ambelokipi, ☎ (30 1) 645 04 04, fax (30 1) 646 65 95, email ausembgr@hol.gr.

New Zealand: c/o Coopers and Lybrand, 24 Xenias Street, Athin, ☎ (30 1) 771 01 12, fax (30 1) 777 73 90 ; or c/o New Zealander Embassy in Rome (Italy), Via Zara 28, Roma, Italia, ☎ (39 6) 441 7171, fax (39 6) 440 29 84, email nzemb.rom@agora.stm.it.

Hungary

GB: Harmincad Utca 6, Budapest (V), ☎ (36 1) 266 28 88, fax (36 1) 266 09 07, email info@britemb.hu.

USA: Szabadság tér 12, Budapest (V), ☎ (36 1) 267 44 00, fax (36 1) 269 93 26, website http://www.usis.hu/embassy.htm.

Canada: Budakeszi utca 32, Budapest (XII), ☎ (36 1) 275 1200, fax (36 1) 275 1210, email bpest@bpest01.x400.gc.ca.

Ireland: Szabadsag ter 7-9, Budapest, ☎ (36 1) 302 9600, fax (36 1) 302 9599.

Australia: Kiralyhago ter 8-9, Budapest, ☎ (36 1) 201 8899, fax (36 1) 201 97 92, email ausembbp@mail.datanet.hu.

New Zealand: Terez krt. 38, Budapest, ☎ and fax (36 1) 331 49 08.

Iceland

GB: Laufásvegur 49, Reykjavík, ☎ (354 55) 158 83, fax (354 55) 051 04, email britemb@centrum.is.

USA: Laufásvegur 21, Reykjavík, ☎ (354 56) 291 00, fax (354 56) 291 18, website http://www.itn.is/america/mainemb.html.

Canada: Canadian Embassy in Oslo (Norway), Wergelandsveien 7, Oslo, Norway, ☎ (47) 22 99 53 00, fax (47) 22 99 53 01, email oslo@oslo01.x400.gc.ca.

Ireland: c/o Irish Embassy in Copenhagen (Denmark), Ostbanegade 21, København, Denmark ☎ (45) 31 42 32 33, fax (45) 35 43 18 58.

Australia: c/o Australian Embassy in Stockholm (Sweden), Sergels Torg 12, Stockholm, Sweden, ☎ (46 8) 613 29 00, fax (46 8) 24 74 14, email info@austemb.se.

Republic of Ireland

GB: 33 Merrion Road, Ballsbridge, Dublin (4), ☎ (353 1) 269 5211, fax (353 1) 205 3893, email Bembassy@internet-ireland.ie

USA: 42 Elgin Road, Ballsbridge, Dublin, ☎ (353 1) 688 8777, fax (353 1) 668 9946, website http://www.indigo.ie/usembassy-usis/.

Canada: 65 St Stephen's Green, Dublin, ☎ (353 1) 478 1988, fax (353 1) 478 1285, email cdnembsy@iol.ie.

Australia: Fitzwilton House, Wilton Terrace, Dublin 2, ☎ (353 1) 676 1517, fax (353 1) 678 5185.

New Zealand: c/o New Zealander Embassy in London (Great Britain), New Zealand House, The Haymarket, London, Great Britain, ☎ (44 171) 973 03 63, fax (44 171) 839 89 29, website http://www.newzealandhc.org.uk.

Italy

GB: via XX settembre 80a, Roma, ☎ (99 6) 482 54 11, fax (39 6) 487 3324, website http://www.grbr.it.

USA: via Venetto 119a, Roma, ☏ (39 6) 467 41, fax (39 6) 48 82 672, website http://www.usis.it/.

Canada: via G.B. de Rossi 27, Roma, ☏ (39 6) 44 59 81, fax (39 6) 44 59 87 50, email rome@rome01.x400.gc.ca, website http://www.canada.it.

Ireland: Piazza di Campitelli 3, Roma, ☏ (39 6) 697 91 21, fax 679 23 54.

Australia: Via Alessandria 215, Roma, ☏ (39 6) 85 27 21, fax (39 6) 85 27 23 00, website agora.stm.it\market\ausembassy.

New Zealand: Via Zara 28, Rome, ☏ (39 6) 441 7171, fax (39 6) 440 29 84, email nzemb.rom@agora.stm.it.

Latvia

GB: 5 Alunana Iela Street, Riga, ☏ (371 7) 338 126 31, fax (371 7) 33 81 32, email british.embassy@apollo.lv.

USA: Raina Blvd 7, Riga, ☏ (371 7) 21 00 05, fax (371 7) 22 65 30, website http://www.usis.bkc.lv/embassy/.

Canada: Doma laukums 4, 4 th Floor, Riga. ☏ (371 7) 83 0141, fax (371 7) 83 0140, email riga@dfait.x400.gc.ca

Ireland: c/o Irish Embassy in Warsaw (Poland), Ul. Humanska 10, Warszawa, Poland, ☏ (48 22) 49 66 33, fax (48 22) 49 84 31.

Australia: c/o Australian Embassy in Stockholm (Sweden), Sergels Torg 12, Stockholm, Sweden, ☏ (46 8) 613 29 00, fax (46 8) 24 74 14, email info@austemb.se.

Lithuania

GB: 2 Antakalnio, Vilnius, ☏ (370 2) 2 20 70, fax (370 2) 2 75 79.

USA: Akmenu g. 6, Vilnius, ☏ (370 2) 22 30 31, fax (370 2) 31 28 19, website http://www.usis.lt/.

Canada: Gedimino pr. 64, Vilnius, ☏ (370 2) 220 898, fax (370 2) 220 884.

Ireland: c/o Irish Embassy in Warsaw (Poland), Ul. Humanska 10, Warszawa, Poland, ☏ (48 22) 49 66 33, fax (48 22) 49 84 31.

Australia: Barboros Radvilaites Str. 1-2, Vilnius, ☏ and fax (370 2) 22 33 69, email aust.con.vilnius@post.omnitel.net.

Luxembourg

GB: 14 boulevard FD Roosevelt, Luxembourg,☏ (352) 22 98 64, fax (352) 22 98 67.

USA: 22 boulevard Emmanuel Servais, Luxembourg, ☏ (352) 460 123, fax (352) 461 401, website http://www.usia.gov/abtusia/posts/LU1/wwwhmain.html.

Canada: c/o Canadian Embassy in Brussels (Belgium), avenue de Tervuren 2, Brussels, Belgium. ☏ (32 2) 741 0611, fax (32 2) 741 0643, email: bru@bru02.x400.gc.ca.

Ireland: 28, route d'Arlon, Luxembourg, ☏ (352) 45 06 10, fax (32 2) 45 88 20.

Australia: c/o Australian Embassy in Brussels (Belgium), Guimard Centre, 6-8 rue Guimard, Brussels, Belgium, ☏ (32 2) 286 05 00, fax (32 2) 230 68 02, website http://ourworld.compuserve.com/homepages/AustralianEmbassyBrussels.

New Zealand: c/o New Zealander Embassy in Brussels (Belgium), 47-48 boulevard du Régent, Brussels, Belgium, ☏ (32 2) 512 1040, fax (32 2) 513 48 56, email nzembbru@compuserve.com.

Macedonia (Former Yugoslavian Republic of Macedonia)

GB: Veljko Vlahovic 26, Skopje, ☏ (389 91) 116 772, fax (389 91) 117 005.

USA: Bul Llinden BB, Skopje, ☏ (389 91) 116 180, fax (389 91) 117 103.

Canada: c/o Canadian Embassy to the Former Yugoslav Republic of Macedonia, Kneza Milosa 75, Belgrade, Yugoslavia, ☏ (381 11) 644 666, fax (381 11) 641 480, email bgrad@bgrad01.x400.gc.ca.

Ireland: c/o Irish Embassy in Berne (Switzlerand), Kirchenfeldstrasse 68, Berne, Switzlerand, ☏ (41 31) 352 14 42, fax (41 31) 352 14 55.

Australia: Motiva, Londonska 11 B, Skopje, ☏ (389 91) 361 114, fax (389 91) 361 834, email motiva@lotus.mpt.com.mk, website www.australia.org.yu.

Malta

GB: 7 St Anne Street, Floriana, ☏ (356) 233134 7, fax (356) 242001, email bhc@dream.vol.net.mt.

USA: 2 Fl., Development House, St Anne St., Floriana, ☏ (356) 235 960, fax (356) 223 322, website http://www.usia.gov/abtusia/posts/MT1/wwwhmain.html.

Canada: c/o Canadian Embassy in Rome (Italy), via G.B. de Rossi 27, Roma (Italia), ☏ (39 6) 44 59 81, fax (39 6) 44 59 87 50, email rome@rome01.x400.gc.ca.

Ireland: c/o Irish Embassy in Rome (Italy), Piazza di Campitelli 3, Roma, Italia, ☏ (39 6) 697 91 21, fax 679 23 54.

Australia: Ta' Xbiex Terrace, MSD 11, Malta, ☏ (356) 33 82 01, fax (356) 34 40 59, aushicom@maltanet.net.

New Zealand: Villa Hampstead, Oliver Agius Street, Attard, ☏ (356) 435 025, fax (356) 437 200.

Netherlands

GB: Lange Voorhout 10, Den Haag, ☏ (31 70) 427 0427, fax (31 70) 427 0345.

USA: Lange Voorhout 102, Den Haag, ☏ (31 70) 310 92 09, fax (31 70) 361 46 88, website http://www.usemb.nl/.

Canada: Sophialaan 7, Den Haag, ☏ (31 70) 311 16 00, fax (31 70) 311 16 20, email hague@hague01.x400.gc.ca, website http://www.dfait-maeci.gc.ca/~thehague/.

Ireland: Lange Vijverberg 9, Den Haag, ☏ (31 70) 363 09 93, fax (31 70) 361 76 04.

Australia: Carnegielaan 4, Den Haag, ☏ (31 70) 310 82 00, fax (31 70) 310 78 63.

New Zealand: Carnegielaan 10, Den Haag, ☏ (31 70) 346 93 24, fax (31 70) 363 29 83, email nzemb@bart.nl.

Norway

GB: Thomas Heftyesgate 8, ☏ (47) 23 13 27 00, fax (47) 23 13 27 27.

USA: Drammensveien 18, Oslo, ☏ (47 22) 448 550, fax (47 22) 443 363, website http://www.usembassy.no/embassy/usembass.htm.

Canada: Wergelandsveien 7, Oslo, Norway, (47) 22 99 53 00, fax (47) 22 99 53 01, email oslo@oslo01.x400.gc.ca.

Ireland: c/o Irish Embassy in Copenhagen (Denmark), Ostbanegade 21, København, Denmark ☏ (45) 31 42 32 33, fax (45) 35 43 18 58.

Australia: Jernbanetorget 2, Oslo, ☏ (47) 22 41 44 33, fax (47) 242 26 83, email australian.consulate@online.no.

New Zealand: Billingstadsletta 19 B, Asker, ☏ (47) 66 84 95 30, (47) 66 84 89 09.

Poland

GB: Aleje Róz No 1, Warszawa, ☏ (48 22) 628 1001, fax (48 22) 621 7161, email britemb@it.com.pl, website http://www.britemb.it.pl/.

USA: aleje Ujazdowskie 29-31, Warszawa, ☏ (48 22) 628 30 41, fax (48 2) 628 82 98, website http://www.usaemb.pl/.

Canada: ul. Matejki 1/5, Warszawa, ☏ (48 22) 629 80 51, fax (48 22) 629 64 57, email: wsaw@wsaw01.x400.gc.ca.

Ireland: Ul. Humanska 10, Warszawa, ☏ (48 22) 49 66 33, fax (48 22) 49 84 31.

Australia: Estonska 3/5, Warsaw, ☏ (48 22) 617 60 81, fax (48 22) 617 67 56, email ausembwa@it.com.pl.

New Zealand: Natpoll Business Centre, Ul. Migdalowa 4, Warszawa, ☏ (48 22) 645 14 07, fax (48 22) 645 12 07.

Portugal

GB: Rua de São Bernardo 33, Lisboa, ☏ (351 1) 292 40 00, fax (351 1) 392 41 85.

USA: Avenida das Forças Armadas, Lisboa, ☏ (351 1) 726 6600, fax (351 1) 726 9109, website http://www.american-embassy.pt/.

Canada: Avenida da Liberdade 144/56, 4 th Floor, Lisboa. ☏ (351 1) 347 4892, fax (351 1) 347 6466, email lsbon@lsbon01.x400.gc.ca.

Ireland: Rua da Imprensa a Estrela 1-4, Lisboa, ☏ (351 1) 39 29 440, fax (351 1) 39 77 389.

Australia: c/o Australian Embassy in Paris (France), 4 rue Jean Rey, Paris (XV), France, ☏ (33 1) 40 59 33 00, fax (33 1) 40 59 33 10, www.austgov.fr.

New Zealand: Avenida Antonio Augusto de Aguiar 122, 9 th Floor, Lisboa, ☏ (351 1) 350 96 90, fax (351 1) 357 20 04.

Romania

GB: 24 Strada Jules Michelet, Bucharest, ☏ (40 1) 312 03 03, fax (40 1) 312 96 52.

USA: Strada Tudor Arghezi 7-9, Bucharest, ☏ (40 1) 210 4042, fax (40 1) 210 0395, website http://www.usembassy.ro/.

Canada: 36 Nicolae lorga, Bucharest, ☏ (40 1) 222 9845, fax (40 1) 312 9680, email bucst@bucst01.x400.gc.ca.

Ireland: c/o Irish Embassy in Athens (Greece), 7 Leoforos Vasileos Konstantinou, Athin, ☏ (30 1) 723 27 71, fax 724 02 17.

Australia: Australian Consulate, Dr Emil Racota, Nr 16/18, Apartment 1, Sector 1, Bucharest, ☏ (40 1) 666 6923, fax (40 1) 212 1424, website www.australia.org.yu.

New Zealand: contact the Great Britain Embassy.

Russia

GB: Sofiyskaya Naberezhnaya 14, Moscow, ☏ (7 503) 956 7200, fax (7 503) 956 7420, email britembppas@glas.apc.org.

USA: 19/23 Novinsky boulevard, Moscow, ☏ (7 095) 252 24 51, fax (7 095) 956 4261, website http://www.usia.gov/posts/moscow.html.

Canada: Starokonyushenny Pereulok, 23, Moscow, ☏ (7 095) 956 66 66, fax (7 095) 232 99 48.

Ireland: Grokholski Pereulok 5, Moscow, ☎ (7 095) 742 09 07, fax (7 095) 975 20 66.

Australia: 13 Kropotkinsky Pereulok, Moscow, ☎ (7 095 or 503) 956 60 70, fax (7 095 or 503) 956 61 70, email austem@dol.ru.

New Zealand: 44 Ulitsa Povarskaya (formerly Voroskovo), Moscow, ☎ (7 095) 956 35 79, fax (7 095) 956 35 83, email nzembmos@glasnet.ru.

Slovakia

GB: Panska 16, Bratislava, ☎ (421 7) 531 96 32, fax (421 7) 531 00 02, email Bebra@internet.sk.

USA: Hviezdoslavovo Namestie 4, Bratislava, ☎ (421 7) 533 0861, fax (421 7) 533 0096, website http://www.usis.sk/.

Canada: Canadian Embassy in Prague (Czech Republic), Mickiewiczova 6, Praha 6, ☎ (420 2) 431 1108, fax (420 2) 431 0294, email prgue@prgue01.x400.gc.ca.
Ireland: c/o Irish Embassy in Vienna (Austria), Hilton Centre, Landstrasse Haupstrasse 2A, Vienna, Austria, ☎ (43 1) 715 42 46, fax (43 1) 713 60 04.

Australia: Mattiellistrasse 2, Vienna, ☎ (43 1) 512 8580, fax (43 1) 513 16 56, email austemb@xpoint.at.

New Zealand: c/o New Zealander Embassy in Bonn (Germany), Bundeskanzlerpl. 2-10, Bonn, Germany, ☎ (49 228) 22 80 70, fax (49 228) 22 16 87, email nzemb.bon@.T-online.de.

Slovenia

GB: Trg republike 3/IV, Ljubljana, ☎ (386 61) 125 7191, fax (386 61) 125 0174, email info@british-embassy.si.

USA: Prazakova 4, Ljubljana, ☎ (386 61) 301 427, fax (386 61) 301 401, website http://www.usis.si/Wwwhemb.htm.

Canada: c/o Canadian Embassy in Budapest (Hungary), Budakeszi utca 32, XII Budapest, ☎ (36 1) 275 1200, fax (36 1) 275 1210, email bpest@bpest01.x400.gc.ca.

Ireland: c/o Irish Embassy in Vienna (Austria), Hilton Centre, Landstrasse Haupstrasse 2A, Vienna, Österreich, ☎ (43 1) 715 42 46, fax (43 1) 713 60 04.

Australia: Trg republike 3/XII, Ljubljana, ☎ (386 61) 125 42 52, fax (386 61) 126 47 21.

Spain

GB: Calle de Fernando el Santo 16, Madrid, ☎ (34 91) 700 82 00, fax (34 91) 700 82 72.

USA: Serrano 75, Madrid, ☎ (34 91) 587 22 00, fax (34 915) 87 23 03, website http://www.embusa.es/indexbis.html.

Canada: Núñez de Balboa 35, Madrid, ☎ (34 91) 431 43 00, fax (34 91) 435 77 98 11, email mdrid@mdrid01.x400.gc.ca, website http://www.canada-es.org.

Ireland: Claudio Coello 73, Madrid, ☎ (34 91) 576 35 00, fax (34 91) 54 35 16 77.

Australia: Plaza del Descubridor Diego de Ordas 3, Santa Engracia 120, Madrid, ☎ (34 91) 441 93 00, fax (34 91) 914 42 53 62, website http://www. embaustralia.es.

New Zealand: 3rd Floor, Plaza de La Lealtad 2, Madrid, ☎ (34 91) 523 02 26, fax (34 91) 523 01 71.

Sweden

GB: Skarpögatan 6-8, Stockholm, ☎ (46 8) 671 90 00, fax (46 8) 671 9100, website http://www.britishembassy.com/.

USA: Strandvägen 101, Stockholm, ☎ (46 8) 783 5300, fax (46 8) 661 1964, website http://www.usis.usemb.se/mission.html.

Canada: Tegelbacken 4, 7th floor, Stockholm, ☎ (46 8) 453 3 000, fax (46 8) 24 24 91, email stkhm@stkhm01.x400.gc.ca. Website http://www.canadaemb.se.

Ireland: Ostermalmsgatan 97 (IV), Stockholm, ☎ (46 8) 661 80 05, (46 8) 660 13 53.

Australia: Sergels Torg 12, Stockholm, ☎ (46 8) 613 29 00, fax (46 8) 24 74 14, email info@austemb.se.

New Zealand: Stureplan 2, Stockholm, ☎ (46 8) 611 26 25, fax (46 8) 611 35 51, email mifr@geddaek.dahl.se.

Switzerland

GB: Thunstrasse 50, Berne, ☎ (41 22) 918 24 00, fax (41 22) 918 23 22, email british@british-embassy-berne.ch, website http://www.british-embassy-berne.ch.

USA: Jubiläumsstrasse 93, Bern, ☎ (41 31) 357 70 11, fax (41 31) 357 73 44, website http://www3.itu.ch/EMBASSY/US-embassy/.

Canada: 88 Kirchenfeldstrasse, Bern, ☎ (41 31) 352 32 00, fax (41 31) 352 32 10, email bern.cda@ping.ch.

Ireland: Kirchenfeldstrasse 68, Bern, ☎ (41 31) 352 14 42, fax (41 31) 352 14 55.

Australia: 56 rue de Moillebeau, Geneva, ☎ (41 22) 918 29 00, fax (41 22) 733 56 64.

New Zealand: 2 chemin des Fins, Grand Saconnex, Genève, ☎ (41 22) 929 03 50, fax (41 22) 929 03 74, email nz@mbox.unicc.org.

Turkey

GB: Sehit Ersan Caddesi 46/A, Cankaya, Ankara, ☎ (90 312) 468 62 30, fax (90 312) 468 32 14.

USA: 110 Ataturk Blvd, Ankara, ☎ (90 312) 468 61 10, fax (90 312) 467 0019, website http://www.usis-ankara.org.tr/main.htm.

Canada: Nenehatun Caddesi 75, Ankara, Gaziosmanpasa, ☎ (90 312) 436 1275, fax (90 312) 446 4437, email ankra@ankra01.x400.gc.ca.

Australia: Nenehatun Caddesi 83, Ankara, Gaziosmanpasa, ☎ (90 312) 446 1180, fax (90 312) 446 1188, email ausemank@ibm.net.

New Zealand: Level 4, Iran Caddesi 13, Kavaklidere, Ankara, ☎ (90 312) 467 90 54, fax (90 312) 467 90 13, email newzealand@superonline.com.

Ukraine

GB: vul. Desyatinna 9, Kiev, ☎ (380 44) 462 0011, fax (380 44) 462 0013, email ukembinf@sovam.com.

USA: vul Yuria Kotsyubinskoho 10, Kiev, ☎ (380 44) 244 73 49, fax (380 44) 244 73 50, website http://www.usemb.kiev.ua/.

Canada: Yaroslaviv Val 31, Kiev, ☎ (380 44) 464 1144, fax (380 44) 464 1133, email: kiev@ kiev01.x400.gc.ca.

Ireland: c/o Irish Embassy in Prague (Czech Republic), Velvyslanectve Irska, Trziste 13, Praha, Czech Republic, ☎ (420 2) 57 53 00 61, fax (420 2) 57 31 14 92.

Australia: 18 Kominterna Ul., Apartment 11, Kyiv, ☎ (38 044) 225 75 86, fax (38 044) 244 3597.

New Zealand: c/o New Zealander Embassy in Moscow (Russia), 44 Ulitsa Povarskaya (formerly Voroskovo), Moscow, Russia ☎, (7 095) 956 35 79, fax (7 095) 956 35 83, email nzembmos@glasnet.ru.

Yugoslavia

GB: Generala Zdanova 46, Belgrade, ☎ (381 11) 645055, fax (381 11) 642293, website http://www.britemb.org.yu.

USA: Kneza Milosa 50, Belgrade, ☎ (381 11) 64 56 55, website http://www.amembbg.co.yu/.

Canada: Kneza Milosa 75, Belgrade, ☎ (381 11) 644 666, fax (381 11) 641 480, email bgrad@bgrad01.x400.gc.ca.

Australia: 13 Cika Ljubina, Belgrade, ☎ (381 11) 624 655, fax (381 11) 624 029, email austemba@eunet.yu, website www.australia.org.yu.

New Zealand: c/o New Zealander Embassy in Bonn (Germany), Bundeskanzlerpl. 2-10, Bonn, Germany, ☎ (49 228) 22 80 70, fax (49 228) 22 16 87, email nzemb.bon@.T-online.de.

Where to stay in Europe

Hotels

The **Michelin Red Guides** Europe, Benelux, Deutschland, España Portugal, France, Great Britain and Ireland, Italia, London, Paris and environs, Switzerland are updated every year and recommend a large choice of hotels indicating class and comfort, location, their facilities and prices. Choices have been made following visits to these places. Establishments with outstanding facilities and tranquillity (unusual decor, location, beautiful or interesting views) are indicated with red symbols.

Carefully read the introduction to these guides so as to understand the meaning of different symbols following the name of each hotel. Likewise in the chapter entitled "Hotel Facilities" you will find symbols indicating: television in room, non-smoking, air-conditioning, telephone with external line in room, tennis courts, sauna, swimming pool etc.

The Red Guides also indicate establishments which accept payment by credit card.

For other European countries, go to tourist offices or travel agencies (they can make reservations for you).

For short trips in the above cities, don't hesitate to consult travel agencies for special deals: train + hotel or plane + hotel and even for car rental.

Hotel vouchers – In certain countries, there are also special deals or vouchers for hotels belonging to the same chain, for example in the Scandinavian countries and Iceland. The vouchers must be purchased prior to departure but do not guarantee room availability. Refunds on unused vouchers can be obtained within specified time limits.

Euro-Guestcheque – Norway, Sweden, Denmark and Finland. Best Western chain.

Scandinavian Hotel Pass – Norway, Sweden and Denmark. Hotels with 5 comfort ratings (supplements payable on arrival).

Pro-Skandinavia – Norway, Sweden, Denmark and Finland. 40 % reduction on the normal price provided you reserve within 24 hrs of arrival.

Finncheque – Finland. Hotels with 3 comfort ratings (supplements payable on arrival).

Dansk Kroferie – Denmark. Comfortable country inns. Suitable for families.

Scandic Holiday Cheque – Norway, Sweden, Denmark, Finland and Germany.

Chèque-Hôtel Manoir – Sweden.

Scandinavian Hotels Checks – Norway and Sweden.

Edda – Iceland. Hotels and guesthouses.

We give below a few adresses and telephone numbers for hotel reservations in some European countries.

Belgium

BTR ☎ (32 2) 513 74 84

Midi Hotel Reservation ☎ (32 2) 522 69 19

Finland

Hotel Booking Centre, Railway Station (West Wing), 00100 Helsinki,
☎ (358 9) 171 133, and (358 9) 22 88 14 00 after the 2.05.99;
email: hotel@helsinki-expert.fi, website http://www.helsinki-expert.fi.
Helsinki Tourist Office, ☎ (358 9) 622 69 90, and (358 9) 22 88 15 00 after the 2.05.99, fax (358 9) 62 26 99 14.

France

Website http://www.hotels.fr/

Relais & Châteaux Relais Gourmands: châteaux and manor houses converted into prestigious hotels and restaurants. ☎ (33 1) 45 72 90 00,
website http://www.relaischateaux.fr/.
Office in USA: Suite 707, 11 East 44th Street, New York, NY 10017,
☎ (1 212) 856 0115, fax (1 212) 856 0193.

Great Britain and North Ireland

Copthorne Hotels ☎ 0800 414 741 (Freephone).
Country Club Hotel group ☎ (44 158) 256 22 56.
De Vere Hotels PLC ☎ (44 192) 526 50 50.
Forte Hotels ☎ 0345 40 40 40 or 0800 40 40 40 (Freephone).
Friendly Hotels ☎ 0800 59 19 10 (Freephone).
Granada Hotels & Lodges ☎ 0800 55 53 00 (Freephone).
Hilton Hotels ☎ 09 90 44 58 66.
Hyatt Hotels ☎ (44 171) 580 81 97.
Intercontinental Hotels Ltd ☎ (44 181) 847 22 77 or calls outside London (44 1703) 455 81 44.

Jarvis Hotels ☎ (44 1703) 455 818 11.
Marriott Hotels ☎ 0800 22 12 22 (Freephone).
Mount Charlotte/Thistle Hotels ☎ 0800 18 17 16 (Freephone)/ (44 113) 243 91 11.
Premier Lodges & Inns ☎ 0800 11 88 33 (Freephone).
Queens Moat Houses PLC ☎ 0500 21 32 14 (Freephone) or (44 170) 876 66 77.
Radisson Edwardian Hotels ☎ 0800 19 19 91 (Freephone).
Ramada International ☎ 0800 18 17 37 (Freephone).
Sheraton Hotel ☎ 0800 35 35 35 (Freephone).
Stakis Hotels ☎ 0800 26 26 26.
Swallow Hotels Ltd ☎ (44 191) 419 46 66.
Travel Inns ☎ (44 158) 241 43 41.
Travelodges ☎ 0800 85 09 50 (Freephone).

Greece

Hellenic Chamber of Hotels, 24 Stadiou, Athens, ☎ (30 1) 323 71 93, fax (30 1) 322 54 49, email grhotels@otenet.gr, website http://users.otenet.gr/~grhotels.

Hungary

IBUSZ Hotel Service, Apaci ut. 1, Budapest 5, ☎ (36 1) 118 57 76, fax (36 1) 117 90 99.

Republic of Ireland

Ryan Hotel Group ☎ (353 1) 878 79 66
Jury's Hotel Group ☎ (353 1) 607 00 70
Holiday Ireland Hotels ☎ (353 1) 874 54 88
Great Southern Hotels ☎ (353 1) 280 80 31
Doyle Hotel Group ☎ (353 1) 660 52 22

Portugal

The state-owned **pousadas** are restored historic monuments (castles, palaces and monasteries) in beautiful sites or excursion centres. They are very comfortable. For further information, contact:
– Enatur, Avenida Santa Joana Princesa 10, 1700 Lisboa, ☎ (351 1) 84 420 01, fax (351 1) 84 420 85, email enatur@mail.telepac.pt, website http://www.pousadas.pt.,
– Abreu Tours, 317 E. 34th St., New York, NY 10016, ☎ 1 800 223 15 80.

Spain

Keytel ☎ (34 91) 542 51 03
Gran Via ☎ (34 91) 732 80 13
Sol Melia ☎ (34 91) 571 16 16
Husa ☎ (34 93) 330 19 19
Tryp ☎ (34 91) 315 32 46
NH Hoteles ☎ (34 93) 417 23 32
Riou Hoteles (Majorque) ☎ (34 971) 74 30 30

Special mention should be made of Spanish **paradors** which can be compared to Portuguese pousadas. They are restored historic monuments (castles, palaces and monasteries) which stand in beautiful sites. For further information, contact:
– Paradores de Turismo, Requena 3, 28013 Madrid, ☎ (34 91) 516 66 66, fax (34 91) 516 66 67 .
– Keytel International, 402 Edgware Road, London W2 IED, ☎ (44 171) 402 81 82, fax (44 171) 72 49 503.
– Marketing Ahead Inc., 433 5th Ave., New York, NY 10016, ☎ 1 800 223 13 56 (freephone) or (1 212) 68 69 213, fax (1 212) 68 60 271.

You can also make reservations at any Best Western, Holiday Inn, Mercure or Novotel-Sofitel Hotels in Europe by calling these numbers (freephones, except *) from your resident country.

Best Western

Website http://www.bestwestern.com, email bw@bestwestern.com (or national domain-name).

☎ from USA and Canada 1800 528 1234, from UK 0800 39 31 30 (for overseas hotels), 0345 73 73 73 for UK hotels, from Republic of Ireland 1800 709 101, from Australia 131 779, from New Zealand 0800 237 883.

Holiday Inn

☎ from USA and Canada 1 800 465 43 29, from UK 0800 897 121, from Republic of Ireland 1 800 55 31 55, from Australia 1 800 533 888, from New Zealand 0800 44 2888.

Mercure

Website http://www.mercure.com.

☎ from USA and Canada 1800 MERCURE, from UK and Republic of Ireland 0181 283 45 80*, from Australia 1 800 642 244, from New Zeland 0 800 44 44 22.

Novotel – Sofitel

Website http://www.novotel.com.

☎ from USA and Canada 1800 NOVOTEL, from UK and Republic of Ireland 0181 283 45 30*, from Australia 1800 642 244, from New Zeland 0800 44 4422.

Homestay programmes

This type of accommodation is becoming favoured by more and more tourists travelling on their own. Tourist offices normally have lists of these addresses and can make immediate reservations. If this is not the case, these rooms are also advertised on sign-boards outside the establishment: "**Chambre d'hôtes**" in France, "**Bed and Breakfast**" in Great Britain, "**Zimmer frei**" in Germany or in Austria, "**Turismo de Habitaçáo**" in Portugal, "**Overnatting**", "**Hytter**", or "**Husrom**" in Norway and "**Varelse**" in Denmark.

Youth hostels

Quality and price varies enormously from one country to the next. They are still much cheaper than hotels and are normally heavily booked up in high season: it is advisable to reserve in advance.
An international youth hostelling association card is recommended, even though certain youth hostels, particularly in the eastern countries don't ask for them. These cards can be purchased from the various associations.

Great Britain – Youth Hostelling Association of England and Wales, Trevelyan House, 8 St Steven's Hill, St Albans, Hertfordshire AL1 2DY, ☎ (44 727) 855 215, fax (44 727) 84 41 26.

USA – Hostelling International-American Youth Hostels, 733 15th Street NW, Suite 840, Washington, DC 20005, ☎ (1 202) 783 61 61, fax (1 202) 783 61 71, email hiayhserv@hiayh.org, http://www.hiayh.org. This association offers the International Guide for Europe to all those who join.

Canada – Hostelling International-Canada, 205 Catherine Street, Suite 400, Ottawa, Ontario, K2P IC3, ☎ (1 613) 237 78 84, fax (1 613) 237 78 68, email info@hostellingintl.ca, website http://www. hostellingintl.ca.

Ireland – An Oige, Irish Youth Hostel Association, 61 Mountjoy Street, Dublin 7, ☎ (353 1) 830 45 55, fax (353 1) 830 58 08, email anoige@iol.ie, website http://www.irelandyha.org.

Australia – Australian Youth Hostels Association, Level 3, 10 Mallet Street, Camperdown NSW 2050, ☎ (61 2) 95 65 16 99, fax (61 2) 95 65 13 25, email yha@yha.org.au.

New Zealand – Youth Hostels Association of New Zealand, PO Box 436, 173 Cashel Street, Christchurch 1, ☎ (64 3) 379 99 70, fax (64 3) 365 44 76, email info@yha.org.nz, website http://www.yha.org.nz.

Youth hostelling association addresses are listed in catalogues and are available at any of the associations. Depending on the establishment, accommodation is either in dormitories, rooms of 2 to 3 people or individual rooms and washrooms are usually communal. Be careful, as some hostels do not provide sheets, though you can rent them. Breakfast is not included.

Camping

Camp-grounds are all over Europe, offering varying degrees of comfort, some even renting bungalows (particularly in countries in northern Europe).
The **Michelin Guide Camping and Caravaning France** suggests a choice of camp-grounds throughout France. Comfort, facilities, number of pitching sights and the telephone number for reservations are listed in each case and a symbol indicates if it is possible to rent caravans, mobile homes, bungalows or chalets in each camp-ground.

What's on the menu in Europe?

Mealtimes

Each country has its own eating habits. However there are distinct trends in types of food eaten in the northern and southern Europe: in Anglo-Saxon countries less time is spent at table, and they are happy with just a sandwich at midday, whereas in southern Europe, there is a strong gastronomic tradition which conditions local eating habits. In eastern countries, the staple diet is often potatoes and ground beef.

North-western Europe

Breakfast is a full meal in Anglo-Saxon countries, including varieties of pork sausage and different cold meats, cheese, eggs and milk products, as well as cereal, different kinds of breads, pastries and sometimes vegetables. Drinks are the same as the rest of Europe: tea, coffee, hot chocolate and milk.
As a result of this heavy breakfast, lunch is a quick, light meal particularly for those who work. In Great Britain meat pies, Ploughman's (cheese, salad pickles, bread and butter); baked potatoes in their jackets with various fillings, sandwiches or fish and chips (fish in batter with French fries). In the Netherlands lunch is a cold meal with coffee, uitsmijer (open sandwiches with butter, ham or roast beef and two fried eggs on top), broodje, soft bread rolls with various fillings. In Scandinavia just a sandwich, drink and a piece of fruit is enough. In Denmark, the national sandwich is smørrebrød made with fillings ranging from salmon or salad to eggs. More is eaten in Germany, Switzerland and Austria: lunch starts with soup, followed by a main dish of meat or fish always accompanied by a salad, then dessert.

Tea-time is sacred in Great Britain: from 4pm onwards, the British have a cup of tea accompanied by mini-sandwiches and pastries.
Those living in Anglo-Saxon countries have dinner very early (from 5pm-6pm or 4pm in Scandinavia) because of very early night-fall in winter. The evening meal is often very simple. In Ireland, the traditional Irish Fry can be for breakfast or as an evening meal. It consists of fried eggs, sausages, blood sausage, potato-cakes, mushrooms and tomatoes. In Germany, an assortment of cheeses and varieties of pork sausage are served with a wide variety of breads. In Scandinavia, dinner can simply be soup or a hot dish. On the other hand it is customary to eat a big meal in the Netherlands: soup, kippers (marinated, smoked herrings), asparagus, and mushrooms for hors-d'œuvres, followed by an main dish of meat or fish and an abundance of fresh vegetables in gravy and salad with mayonnaise, then after this copious meal, maybe dessert (ice-cream, and pastries topped with whipped cream). The day is rounded off with a hot drink and maybe a pastry or a little sandwich.

Southern Europe

Southerners are generally more interested in the pleasures of eating than those living in north-western Europe. This love of fine food is hereditary: they love elaborate, large meals.

Only **breakfast** doesn't follow this rule: it is a quick, light meal. In France their famous, baguette (bread stick), is cut into slices, buttered and dipped in black or white coffee. You can also enjoy French pastries such as *croissants*, *pain au chocolat* and *pain aux raisins*. Elsewhere, bread, butter, jams, honey and hot drinks (tea, coffee, hot chocolate, milk) are breakfast's main ingredients.

Lunch is the main meal of the day unlike the Anglo-Saxon countries. It may be preceded with an **aperitif** designed to give you an appetite. Appetisers are served with an alcoholic beverage: *mezédes* with ouzo (Greece) and *tapas* with *sangría* (Spain). Dinner consists of three, even four courses, starting with soup (common in Portugal) and/or hors-d'œuvres of cooked varieties of pork sausage or raw vegetables, or sometimes fresh cheeses (Portugal). This course is called *primero* in Spain, *antipasto* in Italy, *entrée* in France and *mehzeh* in Turkey. There is an extra course in Italy which is the first main course of rice or pasta. The following course is the most nourishing of the meal, with meat or fish accompanied by vegetables, starchy food or rice (except in Italy where salad is more commonly served); this course is called *segundo* in Spain; *plat de résistance* in France and *secondo* in Italy. To finish the meal, there is dessert, preceded by a selection of cheeses (sometimes served with a green salad) in France and Italy. Desserts are made with fruits, ice-cream, pastries and milk puddings whether you are eating a Spanish *postre*, an Italian or Greek *glika*, or a French *dessert*. The meal is, of course, accompanied by different wines depending on the various dishes. After lunch, the meal is almost invariably rounded off with a small, strong black coffee. In Greece and Turkey, things happen differently: in the same way as Oriental meal, dishes are usually served all at the same time. You can share selections of hors-d'œuvres and main dishes, each person serving him/herself. Dinner can be light or more substantial. You can eat soup or a dish of meat and vegetables. Cheese or dessert round off dinner in the same way as for lunch. In Mediterranean countries (Spain, Greece and Turkey), people eat fairly late in the evening because of the early afternoon heat, when most people have to go and have a siesta (mid-afternoon nap) until 4pm.

After going out, it is time to have **supper.** This is a short meal, consisting very often of soup, as the name suggests. For example, the famous French onion soup, eaten in the small hours, after a wedding or a theatre performance etc.

Eastern Europe

Depending on their geographical location, eating customs in these countries resemble customs either in northern or southern countries. Therefore, Russians and Polish have a substantial breakfast, whereas the Hungarians eat just a little bread with a cup of coffee or tea. The copious **midday meal** and evening meal vary according to whether a smaller quantity is eaten at midday (Russia), or in the evening (other eastern countries). A glass of alcohol is sometimes served before the meal, as in southern Europe: tuica (plum brandy) accompanied by appetisers (tomatoes, cucumbers, cheese, cooked pork meats etc.) in Romania and mézés in Bulgaria, consisting of an assortment of spicy sausages, raw vegetables and cheese. To start off midday meals, there are hors-d'œuvres (salad, little grilled sausages etc.). In Russia, zakouski are little hors d'œuvres served Oriental style (all at the same time): caviar and blinis, pirojki (little savoury tarts), cold meats, fish, raw vegetables, all eaten with rye bread. Winter come summer, soup is the second course, then the meat dish (steaks or boiled meat in gravy) or fish with vegetables, potatoes or mamaliga (in Romania, a variety of polenta). Vegetarian dishes are also quite common: vegetables stuffed with rice, tomatoes and onions are very popular in Hungary as well as Bulgaria. As for desserts, they vary from cakes, pancakes and doughnuts to ice-cream (Russians have an especially sweet tooth), accompanied by a strong coffee or tea. Russians and Polish sometimes have rather surprising eating habits. In Russia, any excuse will do to have a good meal at any time of the day. Polish have no less than four meals per day: breakfast, a second breakfast; (a sandwich around 11am); obiad, the main meal of the day eaten after work at 3pm and 6pm and lastly supper (a substantial meal or a cup of tea and a pastry).

Different types of restaurants

Restaurants – The **Michelin Red Guides** Europe, Benelux, Deutschland, España Portugal, France, Great Britain and Ireland, Italia, London, Paris and environs and Switzerland, are updated each year and recommend a large choice of restaurants where you can taste specialities of the different countries. **Stars** for good cooking (one to three stars) indicate establishments with outstanding quality of cooking. The "**Gourmet Bib**" symbol indicates restaurants offering good quality meals at a reasonable price.
In eastern countries, restaurants are often classed by categories according to the quality of service and food. Of course, prices vary according to their category. In Romania, the gradina de vara are open-air restaurants, situated in either gardens or on lake shores. They are wonderful places to dine in fine weather. Most restaurants in eastern countries provide entertainment of dancing and folk music from 9pm onwards.
All over Europe, restaurants are the most likely places to try the most typical dishes. Full meals are served with hors-d'oeuvres, entrée and dessert depending on different country's customs. Picturesque inns with traditional decor produce plentiful home-style cooking.
In large restaurants and hotel restaurants, menus are printed in the native language and in English (except Great Britain and Ireland).

Fast food restaurants – Snack bars, bars, diners and cafeterias in eastern countries serve simple, quick and cheap meals everywhere, ranging from a sandwich or a salad to a hot dish. Some of them have self-service, others have waiter service.

Cafes and pubs – In all countries, these establishments are where a whole cross-section of the population meet up: friends and colleagues alike, get together to relax, drink and discuss the news of the day. Here, you will find the real character of a country and the people who live there.
In British and Irish **pubs,** you can have food but they are mainly for drinking beer, discussing football and rugby matches (pubs often have a television) and singing popular folk songs (Ireland in particular).
Spanish **bars** are full the whole day long: for an aperitif, for a coffee, when getting out of the office (usually frequented by men talking about current affairs or telling jokes) and at the end of the afternoon, to drink a hot chocolate.
In Central Europe, cafes are places to relax or read newspapers for hours on end, drink a coffee, eat a pastry and chat with your companions. The most famous cafés are in Vienna and Budapest, with its memories of the Austro-Hungarian Empire.

Gourmet Europe

Each country has its culinary specialities, all equally as appetising. We are going to give you some mouth-watering suggestions.

Some good dishes – Austria is known for Wienerschnitzel (veal cutlets); Germany for its wide variety of pork sausage; Italy for an unparalleled selection of pasta (in Tuscany, soups made with little fish, octopus and shell fish dishes such as cucciucco ala livornasa are delicious); Great Britain for steak and kidney pie; the Netherlands for hutspot (stew with ground beef); Ireland for Irish stew (mutton stew); Portugal for soups (caldo verde and gazpacho) and cod dishes; Spain for paëlla; Greece for moussaka and souvlaki (meat kebabs); the eastern countries for their different kinds of goulasch (with paprika in Hungary) and Romania for sarmale (meat balls wrapped in cabbage, sauerkraut or vine leaves); France for its pot-au-feu (stew), choucroute (cabbage and meat dish) and its popular steak and French fries and Belgium for its mussels and French fries.

PRIMA PRESS

Cacciucco alla livornese, Tuscany

Some typical cheeses – Cheeses are produced all over Europe, but the country which still has the greatest variety of cheeses is France (Camembert, Brie, Reblochon, Fourme díAmbert, Crottin de Chavignol, Roquefort, Munster, ...poisse etc.). Amongst others, Switzerland produces Gruyère and Raclette, which makes delicious fondues. Italy uses mozzarella in pizzas, parmesan and gorgonzola in pasta. The Netherlands produce hard cheeses such as Gouda and Edam. Great Britain has its own specialities, Stilton and cheddar. Greek feta is eaten in a salad made with cucumber and tomatoes. Bulgaria is famous for yoghurts, and Romania for Braila and "bourdouf" cheese.

A few sweet things to bring back from vacation – There are certain cakes that are only made for festivals such as Christmas pudding (Great Britain). Vienna is famous throughout the world for its pastries (they are so famous that France adopted the name "viennoiseries" for its croissants, pains au chocolat and pains aux raisins). Germans love their Dresdener Stollen (layered raisin cake). Italy excels in making ice-cream (gianduia, cassata and tiramisu – an alcoholic coffee cheesecake). Ice-creams are also eaten a lot in Russia.
In Turkey and Greece, the locals are very fond of very sweet candies, usually made with honey: baklavas, loukoums and halva. Honey is also used as a main ingredient in French nougat and Spanish turrón.

A selection of national drinks – Many European countries are wine-producing. Wine is drunk during meals, but also as an aperitif. France has many famous vineyards: vintage **St Émilion** (red wine) or **Château d'Yquem** from Bordeaux; Monbazillac (sweet white wine) of Bergerac; vintage **Gevrey-Chambertin**, Nuits St Georges, **Pommard** (red) or Meursault and Chassagne-Montrachet (white wine) from Burgundy; vintage Riesling

and Gewurztraminer (white wine) from Alsace, vintage Châteauneuf du Pape and Côte Rôtie (red and white) from Côtes du Rhône and wine from **Champagne**. Germany produces very good white wines (Riesling from Moselle and Mittelrhein), as well as Switzerland (Fendant and Johannisberg). The most famous Italian wines are Valpolicella (rose and red), Lambrusco (sparkling red wine), **Chianti** (red), Lacryma Cristi (white) and Marsala (red). The favoured drink in Greece is retsina which is a wine preserved by adding pine resin. Portugal (Minho region) produces young, sparkling red and white wines called vinho verde. Romania produces white wines (vintage Cotnari and Tirnaveni).
Alcoholic beverages drunk before the meal range from Scottish **whisky**, Irish **whiskey** to Russian and Polish **vodka**, Portuguese **port** and madeira, French **armagnac**, Bulgarian **rakiya** (fruit brandy), Romanian **tuica** (plum brandy), Czech **becherovka** to Spanish **sherry** and **Malaga wine**.
Aniseed-based alcohol is widespread in southern Europe, whether it is called *anisette* or *pastis* in France, *ouzo* in Greece, *raki* in Turkey and *mastika* in Bulgaria.
Europeans are great beer-lovers. Belgian, Irish and German beers have a great reputation, but there are also other good-quality beers in the Baltic States, Spain, Czech Republic, Great Britain and France.

The best restaurants!

In western Europe, there is a great culinary tradition that has gathered knowledge and experience over the centuries.
Multitudes of restaurants mean it is often difficult to find a restaurant with a good reputation for really high quality cooking. You can always read food columns in your regular newspaper but it is always better to trust the **Michelin Red Guides** before trying out a place and be guided by their stars for good cooking. A three star restaurant is of the highest quality and refinement and worth a trip. You must also make a reservation. Allow plenty of time, as each meal is a veritable feast. First and foremost a feast for your eyes as rooms and tables are decorated with good taste and then a feast for your palate, as the chef here creates and designs the food he serves like a true artist. Let yourself be carried away into realms that surpass the simple idea of a meal. You will be overcome by a great feeling of contentment as expert, stylish and caring personnel look after your every need during this feast fit for a king.
Wines selected by the wine waiter enhance the flavours of the dishes cooked with such finesse.
All Europe's varied gastronomic traditions are sure to leave you with unforgettable memories.

J.-P. Lescourret/EXPLORER

Cheese porters in Alkmaar, Netherlands

Books to discover Europe

The following list gives a selection of books on various aspects of the European continent.

History

The Oxford Illustrated Prehistory of Europe by Barry Cunliffe *(Oxford University Press)*

Exploring the World of the Celts by Simon James *(Thames & Hudson)*

The Oxford History of the Classical World edited by John Boardman Jasper Griffin and Oswyn Murray *(Oxford University Press)*

Encylopedia of the Ancient Greek World by David Sacks *(Constable)*

Cultural Atlas of the Viking World by James Graham-Campbell *(Facts on File)*

The Viking Achievement by PG Foote and DM Wilson

Byzantium: The Early Centuries, The Apogee and The Decline and Fall by John Julius Norwich *(Penguin and Viking)*

The Holy Roman Empire by Friedrich Heer *(Phoenix)*

The Monks of War: The Military Religious Orders by Desmond Seward *(Penguin)*

The Oxford Illustrated History of the Crusades by Jonathan Riley-Smith *(Oxford University Press)*

The Making of Europe: Conquest, Colonisation and Cultural Change 950-1350 by Robert Bartlett *(Viking)*

The Black Death by Philip Ziegeler *(Penguin)*

The Decline and Fall of the Ottoman Empire by Alan Palmer *(John Murray)*

The Civilisation of Europe in the Renaissance by John Hale *(Harper Collins)*

The Mediterranean and the Mediterranean World in the Age of Philip II by Fernand Braudel, translated by Siân Reynolds *(Harper Collins)*

One Hundred Days: Napoleon's Road to Waterloo by Alan Schom *(Michael Joseph)*

The Longman Companion to Napoleonic Europe *(Longman)*

Europe: A History of its People by Jean-Baptiste Duroselle *(Viking)*

Europe, a history by Norman Davies *(Pimlico)*

The Oxford Illustrated History of Modern Europe edited by TCW Blanning *(Oxford University Press)*

The Times Illustrated History of Europe *(Time Books)*

D-Day by Warren Jute *(Pan)*

The Penguin Atlas of D-Day and the Normandy Campaign by John Man *(Penguin)*

Europe in Our Time: A History 1945-1992 by Walter Laqueur *(Penguin)*

Political and social Europe

The Rebirth of History: Eastern Europe in the Age of Democracy by Misha Glenny *(Penguin)*

The Europeans by Luigi Barzini *(Penguin)*

The New Europe: An Encyclopedic Atlas by Hames Hughes and Monika Unger *(Mitchell Beazley)*

The Far Right in Western and Eastern Europe by Luciano Cheles, Ronnie Ferguson, Michalina Vaugham *(Longman)*

Russia Transformed by Dmitry Mikheyev *(Hudson Institute)*

The Penguin Companion to European Union by Timothy Bainbridge with Anthony Teasbale *(Penguin)*

Art

The Essential Gombrich: Selected Writings on Art and Culture by Professor Sir Ernst Gombrich, edited by Richard Woodfield *(Phaidon)*

A History of Western Art by Laurie Schneider Adams *(Abrams)*

Impressionism: The Painters and the Paintings by Bernard Denvir *(Studio Editions)*

The Expresssionists by W-D Dube *(Thames & Hudson)*

Painting and Sculpture in Europe 1880-1940 by George Heard Hamilton *(Yale University Press)*

Art and Civilisation by Edward Lucie-Smith *(Lawrence King Publishing)*

A Concise History Watercolours by Graham Reynolds *(Thames & Hudson)*

The Arts and Crafts Movement by Elizabeth Cumming and Wendy Kaplan *(Thames & Hudson)*

The Medieval Menagerie: Animals in the Art of the Middle Ages by Janetta Rebold Benton *(Abbeville Press)*

Art of the Celts from 700BC to the Celtic Revival by Lloyd and Jennifer Laing *(Thames & Hudson)*

The Renaissance: European Painting 1400-1600 by Charles McCorquodale *(Studio Editions)*

The History of Decorative Arts: The Renaissance and Mannerism in Europe edited by Alain Gruber et al *(Abbeville Press)*

The Traveller's Guide to the Great Art Treasures of Europe by David Lawrence Morton *(Arlington Books)*

Architecture

An Outline of European Architecture by N. Pevsner *(Penguin)*

City and People by Mark Giouard *(Yale University Press)*

The Great Country Houses of Central Europe: Czechoslovakia, Hungary, Poland by Lord Michael Pratt *(Abbeville Press)*

The History of Garden Design: the Western Tradition from the Renaissance to the Present Day edited by Monique Mosser and Georges Teyssot *(Thames & Hudson)*

Architecture in Europe since 1968 by Alexander Tzonis and Liane Lefaivre *(Thames & Hudson)*

Literature and Music

The Western Canon (26 great Western writers) by Harold Bloom *(Macmillan)*

The Faber Book of Modern European Poetry by A Alvarez *(Faber & Faber)*

20th Century Literary Criticism by David Lodge *(Longman)*

The Opera Lover's Guide to Europe by John Philip Couch

Wildlife

Birds of Europe by Lars Jonsson *(Christpher Helm)*

Mammals of Britain & Europe by David Macdonald and Pricella Barret *(Collins Field Guide)*

Insects of Britain & Northern Europe by Michael Chinery *(Collins Field Guide)*

Trees of Britain & Northern Europe by A. Mitchell *(Collins Field Guide)*

Food and drink

Port by George Robertson *(Faber & Faber)*

The Essential Guide to Scotch Whisky by Michael Brander *(Canongate Press)*

The Story of Wine by Hugh Johnson *(Mitchell Beazley)*

Bordeaux by David Peppercorn *(Faber & Faber)*

Travels à la carte by Sophie Grigson and William Black *(Network Books)*

Traditional Italian Food by L. B. Birch *(Fontana)*

Wine Atlas (wines and wine regions in the world) by Oz Clarke *(Little, Brown & Company)*

The Wine Lover's Guide to France by M. Busselle *(Pavilion, Michael Joseph)*

The Great Beers of Belgium by Michael Jackson *(Prion)*

The Millenium Champagne & Sparkling Wine Guide by Tom Stevenson *(Dorling Kindersley)*

The Food Lover's Guide to France by P. Wells *(Eyre and Spottisswoode)*

French cheeses by K. Masui, T. Yamada et R. Hodgson, foreword by Joël Robuchon *(Dorling Kindersley)*

The Food and Cooking of Eastern Europe by Lesley Chamberlain

Travel

On Foot to the Golden Horn by Jason Goodwin *(Chatto & Windus)*

The Way of St James: A Pilgrimage to Santiago de Compostela by James Bentley *(Pavilion Books)*

Stalin's Nose: Across the Face of Europe by Rory Maclean *(Flamingo)*

The Pillars of Hercules: A Grand Tour of the Mediterranean by Paul Theroux *(Hamish Hamilton)*

Among the Russians by Colin Thubron *(Penguin Books)*

The Impossible Country (a journey through the last days of Yugoslavia) by Brian Hall *(Minerva)*

Great European Festivals

In this section information will be given about the great festivals that happen in Europe the whole year round. There are, of course, hundreds of others. To find out about them, go to tourist offices in the respective countries or the organisers.

Religious festivals

19 January

Russia .... Krechtchenie: Feast of the benediction of holy water in churches.

17 March

Ireland .... St Patrick's Day parades.

Holy Week

Braga (Portugal) .... Processions and religious ceremonies.

Cartagena, Cuenca, ... Solemn processions.
Malaga, Murcia, Seville, Valladolid
Zamora (Spain)

Good Friday

Greece............................... Epitafios Procession.

Perpignan (France) .... Sanch Procession.

Sartène (Corsica)................ U Catenacciu Procession.

Easter Sunday

Greece............................... Midnight mass in the open air, Feast of the Paschal Lamb.

April

Chartres (France) .... Students' Pilgrimage.

12-13 May and 12-13 October

Fátima (Portugal)............... Annual processions.

Ascension Day

Bruges (Belgium) .... Procession of the Holy Blood.

21-23 May

Langadas and .... Anastenaria (women dancing in a trance on hot coals,
Agia Eléni (Greece) carrying icons of St Constantine and St Helen).

Late May

Les Stes Maries .... Gypsy Pilgrimage.
de la Mer (France)

24 June

Alicante (Spain) .... Hogueras: fireworks festival in honour of St John.

Scandinavia .... Feast of St John.

3rd Sunday in July

Mont Gaina (Romania) ...... "Targul de fete" (Girls' festival). Big popular festival bringing together the inhabitants of three districts.

25 July

Greece............................... Pilgrimages to the mountain tops in honour of St Elijah.

Last Sunday in July

Furnes (Belgium) .... Penitents' Procession.

15 August

Tinos (Greece) .... Pilgrimage to the miraculous image of the Virgin.

19 September

Naples (Italy) .... Feast of the Miracle of St Januarius in the cathedral.

3rd Sunday before 5 December

Amsterdam .... Official entrance of St Nicholas, Prins Hendrikkade.
(the Netherlands)

Early December

Strasbourg (France)........... Christmas Markets.

Mont St Odile (France)....... Pilgrimage in Alsace.

5 December

Bad Mitterndorf (Austria)... Nikolospiel (Feast of St Nicholas): procession of St Nicholas in the streets with noisy and colourful events.

1st Saturday in December

Fribourg (Switzerland) .... St Nicholas fair and market.

Friday before Advent to 24 December

Nuremberg (Germany) .... Chritkindlesmarkt (Infant Jesus market): sale of Christmas tree decorations; many children's games in the square of the illuminated market.

13 December

Sweden .... Feast of St Lucy (festival of light).

Christmas-Epiphany

Naples (Italy) .... Traditional crèches in the town's churches.

Traditions

6 January

Patrai (Greece) .... Carnival.

February

Venice (Italy)....................... Carnival (close of Mardi Gras).

Nice (France) .... Carnival.

Last week-end before Lent

Mohacs (Hungary) .... Carnival.

During Lent

Breda, Maastricht .... Carnival.
(the Netherlands)

1st Monday in Lent

Basle (Switzerland) .... Carnival (3 days).

Week before Mardi Gras

Loulé (Portugal).................. Carnival and Feast of Almond Trees.

Sunday, Monday and Tuesday (Mardi Gras)

Binche (Belgium) .... Carnival.

Monday and Tuesday

Rottweil (Germany)............ Narrensprung: German carnival including a procession of fools.

Sunday in mid-Lent

Stavelot (Belgium) .... Carnival procession with Blancs Moussis.

1st-8 March

Russia................................ Festival of Russian Winter: troïka (sleigh) races. Beginning of Lent for the Catholics.

Late March-mid or late May

Keukenhof .... National Flower Festival.
(the Netherlands)

April

Seville (Spain) .... Feria (festival).

3rd Monday in April

Zurich................................ Sechseläuten: festival celebrating the end of winter.

30 April

Sweden.............................. Valborgsmässoafton (Evening of the Walpurgis Mass): festival celebrating the end of winter.

Early May

Taormina (Sicily)................. Festival of costumes and Sicilian carts.

Jerez de la Frontera .... Feria de caballo (horses).
(Spain)

Early May-August

Peak District .... Well dressing: floral decoration of wells.

First fortnight in May

Cordoba (Spain).................. Festival of Cordovan patios and national Flamenco competition.

3-5 May

Sesimba (Portugal) .... Do Senhor das Chagas festival: fishermen's festival dating from 16C.

8 May

Helston (Great Britain) .... Flora Day Furry Dance: 5 processional dances at 7am, 8.30am, 10am, midday and 5pm.

2nd week-end in May

Vila Franca do Lima (Portugal) .... Festival of Roses: procession of Mardomas: (mistresses of the household) wearing floral head-dresses, representing the Portuguese regional coats of arms.

15 May

Madrid (Spain) .... Saint Isidora: corridas for several days.

Mid-May to mid-September each Sunday at midday

Hameln (Germany) .... Rattenfängerspiel: festivals recounting the tale of the Pied Piper of Hamlyn.

Whit Monday

Gerpinnes (Belgium) .... Military march.

June

Antrim Glens (Ireland) .... Feis na n Gleann Festival: dancing, music, poetry, arts and crafts and sports started in 19C to preserve the country's old customs, language and sports (hurling – a kind of hockey).

2nd or 3rd Saturday in June

Horse Guards Parade (Great Britain) .... Trooping of the Colour: great procession celebrating Queen Elizabeth II's Birthday.

June-July

Straznice (Czech Republic) .. International meeting for folk groups.

Late June-early July (every other year)

Tomar (Portugal) .... Festival of Tabuleiros.

July-August, Saturday afternoons

Kinderijk (the Netherlands) . Windmill Festival.

July-August

Estoril (Portugal) .... Craft Fair: craftsmen from every region exhibiting their wares.

Vychodna (Slovakia) .... Folk Festival.

Ph. Roy/EXPLORER

The Tabuleiros Festival, Tomar, Portugal

2 July and 16 August

Siena (Italy) .... Pallo delle Contrade.

6-14 July

Pamplona (Spain) .... Sanfermines.

Mid-July

Belfast (Ireland) .... International Rose Competition.

24 July-8 August

Sétubal (Portugal) .... Santiago Festival: touradas and folk groups.

August

Edinburgh (Scotland) .... Military Tattoo: military parades and international festival.

20 August

Debrecen (Hungary) .... Flower Festival.

Nagykallo (Hungary) .... Traditional Arts and Crafts Festival.

1st Sunday after 15 August

Portaria (Crete) .... Reconstruction of traditional marriages.

Ath (Belgium) .... Ducasse Festival.

Last Sunday in August

Wingene (Belgium) .... Breughel Festival: fancy dress parade inspired by Breughel's paintings, followed by a Breughel feast.

Last Sunday in August and 1st Sunday in September

Arezzo (Italy) .... Saracen jousting.

1st Saturday in September

Braemar (Scotland) .... Meeting of clans and Highland Games.

Early September

Lille (France) .... Open air Market.

3rd Sunday in October

Châtel St Denis (Switzerland) .... Bénichon festival celebrating the end of the hard work done in summer: folk procession, traditional Bénichon menus.

Mid-November-6 January

West End – London (Great Britain) .... Christmas Lights.

Early December

Marseille (France) .... Santon Fair.

Music, dance and theatre

1st January

Vienna (Austria) .... New Year's concert by the Vienna Philharmonic Orchestra at Musikverein.

Hans Wiesenhofer/REGINA ANZENBERGER, Vienne

New Year's Day Concert, Vienna Philharmonic Orchestra

March

Budapest (Hungary) Budapest Spring Festival: shows, conferences, exhibitions.

Early April-early May

Bourges (France) Spring in Bourges (rock, folk, jazz music).

Late April-early July

Florence (Italy) Florentine May Music Festival: many musical events (concerts, operas, ballets etc.).

May

Częstochowa (Poland) Gauda Mater: International Religious Music Festival.

Mid May-mid June

Vienna (Austria) Vienna Festival.

May-June

Prague (Czech Republic) ..... Prague Spring Music Festival.

Bergen (Norway) .... Music Festival.

May-August

Glyndebourne (Great Britain) .... The Annual Opera and Music Festival.

June

Amsterdam (the Netherlands) .... Holland Festival (concerts, operas, ballets, theatre etc.).

Opole (Poland) .... Polish Song Festival.

Mid June-early October

Athens (Greece) .... Athens Festival: theatre performances, concerts and ballets.

18-30 June

St Petersburg (Russia)........ White Nights: operas, concerts and ballets.

Late June-early July

Spoleto (Italy) .... Festival dei Due Mondi: international theatre, music and dance festival.

Roskilde (Denmark) .... Roskilde Rock Festival.

June-August

Koszalin (Poland)................ Organ Music Festival.

Chorin (Germany) .... Chorin Summer Music Festival.

Late June-late August

Epidaurus........................... Ancient Theatre Festival.

Verona (Italy) .... Summer Theatre Festival: season of opera in the Roman amphitheatre.

Late June-Early September

Interlaken (Switzerland) .... Open-air performance in German of Schiller's William Tell.

July

Montreux (Switzerland) ...... International Jazz Festival.

Szombathely (Hungary) ...... Bartók Festival.

Savonlinna (Finland) .... Savonlinna Opera Festival.

Aix-en-Provence (France).... Opera Festival.

Beginning July to end August

Avignon (France) .... Theatre Festival.

Juan-les-Pins (France) .... World Jazz Festival.

Orange (France).................. Chorégies d'Orange.

17-18 July

Voni (Crete) .... Cretan Dance and Song Festival.

Late July-late August

Bayreuth (Germany) .... Richard Wagner Festival.

Salzburg (Austria).............. Salzburg Festival.

July-August

Maastricht (the Netherlands) .... Bell concerts at the Town Hall.

Marguerite Island and Szentendre (Hungary) .... Open-air theatre.

3rd week-end in July-late October

Fountains Abbey (Great Britain) .... Illuminations (Friday and Saturday only) from dusk to 10.30pm with Gregorian chants.

August

Oslo (Norway).................... Ibsen International Festival.

Early August

Lorient (France)................. Festival Interceltique.

End August-early September

Utrecht (the Netherlands).... Holland Festival: ancient music.

End August-end September

Montreux, Vevey (Switzerland) .... Montreux-Vevey Classical Music Festival.

September

Carlsbad (Czech Republic)... Antonin Dvórak Autumn Festival.

Kraków (Poland)................. Solo-Duo-Trio: jazz festival.

Warsaw (Poland)................. Autumn in Warsaw: international contemporary festival.

3-11 September

Aarhus (Denmark)............... Music, dance, theatre, literature and cinema festival.

2nd fortnight in September

Lyon (France)...................... Biennial festival: even years, dancing; odd years, music and contemporary arts.

October

Bratislava (Slovakia) .... International Jazz Festival.

November

Belfast (Northern Ireland) ... Queen's Festival, Belfast: folk, jazz, classical music, theatre, ballet and cinema.

Cinema

January

Solothurn (Switzerland) ...... Sololothurn Cinema Festival, dedicated to Swiss cinema.

3rd week in January

Avoriaz (France)................. Festival of Fantasy Films.

February

Budapest (Hungary)........... Budapest Cinema Festival: Hungarian films.

Berlin (Germany) .... Berlin Film Festival.

May

Cannes (France) .... International Film Festival.

July

Carlsbad (Czech Republic)... International Cinema Festival.

Late August-early September

Lido (Venice)....................... International Cinema Festival.

September

Gdańsk (Poland) .... Polish Film Festival.

1st fortnight in September

Deauville (France) .... American Film Festival.

October

Warsaw (Poland) .... Warsaw Cinema Festival.

Sports

1st January

Garmisch-Partenkirchen .... (Germany) New Year's International Ski-jumping Competition.

January

Saalfelden (Austria) .... World Cup in Nordic Skiing.

Early January

Innsbruck (Austria) .... World Cup in Ski-jumping, Bergisel.

Mid-January

Haute région, Maurienne .. (France) Tran' Maurienne-Vanoise: mountain-bike race.

March

Sweden (arrival at Mora)..... Vasaloppet: cross-country skiing competition celebrating the escape of Gustave 1st Vasa in 1521.

Early March

Geneva (Switzerland).......... International Motor Show.

18-21 March

Arèches-Beaufort (France).. Pierra-Menta-Tivoli: top class down-hill ski competition.

April

The Thames River - .... London (Great Britain) Boat Race: annual rowing boat race between the universities of Oxford and Cambridge.

June

Paris (France) .... Roland-Garros Tennis Tournament.

Wimbledon – London .... International Tennis Championships.
(Great Britain)

Mid-June

Le Mans (France)............... The 24-hour Car Race of Le Mans.

3rd week in June

Ascot (Great Britain) .... Ascot Week: horse racing.

July

France .... Tour de France bicycle race.

August

Budapest (Hungary)........... Hungarian Formula 1 Grand Prix.

2nd week in August

Kinvarra, Connemara .... Boat festival: Galway boat regattas.
(Ireland)

Gastronomy

Mid-April-mid-September, Friday

Alkmaar (the Netherlands) .. Cheese Market.

Penultimate week-end in June

Oostuinkerke (Belgium) ...... Prawn Festival.

8 August

Scandinavia .... Crayfish festival.

Mid-August

La Clusaz (France) .... Reblochon Festival.

September

Grevenmacher .... Wine Festival.
(Luxembourg)

1st week in September

Galway .... Oyster Festival (international oyster-opening competition in pubs).

Palmela (Portugal) .... Harvest Festival: blessing of the grapes, releasing of bulls, fireworks etc.

1st Sunday in September

Bad Dürkheim (Germany)... Würstlmarkt (sausage festival), big wine festival.

20-26 September

Logroño (Spain)................. Grape Harvest Festival of Rioja.

Late September-Early October

Munich (Germany) .... Oktoberfest: beer festival.

October

Kinsale .... Week of Gastronomy.
(Republic of Ireland)

1st week in October

Neustadt-an-der- ....Wine Festival: procession and election of the Wine Queen.
Weinstrasse (Germany)

Index

Berlin, *Germany* .... Towns, sights and tourist regions followed by the name of the Province
Chopin, Frédéric .... People, historical events and subjects
Isolated sights (castels, abbeys, caves, etc) are listed under their proper anme.

C

D

E

F – G

H

I

J

K

L

M

N

O – P

Q – R

S

T

U

V – W

Y – Z

Manufacture Française des Pneumatiques Michelin
Société en commandite par actions au capital de 2 000 000 000 de francs
Place des Carmes-Déchaux – 63000 Clermont-Ferrand (France)
R.C.S. Clermont-Fd B 855 200 507

Dépôt légal 11/96 – ISBN 2-06-159101-9 – ISSN 0763-1383

Printed in the EU 06-99
Compogravure : Nord-Compo à Villeneuve-d'Ascq
Impression et brochage : KAPP LAHURE JOMBART, Évreux

Illustration de la couverture par PUBLIMER